Software Management

Fourth Edition

Software Management

FOURTH EDITION

Donald J. Reifer

 IEEE Computer Society Press

 The Institute of Electrical and Electronics Engineers, Inc.

Software Management

Fourth Edition

Donald J. Reifer

IEEE Computer Society Press
Los Alamitos, California

Washington • Brussels • Tokyo

IEEE Computer Society Press Tutorial

Library of Congress Cataloging-in-Publication Data

Software management / [Edited by] Donald J. Reifer. — 4th ed.
        p. cm. — (IEEE Computer Society Press tutorial)
Rev. ed. of: Tutorial, software management / [edited by] Donald J. Reifer. 1986.
Includes bibliographical references and index.
    ISBN 0-8186-3342-5 (hard.). — ISBN 0-8186-3341-7 (fiche).
    1. Computer programming management. 2. Computer software-Development — Management
I. Reifer, Donald J. II. Title: Tutorial, software management. III. Series.
QA76. 6.T888   1993
658.4'038 — dc20

92-27322
CIP

Published by the
IEEE Computer Society Press
10662 Los Vaqueros Circle
PO Box 3014
Los Alamitos, CA 90720-1264

IEEE Computer Society Press Order Number 3342-01
Library of Congress Number 92-27322
ISBN 0-8186-3342-5 (case)
ISBN 0-8186-3341-7 (microfiche)

Additional copies can be ordered from

IEEE Computer Society Press
Customer Service Center
10662 Los Vaqueros Circle
PO Box 3014
Los Alamitos, CA 90720-1264

IEEE Computer Society
13, avenue de l'Aquilon
B-1200 Brussels
BELGIUM

IEEE Computer Society
Ooshima Building
2-19-1 Minami-Aoyama
Minato-ku, Tokyo 107
JAPAN

Technical Editor: Charles Richter
Production Editor: Lisa O'Conner
Copy Editor: Tom Culviner
Cover artist: Joe Daigle
Printed in the United States of America by Braun-Brumfield, Inc.

  THE INSTITUTE OF ELECTRICAL AND ELECTRONICS ENGINEERS, INC.

Foreword

Software management has made great strides since I published the third edition of this tutorial. In response, I have totally revamped this edition in terms of both its organization and content. In addition, I have included several new sections and higher quality papers, and I have woven case studies throughout the chapters. My goal for this fourth edition is to provide managers at all levels of the organization with a clear snapshot of the technology available for managing the process, products, and people involved in software development and maintenance. My real hope is that managers will utilize the papers I have collected in this tutorial to improve their state of the practice.

This tutorial, like the three past editions, is intended to provide both the novice and experienced manager with the materials needed to understand and use the basic theories, concepts, tools, and techniques of software management. It is introductory in the sense that I do not assume that the reader has extensive experience in the field. I have neither attempted to put in all the knowledge a practicing manager might need to know nor covered the many topics involved. That would be too ambitious. Most managers take years to develop the skills, knowledge, and abilities needed to successfully control the delivery of quality products on time and within budget. Rather, I have tried to furnish a framework which my readers can use to organize knowledge so that they can address important issues and key success factors.

This tutorial framework is centered around the five basic functions of management: planning, controlling, organizing, staffing, and directing. Project and technology management are encompassed within these headings. I discuss these five functions along with the importance of software in the introduction. Papers amplify related management theories, concepts, tools, and techniques, and provide guidelines to improve the practice. I treat both commercial and military systems and include case studies to emphasize lessons learned. I give added attention to the topics of process assessment, metrics, and risk management in this edition. I also include two IEEE standards, an annotated bibliography, and a glossary to round out the volume.

As in the third edition, let me stress that management is both an art and a discipline: an art because it takes intuition, innovation, and judgment to practice it well, and a discipline in that a body of knowledge exists to inform, structure, and guide the artist's creative energies. To be successful, managers must develop their people-oriented skills, judgment, and abilities. After all, they must inspire people to accomplish organizational goals smartly with a minimum of waste and effort. Working smarter, not harder, is the theme of the fourth edition of this software management tutorial.

I acknowledge the many helpful suggestions offered by my colleagues, my students, and members of the IEEE Computer Society Editorial Board. I thank my secretary, Diane Dearborn, for her tireless efforts. Last, but by no means least, I thank my wife Carole, son Joseph, and daughter Jessica for their patience and understanding. As in the past, this edition is dedicated to all of those who contributed.

Donald J. Reifer
February, 1993

Preface

The primary goal of this tutorial is to provide managers with much of the information they need to know to be successful in a software venture. To achieve this wide scope, the tutorial must be structured to take into account a number of viewpoints. Project managers need help in delivering acceptable products on time and within budget. Functional managers need to increase demand for their departments' goods and services. Executives and corporate managers need to integrate their software strategies with their enterprises' growth, penetration, and survival plans. All of these needs must be addressed by this tutorial if it is going to succeed in its purpose.

Papers were chosen to communicate first the basics, then the advanced aspects of software management to

- *new managers* who need to understand the basics,
- *experienced managers* who want to know more about what works, when, and under what circumstances,
- *would-be managers* who are interested in what management is all about and what's in it for them,
- *experienced software managers* who are looking to improve their skills, knowledge, and abilities,
- *non-software managers* from fields other than software who want to unravel the mystique and learn how to manage it,
- *software engineers and professionals* who want to understand more about the techniques used to manage software projects and organizations, and
- *teachers and students* teaching or attending classes on the topic of software management.

Every attempt was made to select the best available papers. This was hard because of the diversity of the target audience. In response, I selected a range of papers in each topical area. One normally communicates the basics, while the others treat more advanced topics. To achieve balance, emphasis was placed on practice as well as theory.

This tutorial systematically addresses most of the skills, knowledge, and abilities that managers, at any level of experience, need to have to practice their trade effectively. The key to being a good manager is to understand what I call the "three P's": product, process, and people. Know what it is you want to build, know how to build it, and have skilled people who want to build it, and you will be successful.

The approaches we follow and the tools, techniques, and practices we use for managing software are not unique. They tend to be what good managers use independent of their specialty. The trick to their effective use is knowing how to apply them in a variety of situations. To emphasize application, I have included experience reports and case studies. These have been included to help readers figure out what makes sense for them.

This tutorial contains original materials as well as a collection of papers. Few of the papers that were in the previous three editions have survived. The primary reason for this is that we have made a lot of progress in management during the past five years and these previous papers have become dated. We have focused on process and devised ways of assessing its maturity. We have improved our estimating abilities. We have instituted programs for risk management and total quality management. Most importantly, we have become professional managers who understand that focus on people and people-oriented skills can make a difference.

Papers in this tutorial are organized in four groupings. The first grouping, Chapters 1 through 3, provides general background information. Chapter 1 introduces the reader to the concerns and challenges of software management and provides management models. Chapter 2 looks at process and process assessments, while Chapter 3 looks at project management. Both have papers on theory and experience. Both cover relatively new subject matter.

The second group of papers, Chapters 4 through 8, addresses the five basic functions of management. Each chapter starts with fundamentals before it moves into advanced topics. Chapter 4 emphasizes planning techniques, while Chapter 5 provides insight into organizations and what makes them tick. The former has papers on estimating, while the latter discusses changing concepts of organizational theory. Chapter 6 looks at staffing, while Chapter 7 describes techniques used to communicate, motivate, and keep staff focused. Both focus on people-oriented issues and skills. Chapter 8 discusses control tools and techniques, and includes papers on the topics of configuration management, quality management, inspections, and verification and validation.

The third group of papers, Chapters 9 through 11, discusses more advanced management topics. Chapter 9 contains two good papers on the topics of risk and risk management. Chapter 10 summarizes the progress we have made in the field of software metrics and measurement. Again, papers on both theory and experience are included. Chapter 11 looks at software engineering technology interfaces and the topic of technology transfer. It describes the differences between the software engineering state of the art and state of the practice, and identifies ways to close the gap.

The fourth group of papers provides support material for teachers. The IEEE standards for software life cycle process and project management plans are included in Chapter 12, so this volume could stand by itself and be used as a textbook in software management courses and seminars.

I have included an updated management bibliography and glossary within the tutorial. Both took a great deal of effort to compile. Both build on work of others, and their contributions are acknowledged.

In conclusion, I hope that this tutorial provides my friends, students, and colleagues in the field of software management with the information they need to move the industry ahead. The gains we have made have been tremendous, but so are the challenges. I am excited by the prospects.

Table of Contents

Chapter 1
Introduction

Under any social order from now to Utopia a management is indispensable and all enduring...the question is not: "Will there be a management elite?" but "What sort of elite will it be?"
— Sidney Webb

Overview

The seven papers selected for this introductory chapter provide insight into the concerns and challenges associated with software management and the framework composed to study ways to deal with them. While each makes a unique point, most of them were selected because they searched for the root causes to what many in the industry have called "the software crisis." All too often, managers tend to treat the symptoms and not the root causes of their problems. All too often, they use "gut feel" instead of "hard" data to develop a "quick fix" to the problem. The papers included are significant because they provide readers with help in devising workable solutions to real problems.

The first paper, by Reifer, was prepared to specifically serve as an introduction to this tutorial. It provides an overview of the fundamentals of management. It also provides an organizational framework for the volume which relates management function to product, process, and people variables. The paper reinforces the message that software can be managed using classical approaches and provides the reader with a road map through this tutorial. It also provides 27 principles of software management which have withstood the test of time.

The second paper, by Basili and Musa, summarizes where progress has been made in the fields of software engineering and management. It provides a perceptive look at industry trends and directions. It looks at the technology available and comments on its practicality. It suggests that placing emphasis on technology transfer, customers, and people will pay off. Although much progress has been made, its message is, "There is still much to do."

The third paper, authored by an international team of experts led by R.T. Yeh, describes a three-dimensional management model for software. Their framework extends activity-oriented process models to address communications and infrastructure relationships. The value of the model as a decision-making tool is illustrated using some interesting examples.

The next two papers make a set. In his "Guts Management" dissertation, Bob Glass argues for managers to stand up for estimates they believe in and say "no" to people demanding tasks to be done to impossible deadlines. In "Why is Software Late," von Genuchten substantiates Glass's arguments by his survey, which points to change and optimism being the primary causes for software being late. The "hard" measurement data, observations, and conclusions presented in Genuchten's article are very revealing and should be studied carefully.

The sixth paper, by Hager, is another paper with "hard" measurement data to examine what can be done during development to reduce software maintenance costs. As reported, the data provides insight into design structure in addition to management practices. Although the paper investigated a single system, its results can be generalized and used during start-up of other projects.

The seventh paper on the topic of software acquisition management was authored specifically for this tutorial by John Marciniak and myself. It talks about contracts and the acquisition process. It summarizes the lessons learned on how to deal with contractors or subcontractors. It describes typical problems that occur and solutions that work. The topic has become important because more and more firms are contracting for software development.

References

Although there are many books and articles on management theory, few of them apply this theory within a software context. Therefore, they are of marginal utility when it comes to helping managers solve their day-to-day problems. The texts that I recommend that bridge the gap and provide useful information include DeMarco's book on project control and Youll's text on project management (References 6 and 33 in the Bibliography). In addition, the book on acquisition management by Marciniak and Reifer (Reference 17) is recommended for those looking to improve their management of third-party software acquisitions.

Managing the Three P's: The Key to Success in Software Management

Donald J. Reifer
Reifer Consultants, Inc.

This paper communicates 27 principles devised to improve the way we manage the processes, products, and people that populate software-intensive projects. These principles are based on the fundamental premise that good engineering and management methods, tools, and techniques can be applied in a cost-effective manner to cope with the challenges associated with delivering high-quality software products on schedule and within budget.

Introduction

Producing a large software system is fraught with all the problems inherent in any highly labor-intensive activity. A large work force must be assembled and organized into teams. The engineering and management processes needed to get the job done have to be solidified. Tool systems need to be acquired to support selected methods and to automate tedium. Requirements need to be specified along with the customer's expectations. Plans need to be developed, and budgets and schedules need to be formalized. A variety of controls needs to be put into place as schedules and deliverables are defined. Staff must be acquired, trained, and motivated to perform agreed-upon tasks in a responsive manner. People need to collaborate, communicate, and be held accountable for results. Risk needs to be abated as managers respond, act, and perform their job, which is aimed at making things happen through the actions of others.

Software project management consists of all those technical and management activities required to implement a "high-quality" solution to a user's need according to an agreed-upon budget and schedule. Software process management develops the infrastructure that is used to manage the processes, people, and products which populate these projects. Both types of management address financial, social, political, and technical issues. Both put focus on the following:

- Planning
- Controlling
- Staffing
- Organizing
- Directing
- Integrating

Software management cannot be accomplished by novices using recipes. Its practice requires skill, knowledge, understanding, and the ability to get a job done under extreme pressure. It can be challenging and frustrating. It requires logic, discipline, and compassion for people. Innovation and imagination are needed to cope with the challenges. Sensitivity is needed to drive out the real issues. Experience is needed to figure out what has to be done, by whom, and when.

In contrast to those who write about "software failures," I'd like to focus on "software successes." I believe we know how to successfully manage a software project. Unfortunately, we don't always put this knowledge into action. To help correct this state of affairs, I have prepared this paper. Its goal is to put together in one place the essential prerequisites for success in large-project software management.

Setting the stage

People often ask me, "Why have you succeeded when others have failed?" After considerable thought, the idea of the "three P's" came to light. I then tested the idea against the projects that I have successfully managed. What, then, are the three P's? Simply stated, they are the *processes*, *people*, and *products* that populate today's software projects. To be successful, managers must manage all three and constantly reconcile conflicts among them.

Think about what the three P's mean. The idea suggests that just concentrating on process alone will not be enough to guarantee your success. The people and product aspects of this process must also be addressed as the process is executed. Trade-offs among them need to be made and their psychological, political, and social implications need to be factored into the decisions that result. In other words, the process that you use must be humanized and productized for it to work in practice.

Using the concept of the three P's, I can glean guiding principles of software management with which we can insert success into our future efforts. These principles are descriptive, not prescriptive. They provide a framework that we can use to plan, direct, and control our software developments.

You must understand that the notion of accuracy that applies to the physical sciences does not apply when it comes to the practice of software management. Because software management is a people-intensive activity, improvements to it depend to a large degree on empirical evidence. As a consequence, we must base success in the future on what we have been successful with in the past.

Maturing the process

Producing software involves more than just writing programs. Software should be thought of as a product that must be specified, designed, built, tested, and documented in a disciplined manner.[1] It must be integrated with other products and with the hardware, and you must show your customer that it meets requirements and works in a specific operational environment. Development of the software product progresses through a series of interrelated, time-phased activities called a life cycle process. Many approaches to implementing this life cycle are available. Independent of the option selected, the process must be fully defined, taught, and supported. The following three principles should be adhered to when you implement such a process within your organization:

PC1 — The added value principle: Arm good people with a process that they have a vested interest in, and they will excel. As we have already stated, having either a good process or good people is not enough. You must have both to succeed when faced with the difficulties of producing a product under the pressures of aggressive schedules. Getting the people to use the process is the next challenge. The best approach to achieving this goal is to make the process your people's process. Participatory approaches to developing the process are therefore encouraged.

PC2 — The process maturity principle: Direct your process definition efforts toward institutionalizing a common decision framework. This framework represents the scaffolding on which you build your policy and practice infrastructure. It enables you to share experiences and build on your lessons learned, both positive and negative.

PC3 — The continuous improvement principle: Aim your advanced efforts in process development toward continuously improving the process. Make sure that the process improved is the process that your people use. Be flexible and try to build on the past in a manner that lets you cope with the future. Try to take people and products into account as you plan your improvements.

To emphasize the importance of process, I have inserted a chapter on it in this edition of the tutorial. The chapter highlights the use of the process maturity model developed at the Software Engineering Institute (SEI).[2] This model uses five levels to characterize the maturity of the software processes your people are using to generate their products. This model can be used to benchmark the "effectiveness" of your current process and identify the holes in it. Using this information, you can implement a process improvement program to correct the deficiencies identified.

I would suggest that you get familiar with the SEI process maturity model. It has had a profound impact on the industry. It lets you benchmark your process versus your competition and helps you identify what must be done to improve the manner in which you develop your products. It also suggests the key practices you should focus on to make improvements.

Yet, as the principles suggest, emphasis on the process is just a necessary but not a sufficient condition for project success. The reason for this is simple. Both the product and people implications of the process must be considered for you to make it work in your environment. For example, selection of a process that is not matched with the product that you are building will lead to catastrophe. And the process is doomed to failure if the people who are tasked to use it don't believe in it. To prove this hypothesis, think of the many projects where the people have fielded products on time and within budget without having a good process. Of course, as my principles suggest, a better approach would be to arm good people with a good process that is being continuously improved. This would make the likelihood of success even greater.

Focusing on product issues

Let's now look at the product management issues. To be successful, you really need to understand what you are building. A good process helps you understand how to build, not what to build. It doesn't enable you to focus on form, fit, function, and performance. To build a product that satisfies your customer, you really must understand the application domain, marketplace, and customer expectations. You must also understand the role quality plays in customer satisfaction. The following four principles help you determine what you should concentrate on within the product domain:

PD1 — The performance principle: Focus your product specification and testing activities on performance because that is what makes or breaks your product from a customer's point of view. Normally, 20 percent of the parts are responsible for 80 percent of the action. Know which parts these are and hold them dear. If you are replacing an existing system, baseline its current performance. This will enable you to make quantitative comparisons and, in the future, demonstrate to your customer the performance improvements you have made.

PD2 — The quality makes the difference principle: When faced with a choice, customers will always select quality when the functionality of the options is nearly equivalent. Price/performance is only important to the consumer when the product works when and how it is supposed to.

PD3 — The feature creep avoidance principle: Avoid feature creep at all costs, or it will doom you to failure. You cannot deliver an acceptable product per a promised budget and schedule when your requirements are changing in midstream.

PD4 — The customer is always right principle: Be customer-directed in your choices because the customers are the ones who must use your product. Involve them in the process and do everything you can to tap their knowledge and experience. Aim your quality assurance activities at customer satisfaction, not specification conformance. Understand that needs and expectations may differ, and do everything you can to capture both in your specifications.

As these principles suggest, product development is driven more by marketing than engineering issues. And the principles of total quality management (TQM) must be held true. You really want to build the right product, right, the first time. You want to provide the features and functionality that your customer requires, needs, and expects. You want to embed quality and make the product reliable, maintainable, usable, and supportable in the field. You want to avoid rework. The approach I suggest is to aim your process at resolving conflicts that exist between product and customer satisfaction issues.

Most of my discussion so far has focused on the deliverable products. Yet there are many nondeliverable engineering products that are generated during the process that deserve attention. Most software engineering results in documentation. All too often, we produce too little or too much of this essential commodity. Planning is needed to make sure the documents produced are actually used. This leads us to our fifth and final product principle:

PD5 — The document proliferation principle: Avoid producing paper for the sake of producing paper. Such folly results in unnecessary effort. Understand your documentation needs and devise a plan to meet them. Distinguish between deliverable and nondeliverable documents. Make sure that every document serves a purpose. Make sure documentation costs are justified.

Realize that documentation takes time and effort to generate. It also takes effort to reproduce, distribute, manage, and configuration control. Produce only that needed to address the needs of your user, developer, maintainer, management, and customer communities. Realize that documents come in four varieties: specifications, plans, test documents, and manuals. The code itself should be self-documenting. After all, that is what programmers read.

I augmented this edition with articles on quality assurance and a separate chapter on metrics and measurement to address these product principles. I have made a major distinction between prerelease and postrelease metrics. This has allowed me to clearly separate developmental from customer concerns. I find this distinction important because it permits me to address different viewpoints in my action plans. Perhaps this distinction will prove valuable to others.

Addressing the people-oriented needs

The final "P" revolves around people. They are your most precious commodity because it is through their efforts that you are successful. When people are turned on, stand out of their way. When they are turned off, beware. With good people, anything is possible. They are indeed your key to success.

As a manager, you get things done through the work of others. Your primary job is to stimulate your people to do their best. To do this, you must be sensitive to their needs, understand them, trust them, and enjoy working with them. You must stress teamwork, collaboration, and communications. You must provide a variety of rewards, both tangible and intangible. You must be invisible, but in control of the situation at all times. You will shine when your people shine. Your outward sign of success will be "results." You will act, move, and integrate the work of others so things will happen in predicable ways. Good managers can be likened to coaches. Results occur on the playing field because they direct the action. They understand their people and get the most from them. They adhere to the following five principles:

PE1 — The quality principle: Know who your top performers are and use them effectively. Realize that 70 percent of the work is done by 30 percent of your people. Reward these high producers and make sure they are not stretched too thin. Coach your people and tap their potential.

PE2 — The sensitivity principle: Make an open commitment to personnel development. Know your people and help them achieve their goals through work-related training and assignments. If you help people be what they want to be, they will walk through fire and brimstone to help you.

PE3 — The motivation principle: People will try to do their best when they are given interesting work, growth opportunities, feedback, praise, recognition for a job well done, and the ability to excel. To turn your people on, you must recognize, respect, and respond to their individual needs. You must deal with personalities, tap potential, and get people to try their hardest, especially when the chips are down.

PE4 — The communications principle: Most disputes that occur between people happen because of poor communications. To cope, you must foster a free exchange of information and ideas. You must build teams that can cross organizational boundaries. You must set up vertical and horizontal communications channels. You must avoid the tendency to hold too many meetings. You must manage communications or communications will manage you.

PE5 — The equity principle: Reward competence and incompetence equally. Otherwise, you will foster ineptitude. Set realistic expectations and hold people accountable for results. Be fair but stern in your convictions. Coach your people and teach them to do a good job. Don't be afraid to terminate an employee for poor performance.

As these principles suggest, managers must focus much of their attention on the needs of their people. Many of these needs revolve around structure and direction. When people know what is expected, they will respond accordingly. Everyone wants to do a good job. Management's primary function is to make such performance possible. Managers must provide people with focus and process, so distractions don't interfere with completing the task at hand.

Software managers often have difficulty in dealing with people issues because they come from technical specialties. They must learn to handle the conflicts that arise between logic and emotion fairly and openly. They must also learn to tap the knowledge base of experience others have developed to manage the work of others. This edition contains many papers to simplify this learning process. Many new papers have been included to address the human side of the software management process.

Instituting software engineering project management

In the three previous editions of this tutorial, I had an article entitled "The Nature of Software Management: A Primer."[3] This article introduced the reader to the tutorial and identified 18 principles of software project management, many of which seem as applicable today as when I formulated them over a decade ago. These principles are classified into six areas: planning, organizing, staffing, directing, controlling, and technology change. Each of these areas in turn formed the basis of a chapter in the tutorial. Some discussion of these principles is in order as an introduction to the work that follows and with emphasis on the implications of the three P's.

Planning. Planning is an essential management function. It is deciding in advance what to do, how to do it, when to do it, and who should do it. It encompasses many related disciplines, such as estimating and budgeting. As discussed in Chapter 4 of this tutorial, policies establish a framework for decision making, and project plans provide the foundation against which performance can be determined. From a project management viewpoint, this leads to the following three planning principles:

PM1 — The precedence principle: Planning logically takes precedence over all other management functions. Yet it is difficult to do and time consuming. Managers must be encouraged to devote the time to determine what they should do and when, and how to address contingencies.

PM2 — The effectivity principle: Plans are most effective when they are consistent with the policies and tap the infrastructure used by the firm. This is especially true when the firm has initiated a process improvement program aimed at institutionalizing a single management approach for software development.

PM3 — The living plan principle: Plans must be maintained as living documents or they will quickly lose their value as a control tool. Just like any other road map, they must be updated periodically to add detail and reflect the current situation.

Because of their short time frames, most project plans tend to be tactical (near-term) instead of strategic (long-term). Yet these plans may influence strategic plans, especially when capital and research budgets are impacted. The most basic parts of a project plan are its budgets and schedules. The parts with the highest leverage include the risk management and contingency plans. It is not uncommon for a manager to spend 50 percent of his time early in the project on planning. The higher in management you go, the more strategic the planning becomes. Independent of the level of planning, each plan represents a road map developed to guide future courses of action.

Controlling. Planning and control are inseparable activities. Managers control by tracking actuals against plans and acting on observed deviations. Controls should be diagnostic, therapeutic, accurate, timely, understandable, and economical. They should call attention to significant deviations from the norm and should suggest ways of fixing the problems. They should be forward-looking and emphasize what's needed in the future. Controls that should be imposed throughout the software process are identified in Chapter 8. To be in control, managers must manage risks (see Chapter 9) and take measurements (see Chapter 10). From a project management viewpoint, this leads to the following three control principles:

PM4 — The significance principle: Controls should be implemented to alert managers promptly to significant deviations from plans. The philosophy of "if it isn't broke, don't fix it" should be adhered to. In other words, don't interfere if things are going well.

PM5 — The measurement principle: Effective control requires that we measure performance against standards. Normally, these standards are the budgets and schedules established by the project plan. However, other standards may exist, especially when other indicators of progress are used to measure progress. Independent of the system used, you can't determine where you are going if you don't know where you are.

PM6 — The risk abatement principle: Risk management and abatement must be an integral part of any control system, or else it will cease to work. Identifying obstacles and figuring out ways to avoid them in advance is an essential part of the control process.

Controls close the loop in the feedback system. They provide managers with the visibility and insight they need to make better and more timely decisions. As noted in Chapter 8 of this tutorial, they rely on the related disciplines of configuration management, quality assurance, software inspections, and verification and validation.

Organizing. Managers create organizations to make it possible for people to work together to accomplish agreed-upon goals. Organization provides a structure that lets managers achieve these goals by delegating and holding people accountable for results. Most managers work within an existing organizational structure. As discussed in Chapter 5, their function is to build teams, staff them, direct them, and manage communications. From a project management viewpoint, this leads to the following two organization principles:

PM7 — The early assignment principle: Make one person responsible for software as early in the life of the project as possible. Ensure that he occupies a high enough position in the hierarchy to successfully compete for resources (dollars, staff, etc.).

PM8 — The parity principle: A software manager's responsibility should be commensurate with his authority. Because software managers are not always masters of their own destiny, they shouldn't be held responsible for results when others' actions impact their performance.

Many of the organizational factors that impact the performance of software managers are outside their sphere of control. For example, marketing is often responsible for developing requirements (and their frequent change) and for customer liaison. Influence is the key to gaining control over this untenable situation. The software manager must be able to exercise options within the existing organizational framework. Working groups and cross-functional teams are mechanisms that can be used effectively for this purpose.

Communications must flow both horizontally and vertically. People must know what is going on, or they will lose focus and their efficiency will be negatively impacted. Newsletters, colloquiums, brown bag lunches, weekly team meetings, and monthly "all-hands" meetings are proven mechanisms for improving communications. They should be exploited, along with peer reviews.

Staffing. Staffing refers to recruiting, growing, and keeping the right skills for the job. Organizations are as good as the people who populate them. As discussed in Chapter 6, managers must be able to recognize talent, breed competence, and weed out deadwood. From a project management viewpoint, this leads to the following two staffing principles:

PM9 — The devotion principle: Managers must show their people that they truly care. Because action speaks louder than words, managers must fight for promotions, salary increases, and better working conditions for their people. As a manager, your job is to make your people's jobs easier. Anything you can do along these lines will be appreciated.

PM10 — The dual ladder principle: Promotion should be possible up either a known technical or a managerial career path. Technical people who do not want to move into management should be given equal opportunity for advancement up the career ladder. Chief software engineer slots that are equivalent to middle and upper level software management positions should be made visible on the organization chart.

Dual career paths act as a powerful incentive for technical people. Knowing what is required to progress along dual lines provides the software people with the growth and opportunity they desire. It also makes career counseling easier, especially when people are not satisfied with their current situations.

As in other scientific disciplines, good technical performers are often promoted prematurely to management positions. This is frequently a mistake because the skills required for management differ from those required for engineering. Good software managers must be bred. Training must be provided for those who have demonstrated management potential. New supervisors should be taught the fundamentals of management.

Directing. Managers get things done through the actions of others. They communicate their goals to their subordinates and lead and motivate them so that the goals are achieved. Direction tends to be difficult because software people are highly creative and individualistic. As shown in Chapter 7, leadership is needed to eliminate mistrust and provide focus for work activities. From a project management viewpoint, this leads to the following three direction principles:

PM11 — The motivation principle: Interesting work and the opportunity for growth, achievement, and advancement will motivate people to do their best. Managers need to understand how to channel behavior so that it is directed toward achieving project-related goals.

PM12 — The leadership principle: People will follow those who represent a means of satisfying their own personal goals. Success will come to those managers who make sure personal and project goals are compatible.

PM13 — The fragmentation principle: To keep them focused, avoid giving your good people too many things to do. Too many distractions cause a loss of efficiency that talent alone cannot overcome. Keep your people from getting involved in too many things, or their performance will suffer and the project may not recover.

We would like to populate our organizations with talented, self-motivated professionals. Under such a system, tasks would get done with little or no management interference. Unfortunately, such situations don't exist in most firms. Managers, like coaches, must build synergistic teams and motivate players to perform at their fullest capability. Managers must be able to communicate, lead, and motivate to survive the trials of combat. They must also be able to focus the team, when required, to meet deadlines.

Instituting technology change. The software industry is in a constant state of technology change. Managers need to be aware of what changes are occurring to harness them for their benefit. While new technology may be a risk, a manager must be able to figure out how to put it to work for the project's benefit. Otherwise, his ability to get the job done may be hindered. As discussed in Chapter 11, technology transfer is a major management issue. This gives rise to one additional principle:

PM14 — The technology risk principle: Technology should be used only when the risk associated with its employment is acceptable. For projects on a very tight schedule, the introduction of a new technology may be unacceptable because of the learning curves involved. Yet the use of the same technology may be defensible on another project when there is adequate time to insert it.

I firmly believe that technology transfer is the primary means we have to alleviate most of the software problems the industry has been experiencing. We need to figure out how to tap the benefits of technology without paying too much of a price. We need to work smarter and harder, or we may not be able to handle the work load in the future.

Summary and conclusions

This paper serves as an introduction to those that follow in this tutorial volume. It describes 27 principles that can be applied by managers to plan, control, organize, staff, and direct their software activities and personnel more effectively. It focuses on managing the three P's. It is success-oriented and aimed at providing managers with knowledge, resources, and insight. It is descriptive, as well as prescriptive. My hope is that it motivates you to read many of the excellent papers that follow.

Acknowledgments

I am indebted to the many good managers I have worked with over the years. They have taught me much. Their conduct has influenced my conduct. They have provided me role models and profoundly influenced my style.

I would also like to thank the IEEE Computer Society for motivating me to keep this volume current. We have made great strides forward in the last decade. I hope the next decade will see us make as much progress. Finally, I would like to thank my IEEE reviewers for their many constructive suggestions. These provided polish and were very much appreciated.

References

1. W.S. Humphrey, *Managing the Software Process*, Addison-Wesley, Reading, Mass., 1989.

2. W.S. Humphrey and W.L. Sweet, "A Method for Assessing the Software Engineering Capability of Contractors," Tech. Report CMU/SEI-87-TR-23, Software Engineering Inst., Pittsburgh, 1987.

3. D.J. Reifer, "The Nature of Software Management: A Primer," *Software Management* (third edition), IEEE CS Press, Los Alamitos, Calif., 1986, pp. 42-45.

The Future Engineering of Software: A Management Perspective

Victor R. Basili, University of Maryland

John D. Musa, AT&T Bell Laboratories

There are many perspectives from which to view the future of software. This article focuses on the engineering process that underlies software development. This process is critical in determining what products are feasible. We support a quantitative approach and believe that software engineering must move in this direction to become a true engineering discipline and to satisfy the future demands for software development. Further, we want to spotlight some areas of software engineering that we believe have received less attention than they merit. We begin with a brief summary of how information technology has affected both institutions and individuals in the past few decades.

The past. In the 1960s, information technology penetrated institutions. This decade could be called the functional era, when we learned how to exploit information technology to meet institutional needs. Institutional functions began to interlink with software.

In the 1970s, the need to develop software in a timely, planned, and controlled fashion became apparent. This decade introduced phased life-cycle models and schedule tracking. It could be called the schedule era.

The 1980s might be named the cost era. Hardware costs continued to decrease, as they had from the early days of computing, and the personal computer created a mass market that drove software prices down as well. In this environment, information technology permeated every cranny of our institutions, making them absolutely dependent on it. At the same time, it became available to individuals. Once low-cost applications became practical and widely implemented, the importance of productivity in software development increased substantially. Various cost models came into use and resource tracking became commonplace.

The problem with these approaches to software development is their focus on single, isolated attributes. We did not understand the relations among functionality, schedule, and cost well enough to control trade-offs. We did not effectively define other attributes such as reliability, necessary for engineering a software

In the 1990s, market forces will drive software development into quantitative methods for defining process and product quality.

Reprinted from *Computer*, Vol. 24, No. 9, September 1991, pp. 90-96. Copyright © 1991 by The Institute of Electrical and Electronics Engineers, Inc. All rights reserved.

product that satisfies a user's needs. We did not learn enough about how to engineer and improve products based on experience.

The future. We believe the 1990s will be the quality era, in which software quality is quantified and brought to the center of the development process. This new focus on quality will be driven by the dependence of institutions on information processing. We can also expect software vendors to try to create new demand in the consumer mass market. Thus, home applications might expand rapidly in the nineties, although the time required for cultural acceptance of some applications could delay this past the turn of the century.

The consumer mass market, with its potential for large sales but rather unsophisticated users, increases the demands on quality. These demands, when satisfied, intensify competition in the institutional market because institutions can improve quality for their customers if better quality is available in the information systems they depend on. In the future, this overall intense competition will be international.

In this article we discuss software quality, software engineering that uses models and metrics to achieve quality, the processes needed to achieve software quality, and how to put these processes and technology into practice.

Software quality

Quality is not a single idea, but a multidimensional concept. The dimensions of quality include the entity of interest, the viewpoint on that entity, and the quality attributes of that entity. Entities include the final deliverable, intermediate products such as the requirements document, and process components such as the design phase. Example viewpoints are the final customer's, the developing organization's, and the project manager's. The quality attributes that are relevant in a given situation depend on both the entity and the viewpoint. For example, readability is an important quality attribute of a requirements document from the designer's viewpoint. Elapsed time is an important quality attribute of the design phase from the project manager's viewpoint. It is important to quantify these dimensions wherever possible.

Software quality attributes are not independent; they influence each other.

Product quality. The ultimate quality goal is user satisfaction. Therefore, we will consider quantitative specification of final product attributes that satisfy explicit and implicit user needs. The attributes most often named as significant are functionality, reliability, cost, and product availability date. Reliability often ranks first.

It is possible to reduce the list of attributes to three by taking a broad view of reliability as the probability (over an appropriate time period) that the product will operate without user dissatisfactions (denoted "failures"). In this view, if a function is missing when the user needs it, the event marks a failure. Thus, the attribute of functionality folds into the attribute of reliability.

The degree of quality is the closeness with which the foregoing attributes meet user needs. Competition makes it necessary to improve the match. It will increasingly force joint supplier-user setting of objectives and measurement to compare them with the results.

Software quality attributes are not independent; they influence each other. If we think of reliability in terms of failure intensity or failures per unit time, we can define a quality figure of merit as the reciprocal of the product of failure intensity, cost, and development duration. (The real relationship among the factors is probably somewhat more complex than simply taking their product, but this formulation will serve our purposes here.)

The quality figure of merit always characterizes the state of the art. Consequently, a lower failure intensity (increase in reliability) will generally require an increase in cost or development duration or both. As technology advances, the quality figure of merit increases and the lower failure intensity is achieved at lower cost or less development time or both.

Process quality. Meeting quality objectives in the delivered product requires a suitable quality-oriented development process. You can view this process as a series of stages, each with feedback paths. In each stage, an intermediate supplier develops an intermediate product for an intermediate user — the next stage. Each stage also receives an intermediate product from the preceding stage. Each intermediate product will have certain intermediate quality attributes that affect the quality attributes of the delivered product, but are not necessarily identical to them. For example, in the design stage, designers are the users for the requirements specification. They develop the system architecture and unit specifications, defining them in a design document, which is their intermediate product. Important quality attributes of the design document are readability and completeness in meeting system requirements.

In addition to viewing the development process as a series of stages with intermediate products, we need to look at it as a semistructured cognitive activity of a social group. Human cognitive processes and social dynamics in software development affect product quality. For example, some evidence suggests that informal communication networks have much more impact than documents in the software development process.

We need models of the development process, measures of its characteristics, and practical mechanisms for obtaining those measures. We need to relate the measures to the quality attributes of the deliverable product. Then, we can control the development process and adjust it to meet the attribute objectives. For example, what are the appropriate methods for developing a product that must have high reliability and what leeway in cost or delivery is permissible to achieve it?

Finally, we need models of how users will employ the system and of the relative criticality of the various operations in this context.

Engineering with models and metrics

We have had quantitative approaches to the design and implementation of pure hardware systems for some time. Scheduling, cost estimation, and reliability technologies for hardware were fairly well developed by the 1960s, but similar technologies for software have lagged by 20 to 30 years. We believe this is due to lesser understanding of software development and the essential differences between hardware and software engineering (for example, the differences between production and development).

In spite of the complexity of the task, we must model, measure, and manage software development processes and products if we are to optimize the balance among quality attributes and satisfy user needs. Understanding where the time and effort are going and what processes provide the attributes needed for a more reliable product will help us refine models of quality attributes and the interrelationship between process and product.

To do this we must isolate and categorize the components of the software engineering discipline, define notations for representing them, and specify interrelationships among them as they are manipulated. The discipline's components consist of various processes and process components (for example, life-cycle models and phases, methods, techniques, tools), products (for example, code components, requirements, designs, specifications, test plans), and other forms of experience (for example, resource models, defect models, quality models, economic models).

We need to build descriptive models of the discipline components to improve our understanding of

(1) the nature and characteristics of the processes and products,
(2) the variations among them,
(3) the weaknesses and strengths of both, and
(4) mechanisms to predict and control them.

We have models for some components. For example, there are several mathematical models of programs and modules, such as predicate calculus, functions, and state machines.

Cost and schedule models have moved from research and development into application. There are parameterized cost models for using historical data to predict the project costs. For example, many organizations are using or studying cost models like Cost Constructive Model (Cocomo),[1] Software Life-Cycle Management (Slim), Software Produc-

tivity, Quality, and Reliability Model (SPQR), and Estimacs.[2]

Software reliability engineering models are coming into practice.[2] The exponential and logarithmic nonhomogeneous Poisson models are the most widely used models in the industry today. Japan has made some use of S-curve models.

We have models and modeling notations for various life-cycle processes. These key modeling technologies form the basis for a quantitative approach to the engineering of software-based systems — enough to start the advance of software engineering from craft to science.

However, many more areas require models. For example, little work has been done in organizing and systematizing the practical knowledge accumulating in various application domains.

We need to screen the models that do exist. They often require more formal definition, further analysis, and integration to deepen our understanding of their components and interactions. We need to eliminate models that are not appropriate or useful.

Based upon analysis of these descriptive models, we must build prescriptive models that improve the products and the processes for creating them. Prescriptive models must relate to quality attributes. We must provide feedback for project control and learn to package successful experience.

Because the overall solutions are both technical and managerial, model-building requires the support of many disciplines. The next several sections focus on areas of technology that we believe will play an important role in deepening our understanding and attainment of software quality in the next decade.

Formal methods. To improve our understanding of the software product itself and to enable the abstraction of its functionality, computer scientists have developed product models based on mathematical formalisms. These formalisms include predicate calculus, functions, and state machines (based on the work of R. Floyd, E. Dijkstra, C. Hoare, H. Mills, and others). These models have had theoretical value for many years, but they have not been used effectively in practice. This is largely due to the inability to scale them up to reasonable-size systems.

We are now beginning to see some

practical application of formal methods in software development (for example, the Vienna Development Method, Z, and Cleanroom). They also may add to the associated discipline of correctness-oriented development. For an introduction to formal methods, see Wing.[3]

Design methods. The 1980s brought a major breakthrough in software design with the introduction of object-oriented design methods, technologies, and languages.[4] This approach will continue to have a major effect on software design in the 1990s. For example, we expect object-oriented technologies to play a major part in the definition of integrated support environments. The notion of managing and designing systems by objects will be better defined and will change the way we think about systems. Object-oriented approaches, like functional decomposition approaches, will become part of the software engineer's set of intellectual tools. They have already begun to affect the creation of reusable software, and this effect is expected to increase as we learn more about software engineering and reuse.

Programming languages. Languages that support object-oriented design and programming, in whole or in part, will continue to evolve (for example, Ada, Objective C, C++, Smalltalk). Notations will also evolve for formalizing higher level abstractions, such as requirements and specifications. The higher the level of these languages, the more likely they will become application oriented and specialized. For example, we will continue to see fourth-generation languages introduced for specific applications; we will also see more effective translation of these higher order languages into executable forms. These notations will become basic tools in the engineering process for software.

Measurement approaches. Measurement is associated with modeling. We must base measures on models to determine if they are performing as planned. In the past, measurement has been metric oriented, rather than model oriented. In other words, it has involved collecting data without an explicit goal, model, and context. For example, in analyzing a test process, project managers may collect data such as program size or number of defects. But they may be unable compare the data to other projects unless the models used to specify the size and defect measures are documented with sufficient contextual information to interpret the data.

We have begun to see more organized approaches to measurement — approaches based on models and driven by goals.[5] These approaches integrate goals with models of the software processes, products, and quality perspectives of interest. They tailor these goals and models to the specific needs of the project and the organization. For example, if the goal is to evaluate how well a system test method detects defects, then models of the test process and defects must be available. Information that supports interpretation must be collected and integrated. For example, how effectively was the test method applied? How well did the testers understand the requirements? How many failures occurred after system test compared with similar projects?

Mechanisms for defining measurable goals have come into use. These include the goal/question/metric paradigm, the quality function deployment approach,[6] and the software quality metrics approach.[7] We expect the use of these frameworks to increase in the future.

Usage and reduced-operation software. Software usage will guide software development. An operational profile, the set of expected user operations and their probabilities of occurrence, will be defined at the same time as the system requirements. Operations are akin to functions except that they also incorporate the concept of the environment. Operations are classified by criticality where appropriate. The operational profile, adjusted for criticality, will guide the setting of priorities and allocation of effort for the entire development process.

There is an excellent chance that we will see the emergence of reduced-operation software. ROS is the software analog of reduced instruction-set computing. It is based on the observation that most software has a few operations that are used most of the time and many operations that are used rarely. The rarely used operations eat up a large proportion of development, documentation, and maintenance costs. They also complicate the system, making user training much more difficult. The ROS approach avoids implementing as many of the rarely used operations as possi-

ble. In many cases, they can be replaced by sequences of more basic, frequently used operations. System and software designers might set up these sequences and document them for users or leave them for users to determine, since many users may never require them.

Reuse. In the past, reuse was limited mostly to the code level and based on individual experience. Interest and technology development have recently surged in this area. We can and must reuse all kinds of software experience, but reusing an object requires the concurrent reuse of the objects associated with it. For example, we have seen the development of faceted schemes, templates, and search strategies associated with reusable software components. Objects may have to be tailored for a particular project's needs; hence, reusable objects must be evaluated for reuse potential and processes must be established for enabling reuse.

Reuse will grow in the next decade based on better understanding of its implications and on development of supporting technology. Object-oriented design should make reuse easier.

Cognitive psychology. Cognitive psychology is the study of problem solving. We can use its disciplines to study different intellectual activities in the software development process. To date, very little research based on cognitive psychology has been performed in software engineering, but there is substantial evidence of its promise. Software engineering, after all, is primarily a problem-solving activity. Unfortunately, few researchers are trained and experienced in both fields. The two fields also have significant cultural differences, which can make cross-fertilization difficult. For example, many software researchers pride themselves on the controlled discipline and logic they believe is central

to their approach to problems. Cognitive psychologists sometimes focus on the deficits and weaknesses they find inherent in all human intellectual processes.

Application of cognitive psychology in software engineering has generally focused on the human-computer interface. This focus is implicit in computer-aided software engineering tools. CASE has championed such human-computer interface design principles as protecting users from mistakes, helping them navigate easily through the commands and data, providing for direct manipulation of objects (for example, screen editors), and using metaphors (for example, the "sheets of paper" metaphor of windows).

This tools-oriented work will undoubtedly continue, but we are likely to see more focus on the internal problem-solving activity of the individual and the methodologies and environmental factors that can enhance the quality and efficiency of this activity. For example, people are known to have limited short-term memory. Are there software development methods that deal with this limitation in a way that increases programmer productivity? Does this limitation tend to produce certain types of faults? If so, can we use that information to improve reliability and debug more efficiently?

Early work of Curtis, Krasner, and Iscoe[8] indicates that application domain knowledge is a principal factor in the wide performance differences among software developers. This belies the frequently held concept that software development is a domain-independent activity that can be abstracted and taught totally by itself. The findings argue for a certain degree of specialization among programmers. Attention must be given to organizing, publishing, and advancing knowledge in specific domains and to providing corresponding education, either formal or on-the-job.

A study of expert debuggers[9] shows that the stereotype of these people as isolated software "freaks" is not true. The best debuggers have excellent communication, negotiation, team building, and other social skills. They generally have a clear vision of the system's purpose and architecture. They typically cultivate an extensive network of experts they can call on. The career importance of these social skills indicates that education in these areas should

> We are likely to see more focus on the internal problem-solving activity of individuals and on ways to enhance its quality.

start in the university and continue in the workplace.

Software sociology. Most software projects are group activities, involving all the complexities of group dynamics, communication networks, and organizational politics. The study of group behavior in software development is in its infancy, but like the study of individuals, it promises to improve our understanding of the development process, particularly at the front end. Many observers believe that improving this phase of development could have the most impact on software quality and productivity.

Software developers commonly face inefficiencies and quality degradation that result from highly volatile requirements. Some change is unavoidable because user requirements evolve with time. However, poor communication accounts for much of this problem. Research on this problem[8] has shown that successful software development is a joint process in which the developer learns the application domain and user operations, and the user learns the design realities and available choices.

Negotiation and conflict resolution are inescapable parts of the process. Managing the learning and negotiation processes intelligently is critical to success. So is making decisions in a timely fashion. In fact, there is some indication that the percentage of unresolved design issues at a given point in the project life cycle may be a good indicator of progress and predictor of future trouble. Measures can play an important role in making the negotiation process concrete and the negotiated agreements specific.

Inadequate documentation has been blamed for many project problems that appear to stem from poor communication. However, documentation may not be the real culprit.[8] Many developers do not consider it possible to maintain documentation that is sufficiently current to meet their needs. They get their information through informal networks. This suggests that we devote more effort to encouraging, cultivating, maintaining, and supporting such networks.

Improving software quality

Engineering processes require models of the various entities within a discipline. The models must approximate reality and include a controlled feedback loop to monitor the differences between the models and reality. In software engineering, we have often not had enough models to complete the process. Where we do have models (for example, for costs and schedules), we do not sufficiently understand the relationship between them and the other discipline entities.

Models are necessary for focusing attention on the multiplicity of issues necessary for engineering a product. But so is a process that supports feedback, learning, and the refinement of the models for the environment.

Manufacturing has learned to control production using models and measurements of the process and product. Feedback processes, such as the Plan-Do-Check-Act cycle,[10] have provided quality-oriented processes for manufacturing. The Deming paradigm uses models and measures to control and engineer the characteristics of processes and products. The Plan phase sets up measures of quality attributes as targets and establishes methods for achieving them. The Do phase produces the product in compliance with development standards and quality guidelines. The Check phase compares the product with the quality targets. During the Act phase, problem reports become the basis for corrective action. Achieving the quality target is the gate to the next phase.

Although software development is fundamentally different from manufacturing, at some level the same principles apply. We need a closed-loop process with feedback to the project and the organization. The process must consider the nature of software development. The quality improvement paradigm[5] is an example approach. It can help in applying, evolving, tailoring, and refining various models and ranges of measurements in software development.

In QIP, *planning* requires models of the various software products and product quality attributes, processes and process quality attributes, and environmental factors. The models must be quantifiable and the measures for them must be set. Developers must understand particular project needs with respect to such factors as functionality, schedule, cost, and reliability. Project and corporate goals are set relative to measurements associated with the models. Unlike manufacturing, there is no single model of the process. Developers must choose the process to meet the mix of quality attributes required by a particular product's user.

Doing and *checking* require following the selected process and taking measurements to track conformance with the models. Because many models are primitive, we also need to track whether the model's predictions are valid and, if they are not, modify the models to come closer to reality.

Acting requires a closed-loop project cycle with feedback for modifying models as well as the processes. It involves analyzing and packaging the experience gained on a project so that it is available to other projects. Analysis includes a postmortem review of the feedback data to evaluate the existing models, determine problems, record findings, and recommend future model improvements. Packaging involves implementing model improvements and storing the knowledge gained in an experience database available for future projects. This represents a closed-loop organization cycle that transfers learning from project to project.

Emphasis on the engineering process will help achieve quality goals for software development. It also supports the transfer of technology within and from outside an organization.

Making software engineering technology more transferable

Transferring technology within an organization requires an evolutionary, experimental approach, similar to QIP. Such an approach bases improvements in software products and processes on the continual accumulation of evaluated experience (learning) in a form that can be effectively understood and modified (such as with experience models). Experience models must be integrated into an experience base that can be accessed and modified to meet the needs of new projects (reuse). The evolving process and product models can help in technology transfer. They represent what we know and can apply in the software development process.

This paradigm implies the separation of project development, which we can assign to a project organization, from the systematic learning and packaging of reusable experiences, which we can assign to a so-called *experience factory*.[5] The project organization's role is to deliver the systems required by the user, taking advantage of whatever experience is available. The experience factory's role is to monitor and analyze project developments; to package experience for reuse in the form of knowledge, processes, tools, and products; and to supply these to the project organization upon request.

In this sense, the experience factory is a logical organization, a physical organization, or both. It supports project developments by acting as a repository for experience, analyzing and synthesizing the experience, and supplying it to various projects on demand. The experience factory evaluates experience and builds models and measures of software processes, products, and other forms of knowledge. It uses people, documents, and automated support to do so.

Transferring software technology into an organization

There has been little success to date in transferring new software engineering methodologies and tools into active practice, despite the potential benefits of improving the development process in an industry of software's size and importance. This failure may be partly because software engineering is a process rather than a product. It is an abstract intellectual activity with limited visibility, which makes it much more difficult to transfer.

Also, research and practice in software engineering have been divided, both organizationally and by cultural values, impeding good communication. Most practicing software engineers are not aware of all the possibilities for improvement that exist. Most researchers are not aware of the full range of problems that must be solved before new technologies can be applied in practice. Tools and methodologies are often difficult to learn or to use or both. Although most people realize that improvement means change in practice, few have been willing to deal with the cultural, motivational, and other factors that impede change.

The situation is not likely to change

> **Research and practice in software engineering have been divided, both organizationally and by cultural values, impeding good communication.**

until researchers and practitioners deal explicitly with these factors, rather than leaving them to chance.[11] They must support change proactively.

Practitioners need to address the requirements and possibilities for improvement. Improvement requires widespread education in new methods, closely integrated with education in tools. We need methods and tools that are easy to learn and use. The new technology must evolve and adapt as we gain experience with its use and continually evaluate its successes and failures. A concept like the experience factory can help with this.

A planned approach is necessary. Strategic planning identifies the goals for change and provides a basis for continuing evaluation of activities undertaken to achieve the goals. In general, this approach follows the classic phases of technology transfer: raising awareness, cultivating interest, and persuading someone to try the technology, followed by trial use and full adoption. Raising awareness typically involves the use of publications, talks before organizations, videos, and demonstrations at exhibits and meetings.

Market research is important in finding connections between project requirements and the opportunities offered by new technology. Then, technical research can find solutions to these requirements and extend available technology to seize the opportunities. Thus, technical and market research interact.

The development of training courses requires input from both marketing and technical research. However, courses are only part of the technology transfer process. Experts should present implementation workshops for the new technology. Consultants must be available to solve problems or, if a problem is not currently solvable, to stimulate research aimed at developing the technology needed for resolution.

The development of software tools should be seen as necessary to the application of a new technology and as an integral part of technology transfer.

It is useful for marketing personnel to attend training courses. They can facilitate connections between technical interests and project applications. This may involve uncovering and dealing with technological and cultural barriers to change. Technical marketing personnel can open communication channels, proactively soliciting user feedback that technology transfer personnel can use to improve tools, courses, consulting, research, and the marketing process itself.

These activities require a range of skills difficult to find in one person. Hence, building a team of people whose skills complement each other is essential, as is building trust and good communication within the team. In the future, we expect corporations to create technology transfer organizations specifically to improve and speed up the process of adopting software engineering technologies. These organizations will probably include a diverse group of professionals: researchers, educators, software developers, consultants, and marketing personnel. They will most likely associate closely with a research organization, but also have access to a training organization. They will cultivate extensive networks among practitioners. Technical improvement will depend on much more than technical factors alone.

We have tried to show why and how the 1990s will be the quality era for software. We believe that increasingly intense international competition will make it essential to specify and attain quantitative product characteristics in software-based systems. This will drive software engineering to become a true engineering discipline.

Existing technologies will become either better focused (reduced-operation software), more disciplined (reuse, measurement approaches), or more practical (formal development methods), providing more effective models for software development. The new disciplines of cognitive psychology and software sociology will enrich software technology.

Process and product models and other forms of structured experience will aid in the practical engineering of software. Feedback and learning through measurement based on these models will become fundamental. Software models will become corporate assets, used not only for improving quality but also for transferring technology. Companies will plan for efficient technology transfer.

The justification for any measure is its role in helping satisfy user needs, and the importance of the measure is its correlation with this satisfaction. The presence of measures indicates that a technology is being challenged in a healthy fashion, that it is responding positively, and that it is therefore maturing. ■

Acknowledgments

We are indebted to Dieter Rombach, John Stampfel, Jar Wu, Pamela Zave, Marv Zelkowitz, and the reviewers for their helpful comments.

References

1. B. Boehm, *Software Eng. Economics*, Prentice Hall, Englewood Cliffs, N.J., 1981.

2. J.D. Musa, A. Iannino, and K. Okumoto, *Software Reliability: Measurement, Prediction, Application*, McGraw-Hill, New York, 1987.

3. J.M. Wing, "A Specifier's Introduction to Formal Methods," *Computer*, Vol. 23, No. 9, Sept. 1990, pp. 8-24.

4. B. Stroustrup, "What is Object-Oriented Programming?" *IEEE Software*, Vol. 5, No. 3, May 1988, pp. 10-20.

5. V.R. Basili, "Software Development: A Paradigm for the Future," *Proc. 13th Int'l Computer Software and Applications Conf.*, CS Press, Los Alamitos, Calif., Sept. 1989, pp. 471-485.

6. M. Kogure and K. Akao, "Quality Function Deployment and CWQC in Japan," *Quality Progress*, Vol. 16, Oct. 1983, pp. 25-29.

7. B.W. Boehm, J.R. Brown, and M. Lipow, "Quantitative Evaluation of Software Quality," *Proc. Second Int'l Conf. Software Eng.*, IEEE CS Press, Los Alamitos, Calif., Order No. 104 (microfiche only), 1976, pp. 592-605.

8. B. Curtis, H. Krasner, and N. Iscoe, "A Field Study of the Software Design Process for Large Systems," *Comm. ACM*, Vol. 31, No. 11, pp. 1,268-1,287.

9. T.R. Riedl et al., "Application of a Knowledge Elicitation Method to Software Debugging Expertise," to be presented at the Fifth Conf. Software Eng. Education, Software Eng. Inst., Oct. 1991.

10. W.E. Deming, *Out of the Crisis*, MIT Center for Advanced Eng. Study, MIT Press, Cambridge, Mass., 1986.

11. *Transferring Software Eng. Tool Technology*, S. Przybylinski and P.J. Fowler, eds., IEEE CS Press, Los Alamitos, Calif., Catalog No. 887, 1988.

Victor R. Basili is a professor in the Institute for Advanced Computer Studies and the Computer Science Department at the University of Maryland. He chaired the department for six years. He is one of the founders and principals in the Software Engineering Laboratory, a joint venture between NASA Goddard Space Flight Center, the University of Maryland, and Computer Sciences Corporation. His research interests include measuring and evaluating software development in industrial and government settings.

Basili received a BS from Fordham University and an MS from Syracuse University, both in mathematics. He received a PhD in computer science from the University of Texas at Austin. He is currently the editor-in-chief of *IEEE Transactions on Software Engineering* and serves on the editorial board of the *Journal of Systems and Software*. He is treasurer of the Computing Research Board and an IEEE fellow. He is a former member of the Computer Society Board of Governors. He will chair the International Conference on Software Engineering in 1993.

John D. Musa is supervisor of the Software Reliability Engineering Group at AT&T Bell Laboratories. He has managed or participated in a number of software projects. His research interests include software reliability engineering, software quality, and software metrics.

Musa received a BA in engineering sciences and an MS in electrical engineering from Dartmouth College. He is a senior editor of the Software Engineering Institute book series; an IEEE fellow, elected on the basis of his extensive contributions to the field of software engineering and software reliability engineering over the past 15 years; a former chair of the IEEE Computer Society Technical Committee on Software Engineering and the Steering Committee of the International Conference on Software Engineering; and a founding member of the Editorial Board of *IEEE Software*.

Basili can be contacted at the Department of Computer Science, A.V. Williams Building, Rm. 411, University of Maryland, College Park, MD 20742; and Musa at AT&T Bell Laboratories, Rm. 2D248, 600 Mountain Ave., Murray Hill, NJ 07974.

Reprinted from *IEEE Software*, Vol. 8, No. 6, November 1991, pp. 23-33. Copyright © 1991 by The Institute of Electrical and Electronics Engineers, Inc. All rights reserved.

A COMMONSENSE MANAGEMENT MODEL

Process-management systems often focus on details at the expense of the big picture. The Cosmos model makes long-term objectives explicit, so managers can have both views.

RAYMOND T. YEH
DAVID A. NAUMANN
International Software Systems

ROLAND T. MITTERMEIR
REINHARD A. SCHLEMMER
University of Klagenfurt, Austria

WILLIAM S. GILMORE
Consultant

GEORGE E. SUMRALL
JOHN T. LEBARON
US Army Communications and
Electronics Command

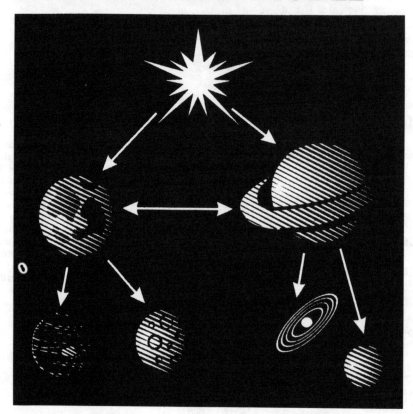

Where is the information we have lost in data? — Hiroshi Inose and J. R. Pierce, *Information Technology and Civilization*

Envisioning, building, deploying, using, and revising a large computer system is an undertaking at least as difficult to manage as any enterprise the system may serve. Essential to managing the evolution of such a system is a conceptual model that guides decisions in all the system's life phases, from creation or purchase to retirement.

We believe a major reason large systems (not to mention large organizations) fail is that formal process and model maps do not adequately inform managers how to navigate in the sea of data that modern communication and reporting tools produce. Without any way to sort out essen-tial information, managers invariably veer off in wrong directions.

The solution is a commonsense management model for systems that incorporates the good practices of successful managers as well as sound software-engineering principles. The system would guide managers toward a system-thinking approach to process modeling — away from the current focus on addressing parts of the process. A shift like that would by nature be difficult, but once managers rise above the clouds to see the whole picture, this type of approach will be much easier and rewarding to use.

In most current practice, decisions are based on a one-dimensional view prescribed by waterfall-like models. This view consists of a single explicit perspective on a set of activities and their interdependencies and schedule — which forms an *activity* structure. In the waterfall model, the activities are sequentially scheduled into phases: requirements analysis, design, code, test, and so on.

Other models suggest adding a second perspective, a *communication* structure. Models like Rapid Iterative Production Prototyping codify good practices in concurrent engineering, such as getting all the stakeholders — customer, user, developer, and so on — involved.[1] It also has explicit role and communication channels to make the project more manageable.

Still other models like the spiral model of software development and enhancement and models based on process-maturity levels suggest including process design and monitoring.

The box on pp. 26-27 describes these models in more detail and provides a detailed comparison.

Forming groups to design and monitor a process is somewhat like establishing a reuse group to design and support reuse. Both these groups, in fact, make up the *infrastructure* that supports the long-term corporate objectives of enhancing quality and improving productivity.

Long-term goals and communication needs should also be part of this infrastructure to reconcile long-term objectives with near-term pressures and the need for control and predictability. Managers can then direct activity structures toward long- and short-term objectives with a priority ranking that is much clearer and more precise.

Our process-management model, called Cosmos, combines the best of these models, incorporating all three perspectives: activity, communication, and infrastructure. Cosmos is designed to manage a large software system from cradle to grave. It builds on earlier work in which six principles were derived for tackling dynamic complexity.[2]

CURRENT PROBLEMS

Somewhere, today, a project is failing!
— Tom DeMarco and Timothy Lister
Peopleware

The most common problems in system development fall into three categories: rigid and ineffective allocation of resources and responsibilities, ineffective communication, and lack of direction. These troubles arise from the characteristics inherent in the system's life process:

♦ Objectives are highly complex and involve complex interaction among disparate groups of people and organizations.

♦ Systems are expensive, large-scale, and long-lasting; the pressure is great to control and predict, but so is the difficulty.

♦ Cost and benefit are very hard to quantify or predict, so the very foundation of decision-making is shaky.

We believe the key to successfully managing system evolution is to balance three essential trade-offs:

♦ Flexibility versus stability. Large-scale, long-life projects have a strong need for schedule predictability and cost control, yet this runs head-on into the characteristics of unpredictability and intangibility of complex problems. In current practice, management depends too much on activity structure and hence on managing in terms of schedules to force stability.

♦ Modularity versus interconnectivity. Designing large-scale systems requires a great deal of modularity in many forms. Yet this is in conflict with the inherent complexity of the system, which demands interactions among diverse stakeholders and the handling of many interrelated concerns.

♦ Broad- versus narrow-scope (long-term versus short-term) objectives. The flexibility/stability and modularity/interconnectivity trade-offs require that managers balance cost and benefit optimiza-

> Designing large-scale systems requires a great deal of modularity in many forms. Yet this is in conflict with these systems' inherent complexity.

tion with predictability and control. Benefit itself must be measured in terms of those objectives. How do we maintain an effective balance among these difficult trade-offs in the face of complex problems?

COMMONSENSE PRINCIPLES

An effective balance starts with six principles[6] for tackling complex problems. These principles are no different from those already used, often unconsciously, by successful managers; good management is essentially making good trade-offs among competing forces.

Separation of concerns. The divide-and-conquer principle focuses on subdivision and decomposition to deal with complexity. However, dividing a problem into subproblems makes sense only if the pieces are less complex than the whole. There is also the complexity of reintegrating solutions to these subproblems.

Coevolution. Many activities in process and system development are closely related, so they must evolve together. Furthermore, separation of concerns predicates the proper coevolution of subdivisions. These two principles are useful when you want to make activities concurrent.

Protoiteration. Protoiteration is a term we coined for repeatedly trying to understand a problem through prototyping. It applies when a single prototyping cycle is unlikely to produce desired results. It also applies to fuzzy goals. Building on successive experience can produce sufficient interim results to better define such goals.

Reification. Successful exchange of information — both to make the basis of judgment explicit and to communicate reasons and rationale — is critical to project success. The more tangibly a need is expressed as an objective, the more easily it is shared by those working to satisfy it.

Inclusion. Systems are built by more than one person, group, or even company —

just as the user may not be a single point but a diverse group of opinions. Therefore, any project should have widespread, ongoing participation. Diverse participation also helps identify problems that might be obvious to one group but subtle to others.

Continual improvement. Continual improvement is the philosophy of getting it right, and then getting it better. It is closely tied to protoiteration because feedback from previous improvements is introduced with each iteration. It is also tied to reification as intangible goals become concrete objectives.

COMMONSENSE MANAGEMENT

These principles can help guide management decisions for the three trade-offs given earlier. In trading off flexibility and stability, for example, managers in charge of projects that are uncertain, ill-defined, and poorly understood need to be more flexible and adaptive until goals and means to those goals are well understood. After that they can apply more rigid advanced planning. Separation of concern, protoiteration, and coevolution can help guide managers in building partial solutions, letting them explore possible directions each time with incrementally small commitments.

In the modularity/interconnectivity trade-off, two needs are at issue: to isolate workers from extraneous distractions and to keep them in touch with relevant information. Separation of concerns, reification, and inclusion help balance these conflicting needs. Separation of concerns helps identify modularity at various levels (process, project management, system architecture). Reification ensures that people communicate rationally by making the issues visible and explicit. Inclusion identifies which stakeholder needs to be involved and thus enables managers to establish proper communication channels.

In current practice, long-term objectives often get only lip service or are confused with short-term objectives. The principle of continual improvement helps managers be aware of long-term objec-

tives by creating concrete infrastructures incrementally to support them. For example, suppose a corporate goal is to increase quality. Managers may implement that goal by establishing a process group to define, train, and measure quality. Reification helps enforce the rationalization of a manager's decision because rationale and background are recorded and communicated appropriately.

Reification of both long- and short-term objectives results in a fault-tolerant process. Managers can save intermediate gains and easily retrace any decisions instead of starting from scratch whenever they must revisit them.

WHY A THREE-DIMENSIONAL MODEL?

By knowing things that exist, you can know that which does not exist.
— Miyamoto Musashi, *A Book of Five Rings*

No process model can dictate the wisest balance in these trade-offs, but the six commonsense principles provide a framework in which managers can rationalize all three explicitly. The framework, which is the basis for Cosmos, encompasses three distinct, but interdependent, views of process modeling: activity, communication, and infrastructure. We chose ACI as the framework for our process-management model because we believe that models based only on one or two dimensions are not as effective in process management.

Activity structure. The activity part of ACI — what activities need to be done and how these activities or tasks are scheduled — is essential in trading off flexibility and stability. This view is what traditional models like the waterfall primarily address. The weakness in these models is that they lead to thinking in terms of a linear cause-and-effect chain. The waterfall model, for example, addresses volumes of detailed complexity through a sequence of

stepwise instructions.

This sequential thinking does not work ultimately because in large software projects many people or organizations come together to understand problems. It takes months to hire and train new people and years to develop the systems and nurture management talent — plus all these processes continually interact. Conventional planning, analysis, and design methods are ill-equipped to deal with this dynamic complexity. The one-dimensional view of a traditional process model suggests that by following a complex set of instructions, in the form of a methodology, you can produce an effective software product. Although this approach is good for handling detailed complexity, it falls short for problems with dynamic complexity.

Communication structure. To tackle these problems, you have to go beyond linear cause and effect and address relationships among various stakeholders, system components, and other significant elements. Only then can you negotiate the modularity versus interconnectivity trade-off.

The communication structure models the communication channels among all parties (customers, developers, users, buyers, and so on). To get things done, people have to exchange information; therefore you have to know who is talking to whom, who should get what information from whom, and in what form. The communication structure includes anyone who influences the system and its acceptance.

Infrastructure. Managers cannot completely address dynamic complexity using activity and communication structures alone. Subtle changes may lead to drastic effects detected too late to avoid project risk. An example is putting a system in the field when maintenance is impractical. To accommodate the impact from these

> In current practice,
> long-term objectives
> often get only
> lip service or
> are confused with
> short-term objectives.

PROCESS MODELS: IN SEARCH OF FLEXIBILITY

George Polya in *Aufgaben und Lehrsätze in der Analysis* (loosely translated *Exercises and Axioms in Analysis*) said "The more general problem is often easier to solve. " This may be surprising, but problem solvers in many fields have come to accept it as true. If you are modeling most any complex problem, you must have a certain degree of flexibility to ensure that you choose the right process as a solution. Unfortunately, many of today's most widely used process models tend to discourage flexibility.

The evolution of process models is a long story of attempts to manage dynamic complexity in system building. The ad hoc approach was of little help in dealing with the three essential trade-offs of system building (see main article). The waterfall model[1] tackled the problem by using a linear sequence of activities composed of requirements analysis, design, implementation, testing, and so on. This linear, one-dimensional perspective cannot balance the trade-offs, and the resulting processes are too rigid to adapt to changing needs and tackle dynamic complexity. It is also too single-project oriented, with little long-term perspective for evolving the system and, moreover, the process itself.

The evolutionary[2] and incremental[3] models introduced a longer term view of the process and met the need to trade off long-term and short-term objectives. Unlike the waterfall model, they build on the premise that good solutions are rarely found in one shot and that needs change as the system is being used. However, both these models still focus mainly on technical activities and do not explicitly consider the necessary managerial activities, communication structure, or infrastructure. Thus, they are ineffective in helping to trade off modularity and interconnectivity or flexibility and stability.

The Rapid Iterative Production Prototyping model[4] introduced communication as an important perspective in the process. But it still did not explicitly consider infrastructure and the need for coevolution.

The spiral model[5] went further than the other models to tackle dynamic complexity. By introducing risk management, it let you add managerial elements to the technical-activity structure. It also introduced dynamic process development, which called for certain infrastructure support. However, the spiral model does not consider either risk management or infrastructure explicitly, nor does it consider coevolution. Therefore, it still does not have the necessarily integrated view for dealing with dynamic complexity.

As Figure A shows, process-modeling approaches have focused mainly on defining the activity structure, which means their effectiveness depends on the type of problem. Explicit definition and the planning of infrastructure and communication structure are mostly omitted.

Many projects have used one of these methods successfully. On the other hand, many projects have failed. Success or failure depends on the fit between actual and needed com-

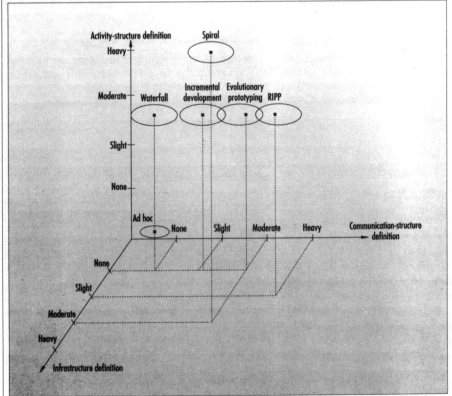

Figure A. *Existing models and their coverage of activity structure, communication structure, and infrastructure.*

munication and/or infrastructure. This dependence is what we call activity myopia.

Viewed from the short-term perspective, activities are very important, but to achieve long-term project objectives, infrastructure and communication structure must have at least equal emphasis with activity structure.

Watts Humphrey, of the Software Engineering Institute, established five levels of process maturity, which he proposed using to assess and improve a process:[6]

♦ **Initial.** The process is ad hoc and chaotic.

♦ **Repeatable.** The process depends on individuals, but rigorous project management has been established to let a predictable process be repeated successfully.

♦ **Defined.** The process has been defined and institutionalized and can be shared to promote consistent implementation and better understanding.

♦ **Managed.** Comprehensive process metrics are collected and analyzed to find opportunities for improvement.

♦ **Optimizing.** Process-data collection is automated, and improvement can continue indefinitely.

Figure B relates these levels to the activity-communication-infrastructure framework of Cosmos (see main article). The coverage of activity and communication structures and the infrastructure grows from none at the lower end to heavily defined at the higher end. The optimized level is a paradigm shift in that the continual improvement is totally embed-

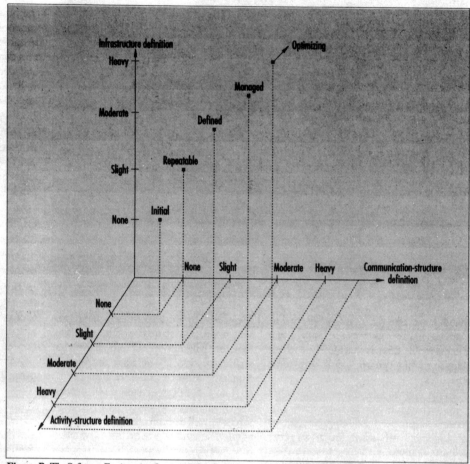

Figure B. *The Software Engineering Institute's five levels of maturity in terms of the ACI framework.*

ded in the process. The infrastructure is not only further enhanced because data is automatically collected and analyzed, but the activity and communication structures are also continually improved. Level 5 (optimizing) is thus a moving point in the ACI space, as the arrow indicates.

We believe that Cosmos is a more general and unifying model than models based on other views. It provides a framework for an organization to move toward the optimizing level of maturity by systemati-

cally making necessary trade-offs.

The lessons learned from concurrent engineering suggest that reengineering business and system development processes will be of great importance in the 1990s. Cosmos is ideal for guiding the implementation of these new processes.

REFERENCES

1. W.W. Royce, "Managing the Development of Large Software Systems: Concepts and Techniques," *Proc. Western Computer Conf.*, IEEE CS Press, Los Alamitos, Calif., 1970.
2. D.D. McCracken and M.A. Jackson, "Life-Cycle Concept Considered Harmful," *ACM Software Eng. Notes*, Apr. 1982, pp. 29-32.
3. C. Floyd, "Outline of a Paradigm Change in Software Engineering," *ACM Software Eng. Notes*, Apr. 1988, pp. 25-38.
4. S. Schultz, *Rapid Iterative Production Prototyping Guide*, DuPont Information Eng. Assoc., 1989 (proprietary document).
5. B.W. Boehm, A Spiral Model of Software Development and Enhancement. *Computer*, May 1988, pp. 61-72.
6. W.S. Humphrey, *Managing the Software Process*, Addison-Wesley, Reading, Mass., 1989.

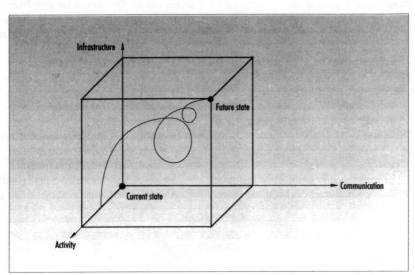

Figure 1. *The coevolving framework of a Cosmos process.*

changes, we added a third perspective in Cosmos — the ability to see change as a process rather than as snapshots — which helps in trading off long- and short- term objectives.

Infrastructure takes into account what is needed to achieve project objectives. For example, a proper food supply is part of the logistical infrastructure to support military operational objectives. Process management is part of the infrastructure to build an organization that can develop a first-rate system.

Infrastructure, therefore, not only supports communication and activities but also helps evolve the process itself. It gets feedback about the process and establishes the implied changes. Furthermore, it supports intangible long-term objectives by transforming them into more concrete goals.

Benefits of ACI. The three-dimensional view of a process model provides the information any manager — whether an army general or a software developer — needs to manage effectively. Some managers now use this view, but they do so mostly by instinct. We want to make this view explicit so that all managers can consciously observe, analyze, and improve a process.

Another benefit of a model based on ACI is that process designers can use the knowledge to produce artifacts that represent a process structure. The resulting structure will support not only analysis but also discussion about what the process should be within a specific context.

The three perspectives of our process model interact and coevolve. Each reinforces as well as limits the others. For example, to change a process from a waterfall process to a spiral approach, an organization may want to build a supporting infrastructure that includes training in the spiral process, support for reuse, and acquisition of the right tools. If, however, it cannot finance infrastructure development, then it either cannot change the activity structure or it must change the structure slowly over time.

Figure 1 shows how activity, communication, and infrastructure coevolve within a cube. To improve the process without degrading the system, organizations should move only within the boundaries of this cube. Different paths from an initial state to a desired state are determined by how the three perspectives are improved.

COEVOLUTION

The coevolutionary perspective of Cosmos's ACI framework is very useful. For example, if you cannot define the ac-

tivity structure at a certain level because the problem is dynamically complex, you can look at the communication structure or infrastructure. Because ACI structures coevolve, managers may be able to clarify and derive a certain activity structure as well as the infrastructure from the communication viewpoint.

A two-level process hierarchy improves the management of coevolution and lets you recursively refine Cosmos into levels. This refinement gives you flexibility and adaptability in dealing with dynamic complexity starting from

◆ A control level to coordinate subprojects and deal with process and project management.

◆ An execution level to perform a subproject's technical activities.

By introducing a control level, Cosmos provides a way to explicitly devote resources to tasks that are usually done as afterthoughts and hence do not get needed attention.

USING COSMOS

In Cosmos, a process starts at an overall control level that encompasses basic activities like problem assessment, merit assessment, and subproblem definition. At this level, the communication structure is defined for the overall process. Subproject teams are seen not as a collection of members who need to communicate but as one point within the communication structure. Because the subproject team's structure is not yet defined, Cosmos cannot model any individual roles and channels.

The same is true for infrastructure. At the highest level Cosmos can model only artifacts that correspond to the project's long-term objectives. At lower levels these objectives may be refined or additional objectives may arise, but they can be modeled only at the level at which they occur.

Cosmos lets you define subprocesses dynamically as the problem is assessed and decomposed into subproblems. If control is handed over to a subproblem and it turns out to be reasonably well understood, you can define the process for solving the subproblem immediately by selecting a specific aspect of the activity structure best fitted for this problem at the execution level. Otherwise, Cosmos reintroduces a control level, which performs the same task as that done in the overall control-level, but it does the task for the subproblem. You can apply decomposition recursively to each subprocess.

The benefit of this approach is that you do not define the process more than you are really able to with the information available. You avoid processes inappropriate to the problem and out of the context of its solution. The process grows with the knowledge you gain about the problem. It also has to coevolve with problem definition and changes in project context.

Figure 2 summarizes the basic information flow and dependencies of a Cosmos process with its three coevolving ACI axes, the unwindings of which closely resemble that of the spiral model.

Activity structure. Cosmos's activity structure, which models the *how* of a process, is expressed mainly by
♦ definition of tasks and work products,
♦ ordering and dependencies among them, and
♦ scheduling, projecting, and tracking of events.

Cosmos includes not only technical, product-related activities but also process-

related tasks that concern managerial duties. The concept of control and execution levels shows this aspect by emphasizing more managerial, process-related tasks at the control levels and mainly technical activities at the execution levels.

At the control level, you can
♦ evaluate a project before it begins,
♦ create a solution strategy and overall activity structure that includes process design and monitoring,
♦ establish a communication structure,
♦ establish an infrastructure,
♦ assess intermediate results, and
♦ integrate and evaluate overall results.

An important issue in establishing an

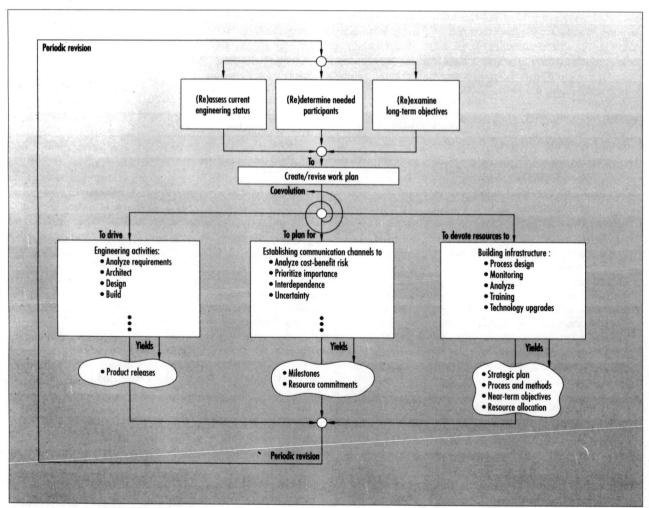

Figure 2. *Information flow in a Cosmos process.*

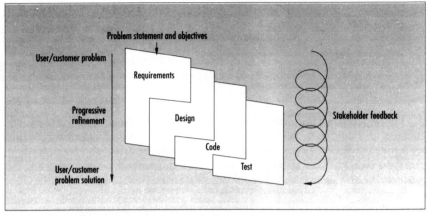

Figure 3. *Proposed engineering activity structure in Cosmos.*

activity structure is how to decompose the overall task of building a system. Of the six commonsense management principles described earlier, three apply to the activity structure: separation of concerns, coevolution, and protoiteration.

You can apply separation of concerns by decomposing tasks not by phases but by subproblems that can be solved more independently. In like fashion, when scheduling tasks, you can decouple events and work products from the activities needed to produce them. Since most project activities are thoroughly interwoven, it is counterproductive to try to put them in a sequence just because the nature of certain work products is sequential.

You also need to apply the principle of coevolution. Because problem complexity is dynamic, you cannot determine requirements totally up front unless you get a greater understanding of the solution. Thus, the requirements have to coevolve with the architecture and design. Coevolution also relates closely to separation of concerns. Once separated, concerns must evolve in like directions to produce a final solution that is consistent with the overall problem and not an assembly of chunks somehow made to fit together. Thus, managers have to install extra activities to ensure that solutions to subproblems coevolve properly. An example is having design subgroups meet to negotiate coordinated decisions.

Protoiteration is another important principle. Good solutions are rarely found in one try. Moreover, the customer's needs change over time and subproblems shift accordingly. Therefore, you have to decompose and schedule tasks in a way that allows for the iterative improvement of separated subproblems that are coevolving with other subproblems.

By applying separation of concerns, coevolution, and protoiteration, you can often make activities concurrent even though their end products occur in sequence. Figure 3 shows a structure for engineering activities in which activities have overlapping phases, are concurrent, and have lots of feedback. Viewing this diagram without also looking at the communication structure and infrastructure is not wise, however. Concurrency almost always requires a strong communication structure. In this case, managers need even more tools to control and predict the activities' outcome.

Cosmos's activity structure can encompass existing activity structures like those in the waterfall and spiral models, depending on the problem's context. For instance, it can behave as a waterfall structure if the problem is tame, or be spiral-like if risk management is a key consideration. You can customize different processes for different subproblems.

Communication structure. The activity structure uses the communication structure as a basis for performing its modeled tasks. How you apply separation of concerns, coevolution, and protoiteration depends on the communication structure's explicit modeling of

♦ roles,
♦ interconnecting communication channels, and
♦ responsibilities and dependencies.

By modeling the different roles in a role map for system development, Cosmos also satisfies the need for inclusion because all stakeholders are part of the process. Reification guides the modeling of information exchanged among roles. An example of this type of information is the intent of a design and the reasoning

behind it. Making what is usually viewed as a by-product of system development more explicit and conveying it as a structure to all parties raises the chances of a project's success. The alternative is ad hoc communication, in which many aspects become so implicit that they risk being lost.

Cosmos captures the communication structure using role maps and their artifacts as well as additional information about the channels. With this information, you can analyze the actual communication structure according to the planned structure, answering questions like what means are available or missing, what communication bottlenecks need special attention, and what disconnections and redundancies exist. If the concerns and roles are sufficiently detailed and well defined, then any needs should surface as you are determining them, and you should also be able to identify the synergistic means available to meet those needs.

A well-designed communication structure should have a concrete infrastructure that lets you judge whether needed communication is practical and predictable. It should also enable you to justify the bridge between strategic objectives and the infrastructure to reach them.

Communication structures provide an information and role view. A project consists of roles or concerns, along with their interconnecting communication channels, responsibilities, and dependencies. From this perspective, projects and organizations are much more stable than from the viewpoint of predicted versus actual events and schedules.

To explicitly analyze the communication structure, you perform the following three steps in sequence when you first develop the structure. Communication is not a one-shot structure; it evolves and undergoes continuous improvement, as does the whole process. Because these steps are being driven by new needs and information as it arises, they do not always remain in the following order.

1. Determine the major stakeholders categories. Categories might include those with significant information needs, those who supply information, those who

can constrain the process, and those who may be affected by the target system. The communication structure comprises the interdependencies among these categories.

2. Determine the major needs for each role/concern like information about application domains, system use, tool use, relevant standards, and common practice. One important need often overlooked is the stakeholders' need to know their role in process design: responsibilities, main interdependencies, and so on.

3. Determine the means for meeting these needs: available communication channels and mechanisms, languages familiar to different stakeholders, scheduling considerations, learning styles, and organizational paths and constraints. In particular, identify participants who can be boundary spanners, bridging gaps between different concerns and roles on different wavelengths. Also identify participants who can evaluate the effectiveness of communication activities.

Figure 4 is an example of a simplified map of likely roles and interdependencies. Such maps are useful both to chart information needs and to chart the means to meet those needs. The roles are generic to any kind of development process, and their names may vary or they may be split up into subroles, depending on the project. People can serve several roles, depending on project size.

Infrastructure. The activity view is concerned with start-stop criteria and input-output artifacts. Although they are essential, these concerns fail to reify the negotiation, analysis, and other information that goes into decisions behind them. Rationale and other information to support decision making may be lost. For instance, a schedule is often a compromise

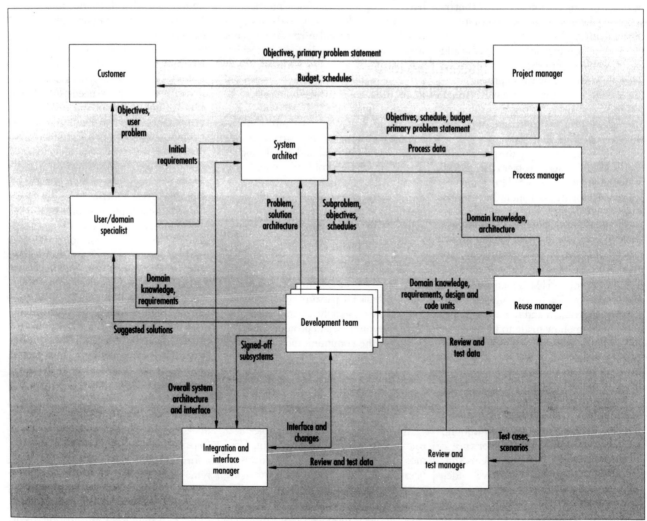

Figure 4. A sample role map.

between parties with conflicting needs. The nature of the conflict may then fade from memory, but not from the actual situation. Documenting this support information is essential when you are building an infrastructure because it becomes part of the corporate and project knowledge that can help you continually improve the overall process.

Infrastructure means "things other than delivered systems that support the meeting of objectives over the life process." Typically, that includes

♦ specification of product and project requirements for specific system versions and projects,

♦ strategic objectives,

♦ communication-structure artifacts,

♦ activity-structure artifacts,

♦ application-domain modules,

♦ reuse strategy and support,

♦ life-process requirements, design, and monitoring, and

♦ databases of test cases and scenarios collected from prototype or actual use.

To achieve long-term objectives, you have to break them down into an explicit design of concrete short-term goals. You then have to establish the infrastructure for accomplishing them and supporting their long-term counterparts. Short-term goals are instantiated through infrastructure. Infrastructure also models elements like effective communication that support process objectives. Thus, it is easy to see how process management is closely related to infrastructure.

Infrastructure is necessary not only for communication and activity performance but also for the evolution of the process itself, because a process needs to continually improve.

Infrastructure can be viewed as intangible or concrete. Intangible infrastructure includes such things as

♦ knowledge, skill, cooperativeness, and other attributes of the relevant stake-holders;

♦ ability of the participants to communicate effectively as needed — for example, a developer knowing how to use application-domain lingo; and

♦ channels for feeding back experience with deployed systems to requirements analysts.

Intangible infrastructure is oriented toward strategic objectives like cooperation, mutual understanding, and consistent requirements.

Concrete infrastructure supports the intangible infrastructure. An example is training users of a certain method to express their needs as inputs to requirements.

Both concrete and intangible infrastructure are designed in accordance with such things as resource constraints.

> **What happened to People Express proves that when system complexity becomes overwhelming, organizations must see the whole picture.**

Small is beautiful.
— Ernst Friedrich Schumacher
Small Is Beautiful: Economics As If People Mattered

Fundamental to the management of any project is to understand the context and scope of considerations you have to deal with. In most large systems, a broad context and long-term objectives are the norm. This, coupled with the complexity and unpredictability of the project and product requirements, usually dictates flexible and adaptive project management. Although Cosmos does not teach managers how to manage, it does model the dynamic complexity of such projects, giving them three interdependent perspectives to base their decisions on.

Cosmos can also provide certain lessons in general management that go beyond software. An example is the demise of People Express airlines, as analyzed by Peter Senge:[5]

"Founded in 1980 to provide low-cost, high-quality airline service to travelers in the eastern United States, People Express grew in five years to be the nation's fifth largest carrier.... Yet, despite its spectacular early success, in September 1986, People Express was taken over by Texas Air Corporation, having lost $133 million in the first six months of 1986 alone."

According to Senge, People Express's fleet size grew rapidly, as did their service personnel, but service capacity failed to keep pace with passenger growth. "People didn't fail to expand the number of service personnel to meet its customer growth," he said, "it failed to build the composite of people, skills, and organizational infrastructure needed to serve customer demand at high levels of quality."

In terms of Cosmos's ACI framework, People Express was very activity-structure oriented when under pressure, changing its fleet size, routes, and so on. It underinvested both in the communication structure — by failing to listen more to customer complaints — and in the infrastructure — by cutting back on personnel training. According to Senge, People Express could have become an enduring success by limiting demand growth while committing to service quality.

What happened to People Express proves that as system complexity becomes overwhelming, organizations must see the whole picture. Cosmos's shift towards system thinking does that, providing a natural stabilizing effect as managers try to balance three essential trade-offs.

We recognize that we need more detailed guidelines for using Cosmos. Many questions remain unanswered, particularly about how Cosmos can encompass existing process models, say in terms of Watts Humphrey's five maturity levels (see box on pp. 26-27): How does each model fit into these levels? How do you go from one level to another? What metrics determine the current state in the three-dimensional ACI space? Can you skip levels?

Despite these questions, we believe that Cosmos reifies successful current practices by explicitly providing a framework that lets the manager see the details of each factor as well as the coevolving whole. What starts out as small steps gradually becomes larger and larger as the reinforcing structures amplify one another. ♦

ACKNOWLEDGMENTS

The work reported here is in part supported by US Army's Communication and Electronics Command under contract DAA B07-88-C-A016. Our work is described in more detail in documentation on the Prism model (R. Yeh et al., *Software Development Process Models and Methods*, DAA B07-88-C-A016, task 6, US Army Cecom, Fort Monmouth, N.J., 1991.)

We are indebted to Mark Longley for his outstanding editing of the original manuscript. We are also grateful to John Morrison and to the *IEEE Software* referees, whose comments were very helpful.

REFERENCES

1. A. Rosenblatt and G.F. Watson, "Concurrent Engineering," *IEEE Spectrum*, June 1991, pp. 22-26.
2. R.T. Yeh, "System Development as a Wicked Problem," *Int'l J. Software Eng. and Knowledge Eng.*, June 1991, pp. 117-130.
3. P.M. Senge, *The Fifth Discipline*, Doubleday/Currency, New York, 1990.

Raymond T. Yeh is cofounder and chairman of International Software Systems, Inc. His current research interest is in building customizable software environments.

Yeh received an MS and a PhD in mathematics from the University of Illinois, Urbana-Champaign, and has published nine books and more than 100 scientific articles. He is an IEEE fellow.

David A. Naumann is an assistant professor of computer science at Southwestern University in Texas. His interests include investigating and implementing verifiably reliable natural-language databases using formal semantics, artificial intelligence, and advanced database technologies.

Naumann received a BA in computer science from the University of Texas at Austin and is currently a PhD candidate in computer science

Roland T. Mittermeir is professor and chairman of the Institute of Computer Science at the University of Klagenfurt, Austria. His research interests include various aspects of software engineering, notably requirements engineering, software design and language design. His recent work focuses on issues of software reusability and object-oriented software design.

Mittermeir holds a Dipl-Ing and a PhD in computer science from the Technical University of Vienna.

Reinhard A. Schlemmer is pursuing graduate studies at the University of Klagenfurt, Austria. His interests include software process modeling and its application to business, which is the topic of his thesis.

William S. Gilmore is an independent consultant working with the University of Pittsburgh. His current research interests include software engineering, process and methods, and organizational development.

Gilmore received a PhD in astronomy from the University of Maryland.

George E. Sumrall is chief of the Software Engineering Technology Branch of the Software Technology Division, which is part of the US Army Communication and Electronics Command's Center for Software Engineering. His interests are software processes, software acquisition; software metrics; software-engineering methods, tools, and techniques; software reengineering, and requirements engineering.

Sumrall received a BS in electrical engineering from the University of Illinois, Urbana-Champaign, and an MS in electrical engineering from New York University.

John T. LeBaron is a computer scientist at the Software Engineering Technology Branch of the Software Technology Division, which is part of the US Army Communication and Electronics Command's Center for Software Engineering. His current interests are software processes and software reengineering.

LeBaron received a BS in computer science from Kean College.

Address questions about this article to Yeh at International Software Systems, Inc., 9430 Research Blvd., Echelon IV, Suite 250, Austin, Texas 78759-6543; Internet issi!yeh@cs.utexas.edu

The "Software Crisis" — Is It a Matter of "Guts Management"?

Robert L. Glass
Computing Trends

Introduction to the "crisis"

I have always been somewhat uncomfortable with the notion of "the software crisis." Part of my reaction is emotional. As an old practicing software professional, I am offended that someone would say that I am not doing a good job. Partly my reaction is logical. If there is truly a software crisis, then how could we be sending vehicles into space? Running our banking systems successfully with computers? Depending on reservation systems for most of our travel? Creating a multibillion dollar software industry? Something about the software crisis just doesn't add up.

My emotion boiled over when I saw how people were using the data from the US General Accounting Office (GAO).[1] You've probably seen the data which shows that a horrendous percentage of the government projects analyzed were never successfully completed. Speakers and writers everywhere use the GAO data to "prove" that there is a software crises. But there is a problem with the data; the projects studied by the GAO were selected *because they were in trouble*. In others words, the GAO study concluded that a fairly high percentage of troubled projects were never successfully completed. This is more self-fulfilling prophecy than it is illuminating new information.

To make matters worse, some writers and speakers have knowingly misused the GAO data. To justify their claims about this elusive software crisis, they seem to be saying that any tactic is fair, even lying.

Some new thoughts on the "crisis"

As time goes by, I have calmed down a little and thought about why we have this "software crisis" mentality. Is it for real? If so, why? I have come to six thoughts, if not conclusions, and I would like to share those with you:

1. The software crisis, although widely described, has neither been proven to exist nor analyzed as to its root causes. Perhaps the research money poured into "solutions" to the crisis should instead be poured into a study of the problem itself. After all, isn't that the first thing we are taught to do when we try to solve a problem?

2. Usually the software crisis is cited as justification for a research study into some technical aspect of the problem. "Give us funding," the researchers say, "and we will automate some portion of the software development process, and that in turn will solve the crisis." It is not at all clear to me — since I believe we understand far too little about the problem — that the solution will be technical.

3. Let us suppose there is a software crisis and that many projects are behind schedule, over budget, and unreliable. Can we suggest a cause? I have a candidate that represents the simplest solution I can think of, because it suggests a single source for all three symptoms. My nominee is that we simply do a bad job of estimating how long it will take to build software. It is obvious that poor estimation could cause poor cost and schedule performance. We can't meet schedule and budget goals because we are working to estimates that were never valid to begin with. But what about unreliability? I would assert that troubled software projects, finding themselves badly behind schedule, skimp on testing and release buggy software because it is their only hope of "catching up."

4. The implications of my thoughts are significant. If I am correct, the software crisis is not about how we actually build software, but how we *think* we build it. That is, it is not the technology of software construction that is the problem; it is the management of that technology. If it is a management problem, it is extremely unlikely that it will be solved by technical solutions. Putting it another way, all those who are crying "software crisis" to obtain funding are crying wolf.

5. If we assume that the software crisis is indeed a management problem, what can we do about it? The first obvious answer is, "Find better ways to estimate schedule and effort for software." At first glance, that throws us neatly back into a technology problem. Can't we find better algorithms for estimation? We have had lots of algorithmic answers to that question for over a decade now. Although some are better than others, and although we are better off using them than if we do not, they have not proved to be accurate in their predictions. Estimation algorithms do not appear to be the solution we need.

6. If estimation algorithms are not the answer, what is? I have a somewhat outrageous answer. I call it "guts management." We need managers who stand up under intense pressure and fight for their beliefs. What do I mean? Let us look at the environment in which software professionals create estimates. Someone conceives of a software product idea. If the idea looks good, everyone seems to want the product yesterday. In some cases, marketing pushes to have the product ready for some window of opportunity. In other cases, engineering pushes to have it available when its interfacing technology is to be available. In yet other cases, corporate management pushes because they are eager to have a win in an important product arena. The schedule pressures, given this type of environment, are enormous. What do we software people do about them? To my way of thinking, we commit the following three serious errors:

   a. We give in to the desired schedule dates rather than hold firm to our own best estimates. In other words, we frequently find the schedule managing us instead of vice versa.

   b. We give estimates at the start of the project that we "don't believe in" and then manage to them throughout the project. We rarely update the estimates to match real activity.

   c. Worst of all, we live or die by estimates generated *before the requirements were even defined* and therefore before we fully understand the problem we are trying to solve!

I believe software management is suffering from the "new kid on the block" syndrome. Wanting to please veteran managers higher in the management chain, we promise to achieve things in an unrealistic time frame arranged before we even know what is to be done! It is time we looked around to see if managers in other disciplines are bound by the same ground rules. For example, do they give estimates before the requirements are understood? I have been told by engineers in several related disciplines (analog design, digital development, mechanical, etc.) that they do not. This suggests that present software managers are being victimized by their own ignorance.

What about the term "guts management"? I think the new kid on the block is folding in the face of pressure. A guts manager is one who stands by his or her guns at the outset, insists on realistic approaches to project budgeting and scheduling, suffers pain at the beginning instead of postponing it until the end, and delivers acceptable products on time and within budget.

All of this is easy to say, of course, and less easy to do. But the route to progress is often charted by the amount of pain in the status quo. What is our present pain? We commit to estimates prematurely, manage to them, fail to achieve them, and then get blamed for a "crisis" based on the results. In this scenario, we are already suffering just about every conceivable pain that could be suffered. Wouldn't it be better to suffer some up-front pain rather than hope for some miracle solution and then suffer even more pain at project's end when the miracle doesn't materialize?

Some academics make an interesting distinction between "hard" and "soft" subjects. Hard subjects, such as the structured methodologies, are those that can be taught through facts and methods, and reinforced by drill and practice. Soft subjects, such as design, are based on ideas. They can be taught through description and reinforced through experience. Academics love hard subjects because they have the reality and/or the illusion of rigor, and because they are easy to teach and grade. But life is made up of more soft subjects than hard ones. This is a case in point. The software crisis, I would assert, is a soft problem with soft solutions. The academics have tried their hand at hard solutions, to little effect. It is time we looked at options.

Conclusions and recommendations

We may not fully understand what causes the software crisis, or even if there really is one. Research into the causes for it, if it exists, is important. Certainly, software's cost and schedule performance is abysmal. I believe that poor management, not poor technology, is the root cause of this "crisis." And I would propose "guts management," management that stands up for what it believes in, as an approach to a solution. I also realize that it is easier to propose such a solution than to implement it. But focusing on the real source of the problem instead of convenient and comfortable alternatives is an important beginning. All too often we treat the symptoms of the problem and not its root cause. Perhaps it is time we opted to redirect our efforts.

Acknowledgment

I want to thank Don Reifer for taking my recent *Computerworld* article on "guts management" and updating it so that it could appear in the latest version of his *Software Management Tutorial*.

Reference

1. "Contracting for Computer Software Development — Serious Problems Require Management Attention to Avoid Wasting Additional Millions," Report FGMSD-80-4, US General Accounting Office, 1979.

Why is Software Late? An Empirical Study of Reasons For Delay in Software Development

Michiel van Genuchten

Abstract—This paper describes a study of the reasons for delay in software development that was carried out in 1988 and 1989 in a Software Engineering Department. The aim of the study was to gain an insight into the reasons for differences between plans and reality in development activities in order to be able to take actions for improvement. A classification was used to determine the reasons. One hundred and sixty activities, comprising over 15 000 hours of work, have been analyzed. Actions have been taken in the Department as a result of the study. These actions should enable future projects to follow the plan more closely. The actions for improvement include the introduction of maintenance weeks. Similar studies in other software development departments have shown that the reasons varied widely from one department to another. It is recommended that every department should gain an insight into its reasons for delay in software development so as to be able to take appropriate actions for improvement.

Index Terms— Analysis of software development, empirical study, improvement, measurement, metrics, project management, reasons for delay, software development, software engineering management.

I. INTRODUCTION

There is frequently a difference between the planned and actual progress of a software project. Why projects do not run according to plan is less clear. This paper describes a study which was carried out in 1988 and 1989 in a Software Development Department. The aim of the study was to obtain information about the differences between plans and reality in software development. The study led to actions for improvement in the department concerned, which should enable future projects to follow the plan more closely.

The aim of this paper is to add to the present knowledge concerning the reasons for overrun and delays in software development. The paper consists of the following sections: Section II describes a number of surveys on delays and reasons for delays, as described in the literature. Section III explains the definition and planning of the study. The results of the study are given in Section IV. The results were interpreted by the project leaders participating in the study. The interpretation of the results is described in Section V. Finally, the conclusions of the study are presented.

Manuscript received February 15, 1990; revised January 10, 1991. Recommended by M. S. Deutsch.

The author is with the Department of Management Information Systems and Automation, Faculty of Industrial Engineering, Paviljoen D3, Eindhoven University of Technology, P.O. Box 513, 5600 MB Eindhoven, The Netherlands.

IEEE Log Number 9144265.

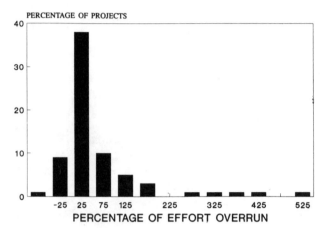

Fig. 1. Distribution of relative effort overruns [7].

II. SURVEYS ON THE OVERRUN OF DEVELOPMENT PROJECTS

Three empirical studies concerning the overrun of development projects will be discussed in this section. These studies will be referred to as "surveys." The definition of the surveys and their results will then be compared with the study described in Sections III through V of this paper.

A. Survey by Jenkins, Naumann, and Whetherbe [7]

Jenkins *et al.* [7] interviewed the developers of 72 information system development projects in 23 major U.S. corporations. The aim of the survey was to collect empirical data on the systems development process in organizations. The average duration of the projects was 10.5 months. Over 70% of the projects took less than 1000 person days to finish. The users of the developed systems stated that they were "satisfied" to "very satisfied" with the result in 72% of the projects. The relative effort overruns are given in Fig. 1.

The average effort overrun was 36%. Fig. 1 shows that 38% of the projects had an overrun of between 0 and 50%. Nine percent of the projects had an underrun of between 0 and 50 %. The relative schedule overruns are given in Fig. 2.

The average schedule overrun was 22%. Fig. 2 shows that 40% of the projects had an overrun of between 0 and 50%. One conclusion of Jenkins *et al.* was that the cost and schedule overruns seem to be uniformly distributed among large, medium, and small projects. They did not look into the reasons for delays and overruns.

B. Survey by Phan, Vogel, and Nunamaker [9], [10]

Researchers at the University of Arizona attempted to

0-8186-3342-5/93 $3.00 © 1991 IEEE

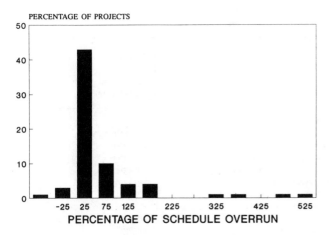

Fig. 2. Distribution of relative schedule overruns [7].

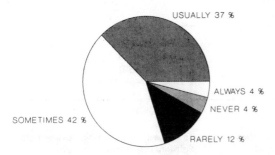

Fig. 3. Prevalence of cost overruns [9].

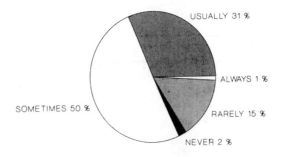

Fig. 4. Prevalence of late deliveries [10].

determine why the planned lead times and costs of information system development projects were overrun [9], [10]. Questionnaires were sent to 827 members of the American Institution of Certification of Computer Professionals. The survey yielded 191 responses. The respondents were involved in projects with an average duration of 102 person months. On average, the lead time was 14 months and 17 people worked on a project. The average cost overrun was 33%, similar to the 36% overrun reported by Jenkins *et al.* [7].

The survey was comprised of 100 questions. In 72 of these the respondents were asked to recall the frequency with which the events occurred as: (a) always; (b) usually; (c) sometimes; (d) seldom/rarely; or (e) never. Over 70% of the respondents claimed that user requirements and expectations were usually met. Fig. 3 shows the prevalence of cost overruns.

Only 16% of the respondents answered that they never or rarely had cost overruns. Cost overruns were usual for 37% of them. Fig. 4 shows the prevalence of schedule overruns.

Fig. 4 shows that more than 80% of the respondents stated that their projects were sometimes or usually late. The survey also addressed the reasons for cost overruns and late deliveries. According to 51% of the respondents, over-optimistic estimation was usually a reason for a cost overrun. Almost 50% stated that frequent changes in design and implementation were usually a reason for a cost overrun. Nine percent stated that these were always a reason. The survey also investigated why the product lead times were overrun. Over-optimistic planning was a reason to which 44% usually attribute the delay. Minor and major changes

were usually a reason for 33 and 36% of the respondents, respectively. The lack of software development tools was only mentioned by 17% as a usual reason.

The four actions most frequently taken to regain control over delayed projects were:

1) Upgrading the priority of the project
2) Shifting part of the responsibility and obligations to other groups
3) Renegotiating the plan and schedule
4) Postponing features and upgrades to the next version.

C. Survey by Thambain and Wilemon [12]

The aim of a field study by Thambain and Wilemon [12] was to investigate the practices of project managers regarding their project control experiences. The scope of the survey was not confined to software engineering projects; the leaders of electronics, petrochemical, construction, and pharmaceutical projects were interviewed. Data was collected from 304 participants in project management workshops or seminars. Those questioned had an average of five years' experience in technical project management. The average lead time for the projects was one year, and on average eight people worked on a project.

Among other things, the survey investigated what the project leaders and their superiors (such as senior functional managers or general managers) believed to be the reasons for cost and lead time overruns. The reasons for overruns were arranged in order of importance by project leaders and general managers. The results are given in Table I.

It is striking to note that the project leaders and general managers do not agree on the importance of 9 of the 15 reasons. According to the researchers, the "practical implication of this finding is that senior management expects proper project planning, organization, and tracking from project leaders. They further believe that the external criteria, such as customer changes and project complexities, impact project performance only if the project had not been defined properly and sound management practices were ignored. On the other hand, management thinks that some of the subtle problems, such as sinking team spirit, priority shifts, and staffing are of lesser importance" [12].

The researchers also investigated the reasons which caused the problems referenced in Table I. These less obvious reasons were called "subtle reasons," which can be classified into five categories:

TABLE I
DIRECTLY OBSERVED REASONS FOR SCHEDULE SLIPS AND COST OVERRUNS

RANK BY		PROBLEM	Agreement between general and project management
General managers	Project managers		
1	10	Insufficient front-end planning	Disagree
2	3	Unrealistic project plan	Strongly agree
3	8	Project scope underestimated	Disagree
4	1	Customer/management changes	Disagree
5	14	Insufficient contingency planning	Disagree
6	13	Inability to track progress	Disagree
7	5	Inability to track problems early	Agree
8	9	Insufficient number of checkpoints	Agree
9	4	Staffing problems	Disagree
10	2	Technical complexity	Disagree
11	6	Priority shifts	Disagree
12	10	No commitment by personnel to plan	Agree
13	12	Uncooperative support groups	Agree
14	7	Sinking team spirit	Disagree
15	15	Unqualified project personnel	Agree

- Problems with organizing the project team
- Weak project leadership
- Communication problems
- Conflict and confusion
- Insufficient upper management involvement.

Obviously, the subtle reasons cited by the project leaders and general managers were not technical reasons, but related to organizational, managerial, and human aspects.

III. DEFINITION AND PLANNING OF THE STUDY

A. Definition of the Study

The framework of experimentation, as proposed by Basili *et al.* [1] will be used to define the study which is described in this paper. According to this framework, a definition consists of six parts: motivation, object, purpose, perspective, domain, and scope. The motivation of this study was to gain an insight into the reasons for delay in order to be able to improve the control of future development projects. This new insight should lead to actions for improvement designed to enable future projects to follow their plan more closely. The object of the study was defined as the primary entity examined [1]. The object in this case was software development activities. Projects can be analyzed on various levels of detail; namely, as a whole (as done by Jenkins *et al.* [7]), at phase level, or at activity level. Data was collected and analyzed at the activity level in this study, because experience has shown that a project generally does not overrun because of one or two main problems, but rather because of a large number of minor problems. According to Brooks [3]: "How does a project get one year late? One day at a time." These small problems could almost certainly be overlooked if data were collected at the project level. In this study an activity was defined as a unit of work that is identified in a plan and can be tracked during its execution. A typical activity may be the specification of a subsystem, the design of a module, or the integration of some modules.

TABLE II
THE DEFINITION OF THE STUDY

Motivation	To increase insight into the reasons for dela
Object	Software engineering activities
Purpose	To evaluate reasons for delay
Perspective	Project leader
Domain	Project
Scope	Six projects in one development department

The purpose of the study was to evaluate the reasons for delay. This was done from the perspective of the project leader. The domain studied was software projects. The scope of the study covered six development projects in one software development department. The definition of the study is summarized in Table II.

B. Planning the Study

The motivation of the study was to gain an insight into the reasons for delay in software development. The kind of questions the study aimed to answer were:

- What are the predominant reasons for delay?
- What is the distribution of the reasons for delay?
- How is the delay distributed over the phases of a project?
- Which actions for improvement can prevent delay in future projects?

The following basic principles were used for data collection:

1) The control of a project refers to the control of quality, effort, and lead time. The study was based on the assumption that an activity is only completed when the (sub)product developed fulfills the specifications. In other words, if the quality of the product developed is adequate. In the department concerned this was monitored by reviews and testing. This assumption allowed attention to be focused on the collection of data relating to time and effort.

TABLE III
DATA DETERMINED FOR EACH ACTIVITY

	PLANNED	ACTUAL	DIFFERENCE	REASON
EFFORT	—	—	—	—
STARTING DATE	—	—	—	—
ENDING DATE	—	—	—	
DURATION	—	—	—	—

2) Data collection focused on the differences between a plan and reality. All planning data were obtained from the most recently approved plan. If a project was officially replanned, the new plan was taken as the starting point for the comparison between the plan and reality. The consequences of a replan will therefore not show up in the measurements. Six projects were studied: one of them was not replanned, four were replanned once, and one was replanned twice during the study. It might be argued that the differences between plan and reality were greater than the measurements will show.

3) The third principle was that data collection should not take the project leaders much time. This was a condition stated by the development department.

The definition of the study and the above principles resulted in a one-page data collection form. This consisted of a table with the data to be collected for each activity and a classification of reasons for delays. The table is shown in Table III.

The planned and actual efforts were expressed in hours. The starting and ending dates were given in weeks. The duration of an activity was defined as the calendar period between the starting and ending dates. All planning data were obtained from the most recently approved plan. The difference column indicated if there was any difference between the plan and reality. The reasons for the three types of differences were distinguished in the final column:

- The reason for a difference between the planned and actual effort
- The reason for a difference between the planned and actual starting date
- The reason for a difference between the planned and actual duration.

A reason for the difference between the planned and actual ending date was not mentioned, because this difference can be explained by the difference in the starting date and the difference in duration.

Obviously, much of the data in Table III was not only kept for the purpose of this study: the planned and actual hours and duration were also required for normal project control purposes. A recent survey [11] showed that in practice, data of this kind are not kept as a matter of course; as many as 50% of the respondents claimed that they did not record progress data during the course of their projects. In this study the project plans provided the planned effort, starting date, and ending date. The clerical office provided the actual data, which were collected on the basis of time sheets. The actual data were

TABLE IV
GROUPS OF REASONS

Group of reasons	Description
	Reason relating to
capacity-related	the availability of the developers
personnel-related	the experience of the developers
input-related	conditions which must be fulfilled
product-related	the software product to be developed
organization-related	the organization in which the development takes place
tools-related	the tools used to develop the software
other	none of the previous categories

validated in interviews with the participating project leaders every other week.

The final column was filled in specially for this study. This was performed by the project leader who, in consultation with the researcher, determined the reasons for differences between planning and reality. A classification was used, for two purposes, to determine a reason: first, the classification gave structure to the reasons identified and allowed results to be compared; and secondly, the classification saved time for thinking up reasons. Six groups of possible reasons for differences were identified in the classification. The division into six groups was based on a discussion with the project leaders concerned and on a previous study [6]. The groups are listed in Table IV.

The division into six groups has proved to be valid for several (software) development departments. In fact, similar studies using the same groups of reasons were applied in a number of departments. About 30 reasons for delay were found within the groups. A first classification of reasons was identified after a discussion with the participating project leaders. A definite classification of reasons was identified after a pilot study. Similar studies in other departments showed that the reasons were specific to the engineering environment in question because of differences among the software engineers, the type of software developed, and the organization of the department. This confirms the measurement principle, which states that metrics must be tailored to their environment, as formulated in [2]. The classification of reasons, as used in this study, is displayed in Table V.

A reason labeled "other" was included in each category, because it was not exactly clear at the start of the study what reasons could be expected. During the study, however, it was found that the reason "other" only needed to be used rarely.

TABLE V
The Classification of Reasons as Used in This Study

CAPACITY-RELATED REASONS
11 capacity not available because of overrun in previous activity
12 capacity not available because of overrun in other activity
13 capacity not available because of unplanned maintenance
14 capacity not available because of unplanned demonstration
15 capacity not available because of other unplanned activities
16 capacity not available because of other causes
19 other

PERSONNEL-RELATED REASONS
21 too little experience with development environment
22 more inexperienced people in team than expected
29 other

INPUT-REQUIREMENTS NOT FULFILLED
31 requirements late
32 requirements of insufficient quality
33 (specs of) delivered software late
34 (specs of) delivered software of insufficient quality
35 (specs of) hardware late
36 (specs of) delivered hardware of insufficient quality
39 other

PRODUCT-RELATED REASONS
41 changing requirements during activity
42 changing of the interfaces during the activity
43 complexity of application underestimated
44 more problems than expected with performance requirements or memory constraints
45 product of insufficient quality developed (redesign necessary)
49 other

ORGANIZATON-RELATED REASONS
51 less continuity in project staffing than expected
52 more interruptions than expected
53 influence of software Quality Assurance
54 bureaucracy
59 other

TOOLS-RELATED REASONS
61 development tools too late or inadequately available
62 test tools too late or inadequately available
69 other

OTHER
71–79

If the actual hours, starting dates, and ending dates were recorded, little time was needed to determine the reason for any difference. In practice, determining the actual hours and starting and ending dates was found in practice to take a great deal more time than determining the reasons. This was done in an interview once every other week with the project leader in question. It was important to analyze the data during the project, because it would have been difficult to collect accurate data after the project had finished, and validating the data would have been almost impossible. Several reasons could be given for each difference, with a maximum of four; in practice, it was found that the difference could usually be ascribed to one reason.

C. Comparison of the Study and Surveys

The study definition which was just described will be compared with the surveys, as in Section II. They will be compared with respect to their motivation, object, scope, and the data collection technique used. The motivation of the survey by Jenkins et al. [7] was to conduct empirical research on the information systems development process in organizations. The survey by Phan et al. [10] aimed to collect factual data with regard to the management and control of software projects. Thambain and Wilemon [12] investigated the practices of project managers in relation to their project control experience. The motivation of the study described in this paper was to gain an insight into reasons for delay.

The object of the three surveys was projects—Jenkins et al. [7] and Phan et al. [10] took information systems development projects as their object, while Thambain and Wilemon's [12] survey was concerned with engineering projects. The object of the study described in this paper is the activities performed within a project. The scope of the surveys covered multiple projects in multiple organizations. This study is limited to six development projects within one department. The last and most obvious difference between the surveys and the study described in this paper is the data collection technique. Jenkins *et al.* conducted interviews on 72 completed projects. Phan *et al.* sent out a questionnaire and received 143 qualified responses. Thambain and Wilemon collected questionnaires from 304 participants in workshops and seminars. In the study described here, data were collected and validated during the execution of the projects on the basis of a number of interviews with the project leaders and the available project data. Because of the differences mentioned, the study and surveys were complementary, rather than similar.

IV. RESULTS

The study took place in a Software Development Department in the second half of 1988 through the first half of 1989. The Department was concerned with the development and integration of system software in the operating system and data communication fields. The Department employed 175 software engineers and covered a range of 300 products. Six representative projects in the Department were selected for the study. A total of 160 activities in the projects were studied. The data in Table III were determined for each activity; these were the planned and actual hours and the starting and ending dates. The average duration of an activity was 4 weeks, and the average effort was close to 100 person hours.

When determining the actual effort and actual starting and ending dates, the existing registration was found to be of limited value, because some of the data on the actual implementation of the project were not available in a usable form. Recording starting and ending dates was no problem, because management emphasized the control of duration. Starting and ending dates were reported at the progress meetings. The number of hours spent on each activity was difficult to determine in the first part of the study for two reasons: first, the lack of reliability of the recorded hours. The validation of the data by project leaders showed that the difference between the recorded hours and the impression of the project leader was sometimes too large to be credible. Second, it was found that the numbering of the activities by the project leaders was found not to be unique in every case. This meant that the hours recorded could not be related to activities. The actual hours were not recorded if the effort could not be related to activities or the validation indicated that something was wrong. As a result, the planned and actual efforts could only be compared for 97 of the 160 activities.

The most important results of the study are presented in the form of four figures. Fig. 5 shows the frequency distribution of the difference between the planned and actual durations of the activities.

Fig. 5 shows that over 30% of the activities were finished according to plan. Nine percent show a one week underrun; 17% show a one-week overrun. Fig. 6 shows the relative difference between the planned and actual efforts for 97 activities. This figure relates to only 97 activities due to the problems which occurred in the recording of hours for each activity.

Fig. 6 shows that about 50% of the activities overran their plan by more than 10%. About 30% underran their plan by

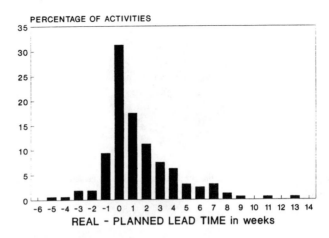

Fig. 5. Frequency distribution of the difference between the planned and actual durations (*N*=160).

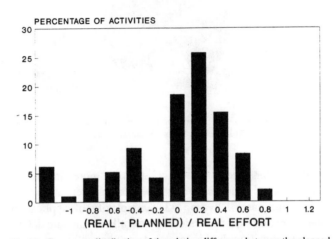

Fig. 6. Frequency distribution of the relative difference between the planned and actual efforts (*N*=97).

more than 10%. The comparison of the planned and actual figures yielded some useful insights. It showed, for instance, that the relative differences between planned and actual efforts increased for the subsequent phases of the project; the delays and overruns increased toward the end of the project. The same result has been found in other engineering environments [4]. This fact makes it possible to discourage the idea that delays can be overcome as the project progresses.

Figs. 7 and 8 present the reasons for the delays and overruns. During the study it was found that many activities started too late. Fig. 7 shows the distribution of the reasons for activities which start too late. These were divided into the groups identified in Section III. Note that when an activity started too late because of a delay in a previous activity, it was recorded as reason 11, a capacity-related reason (see Table V). This explains the large capacity section in Fig. 7.

The input-related reasons had to do with the late delivery of hardware components developed in parallel with the software. The start of the software development activities was also delayed because of this. The reasons for the differences between the planned and actual duration are listed in Fig. 8.

Within the groups identified it was found that the most frequent reasons for differences between the planned and

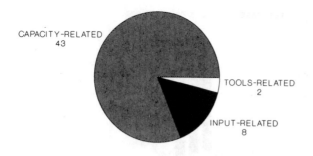

Fig. 7.   Distribution of reasons for differences between the actual and planned starting date ($N = 53$).

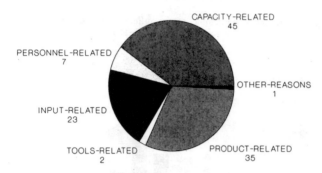

Fig. 8.   Distribution of the reasons for differences between the actual and planned durations ($N = 113$).

actual durations were: reasons 12 to 16: "more time spent on other work than planned" (these reasons were named in 27% of the cases). Reason 43: "complexity of application underestimated." Some outsiders blame all the software delays on underestimation. In this case, underestimation was given as an explanation in about 20% of the cases.

V. Interpretation of the Results

The results were interpreted during a meeting attended by the project leaders taking part, the department manager, and the researcher. In the researcher's opinion, data of this kind should, in the first place, be analyzed together with the people involved in data collection. Six reasons for this are given: first, it is the engineer's, project leader's, and manager's job to control software development. They should be supported with all the available data. Second, those involved represent the knowledge of software development in the department concerned; this knowledge is needed to interpret the results. Third, those involved can assess the feasibility of any actions for improvement. Fourth, actions which are decided on by members of the organization concerned will be accepted more easily, and thus be implemented more quickly, than actions recommended by an outsider. Fifth, interpretation of the results shows the people involved that the data is being used for their benefit. This should motivate them to participate in future analyses. Finally, a meeting like this can contribute to creating a common understanding among project leaders and general managers regarding problems within the department. Collective interpretation of the results can help to prevent

different perceptions of the problems, as was reported by Thambain and Wilemon [12] (see Section II).

During the meeting it was found that the results of the study confirmed and quantified a number of existing impressions of project leaders and the manager. For some of those present, the results provided new information. For instance, it was not clear to everyone that the amount of other work had such a significant effect on duration.

The following are examples of the possible actions for improvement that were discussed at the meeting.

It was found that the amount of "other work" in the projects studied was underestimated. During the meeting it was shown that the other work consisted mainly of maintenance. Those present decided that in future projects, more time and capacity should be set aside for "other work."

During the meeting it was shown that the maintenance activities in particular constantly interrupted development. A number of possible ways of separating development and maintenance was discussed. The possibility of setting up a separate maintenance group was discussed and rejected. It was decided to schedule the maintenance work as far as possible in maintenance weeks, and to include two maintenance weeks in each quarter. It was obvious that not all maintenance can be delayed for a number of weeks. Any defect that affected the customer's operation was resolved immediately, irrespective of the maintenance weeks. Defects of this kind were only a small fraction of the defects, and correcting them involved only a small fraction of the maintenance effort. The vast majority of defects was found in products before they were released to customers. By carrying out most of the maintenance during maintenance weeks, it was hoped that development could proceed more quickly and with fewer interruptions during the other weeks. This suggestion was implemented by the department within one month after the meeting.

The department wanted to gain more insight into the origin of maintenance. Another analysis study started. Its aim was to gain an insight into the origin of maintenance in order to be able to take improvement measures which could reduce future maintenance effort.

At the end of the meeting it was concluded that the study had yielded sufficient results for those involved. A considerable contribution was the fact that ongoing discussions could now be supported by facts.

Comparable studies have been carried out in a number of other software development departments. The result of one of those studies is given for the sake of comparison, and also to discourage unjustified generalizations of the results given so far. Fig. 9 shows the reasons for differences between planned and actual durations, which are given for 80 activities, carried out in a development department which develops systems software and CAM software [8]. The groups of reasons distinguished in Section III were again used here.

The differences between the distribution of reasons given in Fig. 8 should be obvious. Based on ongoing measurements in a number of departments, the author concludes that the distribution of causes varies strongly for each department. Every department should therefore gain an insight into its

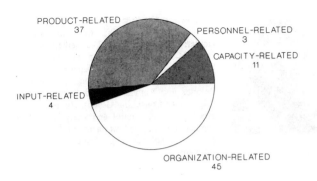

Fig. 9. Distribution of the causes of differences between the actual and planned durations in another department [8].

reasons for delay in software development projects in order to be able to take appropriate actions for improvement.

VI. Conclusions

The conclusions below consist of two parts: first, the study and its results are compared with the surveys discussed in Section II of this paper, after which the main conclusions of the study will be restated.

Three surveys concerned with the investigation of delays and the reasons for delays were presented in Section II of this paper. A comparison of the definition of the surveys and the study presented in this paper was given in Section III. The comparison showed that the surveys on the one hand, and the study on the other, were complementary rather than similar. The comparison of the results of the present study with the surveys described in the literature provides the following information:

The average overruns found in the present study approximated the overruns found by Phan et al. [9], [10] and Jenkins et al. [7]. However, in the present study the relative lead time overrun was greater than the relative effort overrun. Jenkins et al. found the opposite result.

Over-optimistic planning was cited as a probable cause in all the studies which examined reasons for delay. Phan et al. found that 44% of the respondents named over-optimistic planning as a reason. An unrealistic project plan and underestimation of the scope were named as major reasons in Thambain and Wilemon's [12] survey. The study described in this paper recorded underestimation of the complexity as a reason in 20% of the cases.

Thambain and Wilemon's investigation of the subtle reasons for delay indicate that the reasons were not technical in nature, but were related to organizational, managerial, and human aspects. The present study shows a similar result. The product- and tools-related reasons represent most of the technical reasons. They comprise only one-third of the reasons mentioned.

It must still be noted that relatively few studies on delays and their reasons have been described in the literature. Moreover, this statement is generally true for empirical studies of the control of software development.

An empirical study of the control of software projects was presented in this paper. An important advantage of the study definition selected was that, in spite of the limited effort required from the project leaders taking part, results were achieved fairly quickly. The cooperation of the developers and project leaders was vital in carrying out the study. One of the conditions for the cooperation of the project leaders was that it was made clear in advance for what the data collected would and would not be used.

Insight into the predominant reasons for delay enabled actions for improvement to be taken in the department concerned. An important conclusion was that the distribution of reasons for delay varied widely from one department to another. The author recommends that every engineering department should gain an insight into its reasons for delay in order to be able to take adequate actions for improvement.

This study targeted the activities within a project. If a project plan is regarded as a set of agreements concerning the work to be done, it might be said that the study investigated to what extent agreements within projects were fulfilled. External entities also have an influence on the execution of a project plan. One example is the fact that departmental management does not provide the planned resources. Another example is failure of a marketing department to deliver clearly defined requirements on time. The author concludes that to some extent, a project cannot be executed according to plan, because external entities do not fulfil their agreements. Software engineers should continue to investigate how agreements are fulfilled within projects. The author would also recommend a comparable study on the fulfilment of those agreements which influence the execution of a project plan, but are not controlled by the project team.

Acknowledgment

The author would like to thank the following people for their cooperation: E. Buijs, M. Fierst van Wijnandsbergen, E. der Veen, H. Keizers, G. Scholten, L. Hulstman, and E. de Vries, and also T. Bemelmans, F. Heemstra, M. Howard, R. Kusters, and again, M. Fierst van Wijnandsbergen, for their contributions to and comments on an earlier version (see [5]) of this paper.

References

[1] V. R. Basili, R. W. Selby, and D. H. Hutchens, "Experimentation in software engineering," IEEE Trans. Software Eng., vol. SE-12, pp. 733–743, July 1986.
[2] V. R. Basili and H. D. Rombach, "The TAME project: toward improvement-oriented software environments," IEEE Trans. Software Eng., vol. SE-14, pp. 758–773, June 1988.
[3] F. B. Brooks, The Mythical Man-Month: Essays on Software Engineering. London: Addison–Wesley, 1975.
[4] M. J. I. M. van Genuchten, "Towards a software factory," Ph.D. thesis, Eindhoven Univ. Technology, The Netherlands, 1991.
[5] M. J. I. M. van Genuchten and M. Fierst van Wijnandsbergen, "An empirical study on the control of software development," in Proc. Conf. Organization and Information Syst. (Bled, Yugoslavia), Sept. 13–15, 1989, pp. 705–718.
[6] F. J. Heemstra, "Estimation and control of software development projects," Ph.D. thesis, Eindhoven Univ. Technology, Kluwer, Deventer, The Netherlands, 1989.
[7] A. M. Jenkins, J. D. Naumann, and J. C., Wetherbe, "Empirical investigation of systems development practices and results," Inform. Manage., vol. 7, pp. 73–82, 1984.
[8] F. L. G. van Lierop and R. S. A. Volkers, "Controlling software projects: a matter of measurement," Masters thesis, Faculty of Industrial

Eng., Eindhoven Univ. Technology, Kluwer, Deventer, The Netherlands, 1989.

[9] D. Phan, "Information systems project management: an integrated resource planning perspective model," Ph.D. thesis, Dept. Management Inform. Syst., Univ. Arizona, Tucson, 1990.

[10] D. Phan, D. Vogel, and J. Nunamaker, "The search for perfect project management," *Computerworld*, pp. 95–100, Sept. 1988.

[11] W. J. A. M. Siskens, F. J. Heemstra, and H. van der Stelt, "Cost control of automation projects: an empirical study" (in Dutch), *Informatie*, vol. 31, pp. 34–43, Jan. 1989.

[12] H. J. Thambain and D. L. Wilemon, "Criteria for controlling projects according to plan," *Project Management J.*, pp. 75–81, June 1986.

Michiel van Genuchten received the M.Sc. degree in industrial engineering from the Eindhoven University of Technology, The Netherlands.

He is currently employed by the Eindhoven University of Technology, Department of Industrial Engineering, Section Management Information Systems and Automation, and Philips Electronics (Lighthouse Consulting Group). His research interests include the control and analysis of software engineering, the application of production control concepts to software engineering, and the reuse of software.

Software Cost Reduction Methods in Practice: A Post-Mortem Analysis

J. A. Hager

HRB Systems, P.O. Box 60, Science Park, State College, Pennsylvania

Sixty percent of the software costs associated with the design, development, and implementation of computer systems occurs in the maintenance phase. Since change is intrinsic in software, a significant reduction in the maintenance costs can be realized by recognizing the evolutionary aspects of software and integrating a design for change philosophy into the engineering life-cycle. Programs must be designed to be alterable and the resulting change process rigorously planned and controlled.

From 1984 to 1987, the government funded a large, computer-based training effort based on these goals. The training system software provided hands-on training for a large collection/processing system by emulating the man-machine interfaces. The fundamental goal of the design and documentation effort was to minimize the impact of implementing expected system changes to the training system.

Initial maintenance metrics collected during 1988 and 1989 for the effort suggest that several of the project design/documentation and maintenance goals were realized. The purpose of this paper is to revisit the design methodology and goals of the effort by analyzing change data gathered during the system test and early maintenance phases. This data strongly suggests that integrating a design for change philosophy into the software development practices has the potential to significantly reduce full life-cycle costs.

1. INTRODUCTION

In 1984, a contract was initiated to develop a computer-based training system to support several data collection and processing systems developed and maintained by government contractors. A major aspect of the computer-based training contract was the requirement to apply software engineering technology developed previously at the customer facility as part of the Software Cost Reduction (SCR) project. To measure the impact of the SCR technology being applied, Software Problem Reports (SPRs) were modified to collect evaluation data.

This paper is a summary of the SPR data submitted from August 1, 1988 to April 30, 1989, where the dominant activities were software and system integration and test. The focus is mostly on how easy it was to correct errors and to make improvements to the training system software during that time.

The remainder of this paper consists of six sections. Section 2 describes the SCR program, fundamental SCR design and documentation concepts, and the training system program. Section 3 reviews the possible future changes to the training system that were identified early in the development effort (definition and design phases) and that influenced the software module structure, which is discussed in Section 4. Section 5 presents analyses of SPR data. Section 6 is a summary.

2. BACKGROUND

The difficulty of generating software that is easily maintained becomes evident when the full software life-cycle costs are examined. Typically, maintenance, i.e., post-delivery, efforts account for 60% or more of the total life-cycle costs [1]. More importantly, a large percentage (35%) of the total maintenance effort is devoted to software enhancements.

Basically, this situation exists because maintainable software is not a natural byproduct of many currently used development approaches and methodologies. Maintenance is difficult for several reasons:

—maintainability requirements are omitted or not clearly identified in system requirements specifications

—verification of maintainability requirements is imprecise at best

—documentation structures do not provide enough visibility to maintenance concerns

---

Address correspondence to James A. Hager, HRB Systems, P.O. Box 60, Science Park, State College, PA 16804

Reprinted by permission of the publisher from "Software Cost Reduction Methods in Practice: A Post-Mortem Analysis", by J.A. Hager, *Journal of Systems and Software*, Vol. 14, No. 2, February 1991, pages 67-77. Copyright 1991 by Elsevier Science Publishing Co., Inc.

—internal/external review structures do not provide accountability for maintenance concerns

—design methodologies encourage ripple effects when implementing changes.

Controlling software maintenance costs requires changes in both design approaches and supporting documentation structures. During the past few years, several new approaches have been advocated to reduce software life-cycle costs. The underlying strategy has been to focus explicitly on possible changes early on in the software life-cycle and to develop, design, and document systems to accommodate these changes.

In 1978, a Software Cost Reduction (SCR) program was initiated by the government to address control of software life-cycle costs [3, 5]. The methodology developed under the project is different from many methodologies and the supporting documentation structures currently used. Key SCR concepts upon which specification and design techniques are based include:

1) Separation of Concerns
2) Formal Specification
3) Documentation as a Software Design Medium
4) Information Hiding/Abstraction of Interfaces.

Separation of Concerns. Separation of concerns is the grouping together of related information, and intentionally separating unrelated information. The primary goal of separating concerns is to minimize software life-cycle costs by reducing the impact that a desired change will have on an existing system. A secondary goal is to establish a single source for answers to system questions.

Formal Specification. One of the shortcomings of the documentation produced for major systems is the almost total dependence on unstructured text. The English language is powerful and flexible, but inherently ambiguous. Specification languages using formal mathematical notation have been proposed and used to a limited extent. These approaches are successful in terms of producing unambiguous, precise, and concise specifications. The negative aspect of these approaches is their inability to be understood by a wide audience.

The SCR approach is a compromise between very formal techniques and unstructured prose. Motivational material employs prose, while design information relies on semiformal structures. Templates are used to rigorously organize material. Acronyms are employed to avoid redundancy, to aid in understanding, to support automated tracking concerns, and to keep the documents concise. Acronyms are introduced for each of the components of the system (inputs, outputs, functions, modes, etc.). Whenever an acronym is used, it is enclosed in special characters that identify what type of

component it is. Complete examples of the documentation structures based upon this approach are found in Hager [4].

This formalism is applied uniformly throughout the documentation structures. Only limited tailoring and extensions necessary to accommodate the different types of material covered in each document are permitted.

Documentation as a Software Design Medium. Documentation as a software design medium is concerned more with the steps that must be followed to produce a system than with the specification techniques used in that process. Simply stated, this concept requires that information be organized so that it provides a framework of questions to be answered. Answering these questions will produce the documentation necessary to specify and design the system.

Once the type of information needed at each phase of the development process is determined, separation of concerns is employed to organize this collection of information. The templates that are used in each section ask the questions to be answered.

Information Hiding/Abstraction of Interface. Information hiding is a software design principle first introduced in the early 1970s by Parnas. The fundamental idea is that a software "module" is a unit of work and a unit of rework. In other words, a software designer must carefully consider likely future changes when identifying software modules to prevent unpredictable or wide-ranging impacts, i.e., rework, over the module structure in the future.

The first step in effectively applying the information-hiding principle is to identify expected changes early in the system development process, i.e., as part of system requirements. The identification of likely changes is a difficult process that requires significant familiarity with the application. Customer participation in this process is critical. Once the expected changes are agreed upon, they are prioritized based on their likelihood of occurrence. Although all expected changes are important, outside factors may prohibit application of the entire list. Prioritization of the expected changes allows some flexibility in this decision process.

The expected changed are next factored into the design of the system. The general approach is to identify and specify modules that limit the rework required of future changes by trying to confine or "hide" each in separate modules, which are referred to as information-hiding modules.

The concept of information-hiding modules requires special care with their specifications. The capabilities offered by a module must be specified so as to prevent users of its capabilities from becoming dependent upon the "secrets," i.e., the hidden or arbitrary details, of the modules. Such specifications are, thus, abstract interface specifications. That is, not every aspect of a module is specified; details that could change based on changing system requirements or on newly discovered implementation approaches are suppressed or "abstracted out." Abstract interface specifications specify modules having many acceptable implementations.

At a minimum, the goal of information hiding is that only very unlikely changes should be allowed to affect the interfaces of widely-used modules. The software module structure described in Section 4 is an information hiding module structure.

2.1 The Training System Program

The Training System Program started in September, 1984, with the purpose of developing a computer-based training system to support several data collection and processing systems developed and maintained by the government. The initial training system contract was awarded based on the success of a prototype that demonstrated the feasibility of enhancing training by means of computer-aided instruction.

Following a successful System Definition phase, the customer redirected the effort to incorporate SCR concerns. The rationale for the redirection was (1) to reduce risk associated with the history of frequent and significant upgrades experienced with the data collection and processing systems, and (2) to experiment with the SCR technology in the development of a new system. To support the redirection, SCR research publications were provided. Although these documents were not complete from an acquisition point of view, they provided an adequate starting point from which to explore the methodology, which was enhanced and referred to as Software Engineering Principles (SEP) technology.

The training system consists of 26 Zenith 286 microprocessors, networked via Ethernet. System users consist of students, courseware authors, instructors, and administrators. Instructors have the ability to interact with and monitor students as they are actively training.

3.0 EXPECTED CHANGES

The information-hiding principle underlying SCR and SEP technology requires early identification of changes that are expected or that appear to be logical evolutions of the system. The changes should be based on customer inputs, identified and prioritized during the System Definition phase, and be presented for review during the System Requirements Review. Following customer approval, the expected changes are included in standard requirements specifications and designers are held accountable for a design architecture that addresses these concerns.

The following list comprises the expected changes identified during the System Definition phase for the computer-based training system:

—terminal interface

—underlying operating system

—networking environment, e.g., Ethernet

—simulation messages and displays, e.g., menus, queries, prompts

—simulation timing

—simulation commands

—student evaluation criteria and reports

—student monitoring formats

—authoring exchange necessary to create/modify scenarios

—specifications for key data structures

—access policies for key data structures

—run-time environment

—language implementation

—additional authors, students, and instructors

—additional classroom management tools

This list was updated and additional expected changes identified during the Preliminary and Critical Design phases as more of the expected behavior of the target systems was better understood. For example, as the physical data requirements were determined during the Critical Design Phase, detailed access policies were formulated and included as secrets of the appropriate data modules.

The expected change list was generated by reviewing modifications made to the target data collection and processing systems during the previous five years and by extensive interviews with customer representatives. To provide rapid access by maintenance personnel to areas of concern within the documentation, the expected changes were grouped in the following way in the System Specification documentation:

—hardware related

—required-behavior related

—implementation related

These initial groups provided a starting point for architecture efforts.

4.0 SOFTWARE MODULE STRUCTURE

The software module structure is quite similar to the SCR module structure [2]. The structure is hierarchical where each higher-level module hides the design decisions encompassed by its descendents. The first two levels provide a logical road map for identifying what collections of software components might need to be modified and thus probably apply to any system. The lower levels correspond more closely to software packages. There were four levels in the software hierarchy, the first level of which consisted of the following:

—the Hardware-Hiding module

—the Behavior-Hiding module

—the Software Decision-Hiding module

4.1 Hardware-Hiding Module

The Hardware-Hiding module comprises modules that need to be modified when hardware is replaced or modified. The Hardware-Hiding module includes, i.e., is decomposed into, the Extended Computer and the Device Interface modules.

Extended Computer Module. The Extended Computer module hides those characteristics of the hardware/software interface that are likely to change if the computer is modified or replaced. It offers a virtual computer for the remaining software. The major submodule of the Extended Computer module is the Virtual Operating System (VOS) module which hides some of the peculiarities and changeable features of the OS version used initially. It should be noted that the VOS offers features "close" to the original OS; in other words, we were careful not to commit ourselves to the design of a new OS.

Device Interface Module. The Device Interface module comprises two submodules—the Virtual Network Interface (VNI) and the Virtual Terminal (VTM) modules. The VNI module hides the commercial network software being used. The abstract interface specifications written for this module identify abstract network primitives for establishing a circuit, sending a message, and receiving a message. If the technology for establishing a circuit or sending a message changes, other modules using the VNI service routines do not have to be modified.

The Virtual Terminal module insulates the system from changes to the terminal by providing primitives for screen display and keyboard drivers. The display output device is managed as a set of windows, each with characteristics to simulate portions of target screen displays. The virtual interface provides the capability to change screen characteristics without affecting existing software. The Virtual Terminal Interface hides the physical characteristics of the display device, locations of the devices, and windowing mechanisms.

Figure 4.1-1. provides a block diagram of the Hardware-Hiding Module.

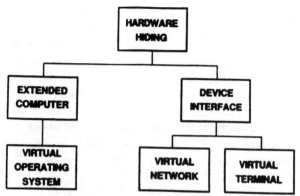

Figure 4.1-1. Hardware-Hiding module.

4.2 Behavior-Hiding Module

The Behavior-Hiding module comprises modules that need to be modified if there are changes to the required system behavior specified in the System Technical Specification. The Behavior-Hiding module is decomposed into two second-level modules: the Application Driver module and the Shared Service module.

Application Driver Module. The Application Driver (AD) module is the sole controller of sets of closely related outputs. Each submodule hides the rules determining the values of the outputs and the data structures and algorithms necessary to implement the outputs. Expected changes dealt with in the AD modules include the authoring exchange necessary to create and maintain scenarios, the system administrator exchange necessary to maintain target system data bases, the system administration classroom management policies, the processing unique to specific target system simulations, the student evaluation processing and criteria, and the student monitoring processing. Changes of this type should be confined to the appropriate submodule.

Shared Service Module. The Shared Service module comprises software that controls required external behavior common to two or more AD modules. The Shared Service modules hide the characteristics of the shared behavior and the algorithms and data structures necessary to implement the shared behavior. Some of the secrets of the Shared Service module include AD module initialization, menu services, and control structures common to the AD modules. A change in any of these areas is isolated to the Shared Service modules, even though the change may affect an external behavior shared by many application modules.

It should be noted that all required system behavior is provided by the Behavior-Hiding modules. During preliminary architecture efforts, design credibility is established by mapping the required system behavior identified in the System Requirements Specification to

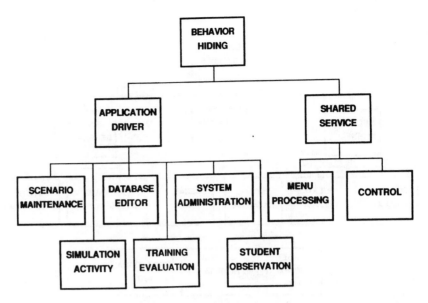

Figure 4.2-1. Behavior-Hiding module.

these modules. Any requirements not mapped to a module or mistakenly mapped to a Hardware-Hiding or Software-Decision Hiding module provide areas to revisit the system architecture. Several discrepancies of this type were found during the design effort.

Figure 4.2-1 provides a block diagram of the Behavior-Hiding modules.

4.3 Software Decision-Hiding Module

The Software Decision-Hiding module comprise the modules that need to be modified if there are changes to designer-generated decisions. For example, the choice of a specific algorithm not specified in the System Requirements Specification is a designer-generated decision.

The Software Decision-Hiding module is decomposed into three second-level modules: the Scenario Interface module, the Data base Utilities module, and the System Generation module.

Scenario Interface Module. The Scenario Interface module hides changes to the scenario validation policies, the translation process from the external scenario language utilized by the authors to the internal scenario primitives, and the execution of those primitives. All algorithms to parse, validate, translate, and execute the scenarios are hidden in these modules. These changes were allocated to Software Decision-Hiding modules because the specific language implementation necessary to support required system behavior was designer-determined.

Data base Utilities Module. The Data base Utilities module consists of software that needs to be modified if

changes are made to the data base management system or to the internal storage, retrieval, or maintenance policies. To insulate application modules from the underlying data base management system, a Virtual Data base Interface module is provided. It provides the file management primitives necessary to support indexed sequential access data retrieval. Any changes to the data access policies are limited to this module.

Scenario Generation Module. The System Generation module hides the expected changes related to the software processing environment and the underlying language. It hides the command structures necessary to compile and link the software, values of system generation parameters that select different implementations of a module, and specialized test software.

The Language Implementation module provides an area to discuss features unique to the specific implementation chosen. Originally, the goal was to abstract out the underlying language implementation. Since this was cost prohibitive, it provided an area to discuss the language specific decisions that might affect program portability.

Figure 4.3-1 provides a block diagram of the Software Decision-Hiding modules.

5.0 DATA ANALYSIS

5.1 General

From August, 1988, until March, 1989, project engineers reported design and code problems found during the integration and testing of the system upgrade. This period coincided with the Software Integration and Test (August, 1988–January, 1989) and the System Integration and Test phases (Feb, 1989–April, 1989). The upgrade consisted of several thousand lines of code,

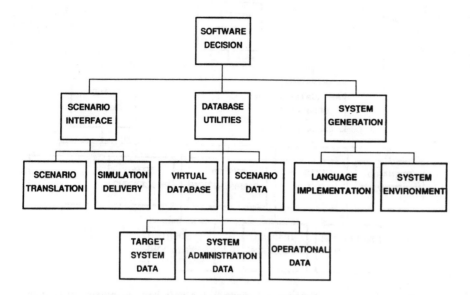

Figure 4.3-1. Software Decision-Hiding module.

spanning several of the expected changes identified in Section 3. Two hundred and thirty software problems were identified, 14 of which were attributed to user error and deleted. The remaining 216 were resolved and the related documentation updated.

Based on the expected change list generated during the System Definition phase and refined during the architecture phases, of the remaining 216 SPRs, 201 were directly related to expected system changes. This was not surprising since the expected change list was not static but evolved as the contractor and customer solidified future system evolutions.

These problems were subsequently logged, reviewed, and a course of action determined by the Configuration Control Board (CCB). The CCB consisted of the program manager, lead system engineer, lead software engineer, system test director, and the configuration manager. The CCB met aperiodically based on the number and magnitude of the problems reported.

SPR Accumulation. Figure 5.1-1 and 5.1-2 are profiles of the resolution activity for the proposed changes.

Although all SPRs required the approval of the CCB before final resolution, Figure 5.1-1 indicates that for the majority of the SPRs, there were no significant delays between submission and resolution. The increased number of SPRs submitted during the December to March time frame is reflected in the increased effort during this period (Figure 5.1-2).

5.2 Data Collection Forms

Figure 5.2-1, 5.2-2, and 5.2-3 show the problem report forms. The Software Problem Report (SPR) in Figure

5.2-1 is filled out by a project engineer and submitted to the configuration manager. The configuration manager logs the SPR and schedules a CCB meeting when a sufficient number of SPRs are collected or the magnitude of a specific SPR requires immediate attention.

The CCB validates the information on the SPR and determines a course of action. In most cases, an engineer is assigned the responsibility for making the necessary modifications to the software and documentation and performing regression testing. Following successful regression testing, the Software Modification Transmittal (SMT) form is completed, logged, and returned to the CCB for disposition.

The SMT form is tailored to collect the information necessary to validate the SEP decomposition strategy and resulting architecture, i.e., minimize the impact of implementing expected changes.

Figure 5.1-1. SPR accumulation.

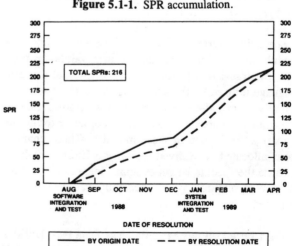

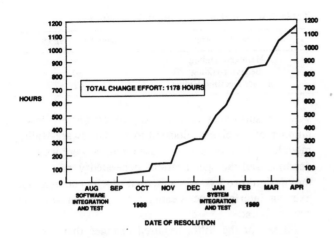

Figure 5.1-2. Cumulative effort in resolving SPRs.

The TYPE OF CHANGE field contains entries for SOFTWARE, SCENARIO, DATA BASE, DOCUMENTATION, and OTHER. During the architecture definition phases, designers were directed to encapsulate several of the high-probability changes in the data structures (scenario/data base). Tools were to be generated and delivered with the system to support updates in these areas.

Other architectural issues related to the number of modules impacted by a change, the total effort required

Figure 5.2-1. Software problem report.

```
                                        SPR NO: _____
         SOFTWARE PROBLEM REPORT        I&T NO: _____
                                        SHEET _____ OF _____
ORIGINATOR/ORG: _____    EXT: ____  DATE: _____
PROBLEM AREA:   SOFTWARE ____  HARDWARE ____  DOCUMENTATION ____
                INTERFACE ____  OTHER ____

PROBLEM WITH:   ROUTINE ____   DATABASE ____  DOCUMENT ____
                SCENARIO ____  TEST FILE ____ OTHER ____

PROBLEM IDENTIFIED DURING:  ANALYSIS ____   DESIGN ____ OTHER ____
                            SOFTWARE TEST _____ SYSTEM TEST ____
IF TEST : THREAD/CATEGORY _____  CASE/SEGMENT _____

BRIEF DESCRIPTION :

DETAILED DESCRIPTION:

PROBABLE CAUSE:

IMPACT:

RECOMMENDATIONS/REMARKS:
MODULES REQUIRED FOR FIX:
DOCUMENT UPDATES REQUIRED:

SETD APPROVAL: _____  DATE: _____

              ** CM USE ONLY **
   DATE LOGGED: _____  PRIORITY: _____
   ACTION ASSIGNEE: _____  CMO: _____
   CCB ACTION: _____  DATE: _____
   RESOLUTION DATE: _____ SMT NO: ____ DOCS UPDATED _____
```

```
                                    SMT NO: _____
SOFTWARE MODIFICATION               DATE: _____
    TRANSMITTAL                     SHEET _____ OF _____
                                    SPR NO: _____
                                    I&T NO: _____

ORIGINATOR/ORG: _____  EXT: ____  DATE: _____

MODULE NAME: _____  BASELINE ID: _____

CLASSIFICATION OF FILES:
TYPE OF CHANGE:  SOFTWARE _____ SCENARIO ____ DATABASE ____
                 DOCUMENTATION ____ OTHER ____

SOFTWARE AFFECTED: _____

DIRECTORY/LOCATION: _____

SOURCE FILE NAME/BRIEF        CHANGED/ADDED    NEW/LAST
  DESCRIPTION OF CHANGE         DELETED        REVISION


DOCUMENTATION AFFECTED:
   DOCUMENT ACCESSION #S        DOCUMENT TITLE/VOLUME/DATE


   FAILURE CAUSE:         TOTAL          LABOR
                          CORRECTION TIME GRADE
                                         09-ENG
___ (1) REQUIREMENT CHANGE               10-AE
___ (2) MISINTERPRETATION OF REQUIREMENT 12-SE
___ (3) CHANGE TO TARGET SYSTEM          14-PE
___ (4) MISINTERPRETATION OF DOCUMENTATION
___ (5) IMPROPER DESIGN           TOTAL NUMBER OF:
___ (6) IMPROPER IMPLEMENTATION OF DESIGN  MODULES CHANGED -
___ (7) TIMING/SIZING                      LOC CHANGED    -
___ (8) DATABASE ERROR
___ (9) INTERFACE ERROR
___ (10) OTHER _____
```

Figure 5.2-2. Software modification transmittal.

Figure 5.2-3. Software modification transmittal (cont).

```
                                    SMT NO: _____
SOFTWARE MODIFICATION               DATE: _____
    TRANSMITTAL                     SHEET _____ OF _____
                                    SPR NO: _____
                                    I&T NO: _____

ADDITIONAL COMMENTS:




FOLLOWING ITEMS UPDATED/DELIVERED:

_____ SOURCE            _____ MDF/TDF
_____ STS               _____ DATABASE
_____ MIMPS             _____ TEST PROCEDURE
_____ MINTS             _____ STREAMING TAPE
_____ USER GUIDE        _____ OTHER: _____


            ** CM/SETD USE ONLY ****
CCB APPROVAL: _____        DATE: _____
CCB APPROVAL/RECORDED: _____     DATE: _____
STATUS OF SOFTWARE CHANGES:  OPEN: ____  CLOSED: _____
STATUS OF DOCUMENTATION CHANGES: OPEN: ____ CLOSED: ____

INTEGRATION AND TEST:  ACCEPTED: ____ YES ____ NO
I&T COMMENTS:




TEST BASELINE: _____
SETD APPROVAL: _____      DATE: _____
MASTER BASELINE UPDATED BY: _____  DATE: _____
COMMENTS:
```

45

Table 5.3-1. Line of Code Relationship

Functional Area	Line of Code
Hardware-Hiding	
Virtual Operating System	2183
Virtual Network	1071
Virtual Terminal	2869
Behavior-Hiding	
Scenario Maintenance	3455
Data Base Editor	1675
System Administration	1740
Simulation Activity	12254
Training Evaluation	1724
Student Observation	946
Menu Processing	4599
Control	718
Software Decision-Hiding	
Scenario Translation	2563
Simulation Delivery	3417
Virtual Data Base	602
System Data	2622
Target Data	2556
System Administration Data	1946
Operational Data	1631

Table 5.3-2. SPR to Functional Area Mapping

Functional Area	Number of SPRS
Hardware-Hiding	9
Behavior-Hiding	80
Software Decision-Hiding	72

to implement a change (software and documentation), and the lines of code required. The LABOR GRADE field was necessary to support the costing analysis associated with the updates.

The FAILURE CAUSE field proved to be extremely difficult to determine. Currently, this data is being reviewed for accuracy by lead engineers and was not used in any of the analysis for this report.

It should be noted that the testing team did not focus on documentation errors; only those documentation updates related to software modifications were performed.

5.3 Analysis

The computer-based training system consisted of approximately 49,000 lines of code and an additional 25,000 data base records. Table 5.3-1 provides the lines of code for each of the modules described in the architecture section. The Simulation Activity module was further decomposed into three fourth-level target system-specific modules.

There was no effort to restructure the architecture based on the size or complexity of a module. The decomposition strategy relied entirely on encapsulating expected changes within logical components of the system. Several of the larger modules were partitioned into lower-level work assignments to satisfy schedule and span of control issues.

Areas of Change. Table 5.3-2 was generated by totaling the number of SPRs written against each of the functional areas. SPRs which spanned more than one functional area were counted for each of the areas. It

was not surprising to see a disproportionately lower number of problems allocated to the Hardware-Hiding modules. The interfaces to these modules were well-understood and the specifications generated very early in the design process. Commercial documentation and existing interface specifications provided an adequate starting point.

Fifteen of the SPRs required changes that spanned two functional areas. Most of these "correlated" changes were to the Simulation Delivery and the Simulation Activity modules. This was to be expected because changes in the required simulations would potentially affect the delivery mechanism as well as the underlying simulation. Changes to the Simulation Delivery module were minor and related more to the control mechanisms necessary to invoke the proper simulation activity function. There were no updates that required changes to modules in all three functional areas.

Table 5.3-3 provides the SPR to module mapping. A significant portion of the SPRs related to changes in the Simulation Activity and the Simulation Delivery modules. There are two reasons for this imbalance: the lack of technical documentation clearly specifying the expected behavior of the target systems and the number of lines of code required to implement the simulations.

Table 5.3-3. SPR to Module Mapping

Functional Area	SPRS
Hardware-Hiding	
Virtual Operating System	3
Virtual Network	1
Virtual Terminal	5
Behavior-Hiding	
Scenario Maintenance	10
Data Base Editor	5
System Administration	6
Simulation Activity	33
Training Evaluation	7
Student Observation	7
Menu Processing	7
Control	5
Software Decision-Hiding	
Scenario Translation	12
Simulation Delivery	40
Virtual Data Base	3
System Data	6
Target Data	3
System Administration Data	1
Operational Data	5

Table 5.3-4. Number of Modules Relationship

Percent of SPRS	Number of Modules Affected
33	0
53	1
11	2
3	> 2

System specification materials for these modules relied heavily on the technical accuracy of the existing target system documentation. In some areas, the documentation was out of date and designers found it necessary to interview operators familiar with the systems. In some cases, the operational software had not been deployed and designers relied on ''informal'' as-built documentation. Designers were aware of the potential problems with this approach and structured the system to accommodate these discrepancies easily.

Updates to these modules usually required updates to the associated target system data bases.

Ease of Change. The structure of the software architecture was optimized to support the implementation of the expected changes identified in Section 3. Although it is difficult to provide an objective measure to gauge the success of this strategy, designers were instructed to minimize the ripple effect of implementing these changes. During the design reviews, each expected change was discussed and its impact on the architecture noted. In some cases, there was a tradeoff between cost and architecture considerations. For example, although the chosen version of PASCAL contained several language extensions, isolating language-dependent features was not possible (cost and schedule) within the scope of the contract. Table 5.3-4 provides a mapping between the percent of SPRs and the number of modules affected by the change. It shows that 86% of the required updates affected one or fewer modules. A change that impacted zero modules was a data base or scenario update. No recompilation of software was required for these updates and tools were provided to simplify the process.

Table 5.3-5 presents the same data restricted to expected changes. There were no SPRs related to expected changes that impacted more than two modules.

Figure 5.3-1 presents the same data in a time line

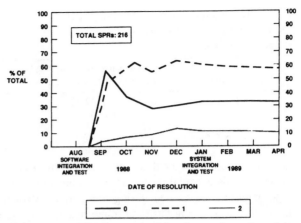

Figure 5.3-1. SPRs categorized by the number of modules changed.

graph. From December through March, the percentage of SPRs that affected one module remained fairly constant at approximately fifty-seven percent. During the same time period, the percentage of SPRs that impacted zero modules was approximately thirty-three percent. There was no significant percentage increase or decrease in the percentage of SPRs that affected two or more modules. The initial increase in zero module impacts can be attributed to the types of problems which would surface most easily during the initial stages of testing. These changes were typically related to the contents of the data bases (screen messages or displays) or scenarios (sequencing of messages and displays).

Effort. Table 5.3-6 shows the relationship between an SPR and the number of hours required to solve the SPR. It shows that 85% of the SPRs required eight or fewer hours to complete. If the SPRs were restricted to only those related to the Expected Change list, then approximately 75% of the required changes were completed in three or fewer hours (Table 5.3-7).

Figures 5.3-2 and 5.3-3 present the effort data in time line graphs. By December, the percentiles found in Table 5.3-6 and Table 5.37 were fairly established; approximately 35% of the SPRs required one or fewer hours to resolve while 48% of the SPRs required between one to two hours to resolve. Figure 5.3-2 suggests that during the later stages of testing, the

Table 5.3-5. SPRs—Number of Modules Relationship Restricted to Expected Changes

Percent of SPRS	Number of Modules Affected
37	0
57	1
6	2
0	> 2

Table 5.3-6. Number of Hours to Implement Change—Percent of SPRs

Number of Hours	Cumulative Percent of SPRS
1	35
2	48
3	57
3 < Hours < 8	85

Table 5.3-7. Number of Hours to Implement Change—Percent of SPRs Restricted to Expected Changes

Number of Hours	Cumulative Percent of SPRS (Restricted to Expected Changes)
1	49
2	67
3	74
3 < hours < 8	96

amount of effort required to solve each SPR was increasing. This is explained by closer examination of the type of testing performed during this period. Most of the test threads during this time frame related to system level transactions designed to expose errors between module interfaces.

Module Size and Error Occurrences. The following tables/graphs relate some of the previous statistics to the module size.

Initially it was thought that there was some relationship between the size of a module and the number of detected errors. To explore this issue, the number of SPRs was mapped to modules normalized in 1000 lines of code increments. If the number of errors/1000 executable lines of code was found to be consistent over module size, this would show size independence. Table 5.3-8 suggests that there is a higher error rate in smaller-sized modules.

There are several potential explanations for this unexpected behavior. One possible explanation is that the larger modules were coded with more care because of their size. On a more pessimistic note, there may be numerous undetected errors within the larger modules due to the scope of the testing required to fully exercise all module paths. If this is the case, then post-deployment maintenance data will reveal numerous additional errors in these modules. One particular data point needs further explanation. The 5000 lines of code and signif-

Figure 5.3-2. Percentage of SPRs in each of the effort categories as a function of time.

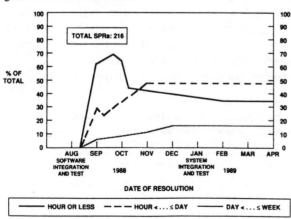

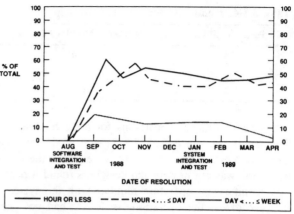

Figure 5.3-3. Percentage of expected change SPRs in each of the effort categories as a function of time.

icantly lower 1.4 error rate data point in Table 5.3-8 relates to the Menu Processing module. This application module was an important part of several system level test threads. Consequently, to reduce the number of problems occurring during system level testing, the module was extensively tested at the unit level.

Table 5.3-9 shows the relationship between the module size and the average number of hours to implement the related SPRs. With the exception of the Menu Processing data point, the trend is toward an increasing effort to resolve SPRs for the larger modules.

Categorizing the data using different module bucket sizes (1000, 2000, 4000, 8000, 16000) did not provide any additional meaningful data.

Table 5.3-10 shows the relationship between the module size and the average number of lines of code for the related SPRs. There is no obvious relationship suggested by the data.

The 21.5 LOC data point corresponds to updates to the Simulation Activity module. The "high" LOC count is mostly based on the need to add functionality

Table 5.3-8. Module Size to Number of Errors

Module Size	Number of Errors/1000
1000	15
2000	12.5
3000	9.6
4000	12.5
5000	1.4
> 5000	2.7

Table 5.3-9. Module Size to Number of Hours to Implement Change

Module Size	Average Number of Hours/Change
1000	4.1
2000	3.4
3000	5.0
4000	6.4
5000	1.5
> 5000	8.3

Table 5.3-10. Module Size—Lines of Code per Change

Module Size	Average Number of Loc/Change
1000	10.3
2000	7.0
3000	3.8
4000	16.0
5000	6.0
> 5000	21.5

not properly specified for the underlying target systems.

Figure 5.3-4 shows the cumulative average hours to resolve each of the SPRs. Separate graphs are plotted for SPRs and SPRs related to expected changes.

CONCLUSIONS

An overview of the project's early change data with respect to project goals revealed some initial trends:

—Generating and prioritizing expected changes early in the definition phases and modularizing the system to encapsulate these changes has the potential to significantly reduce the effort required to implement these changes (Table 5.3-6, Figure 5.3-2, Table 5.3-9, Figure 5.3-4).

—Generating and prioritizing expected changes and modularizing the system to encapsulate these changes has the potential to greatly reduce the rippling effects when implementing changes (Tables 5.3-4, 5.3-5, Figure 5.3-1).

Although it is difficult to quantify these ''reductions'' due to the unavailability of industry-wide metrics, readers are encouraged to compare this data with in-house metrics.

Other results of interest to application developments based on the SCR methodology include:

—The number of problem reports generated against the Hardware-Hiding modules was significantly lower

Figure 5.3-4. Cumulative resolution time as a function of time.

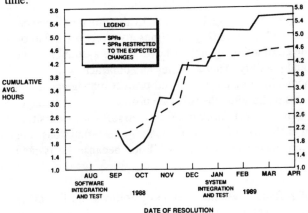

than the Behavior-Hiding and the Software Decision-Hiding modules. This statistic has the potential to affect future testing strategies by focusing efforts on the areas of concern (Table 5.3-3).

—There was no perceivable relationship between a module size and the number of detectable errors attributed to the module (Table 5.3-8).

The computer based training system was deployed in May, 1989. Part of the maintenance effort includes a task to collect and maintain metrics data throughout the life cycle of the product. The additional data points should add credibility to the initial reports by allowing the generation of formal statistical parameters to verify data relationships.

In addition, the Software Modification Transmittal forms are being updated to provide more visibility into the failure cause data.

REFERENCES

1. B. Boehm, Software and its impact: A quantitative assessment, *Datamation*, May (1973).
2. K. Britton and D. Parnas, A7-E software module guide, *NRL Memorandum Report 4702*, 8 December (1981).
3. P. Clements, Software cost reduction through disciplined design, *NRL Memorandum*, 22 Feb (1985).
4. J. A. Hager, Software engineering principles study report, *NRL Report*, April (1988).
5. K. Heninger, Specifying software requirements for complex systems: New techniques and their application, *NRL Memorandum*, April (1979).

Additional Readings

V. Basili and T. Perricone, Software errors and complexity: An empirical investigation, *Communications of the ACM*, January (1984).

Chmura, Norcio, Wicinski, Design changes in the software cost reduction program, *NRL Report 9124*, June 30 (1988).

R. Grady, Measuring and managing software maintenance, *IEEE Proceedings on Quality Assurance*, September 1987.

J. A. Hager, Designing for change, *Proceedings of the 7th NSIA International Conference*, May 1987.

J. A. Hager, Designing for change: An ada design tutorial, *Proceeding of the National Conference on Ada Technology*, March, 1989.

J. A. Hager, Developing maintainable systems: A full life-cycle approach, *Proceedings of the Conference on Software Maintenance*, October 1989.

J. Kmiecik (Principal Investigator), Software cost reduction requirements guideline, *Report No. SRSR-NRL-84-001*, 24 August 1984.

D. Parnas, P. Clements, and D. Weiss, Enhancing reusability with information hiding, *Proceedings of the Workshop on Reusability in Programming*, 7–9 September 1983, pp. 240–247.

J. Stockenberg, DWS/CS emergency preset extensions to the A-7E methodology, March 1983.

Wallace, Stockenberg, Charette, *A Unified Methodology for Developing Systems*, McGraw-Hill, 1987.

Software Acquisition Management

John J. Marciniak, CTA Incorporated
and
Donald J. Reifer, RCI

Software acquisition management is the process of acquiring custom software, usually by contract from some third party. This article introduces you to the topic of software acquisition management and the management and engineering environment in which it takes place. The environment is described in terms of strategies, vehicles, and the processes employed to manage the acquisition of software. Planning and assessment functions that are important to acquiring a capable source are then discussed. Finally, the key assessment methods employed to provide visibility and control over the development as the acquisition unfolds are described.

Introduction

This paper is about acquiring, usually using a contract vehicle, custom software systems. One can immediately see that a caveat has been introduced — the word "custom." Simply stated, a custom system is one that cannot be procured in the commercial off-the-shelf market (Lotus 1-2-3, for example). Although a custom system may contain commercial software packages, it is typically built, or developed, because there are unique customer requirements.

Custom software systems may be developed internally by a firm's programming department. However, such systems are usually bought, or acquired, by hiring an external source (such as a software or systems contractor) because the firm does not have the right resources, skills, or experience to do the job within the desired time period. In either event, a written agreement, or contract, is used as the basis of system acquisition. The developer, or seller, takes a contract from the acquirer, or buyer, to deliver the system based on the cost, schedule, and functional and quality requirements contained within the agreement. The process of arranging for and administering the contract agreement, and managing the performance of the developer, is called acquisition management.

Custom software comes in a variety of categories from stand-alone systems that are totally composed of software to systems that have appreciable hardware content. In all cases, software acquisition management deals with the management of systems where there is extensive software development. These systems may range from those developed by the government for military, space, transportation, and other purposes to systems acquired in the private sector by banks, insurance companies, and a variety of other institutions. Although the development of the space shuttle was dominated by complex hardware, it had a large, critical software component. No matter the nature of the system, the acquisition of custom software follows basic acquisition management tenets.

Acquisition management

Software acquisition management activities include planning, contracting, budgeting, evaluating performance, and providing for future support of the system. As shown in Figure 1, the three organizations involved in acquisition management include the customer or user of the system, the contracting agency or buyer of the system, and the developer or seller. As scoped, there may be many people and possibly many agencies and contractors involved.

Figure 2 illustrates the relationship between software acquisition management and project management and software engineering. While software engineering concentrates on building the software product, project management focuses on managing the engineering development. As shown, there is an overlap between software acquisition management and project management. There are people in each activity who participate in both functions. For example, the software project manager also has acquisition management responsibilities because he is held accountable for meeting contract requirements.

Acquisition management environment. Acquisition of software systems commonly follows the life cycle depicted in Figure 3, which shows the three major phases: concept exploration, source acquisition, and performance management. During concept exploration, the buyer develops requirements, prepares functional specifications, and develops an acquisition management strategy. During source selection, a vendor is chosen to develop the system based on a proposal made by a single seller or multiple set of sellers. During performance management, the buyer monitors the seller's progress and compliance with contract provisions.

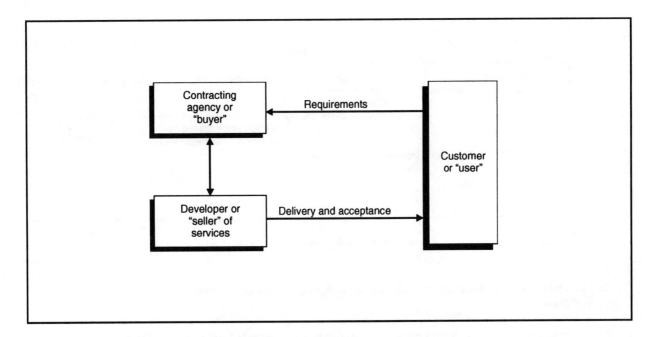

Figure 1: Acquisition Management Players

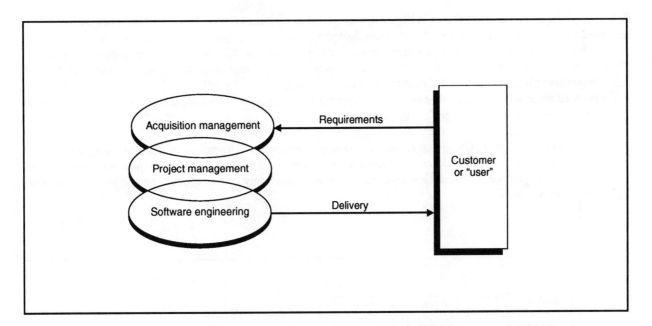

Figure 2: Acquisition Management Relationships

Acquisition management strategies. There are several acquisition strategies commonly used to acquire custom software systems. Selection of the best strategy is based on numerous technical, management, and financial factors. Typical factors that influence the selection process include cost, requirements volatility, risk, schedule, size, and uniqueness. For example, if the development is of low cost and risk, the acquisition strategy may be straightforward. You may select a source purely on price because other factors do not influence the development. If it is not simple, a more complicated strategy may be warranted. The primary goal is to use competitive forces whenever possible to keep the cost under control.

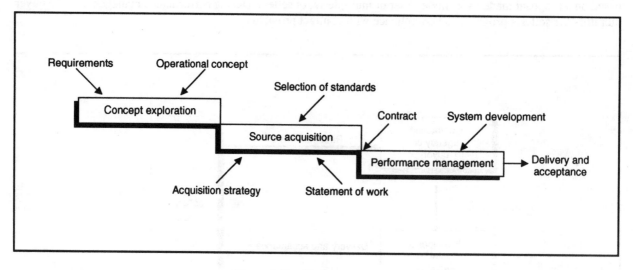

Figure 3: The Acquisition Life Cycle

The three basic types of acquisition strategies are competitive, two-phase, and sole source. Each is explained briefly as follows:

1. *Competitive acquisition.* With this strategy, sources, or sellers, compete for the job based on an open solicitation containing definitive requirements.

2. *Two-phase acquisition.* As shown in Figure 4, the development of the system is preceded by a competitive phase used to define requirements, develop alternate design approaches, or prototype implementations. This strategy is commonly used by the US government. In the initial phase several sellers, usually two to three, are selected to compete with each other against identical conditions (e.g., requirements, cost, schedule). After the competitive phase is concluded, a single source is usually selected for the full-scale development. This strategy places additional management burden on the buyer since the buyer must ensure all teams are treated fairly and none of the sources receives preferential treatment.

3. *Sole source acquisition.* Using this strategy, the buyer negotiates and awards a contract to a single seller. It is used when it is clear that only one supplier can do the job and a competitive procurement would be a waste of time and resources. A sole source contract, however, should only be awarded when it is clear that there is no other alternative.

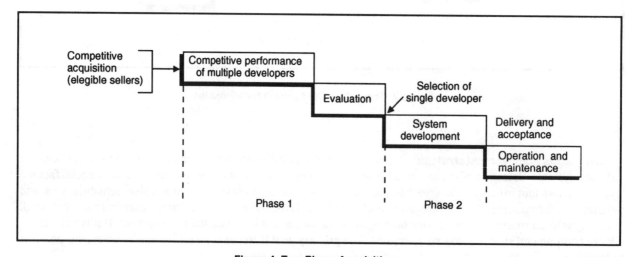

Figure 4: Two Phase Acquisitions

The procurement process. A great deal of work must be done before a source can be selected. Procurement plans must be prepared, management approaches must be developed, visibility and control provisions must be crystallized, documentation needs must be defined, schedule and cost estimates must be developed, and a draft contract must be readied. A key part of the package is the *Statement Of Work* (SOW) because it details the tasks that must be performed, their products, and documentation to be delivered as part of the contract. It also identifies how the management approach will be implemented because it defines the acceptance, configuration management, quality assurance, testing, training, and support processes used by the buyer to gain visibility into and control over the seller's activities.

This work results in a product called the solicitation package. The package typically contains the following items:

- Project Management Plan (PMP)
- System or software specification
- Operational Concept Document (OCD)
- Statement Of Work (SOW)
- Work Breakdown Structure (WBS)
- Documentation list (in US government acquisitions this is known as the contract data requirements list or CDRL)
- Schedule
- Independent cost estimate
- Evaluation criteria for selecting a source (sources are assessed against these criteria and not against each other)
- Draft contract
- Proposal preparation guidelines

To get feedback before the competition, this package may be sent by the buyer to cognizant sources for review and comment. A source list will be prepared to identify qualified bidders. A bidders' conference may be held to answer questions and communicate information to prospective bidders. Every effort is normally made to make the package as complete and comprehensive as possible prior to its release for bid.

The package that hits the street is called the *Request For Proposal* (RFP). Its contents include the procurement package and all those administrative and legal provisions required to comply with the law. For example, the federal and state governments require firms to comply with certain executive orders. Firms have their own requirements, especially when it comes to conflict of interest and accounting standards. Unions and labor contracts place still more constraints on prospective bidders. All of these must be communicated to the bidders so that they may factor them into their offers.

The steps in the procurement process

The five steps in a typical competitive procurement are shown in Figure 5 and detailed as follows:

1. *Reviewing the solicitation.* Once the solicitation package is completed, it is extensively reviewed within the buyer and user organizations. When the procurement is ready to proceed, a request for proposal (RFP) is prepared. The RFP contains everything by source selection sensitive items. As already noted, the buyer might make the draft RFP available to potential sellers prior to formal release to gain useful feedback. As the buyer's acquisition strategy unfolds, the seller evaluates the opportunity and prepares for the procurement. The seller must track the procurement as early as possible to have sufficient lead time to prepare a "winning" proposal. It will "market" the buyer to get the information needed to make a "bid/no bid" decision. If the decision is positive, the seller will acquire the required "bid and proposal" money and dedicate the resources needed to win the competition. Proposals are written only when the firm feels it has a good chance to win.

2. *Issuing RFP.* The RFP is sent to interested sellers. Usually, the list of qualified sellers is used for this purpose. This list may be compiled by formal advertisement in trade publications, journals, or government solicitations such as the *Commerce Business Daily*, or it may be prepared using existing source lists.

3. *Proposal preparation.* Any qualified source may submit a proposal after the RFP package is released. If go-ahead is approved, the seller staffs the proposal effort and goes after the "win." Proposal teams put their "win" strategies, proposal themes, offers, and technical backup on paper to show how they plan to meet the buyer's requirements.

4. *Proposal evaluation.* When the bids are closed and the proposals have been submitted, proposal evaluation and source selection begin. Each proposal is evaluated and scored against the criteria contained in the evaluation guide using standards developed for that purpose. A competitive range is established of those sources that have successfully met the requirements of the RFP. Sources that have not are notified and eliminated from further consideration. At this point the buyer has several options. It may elect to award the job to the offerer with the best price in the competitive range. Or additional information may be solicited to answer questions raised by the proposals, thus allowing bidders to clarify their offers. Proposal scores may be improved based on the answers to the buyer's questions. At this point in the process, several sources or a single source may be selected and negotiations may begin. Sometimes the buyer may solicit a *Best And Final Offer* (BAFO) to allow sellers to refine their cost proposals based on negotiations.

5. *Negotiations.* This is the final step in the process. Negotiations are held to update offers and seek concessions on either the buyer's or seller's part based on events that may have occurred during the source selection process. Technical, cost, legal, and other contract terms and conditions may be altered, as required, to implement the compromises made by both sides.

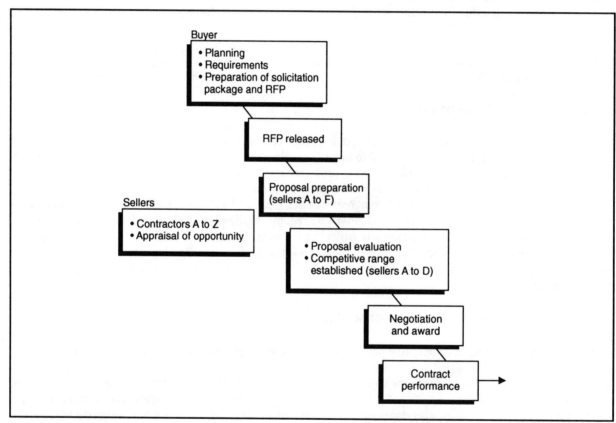

Figure 5: Steps in the Competitive Procurement Process

Contracting. Contracting is an important part of acquisition management. While obscured from most of the development team, the contract is a focus for many managers since it is the basis of all of the development effort. Administration of the contract has impact on the project throughout the life of the development.

There are at least four key people directly involved in contracting: the buyer's *contracting officer* (CO) and program/project manager, typically referred to as the *contracting officer's representative* (COR), and the seller's contracts manager and program/project manager. The CO handles all contract matters, while the COR provides the contractor with technical direction to fill in details, clarify or interpret the technical requirements, implement lines of inquiry, or otherwise serve to accomplish the technical goals of the contract.

For technical direction to be valid, it must meet the following conditions:

• It must be consistent with the scope of work set forth in the contract and its applicable requirements.
• It must not constitute a new assignment of work or change to the terms and conditions of the contract.
• It must not constitute a change in any contract consideration or contract delivery schedule.

To understand what direction can be given, program/project managers must understand contracting fundamentals, their roles, and the roles of the CO. They must also fully understand all of the provisions of their contract.

Types of contracts

The two basic compensation schemes used in contracts are fixed-price and cost reimbursement. Under a fixed-price contract, the buyer pays the seller a fixed sum for the agreed-upon goods and/or services. Because the price is fixed, the seller assumes the bulk of the risk during the development. Under a cost type contract, this risk is shared because the buyer agrees to reimburse the seller's allowable costs plus profit.

Fixed-price contracts. The four basic types of fixed-price contracts are as follows:

1. *Firm fixed-price (FFP).* A contract that is basically an agreement to pay a specified price upon delivery and acceptance of the goods or services.

2. *Fixed-price with economic price adjustment (FPEPA).* A form of fixed-price contract that includes a special clause allowing for economic price adjustments when they are needed to protect either or both parties from significant economic fluctuations in labor or material costs.

3. *Fixed-price incentive (FPI).* A fixed-price contract whose fee is varied and used to motivate the seller to increase efficiency or reduce cost. The incentive relates profits directly to performance goals.

4. *Fixed-price redetermination (FPR).* A fixed-price contract that has a means to shift certain indeterminable risks from the seller to the buyer after an initial price is negotiated. This form of contract could be used when specifications are not firm enough to allow for reasonable estimates of cost. The contract price is adjusted during the acquisition based on factors that were negotiated a priori.

Cost reimbursable contracts. The four basic types of cost reimbursement contracts are as follows:

1. *Cost or cost sharing (CS).* Under a cost or cost sharing contract, the seller receives no fee. In a cost contract, only the seller's allowable costs are reimbursed. In a cost sharing contract, the buyer and the seller agree on the ratio by which they will share costs. CS contracts are used for joint developments where both parties risk in order to share the rewards.

2. *Cost plus incentive fee (CPIF).* Similar to a fixed-price incentive contract, this form uses fee to motivate the seller to control costs. Negotiations set a target cost, a target fee, a ceiling price, and an adjustment formula. A minimum and maximum fee are established and related to performance goals.

3. *Cost plus award fee (CPAF).* The CPAF contract extends CPIF financial incentives into subjective areas by establishing a number of performance criteria whose finite measurements are difficult to quantify (e.g., quality, ease of use). The buyer and seller structure incentives based on the subjective evaluation of performance. The fee structure is then established so that there is a base fee and an award amount directly related to the criteria.

4. *Cost plus fixed fee (CPFF).* This type of contract reimburses the seller's allowable costs and pays a fixed fee. The CPFF contract is normally used for research and development efforts where the parties involved cannot reasonably predict the cost. As a result, the risks associated with the effort need to be shared.

There are several other contractual devices that may be employed in special circumstances.[1]

Selecting the appropriate contract type. Selecting the proper or appropriate contract clearly depends on many factors, the most important of which are as follows:

- Availability of qualified competition
- Availability of firm requirements
- The urgency of the needed system

- The risk associated with development
- The difficulty in assessing performance
- The size of the effort

Because the contract is the sole vehicle upon which the acquisition is based, proper selection of type is essential. Incentives reward diligence and cost avoidance. Risks should be shared and teamwork fostered by them. It should be remembered that neither the buyer nor the seller benefits when the contract is used inappropriately.

Planning for the acquisition

In an acquisition, project planning begins when the requirements start to be prepared. Because of the lead times involved in competitive acquisitions, buyer and seller resources must be put into place well in advance of the contract. The buyer must plan to get ready to manage performance, while the seller must plan on getting the job done.

There are two key planning documents in any software acquisition: the *Program Management Plan* (PMP) and the *Software Development Plan* (SDP). These planning documents set the stage for the project. The PMP sets the tone for the entire development. It establishes the management infrastructure and details how the buyer and seller will interact during the contract. Its focus is visibility and control, and it details how they will be implemented. In contrast, the SDP concentrates on software methods, tools, and resource issues. It provides the detailed information on how the software will be developed. When a PMP and SDP are prepared, redundancy is precluded by referring to relevant portions of each document rather than duplicating information in each.

Program management plan. Both the buyer and the seller typically develop their own PMPs to detail how and when the acquisition will take place and what resources are required to manage the acquisition. Since the buyer's PMP is part of the solicitation package, it is written before the RFP is released. The seller's plans respond to these and are usually prepared as a part of the proposal, or shortly after the contract is awarded. It would be best if these documents were prepared when the effort began. However, this may be difficult since the seller may not have sufficient resources to cover the expenses required to write a "winning" proposal. When the plans have been prepared before the award of the contract, the first task is to update them to incorporate any changes and to enrich areas that deserve further detail.

The plan serves as a road map through the project. It allows everyone to understand what work needs to be done, who is going to do it, and when it is going to get done. The plan helps everyone on the project to do his job by accomplishing the following objectives:

- It communicates the work and expectations to those doing it.
- It establishes a baseline for control over the work in process by establishing intermediate goals and milestones.
- It focuses the efforts of the team toward accomplishment of project-related objectives.
- It integrates the budgets and schedules so that the impact of slippage can readily be determined.
- It permits the seller to exercise control over the many obstacles that can impede acceptable delivery to the buyer and its customer.

An outline for a project management plan developed by the IEEE[2] is illustrated in Figure 6. Although software-oriented, most of the issues addressed within this plan are applicable throughout the full range of systems acquired contractually from third-party sources.

The management systems used to put the plan into action within most seller organizations usually revolve around some form of internal contract, or work package, between the program office and the performer organizations. For each work package, a budget and schedule are established based on the scope of work negotiated between the two functions. The program office establishes the requirements, while the performer organization determines how the work package will be done and who will perform it. The program office then monitors the performing organizations to make sure that the work performed tracks with the work paid for. If it does not, the program manager initiates action to find out why not.

The primary planning tool used by the software project manager is the *work breakdown structure* (WBS). The WBS is a family tree that decomposes the work to be performed hierarchically into its component parts so that short, well-defined tasks, each of which results in a deliverable product, are defined at each level of the decomposition. Assumptions can be made and risks identified as each task is defined in the accompanying WBS dictionary. The more detail included in this tree structure, the better the plan. The summary-level WBS is usually outlined in the RFP. The buyer typically requires the seller to use this structure when authoring a detailed WBS for the project.

Once the WBS has been defined, each of the tasks identified within it can be scheduled and resources can be estimated. Tasks can then be interrelated so that the critical path through the schedule network can be identified. This network and critical path can be used to analyze the impact of varying one task on another.

Software development plan. The single most important document for software development is the *software development plan* (SDP). This document places more emphasis on the technical aspects of the job than the managerial. It requires the developer to define its processes, methods, and tools in advance of doing the work. As shown in Figure 7, the SDP can be prepared incrementally in a just in time (JIT) manner. As one can immediately see by looking at the figure, there is overlap between a PMP and an SDP. In large projects this overlap is often obscured because tasks cross organizational boundaries. In a small project, the buyer and seller may choose to combine both plans into one document.

The manner in which the buyer and seller will interface, interact, and manage the project is defined in depth by these plans. The management infrastructure created by the seller responds directly to requirements contained within the contract. These in turn respond to the requirements that emanate from the buyer's PMP. If this is a government job, the infrastructure must respond to the myriad of regulations that govern acquisitions. If it is a commercial offering, many of the requirements may be simplified, but not eliminated.

Figure 6: Software Project Management Plan Outline

Title Page
Revision Sheet
Preface
Table of Contents
List of Figures
List of Tables

1.   Introduction
    1.1   Project Overview
    1.2   Project Deliverables
    1.3   Evolution of the Plan
    1.4   Reference Materials
    1.5   Definitions and Acronyms

2.   Project Organization
    2.1   Process Model
    2.2   Organizational Structure
    2.3   Organizational Boundaries and Interfaces
    2.4   Project Responsibilities

3.   Managerial Process
    3.1   Management Objectives and Priorities
    3.2   Assumptions, Dependencies, and Constraints
    3.3   Risk Management
    3.4   Monitoring and Controlling Mechanisms
    3.5   Staffing Plan

4.   Technical Process
    4.1   Methods, Tools, and Techniques
    4.2   Software Documentation
    4.3   Project Support Functions

5.   Work Packages, Schedule, and Budget
    5.1   Work Packages
    5.2   Dependencies
    5.3   Resource Requirements
    5.4   Budget and Resource Allocation
    5.5   Schedule

Additional Components
Index
Appendices

————————————

Source: ANSI/IEEE Std 1058.1-1987, *IEEE Standard for Software Project Management Plans,* IEEE, New York, 1987.

Figure 7: Software Development Plan Outline

1.   Scope

2.   Referenced documents

3.   Software development management
        Project organization and resources
        Schedule and milestones
        Risk management
        Security
        Interface with associate contractors
        Interface with IV&V agent(s)
        Subcontractor management
        Formal reviews
        Software development library
        Corrective action process
        Problem/change report

4.   Software engineering
        Organization and resources
        Software standards and procedures
        Nondevelopmental software

5.   Formal qualification testing
        Organization and resources
        Test approach/philosophy
        Test planning assumptions and constraints

6.   Software product evaluations

7.   Software configuration management

8.   Other software development functions

9.   Notes

10.   Appendixes

————————————

This outline is taken from the DOD-STD-2167A Data Item Documentation Standard (DI-MCCR-80030A).

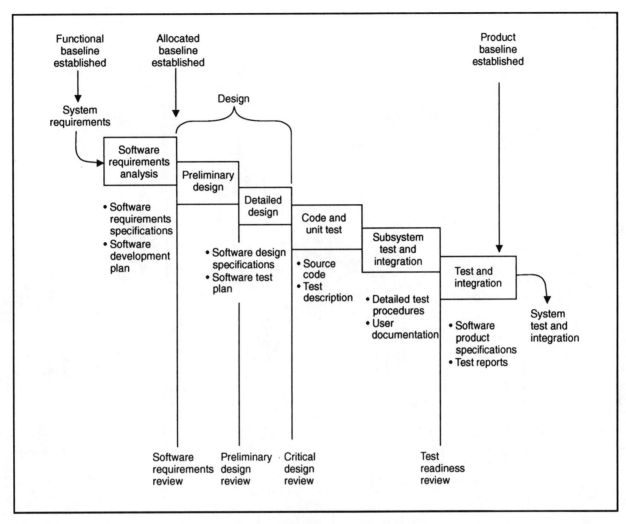

Figure 8: The Waterfall Software Development Process Model

Life cycle standards. Successful software development revolves around managing the processes, products, and people involved in the project. The mechanism used to structure the process and define the major activities associated with it is called a *life cycle model*. This process model serves as a mechanism for communicating what work tasks need to be done, when, and by whom to the managerial, technical, and user personnel associated with the project. Understanding this process is a prerequisite to figuring out how to manage a software acquisition.

The simplest process model for software development is the waterfall life cycle model. While advanced models are often used to structure the work in complex software developments, the waterfall model can be used to communicate the sequence of work that must be completed to develop a software product.

Figure 8 illustrates the software development cycle by defining the sequence of activities performed, the major reviews held, the configuration management baselines, and the typical products (documents and programs) generated in each of its phases. This waterfall model has been institutionalized in a number of standards. Guidelines and procedures have also been published to provide pointers on how to implement the process. These standards provide a basis for management, thus providing an acquisition infrastructure for the project.

In the management process, standards play a stabilizing role because they allow organizations to communicate in common terms with respect to a decision framework that everybody involved understands. Without standard practices and procedures, each management environment would be unique. There would be no consistency across projects, and each project would have to relearn what others have already learned. Both buyer and seller would have to train each project team in a new way of doing business, and the process of continuous improvement would break down because of the lack of continuity of experience.

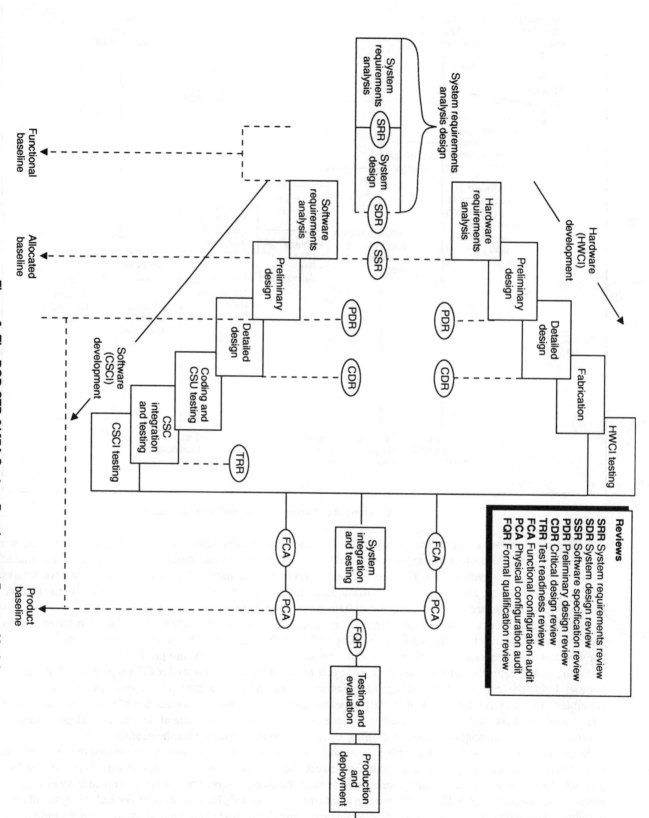

Figure 9: The DOD-STD-2167A System Development Process Model

Many standards have been developed for this reason. The two most popular public sources of life cycle process standards are the following:

1. *Department of Defense (DOD)*. The dominant software standard within the military is DOD-STD-2167A.[3] This standard is a management and engineering standard that sets forth requirements for software development and prescribes a "uniform software development process." It contains requirements in six areas: software development management, software engineering, software configuration management, software product evaluation, formal qualification testing, and transitioning to operational support. It establishes baselines used to control development and documentation that describes the products of development. Figure 9 depicts the sample development life cycle of the standard.

2. *Institute for Electrical and Electronics Engineers (IEEE)*. The IEEE has developed several software engineering standards. From a life cycle management perspective, the most pertinent one is the draft *Standard for Software Life Cycle Processes*.[4] This standard defines life cycle management processes, activities within each process, and the interrelationship of processes and activities. The standard permits the development of a project-specific life cycle. The model on which it is based, shown in Figure 10, has four processes: project management, predevelopment, development, and postdevelopment.

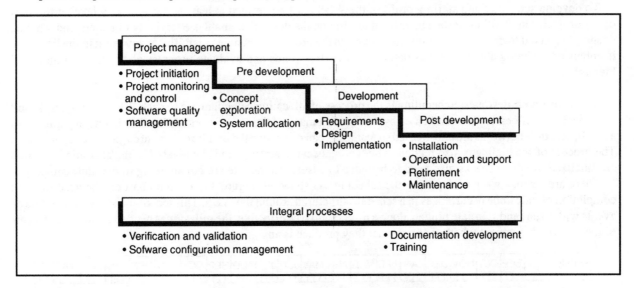

Figure 10: The IEEE Development Process Model

Other standards and life cycle models exist. The trick to using any of these effectively is to tailor and/or scale it to the unique needs of your project. Tailoring means eliminating requirements or document paragraphs. For example, a document is tailored when instructions to delete a section are included. Scaling refers to combining things in a way that makes sense for the project. For example, scaling may have you combine test plans, procedures, and reports using a test notebook instead of generating separate documents.

The project management environment

The PMP and SDP detail the engineering and management approaches to be used during the development. They specify how the project will be organized, what tasks will be performed, what schedules and budgets will be adhered to, what quality controls will be enforced, how configuration management will be done, what specific reviews will be held, how testing will be accomplished, and a host of other things. The key considerations that both of these plans need to address include organization and interfaces, activity structure, schedule and milestones, resources, support contractors, subcontractor management, software methodology, reviews, documentation, software environment, testing, product evaluations, and risk management.

Project organization and interface control. The software organization should be a highly visible part of the project structure. It should report high enough in the hierarchy to command the resources it needs to do its job effectively. Communications paths through the organization should be structured to expedite vertical as well as horizontal flows. Cross-functional teams should be formed to work on problems that cross organizational boundaries.

Working groups should be formed and used to focus resources on solving problems instead of just talking about them. Finally, plans to change the organizational structure as the project moves from definition through testing to operations also need to be made so that the right resources are available, when needed, to do the job.

The key to success in a software acquisition is to structure the organization around function to provide the buyer with visibility into and control over the development at the appropriate level. Balance is needed to avoid having the buyer "micro-manage." Single-point interfaces are also needed to limit the fragmentation that occurs when good people are asked to do too many things. These interfaces are also needed to limit the impact of the many organizations, both internal and external, that are chartered to help software developers to do their job (quality assurance, independent verification and validation, systems engineering, etc.). Focus must be preserved as developers are tasked to perform various work assignments. Administrative as well as technical support is needed so that they don't become overburdened.

Activity structure. As we already discussed, the work breakdown structure (WBS) permits managers to decompose the process of software development into activities, tasks, and work packages. But this decomposition cannot occur in a vacuum. It must relate what is being built to those who are building it. This allows managers to identify responsibility and delegate authority based on what work needs to be done. Budgets and schedules can be developed based on tasking. Using these, managers can hold people and organizations accountable for results.

To develop schedules and staffing profiles, the WBS must be defined at least at the summary level at the start of the project. The WBS must then be refined to provide the detail that enables everybody to understand what he or she is expected to do and how it impacts others and the project as a whole. Visibility at any point in the life cycle is enhanced by being able to use this detail to summarize status and evaluate progress at any level in the WBS hierarchy.

Schedule and milestones. Scheduling is the process of allocating calendar time to each WBS activity, task, and work package. Allocation is complicated by the fact that many of the tasks are interrelated and done in parallel. As a result, schedule networks are constructed so managers can determine the optimum way through the schedule maze. The process of scheduling is also related to budgeting because staffing must be leveled as the allocations of time are finalized. Realism checks also need to be made to ensure that people are not agreeing to the impossible.

There are various ways of depicting the schedule. As shown in Figure 11, a Gantt chart can be used to track completion of milestone occurrences in a schedule structured around the WBS. This technique shows a schedule of events with a start and stop date plotted along a time axis. To be effective, the milestones need to be defined in terms of the criteria that govern whether or not what they produce is any good.

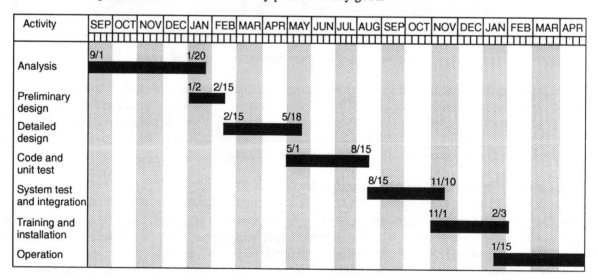

Figure 11: Example Gantt Chart

A popular method used to investigate the interrelationships between tasks is the *Project Evaluation and Review Technique/Critical Path Method* (PERT/CPM). As shown in Figure 12, this technique builds a schedule network that, when analyzed, permits managers to determine the impact of varying task schedules.

Often the schedule provided in the proposal is high level, containing somewhat superficial milestones such as design reviews and testing. While these may satisfy top-level management, they are not adequate for following a complex development project. The degree of visibility achieved is insufficient because the time between milestones is too great. To be effective, the events described should be spaced at fairly close intervals in the project. To accomplish this spacing, many PMPs and SDPs contain tiered schedules and schedule networks. These allow managers at each level of the organization to summarize the task schedule for which they are being held accountable.

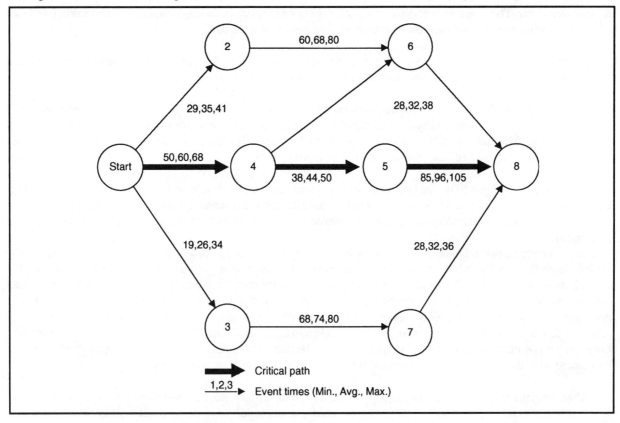

Figure 12: Example PERT/CPM Network Diagram

Resources. Budgeting is the process of allocating available resources (dollars, staff, machines, etc.) to WBS activities. Often what is available is not what was originally estimated or what is needed to do the job. While there may be logical reasons for these cutbacks, they don't make the job of optimizing the allocation of these sparse resources any easier. Even if there are not any cutbacks, staffing a project is difficult because the people with the needed skills just may not be available when the project needs them. No contractor has the full development team in place when the effort begins. Most of the people are committed and must transition off other projects gradually. Add to this the learning curves needed to address the impacts of new technology and the need for adequate machine resources and you will realize the difficulties involved in coming up with a realistic staffing projection as part of the PMP and the SDP.

Support contractors. In cases where suitable resources are not available, the buyer or the seller might consider acquiring the services of a support contractor. The areas considered for support are broad and depend on specific organizational and project needs. Areas in which support contractors could be employed include the following:

- Supplementing the engineering work force of the buyer and, more infrequently, the seller.
- Providing special expertise to the seller in such areas as database engineering, knowledge base engineering, and communications.
- Performing independent or beta testing of the product.
- Providing management support functions such as program control and quality assurance.
- Performing periodic assessments that are independent and focused.
- Preparing user documentation or technical publications.
- Handling distribution, training, and other user services.

Selection of support contractors should be based on competence. Often firms use support contractors to off-load work when there are limits placed on staff levels or when there are specific technical needs that their own staff cannot fulfill.

Types of support contractors. There are three basic categories of support contractors:

1. *Service firms.* These contractors provide a wide variety of support, including general data processing services such as software maintenance and operation of data processing facilities.

2. *System engineering and technical assistance (SETA) contractors.* SETA firms typically provide engineering support on a task order basis, most often to the buyer of the system.

3. *Independent verification & validation contractors.* An IV&V contractor provides an in-depth technical assessment of the software as it is developed and makes sure that the system to be delivered performs all intended operational functions. IV&V is normally performed by some independent third party. Therefore, added resources are required for the contract and for its management.

As part of the PMP and SDP, the impact of these support contractors should be factored into project schedules and budgets. Nothing good comes for nothing. Each of these firms must be managed, and each requires seller support. A tariff for the seller of 10 to 20 percent is not uncommon when a third party is hired by the buyer to keep tabs on its progress.

It is extremely important to define the manner in which the support supplier will interface with all players on the project. Both the seller's and the support firm's contracts should contain language that clearly defines roles and the conditions of involvement. For example, if the support contractor must have access to design documentation that is being issued by the seller, that requirement should be included in the seller's contract. Otherwise, it might not be provided when needed. The enabling clauses should specify what the support contractor needs and when that access is required. They should state the form of the deliverable and access rights of all parties concerned (for information only, for review only, etc.). If there is proprietary data, the support contractor may have to sign a confidentiality agreement with the seller. Access to subcontractor/supplier data should also be permitted.

Subcontractor management. The acquisition environment is often more complicated than a single buyer and single seller. As shown in Figure 13, there may be many players involved in the acquisition. On the buyer's side, there is always a user represented or a user community. In addition, the buyer may utilize support contractors for engineering support or IV&V. On the seller's side, the contractor may have teamed with several cocontractors or subcontractors. It may have hired a services firm to off-load work, and there are always the suppliers.

This complex acquisition environment makes the buyer's management job more difficult. The buyer cannot only manage the prime contract. To determine performance, the buyer must be able to get visibility into the status and progress of the subcontractors, suppliers, and service firms. Again, this visibility must be provided via contractual clauses. In addition, provisions from the prime contract should be passed through to the suppliers so that required controls are invoked by the prime on the subcontractors.

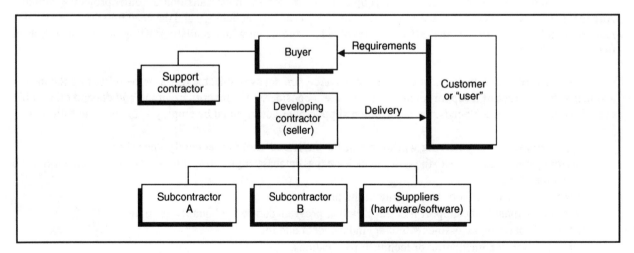

Figure 13: Buyer-Seller Relationships in an Acquisition

The issues associated with subcontractor management in an acquisition environment are many and include the following:

1. *Partition of work.* Often the prime seller dictates the terms of the agreement to the subcontractors. The seller strives to assemble the best possible team to win the contract. After contract award, however, the prime contractor can alter the team, usually to increase its overall proportion of the effort to obtain more direct labor revenue. This can result in a compromised technical effort.

2. *Price.* The prime can dictate pricing to the subcontractors. For example, if a third-party supplier bids on a cost plus fixed fee basis to the prime, while the prime bids on a fixed fee basis to the buyer, the negotiated price of third-party supplier tasks could be immeasurably more than the effort may seem to be worth. This may place the prime in a position of affording the seller a reduced price based on the seller's direct effort. Another problem is the pressure the prime can bring on a subcontractor during cost negotiations. In the need to develop a more cost-competitive price, the prime could pressure a third-party supplier to reduce its price without negotiating a reduction for those tasks assigned to the subcontractor. These situations are normally transparent to the buyer. However, they may show up during contract performance.

3. *Communication and visibility.* Since the buyer's primary interaction is with the prime contractor, subcontractor performance is often hidden from the buyer. The buyer must make sure that the seller provides visibility into its suppliers' progress. This means that suppliers should be asked to participate in reviews and other project activities. When large amounts of subcontracting are planned, the seller should be required to submit a subcontract management plan for buyer approval. Common methods, tools, and training should be emphasized so that the buyer views the seller as one team. The buyer should also make sure that the seller understands that it is held accountable for its team's performance, independent of whatever mechanisms it uses to maintain control over them.

4. *Management mechanisms.* The buyer should require that the management requirements that are placed on the seller's contract be passed through to the subcontractors. For example, project reviews and configuration management controls should be consistently applied throughout the project environment. If the buyer does not impose this requirement, the seller is left to its own desires and management approach. If the subcontractor is small, the seller has to be careful to avoid giving the supplier an unnecessary management burden.

There are many proven approaches to subcontract management available to the seller — for example, resident seller management teams placed in the subcontractor's plant to provide oversight management and make the day-to-day decisions have proven useful on large projects. As another example, tying a geographically dispersed team together via a computer network that exploits a common software environment has also proven effective. The key element of success is to recognize that "one team" needs to be formed and that common tools, methods, and training need to be employed. Both the PMP and SDP should address how this "one team" philosophy will be put into place so that the buyer can rely on the seller to manage its teammates.

Software methodology. Both the PMP and SDP should address the methodology used to develop and manage the overall software effort. The PMP discussion should address methodology from a management viewpoint. It should describe at a high level the software life cycle selected, methods used in each of its phases, reviews held, products prepared, tools employed, documents generated, standards used, and approaches taken for project, risk, configuration, and quality management. Issues that need to be addressed in the PMP include the following:

- Requirements traceability
- Methodology interaction and tool support
- Technology insertion mechanisms
- Approaches used for Total Quality Management (TQM)

Schedules, budgets, networks, and staff-loading diagrams at the program level should be included in the document, keyed to this top-level methodology. In addition, the integrated set of methods should be supported by a mature set of standards, practices, and tools.

The SDP addresses similar topics, but in more detail. The SDP communicates the task-level plans, while the PMP addresses plans at the activity level. The methodology is also described in more detail. Checklists for each life cycle phase are often included in the SDP to communicate to software engineers the engineering that needs to be done to produce acceptable products. Issues that should be addressed in the SDP include, but are not limited to, the following:

- Peer review strategies
- Design and coding standards
- Language conventions
- Reuse strategies
- Method clashes and their resolution
- Tool integration
- Quality controls

Detailed schedules, budgets, networks, and staff-loading at the task level should be included in the document, keyed to the methodology.

Reviews. Reviews are a key ingredient to sound software development. Reviews that should be considered include management reviews, formal project reviews, quality reviews, walk-throughs and inspections, and in-progress reviews. As noted, the review strategy should be described in the plans. Reviews are run for three purposes. First, they are used by management to gain insight into the development process. Second, they are used as an engineering tool to enhance and improve the product. Third, they are used as a consensus building tool to get the buyer and seller to buy into the engineering solution to the specified problem. Each type of review is briefly described as follows:

1. *Management reviews.* Most sellers set up a series of periodic internal management reviews for their projects. These are held to identify and work on problems before they get out of hand. Buyer participation in these reviews is not encouraged as they are held primarily for the seller to get its and its teammates' act together. Often these meetings get "down and dirty," and the real issues, many internal, are discussed.

2. *Formal reviews.* Formal reviews are the most visible type of review on a project. They are normally called out by the contract, which provides the requirements for their conduct. Formal reviews directly support the management of the engineering process and provide both the buyer and seller with insight into the development. Since the completeness of an activity is marked by the engineering products of that activity, project documentation is a prerequisite for the review. Often these reviews provide an opportunity for the buyer and seller to get together. Such communications are encouraged because misconceptions between the two need to be clarified as direction is given to the seller.

3. *In-progress reviews.* Most buyers conduct periodic management reviews on their projects to assess status, determine progress, and identify risks and work issues, both technical and managerial. The buyer helps the seller get the job done by handling those issues that are outside its control (customer meddling, lack of direction, etc.). Team members either are encouraged to participate or hold their own in-progress reviews.

4. *Peer reviews.* The most common type of technical review held within the project is the walk-through. The walk-through is an informal review in which the software engineer leads one or more members of the development team through a segment of design or code that he or she has written. The other team members ask questions and make comments about technique, style, possible errors, and other issues. Follow-up ensures that rework has been satisfactorily accomplished based on an action item list.

There has been a good deal of recent emphasis on formally structuring the walk-through with a process called software inspections.[5] A software inspection is a formal review in which a moderator leads a team of software engineers through a segment of design or code. The review is gauged based on previously defined criteria contained within a checklist. The checklist is based on both general and specific requirements for the project. Defects are documented and analyzed. Because of the rigor of the process, the results are better than those of normal "informal" walk-throughs. More defects are found earlier. As everyone now knows, the earlier that defects are discovered, the easier they are corrected, and the more reliable the system.

Reviews are activities, not just meetings. They take time to prepare for, conduct, and recover from. They must be planned and led, and they require follow-up. Getting ready for the review provides added value. During this time period, the materials for the review are developed, compiled, and assembled, and most of the engineering is accomplished. With walk-throughs, the planning process is also important because it forces participants to get ready for the review. Interaction, however, takes place during the peer meeting itself. After the review is conducted, postreview meeting actions must be documented, assigned, and monitored to ensure completion. Reviews should only be scheduled when they pay for themselves. Having too many is just as bad as not having enough.

Documentation. Documentation describes the results of the engineering process and its products, and provides instructions to the customer on how to use, operate, and maintain the system. Documentation is produced to capture the engineering results so that others can understand and benefit from them. Documentation should be an outgrowth of the process, not an end unto itself. It is important because it takes considerable time, talent, and effort to generate properly. Software documentation can be classified using the following three general categories:

1. *Product documentation* used to describe the engineering process and its products. It consists of specifications, listings, and test documents.

2. *Process documentation* describing the processes used to manage and engineer the system. It includes test plans, configuration management plans, quality assurance plans, and the software development plan.

3. *Support documentation* consisting of items such as manuals, tutorials, and version description documents.

Acquisitions typically produce more documentation because of the buyer's need to have visibility into the seller's progress. The key management issue to be resolved is how much documentation is enough. Typically, an existing standard such as the IEEE or DOD-STD-2167A standard is utilized. The selection of document type and tailoring/scaling of it must be based on the needs of the project. Often the buyer or seller is not smart enough to understand this, and, to try to protect the user, requires the full set of documentation to be delivered. This is most prevalent in the generation of documents for the government. Modern methods, such as object-oriented design, make document preparation easier because of their graphical orientation. Modern tools ease the burden even more. Yet good documentation is essential because it is the means we use to capture the engineering and make it visible to those members of the seller, buyer, and customer communities who are concerned about it.

Software environment. Modern software development is based on both the buyer and seller having an adequate software environment. A software environment consists of the set of hardware, software, and firmware used to perform a development effort. Typical elements of the environment include equipment (workstations, file servers, communications networks, mainframes, etc.), assemblers, compilers, database managers, debuggers, editors, library systems, simulators, and a variety of other tools. In addition, an environment may incorporate Computer-Aided Software Engineering (CASE) tools, which are becoming widely available commercially.

The aim of most software environments is to improve communications and enhance the productivity of the software engineers working on the project by supplying them with selective automation. Communications are enhanced when both buyer and seller have access to the information stored within the environment. Automation is made more meaningful when it is configured to support the project's software methodology and its review and documentation strategies. Criteria for tool selection for the software environment include

- ease of learning and use,
- ease of tool integration,
- functionality, richness, and power,
- portability across platforms,
- quality of training and support, and
- acceptable performance.

An illustration of a modern software environment is shown in Figure 14. It portrays the typical hardware and software components. The repository is the mechanism that links the engineering data that the tools operate on together. The local area network is the communications mechanism that enables users to collaborate and build group products. The host serves as both a compile and file server. Many options are in use in industry today. Selection of the best alternative is a function of many variables, of which cost is primary.

Testing. Testing is an activity that begins when the project starts and continues until the system is retired. Test concepts must be considered as the requirements are formulated, again during implementation, and finally during maintenance. Strategies for testing are integral to the success of the project and should be outlined in both the PMP and SDP.

Testing can be classified as being either formal (qualification) or informal (development). Formal means that the test signifies demonstration of contract requirements and completion of a major activity. Its conduct is monitored, and its results are witnessed by the buyer and customer. Informal testing means that the test is being conducted to provide feedback during and as part of the software engineering process. Typically, the SOW contains requirements for the qualification test program, which are addressed in the PMP. The SDP is used as the common vehicle for describing the informal test program.

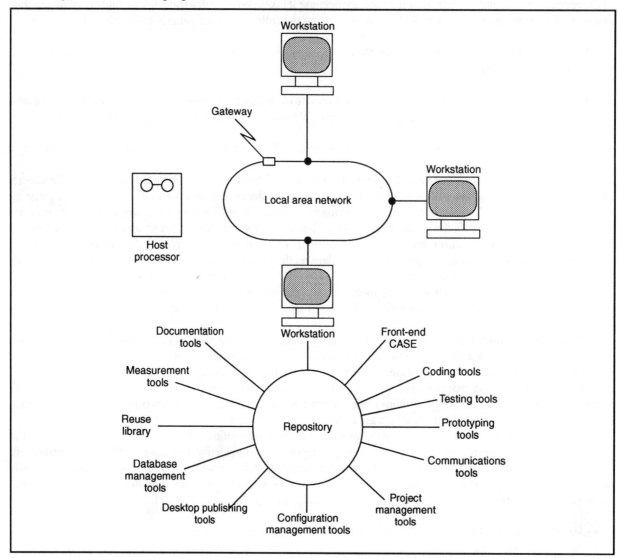

Figure 14: Software Environment Example

Development testing is conducted by the project organization. Formal testing is often conducted by an independent engineering or beta test team. The test team employed by the seller should be an experienced one because the job of testing requires skills that differ from those used during development. An adequate test environment (equipment, facilities, tooling, etc.) should be in place, and the test team should be delegated the authority needed to accomplish its responsibilities. Teamwork should be valued and overlap between groups should be minimized as the test team is put to work to demonstrate that the system fulfills its requirements and works in its operational environment.

Software product evaluations. Evaluations need to be conducted as products are developed to ensure that they achieve acceptable functionality, performance, and quality. These evaluations are conducted using criteria that are developed a priori and documented in the SDP. Evaluations are normally conducted by the project team as a normal part of its engineering activities. Various analytical and review techniques are used to conduct the evaluations. The use of checklists has proven beneficial, especially when they contain enough detail to make a proper determination and finding. These checklists can be effectively used as a focusing tool during a walk-through or inspection.

Risk management. Risk refers to those factors, both technical and managerial, that are threats to success and have the potential to jeopardize the attainment of the specific project objectives, whether from a user, buyer, seller, or support perspective. Risk management is the process of identifying, analyzing, quantifying, and developing plans to eliminate risk before it does any harm on a project. Risk revolves around uncertainty. Therefore, risk analysis is normally performed using statistical techniques.

During the planning phase, risk assessment is focused on issues that impact feasibility. Program risk revolves around time and effort. If either cost or schedule is impacted, the risks surrounding the occurrence should be examined and ways to mitigate the risk to an acceptable level should be investigated. Technical risk revolves around performance and functionality. Technical impacts must be quantified in terms of their costs in time and effort to assess the viability of options defined to mitigate them.

Management's prime emphasis should be problem prevention, not correction. A risk management program provides an efficient way of getting rid of problems before they happen. The basic process for managing risk is as follows:

1. *Identification.* Determining what the risks are is the first step in the process. The techniques employed to identify risks rely on experience, modeling, and decision-driver analysis. Checklists are normally provided to guide the determination. Statistical approaches are used to confirm the cause-effect relationships.

2. *Analysis.* Each risk area should be analyzed to determine its impact, both technical and programmatic. The cost and schedule consequences of the risk need to be quantified for priorities to be set. Cost models, factor sensitivity analysis, and decision chains have proven useful in performing impact assessments.

3. *Evaluation.* The next step in the process is to determine what actions, if any, should be taken to abate/eliminate the risk. Approaches to get rid of the risk should be assembled. If there is no reasonable way to abate the risk, or if the risk is acceptable, then the risk area should be monitored throughout the development effort.

4. *Abatement/Elimination.* The final step in the process is to implement the recommended course of action. As implementation progresses, the risk should be monitored to ensure the recovery plan is working.

Table 1 provides a list of common software risks. Each of these should be guarded against as the risk management program is put into operation.

Source selection

In response to an RFP, the seller prepares a proposal to communicate its offer to the buyer. The proposal is structured to respond to the requirements of the solicitation. Proposals are assessed against proposal evaluation criteria using standards developed for that purpose. They are not rated by comparing one offer to another. That would be unfair. Points are allocated for each of the factors, and scores are tabulated for ranking and rating the offers. Cost and technical factors are normally assessed separately. Typical high-level source selection evaluation criteria include the following:

- Understanding of the problem
- Soundness of the technical approach
- Minimum risk (to the buyer)
- Past performance
- Cost/price realism

An independent cost estimate is normally prepared by the buyer to provide a standard against which offers are judged. This permits the buyer to trade off cost versus technical advantage. It also allows the buyer to penalize sellers whose price is unreasonable (subtract points from their score).

It is not uncommon for the buyer to weight the factors so that preference is given to the best technical offer. In other words, the lowest price might not always win. As a consequence, sellers must try to balance cost and technical factors in their proposals. They might also make the following offers to keep their costs down:

- Purchase equipment for the job out of capital funds.
- Offer cost sharing for some of the R&D in exchange for commercial rights to the technology.

- Suggest that buyer surplus equipment and software be used to reduce the costs.
- Propose reusing existing software assets to reduce the development costs.

Table 1: Common Software Risks

People

1. Personnel shortfalls $\rightarrow$ Staff is not qualified

2. Fragmentation $\rightarrow$ Staff members are doing too many things, causing a lack of focus

Resources

3. Unrealistic schedule $\rightarrow$ The schedule is impossible

4. Inadequate budget $\rightarrow$ The budgets are not reasonable

5. Not enough resources $\rightarrow$ The hardware and software that make up the environment are not capable of supporting peak loads

Requirements

6. Developing the wrong functions $\rightarrow$ The customer has not validated the requirements

7. Poorly defined requirements $\rightarrow$ The requirements are incomplete

8. Gold plating $\rightarrow$ The requirements are overkill

9. Continuing change (feature creep) $\rightarrow$ The requirements are volatile

10. Too little customer involvement $\rightarrow$ The customer's view has not been extracted or incorporated

Receivables

11. Other projects don't deliver $\rightarrow$ Promises made by other projects are not kept

12. Legacy not up to expectation $\rightarrow$ Existing assets are not capable of being used

Technology

13. Technology shortfalls $\rightarrow$ Technology is not mature enough to be exploited

14. Too much change $\rightarrow$ The project is trying to do too much, too quickly

---

Source: B.W. Boehm, *Software Risk Management,* IEEE Computer Society Press, Los Alamitos, Calif., 1988 (adapted).

As noted, the source selection process for large contracts is often long and tedious. In large US government procurements, it may take years to issue a contract. It also requires a great deal of planning and a lot of work. As the decision grows near, every effort is made to be fair and avoid a protest. The reason for this is simple. A protest may force the buyer to recompete the job, thereby adding time and putting contract funds in jeopardy.

A contract can be issued based on a proposal directly. However, the buyer may want to leverage its advantage through negotiations to get concessions from the seller on price, contract terms, or technical approaches. Negotiations may commence with one or more sources at any time during the source selection. The goal is for the buyer and seller to reach agreement on an offer. Both the buyer and seller must be extremely careful. In their zeal to consummate a deal, they may do something rash. For example, they may make concessions that come back to haunt them as the contract proceeds.

Performance management

After the contract is executed, the real task of managing the development effort begins. The buyer must continuously assess the seller's performance to determine what progress payments should be made, whether contract changes are in order, and whether or not all contract terms and conditions are being complied with satisfactorily. It is dangerous to assume that exercising contract provisions will lead to a satisfactory product. The buyer and seller must communicate, aggressively search out problems, and manage risk. Both must take a proactive stance to effectively manage the acquisition.

The key to performance management is providing the buyer and seller with visibility into the process and products of software development. Without visibility, both parties are blind. Neither has insight into whether real progress is being made. To gain visibility, meaningful management reviews need to be held. Configuration management and quality assurance systems need to be put into place, along with a progressive test and evaluation program. Metrics need to be captured and reported to provide management with "hard" evidence or indicators of progress.

Once the contract is under way, it must be administered, monitored, and managed. Compliance with contractual terms must be ensured, and payments, consents, and changes must be regulated. Reports need to be periodically issued detailing equal opportunity, property administration, patent disclosures, and a host of other concerns. To accomplish these tasks, both buyer and seller employ different forms of information and project management systems. Some of these are called out in the contract. Others are part of the infrastructure the company uses to track and control its efforts.

Management reviews. For reviews to provide the seller with meaningful visibility into progress, they must separate fact from fiction. To do this, trust must be built as both the buyer and the seller work together to solve the typical problems that occur during an acquisition. Reviews are useful because they provide a benchmark against which performance can be compared. They provide an opportunity for both sides to share experience and build on lessons learned. They improve communications, highlight teamwork, and permit both sides to buy into solutions. Their practice should be spotlighted.

The frequency and formality of management reviews vary, based on a variety of factors. It is common to hold such reviews monthly on a semiformal basis. However, weekly and daily informal reviews may be warranted when decisions need to be made and direction is needed. Formality may increase when upper management attends. A pragmatic approach should be taken as reviewers do whatever is needed to achieve the intent of the review.

Software configuration management. During the acquisition, numerous products are generated for review by the seller. To determine if these are any good, some form of control over these products needs to be implemented. *Configuration management* (CM) provides this control by uniquely identifying, controlling changes to, and reporting the status of these products throughout the development life cycle.

A comprehensive configuration management system has four functions:

1. *Configuration identification.* Configuration items are identified and program development is controlled through the progressive establishment of baselines, each of which is uniquely identified.

2. *Configuration control.* Once the program is identified, changes to it can be controlled. This is accomplished by instituting procedures that ensure that all those affected by a change are consulted before it is implemented in the delivered system.

3. *Configuration status accounting.* The record keeping part of configuration management ensures that the status of all changes in the system is reported.

4. *Configuration audit.* Audits are held periodically to determine whether the process is working and whether the software contains those changes that have been approved.

An important aspect of configuration management is the support it provides to management through the use of baselines. A baseline is something against which changes are controlled. In the development process, there are many baselines. Some of these mark the completion of major milestone activities and are controlled by the buyer. Others create reference points against which requirements can be tracked. For example, the allocated baseline permits the requirements to be mapped to the design architecture. This permits the impact of changes to be traced from specification into the implementation. The acceptance of the allocated baseline also provides the basis for detailed design. Formal control implies that all changes to the baseline must be approved before they are implemented. For formal baselines, the change authority is normally the buyer, since changes affect the scope of the contract. There are normally three baselines established during a development: the functional, allocated, and product baselines.

Modern configuration management demands the use of automated tools. While file management systems, common to most operating systems, provide a basic capability to place access control on files (and code), they do not provide robust capabilities needed for versioning source code and documentation. They also do not support the required status accounting and reporting capabilities. Many sophisticated packages, many of which are available commercially, have been introduced to fill the void.

Quality assurance. The *Software Quality Assurance* (SQA) function has served as the traditional mechanism to ensure the product quality. This role has expanded with the recent emphasis on process assurance as a total quality management practice. Quality, when used in this context, has a twin meaning: making sure the provisions of the contract are met and achieving customer satisfaction. While sometimes these goals are in conflict, both should be strived for.

The three elements of SQA are shown in Figure 15. The quality assurance role is aimed at making sure that developers don't take shortcuts with the process when they develop deliverable software products. It is the audit function aimed at ensuring compliance with standards and procedures. The quality control role is aimed at making sure that the products are of the highest quality. It is the verification function directed at ensuring the technical integrity of the products themselves. The quality testing role is to ensure that the quality requirements specified in the contract are demonstrated. It is the test function aimed at validating performance from a quality viewpoint.

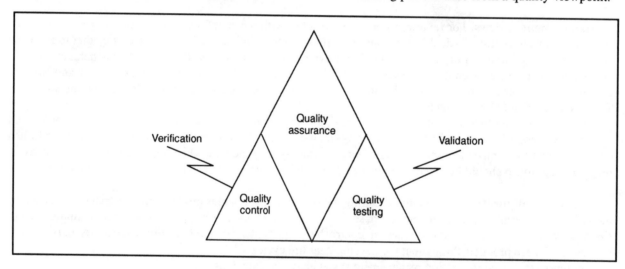

Figure 15: The Quality Triad

SQA is typically implemented by yet another independent organization. To be independent, the SQA organization should report, as shown in Figure 16, up a chain other than via the program manager. This allows disputes over quality to be elevated to top management for resolution. As illustrated, independence does not mean that the SQA organization does not work for the project. That would be suicide in most cases.

Test and evaluation. The test program provides the buyer with a means to get visibility. Early attention to testing and careful use of the test program are necessary to gain needed insight. For the test program to provide realistic measurement of progress, it must be properly planned, carefully documented, and correctly conducted.

There must be a one-for-one correlation between test conduct and contract requirements. Test documentation must be reviewed at appropriate milestones, and tests must be monitored to determine if progress is being made.

Independent testing is often employed to provide an independent assessment of the system. On small projects, this may not be practical. On large projects, it should be mandatory. Independent testing should be used in developments that are complex or carry critical mission operations, or to provide the manager an extra degree of assurance. Independent testing is directed at finding problems instead of proving that the system works. The independent test team tries to define the limits of the product, that is, where and when it will fail. Thus, the independent test team focuses on the fringes.

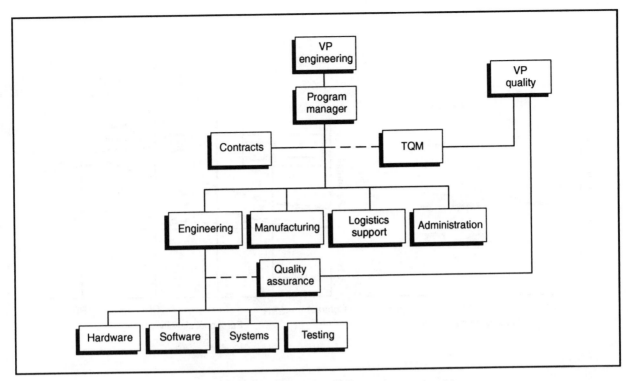

Figure 16: Independent Quality Reporting Relationships

When considering independent testing, you should make sure the following are true:

1. Qualification requirements are part of the specifications.

2. The PMP and the SDP address the testing program.

3. The seller employs a comprehensive environment for testing.

4. A viable test organization is in place with adequate authority and resources for the conduct of the program.

5. Checks and balances have been placed on the testing process so that it will provide the buyer with the visibility and insight desired.

Beta testing is an effective form of independent testing. Here, friendly users are tasked with shaking down a product prior to its release to the general marketplace. Beta testing works well because it tests a system from a user's, not a developer's, viewpoint. Sufficient time should be factored into the schedule to permit the results of beta testing to be incorporated into the product before it is delivered or released for use.

Corrective action system. The problem reporting system used in the development process is an important visibility tool. In addition to keeping track of errors, it helps the quality assurance function track what products are error-prone and where problems in the process are occurring. In addition, it supports configuration and project management by providing them with timely access to needed information.

By monitoring problem reports, the buyer can obtain useful insight into the development process. By evaluating problem reports and their closure rates, visibility into development progress can be gained. In addition, testing progress can be judged by keeping track of the number of defects the process is removing from the product. Problem reports could also be one of the factors used to govern milestone completions. If there are many open problems, the milestone should not be considered closed.

A corrective action system and a measurement program are needed to support a software total quality management (TQM) program. Within the DOD, this concept has been effectively employed to improve the software development process by incremental improvements to the software infrastructure. This TQM process has been aided by the use of a process maturity model.[6] The model defines five levels of process maturity. The contractor climbs the maturity ladder by selectively improving specific parts of the process framework, such as the metrics program. A self-

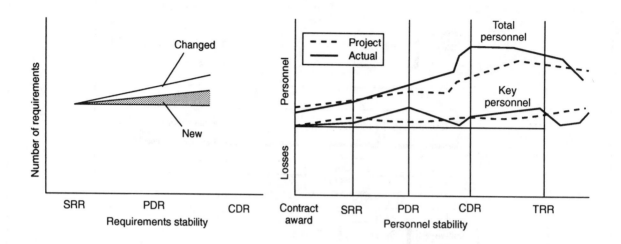

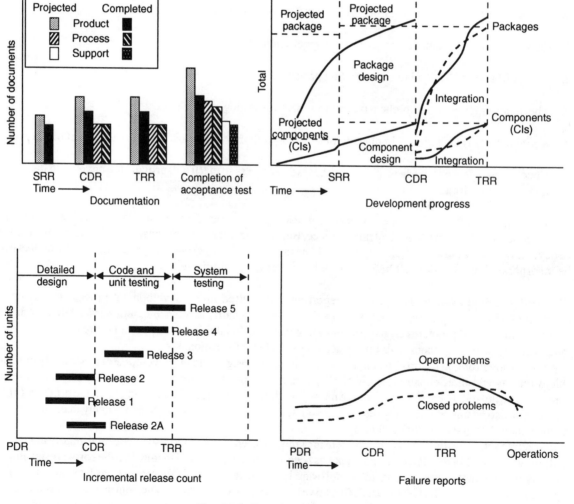

Figure 17: Management Indicators

assessment process, developed by the Software Engineering Institute, provides a common method for assessing the contractor's level of process maturity. This management tool has been effectively applied during the source selection process as a means to qualify a seller's software development capability.[7]

Metrics/management indicators. Metrics and management indicators have proven to be useful in gaining insight into a software acquisition. Metrics are quantitative measures of the degree to which a system, process, or component possesses a given attribute — for example, error density (errors/thousand lines of source code) is a measure of software reliability. In contrast, management indicators are devices that identify a prescribed state of affairs relative to managerial or financial performance — for example, development progress (milestones completed/milestones planned), requirements stability (changes made/calendar time). Metrics are often presented as numbers, while indicators are presented as trends. Management indicators were developed by the MITRE Corporation,[8] examples of which include

- memory utilization,
- personnel stability,
- software size, and
- test progress.

As shown in Figure 17, these management indicators were chosen because they address risks that occur during the entire life cycle of development. They provide insight into the development and can pinpoint causes of many problems. To see how these are used, let us look at the development progress indicator in Figure 17. This indicator tracks key implementation events and provides a level of detail that supplements top-level milestone schedules. Progress is tracked by gauging the headway made in building major software components. In this example, we show Ada packages tracked through their design, coding, and integration. If design completion is not keeping up with the projection, it could mean that a major review, the PDR, will probably slip. Thus, schedule problems can be discovered before they actually occur. The selection of a set of indicators/metrics should be consistent with the contract and resources available to the project. It makes little sense to arbitrarily select and apply a set of indicators when they do not address what the project needs.

The use of metrics and management indicators is gaining wider acceptance as firms try to improve the maturity of their processes. Although the concept of measurement is not new, it is shifting in perspective from arbitrarily applied measures, or metrics, to measurement-centered software development paradigms.

Contracts and financial management

In addition to keeping track of technical progress, the buyer must perform the following myriad of related tasks to properly manage the acquisition:

- Evaluate and process proposed changes to contract requirements.
- Evaluate and process proposed waivers to contract requirements.
- Administer award fee and incentive fee plans.
- Keep track of funds status and process payments.
- Administer warranties, data rights, patents, and property disposals.
- Obtain release of claims and negotiate adjustments.
- Monitor seller direct and indirect costs.
- Provide consent to place subcontracts.
- Monitor compliance of seller systems with contract requirements:
    Accounting
    Financial management
    Labor relations
    Personnel
    Purchasing
    Quality control
    Security
    Wages and benefits
- Provide timely closeout of contracts and settlement of payments.

As illustrated by this list, constant vigilance is needed to make sure the contract's terms and conditions are adhered to. Instead of technical performance, it is conceivable for data rights, patents, or some other contractual issue to become the primary risk factor. All of this points to the difficulties that arise when systems are acquired using third parties. There are many factors to consider when entering into such a relationship.

Summary

As one can see, acquisition management is a very complex subject. It involves numerous personnel and requires a breadth of skills, knowledge, and abilities that cross discipline boundaries (contracts, engineering, legal, etc.). It requires the application of modern management methods (team building, change management, etc.) and a thorough understanding of current engineering methods and thought. It requires enlightened leadership with the ability to make trade-offs and compromises. It requires teamwork between the buyer and the seller. It revolves around trust in everyone's ability to do a good job. The list of desirable characteristics goes on and on. Needless to say, it takes a lot of skill for the buyer to motivate the seller to perform when all you have is a contract at your disposal.

There are many additional topics that we have not touched on in this short article due to the limitations of space. Cost-estimation techniques, training strategies, project management tactics, development paradigm choices, reuse approaches, customer preferences, and emerging technologies like expert systems and object-oriented development all tend to impact the practice of acquisition management greatly. Each deserves a more thorough treatment than we have been able to provide, again due to the limitations of time and space.

Acquisition management is an important, although not a universally recognized, discipline. It has been practiced for many years in the US government, and to a lesser extent elsewhere in industry. As software continues to grow in importance, software acquisition management will become a more pervasive management concern. The key to successful acquisition of custom software systems is the well-founded acquisition management discipline described in this article. Hopefully, we challenged you to put this discipline into practice in your organization.

References

1. J.J. Marciniak and D.J. Reifer, *Software Acquisition Management*, John Wiley and Sons, New York, 1990.

2. ANSI/Std 1058.1-1987, *Standard for Software Project Management Plans*, IEEE, New York, 1987.

3. DOD-STD-2167A, *Defense System Software Development*, Feb. 29, 1988.

4. Standard P1074/D4 (draft), *Standard for Software Life Cycle Processes*, IEEE, New York, 1989.

5. M.E. Fagen, "Design and Code Inspections to Reduce Errors in Program Development," *IBM Systems J.*, No. 3, 1976, pp. 182-211.

6. W.S. Humphrey, *Managing the Software Process*, Addison-Wesley, Reading, Mass., 1989.

7. W.S. Humphrey and W.L. Sweet, "A Method for Assessing the Software Engineering Capability of Contractors," Tech. Report CMU/SEI-87-TR-23, Software Engineering Inst., Pittsburgh, 1987.

8. H.P. Schultz, *Software Management Metrics*, MITRE Corp., 1988.

Chapter 2
Software Process

Order is not pressure which is imposed on society from without, but an equilibrium which is set up from within.

— Jose Ortega y Gasset, *Mirabeau and Politics*

Overview

The Software Engineering Institute's publication of its process maturity framework (W.S. Humphrey, "Characterizing the Software Process: A Maturity Framework," Tech. Report CMU/SEI-87-TR-11, Software Engineering Inst., Pittsburgh, 1987) in the mid-1980s ranks as one of the major developments in the software management field during the past decade. This framework permits organizations to determine where they stand relative to norms so that they can focus their resources and make improvements in those areas where it matters.

The Department of Defense has actively promoted the use of the process maturity framework. It has directed the Software Engineering Institute (SEI) to implement a program to offer assistance to firms embarking on process assessments and evaluations. The SEI has also started to commercialize the program by licensing a number of firms to offer process assessment assistance to third parties on a fee-for-service basis.

The six papers that follow describe experience with the SEI methodology. The first paper, by Humphrey, Kitson, and Kasse, describes the process maturity model and summarizes where most US companies that had been rated by the SEI stood prior to 1989. This article was selected from the many that have been published on the topic because it provides a good overview of the SEI program and benchmark data for use in determining how you compare with others who have conducted assessments. It is interesting to note that recent updates to this database still show most firms at the first level of maturity.

The next paper describes how one division of Hughes Aircraft Company used the SEI process maturity framework to make improvements over a two-year period. It describes the action plan, the costs, the obstacles, and the lessons learned as Hughes implemented it. The authors conclude by stating that they thought the benefits were worth the time and effort expended.

The third paper, by Bollinger and McGowan, critically exams the SEI's process maturity program and points out its strengths and weaknesses. Several serious flaws with the program are identified, along with recommendations for their closure. The authors also discuss the pros and cons of the government's use of evaluations for accrediting potential contractors.

The next two papers, one by Boehm and one by Royce, describe what is involved in defining and implementing a modern software development process. The Boehm paper defines the "spiral development" process and discusses its use as a risk-reduction device. It also provides useful background information on process models. The Royce paper describes how the spiral model in the Boehm paper was implemented on the CCPDS-R project. It summarizes actual experience and discusses metrics data on this demonstrate-as-you-build methodology.

The final paper, by Curtis, points out three major philosophical problems with process models. Curtis also provides some perceptive notions on what needs to be done to correct them. His basic premise is that software processes are continuous and that they can be used to grow both people and reusable assets if they are designed properly.

References

A copy of the *IEEE Standard for Developing Software Life Cycle Processes*, P1074, is provided in Chapter 12 to give you an example of what goes into a process description. For those who want more information on software process assessments, I refer you to Humphrey's landmark text on the topic (Reference 13 in the Bibliography). The Camp benchmarking book (Reference 5) is also suggested because it provides another more quantitative way of rating and ranking competitiveness.

The State of Software Engineering Practice:
A Preliminary Report

Watts S. Humphrey
David H. Kitson
Tim C. Kasse

Software Engineering Institute, Carnegie Mellon University
Pittsburgh, Pennsylvania 15213

Abstract

This is the first in a series of SEI reports to provide periodic updates on the state of software engineering practice in the DoD software community. The SEI has developed, and is refining, a process framework and assessment methodology for characterizing the processes used by software organizations to develop and evolve software products. This report provides a brief overview of the process framework and assessment approach, describes assessment results obtained to date, and discusses implications of the current state of the practice for both customers and suppliers of DoD software.

Executive Summary

The Software Engineering Institute (SEI) was established by the U.S. Department of Defense (DoD) to transition improved software methods into general practice. As part of this mission, work is under way to characterize and report on the state of the practice of software engineering in the DoD software community.* Preliminary results of this work indicate that the majority of the software organizations in this community are operating at an immature level of software process maturity.**

In a mature software process, people, methods, techniques, and technology are effectively and efficiently coupled to consistently produce quality software within the constraints of cost and schedule requirements. In an immature software process, costs and schedules are largely unpredictable, quality is generally marginal, and technology is often used ineffectively. Specifically, organizations with immature processes are often deficient in one or more of the following areas:

- project planning
- project management
- configuration management
- software quality assurance

Software professionals generally need most help in controlling requirements, coordinating changes, managing (and making) plans, managing interdependencies, and getting help on systems design issues. Since these and similar problems generally consume much of every practitioner's time, this is where management can provide the most immediate help. *For low-maturity organizations, technical issues almost never appear at the top of key priority issue lists. This is not because technical issues are not important but simply because so many management problems must be handled first.*

According to the SEI five-level process maturity model,* current software engineering practice is largely at the initial level (level 1, or lowest level) of process maturity. There is a small number of level 2 organizations and a few level 3 projects in some organizations. No projects have been reported or assessed at level 4 or 5.

Nearly all level 1 software organizations urgently need to improve their management system for controlling their software process. Many managers need guidance on how to conduct project reviews, what key indicators to examine, and how to use basic management methods and tools. For project managers, this training should include the methods and procedures for estimating software size, estimating resource needs, and developing schedules. The second area requiring immediate attention for level 1 software organizations is Software Quality Assurance (SQA). SQA, while generally available, is not effectively performing its role because of inadequate resources, inadequate task definition, or inadequate management support. As organizations start to improve their software process, they should also begin gathering data on their code and test errors.

---

* By DoD software community we mean DoD agencies and DoD contractors engaged in the acquisition, production, or maintenance of software.

**Because of the way organizations were selected for inclusion in this study, the data upon which the report is based does not necessarily constitute a statistically valid measure of the state of DoD software community practice.

---

*The maturity model is discussed in Section 1.2.

©1989 ACM 0270-5257/89/0500/0277$00.75

Recommended by: Barry Boehm

"The State of Software Engineering Practice: A Preliminary Report," by W.S. Humphrey, D.H. Kitson, and T.C. Kasse from *Proc. 11th Int'l Conf. Software Engineering*, 1989, pages 277-288. Copyright © 1989 by the Association for Computing Machinery, Inc., reprinted with permission.

Since level 1 organizations are typically high-risk suppliers, we suggest that acquisition authorities that deal with level 1 organizations require aggressive action by these organizations to improve to level 2.

The relatively few level 2 organizations are currently among the most capable software groups in the DoD software community. But even though they have advanced substantially beyond level 1, they still have considerable room for improvement. Many of these organizations are equipped to advance rapidly; a full 69% have a Software Engineering Process Group (SEPG).* Organizations without a SEPG should promptly establish one.

Level 2 organizations typically do not adequately train their software people. A further deficiency in level 2 organizations is the lack of mechanisms to assure that SQA is evaluating representative samples of the software process. The lack of adequate regression testing is also a common problem. This generally leads to late discovery of problems, last-minute testing crises, and poor product quality. While level 2 organizations typically have their costs and schedules under reasonable control, they generally do not have orderly methods for tracking, controlling, and improving the quality of their software or of their software process. Further, few of these organizations have adequate resources or action plans directed at long-term software process improvement.

With the increasing reliance of critical defense systems on complex software, the necessary improvements require aggressive action. Thus, we suggest that acquisition authorities require level 2 organizations to dedicate resources to process improvement and to establish and report on the actions needed to progress to maturity level 3. An appropriate vehicle for doing so might be to provide for such improvement efforts as an allowable cost to the contract, or in the statement of work. We also suggest that acquisition authorities require that contractor SQA organizations be adequately staffed and effectively used.

Because there are only a few level 3 projects in organizations, our sample size is too small to draw meaningful conclusions about their improvement needs.

1. Introduction

This report describes the initial results of a continuing Software Engineering Institute effort to characterize and report on the current state of software engineering practice.

Characterizing, understanding, and facilitating improvement in the practice of software engineering is important to the SEI, the Department of Defense, and the nation. The SEI Software Process Program has the goal of improving the process of developing and evolving software. Our approach emphasizes the following:

1. Developing and validating a software process framework and evaluation methodology for identifying capable contractors.

2. Transitioning the evaluation methodology to DoD software acquisition agencies and their prime contractors.

3. Developing and refining an associated assessment methodology for use by the DoD software community for internally assessing software engineering capability and determining improvement needs.

4. Characterizing and reporting on the state of software engineering practice in the DoD software community.

5. Facilitating software process improvement in the DoD software community.

The focus of this report is the current state of software engineering practice from a software process perspective; that is, the report will characterize the software processes currently used by software managers and practitioners in organizations doing DoD software work. The SEI has considered and our results are generally consistent with the results of a number of prior studies [BAS84, DRU82, REI88, THA82].

This report is organized in three parts. The first section provides the background and framework for collecting the data upon which the report is based. Section 2 describes the data collected and the analyses performed on this data. Section 3 discusses implications and recommendations for customers and suppliers of DoD software.

1.1. Software Process Focus

Since early 1987, the SEI Software Process Program has focused on *software process* as a means of improving the ability of software organizations to produce software products according to plan while simultaneously improving the organization's ability to produce better products. This focus on software process is based on the premises that 1) the process of producing and evolving software products can be defined, managed, measured, and progressively improved and 2) the quality of a software product is largely governed by the quality of the process used to create and maintain it.

The software process is the set of activities, methods, and practices which guide people (with their software tools) in the production of software. An effective process must consider the relationships of the required tasks, the tools and methods, and the skills, training, and motivation of the people involved.

Software process management is the application of process engineering concepts, techniques, and practices to explicitly monitor, control, and improve the software process. It is only one

---

**An SEPG is a group of software professionals specifically chartered to focus on software process improvement.

of several activities which must be effectively performed for software-producing organizations to be consistently successful. Capable and motivated technical people are also needed. Knowledge of the ultimate application environment is critical also, as is detailed understanding of the end user's needs [CUR88]. Even with all these capabilities, however, inattention to the software management problems described in Section 2 will likely result in disappointing organizational performance. [KIT89] provides a more comprehensive discussion of the role and significance of software process and the discipline of software process management.

This view of process and process management has led to the creation of a process maturity model and a related software process assessment instrument, which are important elements of SEI methods for examining software processes. The remainder of Section 1 briefly discusses these elements and some methods of applying them to the software processes of organizations.

1.2. Software Process Maturity Model

The software engineering capability of an organization can be characterized with the aid of the software process maturity model shown in Figure 1.2.1. This model provides five maturity levels, identifies the key improvements required at each level, and establishes a priority order for moving to higher levels of process maturity.

At the initial level (level 1), an organization can be characterized as having an ad hoc, or possibly chaotic, process. Typically, the organization operates without formalized procedures, cost estimates, and project plans. Even if formal project control procedures exist, there are no management mechanisms to ensure that they are followed. Tools are not well integrated with the process, nor are they uniformly applied. In addition, change control is lax, and senior management is not exposed to or does not understand the key software problems and issues. *When projects do succeed, it is generally because of the heroic efforts of a dedicated team rather than the capability of the organization.*

An organization at the repeatable level (level 2) has established basic project controls: project management, management oversight, product assurance, and change control. The strength of the organization stems from its experience at doing similar work, but it faces major risks when presented with new challenges. The organization has frequent quality problems and lacks an orderly framework for improvement.

At the defined level (level 3), the organization has laid the foundation for examining the process and deciding how to improve it. The key actions needed to move from the repeatable level to the defined level are to establish an SEPG within the organization, to establish a software process architecture that describes the technical and management activities required for proper execution of the process, and to introduce a family of software engineering methods and technologies.

The managed level (level 4) builds on the foundation established at the defined level. When the process is defined, it can be examined and improved but there is little data to indicate effectiveness. Thus, to advance to the managed level, an organization should establish a minimum set of measurements for the quality and productivity parameters of each key task. The organization should also establish a process database with resources to manage and maintain it, to analyze the data, and to advise project members on its meaning and use.

Two requirements are fundamental to advance from the managed to the optimizing level (level 5). Data gathering should be automated, and management should redirect its focus from the product to process analysis and improvement. At the optimizing level, the organization has the means to identify the weakest process elements and strengthen them, data are available to justify applying technology to various critical tasks, and numerical evidence is available on the effectiveness with which the process has been applied. The key additional activity at the optimizing level is rigorous defect cause analysis and defect prevention.

These maturity levels have been selected because they do the following:

- Reasonably represent the historical phases of evolutionary improvement of actual software organizations.

- Represent a measure of improvement that is reasonable to achieve from the prior level.

- Suggest interim improvement goals and progress measures.

- Make obvious a set of immediate improvement priorities, once an

While there are many aspects to the transition from one maturity level

Level	Characteristic	Key Problem Areas	Result
Optimizing	Improvement fed back into process	Automation	**Productivity & Quality**
Managed	(quantitative) Measured process	Changing technology Problem analysis Problem prevention	
Defined	(qualitative) Process defined and institutionalized	Process measurement Process analysis Quantitative quality plans	
Repeatable	(intuitive) Process dependent on individuals	Training Technical practices • reviews, testing Process focus • standards, process groups	
Initial	(ad hoc / chaotic)	Project management Project planning Configuration management Software quality assurance	**Risk**

Figure 1.2.1: SEI Software Process Maturity Model

to another, the basic objective is to achieve a controlled and measured process as the scientific foundation for continuous improvement.

It has been our experience (based on ten SEI-assisted assessments conducted since February 1987) that when software organizations are assessed against this maturity framework, the assessment method has enabled us to accurately place them on the maturity scale and identify key improvement needs. We believe software process maturity is a useful indicator of an organization's software engineering capability, e.g., its ability to produce quality software products on time and within budget. We also believe that while the use of tools and technology can enhance software engineering capability, their contribution is often of limited value for organizations with low-maturity software processes.

[HUM88] and [KIT89] provide more comprehensive descriptions of software process management and the maturity model.

1.3. Software Process Assessment Instrument

The assessment instrument is a structured set of yes-no questions which helps to facilitate the conduct of reasonably objective and consistent assessments of software organizations [HUM87]. It has also been designed to assist DoD acquisition organizations in identifying software contractors with acceptable software engineering capabilities. Since the instrument and method for applying it are publicly available, software contractors can use them to identify areas for improvement. The SEI provides training on how to conduct effective assessments for organizations interested in conducting their own assessments.

The questions in the assessment instrument cover three areas:

1. Organization and resource management. This section deals with functional responsibilities, personnel, and other resources and facilities.

2. Software engineering process and its management. This section concerns the scope, depth, and completeness of the software engineering process and the way in which the process is measured, managed, and improved.

3. Tools and technology. This section deals with the tools and technologies used in the software engineering process. It helps determine the effectiveness with which the organization employs basic tools and methodologies.

Some sample questions from the assessment instrument are:

*   Is there a software engineering process group or function?
*   Is a formal procedure used to make estimates of software size?
*   Are code and test errors projected and compared to actuals?

1.4. Examining Software Processes

There are a number of ways the software process framework (software process concepts and principles + maturity model + assessment instrument) can be applied; the SEI has developed, and has experience with, the following:

*   SEI-assisted assessments
*   self-assessments
*   capability evaluations
*   workshop assessments

The paragraphs below briefly discuss each type of application. A more comprehensive discussion of how assessments are conducted and the role of assessment in improving software engineering capability is contained in [KIT89].

1.4.1. SEI-Assisted Assessments   An SEI-assisted assessment is an appraisal, by a trained team of experienced software professionals, of an organization's current de facto software process. Typically, a team is composed of four or five SEI professionals and one to three site professionals. A methodology for conducting assessments has been developed by the SEI [OLS89]. The assessment team receives training in the methodology prior to conducting the actual assessment. The goal for this type of assessment is to facilitate improvement of the organization's software process. The assessment team identifies the most important software process issues currently facing the organization and develops recommendations to deal with these issues. Since the objective is improvement within a given organization, validation of questionnaire responses (e.g., requesting substantiating documents) is limited to those having a direct bearing on transition to the next higher level of process maturity (contrast this with contractor evaluation as discussed in Section 1.4.3).

SEI-assisted assessments are conducted in accordance with an assessment agreement signed by the SEI and the organization being assessed. This written agreement contains provisions for senior management involvement, organizational representation on the assessment team, confidentiality of results, and follow-up actions.

The SEI has been conducting this type of assessment since February 1987 and is using the knowledge and information acquired to refine an emerging picture of the state of the practice of software engineering in the DoD software community.

1.4.2. Self-Assessments   Self-assessments are similar to SEI-assisted assessments, with the primary difference being assessment team composition. Self-assessment teams are composed primarily of software professionals from the organization being assessed, with one or two SEI software professionals optionally present. The context, objective, and degree of validation are the same as for SEI-assisted assessments.

The SEI offers self-assessment training on a limited basis for organizations committed to improving their software engineering capability. Organizations that participate in the SEI-provided training execute a written agreement with the SEI which provides for sharing of assessment results, integrity of the assessment methodology, and optional participation of SEI assessment team members.

1.4.3. Capability Evaluations

Capability evaluations, like SEI-assisted assessments and self-assessments, are appraisals of an organization's current software process; however, the context, purpose, and assessment team composition are different. The context of capability evaluation is the DoD acquisition process, and the purpose is to provide information concerning the organization's software engineering capabilities for the acquisition agency. This information is then considered, along with other relevant information, in the source selection decision. Hence, validation of assessment instrument responses is a greater consideration here than it is in assessments.

Capability evaluations are conducted by trained teams of evaluators from the acquisition agency. The SEI provides the necessary training for the evaluation teams using our methodology, but we do not participate in evaluations. The results of capability evaluations are supplied by the evaluation team to the acquisition agency. Non-attributed, "sanitized" results are provided to the SEI to help us refine the assessment instrument and evaluation methodology; they also contribute to our emerging picture of the status of DoD software engineering capability.

1.4.4. Workshop Assessments

At workshop assessments, professionals from various organizations learn about process management concepts, assessment techniques, and the SEI assessment methodology. They also complete an assessment instrument and supply demographic data based on a project with which they are familiar. This format is designed for people who wish to learn more about the SEI assessment methodology with minimal investment.

The data collected at workshop assessments is added to the SEI assessment database and is used for various analyses. Workshop assessments are typically conducted at conferences and symposia attended by DoD and DoD contractor software professionals (e.g., National Security Industrial Association, Electronic Industries Association, and the annual SEI affiliates symposium).

2. Data Collection and Analysis Methodology

This section provides a characterization of the data used in this report, identifies some of the considerations in using this data, and describes the analyses which were performed to derive the results presented.

2.1. Basis for the Report

This report is based on information of two types:

- Responses to the assessment instrument (the questions in the instrument are yes-no questions). The responses were collected from workshop assessments and SEI-assisted assessments.

- The collective knowledge and experience which the SEI has acquired as a result of our involvement in the development and application of the various assessment methods discussed in Section 1.4.

Assessment participants include software and hardware/software developers from DoD organizations, DoD contractors, and commercial enterprises. Ten organizations participated in SEI-assisted assessments (with 4 to 6 projects involved in each assessment), and over 70 organizations were represented in the workshop assessments, representing 168* data points from assessments across the United States. In every assessment, the SEI signs an agreement that there will be no attribution of the results to a specific company. The implications and recommendations presented in Section 3 of this report, therefore, represent an aggregate view.

2.2. Data Usage Considerations

The results described in this report reflect the state of the software engineering practice based on the data, experience, and knowledge acquired by the SEI since February 1987. This section describes some methodological considerations which we feel are germane to readers of this report.

First, the sample population was not statistically selected. Most of the respondents came from organizations that are affiliated with the SEI. These respondents varied in the type and degree of involvement with the projects they reported on.

Another consideration is the degree of validation of the responses; the extent to which corroboration of responses was requested depended on the type of assessment being conducted. At this time, we have no way of determining the effect of this factor on the responses.

In comparing the question responses received from workshop assessments and from SEI-assisted assessments, several points should be noted:

1. The SEI-assisted assessments were conducted on-site by a trained team, with participation from knowledgeable project managers and technical professionals.

2. The workshop assessment respondents contained a mix of management and non-management professionals, some of whom likely had detailed knowledge of the technical points.

3. For SEI-assisted assessments, many threshold responses were verified; however, no workshop assessment responses were verified.

---

*A data point is one set of yes-no responses to the software process assessment instrument; the scope of these responses is a specific software project.

2.3. Data Analysis

Two views of the data were prepared and analyzed: (1) software process maturity level distribution and (2) percent negative response to key questions.* For the purposes of this report, we separated response data from SEI-assisted assessments and that from workshop assessments, treating them as two distinct data populations. Because of the considerations mentioned in Section 2.2, we do not believe that greater depth of analysis than that presented in this report is justified.

2.3.1. Software Process Maturity Level Distribution

The distribution of software process maturity level across the sample population pro-

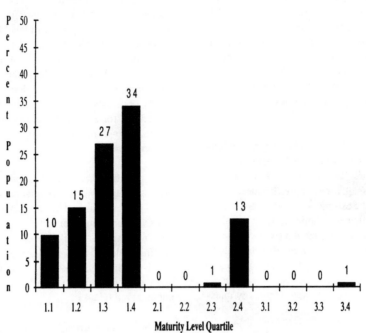

Figure 2.3.1.1: Software Process Maturity Level Distribution - Workshop Assessment Data (113 Data Points)*

vides a high-level view of the state of the practice; Figures 2.3.1.1 and 2.3.1.2 show the software process maturity distributions for workshop assessments and SEI-assisted assessments, respectively.

For both figures, the vertical axis represents the percentage of data points in the population; the horizontal axis represents the software process maturity scale—levels 1 through 5. In order to show additional fine structure, the maturity scale has been further divided into quartiles—four quartiles for each maturity level (for a total of 20 quartiles, or 20 vertical bars). The quartiles are identified in the charts using the notation x.y, where x is the maturity level (1-5),

and y is the quartile (1-4). In Figure 2.3.1.1, for example, 2.4 refers to the fourth (and last) quartile for level 2 and contains approximately 13% of the sample population. Note that since no data points have been observed to date at level 4 or above, that portion of the graph has not been shown.

Each data point was placed in the maturity level distribution based upon a determination of how many additional affirmative responses would have been needed to rate the project at the next higher level of process maturity. The range of these values was then equally divided into four "buckets" or quartiles. Thus, the higher the quartile number, the closer the project is to being rated at the next higher maturity level.

The workshop assessment results, shown in Figure 2.3.1.1, indicate that the majority of the respondents reported projects at the initial level of maturity. Figure 2.3.1.1 shows a large percentage of the respondents to be in the fourth quartile of level 1 (quartile 1.4); with minimal improvement, these projects could be classified as level 2. Fourteen percent of all the workshop respondents reported projects at the repeatable level, and only 1% of those respondents described projects at level 3, the defined level. No workshop respondents reported projects at either the managed or the optimizing level of software process maturity. The maturity level distribution for projects reviewed by SEI-assisted

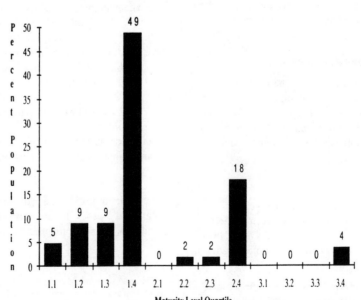

Figure 2.3.1.2: Software Process Maturity Level Distribution - SEI-Assisted Assessment Data (55 Data Points)*

*Key questions are those for which a high percentage of affirmative responses is required to qualify for a particular maturity level. See Section 2.3.2.

*Note that the percentages may not total 100 due to rounding errors.

83

assessments, shown in Figure 2.3.1.2, is very similar to that for the workshop data. Although workshop participants were largely mid- to upper-level managers not currently managing a project (as opposed to the project managers who provided data for SEI-assisted assessments), the profiles of process maturity are surprisingly similar. Some key differences are apparent, however. First, Figure 2.3.1.2 shows that the sample population is skewed slightly towards higher levels of process maturity. Secondly, larger numbers of projects are in quartile 4 of maturity levels 1, 2, and 3, poised for moving to the next higher level of software process maturity.

2.3.2. Profiles of Negative Responses to Key Questions

For the purposes of this report, two attributes of the assessment instrument questions are germane. First, each question is associated with a particular maturity level; for example, the question "Is a formal procedure used to make estimates of software size?" is a level 2 question. This means that an organization that has all of the attributes of a level 2 software organization (with respect to the SEI process maturity model) would respond affirmatively to this question. Second, certain questions are designated as being *key*. In order to qualify at a given level of process maturity, an organization must respond affirmatively to 90% of the key questions for that level.

To analyze the responses to key questions, we determined the percentage of the population responding negatively to each key question for levels 2 and 3 and displayed the results in decreasing order. These computations were performed for both the workshop assessment data and for SEI-assisted assessment data. The results are provided in Appendix A and are referenced in appropriate parts of Section 3. An examination of the results in Appendix A shows a close, though not exact, correlation between the two data samples; for example, for both level 2 and level 3 profiles, four out of the top five questions for SEI-assisted assessments were among the top five questions for the workshop assessment profiles.

3. Implications and Recommendations

This section discusses the implications of the current state of software engineering practice and suggests improvement actions. We discuss implications and recommendations, first for level 1 organizations, then for level 2 organizations. Our views are offered for two audiences: software suppliers and acquisition authorities.

3.1. Level 1 Organizations

3.1.1. Software Suppliers Nearly all level 1 software organizations urgently need to improve their project management methods (CN24, CN42, CN43 ,CN44, CN46, CN77, CN84).*
Many managers need guidance on conducting project reviews,

selecting key indicators to examine, and using basic management methods and tools. For project managers, training should include the methods and procedures for estimating software size, estimating resource needs, and developing schedules. While organizations in the highest quartile of level 1 typically have the ability to make resource and schedule projections, size estimating is a problem for fully 66% (CN42) of level 1 projects.** Software size tracking is also a problem for 64% (CN46) of this group. As a result, projects generally underestimate resources and rely on overly optimistic schedules. The introduction of more formal procedures for estimating and tracking software size will thus substantially contribute to improved project cost and schedule performance.

One of the first steps organizations must take when they start to seriously address software quality is to gather data on the errors found in the product. This area should receive early focus in any process improvement program as it is a prerequisite to significant improvements in overall process quality and productivity. Since the final code and test stages are generally the easiest to measure, this is where data gathering should start. Of the workshop assessment respondents, nearly 60% indicate that such data was not gathered (CN48).

Another area requiring immediate attention for level 1 software organizations concerns the role of Software Quality Assurance (SQA). While 70% of level 1 organizations have reporting channels separate from development for their SQA groups (CN6), 56% of the organizations report that they do not have independent audits of each step in their software development process.† As a result, SQA, while generally available, is not effectively performing its role. The reasons may be a lack of adequate resources, a lack of adequate task definition, or inadequate management support. In any event, effective SQA is required to assure management that its established methods, standards, and procedures are being applied. SQA can only be effective, however, when it addresses clearly identified and stated objectives. Wherever SQA is established merely to meet a contractual provision, it is not likely to contribute significantly to overall performance and may, in fact, detract.

3.1.2. Acquisition Authorities Since level 1 organizations are typically high-risk suppliers, we suggest that acquisition authorities who deal with level 1 organizations require aggressive action by these organizations to improve to level 2.

The key items to examine in determining whether an organization is at level 1 or level 2 are defined in the SEI software maturity model and the software process assessment instrument [HUM88,

---

*CN = control number. The control number uniquely identifies a particular question and is invariant across versions of the assessment instrument. Where conclusions are directly supported by question responses, the relevant assessment instrument question control number is cited. The question text can be found in Appendix A.

*This, and subsequent, percent negative response values are taken from the workshop assessment charts provided in Appendix A.
**The 56% figure is based on responses to question CN30 - a non-key question ("For each project, are independent audits conducted for each step of the software development process?").

HUM87]. If a detailed review is impractical, however, a critical examination of current practices for size and resource estimating and scheduling should identify the most critical exposures. When these are not adequate, improvement commitments should include the establishment of a formal planning and review system as well as comprehensive management training in software project planning.

Acquisition agencies should also be particularly interested in contractor procedures for gathering code and test error statistics since this data provides a good indication of product quality. When the data is available and can be reviewed during the project, it provides early warning of quality problems. Without this data, quality problems are generally first detected in final test, when it is too late to recover without serious schedule and cost consequences. Thus, we suggest that the acquisition agency request code and test error statistics as part of its normal project review process.

We further suggest that software acquisition agencies require the contractor to establish and maintain an effective SQA organization with adequate resources to review the key steps in the process. This SQA role should be clearly defined and documented. SQA responsibilities should be focused on the policies, methods, procedures, and standards for making plans and tracking progress against them. Once these are in place and consistently followed, the SQA role should be expanded to include peer reviews* and test. If the measures above are coupled with a separate management reporting chain to assure that SQA nonconcurrences and issues are resolved, SQA is likely to quickly become effective.

3.2. Level 2 Organizations

3.2.1. Software Suppliers Though organizations at level 2 have advanced substantially beyond level 1, they still have considerable room for improvement.

Across all organizations at all maturity levels, training was found to be the area most needing improvement. Fully 88% of the level 2 organizations in the workshop assessments did not have adequate training for review leaders (CN20) and over half the organizations did not have a required training course for software developers (CN19). Although a lack of training may be acceptable for simple or noncritical applications, training is crucial in organizations responsible for developing advanced software systems. Software practitioners need to be knowledgeable and skilled in the use of languages and organizational procedures, understand the project requirements and the application area, and have a common understanding of the system protocols and architectural design. Without adequate training, projects often

---

*By peer review we mean a review of a software product (specification, design, code, test plan, etc.) by peers of the producer(s) of the product for the purpose of identifying defects and improvements. Peer reviews range from walk-throughs to formal inspections, as described in IEEE standard 1028, "Standard for Software Reviews and Audits."

have serious schedule and cost problems; and they have difficulty ensuring that the requirements and the system architecture are consistently implemented.

A full 69% of the level 2 organizations do have Software Engineering Process Groups (CN15) and, thus, are equipped to advance rapidly to a more mature status. Conversely, 31% of the level 2 organizations have not established SEPGs and, thus, are hindered in planning and implementing significant software process improvement actions. The lack of a process focus is demonstrated by the fact that 50% of level 2 organizations do not track software design errors (CN47).

Regression testing helps to ensure that code changes made to a product baseline which render previously implemented functions inoperable are identified. When regression testing is not adequately performed, such damage is generally not found until later in the process, when it is more expensive and time consuming to fix. Regression testing is a problem for nearly 80% (CN99) of the organizations in the workshop assessment population, indicating that late problem discovery is a common problem. This situation can be substantially reduced with relatively simple regression test procedures.

A further serious need for level 2 organizations carries over from level 1. Almost one-third of these organizations do not have mechanisms in place to assure that SQA is evaluating representative samples of the software process (CN98). It has also been found that many SQA organizations are understaffed, or their role is ill-defined, or they are not adequately supported by management. The continuing lack of adequate SQA generally results in inconsistent use of established methods and procedures. Without effective SQA, organizations will find it difficult, if not impossible, to improve to level 3. Until the basic methods and procedures of level 2 are consistently and effectively applied, further process improvement efforts are likely to be ineffective.

3.2.2. Acquisition Authorities Based on the SEI data and experience to date, the relatively few level 2 organizations are currently among the most capable software groups in the DoD software community. They typically have their costs and schedules under reasonable control; however, they generally do not have orderly methods for tracking, controlling, and improving the quality of either their software or their software process. Further, few of these organizations have adequate resources or action plans directed at long-term software process improvement.

Level 2 organizations should concentrate on establishing SEPGs as a focal point for process improvement. We suggest that acquisition authorities require organizations to dedicate resources to process improvement, including initiating and monitoring the actions needed to progress to maturity level 3. An appropriate vehicle for doing so might be to provide for such improvement efforts as an allowable cost to the contract, or in the statement of work. The key needs are for process standardization; improved methods for design, implementation, and test; and the identification and application of improved tools and technologies. Typically, the lack of an SEPG means that no one is responsible for defining metrics, installing an error tracking system, retaining and analyzing the resulting data, or reporting on progress in quality or process improvement. While the specific improvement priorities vary across organizations, the common need is for resources dedicated to process improvement.

Training is a particularly sensitive problem. Unless the contractor has an experienced team which is already familiar with the system and its application and is fully familiar with the languages and tools they are to use, some training programs are essential. Even with such an experienced team, some training is valuable. Though specific course needs vary among organizations and training involves some expense, the costs are invariably less than the hidden costs of trial-and-error methods. *Training is expensive, but not nearly as expensive as not training.*

Regression testing is essential for any well-run software project. Without selective retesting of the system or component to verify that modifications have not caused unintended effects, there is no assurance that previously integrated functions still perform and that the system or components still comply with the specified requirements. Unless adequate regression testing is routinely performed as changes occur, large numbers of problems are likely to be found when the complete test suite is run at acceptance testing. The time used to fix defects and rerun the tests can be substantial when these activities occur during the final phase of testing. We suggest that acquisition agencies closely examine the regression test plans of their level 2 contractors.

We also suggest that acquisition authorities require their contractors to adequately staff SQA organizations and effectively use them. Although a high percentage of level 2 organizations have SQA organizations in place, only 31% of them have established methods for ensuring that SQA samples are appropriately selected. Thus, it is likely that many SQA groups represent a substantial expense but do not produce measurable benefits for the organization. If the contractor has an SQA group, the acquisition agency should require clear evidence that it is being used effectively. Such evidence should include: an SQA charter signed by a senior executive; approved standards against which SQA conducts audits; and a record of SQA nonconcurrences and the corrective actions taken. If an SQA group is not in place, its effective establishment should be a requirement in the contract.

Acknowledgments

The authors acknowledge the efforts of those individuals (both within the SEI and from organizations which support the SEI) who contributed to the work described in this report. In particular, we acknowledge the contributions of Ken Dymond, who performed various analyses of the assessment data and provided the authors with relevant information and graphics. Also, we acknowledge Linda Pesante, who significantly improved the readability of the report through her technical editing skills. We extend a special thanks to all the individuals and sponsoring organizations that were involved in the various assessments, and to our colleagues at the SEI who reviewed the various drafts leading to this report. We particularly appreciate the efforts of the members of the final technical report review team: Ken Dymond, Ron Higuera, Mark Paulk, Rich Pethia, and Bill Sweet.

References

1. [BAS84] Basili, V.R., Gannon, J.D., Hamlet, R.G., Yeh, R.T., Zelkowitz, M.V., "Software Engineering Practices in the US and Japan," *IEEE Computer*, 1984.

2. [CUR88] Curtis, B., Krasner, H., Iscoe, N., "A Field Study of the Software Design Process for Large Systems," *Communications of the ACM*, November 1988.

3. [DRU82] Druffel, L.E., Lt. Col. USAF, et al, *Report of the DoD Joint Service Task Force on Software Problems*, Department of Defense, July 1982.

4. [HUM87] Humphrey, W.S., Sweet, W., et al., *A Method for Assessing the Software Engineering Capability of Contractors*, Software Engineering Institute, (CMU/SEI-87-TR-23), September 1987.

5. [HUM88] Humphrey, W.S., "Characterizing the Software Process: A Maturity Framework," *IEEE Software*, March 1988.

6. [KIT89] Kitson, D.H., Humphrey, W.S., *The Role of Assessment in Software Process Improvement*, Software Engineering Institute, (CMU/SEI-89-TR-3), February 1989.

7. [OLS89] Olson, T.G., Humphrey, W.S., Kitson, D.H., *Conducting SEI-Assisted Software Process Assessments*, Software Engineering Institute, (CMU/SEI-89-TR-7), February 1989.

8. [REI88] Reifer, D.J., *Final Report: Software Quality Survey*, American Society for Quality Control, 1988.

9. [THA82] Thayer, R.H., Pyster, A., Wood, R.C., "Validating Solutions to Major Problems in Software Engineering Project Management," *IEEE Computer*, August 1982.

Appendix A. Key Questions and Response Profiles

This section of the report provides a view of selected portions of the response data from workshop assessments and SEI-assisted assessments. Figures A.1 and A.2 show negative response profiles (with respect to those projects rated overall to be at level 1) for level 2 key assessment instrument questions. Table A.1 provides the text of the same key questions indexed by control number (CN). For example, Figure A.1 shows that of the workshop assessment projects reported to be at level 1 (96 out of a total of 113 projects), 64% responded negatively to question CN46 ("Are profiles of software size maintained for each software configuration item, over time?"). Question CN46 is a key question for advancing to level 2.

Figures A.3 and A.4 show negative response profiles (with respect to those projects rated overall to be at level 2) for level 3 key assessment instrument questions. Table A.2 provides the text of the same key questions indexed by control number.

Table A.1: Key Questions for Level 2

CN*	Question
6	Does the Software Quality Assurance (SQA) function have a management reporting channel separate from the software development project management?
14	Is there a software configuration control function for each project that involves software development?
24	Is a formal procedure used in the management review of each software development prior to making contractual commitments?
42	Is a formal procedure used to make estimates of software size?
43	Is a formal procedure used to produce software development schedules?
44	Are formal procedures applied to estimating software development cost?
46	Are profiles of software size maintained for each software configuration item, over time?
48	Are statistics on software code and test errors gathered?
77	Does senior management have a mechanism for the regular review of the status of software development projects?
84	Do software development first-line managers sign off on their schedules and cost estimates?
87	Is a mechanism used for controlling changes to the software requirements?
96	Is a mechanism used for controlling changes to the code? (Who can make changes and under which circumstances?)

Table A.2: Key Questions for Level 3

CN	Question
15	Is there a software engineering process group function?
19	Is there a required software engineering training program for software developers?
20	Is a formal training program required for design and code review leaders?
23	Does the software organization use a standardized software development process?
23	Does the software organization use a standardized and documented software development process on each project?
47	Are statistics on software design errors gathered?
59	Are the action items resulting from design reviews tracked to closure?
61	Are the action items resulting from code reviews tracked to closure?
83	Is a mechanism used for ensuring compliance with the software engineering standards?
91	Are internal software design reviews conducted?
92	Is a mechanism used for controlling changes to the software design?
95	Are software code reviews conducted?
98	Is a mechanism used for verifying that the samples examined by Software Quality Assurance are truly representative of the work performed?
99	Is there a mechanism for assuring the adequacy of regression testing?

---

*CN = control number - the control number uniquely identifies a particular question and is invariant across versions of the assessment instrument. These questions are presented here in control number order.

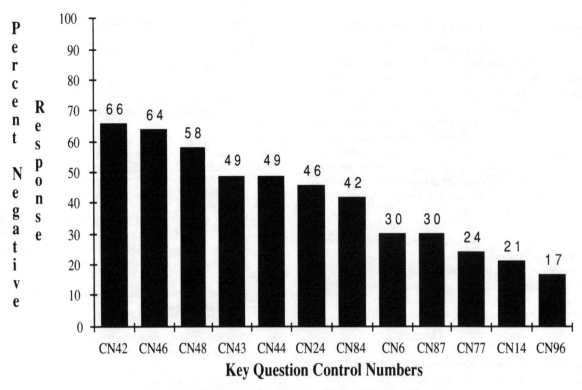

Figure A.1: Percent Negative Response of Level 1 Projects to Level 2
Key Questions - Workshop Assessment Data (96 Data Points)

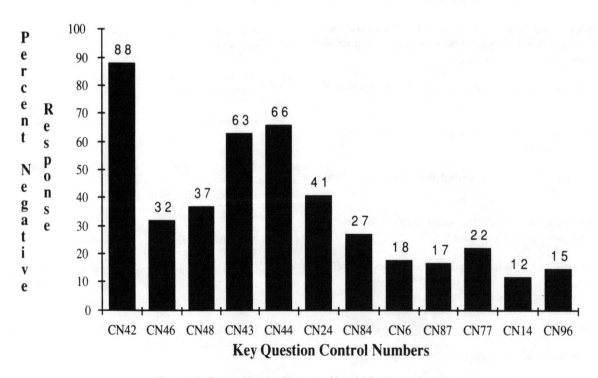

Figure A.2: Percent Negative Response of Level 1 Projects to Level 2
Key Questions - SEI-Assisted Assessment Data (41 Data Points)

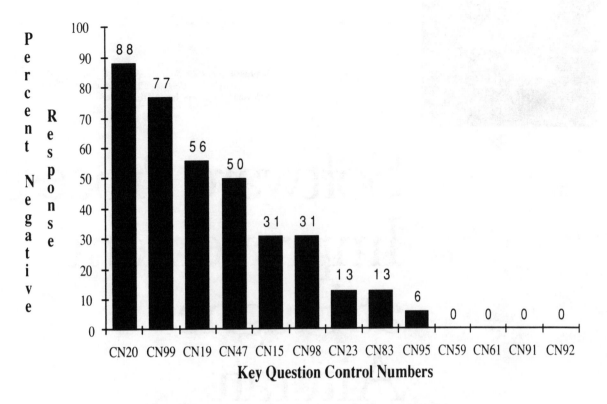

Figure A.3: Percent Negative Response of Level 2 Projects to Level 3 Key
Questions - Workshop Assessment Data (16 Data Points)

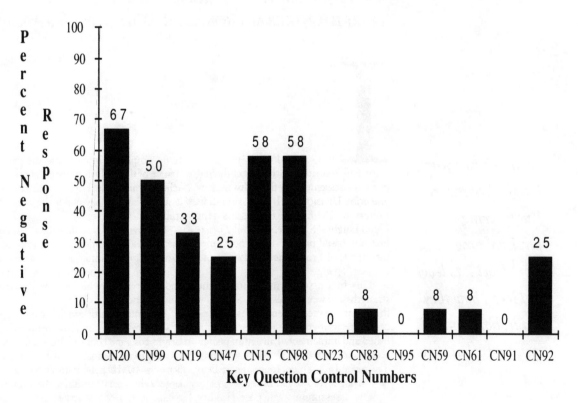

Figure A.4: Percent Negative Response of Level 2 Projects to Level 3 Key
Questions - SEI-Assisted Assessment Data (12 Data Points)

Reprinted from *IEEE Software,* Vol. 8, No. 4, July 1991, pp. 11-23. Copyright © 1991 by The Institute of Electrical and Electronics Engineers, Inc. All rights reserved.

Software Process Improvement at Hughes Aircraft

WATTS S. HUMPHREY, *Software Engineering Institute*
TERRY R. SNYDER *and* RONALD R. WILLIS, *Hughes Aircraft*

❯In just two years, Hughes' Software Engineering Division progressed from level 2 to level 3. Here's how they did it, how much it cost, and what they gained.

I n 1987 and 1990, the Software Engineering Institute conducted process assessments of the Software Engineering Division of Hughes Aircraft in Fullerton, Calif. The first assessment found Hughes' SED to be a level 2 organization, based on the SEI's process-maturity scale of 1 to 5, where 1 is worst and 5 is best.[1]

This first assessment identified the strengths and weaknesses of the SED, and the SEI made recommendations for process improvement. Hughes then established and implemented an action plan in accordance with these recommendations. The second assessment found the SED to be a strong level 3 organization.

The assessment itself cost Hughes about $45,000, and the subsequent two-year program of improvements cost about $400,000. Hughes found that the investment improved working conditions, employee morale, and the performance of the SED as measured in project schedule and cost. Hughes estimates the resulting annual savings to be about $2 million.

In this article, we outline the assessment method used, the findings and recommendations from the initial assessment, the actions taken by Hughes, the lessons learned, and the resulting business and product consequences.

We write this article in the broad interest of software-process improvement, particularly its costs and benefits. Because its assessments are confidential, the SEI cannot publicize costs and benefits until it has amassed a large body of data. So, during the second assessment in 1990, Watts Humphrey and Terry Snyder agreed to write an article – Humphrey to provide material on the assessment process and Hughes to provide material on results and benefits.

Background. The SED is one division in Hughes' Ground Systems Group. Although it is the largest dedicated software organization in the Ground Systems Group and provides contract support for many other divisions, there are other (project-related) software organizations in the group.

The SED, formed in 1978, primarily works on US Defense Dept. contracts. It employs about 500 professionals. Of these, 41 percent have 10 to 20 years experience in software and 12 percent have 20 or more years experience. The assessments described here examined only the work of the SED in Fullerton; the findings and recommendations are pertinent only to that organization. However, Hughes has capitalized on this experience to launch a broader process-improvement effort.

At the time of the 1990 assessment, the SEI had conducted 14 assessments and observed 18 self-assessments. As a result, it had gained a great deal of experience on effective methods for identifying the actual state of practice in software organizations. It is thus our opinion that the overall effect of misunderstandings and errors on these assessments was modest.

ASSESSMENT PROCESS

A process assessment helps an organization characterize the current state of its software process and provides findings and recommendations to facilitate improvement. The box on pp. 14-15 explains the SEI's process-improvement paradigm, its supporting process-maturity structure, and the principles of process assessment.

Hughes assessments. The two Hughes assessments were conducted by teams of SEI and Hughes software professionals. In both assessments, all the team members

> A process assessment helps an organization characterize the current state of its software process and provides findings and recommendations to facilitate improvement.

were experienced software developers. The 1987 assessment was conducted by a team of seven: one from Hughes and six from the SEI. The 1990 assessment team included nine professionals: four from Hughes and five from the SEI. Two of the authors, Watts Humphrey and Ronald Willis, were members of both teams.

The SED team members prepared a list of candidate projects for review by the entire assessment team during training. The entire team then selected projects that it felt reasonably represented the development phases, typical project sizes and applications, and the major organization units. Six projects were reviewed in the 1987 assessment and five in 1990. Only one project was included in both assessments.

Before the assessment, the Hughes SED manager, Terry Snyder, and the SEI's process-program director, Watts Humphrey, signed confidential agreements covering the ground rules for the assessments. The key points in these agreements were:

♦ The SEI and the assessment team members were to keep the assessment results confidential. Hughes could use the assessment results in any way it chose.

♦ The SED manager agreed to participate in the opening and closing assessment meetings.

♦ In addition to the regular team members, the SED manager agreed that Hughes would provide needed support to handle the assessment arrangements and to lead the work on the follow-up action plan.

♦ The SED manager also committed Hughes to developing and implementing appropriate action plans in response to the assessment recommendations. If Hughes deemed that action was not appropriate, it was to explain its reasons to the assessment team.

After the SEI agreed to consider conducting an assessment:

♦ A commitment meeting was held with the SEI and the SED manager and his staff to agree on conducting the assessment and to establish a schedule.

♦ For both assessments, Hughes and the SEI selected the assessment team members, and the SEI trained them in its assessment method. These two-day training programs were held at the SEI, where the entire assessment team was familiarized with the assessment process and prepared for the on-site period.

♦ The on-site assessment was conducted.

♦ A detailed, written report of the assessment findings and recommendations was prepared and a briefing on the recommendations was delivered to the SED management team and all the assessment participants. In both assessments, the SED manager invited senior corporate executives to attend the briefing. Because he did not know the findings in advance, this involved some risk. However, the added understanding provided by these briefings contributed materially to the launching of a Hughes corporate-wide process-improvement initiative modeled on the SED's work.

♦ The SED developed and implemented an action plan based on these recommendations.

Maturity levels. In 1987, the assessments focused on the responses to the level 2 and level 3 questions: Because the assessment period is intentionally limited to four days, we decided to devote our attention to those areas most pertinent to the organization's perceived maturity level. This was possible because the SEI assessment process uses the questionnaire to help focus on the most informative interview topics.

In the 1990 assessment, the team briefly reviewed the level 2 responses and then interviewed the project representatives on the questions at levels 3, 4, and 5. In areas where the project responses differed or where the response pattern was atypical, the team requested more information. Because these discussions were on Tuesday afternoon and the additional materials were needed by Thursday morning, the representatives were told to bring only available working materials and not to prepare anything special.

As a consequence, we believe the team determined an organizational maturity level with a fair degree of accuracy in both the 1987 and 1990 assessments. There is, of course, the possibility that some questions were not discussed in sufficient detail to identify all misunderstandings or errors.

1987 ASSESSMENT

The first SEI assessment of six Hughes projects was conducted November 9-12, 1987. The final report, including recommendations, was presented in January 1988.

Recommendations. The assessment team made seven recommendations.

Quantitative process management. The assessment team found that the professionals working on the assessed projects gathered a significant amount of data on many aspects of the process. While this was important in moving the organization toward a managed software process (level 4), much of the long-term potential value of this data was lost because it was kept in multiple, disparate databases. Furthermore, the lack of a central location for this data made it difficult for project managers and professionals to know what data was available, what data should be gathered, and how it could most effectively be used for product and process improvement.

The team recommended that the SED establish the goal of achieving quantitative process management. To establish the foundation for statistical process management, this goal should include:

◆ Establishing a centralized database to include current and future data on cost estimates, cost experience, error data, and schedule performance. Additional process data should be included as it is gathered.

◆ Establishing uniform data definitions across projects.

◆ Augmenting the process definitions to include those key measures and analyses required at each major project milestone,

together with appropriate responsibilities.

◆ Providing the resources needed and the responsibility assignments required for gathering, validating, entering, accessing, and supporting the projects in analyzing this data.

Process group. The team recommended that the SED establish a technical group to be the focal point for process improvement. This group's initial tasks would be to lead the development of action plans for accomplishing the assessment team's recommendations, to lead, coordinate, and track the implementation of the action plans, and to establish the centralized process database.

Requirements. The team found that the SED generally was not involved in early system definition. Whenever software considerations were not integrated into systems engineering early in the system-definition phase, the software specifications often were ambiguous, inconsistent, untestable, and subject to frequent last-minute changes. Because in general the quality of a software product cannot exceed the quality of its requirements, the team perceived this as a critical problem.

The team recommended that the SED be involved in the specification development for all new Hughes software-intensive projects. It also suggested that systems-engineering groups attend applicable software-engineering courses.

Quality assurance. Although the existing software quality-assurance organization at Hughes performed several necessary functions, it suffered from widely different views of its usefulness and could not fully contribute to the software-development process because it was understaffed and its personnel were not adequately trained.

To strengthen the role of SQA, the

team recommended a training program that would include software-engineering principles, Hughes standard procedures, phases of the life cycle, and the functions of SQA personnel. It was also recommended that the value added by SQA be clarified for program management so it could better understand the need to allocate resources to it.

Training. The team found that Hughes had a comprehensive, company-sponsored software-engineering training program. However, the team also found that certain training categories were either not available or not being used adequately. Key examples were training for assistant project managers, review leaders, and requirements specification.

The team recommended that Hughes review its software-training requirements. The review was to conclude with plans for restructuring the current training programs, providing new subjects, creating a training priority structure, and using new training methods as appropriate. It was also recommended that Hughes consider a required training program.

Review process. Although Hughes had made provision for technical reviews during the development process, they were not performed uniformly across all projects. So the team recommended that Hughes reassess its current review practices and determine how to assure a consistent and uniform review practice at appropriate points in the software-development process. The objective was to improve product quality, reduce reliance on testing, and improve overall project predictability and productivity.

Working relationship. During the assessment, the working relationship with the Defense Dept.'s Defense Contract Administrative Services department was often

> In general the quality of a software product cannot exceed the quality of its requirements, so the team recommended the SED be involved in specification development.

SEI PROCESS ASSESSMENT PROCEDURES

To make orderly improvement, development and maintenance organizations should view their process as one that can be controlled, measured, and improved. This requires that they follow a traditional quality-improvement program such as that described by W. Edwards Deming.[1]

For software, this involves the following six steps:

1. Understand the current status of their process.

2. Develop a vision of the desired process.

3. Establish a list of required process-improvement actions in priority order.

4. Produce a plan to accomplish these actions.

5. Commit the resources and execute the plan.

6. Start over at step 1.

The SEI has developed a framework to characterize the software process across five maturity levels. By establishing their organization's position in this framework, software professionals and their managers can readily identify areas where improvement actions will be most fruitful.

Many software organizations have found that this framework provides an orderly set of process improvement goals and a helpful yardstick for tracking progress. Some acquisition groups in the US Defense Dept. are also using this maturity framework and an associated SEI evaluation method called the Software Capability Evaluation to help select software contractors.

Maturity framework. Figure A shows the SEI's software process-maturity framework. The SEI derived this empirical model from the collective experiences of many software managers and practitioners. The five maturity levels

♦ reasonably represent the historical phases of evolutionary improvement of actual software organizations,

♦ represent a measure of improvement that is reasonable to achieve from the prior level,

♦ suggest interim improvement goals and progress measures, and

♦ make obvious a set of immediate improvement priorities once an organization's status in the framework is known.

While there are many aspects to these transitions from one maturity level to another, the overall objective is to achieve a controlled and measured process as the foundation for continuous improvement.

Assessment. The process-maturity framework is intended to be used with an assessment method. A process assessment is a review of an organization's software process done by a trained team of software professionals. Its purpose is to determine the state of the organiza-

tion, to identify the highest priority process issues, and to facilitate improvement actions.

The assessment process facilitates improvement by involving the managers and professionals in identifying the most critical software problems and helping them agree on the actions required to address these problems.[2] The basic objectives of an assessment are to

♦ learn how the organization works,

♦ identify its major problems, and

♦ enroll its opinion leaders in the change process.[3]

In SEI assessments, five or six projects are typically selected as representative samples of the organization's software process. The guiding principle for selecting projects is that they represent the mainstream software business for the organization.

On-site period. The on-site assessment period is an intense

Level	Characteristics	Key challenges	Result
5 **Optimizing**	• Improvement fed back into process • Data gathering is automated and used to identify weakest process elements • Numerical evidence used to justify application of technology to critical tasks • Rigorous defect–cause analysis and detect prevention	• Still human-intensive process • Maintain organization at optimizing level	**Productivity & quality**
4 **Managed**	(Quantitative) • Measured process • Minimum set of quality and productivity measurements established • Process database established with resources to analyze its data and maintain it	• Changing technology • Problem analysis • Problem prevention	
3 **Defined**	(Qualitative) • Process defined and institutionalized • Software Engineering Process Group established to lead process improvement	• Process measurement • Process analysis • Quantitative quality plans	
2 **Repeatable**	(Intuitive) • Process dependent on individuals • Established basic project controls • Strength in doing similar work, but faces major risk when presented with new challenges • Lacks orderly framework for improvement	• Training • Technical practices (reviews, testing) • Process focus (standards, process groups)	
1 **Initial**	(Ad hoc/chaotic process) • No formal procedures, cost estimates, project plans • No management mechanism to ensure procedures are followed, tools not well integrated, and change control is lax • Senior management does not understand key issues	• Project management • Project planning • Configuration management • Software quality assurance	**Risk**

Figure A. The SEI process-maturity framework.

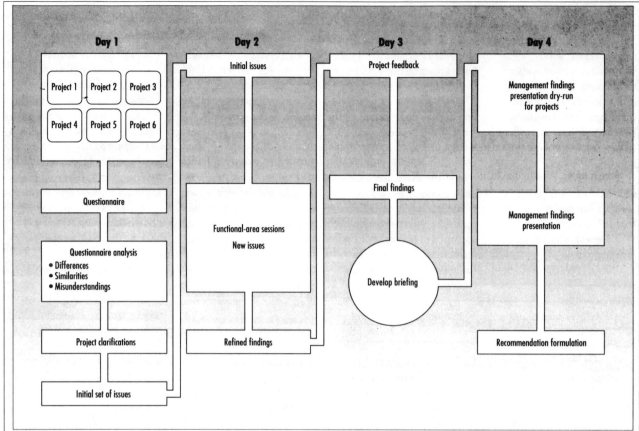

Figure B. *On-site assessment process flow.*

four "half-days": The team members are involved for more than half of each 24 hours, generally starting at 7:30 a.m. and not concluding until 10:00 or 11:00 p.m. No one has time to perform normal duties during this phase.

While this is a potentially stressful activity, the extensive training prepares the team members to make a highly productive effort and to build the cohesion and team spirit required to achieve consensus on the complex issues encountered. The dedication and enthusiasm of the assessment team also significantly contributes to their credibility to the organization and to acceptance of the findings.

Figure B shows the flow of the on-site activities during SEI process assessments. Each on-site assessment starts with a presentation to the manager, staff, and all the assessment participants. This

meeting covers the assessment ground rules, assessment principles, and the schedule.

The assessment team then meets in closed session to review the questionnaire responses in preparation for the first round of discussions with project leaders. Project managers and functional experts are interviewed to clearly determine the key issues behind their responses to an SEI questionnaire.[4]

Next, a private discussion is held with each project leader to clarify any issues identified by the assessment team during its review of project responses and to request explanatory materials, if appropriate.

Next, a full day is devoted to discussions with software practitioners from selected technical areas such as requirements and high-level design, and code and unit test. Typically, about six professionals are selected from across

the organization for each functional area. These functional area representatives are selected with the following criteria:

♦ Be considered an expert in the technical area by his or her peers.

♦ Be assigned to, and working on, one or more mainstream projects at the site (not necessarily a project included in the assessment).

♦ Be considered an opinion leader in the organization.

A second round of individual project leader meetings is then held to review the supporting materials, resolve remaining issues, and review the preliminary assessment findings. On the last day, a findings briefing is presented to senior management and all the assessment participants.

The final assessment activity is the preparation and presentation of a written report

and recommendations to the site manager and staff. The recommendations highlight the assessment team's view of the highest priority items for immediate action. Following the assessment, the organization prepares and implements an action plan. In accordance with the agreement, the SEI reviews and comments on these plans.

REFERENCES

1. W.E. Deming, *Out of the Crisis*, MIT Center Advanced Eng. Study, Cambridge, Mass., 1982.
2. R.A. Radice et al., "A Programming Process Study," *IBM Systems J.*, No. 2, 1985, pp. 91-101.
3. D.H. Kitson and W.S. Humphrey, "The Role of Assessment in Software Process Improvement," Tech. Report CMU/SEI-89-TR-3, Software Eng. Inst., Carnegie Mellon Univ., Pittsburgh, 1989.
4. W.S Humphrey and W. Sweet, "A Method for Assessing the Software Engineering Capability of Contractors," Tech. Report CMU/SEI-87-TR-23, Software Eng. Inst., Carnegie Mellon Univ., Pittsburgh, 1987.

identified as ineffective or counterproductive. It was thus recommended that the SED work to improve this relationship.

Actions taken. Within two months of the January 1988 recommendations briefing, Hughes developed an action plan to implement the recommended improvements. As predetermined, the assessment site coordinator was the primary author for the action plan, although many people contributed to the decision and approval process.

Because implementation of the proposed actions was estimated to require a 2-percent increase in division overhead rate, it took three more months (until June 1988) to get the action plan and required funding approved by Ground Systems Group management. In so doing, top management became committed to the improvement program.

For the most part, the 1988 action plan was implemented on schedule and under budget. It took 18 months and was completed just one month before the 1990 reassessment.

Action plan. The 1988 action plan began with a one-page summary of the assessment life cycle and the projects assessed. It then listed the goals and put the action plan in the context of a Ground Systems

---

3.1 FORM SOFTWARE ENGINEERING PROCESS GROUP

3.1.1 Summary of the SEI Findings. Decentralization of the software organization into geographically isolated projects and even into separate product line divisions has impaired progress in software-technology development. Such decentralization has already affected quality-indicator data collection leading to multiple, disparate databases.

3.1.2 Requirements. The following are necessary attributes of the desired solution.

a. An organizational entity, the software-engineering process group (SEPG), exists and has the following attributes:
- serves as the focal point for software process improvement
- leader has technical credibility and influence
- staff is experienced
- initial staff size is three people
- eventual staff size is 2 percent to 3 percent of software developers
- staff is rotated every 2 to 3 years

b. The SEPG performs the following functions:
- lead development and implementation of the SEI action plan
- define/improve technical and management software practices
- lead definition of standards for software processes/products
- establish and maintain the software-process database
- initiate the definition, collection, analysis of process data
- facilitate periodic assessment of software-engineering process
- identify and promote the organization's technology needs
- establish requirements and plans for training
- research, develop, and transfer new technology
- define requirements for process automation (i.e. tools)
- facilitate periodic management reviews on state of practice

3.1.3 Responsibilities.

Manager, Software Engineering Division, forms SEPG and assigns SEPG leader, approves SEPG charter, provides funding for SEPG activities, and periodically reviews SEPG progress. Leader, Software Engineering Process Group, develops SEPG charter, develops and implements plans to accomplish 3.1.2, and recruits and selects full-time technical staff for the SEPG.

3.2 IMPLEMENT QUANTITATIVE PROCESS MANAGEMENT

3.2.1 Summary of the SEI Findings. Although data on projects is collected, it is kept in multiple, unrelated databases. The lack of a central focal point for data makes it difficult to know what data is available, what data should be gathered, and how it can be most effectively used for product and process improvement.

3.2.2. Requirements. The following are necessary attributes of the desired solution:

a. A centralized database exists that has the following attributes:
- standardized data definitions across all projects
- fed by all projects
- sufficient data element types to statistically manage the software-development process

b. Software process and product standards exist that specify when and what data to collect to be able to statistically manage the software-development process.

c. Software process and product standards exist that specify analyses to be performed at each project milestone, together with appropriate responsibilities, to be able to statistically manage the software-development process.

d. An organization exists (SEPG) that provides the following services:
- gathers, validates, and enters data into the database
- controls access to the database
- supports projects in analyzing the data

e. Formal means exist to enforce these requirements.

3.2.3. Responsibilities.

Leader, Software Engineering Process Group, assigns responsibility for 3.2.2a through 3.2.2.d, ensures implementation of 3.2.2.e.

3.3 FILLS GAPS IN TRAINING PROGRAM

3.3.1 Summary of the SEI Findings. Although there is clear evidence of commitment to training, there are unfilled gaps in certain areas, opportunities for more effective training, and not enough required training (as opposed to optional training).

3.3.2 Requirements. The following are necessary attributes of the desired solution:

a. A report based on review of current training needs and training effectiveness exists and is used to modernize the existing training program. The report contains the following:

Figure 1. Section 3 of Hughes SED 1988 action plan. The action plan lists tasks as process-requirements specifications in the context of the Ground Systems Group.

Group organizational improvement strategy.

The plan then detailed five improvement tasks, written as process-requirement specifications:

♦ Form a software-engineering process group.

♦ Implement quantitative process management.

♦ Fill in the gaps in training.

♦ Standardize an effective review process.

♦ Move toward a software-engineering discipline.

Figure 1 shows a part of the plan's wording. As the figure shows, the plan specified testable conditions for each task that, if met, would satisfy the recommended process improvements. The plan also avoided specifying solutions, to allow implementation flexibility.

Two of the SEI's recommendations were not included in the action plan because they involved organizations not under SED control. The first, to strengthen SQA, dealt with a function that was in another division of Hughes. Although the SED was striving to regain a centralized SQA function that would be under its control, it had not yet achieved that reorganization and therefore could not guarantee the outcome. (Later, the SED did achieve a centralized SQA organization.)

- recommended restructuring of current training program
- unfilled gaps in training curriculum
- training priorities
- recommended changes to existing training methods

b. A training curriculum exists that contains all training that is currently defined plus the following additional training subjects:

- associate program manager (APM)
- review leader (for internal reviews)
- use of engineering techniques in software development
- understanding and using software practices and procedures
- how to write good software-requirements
- how to test at the software-requirements level
- how to test at the unit level
- software quality assurance
- practical guide to the use of performance analysis

c. A directive exists that specifies training requirements in terms of specific subjects versus job position and that these training requirements be considered in annual performance evaluations.

3.3.3 Responsibilities.

Leader, Software Engineering Process Group, leads the effort to accomplish 3.3.2.a, 3.3.2.b, and 3.3.2.c.

Manager, Software Engineering Division, approves and enforces the training practice developed as a result of 3.3.2.c.

3.4 STANDARDIZE AN EFFECTIVE REVIEW PROCESS

3.4.1 Summary of the SEI Findings. While Hughes does include provision for reviews during the development process, reviews do not appear to be uniformly performed across projects.

3.4.2 Requirements. The following are necessary attributes of the desired solution:

a. Review standards exist as part of the directive system. They include the following:

- overall review practice (i.e., what reviews, when, who is responsible)
- specific criteria to be used in each review
- procedures for conducting reviews

- required data collection and reporting from reviews

b. Required training curriculum includes review-leader training.

3.4.3 Responsibilities.

Leader, Software Engineering Process Group, leads the effort to accomplish 3.4.2.a and 3.4.2.b.

Manager, Software Engineering Division, approves and enforces the standards developed as a result of 3.4.2.b.

3.5 MOVE TOWARD SOFTWARE -ENGINEERING DISCIPLINE

3.5.1 Summary of the SEI Findings. Software engineering is not uniformly treated as an engineering discipline. There are several aspects to this problem, including lack of early software involvement in systems definition, lack of the use of experimentation (i.e., prototyping) as an engineering tool, and skipping software-development steps when schedule pressures increase. On several of the projects studied, software engineering is appropriately addressing these systems-engineering concerns, and software engineering is treated as an engineering discipline; however, on other projects, this was found not to be the case.

3.5.2 Requirements. The following are necessary attributes of the desired solution:

a. Software-development plans for all new projects include an approved budget and task for software-engineering participation in system design and software-requirements specification.

b. System engineers are invited and attend appropriate software-engineering training classes.

c. All required software-development steps are carried out, regardless of schedule pressure.

3.5.3 Responsibilities.

Software Associate Program Managers (APMs) implement 3.5.2.a and 3.5.2.c.

Manager, Software Engineering Division, ensures 3.5.2.a and 3.5.2.c.
Leader, Software Engineering Process Group, leads the effort to accomplish 3.5.2.b.

The second recommendation not included, to improve relations with Defense Contract Administrative Services, again dealt with an organization over which the SED had no control. To negotiate an effective interface with the DCAS was not something Hughes could guarantee, so it was excluded from the action plan. (However, an effective interface was later negotiated.)

The action plan then estimated the labor for implementation to be 100 man-months over 18 months, divided into six major functions:

♦ process-group leader: 8 percent,
♦ process definition: 6 percent,
♦ technology development: 28 percent,
♦ quantitative-process management: 41 percent,
♦ training: 16 percent, and
♦ review-process standardization: 1 percent.

Budget cuts later reduced the 100 man-months of labor to 78. Not included in these estimates were other direct charges for such things as computers, office space, and training facilities, and the existence of certain services such as training and central computer facilities.

Process group. In June 1988, the idea of an SEPG was relatively new at the SEI. Although the concept was well-understood, the implementation was assumed to require that certain roles be organized into a separate function focused on process-technology improvement.

At first, Hughes didn't understand the process-group concept very well, so it tried to implement this SEI approach literally. Also, Hughes' experience with centralizing technology improvement was that, over time, walls of miscommunication developed, leading to just the opposite of technology transfer.

However, on further examination, it was found that the SED, a high level 2 organization with significant progress toward level 3, already had formal roles in place for many process-group functions. All but three functions (action-plan implementation, technology transfer, and development of a required training policy) were either in place or being formed independently of the action plan. Hughes just didn't call it a process group.

To implement the action plan, Hughes issued a bulletin that created the process group, named the existing major functions, and named the person responsible for each function. The bulletin was enlightening to those who understood both what already existed and the SEI's concept of a process group because it made the concept tangible.

The process group, however, was not yet complete. Three key additions brought it all together as an effective focus for process improvement:

♦ Technology steering committee. Although the technology steering committee already existed, Hughes did not fully understand its role as a process-group driving function. Given the newly established functions and responsibilities, the process group did not have one person as a leader but instead was directed by the technology steering committee. Thus, it became the committee's job to develop technology road maps, assess current technology, evaluate the overall direction, and make general technology-policy decisions.

♦ Technology management. Hughes' practices and procedures addressed people management, project management, resource management, and management of other *things*, but not management of *technology*. One of the first improvements was to formalize the management of technology, as with any other corporate resource. This was done through brainstorming and consensus decision making. The plans were recorded as a new practice, technology management.

♦ Technology transfer. A new job function, head of technology transfer, was created and staffed with a full-time person. It was soon clear that the establishment of this function was the most profound action in the entire improvement process. It is not clear if the very positive effect of this action was due to the person's abilities, the existence of the function, or just the timing — but without a doubt this function had more effect than any other single improvement.

Among other things, the head of technology transfer coordinated self-assessments, developed a questionnaire glossary, became the local expert in the SEI maturity questionnaire, became a member of the Software Productivity Consortium's technology-transfer advisory group, developed an SPC technology-transfer plan, briefed senior management on the state of process maturity, maintained a database of technology used on each project and an awareness of what technology each project needed, facilitated technology transfer among projects, ran a special-interest group on process improvement, supported the corporate-wide technology-transfer program, and served on the practices and procedures change-review board, the training policy committee, and the technology steering committee.

Two other additions to the process group that were very helpful were a training committee to periodically review training requirements and their effectiveness and a special-interest group on process improvement. These groups met as needed to find and fix process problems.

Quantitative process management. Before the 1988 action plan, the SED collected "quality indicators" in response to a company-wide push for total quality management. These indicators were error or defect counts, categorized into types, shown in bar graphs with descending importance, and used in postanalyses to isolate where improvement was needed. Each project collected its own data in its own format.

> The action plan estimated the labor for implementation to be 100 man-months over 18 months. Budget cuts later reduced the 100 man-months of labor to 78.

The new approach called for senior management to be briefed every month on the health of each project. To do this, information was collected from each project and compiled into a report that included the project's accomplishments, problems, program trouble reports, quality indicators, scope changes, resource needs, and lessons learned. Also presented were plots of actual versus planned values over time to show the project's schedule, milestones, rate chart, earned value, financial/labor status, and target-system resource use.

The SED implemented a new, division-wide quantitative process-management function and selected one person to be its champion. It standardized the data collected and the reports produced with it, centralized its error-and-defect database, and established a technology center for process-data analysis.

This effort firmly ingrained error-and-defect data collection and analysis into the Hughes culture. It provided the capability required for level 3 maturity and serves as a foundation for future improvement. But time and budget constraints caused it to fall short of achieving all the goals. Some capabilities not achieved are

♦ collecting historical data to support predictions,

♦ projecting analyses within the context of division-wide data,

♦ automating data collection and reporting, and

♦ optimizing data collection based on business needs.

Training gaps. The SED also implemented an organizational policy for required training. Although a policy for required training was not achievable the first time it was tried in 1985, by 1988 the time was right to make it work. (Hughes made training a job requirement, not a promotion requirement, thus solving the equal-employment-opportunity problem that stalled the 1985 effort.)

The company's thrust in continuous measurable improvement and total quality management, combined with the SED manager's personal belief in training resulted in a new policy that required training for all software engineers in the divi-

sion. To support the new requirement, the SED implemented a training-records database that recorded the training status of each employee yearly, at about the time of performance appraisals, and it established a training committee to periodically review training requirements and effectiveness.

Before the 1988 action plan, the SED's internal formal training classes included 17 on modern programming practices, 51 on programming languages and CASE tools, and three on job-specific topics. Enrollment was first-come, first-served. Although training was encouraged and well attended, it was not required.

Although the action plan suggested specific additions to the training program, the SED surveyed its employees to establish what new training was needed. Based on that survey, it added classes on project management, internal reviews, requirements writing, requirements- and unit-level testing, and quality assurance. All these courses had been developed and conducted several times by the 1990 reassessment.

The training programs were open to all engineering functions. Attendance was advertised to and encouraged for all engineers. As of November 1989, 20 percent (174) of the attendees at the training classes were from organizations outside the SED.

Standardized reviews. Before the 1988 action plan, Hughes had established an overall technical-review practice, review criteria, review reporting, data-collection procedures, and the requirement to have a quality-evaluation plan for each project.

Despite these practices, the assessment revealed that the review process was inconsistent. The 1988 action plan included a standard procedure for conducting reviews as well as the training of review leaders in how to conduct reviews. Both were

completed in 1989.

Software-engineering discipline. The 1988 action plan required that software engineers be involved in the system-engineering process, that system engineers become more involved with software, and that software engineers use traditional engineering techniques such as prototypes and experimentation.

The SED could not require that the system-engineering organization implement these changes because system engineering was not under its control.

Instead, the plan required that the SED participate in the system-engineering process, with the realization that some system-engineering organizations might be reluctant to accept its help. In those cases where software engineers were involved with system design, considerably fewer problems occurred and better products resulted.

1990 REASSESSMENT

Early in 1989, Hughes asked the SEI to conduct a second assessment of the SED. The SEI's resources are limited and it can conduct only a few assessments per year, but the opportunity to evaluate a major software organization at two points in its process-improvement program interested the SEI greatly.

The findings and recommendations from the second assessment indicated that substantial improvements had been implemented. From level 2 in 1987, Hughes had progressed to being a strong level 3, with many activities in place to take it to level 4 and 5.

Improvements included the formation of a process group, key training actions, and a comprehensive technical review process. The assessment concluded that Hughes had achieved a strong position of

> **The SED implemented a new, division-wide quantitative process-management function and selected one person to be its champion.**

TABLE 1
COMPARISON OF RESPONSES TO LEVEL 2 AND LEVEL 3 QUESTIONS
(PERCENTAGE OF POSITIVE RESPONSES)

Question		1987 assessment	1990 assessment	Average response (from *State of the Practice*)
Level 2				
2.1.4	Is a formal procedure used to make estimates of software size?	50	100	33
2.2.2	Are profiles of software size maintained for each software configuration item over time?	83	100	36
Level 3				
1.1.7	Is there a software-engineering process group or function?	50	100	69
1.2.3	Is there a required software-engineering training program for software developers?	50	100	44
1.2.5	Is a formal training program required for design- and code-review leaders?	0	100	12
2.4.13	Is a mechanism used for controlling changes to the software design?	50	100	100
2.4.19	Is a mechanism used for verifying that the samples examined by software quality assurance are truly representative of the work performed?	33	100	69
2.4.21	Is there a mechanism for assuring the adequacy of regression testing?	33	80	23

software-process leadership and had established the foundation for continuing process improvement.

The assessment team also found that the professional staff was committed to high-quality software work and that it demonstrated disciplined adherence to the established process.

Findings. The SEI made five basic findings in the second assessment:

◆ The SED's role in the Ground Systems Group. The software-engineering process was constrained by lead program managers' misunderstandings of software issues.

◆ Requirements specifications. The SED had become involved in specifying software requirements for some, but not all, projects.

◆ Process data. The SED had made substantial progress in gathering data, but the progress still required solidification. For example, it needed more assistance for data application and analysis. (Although data analysis at the project level was maturing, division-wide data analysis was limited.)

◆ Process automation. The SED had improved its CASE technologies, but the team found that improvement in six areas would reduce the drudgery and labor of recurring tasks: unit-test procedure generation, execution and analysis of regression tests, path-coverage analysis, CASE-tool evaluation, tool expertise, and tool- and method-effectiveness evaluation.

◆ Training. Training was identified as an organizational strength. However, the team found that additional training was needed to help the projects effectively use the process data being gathered.

Recommendations. The team made six recommendations.

Process awareness. Enhance the awareness and understanding of the software process within lead divisions and Ground Systems Group management.

Process automation. Establish a project-oriented mechanism to assess tool needs and effectiveness, develop or acquire automation support where needs assessment justi-

fies its use, provide ongoing information on CASE availability and capabilities, and make tools expertise available to the projects.

Process-data analysis. Expand the process-data analysis technology to include error projection, train employees to analyze project-specific process data, develop a division-wide context for interpreting project-specific data, and ensure that process data is not used to evaluate individuals.

Data-collection/-analysis use. Optimize process data collection and analysis to best benefit product and business results.

Requirements process. Continue efforts to increase participation in the software-requirements process, update SED bidding practice to require SED input and participation in requirements generation, and increase the skill level of software engineers in writing requirements.

Quality assurance. Ensure adequate SQA support for SED software efforts. In particular, it should ensure that Ground Systems Group SQA practices are consistently applied on all efforts in which the SED is responsible for the software and that the level of SQA effort is sufficient to support each project's needs.

ASSESSMENT COMPARISON

The SEI has compiled data on all the assessments it has conducted in its *State of the Software Engineering Practice.* [2] Tables 1 and 2 detail the two Hughes assessment results compared with the state-of-the-practice data for level 2 and level 3 questions. (Because there was insufficient data on level 4 and 5 questions at the time of the state-of-the-practice report, we cannot include this comparison.)

To provide a valid comparison between the two SED assessments, we used the same SEI questionnaire in both assessments. In 1987, the SED met the level 2 criteria in all important aspects. As Table 1 shows, of the six projects assessed, there were only four negative answers to two of the 12 key level 2 questions. In other words, of 72 answers, 68 were yes. In 1987, the SED could not answer yes to many key level 3 questions, as Table 1 also shows. Table 2 shows the more interesting

changes in the key level 4 questions between the two assessments.

We drew several conclusions from these results. First, in 1987 there was not agreement among projects on some organization-wide questions. For example, in Table 1 questions 1.1.7, 1.2.3, and 1.2.5 concern the total organization, not individual projects. In all cases, these responses should have been 0 percent. Similarly, in Table 2, questions 1.3.4, 2.3.1, 2.3.8, and 2.4.2 relate to the entire organization. Here, the numbers should have been 0 percent for the first three and 100 percent for 2.4.2.

Second, the analysis and error-projection activities asked about in the level 4 questions typically are difficult and require extensive training and support. Because the intent is to focus attention on the key error causes, to build understanding of these critical factors, and gradually to establish the means to control them, considerable data analysis and experience is required before proficiency can be expected.

LESSONS LEARNED

Hughes learned 11 important lessons from the SED process-improvement ef-

fort, listed here in order of importance.

Management commitment. The path to improvement requires investment, risk, time, and the pain of cultural change. Delegation is not strong enough to overcome these roadblocks. Commitment is. Process improvement should be tied to the salary or promotion criteria of senior management.

Pride is the most important result. Improvements are one-time achievements, but pride feeds on itself and leads to continuous measurable improvement. When the whole organization buys into the improvement and sees the results unfold, it gains a team esprit de corps and from that, pride. Hughes' people pulled together to improve the entire organization's software process and they all share in the success.

Increases in maturity decrease risk. Another important benefit (and goal) of process maturation is decreased risk of missing cost and schedule estimates. The two concepts of risk and process maturity are closely coupled. As an organization matures, its performance in meeting planned costs and schedules improves.

TABLE 2
COMPARISON OF RESPONSES TO LEVEL 4 QUESTIONS
(PERCENTAGE OF POSITIVE RESPONSES)

Question		1987 assessment	1990 assessment
1.3.4	Is a mechanism used for managing and supporting the introduction of new technologies?	16	100
2.2.5	Are design errors projected and compared to actuals?	16	20
2.2.6	Are code and test errors projected and compared to actuals?	16	20
2.2.14	Is test coverage measured and recorded for each phase of functional testing?	83	100
2.3.1	Has a managed and controlled process database been established for process metrics data across all projects?	50	100
2.3.2	Are the review data gathered during design reviews analyzed?	16	100
2.3.3	Is the error data from code reviews and tests analyzed to determine the likely distribution and characteristics of the errors remaining in the product?	16	20
2.3.4	Are analyses of errors conducted to determine their process-related causes?	83	100
2.3.8	Is review efficiency analyzed for each project?	50	100
2.4.2	Is a mechanism used for periodically assessing the software-engineering process and implementing indicated improvements?	83	100

The indicator the SED uses for cost risk, and the indicator for which there is historical data available, is a cost-performance index, which is calculated as CPI = BCWP/ACWP, where BCWP is the budgeted cost of work performed and ACWP is the actual cost of work performed.

The CPI has shown a steady improvement, from 0.94 in July 1987 to 0.97 in March 1990. In other words, in July 1987 the SED averaged about 6 percent actual costs over budgeted costs; in March 1990 it had reduced this average to 3 percent. This 50-percent reduction nets Hughes about $2 million annually. These values are averages for all SED projects at the time.

When considering all the direct labor, support, overhead, travel, and equipment costs for the assessment and improvement costs, these first-year benefits are five times the total improvement expenditures.

Assuming that the Hughes maturity is at least maintained, these financial benefits should continue to accrue. Furthermore, the improved contract performance makes Hughes' estimates of software cost more credible during contract negotiations.

The benefits are worth the effort and expense. When the improvement effort was begun in 1988, Hughes was not sure what the benefits would be, other than achieving the next higher level on the process-maturity model. However, Hughes received a handsome return on its investment: The quality of work life has improved, and the company's image has benefited from the improved performance.

The SED has experienced very few crises at the Ground Systems Group facility since applying a mature process to each project. Although volatile requirements continue to be a persistent engineering problem, the effect of shifting requirements on cost and schedule is under con-

trol and reliably predictable.

A less quantifiable result of process maturity is the quality of work life. Hughes SED has seen fewer overtime hours, fewer gut-wrenching problems to deal with each day, and a more stable work environment. Even in the volatile aerospace industry in California, software-professional turnover has been held below 10 percent.

Software technology center is key. A software technology center works most effectively when most of the development, project management, administration, technology development, training, and marketing are housed in one organization.

> Hughes SED has seen fewer overtime hours, fewer gut-wrenching problems to deal with each day, and a more stable work environment.

The size and focus of such a central organization makes it possible to afford, for example, an SEPG that focuses on technology improvement, a full-time person in charge of technology transfer, an organization-wide data-collection and -analysis service, independent software research and development, and a CASE center. All these are important contributors to improving process maturity.

A coherent culture exists at level 3. A coherent organizational culture results from the cumulative effect of a long-lived organization with a common purpose, environment, education, and experience base. You can quickly sense the nature of an organization's culture when you hear people speaking in the same technical language, sharing common practices and procedures, and referring to organizational goals as their own.

At level 3, Hughes found that the common culture helped foster an esprit de corps that reinforced team performance. In fact, Hughes concluded it needed to achieve a common process across the organization, to establish an organization-wide training program, and to enable buy-in of organizational goals. Although it is difficult to precisely phrase a question to determine if an organization does or does

not have such a positive culture, an assessment team can agree whether or not team members experienced it during an assessment.

A focal point is essential. Disintegrated, asynchronous improvement is not only inefficient but also ineffective for solving organization-wide problems. Although there is still the need for cell-level improvement teams, there must also be an organizational focal point to plan, coordinate (integrate), and implement organization-wide process improvements. The SEI calls this focal point an SEPG. Hughes calls it the technology steering committee, others might call it an engineering council. Whatever the name, there must be a focal point.

Technology transfer is essential. The establishment of a technology-transfer function was judged the most profound of the actions taken.

Software-process expertise is essential. In 1987, the SEI questionnaire and a few SEI professionals were all the expert help there was. Now there is a growing literature on software process, a draft capability maturity model, and an improved draft questionnaire. Many SEI people are experts in software process, and even more people in industry have become experts in software process.[1]

To understand and use the available knowledge, process-improvement teams must become process experts and they must be able to interpret the assessment questionnaire in the context of the organization. For example, the SED wrestled over the ambiguity of the phrase "first-line managers" in the questionnaire. In the Hughes organization, "manager" is used only for the third promotion level and above in the line-management hierarchy, but this isn't what the SEI meant. After discussions with the SEI over the meaning of the phrase, Hughes concluded that it meant the first supervisory position for software engineers, a position Hughes called group head.

Because group heads did not sign off on schedules and cost estimates, Hughes considered changing their practices to require the heads to do so. However, Hughes found that some software projects have eight people, while others might include an entire lab of 250 people with several sections and many groups. It thus did not always seem appropriate to have group heads approve schedules and cost estimates.

Hughes finally concluded that "first-line manager" in the Hughes culture meant associate project manager, the person who is in charge of software development on a project (no matter what level), and the one who negotiates and approves schedules and cost estimates with the program manager, documenting those agreements in a work authorization and delegation document. Hughes SED thus translated the question "Do software first-line managers sign off on their schedules and cost estimates?" as "Do associate project managers approve work authorization and delegation documents?"

An action plan is necessary. An action plan based on process-maturity assessment recommendations will not necessarily move an organization to the next stage of maturity. Assessment recommendations come from a brainstorming and consensus-building team process that, because of the nature of the process and the time limitations, can address only the top priority recommendations (about 10 out of 36 in the last assessment). Furthermore, action plans tend to not include many people-oriented changes (such as getting people to buy in on changes) that are needed for progress.

The only ones questioning the value of level 2 are those who have not achieved it. To an organization that has achieved it, level 2 capabilities seem obvious and indispensable. It is simply a natural, responsible way of conducting business.

When compared with those of the general population of SEI-assessed organizations, it is clear that the 1987 Hughes improvement efforts started from a very strong base. Based on the SEI data, the Hughes process in 1987 was in approximately the 90th percentile of all organizations studied.[2]

It is also clear that given sufficient management emphasis and competent, skilled, and dedicated professionals, significant improvement in software process is possible. Improvements like those made at Hughes' SED can significantly help a software organization's overall business performance. The SEI assessment of Hughes' SED formed the bases for a sustained improvement effort.

Finally, improvement is reinforcing. As each improvement level is reached, the benefits are demonstrated and the opportunities for further improvement become clear. ◆

Watts S. Humphrey, a reseach scientist at the Software Engineering Institute, founded its software-process program, which helps establish advanced software-engineering processes, metrics, methods, and quality programs for the US government and its contractors. He is the author of three books and holds five US patents.

Humphrey received a BS in physics from the University of Chicago, an MS in physics from Illinois Institute of Technology, and an MBA from the University of Chicago. He is an IEEE fellow, a member of ACM, and a member of the board of examiners for the Malcolm Baldrige National Quality Award.

Terry R. Snyder is manager of Hughes Aircraft's Ground Systems Group. He has more than 30 years experience managing and programming large-scale, real-time systems. The Ground Systems Group develops air defense and air traffic control systems, communication systems, ground and shipboard radar, shipboard electronic systems, and military displays.

Snyder received a BS in math from Penn State and is a graduate of UCLA's Executive Management Program. He serves on Software Productivity Consortium's board of directors, is a member of the Aerospace Industries Association's embedded software committee, and serves on the University of California at Irvine's Computer Science Dept's. advisory board.

Ronald R. Willis is a member of the technical staff of Hughes Aircraft's Ground Systems Group, where he is a chief scientist in the Software Engineering Division. He has coauthored a book, written many technical articles, and has developed systems for discrete-event simulation, graphical modeling and simulation analysis, and software quality engineering.

Willis received a BS in mathematics from California State University at Long Beach and an MS in computer science from the University of Southern California. He is a member of ACM.

Address questions about this article to Humphrey at Software Engineering Institute, Carnegie Mellon University, Pittsburgh, PA 15213; Internet watts@sei.cmu.edu.

ACKNOWLEDGMENTS

We thank Ken Dymond, Larry Druffel, George Pandelious, Jeff Perdue, and Jim Rozum for their helpful review comments. We very much appreciate Dorothy Josephson's support in preparing the manuscript and the able editorial assistance of Linda Pesante and Marie Elm. The comments and suggestions of Carl Chang and the anonymous referees were also a great help in converting our manuscript into a finished article.

This work was sponsored by the US Defense Dept.

REFERENCES

1. W.S. Humphrey, *Managing the Software Process*, Addison-Wesley, Reading, Mass., 1989.
2. W.S. Humphrey, D.H. Kitson, and T.C. Kasse, "The State of Software-Engineering Practice: A Preliminary Report," Tech. Report CMU/SEI-89-TR-1, Software Eng. Inst., Carnegie Mellon Univ., Pittsburgh, 1989.

Reprinted from *IEEE Software*, Vol. 8, No. 4, July 1991, pp. 25-41. Copyright © 1991 by The Institute of Electrical and Electronics Engineers, Inc. All rights reserved.

A Critical Look at Software Capability Evaluations

TERRY B. BOLLINGER, *NEC America*
CLEMENT MCGOWAN, *Software Productivity Consortium*

◆ *The Software Engineering Institute's Software Capability Evaluation program is having a profound effect on the software community.*
However, a critical look reveals serious flaws in SCE methods.

I n recent years, the concept of software process assessment has become increasingly important both to the software community in general and to software developers for the US Defense Dept. in particular. In the most general use of the phrase, a software process assessment is simply a determination of how various parts of a project (such as people, tasks, tools, standards, and resources) interact to produce software. The objectives of a process assessment are to understand and improve how an organization uses its resources to build high-quality software.

One of the most interesting approaches to process assessment comes from the Software Engineering Institute, a Defense Dept.-sponsored research and development center in Pittsburgh. Since about 1987, the SEI has promoted a well-defined approach to process assessment that emphasizes self-evaluation by organizations,

with the SEI providing the necessary training of personnel and various levels of on-site assistance.[1] Results of SEI assessments are kept confidential, and organizations are often surprised at how positively its employees react to such assessments. SEI process assessments are normally done at the request of the assessed organizations, not the government.

There is, however, a curious twist to SEI assessments. Although SEI assessments are valuable in their own right, many organizations are interested in them because of a closely related program called Software Capability Evaluation, which is used by US government agencies to judge how capable companies are at developing software.

The SCE program was developed by the SEI in parallel with its process-assessment program, and the two programs share many concepts and source materials. Unlike SEI assessments, though, SCEs

1. **Sign up.** High-level management agrees to an assessment and commits to improvement.
2. **Training.** A small team from the organization is trained in how to perform assessments.
3. **Preparation.** The trained team prepares to ensure an orderly one-week assessment.
4. **Questionnaire.** Selected projects and groups fill out an SEI questionnaire (101 yes/no answers).
5. **Assessment.** The trained team performs an intensive week of project and group interviews.
6. **Presentation.** The week concludes with the presentation of key findings to management.
7. **Report.** The trained team produces a report on key findings and how to implement them.
8. **Implementation.** Management works to follow through on improvement commitments.

Figure 1. SEI process-assessment steps.

are neither voluntary nor confidential. An agency may require that all its current or potential software contractors undergo an SCE, and it may then use the SCE results to weed out low-scoring organizations from the bidding process. One apt analogy often used by people familiar with the two programs is that having an assessment is like hiring a tax consultant, while having an SCE is like being audited by the US Internal Revenue Service.

The SEI has designed its process assessments to act as preparatory tests for SCEs, so organizations that undergo assessments will have a better idea of what will be expected of them during SCEs. It is this close linkage of SEI assessments with SCE evaluations that helps make SEI process assessments a subject of intense interest to most companies that compete for government software contracts.

SUBSTANTIAL EFFECT

The potential effect of these two associated programs on the software industry is likely to be substantial. Even though they are targeted primarily at the software developers used by the Defense Dept., the competitive effects of low SCE ratings will almost surely spill over into other software-development arenas. For example,

other US government agencies, such as the National Aeronautics and Space Administration, may have difficulty justifying the use of contractors with low SCE scores. Even private industry is likely to follow suit eventually, based on the assumption that a rating system that is good enough for the US government should be good enough for them.

If the effect of these two programs is likely to be that broad, they certainly merit close examination. We have been trained at the SEI in how to perform process assessments, and we have had extensive talks with SEI personnel on both assessments and the SCE program. We have analyzed several key components of the assessment and SCE programs, and our analysis has resulted in some surprising (and in some cases distressing) findings. Finally, we have both participated in several custom, non-SEI assessments within Contel Technology Center (our former employer) and have found from this firsthand experience that many of the assessment concepts taught by the SEI are very effective at helping development groups increase their ability to work efficiently.

We feel that our combined background of training, detailed analysis, and sincere interest and enthusiasm for process assessment provides us with a good basis for the close examination of SCE methods given in this article.

Our overall conclusion is that while the SEI has developed a truly outstanding program for performing process assessments, both its assessment and the SCE program are seriously flawed by their reliance on the SEI's unproven process-maturity model. Furthermore, the methods by which the SCE program determines numeric process-maturity scores for organizations are so riddled with statistical and methodological problems that it appears unlikely that such ratings have any meaningful correlation to the actual abilities of organizations to produce high-quality software on time and within budget. These SCE scoring flaws include a striking degree of indifference to how well (or poorly) a organization uses technology and automation to increase process efficiency, a very weak, sparse-coverage ap-

proach to collecting and analyzing process maturity data, and a failure to deal clearly with the issue of process risk. (As we describe in the box on pp. 35-37, our own work with custom process assessments has led us to conclude that risk understanding and reduction are fundamental issues in defining and optimizing software processes.)

SEI PROCESS ASSESSMENTS

Because SEI assessments are a preparation for SCEs, it is helpful to look at the assessment program first. Figure 1 shows the major steps in an SEI process assessment.

Steps. Preparation for an assessment begins officially when high-level management at the organization signs up to have an assessment. The SEI has focused on this top-down approach as a way of increasing the chances that the recommendations from an assessment will actually be implemented. Furthermore, this approach gives assessment participants more confidence that their input may actually result in changes at the organization. The result is a greater motivation to cooperate.

Next, a carefully selected team of people from the organization is trained in performing assessments. This training is provided either directly by SEI personnel or by private groups that the SEI has accredited for assessment training. Once they have been trained in how to do SEI assessments, the primary responsibility for performing assessments falls on the newly trained team. From that point on, the role of the SEI and its accredited private trainers is strictly to help the newly trained team assess its own organization. This approach greatly facilitates the important objective of keeping results confidential and keeps the SEI training program from being overloaded.

The newly trained team then selects specific projects and functional groups to interview. Representatives from these selected projects and groups are asked to fill out a 101-item, yes/no questionnaire about how they currently develop software. In SEI assessments, this questionnaire turns out to be little more than a starting point for later detailed discussions. However, this process questionnaire has very important implications for an SCE and is therefore described in considerable detail during the SEI assessment training.

The actual assessment takes from three to five days. It consists mostly of intensive interviews and guided group discussions. Due in large part to the SEI's excellent materials and training, these interviews and discussions are usually far more positive in tone and content than you might expect.

Team leaders are trained to encourage an atmosphere of open discussion without fear of repercussions, which is feasible only because the SEI methods place a strong emphasis on confidentiality and non-attribution of data. Team leaders, project representatives, and functional-group representatives are asked to reach a group consensus on how they would recommend that the organization's software processes be changed, and the resulting recommendations are presented to higher level management on the last day of the assessment.

This is an area in which assessments contrast sharply with SCEs. While in SEI assessments the dominant objective of the team leader is to encourage open communication, in SCEs the major objective is to verify that the organization has answered a series of yes/no questions accurately, and that it has documentation to back up those answers. Not too surprisingly, this "prove I can trust you" approach of SCEs makes the kind of free, open communication found in SEI assessments very unlikely.

After the assessment, the team must write a report that describes how those recommendations should be implemented. The chances that the report will actually be implemented (a concern familiar to many software-engineering and quality-assurance groups) is greatly increased by the fact that high-level management has explicitly commissioned the assessment and thus has committed itself publicly to taking action on the resulting report. While this arrangement does not guarantee implementation, it at least ensures that the report cannot easily be forgotten or put aside.

Strong points. What makes SEI assessments truly remarkable is their ability to bring together people from projects and groups that may not even be on speaking terms and, in most cases, to integrate them into a proactive, forward-looking development team. One common result of process assessment is that conflicting groups may realize that their difficulties in working together result from poorly structured processes, rather than from, say, personality conflicts.

Another strong point of SEI assessments is that they introduce standard software-engineering practices in an open, constructive forum that encourages people to take them seriously and try to apply them in their own work. By combining such technology-transfer issues with process issues, people are often better able to see how such practices apply to their own specific circumstances and needs.

The SEI's program for training people in how to do process assessments should also receive high marks: Its well-organized concepts and training methods are instrumental to the success of those who must actually perform process assessments. The SEI training program appears to be highly responsive to feedback from those who have been trained in its methods and from those who have done assessments. This responsiveness and attention to detail has helped the SEI fine-tune its training program so that those trained are thoroughly versed in the details of how to make their process assessments successful.

However, one implication of the mostly people-oriented strengths of SEI assessments is that such assessments are less dependent on the use of a specific maturity model or set of questions than you might expect. For example, in our own custom process assessments we do not use SEI-style questionnaires at all, but instead focus first on building a detailed graphical model of the existing software process.

Despite such a different starting point, our custom process assessments achieve the same types of improvements in process, integration, and team outlook that are the strongest features of SEI assessments. This experience leads us to believe that effective process assessments depend far more on having good methods for recording and analyzing process issues than they do on using the SEI process-maturity model or questionnaire.

Weak points. SEI assessments elicit far more information about processes than they can record. Final reports in the SEI assessments give major recommendations and detailed action plans, but they do not normally include any detailed road maps of how the process is structured and controlled.

Such process-modeling information has great value for defining exactly how and where improvements should be made and for increasing the overall awareness of how the components of a development organization work together. Also, detailed process models can provide invaluable starting points for new projects that otherwise might have to design their processes from scratch.

A second and potentially more serious flaw has to do with the SEI's process-maturity model, which is the basis for much of the SEI assessment approach. While the SEI process-maturity model is clearly intended to help design-intensive organizations become better at developing software, in reality it appears to strongly favor maintenance processes with relatively narrow product definitions. We examine the flaws inherent in this model in more detail later in this article.

SEI CAPABILITY EVALUATIONS

The SCE program was designed by the SEI in close conjunction with its process-assessment program. The stated goal

> Effective process assessments depend far more on good methods for recording and analyzing process issues than they do on using the SEI model.

of the SCE program is to provide the Defense Dept. with a method by which it can rank the overall capability of organizations to produce software in a timely, repeatable fashion.

Training in SCE methods is restricted to government employees, so we verified this information by sending early copies of this article to people involved in both assessment and SCE training. These review copies were followed by extensive phone conversations in which the basic factual information about SCE methods was confirmed, although SEI personnel were reluctant to go into detail. These conversations also demonstrated to us the highly positive role that SCE personnel have played in working to make the program as fair and equitable as possible.

SCE training program. As with process assessment, the SEI has an extensive, highly developed training course in how to apply SCE methods. Attendance at SCE training is available only to US government employees and employees of Mitre Corp., which has a special quasigovernmental status.

By all accounts available, this training program appears to be just as carefully and meticulously done as its assessment counterpart, although its auditing objectives obviously make much of its content unique. For example, one major thrust of the program is to teach SCE trainees how to distinguish genuine answers from attempts at obfuscation or even outright falsification. People are trained for this possibility by interviewing "The Teflon Contractor," an SEI person to whom nearly any question can be asked but from whom very few relevant answers will be received.

A second major theme of SCE training is fairness. SCE trainers make a sincere and concerted effort to ensure that their trainees do not just view an SCE as a rote procedure by which capability ratings can be mechanically cranked out. Instead, they emphasize the importance of looking at and understanding the overall context of software development at an organization.

Given this sincere emphasis on fairness, we were very surprised to discover that the SEI apparently has a standard policy of sidestepping questions about all detailed aspects of its SCE program. Whenever we asked various SEI people questions about any detailed aspects of SCE training, they went to remarkable lengths to either change the subject or give generic answers. At no time did they simply say, "I'm not allowed to answer that." The overall effect was strikingly similar to that of a Teflon Contractor session, except that it was the SEI rather than a contractor who was avoiding the questions.

For example, even though it is public information that the grading templates distributed in SEI assessment training are exactly the same ones used in SCE grading, we were flatly unable to get anyone from SEI to confirm this fact, no matter how explicitly we asked the question. We were never told that this was in any way confidential information — but neither were we ever given a direct answer!

The rationale behind such curious obfuscation presumably is that giving out details on SCE training might give some contractors unfair advantages in SCEs. However, the SEI appears to have placed itself in the highly unusual position of treating some of the same documents (like the grading templates) as public information in assessment training but as confidential information in SCE training. It would seem much more straightforward if it simply specified what aspects of both programs are confidential and what aspects are not, and then to answer questions about such issues directly.

SCE steps. Procedurally, an evaluation resembles a simplified process assessment. The organization is first notified that it will be audited. It then receives and completes the same questionnaire used in the SEI assessments (although an SEI assessment is not a prerequisite for an audit). A team of SEI-trained evaluators (auditors) from the Defense Dept. or other government agency is then sent to the site to carefully review the answers with members of the organization.

This on-site meeting is intended to clear up any misunderstandings about the meanings of questions, to verify the accuracy of responses, and to obtain general information about the organization's process capabilities. The auditors then collect the findings into a report and use the verified information from the questionnaire to develop a process-maturity grade that can range in value from level 1 (low) to level 5 (high).

The detailed information collected in these on-site meetings is known to the agencies that perform the audits, but is not made public. The numeric grades may or may not be made public, depending on the policies of the agencies. Organizations that rate high on the SEI numeric scale are usually anxious to make their numeric scores public, which in turn creates a competitive effect that may force other groups to publicize their scores lest they be assumed to be very low.

SCE grades. Although the total amount of information collected during an SCE is far more than just a number, it is difficult to overstate the psychological and contractual implications of the numeric grade assigned as one result of an SCE. At conferences and meetings where SCE audits are discussed, the level grades are not just the major topic of discussion — they are usually the *only* topic of discussion.

SEI advocates like to focus on how many organizations have moved up how many levels, especially when companies reach one of the higher levels. Contracting agencies are often interested in using SCE grades to flatly bar low-scoring companies from bidding on new contracts — an idea that, by the way, makes SEI advocates very uneasy. The most frequent criterion mentioned in such discussions is that only organizations with scores of level 3 or above should be permitted to bid on new work.

> It is difficult to overstate the psychological and contractual implications of the numeric grade.

As you might expect, private-industry representatives tend to react to such comments with trepidation. One analogy we've heard is that the the SEI grading system is a steamroller that is about to roll right over the software industry. It is a pointed analogy, but one with which many industry people seem to sympathize. SEI advocates usually respond to such comments by pointing out all positive aspects of process assessment, ignoring that for many organizations an assessment is merely a prelude an SCE audit.

Ironically, the SEI seems genuinely opposed to the idea of its numeric grading system becoming such a steamroller. Its position is that using only the numeric grades violates the intent of the SCE program. In the SEI's view, it is the full set of information and recommendations developed during an SCE that is truly important for understanding an organization's maturity, not the numeric grade. When the SEI originally devised the SCE methods, it simply did not anticipate the intense focus that government agencies, private industry, and even the SEI itself would wind up placing on the SCE numeric grades.

Determining SCE grades. Given the high interest in the SCE numeric grades, it is worth taking a close look at how they are derived. The three components are:

♦ SEI process-maturity framework. This is the five-level scale with which the output of the SEI grading templates is associated.

♦ SEI process-maturity questionnaire. This is a standardized yes/no questionnaire used in both assessments and SCEs.

♦ SEI grading templates. These standardized grading templates are also used in both assessments and SCEs.

Framework. This five-level scale is described in detail in *Managing the Software Process* by Watts Humphrey.[2] Figure 2 summarizes the intent of its five levels, as derived from the book and the SCE grading templates.

Questionnaire. The SEI process-maturity questionnaire consists of 101 yes/no ques-

tions on a variety of software-engineering and process issues. Figure 3 shows a subject breakdown for the questionnaire. (The SEI has been working to develop a new questionnaire, but at the time this article was written it had not yet released the new version for use in assessments or SCEs.)

To fully understand its impact on SEI assessments and SCEs, you must view this questionnaire from two perspectives. From the first perspective, it is a tool for introducing a variety of important management, process, and technical issues that are of undisputed importance to developing an efficient software-development organization. From the second perspective, the SEI questionnaire is just a checklist from which the data used to determine the critically important process-maturity grade is mechanically extracted. These two perspectives have strikingly different implications.

When viewed from the first perspective, the SEI questionnaire is simply a launching point for more detailed discussions on management, process, and technical issues. This is precisely how it is used in SEI assessments. The questions provide a starting point for conversations that quickly focus on more specific issues that are unique to an organization. From this perspective, the specific questions used in the SEI questionnaire are less important than the general subject areas they introduce.

However, when viewed from the second perspective of process-maturity grading, the questionnaire can no longer be viewed as just a starting point for wide-ranging process discussions. Instead it becomes one component of a precisely defined grading process in which the relative importance of the questions can vary greatly.

One area in which such differences show up very distinctly is in the use of software tools and technology to improve process efficiency. The SEI questionnaire has 16 questions that directly address the subject of tools and technology, and another five that deal with how new technologies should be acquired, managed, and introduced. These 21 technology ques-

Level 1 — "Initial" processes
♦ SEI: *"Unpredictable and poorly controlled"*
♦ Includes nearly all "unprepared" organizations
♦ No entry requirements, so skills may vary greatly

Level 2 — "Repeatable" processes
♦ SEI: *"Can repeat previously mastered tasks"*
♦ Focus on management and tight project control
♦ Focus on collecting various types of "trend" data

Level 3 — "Defined" processes
♦ SEI: *"Process characterized, fairly well understood"*
♦ Focus on software design skills, design tracking
♦ Focus on various types of traceability

Level 4 — "Managed" processes
♦ SEI: *"Process measured and controlled"*
♦ Focus on technology management and insertion
♦ Focus on estimates/actuals, error-cause analysis

Level 5 — "Optimizing" processes
♦ SEI: *"Focus on process improvement"*
♦ Focus on rapid technology updating, replacement
♦ Focus on process optimization to reduce errors

Figure 2. The SEI process-maturity framework.

Organization and resource management	
Organizational structure	7
Resources, personnel, and training	5
Technology management	5
Total	17
Software-engineering process and its management	
Documented standards and procedures	18
Process metrics	19
Data management and analysis	9
Process control	22
Total	68
Tools and technology (not graded)	16
Total questions	101
Total graded questions	85

Figure 3. Maturity questionnaire subjects by topic.

tions provide a more than adequate base for allowing a process assessment to focus strongly on the need for tools to help automate and streamline the software process.

In contrast to this rich set of technol-

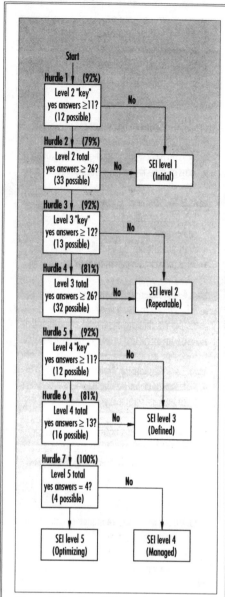

Figure 4. *Grading of SEI questionnaires.*

ogy questions in the questionnaire itself, the importance of technology issues from the perspective of process-maturity grading is negligible. As described in a September 30, 1987, SEI training document, "SEI Assessment Methodology," the 16 direct technology questions are completely ignored during SEI maturity grading. The five remaining general questions on technology management are graded, but are given very low priority until the higher levels (4 and 5) are reached. The net result is that the effect of technology on the software process is very nearly ignored when a company is audited by an SCE.

In the same document, the SEI does define a separate two-stage method for classifying organizations as having "inefficient technology" (stage A) or "basic tech-

nology" (stage B). However, the boundary between these two categories is extremely vague, since the SEI document simply says that stage B organizations should answer yes to "most" of the 16 technology questions in the questionnaire. This technology rating method does not appear to be in general use anyway, since we have never heard it discussed or even mentioned by the SEI or anyone else.

The unfortunate implication of all this is that a company that has made excellent use of automation to streamline its software process would not necessarily be assured of getting a better maturity grade than a similar company that relies heavily on inefficient manual methods. Strictly interpreted, the SEI grading methods would not even be able to detect the process effects of programming business applications in machine code versus a fourth-generation language. As long as a company that uses machine code meets all of the nontechnology criteria of SEI grading, it could easily rank as high or higher than an enormously more more efficient company that uses only fourth-generation language.

Technology can also be used to automate error-prone process steps, rather than just trying to make them more predictable. Automation of this type clearly meets the spirit of the SEI program because it moves the overall process toward greater reliability and lower cost. Such automation also increases control over the process, assures quality, and frees people to concentrate on areas that cannot be automated.

The reason for this remarkable disparity in how technology questions in the SEI questionnaire are handled appears to have its roots in Humphrey's five-level process-maturity model. This model incorporates the assumption that until an organization has its software process firmly under control, it will simply not be able to adequately handle the effects of new technology. This outlook appears to have been firmly held as the official SEI position up until as recently as January 1991.

However, in the last few months, the SEI appears to have adopted a much more positive, proactive approach to process-technology issues. We think this is a very

positive change and hope that it will soon be reflected in the critically important grading policies that the SEI and various government agencies are still using to assign maturity grades to private software organizations.

GRADING TEMPLATES

The exact algorithm for grading the SEI questionnaires is contained in a set of public-domain grading templates that use holes to group answers according to the grading levels. The same algorithm is also described more directly in various SEI training documents.

Figure 4 illustrates the SCE grading algorithm. The best way to look at the algorithm is to think of it as a series of seven hurdles, each of which is really a very small true/false test for a specific set of questions. The total number of questions in this series of hurdles is 85, since the algorithm ignores the 16 technology questions.

Level 1 means "failed." One interesting point that can easily be seen from the figure is that level 1 is really not a level at all, but the logical equivalent of an F — a failing grade. Level 1 is a failing grade because it requires no effort whatsoever to obtain it — you can answer no to every question on the test and still wind up with a level 1 rating.

What this means in practice is that the level 1 category could include a very broad range of organizations, ranging from those that are totally incapable of producing software to those with excellent bottom-line development track records. The breadth of the level 1 failure category will of course depend on how closely the criteria for getting a passing grade (level 2 or above) correspond to the actual productivity and quality of a software organization.

The first SCE hurdle. Figure 5 quotes the 12 first-hurdle questions verbatim from the SEI questionnaire. (All italics are as used in the questionnaire.)

These questions in the first hurdle can be grouped into four major themes:

♦ Management controls. Four questions (1, 3, 9, and 10) deal with an organization's basic management controls and policies.

♦ Configuration controls. Three questions (2, 11, and 12) deal with configuration control at both the code and requirements levels.

♦ Project estimation. Three questions (4, 5, and 6) focus on formal procedures for estimating project-level issues such as sizes, times (schedules), and costs.

♦ Data collection. The remaining questions (7 and 8) deal with data collection on code size and numbers of errors found during testing.

With the possible exception of the fourth theme of data collection, these are certainly reasonable issues to address early in the history of a process. Management and configuration control seem particularly appropriate because they provide an immediate payback by giving the process a structure, reducing confusion, and minimizing lost work. Project estimation also seems to be a reasonable early theme because it safeguards against unrealistic resource commitments.

The last theme of data collection is more surprising because it is not obvious what a supposedly immature software organization should do with a metric such as code size trends after collecting it. Possibly it is intended to get data collection off to an early start, so the organization will have the data available for later use. However, based on *Managing the Software Process*, it would appear that this emphasis is most likely part of an overall theme of gaining statistical control over the software process, much as assembly-line factories use statistical control to ensure product quality. (While this emphasis on a software factory model is by no means unique to the SEI model, the SEI approach in general seems to take the assembly-line model for software development much farther than most other models.)

Artificial ordering. One troublesome feature of multihurdle grading is that it tends to introduce artificial ordering into the test's subject area — an implied order of difficulty that reflects the test structure rather than the structure of the subject area.

1. Does the Software Quality Assurance (SQA) function have a management reporting channel separate from the software development project management? (SEI question 1.1.3)
2. Is there a software configuration control function for each project that involves software development? (1.1.6)
3. Is a *formal process* used in the management review of each software development prior to making contractual commitments? (2.1.3)
4. Is a *formal procedure* used to make estimates of software size? (2.1.14)
5. Is a *formal procedure* used to produce software development schedules? (2.1.15)
6. Are *formal procedures* applied to estimating software development cost? (2.1.16)
7. Are profiles of software size maintained for each software configuration item, over time? (2.2.2)
8. Are statistics on software code and test errors gathered? (2.2.4)
9. Does senior management have a *mechanism* for the regular review of the status of software development projects? (2.4.1)
10. Do software development first-line managers sign off on their schedules and cost estimates? (2.4.7)
11. Is a *mechanism* used for controlling changes to the software requirements? (2.4.9)
12. Is a *mechanism* used for controlling changes to the code? (Who can make changes and under which circumstances?) (2.4.17)

Figure 5. *First-hurdle questions (italics are the SEI's).*

The problem is that, in multihurdle testing, questions in the last hurdle tend to be very hard to reach, even if the questions themselves are easily answered. For example, it is very common in SEI process assessments to hear people complain that although they can honestly answer yes to the majority of the level 3 questions, they are not permitted to grade those answers because they have already missed two or more level 2 questions. Such complaints are often a good indicator of an unfair grading system and should not be dismissed lightly.

Statistical reliability. Another feature of the SCE algorithm is that it is remarkably complex for a method that grades only 85 yes/no questions. A yes/no test of this size would normally be graded by an algorithm that was no more complex than a simple percentage cutoff.

By breaking the test into a multihurdle structure, the statistical reliability of the answer set is reduced in two ways. First, each hurdle, or minitest, will be less reliable simply because it has fewer questions. Second, the way the tests are linked into a chain means that the uncertainty of the individual minitests must be multiplied by each other. Taken together, these effects result in a very rapid escalation of statistical uncertainty as the total number of hurdles is increased.

For SCE grading, this lack of statistical reliability shows up as quirky grading results. An organization with no foreknowl-

edge of the SEI questionnaire or grading system could in principle answer yes to all but two of the 85 graded questions and still end up being rated as a "failed" (level 1) organization. This can happen because the first hurdle in SEI grading requires that at least 11 of its 12 questions be answered correctly. If an organization misses more than one of that key set of 12 questions, it will fail the entire test, regardless of how well it answers any other questions.

Failing the hard way. This possibility of failing an SCE by missing only two questions merits examination. For example, are the questions in the first hurdle sufficiently good data points to indicate that an organization that misses two of them should fail? Unfortunately, the answer appears to be no. An organization that is sincerely committed to all four of the first hurdle themes can still fail the SCE test simply because it does not have exactly the right kind of management controls, configuration controls, project estimation, or data collection.

For example, an organization might have an extensive program for collecting and using data. It might collect data on issues such as the number and type of problems found in walkthroughs, complexity, correlations between complexity and testing difficulty, test results, and total work expended each time a change is implemented in a baselined interface definition. But if that organization happens to believe that the much simpler metric of

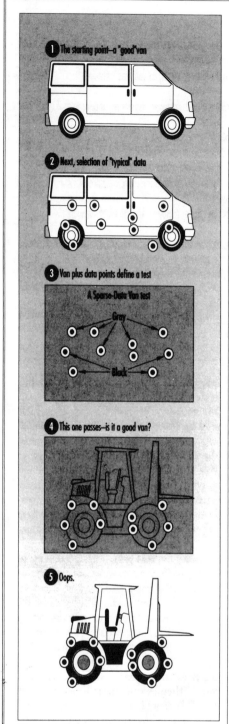

Figure 6. *Ambiguity in sparse-data analysis.*

size trends (question 7 in Figure 5) is neither relevant nor useful, it will be halfway to failing its SCE audit.

Now, suppose the same organization was also very committed to quality assurance, so managers and developers who could not show a clear commitment to quality simply did not get hired. As a result, the organization developed an unusually solid and close working relationship between developers and quality-assurance personnel, one in which developers viewed quality-assurance people as important team members who were responsible for finding problems before they mushroomed into extra work for the developers. Due to this unusually good working relationship, the organization hired quality-assurance people directly into projects so they could focus on the specific quality-assurance needs of each project.

It would be a serious understatement to say that such an organization was in keeping with the spirit of process-level quality assurance. Unfortunately, none of the complex history, reasoning, or even actual quality results of such an organization would show up under the SEI testing scheme, because the organization would answer "no" to question 1 of the first hurdle, which asks whether quality-assurance people have an independent management chain.

So our example organization, despite a serious commitment to quality and reliability and the possibility that it may have done very well on the other questions in the test, has failed the SCE audit.

Such a result is even more interesting if you consider what the SEI literature has to say about the quality and dependability of level 1 organizations. On page 55 of *Managing the Software Process*, Humphrey stated that "the Initial [level 1] Process is the lack of a managed, defined, planned, and disciplined process for developing software." On page 5 he wrote, "until the process is under statistical control, orderly progress in process improvement is not possible."

Descriptions such as these are not going to help the hypothetical organization get new work, since anyone familiar with the SEI's grading scale would tend to assume the SCE audit had proven such descriptions were applicable. After all, once you have an F on your report card, it can be very hard to persuade people that it really would have been a C if you had only answered a couple more questions correctly.

Of course, you might respond that the organization is only hypothetical and thus highly unrealistic, or that any organization that was that good could easily reconfigure details of how it operates so it would be more in line with the structure of the SEI's multihurdle grading system. But this overlooks the main point of the example: When you are developing a testing strategy for analyzing a complex system, using a very sparse set of one-bit data points will expose your test to the significant danger of misinterpreting the real situation.

SPARSE-DATA ANALYSIS

The issue of whether sparse data sets can be used reliably to analyze complex systems such as software processes deserves a closer look, since it addresses the overall approach the SEI has selected for SCE scoring.

Figure 6 shows a graphical example of the general problem of using fixed templates to evaluate a complex, highly variable system. As the figure shows, the central problem with such templates is that they can only pin down a small set of specific features. You generally would not want to define a forklift as a good example of a van, but if the data collected during the analysis is too sparse, it becomes difficult to prevent such definitions.

The forklift dilemma. Of course, there's an obvious solution, which is simply to increase the number of test points. After all, it would only take more probe points in Figure 6 to banish the forklift. However, this "more probes" approach suffers from two significant problems.

The first problem is that adding many such fixed probe points will not only eliminate most nonvans, it will also eliminate most good vans. That is because fixed-point data collection requires not just a template, but also an example of what an ideal van looks like. For example, if someone chose to produce a van that replaces the traditional cargo-oriented sliding doors with people-oriented passenger doors, how would this new van rate under a fixed-template test? The answer is that it would be very likely to fail — not because it is a bad van, but because it is a *different* van, one that deviates from the assumed ideal model.

In the SEI's process testing, such problems are aggravated because its model is based on an ideal organization that never existed. As described in *Managing the Software Process*, the highest levels (4 and 5) of the SEI process-maturity framework are extrapolations from a very small number of isolated projects that were done many years ago at IBM. The book gives little quantitative data on bottom-line productivity and quality results from these projects, so it is difficult to judge how well the proposed methods actually worked.

Even if the model projects did indeed work very well, an extrapolation of this magnitude is clearly risky. In terms of the van analogy, it would be roughly equivalent building one or two small models of a supposedly ideal van, then using extrapolated measurements as criteria for how all future vans should be designed.

Fixed testing of adaptive systems. The second problem with increasing the number of questions is that this solution does not deal directly with the more fundamental problem of how to use fixed data points to analyze adaptive systems — that is, systems that can change their behavior in response to the testing activity.

For example, assume for a moment that the Figure 6 template is testing only for a good paint job. Because very little actual data is collected about the paint job on a van, it will not take the maker long to realize that doing shoddy work or no work at all on surfaces far away from the inspection points will produce a van that is just as acceptable (according to the template) as one that was meticulously painted.

The absurd (but logical) result of this thinking is for the maker to buy very precise, very high-quality spot painters to paint vans only at the inspection points. By investing heavily in high quality where high quality is expected, the maker can build a process that gets very good quality ratings — and saves a bundle on paint costs. Meanwhile, buyers wind up with very high quality polka dots, but little else!

The SEI questionnaire is clearly subject to this type of customization around test criteria, an effect that in contract procurement is known as gaming. For example, the three configuration-control questions (2, 11, and 12) in Figure 5 imply that a configuration-control function must exist for each project and must at least be able to control changes to both requirements and code. However, the questions say nothing about tracking other intermediate products, such as high-level designs, detailed designs, documents, test procedures, and sets of reusable test data.

The intent of these three questions appears to be that the configuration-control system should track changes to a broad range of intermediate products, including such things as changes to requirements, designs, detailed designs, code, and test procedures. But because they are only a partial sampling, they actually specify tracking changes only for requirements and code.

As a result, an organization that is strongly motivated to move to the next higher level of the SEI model may choose to implement only these two aspects of configuration control, rather than dealing with the general concept. Indeed, because it will be unfamiliar with the background of why the SEI chose to focus on those questions, the organization may quite honestly assume that it is supposed to set up only these two aspects of a configuration-control system.

Adaptation and yes/no questions. Well-intentioned adaptation can lead to some amusing grading scenarios, especially if they involve questions that are ambiguous, technically out of date, or just plain irrelevant. Figure 7 shows a self-assessment scenario based on an actual question (question 2.2.12: "Is target computer I/O channel utilization tracked?") from the SEI questionnaire.

The scenario shows how a sincere attempt to answer a badly designed question can lead to responses that have little to do with tackling real productivity problems but that have a good deal to do with getting a better grade.

As Figure 7 illustrates, devising yes/no questions that are both highly specific and at the same time universal in coverage of a topic is by no means a trivial task. Other problems with using yes/no questions as

Figure 7. A worst-case grading scenario.

probes into complex systems are that they
♦ are hard to generalize for a wide audience,
♦ are subject to rapid obsolescence,
♦ encourage fixes of limited scope,
♦ tend to overlook complex problems,
♦ can be unfair to innovative approaches,
♦ can be ambiguous because of oversimplification,
♦ can encourage an overly myopic view, and
♦ tend to use jargon that makes them cryptic.

Information-flow perspective. You can better understand why fixed sets of yes/no questions do not seem to work well for analyzing complex adaptive systems if you

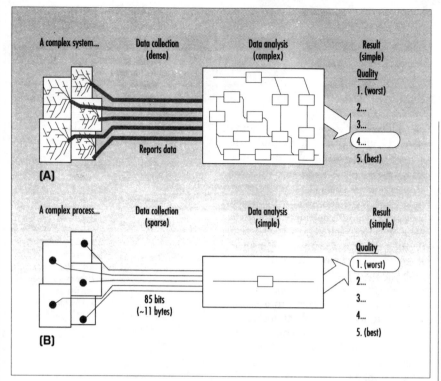

Figure 8. *Systems-analysis methods.*

look at such systems in terms of information flow. Figure 8 shows two very different approaches to analyzing complex systems: a dense-data approach typical of most systems analysis, and a sparse-data approach representing the SEI's yes/no template method.

In dense-data analysis, the data-collection activity is both rich in detail and dynamic in nature. Even if the analysis begins with a general model of what the system will look like, actual data collection will depend greatly on the data itself: Data that indicates problems or important issues may be pursued down to a deeper level, or perhaps taken as a clue that further analysis is needed in some other area that may at first have seemed unrelated.

Thus, the analyst must play the role of a data detective. He must follow leads wherever they go, search for hidden clues, and generally try to expect the unexpected. If the case is simple, it may be possible to wrap up the data-collection activity fairly quickly. But if it is a system involving people, the analyst is likely to uncover a good deal more work that needs to be done.

The results of such a data-collection activity are themselves rich in detail and must be represented in forms that adequately express that complexity. Reports, diagrams, and tables of data are examples

of some of the types of media that may be used to express such output.

Similarly, the analysis step is complex because it must convert this rich set of collected data into some relatively small set of bottom-line recommendations. An analysis task that does not encounter some surprises as this is done is probably not doing its job, because in many cases some of the smaller, less obvious chunks of collected information will turn out to be critical to formulating the final recommendations. Anyone who buys a used car can probably grasp this — it is often the less obvious questions that prove to be the most critical in determining the actual value of a car.

The SCE audit process as a whole does appear to meet the criteria of dense-data systems analysis. SCE auditors apparently collect far more than just questionnaire answers when they go to a site, and the SCE training program apparently emphasizes that this data should be viewed and analyzed as a whole. While the auditing style of an SCE does not produce the free flow of information found in confidential, nonattributed assessments, an SCE does appear to collect and process enough data to classify it as dense-data systems analysis.

The irony is that, while the SCE process as a whole qualifies as dense-data analysis, the process by which the critically important SCE numeric scores are

determined will necessarily converge over time into a sparse-data analysis. The reason is that the basic questionnaire used to collect data for grading is a public-domain document known to all potential bidders for a contract. If one such bidder began to suspect that they lost a contract due to an overly generous interpretation of the SEI questionnaire during the SCE audit of a competitor, it is entirely possible that it might decide to sue the auditing agency and ask for full disclosure of the data that resulted in its competitor getting a higher process-maturity score. Given that the SEI questionnaire is a public document that supposedly tells contractors all the key information they need to know about how to achieve maturity scores, such a lawsuit would have a good chance of succeeding. The net result would be that any anomalies in the interpretation of the SEI questionnaire could wind up being the subject of intense legal and public scrutiny.

The best way to avoid getting into such an unpleasant predicament is to take a very literal approach to interpreting the SEI questionnaire during SCE audits — a point that presumably has not been lost on either the SEI or the agencies it has trained. Such a literal interpretation of the SEI questionnaire would in turn lead to a tightly defined, sparse-data interpretation of the questionnaire, regardless of what other data might be collected during an SCE audit.

The total amount of data collected for transfer to the analysis phase in SCE numeric scoring thus will be only 85 bits, or roughly 11 bytes (characters) of information.

Another point that might be made about the Figure 8 depiction of SEI grading is that it ignores the intensive interviewing and analysis process that occurs before the data is finally wrapped up into a mere 85 bits. Even with literal interpretations of individual questions, isn't it possible that the SCE grading method is simply equivalent to doing most of the necessary analysis at an earlier stage, so that the final algorithm of Figure 4 is really just a minor reformatting of almost finished results?

Data chunks. Unfortunately, no. In data-rich systems analysis, raw data from the data-collection phase is best defined as a set of independent chunks, or pieces of self-consistent data that have not yet been extensively compared or correlated with each other. A data chunk may be very complex, but it is still raw data until it has been correlated against the other chunks in the set, an activity that is the responsibility of the analysis phase.

For example, consider a software-maintenance process being analyzed in hopes of improving its efficiency. One chunk of raw data for such a system might be a traceback of why test schedules are persistently underestimated for one specific type of change requests but are very accurate for other types.

If this input to the analysis phase consisted of little more than the assertion that 10 percent of all test schedules were underestimated, it would be very difficult for the analysis activity to determine what the reason for this might be. Is it a process problem that can only be corrected by re-

THE SEI SOFTWARE FACTORY AND RISK

As seen both in the details of level 4 and level 5 and in numerous statements in *Managing the Software Process*, the SEI maturity model is based largely on the assumption that assembly-line process and quality-control concepts should apply as well to software as they do to physical products such as copper sheeting.

In level 4, the influence of this model shows up as an intense focus on collection and analysis of metrics; in level 5, it shows up as a broad assumption that tracing a defect back to its process (assembly-line) origin should be a sufficiently powerful paradigm for optimizing the ability of that process to produce low-defect software.

Yet when you analyze the detailed implications of levels 4 and 5, unexpected problems pop up. The process-instrumentation approach that works very well for assembly-line quality control seems to cause software processes to fossilize into inflexible configurations. The traceback methods that are good for identifying persistent problems in the manufacture of hard goods seem in the case of software to be belated and poorly focused. What's going wrong here?

Importance of risk. To a large degree, the SEI software-factory analogy does not work well because it fails to recognize that there are different types of process risk and that these different types of risk have different implications about how a process should be structured and optimized.

Specifically, the assembly-line processes on which the SEI model is based are dominated by replication risks, while the vast majority of software processes are instead dominated by design risks. The fact that the SEI model does not distinguish between these risk categories leads to odd and often counter-intuitive results.

API process models. To explain the importance of risk in process design, it helps to have a process representation that shows the effects of risk explicitly. Figure A shows one such method, the allocator-producer-integrator model, which we developed. The diagram in Figure A shows three types of process activities: an allocator, several (unlabeled) producers, and an integrator.

The allocator activity distributes work into distinct, parallel processes. Allocation is crucial to overall process efficiency because it lets you develop parts of a product in parallel. Effective allocation not only speeds development but also reduces the complexity of the individual development tasks.

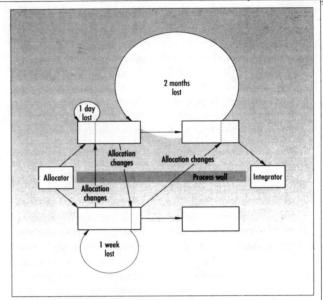

Figure A. *The cost of unplanned interactions.*

The producer activities transform work definitions (which they receive from the allocator) into products, and the integrator activity assembles the results of the producer activities into a single product and reconciles any conflicts that may occur during integration.

Associated with the allocator activity is the abstract process wall. The process wall does not correspond to any physical part of the software process. Instead, it is a measure of how well the allocator activity is performing its task. A strong process wall means that the allocator has been highly effective at setting up distinct, non-interacting work definitions for the producer activities. A weak process wall means it is unlikely that the parallel activities will remain truly separate, and they will probably interact in some (usually unexpected) way before they can finish their assigned tasks.

Lost work. The problem with such interactions is that they are a major source of lost work. Lost work is just that: work that goes into building items that are eventually discarded. When parallel activities interact with each other in unexpected ways, lost work is usually one of the consequences.

To show how unplanned in-

113

placing the current estimation procedures, or is it related to some aspect of the product? If the data chunk is too sparse, it becomes difficult to correlate it with other results about the process and the product.

On the other hand, if the data chunk is rich in its level of detail about the estima- tion problem, it will include a good deal of information about the type of change requests that tend to cause an estimation problem. By correlating that information to data chunks about known problems in the software being maintained, the analyst will be able to identify that the underesti- mated tasks all involve changes to one set of very poorly coded modules. The result- ing process-level recommendations in this case would be that the estimation process be augmented to recognize and estimate these cases more accurately, and that an active program of proactive redevelopment of

teractions can lead to lost work, imagine that Figure A describes bicycle manufacturing. The upper branch of the process corresponds to the manufac- ture of the bicycle frames, and the lower branch corresponds to the manufacture of wheel as- semblies.

Picture what would happen if the maker of the frame unex- pectedly called up the maker of the wheels and requested a change in the diameter of all wheel hubs. In real life, such a request would be met with howls of protest, because it would entail a potentially huge loss of work on components that were assumed to be fin- ished.

Unplanned interactions. In prac- tice, such unplanned interac- tions are very rare in assembly- line manufacturing. The reason is that the design of the product —a bicycle in this case—is ex- tremely stable. The manufac- turer of the bicycle frame knows that if each frame he builds is a sufficiently close match to the predefined design of the bicycle, he can be confi- dent that his own process can proceed smoothly (and inde- pendently) toward the goal of building complete bicycles.

Because of this indepen- dence, the process objectives of the bicycle-frame manufacturer tend to be introspective. It is more important to assure that

each new bicycle matches an exact design than it is to worry about how that design might change in the future. This focus on design replication leads naturally to a process in which quality control means fine-tuning his process to be as predictable as possible.

Another significant effect of the very high per-product stability of assembly-line pro- cesses is that allocator activities in such processes may be very minimal or even nonexistent. This is because the key work needed to make sure that all of the parts of the bicycles will fit together has been done long before the mass-manufacturing process began. By the time the actual manufacture of the bicy- cle has begun, the work remain- ing to be done by the allocator process is usually very small.

Replication risk. Risk in such a process derives mostly from the fact that it is often difficult to guarantee that each new prod- uct will be a sufficiently precise duplicate of the original design. This replication risk stems from the inherent difficulty of working with physical media, rather than any major uncer- tainty about the design itself.

Such risks occur primarily in producer activities, and they are best handled by process op- timizations that focus on uncov- ering how and where physical defects arise each time the de-

sign is replicated.

Design risk. Now take a look at a typical software process. Just like the bicycle-manufac- turing process, this process must be able to allocate work into separate packages that can be done in parallel, and it (usu- ally) must be able to produce multiple products. Thus there are many important similarities between these two types of pro- cesses.

However, there is one strik- ing difference between the bicy- cle and software processes. While the bicycle process can safely assume that there will be no design variation from prod- uct to product, the software process must assume that there will always be significant design variations from product to product. In other words, a soft- ware process has an inherent and unavoidable need to deal with design risk each time it generates a new product.

Why? Part of the answer lies in the fact that the exact replication of software designs is pretty much a solved prob- lem—it amounts to little more than duplication of, say, mag- netic or ROM media. That is not to say exact software repli- cation is a trivial problem, as anyone involved in the manu- facturing of high-quality mag- netic media will attest. But for all practical purposes, the prob- lem of exact replication of soft-

ware is not a significant risk or cost issue in our industry.

What we call a software pro- cess, then, is really an example of a design process, rather than a replication process. It has more in common with the pro- cess by which new bicycles are designed and tested than it does to the process by which bicycle designs are replicated in an as- sembly line. Instead of being dominated by replication risks, software processes are domi- nated by design risks, which are the uncertainties associated with building anything that is new and thus at least partially unknown.

Implications of risk. Given this perspective, an obvious ques- tion is to ask how processes dominated by design risks dif- fer from those dominated by replication risks.

One difference is that, while replication risk is handled pri- marily in producer activities, design risk is handled primarily by allocator activities. The rea- son for this is that when design risk exists, there can be no firm guarantees that an allocation pattern that worked in the past will work in the future. Thus each new software product must be evaluated to ensure that its work allocations will re- sult in strong process walls be- tween activities.

This is by no means a trivial task, and the difficulty of han-

trouble-prone modules might be needed.

Data chunks in SCE grading. In the case of the SEI analysis model, the issues covered by the yes/no questions are far closer to being uncorrelated, raw-data chunks than they are to final conclusions. The SEI questions deal with a very broad range of issues whose exact relationship to each other is very much open to debate. In terms of sparseness, these 85 data chunks represent the ultimate extreme — each is only one bit of information!

Once again, the issue is one of statistical reliability. If the 85-bit filter happens to exactly match the crucial points of a process, it may give reasonable results. But if there are any critical issues that fall outside the expectations of the 85-bit filter, the results can be highly misleading. But, as we've said, because the SEI template is

---

dling design risk increases rapidly as the complexity and novelty of the software become greater. For new, one-of-a-kind software problems, allocator activities can easily become the dominant cost factor. For software problems that are essentially variants of earlier designs, the allocator activities may shrink to the point where they are a fairly minor factor in the overall cost.

One example of how an allocator might approach the problem of defining strong work allocations is prototyping. Prototyping is above all a technique for dealing with risk, since its purpose is to replace large, expensive loops of lost work with much smaller, less costly loops that are fully contained in the boundaries of the allocator activity.

Although they are very similar, there is one interesting difference in emphasis between conventional prototyping and API prototyping. In API, prototyping is viewed more as a technique for developing strong process walls than as a technique for building products per se. The focus on building strong process walls leads to rather distinct objectives for the prototyping activity, and also helps clarify the issue of when a prototyping activity should be considered finished.

Replication is maintenance. If most software processes are dominated by design risks rather than replication risks, what are some of the implications of trying to make a replication-focused model into the overall process objective of the software industry?

To make software fit into the replication-risk model, it is necessary to decrease drastically the size of its allocation activities. One way to do this is to decrease the level of product variability — to make all the products as similar as possible.

This is clearly a special case, since the majority of software problems for both the Defense Dept. and the software industry as a whole are not amenable to such high levels of specialization. Moreover, if a line of software products becomes too similar, it will be increasingly difficult to explain why the whole software process should not be replaced by a fully automated product-configuration tool.

The class of software problems that most resembles the replication model is software maintenance, as Figure B shows. In software maintenance, each new release of a software product is equivalent to the release of a new, slightly updated version of the original product. Design risk is automatically kept at a lower level than start-from-scratch software development because both the software and its application environment tend to be stable.

While maintenance is a fundamental part of the software industry, elevating this class of highly specialized organizations to the position of industry standards for all types of software development could seriously damage both the software industry and the Defense Dept.'s ability to contract for new, complex software systems.

Such disparities are possible in part because the SEI model was never rigorously or even modestly proven before being extrapolated into an industry standard. You need look no further than the main mirror of the Hubble space telescope to get an idea of the dangers of building an ideal test template that turns out not to be ideal at all. The inadvertent Hubble experiment in building a complex system around a flawed test template was a very costly one, but how might it compare to the cost of redesigning the entire software industry around a test template that is later realized to be seriously flawed?

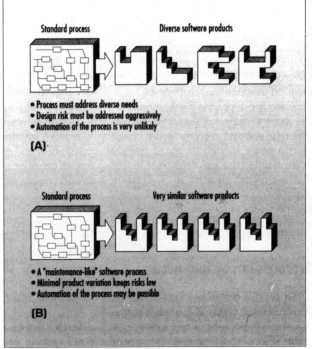

Figure B. *Paths to low-defect software.*

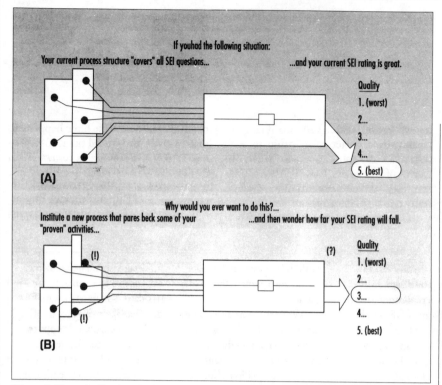

Figure 9. *Process fossilization.*

generally blind to process-automation issues, it could give an excessively labor-dependent group a higher rating simply because that group produces more data of the type expected by the SEI template.

Process fossilization. Another risk factor in using fixed templates to analyze complex processes is that it can lead to process fossilization, as Figure 9 shows. In process fossilization, the way software development is done may become stilted and lethargic due to the constant need to keep the process in line with the expectations of the fixed template used to grade it.

This type of process fossilization is really just a reflection of the fact that when adaptive systems are repeatedly tested against some model, they will quickly begin to reflect the major characteristics of that test model. Because an SCE uses a static, inflexible model for numeric grading, processes graded by that model will naturally start to reflect those same static, inflexible features.

SEI PROCESS-IMPROVEMENT MODEL

So far this article has focused on the statistical reliability of SCE grading methods. But we also want to take a close look at the SEI's overall process-improvement paradigm — that is, the set of goals and directions it is trying to impart to the industry through its assessment and evaluation programs. Where, exactly, is the SEI process-improvement paradigm likely to take the software industry if it is fully accepted and extensively implemented?

This question has broad implications, because, as the box on pp. 35-37 outlines, the SEI has selected an extreme form of the factory model of development as the basis for its software-maturity model. Indeed, we have heard SEI personnel seriously describe software development with an analogy of how high-quality copper sheeting is manufactured. The analogy we heard was that, just as the average number of physical defects on copper sheeting can be reduced by appropriate statistical process-control and quality mechanisms, the average number of software defects per unit of code can similarly be minimized by essentially the same methods, translated appropriately into software terms.

While it is common to hear comparisons of the software process to the factory process, such an exact analogy is unusual. Looking at the SEI process model thus provides a few insights into this version of the software-factory paradigm.

Levels 1 through 3. As we've mentioned, level 1 (initial) of the SCE numeric grade is a failure rating, so it has no real implica-

tions as to how a software process should be structured. Level 2 (repeatable) emphasizes basic project-management controls, and level 3 (defined) promotes a variety of software-engineering and configuration-control methods.

Most of the recommendations in these levels are very similar to techniques that have been advocated and taught for many years in the project-management and software-engineering disciplines. However, levels 2 and 3 do show a strong emphasis on collecting data about product and development trends, and on data traceability. These emphases appear to reflect the SEI's strong factory analogy, in which data about the rate and type of product defects is the starting point for understanding how to reduce those defect rates.

Level 3 also includes the formation of a software-engineering process group, whose role is to take a proactive approach to improving the software process and inserting new software technologies. The process group is one of the more innovative recommendations of the first three levels, and one that clearly has merit as a means for increasing the long-term awareness of process issues in an organization or project.

Levels 4 and 5. If you enjoy precipitating heated debates, one good way is to go to a meeting where software process is being discussed and ask what levels 4 and 5 of the SEI maturity model really mean. Considering that these are the nominal process-improvement goals of the entire SEI process program, there seems to be remarkably little consensus even within the SEI as to what they actually mean. In contrast to levels 2 and 3, the questionnaire offers little help in understanding these higher levels, since only a few general questions are used to define them.

However, levels 4 and 5 are described in detail in *Managing the Software Process*. Thus it is not entirely clear why there is so much public confusion about their meaning. Some of the confusion may stem from trying to understand what the levels mean by looking only at the SEI process questionnaire.

Level 4 (managed) is covered in chapters 15 and 16 of *Managing the Soft-*

wareProcess. Level 4 is intensely focused on data collection and data analysis, and on using such data to estimate, track, and control software quality. The factory paradigm thus is very strong in level 4, since these data-collection and quality-management themes are very similar to those used to improve product quality in assembly lines.

Level 5 (optimizing) is covered mainly in chapter 17 of *Managing the Software Process*. It is centered largely on a method called defect prevention. Although the process group of an organization clearly could implement its own methods for optimizing a software process, this technique of defect prevention appears to be the only such optimization method described in the SEI literature. It is thus instructive to see how this technique works.

Defect prevention. Chapter 17 of the book provides a detailed description of defect prevention that includes examples of actual forms used to perform it. These standard forms are used to help translate defects detected in products into specific error-preventing actions. The method is a product-driven paradigm, which is in keeping with models for assembly-line quality control.

Figure 10 illustrates the SEI optimization model of level 5, based on this description and example forms. Whenever a defect is identified in a software product, the exact nature of that defect is identified and recorded and a traceback (our term, not the SEI's) is initiated.

The purpose of a traceback is to identify as specifically as possible where the defect originated, how it occurred, the underlying (process) cause, and how the process should be changed to prevent that type of defect from occurring in the future.

As defined in the book, the traceback method also provides some context for understanding the role of the data collected in level 4. The impression given in the book is that to make traceback work well, it is necessary to first have a rich set of data about previous steps in the process. By having a detailed set of process data available, level 5 tracebacks will be more easily able to pinpoint the exact locations at

which defects were first introduced. This scenario is again consistent with the assembly-line quality-assurance model.

We use the term "traceback" to emphasize that the fundamental concept of level 5 is neither terribly complex nor hard to understand. Indeed, it is something with which anyone who has debugged a program can claim considerable familiarity. The fact that this debugging method is being applied here to processes rather than programs does not change its key features. Nor does it change some of its fundamental limitations.

The problem with tracebacks is that they are a local, or bottom-up, approach to optimization. They are local in the sense that although they may cross boundaries between activities, they provide little or no insight about how well the process (or program) as a whole is structured. For example, it is possible that process branch X in Figure 10 represents an entire stream of activities that are redundant and should be eliminated. Such redundancies are unlikely to be identified through traceback methods.

Another problem with using traceback as the primary paradigm for process improvement is that, in programming, extensive applications of tracebacks generally result in a gradual degradation of quality, not an enhancement. This is because its focus on fixing isolated defects or bugs encourages traceback to break various tacit agreements in how the program should be structured. Formerly pristine interfaces may be violated, and key information-hiding restrictions may be damaged in subtle, hard-to-analyze ways. Software processes also have tacit agreements and arrangements for sharing data between activities, and are thus subject to a related form of damage where rules and agreements (many of them implicit) that make the process robust and flexible may be replaced with sets of special-case exceptions.

Fossilization. This in turn can lead to a second form of process fossilization. The SEI model requires that organizations that want to reach level 5 must first put into their process an intensive instrumentation that leads to data collection throughout the process. By the time level 5 is reached,

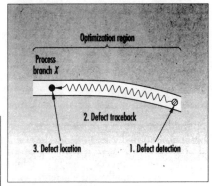

Figure 10. Level-5 optimization paradigm.

each branch of an overall process is likely to have been instrumented to the hilt with procedures and tools for collecting and measuring various aspects of the local process and the quality of its products.

Because each process branch is extensively instrumented, defects are indeed found and methodically corrected by traceback. The result is like a program that has been instrumented with many debugging statements that constantly churn out data that show that the program is working correctly. When new problems occur, this data is used as a resource for uncovering where in the existing structure the problem originated.

However, what all this data is not likely to reveal is that the overall structure of the process (or program) may be fragile and highly disorganized, possibly to the point that it will simply collapse if anyone tries to make a serious change to it. This kind of effect can be seen in programs that have been optimized without regard for the overall design — the act of optimizing in such a way removes most of its original design flexibility, so that major changes can become difficult to implement correctly.

All this can lead to fossilization: Poorly coordinated optimizations result in a fragile, excessively instrumented process that cannot be easily (or in some cases safely) changed in any significant way.

How can such a fossilization effect be reconciled with the very explicit statements in the SEI literature that level 5 is supposed to promote innovation both in the process itself and in the acquisition and use of new software technology? Actually, very easily.

The phenomenon might be termed the Sage effect, in honor of the highly effective (but dated) vacuum-tube computer system that was a key part of our national defense system until the mid-1980s. In a

typical level 5 process, each new technology will be rapidly and efficiently evaluated — but the extensive data available through process instrumentation will then be used to prove conclusively that the technology is inappropriate for that process! Only technologies that result in very minor tweaks to the "nearly perfect" process will be able to squeak through such a daunting data gauntlet.

Another interesting aspect of the SEI level 5 traceback paradigm is that there is no obvious reason why it could not be used effectively at the earliest stages of process improvement. The justification for placing it in level 5 appears to be that an abundant supply of data is needed to make it work. However, traceback is essentially an inductive, detective technique that relies more on insight and the following of clues than it does on does on having masses of data available. Indeed, there are more than a few cases in which large masses of data may obscure the tracing activity.

Another significant danger in relying primarily on traceback optimization is that it can easily lead to *process dithering*. Process dithering is when a project or organization spends most of its time trying to optimize or improve the low-level symptoms of what is actually a high-level flaw in the process. One example would be a project that spends a great deal of time and money to instrument and measure a particular branch of its process, only to discover later that the branch is redundant and should have been removed altogether.

Process dithering is a significant temptation for any kind of process analysis because it can provoke furious activity and produce reams of so-called process-improvement data — all without having much real effect on the efficiency of the process or the quality of the software it produces.

Suggested fix. Fortunately, the various problems associated with process optimi-

zation via traceback can be fairly easily fixed by adapting a global, top-down approach to process optimization. We have applied such methods to our own custom process assessments within Contel, and have found a top-down perspective to be very helpful for identifying key issues and understanding broad relationships between process problems. There does not appear to be any fundamental reason why similar methods cannot easily be inserted into SEI's process model.

The key to global process optimization is to view the entire process as a hierarchy of work activities and product flows that can be elaborated to any level of detail. Because many process problems turn out to have roots very early in the process, global process optimization always begins by looking first at the highest levels of the process structure. Optimization can then proceed recursively down through the lower levels of the model to whatever level of detail is judged to be cost-effective. Process dithering is thus readily avoided, and changes to the process tend to be implemented in the order of highest payback first.

To perform this kind of top-down strategy, it is important to have a good mechanism for recording the details of the process structure as it currently exists. Recommendations for how to modify the process can then be made straightforwardly because they can be phrased in terms of an existing process structure with which the members of the organization are already familiar.

The method we chose to record existing process structures was Structured Analysis and Design Technique, a method with which one of us (McGowan) is especially familiar[3] and one that is already widely used to record processes such as those found in manufacturing facilities. This is by no means the only method we could have used to record processes, but it is an easy technique to learn and has the requisite ability to record multiple levels of

detail about how a process works.

Besides representing the standard input/process activity/output flow, SADT lets you clearly represent constraints (like formats and deadlines) and organizational responsibilities for an activity. For these reasons, SADT is easily understood by members of the organization being analyzed. This is very helpful for verifying the accuracy of the process model and for establishing a general awareness of how individual work activities fit into the overall process.

In many cases, opportunities for global process optimization can be identified simply by inspecting the SADT model. For example, a common problem in poorly planned processes is the existence of activities or sequences of activities that perform very similar work. Due to the use of different terminologies or because of poor communications, project personnel may not be aware that these activities are essentially redundant. Such situations are often easy to spot in SADT models, since they provide a common graphical language in which similar work activities usually wind up with similar SADT representations.

RECOMMENDATIONS

Based both on having seen the SEI's process-assessment program at work and on having done custom process assessments in which we applied many of the SEI's methods, we are convinced that the SEI has made a truly outstanding contribution to the software industry with this program. In addition to having crafted a set of methods that are remarkably consistent in their ability to elicit important process information from members of organizations, the SEI has also succeeded in getting the software industry to look seriously at the importance of understanding and taking control of its processes.

Assessment program. Our only suggestion for the assessment program is that it needs some type of structured, preferably graphical, method for recording the details of an organization's existing processes. Such models would allow for more specific process-improvement recommendations, increase long-term awareness in the

> The current grading system is so seriously and fundamentally flawed that it should be abandoned rather than modified.

organization, and allow better estimation of which recommendations are most likely to achieve significant process payoffs.

However, the current grading system by which five process-maturity numbers are assigned to software organizations is so seriously and fundamentally flawed that it should be abandoned rather than modified or updated.

Although it represents a good initial attempt at dealing with some serious issues in how software processes should be structured and optimized, the SEI's process-maturity model is too incomplete to be viewed as the improvement goal for the software industry.

Two areas in which it is especially weak are its failure to take a global, top-down perspective on how processes should be designed and optimized, and its failure to recognize the effects of different types of risk on the software process. As we describe in the box on pp. 35-37, we believe it should be replaced with methods that focus on designing processes, rather than just modifying them.

Software Capability Evaluations. We do not feel there is anything fundamentally wrong with the idea of a government program for accrediting software organizations. However, the current SCE effort clearly is not such a program, nor will it easily be transformed into one. Just as no government agency would think of using a single test to accredit lawyers, civil engineers, and doctors to do government work, it would seem comparably unwise to try to use a single 85-question yes/no test to accredit organizations for developing all the many types of application software used by the Defense Dept.

During a conference presentation of some of the ideas in this article, one participant asked an interesting question: While the SCE program may be seriously flawed, what else do we have that could be used in its place?

One answer to this important question is very simple: Use the proven track records of the companies for producing quality software on time and within budget. Such an approach would be eminently more fair than the current SCE approach, since it would judge exactly what it is supposed to judge: how good the organization is at producing quality software.

Software engineering is a very young discipline, one that many people feel is not truly an engineering discipline at all. In its present form, it is little more than a hodgepodge collection of ideas, rules, and methods that often appear to have little relationship to one another.

But there may be hope. Consider that physics was once little more than a hodgepodge of ideas, rules, and methods, too. These rules worked after a fashion, but any time a new system was discovered, its properties had to be analyzed anew. Physics became a true science when it began to perceive the existence of unifying themes that could be used to place seemingly disparate pieces of information into a single framework. With these new insights, the incomplete and previously separate lists of properties for such diverse phenomena as light, heat, magnets, lightning, batteries, and radio waves began shifting and merging as new insights were gained, until finally a beautiful and incredibly powerful new framework of electromagnetism was born. It was a framework that allowed deep insights into the nature of the world around us, and permitted us to build a world of technology and innovation.

The SEI's work on software-process and software-capability evaluation is an important part our effort to become a true engineering discipline. Like many early experiments in a new disciplines, these two SEI programs are a curious mixture of strengths and weaknesses that often grate against each other. But nonetheless, they have clearly helped move the software industry toward a better understanding of just what it is we are trying to do and how we should go about doing it — and for that, both of these SEI programs should be applauded. ♦

Terry B. Bollinger manages a software-reuse project at NEC America in Dallas. His hobbies include research into the information aspects of quantum mechanics.

Bollinger received a BS and MS in computer science from the University of Missouri at Rolla. He is a member of IEEE and ACM.

Clement McGowan is manager of the verification project at the Software Productivity Consortium. He recently coauthored a book on Structured Analysis and Design Technique.

McGowan received a PhD in computer science from Cornell University.

Address questions about this article to Bollinger at NEC America, Advanced Switching Laboratory, 1525 Walnut Hill Ln., Irving, TX 75038; Internet terry@asl.dl.nec.com or McGowan at Software Productivity Consortium, 2214 Rock Hill Rd., Herndon, VA 22070; Internet mcgowan@sofware.org.

ACKNOWLEDGMENTS

We thank Bruce H. Barnes of the National Science Foundation for the many discussions in which he contributed to the ideas in this article. We also thank Thomas Reid and Shawn Bohner of the Contel Technology Center for their discussions.

REFERENCES

1. W.S. Humphrey, "Characterizing the Software Process: A Maturity Framework," *IEEE Software*, March 1988, pp. 73-79.
2. W.S. Humphrey, *Managing the Software Process*, Addison-Wesley, Reading, Mass., 1989.
3. D.A. Marca and C.L. McGowan, *SADT: Structured Analysis and Design Technique*, McGraw-Hill, New York, 1988.

A Spiral Model of Software Development and Enhancement

Barry W. Boehm, TRW Defense Systems Group

Reprinted from *Computer*, Vol. 21, No. 5, May 1988, pp. 61-72.

"Stop the life cycle—I want to get off!"
"Life-cycle Concept Considered Harmful."
"The waterfall model is dead."
"No, it isn't, but it should be."

This evolving risk-driven approach provides a new framework for guiding the software process.

These statements exemplify the current debate about software life-cycle process models. The topic has recently received a great deal of attention.

The Defense Science Board Task Force Report on Military Software[1] issued in 1987 highlighted the concern that traditional software process models were discouraging more effective approaches to software development such as prototyping and software reuse. The Computer Society has sponsored tutorials and workshops on software process models that have helped clarify many of the issues and stimulated advances in the field (see "Further reading").

The spiral model presented in this article is one candidate for improving the software process model situation. The major distinguishing feature of the spiral model is that it creates a *risk-driven* approach to the software process rather than a primarily *document-driven* or *code-driven* process. It incorporates many of the strengths of other models and resolves many of their difficulties.

This article opens with a short description of software process models and the issues they address. Subsequent sections outline the process steps involved in the spiral model; illustrate the application of the spiral model to a software project, using the TRW Software Productivity Project as an example; summarize the primary advantages and implications involved in using the spiral model and the primary difficulties in using it at its current incomplete level of elaboration; and present resulting conclusions.

Background on software process models

The primary functions of a software process model are to determine the *order of the stages* involved in software development and evolution and to establish the *transition criteria* for progressing from one stage to the next. These include completion criteria for the current stage plus choice criteria and entrance criteria for the next stage. Thus, a process model addresses the following software project questions:

(1) What shall we do next?
(2) How long shall we continue to do it?

Consequently, a process model differs from a software method (often called a methodology) in that a method's primary focus is on how to navigate through each phase (determining data, control, or "uses" hierarchies; partitioning functions; allocating requirements) and how to represent phase products (structure charts; stimulus-response threads; state transition diagrams).

Why are software process models important? Primarily because they provide guidance on the order (phases, increments, prototypes, validation tasks, etc.) in which a project should carry out its major tasks. Many software projects, as the next section shows, have come to grief because they pursued their various development and evolution phases in the wrong order.

Evolution of process models. Before concentrating in depth on the spiral model, we should take a look at a number of others: the code-and-fix model, the stagewise model and the waterfall model, the evolutionary development model, and the transform model.

The code-and-fix model. The basic model used in the earliest days of software

0-8186-3342-5/93 $3.00 © 1988 IEEE

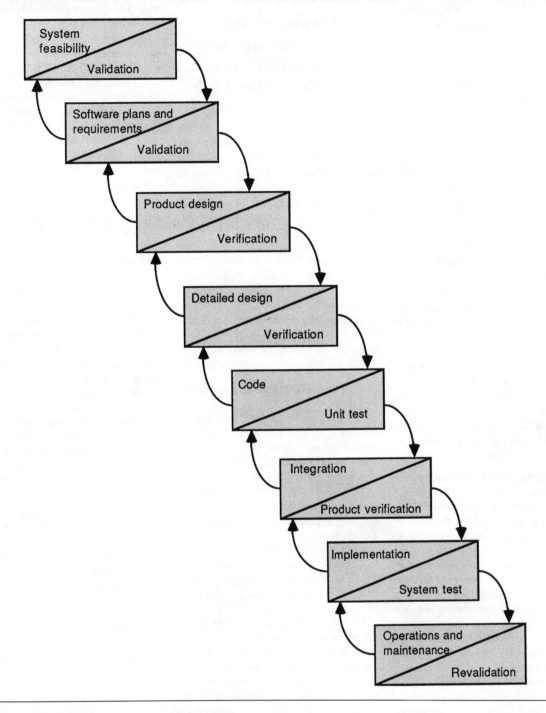

Figure 1. The waterfall model of the software life cycle.

development contained two steps:

(1) Write some code.

(2) Fix the problems in the code.

Thus, the order of the steps was to do some coding first and to think about the requirements, design, test, and maintenance later. This model has three primary difficulties:

(a) After a number of fixes, the code became so poorly structured that subsequent fixes were very expensive. This underscored the need for a design phase prior to coding.

(b) Frequently, even well-designed software was such a poor match to users' needs that it was either rejected outright or expensively redeveloped. This made the need for a requirements phase prior to design evident.

(c) Code was expensive to fix because of poor preparation for testing and modification. This made it clear that explicit recognition of these phases, as well as test-and-evolution planning and preparation tasks in the early phases, were needed.

The stagewise and waterfall models. As early as 1956, experience on large software systems such as the Semi-Automated Ground Environment (SAGE) had led to the recognition of these problems and to the development of a stagewise model[2] to address them. This model stipulated that software be developed in successive stages (operational plan, operational specifications, coding specifications, coding, parameter testing, assembly testing, shakedown, system evaluation).

The waterfall model,[3] illustrated in Figure 1, was a highly influential 1970 refinement of the stagewise model. It provided two primary enhancements to the stagewise model:

(1) Recognition of the feedback loops between stages, and a guideline to confine the feedback loops to successive stages to minimize the expensive rework involved in feedback across many stages.

(2) An initial incorporation of prototyping in the software life cycle, via a "build it twice" step running in parallel with requirements analysis and design.

The waterfall model's approach helped eliminate many difficulties previously encountered on software projects. The waterfall model has become the basis for most software acquisition standards in government and industry. Some of its initial difficulties have been addressed by adding extensions to cover incremental development, parallel developments, program families, accommodation of evolutionary changes, formal software development and verification, and stagewise validation and risk analysis.

However, even with extensive revisions and refinements, the waterfall model's basic scheme has encountered some more fundamental difficulties, and these have led to the formulation of alternative process models.

A primary source of difficulty with the waterfall model has been its emphasis on fully elaborated documents as completion criteria for early requirements and design phases. For some classes of software, such as compilers or secure operating systems, this is the most effective way to proceed. However, it does not work well for many classes of software, particularly interactive

---

The waterfall model has become the basis for most software acquisition standards.

---

end-user applications. Document-driven standards have pushed many projects to write elaborate specifications of poorly understood user interfaces and decision-support functions, followed by the design and development of large quantities of unusable code.

These projects are examples of how waterfall-model projects have come to grief by pursuing stages in the wrong order. Furthermore, in areas supported by fourth-generation languages (spreadsheet or small business applications), it is clearly unnecessary to write elaborate specifications for one's application before implementing it.

The evolutionary development model. The above concerns led to the formulation of the *evolutionary development* model,[4] whose stages consist of expanding increments of an operational software product, with the directions of evolution being determined by operational experience.

The evolutionary development model is ideally matched to a fourth-generation language application and well matched to situations in which users say, "I can't tell you what I want, but I'll know it when I see it." It gives users a rapid initial operational capability and provides a realistic operational basis for determining subsequent product improvements.

Nonetheless, evolutionary development also has its difficulties. It is generally difficult to distinguish it from the old code-and-fix model, whose spaghetti code and lack of planning were the initial motivation for the waterfall model. It is also based on the often-unrealistic assumption that the user's operational system will be flexible enough to accommodate unplanned evolution paths. This assumption is unjustified in three primary circumstances:

(1) Circumstances in which several independently evolved applications must subsequently be closely integrated.

(2) "Information-sclerosis" cases, in which temporary work-arounds for software deficiencies increasingly solidify into

unchangeable constraints on evolution. The following comment is a typical example: "It's nice that you could change those equipment codes to make them more intelligible for us, but the Codes Committee just met and established the current codes as company standards."

(3) Bridging situations, in which the new software is incrementally replacing a large existing system. If the existing system is poorly modularized, it is difficult to provide a good sequence of "bridges" between the old software and the expanding increments of new software.

Under such conditions, evolutionary development projects have come to grief by pursuing stages in the wrong order: evolving a lot of hard-to-change code before addressing long-range architectural and usage considerations.

The transform model. The "spaghetti code" difficulties of the evolutionary development and code-and-fix models can also become a difficulty in various classes of waterfall-model applications, in which code is optimized for performance and becomes increasingly hard to modify. The transform model[5] has been proposed as a solution to this dilemma.

The transform model assumes the existence of a capability to automatically convert a formal specification of a software product into a program satisfying the specification. The steps then prescribed by the transform model are

- a formal specification of the best initial understanding of the desired product;
- automatic transformation of the specification into code;
- an iterative loop, if necessary, to improve the performance of the resulting code by giving optimization guidance to the transformation system;
- exercise of the resulting product; and
- an outer iterative loop to adjust the specification based on the resulting operational experience, and to rederive, reoptimize, and exercise the adjusted software product.

The transform model thus bypasses the difficulty of having to modify code that has become poorly structured through repeated reoptimizations, since the modifications are made to the specification. It also avoids the extra time and expense involved in the intermediate design, code, and test activities.

Still, the transform model has various

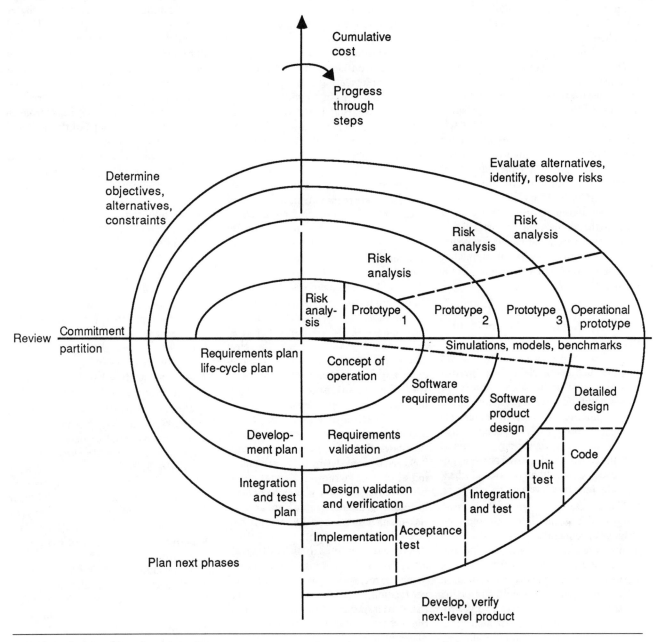

Figure 2. Spiral model of the software process.

difficulties. Automatic transformation capabilities are only available for small products in a few limited areas: spreadsheets, small fourth-generation language applications, and limited computer-science domains. The transform model also shares some of the difficulties of the evolutionary development model, such as the assumption that users' operational systems will always be flexible enough to support unplanned evolution paths.

Additionally, it would face a formidable knowledge-base-maintenance problem in dealing with the rapidly increasing and evolving supply of reusable software components and commercial software products. (Simply consider the problem of tracking the costs, performance, and features of all commercial database management systems, and automatically choosing the best one to implement each new or changed specification.)

The spiral model

The spiral model of the software process (see Figure 2) has been evolving for several years, based on experience with various refinements of the waterfall model as applied to large government software projects. As will be discussed, the spiral model can accommodate most previous models as special cases and further provides guidance as to which combination of previous models best fits a given software situation. Development of the TRW Software Productivity System (TRW-SPS), described in the next section, is its most complete application to date.

The radial dimension in Figure 2 represents the cumulative cost incurred in accomplishing the steps to date; the angular dimension represents the progress made in completing each cycle of the spiral. (The model reflects the underlying concept that each cycle involves a progression that addresses the same sequence of steps, for each portion of the product and for each of its levels of elaboration, from an overall concept of operation document down to the coding of each individual program.) Note that some artistic license has been taken with the increasing cumulative cost dimension to enhance legibility of the steps in Figure 2.

A typical cycle of the spiral. Each cycle of the spiral begins with the identification of

- the objectives of the portion of the product being elaborated (performance, functionality, ability to accommodate change, etc.);
- the alternative means of implementing this portion of the product (design A, design B, reuse, buy, etc.); and
- the constraints imposed on the application of the alternatives (cost, schedule, interface, etc.).

The next step is to evaluate the alternatives relative to the objectives and constraints. Frequently, this process will identify areas of uncertainty that are significant sources of project risk. If so, the next step should involve the formulation of a cost-effective strategy for resolving the sources of risk. This may involve prototyping, simulation, benchmarking, reference checking, administering user questionnaires, analytic modeling, or combinations of these and other risk-resolution techniques.

Once the risks are evaluated, the next step is determined by the relative remaining risks. If performance or user-interface risks strongly dominate program development or internal interface-control risks, the next step may be an evolutionary development one: a minimal effort to specify the overall nature of the product, a plan for the next level of prototyping, and the development of a more detailed prototype to continue to resolve the major risk issues.

If this prototype is operationally useful and robust enough to serve as a low-risk base for future product evolution, the subsequent risk-driven steps would be the evolving series of evolutionary prototypes going toward the right in Figure 2. In this case, the option of writing specifications would be addressed but not exercised. Thus, risk considerations can lead to a project implementing only a subset of all the potential steps in the model.

On the other hand, if previous prototyping efforts have already resolved all of the performance or user-interface risks, and program development or interface-control risks dominate, the next step follows the basic waterfall approach (concept of operation, software requirements, preliminary design, etc. in Figure 2), modified as appropriate to incorporate incremental development. Each level of software specification in the figure is then followed by a validation step and the preparation of plans for the succeeding cycle. In this case, the options to prototype, simulate, model, etc. are addressed but not exercised, leading to the use of a different subset of steps.

This risk-driven subsetting of the spiral model steps allows the model to accommodate any appropriate mixture of a specification-oriented, prototype-oriented, simulation-oriented, automatic transformation-oriented, or other approach to software development. In such cases, the appropriate mixed strategy is chosen by considering the relative magnitude of the program risks and the relative effectiveness of the various techniques in resolving the risks. In a similar way, risk-management considerations can determine the amount of time and effort that should be devoted to such other project activities as planning, configuration management, quality assurance, formal verification, and testing. In particular, risk-driven specifications (as discussed in the next section) can have varying degrees of completeness, formality, and granularity, depending on the relative risks of doing too little or too much specification.

An important feature of the spiral model, as with most other models, is that each cycle is completed by a review involving the primary people or organizations concerned with the product. This review covers all products developed during the previous cycle, including the plans for the next cycle and the resources required to carry them out. The review's major objective is to ensure that all concerned parties are mutually committed to the approach for the next phase.

The plans for succeeding phases may also include a partition of the product into

increments for successive development or components to be developed by individual organizations or persons. For the latter case, visualize a series of parallel spiral cycles, one for each component, adding a third dimension to the concept presented in Figure 2. For example, separate spirals can be evolving for separate software components or increments. Thus, the review-and-commitment step may range from an individual walk-through of the design of a single programmer's component to a major requirements review involving developer, customer, user, and maintenance organizations.

Initiating and terminating the spiral. Four fundamental questions arise in considering this presentation of the spiral model:

(1) How does the spiral ever get started?

(2) How do you get off the spiral when it is appropriate to terminate a project early?

(3) Why does the spiral end so abruptly?

(4) What happens to software enhancement (or maintenance)?

The answer to these questions involves an observation that the spiral model applies equally well to development or enhancement efforts. In either case, the spiral gets started by a hypothesis that a particular operational mission (or set of missions) could be improved by a software effort. The spiral process then involves a test of this hypothesis: at any time, if the hypothesis fails the test (for example, if delays cause a software product to miss its market window, or if a superior commercial product becomes available), the spiral is terminated. Otherwise, it terminates with the installation of new or modified software, and the hypothesis is tested by observing the effect on the operational mission. Usually, experience with the operational mission leads to further hypotheses about software improvements, and a new maintenance spiral is initiated to test the hypothesis. Initiation, termination, and iteration of the tasks and products of previous cycles are thus implicitly defined in the spiral model (although they're not included in Figure 2 to simplify its presentation).

Using the spiral model

The various rounds and activities involved in the spiral model are best understood through use of an example. The spiral model was used in the definition and development of the TRW Software Productivity System (TRW-SPS), an integrated software engineering environment.[6] The initial mission opportunity coincided with a corporate initiative to improve productivity in all appropriate corporate operations and an initial hypothesis that software engineering was an attractive area to investigate. This led to a small, extra "Round 0" circuit of the spiral to determine the feasibility of increasing software productivity at a reasonable corporate cost. (Very large or complex software projects will frequently precede the "concept of operation" round of the spiral with one or more smaller rounds to establish feasibility and to reduce the range of alternative solutions quickly and inexpensively.)

Tables 1, 2, and 3 summarize the application of the spiral model to the first three rounds of defining the SPS. The major features of each round are subsequently discussed and are followed by some examples from later rounds, such as preliminary and detailed design.

Round 0: Feasibility study. This study involved five part-time participants over a two- to three-month period. As indicated in Table 1, the objectives and constraints were expressed at a very high level and in qualitative terms like "significantly increase," "at reasonable cost," etc.

Some of the alternatives considered, primarily those in the "technology" area, could lead to development of a software product, but the possible attractiveness of a number of non-software alternatives in the management, personnel, and facilities areas could have led to a conclusion not to embark on a software development activity.

The primary risk areas involved possible situations in which the company would invest a good deal only to find that

- resulting productivity gains were not significant, or

- potentially high-leverage improvements were not compatible with some aspects of the "TRW culture."

The risk-resolution activities undertaken in Round 0 were primarily surveys and analyses, including structured interviews of software developers and managers, an initial analysis of productivity leverage factors identified by the constructive cost model (Cocomo)[7]; and an analysis of previous projects at TRW exhibiting high levels of productivity.

The risk analysis results indicated that significant productivity gains could be achieved at a reasonable cost by pursuing an integrated set of initiatives in the four major areas. However, some candidate solutions, such as a software support environment based on a single, corporate, maxicomputer-based time-sharing system, were found to be in conflict with TRW constraints requiring support of different levels of security-classified projects. Thus, even at a very high level of generality of objectives and constraints, Round 0 was able to answer basic feasibility questions and eliminate significant classes of candidate solutions.

The plan for Round 1 involved commitment of 12 man-months compared to the two man-months invested in Round 0 (during these rounds, all participants were part-time). Round 1 here corresponded fairly well to the initial round of the spiral model shown in Figure 2, in that its intent was to produce a concept of operation and a basic life-cycle plan for implementing whatever preferred alternative emerged.

Round 1: Concept of operations. Table 2 summarizes Round 1 of the spiral along the lines given in Table 1 for Round 0. The features of Round 1 compare to those of Round 0 as follows:

- The level of investment was greater (12 versus 2 man-months).

- The objectives and constraints were more specific ("double software productivity in five years at a cost of $10,000 a person" versus "significantly increase productivity at a reasonable cost").

- Additional constraints surfaced, such as the preference for TRW products (particularly, a TRW-developed local area network (LAN) system).

- The alternatives were more detailed ("SREM, PSL/PSA or SADT, as requirements tools etc." versus "tools"; "private/shared" terminals, "smart/dumb" terminals versus "workstations").

- The risk areas identified were more specific ("TRW LAN price-performance

Table 1. Spiral model usage: TRW Software Productivity System, Round 0.

Objectives	Significantly increase software productivity
Constraints	At reasonable cost Within context of TRW culture • Government contracts, high tech., people oriented, security
Alternatives	Management: Project organization, policies, planning, control Personnel: Staffing, incentives, training Technology: Tools, workstations, methods, reuse Facilities: Offices, communications
Risks	May be no high-leverage improvements Improvements may violate constraints
Risk resolution	Internal surveys Analyze cost model Analyze exceptional projects Literature search
Risk resolution results	Some alternatives infeasible • Single time-sharing system: Security Mix of alternatives can produce significant gains • Factor of two in five years Need further study to determine best mix
Plan for next phase	Six-person task force for six months More extensive surveys and analysis • Internal, external, economic Develop concept of operation, economic rationale
Commitment	Fund next phase

within a "$10,000-per-person investment constraint" versus "improvements may violate reasonable-cost constraint").

• The risk-resolution activities were more extensive (including the benchmarking and analysis of a prototype TRW LAN being developed for another project).

• The result was a fairly specific operational concept document, involving private offices tailored to software work patterns and personal terminals connected to VAX superminis via the TRW LAN. Some choices were specifically deferred to the next round, such as the choice of operating system and specific tools.

• The life-cycle plan and the plan for the next phase involved a partitioning into separate activities to address management improvements, facilities development, and development of the first increment of a software development environment.

• The commitment step involved more than just an agreement with the plan. It committed to apply the environment to an upcoming 100-person testbed software project and to develop an environment focusing on the testbed project's needs. It also specified forming a representative steering group to ensure that the separate activities were well-coordinated and that the environment would not be overly optimized around the testbed project.

Although the plan recommended developing a prototype environment, it also recommended that the project employ requirements specifications and design specifications in a risk-driven way. Thus, the development of the environment followed the succeeding rounds of the spiral model.

Round 2: Top-level requirements specification. Table 3 shows the corresponding steps involved during Round 2 defining the software productivity system. Round 2 decisions and their rationale were covered in earlier work[6]; here, we will summarize the considerations dealing with risk management and the use of the spiral model:

• The initial risk-identification activities during Round 2 showed that several system requirements hinged on the decision between a host-target system or a fully portable tool set and the decision between VMS and Unix as the host operating system. These requirements included the functions needed to provide a user-friendly front-end, the operating system to be used by the workstations, and the functions necessary to support a host-target

operation. To keep these requirements in synchronization with the others, a special minispiral was initiated to address and resolve these issues. The resulting review led to a commitment to a host-target operation using Unix on the host system, at a point early enough to work the OS-dependent requirements in a timely fashion.

• Addressing the risks of mismatches to the user-project's needs and priorities resulted in substantial participation of the user-project personnel in the requirements definition activity. This led to several significant redirections of the requirements, particularly toward supporting the early phases of the software life-cycle into which the user project was embarking, such as an adaptation of the software requirements engineering methodology (SREM) tools

for requirements specification and analysis.

It is also interesting to note that the form of Tables 1, 2, and 3 was originally developed for presentation purposes, but subsequently became a standard "spiral model template" used on later projects. These templates are useful not only for organizing project activities, but also as a residual design-rationale record. Design rationale information is of paramount importance in assessing the potential reusability of software components on future projects. Another important point to note is that the use of the template was indeed uniform across the three cycles, showing that the spiral steps can be and were uniformly followed at successively detailed levels of product definition.

Table 2. Spiral model usage: TRW Software Productivity System, Round 1.

Objectives	Double software productivity in five years
Constraints	$10,000 per person investment
	Within context of TRW culture
	• Government contracts, high tech., people oriented, security
	Preference for TRW products
Alternatives	Office: Private/modular/. . .
	Communication: LAN/star/concentrators/. . .
	Terminals: Private/shared; smart/dumb
	Tools: SREM/PSL-PSA/. . .; PDL/SADT/. . .
	CPU: IBM/DEC/CDC/. . .
Risks	May miss high-leverage options
	TRW LAN price/performance
	Workstation cost
Risk resolution	Extensive external surveys, visits
	TRW LAN benchmarking
	Workstation price projections
Risk resolution results	Operations concept: Private offices, TRW LAN, personal terminals, VAX
	Begin with primarily dumb terminals; experiment with smart workstations
	Defer operating system, tools selection
Plan for next phase	Partition effort into software development environment (SDE), facilities, management
	Develop first-cut, prototype SDE
	• Design-to-cost: 15-person team for one year
	Plan for external usage
Commitment	Develop prototype SDE
	Commit an upcoming project to use SDE
	Commit the SDE to support the project
	Form representative steering group

Succeeding rounds. It will be useful to illustrate some examples of how the spiral model is used to handle situations arising in the preliminary design and detailed design of components of the SPS: the preliminary design specification for the requirements traceability tool (RTT), and a detailed design rework or go-back on the unit development folder (UDF) tool.

The RTT preliminary design specification. The RTT establishes the traceability between itemized software requirements specifications, design elements, code elements, and test cases. It also supports various associated query, analysis, and report generation capabilities. The preliminary design specification for the RTT (and most of the other SPS tools) looks different from the usual preliminary design specification, which tends to show a uniform level of elaboration of all components of the design. Instead, the level of detail of the RTT specification is risk-driven.

In areas involving a high risk if the design turned out to be wrong, the design was carried down to the detailed design level, usually with the aid of rapid prototyping. These areas included working out the implications of "undo" options and dealing with the effects of control keys used to escape from various program levels.

In areas involving a moderate risk if the design was wrong, the design was carried down to a preliminary-design level. These areas included the basic command options for the tool and the schemata for the requirements traceability database. Here again, the ease of rapid prototyping with Unix shell scripts supported a good deal of user-interface prototyping.

In areas involving a low risk if the design was wrong, very little design elaboration was done. These areas included details of all the help message options and all the report-generation options, once the nature of these options was established in some example instances.

A detailed design go-back. The UDF tool collects into an electronic "folder" all artifacts involved in the development of a single-programmer software unit (typically 500 to 1,000 instructions): unit requirements, design, code, test cases, test results, and documentation. It also includes a management template for tracking the programmer's scheduled and actual completion of each artifact.

An alternative considered during detailed design of the UDF tool was reuse of portions of the RTT to provide pointers to the requirements and preliminary design specifications of the unit being developed. This turned out to be an extremely attractive alternative, not only for avoiding duplicate software development but also for bringing to the surface several issues involving many-to-many mappings between requirements, design, and code that had not been considered in designing the UDF tool. These led to a rethinking of the UDF tool requirements and preliminary design, which avoided a great deal of code rework that would have been necessary if the detailed design of the UDF tool had proceeded in a purely deductive, top-down fashion from the original UDF requirements specification. The resulting go-back led to a significantly different, less costly, and more capable UDF tool, incorporating the RTT in its "uses-hierarchy."

Spiral model features. These two examples illustrate several features of the spiral approach.

• It fosters the development of specifications that are not necessarily uniform, exhaustive, or formal, in that they defer detailed elaboration of low-risk software elements and avoid unnecessary breakage in their design until the high-risk elements of the design are stabilized.

• It incorporates prototyping as a risk-reduction option at any stage of development. In fact, prototyping and reuse risk analyses were often used in the process of going from detailed design into code.

• It accommodates reworks or go-backs to earlier stages as more attractive alternatives are identified or as new risk issues need resolution.

Overall, risk-driven documents, particularly specifications and plans, are important features of the spiral model. Great amounts of detail are not necessary unless the absence of such detail jeopardizes the

Table 3. Spiral model usage: TRW Software Productivity System, Round 2.

Objectives	User-friendly system
	Integrated software, office-automation tools
	Support all project personnel
	Support all life-cycle phases
Constraints	Customer-deliverable SDE ⇒ Portability
	Stable, reliable service
Alternatives	OS: VMS/AT&T Unix/Berkeley Unix/ISC
	Host-target/fully portable tool set
	Workstations: Zenith/LSI-11/. . .
Risks	Mismatch to user-project needs, priorities
	User-unfriendly system
	• 12-language syndrome; experts-only
	Unix performance, support
	Workstation/mainframe compatibility
Risk resolution	User-project surveys, requirements participation
	Survey of Unix-using organizations
	Workstation study
Risk resolution results	Top-level requirements specification
	Host-target with Unix host
	Unix-based workstations
	Build user-friendly front end for Unix
	Initial focus on tools to support early phases
Plan for next phase	Overall development plan
	• for tools: SREM, RTT, PDL, office automation tools
	• for front end: Support tools
	• for LAN: Equipment, facilities
Commitment	Proceed with plans

project. In some cases, such as with a product whose functionality may be determined by a choice among commercial products, a set of weighted evaluation criteria for the products may be preferable to a detailed pre-statement of functional requirements.

Results. The Software Productivity System developed and supported using the spiral model avoided the identified risks and achieved most of the system's objectives. The SPS has grown to include over 300 tools and over 1,300,000 instructions; 93 percent of the instructions were reused from previous project-developed, TRW-developed, or external-software packages. Over 25 projects have used all or portions of the system. All of the projects fully using the system have increased their productivity at least 50 percent; indeed, most have doubled their productivity (when compared with cost-estimation model predictions of their productivity using traditional methods).

However, one risk area—that projects with non-Unix target systems would not accept a Unix-based host system—was underestimated. Some projects accepted the host-target approach, but for various reasons (such as customer constraints and zero-cost target machines) a good many did not. As a result, the system was less widely used on TRW projects than expected. This and other lessons learned have been incorporated into the spiral model approach to developing TRW's next-generation software development environment.

Evaluation

Advantages. The primary advantage of the spiral model is that its range of options accommodates the good features of existing software process models, while its risk-driven approach avoids many of their difficulties. In appropriate situations, the spiral model becomes equivalent to one of the existing process models. In other situations, it provides guidance on the best mix of existing approaches to a given project; for example, its application to the TRW-SPS provided a risk-driven mix of specifying, prototyping, and evolutionary development.

The primary conditions under which the spiral model becomes equivalent to other main process models are summarized as follows:

• If a project has a low risk in such areas

All of the projects fully using the system have increased their productivity at least 50 percent.

---

as getting the wrong user interface or not meeting stringent performance requirements, and if it has a high risk in budget and schedule predictability and control, then these risk considerations drive the spiral model into an equivalence to the waterfall model.

• If a software product's requirements are very stable (implying a low risk of expensive design and code breakage due to requirements changes during development), and if the presence of errors in the software product constitutes a high risk to the mission it serves, then these risk considerations drive the spiral model to resemble the two-leg model of precise specification and formal deductive program development.

• If a project has a low risk in such areas as losing budget and schedule predictability and control, encountering large-system integration problems, or coping with information sclerosis, and if it has a high risk in such areas as getting the wrong user interface or user decision support requirements, then these risk considerations drive the spiral model into an equivalence to the evolutionary development model.

• If automated software generation capabilities are available, then the spiral model accommodates them either as options for rapid prototyping or for application of the transform model, depending on the risk considerations involved.

• If the high-risk elements of a project involve a mix of the risk items listed above, then the spiral approach will reflect an appropriate mix of the process models above (as exemplified in the TRW-SPS application). In doing so, its risk-avoidance features will generally avoid the difficulties of the other models.

The spiral model has a number of additional advantages, summarized as follows:

It focuses early attention on options involving the reuse of existing software. The steps involving the identification and evaluation of alternatives encourage these options.

It accommodates preparation for life-cycle evolution, growth, and changes of the software product. The major sources of product change are included in the product's objectives, and information-hiding approaches are attractive architectural design alternatives in that they reduce the risk of not being able to accommodate the product-charge objectives.

It provides a mechanism for incorporating software quality objectives into software product development. This mechanism derives from the emphasis on identifying all types of objectives and constraints during each round of the spiral. For example, Table 3 shows user-friendliness, portability, and reliability as specific objectives and constraints to be addressed by the SPS. In Table 1, security constraints were identified as a key risk item for the SPS.

It focuses on eliminating errors and unattractive alternatives early. The risk-analysis, validation, and commitment steps cover these considerations.

For each of the sources of project activity and resource expenditure, it answers the key question, "How much is enough?" Stated another way, "How much of requirements analysis, planning, configuration management, quality assurance, testing, formal verification, etc. should a project do?" Using the risk-driven approach, one can see that the answer is not the same for all projects and that the appropriate level of effort is determined by the level of risk incurred by not doing enough.

It does not involve separate approaches for software development and software enhancement (or maintenance). This aspect helps avoid the "second-class citizen" status frequently associated with software maintenance. It also helps avoid many of the problems that currently ensue when high-risk enhancement efforts are approached in the same way as routine maintenance efforts.

It provides a viable framework for integrated hardware-software system development. The focus on risk-management and on eliminating unattractive alternatives early and inexpensively is equally applicable to hardware and software.

Difficulties. The full spiral model can be successfully applied in many situations, but some difficulties must be addressed before it can be called a mature, universally applicable model. The three primary challenges involve matching to contract software, relying on risk-assessment expertise, and the need for further elaboration of spiral model steps.

Matching to contract software. The spiral model currently works well on internal software developments like the TRW-SPS, but it needs further work to match it to the world of contract software acquisition.

Internal software developments have a great deal of flexibility and freedom to accommodate stage-by-stage commitments, to defer commitments to specific options, to establish minispirals to resolve critical-path items, to adjust levels of effort, or to accommodate such practices as prototyping, evolutionary development, or design-to-cost. The world of contract software acquisition has a harder time achieving these degrees of flexibility and freedom without losing accountability and control, and a harder time defining contracts whose deliverables are not well specified in advance.

Recently, a good deal of progress has been made in establishing more flexible contract mechanisms, such as the use of competitive front-end contracts for concept definition or prototype fly-offs, the use of level-of-effort and award-fee contracts for evolutionary development, and the use of design-to-cost contracts. Although these have been generally successful, the procedures for using them still need to be worked out to the point that acquisition managers feel fully comfortable using them.

Relying on risk-assessment expertise. The spiral model places a great deal of reliance on the ability of software developers to identify and manage sources of project risk.

A good example of this is the spiral model's risk-driven specification, which carries high-risk elements down to a great deal of detail and leaves low-risk elements to be elaborated in later stages; by this time, there is less risk of breakage.

However, a team of inexperienced or low-balling developers may also produce a specification with a different pattern of variation in levels of detail: a great elaboration of detail for the well-understood, low-risk elements, and little elaboration of the poorly understood, high-risk elements. Unless there is an insightful review of such a specification by experienced development or acquisition personnel, this type of project will give an illusion of progress during a period in which it is actually heading for disaster.

Another concern is that a risk-driven specification will also be people-dependent. For example, a design produced by an expert may be implemented by non-experts. In this case, the expert, who does not need a great deal of detailed documentation, must produce enough additional documentation to keep the non-experts from going astray. Reviewers of the specification must also be

Table 4. A prioritized top-ten list of software risk items.

Risk item	Risk management techniques
1. Personnel shortfalls	Staffing with top talent, job matching; teambuilding; morale building; cross-training; pre-scheduling key people
2. Unrealistic schedules and budgets	Detailed, multisource cost and schedule estimation; design to cost; incremental development; software reuse; requirements scrubbing
3. Developing the wrong software functions	Organization analysis; mission analysis; ops-concept formulation; user surveys; prototyping; early users' manuals
4. Developing the wrong user interface	Task analysis; prototyping; scenarios; user characterization (functionality, style, workload)
5. Gold plating	Requirements scrubbing; prototyping; cost-benefit analysis; design to cost
6. Continuing stream of requirement changes	High change threshold; information hiding; incremental development (defer changes to later increments)
7. Shortfalls in externally furnished components	Benchmarking; inspections; reference checking; compatibility analysis
8. Shortfalls in externally performed tasks	Reference checking; pre-award audits; award-fee contracts; competitive design or prototyping; teambuilding
9. Real-time performance shortfalls	Simulation; benchmarking; modeling; prototyping; instrumentation; tuning
10. Straining computer-science capabilities	Technical analysis; cost-benefit analysis; prototyping; reference checking

Table 5. Software Risk Management Plan.

1.	Identify the project's top 10 risk items.
2.	Present a plan for resolving each risk item.
3.	Update list of top risk items, plan, and results monthly.
4.	Highlight risk-item status in monthly project reviews. • Compare with previous month's rankings, status.
5.	Initiate appropriate corrective actions.

sensitive to these concerns.

With a conventional, document-driven approach, the requirement to carry all aspects of the specification to a uniform level of detail eliminates some potential problems and permits adequate review of some aspects by inexperienced reviewers. But it also creates a large drain on the time of the scarce experts, who must dig for the critical issues within a large mass of non-critical detail. Furthermore, if the high-risk elements have been glossed over by impressive-sounding references to poorly understood capabilities (such as a new synchronization concept or a commercial DBMS), there is an even greater risk that the conventional approach will give the illusion of progress in situations that are actually heading for disaster.

Need for further elaboration of spiral model steps. In general, the spiral model process steps need further elaboration to ensure that all software development participants are operating in a consistent context.

Some examples of this are the need for more detailed definitions of the nature of spiral model specifications and milestones, the nature and objectives of spiral model reviews, techniques for estimating and synchronizing schedules, and the nature of spiral model status indicators and cost-versus-progress tracking procedures. Another need is for guidelines and checklists to identify the most likely sources of project risk and the most effective risk-resolution techniques for each source of risk.

Highly experienced people can successfully use the spiral approach without these elaborations. However, for large-scale use in situations where people bring widely differing experience bases to the project, added levels of elaboration—such as have been accumulated over the years for document-driven approaches—are important in ensuring consistent interpretation and use of the spiral approach across the project.

Efforts to apply and refine the spiral model have focused on creating a discipline of software risk management, including techniques for risk identification, risk analysis, risk prioritization, risk-management planning, and risk-element tracking. The prioritized top-ten list of software risk items given in Table 4 is one result of this activity. Another example is the risk management plan discussed in the next section.

Implications: The Risk Management Plan. Even if an organization is not ready to adopt the entire spiral approach, one characteristic technique that can easily be adapted to any life-cycle model provides many of the benefits of the spiral approach. This is the Risk Management Plan summarized in Table 5. This plan basically ensures that each project makes an early identification of its top risk items (the number 10 is not an absolute requirement), develops a strategy for resolving the risk items, identifies and sets down an agenda to resolve new risk items as they surface, and highlights progress versus plans in monthly reviews.

The Risk Management Plan has been used successfully at TRW and other organizations. Its use has ensured appropriate focus on early prototyping, simulation, benchmarking, key-person staffing measures, and other early risk-resolution techniques that have helped avoid many potential project "show-stoppers." The recent US Department of Defense standard on software management, DoD-Std-2167, requires that developers produce and use risk management plans, as does its counterpart US Air Force regulation, AFR 800-14.

Overall, the Risk Management Plan and the maturing set of techniques for software risk management provide a foundation for tailoring spiral model concepts into the more established software acquisition and development procedures.

W e can draw four conclusions from the data presented:

(1) The risk-driven nature of the spiral model is more adaptable to the full range of software project situations than are the primarily document-driven approaches such as the waterfall model or the primarily code-driven approaches such as evolutionary development. It is particularly applicable to very large, complex, ambitious software systems.

(2) The spiral model has been quite successful in its largest application to date: the development and enhancement of the TRW-SPS. Overall, it achieved a high level of software support environment capability in a very short time and provided the flexibility necessary to accommodate a high dynamic range of technical alternatives and user objectives.

(3) The spiral model is not yet as fully elaborated as the more established models. Therefore, the spiral model can be applied by experienced personnel, but it needs further elaboration in such areas as contract-ing, specifications, milestones, reviews, scheduling, status monitoring, and risk-area identification to be fully usable in all situations.

(4) Partial implementations of the spiral model, such as the Risk Management Plan, are compatible with most current process models and are very helpful in overcoming major sources of project risk.□

Acknowledgments

I would like to thank Frank Belz, Lolo Penedo, George Spadaro, Bob Williams, Bob Balzer, Gillian Frewin, Peter Hamer, Manny Lehman, Lee Osterweil, Dave Parnas, Bill Riddle, Steve Squires, and Dick Thayer, along with the *Computer* reviewers of this article, for their stimulating and insightful comments and discussions of earlier versions of the article, and Nancy Donato for producing its several versions.

References

1. F.P. Brooks et al., *Defense Science Board Task Force Report on Military Software*, Office of the Under Secretary of Defense for Acquisition, Washington, DC 20301, Sept. 1987.

2. H.D. Benington, "Production of Large Computer Programs," *Proc. ONR Symp. Advanced Programming Methods for Digital Computers*, June 1956, pp. 15-27. Also available in *Annals of the History of Computing*, Oct. 1983, pp. 350-361, and *Proc. Ninth Int'l Conf. Software Engineering*, Computer Society Press, 1987.

3. W.W. Royce, "Managing the Development of Large Software Systems: Concepts and Techniques," *Proc. Wescon*, Aug. 1970. Also available in *Proc. ICSE 9*, Computer Society Press, 1987.

4. D.D. McCracken and M.A. Jackson, "Life-Cycle Concept Considered Harmful," *ACM Software Engineering Notes*, Apr. 1982, pp. 29-32.

5. R. Balzer, T.E. Cheatham, and C. Green, "Software Technology in the 1990s: Using a New Paradigm," *Computer*, Nov. 1983, pp. 39-45.

6. B.W. Boehm et al., "A Software Development Environment for Improving Productivity," *Computer*, June 1984, pp. 30-44.

7. B.W. Boehm, *Software Engineering Economics*, Prentice-Hall, 1981, Chap. 33.

Further reading

The software process model field has an interesting history, and a great deal of stimulating work has been produced recently in this specialized area. Besides the references that appear at the end of the accompanying article, here are some additional good sources of insight:

Overall process model issues and results

Agresti's tutorial volume provides a good overview and set of key articles. The three recent *Software Process Workshop Proceedings* provide access to much of the recent work in the area.

Agresti, W.W., *New Paradigms for Software Development*, IEEE Catalog No. EH0245-1, 1986.

Dowson, M., ed., *Proc. Third Int'l Software Process Workshop*, IEEE Catalog No. TH0184-2, Nov. 1986.

Potts, C., ed., *Proc. Software Process Workshop*, IEEE Catalog No. 84CH2044-6, Feb. 1984.

Wileden, J.C., and M. Dowson, eds., Proc. Int'l Workshop Software Process and Software Environments, *ACM Software Engineering Notes*, Aug. 1986.

Alternative process models

More detailed information on waterfall-type approaches is given in:

Evans, M.W., P. Piazza, and J.P. Dolkas, *Principles of Productive Software Management*, John Wiley & Sons, 1983.

Hice, G.F., W.J. Turner, and L.F. Cashwell, *System Development Methodology*, North Holland, 1974 (2nd ed., 1981).

More detailed information on evolutionary development is provided in:

Gilb, T., *Principles of Software Engineering Management,* Addison Wesley, 1988 (currently in publication).

Some additional process model approaches with useful features and insights may be found in:

Lehman, M.M., and L.A. Belady, *Program Evolution: Processes of Software Change*, Academic Press, 1985.

Osterweil, L., "Software Processes are Software, Too," *Proc. ICSE 9*, IEEE Catalog No. 87CH2432-3, Mar. 1987, pp. 2-13.

Radice, R.A., et al., "A Programming Process Architecture," *IBM Systems J.*, Vol. 24, No.2, 1985, pp. 79-90.

Spiral and spiral-type models

Some further treatments of spiral model issues and practices are:

Belz, F.C., "Applying the Spiral Model: Observations on Developing System Software in Ada," *Proc. 1986 Annual Conf. on Ada Technology,* Atlanta, 1986, pp. 57-66.

Boehm, B.W., and F.C. Belz, "Applying Process Programming to the Spiral Model," *Proc. Fourth Software Process Workshop*, IEEE, May 1988.

Iivari, J., "A Hierarchical Spiral Model for the Software Process," *ACM Software Engineering Notes,* Jan. 1987, pp. 35-37.

Some similar cyclic spiral-type process models from other fields are described in:

Carlsson, B., P. Keane, and J.B. Martin, "R&D Organizations as Learning Systems," *Sloan Management Review,* Spring 1976, pp. 1-15.

Fisher, R., and W. Ury, *Getting to Yes*, Houghton Mifflin, 1981; Penguin Books, 1983, pp. 68-71.

Kolb, D.A., "On Management and the Learning Process," MIT Sloan School Working Article 652-73, Cambridge, Mass., 1973.

Software risk management

The discipline of software risk management provides a bridge between spiral model concepts and currently established software acquisition and development procedures.

Boehm, B.W., "Software Risk Management Tutorial," Computer Society, Apr. 1988.

Risk Assessment Techniques, Defense Systems Management College, Ft. Belvoir, Va. 22060, July 1983.

Barry W. Boehm is the chief scientist of the TRW Defense Systems Group. Since 1973, he has been responsible for developing TRW's software technology base. His current primary responsibilities are in the areas of software environments, process models, management methods, Ada, and cost estimation. He is also an adjunct professor at UCLA.

Boehm received his BA degree in mathematics from Harvard in 1957 and his MA and PhD from UCLA in 1961 and 1964, respectively.

Readers may write to Boehm at TRW Defense Systems Group, One Space Park, R2/2086, Redondo Beach, CA 90278.

TRW's Ada Process Model for Incremental Development of Large Software Systems

Walker Royce

TRW Systems Integration Group
Space & Defense Sector
Redondo Beach, CA 90278

ABSTRACT

TRW's Ada Process Model has proven to be key to the Command Center Processing and Display System-Replacement (CCPDS-R) project's success to date in developing over 300,000 lines of Ada source code executing in a distributed VAX VMS environment.

The Ada Process Model is, in simplest terms, a uniform application of incremental development coupled with a demonstration-based approach to design review for continuous and insightful thread testing and risk management. The use of Ada as the life-cycle language for design evolution provides the vehicle for uniformity and a basis for consistent software progress metrics. This paper provides an overview of the techniques and benefits of the Ada Process Model and describes some of the experience and lessons learned to date.

Project Background

The Command Center Processing and Display System-Replacement (CCPDS-R) project will provide display information used during emergency conferences by the National Command Authorities; Chairman, Joint Chiefs of Staff; Commander in Chief, North American Aerospace Command; Commander in Chief, United States Space Command; Commander in Chief, Strategic Air Command, and other nuclear-capable commanders in chief. It is the missile warning element of the new Integrated Tactical Warning/Attack Assessment system architecture developed by North American Aerospace Defense Command/Air Force Space Command.

The CCPDS-R project is being procured by Air Force Systems Command Headquarters, Electronic Systems Division (ESD) at Hanscom AFB and was awarded to TRW Defense Systems Group in June 1987. TRW will build three subsystems. The first, identified as the Common Subsystem, is 27 months into development. The Common Subsystem consists of over 300,000 source lines of Ada with a development schedule of 38 months. It will be a highly reliable, real-time distributed system with a sophisticated user interface and stringent performance requirements implemented entirely in Ada. CCPDS-R Ada risks were originally a very serious concern. At the time of contract definition, Ada host and target environments and Ada-trained personnel availability were questionable.

The genesis of the Ada Process Model was a TRW Independent Research and Development project which pioneered the technology from 1984–1987 and provided the key software personnel for CCPDS-R startup.

The CCPDS-R architecture consists of approximately 300 tasks executing in a network of 10 VAX family processors with over 1,000 task-to-task software interfaces. This large distributed network was developed primarily on the VAX Ada environment augmented with a Rational R1000 host. Currently, CCPDS-R is immersed in formal testing of most of the software builds with the last build still in development. To date, the software effort (75 people) has flowed smoothly on schedule and on budget.

Conventional Software Process Shortfalls

All large software products require multiple people to *converge* individual ideas into a single solution for a *vaguely* stated problem. The real difficulties in this process are twofold:

1. *Convergence of individual solutions* into an integrated product implies that multiple people must communicate capably.

2. *Vaguely stated problems* stem from the use of ambiguous human communication techniques (e.g., English) as well as numerous unknown criteria at the time of requirements definition.

Conventional methods of software engineering focused on explicit separation of the problem (requirements), the abstract solution (design), and the final product (code and documentation). No single representation format was suitable for requirements and design, or design and code, or all three. The tools supporting these phases were very different, and the cost of change increased exponentially from one phase to the next. This lack of evolving flexibility forces the industry into a mode of "perfecting" one phase prior to the next; hence, no design was permitted until requirements were baselined and no coding was permitted until the design was baselined, etc.

The inherent problem with different representation formats for the products of each phase is that translation, interpretation, and communication in transitioning to the next phase is very error prone. "Representers" were frequently not the "translators" throughout the life cycle and basic intentions were often corrupted. Furthermore, the evaluation of each intermediate phase was typically based on paper review, simulation, and for the most part, engineering judgment and conjecture. Given a complex software system, there are far too many subtle interactions, miscommunications, and complex relationships to predictably achieve quality design verification without actually building subsets of the product and getting *factual* feedback. The "real"

Reprinted from *Proceedings of the 12th Int'l Conf. Software Engineering,* 1990, pp. 2-11. Copyright © 1990 by The Institute of Electrical and Electronics Engineers, Inc. All rights reserved.

evaluation of goodness occurred very late in conventional programs when components were integrated and executed in the target environment *together* for the first time. This usually resulted in excessive rework and caused late "shoehorning" of less than desirable solutions into the final product. These late, reactive changes resulted in added fragility and reduced product quality.

Figure 1 identifies the result of a typical conventional project when integration of components is delayed until late in the life cycle: substantial rework. The figure plots "Development Progress" against schedule. Development progress here is defined to be the percentage of the software product coded, compiled, and informally tested in its target language (i.e., demonstrable). Although conventional projects operated under the guise "no coding prior to CDR," we have displayed the conventional project's development progress assuming some standalone prototypes are done prior to CDR and that much of conventional Program Design Language (PDL) is directly translatable into the target language (i.e., demonstrable). In the figure, the conventional project is characterized by: an early PDR supported by small prototypes and a foreign PDL, no substantial coding until after CDR, risk management by conjecture, paper design reviews, protracted integration, and unlikely adherence to the planned completion schedule.

CCPDS-R is characterized in Figure 1 by a later PDR with a more tangible definition of what constitutes a preliminary design, demonstrations of incremental capabilities coupled with each design review, continuous integration during the design phase rather than the test phase, systematic risk management based on factual early feedback, and a higher probability of meeting an end-item schedule with a higher quality product.

Ada Process Model Goals

TRW's Ada Process Model recognizes that all large, complex software systems will suffer from design breakage due to early unknowns. It strives to accelerate the resolution of unknowns and correction of design flaws in a systematic fashion which permits prioritized management of risks. *The dominant mechanism for achieving this goal is a disciplined approach to incremental development.* The key strategies inherent in this approach are directly aimed at the three main contributors to software diseconomy of scale: minimizing the overhead and inaccuracy of interpersonal communications, eliminating rework and converging requirements stability as quickly as possible in the life cycle. These objectives are achieved by:

1. Requiring continuous and early convergence of individual solutions in a homogeneous life-cycle language (Ada).

2. Eliminating ambiguities and unknowns in the problem statement and the evolving solution as rapidly as practical through prioritized development of tangible increments of capability.

Although many of the disciplines and techniques presented herein can be applied to non-Ada projects, the expressiveness of Ada as a design and implementation language and support for partial implementation (abstraction) provide a strong platform for implementing an effective, uniform approach.

Many of the Ada Process Model strategies (summarized in Figure 2) have been attempted, in part, on other software development efforts; however, there are fundamental differences in this approach with respect to conventional software development models.

Uniform Ada Life-Cycle Representation

The primary innovation in the Ada Process Model is the use of a single language for the entire software life cycle, including, to some degree, the requirements phase. All of the remaining techniques rely on the ability to equate design with code so that the only variable during development is the level of abstraction. This provides two essential benefits:

1. *The ability to quantify units of software (design/development/test) work in **one dimension**, Source Lines of Code (SLOC).* While it is certainly true that SLOC is not a perfect

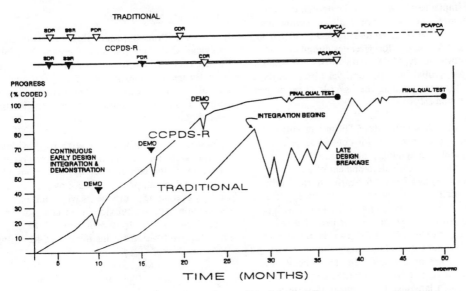

Figure 1. Software Development Progress

Process Model Strategy		Conventional Counterpart
Uniform Ada Lifecycle Representation	$\Longrightarrow$	PDL/HOL
Incremental Development	$\Longrightarrow$	Monolithic Development
Design Integration	$\Longrightarrow$	Integration and Test
Demonstration Based Design Review	$\Longrightarrow$	Documentation Based Design Review
Total Quality Management	$\Longrightarrow$	Quality by Inspection

Figure 2. New Techniques vs. Conventional Techniques

absolute measure of software, with consistent counting rules [3], it has proven to be the best normalized measure and provides an objective, consistent basis for assessing relative trends across the project life cycle.

2. *A formal syntax and semantics for life-cycle representation with automated verification by an Ada compiler.* Ada compilation does not provide complete verification of a component. It does go a long way, however, in verifying configuration consistency and ensuring a standard, unambiguous representation.

Incremental Development

Although risk management through incremental development is emphasized as a key strategy of the Ada Process Model, it was (or always should have been) a key part of most conventional models. Without a uniform life-cycle language as a vehicle for incremental design/code/test, conventional implementations of incremental development were difficult to manage. This management is highly simplified by the integrated techniques of the Ada Process Model [8].

Design Integration

In this discussion, we will take a simpleminded view of "design" as the partitioning of software components (in terms of function and performance) and definition of their interfaces. At the highest level of design we could be talking about conventional requirements definition; at the lowest level, we are talking about conventional coding. Implementation is then the development of these components to meet their interface while providing the necessary functional performance. *Regardless of level, the activity being performed is Ada coding.* Top-level design means coding the top-level components (Ada main programs, task executives, global types, global objects, top-level library units, etc.). Lower-level design means coding the lower-level program unit specifications and bodies.

The postponement of all coding until after CDR in conventional software development approaches also postponed the primary indicator of design quality: integrability of the interfaces. The Ada Process Model requires the early development of a Software Architecture Skeleton (SAS) as a vehicle for early interface definition. The SAS essentially corresponds to coding the top-level components and their interfaces, compiling them, and providing adequate drivers/stubs so that they can be executed. This early development forces early baselining of the software interfaces to best effect smooth development, evaluate design quality early, and avoid/control downstream breakage. In this process, we have made integration a design activity rather than a test activity. To a large degree, the Ada language forces integration through its library rules and consistency of compiled components. It also supports the concept of separating structural design (specifica-

tions) from runtime function (bodies). The Ada Process Model expands this concept by requiring structural design (SAS) prior to runtime function (executable threads). Demonstrations provide a forcing function for broader runtime integration to augment the compile time integration enforced by the Ada language.

Demonstration-Based Design Review

Many conventional projects built demonstrations or benchmarks of standalone design issues (e.g., user system interface, critical algorithms, etc.) to support design feasibility. However, the design baseline was represented on paper (PDL, simulations, flowcharts, vugraphs). These representations were vague, ambiguous and not amenable to configuration control. The degree of freedom in the design representations made it very difficult to uncover design flaws of substance, especially for complex systems with concurrent processing. Given the typical design review attitude that a design is "innocent until proven guilty," it was quite easy to assert that the design was adequate. This was primarily due to the lack of a tangible design representation from which true design flaws were unambiguously obvious. Under the Ada Process Model, design review demonstrations provide some proof of innocence and are far more efficient at identifying and resolving design flaws. The subject of the design review is not only a briefing which describes the design in human understandable terms but also a demonstration of important aspects of the design *baseline* which verify design quality (or lack of quality).

Total Quality Management

In the Ada Process Model there are two key advantages for applying TQM. The first is the common Ada format throughout the life cycle, which permits consistent software metrics across the software development work force. Although these metrics do not all pertain to quality (many pertain to progress), they do permit a uniform communications vehicle for achieving the desired quality in an efficient manner.

Secondly, the demonstrations serve to provide a common goal for the software developers. This "integrated product" is a reflection of the complete design at various phases in the life cycle for which all personnel have ownership. Rather than individually evaluating components which are owned by individuals, the demonstrations provide a mechanism for reviewing the team's product. This team ownership of the demonstrations is an important motivation for instilling a TQM attitude.

Incremental Development

Incremental development is a well-known software engineering technique which has been used for many years [1],[2]. The Ada

134

Process Model simply extends the discipline of incremental development into three dimensions:

Subsystem Increments, called *builds*, are selected subsets of software capability which implement a specific risk management plan. These increments represent a cross section of components which provide a demonstrable thread of capability. Integration across builds is mechanized by constructing major milestone (SSR, PDR, CDR) demonstrations of capabilities which span multiple builds.

Build Increments, called *design walkthroughs*, are sets of partially implemented components within a build which permit evolutionary insight into the allocated build components' structure, operation, and performance as an integrated set. Integration of components within builds is mechanized by constructing small scale design walkthrough (PDW and CDW) demonstrations composed of capabilities which span multiple components.

Component Increments, called *Ada Design Language*, or ADL, are partial implementations of Ada program units maintained in a compilable Ada format with placeholders for pending design detail. Integration of Ada program units is enforced to a large degree through compilation.

The paramount advantage of Ada in supporting incremental development is its support for partial implementations. Separation of specifications and bodies, packages, powerful data typing, and Ada's expressiveness and readability are features which can be exploited to provide an effective development approach and insightful development progress metrics for continuous assessment of project health from multiple perspectives. These development progress metrics are described later in this paper and in [8].

Figure 3 is an overview of a generic definition of project "builds" for insightful risk management. This definition has been abstracted from CCPDS-R experience where a similar build content/schedule has been extremely successful. The key features of the proposed build definition are:

Risk Management

Planning the content and schedule for each of the builds is perhaps the first and foremost risk management task. This activity essentially will define the risk management plan for the project. The importance of a good build content and schedule plan cannot be overemphasized, the efficiency of the software development depends on its initial quality *and the ability for the*

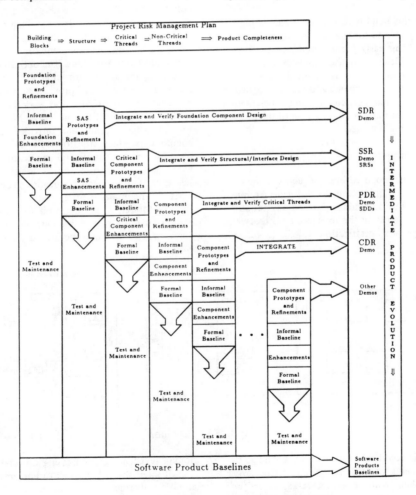

Figure 3. Incremental Development under the Ada Process Model

project to react to changes as the development progresses. The last point is important (as we have learned on CCPDS-R) because of the need to adjust build content and schedule as more accurate assessments of complexity, risk, personnel, and value engineering are achieved. Applying the underlying theory of this process model, the incremental development of the risk management plan must also provide some flexibility during the early builds as conjecture starts evolving into fact.

Pioneering an Early Build

The first build is identified in the figure as the foundation components. This build is critical to the Ada Process Model for two reasons: it must provide the prerequisite components for smooth development as well as a vehicle for early prototyping of the development process itself. There are always components which can be deemed "mission requirements independent" that fall into the category of foundation components.

The foundation software build represents components which are likely to be depended on by large numbers of development personnel. Their early availability, usage, feedback, and stabilization represent a key asset in avoiding downstream breakage and rework.

The second purpose of this build is to provide a guinea pig for exercising the process to be used for the subsequent mainstream builds. The existence of this early pioneer build on CCPDS-R was key to uncovering inefficiencies in the standards, procedures, tools, and techniques in a small scale where breakage was controllable and incorporating improvements and lessons learned in time to support later builds more efficiently. This "incremental development" of the process itself is important until the process matures into a truly reusable state itself.

Requirements/Design Concurrence

An interesting aspect of the proposed build sequence is the concurrency of requirements definition and the Software Architecture Skeleton (SAS) build. This concurrency ensures design/requirements consistency at the interface level described in the Software Requirements Specifications (SRS). In general,

we are prescribing that this level be the set of interfaces which are inherent in the Software Architecture Skeleton. The purpose of this concurrency is twofold: to ensure that the requirements are validated (to some degree) by a design representation and to eliminate ambiguities and identify holes in the requirements through experience in constructing the candidate solution's structure. This approach explicitly admits that the difference between requirements and design is a subtle one. The extent to which a project defines its software requirements will depend on both contractor and customer desires. The purpose of this approach is not to define that extent, but rather to provide enough early information in both the design and requirements representations to converge on an SRS baseline which is suitable to both parties. This subject is treated further in [5].

Software Architecture Skeleton (SAS)

The concept of a software architecture skeleton (SAS) is fundamental to effective evolutionary development. Although different applications domains may define the SAS differently, it should encompass *the declarative view of the solution which identifies all top-level executable components (Ada Main Programs and Tasks), all control interfaces between these components, and all type definitions for data interfaces between these components*. Although a SAS should compile, it will not necessarily execute without software which provides data stimuli and responses. The purpose of the SAS is to provide the structure/interface baseline environment for integrating evolving components into demonstrations. The definition of the SAS (Figure 4) represents the forum for interface evolution between components. In essence, a SAS provides only software potential energy: a framework to execute and a definition of the stimulus/response communications network. Software work is only performed when stimuli are provided along with applications components which transform stimuli into responses. If an explicit subset of stimuli and applications components are provided, a system thread can be made visible. The incremental selection of stimuli and applications components constitutes the basis of the build a little, test a little approach of the Ada Process Model. It is important to construct a candidate SAS early, evolve it into a stable baseline, and continue to enhance, augment, and maintain the SAS as the remaining design evolves.

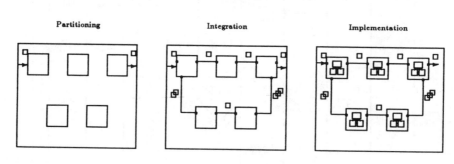

Figure 4. SAS Definition

In Figure 4, the symbols could take on different meanings depending on the object being defined. For example, the larger boxes could represent Ada main programs, tasks, or subprograms. The smaller boxes tagged to interface lines could represent types, packages of types, or other objects. The important message of the figure is that all SAS objects evolve from parti-

tioning (existence of processing objects) to integration (definition of inter-object behavior) to implementation (completion of all object abstractions) in a compilable Ada format. This evolution should occur in a combination of breadth-first and depth-first design activities which best match the risk management plan of the project.

The PDR Milestone

In Figure 3, the Preliminary Design Review (PDR) takes on a different meaning than in conventional process models. In the context of the Ada Process Model, PDR is the review and formal baselining of the SAS. The PDR reviews this candidate baseline with a supporting demonstration of some capability subset exercising the SAS to the extent that the structure can be deemed an acceptable baseline. The definition of the capability subset to be demonstrated at PDR is application dependent, but certainly should include the potential performance drivers (in space, time, throughput, or whatever), risky functional implementations, and design breakage drivers (i.e., components which are "withed" by many other components). With the exception of the SAS, PDR has been intentionally defined generically, to be instantiated appropriately for each project.

Conventional software PDRs define standards for review topics that result in tremendous breadth of review, with only a minimal amount that is really important or understood by the large, diverse audience. Reviewing all requirements in equal detail at a PDR is inefficient and unproductive. Not all requirements are created equal; some are critical to design evolution, some are don't cares. The Ada Process Model attempts to improve the effectiveness of design review by allocating the technical software review to smaller scale design walkthroughs and focusing the major milestone reviews on the globally important design issues. Furthermore, focusing the design review on a demonstration provides a more understandable representation of design perspectives for the diverse PDR audience (procurement, user, technical assistance personnel), most of whom are not familiar with Ada or detailed software engineering tradeoffs.

Demonstrations as Primary Products

Traditional software developments under the current Military Standards focus on documentation as intermediate products. To some extent, this is certainly useful and necessary [6]. However, by itself it is inadequate for large systems. Fundamental in the Ada Process Model is forcing design review to be more tangible via visibly demonstrated capabilities. These demonstrations serve two key objectives:

1. The generation/integration of the demonstration provides tangible feedback on integrability, flexibility, performance, interface semantics, and identification of design and requirements unknowns. It satisfies the software designer/developer by providing first hand knowledge of the impact of individual design decisions and their usage/interpretation by others. *The generation of the demonstration is the real design review.* This activity has proven to provide the highest return on investment in CCPDS-R by uncovering design interface deficiencies early.

2. The finished demonstration provides the monitors of the development activity (users, managers, customers, and other indirectly involved engineering performers) tangible insight into functionality, performance, and development progress. One sees an executing Ada implementation of understandable and relevant capability subsets.

On CCPDS-R, lessons learned from informal design walkthrough demonstrations are tracked via action items. For major milestone demonstrations, a demonstration plan is developed which identifies the capabilities planned to be demonstrated, how the capabilities will be observed, and explicit pass/fail criteria. Pass/fail criteria should be defined as a threshold for generating an action item; they need not be derived directly from requirements. The pass/fail criteria should trigger an action based on exceeding a certain threshold of concern as negotiated by the responsible engineering authorities for both contractor and customer.

With early demonstrations (whether on the target hardware or host environment), significantly more accurate assessments of performance issues can be obtained and resolved *inexpensively*. An important difference in the Ada Process Model, however, is that these demonstrations may tend to start out showing performance issues as immature designs are assessed. Whereas traditional projects started out with optimistic assessments that matured into problems, this approach may start pessimistic and mature into solutions.

Build Chronology

The individual milestones within a build need to be integrated into (or flowed down from) the higher-level project milestones. There is a tradeoff between the number of builds and the integration of concurrent build activities into a higher-level milestone plan. In general, an increased number of builds provides for more detailed development risk control. However, it also increases the management overhead and complexity of scheduling concurrent builds, managing personnel, and supporting an increased number of design walkthroughs. For any given project, these criteria need to be carefully evaluated. As general lessons learned, CCPDS-R defined small but complex early builds where detailed technical control and insight were necessary, and larger, less complex, later builds where the management focus was on production volume rather than on technical risks.

Within an individual build (Figure 5), a well-defined sequence of design walkthroughs takes place, Design walkthroughs are informal, detailed technical peer reviews of intermediate design products with attendance by interested reviewers including other designers, testers, QA, and customer personnel. Typically, the audience is restricted to a small knowledgeable group. However, other attendance is useful for the purposes of training. On CCPDS-R, design walkthrough attendance averaged 20–30 people. Design walkthroughs must be informal and highly interactive with open critique. A contractor or customer who forces too much formality into the walkthrough process will slow down the design evolution, or stifle the openness of raising issues; both are counterproductive (e.g., dry runs should be unnecessary). Likewise, followthrough must be effective and timely to maintain development continuity and capture issue resolution. Design walkthrough standards for format and content are needed early and should be evolved with experience.

Initial prototyping and design work is iterated primarily for the purpose of presenting a Preliminary Design Walkthrough (PDW) and associated capability demonstration. The focus of the PDW should be on reviewing the structure of the components which make up the build., with the demonstration focused on integrated components in an environment which exercises intercomponent interfaces in a visible manner. In simple terms, the PDW is focusing on a review of the declarative view of the components with enough executable capability to evaluate the goodness of the structure and interfaces.

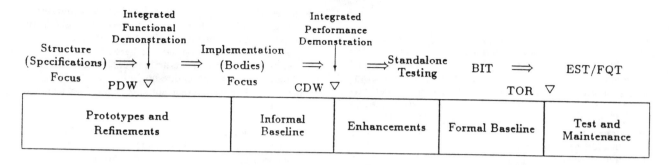

Figure 5. Incremental Development within a Build

Following the PDW, design lessons learned from both the PDW and the demonstration (tracked via informal action items on CCPDS-R) are incorporated into the evolving components, and further refinements of the design are performed en route to a Critical Design Walkthrough (CDW). The focus of the CDW should be on reviewing the operation of the components which make up the build, with the demonstration focused on integrated components in an environment which exercises intercomponent performance in a visible manner. The CDW is focusing on a review of the executable view of the components with enough capability to evaluate the performance of the *integrated* component subset. CDW demonstrations should be defined so that the important aspects of execution performance are visible (e.g., space, response time, accuracy, throughput, etc.), and the subset of partial implementations provides coverage of the components expected to be drivers in any performance criteria of interest.

The next phase is to incorporate the action items from CDW and the CDW demonstration's lessons learned into the build components, and refine and enhance those components into complete implementations. These components are then standalone tested for complete coverage of allocated requirements and boundary conditions in preparation for delivery to an independent test team. These informal tests perform the lowest levels of *integrated test* so that complete library units are turned over for formal requirements verification tests. Note the use of the term "integrated test" which implies that most integration has occurred in the process of providing working demonstrations. One still must account for some future integration effort, however, since incorporation of action items and demonstration lessons learned could result in interface breakage which must be re-integrated.

The final activity is the process of software turnover where the standalone tested units are placed under configuration control. These activities must be carefully planned so that the intercomponent dependencies within a build are accommodated in the turnover sequence. The build integration test phase (described below) is conducted during the turnover activity as an informal verification of configuration consistency, interface integrity, and standalone test completeness. These activities are logically just regression tests of previous demonstrations to ensure that all previously identified issues have been rectified and previously untested interfaces are accounted for prior to formal testing.

Incremental Test

Another benefit of this process model is the partitioning of the software into manageable increments for software test with planned software maintenance time. Although substantial informal testing occurs as a natural by-product of demonstration development, it is by no means complete, nor is it intended to demonstrate requirements satisfaction. Software test under this Process Model includes:

SAT. Standalone Test is an integrated set of Ada program units (typically a complete library unit) tested in a standalone environment. This level of testing corresponds to completeness and boundary condition testing to the extent possible in a standalone environment prior to delivery as a configuration baseline. Most SATs are informal in that they do not verify requirements; however, requirements verification in a standalone test (e.g., algorithm accuracy) can be performed after the components are installed into a controlled configuration baseline.

BIT. Where conventional projects typically suffer extensive design breakage during integration, build integration testing in the Ada Process Model is straightforward and rapid. It is essentially a regression test of previous demonstrations which should have resolved the major interface issues. It is still a necessary step, however, since it corresponds to the "Quality Evaluation" associated with installation of a standalone tested configuration baseline. BIT serves to validate that the previously demonstrated threads can be repeated, that previously defined deficiencies have been fixed, and that the configuration installation does not break any previous configurations. Furthermore, it does provide completeness of interface exercise not provided in the demonstrations.

EST. Engineering String Tests represent test cases which are focused on verifying specific subsets of requirements from possibly multiple CSCIs through demonstration and test of capability threads.

FQT. Formal Qualification Tests require a complete software subsystem for requirements verification. For example, a requirement such as "50% reserve capacity" cannot be verified until all components are present. The subject of this incremental test approach is treated more fully in [7].

Ada as a Design Language

The use of compilable Ada as a Design Language (ADL) is one of the primary facets of the Ada Process Model which provides uniformity of representation format. As will be described in the next section, the uniformity and Ada/ADL standards permit insight via software development progress metrics. Note that the terms Ada and ADL are virtually interchangeable with respect to our usage standards; the standards which apply to our final Ada products are the same as those that apply to earlier design representations. This approach best supports our technique of *evolving* designs into implementations without translating between two sets of standards.

The foundation of Ada Design Language is the use of Ada, comments, and predefined TBD Ada objects to evolve a continuously compilable design representation from a high-level abstraction into a complete Ada implementation. *ADL statements* are Ada statements which contain placeholders from the predefined set of TBD Ada objects. A package called **TBD_Types** defines TBD types, TBD constants, TBD values, and a TBD procedure for depicting statement counts associated with comments which together act as placeholders for TBD processing.

The use of objects from package **TBD_Types** constitutes a program unit or statement being identified as "ADL" (i.e., incom-

plete). Program units or statements which have no references to TBD objects are identified as "Ada" (i.e., complete) for the purposes of metrics collection.

Figure 6 shows a typical transition of ADL to Ada for a specific library unit from CCPDS-R. Although this evolution identifies a fairly uniform transition to Ada across all program units at PDW and CDW, a more typical evolution would have more individual program units being 100 percent complete while others being essentially zero percent complete. In other words, most designers on CCPDS-R tend to focus on completing sets of individual program units rather than portions of all program units. Given the flexibility of Ada packaging and structure, either technique has proven to be equally useful and should be left as designer's choice. However, the general transition trend has still been approximately 30 percent done by PDW, 70 percent done by CDW, and 100 percent done by Turnover.

	Program Unit	Type	Ada	ADL	Cplx	Total	%
	Inm_Erm_Procedures	TLCSC	6	122	4.0	128	4.7
		Package	2	122	4.0	124	1.6
	Create_Inm_Erm_Circuits	Proc	1	0	3.0	1	100.0
	Perform_Reconfiguration	Proc	1	0	4.0	1	100.0
Initial	Perform_Shutdown	Proc	1	0	3.0	1	100.0
View	Process_Error_Messages	Proc	1	0	4.0	1	100.0
	Inm_Erm_Procedres	TLCSC	47	101	3.9	148	31.8
		Package	24	19	4.0	43	55.8
	All_Node_Connections	Proc	3	19	4.0	22	13.6
PDW	Create_Inm_Erm_Circuits	Proc	4	8	3.0	12	33.3
View	On_Node_Connections	Proc	3	7	4.0	10	30.0
	Perform_Reconfiguration	Proc	6	2	4.0	8	75.0
	Perform_Shutdown	Proc	4	3	3.0	7	57.1
	Process_Error_Messages	Proc	3	43	4.0	46	6.5
	Inm_Erm_Procedures	TLCSC	87	48	3.9	135	64.4
		Package	30	11	4.0	41	73.2
	All_Node_Connections	Proc	16	0	4.0	16	100.0
CDW	Create_Inm_Erm_Circuits	Proc	8	4	3.0	12	66.7
View	On_Node_Connections	Proc	9	0	4.0	9	100.0
	Perform_Reconfiguration	Proc	6	2	4.0	8	75.0
	Perform_Shutdown	Proc	6	1	3.0	7	85.7
	Process_Error_Messages	Proc	12	30	4.0	42	28.6
	Inm_Erm_Procedures	TLCSC	137	0	3.9	137	100.0
		Package	42	0	4.0	42	100.0
	All_Node_Connections	Proc	16	0	4.0	16	100.0
	Create_Inm_Erm_Circuits	Proc	12	0	3.0	12	100.0
Turnover	On_Node_Connections	Proc	9	0	4.0	9	100.0
View	Perform_Reconfiguration	Proc	8	0	4.0	8	100.0
	Perform_Shutdown	Proc	7	0	3.0	7	100.0
	Process_Error_Messages	Proc	43	0	4.0	43	100.0

Figure 6. Incremental Development within a Component: ADL

Software Metrics

One of the by-products of our definition of ADL is the uniform representation of the design with a complete estimate of the work accomplished (source lines of Ada) and the work pending (source lines of ADL) embedded in the evolving source files in a compilable format. Although the Ada source lines are not necessarily complete (further design evolution may cause change), they do represent an accurate assessment of work accomplished. Given this life-cycle standard format, the complete set of design files can be processed at any point in time to gain insight into development progress. On CCPDS-R, a metrics tool was developed which scans Ada/ADL source files and compiles statistics

automatically. Figure 7 identifies example statistics which are produced by CSCI, by CSCI build, by build, and by subsystem. The metrics collection process is performed monthly for detailed management insight into development progress, code growth, and other indicators of potential problems [8].

The monthly metrics are collected by build, and by CSCI so that high-level trends and individual contributions can be assessed. Individual CSCI managers collect their metrics and assess their situation prior to incorporation into project-level views and are held accountable for monthly explanations of anomalous circumstances.

NAS CSCI Metrics (Month 10)			
	Designed	Coded	Total
TLCSCs	39	33	40
LLCSCs	13	10	13
Units	484	459	494
	ADL	Ada	Total
SLOC	1858	16636	18494
% Coded			90.0%
CPLX			3.8

Figure 7. Summary Metrics for CSCI

This process provides objectivity, consistency, and insight into progress assessment. Although the lowest level assessments of ADL statements are certainly still somewhat subjective, they are determined by the most knowledgeable people, the designers, and are therefore more likely to be accurate. Furthermore, the CSCI manager assesses his own situation based on the combined influence of his design team communicating to him in a uniform format. This consistency is even more valuable to the software management team since all of the responsible managers are communicating progress in the same language and the assessment of

CSCI progress, Build progress, and Subsystem progress are also consistent. The software management team can assess trends early, identify potential problems early, and communicate with higher-level management and customer personnel in an objective manner. This definition of development progress makes the development effort more tangible so that decision making and management can be based on fact rather than conjecture.

CCPDS-R Experience

At the time of this writing CCPDS-R is in month 27 of development. Five out of six builds have been developed and are currently maintained in a configuration-controlled baseline. This represents about 97 percent of the total Common Subsystem product being developed, integrated, and standalone tested. We are currently immersed in the formal requirements verification activities. As displayed in Figure 8, the design and development has flowed smoothly *as planned*, and there is a high probability of finishing on schedule, and on budget. The program is currently about 3 months past "System CDR." This is misleading, however, since contractually we were required to hold CDR after our final build's CDW. The success of CCPDS-R to date under the Ada Process Model described in this paper has not been easily attained. There has been high commitment on the part of the CCPDS-R project team, the CCPDS-R customer, and TRW management to make sure that the process was followed and that lessons learned were incorporated along the way.

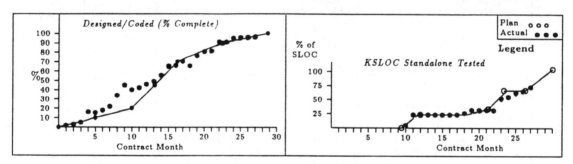

Figure 8. Common Subsystem Development Progress

Summary

Under careful scrutiny by managers, customers, developers, and testers, this Ada Process Model has matured into a powerful technique embraced by all levels. Developers and designers prefer working in the Ada language with demonstrations as products. Managers and customers appreciate the tangible insight into progress and technical risk evaluation and reduction. Testers have benefited from early involvement, better intermediate products, and the ability to focus on testing rather than integration. But most of all, users should ultimately receive a better product on schedule for a reasonable cost.

In the face of early Ada risks (compiler maturity, trained personnel, etc.), the CCPDS-R software development has been exemplary. We have continuously resolved issues as early as possible in the life cycle and the likelihood of confronting any serious problems in the future seems small. All in all, CCPDS-R represents an outstanding first generation Ada project from which many lessons have been learned. Second generation projects should be better.

Acknowledgments

The success of the Ada Process Model on CCPDS-R to date is due to multiple contributions including the TRW Systems Engineering & Development Division's management commitment to follow through on a risky new technology insertion with strong support as well as the entire CCPDS-R Software and Systems Engineering team. Explicit acknowledgments are due to Don Andres, Joan Bebb, Chase Dane, Charles Grauling, Tom Herman, Bruce Kohl, Steve Patay, Patti Shishido, and Mike Springman, whose day to day involvement and commitment have transformed some common sense ideas into tangible successes.

Biography

Walker Royce is the Software Chief Engineer on the CCPDS-R Project. He received his BA in Physics at the University of California, Berkeley, in 1977; an MS in Computer Information and Control Engineering at the University of Michigan in 1978, and has an additional 3 years of post-graduate study in Computer Science at UCLA. Mr. Royce has been at TRW for 10 years, dedicating the last five years to advancing Ada technologies in support of CCPDS-R. He served as the principal investigator of SEDD's Ada Applicability for C^3 Systems Independent Research and Development Project from 1984–1987. This IR&D project resulted in the Ada Process Model and the Network Architecture Services Software, technologies which earned TRW's Chairman's Award for Innovation and have since been transitioned from research into practice on real projects.

REFERENCES

[1] B.W. Boehm, *Software Engineering Economics*, Prentice-Hall, 1981.

[2] B.W. Boehm, "The Spiral Model of Software Development and Enhancement," *Proceedings of the International Workshop on the Software Process and Software Environments*, Coto de Caza, CA, March 1985.

[3] B.W. Boehm and W.E. Royce, "TRW IOC Ada COCOMO: Definition and Refinements," *Proceedings of the 4th COCOMO Users Group*, Pittsburgh, PA, November 1988.

[4] W.E. Royce, "Reliable, Reusable Ada Components for Constructing Large, Distributed Multi-Task Networks: Network Architecture Services (NAS)," *TRI-Ada Proceedings*, Pittsburgh, PA, October 1989.

[5] C.G. Grauling, "Requirements Analysis for Large Ada Programs: Lessons Learned on CCPDS-R," *TRI-Ada Proceedings*, Pittsburgh, PA, October 1989.

[6] M.C. Springman, "Software Design Documentation Approach for DoD-STD-2167A Ada Projects," *TRI-Ada Proceedings*, Pittsburgh, PA, October 1989.

[7] M.C. Springman, "Incremental Software Test Approach for a DoD-STD-2167A Ada Project," *TRI-Ada Proceedings*, Pittsburgh, PA, October 1989.

[8] D.H. Andres, "Software Project Management Using Effective Process Metrics: The CCPDS-R Experience," *To be presented at the AFCEA Military/Government Computing Conference*, Washington, DC, January 1990.

Three Problems Overcome with Behavioral Models of the Software Development Process

Bill Curtis

MCC Software Technology Program
P.O. Box 200195, Austin, Texas 78720

Software development processes are usually modeled by manifestations of the software artifact at given stages in its evolution and the nature of the transformations being applied to it during these stages. Thus, the software process is purported to begin with a stage called something like *requirements development*, or in some cases with the even the earlier step of a *feasibility study*. Such models vary the ordering of process stages (eg., prototyping vs. a traditional waterfall vs. incremental building and releasing). Yet, in all such models the software process is bounded by those activities that initiate and terminate the development of a specific software product.

There are three mistakes that can be made if the software development process is analyzed only with models that focus on stages of transforming the artifact:

1) the progression of stages through which the artifact evolves gets confused with the organization of the processes through which people develop software,

2) project processes that do not directly transform the artifact are not analyzed for their productivity and quality implications,

3) the process is treated as discrete rather than continuous in time (i.e., each project invokes a separate process).

These three problems can only be overcome by making a behavioral analysis of software development and the factors that control its productivity and quality. Such an analysis does not replace traditional models of software product evolution, rather they supplement them with much greater understanding of what controls project outcomes. For instance, Figure 1 presents the *layered behavioral model* used by Curtis, Krasner, and Iscoe (1988) to analyze problems experienced in developing large software systems. The three problems described above result in analytic shortfalls at different levels of this model.

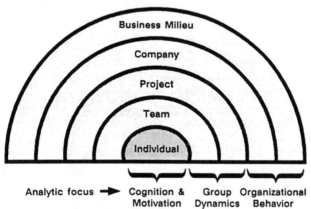

Figure 1. The layered behavioral model of software development processes (Curtis et al., 1988).

Confusing project stages with development processes – Since most software engineering textbooks order their chapters to progress through stages of the traditional waterfall model, development is usually depicted as a sequential, top down, balanced process. Many development standards have been written to stabilize this process. One alternative to this model is *prototyping*, in which there is an initial phase of exploratory programming followed by a phase of assessing the resulting program. This sequence of building something and trying it out can be repeated iteratively with each cycle involving the possibility of inserting more structure into the process. At any point in any of these iterative cycles it is possible to shift into the more traditional waterfall process. An interesting application of the cyclic model to assess and control project risk appears in Boehm's (1988) *spiral model*.

These process models for ordering the stages of the software development process are often used to guide the design of software development methods and tools. Since the stages through which the project progresses are ordered either linearly or cyclically, developers are assumed to perform their development tasks in the same order. Thus, the sequence of processes used to guide development at the project level of the layered behavioral model is mapped onto behavior occurring at the individual level. Unfortunately, no one has ever shown empirically that the disaggregation of project level stages had to result in an identical set of staged processes at the individual level.

The grafting of project level stages onto individual level behaviors assumes that mechanisms underlying both project and individual activities are identical. There is currently no theoretical or empirical basis for supporting this assumption. There is no reason to assume that mechanisms governing cognitive processes are controlled in the same fashion as those governing behavior at the project level. Behavior at the project level is affected by an amalgam of factors that involve group dynamics occurring at the team level and organizational behavior occurring at the company level. The project level represents a process abstraction in which management establishes a means of ordering, monitoring, and accounting for what is happening on a project. Traditional software process models provide management with the abstractions necessary to describe behavior at this level.

In research performed at MCC, Raymonde Guindon (Guindon & Curtis, 1988) has demonstrated that the software design behavior of individual designers is better characterized as an *opportunistic process*. These processes are characteristic of those observed in the cognitive literature on planning, and have been modeled in the blackboard architectures used in artificial intelligence research. Guindon has shown that in making design decisions, designers move back and forth across levels of abstraction ranging from application domain issues to detailed design and even coding issues. Decisions to be made at one level of abstraction are compared against their implications for decisions or implementations to be made at other levels. This process is neither sequential nor cyclic, since design behaviors are initiated by the recognition of issues that may occur at any level of abstraction.

"Three Problems Overcome with Behavioral Models of the Software Development Process," by B. Curtis from *Proc. 11th Int'l Conf. Software Engineering*, 1989, pages 398-399. Copyright © 1989 by the Association for Computing Machinery, Inc., reprinted with permission.

If software tools and methods are to provide useful support to software engineers while they are actually performing their tasks, they must be capable of being used in a way that is consistent with how software engineers make their decisions and work with software artifacts. For instance, Curtis, Sheppard, Kruesi-Bailey, Bailey, and Boehm-Davis (1989) have shown how little of the variation in performance is affected by specification formats compared to the enormous impact of individual differences among the software engineers using them. Currently, different levels of abstraction (eg., requirements, software architecture, detailed design, etc.) are usually contained in different documents and are not easily accessed simultaneously in most tools. Next generation design tools must allow software engineers to rapidly switch levels of abstraction in the artifact and support the opportunistic exploration of design decisions.

Ignoring non-transformational processes – Since the software development process is typically described in terms of the transformational stages of the software artifact's evolution, the activities on which these models focus are those that directly serve the transformational process. However, in studying design processes on large software projects in actual development settings, Curtis et al. (1988) found a range of critical problems involving behaviors that are talked about rarely in either software engineering textbooks or models. These activities involve human responses to the situations and conditions under which software development is performed, and involve behaviors at all levels of the layered behavioral model.

The three problems discussed by Curtis et al. (1988) affect cognitive, social, and organizational processes. Since they are based in the behavior of customers and developers, they must be analyzed in behavioral rather than artifactual terms. These problems involve:

1) the thin spread of application domain knowledge,
2) fluctuating and conflicting requirements, and
3) communication and coordination breakdowns.

The first problem recognizes that computer science knowledge alone is not sufficient for building most large systems, since the domain of application can be as complex as the domain of computation. Thus, a software project involves a significant learning component for any project member not already familiar with the application domain. If this learning process is not taken into account in project planning, the time required to build the system will be underestimated. People rarely remember how long it took to learn things before they could actually start doing something. Further, no plan for how to provide the required training will be formulated, leaving software engineers to scavenge for application knowledge wherever they may.

The second problem occurs for many reasons, and frequently because the customer for a computer system is also in a learning process. Far from being able to provide a stable set of requirements, many customers are seeing a range of possibilities unfold before them as developers discuss the implications of the requirements. This learning process continues throughout development, and as a result, these fluctuations perturb the process of transforming the artifact throughout the process.

The third problem involves the enormous amount of time spent by software engineers in communication with each other and the customer. Tools that improve the coordination or collaboration among software project members should have dramatic impact on software development productivity and quality, even though these tools are not actually used to transform the software artifact. The more consistent the understanding of design decisions and constraints are across project personnel, the more consistent the design and implementation will be. Few process models discuss how to organize and manage large development groups to maximize their coordination, but this is as important as managing the transformation process.

Discrete versus continuous process models – Perhaps the most serious shortcoming of most software process models is that they treat software development as a discrete process invoked at the beginning of a project and terminating at the end of a program's useful life. However, the behavioral factors that have been shown to exert so much influence over software productivity and quality are in many cases not factors that can be managed within the space of a single project.

Boehm (1981) and Valett and McGarry (1989) have demonstrated the dramatic impact differences in personnel capability can have on project performance. These talents are mostly in place before a project begins, and managers scramble to get the most talented people available. However, when queried as to how they are improving the level of talent available to a project, they will reply, "Listen, we hire the best people we can, and there isn't much more we can do to improve the people side of the equation." This attitude is a severe impediment to their productivity on two accounts. First, they assuredly are not doing all they can to hire the best people available. Second, they probably are not doing anything systematic to ensure that they grow and retain the talent they have attracted. The few companies that take recruiting, selection, growth, and retention seriously are noted for their outstanding staff and performance.

A second problem with having a discrete single project model of the software process is that it becomes difficult to argue for the added cost of creating well-designed, highly reliable reusable software components. The cost of tooling up for effective reuse must be paid up front to be reaped out back. If performance (productivity, quality, costs, etc.) is to be accounted for on a single project basis, few managers will volunteer to absorb the costs of providing for future reusability on their watch.

In order to improve the quality of the staff and the availability of reliable reusable parts, the software process must be thought of as a continuous process. It must be reconceived as a process of growing both people and the base of reusable software assets. Rather than squandering the learning that has been paid for so dearly, a plan for a software business will be put in place that projects the growth of business performance in conjunction with the growth of knowledge in the staff and in the component library. Projects are conceived as occurrences in the larger business process that measure the maturation achieved at a particular time through their performance. Thus, the software process is modeled as a set of processes at the company level rather than at the project level. The software process is the continuous growth of the business assets, and their value over time is measured in a series of discrete events constituting software development projects.

References

Boehm, B. W. (1981). *Software Engineering Economics*. Englewood Cliffs, NJ: Prentice-Hall.

Boehm, B. W. (1988). A spiral model of software development and maintenance. *IEEE Computer*, 21 (5), 61-72.

Curtis, B., Krasner, H., & Iscoe, N. A field study of the software design process for large systems. *Communications of the ACM*, 31 (11), 1988, 1268-1287.

Curtis, B., Sheppard, S.B., Kruesi-Bailey, E., Bailey, J., & Boehm-Davis, D. Experimental evaluation of software specification formats. *Journal of Systems and Software*, 1989, 9 (2), 167-207.

Guindon, R. & Curtis, B. (1988). Control of cognitive processes during design: What tools would support software designers? In *Proceedings of CHI'88*. New York: ACM, 263-268.

Valett, J.D. & McGarry, F.E. (1989). A summary of software measurement experiences in the Software Engineering Laboratory. *Journal of Systems and Software*, 1989, 9 (2), 137-148.

Chapter 3
Project Management

Project management is the art of creating the illusion that any outcome is the result of a series of predetermined, deliberate acts when, in fact, it was dumb luck.
— Kerzner, *Project Management*

Overview

This chapter contains four papers on the topic of project management. Project management directs resources toward delivery of acceptable products per agreed-upon specifications, budgets, and schedules. It requires trade-offs between functionality, quality, cost, and schedules. Its practice takes guts, patience, smarts, skill, understanding, and perseverance. Its potential is large, as are its heartaches.

You can define a project by the following recognizable characteristics:

- There is a well-defined objective and deliverable.
- There are agreed-upon start and stop dates.
- The endeavor results in something unique.
- There are resource limitations (time, staff, dollars, etc.).
- It requires focus and leadership to be successful.

You can then use project management techniques to plan and control your software project so that its objectives are met and suitable products are delivered to the customer on schedule and per the agreed-upon budget.

The first paper, by Carter, Clare, and Thorogood, introduces you to project management techniques and discusses their application to computer projects. This article surveys the basic tools and techniques used in project planning and control. It describes the use of PERT/CPM and other networking techniques to develop, allocate, and schedule resource estimates for the project.

The second paper, by Brooks, is one of the true classics in the field. I debated a long time on whether or not to leave it in this edition. After much thought, I opted to include it because of its wit and the wisdom it imparts. In addition, it permits newcomers to the field to read the original "Brooks Law" in the context where it was born.

The next paper, by Tom Gilb, is one of my favorites. It advocates the use of a "guts management" philosophy to cope with short deadlines, low budgets, and insufficient staffing levels. It is witty and full of good advice. Tom's 10 guiding principles make a lot of sense, as does much of his commentary.

The fourth paper, by Boehm and Ross, explains and defends a new theory of software project management called Theory W. The paper describes the principles behind and the steps involved in this theory, whose underlying premise is that you must make everyone a winner to succeed in project management. The paper goes on to present a case study that illustrates the application of the theory on an attempt to introduce a new information system in a large company.

References

For those interested, Chapter 12 contains the *Standard for Software Project Management Plans,* ANSI/IEEE Std 1058.1-1987. This standard contains an outline for and describes the contents of what many in the industry believe is a "good" project plan.

Probably the best general text that I have read on the topic of project management was authored by Kerzner (Reference 16 in the Bibliography). Although dated, another good reference is Metzger's book (Reference 19). Many other textbooks that will serve you well are available.

Engineering project management techniques and their application to computer projects

by Guy D. Carter, C. P. Clare and D. C. J. Thorogood

Project management is a topic which occurs on an increasing number of college and university courses in engineering and computing. Inspection of syllabuses will reveal the same tools and techniques being covered in both 'hard' engineering disciplines (such as mechanical engineering) and 'soft' engineering (such as computing science). This paper describes those tools and techniques and looks at the difficulties in applying them successfully to projects concerned with building computer-based information systems.

1 Introduction

The modern commercial environment is extremely competitive, and so all aspects of an organisation must be carefully managed to maximise profits and meet objectives. This is true in all spheres of business whether it is a factory, a construction company or a software house.

When a company considers undertaking a project, a number of decisions must be made regarding the venture. One of the fundamental questions is to ascertain whether or not it will be profitable, and a significant variable here is the time scale: 'time is money'. Thus a high degree of control must be exercised to ensure that a project does not run over time (and consequently budget). This control is part of a science termed 'project management'. In the world of engineering a number of techniques have been developed which assist in project management, from the initial realisation of a scheme right through its subsequent life cycle.

As computer projects become more numerous, both within the commercial environment, where computers are used as tools, and in the area of computer package development, i.e. software houses, it has become apparent that control of computer projects is an enigma to all levels of management. Projects are commenced without accurate estimates as to the cost, time scale or resources necessary. Thus adequate control is virtually impossible, resulting in poor products, which are delivered late and cost far more than was expected.

The aim of this paper is to collect together, and clarify, those techniques that have been successfully applied to engineering projects, and to determine whether these techniques can be successfully applied to computer projects.

2 Project management

Project management is intended to be a tool which will provide management with control over, and the flexibility to change, a project. Project management should give management:

● the ability to plan the best possible use of resources to meet a goal, given limits on time and cost

● the chance to plan 'one-off' projects, where experience cannot be gained from previous repetition or where standard time/cost information is unavailable

● information presented in a particularly easy to use fashion, for example time schedules, areas of slack time etc.

As in all areas of management, there are many aspects to project management. However, this paper restricts its attention to those areas which relate directly to the quantitative aspects of the control of a project. Other areas of concern, such as staff management and equipment, are only considered when strictly relevant to a project as resources. Management must be involved with a project throughout its life cycle, and as an aid to the necessary control each project may be divided into three specific areas of operation.

2.1 Feasibility

Initially every project comes to life as an idea, a vague plan to create a product or develop a situation. The original idea is subsequently massaged into shape until the final end-product, and development scheme, is envisaged. Once the end-product has been completely specified, in the form of agreed terms of reference, the control offered by project management may be applied to the project.

So that decisions may be made regarding the viability of the product, all areas affected by the project must be considered. Intensive research must be undertaken, so that management may have accurate answers to questions con-

"Engineering Project Management Techniques and Their Application to Computer Projects," by G.D. Carter, C.P. Clare, and D.C.J. Thorogood from *Software Engineering Journal*, Vol. 2, No. 1, Jan. 1987, pages 15-20. Copyright © 1987 Institution of Electrical Engineers, reprinted with permission.

cerning the proposed product, such as: 'Is it profitable/necessary/desirable/in the interest of the company?' In other words, does the project fit in with the strategic plans of the organisation? These answers, together with the estimated overall cost of the project, must be carefully considered. Only when sufficient research and investigation into the costs and benefits have provided management with a positive indication as to the feasibility of the project should the commencement of that project be considered.

2.2 Planning

Subsequent to its approval a project must be subjected to further control, as part of project management, before it is physically commenced. The complete life cycle of the project must be considered, specified and planned. Ideally the complete scheme will be defined as a number of inter-related modular tasks. Each of these tasks must be assigned a time scale, a cost, resource requirements and priority.

Once the project has been defined in this manner a reasonably accurate prediction may be made as to the total cost and time scale of production (results from this planning may necessitate a return to the feasibility considerations, for further deliberation). This project plan will allow the definition of start and finish dates, the identification of tasks which must be completed before others are commenced, and the scheduling of all necessary resources.

It is only by applying this type of control that a project may be commenced with confidence. Management will know exactly the manner in which a project is expected to proceed and may start a project with the knowledge that all areas of difficulty have been foreseen and allowances have been made.

2.3 Control during the life cycle

It is, perhaps, somewhat idealistic to assume that a well planned project will adhere to a schedule throughout its life cycle. It is an unfortunate fact of life that even the best of plans never runs smoothly. Every project will have a large number of possible variables, any or all of which may change during the project's life cycle. Equipment may malfunction, materials may not arrive on time, personnel may be taken ill — these few examples indicate the diversity of problems that may beset the management plan.

However, some degree of control may be exercised over a 'rogue' project. If, for instance, a task is running over its allocated time span, by dextrous manipulation of the original plan, devised as the

ideal life cycle of the project, new time scales may be calculated for all tasks affected by the late running, or, if possible, resources may be transferred to alleviate the problem. In either case the revised costs and completion dates can be readily calculated.

Use of the original plan, together with the latest information regarding the project, allows management to produce a new estimate of the project life cycle when necessary, and thus ensure that continual optimal use is made of all resources — resulting in minimum costs. However, the fact that this degree of control is available does not negate the possibility that, owing to unfavourable circumstances, a project may become infeasible, through the occurrence of extra costs or time span.

Being in an informed position and thus able, if necessary, to terminate a project during its life cycle may be considered the ultimate level of control.

3 Techniques available

There are a number of well established techniques available which assist in project management. These techniques have been developed primarily in the engineering field and thus relate particularly well to that environment. It will be seen that some of these techniques relate specifically to the areas of project management outlined previously, and others are concerned with the same areas, but differ widely in the number of project variables that they address. No attempt has been made to give a full description of any of the techniques listed below; any further information may be obtained from Refs. 1–4.

3.1 Decision criteria

The theories of decision are used solely during the feasibility study of a project. Their use requires estimations of the expected profitability of, or benefit to be gained from, the end-product of a project and of the cost of the project overall.

Decision criteria encompass a number of differing techniques, for example decision theory, maximin criteria, regret criteria (Ref. 4). Each allows the user to place emphasis on his own expectations of the market situation, and thus decisions are made with the user having taken note of the real possibilities of fluctuating markets. By using decision criteria, together with management experience, optimal courses of action may be calculated from the estimated figures provided. Hence conclusions as to the real viability of a project may be reached.

It should be noted that other project management techniques may need to be applied to a project before any decision

criteria are used, owing to the requirement of an accurate estimation of total project cost, for use as input to the decision theories in use.

3.2 Milestone charts

The use of milestone charts involves the division of a project into separate, self-contained tasks. A table, or chart, is then drawn up listing these tasks plus relevant information concerning each task. Each entry of the table will contain such items as the task title, employee or team assigned, a review date and the completion date.

The milestone charts thus constructed provide a convenient and easily prepared and understood reference table. A quick glance at the table will provide management with basic information about each modular task. However, while use of the chart will indicate whether a job has overrun its expected completion date, there is no way that this can be used to assess the overall effect that this will have on the project as a whole.

In fact, milestone charts do not indicate the inter-relationships between tasks, i.e. overlap of tasks or tasks which must be completed before another can be commenced. A further limitation of milestone charts can be seen as their lack of provision for any variables other than time; resource scheduling or costs are not catered for.

3.3 Gantt charts

Gantt charts, named after their originator, are very similar to milestone charts. Tasks are defined in the same manner and tabulated on the chart. The time span of each task is indicated by the length of a line drawn on an adjacent calendar. The calendar is defined in the scale chosen to be the most appropriate by the project manager, i.e. hours, days, weeks etc.

The advantages and disadvantages of Gantt charts are similar to those specified for milestone charts. They are easy to prepare and understand, but, although they can illustrate the overlap of tasks, by the definition of start and finish times on the calendar, predecessor tasks are still not identified; nor can the effect of delays be related to the project as a whole.

3.4 Networks

Networking is a generic name for a number of techniques which utilise what is termed 'time network analysis' as a basis for the control of manpower, resources and capital used in a project.

The indiscriminate switching of one technique name for another in many publications has resulted in much confusion as to which name refers to which technique. Before giving a description of the networking technique, a brief recount of its history may help alleviate this problem.

In 1958 the Special Projects Office of the US Navy, concerned with performance in large development projects, introduced a 'Project evaluation and review technique' (PERT) on the Polaris weapon system. At about the same time the US Air Force developed a similar system called 'Project evaluation procedure' (PEP), although this was subsequently dropped in favour of PERT. Dupont, the large chemical concern, in an effort to shorten the length of time between product research and production, initiated a study which resulted in a technique known as 'Critical path method, or analysis' (CPM/CPA).

At the time of their conception both PERT and CPA were virtually the same system. Both these project management techniques were concerned solely with the time span of a project's tasks, their inter-relation, and hence the life cycle of the project as a whole.

As the engineering community became aware of the obvious benefits of PERT/CPA, they were further developed so that the control offered by these techniques could encompass more of the variables that exist as part of a large project. It is at this point that the beginning of the differentiation between PERT and CPA can be identified. While CPA was to remain unchanged, i.e. dealing with time factors only, PERT was developed by various academic and commercial bodies to encompass an increasing number of other project variables. The decision regarding which of the two techniques to work on was, apparently, quite arbitrary.

The development of PERT has been described as a number of successive generations:

• *First generation:* PERT/TIME — the original specification, virtually identical to CPA.
• *Second generation:* PERT/COST — the effects and consequences of any divergence from the planned time scale are related to overall costings.
• *Third generation:* PERT/LOB (line of balance) — the utilisation of a time-orientated network is used for planning the project, but more specifically as a management information system during the production phase of the project.
• *Fourth generation:* PERT/LOB/COST — used to take into account time, cost and resource scheduling: one published fourth-generation PERT known as CSPC ('Cost and schedule planning and control') (Ref. 5) is claimed not only to serve as a control mechanism for project managers, but is also designed to enhance an executive's visibility of the project.'

While definitions of the later generations of PERT are not always as rigorous as one would hope, the general concept of PERT being developed in order to accommodate an increasing number of project factors under its umbrella of control is fairly clear.

Having highlighted these variations in network techniques it should be noted that, however high one climbs on the PERT generation ladder, the basic networking procedure remains the same; in particular all define a critical path. As the complexity of the technique increases, more parameters are simply included in the basic scheme. For this reason it is deemed prudent to include all the networking systems, i.e. CPA and all the PERT generations, under the banner of PERT (an arbitrary choice). Hopefully this will dispel confusion. When the term PERT is used in the remainder of this paper, the degree of complexity of the technique will either be apparent from the text, or it will be a generalisation to cover any variations deemed appropriate.

As indicated above the basic PERT technique relates solely to time scales. In order to apply PERT to a project the complete scheme must initially be split into a number of self-contained tasks. Predictions as to the time span of each task must then be made, tasks which must be finished before others may be commenced must be identified (task inter-relationships must be defined), and either a start date or target date for the finish of the complete project must be set (one is set, the other is obviously governed by the total life cycle of the project, calculated with the aid of the completed network).

The heart of any PERT analysis is the network, or arrow diagram. This differs significantly from the Gantt charts. The diagram consists of a number of circles (events) which indicate the start or completion of a task, and arrows (activities) representing the tasks themselves.

Having introduced the network diagram, and before further description, a concept is introduced here which is developed in a later section: the comparison of structured analysis and design with PERT techniques.

The arrow diagram can be said to follow similar principles to the data flow diagram (DFD) occurring in structured systems analysis and design methodologies (Ref. 5). Each event is displayed as a circle, with vectors 'input' to and 'output' from that event. The diagram shows, at each point, the status of a project in that an event relies upon a certain number of activities (inputs) which themselves rely on pre-vious events. Furthermore, subsequent activities (shown as outputs from a particular event) cannot commence until that event has occurred. DFDs involve the use of circles to represent processes which require and produce input and output data flows. A process cannot start until all its inputs are present, and no outputs can occur until the process is activated.

The parallel between the network and the DFD is rather more than just appearance. Both are static diagrammatic representations of a dynamic system, representing that system as a series of sub-systems, each with well defined inputs and outputs. Because of the structure of the diagrams, the effects of modification of inputs and outputs to a particular node (circle) can be related to the entire structure, which in PERT terms means the entire project span.

Both techniques also suffer from the fact that the more complex the project, the more difficult is the construction of the diagram. With DFDs this problem is overcome by the technique of 'levelling' the diagram. The first stage is to create a context level diagram showing one large process with a mass of data input flows and a mass of outputs. The context diagram is then sub-divided into levels of refinement, where each circle is successively replaced by a number of linked circles reflecting the refinement of one process into a number of sub-processes. This technique is well documented by De Marco (Ref. 6).

It is probable that this levelling technique could be adapted for the construction of a PERT network diagram. The main difference would be that the successive refinement process would be concentrated more on the lines (activities) than the circles (events). Levelling DFDs, although concentrating on the circles (processes), necessarily carries along the sub-division of the lines (data flows) as an integral part of the exercise. PERT diagram 'levelling' would be, in a sense, the reverse of this, but if successful would result in a properly structured system of activities and events. The levelling methodology for PERT is an area for further research.

Having brought the apparent similarities between structured analysis and design and PERT techniques to the fore, there now follows a more complete description of the network analysis.

Two events are linked by means of an activity; the arrows are now drawn to any scale, but the time span of the activity is included, as a figure, above the arrow. By careful construction of the diagram the interdependence of one task upon another is illustrated; i.e. for a task (activity) to be shown as being the predecessor of another an arrow is drawn linking the circle which indicated the start of the predecessor to the circle indicating the start of its dependent. 'Dummy' activities are used to distinguish between the activities associated with an event which has more than one dependent. These 'dummy activities' are normally of zero duration.

With the diagram constructed and activity time spans indicated, the network is subjected to forward analysis, when each event is given an earliest start time — earliest event time (EET) — based on the duration of the activities preceding it. The critical path (CP) may now be identified. The CP is the longest, direct route through the network; i.e. lengthening the time span of any of the activities on the CP would extend the EET of the final event. The network can now be reverse analysed, calculating the latest event time (LET) for each event, i.e. the latest an event may occur without affecting the EET of the final event (this would in fact alter the route of the CP). The network can now be said to be 'time-analysed'.

Reference to this time-analysed network supplies immediate information as to the effect of a task over-run. Those tasks on the CP will, obviously, have a direct effect on the complete project time span. Such tasks are practically identified as those whose EET and LET coincide. However, all other tasks will have a 'float', or 'slack quantity', which is the amount of time that their LET differs from their EET; i.e. any over-run that is less than or equal to their slack quantity will not alter the project life span.

Any alteration to a task's estimated time span can conveniently be checked against the network, and the network can easily be re-calculated to compensate for any unexpected occurrences. The effect of resource re-scheduling is also readily modelled; 'what if?' type enquiries may be posed and readily answered by appropriately re-structuring the network.

Although this description has dealt solely with the consideration of time spans, it is evident that factors such as cost and resource scheduling can be incorporated into this technique, forming an extremely powerful, albeit complex, project management tool.

Network analysis would appear to offer the facility of comprehensive project planning and control, and it is to this technique that the attention of this paper now turns.

4 Software available

In November 1982 *Engineering Computers* (Ref. 7) declared that computer manufacturers had 'at last' realised the potential in the engineering field and published a synopsis of available management packages, several of these being specifically for project management.

The range of software would appear to be comprehensive, starting with cheap packages for microcomputers and extending to systems with prices in the five-figure bracket. Some industries have developed software specific to their own field, while others have the advantage of packages from software houses catering for a particular industrial field, or a particular aspect of project management.

It would appear that, in common with most commercial purchases, the more expensive products provide a more complete and complex service. So while the cheaper microcomputer-based packages may provide only the basic PERT (time analysis), and place restrictions on the number of events and activities specified, the more costly software designed for larger machines will offer increasing levels of processing features, for example cost, resources, dates, holiday factors etc. Similarly, graphical output will improve from basic network drawing to include graphs, bar charts and histograms.

It should be noted that there is, apparently, no software available to support decision criteria, although a number of algorithms have been published (Ref. 8) for completing this task. Being iterative, the majority of tasks are ideally suited for interaction between the decision maker, the analyst and a computer. Although the computer software industry has only recently become aware of the market for project management packages, the range of products now available allows management the opportunity to make full use of the established PERT technique. The speed and ease with which computer-based networks may be set up, adjusted and re-analysed allows general 'what if?' queries and run-time control to become a real real-time possibility.

5 Tailoring an engineering project to PERT

As indicated previously, all references to network analysis techniques shall be couched under the general heading of PERT. The number of parameters used in specifying a project will be the means of identifying the level of PERT to be used.

For a project to be controlled in the most effective manner, it must be analysed and tailored to suit the management technique. Initially, once defined, a project must be divided into a number of tasks. Each task should ideally be small enough to allow the reliable estimation of time, cost etc., but large enough to be seen as a complete activity with well defined start and finish points. This part of the project analysis is perhaps the most critical, as the omission of an activity will nullify any accuracy of the final plan and addition of a task at a later date would necessitate the complete re-working of the network. Thus care must be taken to include all tasks which are ancillary to those more easily recognised. These might include:

- preparation of materials
- ordering and delivery of materials
- testing of completed parts
- training of end-product users
- writing of manuals
- clearing away of waste materials.

Once all tasks which make up the total project have been identified, each must be allocated a time scale. Many jobs within the engineering and construction industries are well practiced, and hence estimates as to their time span may be performed accurately, based on experience.

However, when previous knowledge is non-existent, or not reliable, algorithms exist which enable the calculation of reasonably accurate estimations.

In order to complete the basic network, tasks which are predecessors of others must be identified. Once these processes have been completed the network may be drawn up and time analysis performed on the project as a whole. Thus prepared, the network will allow identification of the CP (the path linking all those tasks whose time scales control the overall project time scale) and the slack areas (the tasks which may over-run their estimated time scale without delaying the end-point of the project).

This is the most basic PERT technique: planning and control are catered for, but purely with respect to time. Further parameters may be added to each task, so that costs and various resources may be accounted for. Cost may be related to a number of aspects of a task, including manpower, materials, use of machinery and use of space.

Consideration must also be given to inflation if the project life cycle extends over one year. By careful manipulation of resources, extra costs, due to a project running behind schedule, may be minimised. This is the concept termed resource scheduling, where resources (labour, capital, materials, working area etc.) are moved from one task to another. For instance a task which is over-running may be allocated resources from a task which has a large slack period. The network will assist in ensuring that any manipulations result in as little cost effect as possible.

It can be seen that an engineering project with tasks conveniently specified and time scales accurately estimatable, as a result of long-term repetition and experience, is ideally suited to the PERT techniques of project planning and control.

6 Tailoring a computer project to PERT

Computer projects have been in existence for a relatively short time, and consequently management has little intuitive reasoning or expertise to apply to them. Whereas long-term repetition, and subsequent experience, in construction and similar industries allows the reasonably accurate estimation of project variables such as time, cost and resources required, faced with an equivalent computer project, management apparently has little idea of time scales or cost. Thus project control is to all intents and purposes practically non-existent, leading to inadequate communication between those involved, over-extended time scales and costs and the eventual high probability of inadequate end-product delivery.

It is obvious that some form of project management is required for application to computer projects, and, as PERT is successfully used by engineering management, investigations should be made into the suitability of PERT for computer projects. A computer project will need to undergo the same analysis to be fitted to PERT as has been previously identified as necessary for an engineering project.

6.1 Division into tasks

The primary concern must be to split the whole project into tasks, using the same criteria to judge the size of each, i.e. small enough to allow accurate time scale estimation but large enough to be identified as a complete and definable job.

The advent and promotion of structured analysis and programming may well be viewed as an aid to defining a project in the required manner. The benefits of the various methods of structured analysis and design (Refs. 6 and 9–11) have mainly been expressed with a view to the quality of the end-product. By taking the overall 'problem' of the need for a new information system, and proceeding through the process of successive refinement, the analyst eventually ends up with a series of sub-problems, all with clearly defined interfaces. This 'divide and conquer' approach allows the sub-problems to be tackled systematically in the knowledge that as each sub-problem is solved, providing the interface definitions have been maintained, the aggregation of the solutions should lead to a correct comprehensive solution to the initial problem.

The structured approach can (and should) be applied at all stages throughout the analysis, design and development of an information system. The end-product of this approach is usually more reliable in its operation and, more importantly, it is more flexible as regards the ease of maintenance and enhancement. Thus the structured methodologies result in considerable cost savings over the life time of an information system.

These benefits provide a strong enough argument for the use of structured methodologies, but the project manager can further exploit the approach. The process of successive refinement naturally produces self-contained modules of work, whether at the analysis, design or development stages. Such modules fit the requirements of the first stage of PERT, in that the content of the modules (tasks) is established, as well as the control aspects such as preparation and reviews being specified. As in engineering projects care must be taken so that no tasks are overlooked. Processes such as making appointments for interviews, preparations for presentations and walkthroughs (at specific stages in the life cycle of the project) must not be overlooked, and must be carefully included in the list of tasks.

While it may be seen as a pains-taking and tedious process, the sectioning of a computer project into separately defined tasks may be seen as relatively problem free, given the tools available and a stoical approach to the problem.

6.2 Estimation of time scales

The next stage in the PERT process is to estimate task time scales, and, while the specifying of the tasks themselves may be expected to present few problems, the accurate estimations of their times will be seen to be fraught with difficulties. De Marco notes the difficulties inherent in these estimations, pointing out that data regarding past projects is rarely collected, and admitting that estimating within structured analysis is heuristic. This is far from the accuracy required for PERT to be successful.

Many formal approaches at estimating time scales for computer system projects have been tried over the past 20 years. Unfortunately, very few have met with any success, although as an aid in estimating the time scale of an activity the engineering users of PERT developed a method for providing an 'accurate estimate' (Ref. 3). However, most practitioners tend to favour 'guesstimating' rather than estimating. This usually involves combining a hunch for the 'feel' of the particular project with some form of comparison with similar jobs undertaken in the past.

This approach was often acceptable in the second and third generation of computer information systems. Then, most projects were concerned with the computerisation of a specific task or of the work of a specific department within an organisation. For example, a project would be to develop a computerised payroll system. If the project manager had had previous experience of computerising payrolls, then the previous development times (possibly adjusted for the size of the organisation) were regarded as a good an estimate as any.

This somewhat sloppy approach is very dangerous with fourth-generation information systems, where the entire corporate information system is the scope of the project. Under these circumstances, payroll is but a part of a complete information system which will have many aspects peculiar to the organisation in question. Clearly the 'wet finger in the air' approach is not acceptable.

Data collection:

A large part of analysis consists of data collection. Often this is effected by interviewing the personnel with direct knowledge of the information required. The situation where an interviewer is able to specify his requirements and the interviewee understands exactly what is required from him will result in a shorter interview than the equivalent situation when the interviewee is at a loss as to what is required from him and the interviewer is unable to convey his needs.

A further difficulty with estimating the time required for fact-finding concerns the attitudes and reactions of the user staff to be interviewed. Much depends on the formal and informal industrial relations atmosphere within the organisation, and this in turn depends on the management style in operation. People are naturally resistant to any change unless they are convinced that they, personally, will benefit from that change. The whole idea of 'computerisation' represents a major change and, moreover, it has to be said that computerisation does not have a good record in terms of publicity. Many people tend to regard computers as a threat and will consciously or sub-consciously withhold information, mislead the interviewer or make the interview difficult. This will result in interviews taking much longer than was estimated.

Coding:

In complete contrast to the problems encountered in data collection, the process of coding a program, or program module, may be completely structured.

However, difficulties in estimating time scales still abound. In estimating the time for a section of code, the project manager/leader may make an un-realistic estimate if the task is to be processed by an inexperienced programmer.

With the development of software for a computerised information system the problems of producing a good product are well researched and documented. The whole area of software engineering aims to provide methodologies designed to ensure that a software product is proven prior to its completion, and hence rigorous testing should confirm that the software meets its specification. Thus the aim is to produce software of good quality, and this is an area of debate. The quality of software is difficult to measure; attempts have been made to define quality at a number of levels (Ref. 12) but there are a wide range of views within the software engineering fraternity as to what such measures should be.

The research on software engineering aims at easing this problem by defining the ways in which quality code can be produced. Until such standards are widely adopted the estimating of time (and hence resources) will still be difficult.

With second- and third-generation computing, the standard measure used in estimating time requirements was the number of lines of code, combined with a programmer productivity rate of ten lines of working, tested code per day.

Two examples of formulas which profess to give an estimate of coding time are provided by Wooldridge (Ref. 2) and the Cocomo model of Boehm (Ref. 13). It is interesting to note that, before any of these formulas can be used, a number of estimates have to be made, such as files to be handled, records accessed or lines of code. Any inaccuracies in these figures will of course affect the final result — erroneous estimates compounding to form an inaccurate estimate. These methods of estimating time scales are regarded with suspicion and are generally considered as purely academic.

Resource scheduling:

The primary resource of a computer project is manpower. Resource scheduling is employed in project management in two ways: initially when decisions are made as to teams that will work on various tasks, and secondly when control of a project during its life cycle makes re-scheduling necessary.

In some forms of 'hard' engineering projects it is possible to increase resources on a particular task with a view to shortening the elapsed time for that task. This can be achieved for certain types of work, for example construction, but it is by no means universal. Moreover, there are many projects (including all

software development projects) where adding twice as many people does not halve the time. The man-month as a unit of 'currency' is in fact a myth (Ref. 14).

Deliverable items:

The first stage in the division of a project is to define the major stages of the life cycle and then to apply the successive refinement approach to work within the stages. There are a vast number of life cycle models currently in use, each with different views as to what a phase is called and what it consists of. One thing that is common to all good models, and is essential for effective project management, is the identification of milestones to indicate the end-point of each phase. If possible, these milestones should be tangible deliverable items such as coded modules, reports, specification documents etc. A view of one such model is given by Rook (Ref. 15).

The advantages to the project manager of such deliverable items are two-fold. First, each specified deliverable item indicates the end of a particular phase; that phase is ended if, and only if, the deliverable is present. Secondly, by requesting the customer (or project steering committee) to 'sign off' each deliverable item, the project manager is able to proceed on the understanding that all work to date had been acceptance tested.

6.3 Costing

Given a task, the length of time to complete it, and the resources necessary, the costing of that task is a straightforward process. However, as has been indicated, arriving at relevant, accurate estimates is far from easy. Unfortunately, the accuracy of project costings is heavily reliant on

these estimates, and thus becomes yet another problem area.

7 Conclusion

Project management has been applied to engineering projects for a considerably long time, and the experience and expertise gained has encouraged the development of a number of techniques to assist in this management. With regard to project planning and subsequent control, the most successful of these techniques has been network analysis. The generic term network analysis encompasses a number of specific theories which, in order to save terminology confusion, this paper has grouped under the more commonly used name, PERT.

The PERT technique is based on the premise that a large project may be specified as a number of small, individual tasks, each of these tasks being analysed in order to assign time scales, costs, resources required and to identify those that are predecessors of others. Engineering projects are conveniently simple to break down in this manner.

With the advances currently being experienced in the application of structured analysis and design methodologies to computer projects, it might appear, at first glance, that the success of the PERT technique in the planning and control of computer projects would equal that of its application in the engineering world. However, while this structured approach to computer projects may assist in specifying a project as a number of tasks, the accurate estimation of time scales and costs creates fundamental problems that require considerable research before the network analysis techniques can realise their full potential in the successful control of computer projects.

8 References

1 LEVY, F. K., THOMPSON, G. L., and WIEST, J. D.: 'The ABCs of the critical path method', *Harvard Business Review*, 1963, Sept./Oct.
2 WOOLDRIDGE, S.: 'Project management in data processing' (Petrocelli/Charter, 1976)
3 LOCK, D.: 'Project management' (Gower, 1984)
4 MOORE, P. G., and THOMAS, H.: 'The anatomy of decisions' (Penguin, 1976)
5 SAITOW, A. R.: 'CSPC: reporting project progress to the top', *Harvard Business Review*, 1969, Jan./Feb.
6 De MARCO, T.: 'Structured analysis and system specification' (Yourdon, 1978)
7 POTTS, D.: 'Engineering comes in from the cold', *Engineering Computers*, 1982, **1**, (5)
8 MEHREZ, A., and SINUANY-STERN, Z.: 'An interactive approach for project selection', *Journal of Operational Research Society*, 1983, **34**, (7)
9 GANE, C., and SARSON, T.: 'Structured methodology: what have we learned?', *Computer World*, 1980, Sept.
10 YOURDON, E., and CONSTANTINE, L.: 'Structured design' (Yourdon, 1978)
11 JACKSON, M. A.: 'System design' (Academic Press, 1983)
12 LEHMANN, M. M.: 'System dynamics', Pergamon Infotech State of Art Report, April 1978
13 BOEHM, B. W.: 'Software engineering economics' (Prentice-Hall, 1981)
14 BROOKS, F. P.: 'Mythical man-months', *Datamation*, 1974, **20**, (12), pp. 44–52
15 ROOK, P.: 'Controlling software projects', *Software Engineering Journal*, 1986, **1**, (1), pp. 7–16

G. D. Carter, C. P. Clare and D. C. J. Thorogood are with the Department of Mathematical Sciences & Computing, Polytechnic of the South Bank, Borough Road, London SE1 0AA, England.

THE MYTHICAL MAN-MONTH

HOW DOES A PROJECT GET TO BE A YEAR LATE? . . . . . . ONE DAY AT A TIME.

By Frederick P. Brooks, Jr.

Dr. Brooks was part of the management team charged with developing the hardware for the IBM 360 system. In 1964 he became the manager of the Operating System/ 360 project; this trial by fire convinced him that managing a large software project is more like managing any other large undertaking than programmers believe and less like it than professional managers expect.

About his OS/360 project, he says: "Managing OS/360 development was a very educational experience, albeit a very frustrating one. The team, including F. M. Trapnell who succeeded me as manager, has much to be proud of. The system contains many excellences in design and execution, and it has been successful in achieving widespread use. Certain ideas, most noticeably device-independent input/ output and external library management, were technical innovations now widely copied. It is now quite reliable, reasonably efficient, and very versatile.

The effort cannot be called wholly successful, however. Any OS/ 360 user is quickly aware of how much better it should be. The flaws in design and execution pervade especially the control program, as distinguished from language compilers. Most of the flaws date from the 1964-1965 design period and hence must be laid to my charge. Furthermore, the product was late, it took more memory than planned, the costs were several times the estimate, and it did not perform very well until several releases after the first."

Analyzing the OS/360 experiences for management and technical lessons, Dr. Brooks put his thoughts into book form. Addison-Wesley Publishing Company (Reading, Mass.) will offer "The Mythical Man-Month: Essays on Software Engineering", from which this article is taken, sometime next month.

NO SCENE FROM PREHISTORY is quite so vivid as that of the mortal struggles of great beasts in the tar pits. In the mind's eye one sees dinosaurs, mammoths, and saber-toothed tigers struggling against the grip of the tar. The fiercer the struggle, the more entangling the tar, and no beast is so strong or so skillful but that he ultimately sinks.

Large-system programming has over the past decade been such a tar pit, and many great and powerful beasts have thrashed violently in it. Most have emerged with running systems—few have met goals, schedules, and budgets. Large and small, massive or wiry, team after team has become entangled in the tar. No one thing seems to cause the difficulty—any particular paw can be pulled away. But the accumulation of simultaneous and interacting factors brings slower and slower motion. Everyone seems to have been surprised by the stickiness of the problem, and it is hard to discern the nature of it. But we must try to understand it if we are to solve it.

More software projects have gone awry for lack of calendar time than for all other causes combined. Why is this case of disaster so common?

First, our techniques of estimating are poorly developed. More seriously, they reflect an unvoiced assumption which is quite untrue, i.e., that all will go well.

Second, our estimating techniques fallaciously confuse effort with progress, hiding the assumption that men and months are interchangeable.

Third, because we are uncertain of our estimates, software managers often

lack the courteous stubbornness required to make people wait for a good product.

Fourth, schedule progress is poorly monitored. Techniques proven and routine in other engineering disciplines are considered radical innovations in software engineering.

Fifth, when schedule slippage is recognized, the natural (and traditional) response is to add manpower. Like dousing a fire with gasoline, this makes matters worse, much worse. More fire requires more gasoline and thus begins a regenerative cycle which ends in disaster.

Schedule monitoring will be covered later. Let us now consider other aspects of the problem in more detail.

Optimism

All programmers are optimists. Perhaps this modern sorcery especially attracts those who believe in happy endings and fairy godmothers. Perhaps the hundreds of nitty frustrations drive away all but those who habitually focus on the end goal. Perhaps it is merely that computers are young, programmers are younger, and the young are always optimists. But however the selection process works, the result is indisputable: "This time it will surely run," or "I just found the last bug."

So the first false assumption that underlies the scheduling of systems programming is that *all will go well*, i.e., that *each task will take only as long as it "ought" to take*.

The pervasiveness of optimism among programmers deserves more than a flip analysis. Dorothy Sayers, in her excellent book, *The Mind of the*

Maker, divides creative activity into three stages: the idea, the implementation, and the interaction. A book, then, or a computer, or a program comes into existence first as an ideal construct, built outside time and space but complete in the mind of the author. It is realized in time and space by pen, ink, and paper, or by wire, silicon, and ferrite. The creation is complete when someone reads the book, uses the computer or runs the program, thereby interacting with the mind of the maker.

This description, which Miss Sayers uses to illuminate not only human creative activity but also the Christian doctrine of the Trinity, will help us in our present task. For the human makers of things, the incompletenesses and inconsistencies of our ideas become clear only during implementation. Thus it is that writing, experimentation, "working out" are essential disciplines for the theoretician.

In many creative activities the medium of execution is intractable. Lumber splits; paints smear; electrical circuits ring. These physical limitations of the medium constrain the ideas that may be expressed, and they also create unexpected difficulties in the implementation.

Implementation, then, takes time and sweat both because of the physical media and because of the inadequacies of the underlying ideas. We tend to blame the physical media for most of our implementation difficulties; for the media are not "ours" in the way the ideas are, and our pride colors our judgment.

Computer programming, however, creates with an exceedingly tractable medium. The programmer builds from pure thought-stuff: concepts and very flexible representations thereof. Because the medium is tractable, we expect few difficulties in implementation; hence our pervasive optimism. Because our ideas are faulty, we have bugs; hence our optimism is unjustified.

In a single task, the assumption that all will go well has a probabilistic effect on the schedule. It might indeed go as planned, for there is a probability distribution for the delay that will be encountered, and "no delay" has a finite probability. A large programming effort, however, consists of many tasks, some chained end-to-end. The probability that each will go well becomes vanishingly small.

The mythical man-month

The second fallacious thought mode is expressed in the very unit of effort used in estimating and scheduling: the man-month. Cost does indeed vary as

the product of the number of men and the number of months. Progress does not. *Hence the man-month as a unit for measuring the size of a job is a dangerous and deceptive myth.* It implies that men and months are interchangeable.

Men and months are interchangeable commodities only when a task can be partitioned among many workers *with no communication among them* (Fig. 1). This is true of reaping wheat or picking cotton; it is not even approximately true of systems programming.

When a task cannot be partitioned

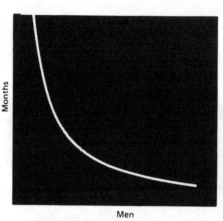

Fig. 1. The term "man-month" implies that if one man takes 10 months to do a job, 10 men can do it in one month. This may be true of picking cotton.

because of sequential constraints, the application of more effort has no effect on the schedule. The bearing of a child takes nine months, no matter how many women are assigned. Many software tasks have this characteristic because of the sequential nature of debugging.

In tasks that can be partitioned but which require communication among the subtasks, the effort of communication must be added to the amount of work to be done. Therefore the best that can be done is somewhat poorer than an even trade of men for months (Fig. 2).

The added burden of communication is made up of two parts, training and intercommunication. Each worker must be trained in the technology, the goals of the effort, the overall strategy, and the plan of work. This training cannot be partitioned, so this part of the added effort varies linearly with the number of workers.

V. S. Vyssotsky of Bell Telephone Laboratories estimates that a large project can sustain a manpower build-up of 30% per year. More than that strains and even inhibits the evolution of the essential informal structure and its communication pathways. F. J.

Corbató of MIT points out that a long project must anticipate a turnover of 20% per year, and new people must be both technically trained and integrated into the formal structure.

Intercommunication is worse. If each part of the task must be separately coordinated with each other part, the effort increases as $n(n-1)/2$. Three workers require three times as much pairwise intercommunication as two; four require six times as much as two. If, moreover, there need to be conferences among three, four, etc., workers to resolve things jointly, matters get worse yet. The added effort of communicating may fully counteract the division of the original task and bring us back to the situation of Fig. 3.

Since software construction is inherently a systems effort—an exercise in complex interrelationships—communication effort is great, and it quickly

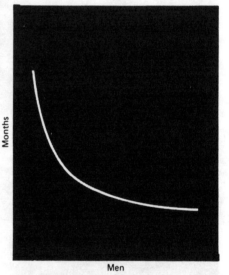

Fig. 2. Even on tasks that can be nicely partitioned among people, the additional communication required adds to the total work, increasing the schedule.

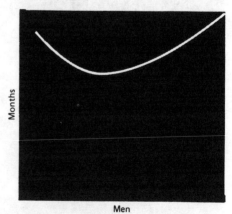

Fig. 3. Since software construction is complex, the communications overhead is great. Adding more men can lengthen, rather than shorten, the schedule.

dominates the decrease in individual task time brought about by partitioning. Adding more men then lengthens, not shortens, the schedule.

Systems test

No parts of the schedule are so thoroughly affected by sequential constraints as component debugging and system test. Furthermore, the time required depends on the number and subtlety of the errors encountered. Theoretically this number should be zero. Because of optimism, we usually expect the number of bugs to be smaller than it turns out to be. Therefore testing is usually the most mis-scheduled part of programming.

For some years I have been successfully using the following rule of thumb for scheduling a software task:

⅓ planning
⅙ coding
¼ component test and early system test
¼ system test, all components in hand.

This differs from conventional scheduling in several important ways:
1. The fraction devoted to planning is larger than normal. Even so, it is barely enough to produce a de-

of the schedule.

In examining conventionally scheduled projects, I have found that few allowed one-half of the projected schedule for testing, but that most did indeed spend half of the actual schedule for that purpose. Many of these were on schedule until and except in system testing.

Failure to allow enough time for system test, in particular, is peculiarly disastrous. Since the delay comes at the end of the schedule, no one is aware of schedule trouble until almost the delivery date. Bad news, late and without warning, is unsettling to customers and to managers.

Furthermore, delay at this point has unusually severe financial, as well as psychological, repercussions. The project is fully staffed, and cost-per-day is maximum. More seriously, the software is to support other business effort (shipping of computers, operation of new facilities, etc.) and the secondary costs of delaying these are very high, for it is almost time for software shipment. Indeed, these secondary costs may far outweigh all others. It is therefore very important to allow enough system test time in the original schedule.

two choices—wait or eat it raw. Software customers have had the same choices.

The cook has another choice; he can turn up the heat. The result is often an omelette nothing can save—burned in one part, raw in another.

Now I do not think software managers have less inherent courage and firmness than chefs, nor than other engineering managers. But false scheduling to match the patron's desired date is much more common in our discipline than elsewhere in engineering. It is very difficult to make a vigorous, plausible, and job-risking defense of an estimate that is derived by no quantitative method, supported by little data, and certified chiefly by the hunches of the managers.

Clearly two solutions are needed. We need to develop and publicize productivity figures, bug-incidence figures, estimating rules, and so on. The whole profession can only profit from sharing such data.

Until estimating is on a sounder basis, individual managers will need to stiffen their backbones, and defend their estimates with the assurance that their poor hunches are better than wish-derived estimates.

Regenerative disaster

What does one do when an essential software project is behind schedule? Add manpower, naturally. As Figs. 1 through 3 suggest, this may or may not help.

Let us consider an example. Suppose a task is estimated at 12 man-months and assigned to three men for four months, and that there are measurable mileposts A, B, C, D, which are scheduled to fall at the end of each month.

Now suppose the first milepost is not reached until two months have elapsed. What are the alternatives facing the manager?
1. Assume that the task must be done on time. Assume that only the first part of the task was misestimated. Then 9 man-months of effort remain, and two months, so 4½ men will be needed. Add 2 men to the 3 assigned.
2. Assume that the task must be done on time. Assume that the whole estimate was uniformly low. Then 18 man-months of effort remain, and two months, so 9 men will be needed. Add 6 men to the 3 assigned.
3. Reschedule. In this case, I like the advice given by an experienced hardware engineer, "Take no small slips." That is, allow enough time in the new schedule to ensure that the work can be carefully and

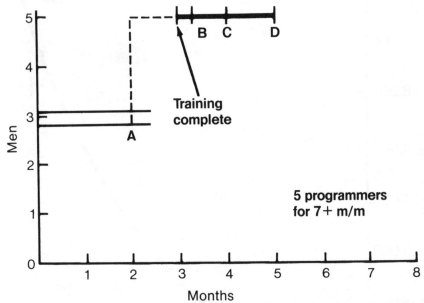

Fig. 4. Adding manpower to a project which is late may not help. In this case, suppose three men on a 12 man-month project were a month late. If it takes one of the three an extra month to train two new men, the project will be just as late as if no one was added.

tailed and solid specification, and not enough to include research or exploration of totally new techniques.
2. The *half* of the schedule devoted to debugging of completed code is much larger than normal.
3. The part that is easy to estimate, i.e., coding, is given only one-sixth

Gutless estimating

Observe that for the programmer, as for the chef, the urgency of the patron may govern the scheduled completion of the task, but it cannot govern the actual completion. An omelette, promised in ten minutes, may appear to be progressing nicely. But when it has not set in ten minutes, the customer has

thoroughly done, and that rescheduling will not have to be done again.

4. Trim the task. In practice this tends to happen anyway, once the team observes schedule slippage. Where the secondary costs of delay are very high, this is the only feasible action. The manager's only alternatives are to trim it formally and carefully, to reschedule, or to watch the task get silently trimmed by hasty design and incomplete testing.

In the first two cases, insisting that the unaltered task be completed in four months is disastrous. Consider the regenerative effects, for example, for the first alternative (Fig. 4 preceding page). The two new men, however competent and however quickly recruited, will require training in the task by one of the experienced men. If this takes a month, *3 man-months will have been devoted to work not in the original estimate.* Furthermore, the task, originally partitioned three ways, must be repartitioned into five parts, hence some work already done will be lost and system testing must be lengthened. So at the end of the third month, substantially more than 7 man-months of effort remain, and 5 trained people and one month are available. As Fig. 4 suggests, the product is just as late as if no one had been added.

To hope to get done in four months, considering only training time and not repartitioning and extra systems test, would require adding 4 men, not 2, at the end of the second month. To cover repartitioning and system test effects, one would have to add still other men. Now, however, one has at least a 7-man team, not a 3-man one; thus such aspects as team organization and task division are different in kind, not merely in degree.

Notice that by the end of the third month things look very black. The March 1 milestone has not been reached in spite of all the managerial effort. The temptation is very strong to repeat the cycle, adding yet more manpower. Therein lies madness.

The foregoing assumed that only the first milestone was misestimated. If on March 1 one makes the conservative assumption that the whole schedule was optimistic one wants to add 6 men just to the original task. Calculation of the training, repartitioning, system testing effects is left as an exercise for the reader. Without a doubt, the regenerative disaster will yield a poorer product later, than would rescheduling with the original three men, unaugmented.

Oversimplifying outrageously, we state Brooks' Law:

Adding manpower to a late software project makes it later.

This then is the demythologizing of the man-month. The number of months of a project depends upon its sequential constraints. The maximum number of men depends upon the number of independent subtasks. From these two quantities one can derive schedules using fewer men and more months. (The only risk is product obsolescence.) One cannot, however, get workable schedules using more men and fewer months. More software projects have gone awry for lack of calendar time than for all other causes combined.

Calling the shot
How long will a system programming job take? How much effort will be required? How does one estimate?

I have earlier suggested ratios that seem to apply to planning time, coding, component test, and system test. First, one must say that one does *not* estimate the entire task by estimating the coding portion only and then applying the ratios. The coding is only one-sixth or so of the problem, and errors in its estimate or in the ratios could lead to ridiculous results.

Second, one must say that data for building isolated small programs are not applicable to programming systems products. For a program averaging about 3,200 words, for example, Sackman, Erikson, and Grant report an average code-plus-debug time of about 178 hours for a single programmer, a figure which would extrapolate to give an annual productivity of 35,800 statements per year. A program half that size took less than one-fourth as long, and extrapolated productivity is almost 80,000 statements per year.[1]. Planning, documentation, testing, system integration, and training times must be added. The linear extrapolation of such spring figures is meaningless. Extrapolation of times for the hundred-yard dash shows that a man can run a mile in under three minutes.

Before dismissing them, however, let us note that these numbers, although not for strictly comparable problems, suggest that effort goes as a power of size *even* when no communication is involved except that of a man with his memories.

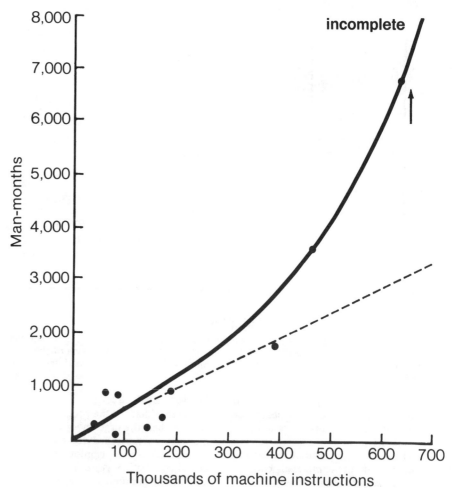

Fig. 5. As a project's complexity increases, the number of man-months required to complete it goes up exponentially.

Fig. 5 tells the sad story. It illustrates results reported from a study done by Nanus and Farr[2] at System Development Corp. This shows an exponent of 1.5; that is,

effort = (constant) × (number of instructions)[1.5]

Another SDC study reported by Weinwurm[3] also shows an exponent near 1.5.

A few studies on programmer productivity have been made, and several estimating techniques have been proposed. Morin has prepared a survey of the published data.[4] Here I shall give only a few items that seem especially illuminating.

Portman's data

Charles Portman, manager of ICL's Software Div., Computer Equipment Organization (Northwest) at Manchester, offers another useful personal insight.

He found his programming teams missing schedules by about one-half—each job was taking approximately twice as long as estimated. The estimates were very careful, done by experienced teams estimating man-hours for several hundred subtasks on a PERT chart. When the slippage pattern appeared, he asked them to keep careful daily logs of time usage. These showed that the estimating error could be entirely accounted for by the fact that his teams were only realizing 50% of the working week as actual programming and debugging time. Machine downtime, higher-priority short unrelated jobs, meetings, paperwork, company business, sickness, personal time, etc. accounted for the rest. In short, the estimates made an unrealistic assumption about the number of technical work hours per man-year. My own experience quite confirms his conclusion.

An unpublished 1964 study by E. F. Bardain shows programmers realizing only 27% productive time.[5]

Aron's data

Joel Aron, manager of Systems Technology at IBM in Gaithersburg, Maryland, has studied programmer productivity when working on nine large systems (briefly, *large* means more than 25 programmers and 30,000 deliverable instructions). He divides such systems according to interactions among programmers (and system parts) and finds productivities as follows:

Very few interactions	10,000 instructions per man-year
Some interactions	5,000
Many interactions	1,500

The man-years do not include support and system test activities, only design and programming. When these figures are diluted by a factor of two to cover system test, they closely match Harr's data.

Harr's data

John Harr, manager of programming for the Bell Telephone Laboratories' Electronic Switching System, reported his and others' experience in a paper at the 1969 Spring Joint Computer Conference.[6] These data are shown in Table 1 and Figs. 6 and 7.

Of these, Fig. 6 is the most detailed and the most useful. The first two jobs are basically control programs; the second two are basically language translators. Productivity is stated in terms of debugged words per man-year. This includes programming, component test, and system test. It is not clear how much of the planning effort, or effort in machine support, writing, and the

	Prog. units	Number of programmers	Years	Man-years	Program words	Words/man-yr.
Operational	50	83	4	101	52,000	515
Maintenance	36	60	4	81	51,000	630
Compiler	13	9	2¼	17	38,000	2230
Translator (Data assembler)	15	13	2½	11	25,000	2270

Table 1. Data from Bell Labs indicates productivity differences between complex problems (the first two are basically control programs with many modules) and less complex ones. No one is certain how much of the difference is due to complexity, how much to the number of people involved.

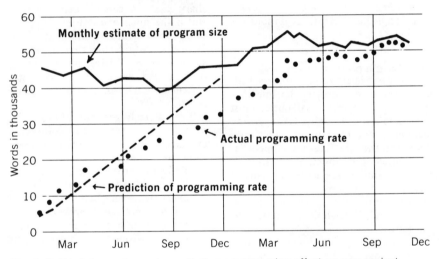

Fig. 6. Bell Labs' experience in predicting programming effort on one project.

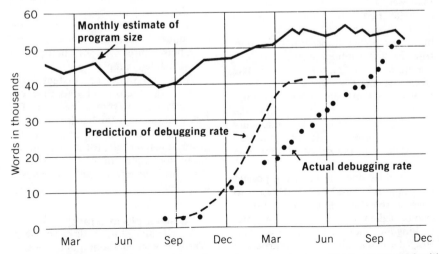

Fig. 7. Bell's predictions for debugging rates on a single project, contrasted with actual figures.

like, is included.

The productivities likewise fall into two classifications: those for control programs are about 600 words per man-year; those for translators are about 2,200 words per man-year. Note that all four programs are of similar size—the variation is in size of the work groups, length of time, and number of modules. Which is cause and which is effect? Did the control programs require more people because they were more complicated? Or did they require more modules and more man-months because they were assigned more people? Did they take longer because of the greater complexity, or because more people were assigned? One can't be sure. The control programs were surely more complex. These uncertainties aside, the numbers describe the real productivities achieved on a large system, using present-day programming techniques. As such they are a real contribution.

Figs. 6 and 7 show some interesting data on programming and debugging rates as compared to predicted rates.

OS/360 data

IBM OS/360 experience, while not available in the detail of Harr's data, confirms it. Productivities in range of 600-800 debugged instructions per man-year were experienced by control program groups. Productivities in the 2,000-3,000 debugged instructions per man-year were achieved by language translator groups. These include planning done by the group, coding component test, system test, and some support activities. They are comparable to Harr's data, so far as I can tell.

Aron's data, Harr's data, and the OS/360 data all confirm striking differences in productivity related to the complexity and difficulty of the task itself. My guideline in the morass of estimating complexity is that compilers are three times as bad as normal batch application programs, and operating systems are three times as bad as compilers.

Corbató's data

Both Harr's data and OS/360 data are for assembly language programming. Little data seem to have been published on system programming productivity using higher-level languages. Corbató of MIT's Project MAC reports, however, a mean productivity of 1,200 lines of debugged PL/I statements per man-year on the MULTICS system (between 1 and 2 million words)[7]

This number is very exciting. Like the other projects, MULTICS includes control programs and language transla-

tors. Like the others, it is producing a system programming product, tested and documented. The data seem to be comparable in terms of kind of effort included. And the productivity number is a good average between the control program and translator productivities of other projects.

But Corbató's number is *lines* per man-year, not *words!* Each statement in his system corresponds to about three-to-five words of handwritten code! This suggests two important conclusions:

- Productivity seems constant in terms of elementary statements, a conclusion that is reasonable in terms of the thought a statement requires and the errors it may include.
- Programming productivity may be increased as much as five times when a suitable high-level language is used. To back up these conclusions, W. M. Taliaffero also reports a constant productivity of 2,400 statements/year in Assembler, FORTRAN, and COBOL.[8] E. A. Nelson has shown a 3-to-1 productivity improvement for high-level language, although his standard deviations are wide.[9]

Hatching a catastrophe

When one hears of disastrous schedule slippage in a project, he imagines that a series of major calamities must have befallen it. Usually, however, the disaster is due to termites, not tornadoes; and the schedule has slipped imperceptibly but inexorably. Indeed, major calamities are easier to handle; one responds with major force, radical reorganization, the invention of new approaches. The whole team rises to the occasion.

But the day-by-day slippage is harder to recognize, harder to prevent, harder to make up. Yesterday a key man was sick, and a meeting couldn't be held. Today the machines are all down, because lightning struck the building's power transformer. Tomorrow the disc routines won't start testing, because the first disc is a week late from the factory. Snow, jury duty, family problems, emergency meetings with customers, executive audits—the list goes on and on. Each one only postpones some activity by a half-day or a day. And the schedule slips, one day at a time.

How does one control a big project on a tight schedule? The first step is to *have* a schedule. Each of a list of events, called milestones, has a date. Picking the dates is an estimating problem, discussed already and crucially dependent on experience.

For picking the milestones there is

only one relevant rule. Milestones must be concrete, specific, measurable events, defined with knife-edge sharpness. Coding, for a counterexample, is "90% finished" for half of the total coding time. Debugging is "99% complete" most of the time. "Planning complete" is an event one can proclaim almost at will.[10]

Concrete milestones, on the other hand, are 100% events. "Specifications signed by architects and implementers," "source coding 100% complete, keypunched, entered into disc library," "debugged version passes all test cases." These concrete milestones demark the vague phases of planning, coding, debugging.

It is more important that milestones be sharp-edged and unambiguous than that they be easily verifiable by the boss. Rarely will a man lie about mile-

> None love
>   the bearer of bad news.
> *Sophocles*

stone progress, *if* the milestone is so sharp that he can't deceive himself. But if the milestone is fuzzy, the boss often understands a different report from that which the man gives. To supplement Sophocles, no one enjoys bearing bad news, either, so it gets softened without any real intent to deceive.

Two interesting studies of estimating behavior by government contractors on large-scale development projects show that:

1. Estimates of the length of an activity made and revised carefully every two weeks before the activity starts do not significantly change as the start time draws near, no matter how wrong they ultimately turn out to be.
2. *During* the activity, *over*estimates of duration come steadily down as the activity proceeds.
3. *Underestimates* do not change significantly during the activity until about three weeks before the scheduled completion.[11]

Sharp milestones are in fact a service to the team, and one they can properly expect from a manager. The fuzzy milestone is the harder burden to live with. It is in fact a millstone that grinds down morale, for it deceives one about lost time until it is irremediable. And chronic schedule slippage is a morale-killer.

"The other piece is late"

A schedule slips a day; so what? Who gets excited about a one-day slip? We can make it up later. And the other piece ours fits into is late anyway.

156

A baseball manager recognizes a nonphysical talent, *hustle,* as an essential gift of great players and great teams. It is the characteristic of running faster than necessary, moving sooner than necessary, trying harder than necessary. It is essential for great programming teams, too. Hustle provides the cushion, the reserve capacity, that enables a team to cope with routine mishaps, to anticipate and forfend minor calamities. The calculated response, the measured effort, are the wet blankets that dampen hustle. As we have seen, one *must* get excited about a one-day slip. Such are the elements of catastrophe.

But not all one-day slips are equally disastrous. So some calculation of response is necessary, though hustle be dampened. How does one tell which slips matter? There is no substitute for a PERT chart or a critical-path schedule. Such a network shows who waits for what. It shows who is on the critical path, where any slip moves the end date. It also shows how much an activity can slip before it moves into the critical path.

The PERT technique, strictly speaking, is an elaboration of critical-path scheduling in which one estimates three times for every event, times corresponding to different probabilities of meeting the estimated dates. I do not find this refinement to be worth the extra effort, but for brevity I will call any critical path network a PERT chart.

The preparation of a PERT chart is the most valuable part of its use. Laying out the network, identifying the dependencies, and estimating the legs all force a great deal of very specific planning very early in a project. The first chart is always terrible, and one invents and invents in making the second one.

As the project proceeds, the PERT chart provides the answer to the demoralizing excuse, "The other piece is late anyhow." It shows how hustle is needed to keep one's own part off the critical path, and it suggests ways to make up the lost time in the other part.

Under the rug

When a first-line manager sees his small team slipping behind, he is rarely inclined to run to the boss with this woe. The team might be able to make it up, or he should be able to invent or reorganize to solve the problem. Then why worry the boss with it? So far, so good. Solving such problems is exactly what the first-line manager is there for. And the boss does have enough real worries demanding his action that he doesn't seek others. So all the dirt gets swept under the rug.

But every boss needs two kinds of information, exceptions for action and a status picture for education.[12] For that purpose he needs to know the status of all his teams. Getting a true picture of that status is hard.

The first-line manager's interests and those of the boss have an inherent conflict here. The first-line manager fears that if he reports his problem, the boss will act on it. Then his action will preempt the manager's function, diminish his authority, foul up his other plans. So as long as the manager thinks he can solve it alone, he doesn't tell the boss.

Two rug-lifting techniques are open to the boss. Both must be used. The first is to reduce the role conflict and inspire sharing of status. The other is to yank the rug back.

Reducing the role conflict

The boss must first distinguish between action information and status information. He must discipline himself *not* to act on problems his managers can solve, and *never* to act on problems when he is explicitly reviewing status. I once knew a boss who invariably picked up the phone to give orders before the end of the first para-

SYSTEM/360 SUMMARY STATUS REPORT
05/369 LANGUAGE PROCESSORS + SERVICE PROGRAMS
AS OF FEBRUARY 01 • 1965

A=APPROVAL
C=COMPLETED

•= REVISED PLANNED DATE
NE=NOT ESTABLISHED

PROJECT	LOCATION	COMMITMNT ANNOUNCE RELEASE	OBJECTIVE AVAILABLE APPROVED	SPECS AVAILABLE APPROVED	SRL AVAILABLE APPROVED	ALPHA TEST ENTRY EXIT	COMP TEST START COMPLETE	SYS TEST START COMPLETE	BULLETIN AVAILABLE APPROVED	BETA TEST ENTRY EXIT
OPERATING SYSTEM										
12K DESIGN LEVEL (E)										
ASSEMBLY	SAN JOSE	04/--/4 C 12/31/5	10/28/4 C	10/13/4 C 01/11/5	11/13/4 C 11/16/4 A	01/15/5 C 02/22/5				09/01/5 11/30/5
FORTRAN	POK	04/--/4 C 12/31/5	10/28/4 C	10/21/4 C 01/22/5	12/17/4 C 12/19/4 A	01/15/5 C 02/22/5				09/01/5 11/30/5
COBOL	ENDICOTT	04/--/4 C 12/31/5	10/25/4 C	10/15/4 C 01/20/5 A	11/17/4 C 12/08/4 A	01/15/5 C 02/22/5				09/01/5 11/30/5
RPG	SAN JOSE	04/--/4 C 12/31/5	10/28/4 C	09/30/4 C 01/05/5 A	12/02/4 C 01/18/5 A	01/15/5 C 02/22/5				09/01/5 11/30/5
UTILITIES	TIME/LIFE	04/--/4 C 12/31/5	06/24/4 C		11/20/4 C 11/30/4 A					09/01/5 11/30/5
SORT 1	POK	04/--/4 C 12/31/5	10/28/4 C	10/19/4 C 01/11/5	11/12/4 C 11/30/4 A	01/15/5 C 03/22/5				09/01/5 11/30/5
SORT 2	POK	04/--/4 C 06/30/6	10/28/4 C	10/19/4 C 01/11/5	11/12/4 C 11/30/4 A	01/15/5 C 03/22/5				03/01/6 05/30/6
44K DESIGN LEVEL (F)										
ASSEMBLY	SAN JOSE	04/--/4 C 12/31/5	10/28/4 C	10/13/4 C 01/11/5	11.13.4 C 11/18/4 A	02/15/5 C 03/22/5				09/01/5 11/30/5
COBOL	TIME/LIFE	04/--/4 C 06/30/6	10/28/4 C	10/15/4 C 01/20/5 A	11/17/4 C 12/06/4 A	02/15/5 C 03/22/5				03/01/6 05/30/6
NPL	HURSLEY	04/--/4 C 03/31/6	10/28/4 C							
2250	KINGSTON	03/30/4 C 03/31/6	11/05/4 C	10/06/4 C 01/04/5	01/12/5 C 01/29/5	01/04/5 C 01/29/5				01/03/6 NE
2280	KINGSTON	06/30/4 C 09/30/6	11/05/4 C			04/01/5 04/30/5				01/28/6 NE
200K DESIGN LEVEL (H)										
ASSEMBLY	TIME/LIFE		10/28/4 C							
FORTRAN	POK	04/--/4 C 06/30/6	10/28/4 C	10/16/4 C 01/11/5	11/11/4 C 12/10/4 A	02/15/5 C 03/22/5				03/01/6 05/30/6
NPL	HURSLEY	04/--/4 C	10/28/4 C			07/--/5				01/--/7
NPL H	POK	04/--/4 C	03/30/4 C			02/01/5 04/01/5				10/15/5 12/15/5

Fig. 8. A report showing milestones and status in a key document in project control. This one shows some problems in OS development: specifications approval is late on some items (those without "A"); documentation (SRL) approval is overdue on another; and one (2250 support) is late coming out of alpha test.

157

graph in a status report. That response is guaranteed to squelch full disclosure.

Conversely, when the manager knows his boss will accept status reports without panic or preemption, he comes to give honest appraisals.

This whole process is helped if the boss labels meetings, reviews, conferences, as *status-review* meetings versus *problem-action* meetings, and controls himself accordingly. Obviously one may call a problem-action meeting as a consequence of a status meeting, if he believes a problem is out of hand. But at least everybody knows what the score is, and the boss thinks twice before grabbing the ball.

Yanking the rug off

Nevertheless, it is necessary to have review techniques by which the true status is made known, whether cooperatively or not. The PERT chart with its frequent sharp milestones is the basis for such review. On a large project one may want to review some part of it each week, making the rounds once a month or so.

A report showing milestones and actual completions is the key document. Fig. 8 (preceding page), shows an excerpt from such a report. This report shows some troubles. Specifications approval is overdue on several components. Manual (SRL) approval is overdue on another, and one is late getting out of the first state (ALPHA) of the independently conducted product test. So such a report serves as an agenda for the meeting of 1 February. Everyone knows the questions, and the component manager should be prepared to explain why it's late, when it will be finished, what steps he's taking, and what help, if any, he needs from the boss or collateral groups.

V. Vyssotsky of Bell Telephone Laboratories adds the following observation:

I have found it handy to carry both "scheduled" and "estimated" dates in the milestone report. The scheduled dates are the property of the project manager and represent a consistent work plan for the project as a whole, and one which is a priori a reasonable plan. The estimated dates are the property of the lowest level manager who has cognizance over the piece of work in question, and represents his best judgment as to when it will actually happen, given the resources he has available and when he received (or has commitments for delivery of) his prerequisite inputs. The project manager has to keep his fingers off the estimated dates, and put the emphasis on getting accurate, unbiased estimates rather

than palatable optimistic estimates or self-protective conservative ones. Once this is clearly established in everyone's mind, the project manager can see quite a ways into the future where he is going to be in trouble if he doesn't do something.

The preparation of the PERT chart is a function of the boss and the managers reporting to him. Its updating, revision, and reporting requires the attention of a small (one-to-three-man) staff group which serves as an extension of the boss. Such a "Plans and Controls" team is invaluable for a large project. It has no authority except to ask all the line managers when they will have set or changed milestones, and whether milestones have been met. Since the Plans and Controls group handles all the paperwork, the burden on the line managers is reduced to the essentials—making the decisions.

We had a skilled, enthusiastic, and diplomatic Plans and Controls group on the os/360 project, run by A. M. Pietrasanta, who devoted considerable inventive talent to devising effective but unobtrusive control methods. As a result, I found his group to be widely respected and more than tolerated. For a group whose role is inherently that of an irritant, this is quite an accomplishment.

The investment of a modest amount of skilled effort in a Plans and Controls function is very rewarding. It makes far more difference in project accomplishment than if these people worked directly on building the product programs. For the Plans and Controls group is the watchdog who renders the imperceptible delays visible and who points up the critical elements. It is the early warning system against losing a year, one day at a time.

Epilogue

The tar pit of software engineering will continue to be sticky for a long time to come. One can expect the human race to continue attempting systems just within or just beyond our reach; and software systems are perhaps the most intricate and complex of man's handiworks. The management of this complex craft will demand our best use of new languages and systems, our best adaptation of proven engineering management methods, liberal doses of common sense, and a God-given humility to recognize our fallibility and limitations.

References

1. Sackman, H., W. J. Erikson, and E. E. Grant, "Exploratory Experimentation Studies Comparing Online and Offline Programming Performance," *Communications of the ACM*, 11 (1968), 3-11.

2. Nanus, B., and L. Farr, "Some Cost Contributors to Large-Scale Programs," *AFIPS Proceedings, SJCC*, 25 (1964), 239-248.

3. Weinwurm, G. F., *Research in the Management of Computer Programming*. Report SP-2059, 1965, System Development Corp., Santa Monica.

4. Morin, L. H., *Estimation of Resources for Computer Programming Projects*, M. S. thesis, Univ. of North Carolina, Chapel Hill, 1974.

5. Quoted by D. B. Mayer and A. W. Stalnaker, "Selection and Evaluation of Computer Personnel," *Proceedings 23 ACM Conference*, 1968, 661.

6. Paper given at a panel session and not included in the *AFIPS Proceedings*.

7. Corbató, F. J., *Sensitive Issues in the Design of Multi-Use Systems*. Lecture at the opening of the Honeywell EDP Technology Center, 1968.

8. Taliaffero, W. M., "Modularity the Key to System Growth Potential," *Software*, 1 (1971), 245-257.

9. Nelson, E. A., *Management Handbook for the Estimation of Computer Programming Costs*. Report TM-3225, System Development Corp., Santa Monica, pp. 66-67.

10. Reynolds, C. H., "What's Wrong with Computer Programming Management?" in *On the Management of Computer Programming*. Ed. G. F. Weinwurm. Philadelphia: Auerbach, 1971, pp. 35-42.

11. King, W. R., and T. A. Wilson, "Subjective Time Estimates in Critical Path Planning—a Preliminary Analysis," *Management Sciences*, 13 (1967), 307-320, and sequel, W. R. King, D. M. Witterrongel, and K. D. Hezel, "On the Analysis of Critical Path Time Estimating Behavior," *Management Sciences*, 14 (1967), 79-84.

12. Brooks, F. P., and K. E. Iverson, *Automatic Data Processing, System/360 Edition*. New York: Wiley, 1969, pp. 428-430. □

Dr. Brooks is presently a professor at the Univ. of North Carolina at Chapel Hill, and chairman of the computer science department there. He is best known as "the father of the IBM System/360," having served as project manager for the hardware development and as manager of the Operating System/360 project during its design phase. Earlier he was an architect of the IBM Stretch and Harvest computers.

At Chapel Hill he has participated in establishing and guiding the Triangle Universities Computation Center and the North Carolina Educational Computing Service. He is the author of two editions of "Automatic Data Processing" and "The Mythical Man-Month: Essays on Software Engineering" (Addison-Wesley), from which this excerpt is taken.

DEADLINE PRESSURE: HOW TO COPE WITH SHORT DEADLINES, LOW BUDGETS AND INSUFFICIENT STAFFING LEVELS

Tom GILB
Independent Consultant
Iver Holtersvei 2, N-1410 Kolbotn, Norway

All industrial software engineering environments are usually under very tight pressure to meet calender deadlines. The pressure is so intense as to tempt software professionals to follow primitive software practices, resulting in poor product quality, and even more real delays in getting satisfactory products to the market. This paper reviews a number of realistic strategies, with reference to practical experience, in dealing with this problem. The solutions are both common sense, political and technical in nature. They involve software metrics to define the real problem, evolutionary delivery and Fagan's Inspection method to correct process failures using early feedback. Ten guiding principles summarize the paper.

1. THE PROBLEM

1.1 The problem as viewed by the project manager's manager.

The big boss wants it.
A deadline has been established.
The pressure to deliver something, on time, is on.

There may well be some clear reason for the particular date chosen. It may be specified in a contract. It may be synchronized with other product developments. But, it could just be an arbitrary guesstimate. It could have simply been a rash promise by the project manager, made to impress his boss.

It is probable that the big boss really:

     - would like to get even earlier delivery - of something, - has no clear unambiguous definition of what is to be delivered, - might accept later delivery of parts of the package, - has been misunderstood, as to what and when, - hasn't told the project manager what he really wants, yet, - is in the process of deciding differently about what and when.

All of these represent potential opportunities for relief of deadline pressure.

1.2 The problem as viewed by the project manager.

The project manager is caught between the pressures from above, and the finite productive capacity below him. You might wonder how intelligent people can voluntarily accept such lack of control over both their destiny and reputation.

The project manager feels that the demands from above are unreasonable. Further, that the resources, in terms of people, talent, budget, machinery and time for getting the job done, are inadequate.

But, the project manager is there to do as well as can be expected under the circumstances. And he will try to do so with the least pain to himself.

The project manager, either through ineptitude, or experience and cunning, has made sure that the exact nature of the project deliveries are perfectly unclear. This has the effect of allowing him to deliver something, really anything that is ready by the "deadline", and claim on-time delivery. Who can prove otherwise?

1.3 The problem as viewed by the project professional.

The people working for the project manager - the ones that have to do the real work - are perfectly prepared to let their boss worry about deadlines, as long as they can do whatever they most enjoy doing, the way they enjoy doing it. They realize that the project manager doesn't dare fire them or take similar drastic action (like training them) because that would destroy the project schedule.

Of course, as individuals each one of them would very much like to make a brilliant recognized contribution to the project. The problem is they are not sure what the project is all about, and they are pretty sure that somebody else will snatch the glory from them anyway. Better to save those brilliant efforts for when one starts ones own company.

If the project fails, they might get promoted to project manager. But the important thing is to not be seen to threaten the project.

1.4 The problem as viewed by the customer/user.

The recipient of the project output probably needs the results "yesterday". Your deadline, as project manager, is probably viewed as the longest acceptable wait time until the product is ready.

The "customer" might very well be willing to wait longer for 90% of the project results, if only 10% were delivered on time. They might even be willing to let some of that 10% be delivered later if 1% were delivered much earlier. It is perfectly possible that they really don't need 99% of what has been asked for. There are a lot of people out there who have a vested interest in building new systems, rather than improving old ones.

2. THE SOLUTIONS

2.1 Redefine the problem.

I have never yet walked into a project of any kind, anywhere in the world where I felt that the project deliveries were fully and completely defined.

I'm not saying that all projects should be perfectly defined in advance. There are both good and bad reasons for incomplete requirements specification. However, this lack-of-specification situation gives us a powerful tool for relieving deadline pressure, because it can put us in a position to "clarify" or "detail" the specifications in such a way as to make the delivery task easier.

Gerald M. Weinberg, in our book "Humanized Input"[1] made use of this principle when he formulated his "Zeroth Law of Unreliability".

" If a system doesn't have to be reliable, it can meet any other objective"

If a quality, like reliability, is not clearly specified - you can deliver the project earlier - if you "interpret" the quality requirement as "whatever it happens to be when the deadline arrives". This, coupled with an innocent "Ohhh ! You wanted more than two minutes between failures!", after the first complaints arrive, will solve the deadline problem initially. You are of course prepared to discuss a new schedule and project for enhancing

quality to the required levels - now clarified for the first time.

Whether or not "reliability" is defined is irrelevant. There are a large number of quality attributes [2]which probably have a dramatic influence on cost and schedule. You only need one of them to be unclearly specified to give you the opening you need.

The more quality requirement specifications that are added, the more uncertainty is introduced into the schedule estimation problem. In fact with ten or more demanding state-of-the-art quality requirements - you can be certain that the project can never be delivered.

The trick is to get the client to specify what they "dream of", rather than what they will want to pay for or wait for. They will always be tempted into this trap, and you will always have an excuse for non-delivery.

2.2 Don't work harder, work smarter.

It is natural, when faced with deadline pressure, to consider various ways of working harder. More overtime, reducing employee vacations, working weekends. Such a response designed to give the impression of trying to meet the deadlines. But, lets face it, working harder defeats the real purpose of life, whatever it is.

There is no certainty that hard work will help the deadline at all. The real problem is the individual who made a promise for a deadline, without considering whether it was realistic at all. Unfortunately, this person is often the Chief Executive of the company.

So, you have to work smarter. This involves doing things mentioned elsewhere in this paper, such as,
- redesigning for evolutionary delivery,
- using Inspection of requirements and high-level design to find problems while they are small ones,
- formally identifying the real goals, measurably,
- sub-contracting the work to someone else.

2.3 Refuse! Make Counter-threats

Have you ever considered refusing to accept the deadline which someone is trying to impose upon you ? You can do so under the guise of loyalty to your boss. But do it in writing. An oral refusal can too easily be misunderstood or misused. Here is an example of a diplomatic formulation:

" I must unfortunately decline, at the present moment, to accept full responsibility for meeting the suggested deadline. I sincerely believe that this would result in you (your boss!) getting blamed for non-delivery at a later date. The project is as yet not clearly defined (it never is) and it is by no means clear that we have the resources (you never will) to complete it on the suggested schedule to the quality expected by the customer. We must not be caught making promises we cannot keep, no matter how great the pressure. What we will promise is to do the very best we can to deliver as early as possible, with the resources we have or are later granted."

If this diplomatic attempt to avoid responsibility doesn't work. Don't worry. The project is sure to be late, or some kind of a disaster. You can then prove that you were wise enough to disclaim responsibility in advance. If, by some miracle everything succeeds, you can safely assume that your disclaimer will be forgotten in the euphoria of success. And if it is remembered, you can safely say that it was luck or that certain factors became clearer after it was written.

2.4 If necessary, use the Counter-Threat.

A diplomatic disclaimer might not be enough to fool your boss. The "counter-threat" ploy may be necessary. The objective is to scare people into not imposing a really serious deadline. It might be along the following lines. (do not copy this text exactly each time - someone might get suspicious).

"I cannot but note the deadline that you have felt it necessary to impose. We will naturally do our very best to meet it. However, in your own interest please note the following problems which may occur as a result.

1. There is very little real chance of meeting this deadline. Can we afford the damage to our reputation?

2. If we do try to deliver something by this date it will most certainly have a quality level below what people will expect. Can we afford this damage to our reputation?

3. The attempt to meet an impossible deadline, upon which we have not been consulted or agreed to, will result in severe stress to our staff. We risk that our best people (who do all the real work) leaving us in frustration.

We do of course want to co-operate in any way we can to make a realistic plan, and to help estimate realistic resources for doing a job which will not threaten our standing as responsible professionals in the eyes of customers or the public."

2.5 Redefine the Solution.

If these tactics fail, don't despair! There are many avenues of rescue open to you. One is to redefine the solution so that it is easier to achieve than the one you were landed with.

This can be a dangerous path because solutions are often "Holy Cows" for somebody. However - just as often - the solutions are accidental and nobody really cares about the detailed solution type - as long as they achieve their real objectives. Somebody (you of course,) has to take the initiative to change the solution so that the deadline can be met.

The steps are as follows:

1. Trap your boss or customer into declaring that the proposed deadline is extremely critical (if it is not, your problem dissolves anyway).

2. Entice them into agreeing that the results of the project are more critical than the means by which it is accomplished. Few managers will admit to anything else. Establish in formal measurable terms the results to be accomplished (savings of time and money, improved service or sales etc.).

3. Show them that the presently suggested solution does not guarantee the achievement of these results. (No solution is ever guaranteed anyway).

4. Then, find an alternative solution which at least looks far more safe in terms of getting the results. For example such a solution is likely to be based on existing and known products or technologies, modified for your purposes. Possibly you can get some outside instance to guarantee the deadline for the modifications - in which case the monkey is off your back.

Naturally, you offer to manage the new effort. This gets you a reputation for sheer heroism in the face of impossible odds. When its all over, you can take the credit for the successful solution.

2.6 Define the solution yourself

Of course "redefining" the solution might seem a bit too much for the cases where no clear

161

solution has yet been defined. In this case you should make use of such an opportunity to get control over the solution definition before others do. They might suggest something which <u>cannot</u> be achieved within the deadline.

There is one <u>cardinal rule</u> when defining <u>solutions</u>. Make sure you have a <u>clear idea of the objectives</u> which <u>top management</u> has. This is likely to be <u>different</u> from what you boss told you the goals were.

Next, you want to do what engineers call "design to cost". This simply means that you must find a solution architecture which ensures that you deliver the results as expected. It is vital that you are prepared to go outside your normal specialty discipline to achieve this.

For example you may be a software engineer. The requirement may be for "zero defects" software. You may not feel capable of producing that within the deadline. So, you must be prepared to swallow your pride - but deliver a solution.

You must for example find a ready-made solution with "zero defect" (or near to it, because perfection is mighty hard to find in practice). Or, you need to find some reputable sub-supplier who will guarantee the result on time.

They will not of course be able to do it - but you can blame them afterwards. <u>Your</u> job amounts to writing a clear specification of what they will be attempting to deliver by the deadline. You should get them to guarantee this in a contract, or at least a letter or in writing.

You might feel more like a legal person than a technical person at this point, but remember - legal people cannot write technical specifications - and they don't care about your deadline pressure.

<u>2.7 Get somebody else to do it.</u>

There is an important strategy of making sure it is <u>someone else</u> who is under the deadline pressure. Remember, management doesn't really care who does things, as long as they get done. If you can, make a strong case for letting somebody else do the job - then pressure is off your back.

It is important that you consider taking main contractor responsibility. That is, you find, then you control, the sub-contractor. This gives you something to do and to look busy with - but of course the sub-contractor does all the real work. You just sit there with a whip.

3. THE TECHNOLOGIES OF THE SOLUTIONS

3.1 Evolutionary Delivery

The most powerful practical technique I have experienced for getting control over deadline pressure is evolutionary delivery[3]. The evolutionary delivery method is based on the simple observation that not everything is needed all at one initial delivery or deadline.

An example: The New Taxation System.

In one concrete case, a national taxation on-line system - we had a deadline six months hence. The initial project plan was to use a staff of one hundred technical people (programmers) for probably (nobody knew) three years to complete delivery of a totally new design. I worked out an alternative design based on making use of all the <u>old data and programs</u>, with a few politically interesting frills thrown in.

This idea alone, guarantees you will meet any deadline - but it is not nearly as much fun for the technologists who want to play with new toys. In this case there were ninety-eight programmers who wanted to learn a totally new programming language.

I made sure that I kept my eye on the essential <u>deadline</u> idea - that the Finance Minister was to see the new system in action personally in exactly six months. The new system was the old system, on a new computer mainly. Secondarily a "while-you-wait" access to their base of taxation data was desired. We provided a way using a copy of their current data. The Finance Minister had to wait one full second to get the data, using binary search on disks, with my modified solution, as opposed to 1/10th of a second with the previously committed 300 work-year solution.

They argued for a full three months about whether my simplistic solution could possibly work in such a large and complex environment. Then, using a handful of people they actually delivered successfully in three months.

3.2 USING FAGAN'S INSPECTION METHOD

"A stitch in time saves nine" says the old folk wisdom. Many of the problems in meeting deadlines for large projects are caused by the tail end backlash. This is the penalty you pay for <u>poor quality control in the early stages of design and planning</u>. The small details that were overlooked come back to haunt you - as you desperately try to fix the problems that pop up when you try to meet required quality levels or performance levels for delivery.

Conventional quality control [4] methods insist that "inspection" of product and process quality is a vital pre-requisite for being able to maintain the required cost and quality attributes of almost any development. Around 1972 Michael E. Fagan, of IBM in Kingston New York, began to transfer these methods to quality control of IBM software products. Nobody had tried to do this until then. In fact it was his training as a quality control hardware engineer which gave him the basic idea of applying "inspection" to software. It was an uphill battle at IBM, but very successful [5]. Although the method is widely recognized internationally, it will still take many more years before it is widely used.

The aspect of Inspection which is interesting in connection with deadline pressure is that it seems to have these repeatable general characteristics:

1. Delivery of major software projects is achieved in about 15% to 35% [6] less calender time than otherwise. This saving can also be translated into cost or work-power savings if desired[7].

2. The quality (in terms of defects removed) is measurably improved (by as much as one or two orders of magnitude) while this saving is made.

3. Improvements are cumulative, for several years. This is due to a process of management analysis of the time and defect statistics generated by inspection - combined with management taking change action to improve productivity [8].

Why does inspection save time and cost ?

It would be too much to explain all the details of inspection here. But, the basic reason why inspection saves resources is simple.

1. It can be used at early stages of design and planning - before conventional product testing can be used. Sixty percent of software bugs exist already at this stage, according to a TRW Study [9]. It identifies and cleans up defects which would cause much larger later repair costs. IBM data indicates as much as eighty-two times[10] more to correct software errors found late at the customer site, as opposed to early at design stages, if they were not found until much later.

2. The statistical data collected during the inspection process is carefully analyzed. This is much like Financial Directors analyze accounting data to get insights into a companies operational weaknesses. It is then used to suggest, and confirm the results of, major changes to the entire development or production process.

If the changes are implemented early enough in a project, they can impact the deadline of that project. If the changes are implemented late, or even after the project is completed - they can at least improve your ability to perform better on the following projects.[11].

3.3 Attribute Specification

Another technology for getting some control over deadlines and other resource constraints is, as indicated above, setting formal objectives for quality and resources in a formal measurable way.

The major reason why this impacts resources is that at the high levels of qualities desired by any user, even small improvements in a quality level, can cost disproportional resources.

So for example it took Bell Labs several years to move the best levels of availability they could report [12] from 99.9% to 99.98% for computerized telephone switching systems. The difference "0.08%" does not seem like a significant number in considering a project deadline. Both the above measures of system availability are "extremely high state of the art levels" if described in mere words. But that"little difference" cost Bell Labs (or AT&T) about eight years of research and development.

It is obviously vital for management to know exactly what levels their projects are aiming for in relation to the state of the art limits. If they don't have full control over those factors, then they do not have control over meeting deadlines.

Here are some principles of attribute specification:

1. All critical attributes of quality and resources should be established as measurable and testable requirements.
2. Any single critical attribute which management fails to control, is likely to be the Achilles Heel of the project - threatening cost and time resources.
3. All attributes should be specified at at least two parameters. The worst acceptable case for any system delivery - and the "planned level" - the one you hope to get to together with the others.

4. It is also quite useful to document, for all critical attributes, the "present system levels" and the known engineering limits or "state of the art limits". It is particularly these which give management a warning of unreasonable planned levels - and thus of impending schedule or cost problems.

5. Even with a first attempt at specification, be prepared to iterate towards a balanced specification of all the demands throughout the design and development process.

AN EXAMPLE OF ACTUAL APPLICATION OF THE PRINCIPLES OF THIS PAPER ON A LARGE PROJECT

One large (multi-thousand work-years, years of effort, $100 million dollars cost) software project in Europe asked me what they could do to avoid overrunning their deadline, a year from then, by more than two years.

Part of my advice was to break the project down, even at this late stage, into evolutionary deliveries. In this case the software critical to the initial and high-volume products to go before the very low volume product software which had been coupled to the same deadline.

Another part of my advice was to use Fagan's Inspection method on their work.

A third component of my advice was to define the worst case quality levels and performance levels more precisely. They had to differentiate between those software components which needed high quality levels, and those that were not as critical. Most of the volume of the software was not as critical as the central "real-time" components - and they had failed to make that distinction in their planning! They were quite simply committed to far too high a quality level, too early, for too much of their project product.

THE RESULTS
After eleven months, in November 1985, one month before the "impossible deadline", this group reported to me that their first useful delivery had been operating for two continuous weeks without any problems. There were certainly many reasons for this , not all of which I have depth knowledge. But evolutionary extraction was certainly a key element.

4.0 SUMMARY

Let me sum up what I have tried to say, as guiding principles of resisting deadline pressure.

1. The Deadline Mirage.
Rethink the deadline given to you - it may not be real.

2. The Solution Mirage.
Rethink the solution handed to you - it may be in the way of on-time delivery.

3. The Other Viewpoint.
Rethink the problem from other peoples point of view -it will help you simplify your problem and convince them to agree with you.

4. The Expert Trap.
Don't trust the experts blindly - they will cheerfully lead you to disaster.
Be sceptical and insist on proof and guarantees.

5. The All-at-once Trap.
Remember, nobody needs all of what they asked for by the deadline - they would simply like you to provide the miracle if possible.

6. The Real-Needs Principle.
Don't damage your credibility by bowing to pressure to make impossible promises. Increase your credibility by fighting for solutions which solve the real needs of your bosses and clients.

7. The Ends Dictate The Means.
If the deadline is critical and seems impossible otherwise - don't be afraid to change the solution.

8. The Principle of Conservation of Energy.
If deadlines are critical, make maximum use of existing systems and "known technology" - avoid research-into-unknowns during your project.

9. The Evolutionary Delivery Principle.
Any large project can be broken down into a series of earlier and smaller deliverables - don't give up - even if you have to change the technical solution to make it happen.
Keep your eye on results - not technologies.

10. The "don't blame me" Principle.
If you succeed using these principles, take the credit - give your boss and these ideas some credit in a footnote. If you fail - you obviously didn't apply these principles correctly (don't mention my name, mention your boss's, if you must blame somebody. Management is always at fault.)

REFERENCES

[1] T. Gilb & G. M. Weinberg, Humanized Input: Techniques for Reliable Keyed Input, QED Information Sciences, Inc., 170 Linden St., Wellesley Mass USA 02181. ISBN 0-89435-073-0, 1984

[2] Gilb, T., Principles Of Software Engineering Management, Addison-Wesley, ca. 1987. This contains chapters on quantitative definitions of software qualities, as well as chapters on Inspection and Evolutionary Delivery discussed in this paper.

[3] Tom Gilb, Evolutionary Delivery versus the Waterfall Model, ACM Software Engineering Notes, July 1985, p. 49-61

[4] See for example J M Juran (Editor), Quality Control Handbook, Third Edition, McGraw Hill, ISBN 0-07-033175-8, 1974.

[5] In 1979 Fagan was awarded a $50 thousand personal "Outstanding Contribution Award" by IBM in recognition of the success of his variant of the method in improving IBM software quality and cost.

[6] See for example the 35% difference measured on about 30 of 60 projects at IBM Federal Systems Division, as reported in IBM Systems Journal Number One 1977 (Felix and Walston article).

[7] Other examples of savings are reported in M E Fagan, "Design and code inspections to reduce errors in program development", IBM Systems Journal Number Three 1976, page 182-211.

[8] These points are supported by various IBM Technical publications authored by Horst Remus of IBM San Jose from 1978 to 1983.

[9] T. A. Thayer et al, Software Reliability, North-Holland, TRWSeries 2. 1978, ISBN 0-444-85217-4. Page 80.

[10] According to data collected by the author at IBM Santa Teresa Labs from Ken Christiansen in 1979. Another factor observed by IBM earlier was 62 x. Same principle as "An ounce of prevention is worth a pound of cure".

[11] R. A. Radice et al, A Programming Process Architecture, IBM SJ Vol. 24, No. 2, p.79-90. also, C. L. Jones, A process-integrated approach to defect prevention, p.151-167.

[12] Communications of ACM about mid 1984, as I recall.

Theory-W Software Project Management: Principles and Examples

BARRY W. BOEHM, SENIOR MEMBER, IEEE, AND RONY ROSS

Abstract—A good software project management theory should be simultaneously simple, general, and specific. To date, those objectives have been difficult to satisfy. This paper presents a candidate software management theory and shows that it satisfies those objectives reasonably well. Reflecting various alphabetical management theories (X, Y, Z), it is called the Theory W approach to software project management.

Theory W: Make Everyone a Winner

The paper explains the key steps and guidelines underlying the Theory W statement and its two subsidiary principles: *plan the flight and fly the plan*; and, *identify and manage your risks*.

Several examples illustrate the application of Theory W, and an extensive case study is presented and analyzed: the attempt to introduce new information systems to a large industrial corporation in an emerging nation. The case may seem unique, yet it is typical. The analysis shows that Theory W and its subsidiary principles do an effective job both in explaining why the project encountered problems, and in prescribing ways in which the problems could have been avoided.

Index Terms—Project management, software case studies, software development, software maintenance, software management, software personnel management, software planning and control.

I. Introduction

SOFTWARE project management today is an art. The skillful integration of software technology, economics and human relations in the specific context of a software project is not an easy task. The software project is a highly people-intensive effort that spans a very lengthy period, with fundamental implications on the work and performance of many different classes of people.

A. The Software Project Manager's Problem

The software project manager's primary problem is that a software project needs to simultaneously satisfy a variety of constituencies: the users, the customers, the development team, the maintainance team, the management. As seen in Fig. 1, each of these constituencies has its own desires with respect to the software project. The *users*—sometimes too enthusiastic, sometimes too skeptical—desire a robust, user-friendly system with many functions supporting their mission. The *customers* desire a product delivered reliably to a short schedule and low budget. The *bosses* of the project manager desire a project with am-

Manuscript received October 30, 1987; revised February 29, 1988.

B. W. Boehm is with TRW Defense Systems Group, One Space Park, Redondo Beach, CA 90278, and the Department of Computer Science, University of California, Los Angeles, CA 90024.

R. Ross is with the Department of Computer Science, University of California, Los Angeles, CA 90024.

IEEE Log Number 8928293.

bitious goals, no overruns, and no surprises. The *maintainers* of the product desire a well-documented, easy-to-modify system with no bugs. The *development team* members—often brilliant, sometimes unmanageable—desire interesting technical challenges and fast career paths, generally with a preference for design and an inclination to defer documentation.

These desires create fundamental conflicts when taken together (e.g., many functions versus a low budget and no overruns). These conflicts are at the root of most software project management difficulties—both at the strategic level (setting goals, establishing major milestones and responsibilities) and at the tactical level (resolving day-to-day conflicts, prioritizing assignments, adapting to changes).

B. The Software Management Theory Problem

A good software management theory should help the project manager navigate through these difficulties. As seen in Fig. 2, a software management theory has a similar challenging set of simultaneous objectives to satisfy. It should be simple to understand and apply; general enough to cover all classes of projects and classes of concerns (procedural, technical, economic, people-oriented); yet specific enough to provide useful, situation-specific advice.

Several attempts have been made to provide a relatively small set of software project management principles which can be easily recalled and applied, and which cover all of the important aspects. Thayer *et al.* [21] and Reifer [18] provide sets of principles largely organized around the five overall management principles in Koontz–O'Donnell [12] of planning, staffing, organizing, controlling, and directing. Boehm [3] provides a set of seven fundamental principles of software development. Although these have been very useful in many situations, none of these to date have produced a sufficient combination of simplicity, generality and specificity to have stimulated widespread use.

This paper presents a candidate fundamental principle for software project management developed by one of the authors (Boehm), and shows how it would apply in avoiding the software project management problems encountered in a case study analyzed by the other author (Ross).

The fundamental principle is called the Theory W approach to software project management.

Theory W: Make Everyone a Winner.

Reprinted from *IEEE Transactions on Software Engineering*, Vol. 15, No. 7, July 1989, pp. 902–916. Copyright © 1989 by The Institute of Electrical and Electronics Engineers, Inc. All rights reserved.

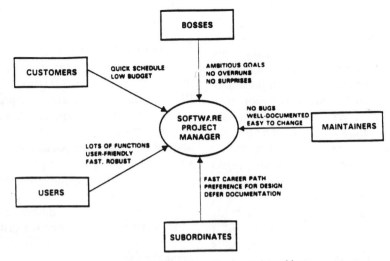

Fig. 1. The software project manager's problem.

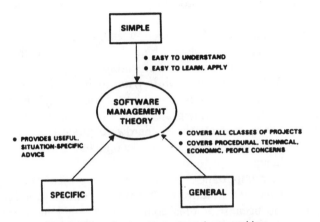

Fig. 2. The software management theory problem.

It holds that the primary job of the software project manager is to make winners of each of the parties involved in the software process: the project manager's subordinates and managers; the customers; the users and maintainers of the resulting product; and any other significantly affected people, such as the developers or users of interfacing products.

Making everyone a winner has a number of implications which will be discussed below, including the use of two subsidiary principles:

- Plan the flight and fly the plan.
- Identify and manage your risks.

Section II of this paper elaborates on the overall Theory W approach and the software project implications of making everyone a winner. Section III elaborates on the two subsidiary principles. Section IV provides the history of the system involved in the case study. Section V analyzes the case study with respect to Theory W and the subsidiary principles, and Section VI presents the resulting conclusions.

II. THEORY W: MAKE EVERYONE A WINNER

This section elaborates on Theory W's major principle. We begin in Section II-A by placing Theory W in the context of other management theories, particularly Theories X, Y, and Z. Section II-B presents the key concept involved in Theory W: the distinction between win–win, win–lose, and lose–lose situations. Section II-C summarizes the three primary steps suggested to achieve the desired goal of making everyone a winner, and the nine substeps involved in implementing Theory W. Section II-C also elaborates on the first three substeps: those that deal with creating win–win situations, the strongest distinguishing feature of Theory W as a management approach. Section II-D elaborates on all of the substeps, and shows how a set of strategic principles for software project management can be generated by applying each of the substeps to each of the project manager's constituencies identified in Fig. 1 above. Section II-E shows via an example how the Theory W steps can be used to solve day-to-day tactical project management problems as well as strategic problems.

A. Comparison to Theories X, Y and Z

The Theory X approach to management built largely on the "scientific management" ideas of Frederick Taylor [20]. It held that the most efficient way to get a job done was to do more and more precise time and motion studies, and to organize jobs into well-orchestrated sequences of tasks in which people were as efficient and predictable as machines. Management consisted of keeping the system running smoothly, largely through coercion.

Theory Y, introduced in [8], held that Theory X was a poor long-term strategy because it stunted people's creativity, adaptiveness, and self esteem, making the people and their organizations unable to cope with change. Theory Y held that management should stimulate creativity and individual initiative. This led to organizations which were much more adaptive and personally satisfying, but created difficulties in dealing with conflict. This was not a problem in Theory X, but became a major concern in Theory Y organizations, with many individual initiatives competing for resources and creating problems of coordination.

Theory Z, described in [10], holds that much of the conflict resolution problem can be eliminated by up-front investment in developing shared values and arriving at major decisions by consensus. It focuses largely on doing this within an organization, and does not say much about how to deal with other organizations with different objectives and cultures—a particularly common situation with software managers and their diverse constituencies (developers, customers, users, etc.). Overall, Theory Z's primary emphasis is at the corporate-culture level rather than at the intercompany level or the individual project level.

Theory W's fundamental principle is well-matched to the problems of software project management. It holds that software project managers will be fully successful if and only if they make winners of all the other participants in the software process: superiors, subordinates, customers, users, maintainers, etc. This principle is particularly relevant in the software field, which is a highly people-intensive area whose products are largely services or decision aids, and whose performers are often unfamiliar with user and management concerns. However, Theory W can be applied to other fields as well.

Rather than characterizing a manager as an autocrat (Theory X), a coach (Theory Y), or a facilitator (Theory Z), Theory W characterizes a manager's primary role as a negotiator between his various constituencies, and a packager of project solutions with win conditions for all parties. Beyond this, the manager is also a goal-setter, a monitor of progress towards goals, and an activist in seeking out day-to-day win–lose or lose–lose project conflicts, confronting them, and changing them into win–win situations.

B. Win–Win, Win–Lose, and Lose–Lose Situations

Making everyone a winner may seem like an unachievable objective. Most situations tend to be zero-sum, win–lose situations. Building a quick and sloppy product may be a low-cost, near-term "win" for the software developer and customer, but it will be a "lose" for the user and the maintainer. Adding lots of marginally useful software "bells and whistles" to a product on a cost-plus contract may be a win for the developer and some users, but a lose for the customer.

At worst, software projects can be lose–lose situations. Setting unrealistic schedule expectations; staffing with incompatible people; poor planning; or trying to catch up on a schedule by adding more people will generally make losers of all the participants.

Nonetheless, win–win situations exist, and often they can be created by careful attention to people's interests and expectations. Creating a profit-sharing arrangement for a software subcontractor provides the subcontractor with a motivation to develop a high-quality, widely-sold product, thus increasing the size of the profit pie for both the subcontractor and the top-level product developer. Using better software technology such as structured programming, early error detection techniques, or information hiding will also create wins for all parties.

C. Creating Win–Win Situations

The best work on creating win–win situations has been done in the field of negotiation. The book *Getting to Yes* [9] is a classic in the area. Its primary thesis is that successful negotiations are not achieved by haggling from preset negotiating positions, but by following a four-step approach whose goal is basically to create a win–win situation for the negotiating parties:

1) Separate the people from the problem.
2) Focus on interests, not positions.
3) Invent options for mutual gain.
4) Insist on using objective criteria.

The Theory W approach to software project management expands on these four steps to establish a set of win–win preconditions, and some further conditions for structuring the software process and the resulting software product, as shown in Table I.

The remainder of this section elaborates on the first three substeps in Table I which deal primarily with the process of creating win–win situations.

1) Understand How People Want to Win: One important subprinciple here is to *make sure you identify the key people*. Often, software projects have failed because a key constituency (users' bosses, hardware procurement personnel, subcontractors) has not been included in the win–win scheme.

Another important subprinciple is to *project yourself into others' win situations*. This is often difficult for people to do because it runs counter to strongly implanted notions of goodness such as the Golden Rule: "Do unto others as you would have others do unto you." But, others may not want what you want as win conditions. Some frequent examples:

• Managers frequently assume that software professionals win by getting "promoted" to management. However, the motivating-factors studies done by Couger and Zawacki [6] indicate that the typical data processing professional has a much stronger need for professional growth than for social interaction, while the average manager has the opposite profile. Thus, promotions to management can be quite harmful to software people's careers, and dual-track (technical and managerial) career-path ladders can be much more successful in software organizations.

• Computer-science majors brought up on canonical applications such as compilers and operating systems, where users are programmers, implicitly build up a set of assumptions about software users: that software users like to program, and prefer powerful and terse (but perhaps obscure) command languages and users' manuals. Well-meaning attempts to apply those assumptions to such software users as nurses, doctors, pilots and bank tellers have led to numerous software disasters.

Thus, Theory W suggests a modified form of the Golden Rule: "Do unto others as you would have others do unto you—if you were like them."

TABLE I
THEORY W WIN–WIN STEPS

1. Establish a set of win-win preconditions

a. Understand how people want to win;
   b. Establish reasonable expectations;
   c. Match people's tasks to their win conditions;
   d. Provide a supportive environment.

2. Structure a win-win software process.

a. Establish a realistic process plan;
   b. Use the plan to control the project;
   c. Identify and manage your win-lose or lose-lose risks;
   d. Keep people involved;

3. Structure a win-win software product.
a. Match product to users', maintainers' win conditions.

Another key subprinciple is the Peters–Waterman [17] maxim to *get close to the customer*. This involves getting software people to operate more like marketing personnel than like people who wait around to code up whatever specification is provided. It involves much more proactive use of interviews, surveys, tours of duty, prototypes, scenarios, operations analysis, user-culture analyses, and understanding of users' previous experiences with automation (scars, bruises, traumas, triumphs).

Overall, the field of motivational analysis provides the most comprehensive set of insights on understanding how people want to win. Gellerman [10] provides a good early survey of the field; more recently, Couger and Zawacki [6] have provided a good set of insights related specifically to data processing people.

2) Establish Reasonable Expectations: Many software problems stem from the fact that software customers and users frequently have little feel for what is easy and what is hard to achieve with computers and software. This leads to a set of unrealistic expectations: either thinking things are too hard to implement (complex scheduling or file management) or too easy (pattern recognition or building 150 man-months worth of software in 6 months). Similarly, software people often have unrealistic expectations of what is easy and what is hard for users to do.

Some important subprinciples here are:

• Bring your constituencies together to identify and resolve expectation mismatches.

• Have people look at issues from the other constituents' viewpoints.

• Have people look for objective, mutually relevant solution criteria.

• Relate people's expectations to experience: benchmarks, reference checks, expert judgment.

• Relate people's expectations to well-calibrated models: computer-performance models, software project cost and schedule estimation models.

A related management insight is that "hard–soft works better than soft–hard." A manager who overpromises to his various constituencies and then has to deflate their expectations has an easier time initially, but a much rougher time in the long run, than a manager who deflates initial expectations and provides some management reserve to soften his position later where necessary.

A good recent example of establishing reasonable soft-

ware project expectations involved the need for improvements in the on-board software of the F-16 aircraft. The aircraft users expected a long list of additional software capabilities to be delivered in 12 months. The developers' expectations were in terms of previous software productivity rates, and indicated a much longer development period. Rather than conduct a positional bargaining exercise resulting in unsatisfied expectations on both sides, the users and developers decided to explore their options using COCOMO, a software cost and schedule estimation model calibrated to experience in similar projects [2].

As a result, both groups developed a much better understanding of the relationships between software functionality, cost, and schedule. The developers found options to increase their software productivity capabilities and expectations. The users were able to establish a series of prioritized annual software increments whose achievability was keyed to their developer-shared productivity expectations. After two years of software deliveries, both groups have experienced satisfactory results relative to their revised expectations.

Overall, the process of reconciling people's expectations is dealt with in the fields of conflict resolution and teambuilding. Walton [22], Kirchof and Adams [11], and Dyer [7] are good sources of additional insight.

3) Match People's Tasks to Their Win Conditions: The key principles here involve *searching out win–win situations* and *expanding the option space to create win–win situations.*

Some effective techniques available to the software project manager for searching out win–win situations include:

• Breaking options into parts (functions, activities, increments, phases), and configuring combinations of suboptions into win packages for each participant. For example, under some conditions, establishing a separate leader for successive software increments has worked well, particularly if the increments are large, with different technical and/or organizational centers of gravity.

• Realigning options along win–win axes. For example, some projects have successfully shifted the authority and responsibility for software quality assurance from the developer (who may consider it a bore) to the maintainer, who has considered it a major win-leverage opportunity.

Some effective techniques available to the software project manager for expanding the option space to create win–win situations are:

• Linking tasks to future options and career paths ("Quality assurance may be a bore, but it's a ticket to a fast-track career path").

• Expanding the scope of a task ("Quality Assurance should not be a bore. I think you could lead the way in helping us make quality assurance a more proactive function in getting us quality products. That would be a real achievement").

• Linking tasks to extra rewards ("Rescuing this integration and test mess will be a killer, but I'll make sure you get a good bonus and lots of kudos if you succeed").

• Providing extra support ("This schedule is very ambitious, but I'll provide your team with the first-class workstations and facilities you'll need to meet it'').

• Surfacing new options (''We can't develop all the functions in 12 months, but if we do an incremental development, we can satisfy your top-priority needs in 12 months'').

Overall, the field of negotiation provides the best additional sources of insight in matching tasks to win conditions. Some good books are Fisher and Ury [9] and Nierenberg [15].

D. Deriving Strategic Project Guidelines from Theory W Win–Win Steps

Most current software management directives, and many of the textbooks, present strategic software management guidelines as a series of relatively unconnected what-to-do lists of activities to perform (e.g., prototype the user interface, configuration-manage the baselined items, set up and follow a set of programming standards).

The power of Theory W becomes evident in Tables II and III, which show that one can derive most of the apparently unconnected what-to-do activities by applying the Theory W win–win steps in Table I to the various constituencies involved in the software process. Prototyping is a way of understanding the users' win conditions (Table II). Configuration management is partly establishing a supportive environment for the developers and maintainers, and partly participation in change control by all parties impacted by a proposed change (Table II). Programming standards contribute to structuring a software product so that its maintainers will be winners (Table III).

Further, Tables II and III provide stronger guidance than usual for allocating life-cycle responsibilities to the various software parties. An example is the allocation of the quality assurance responsibility to the maintainers, as their win conditions are most strongly affected by product quality.

Tables II and III also show that Theory W provides not just a ''what'' for the process activities, but also the underlying ''why.'' This is very important in the frequent situations of tailoring the process activities to special circumstances, and determining how much of a given process activity is enough. For example, if the inclusion of machine-generated flowcharts in the maintainance documentation does not help the maintainers become winners, it is not necessary to require their delivery.

E. Theory W: A Tactical Management Example

Theory W provides specific useful guidance in tactical as well as strategic project management situations. The resulting solutions are often preferable to those derived from previous management theories. Consider the following example:

XYZ Corp. has been developing a large financial system for a Boston bank. A new position on the project is being created to lead a system analysis ef-

TABLE II
STRATEGIC GUIDELINES DERIVED FROM WIN–WIN PRECONDITIONS

Win-Win Precondition	Users	Maintainers	Customers	Developer Team
Understand win conditions	Mission anal. Ops. concept Prototyping Rqts. spec Early users' manual	Ops. concept Ops. procedures	Cost-benefit analysis	Career path develop.
Reasonable expectations	*Teambuilding, Negotiating, Conflict resolution*			
	Rqts. scrub	*Resource allocation*		
Match tasks to win conditions	*Change control participation*			
	User-spec reviews Prototype exercise	Quality assurance	Status tracking	Staffing, organizing
			Early Error Detection	
Supportive environment preparation	User training Cutover preparation	Maint. training Conversion Deliverable support envir. Config. mgmt.	Customer training	Developer training Support envir. Config. mgmt.
	Modern programming practices			

TABLE III
STRATEGIC GUIDELINES DERIVED FROM PRODUCT, PROCESS GUIDELINES

Guideline	Users	Maintainers	Customers	Developers
Process planning	Operational plan Installation & training plans	Life-cycle support plan	*Development plans*	
Process control	*Teambuilding, Negotiating, Communicating*			
	Reviews	Reviews	Status tracking, Controlling Perform. feedback	
Risk management	*Sensitivity analysis*			
	Risk management plans			
	User rqts. validation, stability	Quality assurance	Budget, schedule Validation	staffing
Process involvement	Sys. engr, plan participation Review participation Prototype exercise	Sys. engr, plan participation Review participation Quality assurance	Cost-benefit reviews, approvals	Delegation Planning particip.
Product structuring	Service oriented Efficient Easy to learn Easy to use Tailorable	Easy to modify Prog. standards	Efficient Correct Feasible	Easy to Modify Balanced Correct

fort. George and Ann are the two primary candidates for the job. They are equally well qualified: George has somewhat more overall experience, while Ann has more experience specific to this type of application. The project manager must decide whom to chose.

Using Theory X, the manager would make a choice, based on some arbitrary criterion such as seniority. Using Theory Y, the manager would likely ask George and Ann for proposals on how they would do the job, and pick the most ambitious one. Using Theory Z, the manager would likely concentrate on prebuilding a consensus on team objectives, and make a choice based on team priorities.

Theory W would try to avoid the above situations, each of which creates a win-lose situation between George and Ann. By following the Theory W steps in Table I, the manager would try to create a win-win situation as follows:

1) Understand how people want to win. In talking with George and Ann, the manager finds that George greatly wants the job because of the extensive travel to Boston, where he has a daughter in college. Ann greatly wants the job because it would provide a career path toward marketing.

2) Match people's tasks to their win conditions. The manager expands the option space by considering comparable jobs with Boston travel for George and comparable marketing-oriented jobs for Ann.

Frequently, the Theory W approach will help the manager to find and establish such win-win solutions, creating more satisfaction and personal commitment among the participants, fewer disaffected and uncooperative participants, and more satisfactory all-around outcomes.

F. Connections between Theory W and Game Theory

Theory W also has fruitful connections to game theory. For example, the case of George and Ann can be formulated as a nonzero-sum game involving three players: George, Ann, and the customer. By using the concept of Rational Offer Groups formulated by Rosenschein and Genesereth [19], one can analyze the conditions under which the expansion of George's and Ann's option spaces will produce a win-win-win situation for George, Ann, and the customer. An example result is that if the project manager is too successful in finding alternate jobs for George and Ann, neither will take the systems analysis job, and the customer will become a loser.

III. Theory W Subsidiary Principles

Because of their particular importance to the management of the software process, the first three Theory W win-win process substeps in Table I are highlighted and combined into two key Theory W subsidiary principles. These are:
- Plan the flight and fly the plan (steps 2a, 2b).
- Identify and manage your risks (step 2c).

A. Planning the Flight

Establishing a realistic process plan is crucial to the success of the project. As indicated in Table III, there are several types of plans involved in making everyone a winner: operational plans, installation and training plans, life-cycle support plans, and development plans. Each of these may have a number of subsidiary plans: configuration management plans, quality assurance plans, test plans, conversion plans, etc.

Plans are important in Theory W because:
- They record the mutual commitment of the project participants to a set of win-win conditions and their implications.

- They provide a framework for detecting deviations from the win-win conditions which require corrective action.

Frequently, each software subplan is organized around a totally different outline, making the various plans more difficult to develop, assimilate, and query. Each Theory W plan is organized around a common outline, reflecting a small number of universal interrogatives (why, what, when, who, where, how, and how much):
1) Objectives (*Why* is the activity being pursued?)
2) Products and Milestones (*What* is being produced by when?)
3) Responsibilities (*Who* is responsible for each result? *Where* are they located organizationally?)
4) Approach (*How* is each result being achieved?)
5) Resources (*How much* of each scarce resource is required to achieve the results?)

Fig. 3 presents the outline for one of the key software management plans: the software development plan. It shows that the subsections of the plan are particular to software development issues (requirements, product design, programming, configuration management, quality assurance, etc.), but that the major sections of the plan follow the common Theory W outline.

Space limitations preclude further discussion of software project planning here; some good references are [8] and [14]. Also, some similar concepts are being developed in the draft IEEE Standard for Software Project Management Plans.

B. Flying the Plan

Developing a plan which satisfies everyone's win conditions is not enough to make everyone a winner. You also need to use the plan to manage the project.

This involves making a particular effort to monitor the project's progress with respect to the plan. The nature of this effort should be specified in the plan; see section 5.3 of the plan outline in Fig. 3. If the project's progress continues to match its plans, the project is in good shape. But usually, there will be some mismatches between the progress and the plans. If so, the manager needs to assess the reasons for the mismatches. It may be that the plans are flawed or out of date, in which case the plans need to be modified. Or the project's progress may be deficient, in which case the project manager needs to apply corrective action.

Applying corrective action is one of the most critical situations for using the "make everyone a winner" principle. It is all too easy to apply snap-judgment corrective actions with win-lose or lose-lose outcomes, or to heap public blame on people so that they feel like losers rather than winners. But it is generally possible to follow the Theory W win-win steps in Table I to find a corrective action strategy which either preserves everyone as winners, or convinces them that their losses are minimal with respect to other strategies. (An example is provided in the case study analysis in Section V-A.) And it is generally possible to reprimand people's behavior without making

1. Objectives (the "why")

   1.1. Software Product Objectives

   1.2. Development Plan Objectives

2. Milestones and Products (the "what" and "when")

   2.1. Overall Development Strategy

   2.2. Detailed Schedule of Deliverables

   2.3. Detailed Development Milestones and Schedules

3. Responsibilities (the "who" and "where")

   3.1. Organizational Responsibilities

      3.1.1. Global Organization Charts

      3.1.2. Organizational Commitment Responsibilities

   3.2. Development Responsibilities

      3.2.1. Development Organization Charts

      3.2.2. Staffing

      3.2.3. Training

4. Approach (the "how")

   4.1. Risk Management

   4.2. Development Phases

      4.2.1. Plans and Requirements Phase

      4.2.2. Product Design Phase

      4.2.3. Programming Phase

      4.2.4. Integration and test Phase

      4.2.5. Implementation Phase

   4.3. Reviews

   4.4. Documentation

   4.5. Configuration Management

   4.6. Quality Assurance

   4.7. Facilities and Related Concerns

5. Resources (the "how much")

   5.1. Work Breakdown Structure

   5.2. Budgets

   5.3. Status Monitoring and Control

Fig. 3. Theory W outline for the software development plan.

them feel like losers. A good example is the "one-minute reprimand" in the book *The One-Minute Manager* [1].

C. Risk Management

Planning the flight and flying the plan will make everyone a winner if the plans reflect the participants' win conditions and if the plans are realistic. Ensuring that the plans are realistic is the province of risk management.

Risk management focuses the project manager's attention on those portions of the project most likely to cause trouble and to compromise the participants' win conditions. Risk management considerations can also help the project manager to determine the appropriate sequence of performing project activities. The spiral model of software development [4] discusses risk-driven sequencing of project activities in more detail.

Webster defines "risk" as "the possibility of loss or injury." The magnitude of a risk item is generally defined as a quantity called Risk Exposure *RE*:

$$RE = (LP) * (LM).$$

The Loss Probability factor *LP* represents the probability of an unsatisfactory outcome. The Loss Magnitude factor *LM* represents the magnitude of the loss if the outcome is unsatisfactory. The magnitude of the loss is best expressed in terms of the participants' utility functions, which measure the degree to which the participants become losers rather than winners.

There are two primary classes of project risk:

1) *Generic risks*, which are common to all projects, and which are covered by standard development plan techniques.

2) *Project-specific risks*, which reflect a particular aspect of a given project, and which are addressed by project-specific risk management plans. The most common project-specific risks are personnel shortfalls, unrealistic schedules and budgets, inappropriate requirements, shortfalls in external components and tasks, and technology shortfalls or unknowns.

D. Risk Management Steps

The practice of risk management involves two primary steps, Risk Assessment and Risk Handling, each with three subsidiary steps. Risk Assessment involves risk identification, risk analysis, and risk prioritization. Risk Handling involves risk management planning, risk management execution, and risk monitoring and control.

Risk Identification produces lists of the project-specific items likely to compromise a project's win–win conditions. Typical risk identification techniques include checklists, decomposition, comparison with experience, and examination of decision drivers.

Risk Analysis produces assessments of the loss-probability and loss-magnitude associated with each of the identified risk items, and assessments of compound risks involved in risk-item interactions. Typical techniques include network analysis, decision trees, cost models, and performance models.

Risk Prioritization produces a prioritized ordering of the risk items identified and analyzed. Typical techniques include risk leverage analysis and Delphi or group-consensus techniques.

Risk Management Planning produces plans for addressing each risk item, including the coordination of the individual risk-item plans with each other and with the overall project plan (e.g., to ensure that enough up-front schedule is provided to properly develop, exercise, and learn from a prototype). Typical techniques include risk-resolution checklists such as the one in Table IV, showing the top 10 primary sources of software project risk and the most effective approaches for resolving them. Other techniques include cost-benefit analysis and statistical decision analysis of the relative cost and effectiveness of alternative risk-resolution approaches. The best form for a risk management plan is the general "why, what, when, who, where, how, how much" plan template discussed above.

Risk Management Execution produces a resolution of the risk items. Typical techniques are the ones shown in Table IV.

Risk Monitoring and Control completes the "flying the plan" counterpart of risk management planning. It involves tracking the progress toward resolving high-risk items and taking corrective action where appropriate. A most effective technique is a Top Ten Risk Item list which

TABLE IV
A TOP TEN LIST OF SOFTWARE RISK ITEMS

A Top Ten List of Software Risk Items	
RISK ITEM	RISK MANAGEMENT TECHNIQUES
1. Personnel shortfalls	-Staffing with top talent; job matching; teambuilding; key-personnel agreements; cross-training; prescheduling key people
2. Unrealistic schedules and budgets	-Detailed multisource cost & schedule estimation; design to cost; incremental development; software reuse; requirements scrubbing
3. Developing the wrong software functions	-Organization analysis; mission analysis; ops-concept formulation; user surveys; prototyping; early users' manuals
4. Developing the wrong user interface	-Prototyping; scenarios; task analysis; user characterization (functionality, style, workload)
5. Gold plating	-Requirements scrubbing; prototyping; cost-benefit analysis; design to cost
6. Continuing stream of requirements changes	-High change threshold; information hiding; incremental development (defer changes to later increments)
7. Shortfalls in externally furnished components	-Benchmarking; inspections; reference checking; compatibility analysis
8. Shortfalls in externally performed tasks	-Reference checking; pre-award audits; award-fee contracts; competitive design or prototyping; teambuilding
9. Real-time performance shortfalls	-Simulation; benchmarking; modeling; prototyping; instrumentation; tuning
10. Straining computer science capabilities	-Technical analysis; cost-benefit analysis; prototyping; reference checking

is highlighted at each weekly, monthly, or milestone project review.

These steps are supported by a variety of techniques. Space limitations preclude further discussion of the issues here. Further details on each of the software risk management steps are given in [5].

IV. THE CASE STUDY

A. Corporate Background

BBB Industries is one of the largest manufacturers in the small, yet advanced emerging nation named Optimia. The company started out in the 1950's as a privately owned workshop, and has gone through periods of prosperity and periods of recession. During one of the recession periods in the early seventies, the owners sold their shares to MMM corporation, one of Optimia's largest investment corporations.

In 1983, BBB Industries' sales volume reached $100 million a year, with over 3000 employees. The manufacturing was carried out in several factories while the Marketing, Production Planning, and Financial Services functions were all concentrated at the company's headquarters. BBB Industries manufactured various consumer products that were marketed through diverse distribution channels, including the company's own store. Over half of the sales were directed to export markets in the USA and Europe.

The profitability of the company was very unstable: the world demand for BBB's product line is subject to frequent ups and downs, and BBB Industries was unable to adjust in time to these dynamic changes. This inability was attributed mainly to BBB's old-fashioned production and organizational methods.

BBB's Information Systems in 1983 were of the most archaic type. In the early 1970's a major effort was made to computerize the production and control systems by using a card-operated computer. This effort failed, and a decision was made to transfer the information processing to a service bureau. For technical and political reasons, the various departments adopted different service bureaus, so that in 1983 each of the General-Ledger, Accounts-Receivables, Payroll and Inventory systems used the services of a different service bureau.

B. The New Management's Attitude

In 1984, a new General Manager was appointed to BBB Industries. The business results of 1984 were good, and the General Manager decided that the time had come to do something about BBB's Information Systems. To achieve that result, he hired a new manager for the Data Processing department, Mr. Smith.

"It's not going to be an easy job," he told Mr. Smith, "But this is a big challenge. I know this company cannot go on without proper information systems. However, my middle management does not understand information systems concepts. It is up to you to show us the way, and to help me convince the other managers in this company to give a hand to this effort. However—you should not forget that BBB's budget is limited, and that 1985 is not going to be as profitable as 1984. So, we shall have to do our best with a minimal budget. And, of course, since I am trying to cut down on all personnel, you cannot hire any more people to the data processing department right now. First, I want to see some results, and then—the sky is the limit."

C. The Initial Survey

The initial survey was done by Mr. Smith himself. The survey consisted of two parts:

a) A study of BBB's existing systems.

b) An outline of BBB's requirements for new Information Systems.

The survey's findings can be summed up as follows:

• Except for the Payroll system, all the existing data-processing systems of BBB did not serve their purposes. These systems were not used in the day-to-day operations, their accuracy was very low, and they therefore required a lot of manual processing.

• The vital Production Design and Control operation could not benefit at all from any of the computer systems, and therefore was slow, inflexible, and inefficient.

• There was practically no integration between the different systems, and each served the specific, limited needs of the department that was in charge of it.

• BBB's productivity, manageability, and profitability depended on the replacement of these systems by new, better ones.

• The potential users of the systems were quire ignorant of what modern information systems concepts are, and how they could be of use for them in their daily activities. Furthermore, the factory workers had little faith in BBB's ability to adopt new, modern methods.

The survey's recommendations were:

• There is immediate need to replace the existing systems by on-line, interactive systems, based on in-house computers, that will supply the information by both operational and management levels in a timely, accurate, and comprehensive fashion. This effort can be done in stages, and the first system to be implemented should be a relatively simple, low-risk system. The success of this implementation will improve the ability to continue with other, more complex systems.

• The development of the first system should be done by an outside contractor, preferably a software house that already has a package for that purpose.

• BBB's middle management personnel should receive special training that will enable them to better understand the potential of on-line computer systems and their applicability to their own problems.

• The problems of the factories are complex, and require more detailed research to analyze and define the information systems requirements of the factories and to evaluate the various modes of operations that are amenable for this problem (distributed processing versus centralized processing, interactive versus autonomous, data collection techniques, etc.).

• Even though the task of computerizing BBB is complex, such projects are common nowadays, and the overall timetable should not exceed three years.

The survey was presented to BBB's management, and its conclusions were approved enthusiastically. The Finished-Goods Sales and Marketing system (FGSM) was chosen for first implementation, primarily because it was the easiest to implement, and because the FGSM managers were the strongest in expressing their need for and support of a new system. Mr. Smith was charged with preparing a Request for Proposal that would be presented to potential suppliers of software and hardware. There was no discussion of the required budget, nor additional personnel.

D. The Request for Proposal (RFP)

The RFP was based on the initial survey and on the findings of a subsequent two-week survey of the Finished-Goods Sales and Marketing organization. It consisted of the following parts:

a) A general description of BBB, its organization, operations, and goals.

b) A thorough, although not detailed, description of the Finished-Goods Marketing and Sales Organization.

c) A list of the requirements for the new system for FGSM:

• The system should be an on-line, interactive system.

• The system shall handle all the different types of items and incorporate all the different types of Catalog Codes that are in current use.

• The system shall handle the Finished Goods inventory in various levels of detail.

• The system shall handle the various types of clients (retailers, wholesalers, department stores, company-owned stores).

• The system shall produce automatic billings to the various clients (some of the department stores required predefined forms).

• The system shall be able to produce different sales and inventory reports.

• The system shall be able to integrate in the future into the General Ledger and Accounts Receivable Systems

d) A four-page outline of the requirements for the new Financial Systems for BBB.

The RFP was presented to the three leading hardware suppliers in Optimia, and to five software companies that had previous experience in similar systems.

E. The Proposals

After the first elimination process, three proposals were left in the game. Since the RFP was rather open-ended, the proposals varied in their scopes and in the extent to which they covered the requirements mentioned. The price quotations ranged from $70,000 to $450,000. The final competitors were as follows.

1) Colossal Computers: The leading hardware distributor in Optimia. Colossal Computers proposed their popular System C computer, and recommended the software packages of SW1 Software as the basis for the implementation. (Colossal refused to take full commitment for both hardware and software.)

2) Big Computing Computers: The second largest hardware distributor in Optimia, distributors of Big computers, with their own Financial and Marketing packages.

3) Fast Computing Computers: The distributors of world renowned Fast computers. There were only few installations of Fast computers in Optimia, even though the equipment was excellent. As a result, there were no software packages available on Fast Computers. The owners of Fast Computing Computers was MMM Corp., the owners of BBB Industries. MMM Corp. was deliberating at the time how to increase the sales of Fast Computers.

Table V summarizes the results of the evaluation process among the three competitors, as presented to BBB's management.

Mr. Smith's recommendation was to buy Colossal's equipment and to engage SW1 Software as subcontractor for the Marketing and Financial Systems, relying on SW1's existing Financial package. Mr. Smith had met with two of SW1's executives and was very impressed with their familiarity with Sales and Marketing Systems. It turned out that SW1 had considerable previous experience in developing Marketing systems similar to that required by BBB.

BBB's management informed the three competitors of BBB's choice, and started final negotiations with Colossal Computers.

TABLE V
PROPOSALS EVALUATION—THE FGSM SYSTEM FOR BBB INDUSTRIES

	Colossal	Big Computing	Fast Computing
HARDWARE EVALUATION			
Speed Factor	Average	Average	V. Good
Memory Factor	Average	Low	V. Good
# of installations (Optimia)	200	50	5
Growth Factor	Average	Low	High
PROPOSED SW SOLUTION			
Financial Package	SW1's package	Own Package	To be developed
Marketing System	SW1	Own devlp.	BBB devlp.
SOFTWARE EVALUATION			
Financial Package	Good	Good	?
Marketing Solution	Good	Average	None
Addt'l Packages	Many	A few	None
GENERAL FACTORS			
Familiarity with Equip.	High	Low	Low
Compatibility with BBB's Inventory Sys.	None	None	High
# of SW houses	15	5	2
COMPANY FACTORS			
Company Stability	High	Average	Average
Maintenance Organization	High	Low	Average
Company Commitment	Average	Average	High
ESTIMATED COSTS			
Hardware	$170K	$130K	$140K
Marketing System	$50K	$40K	?
Financial Package	$30K	$30K	$40K
Estimated Modifications to Financial Package	$20K-$40K	$30K-$50K	?
TOTAL COSTS	$270K-$290K	$240K-$260K	$180K+?

The next day, BBB's General Manager got a call from Fast Computing Computers' General Manager, and a meeting was set where BBB was asked to clarify why Colossal was chosen. Fast Computing's General Manager explained that the BBB account had a crucial significance to Fast Computing's future. "If in-house companies (that is—MMM owned) won't buy our equipment, who will? Colossal will use this fact as a weapon to beat us even in places where they don't have such an advantage," he said.

"The solution offered by Colossal answers most of our needs," replied BBB's General Manager, "Your equipment may be good, but you simply do not have enough software packages to attract new clients in our line of business."

The following day, BBB's General Manager got a call from MMM's Chairman: "I would hate to interfere with BBB's internal management, but will you please give Fast Computers another chance? There must be a way for them to get this account."

BBB's General Manager's reply to that was simple: "Only if we can get the same solution as is available on Colossal equipment, within no more than two months delay, and provided that the software is developed by SW1 and that we get all the required modifications to the financial package for free."

When informed by BBB's General Manager of this conversation, Mr. Smith protested: "This is an infeasible solution! It is too expensive for Fast Computing, and I don't believe we will get our system within this time frame."

"Are you sure it cannot be done?" asked BBB's manager.

"Well—It's not impossible, but it sure requires an extraordinary effort," replied Mr. Smith.

"So, we must make sure that Fast Computing does this extraordinary effort."

"If that's what you want, we can put a clause in the agreement that we will not pay unless we get satisfactory results within a predescribed timeframe. However—I still recommend that we take Colossal's proposal," said Mr. Smith.

A couple of days later BBB signed an agreement with Fast Computing Computers. One of the preconditions for payments for both Hardware and Software was that BBB must receive a software solution that satisfied its needs, within the outlined timetable. The total cost of the project to BBB (Hardware, Marketing System, Financial Package and all the required modifications to the Financial Package) was to be $230,000.

F. The Detailed Requirements Specifications for the FGSM System

Fast Computing Computers engaged SW1 Software to develop both the Marketing and the Financial Systems. The Marketing system was to be developed according to BBB's requirements, and the Financial System was to be converted from the Colossal Computer version.

Since the project was to be carried out on Fast computers, SW1 decided not to allocate the same project manager that was proposed to manage the development on Colossal computers (Mr. Brown). A new project manager was recruited to SW1—Mr. Holmes. Mr. Smith was disappointed, since his decision to choose SW1 as software developer was based partly on Mr. Brown's capabilities and familiarity with marketing systems. But, SW1 insisted (they did not want to waste Mr. Brown's familiarity with Colossal equipment).

A Technical Committee was formed: Mr. Smith, Mr. Holmes and Mr. Watson, the representative of Fast Computing Computers. The Committee agreed upon the timetable outlined in Table VI for the development of the FGSM system. It was further agreed that, if feasible, the design and development would be divided into modules (increments), thus enabling starting 1986 with the new inventory system for FGSM (the beginning of the 10th month from the start of the project).

The analysis of FGSM's requirements specifications started off on the right foot. The Specifications Document was ready in time for the Design Review scheduled for month 4. The Design Review lasted two whole days: on top of the technical and supervisory committee members, additional representatives from FGSM's organization participated and contributed their comments and clarifications. However, Mr. Holmes expressed his concern regarding the difficulty in handling the complex form required for the Catalog Number. He complained about the lack of appropriate software tools on Fast Computers: his people were having difficulties in adjusting to the new development environment. They were very hopeful that the new version of operating system, due to be released the next month, would solve these problems. When the discussion narrowed down on the format of the sales reports, it turned out that there was no easy way to develop a report-writer similar to report-writers found in Colossal applications, and SW1 refused to commit to develop a report-writer within the existing budget for the FGSM system. They were willing to commit only to 4 predefined

TABLE VI
Original Timetable for the FGSM Project

Months	Subject
1 - 3	Detailed System Requirements Document for FGSM
4	Requirements Review
5 - 6	Detailed Design of FGSM
7 - 9	Programming
10	Acceptance Tests
11-12	New and Old Systems running concurrently

TABLE VII
Updated Timetable for the Incremental Development of the FGSM System

Months (From beginning of Project)	Subject
5 - 6	Module # 1 - Detailed Design
7 - 9	Module # 1 - Programming and Test
10	Module # 1 - Acceptance Tests
7 - 9	Module # 2 - Detailed Design
10 - 11	Module # 2 - Programming and Test
12	Module # 2 - Acceptance Tests
10	Module # 3 - Detailed Design
11 - 12	Module # 3 - Programming and Test
13	Module # 3 - Acceptance Test

sales reports. Mr. Smith would not agree, and the issue remained unsolved. A similar problem arose regarding the development of special reports to Department-Stores, and this issue remained unsolved as well.

The disagreements were outlined in the document that summarized the Design Review.

G. The Design and Development of the FGSM System

The real problems started at the detailed design phase. SW1's people discovered that the differences between the Fast computer and other computers were more than they had planned for. SW1 did not have people with previous experience in Fast computers, and so the original estimates, that were prepared for the Colossal computer, were not accurate. So as to enable BBB to start 1986 with a new Inventory system, the development was partitioned into 3 increments. The Inventory Module, the Operations Module, the Sales Reports Module. Mr. Holmes presented to Mr. Smith the updated timetable outlined in Table VII.

Mr. Smith pointed out that even though he understood the difficulties SW1 had run into, these problems should be addressed to Fast Computing, and they should be able to help SW1 to keep the original timetables. BBB was willing to accept only one month of delay in the delivery of the total system, and had agreed to break the system into increments so as to receive the first module sooner, not later, than the original timetable. After a couple of meetings between Mr. Smith, Mr. Holmes and Mr. Watson, the parties agreed that it was possible to improve the timetables by 6 weeks, delivering the first module to BBB before the end of the 8th month.

Meanwhile, the people of FGSM were full of enthusiasm towards the prospect of the forthcoming installation. Being aware that once the system was installed, it would be hard to request changes and improvements, they began asking for all sorts of small improvements and minor changes. Both Mr. Holmes and Mr. Smith were very satisfied with the users' attitude, and made every possible effort to please the people of FGSM, by incorporating most of these changes into the design.

H. The Installation of Module #1

Module #1 was installed in the middle of the 9th month—two weeks before the beginning of the New Year. Mr. Holmes, Mr. Smith, and the people of FGSM exerted enormous efforts to have the system up and running in time for the New Year. It turned out, however, that the

acceptance tests were not comprehensive enough, and after the system was already installed and running, many problems and bugs would still pop up during operations. The many minor design changes that had accumulated in the last 3 months did not help the SW1 programmers to correct these bugs and problems in time, and it was hard to tell which was the latest version of every program. Though the FGSM people were pleased with having an on-line system, they began to feel pretty uneasy about the system when it went through a whole series of corrections, errors, and crashes.

By early 1986, the development of Module #2 was almost complete, but the amount of man-months invested by SW1 had already exceeded the original estimates that were presented to Fast Computing. When SW1's General Manager discussed this problem with Mr. Watson, Mr. Watson explained that there was not much they could do for the time being: Fast Computing still had not received any money from BBB, and its own investments in support and management attention to this project were very high. Mr. Watson's recommendation was to wait for the successful installation of the 2nd and 3rd module before approaching BBB's higher management.

Mr. Holmes discussed these problems with Mr. Smith. Mr. Smith expressed his opinion, that Fast Computing had misled his management into believing that an impossible effort was possible, and that now Fast Computers were not doing their very best to keep their promise. Mr. Holmes remarked that his company did not like to be in such a situation either: lagging behind timetables and exceeding cost estimates. Both felt pretty bitter about the situation they found themselves in. Mr. Holmes, who was not party to the original cost estimates, began to feel that he was going to be blamed for something that was not of his doing, and secretly began looking for another job. One month later Mr. Holmes announced his decision to resign from SW1. One of SW1's senior Systems Analysts who participated in the project was made Project Manager.

I. The Installation of Modules #2 and #3

The installation of Module #2, though two months later than scheduled, was smoother than the installation of Module #1: the acceptance tests were ready, and were carried out properly. However the integration with Module #1 was not an easy task: it was hard to locate the latest versions of the software that were currently in use. Thus, the installation required a lot of time from SW1 programmers. It became evident that Module #3 would not be ready on time; in fact, the delay was estimated at 6 months.

All the partners to the effort were in bad shape. On one hand, the expenses of SW1 and Fast Computing exceeded even the worst projections, and it was obvious that both companies were going to lose money on this project. On the other hand, BBB was not getting the systems according to the promised timetables, and people started to compare the project to former unsuccessful attempts to introduce new systems to BBB.

The disagreements regarding the contents and form of the Sales Reports now surfaced. FGSM was not willing to settle for the 4 reports suggested by SW1. "The system is completely useless unless we get the reports we want," said Mr. Jones. "Not only that, but the Department Stores are threatening to close their account with us unless we automate the special reports they required, like all their other customers."

SW1 claimed that these reports were not part of their original agreement with Fast Computing. In fact, they blamed the Initial Survey for being vague on these points. "Heaven knows how much money we are going to lose in this project," said their General Manager to Mr. Smith, "Either BBB or Fast Computing must make it up to us."

J. The Financial Systems Design

The problems of the FGSM system were minor relative to the problems that arose during the analysis of BBB's requirements for the Financial Systems. Fast Computing's commitment was to deliver a complete system, tailored to BBB's requirements, and at the price of an "off-the-shelf" product. An initial survey of BBB's requirements, carried out by SW1's professionals, estimated the cost of this project at $150K.

The three General Managers of the three companies were summoned by Mr. Watson to a special meeting. BBB was asked to lower its level of requirements from the Financial System, so as to minimize the projected expenses. BBB's General Manager was furious: "We could have had a working system by now, had we purchased Colossal equipment," he exclaimed. "My people want nothing but the best. It took me a great effort to raise their expectations, and I am not going to let them down. Fast Computers knew exactly what they were up against when they signed the agreement with us. They cannot disregard their commitments now!"

"Our original estimates regarding the scope of the project were based upon the prices quoted by SW1 Software," replied Fast Computing's General Manager "We never intended to make money on this project, but we also never intended to lose that much."

"We based our estimates on BBB's initial survey," retorted SW1's General Manager. "As it turned out, there were too many TBD's, and the problem was that BBB's people wanted the maximum in every case, and would not settle for anything less. They kept coming with more requirements and endless modifications. One of my people has already resigned. We will not take the responsibilities that you two should have taken."

The meeting lasted for four hours, but the parties could not reach an agreement on how to proceed.

V. Case Study Analysis

Clearly, in this case, none of the parties came out a winner. BBB Industries ended up with unsatisfied users, mistrust in information systems, delays, partial systems, low morale, and major unresolved problems. Fast Computing ended up with significant unreimbursed expenditures, a poor reputation in the Sales Information Systems marketplace, and some useless partial products. SW1 also ended up with unreimbursed expenditures, and also a tarnished reputation in Sales Information Systems and poor prospects for future business in the Fast computer user community.

Below is an analysis of how these problems can be traced to lack of responsiveness to the Theory W fundamental principle (*make everyone a winner*) and to the two subsidiary principles (*identify and manage your risks*, and *plan the flight and fly the plan*). The analysis also indicates ways in which the principles could have been used to avoid the problems and to make the participants winners.

A. Make Everyone a Winner

The major source of difficulty was the win-lose contract established between BBB and Fast Computing: no payment unless BBB got everything it asked for, on schedule (Section IV-E). Fast Computing should have made a more thorough analysis of their overrun potential (risk assessment), and a thorough assessment of the benefits of entering the Sales Information System market. If the benefits were high enough, they should have approached MMM's Chairman to authorize their spending additional profit dollars to cover the added costs of software development. Otherwise, they should have dropped out. BBB's General Manager should have heeded Mr. Smith's cautions, and either required a more detailed and realistic plan and cost estimate from Fast Computers, or gone ahead with Colossal. BBB could have made a better win-win situation by not coupling system delivery and cutover to the New Year at a time when the likely development schedules were not well known.

Another major difficulty was SW1's use of Mr. Holmes. If SW1 seriously wanted to penetrate the Fast Computers market, they should have used Mr. Brown (Section IV-F). Holmes should not have accepted responsibility for making people winners until he understood the situation better (Section IV-F). SW1 management should have done more to make Holmes a winner: apprised him of the risks, done a better job of recognizing his good work in getting Module 1 running (Section IV-H), and of monitoring his frustration level and likelihood of leaving SW1 (Section IV-H).

As indicated in Section II, making people winners involves seeking out day-to-day conflicts and changing them into win–win situations. An excellent opportunity to do this occurred at the Design Review (Section IV-F), when SW1 balked at producing more than four sales reports, and at producing any Department Store reports at all. However, the conflict was not addressed, and the project continued to inflate users' expectations without any attempt to get SW1 to provide the promised capabilities.

A Theory W solution to this problem would consider the conditions necessary to make winners of each of the interested parties:

• *BBB and Its Customers:* Furnish the most important reports in the initial delivery, with the other reports as soon as possible thereafter.

• *SW1:* Provide a realistic schedule and budget for producing the desired reports (and other capabilities).

• *Fast Computing:* Develop a strong system with further sales potential, within a realistic and affordable budget and schedule.

Subsequently, a much more thorough analysis would be done to determine realistic budget and schedule estimates as functions of the amount of functionality to be delivered at each increment. These levels of functionality, their associated schedules, and Fast Computing's definition of "affordability" provide some degrees of freedom within which may be possible to define a win–win solution. If so, the project can go forward on such a basis. If not, the project should be disbanded: everyone would not be a winner, but they would minimize their losses.

A similar day-to-day problem which was deferred rather than addressed was the Fast Computing payments problem (Section IV-H). A related problem was the addition of changes and improvements to the system without changing the budget or schedule (Section IV-G). This usually leads to a lose–lose situation when the budget and schedule give out and all the original and new capabilities are not completed. A Theory W solution would involve prioritizing the proposed changes with respect to the original desired capabilities, reallocating the top priority capabilities to remain consistent with the three scheduled increments; then defining an Increment 4 and assuring the users that their remaining features would definitely be incorporated in Increment 4 if BBB's management agreed to provide the budget for them.

Some other problems were created by establishing unrealistic expectations. Issuing vague Requests for Proposal (Section IV-D) is a classical example: users tend to interpret the requirements expansively, while developers interpret them austerely, creating an inevitable lose–lose situation. The cost underestimate and specification interpretation for the Financial System is another example (Section IV-J).

On the other hand, some Theory W principles were followed well. The BBB General Manager's initial conversation with Mr. Smith (Section IV-B) established a realistic climate of expectations. The choice of FGSM as the initial system to implement (Section IV-C) was good, given that FGSM's managers were enthusiastic product champions. Had the other situations been handled in similar ways, with the participants trying harder to accommodate the others' interests, the project could have had a good chance of making the participants winners.

B. Plan the Flight and Fly the Plan

The project's planning was seriously deficient with respect to the elements of a Software Development Plan shown in Fig. 3. Some top-level milestones were established, but no attempt was made to identify dependencies and critical-path items. As discussed in the previous section, the imprecise allocation of responsibilities (e.g., SW1's responsibilities for sales reports) led to serious problems downstream. Several approach and resources problems (configuration management, verification, and validation planning, reviews, resource control) will be discussed further below.

But the major problem here was in putting the plans on a realistic basis. Budgets and schedules were determined more from optimistic target figures than from any rationale based on cost estimation techniques or task dependency analyses. Thus, although more elaborate approach plans would have avoided some problems, they would not have cured the budget-schedule-functionality mismatch problems.

For example, SW1's projected productivity for the Fast Computer development was considered to be equal to their productivity on Colossal Computer projects. Even a rough analysis using the COCOMO cost model [2] indicated a factor of 3 likely reduction in productivity due to personnel capability and experience, support system volatility, reduced tool support, and schedule compression.

1) Configuration Management: In this area, we can easily count the following shortcomings from the part of the project management:

• No change control system.

• No configuration management and control.

• No baselined master version of the specs or programs.

• No quality assurance (project standards, technical audits).

All those led to confusion, multiple bugs, problems in integration, installation, unmaintainability of the system, additional costs, and errors. There was no controlled mechanism for product changes, no track of product status, and no product integrity.

2) Verification and Validation Planning:

Most of the basic principles of V&V planning were not implemented in this case:

• No verification of the initial survey or the detailed design.

• Insufficient, late test plans (due to untimely, careless preparation).

• No acceptance criteria.

• No integration and test plans.

• Test phase and system acceptance combined.

As a result, the users got their system before it was completely verified, and were confronted with bugs and problems. The system's reliability was undermined, and the operations forced into a haphazard process.

3) Review Plans: No product review was held, only a requirements review. However, the problems that arose in the review were not assigned, nor tracked. It is no wonder that most problems were left unattended. The results were that on one hand there were missing capabilities, and on the other that some of the requirements were not really needed. The users were not committed to the final product. Attempts to correct the problems of missing capabilities at later stages were very expensive. A proper treatment of the problem at an earlier stage would have been less costly.

4) Resources, Status Monitoring, and Control: The main problems in the area were:
- Only high-level milestone charts were available.
- No work breakdown structure was prepared.
- No budget allocations were established.

Therefore, no cost versus progress monitoring and control was possible, and only when the overall budget was exceeded were the problems surfaced. Problems of insufficient personnel and inappropriate budget were discovered only when it was too late. In short, the visibility was poor, both at the overall progress level and the individual trouble-spot level.

C. Identify and Manage Your Risks

In some cases, the participants did a good job of identifying and managing risks. In particular, Mr. Smith's recommendation in Section IV-C to start and pursue an incremental development was very good. But there were many situations in which the lack of risk management caused serious problems.

Allowing two weeks to prepare the RFP (Section IV-D) reflects a serious neglect of risk management. BBB's General Manager should have done a risk analysis on hearing Mr. Smith assess Fast Computing's need for "extraordinary effort" to succeed (Section IV-E); in particular, to carry out an independent estimate of the development cost and schedule.

BBB also did not risk assessment by looking behind the interface between Fast Computing and SW1. They did not investigate whether SW1 would use Mr. Brown on their job, and were taken by surprise when SW1 assigned the unknown Mr. Holmes. Holmes himself did very little analysis of the risks he was getting into.

BBB did not assess the risk of the highly optimistic, highly overlapped incremental development schedule proposed by SW1 (Table V, Section IV-G). They were too preoccupied with establishing an ambitious schedule for Increment 1 to meet their New Year deadline. Such overlapping increments are major sources of risk, as changes in the earlier increments usually have serious ripple effects on the later increments under development.

In one case, risk avoidance caused an "everyone a winner" problem. Mr. Smith identified several risks due to lack of user management commitment, and addressed these by a strong effort to sell the users on the advantages of information technology. This backfired when the users compared their unrealistic expectations to the project's results. A preferred Theory W solution would be to couch user benefit projections more realistically in terms of expected near-term and long-term benefits, and to involve the users more closely in analyzing and preparing for the benefits.

VI. Conclusions

When applied to a project case study, a good management theory should be able to do two things:

1) To explain why the project encountered problems.

2) To prescribe improved approaches which would have avoided the problems.

Analysis of the BBB case study indicates that the Theory W fundamental principle (*Make everyone a winner*) and its two subsidiary principles (*Plan the flight and fly the plan; identify and manage your risks*) did a good job on both counts. The case study and the other examples provided earlier also indicate that Theory W does a reasonably good job in satisfying the management theory objectives of being simultaneously simple, general, and specific.

References

[1] K. Blanchard and S. Johnson, *The One Minute Manager*. Berkeley, CA: Berkeley Books, 1982.

[2] B. W. Boehm, *Software Engineering Economics*. Englewood Cliffs, NJ: Prentice-Hall, 1981.

[3] ——, "Seven basic principles of software engineering," *J. Syst. Software*, vol. 3, pp. 3-24, 1983.

[4] ——, "A spiral model of software development and enhancement," *Computer*, pp. 61-72, May 1988.

[5] ——, "Tutorial volume: Software risk management," IEEE Computer Society, 1989 (in publication).

[6] J. D. Couger and R. A. Zawacki, *Motivating and Managing Computer Personnel*. New York: Wiley, 1980.

[7] W. G. Dyer, *Team Building*. Reading, MA: Addison-Wesley, 1987.

[8] M. W. Evans, P. Piazza, and B. Dolkas, *Principles of Productive Software Management*. New York: Wiley, 1983.

[9] R. Fisher and W. Ury, *Getting to Yes*. Boston, MA: Houghton-Mifflin, 1981; also, Baltimore, MD: Penguin Books, 1983.

[10] S. W. Gellerman, *Motivation and Productivity*. New York: American Books, 1978.

[11] N. J. Kirchof and J. R. Adams, *Conflict Management for Project Managers*, Project Management Inst., Feb. 1986.

[12] H. Koontz and C. O'Donnell, *Principles of Management: An Analysis of Managerial Functions*, 5th ed. New York: McGraw-Hill, 1972.

[13] D. McGregor, *The Human Side of Enterprise*. New York: McGraw-Hill, 1960.

[14] P. W. Metzger, *Managing a Programming Project*, 2nd ed. Englewood Cliffs, NJ: Prentice-Hall, 1981.

[15] G. I. Nierenberg, *The Art of Negotiating*, Pocket Books, 1984.

[16] W. G. Ouchi, *Theory Z*. Reading, MA: Addison-Wesley, 1981; also Avon, 1981.

[17] T. J. Peters and R. H. Waterman, *In Search of Excellence*. New York: Harper & Row, 1982.

[18] D. J. Reifer, *Tutorial: Software Management*, 3rd ed., IEEE Catalog No. EHO 189-1, 1986.

[19] J. S. Rosenschein and M. R. Genesereth, "Deals among rational agents," in *Proc. IJCAI-85*, pp. 91-99.

[20] F. W. Taylor, *The Principles of Scientific Management*. New York: Harper and Brothers, 1911.

[21] R. H. Thayer, A. Pyster, and R. C. Wood, "The challenge of software engineering project management," *Computer*, pp. 51-59, Aug. 1980.

[22] R. E. Walton, *Managing Conflict*. Reading, MA: Addison-Wesley, 1987.

Barry W. Boehm (SM'84) received the B.A. degree in mathematics from Harvard University, Cambridge, MA, in 1957, and the M.A. and Ph.D. degrees in mathematics from the University of California, Los Angeles, in 1961 and 1964, respectively.

He is an Adjunct Professor of Computer Science at UCLA, and also Chief Scientist of TRW's Defense Systems Group. He has served as the manager of several TRW software development projects, and also directed the development of TRW's software management policies and standards.

Within the IEEE Computer Society, Dr. Boehm has served as Chairman of the Technical Committee on Software Engineering, a member of the Governing Board, and an editorial board member of *Computer*, *IEEE Software*, and IEEE TRANSACTIONS ON SOFTWARE ENGINEERING.

Rony Ross was born in Tel Aviv. She received the B.Sc. degree in mathematics from Tel Aviv University in 1972, the M.Sc. degree in computer science from the Weizmann Institute of Science, Rehovot, Israel, in 1976, and the M.B.A. degree in business administration from the Graduate School of Management, Tel Aviv University, in 1980.

From 1971 to 1980, she was a Teaching Assistant at Tel Aviv University Department of Computer Science. From 1975 to 1980, she was employed by Mini-Systems Computers Ltd. as a Systems Analyst and Real-Time Programmer, working for Sci-Tex Corp. From 1980 to 1983, she was Manager of Data Processing and Information Systems Department of Kitan Ltd. From 1983 to 1986, she was in charge of new business development for Contahal Ltd. Currently, she is studying toward the Ph.D. degree in the Department of Computer Science at the University of California, Los Angeles.

Chapter 4
Planning Fundamentals

But since the affairs of men rest still uncertain, let us reason with the worst that may befall.
— Shakespeare, *Julius Caesar*

Overview

Planning is the most basic function of management. It is deciding in advance what to do, how to do it, when to do it, and who is to do it. It is setting objectives, breaking the work into tasks, establishing schedules and budgets, allocating resources, setting standards, and selecting future courses of action. It bridges the gap from where we are to where we want to be. Plans tend to be strategic when done by upper management and tactical when done by middle management and line supervision. Both project and functional managers prepare plans. The six papers that follow focus attention on the concepts, tools, and techniques needed by management to generate plans.

This chapter was included to emphasize the importance of planning. There are many types of plans. Some are strategic, others are tactical. Some are financial, others are technical. There are marketing plans and support plans. There are development and maintenance plans. To communicate the differences, I have authored the first paper. It creates the hierarchy under which project plans operate. This hierarchy is summarized as follows:

- *Strategies.* Long-term plans aimed at achieving corporate goals.
- *Business plans.* Medium-term plans that formulate business objectives and ways of realizing them.
- *Operational plans.* Tactical plans aimed at keeping the business operating efficiently.
- *Project plans.* Tactical plans aimed at developing goods and services needed by marketing or operations.
- *Work plans.* Short-term plans that provide structure for smaller groups.

The second paper, by Wilson and Sifer, homes in on project planning approaches. It discusses work structuring, partitioning, and flow analysis in both a static and dynamic context. It introduces the reader to the concept of a *Work Breakdown Structure* (WBS). It then discusses how the WBS can be used as a foundation for project planning and control. It is a basic article that focuses on the fundamentals involved in planning.

The third paper, by Tausworthe, explains the WBS concepts in more depth. The WBS interrelates the work to be accomplished to the products that will be built. Work is arranged as family trees of subprojects, tasks, subtasks, and work packages. Products are decomposed using a delivery, software item, build, component, and unit hierarchy. The magic of the WBS is revealed by Tausworthe as he shows how to use the WBS to manage the delivery of "root" level milestones, those at the work package/unit level.

The fourth paper, by Boehm, is a classic that discusses the topic of software engineering economics. Being able to estimate resources (time, budget, staff, capital, etc.) accurately is a skill managers at every level of the organization need. The paper surveys the available methods of estimating and rates their relative strengths and weaknesses. It introduces the reader to cost-estimating models. Then it provides general background information on several models and discusses how they work. Details are then provided for the popular COCOMO software cost-estimation model, along with guidance in its use for the conduct of cost-benefit and risk analysis.

The fifth paper, by Albrecht and Gaffney, provides the reader with an alternative approach to software resource estimation. The authors show how to quantify the amount of effort needed, based on the amount of function to be delivered instead of the size of the application. The volume of function is determined using a specification-based metric called *function points*, which are computed as the weighted sum of the number of inputs, outputs, inquiries, interfaces, and master files in the application under study.

The sixth paper, by Ferens and Daly, describes traditional scheduling tools available to the software manager. These include Gantt charts, milestone charts, Swan charts, and PERT/CPM (Program Evaluation and Review Technique/Critical Path Method) networks. It then discusses the scheduling algorithms provided in several of the more popular software cost-estimating packages and assesses their accuracy using actual data and standard statistical techniques.

References

Those interested in software cost estimating and control are referred to the textbooks on the topic by Boehm and Putnam (References 2 and 22 in the Bibliography, respectively). As already stated, the *Standard for Software Project Management Plans* in Chapter 12 details the format and content of this important project planning document.

The Planning Hierarchy

Donald J. Reifer
Reifer Consultants, Inc.

This short article shows the interrelationships that exist between different types of plans via a hierarchy constructed for that purpose. First, each level of plan, its typical contents, and how it is used to structure future events are described. Then, criteria for determining the acceptability of each of the plans are provided. Finally, several recommendations aimed at improving planning in the future are offered.

Introduction

Plans are by their nature concerned with the future. They identify a goal and sketch out a course of action designed to meet it. They scope a solution and identify the what, who, when, where, and how. They bound risk and address contingencies. They provide a road map that can be used to structure the work and control its execution.

Generating plans is an integral part of every manager's job. Time, talent, and effort must be expended to sift through alternatives and select an option. Requirements need to be determined, operational concepts devised, players named, tasks defined, budgets developed, and schedules agreed upon. Constraints need to be crystallized, along with contingencies. Then the details need to be added, and those tasked with implementation have to be sold on the plan's provisions. As such, a lot of work needs to be completed before a plan comes out the door.

If every manager does planning, why do we need a planning hierarchy? The answer is simple. There are so many different plans being developed that sometimes we get confused as to where our plan fits into the scheme of things. A hierarchical framework is required to define the relationship between plans.

Layered planning hierarchy

The three-layered planning hierarchy illustrated in Figure 1 provides us with the framework we need to reduce confusion over plan interrelationships. The structure was selected to be compatible with the timing considerations of most corporate planning horizons. It uses the software engineering principle of separation of concerns to clearly organize plans along temporal lines.

The top layer of the hierarchy is strategic in nature and looks three to eight years into the future. These plans are typically drafted by top executives and their staffs. As Figure 2 illustrates, plans in this layer focus on what needs to be done to meet the long-term goals of the organization. Such plans could develop market penetration or capital acquisition strategies.

The middle layer contains tactical plans that look one to three years into the future. These plans are aimed at developing what is needed to implement the longer range business strategies defined by the top level of the hierarchy. These plans are typically generated by middle management. They tend to be business-based and operationally oriented. They may define specific projects or financing approaches.

The bottom layer focuses on mechanization plans that are implemented in the near term (less than a year). These plans are typically produced by first-line supervisors to structure the work of teams. These plans tend to be task oriented. They may include project plans when the projects are small.

Acceptability criteria

The criteria we suggest that you use to assess the acceptability of plans are as follows:

- *Completeness.* All of the parts of the plan should be present and each of the parts should be fully developed.
- *Conciseness.* The plan should not have excessive information. Excessive verbosity and repetition should be avoided.
- *Consistency.* The plan should be internally consistent in that it contains uniform notation, terminology, and symbology.
- *Feasibility.* The plan must be technically and economically feasible. In other words, it must be sound and make business sense to pursue the course of action it recommends.
- *Traceability to requirements.* The plan must be able to accomplish its goals quickly and efficiently within its established scope and subject to any constraints listed.

The checklists illustrated in Figure 3 have been developed using these criteria to assess the acceptability of software plans at each level of our planning hierarchy. They are not intended to be used like cookbooks. Rather, they are aimed at reminding you of things that you should not overlook when you develop a plan. The checklists are presented as compendiums of questions. Answers to these questions provide you with insight into planning risks.

Checklists are provided in question and answer form. If the answer to the question posed is "yes," place a check in the corresponding box. If you don't know the answer, leave the box blank and fill it in at a later time. Finally, cross out any questions that you believe are not applicable. After you have completed the checklist, review those items with no check mark to determine what action, if any, you should take to remedy noted discrepancies.

Summary, conclusions, and recommendations for improvement

This article was written to illustrate the interrelationships that exist between plans via a layered hierarchy constructed for that purpose. Three levels of plans have been described, along with criteria for determining their acceptability. Checklists have been provided which relate to these evaluation criteria.

To improve the planning process, we recommend the following:

- Use the software engineering principle of separation of concerns to clearly organize plans along strategic, tactical, and mechanization lines. This lets you focus on the timing associated with goal achievement.
- Prepare plans with the interrelationships noted between strategy, tactics, and mechanization layers in mind. In other words, plans should not be written to stand alone. They should be prepared with overall business strategies and tactics in mind.
- Take advantage of the concept of strategy deployment in the planning process. This lets you move from the strategy to mechanization layer of the hierarchy in a systematic manner.
- Write plans to be read. More effort should be expended to make sure that plans are concise, readable, and focused.

I would like to thank the IEEE for encouraging me to write this brief article. Hopefully, it makes it easy for the reader to clearly interrelate plans that have different timetables.

Bibliography

1. Peter F. Drucker, *Management: Tasks, Responsibilities and Practices,* Harper and Row, 1974.

2. Andrew S. Grove, *High Output Management,* Random House, 1983.

3. Donald J. Reifer, "Software Checklists," Tech. Report RCI-TR-017 (Revision 1), Reifer Consultants, Inc., Torrance, Calif., 1988.

4. George A. Steiner, *Top Management Planning,* MacMillan Publishing Co., 1969.

Figure 1: The Layered Planning Hierarchy

Strategy Layer
Strategies → Long-term plans aimed at achieving corporate goals

Tactics Layer
Business plans → Medium-term plans that formulate business objectives and ways of realizing them

Operational plans → Tactical plans aimed at keeping the business operating efficiently

Project plans → Intermediate plans aimed at creating goods and services needed by marketing or operations

Mechanization Layer
Work plans → Short-term plans that provide structure for smaller groups

Figure 2: Types of Plans

Strategic	Tactical	Mechanization
Marketing plan	Sales plan	Task plan
Acquisition plan	Development plan	Purchasing plan
Capital plan	Financial plan	Schedule/budget
Staffing plan (3-8 years)	Staffing plan (1-3 years)	Staffing plan (1-12 months)
New product introduction plan	Product line/project plan	Test and evaluation plan
Total quality management plan	Institutional management plans (CM, PM, QM, etc.)	Risk management plan

Plans revolve around an infrastructure that defines the processes, procedures, and standards employed by the firm.

Figure 3: Software Planning Checklist

General Questions

[ ]   Are your plans concise, consistent, complete, and understandable?

[ ]   Have you involved all those parties affected by the plan in the planning process?

[ ]   Are the goals of the plan specific and has the scope been limited?

[ ]   Do your plans hold people/organizations accountable for results?

[ ]   Have you ensured that you have not overplanned or underplanned?

[ ]   Are your plans periodically updated and treated as living documents?

[ ]   Have you critically examined the feasibility of your plans prior to their approval?

Strategic Plans

[ ]   Has the strategy been described and is the timetable associated with realizing it realistic?

[ ]   Has the vision behind the strategy been explained?

[ ]   Has the context of the plan been delineated, along with any constraints that potentially could limit goal achievement?

[ ]   Have you ensured that the goals established are not too aggressive (or not aggressive enough)?

[ ]   Is the technology needed to achieve the goals mature and stable?

[ ]   Have all of the available options been thoroughly examined in light of the economic, political, and business environment?

[ ] Has an operational concept been developed, along with a means to deploy the strategy?

[ ] Is the organization ready for the strategy?

[ ] Do you have the right people and organizations in place to deploy the strategy? If not, does the plan address how to acquire them?

[ ] Do your software policies and practices support the strategy? If not, does your plan consider whether and how to modify them?

[ ] Is additional capitalization (facilities, workstations, equipment, tools, etc.) needed to deploy the strategy?

[ ] Have you benchmarked your software capacity/capabilities to establish a baseline for measuring improvement?

[ ] Are the schedules and budgets in the plan reasonable and achievable?

Tactical Plans

[ ] Does the plan focus on near-term achievement of goals?

[ ] Does the plan comply with existing software policies and practices? If not, why not? Has a waiver been solicited?

[ ] Does the plan take advantage of the process improvement activities that are under way?

[ ] Are there multiyear performance goals for affected organizations and have they been empowered to achieve them?

[ ] Has the work been broken down using a work breakdown structure (WBS)?

[ ] Have all receivables, deliverables, and inheritables been defined for each WBS task?

[ ] Are the budgets and schedules in the plan reasonable and achievable?

[ ] Have the budgets and schedules been related to WBS tasks?

[ ] Is there a schedule network in the plan and has the critical path through it been identified?

[ ] Does the budgetary system encompass multiple-year time periods?

[ ] Are risks identified, analyzed, and mitigated in the plan?

[ ] Are staffing forecasts made and actions initiated to see that places are filled by qualified candidates?

[ ] Are there contingency plans should key staff not be made available when needed?

[ ] Is there a training plan and does it address the development of job-related skills, knowledge, and abilities?

[ ] Is there a release plan to enhance and improve current products and product lines?

[ ] Is there a plan to cement strategic alliances that have already been initiated with partners and subcontractors?

[ ] Does the plan address interfaces with nonsoftware organizations?

[ ] Is there a well-defined process in use and has it been supplemented with standards and procedures for configuration, financial, project, and quality management that all of your organizations and projects use in the performance of their jobs?

[ ]   Are the R&D issues being worked on in parallel with the product development activities?

Mechanization Plans

[ ]   Have the appropriate task-level plans been prepared?

[ ]   Are these plans consistent with the firm's established process and management infrastructure?

[ ]   Has the software methodology been defined in detail, along with the associated delivery milestones?

[ ]   Are the milestones/budgets established within these plans reasonable in that they represent aggressive, but realizable objectives?

[ ]   Do the plans identify necessary technical and management controls and have they been made as quantifiable as possible?

[ ]   Have procedures for configuration management and quality assurance been issued and are they responsive to the needs of the project?

[ ]   Have the staffing requirements been identified within the plans, along with sources and key personnel lists?

[ ]   Have contingency plans been made to handle the "what-if" situations?

[ ]   Are classical project management techniques (work breakdown structure, Gantt charts, PERT/CPM, etc.) used to track and assess performance and provide visibility into progress?

[ ]   Are the interface agreements essential for success spelled out and have commitments been made to realize them?

[ ]   Are the software people involved held accountable via the plan for their work products?

[ ]   Are the metrics being used compatible with those used at the corporate level?

[ ]   Are peer reviews and participatory approaches to software management employed?

[ ]   Does your planning process allow your people to set challenging, but realizable goals that are compatible with those of your organization?

[ ]   Does your planning process allow people to take pride in their work and in goal achievement?

[ ]   Does your planning process encourage your people to do software jobs composed of several work elements, each of which requires the use of a number of different skills?

[ ]   Does your planning process encourage your people to complete highly visible pieces of work which they can take pride in and can accomplish from beginning to end?

Structured planning — project views

by David N. Wilson and Mark J. Sifer

The quality of software products may be improved by enhancing the performance of any of the varied activities associated with the production of the software. One such activity is 'project planning'. Project planning may be a small part of the total project effort, but will have a large effect on all activities in the project and, therefore, a major impact on the final software quality. Thus the cost benefits that can be expected from effective project planning are substantial. This paper discusses 'structured planning' — the integration of many aspects of planning, such as work breakdown, scheduling, resource allocation and change/defect tracking, into a single project model, which could be the basis of a structured planning software tool.

1 Introduction

Modern software development is characterised by two conflicting factors: first, an increase in the size and complexity of the systems being developed, and, secondly, a need for high-quality software (i.e. software with minimum defects). The controls necessary to satisfy the need for quality, while developing systems which are tending to become larger and more complex, can be provided by improved project planning tools and techniques.

Existing methods of project planning are all based on one approach. In this approach, the project tasks are successively partitioned, and then the dependencies between subtasks are identified, producing a quantified network of tasks. This paper introduces structured planning, a method of combining these two activities. Tasks and dependencies are described by levelled work flow diagrams, where the 'flows' between tasks are the task inputs and the task deliverables. These work flow diagrams are similar to the data flow diagrams of structured analysis, with tasks replacing processes and task inputs and task deliverables (work flows) replacing data flows. Just as data types are described in a data dictionary, work flows can be described in a work flow dictionary, which is built by partitioning the work flows associated with each high-level task, producing work flow sets to be associated with lower-level tasks.

Structured planning will produce a balanced partitioning of tasks and deliverables and will allow the tasks and their dependencies to be viewed at varying levels of detail. The method will describe a project model which enables:

- project estimates (such as costs, resources etc.) to be tracked
- changes and defects to be supervised
- scheduling/rescheduling to be performed.

The project model will be the standard description of any project, with collections of past project models forming an accessible historical database.

2 The traditional work breakdown structure

Project planning is traditionally approached in a sequence of steps:

- partitioning the project into tasks
- quantifying these tasks
- identifying the dependencies between tasks
- preparing a preliminary schedule
- balancing resources.

Partitioning, as the initial stage, is the most critical step in planning and is applied successively to produce a tree of manageable subtasks; this tree, or work breakdown structure (Ref. 1), may be visualised as growing downwards from the root node, which represents the project (Ref. 2). The first level shows the initial partitioning of the project which, in the software engineering field, represents the traditional life cycle development phases : requirements definition, the design phases, program and procedure development, testing and implementation. The second level represents the standard tasks that have been identified for each of these phases (Ref. 3); standard tasks are common for mos projects and enable a common language to be used for communication between the project team, the users or the client and management. Standard tasks are often sizable portions of work and are successively partitioned into a third level of work packages. Work packages are subtasks which can be allocated to individuals or small teams. The partitioning of the standard tasks is project-specific and will vary greatly from project to project.

The reasons for partitioning a project to the level of work packages are as follows:

- Short-term, well defined goals provide motivation for

professional project staff, as close supervision is not required (Refs. 4 and 5).

● Estimation of duration and cost tends to be more accurate for small tasks than for large tasks; thus, long term, the variance in meeting the deadline of a project becomes smaller as the number of estimated detailed tasks becomes larger (Ref. 3).

● A good measure of project progress is the number of work packages completed, each work package being measured as either 100% complete or 0% complete; large tasks require an estimate of the percentage of required work to completion and such estimates tend to be inherently unreliable (Ref. 6).

The fully detailed work breakdown structure (WBS) is produced as the project progresses. At the beginning of the project only the first development phase may be planned to the work package level. As the detailed tasks of later phases will be to some extent determined by the results of the earlier stages, later phases may initially be detailed only to the standard task level. The work packages are commonly defined for a three- to six-month window in advance of the current date.

Thus we have seen that, through the WBS, a project is partitioned into manageable pieces of work by the delineation of tasks/subtasks/activities/work packages. Traditional project management tools utilise the concept of network analysis (Refs. 7 – 11) at the work package level. In contrast, structured planning applies the techniques of network analysis at all task levels.

3 Deliverables and dependencies

The project's product quality is measured by how closely the product matches the original specification; this can be difficult to gauge for all but the smallest projects. After the project is partitioned into a collection of tasks, the quality of the product is ensured when the output of each task matches the specification of that task and the integrated function of all the tasks matches the specified overall function of the project. Ensuring a match between the output of a task and its specification is less difficult than ensuring this match for the whole project, because the requirements of a task are smaller; ensuring this match for a project is a problem of finding an appropriate work breakdown for the project.

The product of a project is defined by the statement of project deliverables. Only after all the project deliverables are produced is the project considered to be finished. As described in Section 2, the project is partitioned successively to the level of work packages. Each work package produces deliverables and is to be defined by those deliverables; the goal for the person assigned to the work package is to produce its deliverables. As a deliverable has either been produced or has not been produced, the completion criteria for a work package are well defined: the work package is considered complete when all its deliverables have been produced (i.e. when the last deliverable for that task is finished). This is the concept of the binary deliverable (Ref. 12).

Tasks can, then, be defined by the deliverables produced rather than by a functional description in terms of a work process. The problem of defining the task process is changed to the problem of defining the task deliverables; the task process becomes the application of people skills to the task inputs (deliverables of a previous task) to produce the task deliverables. Task deliverables can be difficult to define; at higher levels of the WBS the standard phases and standard tasks will have standard deliverables, but work packages may

have to be re-partitioned until well defined deliverables are identified. Once this is achieved, communication between the project team and management is improved, as visible, well defined deliverables appear during the project rather than only on completion (Ref. 13).

When every task in a project has well defined inputs and deliverables, the dependencies between tasks can be identified. With the exception of the project inputs and deliverables (some tasks will have inputs which are sourced from outside the project and some tasks produce deliverables which are used outside the project), the deliverable produced by one task will become the input of another task. A task input is either a project input or a deliverable produced by another task. Deliverables become a means of identifying the dependencies between tasks (Refs. 14 and 15). Predecessor tasks produce the deliverables which input to a task, and successor tasks accept as input the deliverables which a task produces. Dependencies of a task are found by identifying the predecessor and successor tasks.

4 Work flow diagrams and work flow systems

As described, a project can be partitioned into a series of high-level tasks (parent tasks); these high-level tasks are further partitioned into a collection of low-level tasks (child

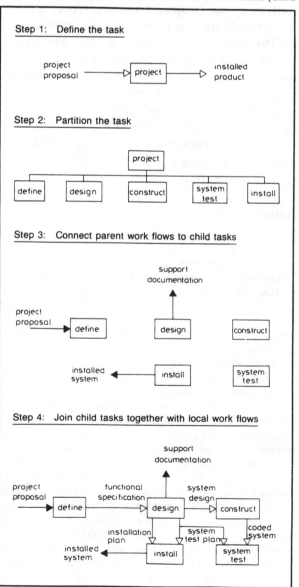

Fig. 1 Building a work flow diagram

tasks), where all the work associated with a task is performed in the child tasks. This creates the WBS for the project. Each task is defined in terms of its deliverables, and the dependencies between tasks are identified by the relationships between the deliverables (the deliverable of one task being the input to another). This model is analogous to the data flow diagrams (DFDs) of structured analysis (Refs. 16 and 17); the tasks replace processes and the deliverables replace the data flows.

Structured planning describes work flow diagrams (WFDs), which are a means of graphically representing groups of tasks using a standard notation. The partitioning of a task (the parent) produces a set of child tasks; this set of tasks with a common parent will be called a 'local task set'. Each task in the local task set will have input and output work flows which connect to other local tasks or to tasks outside the local task set (external tasks). The task outputs are called deliverables; the deliverable of a task becomes an input to another task and/or a deliverable of the project. Joining all the local work flow connections creates a directed network of tasks, the WFD. The input and deliverable work flows of the parent task will be the external input and deliverable work flows for the WFD being created.

Creating a WFD starts from a single task description. This task is partitioned into child tasks; the external work flows

are associated with the relevant child tasks and the local work flows are added (Fig. 1). During this process, a work flow of the parent may be represented by several work flows to/from separate child tasks; when a task is partitioned into a local task set, the inputs and deliverables of the parent task may also be partitioned within the local task set. Input work flows of the parent may be shared among several child tasks or be divided into several separate inputs to individual child tasks; the deliverables of a parent task may be represented by the deliverables of individual child tasks or by several composite deliverables of several child tasks (Fig. 2). These relationships are described in the work flow dictionary (Fig. 2).

A work flow system (WFS) is the collection WFDs which describe an entire project and the dependencies between all levels of tasks in the project (Fig. 3). The parent task (WFD 0) is partitioned into a local task set (WFD 1); tasks 1, 3 and 5 are then further partitioned into a group of local task sets at a lower level (WFDs 2, 3 and 4, respectively). This partitioning of tasks continues until all tasks are reduced to the level of work packages. External work flows (solid black arrows) are shown with a suffix to denote the composite work flows of a parent work flow which has been divided; the relationships between work flows are described in the work flow dictionary (Fig. 4). To allow compact graphical

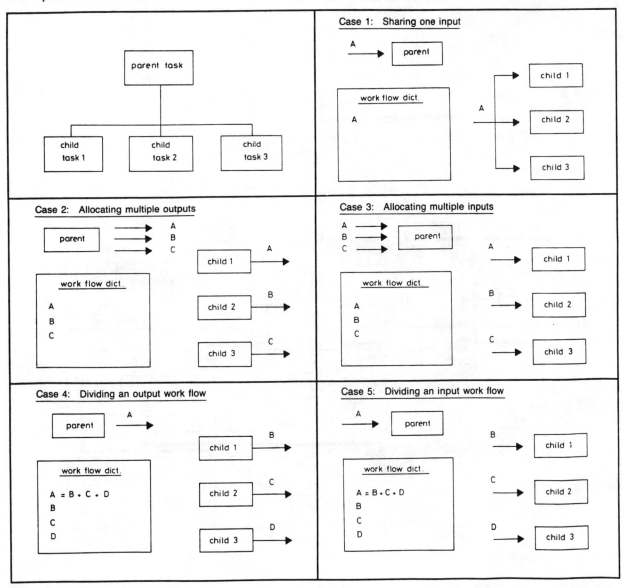

Fig. 2   Partitioning of task work flows

189

representation, the WFS can be presented as a tree of relationships, called the WBS (Fig. 5); the hierarcnical numbering sytem allows easy identification of equivalent tasks. There are no hard and fast rules as to the level to which partitioning should continue; however, as a guideline, work packages should represent one or two weeks of effort (Ref. 3) and should have obvious input and output deliverables (Ref. 12).

5 Viewing a work breakdown structure

Viewing is the presentation or display of a WFS. A view is defined by a subtree of the WFS and the set of tasks which collectively represent the activity described by the WFS; the WFS is identified by the parent task. Four ways of viewing a project structure will be described: a baseline view, a summary view, a context view and a partial view.

5.1 The baseline view of a project

Structured planning enables a project to be described by a collection of WFDs. Each diagram describes a portion of the work to be done and is also related to other diagrams via parent-child relationships; thus a project is represented by progressive levels of diagrams. The baseline view presents a network of tasks at the lowest level (i.e. work packages), showing their dependencies on other tasks (both local and external) at this lowest level. This view is equivalent to that presented by traditional project planning methods. The baseline view is created by identifying those tasks which do not have child WFDs, called leaf tasks (shaded boxes in Fig. 5), and producing a WFS showing only such leaf tasks and their dependencies.

5.2 The summary view of a project

The baseline view can become unmanageable as even a medium-sized project will contain hundreds of work packages. The project model needs to be condensed or summarised to provide a workable view of the project. The aim is to remove child tasks, according to some algorithm, to produce a WFS showing only high-level parent tasks (Fig. 6 shows such a WFS for the summarised WBS presented in Fig. 5). Two procedures are described for summarising the

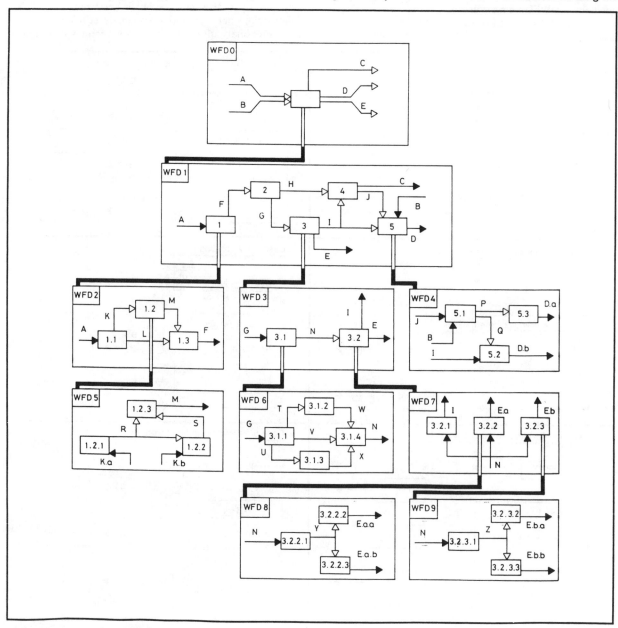

Fig. 3   A tree of work flow diagrams which constitute a work flow system

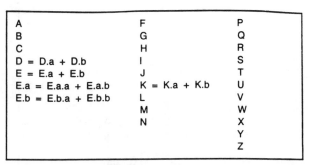

```
A               F               P
B               G               Q
C               H               R
D = D.a + D.b   I               S
E = E.a + E.b   J               T
E.a = E.a.a + E.a.b   K = K.a + K.b   U
E.b = E.b.a + E.b.b   L               V
                M               W
                N               X
                                Y
                                Z
```

Fig. 4   Work flow dictionary

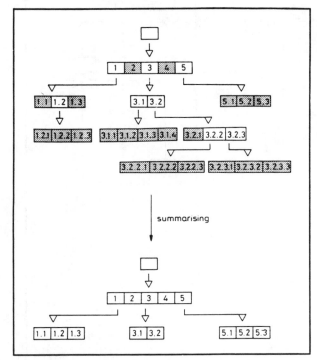

Fig. 5   Work breakdown structures

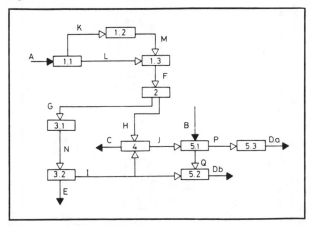

Fig. 6   A summarised view of a work flow system

project model: value trimming and proportional depth reduction:

●   *Summarising by value trimming:* The project planner assigns a value (in accordance with the cost, resource and/or duration of the task) to each leaf task; the value of each non-leaf task is calculated as:

$$\text{Value (N)} = \sum \text{Value (N}_{\text{child}})$$

where N is a task or WFD within the WFS. All leaf networks with the lowest value are progressively removed until the desired level of summarisation is achieved.

●   *Summarising by proportional depth reduction:* The progressive levels of diagrams (or depth of the WFD) describing a project will vary across the project model; summarising by this method reduces the model in proportion to the depth of a particular part. The algorithm for proportional depth reduction is:

$$\text{Depth Ratio (N)} = (L - D + 1)/L$$

where N is a task or WFD within the WFS, D is the current depth of N in the WFS, and L is the length of the longest path through N. The network with the smallest depth ratio is trimmed from the WFS; if there are several WFDs with the same value, the one with the greatest value L is trimmed.

5.3   The context view of a project

When working with a WFS, interest is often focused on a particular task and how that task fits into the context of the whole project; the context of a task is the WFD to which the task belongs, together with all the ancestor WFDs. This context will form a complete view of the project, with the greatest detail focused on a particular task. The WFS is expanded to show only child tasks for the network containing the task of interest; other networks are represented only by a high-level parent.

5.4   The partial view of a project

The views described above have involved merging WFDs in the WFS together, so producing a view of the entire project. The domain of interest in a WFS is not always the whole project, but often only a portion of it (a particular phase, for example). A partial view is a subtree of the WFS, where the root task of the subtree is any non-leaf task within the project (in contrast, the root task of other views is the project parent of the entire WFS).

6   Example of structured planning

The structured planning methodology, described above, is illustrated by the example of a project to build a house (Fig. 7). A specific project view, the context view of task 4 : 'fitting out', is shown in Fig. 8.

7   Dynamic project views

During the progress of the project, the state of any particular task will vary as a function of time: a task may be complete, in progress, or yet to start at any point in time. A leaf task is straightforward and is considered to be in progress once all the inputs are available and is considered to be complete once all its deliverables have been produced. A non-leaf task is more complex, because the activity of all the related child tasks is summarised by the non-leaf task. A non-leaf task is considered to be in progress when any of its child tasks are in progress and is considered to be complete only when all its child tasks are complete.

Each leaf task in a WFS is given a duration value (the time required to complete the leaf task once all task inputs are available) by the project planner. To calculate the duration of a non-leaf task, a baseline view of the related child tasks is created and is used as a scheduling network from which the critical path can be calculated; the value of the critical path becomes the duration of the non-leaf task. The model can be analysed to compare task states (determined by the availability of inputs and the completion of deliverables) with the actual and expected duration of individual tasks or the project to date.

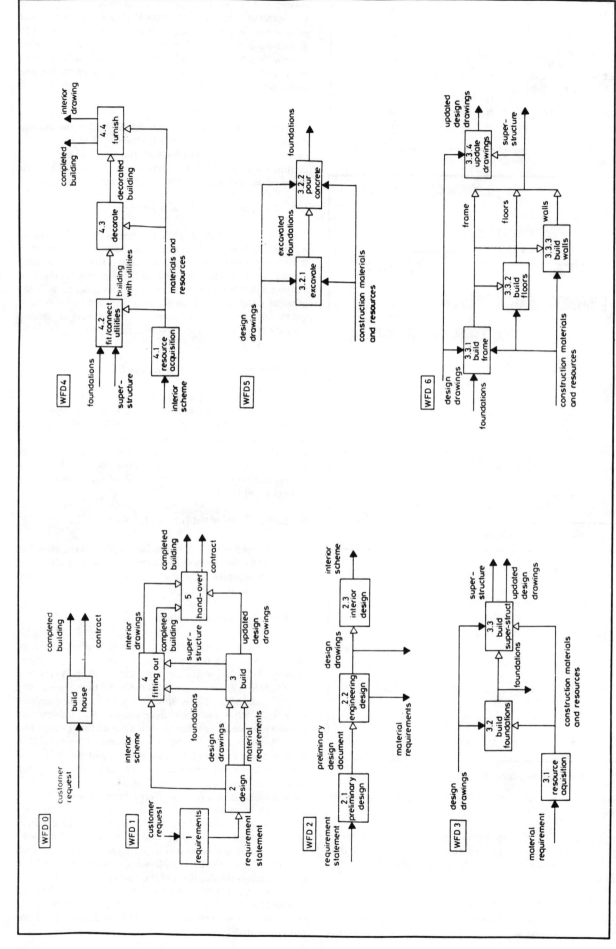

Fig. 7 Example of a work flow system

192

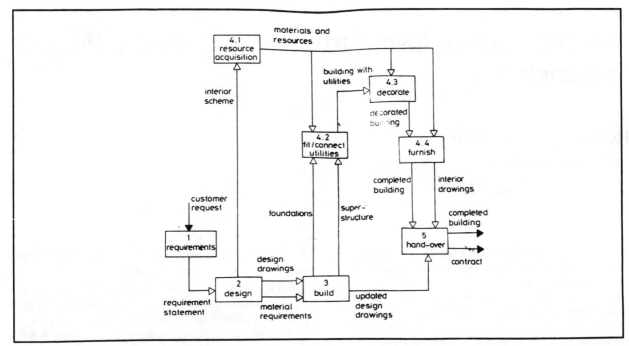

Fig. 8 Example of a context view of 'fitting out' task

8 Conclusion

The parallels between project planning techniques and DFDs are well documented (Ref. 18) but have not been formally developed; this paper describes a methodology and technique for project management based on the ideas of structured analysis. The methodology defines a model which could be the basis of an automated project management tool. This tool could allow the project to be viewed in a variety of ways (the baseline view, the summary view, the context view and the partial view), rather than only at the baseline level as with traditional project management techniques.

The initial aim of the WBS is to create a baseline task list for a project; however, the WBS can be used to manipulate a variety of project- or task-related information. Typically, the model could contain details of estimated/actual resource usage, estimated/actual costs, duration, task status and change/defect status. The project planner assigns a value to each leaf task; the value of non-leaf tasks is calculated according to a specific algorithm (summation for costs, critical path method for durations etc.).

9 Acknowledgments

The authors wish to acknowledge the support for this work by Stowe Computing Australia and the Department of Industry and Commerce under the Teaching Companies Scheme of the Federal Government of Australia. The authors also wish to thank Dr. John Debenham, David Smiley and Andrew Stark for their helpful comments on the initial draft and the two anonymous referees for their constructive comments in improving this paper.

10 References

1 HAJEK, V. G.: 'Management of engineering projects' (McGraw-Hill, 1977)
2 MORREALE, R.: 'Project planning and control', *Data Processing*, 1985, **27**, (3), pp. 19–21
3 TAUSWORTHE, R. C.: 'The work breakdown structure in software project management', *Journal of Systems & Software*, 1980, 1, pp. 181–186
4 HACKMAN, J. R., OLDAM, G., JANSON, R., and PURDY, K.: 'A new strategy for job enrichment', *California Management Review*, **17**, (4), pp. 57–71
5 DESSLER, G.: 'Management fundamentals: modern principles and practices' (Reston, 1979) (Second Edition), chap. 16
6 BURRILL, C. W., and ELLSWORTH, L. W.: 'Modern project management: foundations for quality and productivity' (Burrill-Ellsworth Associates, 1980), pp. 137–139
7 LEVY, F. K., THOMPSON, G. L., and WEIST, J. D.: 'The ABCs of the critical path method', *Harvard Business Review*, 1963, Sept./Oct.
8 WOOLDRIDGE, S.: 'Project management in data processing' (Petrocelli/Charter, 1976)
9 LOCK, D.: 'Project management' (Gower, 1984)
10 O'BRIEN, J. J.: 'Project management: an overview', in ADAMS, J. R., and KIRCHOF, N. (Ed.): 'A decade of project management' (Drexel Hill: Project Management Institute, 1981)
11 MATTHEWS, M. D.: 'Networking as a tool and methodology for information management: outlines of a discipline'. Proceedings of Annual Seminar/Symposium of the Project Management Institute, 1984
12 De MARCO, T.: 'Controlling software project: management, measurement and estimation' (Yourdon Press, 1982)
13 BRYAN, W., and SIEGEL, S.: 'Making software visible, operational and maintainable in a small project environment', *IEEE Transactions on Software Engineering*, 1984, **SE-10**, (1), pp. 59–67
14 BERSOFF, E. H.: 'Elements of software configuration management', *IEEE Transactions on Software Engineering*, 1984, **SE-10**, (1), pp. 79–87
15 COOPER, J.: 'Software development management planning', *IEEE Transactions on Software Engineering*, 1984, **SE-10**, (1), pp. 22–26
16 De MARCO, T.: 'Structured analysis and systems specification' (Yourdon Press, 1978)
17 YOURDON, E., and CONSTANTINE, L.: 'Structured design' (Yourdon Press, 1978)
18 CARTER, G. D., CLARE, C. P., and THOROGOOD, C. J.: 'Engineering project management techniques and their application to computer projects', *Software Engineering Journal*, 1987, **2**, (1), pp. 15–20

D. N. Wilson is with the School of Computing Sciences, University of Technology, Sydney, PO Box 123, Broadway, NSW 2007, Australia, and M. J. Sifer is with Computer Sciences of Australia, 460 Pacific Highway, St. Leonards, NSW 2065, Australia.

The Work Breakdown Structure in Software Project Management*

Robert C. Tausworthe

Jet Propulsion Laboratory

The work breakdown structure (WBS) is a vehicle for breaking an engineering project down into subproject, tasks, subtasks, work packages, and so on. It is an important planning tool which links objectives with resources and activities in a logical framework. It becomes an important status monitor during the actual implementation as the completions of subtasks are measured against the project plan. Whereas the WBS has been widely used in many other engineering applications, it has seemingly only rarely been formally applied to software projects, for various reasons. Recent successes with software project WBSs, however, have clearly indicated that the technique can be applied and have shown the benefits of such a tool in management of these projects.

This paper advocates and summarizes the use of the WBS in software implementation projects. It also identifies some of the problems people have had generating software WBSs, and the need for standard checklists of items to be included.

INTRODUCTION

If one were to be given the task of writing a program, such as that structurally illustrated in Figure 1, in which the target language instruction set was not intended to be executed by some dumb computer, but, instead, by intelligent human beings, then one might be thought to have an easier job than colleagues who write their programs for machines. However, a little reflection will show that this job is much more difficult

for a number of reasons, among which are ambiguities in the English language and a multitude of human factors [1]. However, such a program, often named the PLAN (Figure 2), is an essential part of almost every industrial project slated for success.

One of the difficulties in writing this program is the supplying of enough detail so as to be executable without allowing ambiguity. Another is getting the right controls into the program so that the programees perform as stated in the PLAN. Still another is making the PLAN complete, with all contingencies covered and a proper response to each supplied. One final problem of note here is making the plan bug-free, or reliable, so that once execution starts, if everything proceeds according to the PLAN, there is no need to deviate.

Programmers well-schooled in modern techniques [2] would approach the writing of this PLAN in a structured way, using top–down design methodology, modular development, stepwise refinement, hierarchic layering of detail, structurally sound constructions, and semantically definite documentation. Such an approach would tend to bring a measure of organization to the PLAN, understandability to its documentation, and reliability to its execution. If created in this way, the resulting format of the PLAN work tasks would have the attributes of what is known in the engineering industry as a "work breakdown structure" [3], structurally illustrated in Figure 3.

The work breakdown structure (WBS) is an enumeration of all work activities in hierarchic refinements of detail, which organizes work to be done into short, manageable tasks with quantifiable inputs, outputs, schedules, and assigned responsibilities. It may be used for project budgeting of time and resources down to the individual task level, and, later, as a basis for progress reporting relative to meaningful management milestones. A software management plan based

*The work reported in this paper was carried out at the Jet Propulsion Laboratory of the California Institute of Technology under contract NAS 7-100, sponsored by the National Aeronautics and Space Administration.

Address correspondence to Robert C. Tausworthe. Jet Propulsion Laboratory. 4800 Oak Grove Drive. Pasadena. California 91103.

The Journal of Systems and Software 1, 181–186 (1980)

© Elsevier North Holland. Inc.. 1980

0164-1212/80/030181-06$02.25

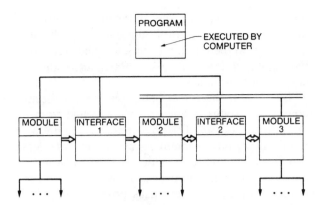

Figure 1. The modular hierarchy of a program.

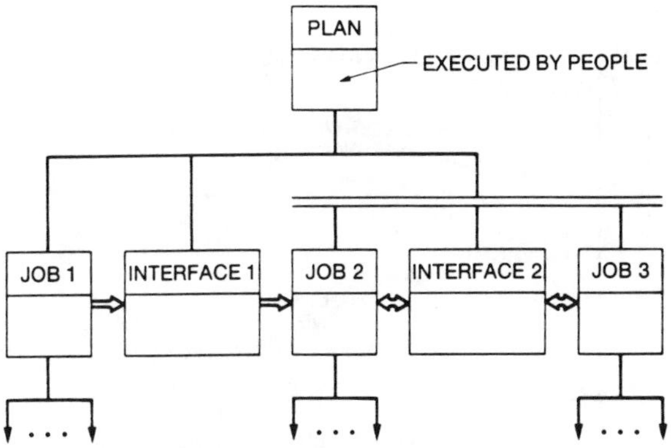

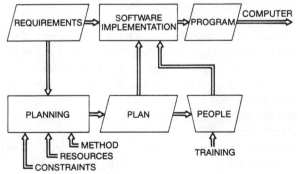

Figure 3. The work breakdown structure (WBS).

on a WBS contains the necessary tools to estimate costs and schedules accurately and to provide visibility and control during production.

Such a plan may be structured to evaluate technical accomplishments on the basis of task and activity progress. Schedules and PERT/CPM [4] networks may be built upon technical activities in terms of task milestones (i.e., accomplishments, outputs, and other quantifiable work elements). Projected versus actual task progress can be reviewed by technical audit and by progress reviews on a regular (say, monthly or biweekly) basis. Formal project design reviews are major checkpoints in this measurement system.

But knowing modern programming theory does little good if one does not also have the programming experience to which to apply it. Similarly, the knowledge of what a WBS is, what its goals are, what its benefits are, and what its structure is supposed to be like, does not necessarily instruct one in how to apply that knowledge toward developing a WBS for a particular project.

In the following sections of this paper, I shall review some of the characteristics and benefits of the

WBS and discuss how these can be developed and applied in software implementation projects. This material will be oriented principally toward new-software production tasks, although many of the concepts will be applicable also to continuing maintenance and operations tasks.

THE WORK BREAKDOWN STRUCTURE

The goals assumed here for generating the WBS are to identify work tasks, needed resources, implementation constraints, and so on, to that level of detail which yields the accuracy stipulated in the original PLAN, and to provide the means for early calibration of this accuracy and corrective replanning, if required, during the actual implementation.

How refined should this WBS be? Let me answer this question by showing how the WBS and schedule projection accuracy are interrelated.

If a project has identified a certain number of equal-effort "unit" milestones to be achieved during the course of implementation, then the mere number of such milestones achieved by a certain date is an indicator of the progress toward that goal. A graph of accumulated milestones as a function of time, sometimes called a "rate chart," permits certain predictions to be made about the future completion date rather handily and with quantifiable accuracy, especially if the milestones are chosen properly. Figure 4 shows a rate chart of a hypothetical software project.

Let it be supposed that it is known a priori, as a result of generating the WBS, that a project will be completed after M milestones have been met. These milestones correspond to all the tasks that have to be accomplished, and can be accomplished once and for all (i.e., some later activity does not reopen an already completed task; if one does, it can be accommodated by making M larger to include all such milestones as

Figure 2. The PLAN is a people program.

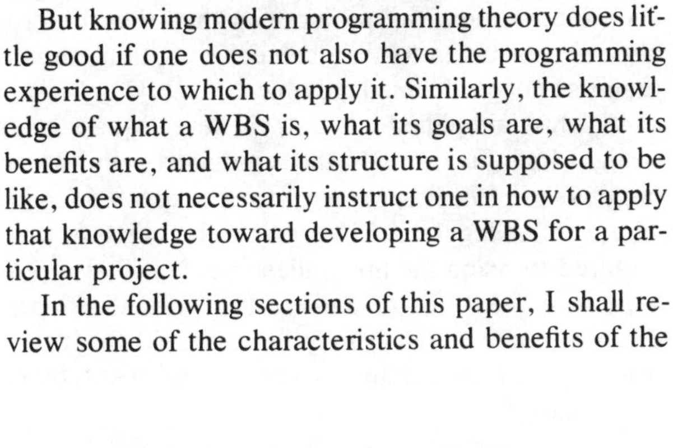

195

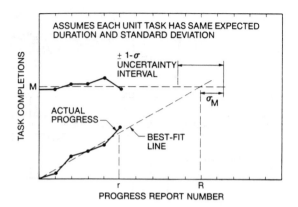

Figure 4. Conceptual progress rate chart.

separate events). The number M, of course, may not be precisely known from the first, and any uncertainty in M is certainly going to affect the accuracy of estimated completion date. Such uncertainties can be factored in as secondary effects later, when needed for refinement of accuracy.

Now, let it be further supposed that it has been possible to refine the overall task into these M milestones in such a way that each task is believed to require about the same amount of effort and duration to accomplish (Figure 5). Viewed at regular intervals (e.g., biweekly or monthly), a plot of the cumulative numbers of milestones reported as having been completed should rise linearly [5] until project completion.

More quantitatively, let m be the average number of tasks actually completed during each reporting period, and let σ be the standard deviation of the actual number of milestones completed each reporting period about this mean value (the values of m and σ are presumed to be constant over the project duration). The value of m is a reflection of the team average pro-

Figure 5. The unit task.

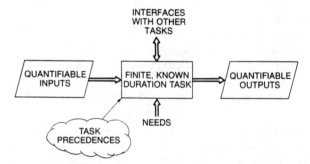

- SIZED FOR A SINGLE INDIVIDUAL
- NO FURTHER BREAKDOWN INTO SUBTASKS

ductivity and σ is a measure of the ability to estimate their production rate. Both attest to team effectiveness: first, in their ability to produce and, second, in their ability to create a work plan that adequately accounts for their time.

By design, the mean behavior of the milestone completion status is linear, a straight line from the origin with slope m. The project should require M/m reporting periods to complete, which time, of course, should not depend on whether a WBS was made (I am discounting, in this discussion, whether WBS generation increases or decreases productivity). Thus, M/m should be a constant value, relatively speaking. If M is made large, tasks are smaller and shorter, so proportionately more of them are completed each reporting period. The project schedule will, in fact, assume some productivity or mean accomplishment rate, but an actual performance value will generally be unknown until progress can be monitored for some period of time.

However, although the numbers M and σ may not affect team productivity, they do directly influence the effectiveness with which a project can monitor its progress and predict its future accomplishments. Generation of a WBS, of course, gives (or estimates) the parameter M. Monitoring the completion of milestones provides estimates for m and σ. From these, projections of the end date and calculations for the accuracy of this prediction can be made. Based on such information, the project can then divert or reallocate resources to take corrective action, should progress not be deemed suitable.

In this simplified model, a least-square-error straight-line fit through the cumulative milestone progress over the first r reports (of an expected $R = M/m$ reports) at regular ΔT intervals will predict the time required to reach the final milestone. It will also provide an estimate of m and σ. The normalized predicted completion date may be expected to deviate from the projected value (as a one-sigma event) by no more than [5]

$$\sigma_M \le 1.48 \, \sigma_1 \, (R/rM)^{1/2}$$

within first-order effects. The value $\sigma_1 = \sigma/m^{1/2}$ represents the normalized standard deviation of an individual task milestone (it is limited to values of less than unity in the underlying model), and σ_M represents the deviation in time to reach milestone M.

The bound permits the specification of WBS characteristics that enable accurate early predictions of future progress. High overall accuracy depends on a combination of low σ_1 and large M. One may compensate for inaccurate appraisals of productivity only by generating a very detailed WBS.

As an example, suppose that a 10% end-date prediction accuracy is required (i.e., $\sigma_M = 0.1$) by the end of the first quarter ($r/R = 0.25$) of a project. Then, as shown in Figure 6, the trade-off figure is $M/\sigma_1^2 = 876$. Hence, if the WBS is highly uncertain ($\sigma_1 = 1$), that WBS should contain 876 unit milestones. If the project is confident that it can hold more closely to its average productivity (and has most contingencies provided for) with $\sigma_1 = 0.5$, then it needs only about 220 milestones. A 1-person-year project with biweekly reporting, one milestone per report (26 milestones in all), must demonstrate a $\sigma_1 = 0.17$ level of task prediction accuracy.

It is therefore both necessary and important to generate a detailed WBS rather carefully and to monitor milestone achievements relative to this WBS very faithfully, if accuracy in predicting the future progress of a project is of great importance.

REASONABLE SCHEDULE ACCURACY

A project engineer on a 2-year, 10-person task may perhaps be able to manage as many as 876 subtasks, each formally assigned and reported on. That amounts to about one subtask completion per week from each of the other nine workers; but the generation of the descriptions for the 876 tasks will require considerable effort. Moreover, it is unlikely that such a detailed plan would have a σ as large as one week; if the project engineer is able to break the work accurately into 876 week-long subtasks, task deviations can probably be estimated to well within a week.

The ability of the project engineer (or planning staff) to generate a clear and accurate WBS will determine the level to which the WBS must be taken. Greater accuracy of the work breakdown definition produces greater understanding and clarity of the actions necessary to complete task objectives. If the work is understood, readily identified, and achievable

as discerned, the confidence of reaching the objectives is high. Thus, the further the subtask descriptions become refined, the better the estimator is able to assess the individual subtask durations and uncertainties. Refinement ceases when the appropriate M/σ_1^2 is reached.

Practically speaking, a work plan with tasks shorter than 1 week in duration will usually require too much planning and management overhead to be worthwhile. On the other hand, a work plan with tasks longer than 1 or 2 weeks will probably suffer from a large σ_1. Thus, a breakdown into 1- or 2-week subtasks is probably the most reasonable target for planning purposes.

A work year consists of about 47 actual weeks of work (excluding vacation, holidays, sick leave, etc.). Therefore, a project of w workers can reasonably accommodate only about $47w/d$ tasks per year (including management tasks) each of duration d weeks; spread over y years, the total number of milestones can reach $M = 47wy/d$, so that the practical accuracy limit one may reasonably expect at the one-quarter point in a project ($r/R = 0.25$) is about

$$\sigma_M \leq 0.432\sigma_1(d/wy)^{1/2}.$$

Note that accuracy is related to the total person-year effort in a project, other things being equal. A 3-person-year project completing 1 task per person-week can expect to have $\sigma_M \leq 0.216\sigma_1$. With a $\sigma_1 = 0.4$ (± 2 days per weekly task), the end-date estimation accuracy is within 10%.

GENERATING THE WBS

There is no mystery about making a WBS. People do it all the time, although they seldom call the result a WBS. Most of the things we do, in fact, are probably first organized in our heads, and for small undertakings, most of the time that works out well. For more complex undertakings, especially those involving other people, it becomes necessary to plan, organize, document, and review more formally.

The general algorithm for generating a WBS is even fairly simple to state. It goes something like this:

1. Start with the project statement of work, and put this TASK on top of the "working stack."
2. Consider the TASK at the top of the working stack. Define technical performance objectives, end-item objectives, reliability and quality objectives, schedule constraints, and other factors, as appropriate; inputs and materials required for starting the task; accomplishments and outputs that signal the completion of the task; known prec-

Figure 6. WBS unit milestones and variance ratio.

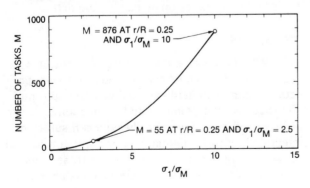

edent tasks or milestones; known interfacing tasks; and resources required, if known. Determine whether this task can be accomplished within the duration (or cost) accuracy goal.

3. If the goal is achieved, skip to the next step; otherwise, partition the current TASK into a small number of comprehensive component subtasks. Include interfacing tasks and tasks whose output is a decision regarding substructuring of other subtasks. Mark the current TASK as a "milestone," pull its description off the working stack, push it onto the "finished stack," and push each of the subtask descriptions onto the working stack.

4. Repeat from step 2 until the working stack is empty.

5. Sequence through all items from the "finished" stack and accumulate durations (costs) into the proper milestones.

The steps in this algorithm are not always simple to perform and cannot always be done correctly the first time or without sometimes referring to items already put into the "finished" list. The process is one of creation and thus requires judgment, experience, identification of alternatives, trade-offs, decisions, and iteration. This last is required since, as the project statement of work is refined, eventually the implementation of the program itself appears as one of the subtasks to be refined. When this subtask is detailed into component parts, the work descriptions begin to follow the influences of the program architecture, organizational matters, chronological constraints, work locations, and "whatever makes sense."

Therefore, the formation of the WBS, the detailed planning, and the architectural design activity are all mutually supportive. The architecture indicates how to structure the tasks, and the WBS goals tell when the architectural phase of activity has proceeded far enough. Scheduling makes use of the WBS as a tool and in turn influences the WBS generation by resolving resource conflicts.

There are many subtasks in a software project, however, that are not connected with the architecture directly, such as requirements analysis, project administration and management, and preparations for demonstration and delivery. The structure of these subtasks, being independent of the program architecture, can be made fairly standard within a given organization for all software productions. However, since there is no automatic or closed-loop means to guarantee that all the planning factors needed in the WBS actually get put into it, a standard WBS checklist can be a significant boon to proper software project planning, to decrease the likelihood of something "dropping through the cracks."

STANDARD WBS CHECKLIST

Previous experience [6] at the Jet Propulsion Laboratory with WBS methodology has permitted moderately large software implementation projects to detect schedule maladies and to control project completions within about 6% of originally scheduled dates and costs. The WBSs were formed by individuals with extensive software experience, overseen by an expert manager. None of the software individuals had ever made a WBS before, and the manager had never tried one on a software project. Together, with much travail, they assembled ad hoc items into a workable system.

A candidate standard WBS outline and checklist is currently being assembled and evaluated within the Deep Space Network (DSN) at the Jet Propulsion Laboratory. This standard WBS checklist includes many factors gained from previous successes and contains items to avert some of the identified shortcomings. Table 1 shows the upper-level structure of this WBS checklist. Detailed task descriptions are also in the process of documentation and evaluation. A short application guidebook is planned, to instruct cognizant individuals in the method, approach, and practice.

Such a checklist and guidebook, together with useful automated WBS entry, update, processing, and report generation aids, impose standards on software projects that are intended to facilitate the project management activity and make it more effective. Initial scheduling and downstream rescheduling of subtasks are aided by a WBS data base that contains precedence relationships, durations, costs, resource requirements, resource availability, and similar constraints on each subtask. PERT and critical-path methods (CPM) are applied directly to the WBS database, resulting in a preliminary schedule. Alterations of this schedule are then effected by editing the WBS via additional constraints recorded into the data base. Actual production progress is measured by marking milestone completions. These are then plotted into a rate chart and all significant milestones are projected to a best-estimate completion date.

PROBLEMS

The WBS is a well-known, effective project engineering tool. It has not been applied to software projects as often as to hardware and construction, probably because the planning and architectural design tasks in software have not always been sufficiently integrated as to be mutually supportive for several reasons: all of the management, support, and miscellaneous tasks were seldom fully identifiable and de-

Table 1. SOFTWARE IMPLEMENTATION PROJECT: Outline of Detailed Work Breakdown Structure

1. ANALYZE SOFTWARE REQUIREMENTS
   1.1 Understand functional and software requirements
   1.2 Identify missing, vague, ambiguous, and conflicting requirements
   1.3 Clarify stated requirements
   1.4 Verify that stated requirements fulfill requestor's goals
   1.5 Assess technology for supplying required software
   1.6 Propose alternate requirements or capability
   1.7 Document revised requirements
2. DEVELOP SOFTWARE ARCHITECTURE
   2.1 Determine architectural approach
   2.2 Develop external functional architecture
   2.3 Develop software internal architecture
   2.4 Assess architected solution vs. requirements
   2.5 Revise architecture and/or renegotiate requirements
   2.6 Document architecture and/or changed requirements
3. DEVELOP EXTERNAL FUNCTIONAL SPECIFICATION
   3.1 Define functional specification standards and conventions
   3.2 Formalize external environment and interface specifications
   3.3 Refine, formalize, and document the architected external operational view of the software
   3.4 Define functional acceptance tests
   3.5 Verify compliance of the external view with requirements
4. PRODUCE AND DELIVER SOFTWARE ITEMS
   4.1 Define programming, test and verification, QA, and documentation standards and conventions
   4.2 Formalize internal environment and interface specifications
   4.3 Obtain support tools
   4.4 Refine and formalize the internal design
   4.5 Define testing specifications to demonstrate required performance
   4.6 Define QA specifications
   4.7 Code and check the program
   4.8 Demonstrate acceptability and deliver software
5. PREPARE FOR SOFTWARE SUSTAINING AND OPERATIONS
   5.1 Train cognizant sustaining and maintenance personnel
   5.2 Train cognizant operations personnel
   5.3 Deliver sustaining tools and materials
   5.4 Deliver all software and data deliverables to operations
   5.5 Install the software and data into its operational environment
   5.6 Prepare consulting agreement between implementation and operations
6. PERFORM PROJECT MANAGEMENT FUNCTIONS
   6.1 Define project goals and objectives
   6.2 Scope and plan the project
   6.3 Administrate the implementation
   6.4 Evaluate performance and product
   6.5 Terminate the project

tailable during the planning phase; because separation of work into manageable packets quite often requires design decisions properly a part of the detailed design phase; because a basis for estimating subtask durations, costs, and other constraints has not existed or been known; and because software managers have not been trained in WBS methodology. Modern software engineering studies of phenomenology and methodology are beginning to close the gaps, however.

The existence of useful tools and methods does not ensure their acceptance; nor does their acceptance ensure project success. Plans and controls are essential project aids but unfortunately do not guarantee success either. The WBS is a planning, monitor, and control tool whose potential for successful application within a software project has been demonstrated. However, further research and demonstrations are necessary before a WBS-oriented software planning and control methodology and system are as well integrated into the software industry as structured programming has only recently become. Fortunately, many organizations and individuals are sensitive enough to the software management crisis of past years that headway is being made [7].

Happily, the solutions will almost certainly not be unique, but will range over limits that accommodate management and programming styles, organizational structures, levels of skill, areas of expertise, cost and end-date constraints, and human and technical factors.

REFERENCES

1. I. Avots, Why Does Project Management Fail? *California Management Review* XII (1), 77–82, Fall 1969.
2. Robert C. Tausworthe, *Standardized Development of Computer Software*, Prentice-Hall, Englewood Cliffs, N.J., 1977.
3. V. G. Hajek, *Management of Engineering Projects*, McGraw-Hill, New York, 1977.
4. DoD and NASA Guide, PERT/COST, Office of The Secretary of Defense and NASA, Washington, D.C., June, 1962.
5. Robert C. Tausworthe, Stochastic Models for Software Project Management, Deep Space Network Progress Report No. 42–37, Jet Propulsion Laboratory, Pasadena, California, February 1977, pp. 118–126.
6. M. McKenzie and A. P. Irvine, Evaluation of the DSN Software Methodology, Deep Space Network Progress Report No. 42–46, Jet Propulsion Laboratory, Pasadena, California, August, 1978.
7. M. M. Lehman et. al., *Software Phenomenology*, working papers of The Software Life Cycle Management Workshop, U.S. Army Institute for Research in Management Information and Computer Science, Atlanta, Georgia, August 1977.

Software Engineering Economics

BARRY W. BOEHM

Abstract—This paper summarizes the current state of the art and recent trends in software engineering economics. It provides an overview of economic analysis techniques and their applicability to software engineering and management. It surveys the field of software cost estimation, including the major estimation techniques available, the state of the art in algorithmic cost models, and the outstanding research issues in software cost estimation.

Index Terms—Computer programming costs, cost models, management decision aids, software cost estimation, software economics, software engineering, software management.

I. INTRODUCTION

Definitions

The dictionary defines "economics" as "a social science concerned chiefly with description and analysis of the production, distribution, and consumption of goods and services." Here is another definition of economics which I think is more helpful in explaining how economics relates to software engineering.

Economics is the study of how people make decisions in resource-limited situations.

This definition of economics fits the major branches of classical economics very well.

Macroeconomics is the study of how people make decisions in resource-limited situations on a national or global scale. It deals with the effects of decisions that national leaders make on such issues as tax rates, interest rates, foreign and trade policy.

Microeconomics is the study of how people make decisions in resource-limited situations on a more personal scale. It deals with the decisions that individuals and organizations make on such issues as how much insurance to buy, which word processor to buy, or what prices to charge for their products or services.

Economics and Software Engineering Management

If we look at the discipline of software engineering, we see that the microeconomics branch of economics deals more with the types of decisions we need to make as software engineers or managers.

Clearly, we deal with limited resources. There is never enough time or money to cover all the good features we would like to put into our software products. And even in these days of cheap hardware and virtual memory, our more significant software products must always operate within a world of limited computer power and main memory. If you have been in the software engineering field for any length of time, I am sure

you can think of a number of decision situations in which you had to determine some key software product feature as a function of some limiting critical resource.

Throughout the software life cycle,[1] there are many decision situations involving limited resources in which software engineering economics techniques provide useful assistance. To provide a feel for the nature of these economic decision issues, an example is given below for each of the major phases in the software life cycle.

- *Feasibility Phase:* How much should we invest in information system analyses (user questionnaires and interviews, current-system analysis, workload characterizations, simulations, scenarios, prototypes) in order that we converge on an appropriate definition and concept of operation for the system we plan to implement?
- *Plans and Requirements Phase:* How rigorously should we specify requirements? How much should we invest in requirements validation activities (automated completeness, consistency, and traceability checks, analytic models, simulations, prototypes) before proceeding to design and develop a software system?
- *Product Design Phase:* Should we organize the software to make it possible to use a complex piece of existing software which generally but not completely meets our requirements?
- *Programming Phase:* Given a choice between three data storage and retrieval schemes which are primarily execution time-efficient, storage-efficient, and easy-to-modify, respectively; which of these should we choose to implement?
- *Integration and Test Phase:* How much testing and formal verification should we perform on a product before releasing it to users?
- *Maintenance Phase:* Given an extensive list of suggested product improvements, which ones should we implement first?
- *Phaseout:* Given an aging, hard-to-modify software product, should we replace it with a new product, restructure it, or leave it alone?

Outline of This Paper

The economics field has evolved a number of techniques (cost-benefit analysis, present value analysis, risk analysis, etc.)

---

[1] Economic principles underlie the overall structure of the software life cycle, and its primary refinements of prototyping, incremental development, and advancemanship. The primary economic driver of the life-cycle structure is the significantly increasing cost of making a software change or fixing a software problem, as a function of the phase in which the change or fix is made. See [11, ch. 4].

Manuscript received April 26, 1983; revised June 28, 1983.

The author is with the Software Information Systems Division, TRW Defense Systems Group, Redondo Beach, CA 90278.

Reprinted from *IEEE Transactions on Software Engineering*, Volume SE-10, Number 1, January 1984, pages 4-21. Copyright © 1984 by The Institute of Electrical and Electronics Engineers, Inc.

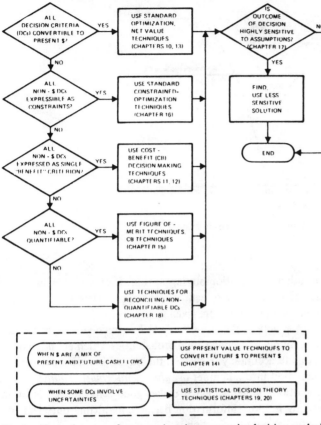

MASTER KEY
TO SOFTWARE ENGINEERING ECONOMICS
DECISION ANALYSIS TECHNIQUES

Fig. 1. Master key to software engineering economics decision analysis techniques.

for dealing with decision issues such as the ones above. Section II of this paper provides an overview of these techniques and their applicability to software engineering.

One critical problem which underlies all applications of economic techniques to software engineering is the problem of estimating software costs. Section III contains three major sections which summarize this field:

III-A: Major Software Cost Estimation Techniques

III-B: Algorithmic Models for Software Cost Estimation

III-C: Outstanding Research Issues in Software Cost Estimation.

Section IV concludes by summarizing the major benefits of software engineering economics, and commenting on the major challenges awaiting the field.

II. SOFTWARE ENGINEERING ECONOMICS ANALYSIS TECHNIQUES

Overview of Relevant Techniques

The microeconomics field provides a number of techniques for dealing with software life-cycle decision issues such as the ones given in the previous section. Fig. 1 presents an overall master key to these techniques and when to use them.[2]

---

[2] The chapter numbers in Fig. 1 refer to the chapters in [11], in which those techniques are discussed in further detail.

As indicated in Fig. 1, standard optimization techniques can be used when we can find a single quantity such as dollars (or pounds, yen, cruzeiros, etc.) to serve as a "universal solvent" into which all of our decision variables can be converted. Or, if the nondollar objectives can be expressed as constraints (system availability must be at least 98 percent; throughput must be at least 150 transactions per second), then standard constrained optimization techniques can be used. And if cash flows occur at different times, then present-value techniques can be used to normalize them to a common point in time.

More frequently, some of the resulting benefits from the software system are not expressible in dollars. In such situations, one alternative solution will not necessarily dominate another solution.

An example situation is shown in Fig. 2, which compares the cost and benefits (here, in terms of throughput in transactions per second) of two alternative approaches to developing an operating system for a transaction processing system.

- *Option A:* Accept an available operating system. This will require only $80K in software costs, but will achieve a peak performance of 120 transactions per second, using five $10K minicomputer processors, because of a high multiprocessor overhead factor.
- *Option B:* Build a new operating system. This system would be more efficient and would support a higher peak throughput, but would require $180K in software costs.

The cost-versus-performance curve for these two options are shown in Fig. 2. Here, neither option dominates the other, and various cost-benefit decision-making techniques (maximum profit margin, cost/benefit ratio, return on investments, etc.) must be used to choose between Options A and B.

In general, software engineering decision problems are even more complex than Fig. 2, as Options A and B will have several important criteria on which they differ (e.g., robustness, ease of tuning, ease of change, functional capability). If these criteria are quantifiable, then some type of figure of merit can be defined to support a comparative analysis of the preferability of one option over another. If some of the criteria are unquantifiable (user goodwill, programmer morale, etc.), then some techniques for comparing unquantifiable criteria need to be used. As indicated in Fig. 1, techniques for each of these situations are available, and discussed in [11].

Analyzing Risk, Uncertainty, and the Value of Information

In software engineering, our decision issues are generally even more complex than those discussed above. This is because the outcome of many of our options cannot be determined in advance. For example, building an operating system with a significantly lower multiprocessor overhead may be achievable, but on the other hand, it may not. In such circumstances, we are faced with a problem of *decision making under uncertainty*, with a considerable *risk* of an undesired outcome.

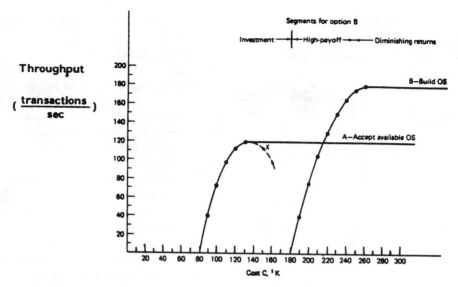

Fig. 2. Cost-effectiveness comparison, transaction processing system options.

The main economic analysis techniques available to support us in resolving such problems are the following.

1) Techniques for decision making under complete uncertainty, such as the maximax rule, the maximin rule, and the Laplace rule [38]. These techniques are generally inadequate for practical software engineering decisions.

2) Expected-value techniques, in which we estimate the probabilities of occurrence of each outcome (successful or unsuccessful development of the new operating system) and complete the expected payoff of each option:

$$EV = Prob(success) * Payoff(successful OS)$$

$$+ Prob(failure) * Payoff(unsuccessful OS).$$

These techniques are better than decision making under complete uncertainty, but they still involve a great deal of risk if the Prob(failure) is considerably higher than our estimate of it.

3) Techniques in which we reduce uncertainty by *buying information*. For example, *prototyping* is a way of buying information to reduce our uncertainty about the likely success or failure of a multiprocessor operating system; by developing a rapid prototype of its high-risk elements, we can get a clearer picture of our likelihood of successfully developing the full operating system.

In general, prototyping and other options for buying information[3] are most valuable aids for software engineering decisions. However, they always raise the following question: "how much information-buying is enough?"

In principle, this question can be answered via statistical decision theory techniques involving the use of Bayes' Law, which allows us to calculate the expected payoff from a software project as a function of our level of investment in a prototype

or other information-buying option. (Some examples of the use of Bayes' Law to estimate the appropriate level of investment in a prototype are given in [11, ch. 20].)

In practice, the use of Bayes' Law involves the estimation of a number of conditional probabilities which are not easy to estimate accurately. However, the Bayes' Law approach can be translated into a number of *value-of-information guidelines*, or conditions under which it makes good sense to decide on investing in more information before committing ourselves to a particular course of action.

Condition 1: There exist attractive alternatives whose payoff varies greatly, depending on some critical states of nature. If not, we can commit ourselves to one of the attractive alternatives with no risk of significant loss.

Condition 2: The critical states of nature have an appreciable probability of occurring. If not, we can again commit ourselves without major risk. For situations with extremely high variations in payoff, the appreciable probability level is lower than in situations with smaller variations in payoff.

Condition 3: The investigations have a high probability of accurately identifying the occurrence of the critical states of nature. If not, the investigations will not do much to reduce our risk of loss due to making the wrong decision.

Condition 4: The required cost and schedule of the investigations do not overly curtail their net value. It does us little good to obtain results which cost more than they can save us, or which arrive too late to help us make a decision.

Condition 5: There exist significant side benefits derived from performing the investigations. Again, we may be able to justify an investigation solely on the basis of its value in training, team-building, customer relations, or design validation.

Some Pitfalls Avoided by Using the Value-of-Information Approach

The guideline conditions provided by the value-of-information approach provide us with a perspective which helps us avoid some serious software engineering pitfalls. The pitfalls

---

[3] Other examples of options for buying information to support software engineering decisions include feasibility studies, user surveys, simulation, testing, and mathematical program verification techniques.

below are expressed in terms of some frequently expressed but faulty pieces of software engineering advice.

Pitfall 1: Always use a simulation to investigate the feasibility of complex realtime software. Simulations are often extremely valuable in such situations. However, there have been a good many simulations developed which were largely an expensive waste of effort, frequently under conditions that would have been picked up by the guidelines above. Some have been relatively useless because, once they were built, nobody could tell whether a given set of inputs was realistic or not (picked up by Condition 3). Some have been taken so long to develop that they produced their first results the week after the proposal was sent out, or after the key design review was completed (picked up by Condition 4).

Pitfall 2: Always build the software twice. The guidelines indicate that the prototype (or build-it-twice) approach is often valuable, but not in all situations. Some prototypes have been built of software whose aspects were all straightforward and familiar, in which case nothing much was learned by building them (picked up by Conditions 1 and 2).

Pitfall 3: Build the software purely top-down. When interpreted too literally, the top-down approach does not concern itself with the design of low level modules until the higher levels have been fully developed. If an adverse state of nature makes such a low level module (automatically forecast sales volume, automatically discriminate one type of aircraft from another) impossible to develop, the subsequent redesign will generally require the expensive rework of much of the higher level design and code. Conditions 1 and 2 warn us to temper our top-down approach with a thorough top-to-bottom software risk analysis during the requirements and product design phases.

Pitfall 4: Every piece of code should be proved correct. Correctness proving is still an expensive way to get information on the fault-freedom of software, although it strongly satisfies Condition 3 by giving a very high assurance of a program's correctness. Conditions 1 and 2 recommend that proof techniques be used in situations where the operational cost of a software fault is very large, that is, loss of life, compromised national security, major financial losses. But if the operational cost of a software fault is small, the added information on fault-freedom provided by the proof will not be worth the investment (Condition 4).

Pitfall 5: Nominal-case testing is sufficient. This pitfall is just the opposite of Pitfall 4. If the operational cost of potential software faults is large, it is highly imprudent not to perform off-nominal testing.

Summary: The Economic Value of Information

Let us step back a bit from these guidelines and pitfalls. Put simply, we are saying that, as software engineers:

"It is often worth paying for information because it helps us make better decisions."

If we look at the statement in a broader context, we can see that it is the primary reason why the software engineering field exists. It is what practically all of our software customers say when they decide to acquire one of our products: that it is worth paying for a management information system, a weather forecasting system, an air traffic control system, an inventory control system, etc., because it helps them make better decisions.

Usually, software engineers are *producers* of management information to be consumed by other people, but during the software life cycle we must also be *consumers* of management information to support our own decisions. As we come to appreciate the factors which make it attractive for us to pay for processed information which helps *us* make better decisions as software engineers, we will get a better appreciation for what our customers and users are looking for in the information processing systems we develop for *them*.

III. SOFTWARE COST ESTIMATION

Introduction

All of the software engineering economics decision analysis techniques discussed above are only as good as the input data we can provide for them. For software decisions, the most critical and difficult of these inputs to provide are estimates of the cost of a proposed software project. In this section, we will summarize:

1) the major software cost estimation techniques available, and their relative strengths and difficulties;

2) algorithmic models for software cost estimation;

3) outstanding research issues in software cost estimation.

A. Major Software Cost Estimation Techniques

Table I summarizes the relative strengths and difficulties of the major software cost estimation methods in use today.

1) *Algorithmic Models:* These methods provide one or more algorithms which produce a software cost estimate as a function of a number of variables which are considered to be the major cost drivers.

2) *Expert Judgment:* This method involves consulting one or more experts, perhaps with the aid of an expert-consensus mechanism such as the Delphi technique.

3) *Analogy:* This method involves reasoning by analogy with one or more completed projects to relate their actual costs to an estimate of the cost of a similar new project.

4) *Parkinson:* A Parkinson principle ("work expands to fill the available volume") is invoked to equate the cost estimate to the available resources.

5) *Price-to-Win:* Here, the cost estimate is equated to the price believed necessary to win the job (or the schedule believed necessary to be first in the market with a new product, etc.).

6) *Top-Down:* An overall cost estimate for the project is derived from global properties of the software product. The total cost is then split up among the various components.

7) *Bottom-Up:* Each component of the software job is separately estimated, and the results aggregated to produce an estimate for the overall job.

The main conclusions that we can draw from Table I are the following.

• None of the alternatives is better than the others from all aspects.

• The Parkinson and price-to-win methods are unacceptable and do not produce satisfactory cost estimates.

TABLE I
STRENGTHS AND WEAKNESSES OF SOFTWARE
COST-ESTIMATION METHODS

Method	Strengths	Weaknesses
Algorithmic model	• Objective, repeatable, analyzable formula • Efficient, good for sensitivity analysis • Objectively calibrated to experience	• Subjective inputs • Assessment of exceptional circumstances • Calibrated to past, not future
Expert judgment	• Assessment of representativeness, interactions, exceptional circumstances	• No better than participants • Biases, incomplete recall
Analogy	• Based on representative experience	• Representativeness of experience
Parkinson Price to win	• Correlates with some experience • Often gets the contract	• Reinforces poor practice • Generally produces large overruns
Top-down	• System level focus • Efficient	• Less detailed basis • Less stable
Bottom-up	• More detailed basis • More stable • Fosters individual commitment	• May overlook system level costs • Requires more effort

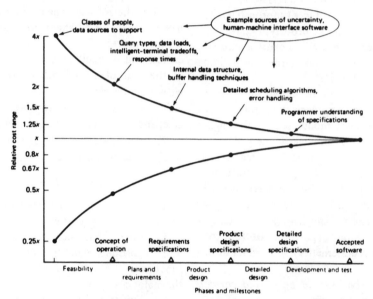

Fig. 3.   Software cost estimation accuracy versus phase.

• The strengths and weaknesses of the other techniques are complementary (particularly the algorithmic models versus expert judgment and top-down versus bottom-up).

• Thus, in practice, we should use combinations of the above techniques, compare their results, and iterate on them where they differ.

Fundamental Limitations of Software Cost Estimation Techniques

Whatever the strengths of a software cost estimation technique, there is really no way we can expect the technique to compensate for our lack of definition or understanding of the software job to be done. Until a software specification is fully defined, it actually represents a range of software products, and a corresponding range of software development costs.

This fundamental limitation of software cost estimation technology is illustrated in Fig. 3, which shows the accuracy within which software cost estimates can be made, as a function of the software life-cycle phase (the horizontal axis), or of the level of knowledge we have of what the software is intended to do. This level of uncertainty is illustrated in Fig. 3

with respect to a human–machine interface component of the software.

When we first begin to evaluate alternative concepts for a new software application, the relative range of our software cost estimates is roughly a factor of four on either the high or low side.[4] This range stems from the wide range of uncertainty we have at this time about the actual nature of the product. For the human–machine interface component, for example, we do not know at this time what classes of people (clerks, computer specialists, middle managers, etc.) or what classes of data (raw or pre-edited, numerical or text, digital or analog) the system will have to support. Until we pin down such uncertainties, a factor of four in either direction is not surprising as a range of estimates.

The above uncertainties are indeed pinned down once we complete the feasibility phase and settle on a particular concept of operation. At this stage, the range of our estimates diminishes to a factor of two in either direction. This range is

[4] These ranges have been determined subjectively, and are intended to represent 80 percent confidence limits, that is, "within a factor of four on either side, 80 percent of the time."

reasonable because we still have not pinned down such issues as the specific types of user query to be supported, or the specific functions to be performed within the microprocessor in the intelligent terminal. These issues will be resolved by the time we have developed a software requirements specification, at which point, we will be able to estimate the software costs within a factor of 1.5 in either direction.

By the time we complete and validate a product design specification, we will have resolved such issues as the internal data structure of the software product and the specific techniques for handling the buffers between the terminal microprocessor and the central processors on one side, and between the microprocessor and the display driver on the other. At this point, our software estimate should be accurate to within a factor of 1.25, the discrepancies being caused by some remaining sources of uncertainty such as the specific algorithms to be used for task scheduling, error handling, abort processing, and the like. These will be resolved by the end of the detailed design phase, but there will still be a residual uncertainty about 10 percent based on how well the programmers really understand the specifications to which they are to code. (This factor also includes such consideration as personnel turnover uncertainties during the development and test phases.)

B. Algorithmic Models for Software Cost Estimation
Algorithmic Cost Models: Early Development

Since the earliest days of the software field, people have been trying to develop algorithmic models to estimate software costs. The earliest attempts were simple rules of thumb, such as:

- on a large project, each software performer will provide an average of one checked-out instruction per man-hour (or roughly 150 instructions per man-month);

- each software maintenance person can maintain four boxes of cards (a box of cards held 2000 cards, or roughly 2000 instructions in those days of few comment cards).

Somewhat later, some projects began collecting quantitative data on the effort involved in developing a software product, and its distribution across the software life cycle. One of the earliest of these analyses was documented in 1956 in [8]. It indicated that, for very large operational software products on the order of 100 000 delivered source instructions (100 KDSI), that the overall productivity was more like 64 DSI/man-month, that another 100 KDSI of support-software would be required; that about 15 000 pages of documentation would be produced and 3000 hours of computer time consumed; and that the distribution of effort would be as follows:

Program Specs:	10 percent
Coding Specs:	30 percent
Coding:	10 percent
Parameter Testing:	20 percent
Assembly Testing:	30 percent

with an additional 30 percent required to produce operational specs for the system. Unfortunately, such data did not become well known, and many subsequent software projects went through a painful process of rediscovering them.

During the late 1950's and early 1960's, relatively little progress was made in software cost estimation, while the frequency and magnitude of software cost overruns was becoming critical to many large systems employing computers. In 1964, the U.S. Air Force contracted with System Development Corporation for a landmark project in the software cost estimation field. This project collected 104 attributes of 169 software projects and treated them to extensive statistical analysis. One result was the 1965 SDC cost model [41] which was the best possible statistical 13-parameter linear estimation model for the sample data:

$$MM = -33.63$$
$$+9.15 \text{ (Lack of Requirements) (0-2)}$$
$$+10.73 \text{ (Stability of Design) (0-3)}$$
$$+0.51 \text{ (Percent Math Instructions)}$$
$$+0.46 \text{ (Percent Storage/Retrieval Instructions)}$$
$$+0.40 \text{ (Number of Subprograms)}$$
$$+7.28 \text{ (Programming Language) (0-1)}$$
$$-21.45 \text{ (Business Application) (0-1)}$$
$$+13.53 \text{ (Stand-Alone Program) (0.1)}$$
$$+12.35 \text{ (First Program on Computer) (0-1)}$$
$$+58.82 \text{ (Concurrent Hardware Development) (0-1)}$$
$$+30.61 \text{ (Random Access Device Used) (0-1)}$$
$$+29.55 \text{ (Difference Host, Target Hardware) (0-1)}$$
$$+0.54 \text{ (Number of Personnel Trips)}$$
$$-25.20 \text{ (Developed by Military Organization) (0-1).}$$

The numbers in parentheses refer to ratings to be made by the estimator.

When applied to its database of 169 projects, this model produced a mean estimate of 40 MM and a standard deviation of 62 MM; not a very accurate predictor. Further, the application of the model is counterintuitive; a project with all zero ratings is estimated at minus 33 MM; changing language from a higher order language to assembly language adds 7 MM, independent of project size. The most conclusive result from the SDC study was that there were too many nonlinear aspects of software development for a linear cost-estimation model to work very well.

Still, the SDC effort provided a valuable base of information and insight for cost estimation and future models. Its cumulative distribution of productivity for 169 projects was a valuable aid for producing or checking cost estimates. The estimation rules of thumb for various phases and activities have been very helpful, and the data have been a major foundation for some subsequent cost models.

In the late 1960's and early 1970's, a number of cost models were developed which worked reasonably well for a certain restricted range of projects to which they were calibrated. Some of the more notable examples of such models are those described in [3], [54], [57].

The essence of the TRW Wolverton model [57] is shown in Fig. 4, which shows a number of curves of software cost per object instruction as a function of relative degree of difficulty

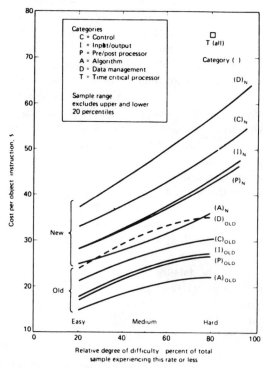

Fig. 4.   TRW Wolverton model: Cost per object instruction versus relative degree of difficulty.

(0 to 100), novelty of the application (new or old), and type of project. The best use of the model involves breaking the software into components and estimating their cost individually. This, a 1000 object-instruction module of new data management software of medium (50 percent) difficulty would be costed at $46/instruction, or $46 000.

This model is well-calibrated to a class of near-real-time government command and control projects, but is less accurate for some other classes of projects. In addition, the model provides a good breakdown of project effort by phase and activity.

In the late 1970's, several software cost estimation models were developed which established a significant advance in the state of the art. These included the Putnam SLIM Model [44], the Doty Model [27], the RCA PRICE S model [22], the COCOMO model [11], the IBM-FSD model [53], the Boeing model [9], and a series of models developed by GRC [15]. A summary of these models, and the earlier SDC and Wolverton models, is shown in Table II, in terms of the size, program, computer, personnel, and project attributes used by each model to determine software costs. The first four of these models are discussed below.

The Putnam SLIM Model [44], [45]

The Putnam SLIM Model is a commercially available (from Quantitative Software Management, Inc.) software product based on Putnam's analysis of the software life cycle in terms of the Rayleigh distribution of project personnel level versus time. The basic effort macro-estimation model used in SLIM is

$$S_s = C_k K^{1/3} t_d^{4/3}$$

where

S_s = number of delivered source instructions
K = life-cycle effort in man-years
t_d = development time in years
C_k = a "technology constant."

Values of C_k typically range between 610 and 57 314. The current version of SLIM allows one to calibrate C_k to past projects or to past projects or to estimate it as a function of a project's use of modern programming practices, hardware constraints, personnel experience, interactive development, and other factors. The required development effort, DE, is estimated as roughly 40 percent of the life-cycle effort for large systems. For smaller systems, the percentage varies as a function of system size.

The SLIM model includes a number of useful extensions to estimate such quantities as manpower distribution, cash flow, major-milestone schedules, reliability levels, computer time, and documentation costs.

The most controversial aspect of the SLIM model is its tradeoff relationship between development effort K and between development time t_d. For a software product of a given size, the SLIM software equation above gives

$$K = \frac{\text{constant}}{t_d^4}.$$

For example, this relationship says that one can cut the cost of a software project in half, simply by increasing its development time by 19 percent (e.g., from 10 months to 12 months). Fig. 5 shows how the SLIM tradeoff relationship com-

TABLE II
FACTORS USED IN VARIOUS COST MODELS

GROUP	FACTOR	SDC, 1965	TRW, 1972	PUTNAM, SLIM	DOTY	RCA, PRICE S	IBM	BOEING, 1977	GRC, 1979	COCOMO	SOFCOST	DSN	JENSEN
SIZE ATTRIBUTES	SOURCE INSTRUCTIONS			X	X		X	X		X	X	X	X
	OBJECT INSTRUCTIONS	X	X		X	X							
	NUMBER OF ROUTINES	X				X					X		
	NUMBER OF DATA ITEMS						X			X	X		
	NUMBER OF OUTPUT FORMATS								X			X	
	DOCUMENTATION				X		X				X		X
	NUMBER OF PERSONNEL			X			X	X			X		X
PROGRAM ATTRIBUTES	TYPE	X	X	X	X	X	X	X			X		
	COMPLEXITY		X	X		X	X			X	X	X	X
	LANGUAGE	X		X				X	X	X	X	X	X
	REUSE			X		X		X	X	X	X	X	X
	REQUIRED RELIABILITY			X		X				X	X		X
	DISPLAY REQUIREMENTS				X						X		X
COMPUTER ATTRIBUTES	TIME CONSTRAINT		X	X	X	X	X	X		X	X	X	X
	STORAGE CONSTRAINT			X	X	X	X			X	X	X	X
	HARDWARE CONFIGURATION	X				X							
	CONCURRENT HARDWARE DEVELOPMENT	X			X	X	X			X	X	X	X
	INTERFACING EQUIPMENT, S/W										X	X	
PERSONNEL ATTRIBUTES	PERSONNEL CAPABILITY			X		X	X			X	X	X	X
	PERSONNEL CONTINUITY						X				X		
	HARDWARE EXPERIENCE	X		X	X	X	X		X	X	X	X	X
	APPLICATIONS EXPERIENCE		X	X		X	X	X	X	X	X	X	X
	LANGUAGE EXPERIENCE			X		X	X		X	X	X	X	X
PROJECT ATTRIBUTES	TOOLS AND TECHNIQUES			X		X	X	X		X	X	X	X
	CUSTOMER INTERFACE	X					X				X	X	
	REQUIREMENTS DEFINITION	X			X		X				X	X	X
	REQUIREMENTS VOLATILITY	X			X	X	X		X	X	X	X	X
	SCHEDULE			X		X				X	X	X	X
	SECURITY						X				X	X	
	COMPUTER ACCESS			X	X		X	X		X	X	X	X
	TRAVEL/REHOSTING/MULTI-SITE	X			X	X					X	X	X
	SUPPORT SOFTWARE MATURITY									X	X	X	
CALIBRATION FACTOR					X	X				X			
EFFORT EQUATION	$MM_{NOM} = C(DSI)^X$, X =		1.0		1.047		0.91	1.0		1.05 – 1.2		1.0	1.2
SCHEDULE EQUATION	$t_D = C(MM)^X$, X =						0.35			0.32 – 0.38		0.356	0.333

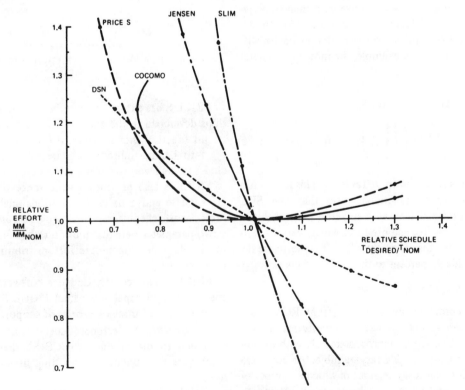

Fig. 5.   Comparative effort-schedule tradeoff relationships.

TABLE III
DOTY MODEL FOR SMALL PROGRAMS*

$$MM = 2.060 \, I^{1.047} \prod_{i=1}^{i=14} f_i$$

Factor	f_i	Yes	No
Special display	f_1	1.11	1.00
Detailed definition of operational requirements	f_2	1.00	1.11
Change to operational requirements	f_3	1.05	1.00
Real-time operation	f_4	1.33	1.00
CPU memory constraint	f_5	1.43	1.00
CPU time constraint	f_6	1.33	1.00
First software developed on CPU	f_7	1.92	1.00
Concurrent development of ADP hardware	f_8	1.82	1.00
Timeshare versus batch processing, in development	f_9	0.83	1.00
Developer using computer at another facility	f_{10}	1.43	1.00
Development at operational site	f_{11}	1.39	1.00
Development computer different than target computer	f_{12}	1.25	1.00
Development at more than one site	f_{13}	1.25	1.00
Programmer access to computer	f_{14}	Limited / Unlimited	1.00 / 0.90

* Less than 10,000 source instructions

pares with those of other models; see [11, ch. 27] for further discussion of this issue.

On balance, the SLIM approach has provided a number of useful insights into software cost estimation, such as the Rayleigh-curve distribution for one-shot software efforts, the explicit treatment of estimation risk and uncertainty, and the cube-root relationship defining the minimum development time achievable for a project requiring a given amount of effort.

The Doty Model [27]

This model is the result of an extensive data analysis activity, including many of the data points from the SDC sample. A number of models of similar form were developed for different application areas. As an example, the model for general application is

$$MM = 5.288 \, (KDSI)^{1.047}, \quad \text{for } KDSI \geq 10$$

$$MM = 2.060 \, (KDSI)^{1.047} \left(\prod_{j=1}^{14} f_j \right), \quad \text{for } KDSI < 10.$$

The effort multipliers f_i are shown in Table III. This model has a much more appropriate functional form than the SDC model, but it has some problems with stability, as it exhibits a discontinuity at KDSI = 10, and produces widely varying estimates via the f factors (answering "yes" to "first software developed on CPU" adds 92 percent to the estimated cost).

The RCA PRICE S Model [22]

PRICE S is a commercially available (from RCA, Inc.) macro cost-estimation model developed primarily for embedded system applications. It has improved steadily with experience; earlier versions with a widely varying subjective complexity factor have been replaced by versions in which a number of computer, personnel, and project attributes are used to modulate the complexity rating.

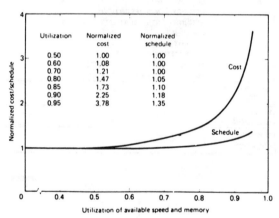

Utilization	Normalized cost	Normalized schedule
0.50	1.00	1.00
0.60	1.08	1.00
0.70	1.21	1.00
0.80	1.47	1.05
0.85	1.73	1.10
0.90	2.25	1.18
0.95	3.78	1.35

Fig. 6. RCA PRICE S model: Effect of hardware constraints.

PRICE S has extended a number of cost-estimating relationships developed in the early 1970's such as the hardware constraint function shown in Fig. 6 [10]. It was primarily developed to handle military software projects, but now also includes rating levels to cover business applications.

PRICE S also provides a wide range of useful outputs on gross phase and activity distributions analyses, and monthly project cost-schedule-expected progress forecasts. Price S uses a two-parameter beta distribution rather than a Rayleigh curve to calculate development effort distribution versus calendar time.

PRICE S has recently added a software life-cycle support cost estimation capability called PRICE SL [34]. It involves the definition of three categories of support activities.

• *Growth:* The estimator specifies the amount of code to be added to the product. PRICE SL then uses its standard techniques to estimate the resulting life-cycle-effort distribution.

• *Enhancement:* PRICE SL estimates the fraction of the existing product which will be modified (the estimator may provide his own fraction), and uses its standard techniques to estimate the resulting life-cycle effort distribution.

- *Maintenance:* The estimator provides a parameter indicating the quality level of the developed code. PRICE SL uses this to estimate the effort required to eliminate remaining errors.

The COnstructive COst MOdel (COCOMO) [11]

The primary motivation for the COCOMO model has been to help people understand the cost consequences of the decisions they will make in commissioning, developing, and supporting a software product. Besides providing a software cost estimation capability, COCOMO therefore provides a great deal of material which explains exactly what costs the model is estimating, and why it comes up with the estimates it does. Further, it provides capabilities for sensitivity analysis and tradeoff analysis of many of the common software engineering decision issues.

COCOMO is actually a hierarchy of three increasingly detailed models which range from a single macro-estimation scaling model as a function of product size to a micro-estimation model with a three-level work breakdown structure and a set of phase-sensitive multipliers for each cost driver attribute. To provide a reasonably concise example of a current state of the art cost estimation model, the intermediate level of COCOMO is described below.

Intermediate COCOMO estimates the cost of a proposed software product in the following way.

1) A nominal development effort is estimated as a function of the product's size in delivered source instructions in thousands (KDSI) and the project's development mode.

2) A set of effort multipliers are determined from the product's ratings on a set of 15 cost driver attributes.

3) The estimated development effort is obtained by multiplying the nominal effort estimate by all of the product's effort multipliers.

4) Additional factors can be used to determine dollar costs, development schedules, phase and activity distributions, computer costs, annual maintenance costs, and other elements from the development effort estimate.

Step 1—Nominal Effort Estimation: First, Table IV is used to determine the project's development mode. Organic-mode projects typically come from stable, familiar, forgiving, relatively unconstrained environments, and were found in the COCOMO data analysis of 63 projects have a different scaling equation from the more ambitious, unfamiliar, unforgiving, tightly constrained embedded mode. The resulting scaling equations for each mode are given in Table V; these are used to determine the nominal development effort for the project in man-months as a function of the project's size in KDSI and the project's development mode.

For example, suppose we are estimating the cost to develop the microprocessor-based communications processing software for a highly ambitious new electronic funds transfer network with high reliability, performance, development schedule, and interface requirements. From Table IV, we determine that these characteristics best fit the profile of an embedded-mode project.

We next estimate the size of the product as 10 000 delivered

TABLE IV
COCOMO SOFTWARE DEVELOPMENT MODES

Feature	Mode		
	Organic	Semidetached	Embedded
Organizational understanding of product objectives	Thorough	Considerable	General
Experience in working with related software systems	Extensive	Considerable	Moderate
Need for software conformance with pre-established requirements	Basic	Considerable	Full
Need for software conformance with external interface specifications	Basic	Considerable	Full
Concurrent development of associated new hardware and operational procedures	Some	Moderate	Extensive
Need for innovative data processing architectures, algorithms	Minimal	Some	Considerable
Premium on early completion	Low	Medium	High
Product size range	<50 KDSI	<300 KDSI	All sizes
Examples	Batch data reduction	Most transaction processing systems	Large, complex transaction processing systems
	Scientific models	New OS, DBMS	Ambitious, very large OS
	Business models	Ambitious inventory, production control	Avionics
	Familiar OS, compiler	Simple command-control	Ambitious command-control
	Simple inventory, production control		

TABLE V
COCOMO NOMINAL EFFORT AND SCHEDULE EQUATIONS

DEVELOPMENT MODE	NOMINAL EFFORT	SCHEDULE
Organic	$(MM)_{NOM} = 3.2(KDSI)^{1.05}$	$TDEV = 2.5(MM_{DEV})^{0.38}$
Semidetached	$(MM)_{NOM} = 3.0(KDSI)^{1.12}$	$TDEV = 2.5(MM_{DEV})^{0.35}$
Embedded	$(MM)_{NOM} = 2.8(KDSI)^{1.20}$	$TDEV = 2.5(MM_{DEV})^{0.32}$

(KDSI = thousands of delivered source instructions)

source instructions, or 10 KDSI. From Table V, we then determine that the nominal development effort for this Embedded-mode project is

$$2.8(10)^{1.20} = 44 \text{ man-months (MM)}.$$

Step 2—Determine Effort Multipliers: Each of the 15 cost driver attributes in COCOMO has a rating scale and a set of effort multipliers which indicate by how much the nominal effort estimate must be multiplied to account for the project's having to work at its rating level for the attribute.

These cost driver attributes and their corresponding effort multipliers are shown in Table VI. The summary rating scales for each cost driver attribute are shown in Table VII, except for the complexity rating scale which is shown in Table VIII (expanded rating scales for the other attributes are provided in [11]).

The results of applying these tables to our microprocessor communications software example are shown in Table IX. The effect of a software fault in the electronic fund transfer system could be a serious financial loss; therefore, the project's RELY rating from Table VII is High. Then, from Table VI, the effort multiplier for achieving a High level of required reliability is 1.15, or 15 percent more effort than it would take to develop the software to a nominal level of required reliability.

TABLE VI
INTERMEDIATE COCOMO SOFTWARE DEVELOPMENT EFFORT MULTIPLIERS

Cost Drivers	Very Low	Low	Nominal	High	Very High	Extra High
Product Attributes						
RELY Required software reliability	.75	.88	1.00	1.15	1.40	
DATA Data base size		.94	1.00	1.08	1.16	
CPLX Product complexity	.70	.85	1.00	1.15	1.30	1.65
Computer Attributes						
TIME Execution time constraint			1.00	1.11	1.30	1.66
STOR Main storage constraint			1.00	1.06	1.21	1.56
VIRT Virtual machine volatility*		.87	1.00	1.15	1.30	
TURN Computer turnaround time		.87	1.00	1.07	1.15	
Personnel Attributes						
ACAP Analyst capability	1.46	1.19	1.00	.86	.71	
AEXP Applications experience	1.29	1.13	1.00	.91	.82	
PCAP Programmer capability	1.42	1.17	1.00	.86	.70	
VEXP Virtual machine experience*	1.21	1.10	1.00	.90		
LEXP Programming language experience	1.14	1.07	1.00	.95		
Project Attributes						
MODP Use of modern programming practices	1.24	1.10	1.00	.91	.82	
TOOL Use of software tools	1.24	1.10	1.00	.91	.83	
SCED Required development schedule	1.23	1.08	1.00	1.04	1.10	

* For a given software product, the underlying virtual machine is the complex of hardware and software (OS, DBMS, etc.) it calls on to accomplish its tasks.

TABLE VII
COCOMO SOFTWARE COST DRIVER RATINGS

Cost Driver	Very Low	Low	Nominal	High	Very High	Extra High
Product attributes						
RELY	Effect: slight inconvenience	Low, easily recoverable losses	Moderate, recoverable losses	High financial loss	Risk to human life	
DATA		$\frac{\text{DB bytes}}{\text{Prog. DSI}} < 10$	$10 \leq \frac{D}{P} < 100$	$100 \leq \frac{D}{P} < 1000$	$\frac{D}{P} \geq 1000$	
CPLX	See Table 8					
Computer attributes						
TIME			≤ 50% use of available execution time	70%	85%	95%
STOR			≤ 50% use of available storage	70%	85%	95%
VIRT		Major change every 12 months Minor: 1 month	Major: 6 months Minor: 2 weeks	Major: 2 months Minor: 1 week	Major: 2 weeks Minor: 2 days	
TURN		Interactive	Average turnaround <4 hours	4–12 hours	>12 hours	
Personnel attributes						
ACAP	15th percentile*	35th percentile	55th percentile	75th percentile	90th percentile	
AEXP	≤4 months experience	1 year	3 years	6 years	12 years	
PCAP	15th percentile*	35th percentile	55th percentile	75th percentile	90th percentile	
VEXP	≤1 month experience	4 months	1 year	3 years		
LEXP	≤1 month experience	4 months	1 year	3 years		
Project attributes						
MODP	No use	Beginning use	Some use	General use	Routine use	
TOOL	Basic microprocessor tools	Basic mini tools	Basic midi/maxi tools	Strong maxi programming, test tools	Add requirements, design, management, documentation tools	
SCED	75% of nominal	85%	100%	130%	160%	

* Team rating criteria: analysis (programming) ability, efficiency, ability to communicate and cooperate

TABLE VIII
COCOMO MODULE COMPLEXITY RATINGS VERSUS TYPE OF
MODULE

Rating	Control Operations	Computational Operations	Device-dependent Operations	Data Management Operations
Very low	Straightline code with a few non-nested SP[a]operators: DOs, CASEs, IFTHENELSEs. Simple predicates	Evaluation of simple expressions: e.g., $A = B + C \cdot (D - E)$	Simple read, write statements with simple formats	Simple arrays in main memory
Low	Straightforward nesting of SP operators. Mostly simple predicates	Evaluation of moderate-level expressions, e.g., $D = SQRT (B^{**}2-4.\cdot A\cdot C)$	No cognizance needed of particular processor or I/O device characteristics. I/O done at GET/PUT level. No cognizance of overlap	Single file subsetting with no data structure changes, no edits, no intermediate files
Nominal	Mostly simple nesting. Some inter-module control. Decision tables	Use of standard math and statistical routines. Basic matrix/vector operations	I/O processing includes device selection, status checking and error processing	Multi-file input and single file output. Simple structural changes, simple edits
High	Highly nested SP operators with many compound predicates. Queue and stack control. Considerable intermodule control.	Basic numerical analysis: multivariate interpolation, ordinary differential equations. Basic truncation, roundoff concerns	Operations at physical I/O level (physical storage address translations; seeks, reads, etc). Optimized I/O overlap	Special purpose subroutines activated by data stream contents. Complex data restructuring at record level
Very high	Reentrant and recursive coding. Fixed-priority interrupt handling	Difficult but structured N.A.: near-singular matrix equations, partial differential equations	Routines for interrupt diagnosis, servicing, masking. Communication line handling	A generalized, parameter-driven file structuring routine. File building, command processing, search optimization
Extra high	Multiple resource scheduling with dynamically changing priorities. Microcode-level control	Difficult and unstructured N.A.: highly accurate analysis of noisy, stochastic data	Device timing-dependent coding, micro-programmed operations	Highly coupled, dynamic relational structures. Natural language data management

[a] SP = structured programming

TABLE IX
COCOMO COST DRIVER RATINGS: MICROPROCESSOR
COMMUNICATIONS SOFTWARE

Cost Driver	Situation	Rating	Effort Multiplier
RELY	Serious financial consequences of software faults	High	1.15
DATA	20,000 bytes	Low	0.94
CPLX	Communications processing	Very High	1.30
TIME	Will use 70% of available time	High	1.11
STOR	45K of 64K store (70%)	High	1.06
VIRT	Based on commercial microprocessor hardware	Nominal	1.00
TURN	Two-hour average turnaround time	Nominal	1.00
ACAP	Good senior analysts	High	0.86
AEXP	Three years	Nominal	1.00
PCAP	Good senior programmers	High	0.86
VEXP	Six months	Low	1.10
LEXP	Twelve months	Nominal	1.00
MODP	Most techniques in use over one year	High	0.91
TOOL	At basic minicomputer tool level	Low	1.10
SCED	Nine months	Nominal	1.00
	Effort adjustment factor (product of effort multipliers)		1.35

The effort multipliers for the other cost driver attributes are obtained similarly, except for the Complexity attribute, which is obtained via Table VIII. Here, we first determine that communications processing is best classified under device-dependent operations (column 3 in Table VIII). From this column, we determine that communication line handling typically has a complexity rating of Very High; from Table VI, then, we determine that its corresponding effort multiplier is 1.30.

Step 3—Estimate Development Effort: We then compute the estimated development effort for the microprocessor communications software as the nominal development effort (44 MM) times the product of the effort multipliers for the 15 cost driver attributes in Table IX (1.35, in Table IX). The resulting estimated effort for the project is then

(44 MM) (1.35) = 59 MM.

Step 4—Estimate Related Project Factors: COCOMO has additional cost estimating relationships for computing the resulting dollar cost of the project and for the breakdown of cost and effort by life-cycle phase (requirements, design, etc.) and by type of project activity (programming, test planning, management, etc.). Further relationships support the estimation of the project's schedule and its phase distribution. For example, the recommended development schedule can be obtained from the estimated development man-months via the embedded-mode schedule equation in Table V:

$$T_{DEV} = 2.5(59)^{0.32} = 9 \text{ months.}$$

As mentioned above, COCOMO also supports the most common types of sensitivity analysis and tradeoff analysis involved in scoping a software project. For example, from Tables VI and VII, we can see that providing the software developers with an interactive computer access capability (Low turnaround time) reduces the TURN effort multiplier from 1.00 to 0.87, and thus reduces the estimated project effort from 59 MM to

(59 MM) (0.87) = 51 MM.

The COCOMO model has been validated with respect to a sample of 63 projects representing a wide variety of business, scientific, systems, real-time, and support software projects. For this sample, Intermediate COCOMO estimates come within 20 percent of the actuals about 68 percent of the time (see Fig. 7). Since the residuals roughly follow a normal distribution, this is equivalent to a standard deviation of roughly 20 percent of the project actuals. This level of accuracy is representative of the current state of the art in software cost models. One can do somewhat better with the aid of a calibration coefficient (also a COCOMO option), or within a limited applications context, but it is difficult to improve significantly on this level of accuracy while the accuracy of software data collection remains in the "±20 percent" range.

A Pascal version of COCOMO is available for a nominal distribution charge from the Wang Institute, under the name WICOMO [18].

Recent Software Cost Estimation Models

Most of the recent software cost estimation models tend to follow the Doty and COCOMO models in having a nominal

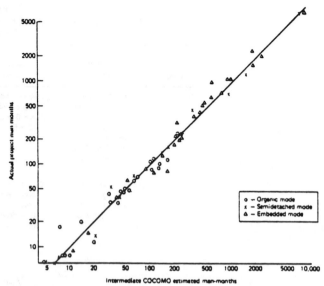

Fig. 7. Intermediate COCOMO estimates versus project actuals.

scaling equation of the form $MM_{NOM} = c(KDSI)^x$ and a set of multiplicative effort adjustment factors determined by a number of cost driver attribute ratings. Some of them use the Rayleigh curve approach to estimate distribution across the software life-cycle, but most use a more conservative effort/schedule tradeoff relation than the SLIM model. These aspects have been summarized for the various models in Table II and Fig. 5.

The Bailey-Basili meta-model [4] derived the scaling equation

$$MM_{NOM} = 3.5 + 0.73 (KDSI)^{1.16}$$

and used two additional cost driver attributes (methodology level and complexity) to model the development effort of 18 projects in the NASA-Goddard Software Engineering Laboratory to within a standard deviation of 15 percent. Its accuracy for other project situations has not been determined.

The Grumman SOFCOST Model [19] uses a similar but unpublished nominal effort scaling equation, modified by 30 multiplicative cost driver variables rated on a scale of 0 to 10. Table II includes a summary of these variables.

The Tausworthe Deep Space Network (DSN) model [50] uses a linear scaling equation ($MM_{NOM} = a(KDSI)^{1.0}$) and a similar set of cost driver attributes, also summarized in Table II. It also has a well-considered approach for determining the equivalent KDSI involved in adapting existing software within a new product. It uses the Rayleigh curve to determine the phase distribution of effort, but uses a considerably more conservative version of the SLIM effort-schedule tradeoff relationship (see Fig. 5).

The Jensen model [30], [31] is a commercially available model with a similar nominal scaling equation, and a set of cost driver attributes very similar to the Doty and COCOMO models (but with different effort multiplier ranges); see Table II. Some of the multiplier ranges in the Jensen model vary as functions of other factors; e.g., increasing access to computer resources widens the multiplier ranges on such cost drivers as personnel capability and use of software tools. It uses the Rayleigh curve for effort distribution, and a somewhat more conservative effort-schedule tradeoff relation than SLIM (see Fig. 5). As with the other commercial models, the Jensen model produces a number of useful outputs on resource expenditure rates, probability distributions on costs and schedules, etc.

C. Outstanding Research Issues in Software Cost Estimation

Although a good deal of progress has been made in software cost estimation, a great deal remains to be done. This section updates the state-of-the-art review published in [11], and summarizes the outstanding issues needing further research:
1) Software size estimation;
2) Software size and complexity metrics;
3) Software cost driver attributes and their effects;
4) Software cost model analysis and refinement;
5) Quantitative models of software project dynamics;
6) Quantitative models of software life-cycle evolution;
7) Software data collection.

1) Software Size Estimation: The biggest difficulty in using today's algorithmic software cost models is the problem of providing sound sizing estimates. Virtually every model requires an estimate of the number of source or object instructions to be developed, and this is an extremely difficult quantity to determine in advance. It would be most useful to have some formula for determining the size of a software product in terms of quantities known early in the software life cycle, such as the number and/or size of the files, input formats, reports, displays, requirements specification elements, or design specification elements.

Some useful steps in this direction are the function-point approach in [2] and the sizing estimation model of [29], both of which have given reasonably good results for small-to-medium sized business programs within a single data processing organization. Another more general approach is given by DeMarco in [17]. It has the advantage of basing its sizing estimates on the properties of specifications developed in conformance with DeMarco's paradigm models for software specifications and designs: number of functional primitives, data elements, input elements, output elements, states, transitions between states, relations, modules, data tokens, control tokens, etc. To date, however, there has been relatively little calibration of the formulas to project data. A recent IBM study [14] shows some correlation between the number of variables defined in a state-machine design representation and the product size in source instructions.

Although some useful results can be obtained on the software sizing problem, one should not expect too much. A wide range of functionality can be implemented beneath any given specification element or I/O element, leading to a wide range of sizes (recall the uncertainty ranges of this nature in Fig. 3). For example, two experiments, involving the use of several teams developing a software program to the same overall functional specification, yielded size ranges of factors of 3 to 5 between programs (see Table X).

The primary implication of this situation for practical software sizing and cost estimation is that *there is no royal road to software sizing.* This is no magic formula that will provide an easy and accurate substitute for the process of thinking through and fully understanding the nature of the software product to be developed. There are still a number of useful

TABLE X
SIZE RANGES OF SOFTWARE PRODUCTS PERFORMING SAME FUNCTION

Experiment	Product	No. of Teams	Size Range (source-instr.)
Weinberg & Schulman [55]	Simultaneous linear equations	6	33–165
Boehm, Gray, & Seewaldt [13]	Interactive cost model	7	1514–4606

things that one can do to improve the situation, including the following.
- Use techniques which explicitly recognize the ranges of variability in software sizing. The PERT estimation technique [56] is a good example.
- Understand the primary sources of bias in software sizing estimates. See [11, ch. 21].
- Develop and use a corporate memory on the nature and size of previous software products.

2) Software Size and Complexity Metrics: Delivered source instructions (DSI) can be faulted for being too low-level a metric for use in early sizing estimation. On the other hand, DSI can also be faulted for being too high-level a metric for precise software cost estimation. Various complexity metrics have been formulated to more accurately capture the relative information content of a program's instructions, such as the Halstead Software Science metrics [24], or to capture the relative control complexity of a program, such as the metrics formulated by McCabe in [39]. A number of variations of these metrics have been developed; a good recent survey of them is given in [26].

However, these metrics have yet to exhibit any practical superiority to DSI as a predictor of the relative effort required to develop software. Most recent studies [48], [32] show a reasonable correlation between these complexity metrics and development effort, but no better a correlation than that between DSI and development effort.

Further, the recent [25] analysis of the software science results indicates that many of the published software science "successes" were not as successful as they were previously considered. It indicates that much of the apparent agreement between software science formulas and project data was due to factors overlooked in the data analysis: inconsistent definitions and interpretations of software science quantities, unrealistic or inconsistent assumptions about the nature of the projects analyzed, overinterpretation of the significance of statistical measures such as the correlation coefficient, and lack of investigation of alternative explanations for the data. The software science use of psychological concepts such as the Stroud number have also been seriously questioned in [16].

The overall strengths and difficulties of software science are summarized in [47]. Despite the difficulties, some of the software science metrics have been useful in such areas as identifying error-prone modules. In general, there is a strong intuitive argument that more definitive complexity metrics will eventually serve as better bases for definitive software cost estimation than will DSI. Thus, the area continues to be an attractive one for further research.

3) Software Cost Driver Attributes and Their Effects: Most of the software cost models discussed above contain a selection of cost driver attributes and a set of coefficients, functions, or tables representing the effect of the attribute on software cost (see Table II). Chapters 24-28 of [11] contain summaries of the research to date on about 20 of the most significant cost driver attributes, plus statements of nearly 100 outstanding research issues in the area.

Since the publication of [11] in 1981, a few new results have appeared. Lawrence [35] provides an analysis of 278 business data processing programs which indicate a fairly uniform development rate in procedure lines of code per hour, some significant effects on programming rate due to batch turnaround time and level of experience, and relatively little effect due to use of interactive operation and modern programming practices (due, perhaps, to the relatively repetitive nature of the software jobs sampled). Okada and Azuma [42] analyzed 30 CAD/CAM programs and found some significant effects due to type of software, complexity, personnel skill level, and requirements volatility.

4) Software Cost Model Analysis and Refinement: The most useful comparative analysis of software cost models to date is the Thibodeau [52] study performed for the U.S. Air Force. This study compared the results of several models (the Wolverton, Doty, PRICE S, and SLIM models discussed earlier, plus models from the Boeing, SDC, Tecolote, and Aerospace corporations) with respect to 45 project data points from three sources.

Some generally useful comparative results were obtained, but the results were not definitive, as models were evaluated with respect to larger and smaller subsets of the data. Not too surprisingly, the best results were generally obtained using models with calibration coefficients against data sets with few points. In general, the study concluded that the models with calibration coefficients achieved better results, but that none of the models evaluated were sufficiently accurate to be used as a definitive Air Force software cost estimation model.

Some further comparative analyses are currently being conducted by various organizations, using the database of 63 software projects in [11], but to date none of these have been published.

In general, such evaluations play a useful role in model refinement. As certain models are found to be inaccurate in certain situations, efforts are made to determine the causes, and to refine the model to eliminate the sources of inaccuracy.

Relatively less activity has been devoted to the formulation, evaluation, and refinement of models to cover the effects of more advanced methods of software development (prototyping, incremental development, use of application generators, etc.) or to estimate other software-related life-cycle costs (conversion, maintenance, installation, training, etc.). An exception is the excellent work on software conversion cost estimation performed by the Federal Conversion Support Center [28]. An extensive model to estimate avionics software support costs using a weighted-multiplier technique has recently been developed [49]. Also, some initial experimental results have been obtained on the quantitative impact of prototyping in [13] and on the impact of very high level nonprocedural languages in [58]. In both studies, projects using prototyping and VHLL's were completed with significantly less effort.

5) Quantitative Models of Software Project Dynamics: Current software cost estimation models are limited in their ability to represent the internal dynamics of a software project, and to estimate how the project's phase distribution of effort and schedule will be affected by environmental or project management factors. For example, it would be valuable to have a model which would accurately predict the effort and schedule distribution effects of investing in more thorough design verification, of pursuing an incremental development strategy, of varying the staffing rate or experience mix, of reducing module size, etc.

Some current models assume a universal effort distribution, such as the Rayleigh curve [44] or the activity distributions in [57], which are assumed to hold for any type of project situation. Somewhat more realistic, but still limited are models with phase-sensitive effort multipliers such as PRICE S [22] and Detailed COCOMO [11].

Recently, some more realistic models of software project dynamics have begun to appear, although to date none of them have been calibrated to software project data. The Phister phase-by-phase model in [43] estimates the effort and schedule required to design, code, and test a software product as a function of such variables as the staffing level during each phase, the size of the average module to be developed, and such factors as interpersonal communications overhead rates and error detection rates. The Abdel Hamid–Madnick model [1], based on Forrester's System Dynamics world-view, estimates the time distribution of effort, schedule, and residual defects as a function of such factors as staffing rates, experience mix, training rates, personnel turnover, defect introduction rates, and initial estimation errors. Tausworthe [51] derives and calibrates alternative versions of the SLIM effort-schedule tradeoff relationship, using an intercommunication-overhead model of project dynamics. Some other recent models of software project dynamics are the Mitre SWAP model and the Duclos [21] total software life-cycle model.

6) Quantitative Models of Software Life-Cycle Evolution: Although most of the software effort is devoted to the software maintenance (or life-cycle support) phase, only a few significant results have been obtained to date in formulating quantitative models of the software life-cycle evolution process. Some basic studies by Belady and Lehman analyzed data on several projects and derived a set of fairly general "laws of program evolution" [7], [37]. For example, the first of these laws states:

> "A program that is used and that as an implementation of its specification reflects some other reality, undergoes continual change or becomes progressively less useful. The change or decay process continues until it is judged more cost effective to replace the system with a re-created version."

Some general quantitative support for these laws was obtained in several studies during the 1970's, and in more recent studies such as [33]. However, efforts to refine these general laws into a set of testable hypotheses have met with mixed results. For example, the Lawrence [36] statistical analysis of the Belady-Lahman data showed that the data supported an even stronger form of the first law ("systems grow in size over their useful life"); that one of the laws could not be formulated precisely enough to be tested by the data; and that the other three laws did not lead to hypotheses that were supported by the data.

However, it is likely that variant hypotheses can be found that are supported by the data (for example, the operating system data supports some of the hypotheses better than does the applications data). Further research is needed to clarify this important area.

7) Software Data Collection: A fundamental limitation to significant progress in software cost estimation is the lack of unambiguous, widely-used standard definitions for software data. For example, if an organization reports its "software development man-months," do these include the effort devoted to requirements analysis, to training, to secretaries, to quality assurance, to technical writers, to uncompensated overtime? Depending on one's interpretations, one can easily cause variations of over 20 percent (and often over a factor of 2) in the meaning of reported "software development man-months" between organizations (and similarly for "delivered instructions," "complexity," "storage constraint," etc.) Given such uncertainties in the ground data, it is not surprising that software cost estimation models cannot do much better than "within 20 percent of the actuals, 70 percent of the time."

Some progress towards clear software data definitions has been made. The IBM FSD database used in [53] was carefully collected using thorough data definitions, but the detailed data and definitions are not generally available. The NASA-Goddard Software Engineering Laboratory database [5], [6], [40] and the COCOMO database [11] provide both clear data definitions and an associated project database which are available for general use (and reasonably compatible). The recent Mitre SARE report [59] provides a good set of data definitions.

But there is still no commitment across organizations to establish and use a set of clear and uniform software data definitions. Until this happens, our progress in developing more precise software cost estimation methods will be severely limited.

IV. Software Engineering Economics Benefits and Challenges

This final section summarizes the benefits to software engineering and software management provided by a software engineering economics perspective in general and by software cost estimation technology in particular. It concludes with some observations on the major challenges awaiting the field.

Benefits of a Software Engineering Economics Perspective

The major benefit of an economic perspective on software engineering is that it provides a balanced view of candidate software engineering solutions, and an evaluation framework which takes account not only of the programming aspects of a situation, but also of the human problems of providing the best possible information processing service within a resource-limited environment. Thus, for example, the software engineering economics approach does not say, "we should use these structured structures because they are mathematically elegant" or "because they run like the wind" or "because they are part of the structured revolution." Instead, it says "we should use these structured structures because they provide people with more benefits in relation to their costs than do other approaches." And besides the framework, of course, it also provides the techniques which help us to arrive at this conclusion.

Benefits of Software Cost Estimation Technology

The major benefit of a good software cost estimation model is that it provides a clear and consistent universe of discourse within which to address a good many of the software engineering issues which arise throughout the software life cycle. It can help people get together to discuss such issues as the following.

• Which and how many features should we put into the software product?

• Which features should we put in first?

• How much hardware should we acquire to support the software product's development, operation, and maintenance?

• How much money and how much calendar time should we allow for software development?

• How much of the product should we adapt from existing software?

• How much should we invest in tools and training?

Further, a well-defined software cost estimation model can help avoid the frequent misinterpretations, underestimates, overexpectations, and outright buy-ins which still plague the software field. In a good cost-estimation model, there is no way of reducing the estimated software cost without changing some objectively verifiable property of the software project. This does not make it impossible to create an unachievable buy-in, but it significantly raises the threshold of credibility.

A related benefit of software cost estimation technology is that it provides a powerful set of insights on how a software organization can improve its productivity. Many of a software cost model's cost-driver attributes are management controllables: use of software tools and modern programming practices, personnel capability and experience, available computer speed, memory, and turnaround time, software reuse. The cost model helps us determine how to adjust these management controllables to increase productivity, and further provides an estimate of how much of a productivity increase we are likely to achieve with a given level of investment. For more information on this topic, see [11, ch. 33], [12] and the recent plan for the U.S. Department of Defense Software Initiative [20].

Finally, software cost estimation technology provides an absolutely essential foundation for software project planning and control. Unless a software project has clear definitions of its key milestones and realistic estimates of the time and money it will take to achieve them, there is no way that a project manager can tell whether his project is under control or not. A good set of cost and schedule estimates can provide realistic data for the PERT charts, work breakdown structures, manpower schedules, earned value increments, etc., necessary to establish management visibility and control.

Note that this opportunity to improve management visibility and control requires a complementary management commitment to define and control the reporting of data on software progress and expenditures. The resulting data are therefore worth collecting simply for their management value in comparing plans versus achievements, but they can serve another valuable function as well: they provide a continuing stream of calibration data for evolving a more accurate and refined software cost estimation models.

Software Engineering Economics Challenges

The opportunity to improve software project management decision making through improved software cost estimation, planning, data collection, and control brings us back full-circle to the original objectives of software engineering economics: to provide a better quantitative understanding of how software people make decisions in resource-limited situations.

The more clearly we as software engineers can understand the quantitative and economic aspects of our decision situations, the more quickly we can progress from a pure seat-of-the-pants approach on software decisions to a more rational approach which puts all of the human and economic decision variables into clear perspective. Once these decision situations are more clearly illuminated, we can then study them in more detail to address the deeper challenge: achieving a quantitative understanding of how people work together in the software engineering process.

Given the rather scattered and imprecise data currently available in the software engineering field, it is remarkable how much progress has been made on the software cost estimation problem so far. But, there is not much further we can go until better data becomes available. The software field cannot hope to have its Kepler or its Newton until it has had its army of Tycho Brahes, carefully preparing the well-defined observational data from which a deeper set of scientific insights may be derived.

REFERENCES

[1] T. K. Abdel-Hamid and S. E. Madnick, "A model of software project management dynamics," in *Proc. IEEE COMPSAC 82*, Nov. 1982, pp. 539–554.

[2] A. J. Albrecht, "Measuring Application Development Productivity," in *SHARE-GUIDE*, 1979, pp. 83–92.

[3] J. D. Aron, "Estimating resources for large programming systems." NATO Sci. Committee, Rome, Italy, Oct. 1969.

[4] J. J. Bailey and V. R. Basili, "A meta-model for software development resource expenditures," in *Proc. 5th Int. Conf. Software Eng.*, IEEE/ACM/NBS, Mar. 1981, pp. 107–116.

[5] V. R. Basili, "Tutorial on models and metrics for software and engineering," IEEE Cat. EHO-167-7, Oct. 1980.

[6] V. R. Basili and D. M. Weiss, "A methodology for collecting valid software engineering data," Univ. Maryland Technol. Rep. TR-1235, Dec. 1982.

[7] L. A. Belady and M. M. Lehman, "Characteristics of large systems," in *Research Directions in Software Technology*, P. Wegner, Ed. Cambridge, MA: MIT Press, 1979.

[8] H. D. Benington, "Production of large computer programs," in *Proc. ONR Symp. Advanced Programming Methods for Digital Computers*, June 1956, pp. 15–27.

[9] R. K. D. Black, R. P. Curnow, R. Katz, and M. D. Gray, "BCS software production data," Boeing Comput. Services, Inc., Final Tech. Rep., RADC-TR-77-116, NTIS AD-A039852, Mar. 1977.

[10] B. W. Boehm, "Software and its impact: A quantitative assessment," *Datamation*, pp. 48–59, May 1973.

[11] ——, *Software Engineering Economics*. Englewood Cliffs, NJ: Prentice-Hall, 1981.

[12] B. W. Boehm, J. F. Elwell, A. B. Pyster, E. D. Stuckle, and R. D. Williams, "The TRW software productivity system," in *Proc. IEEE 6th Int. Conf. Software Eng.*, Sept. 1982.

[13] B. W. Boehm, T. E. Gray, and T. Seewaldt, "Prototyping vs. specifying: A multi-project experiment," *IEEE Trans. Software Eng.*, to be published.

[14] R. N. Britcher and J. E. Gaffney, "Estimates of software size from state machine designs," in *Proc. NASA-Goddard Software Eng. Workshop*, Dec. 1982.

[15] W. M. Carriere and R. Thibodeau, "Development of a logistics software cost estimating technique for foreign military sales," General Res. Corp., Rep. CR-3-839, June 1979.

[16] N. S. Coulter, "Software science and cognitive psychology," *IEEE Trans. Software Eng.*, pp. 166–171, Mar. 1983.

[17] T. DeMarco, *Controlling Software Projects*. New York: Yourdon, 1982.

[18] M. Demshki, D. Ligett, B. Linn, G. McCluskey, and R. Miller, "Wang Institute cost model (WICOMO) tool user's manual," Wang Inst. Graduate Studies, Tyngsboro, MA, June 1982.

[19] H. F. Dircks, "SOFCOST: Grumman's software cost eliminating model," in *IEEE NAECON 1981*, May 1981.

[20] L. E. Druffel, "Strategy for DoD software initiative," RADC/DACS, Griffiss AFB, NY, Oct. 1982.

[21] L. C. Duclos, "Simulation model for the life-cycle of a software product: A quality assurance approach," Ph.D. dissertation, Dep. Industrial and Syst. Eng., Univ. Southern California, Dec. 1982.

[22] F. R. Freiman and R. D. Park, "PRICE software model—Version 3: An overview," in *Proc. IEEE-PINY Workshop on Quantitative Software Models*, IEEE Cat. TH0067-9, Oct. 1979, pp. 32–41.

[23] R. Goldberg and H. Lorin, *The Economics of Information Processing*. New York: Wiley, 1982.

[24] M. H. Halstead, *Elements of Software Science*. New York: Elsevier, 1977.

[25] P. G. Hamer and G. D. Frewin, "M. H. Halstead's software science—A critical examination," in *Proc. IEEE 6th Int. Conf. Software Eng.*, Sept. 1982, pp. 197–205.

[26] W. Harrison, K. Magel, R. Kluczney, and A. DeKock, "Applying software complexity metrics to program maintenance," *Computer*, pp. 65–79, Sept. 1982.

[27] J. R. Herd, J. N. Postak, W. E. Russell, and K. R. Stewart, "Software cost estimation study—Study results," Doty Associates, Inc., Rockville, MD, Final Tech. Rep. RADC-TR-77-220, vol. 1 (of two), June 1977.

[28] C. Houtz and T. Buschbach, "Review and analysis of conversion cost-estimating techniques," GSA Federal Conversion Support Center, Falls Church, VA, Rep. GSA/FCSC-81/001, Mar. 1981.

[29] M. Itakura and A. Takayanagi, " A model for estimating program size and its evaluation," in *Proc. IEEE 6th Software Eng.*, Sept. 1982, pp. 104–109.

[30] R. W. Jensen, "An improved macrolevel software development resource estimation model," in *Proc. 5th ISPA Conf.*, Apr. 1983, pp. 88–92.

[31] R. W. Jensen and S. Lucas, "Sensitivity analysis of the Jensen software model," in *Proc. 5th ISPA Conf.*, Apr. 1983, pp. 384–389.

[32] B. A. Kitchenham, "Measures of programming complexity," *ICL Tech. J.*, pp. 298–316, May 1981.

[33] ——, "Systems evolution dynamics of VME/B," *ICL Tech. J.*, pp. 43–57, May 1982.

[34] W. W. Kuhn, "A software lifecycle case study using the PRICE model," in *Proc. IEEE NAECON*, May 1982.

[35] M. J. Lawrence, "Programming methodology, organizational environment, and programming productivity," *J. Syst. Software*, pp. 257–270, Sept. 1981.

[36] ——, "An examination of evolution dynamics," in *Proc. IEEE 6th Int. Conf. Software Eng.*, Sept. 1982, pp. 188–196.

[37] M. M. Lehman, "Programs, life cycles, and laws of software evolution," *Proc. IEEE*, pp. 1060–1076, Sept. 1980.

[38] R. D. Luce and H. Raiffa, *Games and Decisions*. New York: Wiley, 1957.

[39] T. J. McCabe, "A complexity measure," *IEEE Trans. Software Eng.*, pp. 308–320, Dec. 1976.

[40] F. E. McGarry, "Measuring software development technology: What have we learned in six years," in *Proc. NASA-Goddard Software Eng. Workshop*, Dec. 1982.

[41] E. A. Nelson, "Management handbook for the estimation of computer programming costs," Syst. Develop. Corp., AD-A648750, Oct. 31, 1966.

[42] M. Okada and M. Azuma, "Software development estimation study—A model from CAD/CAM system development experiences," in *Proc. IEEE COMPSAC 82*, Nov. 1982, pp. 555–564.

216

[43] M. Phister, Jr., "A model of the software development process," *J. Syst. Software*, pp. 237–256, Sept. 1981.

[44] L. H. Putnam, "A general empirical solution to the macro software sizing and estimating problem," *IEEE Trans. Software Eng.*, pp. 345–361, July 1978.

[45] L. H. Putnam and A. Fitzsimmons, "Estimating software costs," *Datamation*, pp. 189–198, Sept. 1979; continued in *Datamation*, pp. 171–178, Oct. 1979 and pp. 137–140, Nov. 1979.

[46] L.H. Putnam, "The real economics of software development," in *The Economics of Information Processing*, R. Goldberg and H. Lorin. New York: Wiley, 1982.

[47] V. Y. Shen, S. D. Conte, and H. E. Dunsmore, "Software science revisited: A critical analysis of the theory and its empirical support," *IEEE Trans. Software Eng.*, pp. 155–165, Mar. 1983.

[48] T. Sunohara, A. Takano, K. Uehara, and T. Ohkawa, "Program complexity measure for software development management," in *Proc. IEEE 5th Int. Conf. Software Eng.*, Mar. 1981, pp. 100–106.

[49] SYSCON Corp., "Avionics software support cost model," USAF Avionics Lab., AFWAL-TR-1173, Feb. 1, 1983.

[50] R. C. Tausworthe, "Deep space network software cost estimation model," Jet Propulsion Lab., Pasadena, CA, 1981.

[51] ——, "Staffing implications of software productivity models," in *Proc. 7th Annu. Software Eng. Workshop*, NASA/Goddard, Greenbelt, MD, Dec. 1982.

[52] R. Thibodeau, "An evaluation of software cost estimating models," General Res. Corp., Rep. T10-2670, Apr. 1981.

[53] C. E. Walston and C. P. Felix, "A method of programming measurement and estimation," *IBM Syst. J.*, vol. 16, no. 1, pp. 54–73, 1977.

[54] G. F. Weinwurm, Ed., *On the Management of Computer Programming*. New York: Auerbach, 1970.

[55] G. M. Weinberg and E. L. Schulman, "Goals and performance in computer programming," *Human Factors*, vol. 16, no. 1, pp. 70–77, 1974.

[56] J. D. Wiest and F. K. Levy, *A Management Guide to PERT/CPM*. Englewood Cliffs, NJ: Prentice-Hall, 1977.

[57] R. W. Wolverton, "The cost of developing large-scale software," *IEEE Trans. Comput.*, pp. 615–636, June 1974.

[58] E. Harel and E. R. McLean, "The effects of using a nonprocedural computer language on programmer productivity," UCLA Inform. Sci. Working Paper 3-83, Nov. 1982.

[59] R. L. Dumas, "Final report: Software acquisition resource expenditure (SARE) data collection methodology," MITRE Corp., MTR 9031, Sept. 1983.

Barry W. Boehm received the B.A. degree in mathematics from Harvard University, Cambridge, MA, in 1957 and the M.A. and Ph.D. degrees from the University of California, Los Angeles, in 1961 and 1964, respectively.

From 1978 to 1979 he was a Visiting Professor of Computer Science at the University of Southern California. He is currently a Visiting Professor at the University of California, Los Angeles, and Chief Engineer of TRW's Software Information Systems Division. He was previously Head of the Information Sciences Department at The Rand Corporation, and Director of the 1971 Air Force CCIP-85 study. His responsibilities at TRW include direction of TRW's internal software R&D program, of contract software technology projects, of the TRW software development policy and standards program, of the TRW Software Cost Methodology Program, and the TRW Software Productivity Program. His most recent book is *Software Engineering Economics*, by Prentice-Hall.

Dr. Boehm is a member of the IEEE Computer Society and the Association for Computing Machinery, and an Associate Fellow of the American Institute of Aeronautics and Astronautics.

Software Function, Source Lines of Code, and Development Effort Prediction: A Software Science Validation

ALLAN J. ALBRECHT AND JOHN E. GAFFNEY, JR., MEMBER, IEEE

Abstract—One of the most important problems faced by software developers and users is the prediction of the size of a programming system and its development effort. As an alternative to "size," one might deal with a measure of the "function" that the software is to perform. Albrecht [1] has developed a methodology to estimate the amount of the "function" the software is to perform, in terms of the data it is to use (absorb) and to generate (produce). The "function" is quantified as "function points," essentially, a weighted sum of the numbers of "inputs," "outputs," master files," and "inquiries" provided to, or generated by, the software. This paper demonstrates the equivalence between Albrecht's external input/output data flow representative of a program (the "function points" metric) and Halstead's [2] "software science" or "software linguistics" model of a program as well as the "soft content" variation of Halstead's model suggested by Gaffney [7].

Further, the high degree of correlation between "function points" and the eventual "SLOC" (source lines of code) of the program, and between "function points" and the work-effort required to develop the code, is demonstrated. The "function point" measure is thought to be more useful than "SLOC" as a prediction of work effort because "function points" are relatively easily estimated from a statement of basic requirements for a program early in the development cycle.

The strong degree of equivalency between "function points" and "SLOC" shown in the paper suggests a two-step work-effort validation procedure, first using "function points" to estimate "SLOC," and then using "SLOC" to estimate the work-effort. This approach would provide validation of application development work plans and work-effort estimates early in the development cycle. The approach would also more effectively use the existing base of knowledge on producing "SLOC" until a similar base is developed for "function points."

The paper assumes that the reader is familiar with the fundamental theory of "software science" measurements and the practice of validating estimates of work-effort to design and implement software applications (programs). If not, a review of [1]–[3] is suggested.

Index Terms—Cost estimating, function points, software linguistics, software science, software size estimation.

"FUNCTION POINTS" BACKGROUND

ALBRECHT [1] has employed a methodology for validating estimates of the amount of work-effort (which he calls work-hours) needed to design and develop custom application software. The approach taken is ". . . to list and count the number of external user inputs, inquiries, outputs, and master files to be delivered by the development project." As pointed out by Albrecht [1], "these factors are the outward manifestations of any application. They cover all the functions in an application." Each of these categories of input and output are counted individually and then weighted by

Manuscript received May 12, 1982; revised September 9, 1982.

A. J. Albrecht is with the IBM Corporate Information Systems and Administration, White Plains, NY 10601.

J. E. Gaffney, Jr., is with the Federal Systems Division, IBM, Gaithersburg, MD.

numbers reflecting the relative value of the function to the user/customer. The weighted sum of the inputs and outputs is called "function points." Albrecht [1] states that the weights used were "determined by debate and trial." They are given in the section "Selection of Estimating Formulas."

The thesis of this work is that the amount of function to be provided by the application (program) can be estimated from an itemization of the major components of data to be used or provided by it. Furthermore, this estimate of function should be correlated to both the amount of "SLOC" to be developed and the development effort needed.

A major reason for using "function points" as a measure is that the point counts can be developed relatively easily in discussions with the user/customer at an *early* stage of the development process. They relate directly to user/customer requirements in a way that is more easily understood by the user/customer than "SLOC."

Another major reason is the availability of needed information. Since it is reasonable to expect that a statement of basic requirements includes an itemization of the inputs and outputs to be used and provided by the application (program) from the user's external view, an estimate may be validated early in the development cycle with this approach.

A third reason is that "function points" can be used to develop a general measure of development productivity (e.g., "function points per work-month" or "work-hours per function point"), that may be used to demonstrate productivity trends. Such a measure can give credit for productivity relative to the amount of user function delivered to the user/customer per unit of development effort, with less concern for effects of technology, language level, or unusual code expansion occasioned by macros, calls, and code reuse.

It is important to distinguish between two types of work-effort estimates, a primary or "task-analysis" estimate and a "formula" estimate. The primary work-effort estimate should always be based on an analysis of the tasks to be done, thus providing the project team with an estimate *and a work plan*. This paper discusses "formula" estimates which are based solely on counts of inputs and outputs of the program to be developed, and not on a detailed analysis of the development tasks to be performed. It is recommended that such "formula" estimates be used only to validate and provide perspective on primary estimates.

"SOFTWARE SCIENCE" BACKGROUND

Halstead [2] states that the number of tokens or symbols N constituting a program is a function of η, the "operator"

Reprinted from *IEEE Transactions on Software Engineering*, Vol. SE-9, No. 6, November 1983, pp. 639–648. Copyright © 1983 by The Institute of Electrical and Electronics Engineers, Inc. All rights reserved.

TABLE I
DP Service Project Data

Custom Application Number	Language	Input/Output Element Counts				Function Points	Source Lines of Code (SLOC)	Work-Hours
		IN	OUT	FILE	INQ			
1	COBOL	25	150	60	75	1750	130K	102.4K
2	COBOL	193	98	36	70	1902	318K	105.2K
3	COBOL	70	27	12	--	428	20K	11.1K
4	PL/1	40	60	12	20	759	54K	21.1K
5	COBOL	10	69	9	1	431	62K	28.8K
6	COBOL	13	19	23	--	283	28K	10.0K
7	COBOL	34	14	5	--	205	35K	8.0K
8	COBOL	17	17	5	15	289	30K	4.9K
9	COBOL	45	64	16	14	680	48K	12.9K
10	COBOL	40	60	15	20	794	93K	19.0K
11	COBOL	41	27	5	29	512	57K	10.8K
12	COBOL	33	17	5	8	224	22K	2.9K
13	COBOL	28	41	11	16	417	24K	7.5K
14	PL/1	43	40	35	20	682	42K	12.0K
15	COBOL	7	12	8	13	209	40K	4.1K
16	COBOL	28	38	9	24	512	96K	15.8K
17	PL/1	42	57	5	12	606	40K	18.3K
18	COBOL	27	20	6	24	400	52K	8.9K
19	COBOL	48	66	50	13	1235	94K	38.1K
20	PL/1	69	112	39	21	1572	110K	61.2K
21	COBOL	25	28	22	4	500	15K	3.6K
22	DMS	61	68	11	--	694	24K	11.8K
23	DMS	15	15	3	6	199	3K	0.5K
24	COBOL	12	15	15	--	260	29K	6.1K

Note: (1) "IN" = No. of inputs; "OUT" = No. of outputs; "FILE" = No. of master files; "INQ" = No. of inquires

vocabulary size, and η, the "operand" vocabulary size. His software length equation is

$$N = \eta_1 \log_2 \eta_1 + \eta_2 \log_2 \eta_2.$$

This formula was originally derived to apply to a small program (or one procedure of a large program) or function, that is, to apply to the program expression of an algorithm. Thus, the number of tokens in a program consisting of a multiplicity of functions or procedures is best found by applying the size equation to each function or procedure individually, and summing the results.

Gaffney [3] has applied the software length equation to a single address machine in the following way. A program consists of data plus instructions. A sequence of instructions can be thought of as a string of "tokens." At the machine code level, for a single address machine, "op. code" tokens, generally alternate with "data label" tokens. Exceptions do occur due to instructions that require no data labels. The "op. codes" may be referred to as "operators" and the "data labels" as "operands." Thus, in an instruction of the form "LA X", meaning, load accumulator with the content of location X, "LA" is the operator, and "X" is the operand. For single address machine level code, the case Gaffney [3] analyzes, one would expect to have approximately twice as many tokens (N) as instructions (I). That is, $I = 0.5N$. Gaffney [3] applied the Halstead software length equation to object code for the AN/UYK-7 military computer (used in the Trident missile submarine's sonar system, as well as other applications). He determined a value for the coefficient "b" in the equation "$I = bN$." It was $b = 0.478$, and the correlation between the estimate $I = 0.478N$ (where the estimate $\hat{N} = \eta_1 \log_2 \eta_1 + \eta_2 \log_2 \eta_2$), and the actual instruction count I, was 0.916. Thus, the data correlated closely with the estimate from the software length equation.

Gaffney's work presumed that the number of unique instruction types (η_1), or operator vocabulary size employed, as well

as the number of unique data labels (η_2) or operand vocabulary size used, was known. However, η_1 need not be known in order for one to estimate the number of tokens N or the number of instructions I. An "average" figure for η_1 (and thus for $\eta_1 \log_2 \eta_1$) can be employed, or the factor $\eta_1 \log_2 \eta_1$ can be omitted, inducing some degree of error, of course. Indeed, Christiansen et al. [4] have observed that ". . . program size is determined by the data that must be processed by the program." Thus one could take several different approaches to estimating software (code) size. The data label vocabulary size (η_2) could be estimated. Alternatively, it is suggested that (η_2^*), the number of conceptually unique inputs and outputs, can be used as a surrogate for (η_2). The estimate for (η_2^*) should be relatively easy to determine early in the design cycle, from the itemization of external inputs and outputs found in a complete requirements definition or external system design.

Some data by Dekerf [5] supports the idea that I (and N) can be estimated as multiples of the variates $\eta_2 \log_2 \eta_2$ and $\eta_2^* \log_2 \eta_2^*$ (for example: $I = A \eta_2 \log_2 \eta_2$, where ($A$) is some constant). Dekerf counted tokens (N), operands (η_2), and conceptually unique inputs and outputs (η_2^*) in 29 APL programs found in a book [6] by Allen of the IBM System Science Institute in Los Angeles. Using Dekerf's data, we have found that the sample correlation between N and $\eta_2^* \log_2 \eta_2^*$ is 0.918, and between N and $\eta_2 \log_2 \eta_2$ is 0.988.

In the next sections, we demonstrate that these (and other) software science formulas originally developed for (small) algorithms only can be applied to large applications (programs), where (η_2^*) is then interpreted to mean the sum of overall external inputs and outputs to the application (program). "Function points" [1] can be interpreted as a weighted sum of the top level input/output items (e.g., screens, reports, files) that are equivalent to (η_2^*). Also, as is shown subsequently, a number of variates based on "function points" can be used as the measure of the function that the application (program) is to provide.

219

TABLE II
Estimating Variates Explored

Independent Variate	Formula Basis	Dependent Variable Explored Source Lines of Code		Work-Hours
		PL/I	COBOL	
1. Function Points	F	X	X	X
2. Function Sort Content	$(F/2) \log_2 (F/2)$	X		X
3. Function Potential Volume	$(F+2) \log_2 (F+2)$	X		
4. Function Information Content	$F \log_2 F$	X		X
5. I/O Count	V			X
6. Sort Count	$(V/2) \log_2 (V/2)$			X
7. Count Information Content	$V \log_2 V$			X
8. Source Lines of COBOL	SLOC			X
9. Source Lines of PL/I	SLOC			X

DP Services Data

Table I provides data on 24 applications developed by the IBM DP Services organization. The language used in each application is cited. The counts of four types of external input/output elements for the application as a whole are given. The number of "function points" for each program is identified. The number of "SLOC," including comments (all the "SLOC" was new) that implemented the function required is identified. Finally, the number of work-hours required to design, develop, and test the application is given.

Selection of Estimating Formulas

Using the DP Services data shown in Table I, 13 estimating formulas were explored as functions of the 9 variates listed in Table II. A basis for their selection is now provided. "Function points" count (F) is the variable determined using Albrecht's methodology [1]. Albrecht uses the following average weights to determine "function points": number of inputs $\times$ 4; number of outputs $\times$ 5; number of inquiries $\times$ 4; number of master files $\times$ 10. Interfaces are considered to be master files. As stated in [1], the weighted sum of inputs, outputs, inquiries, and master files can be adjusted within a range of +/- 25 percent, depending upon the estimator's assessment of the complexity of the program. As an example of the calculation of the number of "function points," consider the data for "custom application one" in Table I. The number of function points is equal to

$$F = (25 \times 4) + (150 \times 5) + (75 \times 4) + (60 \times 10) = 1750.$$

The current "Function Points Index Worksheet" being used in the IBM I/S organization is shown in Appendix A. The major changes from [1] are as follows.

1) Interfaces are separately identified and counted.

2) Provision is made for above average and below average complexities of the elements counted.

3) A more objective measure of processing complexity is provided.

"I/O count" (V) is the total program input/output count without the weights and processing complexity adjustment applied in "function points." Both function points and I/O count are treated as equivalent to Halstead's η_2^*, the unique input/output (data element) count. The "potential volume" formula $(F + 2) \log_2 (F + 2)$ was developed by Halstead [2]. The "information content" formula ($F \log_2 F$), also used as a variate here, corresponds to $\eta_2^* \log_2 \eta_2^*$, an approximation to the factor $\eta_2 \log_2 \eta_2$ in Halstead's software length equation.

The origin of the "sort count" variate $(F/2) \log_2 (F/2)$ is as follows. Gaffney [7] estimated the number of conditional jumps in a program to be

$$J = (\eta_2^*/2) \log_2 (\eta_2^*/2)$$

if it is assumed that the η_2^* (total number of conceptually unique inputs and outputs) are equally divided between inputs and outputs. This is in keeping with the following observations: if $\eta_2^*/2$ were to symbolize the number of items to be sorted (by a data processing program), then the number of comparisons (and hence conditional jumps) required would be on the order of J, as just defined [8]. This form is used subsequently as the "sort content" where either the variable "F" ("function point") or "V" (I/O count) is employed in the place of η_2^*.

Development and Application of Estimating Formulas

This section provides a number of formulas for estimating work hours and "SLOC" as functions of "function points" (F), "input/output count" (V), and several of the variates cited in Table II, which themselves are functions of (F) and (V), as described in the previous section).

To demonstrate the equivalency of the various measures and also to show their effectiveness as estimators, correlations were performed on the combinations of variates checked in Table II. Table III summarizes the results of using the variates checked to estimate "SLOC" in the Cobol and PL/1 applications (see Table I) as indicated. The estimating model relating

TABLE III
Summary Comparison of the SLOC Estimation Approaches

Estimators of SLOC (1) Variables Used Were:	Relative Error (2)		Sample Correlation Between the Variables And Actual SLOC
	Avg.	Standard Deviation	
1. Function Points (COBOL)	.229	.736	.854
2. Function Points (PL/1)	.003	.058	.997
3. Function Sort Content (PL/1)	.007	.057	.997
4. Function Potential Volume (PL/1)	-.002	.057	.997
5. Function Information Content (PL/1)	-.002	.057	.997

Notes:

(1) The formulas used were:

1. $\hat{S} = 118.7\ (F) - 6,490$
2. $\hat{S} = 73.1\ (F) - 4,600$
3. $\hat{S} = 13.9\ (F/2)\ \log_2\ (F/2) + 5,360$
4. $\hat{S} = 6.3\ (F+2)\ \log_2\ (F+2) + 4,370$
5. $\hat{S} = 6.3\ (F\ \log_2\ F) + 4,500$

(2) $\dfrac{\hat{S}-S}{S}$, where $\hat{S}$ = estimate and S = actual SLOC

TABLE IV
Summary Comparison of the Work-Hours Estimation Approaches

Estimators of Work-hours (1) Variables Used Were:	Relative Error (2)		Sample Correlation Between the Variables And Actual Work-Hours
	Avg.	Standard Deviation	
1. Function Points	.242	.848	.935
2. Function Sort Content	.192	.759	.945
3. Function Information Content	.194	.763	.944
4. I/O Count	.206	.703	.945
5. I/O Count Sort Content	.195	.630	.954
6. I/O Count Information Content	.195	.637	.954
7. Source Lines of Code (PL/1)	.023	.213	.988
8. Source Lines of Code (COBOL)	.323	.669	.864

Notes:

(1) The formulas used were:

1. $\hat{W} = 54\ (F) - 13,390$
2. $\hat{W} = 10.75\ (F/2)\ \log_2\ (F/2) - 8,300$
3. $\hat{W} = 4.89\ (F\ \log_2\ F) - 8,762$
4. $\hat{W} = 309\ (V) - 15,780$
5. $\hat{W} = 79\ (V/2)\ \log_2\ (V/2) - 8,000$
6. $\hat{W} = 35\ (V\ \log_2\ V) - 8,900$
7. $\hat{W} = 0.6713\ (S) - 13,137$, PL/1
8. $\hat{W} = 0.3793\ (S) - 2,913$ COBOL

(2) $\dfrac{\hat{W}-W}{S}$, where $\hat{W}$ = estimated and W = actual work-hours

"function points" to PL/1 "SLOC" was found to be quite different from the model for Cobol. Significantly more Cobol "SLOC" are required to deliver the same amount of "function points" than are required with PL/1 "SLOC." The PL/1 data in particular closely approximate a straight line for all the measures. Any of the measures shown should be a good estimator for PL/1 "SLOC." In the next section, these measures are further validated using additional data from three other application development sites.

Table IV summarizes the results of using the variables checked in Table II and SLOC to estimate work-effort. The correlations and standard deviations of the data for the estimating formulas, using I/O count (V) and function point count (F), shown suggest that any of them would be an effective "formula" estimate. The measures based on "I/O count" show slightly, but not significantly, better statistics than those based on "function points." The last two rows of Table IV summarize the results of using "SLOC" to estimate work-effort. It is

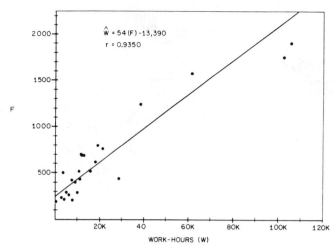

Fig. 1. Function points versus work-hours.

TABLE V
SOME VALIDATION STATISTICS

SLOC Estimating Formula (2)	Relative Error (3)		Sample Correlation Between $\hat{S}$ and S
	Avg.	Standard Deviation	
$\hat{S}_1$	-.0753	.5438	.9367
$\hat{S}_2$	.2406	.5174	.9367
$\hat{S}_3$	-.0182	.4151	.9374
$\hat{S}_4$	.0629	.3983	.9289

Notes:
(1) For 'validation sites' 2, 3, 4, see detailed data in Table 6.

(2) $\hat{S}_1$ = 73.1F - 4600 (based on the PL/1 cases)

$\hat{S}_2$ = 53.2F + 12773 (based on all 24 cases) } derived from the

$\hat{S}_3$ = 66F (a simplified model) } DPS data

$\hat{S}_4$ = 6.3F log F + 4500 (based on the PL/1 cases)

(3) $\dfrac{\hat{S}-S}{S}$, where S = actual SLOC and $\hat{S}$ = estimated SLOC

shown that the estimating model based on the Cobol data is quite different from the model based on PL/1 data. Almost twice as much work-effort is required to produce a "SLOC" of PL/1 as is required to produce a "SLOC" of Cobol. However, Table III shows that almost twice as much "function" is estimated to be delivered by an "SLOC" of PL/1 as is estimated to be delivered by an "SLOC" of Cobol. Therefore, it is advisable to keep these languages separated in estimating models based on "SLOC."

Fig. 1 is a scatter plot of actual "function points" and work-hours data and estimation formula number 1 from Table IV plotted on the same graph.

The correlations and standard deviations of linear models of "function points," "function sort content," "function information content," "I/O count," "I/O count," "I/O count sort content," and "I/O count information content," and "SLOC" are shown in Table IV. Each model could be an effective tool for validating estimates. The early availability of elements that comprise "function points" and "I/O count" for an application suggest that this validation could be done earlier in the development schedule than validations based on estimated "SLOC."

VALIDATION

The previous section, and the related figure and tables, developed several estimating formulas and explored their consistency within the DP Services data used to develop the formulas. This section validates several SLOC estimation formulas developed from the DP Services data presented in Table I against three *different* development sites. While it is *interesting* to note relations between "function points" and SLOC, it is *significant* to know that these relations hold also on a *different* set of data than that employed to develop them originally. The excellent degree of fit obtained would tend to support the view that these (and the other) formulas not validated here have some degree of universality. Table V presents four formulas developed from the DP Services data and the statistics of their validation on the data form the other three sites. Table VI provides the data from the three sites from which the statistics in Table V are derived. The very high values of sample correlation between the estimated and actual SLOC for the 17 validation sites, listed in Table V (i.e., >0.92) are most encouraging.

TABLE VI
VALIDATION OF SOME SLOC ESTIMATING EQUATIONS

Application Number	Function Points F	PL/I SLOC S	$\hat{S}_1$ KSLOC	$\hat{S}_2$ KSLOC	$\hat{S}_3$ KSLOC	$\hat{S}_4$ KSLOC
1. DPS - 4	759	54K	50.9	53.2	50.1	50.2
2. 14	682	42K	45.2	49.1	45.0	44.9
3. 17	606	40K	39.7	45.0	40.0	39.8
4. 20	1,572	110K	110.3	96.4	103.8	109.7
5. Site 2-1	803	31.0K	54.1	55.5	53.0	53.3
6. 2	335	31.4K	19.9	30.6	22.1	22.2
7. 3	685	23.3K	45.5	49.2	45.2	45.2
8. 4	1,119	126.6K	77.2	72.3	73.9	75.9
9. 5	712	40.9K	47.4	50.7	47.0	47.0
10. 6	261	19.9K	14.5	26.7	17.2	17.7
11. Site 3-1	1,387	120K	96.8	86.6	91.5	95.7
12. 2	1,728	120K	121.7	104.7	114.0	121.6
13. 3	2,878	150K	205.8	165.9	190.0	212.8
14. Site 4-1	2,165	123.2K	153.7	128.0	142.9	155.6
15. 2	236	16.3K	12.7	25.3	15.6	16.2
16. 3	3,694	195.0K	265.4	209.3	243.8	280.3
17. 4	224	41.0K	11.8	24.7	14.8	15.5
18. 5	42	6.5K	-1.5	15.0	2.8	5.9
19. 6	1,629	102.0K	114.5	99.4	107.5	114.0
20. 7	105	9.8K	3.1	18.4	6.9	8.9
21. 8	581	45.9K	37.9	43.7	38.3	38.1
Average Relative Error			-.060	.186	-.024	.051
Std. Deviation of Relative Error			.488	.480	.372	.358
Correlation With S			.938	.938	.938	.997

CONCLUSION

The "function point" software estimation procedure appears to have a strong theoretical support based on Halstead's software science formulas. Apparently, some of Halstead's formulas are extremely robust and can be applied to the major inputs and outputs of a software product at the top level. At least for the applications analyzed, both the development work-hours and application size in "SLOC" are strong functions of "function points" and "input/output data item count." Further, it appears that basing applications development effort estimates on the amount of function to be provided by an application rather than an estimate of "SLOC" may be superior.

The observations suggest a two-step estimate validation process, which uses "function points" or "I/O count" to estimate, early in the development cycle, the "SLOC" to be produced. The work-effort would then be estimated from the estimated "SLOC." This approach can provide an early bridge between "function points," software science," and "SLOC," until "function points" and "software science" have a broader supporting base of productivity data.

APPENDIX

A. Function Points Definitions

This section provides the basic definitions supporting the measurement, recording, and analysis of function points, work-effort, and attributes.

B. General

The following considerations are generally applicable to the specific definitions of function points, work-effort, and attributes in later paragraphs in this section.

1) Development Work-Product versus Support Work-Product: Development productivity should be measured by counting the function points added or changed by the development or enhancement project. Therefore, we have the following.

Development Work-Product: The absolute value sum of all function points added or changed by the development or enhancement project. (Deleted function points are considered to be changed function points.)

Support productivity should be measured by counting the total function points supported by the support project during the support period. Therefore, we have the following.

Support Work-Product: The original function points of the application, adjusted for any changes in complexity introduced, plus any function points added, minus any function points deleted by subsequent enhancement projects.

2) Measurement Timing: To provide the work-product, work-effort, and attributes measures needed for each development project, enhancement project, and support project to be measured, the indicated measures should be determined at the following times in the application life cycle.

• The development work-product and attributes measures should be determined at the completion of the *external design phase* for each development and enhancement project (when the user external view of the application has been documented).

• The development work-product, work-effort, and attributes measures should be determined at the completion of the *installation phase* for each development and enhancement project (when the application is ready for use).

• The support work-product, work-effort, and attributes measures should be determined at the end of *each year* of support and use for each support project.

3) Application Boundaries: Normally, as shown in Fig. 1, a single continuous external boundary is considered when counting function points. However, there are two general situations where counting function points for an application in parts, is necessary.

a) The application is planned to be developed in multiple stages, using more than one development project.

This situation should be counted, estimated, and measured as *separate projects*, including all inputs, outputs, interfaces, and inquiries crossing *all* boundaries.

b) The application is planned to be developed as a single application using one development project, but it is so large that it will be necessary to divide it into subapplications for counting function points.

The internal boundaries are arbitrary and are for counting purposes only. The subapplications should be counted separately, but *none* of the inputs, outputs, interfaces, and inquiries crossing the *arbitrary internal* boundaries should be counted. The function points of the subapplications should then be summed to give the total function points of the application for estimation and measurement.

4) Brought-In Application Code: Count the function points provided by brought-in application code (reused code), such as: an IBM, IUP, PP, or FDP; an internal shared application; or a purchased application if that code was selected, modified, integrated, tested, or installed by the project team. However, do *not* count the function points provided by the brought-in code that provided user function beyond that stated in the approved requirements.

Some examples are the following.

a) Do count the function points provided by an application picked up from another IBM site, or project, and installed by the project team.

b) Do *not* count the function points provided by software, such as IMS or a screen compiler, if that software had been made available by another project team.

c) Do *not* count ADF updates of *all* files if the user only required updates of *three* files, even though the capability may be automatically provided.

5) Consider All Users: Consider *all* users of the application, since each application may have provision for many specified user functions, such as:
- end user functions (enter data, inquire, etc.)
- conversion and installation user functions (file scan, file compare discrepancy list, etc.)
- operations user functions (recovery, control totals, etc.).

C. Function Points Measure

After the general considerations described in the preceding paragraphs have been decided, the function points measure is accomplished in three general steps:

a) classify and count the five user function types;

b) adjust for processing complexity;

c) make the function points calculation.

The paragraphs in this section define and describe each of these steps. The first step is accomplished as follows.

Classify, to three levels of complexity, the following user functions that were made available to the user through the design, development, testing, or support efforts of the development, enhancement, or support project team:

a) external input types;

b) external output types;

c) logical internal file types;

d) external interface file types;

e) external inquiry types.

Then *list* and *count* these user functions. The counts should be recorded for use in the function points calculation, on an appropriate work-sheet. Examples of the useful function points work-sheets are provided in Section IV, function points work-sheets.

The definitions of each of the user functions to be counted, and the levels of complexity, are provided in the following paragraphs.

1) External Input Type: Count each unique user *data* or user *control* input type that enters the external boundary of the application being measured, and *adds* or *changes* data in a logical internal file type. An external input type should be considered unique if it has a different *format*, or if the external design requires a *processing logic* different from other external input types of the same format. As illustrated in Fig. 1, include external input types that enter directly as transactions from the user, and those that enter as transactions from other applications, such as, input files of transactions.

Each external input type should be classified within three levels of complexity, as follows.

- *Simple:* Few data element types are included in the external input type, and few logical internal file types are referenced by the external input type. User human factors considerations are not significant in the design of the external input type.

- *Average:* The external input type is not clearly either simple or complex.

- *Complex:* Many data element types are included in the external input type, and many logical internal file types are referenced by the external input type. User human factors considerations significantly affect the design of the external input type.

Do *not* include external input types that are introduced into the application only because of the technology used.

Do *not* include input files of records as external input types, because these are counted as external interface file types.

Do *not* include the input part of the external inquiry types as external input types, because these are counted as external inquiry types.

2) External Output Type: Count each unique user *data* or *control* output type that leaves the external boundary of the application being measured. An external output type should be considered unique if it has a different *format*, or if the external design requires a *processing logic* different from other external output types of the same format. As illustrated in Fig. 1, include external output types that leave directly as reports and messages to the user, and those that leave as reports and messages to other applications, such as, output files of reports and messages.

Each external output type should be classified within three

levels of complexity, using definitions similar to those for the external input types [paragraph C1]. For reports, the following additional complexity definitions should be used.

- *Simple:* One or two columns. Simple data element transformations.
- *Average:* Multiple columns with subtotals. Multiple data element transformations.
- *Complex:* Intricate data element transformations. Multiple and complex file references to be correlated. Significant performance considerations.

Do *not* include external output types that are introduced into the application only because of the technology used.

Do *not* include output files of records as external output types, because these are counted as external interface file types.

Do *not* include the output response of external inquiry types as external output types, because these are counted as external inquiry types.

3) Logical Internal File Type: Count each major logical group of user *data* or *control* information in the application as a logical internal file type. Include each logical file, or within a data base, each logical group of data from the viewpoint of the user, that is *generated*, *used*, and *maintained* by the application. Count logical files as described in the external design, not physical files.

The logical internal file types should be classified within three levels of complexity as follows.

- *Simple:* Few record types. Few data element types. No significant performance or recovery considerations.
- *Average:* The logical internal file type is not clearly either simple or complex.
- *Complex:* Many record types. Many data element types. Performance and recovery are significant considerations.

Do *not* include logical internal files that are *not* accessible to the user through external input, output, interface file, or inquiry types.

4) External Interface File Type: Files *passed* or *shared* between applications should be counted as external interface file types within *each* application. Count each major logical group of user *data* or *control* information that enters or leaves the application, as an external interface file type. External interface file types should be classified within three levels of complexity, using definitions similar to those for logical internal file types [paragraph C3].

Outgoing external interface file types should also be counted as logical internal file types for the application.

5) External Inquiry Type: Count each unique input/output combination, where an input causes and generates an immediate output, as an external inquiry type. An external inquiry type should be considered unique if it has a *format* different from other external inquiry types in either its input or output parts, or if the external design requires a *processing logic* different from other external inquiry types of the same format. As illustrated in Fig. 1, include external inquiry types that enter directly from the user, and those that enter from other applications.

The external inquiry types should be classified within three levels of complexity as follows.

a) Classify the input part of the external inquiry using definitions similar to the external input type [paragraph C1].

b) Classify the output part of the external inquiry type using definitions similar to the external output type [paragraph C2].

3) The complexity of the external inquiry type is the greater of the two classifications.

To help distinguish external inquiry types from external input types, consider that the input data of an external inquiry type is entered only to direct the search, and no update of logical internal file types should occur.

Do *not* confuse a query facility as an external inquiry type. An external inquiry type is a direct search for specific data, usually using only a single key. A query facility provides an organized structure of external input, output, and inquiry types to compose many possible inquiries using many keys and operations. These external input, output, and inquiry types should *all* be counted to measure a query facility.

6) Processing Complexity: The previous paragraphs define the external input, external output, internal file, external interface file, and external inquiry types to be listed, classified, and counted. The function points calculation [paragraph C7] describes how to use these counts to measure the standard processing associated with those user functions. This paragraph describes how to apply some general application characteristics to adjust the standard processing measure for processing complexity.

The adjustment for processing complexity should be accomplished in three steps, as follows.

a) The *degree of influence* of each of the 14 general characteristics, on the value of the application to the users, should be estimated.

b) The 14 degree of influence(s) should be summed, and the total should be used to develop an *adjustment factor* ranging from 0.65 to 1.35 (this gives an adjustment of +/- 35 percent).

c) The *standard processing measure* should be multiplied by the adjustment factor to develop the work-product measure called function points.

The first step is accomplished as follows.

Estimate the degree of influence, on the application, of each of the 14 general characteristics that follow. Use the degree of influence measures in the following list, and record the estimates on a work-sheet similar to Fig. 2.

Degree of Influence Measures:

- Not present, or no influence if present   = 0
- Insignificant influence   = 1
- Moderate influence   = 2
- Average influence   = 3
- Significant influence   = 4
- Strong influence, throughout   = 5.

General Application Characteristics:

a) The *data* and control information used in the application are sent or received over *communication* facilities. Terminals connected locally to the control unit are considered to use communication facilities.

b) *Distributed* data or processing *functions* are a characteristic of the application.

4.1 FUNCTION POINTS CALCULATION

Application: _____. Appl ID: _____.

Prepared by: _____ __/__/__. Reviewed by: _____ __/__/__.

Notes: _____

o Function Count:

Type ID	Description	Complexity			Total
		Simple	Average	Complex	
IT	External Input	__ x 3 = __	__ x 4 = __	__ x 6 = __	__
OT	External Output	__ x 4 = __	__ x 5 = __	__ x 7 = __	__
FT	Logical Internal File	__ x 7 = __	__ x10 = __	__ x15 = __	__
EI	Ext Interface File	__ x 5 = __	__ x 7 = __	__ x10 = __	__
QT	External Inquiry	__ x 3 = __	__ x 4 = __	__ x 6 = __	__
FC		Total Unadjusted Function Points			__

o Processing Complexity:

ID	Characteristic	DI	ID	Characteristic	DI
C1	Data Communications	__	C8	Online Update	__
C2	Distributed Functions	__	C9	Complex Processing	__
C3	Performance	__	C10	Reuseability	__
C4	Heavily Used Configuration	__	C11	Installation Ease	__
C5	Transaction Rate	__	C12	Operational Ease	__
C6	Online Data Entry	__	C13	Multiple Sites	__
C7	End User Efficiency	__	C14	Facilitate Change	__
PC		Total Degree of Influence			__

o DI Values:

- Not present, or no influence = 0
- Insignificant influence = 1
- Moderate influence = 2
- Average influence = 3
- Significant influence = 4
- Strong influence, throughout = 5

PCA Processing Complexity Adjustment = 0.65 + (0.01 x PC) = _____.

FP Function Points Measure = FC x PCA = _____.

Fig. 2. Function points calculation worksheet.

c) Application *performance* objectives, in either response or throughput, influenced the design, development, installation, and support of the application.

d) A *heavily used* operational *configuration* is a characteristic of the application. The user wants to run the application on existing or committed equipment that will be heavily used.

e) The *transaction rate* is high and it influenced the design, development, installation, and support of the application.

f) *On-line data entry* and control functions are provided in the application.

g) The on-line functions provided, emphasize *end user efficiency*.

h) The application provides *on-line update* for the logical internal files.

i) *Complex processing* is a characteristic of the application. Examples are:

- many control interactions and decision points
- extensive logical and mathematical equations
- much exception processing resulting in incomplete transactions that must be processed again.

j) The application, and the code in the application, has been specifically designed, developed, and supported for *reusability* in other applications, and at other sites.

k) Conversion and *installation ease* are characteristics of the application. A conversion and installation plan was provided, and it was tested during the system test phase.

l) *Operational ease* is a characteristic of the application. Effective start-up, back-up, and recovery procedures were provided, and they were tested during the system test phase. The application minimizes the need for manual activities, such as, tape mounts, paper handling, and direct on-location manual intervention.

m) The application has been specifically designed, developed, and supported to be installed at *multiple sites* for multiple organizations.

n) The application has been specifically designed, developed, and supported to *facilitate change*. Examples are:

- flexible query capability is provided
- business information subject to change is grouped in tables maintainable by the user.

7) Function Points Calculation: The previous paragraphs described how the function types are listed, classified, and counted; and how the processing complexity adjustment is determined. This paragraph describes how to make the calculations that develop the function points measures.

Using the definitions in paragraph C1), two equations have been developed to more specifically define the *development work-product* measure and the *support work-product* measure:

Development Work-Product FP Measure = (Add + ChgA) PCA2 + (Del) PCA1 = _____.

Support Work-Product FP Measure = Orig FP + (Add + ChgA) PCA2 - (Del + ChgB) PCA1 = _____.

Orig FP = adjusted FP of the application, evaluated as they were before the project started.

Add = unadjusted FP added to the application, evaluated as they are expected to be at the completion of the project.

ChgA = unadjusted FP changed in the application, evaluated as they are expected to be at the completion of the project.

Del = unadjusted FP deleted from the application, evaluated as they were before the project started.

ChgB = unadjusted FP changed in the application, evaluated as they were before the project started.

PCA1 = the processing complexity adjustment pertaining to the application before the project started.

PCA2 = the processing complexity adjustment pertaining to the application after the project completion.

REFERENCES

[1] A. J. Albrecht, "Measuring application development productivity," in *Proc. IBM Applications Develop. Symp.*, Monterey, CA, Oct. 14-17, 1979; GUIDE Int. and SHARE, Inc., IBM Corp., p. 83.

[2] M. H. Halstead, *Elements of Software Science.* New York: Elsevier, 1977.

[3] J. E. Gaffney, "Software metrics: A key to improved software development management," presented at the Conf. Comput. Sci. Statist., 13th Symp. on Interface, Pittsburgh, PA, Mar. 1981; also Proceedings, Springer-Verlag, 1981.

[4] K. Christensen, G. P. Fitsos, and C. P. Smith, "A perspective on software science," *IBM Syst. J.*, vol. 20, no. 4, pp. 372-387, 1981.

[5] J.L.F. Dekerf, "APL and Halstead's theory of software metrics," in *APL81 Conf. Proc. ACM* (APL Quote Quad), vol. 12, Sept. 1981, pp. 89-93.

[6] A. O. Allen, "Probability, statistics, and queueing theory—With computer science applications," in *Computer Science and Applied Mathematics Series.* New York: Academic, 1978.

[7] J. E. Gaffney, "A comparison of a complexity—Based and Halstead program size estimates," presented at the 1979 ACM Comput. Sci. Conf., Dayton, OH, Feb. 1979.

[8] D. F. Stanat and D. F. McAllister, *Discrete Mathematics in Computer Science.* Englewood Cliffs, NJ: Prentice-Hall, 1977, p. 265.

[9] N. Pippenger, "Complexity theory," *Scientific Amer.*, p. 120, June 1978.

Allan J. Albrecht received the B.S.E.E. degree from Bucknell University, Lewisburg, PA, in 1949.

He is currently the Program Manager of the Application Development and Maintenance (AD/M) Measurement Program for IBM. The program objective is to measure, establish, and improve the effectiveness and efficiency of the development of application programs in the company. Before this assignment, he was on the staff of the Director of IBM's DP Services Organization (now known as Information System Services). In addition to providing software project management advice and consultation to the Director, he was responsible for reviewing, developing, and revising the processes used to propose, manage, and review their contracts. He has had about 25 years of project management experience. The software projects he has managed have included missile range control systems, an insurance medical claims processing system, and a motor freight company management system. His experience has included development of hardware, development of software for internal use, development of software for license to customers, and development of software under contract to customers.

John E. Gaffney, Jr. (M'55) received the A.B. degree from Harvard University, Cambridge, MA, in 1955 and the M.S. degree from Stevens Institute of Technology, Hoboken, NJ, in 1957. He has done additional graduate work at The American University, Washington, DC.

He joined IBM, Ossining, NY, in 1957 in the Research Division, working on the SABRE airlines reservation system. Subsequently, he had assignments in Poughkeepsie, NY, San Jose, CA, Stockhom, Sweden, Bethesda and Gaithersburg, MD, and Manassas, VA. He has worked in process control, image processing, artificial intelligence, sonar systems, and in recent years in software and cost engineering. He spent the period July 1982 to July 1983 on sabbatical with the National Weather Service, U.S. Department of Commerce, Silver Spring, MD, working on systems requirements and the application of artificial intelligence to weather forecasting. Currently, he is working in the Advanced Technology Department at IBM, FSD, Gaithersburg, MD.

Mr. Gaffney is a Registered Professional Engineer (electrical engineering) in the District of Columbia.

A Comparison Of Software Scheduling Models

Daniel V. Ferens
Air Force Institute of Technology (AFIT/LSY)
Wright-Patterson AFB, OH 45433-6583

and

Captain Bryan A. Daly, USAF
Ballistic Missile Office (BMO/MGPO)
Norton AFB, CA 92409-6468

Introduction

Schedule delays can be very costly for software projects; yet, they are commonplace for many software efforts. A top Air Force General recently stated that his command had a perfect record for meeting software schedules — not one had yet been met! Fortunately, there are numerous models and techniques to help obtain reasonable software schedule estimates early in a program, but it is uncertain which models, if any, can accurately predict software schedules for a given situation. This paper assesses the current status of software scheduling models and techniques, and features a recent study performed at the Air Force Institute of Technology (AFIT) to assess the expected accuracy of five software scheduling models.

The first part of this paper describes software scheduling techniques and algorithms, emphasizing those included in currently popular software parametric cost models. This part also summarizes the results of some quantitative studies to assess the accuracy of these models. The specific findings of each of the studies are described, along with an assessment of the strengths and limitations of the studies themselves. The second part of this paper is an in-depth discussion of a study performed at AFIT to analyze the expected accuracy of the scheduling algorithms for five software cost models using a 26-program database developed by The MITRE Corporation for the Air Force's Electronic Systems Division. Conclusions from this study and recommendations for future work are presented.

Survey of current software scheduling techniques

Fortunately for the software analyst, there are many scheduling models and techniques available for software development. Almost all cost models include scheduling algorithms, and there are some traditional system-level scheduling techniques that may be applied to software. These traditional techniques and scheduling algorithms, along with some independent assessments of these techniques and algorithms, are discussed.

Traditional Scheduling Techniques. According to (Rosenau and Lewin, 1984), traditional scheduling techniques, which have been used in system project scheduling endeavors, are sometimes applied to software projects. These techniques include Gantt charts, milestone charts, and Program Evaluation Review Technique/Critical Path Method (PERT/CPM) networks. Although these techniques are seldom used alone for software schedule estimation, they are frequently output by software cost models as an aid in schedule estimation and tracking. These techniques are not discussed further in this paper since most readers are already familiar with their general characteristics. Additional information may be found in many sources such as (Ferens, 1990).

Cost Model Scheduling Algorithms. Although most software cost models address scheduling, the scheduling algorithms and outputs vary among cost models. Scheduling algorithms of seven popular cost models are briefly explained to demonstrate how these models address schedule estimation. The models, considered for the AFIT study described later in this paper, are listed in their approximate chronological order.

a. PRICE-S: A paper published by GE PRICE Systems (PRICE, 1988) describes scheduling algorithms for this cost model. First introduced in 1977, PRICE-S is chiefly a scheduling model that estimates cost only after a schedule is estimated. The schedule estimate is primarily based on software size, application, complexity, and degree of software reuse. Other inputs are used to make adjustments to the estimate. PRICE-S uses three Beta curves, as shown in Figure 1, to estimate the times for the design, coding, and testing phases of a software development effort. The shapes of these Beta curves are dependent, in part, on the unique inputs for a software project. Some of the input parameters that affect schedule can be calibrated.

PRICE-S estimates an optimal schedule for a software project, and can compare the optimal schedule to a user-specified schedule to assess penalties for schedule compression or expansion. Figure 2 illustrates a generalized cost-schedule trade-off curve that is used by PRICE-S and several other models. This curve assumes that compressing a schedule relative to the optimal time (T_{OPT}) requires more effort, and there is a minimum time (T_{MIN}) beyond which a schedule can not be further compressed. Also, expanding a schedule relative to T_{OPT} will require more effort because personnel time is wasted.

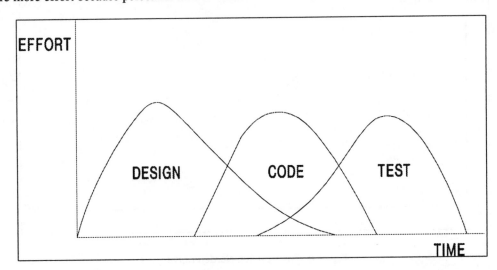

Figure 1: Beta Curves

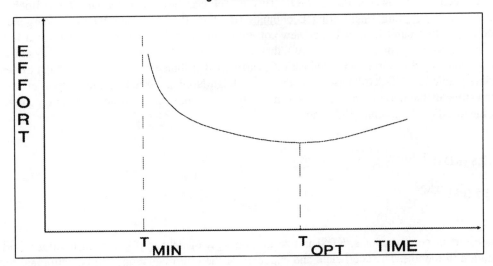

Figure 2: Cost-Schedule Trade-off Curve

b. Software Life Cycle Management (SLIM): This model was originally developed by Lawrence Putnam in the late 1970s. The SLIM user's manual (QSM, 1987) describes some scheduling information for the model. Program size, a calibratible productivity index, and a calibratible manpower build-up index are the primary inputs to the SLIM scheduling algorithm, which uses Putnam's software equation derived from the popular Rayleigh-Norden curve illustrated in Figure 3. The software equation used in SLIM is:

$$S_s = C_k \times K^{1/3} \times T_d^{4/3} \qquad (1)$$

where S_s is the number of source statements, C_k is a technology constant, K is the person-months of effort required, and T_d is the development time, in months (Putnam, 1992). Unlike most software cost models, SLIM first computes a minimum time solution, then allows the user to specify a longer schedule within a relevant range. The effort required for the longer schedule is less than that of the minimum time solution; no "optimum" time solution is provided. Schedule outputs for SLIM include a milestone chart and a Gantt chart for the specified project.

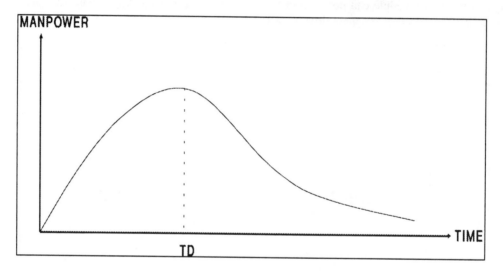

Figure 3: The Rayleigh-Norden Curve

c. The Constructive Cost Model (COCOMO): This model was developed by Dr. Barry Boehm and first published in his text, Software Engineering Economics (Boehm, 1981). COCOMO has undergone numerous updates since it was first published, including new equations for the Ada language and additional input factors. Numerous computerized versions of COCOMO that contain the latest updates are now available such as COSTAR, distributed by Softstar Systems and REVIC, currently distributed by the Air Force Cost Center.

For schedule prediction, COCOMO uses a modified Rayleigh-Norden curve to estimate total effort in person-months, then estimates the duration of the project in months. The nominal effort and schedule equations for the COCOMO embedded mode (Boehm, 1981), are:

$$PM = 2.8 \, (KDSI)^{1.20} \qquad (2)$$

$$M = 2.5 \, (PM)^{0.32} \qquad (3)$$

where PM is effort in person-months, KDSI is size in thousands of delivered source instructions, and M is the schedule duration in months. The coefficient and exponent of the effort equations can be calibrated to the user's database. Also, for the intermediate and detailed versions of COCOMO, a set of product multipliers is used to adjust person-months for various software development environment attributes. Some of the more significant attributes include personnel capabilities and experience, complexity, and reliability requirements. In addition to providing an estimate of project duration, many computerized editions of COCOMO, including COSTAR and REVIC, provide milestone charts and schedule trade-off capabilities.

d. SPQR/20: This model was developed by Software Productivity Research (SPR) during the middle 1980s, and is based on the work of Capers Jones. SPQR/20 was one of the first models that allowed the use of function points as a measure of size in lieu of source lines of code (SPR, 1986). Other key SPQR/20 inputs which affect schedule include project type and class, language, and several environmental inputs. The model has several scheduling options, including normal average time, shortest time, and minimum time with high quality. The model does not use the Rayleigh-Norden curve shown in Figure 3, but uses a variety of algorithms dependent on the project type and class chosen. The model's outputs include a milestone chart for scheduling.

It should be noted that SPR also has a model called Checkpoint which is much more detailed than SPQR/20 (SPR, 1990), but was not available to AFIT at the time of this study. Like SPQR/20, CHECKPOINT uses a variety of scheduling algorithms dependent on project type and class chosen.

e. SEER: This model, marketed by Galorath Associates, is based on the work of Dr. Randall Jensen, whose papers appear in the SEER User's Manual (Galorath, 1989). The model uses Jensen's equation, derived from the Rayleigh-Norden curve, to estimate either a minimum time or minimum effort schedule based on a multitude of inputs including size, complexity, and personnel capabilities. Jensen's scheduling equation is:

$$T_d = S_e^{0.4} \times C_{te}^{-0.4} \times D^{-0.2} \qquad (4)$$

where t_d is development time in years, S_e is effective source lines of code, C_{te} is an effective development technology constant, and D is a measure of software complexity. Schedule outputs for SEER include milestone charts and schedule risk analyses.

f. SYSTEM-4: This model is the latest in a succession of models developed by Computer Economics, Inc. (CEI) which included the Jensen-1, Jensen-2, and SYSTEM-3 models (CEI, 1989). The scheduling algorithms for SYSTEM-4 are not published in (CEI, 1989); however, since SYSTEM-4 is a successor to the Jensen models, it probably uses the Jensen equation or a variant. SYSTEM-4 estimates a minimum effort schedule, although a minimum time schedule is an option. Key inputs to the model include size, developer technology factors, and many environmental parameters. Model outputs include milestone charts and schedule risk analyses. SYSTEM-4 also contains a schedule adjustment factor which may be calibrated by the user.

g. SASET: This model was developed for the Department of Defense by Martin Marietta Corporation during the late 1980s. As explained in the SASET manual (Silver, 1990), the model uses three tiers of inputs to estimate development schedule, system environment, system complexity, and functionality. For functionality, the user can either directly input program size or allow SASET to compute size based on function-related inputs. The model also has an extensive calibration file in which the user can adjust many parameters. A scheduling equation contained in the model is derived from the inputs and calibration values selected by the user. Schedule outputs for SASET include milestone charts and a Gantt chart.

Quantitative Scheduling Study Results. There have been few, if any, studies to validate traditional scheduling techniques; however, there have been some independent studies to assess the probable accuracy or validity of the schedules computed by cost models. These studies, including a discussion of the results, are described below.

a. Model developer assertions: In Chapter 6 (Boehm, 1981), Boehm states that the COCOMO scheduling equations are within 20% of actuals 58% of the time. Some model developers claim even better accuracies for cost or schedule results, or make statements such as, "This model has been validated for over a thousand projects." These accuracies, however, are usually obtained from the model databases (at best), and not from independent assessments.

b. Blalock's study: This study involved an independent comparison of estimated and actual development schedules for five models, COCOMO, PRICE-S, SYSTEM-3 (the predecessor to SYSTEM-4), SoftCost-R, and SPQR/20, using a single project from a 31-point database (Daly, 1990). All models except COCOMO provided an estimate that was within 20% of the actual development time, and SYSTEM-3 was the most accurate. The obvious limitation of this study is that it used only one project; however, it did provide impetus for further work.

c. The IIT Research Institute (IITRI) study: This study (IIT, 1989) used a database of eight Ada language projects to assess overall accuracy, including schedule accuracy, for six models: COSTMODL (a computerized edition of the Ada version of COCOMO), PRICE-S, SASET, SPQR/20, SYSTEM-3, and SoftCost-Ada, a special edition of SoftCost-R (Reifer, 1989). For software schedule accuracy, the models were run for a complete set of inputs derived from the database and for a "nominal" case where only inputs that could be determined early in a program were used (the rest were either not used or allowed to assume nominal values). The six models were evaluated for accuracy to within 30% of actual schedules and for consistency, a measure of the models' percentage departures from the mean value of the estimates for all eight projects, to within 30% of that mean. A summary of the results are as follows (only the top two models for each category are listed):

1. For project schedule accuracy, SYSTEM-3 was accurate within 30% for 5 of 8 projects, and PRICE-S for 4 of 8 projects.
2. For project schedule consistency, SYSTEM-3 and PRICE-S were within 30% for 5 of 8 projects.
3. For nominal schedule accuracy, SPQR/20 was accurate to within 30% for 6 of 8 projects, and PRICE-S for 4 of 8 projects.
4. For nominal schedule consistency, SPQR/20 was accurate to within 30% for 6 of 8 projects, and PRICE-S for 5 of 8 projects.

From this study, SYSTEM-3, SPQR/20, and PRICE-S gave the best scheduling results for the eight Ada projects. However, the small database of eight projects prohibits generalizing the results of the IITRI study to other Ada projects.

d. The Army Aviation Systems Command study: This study (Greathouse and Shipley, 1990) contains a preliminary analysis of the scheduling accuracy of four cost models: PRICE-S, REVIC, SASET, and SECOMO (a computerized edition of COCOMO). The study used a database of twelve Department of Defense weapon system software programs, and concluded that, overall, SASET was the most accurate model. Although percentage values were not provided in the study, a graph included in the study shows that SASET was almost always "very close" to the actual schedule, while PRICE-S and REVIC consistently overestimated the schedule and SECOMO consistently underestimated the schedule. However, the accuracy of PRICE-S and REVIC improved substantially if adjustments were made to the models' estimates for the preliminary design phase. Of all studies discussed so far, this has the most data points. However, some of the statistical methods used in the study were not explained, and the study is stated to be "preliminary".

The results of studies performed to date seem to indicate that certain models appear to be relatively more accurate schedule estimators for selected applications than other models. However, the studies are limited in several respects, and no one model was shown to be accurate for a wide range of applications.

The AFIT software scheduling study

This study (Daly, 1990) used twenty-one data points and five well-known statistical methods to assess the accuracy of five models for the database.

a. Database: The database was supplied by The MITRE Corporation, a Federally Funded Research and Development Center for the Department of Defense that supports the Air Force's Electronic Systems Division and the Army's Communications and Electronics Command. This database, which contains twenty-six subsystems with data supplied by defense contractors, was the most comprehensive Air Force database available at the time of this study. The programs are primarily for command and control and radar systems, although some simulation programs are also included. For the twenty-one programs which have historical schedule data, schedules ranges from 13 to 84 months. Because of contractor-proprietary data restrictions, the database can not be described further in this paper nor can detailed output runs be presented.

b. Models: The five models selected; PRICE-S, SEER, SPQR/20, SYSTEM-4, and REVIC (a computerized edition of COCOMO); are among the seven models discussed earlier in this paper. These were made available to the researchers by model developers or the managing agencies. The researchers did not have access to SLIM; and SASET, although available, was not selected because it is difficult to learn and is not available outside the Department of Defense.

c. Statistical methods: The five statistical tests used in this study were the Linear Least-Squares Best Fit, Log-Log Linear Least-Squares Best Fit, Wilcoxon Sign Test, Friedman Rank-Sum Test, and Percentage Method at 95% and 99% confidence levels. A further description of each test is provided in the study document (Daly, 1990), although some additional information about each test is included in the findings.

TABLE 1
AFIT STUDY: RESULTS OF STATISTICAL TESTS

Test	Result
Linear least squares best fit	Low coefficients of determination for all models
Log-Log linear least squares best fit	Low coefficients of determination for all models
Wilcoxon test	At 95% level, only SYSTEM-4 was unbiased
Friedman rank-sum test	At 95% level, SYSYEM-4 and PRICE-S pass; REVIC passes at 99% level
Percentage tests – 20% unadjusted	No model better than 33%
– 30% unadjusted	SYSTEM-4 highest at 71%. REVIC and SEER at 33%
– 30% adjusted for percentage error	REVIC best at 62%. SYSTEM-4 and SEER at 57%

Findings

The models were run for the twenty-one programs in the MITRE database using either values supplied from the database, or typical default values when necessary; no calibration was done for this study due to time constraints involved in learning all five models. Estimated schedules from the five models were then compared to the actual schedules using the five statistical tests listed above. The results of each test are summarized in Table 1. Tables of actual results are attached in Appendices A through E.

a. Linear Least Squares Best Fit: Results were assessed in terms of an F-Ratio, which indicates significance, and Coefficient of Determination (R^2), which is a measure of how much variance among results is explained by the model. All models had significant F-Ratios (at the 95% confidence level), which indicated that the models are better predictors than historical averages. However, R^2 values of less than 0.45 for all models indicated that the resultant regression line explained less than half of the variance.

b. Log-Log Linear Least Squares Best Fit: This test uses the same ratios as the test above, but uses the logarithms of the estimates and actuals instead of the values themselves. This test was used because Log-Log is a fairly typical relationship for software modeling. The results were not much better. There were significant F-Ratios for all models, but all models had R^2 values of less than 0.50.

c. Wilcoxon Sign Test: This test is used to investigate the models for bias. The differences between estimated and actual results are ranked; the ranks are divided into positive and negative columns; and the ranks for both columns are summed. A T-statistic which compares the sums is computed. If there is a large difference between the sums, bias is indicated. At the 95% confidence level, only SYSTEM-4 showed no bias.

d. Friedman Rank Sum Test: This test is used to show whether all data sets (i.e., the set of 21 actuals and the five sets of 21 estimates) are relatively equivalent, and whether any specific data set is relatively equal to the set of actual values. The first portion of the test failed at the 95% confidence level; the data sets were not all equivalent. However, for the specific data sets, SYSTEM-4 was well within the 95% confidence level, and PRICE-S was barely within the 95% confidence level. REVIC passed at the 99% confidence level. This means that, for these models, the ranking of the estimated and actual values may be considered equivalent.

e. Percentage method: This method was used in several different ways. First, the estimates of the five models were compared with actuals to discover how many estimates were within twenty or thirty percent of the actuals. Next, an average percentage of overestimation was computed for all five models (all five tended to overestimate schedule), and the thirty percent test was re-run by multiplying all estimates for each model by the average percentage deviation for that model. For the 30% range, SYSTEM-4 stood out as the most accurate with 15 out of 21 (71%) of the estimates within 30% of the actuals. No other model was better than 33%. For the 20% range, no model was outstanding; SYSTEM-4 and SEER were best at 33%. When the values were adjusted by the inverse of the average percentage of overestimation, they were generally more accurate at the 30% level. REVIC had 13 of 21 within 30%, while PRICE-S, SEER, and SYSTEM-4 each had 12 of 21 within 30%. It is interesting to note that SYSTEM-4 was worse after being adjusted than before. This is due to the effect of outlying values in the computation of the percentage of overestimation.

Another analysis was performed on the individual phases of the estimated and actual schedules of the models. The average deviation from the actuals by life cycle segment by model is shown in Figure 4. The acronyms used are explained as follows: PD is Preliminary Design, DD is Detailed Design, CUT is Code and Unit Test, and IT is Integration and Test.

The results were similar to those of the Army Aviation Systems Command study in that the accuracy of REVIC and PRICE-S may be improved substantially if adjustments can be made to those models' predictions during the preliminary design phase of software development. Much of the estimating error for these two models was confined to this phase.

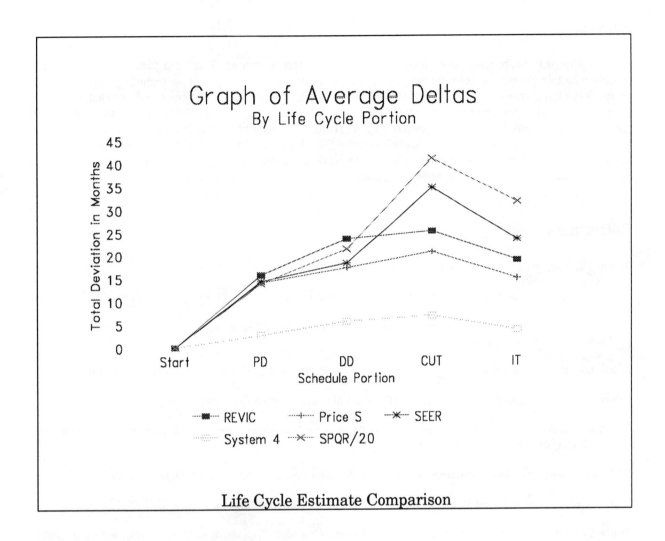

Life Cycle Estimate Comparison

Conclusions and recommendations

For this study, SYSTEM-4 performed much better than the other models in the Wilcoxon, Friedman, and the percentage tests (when the percentage was set at 30%), and appears to be the most accurate for the projects represented in the MITRE database. However, PRICE-S and REVIC may produce similar results if they can be calibrated to eliminate over-estimation during the software preliminary design phase. This can be done relatively easily in PRICE-S, which contains adjustable phase multipliers, but is difficult to accomplish in REVIC, which does not currently have phase adjustment capability.

A comparison with some of the other studies discussed shows that SYSTEM-4 and its predecessor, SYSTEM-3, have done relatively well when schedule estimates have been compared to actuals. A common characteristic of all studies described, however, is that the models have used default values in determination of inputs; they were not calibrated. An idea for future research is to calibrate models from one portion of a database such as the MITRE database used in the AFIT study, then test the accuracy of the models by comparing model results to actual schedules for the remainder of the database. A further effort may involve running the models on a different database to examine whether any models could be applied more generally across projects. Additionally, it would be interesting to test some other models such as SoftCost-R or SASET against the MITRE database or other databases.

Summary

The status of software schedule estimation may be summarized as follows: There is a panoply of software cost models available to estimate software development time. They use various algorithms, including equations based on the Rayleigh-Norden curve, Beta curves, and others. Various models have different features that may make them more suitable for certain applications. Several studies have been conducted to assess the accuracy of scheduling algorithms on various databases. The AFIT study stands out in that it used a relatively large (21-program) database and several different statistical techniques. However, no study has proven the superiority of any models except for limited applications. Much more work is needed in this area to study the applicability of available models to a wide range of software applications.

References

Boehm, Dr. Barry W., *Software Engineering Economics*, Englewood Cliffs, NJ, Prentice-Hall, 1981.

Computer Economics, Inc. (CEI), *SYSTEM-4 User's Manual*, Marina del Rey, CA, CEI, 1989.

Daly, Bryan A., *A Comparison of Software Schedule Estimators* (AFIT Thesis GCA/LSQ/90S-1), Dayton, OH, Air Force Institute of Technology, 1990.

Ferens, Daniel V., *Defense System Software Project Management*, Dayton, OH, Government Printing Office, 1990.

Galorath Associates, *SEER/SEM User's Manual*, Marina del Rey, CA, Galorath Associates, 1989.

Greathouse, Richard M., and Kelly L. Shipley, *Current Research on Schedulers for Aerospace Industry Software*, Dayton, OH, Society of Automotive Engineers, 1990.

IIT Research Institute (IITRI), *Estimating the Cost of Ada Software Development*, Lanham, MD, IITRI, 1989.

Putnam, Lawrence H., and Ware Myers, *Measures of Excellence,* Englewood Cliffs, NJ, Prentice-Hall, 1992.

PRICE Systems, "The Central Equations of the PRICE Software Cost Model", *Proceedings of the Fourth Annual COCOMO User's Group Meeting*, Pittsburgh, PA, Software Engineering Institute, November, 1988.

Quantitative Software Management (QSM), *SLIM User's Manual, Version 2.0*, McLean, VA, QSM, 1987.

Reifer, Donald J., *SoftCost-R User's Manual*, Torrance, CA, Reifer Consultants, 1989.

Rosenau, Milton D., and Marsha D. Lewin, *Software Project Management: Step By Step*, Belmont, CA, Wadsworth, 1984.

Silver, Dr. Aaron N., et al, *SASET User's Guide, Version 1.7*, Denver, CO, Martin Marietta, 1990.

Software Productivity Research (SPR), *SPQR/20 User's Guide*, Boston, MA, SPR, 1986.

Biographical Sketches

Daniel V. Ferens is an Associate Professor of Systems Management at the Air Force Institute of Technology (AFIT) School of Systems and Logistics at Wright-Patterson Air Force Base in Dayton, Ohio. He is currently the course director for a graduate-level course in software cost estimation and a short course in software project management. He has delivered numerous presentations at local, national, and international conference on software-related subjects. He has a Master's Degree in Electrical Engineering from Rensselaer Polytechnic Institute, and a Master's Degree in Business from University of Northern Colorado. Mr. Ferens is a life member of ISPA, and was a member of the founding ISPA Board of Directors. He was the winner of the 1990 ISPA "Arametrician of the Year" award.

Captain Bryan A. Daly graduated from Air Force Institute of Technology in 1990 with a Master's Degree in Management Science specializing in cost analysis. Prior to this assignment, he served for three years as a cost analyst at Electronic Systems Division, and, previously, served as a Cost/Schedule Control Systems Criteria monitor at the Air Force Plant Representative Office at the General Electric Company's Evendale, Ohio office. He is now a cost estimator for the Small ICBM program office at Norton Air Force Base, California.

Appendix A: LSBF Analysis

Input Data

Project #	REVIC	SPQR/20	System 4	SEER	PRICE-S	Actuals
1	32.3	36.9	28.5	31.6	45.7	29.0
2	19.7	35.7	19.0	22.2	22.8	27.0
3	28.0	29.7	23.0	30.8	30.4	18.0
4	25.6	28.2	24.1	30.3	36.9	33.0
5	25.9	39.9	13.5	26.8	29.3	13.0
8	61.1	86.1	44.6	66.7	48.0	68.0
9	62.0	109.9	44.9	62.7	43.9	71.0
10	141.9	116.1	107.3	158.0	131.6	84.0
11	51.9	73.0	30.4	55.3	39.2	22.0
12	61.8	77.1	45.9	68.0	53.2	75.0
13	71.1	103.1	52.6	62.5	62.7	43.0
14	54.7	83.7	55.2	54.1	42.6	23.0
15	143.3	83.4	99.9	165.2	114.9	41.0
17	42.8	68.9	27.0	45.7	44.1	22.0
18	52.8	69.9	34.6	56.7	48.8	31.0
19	53.5	74.2	30.0	66.7	50.0	40.0
20	40.3	84.0	26.1	48.7	54.9	26.0
21	42.3	64.5	30.9	42.6	34.2	33.0
22	46.1	70.9	31.4	50.6	44.8	25.0
23	56.3	71.6	25.4	69.2	55.1	33.0
24	39.5	30.9	23.2	46.1	36.3	26.0

LSBF Results

REVIC :   Regression Output:

Constant	16.67358	
Std Err of Y Est	16.40234	SSE = 5111.696
R Squared	0.364714	SST = 8046.286
No. of Observations	21	SSR = 2934.59
Degrees of Freedom	19	
		F = 10.90777
X Coefficient(s)	0.375546	
Std Err of Coef.	0.113709	F(.95,1,19) 4.38
		F(.99,1,19) 8.19

SPQR/20 :   Regression Output:

Constant		3.031709			
Std Err of Y Est		15.55677	SSE	=	4598.251
R Squared		0.428525	SST	=	8046.286
No. of Observations		21	SSR	=	3448.035
Degrees of Freedom		19			
			F	=	14.2473
X Coefficient(s)	0.50034				
Std Err of Coef.	0.132556		F(.95,1,19)		4.38
			F(.99,1,19)		8.19

System 4:   Regression Output:

Constant		17.17003			
Std Err of Y Est		16.12817	SSE	=	4942.24
R Squared		0.385774	SST	=	8046.286
No. of Observations		21	SSR	=	3104.045
Degrees of Freedom		19			
			F	=	11.93322
X Coefficient(s)	0.51686				
Std Err of Coef.	0.149621		F(.95,1,19)		4.38
			F(.99,1,19)		8.19

SEER :   Regression Output:

Constant		18.26531			
Std Err of Y Est		16.76138	SSE	=	5337.936
R Squared		0.336596	SST	=	8046.286
No. of Observations		21	SSR	=	2708.35
Degrees of Freedom		19			
			F	=	9.640177
X Coefficient(s)	0.357162				
Std Err of Coef.	0.115033		F(.95,1,19)		4.38
			F(.99,1,19)		8.19

Price-S :   Regression Output:

Constant		15.42216			
Std Err of Y Est		17.09459	SSE	=	5552.277
R Squared		0.309958	SST	=	8046.286
No. of Observations		21	SSR	=	2494.009
Degrees of Freedom		19			
			F	=	8.534546
X Coefficient(s)	0.429338				
Std Err of Coef.	0.146964		F(.95,1,19)		4.38
			F(.99,1,19)		8.19

Appendix B: Log-Log Analysis

Project #	REVIC	SPQR/20	System 4	SEER	PRICE-S	Actuals
1	1.509	1.567	1.455	1.499	1.660	1.462
2	1.294	1.553	1.279	1.347	1.358	1.431
3	1.447	1.472	1.362	1.488	1.483	1.255
4	1.408	1.451	1.382	1.481	1.567	1.519
5	1.413	1.601	1.130	1.428	1.467	1.114
8	1.786	1.935	1.649	1.824	1.681	1.833
9	1.792	2.041	1.652	1.797	1.642	1.851
10	2.152	2.065	2.031	2.199	2.119	1.924
11	1.715	1.863	1.483	1.742	1.593	1.342
12	1.791	1.887	1.662	1.832	1.726	1.875
13	1.852	2.013	1.721	1.796	1.797	1.633
14	1.738	1.923	1.742	1.733	1.629	1.362
15	2.156	1.921	2.000	2.218	2.060	1.613
17	1.631	1.838	1.431	1.660	1.644	1.342
18	1.723	1.844	1.539	1.753	1.688	1.491
19	1.728	1.870	1.477	1.824	1.699	1.602
20	1.605	1.924	1.417	1.688	1.740	1.415
21	1.626	1.809	1.490	1.630	1.534	1.519
22	1.664	1.851	1.497	1.704	1.651	1.398
23	1.751	1.855	1.405	1.840	1.741	1.519
24	1.597	1.490	1.365	1.664	1.560	1.415

REVIC :   Regression Output:

Constant	0.435903	
Std Err of Y Est	0.164697	SSE = 0.515375
R Squared	0.42555	SST = 0.897162
No. of Observations	21	SSR = 0.381787
Degrees of Freedom	19	
		F = 14.07511
X Coefficient(s)	0.643387	
Std Err of Coef.	0.171493	F(.95,1,19) 4.38
		F(.99,1,19) 8.19

SPQR/20 :   Regression Output:

Constant	0.359679	
Std Err of Y Est	0.17594	SSE = 0.588145
R Squared	0.344438	SST = 0.897162
No. of Observations	21	SSR = 0.309017
Degrees of Freedom	19	
		F = 9.982782
X Coefficient(s)	0.644941	
Std Err of Coef.	0.204124	F(.95,1,19) 4.38
		F(.99,1,19) 8.19

System 4   Regression Output:

Constant	0.478035	
Std Err of Y Est	0.155078	SSE = 0.456933
R Squared	0.490691	SST = 0.897162
No. of Observations	21	SSR = 0.44023
Degrees of Freedom	19	
		F = 18.30547
X Coefficient(s)	0.680146	
Std Err of Coef.	0.158969	F(.95,1,19) 4.38
		F(.99,1,19) 8.19

SEER :   Regression Output:

Constant	0.461073	
Std Err of Y Est	0.165378	SSE = 0.519645
R Squared	0.420791	SST = 0.897162
No. of Observations	21	SSR = 0.377517
Degrees of Freedom	19	
		F = 13.80334
X Coefficient(s)	0.634176	
Std Err of Coef.	0.170694	F(.95,1,19) 4.38
		F(.99,1,19) 8.19

Price-S :   Regression Output:

Constant	0.314083	
Std Err of Y Est	0.174601	SSE = 0.579226
R Squared	0.35438	SST = 0.897162
No. of Observations	21	SSR = 0.317937
Degrees of Freedom	19	
		F = 10.42909
X Coefficient(s)	0.722572	
Std Err of Coef.	0.223747	F(.95,1,19) 4.38
		F(.99,1,19) 8.19

Appendix C: Wilcoxon Test

Wilcoxon Test - REVIC

Project #	REVIC	Actuals	Delta	Rank +	Rank –
1	32.3	29.0	3.3	1	
2	19.7	27.0	-7.3		3
3	28.0	18.0	10	7	
4	25.6	33.0	-7.4		4
5	25.9	13.0	12.9	8	
8	61.1	68.0	-6.9		2
9	62.0	71.0	-9		5
10	141.9	84.0	57.9	19	
11	51.9	22.0	29.9	18	
12	61.8	75.0	-13.2		9
13	71.1	43.0	28.1	17	
14	54.7	23.0	31.7	20	
15	143.3	41.0	102.3	21	
17	42.8	22.0	20.8	13	
18	52.8	31.0	21.8	15	
19	53.5	40.0	13.5	11	
20	40.3	26.0	14.3	12	
21	42.3	33.0	9.3	6	
22	46.1	25.0	21.1	14	
23	56.3	33.0	23.3	16	
24	39.5	26.0	13.5	10	
		SUMS		208	23

Wilcoxon T   =   23

H_0 = center of paired differences of population distributions = 0
        (i.e. no differences in the distributions)

$\mu(T) = n(n+1)/4 =$ 115.5 Number of non-zero deltas >=20
                        therefore approximates normal curve
$\sigma^2(T) = n(n+1)(2n+1) / 24 =$ 827.75

Test stat = $(T - \mu) / \sigma =$ -3.21508

z (.95) =   1.645
z (.99) =   2.33

Results of test   =   fail at both levels

Wilcoxon Test - SPQR/20

Project #	SPQR/20	Actuals	Delta	Rank +	Rank -
1	36.9	29.0	7.91	4	
2	35.7	27.0	8.71	5	
3	29.7	18.0	11.67	6	
4	28.2	33.0	-4.77		2
5	39.9	13.0	26.9	8	
8	86.1	68.0	18.13	7	
9	109.9	71.0	38.93	14	
10	116.1	84.0	32.07	10	
11	73.0	22.0	50.99	18	
12	77.1	75.0	2.08	1	
13	103.1	43.0	60.13	20	
14	83.7	23.0	60.69	21	
15	83.4	41.0	42.4	15	
17	68.9	22.0	46.9	17	
18	69.9	31.0	38.88	13	
19	74.2	40.0	34.2	11	
20	84.0	26.0	57.98	19	
21	64.5	33.0	31.49	9	
22	70.9	25.0	45.88	16	
23	71.6	33.0	38.59	12	
24	30.9	26.0	4.93	3	
		SUMS		229	2

Wilcoxon T = 2

H_o = center of paired differences of population distributions = 0
        (ie no differences in the distributions)

$\mu(T) = n(n+1)/4 =$ 115.5 Number of non-zero deltas >=20
                therefore approximates normal curve
$\sigma^2(T) = n(n+1)(2n+1)/24 =$ 827.75

Test stat = $(T - \mu)/\sigma =$ -3.94499

z (.95) =   1.645
z (.99) =   2.33

Results of test =   fail at both levels

Wilcoxon Test - System-4

Project #	System 4	Actuals	Delta	Rank +	Rank -
1	28.5	29.0	-0.5		2.5
2	19.0	27.0	-8		11
3	23.0	18.0	5	7	
4	24.1	33.0	-8.9		13
5	13.5	13.0	0.5	2.5	
8	44.6	68.0	-23.4		17
9	44.9	71.0	-26.1		18
10	107.3	84.0	23.3	16	
11	30.4	22.0	8.4	12	
12	45.9	75.0	-29.1		19
13	52.6	43.0	9.6	14	
14	55.2	23.0	32.2	20	
15	99.9	41.0	58.9	21	
17	27.0	22.0	5	8	
18	34.6	31.0	3.6	6	
19	30.0	40.0	-10		15
20	26.1	26.0	0.1	1	
21	30.9	33.0	-2.1		4
22	31.4	25.0	6.4	9	
23	25.4	33.0	-7.6		10
24	23.2	26.0	-2.8		5
			SUMS	116.5	114.5

Wilcoxon T =   114.5

H_0 = center of paired differences of population distributions = 0
        (ie no differences in the distributions)

$\mu(T) = n(n+1)/4 =$ 115.5 Number of non-zero deltas >=20
        therefore approximates normal curve
$\sigma^2(T) = n(n+1)(2n+1)/24 =$ 827.75

Test stat = $(T - \mu)/\sigma =$ -0.03476

z (.95) =   1.645
z (.99) =   2.33

Results of test   =   pass at both levels

244

Wilcoxon Test - SEER

Project #	SEER	Actuals	Delta	Rank +	Rank –
1	31.6	29.0	2.56		1
2	22.2	27.0	-4.77		4
3	30.8	18.0	12.79	6	
4	30.3	33.0	-2.7		3
5	26.8	13.0	13.82	7	
8	66.7	68.0	-1.35		5
9	62.7	71.0	-8.35	11	
10	158.0	84.0	73.97	20	
11	55.3	22.0	33.27	18	
12	68.0	75.0	-7.01		9
13	62.5	43.0	19.46	8	
14	54.1	23.0	31.12	17	
15	165.2	41.0	124.16	21	
17	45.7	22.0	23.7	13	
18	56.7	31.0	25.66	15	
19	66.7	40.0	26.69	14	
20	48.7	26.0	22.73	12	
21	42.6	33.0	9.64	2	
22	50.6	25.0	25.56	16	
23	69.2	33.0	36.22	19	
24	46.1	26.0	20.1	10	
		SUMS		209	22

Wilcoxon T =   22

H_o = center of paired differences of population distributions = 0
        (ie no differences in the distributions)

$\mu(T) = n(n+1)/4 =$ 115.5 Number of non-zero deltas >=20
        therefore approximates normal curve
$\sigma^2(T) = n(n+1)(2n+1)/24 =$ 827.75

Test stat = $(T - \mu)/\sigma =$ -3.24984

z (.95) =   1.645
z (.99) =   2.33

Results of test   =   fail at both levels

Wilcoxon Test - Price-S

Project #	PRICE-S	Actuals	Delta	Rank +	Rank –
1	45.7	29.0	16.7	8	
2	22.8	27.0	-4.2		3
3	30.4	18.0	12.4	6	
4	36.9	33.0	3.9	2	
5	29.3	13.0	16.3	7	
8	48.0	68.0	-20		14
9	43.9	71.0	-27.1		18
10	131.6	84.0	47.6	20	
11	39.2	22.0	17.2	9	
12	53.2	75.0	-21.8		15
13	62.7	43.0	19.7	12	
14	42.6	23.0	19.6	11	
15	114.9	41.0	73.9	21	
17	44.1	22.0	22.1	16.5	
18	48.8	31.0	17.8	10	
19	50.0	40.0	10	4	
20	54.9	26.0	28.9	19	
21	34.2	33.0	1.2	1	
22	44.8	25.0	19.8	13	
23	55.1	33.0	22.1	16.5	
24	36.3	26.0	10.3	5	
		SUMS		181	50

Wilcoxon T = 50

H_0 = center of paired differences of population distributions = 0
(ie no differences in the distributions)

$\mu(T) = n(n+1)/4 =$ 115.5 Number of non-zero deltas >=20
therefore approximates normal curve
$\sigma^2(T) = n(n+1)(2n+1)/24 =$ 827.75

Test stat = $(T - \mu)/\sigma =$ -2.27663

z (.95) = 1.645
z (.99) = 2.33

Results of test = fail at .95, pass at .99

246

Appendix D: Friedman Rank Sum

(Ranks in Parentheses)

Proj #	Actuals		REVIC		SPQR/20		System 4		SEER		PRICE-S	
1	29	(2)	32.3	(4)	36.9	(5)	28.5	(1)	31.6	(3)	45.7	(6)
2	27	(5)	19.7	(2)	35.7	(6)	19.0	(1)	22.2	(3)	22.8	(4)
3	18	(1)	28.0	(3)	29.7	(4)	23.0	(2)	30.8	(6)	30.4	(5)
4	33	(5)	25.6	(2)	28.2	(3)	24.1	(1)	30.3	(4)	36.9	(6)
5	13	(1)	25.9	(3)	39.9	(6)	13.5	(2)	26.8	(4)	29.3	(5)
8	68	(5)	61.1	(3)	86.1	(6)	44.6	(1)	66.7	(4)	48.0	(2)
9	71	(5)	62.0	(3)	109.9	(4)	44.9	(2)	62.7	(4)	43.9	(1)
10	84	(1)	141.9	(5)	116.1	(3)	107.3	(2)	158.0	(6)	131.6	(4)
11	22	(1)	51.9	(4)	73.0	(6)	30.4	(2)	55.3	(5)	39.2	(3)
12	75	(5)	61.8	(3)	77.1	(6)	45.9	(1)	68.0	(4)	53.2	(2)
13	43	(1)	71.1	(5)	103.1	(6)	52.6	(2)	62.5	(3)	62.7	(4)
14	23	(1)	54.7	(4)	83.7	(6)	55.2	(5)	54.1	(3)	42.6	(2)
15	41	(1)	143.3	(5)	83.4	(2)	99.9	(3)	165.2	(6)	114.9	(4)
17	22	(1)	42.8	(3)	68.9	(6)	27.0	(2)	45.7	(5)	44.1	(4)
18	31	(1)	52.8	(4)	69.9	(6)	34.6	(2)	56.7	(5)	48.8	(3)
19	40	(2)	53.5	(4)	74.2	(6)	30.0	(1)	66.7	(5)	50.0	(3)
20	26	(1)	40.3	(3)	84.0	(6)	26.1	(2)	48.7	(4)	54.9	(5)
21	33	(2)	42.3	(4)	64.5	(6)	30.9	(1)	42.6	(5)	34.2	(3)
22	25	(1)	46.1	(4)	70.9	(6)	31.4	(2)	50.6	(5)	44.8	(3)
23	33	(2)	56.3	(4)	71.6	(6)	25.4	(1)	69.2	(5)	55.1	(3)
24	26	(2)	39.5	(5)	30.9	(3)	23.2	(1)	46.1	(6)	36.3	(4)
Rank Sums	46		77		108		37		95		76	

Avg for 5   72.6

H_o: All data sets are the same
H_a: Not all data sets are the same

$S =$ 47.14966

$\chi^2 (5, .05) =$ 11
$\chi^2 (5, .01) =$ 15

Fails, therefore not equivalent at both levels

Actuals	REVIC	SPQR/20	System 4	SEER	PRICE-S
Rank Sums 46	77	108	37	95	76
R1 vs Rn =	31	62	9	49	30

H_o: Both compared data sets are equal
H_a: The compared data sets are not equal

m (.05,5,.5) = 2.51, therefore test statistic m* = 30.4321
m (.01,5,.5) = 3.06, therefore test statistic m* = 37.1005

at .05 level:	Different	Different	Same	Different	Same
at .01 level:	Same	Different	Same	Different	Same

Appendix E: Percentage Method

Project #	REVIC	SPQR/20	System 4	SEER	PRICE-S
1	1.11	1.27	0.98	1.09	1.58
2	0.73	1.32	0.70	0.82	0.84
3	1.56	1.65	1.28	1.71	1.69
4	0.78	0.86	0.73	0.92	1.12
5	1.99	3.07	1.04	2.06	2.25
8	0.90	1.27	0.66	0.98	0.71
9	0.87	1.55	0.63	0.88	0.62
10	1.69	1.38	1.28	1.88	1.57
11	2.36	3.32	1.38	2.51	1.78
12	0.82	1.03	0.61	0.91	0.71
13	1.65	2.40	1.22	1.45	1.46
14	2.38	3.64	2.40	2.35	1.85
15	3.50	2.03	2.44	4.03	2.80
17	1.95	3.13	1.23	2.08	2.00
18	1.70	2.25	1.12	1.83	1.57
19	1.34	1.86	0.75	1.67	1.25
20	1.55	3.23	1.00	1.87	2.11
21	1.28	1.95	0.94	1.29	1.04
22	1.84	2.84	1.26	2.02	1.79
23	1.71	2.17	0.77	2.10	1.67
24	1.52	1.19	0.89	1.77	1.40

Note: The values above are the estimated schedule divided by the actual schedule. For example, on project #1, REVIC estimated a schedule 11% longer than the actual schedule.

Is the estimate within 30%?

Project #	REVIC	SPQR/20	System 4	SEER	PRICE-S
1	Pass	Pass	Pass	Pass	Fail
2	Pass	Fail	Pass	Pass	Pass
3	Fail	Fail	Pass	Fail	Fail
4	Pass	Pass	Pass	Pass	Pass
5	Fail	Fail	Pass	Fail	Fail
8	Pass	Pass	Fail	Pass	Pass
9	Pass	Fail	Fail	Pass	Fail
10	Fail	Fail	Pass	Fail	Fail
11	Fail	Fail	Fail	Fail	Fail
12	Pass	Pass	Fail	Pass	Pass
13	Fail	Fail	Pass	Fail	Fail
14	Fail	Fail	Fail	Fail	Fail
15	Fail	Fail	Fail	Fail	Fail
17	Fail	Fail	Pass	Fail	Fail
18	Fail	Fail	Pass	Fail	Fail
19	Fail	Fail	Pass	Fail	Pass
20	Fail	Fail	Pass	Fail	Fail
21	Pass	Fail	Pass	Pass	Pass
22	Fail	Fail	Pass	Fail	Fail
23	Fail	Fail	Pass	Fail	Fail
24	Fail	Pass	Pass	Fail	Fail

	REVIC	SPQR/20	System 4	SEER	PRICE-S
	Pass	Pass	Pass	Pass	Pass

	REVIC	SPQR/20	System 4	SEER	PRICE-S
	Fail	Fail	Fail	Fail	Fail

	REVIC	SPQR/20	System 4	SEER	PRICE-S
Pass	7	5	15	7	6
Fail	14	16	6	14	15
% Pass	33.3%	23.8%	71.4%	33.3%	28.6%

Is the estimate within 20%?

Project #	REVIC	SPQR/20	System 4	SEER	PRICE-S
1	Pass	Fail	Pass	Pass	Fail
2	Fail	Fail	Fail	Pass	Pass
3	Fail	Fail	Fail	Fail	Fail
4	Fail	Pass	Fail	Pass	Pass
5	Fail	Fail	Pass	Fail	Fail
8	Pass	Fail	Fail	Pass	Fail
9	Pass	Fail	Fail	Pass	Fail
10	Fail	Fail	Fail	Fail	Fail
11	Fail	Fail	Fail	Fail	Fail
12	Pass	Pass	Fail	Pass	Fail
13	Fail	Fail	Fail	Fail	Fail
14	Fail	Fail	Fail	Fail	Fail
15	Fail	Fail	Fail	Fail	Fail
17	Fail	Fail	Fail	Fail	Fail
18	Fail	Fail	Pass	Fail	Fail
19	Fail	Fail	Fail	Fail	Fail
20	Fail	Fail	Pass	Fail	Fail
21	Fail	Fail	Pass	Fail	Pass
22	Fail	Fail	Fail	Fail	Fail
23	Fail	Fail	Fail	Fail	Fail
24	Fail	Pass	Pass	Fail	Fail
	REVIC	SPQR/20	System 4	SEER	PRICE-S
	Pass	Pass	Pass	Pass	Pass
	REVIC	SPQR/20	System 4	SEER	PRICE-S
	Fail	Fail	Fail	Fail	Fail
Pass	4	3	6	6	3
Fail	17	18	15	15	18
% Pass	19.0%	14.3%	28.6%	28.6%	14.3%

Chapter 5
Organizing for Success

We trained hard...but it seemed that every time we were beginning to form into teams we would be reorganized... I was to learn later in life that we tend to meet any new situation by reorganizing; and a wonderful method it can be for creating the illusion of progress while producing confusion, inefficiency and demoralization.

— Petronius Arbiter, 210 BC

Overview

For most managers, the term "organization" implies some formalized structure of roles or positions within which they must operate to get their jobs done. To arrive at this structure, a firm must define management's span of control and authority-responsibility, staff-project-line, and departmental relationships. Most middle managers don't have much to say about the way a firm organizes itself. Instead, their influence is directed toward creating structures that enable the teams doing the work to function within and across operational units. In addition, they focus on interdisciplinary teams to work on problems that cross technical bounds.

This chapter provides five papers on organization. General organization theory is changing because management emphasis has shifted to quality. The hierarchies of the past are being replaced by flatter organizations where premiums are placed on teamwork, communication, and core competency. In response, I have selected papers that describe these changes, why they are being made, and what effects they are having on software organizations. The intent of this chapter is to discuss trends, identify options, and let readers make logical choices.

The first paper, by Baatz, discuss the underlying motivation behind the organizational changes we are seeing in the industry. The article reports the results of a survey conducted by *Electronic Business* and Ernst & Young to identify strategies for quality improvement. The survey shows that organizations have flattened to focus on customer satisfaction and quality. The comments by CEOs on organization, management structure and style, empowerment, teamwork, and globalization are well worth reading.

The next paper, by Prahalad and Hamel, has had far-reaching effects on industry in the United States. The concept of core competency has made many in this country rethink how to structure their corporations. In essence, the organizational practice that this sparks is vertical integration of business units. When viewed from a global context, this implies that cross-functional teams of geographically dispersed units must cooperate to develop strategies at more of a corporate level. Globalization and groupware have become interwoven as firms structure teams that cross business unit boundaries to put into practice the concepts involved.

The third paper, by Daly, is more relevant to the software manager. While the previous papers discuss why organizations are changing, this one describes the options available that respond to these trends. The paper provides a good introduction to matrix, project, and functional forms of organization. Daly highlights strengths and weaknesses of each and its impact on software productivity and efficiency.

The fourth paper, by DeFiore and Gorewitz, describes what firms are doing to cope with these changes in orientation and organizational theory. Service and viewing the user as the client are the themes of this piece, which discusses a formula for change. The paper defines customer satisfaction:

$$\text{Customer satisfaction} = \text{performance/expectation}$$

It then goes on to discuss how to use modern management concepts to match or exceed expectations with suitable performance.

The final paper, by Carlyle, takes a look at tomorrow's organization. It describes current trends toward centralization and the conflicts that occur as multidisciplinary teams and globalization concepts are introduced into the firm. Its 10 organizational commandments fully implement tendencies toward customer satisfaction and quality. The paper is perceptive when it states that software is often set up to mirror the organizational tendencies of the firm as a whole.

References

Semprevivo's treatment of teams and their use in software development is well worth reading (Reference 28 in the Bibliography). I have yet to find a good text to recommend on organization. The reason is simple. As I said in my opening statements, organization theory is changing and the texts are in the process of being updated to reflect the change.

Reprinted from ELECTRONIC BUSINESS, March 18, 1991. © 1991 by Cahners Publishing Company.

The changing face of the ORGANIZATION

BY ELIZABETH B.BAATZ

KEY FINDINGS:

☐ *Commitment to quality and customer satisfaction are the keys to organizational excellence*

☐ *CEOs lack reliable tools for gauging the effects of their companies' quality programs*

☐ *The successful corporation demands motivated, well-trained workers and excellence at the very top*

☐ *CEOs rank training and education as top priorities*

Given fierce global and domestic competition and the blistering pace of technological change, organization is more critical than ever for today's electronics company. What are today's CEOs doing to manage their organizations for survival and success?

Not surprisingly, the ELECTRONIC BUSINESS/Ernst & Young survey revealed no clear consensus on a single most critical strategy for companies to reach or sustain exceptional organizational performance. In other words, there is no magic answer. Most executives, however, offered two suggestions for helping to achieve organizational excellence: measuring customer satisfaction and committing the entire company to quality. Ironically, less than one-third of our CEOs agreed that either of these suggestions are very important to their strategies.

Not measuring up

Measuring customer satisfaction may be strategically important, but a significant number of CEOs in the survey are less than satisfied with their company's measurement techniques.

Although only a handful of companies in the survey have applied or plan to apply for the Malcolm Baldrige National Quality Award, over three-quarters of the CEOs surveyed said their company has a quality improvement program underway. In fact, a full 90% of midsize companies and nearly 95% of all large and top-tier companies in the survey have some form of quality improvement plan in the works.

But two-thirds of the CEOs admit to inadequate techniques for measuring product quality throughout the development process. Even among the largest companies with the deepest pockets, 20% are dissatisfied with their measurement process. By industry segment, companies in the area of industrial electronics, communications, and software expressed the most dissatisfaction with their product quality yardsticks.

As for measuring customer satisfaction specifically, only 29% of the respondents said that providing a system for measurement would be the most important part of the plan to ensure customer satisfaction. Also, only 15% indicated that linking employee incentive plans to customer satisfaction measures would be most important; instead, nearly three-quarters of the respondents said their most important initiative in order to ensure customer satisfaction was "to commit management to build a customer-driven organization."

The most popular method CEOs use to measure customer satisfaction may be considered a bit old-fashioned. Over 66% of the CEOs ranked personal visits to product users as

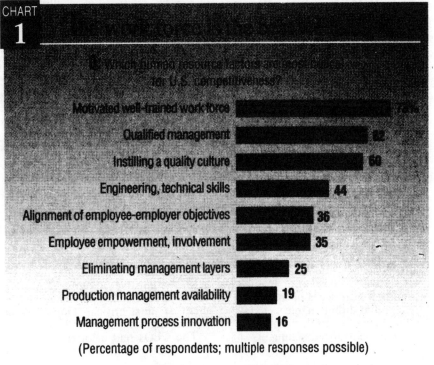

CHART 1

The workforce is the...

Which human resource factors are most critical for U.S. competitiveness?

Motivated well-trained work force	76%
Qualified management	62
Instilling a quality culture	60
Engineering, technical skills	44
Alignment of employee-employer objectives	36
Employee empowerment, involvement	35
Eliminating management layers	25
Production management availability	19
Management process innovation	16

(Percentage of respondents; multiple responses possible)

their most useful measurement technique. Another 49% said interaction with upper management in the customer's company was most useful.

The more scientific methods of measuring performance ranked lowest. Customer-service tracking systems, market research surveys, and field audits each were marked by less than one-third of the respondents as most useful. While electronics companies have become more market-driven, the industry's adoption of formal measures of customer satisfaction appears to be lagging.

Every CEO worships at the altar

Leon Machiz,
Chairman, CEO and President, Avnet Inc.

On reorganizing for efficiency. . .

"The biggest challenge Avnet faces is efficiency. Starting a few years ago, it was apparent that an aggressive posture with regard to efficiency was necessary. That was the reason I adopted the concept of 'hubbing.' I realized that just because we had a huge number of outlets, it didn't mean that we were necessarily structured correctly. Hubbing evolved as a result of addressing the bottom line and making sure that we're doing a sufficiently good job of keeping our suppliers happy.

"Hubbing just means moving out administration into centralized areas—centralized inventory, centralized product management, and centralized purchasing. There are two advantages: We can buy more effectively by buying in larger quantities and, by buying larger quantities, we found that we could collectively offer better terms.

"In looking at our organization, it was apparent that a number of facilities were not profitable. It also became apparent that we were really not allowing ourselves the advantage of critical mass. By being so disbursed we were, in effect, running a huge series of small businesses that didn't enable us to take advantage of centralized purchasing and centralized selling."   □

of customer satisfaction and product quality; pressure from foreign competitors has made this a must. But moving to actual implementation of measurement and controls still needs to happen by electronics companies.

Instead of measuring, executives are busy motivating, educating, training, communicating, hiring, and keeping talent. While the survey asked many questions about quality goals, measurement, and customer satisfaction, the most clear-cut consensus in the survey, the interviews, and the roundtable discussions were the issue of people. But electronics CEOs say employees are clearly the power behind any company's competitive edge and organizational excellence.

The survey asked CEOs to rank nine human-resource factors on importance in affecting their company's competitiveness. The number-one answer, with 73% ranking it most critical: a motivated, well-trained work force. Every industry segment except industrial electronics put the work force at the top of their list. By size, 85% of top-tier companies ranked the work force as their most critical competitive advantage.

After a motivated work force, the CEOs ranked qualified management as a competitive advantage. Among all companies, 62% ranked management as most critical. Only 51% of developing companies did so.

The CEOs had a lot to say about motivating employees. The methods

Finis F. Conner,
Chairman and CEO, Conner Peripherals Inc.

On management structure and style. . .

"I was determined to have a company that was successful, not because of how much one or two people contribute, but because it has multiple functions and multiple strengths. If you look at Seagate today there are two key people. And if either one left or was hit by a truck, where would they be? So our success is to continue to build. We have the most senior, successful managers in the business. But we can't stop, we have to add more. . .

"[The decision-making process is] a mixture of disciplines. We are not a traditional organization where everyone brings their argument to the party. We vote on it. And I have one more vote than everyone else. But neither are we so loose. Instead we talk about it. We have a group called the corporate management committee that has all the key individual contributors in it—Squires, Schroeder, Holt, Neun, Almon, myself. We bring that group together on anything that has to do with strategic direction. We have to meet and agree on where we are going.

"You have to have the trust and confidence [in each other]. I guess if there is one phrase to describe my management style it is mutual trust. I have to trust John Squires who knows more technical information than I ever will. If we are making a technical decision, he has the lead, he has one more vote. When it comes to an operations decision, we turn to Bill Almon. For marketing, Scott Holt. I have input into all those. If I think it is contradictory to what I think is right, I will try to convey my views and why. At the corporate management committee we are all equal. We have never had a situation, with the exception of one, where I had to make a decision contrary to the consensus."   □

range from the absurd (one CEO jumped into a vat of Jell-o in the company parking lot) to the sublime (another motivates by sharing the company financial statements with every employee). In the end, personal style becomes a very real factor in the race to hire the best and to motivate them.

For Peter Cherry president and CEO of The Cherry Corp., personal style is precisely what he looks for in his top staff. Says Cherry, "I'm not looking for someone who is book smart. I want someone who has that entrepreneurial spark; someone who is constantly challenging the organization and the status quo; someone who suggests improvement, whether it's a new technology in assembly, a new product, a new selling technique, or a new accounting method. That's the kind of person who gives the company its culture, its stature."

Keeping those key employees after you have found them is another matter altogether. During the '90s this issue will become even more critical as demographic trends point to a labor shortage of U.S. entry-level engineers and other young employees. Competition for the best employees is already cutthroat and most employees switch jobs much more often than the employees of 30 years ago. So electronics companies may buy fewer gold watches for the 25-year

Donald F. McGuinness,
Chairman, Electronic Designs Inc.

On empowering employees and cycle-time reduction. . .

"I think that management's role is to empower people and not much else. When the management gets involved and starts saying the way it should be, almost invariably the people say, 'Well, I'll show you another way it's going to be.' The Japanese are pretty good at it. Culturally they're better at team playing and getting together than our culture is. So the trick is empowering people constantly in the organization.

"The other issue is a cross-divisional issue. Take cycle time. Cycle time involves all of [the employees] together, from sales to accounting. But everyone looks at their own piece, and it can be very difficult to see how it fits in with the total picture. So the big issue for my company is how to manage across the departments, because that is where the big breakthroughs are. One partial solution to both problems is to set up some kind of reward system for our employees. This is what we are working on." □

veteran, but the costs of getting and keeping good employees will be higher.

Corporate culture and stimulating, challenging work are paramount to keeping good employees. Most executives agree with Michael Cope, CEO of Interphase Corp. "Salary is way down the list in terms of attracting and retaining really qualified people," according to Cope.

For Robert Paluck of Convex Computer Corp., maintaining that special corporate culture takes a lot of work. "Maintenance of the culture is totally a function of the energy you pour into it," he says. "The whole driving force behind this is that you don't believe you can have an intensely happy customer unless you have intensely happy employees. You can't have one without the other."

Productivity pundits

Along with improving product quality, improving productivity remains a top goal with the CEOs who were interviewed. The success story of one large electronics company, Rockwell International Corp., inspires even the smallest electronics company. From 1980 to 1989 the number of people employed at Rockwell rose just 1,000, from 108,000 to 109,000. Yet over this same time period, revenue doubled.

Rockwell's COO, Kent Black, explains his productivity success story as "a lot of small ways of learning how to do things better and how to buy material better." One of Rockwell's improvements has been to set up a system of preferred buyers from whom Rockwell demands the highest quality.

By concentrating the buying power

Elton White,
Executive VP of marketing, NCR Corp.

On project teams and decision making. . .

"For every new program, we put together a planning team which includes development, product management, and marketing. We put together what we call an integrated business plan which includes the marketing and development aspects. We've been doing this for about five years.

"NCR has had a management philosophy for some time that involves moving decision-making as far down the organization as possible. So one of the things we do is put together an organization that is responsible, that has a product charter. [The team] has a final decision on what the product should be that satisfies the market requirements. For that chartered area they have that responsibility. To facilitate this, we put together teams that work to get the right information and get the product to market fast. It's not the team's decision, but the organization's decision, on what the product is and the content of that product.

"So one of our objectives has been to move the decision-making down the organization. There are two conditions on that: [The decision maker] has to be at a level where the information is available to make that decision and at a level where the decision can be measured." □

of all their operations into one corporate purchase agreement, by hiring purchasing people who are engineers, and by doing a multitude of small things better, Rockwell's productivity has soared. For example, at Rockwell's Tactical Systems Division in Atlanta, parts are no longer inspected on receipt; that responsibility belongs to the supplier. "In that way," says Black, "we've cut the hours to build a missile in half, and we've increased production about two and a half times. I think the head count in the division is down 40%."

The changing nature of the relationship with both suppliers and with customers has slowly but inexorably exerted its influence on the organizational structure of the electronics company. The trends of the '80s are changing the electronics company in the '90s: faster time to market; smarter, more quality-conscious consumers; increased foreign competition. The list continues on and on. But above all, the employee remains the key to the future success of the organization.

When asked which of eight techniques have been most successful in improving product quality, 76% of the survey respondents answered "employee involvement." The next most popular answer, with just 33% marking it as a most effective technique, was "improved customer communications."

With employee involvement so critical to the success of today's electronics company, training and education now rank as top priorities for the nation and the electronics CEO. Says Gary Tooker, president and COO of Motorola Inc., "There is a shrinking supply of technical talent, so one of the things we have to do is nurture the raw material. That's why we work on education. We spend about $60 million a year on education internally."

For electronics companies, which rely on a highly trained work force, the current state of the U.S. education system is a serious problem that many executives confront all the time. Some companies, like Motorola and Rockwell, have responded to the problem by increasing the amount of time and money spent on training. Others have begun more extensive testing of their work force before moving them into new positions that require more skills. And still others are importing their manufacturing

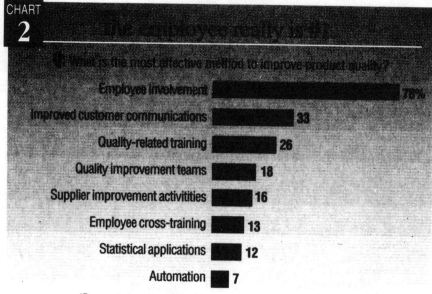

CHART 2 — The employee really is #1

What is the most effective method to improve product quality?

Method	%
Employee involvement	76
Improved customer communications	33
Quality-related training	26
Quality improvement teams	18
Supplier improvement activitities	16
Employee cross-training	13
Statistical applications	12
Automation	7

(Percentage of respondents; multiple responses possible)

Frederick A. Krehbiel,
Vice chairman and CEO, Molex Inc.

On the global employee...

"We need more people with global experience. Without it, Molex managers and employees are limited in their opportunities. You can only go so far up the ladder without international experience. It is expensive sending people overseas, but you have to do it.

"I worry about finding the right people to assemble the global network, making sure things fit together. Whenever possible, don't centralize your operations. It is too easy to lose flexibility with your customers." □

engineers from abroad when they cannot find qualified American-born engineers.

Talk is not cheap

In the electronics industry, change shapes every CEO's day. While more traditional industries react slowly to a changing global environment, the electronics industry itself is predicated on the value of rapid technological change. Anticipating, managing, and communicating that change is a big part of every CEO's job.

David Feldman, chairman and CEO of Ampro Computers, sees communication as paramount. Last year, after a trip to the Far East, Feldman decided he needed to make some basic changes in his company in order to compete. He came back from his trip, cut his company's price list from eight to two and a half pages, and rewrote the business plan.

But it didn't stop there. Next Feldman sent out the new plan to every manager in the company and requested their comments. Communication, both to and from the CEO, gets Ampro's employees intimately involved with the changes and the success of those changes.

For small, domestic companies, the task of communicating is ingrained in their corporate culture. James Donald, CEO of DSC says, "Employees can come see me any time they

want." However, he admits, "It's getting a little bit more difficult these days because I can't find a place big enough to get everybody together every quarter."

Once the company gets larger and goes global, communication becomes a much more difficult task. For Robert Todd of Flextronics, the cost of communicating well is high because it necessitates frequent trips to see his operations and engineering staff in Asia. In fact, face-to-face communication remains key, say the executives, no matter where staff is located or how big a staff you've got.

CEOs of the larger electronics companies make it part of their job to find ways to get the benefits of size while minimizing the costs. For Rockwell International, that has meant eliminating excess management layers. For Cypress Semiconductor, nurturing smaller, focused business groups within the large corporation has been successful. For Motorola, cross-functional teams of engineering, manufacturing, and marketing has made communication more efficient.

Managing change and preparing their organizations to fight the business battles of the '90s, electronic industry executives have their work cut out for them. To survive, all CEOs will be striving for organizational excellence as never before. □

The Core Competence of the Corporation

by C.K. Prahalad and Gary Hamel

The most powerful way to prevail in global competition is still invisible to many companies. During the 1980s, top executives were judged on their ability to restructure, declutter, and delayer their corporations. In the 1990s, they'll be judged on their ability to identify, cultivate, and exploit the core competencies that make growth possible – indeed, they'll have to rethink the concept of the corporation itself.

Consider the last ten years of GTE and NEC. In the early 1980s, GTE was well positioned to become a major player in the evolving information technology industry. It was active in telecommunications. Its operations spanned a variety of businesses including telephones, switching and transmission systems, digital PABX, semiconductors, packet switching, satellites, defense systems, and lighting products. And GTE's Entertainment Products Group, which pro-

C.K. Prahalad is professor of corporate strategy and international business at the University of Michigan. Gary Hamel is lecturer in business policy and management at the London Business School. Their most recent HBR article, "Strategic Intent" (May-June 1989), won the 1989 McKinsey Award for excellence. This article is based on research funded by the Gatsby Charitable Foundation.

duced Sylvania color TVs, had a position in related display technologies. In 1980, GTE's sales were $9.98 billion, and net cash flow was $1.73 billion. NEC, in contrast, was much smaller, at $3.8 billion in sales. It had a comparable technological base and computer businesses, but it had no experience as an operating telecommunications company.

Yet look at the positions of GTE and NEC in 1988. GTE's 1988 sales were $16.46 billion, and NEC's sales were considerably higher at $21.89 billion. GTE has, in effect, become a telephone operating company with a position in defense and lighting products. GTE's other businesses are small in global terms. GTE has divested Sylvania TV and Telenet, put switching, transmission, and digital PABX into joint ventures, and closed down semiconductors. As a result, the international position of GTE has eroded. Non-U.S. revenue as a percent of total revenue dropped from 20% to 15% between 1980 and 1988.

NEC has emerged as the world leader in semiconductors and as a first-tier player in telecommunications products and computers. It has consolidated its position in mainframe computers. It has moved beyond public switching and transmission to include

Copyright © 1990 by the President and Fellows of Harvard College. All rights reserved.

Reprinted with permission from *Harvard Business Review*, May-June 1990, pages 79-91.

such lifestyle products as mobile telephones, facsimile machines, and laptop computers – bridging the gap between telecommunications and office automation. NEC is the only company in the world to be in the top five in revenue in telecommunications, semiconductors, and mainframes. Why did these two companies, starting with comparable business portfolios, perform so differently? Largely because NEC conceived of itself in terms of "core competencies," and GTE did not.

Rethinking the Corporation

Once, the diversified corporation could simply point its business units at particular end product markets and admonish them to become world leaders. But with market boundaries changing ever more quickly, targets are elusive and capture is at best temporary. A few companies have proven themselves adept at inventing new markets, quickly entering emerging markets, and dramatically shifting patterns of customer choice in established markets. These are the ones to emulate. The critical task for management is to create an organization capable of infusing products with irresistible functionality or, better yet, creating products that customers need but have not yet even imagined.

This is a deceptively difficult task. Ultimately, it requires radical change in the management of major companies. It means, first of all, that top managements of Western companies must assume responsibility for competitive decline. Everyone knows about high interest rates, Japanese protectionism, outdated antitrust laws, obstreperous unions, and impatient investors. What is harder to see, or harder to acknowledge, is how little added momentum companies actually get from political or macroeconomic "relief." Both the theory and practice of Western management have created a drag on our forward motion. It is the principles of management that are in need of reform.

NEC versus GTE, again, is instructive and only one of many such comparative cases we analyzed to understand the changing basis for global leadership. Early in the 1970s, NEC articulated a strategic intent to exploit the convergence of computing and communications, what it called "C&C."[1] Success, top management reckoned, would hinge on acquiring *competencies*, particularly in semiconductors. Management adopted an appropriate "strategic architecture," summarized by C&C, and then communicated its intent to the whole organization and the outside world during the mid-1970s.

NEC constituted a "C&C Committee" of top managers to oversee the development of core products and core competencies. NEC put in place coordination groups and committees that cut across the interests of individual businesses. Consistent with its strategic architecture, NEC shifted enormous resources to strengthen its position in components and central processors. By using collaborative arrangements to multiply internal resources, NEC was able to accumulate a broad array of core competencies.

NEC carefully identified three interrelated streams of technological and market evolution. Top management determined that computing would evolve from large mainframes to distributed processing, components from simple ICs to VLSI, and communications from mechanical cross-bar exchange to complex digital systems we now call ISDN. As things evolved further, NEC reasoned, the computing, communications, and components businesses would so overlap that it would be very hard to distinguish among them, and that there would be enormous opportunities for any company that had built the competencies needed to serve all three markets.

NEC top management determined that semiconductors would be the company's most important

> Why did NEC enter myriad alliances between 1980 and 1988? To learn and absorb other companies' skills.

"core product." It entered into myriad strategic alliances – over 100 as of 1987 – aimed at building competencies rapidly and at low cost. In mainframe computers, its most noted relationship was with Honeywell and Bull. Almost all the collaborative arrangements in the semiconductor-component field were oriented toward technology access. As they entered collaborative arrangements, NEC's operating managers understood the rationale for these alliances and the goal of internalizing partner skills. NEC's director of research summed up its competence acquisition during the 1970s and 1980s this way: "From an investment standpoint, it was much quicker and cheaper to use foreign technology. There wasn't a need for us to develop new ideas."

No such clarity of strategic intent and strategic architecture appeared to exist at GTE. Although senior executives discussed the implications of the evolving information technology industry, no commonly accepted view of which competencies would be re-

---

1. For a fuller discussion, see our article, "Strategic Intent," HBR May-June 1989, p. 63.

quired to compete in that industry were communicated widely. While significant staff work was done to identify key technologies, senior line managers continued to act as if they were managing independent business units. Decentralization made it difficult to focus on core competencies. Instead, individual businesses became increasingly dependent on outsiders for critical skills, and collaboration became a route to staged exits. Today, with a new management team in place, GTE has repositioned itself to apply its competencies to emerging markets in telecommunications services.

The Roots of Competitive Advantage

The distinction we observed in the way NEC and GTE conceived of themselves – a portfolio of competencies versus a portfolio of businesses – was repeated across many industries. From 1980 to 1988, Canon grew by 264%, Honda by 200%. Compare that with Xerox and Chrysler. And if Western managers were once anxious about the low cost and high quality of Japanese imports, they are now overwhelmed by the pace at which Japanese rivals are inventing new markets, creating new products, and enhancing them. Canon has given us personal copiers; Honda has moved from motorcycles to four-wheel off-road buggies. Sony developed the 8mm camcorder, Yamaha, the digital piano. Komatsu developed an underwater remote-controlled bulldozer, while Casio's latest gambit is a small-screen color LCD television. Who would have anticipated the evolution of these vanguard markets?

In more established markets, the Japanese challenge has been just as disquieting. Japanese companies are generating a blizzard of features and functional enhancements that bring technological sophistication to everyday products. Japanese car producers have been pioneering four-wheel steering, four-valve-per-cylinder engines, in-car navigation systems, and sophisticated electronic engine-management

systems. On the strength of its product features, Canon is now a player in facsimile transmission machines, desktop laser printers, even semiconductor manufacturing equipment.

In the short run, a company's competitiveness derives from the price/performance attributes of current products. But the survivors of the first wave of global competition, Western and Japanese alike, are all converging on similar and formidable standards for product cost and quality – minimum hurdles for continued competition, but less and less important as sources of differential advantage. In the long run, competitiveness derives from an ability to build, at lower cost and more speedily than competitors, the core competencies that spawn unanticipated products. The real sources of advantage are to be found in management's ability to consolidate corporatewide technologies and production skills into competencies that empower individual businesses to adapt quickly to changing opportunities.

Senior executives who claim that they cannot build core competencies either because they feel the autonomy of business units is sacrosanct or because

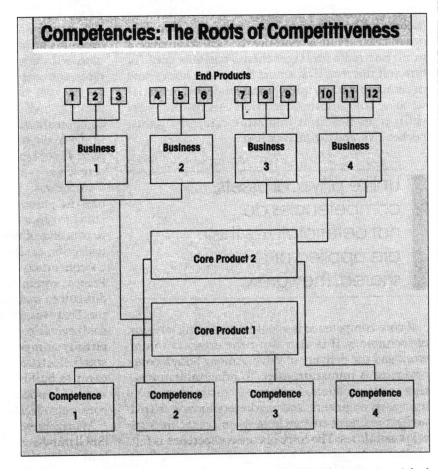

Competencies: The Roots of Competitiveness

The corporation, like a tree, grows from its roots. Core products are nourished by competencies and engender business units, whose fruit are end products.

their feet are held to the quarterly budget fire should think again. The problem in many Western companies is not that their senior executives are any less capable than those in Japan nor that Japanese companies possess greater technical capabilities. Instead, it is their adherence to a concept of the corporation that unnecessarily limits the ability of individual businesses to fully exploit the deep reservoir of technological capability that many American and European companies possess.

The diversified corporation is a large tree. The trunk and major limbs are core products, the smaller branches are business units; the leaves, flowers, and fruit are end products. The root system that provides nourishment, sustenance, and stability is the core competence. You can miss the strength of competitors by looking only at their end products, in the same way you miss the strength of a tree if you look only at its leaves. (See the chart "Competencies: The Roots of Competitiveness.")

Core competencies are the collective learning in the organization, especially how to coordinate diverse production skills and integrate multiple streams of technologies. Consider Sony's capacity to miniaturize or Philips's optical-media expertise. The theoretical knowledge to put a radio on a chip does not in itself assure a company the skill to produce a miniature radio no bigger than a business card. To bring off this feat, Casio must harmonize know-how in miniaturization, microprocessor design, material science, and ultrathin precision casing—the same skills it applies in its miniature card calculators, pocket TVs, and digital watches.

> **Unlike physical assets, competencies do not deteriorate as they are applied and shared. They grow.**

If core competence is about harmonizing streams of technology, it is also about the organization of work and the delivery of value. Among Sony's competencies is miniaturization. To bring miniaturization to its products, Sony must ensure that technologists, engineers, and marketers have a shared understanding of customer needs and of technological possibilities. The force of core competence is felt as decisively in services as in manufacturing. Citicorp was ahead of others investing in an operating system that allowed it to participate in world mar-

kets 24 hours a day. Its competence in systems has provided the company the means to differentiate itself from many financial service institutions.

Core competence is communication, involvement, and a deep commitment to working across organizational boundaries. It involves many levels of people and all functions. World-class research in, for example, lasers or ceramics can take place in corporate laboratories without having an impact on any of the businesses of the company. The skills that together constitute core competence must coalesce around individuals whose efforts are not so narrowly focused that they cannot recognize the opportunities for blending their functional expertise with those of others in new and interesting ways.

Core competence does not diminish with use. Unlike physical assets, which do deteriorate over time, competencies are enhanced as they are applied and shared. But competencies still need to be nurtured and protected; knowledge fades if it is not used. Competencies are the glue that binds existing businesses. They are also the engine for new business development. Patterns of diversification and market entry may be guided by them, not just by the attractiveness of markets.

Consider 3M's competence with sticky tape. In dreaming up businesses as diverse as "Post-it" notes, magnetic tape, photographic film, pressure-sensitive tapes, and coated abrasives, the company has brought to bear widely shared competencies in substrates, coatings, and adhesives and devised various ways to combine them. Indeed, 3M has invested consistently in them. What seems to be an extremely diversified portfolio of businesses belies a few shared core competencies.

In contrast, there are major companies that have had the potential to build core competencies but failed to do so because top management was unable to conceive of the company as anything other than a collection of discrete businesses. GE sold much of its consumer electronics business to Thomson of France, arguing that it was becoming increasingly difficult to maintain its competitiveness in this sector. That was undoubtedly so, but it is ironic that it sold several key businesses to competitors who were already competence leaders—Black & Decker in small electrical motors, and Thomson, which was eager to build its competence in microelectronics and had learned from the Japanese that a position in consumer electronics was vital to this challenge.

Management trapped in the strategic business unit (SBU) mind-set almost inevitably finds its individual businesses dependent on external sources for critical components, such as motors or compressors. But these are not just components. They are core products that contribute to the competitiveness of a wide range of end products. They are the physical embodiments of core competencies.

How Not to Think of Competence

Since companies are in a race to build the competencies that determine global leadership, successful companies have stopped imagining themselves as bundles of businesses making products. Canon, Honda, Casio, or NEC may seem to preside over portfolios of businesses unrelated in terms of customers, distribution channels, and merchandising strategy. Indeed, they have portfolios that may seem idiosyncratic at times: NEC is the only global company to be among leaders in computing, telecommunications, and semiconductors *and* to have a thriving consumer electronics business.

But looks are deceiving. In NEC, digital technology, especially VLSI and systems integration skills, is fundamental. In the core competencies underlying them, disparate businesses become coherent. It is Honda's core competence in engines and power trains that gives it a distinctive advantage in car, motorcycle, lawn mower, and generator businesses. Canon's core competencies in optics, imaging, and

> Cultivating core competence does *not* mean outspending rivals on R&D or getting businesses to become more vertically integrated.

microprocessor controls have enabled it to enter, even dominate, markets as seemingly diverse as copiers, laser printers, cameras, and image scanners. Philips worked for more than 15 years to perfect its optical-media (laser disc) competence, as did JVC in building a leading position in video recording. Other examples of core competencies might include mechantronics (the ability to marry mechanical and electronic engineering), video displays, bioengineering, and microelectronics. In the early stages of its competence building, Philips could not have imagined all the products that would be spawned by its optical-media competence, nor could JVC have anticipated miniature camcorders when it first began exploring videotape technologies.

Unlike the battle for global brand dominance, which is visible in the world's broadcast and print media and is aimed at building global ''share of mind,'' the battle to build world-class competencies is invisible to people who aren't deliberately looking for it. Top management often tracks the cost and quality of competitors' products, yet how many managers untangle the web of alliances their Japanese competitors have constructed to acquire competencies at low cost? In how many Western boardrooms is there an explicit, shared understanding of the competencies the company must build for world leadership? Indeed, how many senior executives discuss the crucial distinction between competitive strategy at the level of a business and competitive strategy at the level of an entire company?

Let us be clear. Cultivating core competence does *not* mean outspending rivals on research and development. In 1983, when Canon surpassed Xerox in worldwide unit market share in the copier business, its R&D budget in reprographics was but a small fraction of Xerox's. Over the past 20 years, NEC has spent less on R&D as a percentage of sales than almost all of its American and European competitors.

Nor does core competence mean shared costs, as when two or more SBUs use a common facility—a plant, service facility, or sales force—or share a common component. The gains of sharing may be substantial, but the search for shared costs is typically a post hoc effort to rationalize production across existing businesses, not a premeditated effort to build the competencies out of which the businesses themselves grow.

Building core competencies is more ambitious and different than integrating vertically, moreover. Managers deciding whether to make or buy will start with end products and look upstream to the efficiencies of the supply chain and downstream toward distribution and customers. They do not take inventory of skills and look forward to applying them in nontraditional ways. (Of course, decisions about competencies *do* provide a logic for vertical integration. Canon is not particularly integrated in its copier business, except in those aspects of the vertical chain that support the competencies it regards as critical.)

Identifying Core Competencies—And Losing Them

At least three tests can be applied to identify core competencies in a company. First, a core competence provides potential access to a wide variety of markets. Competence in display systems, for example, enables a company to participate in such diverse businesses as calculators, miniature TV sets, monitors for laptop computers, and automotive dashboards – which is why Casio's entry into the handheld TV market was predictable. Second, a core competence should make a significant contribution to the perceived customer benefits of the end product. Clearly, Honda's engine expertise fills this bill.

Finally, a core competence should be difficult for competitors to imitate. And it *will* be difficult if it is a complex harmonization of individual technologies and production skills. A rival might acquire some of the technologies that comprise the core competence, but it will find it more difficult to duplicate the more or less comprehensive pattern of internal coordination and learning. JVC's decision in the early 1960s to pursue the development of a videotape competence passed the three tests outlined here. RCA's decision in the late 1970s to develop a stylus-based video turntable system did not.

Few companies are likely to build world leadership in more than five or six fundamental competencies. A company that compiles a list of 20 to 30 capabilities has probably not produced a list of core competencies. Still, it is probably a good discipline to generate a list of this sort and to see aggregate capabilities as building blocks. This tends to prompt the search for licensing deals and alliances through which the company may acquire, at low cost, the missing pieces.

Most Western companies hardly think about competitiveness in these terms at all. It is time to take a tough-minded look at the risks they are running. Companies that judge competitiveness, their own and their competitors', primarily in terms of the price/performance of end products are courting the erosion of core competencies – or making too little effort to enhance them. The embedded skills that give rise to the next generation of competitive products cannot be "rented in" by outsourcing and OEM-supply relationships. In our view, too many compa-

> ## Unlike Chrysler, Honda would never yield manufacturing responsibility for its engines – much less design of them.

nies have unwittingly surrendered core competencies when they cut internal investment in what they mistakenly thought were just "cost centers" in favor of outside suppliers.

Consider Chrysler. Unlike Honda, it has tended to view engines and power trains as simply one more component. Chrysler is becoming increasingly dependent on Mitsubishi and Hyundai: between 1985

and 1987, the number of outsourced engines went from 252,000 to 382,000. It is difficult to imagine Honda yielding manufacturing responsibility, much less design, of so critical a part of a car's function to an outside company – which is why Honda has made such an enormous commitment to Formula One auto racing. Honda has been able to pool its engine-related technologies; it has parlayed these into a corporatewide competency from which it develops world-beating products, despite R&D budgets smaller than those of GM and Toyota.

Of course, it is perfectly possible for a company to have a competitive product line up but be a laggard in developing core competencies – at least for a while. If a company wanted to enter the copier business today, it would find a dozen Japanese companies more than willing to supply copiers on the basis of an OEM private label. But when fundamental technologies changed or if its supplier decided to enter the market directly and become a competitor, that company's product line, along with all of its investments in marketing and distribution, could be vulnerable. Outsourcing can provide a shortcut to a more competitive product, but it typically contributes little to building the people-embodied skills that are needed to sustain product leadership.

Nor is it possible for a company to have an intelligent alliance or sourcing strategy if it has not made a choice about where it will build competence leadership. Clearly, Japanese companies have benefited from alliances. They've used them to learn from Western partners who were not fully committed to preserving core competencies of their own. As we've argued in these pages before, learning within an alliance takes a positive commitment of resources – travel, a pool of dedicated people, test-bed facilities, time to internalize and test what has been learned.[2] A company may not make this effort if it doesn't have clear goals for competence building.

Another way of losing is forgoing opportunities to establish competencies that are evolving in existing businesses. In the 1970s and 1980s, many American and European companies – like GE, Motorola, GTE, Thorn, and GEC – chose to exit the color television business, which they regarded as mature. If by "mature" they meant that they had run out of new product ideas at precisely the moment global rivals had targeted the TV business for entry, then yes, the industry was mature. But it certainly wasn't mature in the sense that all opportunities to enhance and apply video-based competencies had been exhausted.

In ridding themselves of their television businesses, these companies failed to distinguish be-

---

2. "Collaborate with Your Competitors and Win," HBR January-February 1989, p. 133, with Yves L. Doz.

tween divesting the business and destroying their video media-based competencies. They not only got out of the TV business but they also closed the door on a whole stream of future opportunities reliant on video-based competencies. The television industry, considered by many U.S. companies in the 1970s to be unattractive, is today the focus of a fierce public policy debate about the inability of U.S. corporations to benefit from the $20-billion-a-year opportunity that HDTV will represent in the mid- to late 1990s. Ironically, the U.S. government is being asked to fund a massive research project—in effect, to compensate U.S. companies for their failure to preserve critical core competencies when they had the chance.

In contrast, one can see a company like Sony reducing its emphasis on VCRs (where it has not been very successful and where Korean companies now threaten), without reducing its commitment to video-related competencies. Sony's Betamax led to a debacle. But it emerged with its videotape recording competencies intact and is currently challenging Matsushita in the 8mm camcorder market.

There are two clear lessons here. First, the costs of losing a core competence can be only partly calculated in advance. The baby may be thrown out with the bath water in divestment decisions. Second, since core competencies are built through a process of continuous improvement and enhancement that may span a decade or longer, a company that has failed to invest in core competence building will find it very difficult to enter an emerging market, unless, of course, it will be content simply to serve as a distribution channel.

American semiconductor companies like Motorola learned this painful lesson when they elected to forgo direct participation in the 256k generation of DRAM chips. Having skipped this round, Motorola, like most of its American competitors, needed a large infusion of technical help from Japanese partners to rejoin the battle in the 1-megabyte generation. When it comes to core competencies, it is difficult to get off the train, walk to the next station, and then reboard.

From Core Competencies to Core Products

The tangible link between identified core competencies and end products is what we call the core products—the physical embodiments of one or more core competencies. Honda's engines, for example, are core products, linchpins between design and development skills that ultimately lead to a proliferation of end products. Core products are the components or subassemblies that actually contribute to the value of the end products. Thinking in terms of core products forces a company to distinguish between the brand share it achieves in end product markets (for example, 40% of the U.S. refrigerator market) and the manufacturing share it achieves in any particular core product (for example, 5% of the world share of compressor output).

Canon is reputed to have an 84% world manufacturing share in desktop laser printer "engines," even though its brand share in the laser printer business is minuscule. Similarly, Matsushita has a world manufacturing share of about 45% in key VCR components, far in excess of its brand share (Panasonic, JVC, and others) of 20%. And Matsushita has a commanding core product share in compressors worldwide, estimated at 40%, even though its brand share in both the air-conditioning and refrigerator businesses is quite small.

> **Maintain world manufacturing dominance in core products, and you reserve the power to shape the evolution of end products.**

It is essential to make this distinction between core competencies, core products, and end products because global competition is played out by different rules and for different stakes at each level. To build or defend leadership over the long term, a corporation will probably be a winner at each level. At the level of core competence, the goal is to build world leadership in the design and development of a particular class of product functionality—be it compact data storage and retrieval, as with Philips's optical-media competence, or compactness and ease of use, as with Sony's micromotors and microprocessor controls.

To sustain leadership in their chosen core competence areas, these companies *seek to maximize their world manufacturing share in core products*. The manufacture of core products for a wide variety of external (and internal) customers yields the revenue and market feedback that, at least partly, determines the pace at which core competencies can be enhanced and extended. This thinking was behind JVC's decision in the mid-1970s to establish VCR supply relationships with leading national consumer electronics companies in Europe and the United States. In supplying Thomson, Thorn, and Telefunken (all independent companies at that time) as well as U.S. partners, JVC was able to gain the cash and the diversity of market experience that ultimately enabled it to outpace Philips and Sony. (Philips developed videotape competencies in parallel with JVC, but it failed to build a worldwide network of OEM relationships that would have allowed it to accelerate the refinement of its videotape competence through the sale of core products.)

JVC's success has not been lost on Korean companies like Goldstar, Sam Sung, Kia, and Daewoo, who are building core product leadership in areas as diverse as displays, semiconductors, and automotive engines through their OEM-supply contracts with Western companies. Their avowed goal is to capture investment initiative away from potential competitors, often U.S. companies. In doing so, they accelerate their competence-building efforts while "hollowing out" their competitors. By focusing on competence and embedding it in core products, Asian competitors have built up advantages in component markets first and have then leveraged off their superior products to move downstream to build brand share. And they are not likely to remain the low-cost suppliers forever. As their reputation for brand leadership is consolidated, they may well gain price leadership. Honda has proven this with its Acura line, and other Japanese car makers are following suit.

Control over core products is critical for other reasons. A dominant position in core products allows a company to shape the evolution of applications and end markets. Such compact audio disc-related core products as data drives and lasers have enabled Sony and Philips to influence the evolution of the computer-peripheral business in optical-media storage. As a company multiplies the number of application arenas for its core products, it can consistently reduce the cost, time, and risk in new product development. In short, well-targeted core products can lead to economies of scale *and* scope.

The Tyranny of the SBU

The new terms of competitive engagement cannot be understood using analytical tools devised to manage the diversified corporation of 20 years ago, when competition was primarily domestic (GE versus Westinghouse, General Motors versus Ford) and all the key players were speaking the language of the same business schools and consultancies. Old prescriptions have potentially toxic side effects. The need for new principles is most obvious in companies organized exclusively according to the logic of SBUs. The implications of the two alternate concepts of the corporation are summarized in "Two Concepts of the Corporation: SBU or Core Competence."

Obviously, diversified corporations have a portfolio of products and a portfolio of businesses. But we believe in a view of the company as a portfolio of competencies as well. U.S. companies do not lack the technical resources to build competencies, but their top management often lacks the vision to build them and the administrative means for assembling resources spread across multiple businesses. A shift in commitment will inevitably influence patterns of diversification, skill deployment, resource allocation priorities, and approaches to alliances and outsourcing.

We have described the three different planes on which battles for global leadership are waged: core competence, core products, and end products. A corporation has

---

Two Concepts of the Corporation: SBU or Core Competence

	SBU	Core Competence
Basis for competition	Competitiveness of today's products	Interfirm competition to build competencies
Corporate structure	Portfolio of businesses related in product-market terms	Portfolio of competencies, core products, and businesses
Status of the business unit	Autonomy is sacrosanct; the SBU "owns" all resources other than cash	SBU is a potential reservoir of core competencies
Resource allocation	Discrete businesses are the unit of analysis; capital is allocated business by business	Businesses and competencies are the unit of analysis: top management allocates capital and talent
Value added of top management	Optimizing corporate returns through capital allocation trade-offs among businesses	Enunciating strategic architecture and building competencies to secure the future

to know whether it is winning or losing on each plane. By sheer weight of investment, a company might be able to beat its rivals to blue-sky technologies yet still lose the race to build core competence leadership. If a company is winning the race to build core competencies (as opposed to building leadership in a few technologies), it will almost certainly outpace rivals in new business development. If a company is winning the race to capture world manufacturing share in core products, it will probably outpace rivals in improving product features and the price/performance ratio.

Determining whether one is winning or losing end product battles is more difficult because measures of product market share do not necessarily reflect various companies' underlying competitiveness. Indeed, companies that attempt to build market share by relying on the competitiveness of others, rather than investing in core competencies and world core-product leadership, may be treading on quicksand. In the race for global brand dominance, companies like 3M, Black & Decker, Canon, Honda, NEC, and Citicorp have built global brand umbrellas by proliferating products out of their core competencies. This has allowed their individual businesses to build image, customer loyalty, and access to distribution channels.

When you think about this reconceptualization of the corporation, the primacy of the SBU – an organizational dogma for a generation – is now clearly an anachronism. Where the SBU is an article of faith, resistance to the seductions of decentralization can seem heretical. In many companies, the SBU prism means that only one plane of the global competitive battle, the battle to put competitive products on the shelf *today*, is visible to top management. What are the costs of this distortion?

Underinvestment in Developing Core Competencies and Core Products. When the organization is conceived of as a multiplicity of SBUs, no single business may feel responsible for maintaining a viable position in core products nor be able to justify the investment required to build world leadership in some core competence. In the absence of a more comprehensive view imposed by corporate management, SBU managers will tend to underinvest. Recently, companies such as Kodak and Philips have recognized this as a potential problem and have begun searching for new organizational forms that will allow them to develop and manufacture core products for both internal and external customers.

SBU managers have traditionally conceived of competitors in the same way they've seen themselves. On the whole, they've failed to note the emphasis Asian competitors were placing on building leadership in core products or to understand the criti-cal linkage between world manufacturing leadership and the ability to sustain development pace in core competence. They've failed to pursue OEM-supply opportunities or to look across their various product divisions in an attempt to identify opportunities for coordinated initiatives.

Imprisoned Resources. As an SBU evolves, it often develops unique competencies. Typically, the people who embody this competence are seen as the sole property of the business in which they grew up. The manager of another SBU who asks to borrow talented people is likely to get a cold rebuff. SBU managers are not only unwilling to lend their competence carriers but they may actually hide talent to prevent its redeployment in the pursuit of new opportunites. This may be compared to residents of an underdeveloped country hiding most of their cash under their mattresses. The benefits of competencies, like the benefits of the money supply, depend on the velocity of their circulation as well as on the size of the stock the company holds.

Western companies have traditionally had an advantage in the stock of skills they possess. But have they been able to reconfigure them quickly to re-

> **How strange that SBU managers should be made to compete for corporate cash but never for key people.**

spond to new opportunites? Canon, NEC, and Honda have had a lesser stock of the people and technologies that compose core competencies but could move them much quicker from one business unit to another. Corporate R&D spending at Canon is not fully indicative of the size of Canon's core competence stock and tells the casual observer nothing about the velocity with which Canon is able to move core competencies to exploit opportunities.

When competencies become imprisoned, the people who carry the competencies do not get assigned to the most exciting opportunities, and their skills begin to atrophy. Only by fully leveraging core competencies can small companies like Canon afford to compete with industry giants like Xerox. How strange that SBU managers, who are perfectly willing to compete for cash in the capital budgeting process, are unwilling to compete for people – the company's most precious asset. We find it ironic that top management devotes so much attention to the capital budgeting process yet typically has no comparable mechanism for allocating the human skills that embody core competencies. Top managers are sel-

Vickers Learns the Value of Strategic Architecture

The idea that top management should develop a corporate strategy for acquiring and deploying core competencies is relatively new in most U.S. companies. There are a few exceptions. An early convert was Trinova (previously Libbey Owens Ford), a Toledo-based corporation, which enjoys a worldwide position in power and motion controls and engineered plastics. One of its major divisions is Vickers, a premier supplier of hydraulics components like valves, pumps, actuators, and filtration devices to aerospace, marine, defense, automotive, earth-moving, and industrial markets.

Vickers saw the potential for a transformation of its traditional business with the application of electronics disciplines in combination with its traditional technologies. The goal was "to ensure that change in technology does not displace Vickers from its customers." This, to be sure, was initially a defensive move: Vickers recognized that unless it acquired new skills, it could not protect existing markets or capitalize on new growth opportunities. Managers at Vickers attempted to conceptualize the likely evolution of (a) technologies relevant to the power and motion control business, (b) functionalities that would satisfy emerging customer needs, and (c) new competencies needed to creatively manage the marriage of technology and customer needs.

Despite pressure for short-term earnings, top management looked to a 10- to 15-year time horizon in developing a map of emerging customer needs, changing technologies, and the core competencies that would be necessary to bridge the gap between the two. Its slogan was "Into the 21st Century." (A simplified version of the overall architecture developed is shown here.)

Vickers is currently in fluid-power components. The architecture identifies two additional competencies, electric-power components and electronic controls. A systems integration capability that would unite hardware, software, and service was also targeted for development.

The strategic architecture, as illustrated by the Vickers example, is not a forecast of specific products or specific technologies but a broad map of the evolving linkages between customer functionality requirements, potential technologies, and core competencies. It assumes that products and systems cannot be defined with certainty for the future but that preempting competitors in the development of new markets requires an early start to building core competencies. The strategic architecture developed by Vickers, while describing the future in competence terms, also provides the basis for making "here and now" decisions about product priorities, acquisitions, alliances, and recruitment.

Since 1986, Vickers has made more than ten clearly targeted acquisitions, each one focused on a specific component or technology gap identified in the overall architecture. The architecture is also the basis for internal development of new competencies. Vickers has undertaken, in parallel, a reorganization to enable the integration of electronics and electrical capabilities with mechanical-based competencies. We believe that it will take another two to three years before Vickers reaps the total benefits from developing the strategic architecture, communicating it widely to all its employees, customers, and investors, and building administrative systems consistent with the architecture.

Vickers Map of Competencies

Electronic Controls
Valve amplifiers
Logic
Motion
Complete machine and vehicle

Fluid Power
Electrohydraulic
Pumps
Control valves
Cartridge valves
Actuators
Package systems
Pneumatic products
Fuel/Fluid transfer
Filtration

Electric Power
AC/DC
Servo
Stepper

Sensors
Valve/Pump
Actuator
Machine

System Engineering
Application focus
Power/Motion
Control
Electronics
Software

Electric Products
Actuators
Fan packages
Generators

Offering
Systems   Packages   Components   Service
Training

Focus Markets
Factory automation   Off-highway   Missiles/Space
Automotive systems   Commercial aircraft   Defense vehicles
Plastic process   Military aircraft   Marine

dom able to look four or five levels down into the organization, identify the people who embody critical competencies, and move them across organizational boundaries.

Bounded Innovation. If core competencies are not recognized, individual SBUs will pursue only those innovation opportunities that are close at hand — marginal product-line extensions or geographic expansions. Hybrid opportunities like fax machines, laptop computers, hand-held televisions, or portable music keyboards will emerge only when managers take off their SBU blinkers. Remember, Canon appeared to be in the camera business at the time it was preparing to become a world leader in copiers. Conceiving of the corporation in terms of core competencies widens the domain of innovation.

Developing Strategic Architecture

The fragmentation of core competencies becomes inevitable when a diversified company's information systems, patterns of communication, career paths, managerial rewards, and processes of strategy development do not transcend SBU lines. We believe that senior management should spend a significant amount of its time developing a corporatewide strategic architecture that establishes objectives for competence building. A strategic architecture is a road map of the future that identifies which core competencies to build and their constituent technologies.

By providing an impetus for learning from alliances and a focus for internal development efforts, a strategic architecture like NEC's C&C can dramatically reduce the investment needed to secure future market leadership. How can a company make partnerships intelligently without a clear understanding of the core competencies it is trying to build and those it is attempting to prevent from being unintentionally transferred?

Of course, all of this begs the question of what a strategic architecture should look like. The answer will be different for every company. But it is helpful to think again of that tree, of the corporation organized around core products and, ultimately, core competencies. To sink sufficiently strong roots, a company must answer some fundamental questions: How long could we preserve our competitiveness in this business if we did not control this particular core competence? How central is this core competence to perceived customer benefits? What future opportunities would be foreclosed if we were to lose this particular competence?

The architecture provides a logic for product and market diversification, moreover. An SBU manager would be asked: Does the new market opportunity add to the overall goal of becoming the best player in the world? Does it exploit or add to the core competence? At Vickers, for example, diversification options have been judged in the context of becoming the best power and motion control company in the world (see the insert "Vickers Learns the Value of Strategic Architecture").

The strategic architecture should make resource allocation priorities transparent to the entire organization. It provides a template for allocation decisions by top management. It helps lower level managers understand the logic of allocation priorities and disciplines senior management to maintain consistency. In short, it yields a definition of the company and the markets it serves. 3M, Vickers, NEC, Canon, and Honda all qualify on this score. Honda *knew* it was exploiting what it had learned from motorcycles — how to make high-revving, smooth-running, lightweight engines — when it entered the car business. The task of creating a strategic architecture forces the organization to identify and commit to the technical and production linkages across SBUs that will provide a distinct competitive advantage.

It is consistency of resource allocation and the development of an administrative infrastructure appropriate to it that breathes life into a strategic architecture and creates a managerial culture, teamwork, a capacity to change, and a willingness to share resources, to protect proprietary skills, and to think long term. That is also the reason the specific architecture cannot be copied easily or overnight by competitors. Strategic architecture is a tool for communicating with customers and other external constituents. It reveals the broad direction without giving away every step.

Redeploying to Exploit Competencies

If the company's core competencies are its critical resource and if top management must ensure that competence carriers are not held hostage by some particular business, then it follows that SBUs should bid for core competencies in the same way they bid for capital. We've made this point glancingly. It is important enough to consider more deeply.

Once top management (with the help of divisional and SBU managers) has identified overarching competencies, it must ask businesses to identify the projects and people closely connected with them. Corporate officers should direct an audit of the location, number, and quality of the people who embody competence.

This sends an important signal to middle managers: core competencies are *corporate* resources and may be reallocated by corporate management. An in-

> Send a message to your middle managers: the people critical to core competencies are *corporate* assets to be deployed by corporate management.

dividual business doesn't own anybody. SBUs are entitled to the services of individual employees so long as SBU management can demonstrate that the opportunity it is pursuing yields the highest possible pay-off on the investment in their skills. This message is further underlined if each year in the strategic planning or budgeting process, unit managers must justify their hold on the people who carry the company's core competencies.

Elements of Canon's core competence in optics are spread across businesses as diverse as cameras, copiers, and semiconductor lithographic equipment and are shown in "Core Competencies at Canon." When Canon identified an opportunity in digital laser printers, it gave SBU managers the right to raid other SBUs to pull together the required pool of talent. When Canon's reprographics products division undertook to develop microprocessor-controlled copiers, it turned to the photo products group, which had developed the world's first microprocessor-controlled camera.

Also, reward systems that focus only on product-line results and career paths that seldom cross SBU boundaries engender patterns of behavior among unit managers that are destructively competitive. At NEC, divisional managers come together to iden-

tify next-generation competencies. Together they decide how much investment needs to be made to build up each future competency and the contribution in capital and staff support that each division will need to make. There is also a sense of equitable exchange. One division may make a disproportionate contribution or may benefit less from the progress made, but such short-term inequalities will balance out over the long term.

Incidentally, the positive contribution of the SBU manager should be made visible across the company. An SBU manager is unlikely to surrender key people if only the other business (or the general manager of that business who may be a competitor for promotion) is going to benefit from the redeployment. Cooperative SBU managers should be celebrated as team players. Where priorities are clear, transfers are less likely to be seen as idiosyncratic and politically motivated.

Core Competencies at Canon

	Precision Mechanics	Fine Optics	Micro-electronics
Basic camera	■	■	
Compact fashion camera	■	■	
Electronic camera	■	■	
EOS autofocus camera	■	■	■
Video still camera	■	■	■
Laser beam printer	■	■	■
Color video printer	■		■
Bubble jet printer	■		■
Basic fax	■		■
Laser fax	■		■
Calculator			■
Plain paper copier	■	■	■
Battery PPC	■	■	■
Color copier	■	■	■
Laser copier	■	■	■
Color laser copier	■	■	■
NAVI	■	■	■
Still video system	■	■	■
Laser imager	■	■	■
Cell analyzer	■	■	■
Mask aligners	■		■
Stepper aligners	■		■
Excimer laser aligners	■	■	■

Every Canon product is the result of at least one core competency.

Transfers for the sake of building core competence must be recorded and appreciated in the corporate memory. It is reasonable to expect a business that has surrendered core skills on behalf of corporate opportunities in other areas to lose, for a time, some of its competitiveness. If these losses in performance bring immediate censure, SBUs will be unlikely to assent to skills transfers next time.

Top management's real responsibility is a strategic architecture that guides competence building.

Finally, there are ways to wean key employees off the idea that they belong in perpetuity to any particular business. Early in their careers, people may be exposed to a variety of businesses through a carefully planned rotation program. At Canon, critical people move regularly between the camera business and the copier business and between the copier business and the professional optical-products business. In mid-career, periodic assignments to cross-divisional project teams may be necessary, both for diffusing core competencies and for loosening the bonds that might tie an individual to one business even when brighter opportunities beckon elsewhere. Those who embody critical core competencies should know that their careers are tracked and guided by corporate human resource professionals. In the early 1980s at Canon, all engineers under 30 were invited to apply for membership on a seven-person committee that was to spend two years plotting Canon's future direction, including its strategic architecture.

Competence carriers should be regularly brought together from across the corporation to trade notes and ideas. The goal is to build a strong feeling of community among these people. To a great extent, their loyalty should be to the integrity of the core competence area they represent and not just to particular businesses. In traveling regularly, talking frequently to customers, and meeting with peers, competence carriers may be encouraged to discover new market opportunities.

Core competencies are the wellspring of new business development. They should constitute the focus for strategy at the corporate level. Managers have to win manufacturing leadership in core products and capture global share through brand-building programs aimed at exploiting economies of scope. Only if the company is conceived of as a hierarchy of core competencies, core products, and market-focused business units will it be fit to fight.

Nor can top management be just another layer of accounting consolidation, which it often is in a regime of radical decentralization. Top management must add value by enunciating the strategic architecture that guides the competence acquisition process. We believe an obsession with competence building will characterize the global winners of the 1990s. With the decade underway, the time for rethinking the concept of the corporation is already overdue.

Reprint 90311

Software managers who succeed in establishing effective organizations will enjoy development rates 1,200% better than managers who fail.

ORGANIZING FOR SUCCESSFUL SOFTWARE DEVELOPMENT

by Edmund B. Daly

Software development requires competent technologists, competent managers and an effective organization structure. The synergistic effect of these three elements differentiates successful development organizations from those forced to operate in a chaotic environment. A good organization structure is meaningless without a well-defined design methodology and without effective management practices. The organization structure brings together technologists and management, but the structure must work within the culture of the organization.

An organization can be described by the way it handles information flow, or by its hierarchical structure—the way it looks on an organization chart. In either case, one must first consider an organization as a group of managers and technologists and then attempt to decompose these personnel in a manner best fitting the projects to be developed. *Organization structures must be dynamic and must be modified to accommodate the project (or work activity) environment.*

An interesting analogy can be established between concepts employed in organizational decomposition and concepts employed in software decomposition. In fact, if one employs the same decomposition rules for both the job to be performed and the people who are to perform the job, a very effective organizational decomposition can be achieved. The common decomposition rules are:

Software: Each software segment should be small so that it can be easily understood (20 source lines).
Organization: Each software team should be small so that it can be effectively controlled (Chief Programmer Group).

Software: Each software segment should be loosely coupled from other software segments.
Organization: Each software team should be assigned a unit of work which allows for minimal coupling among software teams.

Software: Each software segment should enjoy high cohesion (performs one function).
Organization: Each software team should be assigned a work unit that is highly cohesive. (One team should not design diagnostic software and supporting software, such as compilers.)

Software: The scope of effect of a software segment should be a subset of scope of control.
Organization: Software teams should be grouped together (reporting to one manager) in such a manner so that the decisions made within the manager group have minimal effect on the work of other managerial groups.

Software: As software is decomposed into a hierarchy of segments, higher level segments perform decision-making and lower level segments do the actual work.
Organization: In an organization structure the managerial hierarchy performs decision-making (more abstract and longer range decisions at higher levels of management) and the lower organization levels perform the actual work.

Software: Pathological connections should be avoided, or if not, at least fully documented. A pathological connection is a communication link not following the hierarchical software structure.
Organization: Pathological connections should be avoided among programmers in an organizational structure.

Fig. 1 illustrates the similarity between a software hierarchy and an organizational hierarchy when one applies the same rules to the decomposition of both work and people. This hierarchy is a basic entity in GTE's software development methodology.

The correlation depicted in Fig. 1 shows that interfaces between modules within a subprogram are controlled by the chief programmer, who is assigned the responsibility for developing one or more subprograms. Interfaces between subprograms within a class are controlled by the first line manager (or an appointee), who is responsible for the development of a software class. Note that in a matrix organization structure (which will be described in detail later), the technical coordination among subprograms will be performed by the project manager.

Let us assume the new development organization is required to develop two projects: Project A and Project B. Each project has three major functions to perform: real-time software development (operating systems), support software development (compilers), and hardware development (computers).

Fig. 2 shows six separate organizational entities, one entity for each technology for each project. The lower levels of the hierarchies shown in Fig. 1 can be viewed as existing within each box in Fig. 2. Now the manner in which we combine these separate organizations will give us a project organization structure (Fig. 3), a functional organization structure (Fig. 4), or a matrix organization structure (Fig. 5).

FACTORS IN SELECTING STRUCTURES

A combination of both matrix and project structures (where small project teams are created within the environment of a larger matrix superstructure) is the most advanta-

Reprinted from DATAMATION, December 1979. © 1979 by Cahners Publishing Company.

The matrix organization has the capability of exhibiting concern both for people and for projects.

geous for organizations responsible for developing both large and small projects. In most practical situations, the organizational structure selected is dependent on the following factors:

1. *Size of each software development.* Number of programmers/ engineers whose output must be combined to make up one working system.

2. *Number of projects.* Few larger projects (above 30 people) or many small projects (under 10 people).

3. *Scope of development.* Types of work activity being performed at any one time. Are all programmers involved in active development? Are some involved in planning for new projects, some involved in new design, and some involved in software maintenance?

4. *Environment.* A laboratory organization structure must recognize and be able to cope with the corporate culture and structure in which it exists. There is no such entity as a "project organization" in a development environment when the project organization controls only 30% of the resources needed to complete the project and the external environment is functionally structured and controls the remaining 70%.

5. *Physical limitations.* Is the project being developed in one location or in many locations, possibly in different countries?

6. *Organizational culture.* What style of manager exists within the organization? And more importantly, what organization structure does the organization's chief officer feel comfortable with?

Project Organization. This structure can be most effectively employed when an organization has many small projects to develop and when each project is developed at one location. The project structure requires that at least 70% of the resources needed to bring a project to completion is under the direct control of one line manager. This one person performs both the functions of project manager (technical) and line manager (administrative).

The advantages of the project organization are:

- Project and administrative decisions are made at the lowest possible organizational level thus allowing quicker decisions and better project control.
- Since full authority for the project is under the control of one person, interfaces are minimized and project responsibility is strictly defined (in case something goes wrong).
- This structure tends to mold system generalists and management personnel who are not assigned to functional specialties.

- Motivation is high during the active development period—programmers tend to identify with the project.

The disadvantages are:

- Projects must be kept small.
- Higher level management often loses track of project progress since their immediate involvement is not required.
- Economics of scale for critical resources can not be achieved. It is difficult to assign one "compiler" expert to three different projects. At least the project structure does not help cope with this problem.
- Training is costly since experts in all phases of development are required on each project. As an example, if one system software load must be generated for a given project, a member of the project organization must be trained in the techniques of generating a load. He may only utilize this training for a few weeks.
- Movement of programmers, especially good ones, from one project to another is difficult.
- Attrition is low during the active project development but often becomes excessive when the project is completed. Either programmers feel a loss of identity or alternative positions on other projects are not attractive.
- Probably the most serious flaw in this structure is that it inhibits both commonality among projects and generation of good software development standards and methodologies.

Functional Organization. This, the oldest form of organizational structure, is seldom used in medium to large development organizations. The concepts associated with a functional organizational structure are important only in so far as they serve as a base behind the more complex matrix structure. The basic problem is that all decisions that cross functional boundaries are made by one individual—the administrative and technical head of the functional organization. Very few managers are able to deal effectively with this much authority and often bottlenecks result, such as schedule slippages, project overruns, and poor quality. Also, the superhuman manager on top of the functional organization often gets bogged down in today's problems, leaving the organization's future to chance.

The advantages of a functional organization are:

- For a strong manager (hopefully free from megalomania) this organization sets a stage for very tight, centralized control.
- Since all the people associated with one specialty are centralized under a func-

tional manager (e.g., one functional manager controls all real-time software development for all projects), commonality among projects can be effectively controlled. Also, selected personnel can be set aside to establish standards and advanced development methodologies, and ensure that industry-wide technological advancements are effectively included in the functional manager's internal operation.

- People establish affinity to a profession or to an organization rather than to a project, thus eliminating the attrition many development organizations face when the project technologists are assigned to nears completion.
- Adapts effectively to the long-range aspects—acquiring advanced technologies, and training and retaining personnel. This structure is capable of concentrating on the individual rather than the project.

The disadvantages of this form of organization are:

- Resolution of interface problems are made by one manager for all projects.
- Limits the creation of system generalists since all technologists are assigned to one functional specialization.
- Exhibits poor project control in terms of meeting development costs, schedules, and quality.

Matrix Organization. The project structure and the functional structure attempt to optimize one organizational constraint. Project structures tend to force an organization to concentrate on *short-term project goals* such as schedule, cost, and project quality. Functional structures tend to force concentration on *long-term goals* such as commonality among projects, technological advancement, improved standards of operation, and critical skills economics of scale.

The matrix operation is a complex organizational structure that attempts to optimize two or more organizational constraints simultaneously. Some matrix structures have been grown in an attempt to optimize multiple organizational constraints. Dow Corning, for example, has instituted a four-dimensional structure aimed at simultaneously optimizing project, function, territory, and strategy. Simple matrix structures are two-dimensional (Fig. 6). Here we see a structure that attempts the advantages of the two simpler structures, project and functional. The project side of the matrix concentrates on short term project objectives. The functional side of the matrix concentrates on longer term organizational objectives.

Probably the major disadvantage

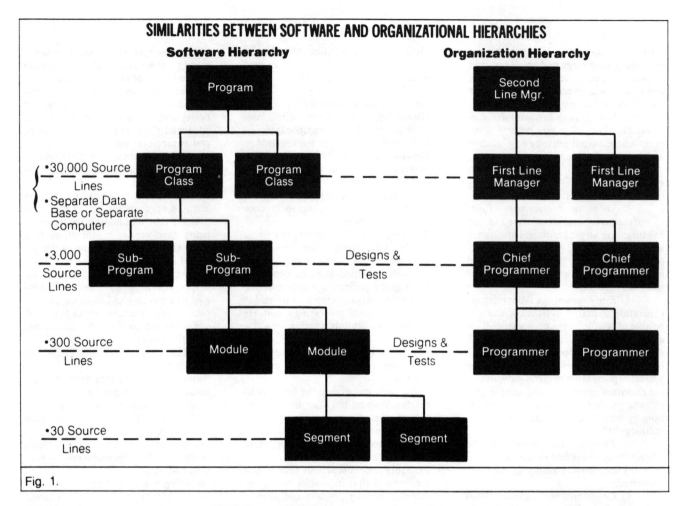

SIMILARITIES BETWEEN SOFTWARE AND ORGANIZATIONAL HIERARCHIES

Software Hierarchy

Organization Hierarchy

Program

Second Line Mgr.

•30,000 Source Lines
•Separate Data Base or Separate Computer

Program Class

Program Class

First Line Manager

First Line Manager

•3,000 Source Lines

Sub-Program

Sub-Program

Designs & Tests

Chief Programmer

Chief Programmer

•300 Source Lines

Module

Module

Designs & Tests

Programmer

Programmer

•30 Source Lines

Segment

Segment

Fig. 1.

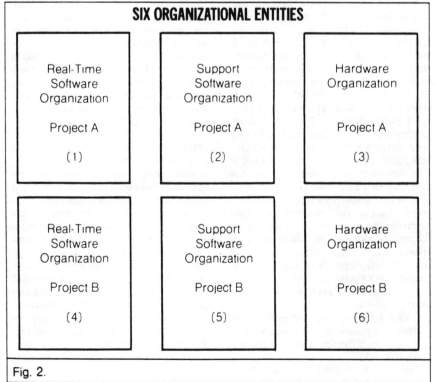

SIX ORGANIZATIONAL ENTITIES

Real-Time Software Organization

Project A

(1)

Support Software Organization

Project A

(2)

Hardware Organization

Project A

(3)

Real-Time Software Organization

Project B

(4)

Support Software Organization

Project B

(5)

Hardware Organization

Project B

(6)

Fig. 2.

Fig. 1 shows that there is a similarity between the software and organization hierarchies when the same rules are applied to the decomposition of work and people. The lower levels of the hierarchies in Fig. 1 can be viewed as existing within each box in Fig. 2.

to a matrix operation is that there is no single person responsible for the success of each project; the responsibility is truly shared between the functional line managers and the project managers. In the matrix philosophy, the functional manager decides *how* to do the job. He supplies all resources for development to take place. The project manager decides *what* to do. He controls the dollars. Dollars are allocated to the functional manager as part of a contractual agreement to perform work.

I have found that not all managers can work effectively in a matrix organization; many managers do not like the division of project responsibility. Unlike project organizations, the matrix does not have, and cannot tolerate, either a bureaucratic manager (must follow the rules) nor an autocratic manager (must do it my way).

In the face of conflict, the method of management operation in a matrix structure is for the project side and functional side to:

- Trust each other.
- Put all the facts on the table.
- Agree to a resolution. If this cannot be accomplished, both sides should compromise. As a last resort (admitting defeat) the problem should be brought to the "boss" who presides over both sides.

An often discussed disadvantage of the matrix is that it is a "two-boss system," meaning that a certain number of people in the organization have two bosses. However, I believe that if authority is properly defined and projects properly planned, the "two-boss" problem can be beneficial rather than detrimental.

MATRIX PROJECT PLANNING

If a development group decides to implement a matrix organization, top management must first define, in detail, the responsibility and authority of both the functional and project sides of the matrix. This is often done. What is overlooked in many situations is projects must be planned differently in a matrix environment. The matrix is a very powerful structure. Unlike either a project or functional structure, the matrix has an inherent capability to properly control "single project" development taking place in diversely located facilities or multiple companies. In a matrix environment, all work is effectively subcontracted rather then passed down through multiple levels of management.

For software design to take place properly within a matrix structure, one must ensure that project planning allows for subcontracting. To ensure this, the project group (usually expanded by temporary assignment of funtional chief programmers and group leaders) will decompose the total project (using work breakdown structure techniques if necessary) into small subprojects. In software, a small project would be one subprogram (3,000 source lines). Each subproject is then fully defined by the project group prior to subcontracting. The resulting package is called a "cost account," and it is this package which will be subcontracted to the functional software development line organization.

Sitting on the functional side of the fence, the functional manager sees his responsibility as one of developing many small projects (cost accounts). The functional software group will be contracting for these cost accounts with many different project groups. The important con-

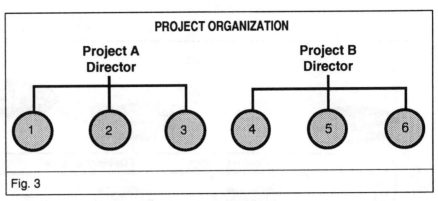

Fig. 3

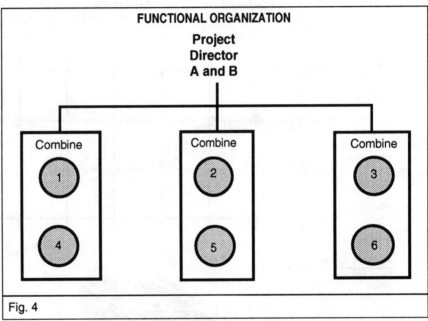

Fig. 4

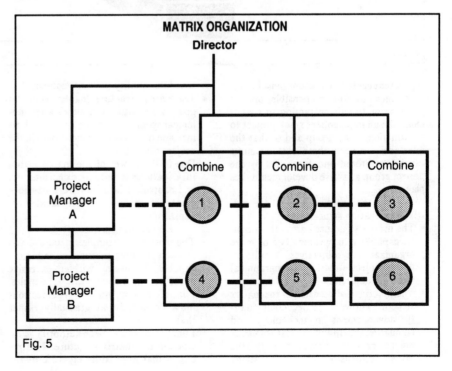

Fig. 5

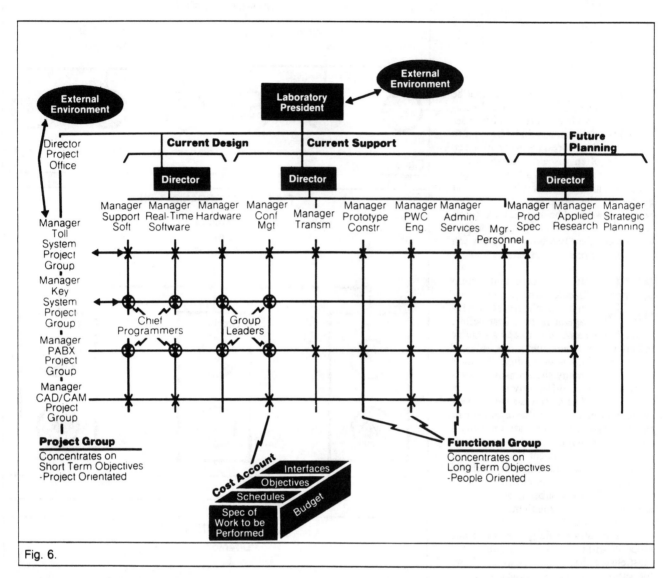

Fig. 6.

cept is that each cost account must be fully defined by the responsible project group prior to subcontracting so that it looks like an independent small project to the functional line group and so that the interfaces between these cost accounts can be monitored and controlled by the project group as active development takes place.

The major advantages of the matrix organization structure are:

- The matrix structure enjoys the intrinsic capability to optimize two or more organizational objectives simultaneously: project, functional, geographical strategic objectives.
- The functional dimension of the matrix structure allows for project commonality, advancement in technology and standards, sharing of critical resources among projects. Simultaneously, the project dimension allows for string

schedule, quality and cost control.
- The matrix structure enables technologists to be matured in either a technological speciality via the functional dimension or as system generalists via the project dimension.
- Due to the power of the matrix structure, it allows for effective coordination and control of large software development performed in diversely located organizations.

Disadvantages are:
- The matrix is a complex structure and as such requires mature management capable of working without excessive autocratic or bureaucratic tendencies. For this reason, matrix organizations must be introduced gradually rather than installed.
- Functional and project authority is divided in the matrix structure. This requires that approximately 15% of the

development staff (the chief programmers) must work for two bosses. Often this two boss system imposes conflicting demands on Chief Programmers.
- A matrix structure requires more formal project planning and control techniques than does a project structure. This is due to the "subcontracting" philosophy utilized in matrix organizations.
- Small developments and some medium-sized developments cannot be effectively managed utilizing the matrix due to overhead costs and division of responsibility. Thus, in most development environments utilizing the matrix, a Project organization philosophy should be employed as a substructure. As a general rule, those projects requiring less than 10 programmers should not be placed into a matrix unless there is excessive commonality with other projects being

Software management's objective: an environment in which high quality software can be developed with minimal resources.

developed or maintained within the organization.

The Management Grid. A popular tool for measuring management style is based on a concept developed by R. R. Blake and J. S. Mouton. This tool is referred to as the management grid. The grid, shown in Fig. 7, represents a two-dimensional analysis of managerial behavior: concern for production and concern for people. A manager who demonstrates extensive concern for people will score high on the vertical axis. A manager who demonstrates extensive concern for production will score high on the horizontal scale. An ideal manager will exhibit behavior characteristics which place him high on both scales, thereby approaching 9.9 on the managerial grid. I have found that the management grid applies to management styles exhibited by organizations as well as by individual managers.

By applying the management grid to organization theory we can see that the characteristics of a project structure tend to force the management style exhibited by the total organization into the lower right-hand quadrant of the grid since this structure stresses project objectives. On the other hand, a functional organization structure tends to force the exhibited management style into the top left-hand quadrant since this structure stresses people rather than projects.

The matrix organization, properly implemented, can now be shown to have a very powerful advantage over either of the two simpler structures (project or functional) since it has the capability of exhibiting concern for people via its functional dimension and concern for projects via its project dimension.

It is extremely rare to find an organization where all the managers fall in the 9.9 quadrant of the management grid. It is, however, easier to find managers who exhibit personality characteristics which place them in the 1.9 quadrant. It is also not too difficult to find managers who fall within the 9.1 quadrant.

By placing the 9.1 type managers in the project side of the matrix structure and the 1.9 type managers in the functional side, a synergistic effect occurs whereby the organization, as a whole, can be seen as exhibiting 9.9 quadrant management.

ORGANIZATION AND SOFTWARE PRODUCTIVITY

We have looked at various heuristics that can be used to decompose a software organization into manageable parts, and have shown that these parts can then be put together in one of three basic struc-

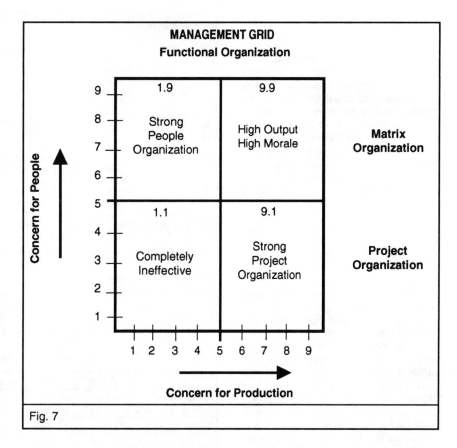

Fig. 7

tures: functional, project or matrix. Now let us analyze a third facet, organizational efficiency. Organizational efficiency is the intrinsic ability of an organization to generate quality software in minimal time with minimal resources. Once the efficiency of an organization has been determined, we can begin to solve a problem that plagues all software management: how to accurately estimate software development effort.

Software development rates are normally measured in "executable source lines generated per programmer hour." The major factors which influence software development rates are the complexity of the software being designed (see Table 1 for a condensed complexity model which has been shown to be effective for our developments); the capability of the programming staff hired to perform the development; the activities required to generate and support commercial software (Table 2); and the efficiency of the organization within which the development is performed.

Experience we have gained in GTE has indicated that the effort required to develop a commerical software package (measured in executable source lines developed per hour) can vary by 6 to 1 depending on the software complexity (see Table 1); by 2 to 1 depending on program-

mer capability (this ratio is lower than that experienced by other organizations, because all programmers must follow a well-defined methodology for software development and, more importantly, the talented programmers have been assigned the more complex software tasks); by 12 to 1 depending on the management and technological methodologies utilized within the organization structure.

Although a significant amount of literature is available describing software complexity models and the effect of programmer capability on software productivity, too little attention has been given to the effects that an organization (along with its engrained methodologies) has on software development rates.

Organizations affect software productivity in three ways: first, the structure used to organize programmers; second, the systems used to plan and control the software development; and third, the management/technical methodologies employed.

Organizations manage these factors with different levels of effectiveness. The most effective organizations can develop high quality commercial software at rates approaching 12 to 1 better than organizations that do not contain the necessary talent to properly manage software development activities.

Based on this dichotomy of management styles, we can segregate software development organizations into one of three categories: dated software organizations, modern software organizations, and state-of-art software organizations.

Dated Software Organization. We have found that development groups using dated organizational techniques have a low software productivity rate. These organizations do not employ composite design techniques nor do they follow a rigid methodology for software implementation. If documentation standards exist at all, they are poor, not formally defined, and poorly planned. Attrition is usually high and the feeling of software professionalism is not a significant aspect of the programming environment. The first four systems in Table 3 illustrate development rates of systems utilizing these concepts.

Modern Software Organization. As a software development organization matures, it establishes stricter controls over the development process. These organizations have enjoyed an improvement in software development rates of 300% over organizations using ineffective techniques for the same type of software listed above. System E in Table 3 illustrates the development rate of a large software system utilizing these more advanced design and management techniques.

Some of the techniques employed by these more efficient organizations:

1. Organizational structures are optimized around the projects being developed. Project structure and matrix structure are both used.

2. Organization hierarchy includes both chief programmers and feature chiefs, as well as a thoroughly documented and enforced design methodology.

3. Standard techniques are employed for decomposing software into functional entities. Techniques employed are transaction analysis, transform analysis, pseudo code, Jackson technique.

4. Strict software documentation standards are established and rigorously enforced. These standards are established to meet the following objectives: documentation is completely computer generated; documentation is a direct output of the design process and is the entity which undergoes design and code reviews; documentation defines software function, inputs and outputs; documentation is structured and accompanied by a hierarchy chart.

COMPLEXITY MODEL

Raw Software Design Hours (RDH) equals the product of (E) which represents organizational efficiency; (B) which represents program specific variables and (N) which represents number of executable instructions.

Thus $RDH = E \cdot B \cdot N$

The complexity model is employed to estimate the variable (B) where B is the product of B_1 times $B_2 ... B_9$.

B_1	=	.8	If the product development is aided by a set of interactive support tools. Else B_1 = 1.0.
B_2	=	.95	If the program is developed by one programmer.
	=	1.15	If the program is developed by more than 15 programmers.
B_3	=	1.0	If the number of independent module inputs and output items is less than five.
	=	1.1	If greater than five.
	=	1.2	If greater than 10.
B_4	=	1.25	If this module has been specified as real-time critical.
B_5	=	1.5	If the module contains a very complex algorithm or has a significant hardware interface.
	=	1.0	If the module is purely data manipulative.
B_6	=	1.2	If the module algorithm is not similar to previous work.
	=	1.0	If the algorithm is similar.
B_7	=	1.5	If the module is modified from an existing module and only new or changed instructions are included in the instruction count.
	=	1.0	Is a new module.
B_8	=	1.25	If the module has been specified as memory size critical.
B_9	=	1.1	If batch is employed and turnaround is greater than four hours.

Table 1.

SUPPORT REQUIREMENTS

$$S = \frac{\text{Raw Software Design Hours (RDH)*}}{\text{Total development hours up to one year after turnover to customer**}}$$

Based on 3,000,000 Hours of Historical Statistics		
Software Design Hours — Project Size —	Value of "S"	Type of Design
400,000 Hours	1.9	New design — no existing base
100,000 Hours	2.0	
20,000 Hours	1.7	
200,000 Hours	2.1	Modified design using existing base
20,000 Hours	2.2	
50,000 Hours	1.5	Design Maintenance after first year
10,000 Hours	1.9	

* Includes only software design hours required to decompose predefined subprograms into modules and segments, code, unit test, string test, integration test and all design documentation.

** Includes configuration management, supervision, laboratory support, evaluation, general project support, field support and design maintenance to one year after turnover to customer plus software design hours and planning hours leading to high level design.

Table 2.

DEVELOPMENT STATISTICS

System	Commercially Available to Customer	Size of Program (New Instructions)	Development Rate Instructions Per Hour
A	1972	160,000	.33*
B	1973	117,000	.43
C	1974	111,000	.53*
D	1977	220,000	.52*
E	1979	131,000	1.2 *

*Executable object

Table 3.

5. Design walkthroughs are held at each level of software decomposition. Preestablished review formats are employed with standard reports generated. Reviews are formally scheduled to ensure programmer time is made available. Only commercial documentation is reviewed at these meetings. Adherence to design standards, documentation standards, and quality, inter cost account interfaces are ensured by these reviews.

6. Walkthroughs are conducted for each feature prior to system testing. During feature review the customer's requirement specification is validated against evaluation test plans and the software functional designs.

7. Structured code is employed, embodied within a medium high level compiler such as PASCAL. Code reviews and code walkthroughs are conducted following a predefined process. The chief programmer and at least one peer programmer read each module of code.

8. Strong management planning and control systems are employed. These systems help plan and control software quality, time, and cost. An ideal system combines PERT networks and the concepts of C/SCSC (a cost/schedule control system developed by the U. S. Department of Defense).

9. All major software interfaces and data structures are defined before detail design begins. Data structures and software interfaces form a contract which is monitored and controlled throughout design and testing.

10. Management attempts to hire and retain the correct mix of software personnel: 30% with more than six years' experience, 40% with between three and six years' experience, and 30% with college degrees and less than three years' experience.

State-of-Art Software Organization. Organizations which are at the state of art in software development should enjoy productivity of from 200% to 400% over modern software organizations. The higher percentage prevails in larger, very complex software developments. These organizations employ all the techniques described above and in addition utilize advanced concepts of a "software factory." This concept is a consolidated set of powerful development tools which allow software managers and programmers to perform the innovative aspects of software development and automate most of the more rudimentary tasks. Projects which have used this consolidated set of supporting tools have experienced significant improvement in developing rates.

The types of tools which have been shown to be most promising in improving development efficiency are described below:

1. A program which accepts rough software documentation as input and performs the following four processes: checks that all data variables have been defined and inserts a definition of each data element into the software documentation package; formats documentation according to predefined standards; generates data base maps and flow charts from data declarations and structured code; generates hierarchy chart from raw software documentation.

2. A requirement language processor and a design language processor. These processors allow the support system to understand constraints in both the system requirements documentation and the commercial software design documentation. This process allows for cross-correlation between the system specification and the design documentation and also allows for check of completeness.

3. A software library concept which allows for effective storage and subsequent retrieval of functional software modules. This process allows for extensive reuse of software modules both within a given development as well as allowing for the reuse of functional modules among different developments.

4. Utilization of an ultrahigh-level programming language. This language allows for automatic code generation from a source language that describes operational processes.

5. Other less important tools, which include a design integrity analyzer, a software interface processor, a functional test plan generator, and various configuration control, design maintenance, and project management processors.

The objective of software management is to establish an environment in which high quality software can be developed using minimal resources. To achieve this objective, we must not only consider the organizational structure but also the control systems and management/technical methodologies employed within the organizational structure. Those software managers who suceed in establishing an effective organization will enjoy software development rates 1,200% better than those managers who fail. ✵

EDMUND B. DALY

Mr. Daly was recently appointed executive director-electronic switching of GTE Automatic Electric Laboratories, where during the past 10 years he has held the positions of assistant to the executive director, director-Advanced Development Laboratory, and director-EAX Operations Laboratory. He holds a BSEE and MSEE from the University of Illinois, Urbana, and a BA and MBA from the University of Chicago.

Excellence In Action: Building A Competitive IS Organization

BY BY RICH DEFIORE AND ANN GOREWITZ

Executive Summary

There is no magic in building a "competitive IS organization." IS professionals must earn the right to be viewed as a business partner within the corporation. Achieving this requires viewing users as clients and managing that relationship more effectively. The corporation now has real and perceived alternatives to the IS department. Outsourcing is only one of them.

To remain competitive, the IS organization has to provide excellent service. To do this, IS professionals must understand the client's business and be constantly aware of client expectations and perceptions. Customer satisfaction is a result of performance meeting or exceeding expectations. Building a relationship is imperative for understanding client needs and expectations.

The information systems (IS) departments in the *Fortune* 500 companies are going through tremendous changes as we approach the 21st century. The pressure to improve return on investment, coupled with the spending of hundreds of millions of dollars per year on technology and related support, has increased the focus on profitability and bottom-line accountability for IS executives. CEOs and managers of business units are looking toward either cutting IS costs or ensuring that they are getting an acceptable return on their sizeable investment.

The purpose of this article is to analyze the structure and interaction of IS departments with users in the past and to identify the skills needed to build a competitive IS organization that will support today's more demanding IS clients.

Data Processing In The Mid-1970s

The mid-1970s were less than 20 years ago, yet the face of the DP organization has changed dramatically.

Technology

The state of the art mainframe was an IBM 370, 135 or 145 with one megabyte of memory. CICS was still state of the art and only being planned in most companies. Terminals were in tech support or systems programming. In development functions it was not uncommon for one terminal to be shared by 20 individuals. Processing data more efficiently was the objective. Microcomputers were non-existent.

Today, almost all employees either have their own computers or terminals. Many employees have personal computers at home and new employees have learned to use personal computers as part of their studies in school, beginning in elementary school.

IS Applications

There was a concentration on automation of back office functions and the DP department had a monopoly on automation support. There were no alternatives such as those that exist now in the forms of time-sharing, minicomputers and personal computers.

Today, applications are plentiful from back office to front office to home use. Employees can write simple and often more complex applications using inexpensive off-the-shelf software.

IS Relationship With Users

People who used the system were called "end users." This term is revealing. DP professionals permitted the people to "use" their systems. Computers intimidated most people outside of the DP department and the IS professional was viewed as a technical guru. On the other hand, IS personnel perceived users as not knowing what they wanted and rarely consulted with or involved users in the implementation of systems. IS personnel focused more on their technical expertise to the detriment of their people skills. Often users felt alienated.

Today, users are more educated and expect to be treated as clients. They view technology as a tool for competitive advantage in their field. They want to be included in decisions and seek solutions that are cost effective. If the internal IS department cannot meet their needs, they seek outside alternatives.

IS In The 1990s

With the 1990s upon us, there has been a growing recognition that IS needs not only a technical focus but also a business focus. IS personnel, used to working from a technical position developed and practiced during the last 20 years, often operates in a manner that no longer works. Many corporations have turned to outsourcing or, as some others have called it, "right sourcing" as a way to satisfy their computing needs.

Vendors are now going directly to CEOs and presidents of large companies and selling their services rather than to the IS departments, as they might have done in the past. The pitch of the outsourcing vendor is aimed at convincing upper management that they can do the job better and cheaper. In too many cases, they are getting the job to the exclusion of the internal IS staff.

The New IS

To succeed in the present and future, IS practitioners must rid themselves of their technical image, not their technical expertise. The present IS method of interaction is no longer working. IS practitioners must develop customer service skills and a greater business perspective to help their organization meet the challenges and take advantage of the opportunities the advancing technology offers.

The new information systems professional must be a technician, planner, strategist, sales person, consultant and enabler. The goal for the IS professional is to encourage business units to depend on IS but not be dependent on IS. Most importantly, the new IS professional must be viewed as a business partner.

Conditions Needed For Change

ACTION is the acronym we have coined for six necessary conditions that, when focused on quality customer service, lead to a competitive and successful IS department. Initially developed more than eight years ago, the six ACTION values have been time-tested with dozens of information services clients.

The ACTION values are as follows:
1. Attitude
2. Close to Client
3. Teamwork
4. Individual Initiative
5. Open Communication
6. New Ideas.

Attitude
Attitude is the foundation on which all else rides. If a person's attitude is negative, that attitude will pervade and sour a relationship. Attitudes are self-fulfilling prophecies. A person's attitude causes him to act in ways that tend to be consistent with what the person believes will happen. The way in which the person behaves creates the scenario that the person initially believed would occur. If an IS professional enters a relationship with a client with a negative attitude, the project takes longer to be completed and is filled with problems.

IS professionals need a positive, "can do" attitude. Displaying a sincere desire to help and aggressively working toward meeting clients' needs is the required attitude. IS is the service provider and the client is the customer. With this idea in mind, the attitudes of helpfulness, empathy and enthusiasm naturally follow.

Close To Client
Being close to the client means building a partnership with a client. Make it a priority to know a client's business and define problems in terms the client will understand. This means avoiding jargon and keeping a client's business goals in mind. Educate the client on realistic capabilities of the systems development team. If a client has some understanding of the IS business, he will be more understanding at later dates for deliverables. Getting close to the client means working together to achieve objectives and maintaining a proactive posture.

Teamwork
The IS function needs to work as a team within the IS department and outside the department to serve the client community. As technology becomes more complicated, no one person can keep abreast of the many technologies and their applications. It is necessary to call on various functional areas within the information services department. It is also important for those areas to work together to develop and implement optimal solutions as efficiently as possible. In this way, members of the team have an opportunity to contribute according to their strengths and technical expertise. There must be a participatory environment and mutual respect among team members. This team concept is lacking in many IS departments. There is too much finger pointing to other internal IS units (e.g., applications, operations, tech support, etc.). IS professionals must be sensitized to the fact that they are all working on the same team.

Individual Initiative
The IS professional must constantly search for improvement in the quality and timeliness of the services offered. This may involve becoming a champion of a new idea and selling that idea to upper management. The IS professional must maintain a restless discontent of never being satisfied but always searching for ways to improve, raising issues and making suggestions. IS managers must create an environment that encourages individual initiative.

Open Communication
A precondition to an effective IS organization is open communication. Communication is the life blood of an organization; it builds and nourishes healthy relationships and allows for organizational productivity. An environment or culture of an organization must encourage open communication. The business issues should be the focal point, not the personalities.

To encourage open communication, an organization should strive toward resolving conflicts constructively. Too often an unresolved conflict creates resentment that builds up out of proportion to the detriment of reaching goals.

For IS professionals to achieve open communication, it is important for them to challenge up and support down. It is not enough for people to see themselves as part of the IS team; they should also be encouraged to give input before decisions are made to effectively utilize the IS department's expertise.

New Ideas
This is an outgrowth of the five other conditions from ACTION. The IS professional should positively impact the business area he supports with creative solutions that can help achieve business goals. Business managers seek new ideas that will help them meet business objectives, but often do not get innovative solutions from information services. IS professionals have had the tendency to focus on the technology. To get creative business solutions, IS professionals must integrate business perspective with a technological view.

Providing Excellent Service

To help their companies take advantage of the opportunities new technologies offer, IS organizations must make a commitment to providing high-quality customer service. We are defining quality service as being proactive, not only satisfying client needs, but also helping clients define needs, identifying opportunities and using information technology as a competitive weapon in the market place.

Providing excellent service is the cornerstone of a business relationship and the way for IS to earn the business partnership. In a firm, the IS professional is the service provider and the end-user is the customer or client. As in any service relationship, the client has to be the hub of the service wheel in order for those services to be truly effective.

Looking at Figure 1, we can see that the service wheel includes people, systems, management and strategy. *People* are the IS department providers of services with whom the client interfaces, (i.e., data center manager, computer operator, applications developer, trainers, etc.). *Systems* refers to the processes that constitute the service or that support the delivery of the service (i.e., on-line systems, systems development methodology, info centers, project life cycle, telephone, etc.). *Management* is responsible for making excellent service a goal and priority. *Strategy* is the overall game plan for providing excellent service to clients. It includes training IS staff in customer service skills, creating a help desk and reviewing policies and procedures.

An effective management team must see the benefit in providing quality service. If they don't, clients will force the issue but the credibility of the IS department will be damaged. Within a service organization, striving to be proactive rather than reactive will help the IS department change its image from putting out fires to offering creative solutions to business needs. Being proactive means seeking ways and places to apply information technology to the solution of business problems and allocating resources where they will do the most good for the company. Customer satisfaction is the goal.

The IS Service Chart (Figure 2) contains four boxes with ratings from 1 to 4. Client perception of IS services is viewed along the vertical portion of the grid. Actual service level is viewed along the horizontal portion. The goal of the IS department is to provide what it deems "good" services that are also perceived by the client as being "good." The chart illustrates the differences between perception and actual service rating.

In the box rated 4, a situation in which many IS organizations find themselves, the actual service level is good but the client perception is that it is "bad." Here, clients have unrealistic expectations of what they

may be receiving and perception management/education is needed to help the clients have more realistic expectations.

In the box rated 3, both the client's perception and the actual service level are rated as "bad." In this case, both need to be addressed. In the box rated 2, the client's perception is that the services are "good" actual service level is "bad." In this case, the IS professional can help raise the client's expectations about the quality of the services that can be expected. The box rated 1 is the ideal situation. The client perceives the services as "good" and the actual service is "good." IS departments should not be satisfied in this position. If the client is truly the hub of the service wheel, then the IS professional will continually search for ways to improve service -- even if clients are satisfied.

Formula For Customer Satisfaction

Customer satisfaction can be viewed as an equation (Figure 3) in which satisfaction equals performance divided by expectations. Before the IS department can provide a higher quality of service, it is imperative to get a baseline of how the client perceives the current level of service. This is the perception piece of the formula. It can be achieved through surveys, suggestion boxes, interviews, focus groups, task forces, meeting informally with clients during lunch, etc. The aim is to find out as much information as possible about the client's perception of what is currently working and what needs improvement.

If this equation is equal to or greater than 1, then the IS department is doing a "good" job in providing customer service. If the results of the equation are less than 1, then client service is not adequate and measures must be taken for improvement. Unless IS professionals have an understanding of clients' perceptions of the current level of service and of their expectations for what they should be receiving, it is impossible to improve the level of service.

From the IS perspective, much time is spent in increasing functionality; lowering response time, doing analyses quicker. It is often thought that this will be seen as providing a higher quality service. The client's view

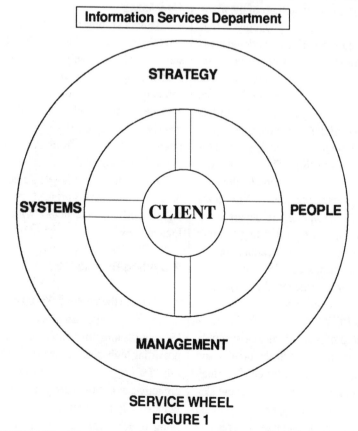

Information Services Department

SERVICE WHEEL
FIGURE 1

of high-quality service may be totally different. The client may be more concerned with how many times the phone rings before it is picked up by an IS professional than with the speeding up the calculation in the new accounting application.

The client's perspective is most important. Through a continuous, open dialogue the client's needs and expectations can be found. IS professionals must spend time with clients. Establishing service level agreements between clients and IS staff is crucial for success. Know what the client wants and needs and let the client know what level of service can be expected given current staffing and budgetary restraints.

Developing strategies to get high customer service ratings is important. Sometimes shifting resources from one area that is of little importance to a client to another that is of high importance can make a significant difference in customer satisfaction. The client's perception of the service level must be constantly reevaluated to determine where gaps occur.

New Skills

Many IS professionals have over the years developed certain skills, attitudes and ways of doing business that, in today's more demanding and computer literate businesses, are no longer acceptable. Ten years ago, the skills an IS professional needed for success were technological skills; learning new systems, learning new programming languages, systems maintenance. There has been a shift in the paradigm for success in IS. The new paradigm is measured by client satisfaction, as well as ability and willingness of IS to become a business partner within the firm.

With "users" more adept at using technology, the IS professional's role has dramatically changed. Like the dinosaurs that became extinct when they could not adapt to the changing environment, IS professionals who are unable to adapt to this rapidly changing world will either be terminated or need major retraining. If a company is to succeed the IS organization must succeed. IS departments must develop a strong, well trained staff and organizational climate that delivers only the highest quality service and products.

The focus for skill development in most IS departments has been on training staff on new advances in technology. To be an effective service provider, other skills are needed, particularly skills to facilitate working more closely and effectively with other people.

Several of these crucial skills are identified in the following paragraphs:

Customer Service Skills

Many projects fail because IS professionals and managers did not adequately assess the client's expectations for success. Helping clients determine realistic expectations, defining roles and responsibilities related to the project, and establishing rapport is critical to project success. The IS professional must also know what support is in existence and what support is still needed to meet the client's needs.

Many times, IS professionals do not market their capabilities to clients enough. It is important for the IS organization to see itself in competition with external consulting firms and outsourcing vendors, and develop ways to promote itself and its successes.

Building Relationships

Feeling comfortable with clients and having clients feel more comfortable with IS professionals is an important goal. To break down barriers and build personal relationships, IS professionals need more contact with clients. Acknowledge client contributions and interactions and enjoy working together. This can be done informally, such as lunch meetings or through team events, golf tournaments or other outings. Understand the client's business and help the client understand technology better, its limits and capabilities, through trade shows and subscribing to trade publications and business journals.

Effective Communication Skills

Words can be misunderstood. "This is an important project. Let's put a rush on it." can easily mean different things to different people. IS professionals have to make commitments to assess that they are dealing on the same level of meaning in their communications with clients. If an IS professional doesn't receive or send a message accurately, words can become very confusing and potential problems are likely to occur. Basic communications skills training such as active listening is very important for being an effective communicator.

Interviewing Skills

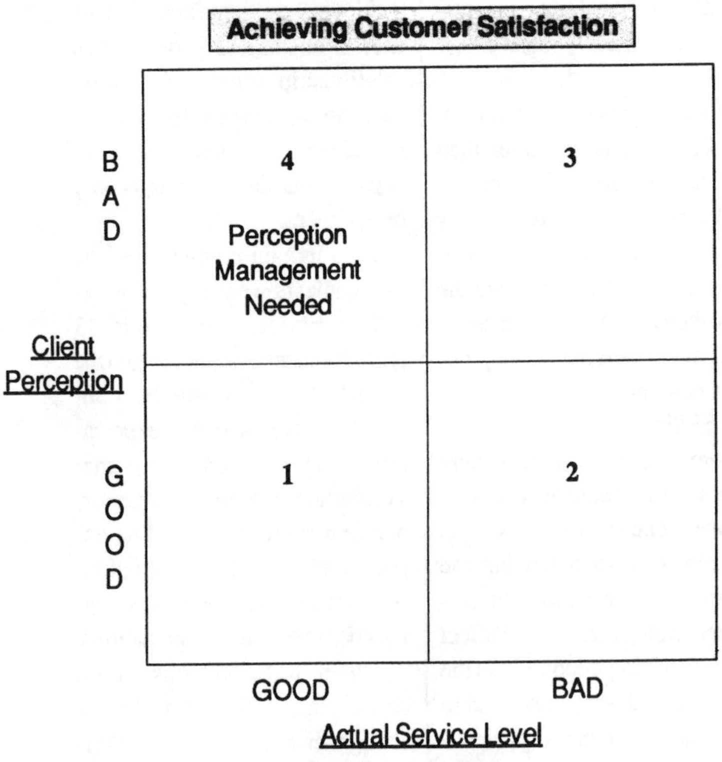

Achieving Customer Satisfaction

I/S SERVICE CHART
FIGURE 2

IS professionals are constantly expected to obtain pertinent information from many different people within the organization (client management, auditors, clerical staff, corporate management, etc.) for an application under development, yet little training is given

---

Customer
Satisfaction =

$$\text{Customer Satisfaction} = \frac{\text{Performance}}{\text{Expectation}}$$

**CUSTOMER SATISFACTION
EQUATION
FIGURE 3**

---

in interviewing techniques. Effective questioning skills can help identify requirements as well as give a greater understanding of needs.

Effective Presentation Skills

Throughout systems development the IS professional presents information to clients and upper management on the progress of a system or application. The person must be able to give an effective presentation or he will quickly lose credibility for himself, the project and the IS function. Training in small and large group presentation skills is essential. It is not only the informational content that is important but also the style in which it is given that can determine whether information or a new idea is positively received.

Negotiating Skills

Often technology users and IS practitioners appear to be adversaries rather than companions in the systems development effort. The use of negotiating skills can very quickly change a win-lose situation to win-win. Often it is not the conflicts that are the problem but how they are handled that determines the extent of cooperation among clients and systems personnel.

Management Skills

The most common use of management skills training is to train managers how to supervise employees better. In this instance, management skills refer to managing the client relationship. This may include educating the client on technology trends that affect his business and identifying trends within the industry in which technology can be used to solve business problems. Technology can be then seen as a competitive weapon in the marketplace. Learning skills for accomplishing this will not only change the relationship of the IS professional with clients outside of the IS department, but also will change the entire image of IS within the company.

Being Part Of The Corporate Culture

Too often, IS professionals seem to be a separate entity within a firm, with its own set of procedures on dress, language and customs. Dress is often more casual than that of other people in the firm. IS professionals are often accused of speaking "computerese" or speech so filled with jargon that no one else can understand what they are talking about. Customs such as people who are highly technical getting promoted to management without proper management training is rampant.

To become a business partner in the firm, IS professionals have to operate within the same corporate culture.

Conclusion

There is no magic in building a "competitive IS organization." IS professionals must earn the right to be viewed as a business partner within the corporation. Achieving this requires viewing users as clients and managing that relationship more effectively. The corporation now has real and perceived alternatives to the IS department. Outsourcing is only one of them.

To remain competitive, the IS organization has to provide excellent service. To do this, IS professionals must understand the client's business and be constantly aware of client expectations and perceptions. Customer satisfaction is a result of performance meeting or exceeding expectations. Building a relationship is imperative for understanding client needs and expectations.

In the past, the focus was on cost savings. This is no longer enough. In a competitive marketplace, a focus toward differenti-ated products for competitive advantage is essential. Development of skills in customer service, interviewing, effective communication techniques, negotiating, management and becoming an integral part of the corporate structure will help the IS professional increase effectiveness. A solid knowledge of advances in technology and how those advances can help the business of the firm will result in the IS professional's earning the right to be a business partner. JSM

Rich DeFiore is president of Interpersonal Technology Group (ITG), a Lynbrook, NY-based consulting and training firm specializing in the organizational and people issues of information services functions. He has more than 15 years of experience in IS training and holds a Ph.D. in organizational psychology.

Ann Gorewitz is a senior consultant for ITG. Formerly vice president of training at Goldman Sachs, she received her Ph.D. in education from Columbia University.

THE TOMORROW ORGANIZATION

How do you decentralize and establish strong central controls simultaneously? Through a combination of IT, entrepreneurial teams, multidisciplinary workers and the trusty old management hierarchy.

BY RALPH CARLYLE

Science fiction writer Isaac Asimov once said that it's easier to foresee the automobile than the traffic jam, the atom bomb than nuclear stalemate, the birth control pill than women's liberation. Put another way, the march of technology is inexorable and, to some extent, predictable. But the resulting corporate organizational and managerial ramifications are much harder to imagine.

A case in point is the corporate organization of tomorrow. Or, as futurists would have us believe, the "unorganization" of tomorrow. The popular conception is that information technology will eliminate bureaucracy within organizations. Advances in IT, coupled with the need to respond quickly to fast-changing global markets, will cause the hierarchy to wither away, leaving small, entrepreneurial teams of specialists that will network to accomplish business critical tasks. These teams will be made up of equals or peers.

Once more, the futurists have foreseen the automobile—IT's ability to span space and time to bring teams together electronically—but not the traffic jam—the resulting human and social response. Curiously, peer-based organizations don't do away with hierarchy, they hunger for it.

A little-known example is the peer network of research staffs that arose spontaneously within IBM during the early 1980s. The researchers quickly reorganized around coalitions, cliques and power bases—around electronic hierarchies. In other words, when hierarchy doesn't exist, people feel compelled to invent it.

Instead of a perfectly egalitarian peer network, the picture of the organization that is really emerging is more in line with what theorist and peer organization proponent Peter Drucker said might occur: namely, teams and a hierarchy of would-be team leaders.

Hierarchy, it seems, is essential not only to coordinate peer groups of specialists but to define their rights and responsibilities. Hierarchy instills discipline by setting objectives, conveying the corporate mission and instilling cultural values. And it fulfills a yearning in many for position and title.

Business leaders say the prevailing compensation structure and systems of corporate ownership will endure through the 1990s and with it hierarchy—and even the much-maligned bureaucracy. As the companies reorganize for the '90s, they are also exploding some other myths. Chief among these is the notion that decentralization, the theme of the 1980s, will be the favored organizational approach to the emerging global marketplace.

The Return of Centralization

The pundits couldn't be more wrong, the executives reveal. Centralized control will increase, new centralized functions and entrepreneurial teams will arise. The freedom of autonomous business units will be curtailed within the context of hierarchy; such units will not exist as an organizational form in its own right. And although there will always be specialists, what the organization will be eager to spawn in the '90s will be multidisciplinary generalists.

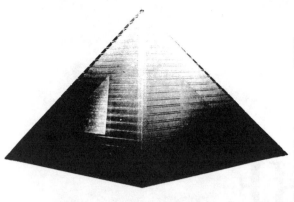

through partners, both value-added resellers (VARs) and original equipment manufacturers (OEMs). The less time a company's own sales force spends in direct contact with end users, the more it must emphasize marketing, promotion, advertising and public relations—all central functions. Why central? "Because we must keep our name before the end user. And we must present a single, united face to the marketplace." explains Bill Conlin, president of Anaheim, Calif.-based CalComp, a division of Lockheed Corp. CalComp is a flat organization of three lines of business—plotters, digitizers and displays—coordinated by centralized marketing-oriented management.

IBUs focus intently on a particular aspect of a company's business and thus can never be a window on the whole corporation. The broad view is difficult to achieve unless the IBUs become integrated business units, a key theme in the current reorganization of the engineering and construction giant, Bechtel Group of Companies. The company's culture historically has leaned toward highly autonomous lines of business, each responsible for its own field operations. Now, however, competitive pressures and the need to cut costs are driving the San Francisco-based enterprise to scale back and better coordinate the activities of its LOBs.

CALCOMP'S CONLIN: Assembly line workers are cross-trained so they can do every job on the line.

If this smacks of turning back the clock, it isn't meant to. "People will still be decentralizing," says Willem Roelandts, vice president and general manager of Hewlett-Packard Co.'s Computer System's Group in Cupertino, Calif., "but with more limited degrees of freedom." HP's own organizational structure is an example of what Roelandts describes. HP is simultaneously shifting to an organizational structure of smaller groups often geographically dispersed but with increased centralized control and coordination of their activities.

The limits that Roelandts refers to will be organizational restraints and IT-related standards. And they will be designed, as one Businessland Inc. executive says colorfully, "to put Humpty Dumpty back together again." This, explains Glenn Miller, the San Jose, Calif.-based company's director of strategic planning, is the downside of the decentralizing '80s. He notes that after a decade of allowing independent business units (IBUs) to call their own IS shots, many companies are realizing that they are stuck with a variety of inconsistent technologies and no way to forge enterprisewide applications.

While Humpty is in pieces, managers can't get a unified view of their business, an essential requirement for a market-driven company and a global competitor. Companies are increasingly selling through indirect channels of distribution and

Bechtel is reorganizing its branch offices so that individually they can sell and deliver all of the company's product lines. The branch offices, however, all are managed by a single, centralized organization. The idea, says John Campbell, manager of management information planning and reporting in the Office of the Controller, is to cut costs by eliminating duplicated branch office management functions. Bechtel also hopes to be more responsive to customers by no longer requiring them to do business only with a certain office.

Peer-based organizations don't do away with hierarchy, they hunger for it.

The '90s corporation isn't just lusting after an enterprisewide view, it wants a global view, argues one Ford Motor Co. executive.

"A multinational can't achieve such a [global] view," insists Norman Lewis, director of the car giant's North American Systems Group in Dearborn, Mich. "Only a global company can." What's the difference? "Multinationals develop products in each market for each market. Global companies start by looking at the marketplace as a whole and finding what is common. They then find ways to address the needs of individual markets with a global product," he explains. The global approach requires common business procedures, common products and unify-

Photograph by Warren Faubel

SYSTEMS & STRATEGIES

ing standards, both IT-based and cultural. Ford, says Lewis, has not yet achieved a global orientation, but is working toward that model.

"That's the way the Japanese do it," says Lewis, "and that's the way we must do it, too."

In multinational corporations, decision making is typically localized by geographic area. Generally, there are separate strategies for Europe, the Far East, the United States and so on. But as companies look more and more at costs and unifying global standards, managers of overseas subsidiaries will

UNUM'S ALEXANDER: Once information technology becomes an enabler, the corporate culture takes over. The culture determines the shape of the organization.

lose some of their independence, the same executive predicts. In some ways, IBUs will be integrated into the main company.

The most fascinating thing about the integration wave is that it embraces not only individual firms but entire industries. The financial services industry is integrating. So, too, is the travel business. Richard G. Grady, vice president and operations manager of information systems for The Liberty Mutual Insurance Group in Boston reckons the integration of banking, brokerage and insurance will create new distribution systems in the '90s and alter the face of financial services.

In airlines, major carriers and regionals have merged into large, integrated systems like Texas Air Corp. Further combinations are possible among airlines, hotels, auto rental firms and travel agents, as the American Airlines-anchored CONFIRM system demonstrates. The idea is that one on-line transaction activates a multitude of services: an airline seat

is reserved, a hotel room is booked, a car rented, etc.

Airlines disaggregated following deregulation. There was rapid growth in specialized, regional and low-cost carriers. Now airlines are reorganizing through a series of mergers and acquisitions and are reintegrating into a new industry structure. Financial services have followed a similar cycle.

Today, it's the manufacturing industry that is disaggregating for competitive reasons. Many believe that this is just a prelude to the type of reintegration that occurred in the automotive industry. When reintegration occurs, it will be global in scale, even down to ownership. The reassembled computer maker, Bull HN Information Systems Inc., for example, has French, Japanese and U.S. owners.

"Our company is much more fleet of foot than it used to be, but not necessarily as a result of its new ownership structure," says David Dotlich, executive vice president of corporate relations for Bull HNIS. "It's due to desktop systems and networks. It's evolving into a programs/missions-oriented company organized on a global basis. That requires a new breed of manager—somebody who we can say can wear the sweat band, meaning a person who takes responsibility for a project's end result."

The Individual as Integrator

What's occurring in a macro sense—integrated industries, companies, business units—is occurring at the individual level, too. People are becoming integrators aided by new organizational forms and technologies. Each worker on Cal-Comp's high-tech assembly line, for example, is cross-trained so that he or she can do every job on that line. The way Bill Conlin tells it is that even his sales personnel are beginning to resemble the multiheaded hydra of mythology. "Each must simultaneously handle end users, OEMs, VARs and distributors," he says. "Formerly, we had to have a manager for each of these functions and a staff."

The story is no different in the factory. A teamwork approach coupled with computer-aided design, engineering and manufacturing is compressing and integrating the value-added chain that exists between suppliers and customers. But the trend won't stop there. Conlin says that with multitasking software there is no reason a single person couldn't act as a designer, engineer, purchasing agent or even a salesperson.

When firms downsize and prune the work force, those people that remain must do more, Conlin says. "The way companies will measure progress in the future is to determine whether an individual's span of responsibility has increased."

This organization of multidisciplinary individuals is a far cry from the specialist-based company beloved of many theorists. But isn't it still a peer-based organization, albeit peers who are generalists? Conlin says yes and no. He says that, for example, engineers can grow laterally by taking on more functions, but a hierarchy will still exist for promotions into sales and especially marketing, "the things that really run the company." In addition, functions such as public relations, advertising, promotion and human resource management will have to be centralized. And the need for these central functions gets stronger the more decentralized or global a company gets.

The upshot is that even the flattest of organizations needs people managers. But since horizontal networking will come of age within the management hierarchy, such leadership will be essentially cooperative and coaching, rather than iron fisted. Even that most charismatic and, some would say, autocratic of company heads, Computer Associates International Inc. chairman Charles Wang, tells DATAMATION that his job is to be a cheerleader.

HP's Roelandts believes a new class of company manager will emerge on a technical and business dimension. These executives won't manage people; they will manage a program or technology and make strategic decisions. They could be recruited from the ranks of the multitasking generalists Conlin referred to. Their challenge will be to create a window to the operational side of the business.

This new breed of manager was not possible before information was integrated. "Now they can sit and access databases," says Roelandts. The business-and-technical manager appears to be the new target of executive information systems (EIS) vendors, which are now saying that their products are better suited to operational types than to the occupants of the boardroom.

Thus, what Conlin, Roelandts and the others are describing is an organization of multidisciplinary teams and multifaceted individuals operating within a hierarchical context and within the wider context of the global market itself. "The measure of such a company's success," says James E. Short, a research associate at the Center for Information Systems, part of Massachusetts Institute of Technology's Sloan School of Management in Cambridge, Mass., "will be how well it achieves concurrency of effort between its functions, products and geographic units. And how closely the results match the needs of the marketplace."

The Need To Tightly Couple Processes

Short says that coordination of the enterprise is more vital today than it has ever been. He believes that competitive pressures are forcing all major firms to become global in scope, to decrease time to market and to redouble their efforts to manage risk, costs and customer service on a truly international scale.

The only solution, he believes, is for firms to tightly couple their core internal and external business processes. "As firms begin to draw these processes together, slack resources [such as inventory, redundant personnel] are being reduced," he says.

People organized in hierarchies and teams, and individuals performing as multidisciplinary workers

Ten Organizational Commandments

Success in the 90's will involve striking a balance between autonomy and control through the following:

- Centralized control of key functions
- Well-defined data
- Cross disiplinary, entrepreneurial teams
- Peer-to-peer networks
- Multidisiplinary generalists
- Integrated business units
- Development of global products
- Tightly coupled operations, running concurrently
- A unified business view
- Cooperative leadership

will help to achieve this coupling. But to be a global competitor requires increased levels of integration not only across the enterprise but even within industries. Rising personnel costs demand the same thing.

"Sharing," says Bill Kerwin, program director for Personal Computing Services at the Gartner Group Inc. research firm in Stamford, Conn., "has become an economic necessity both within organizations and between them." That's why technology exchanges are now commonplace, even between competitors. Literally hundreds of companies have developed systems and written programs for the same types of applications. The duplication of effort has been enormous. So rather than tie up expensive IS talent in recreating the wheel, companies are sharing.

Three Wall Street firms are building business critical systems with the same set of computer-aided software engineering (CASE) tools. New York City-based brokerage house First Boston Corp. developed the tools, and, to defray its enormous develop-

ment costs, sold the technology to Bear Sterns & Co. Inc. of Atlanta and Kidder Peabody & Co. Inc. of New York City. As a result, First Boston's IS workers have added to the growing integration trend within financial services.

The financial services market demands integration, and technology supplies the means. The two are finally moving together hand in hand.

"Perhaps the most potent enabler of all," emphasizes MIT's Short, "is the technology itself: well-defined data and a transparent network."

The idea that IT can truly be an enabler and an asset to the organization is of recent vintage. In the past, business priorities and organizational form were limited by technology, not enhanced. Business people couldn't work as they wished. "The technol-

ogy and the IS department were a barrier," says John Goodfellow, general manager of the Skipton Building Society, a U.K. financial institution similar to a credit union, which is based in Skipton, Yorkshire. "They were blocking the critical business path we want to go down. But that's changing."

Goodfellow says that networking technologies, both communications and database, "offer an array of possibilities. Organizations can either decentralize or centralize as they choose." Because of this array of options, HP's Roelandts expects to see all kinds of organizations in the '90s, a sort of "have it your way [with apologies to Burger King] with IT."

The elevation of IS, and IS professionals, reflects another fact. IS is so much a part of the fabric of the corporation that one cannot be changed without simultaneously changing the other. The pair of contradictory trends that have been a feature of the organization—empowering people through decentralization while at the same time establishing greater central controls—has been a feature of the IS world, too. IS workers have been dispersed into IBUs, but they are also emerging as centralized architects of data, communications and standards, as well. Decentralization typically goes hand in hand with the creation of a technology research group that decides on standards. (See "Advanced Technology Groups," November 1, 1988, p. 18.)

IS, too, is split into people managers and technical managers, and both, like the multiheaded hydras, "will grow in proportion to how much they take on," says Stratton Sclavos, director of channel marketing for MIPS Computer Systems Inc. in Sunnyvale, Calif.

Sclavos believes that systems analysts can grow from being purely technical managers to becoming business-and-technical managers. "There is a need for people who can look at the worldwide picture and analyze the various pieces."

Here, again, technology will be an enabler. The IS organization now has CASE to sharpen and extend its skills, just as CalComp's designers and engineers have computer-aided design and engineering.

IS mirrors the whole corporation in another sense; namely, in having to address the make-or-buy decision that must be made for all materials and services. As companies downsized, the IS budget was cut, mercilessly in some cases. "Managers have been asking IS to go through make-or-buy analyses on practically every one of its activities," says Businessland's Miller. Independent software vendors (ISVs) often have more business savvy and specialized knowledge than can be found in the IS department and can get the job done for much less. As a result, they have

The Technologies of Concurrency

A perfect metaphor for what corporate organization in the 1990s is all about is the multitasking window. When desktop software first emerged, it could only handle one task at a time. Managers could massage financial data or build a graphics presentation or store and retrieve data. They couldn't do all three at once because the data had to be reentered for each task.

Lotus Development Corp.'s best selling 1-2-3 spreadsheet software was great if all a manager wanted to do was play with numbers. But what about text, image, voice? What was really needed was a window on the whole company. -

That's the story of the '90s. The technologies that succeed in the '90s, say experts, will be the combinational technologies such as windows-like interfaces that enable the user to make the computer do four or five different things at the same time. Other enabling technologies are operating systems that support talking help screens and link together to allow users to access information wherever it's stored without regard to conventions or interfaces. Relational databases that link text, full motion video and audio objects are also critical.

"That's what technology in the '90s is all about," says Norm Weizer, a senior consultant at Arthur D. Little Inc. in Cambridge, Mass. That's why 1-2-3 will become 4-5-6 or some other name as it embraces multimedia. That's why automated teller machines are now selling stamps and will soon be selling airline tickets. That's also why uniprocessors have become parallel processors and federations of processors. It's also why IBM is now peddling a global data repository as opposed to the back office kind. And that's also why the integrated services digital network (ISDN) is emerging as a carrier of different forms of information: data, text, sound and image. It's simply not enough just to carry telephone calls.

The essence of technologies in the '90s, says Weizer, "is their inclusiveness and their ability to allow a multitude of things to happen simultaneously, rather than serially as in the past."

Electronic document-imaging is a good example. Weizer says that, 95% of the time, office memos aren't actually being read or acted upon. "They are just moving around." Acres of direct access storage devices, wideband communications and document imaging changes all that. "Now a compound document [i.e., one combining multimedia] can be created electronically and worked on by a number of people simultaneously." In one fell swoop, the technology makes multimedia, multitasking and teamwork possible.

Computer-aided design, engineering and manufacturing are helping to integrate and compress the value-added chain between suppliers and customers, allowing them to act together in parallel. Suppliers are now sitting in on the initial product design and planning meetings of their customers, as valued members of the team. And the reverse also applies. The technology is having a bonding effect.

Of course, the ultimate symbol of inclusiveness is the network. And perhaps this is why many observers are already referring to the new decade as the "networked '90s."

become a big favorite of budget-constrained IBU managers.

As more companies consider buying IS services from outside sources, someone has to negotiate and manage the resulting vendor relationships. The IS department figures to fill that role: now that Humpty is in pieces, both the IS department and outside IT professionals should gain by putting him back together again.

The New Job for IS

The IS organization's changing role as integrator and coordinator is already reflected in new jobs and responsibilities. The Toronto steel giant Stelco Inc. last year created the first known data repository-related position: Supervisor, Repository Administration. Growing electronic trade is reflected in the title Supervisor of Trade Systems (or Supervisor, Electronic Data Interchange, as it is also known) at Bearings Inc. of Cleveland. Numerous other new titles have emerged, including Director of AI and Director, Worldwide Architecture. Companies can't get enough network engineers, quality control and assurance engineers, and database managers. Titles with the words *telecommunications*, *data communications* or *connectivity* in them are propagating like crazy.

The new skills represented in these new titles should enable IS to regain some of its lost authority. "I see the pendulum swinging back to some degree," says Businessland's Miller.

As IT becomes seen as an enabler of business success, IT professionals in the '90s may once again achieve the status formerly enjoyed in the heyday of mainframes. But the situation will not be exactly the same. The IT professionals will not remain outside the mainstream of business as they had in the past, and technology will not remain separate from corporate culture. "Once IT becomes an enabler, the corporate culture takes over," says John Alexander Jr., senior vice president and chief information officer at Unum Life Insurance Co. in Portland, Maine. "The culture determines the shape of the organization."

Organizational theorists have assumed that IT will determine the shape of the '90s enterprise. And in a sense they are right because technology will allow professionals throughout an organization to communicate with each other via networked computers, forming peer links that would otherwise not exist. These are, of course, informal links rather than the more formal reporting relationships or traditional team relationships. People help each other, share advice, philosophies, information and so on.

Such informal organizations have always existed in corporations. The old boys network is a good

SLOAN SCHOOL'S SHORT: The measure of a company's success will be how well it achieves concurrency of effort between its functions, products and geographic units.

example. But today the old boys network, or any other informal grouping, can be global, spanning time and space limitations. That's IS's contribution. People do what they want to do, but in a more amplified way.

It is important to resist overstating the importance of technology, as some futurists have done. There is always a wild card in the IS impact prediction deck, namely human nature. IS will not determine the shape of the '90s organization, as theorists have predicted, even though, as builders of the data and communications highways of the '90s organization, IT practitioners will, in a very real sense, be the architects of the future. But it will be the future that business professionals want. ▭

Contributors to this article were Bob Francis, Susan Kerr, Jane Majkiewicz, Tom McCusker, John McMullen, Jeff Moad and Chris Sivula.

Photograph by David Bradley

Chapter 6
Staffing Essentials

One-tenth of the participants produce at least one-third of the output, and increasing the number of participants merely reduces the average output.
— Norman R. Augustine, *Augustine's Laws*

Overview

Staffing means recruiting the right people, growing their capabilities, and keeping them focused. It is not a function that can be delegated to the personnel department. Because good people are the key to a company's success, it is management's responsibility to recruit, train, coach, grow, appraise, and reward them. Sensitivity and compassion are needed, as are discipline and direction. Teamwork must be emphasized in addition to individual performance.

This chapter contains four papers on the subject of staffing. These papers concentrate on topics that often prove difficult for engineers and engineering managers. Engineers are used to dealing with logic and physical laws. People sometimes defy logic and do irrational things. Different skills are needed for managers to effectively deal with people. These skills must be built in order for managers to perform effectively.

The first paper, by Abdel-Hamid, discusses the dynamics of software project staffing. The author uses a systems dynamics model to research staffing policies used to manage human resources throughout the software development life cycle. The impacts of these policies on project behavior are illustrated using examples and a NASA case study. The paper provides interesting insights into the relationships that exist between staffing, scheduling, training, and other project management functions. This paper sets the stage for the three others that follow it.

In the next paper, Cheney, Hale, and Kasper identify the skills senior managers believe that project managers, system analysts, and programmers need to have to perform their jobs efficiently in the 1990s. They report the findings of a survey taken across 58 firms of varying size. The results are interesting because they suggest emphasis should be placed on statistics, security, legal, and telecommunications aspects rather than the computer science curriculum advanced by the Association for Computing Machinery.

The third paper, by Schulmeyer, describes what to do about "Net Negative Producing Programmers" (NNPPs). It provides insights into why performance degrades as teams are built and shows how behavior can be directed toward achievement of project-related goals. Guidelines are offered on how to counter poor performance. Remedial actions that can be taken and counseling tips are reviewed, as the article focuses on what can be done to improve the situation.

The final paper, by Lyon, looks at the appraisal process. It emphasizes the need to rely on fact, not emotion, when assessing performance. It suggests use of a goal-oriented approach to appraisal, where employees are ranked and rated using key performance indicators. It summarizes the steps involved in the appraisal process. It also describes how to use appraisals as vehicles for employee performance improvement.

References

I am at a loss. I cannot think of a text that I would recommend on staffing. There has to be one out there. But I just cannot find one that goes beyond the obvious. The available works are the textbooks used by business schools to teach the basics of staffing. What's missing is one that describes the practice.

The Dynamics of Software Project Staffing: A System Dynamics Based Simulation Approach

TAREK K. ABDEL-HAMID, MEMBER, IEEE

Abstract—People issues have gained recognition, in recent years, as being at the core of effective software project management. In this paper we focus on the dynamics of software project staffing throughout the software development lifecycles. Our research vehicle is a comprehensive system dynamics model of the software development process. A detailed discussion of the model's structure as well as its behavior is provided. The results of a case study in which the model is used to simulate the staffing practices of an actual software project is then presented. The experiment produces some interesting insights into the policies (both explicit and implicit) for managing the human resource, and their impact on project behavior. The decision-support capability of the model to answer what-if questions is also demonstrated. In particular, the model is used to test the degree of interchangeability of men and months on the particular software project.

Index Terms—Simulation, software engineering, software project management, staffing, system dynamics.

INTRODUCTION

PEOPLE issues have gained recognition, in recent years, as being at the core of effective software project management [20]. For several reasons:

Personnel costs are skyrocketing relative to hardware costs. Chronic problems in software development and implementation are more frequently traced to personnel shortcomings. Information systems staff sizes have mushroomed with little time for adequate selection and training. It is little wonder, then, that software project managers find themselves focusing increasing amounts of attention on human resource issues [36].

Along with this growing interest in human resource management there are, however, some serious and legitimate concerns. Chief among them is the belief that, as of yet, we still lack the fundamental understanding of the software development process, and that without such an understanding the likelihood of any significant improvements in this area are questionable [37], [38].

This is no trivial impediment. But, if it is any solace, it is one that is not unique to this young field:

Any worthwhile human endeavor emerges first as an art . . . Over the centuries, management as an art has progressed by the acquisition and recording of hu-

man experience. But as long as there is no orderly underlying scientific base, the experiences remain as special cases. The lessons are poorly transferrable either in time or in space . . . (And) in time (the art) ceases to grow because of the disorganized state of its knowledge . . .
The management of the underlying science (is then) motivated by the need to understand better the foundation on which the art rested . . .
When the need and necessary foundation coincide, a science develops to explain, organize, and distill experience into a more compact and usable form . . .
Such a base of applied science would permit experience to be translated into a common frame of reference from which they could be transferred from the past to the present or from one location to another, (and) to be effectively applied in new situations . . . [15].

That we lack a scientific base is demonstrated by examining one example ''lesson'' in the ''art'' of managing the human resource in software development, namely, Brooks' Law. Brooks' Law states that adding manpower to a late software project makes it later [6]. Since its publication, Brooks' Law has been widely endorsed in the literature. This, in spite the fact that it has *not* been formally tested. Furthermore, it has often been endorsed indiscriminately, e.g., for systems programming-type projects as well as applications-type projects, both large and small [22], even though Brooks [6] was quite explicit in specifying the domain of applicability of his insights, i.e., to what he called ''jumbo systems programming projects.''

Later in the paper we will investigate the applicability of Brooks' Law to a real software project, namely, NASA's DE-A software development project. The project's uncharacteristic workforce staffing pattern is portrayed in Fig. 1. (Further details on the NASA DE-A project are provided in the Appendix.) The behavior indicates that management is (implicitly if not explicitly) oblivious to the lesson of Brooks' Law. Because NASA's launch of the DE-A satellite was tied to the completion of the DE-A software, serious schedule slippages could not be tolerated. Specifically, all software was required to be accepted and frozen 90 days before launch. As the project slipped and this date approached, management reacted (or overreacted) by adding new people to the project to meet

Manuscript received September 30, 1986; revised November 30, 1987.
The author is with the Department of Administrative Sciences, Naval Postgraduate School, Monterey, CA 93943.
IEEE Log Number 8825078.

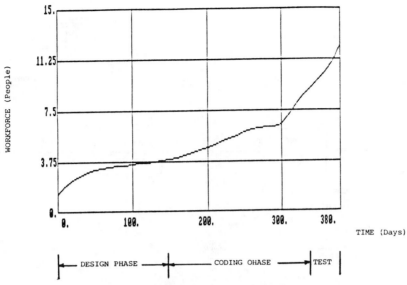

Fig. 1. Project DE-A's workforce level.

the strict launch deadline, as evidenced by the rising workforce curve in the final stages of the project.

The lesson of Brooks' Law would, of course, suggest that by adding new people to the late DE-A project, management actually delayed it further. This raises the set of intruiging questions: *What-if* new people were in fact not added at the later stages of the DE-A project? Would the DE-A project have completed earlier? And, why (or why not)?

The research vehicle we utilize to study the dynamics of the human resource management activity is a comprehensive system dynamics model of the software development process. The model was developed as part of an ongoing research effort for the purpose of studying, gaining insight into, and making predictions about the dynamics of the software development process. We begin our presentation, in the next section, with a discussion of the model's structure.

An Integrative System Dynamics Model of Software Development

A major deficiency in much of the research to date on software project management has been its inability to integrate our knowledge of the microcomponents of the software development process such as scheduling, progress measurement, productivity, and staffing to derive implications about the behavior of the total sociotechnical system in which the micro components are embedded [31]. In the words of Jensen and Tonies [17]: "There is much attention on individual phases and functions of the software development sequence, but little on the whole lifecycle as an integral, continuous process—a process that can and should be optimized."

The model we are presenting in this paper provides such an integrative perspective. It integrates the multiple functions of the software development process, including both the management-type functions (e.g., planning, control-

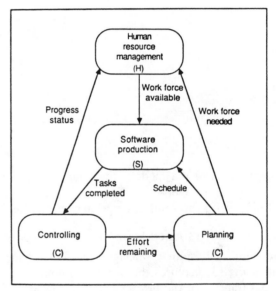

Fig. 2. Overview of the model's four subsystems.

ling, staffing) as well as the software production-type activities (e.g., designing, coding, reviewing, testing).

The model was developed on the basis of a battery of 27 field interviews of software project managers in five software producing organizations, supplemented by an extensive database of empirical findings from the literature. Fig. 2 depicts the model's four subsystems, namely: 1) The Human Resource Management Subsystem; 2) The Software Production Subsystem; 3) The Control Subsystem; and 4) The Planning Subsystem. The figure also illustrates some of the interrelationships among the four subsystems.

Because the model is quite comprehensive and highly detailed, it is infeasible to fully explain it in the limited space of this paper. We will, therefore, provide a detailed description for only the Human Resource Management Subsystem (our focus in this discussion), while limiting

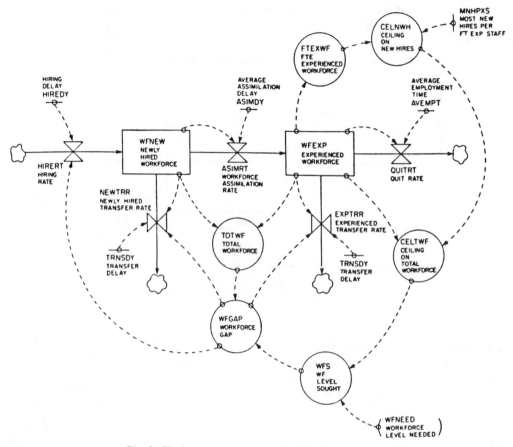

Fig. 3. The human resource management subsystem.

our descriptions of the model's three remaining subsystems to high level overviews. The interested reader can refer to [1] or [2] for a full description of the model.

THE HUMAN RESOURCE MANAGEMENT SUBSYSTEM

The Human Resource Management Subsystem, depicted in Fig. 3, captures the hiring, training, assimilation, and transfer of the project's human resource. (The schematic conventions used in Fig. 3 are the standard conventions used in System Dynamics models.) Such actions are not carried out in a vacuum, but, as Fig. 2 suggests, they are affected by the other subsystems. For example, the project's hiring rate is a function of the workforce level needed to complete the project on a certain *planned* completion data. Similarly, what workforce is available has direct bearing on the allocation of manpower among the different software *production* activities.

Returning back to Fig. 3, notice that the project's total workforce is comprised of two separate workforce levels, namely, "Newly Hired Workforce" and "Experienced Workforce." (In the model, workforce is actually more finely divided into four, not two, levels. However, for this presentation the simpler structure of Fig. 3 is quite sufficient to demonstrate the basic ideas.)

Segregating the workforce into these two categories of employees is needed for two reasons. First, newly hired project members pass through an "orientation phase"

during which they are less than fully productive. The orientation process has both technical as well as social dimensions. On the technical side,

> . . . (newly hired) personnel often require considerable training to become familiar with an organization's unique mix of hardware, software packages, programming techniques, project methodologies and so on [34].

As for "social orientation:"

> . . . (it) refers to the processes of teaching the new recruit how to get along in the organization, what the key norms and rules of conduct are, and how to behave with respect to others in the organization. The new recruit must learn where to be at specified times, what to wear, what to call the boss, whom to consult if he or she has a question, how carefully to do the job, and endless other things which insiders have learned over time [25].

Of course, not all new project members are necessarily recruited from *outside* the organization; some might be recruited from within, e.g., transferred from other projects. For this type of employee, there will still be a project orientation period, e.g., to learn the project's ground rules, the goals of the effort, the plan of the work, and all the details of the system [32]. Although obviously less costly than the full orientation needed by an out-of-company recruit, such project orientation is still a significant drag on productivity.

Capturing the productivity differential that exists between the "Newly Hired Workforce" and the "Experienced Workforce" was, therefore, the first reason for disaggregating the workforce. The second reason arose from the need to capture the *training processes* involved in adding new members to the project. This training of newcomers, both technical and social, is usually carried out by the "oldtimers" [5], [10], [34]. This is costly, because while the oldtimer is helping the new employee learn the job, his/her own productivity is reduced.

The determination of the amount of effort to commit to the training of new employees is typically based on organizational custom. There are no proposed formulas in the literature, nor did we find any in the organizations we studied. We did find, however, rules-of-thumb, and these ranged from committing 15 percent of an experienced employee's time (per new employee) to a 25 percent committment.

The "Average Assimilation Delay" is the average time it takes a new recruit to be trained, i.e., to attain the "Experienced Employee" status. The assimilation delay is formulated in the model as a first-order exponential delay. Such delays are primary building-blocks of system dynamics models.

Besides the direct training overhead, adding people to a software project can dilute overall project productivity in a perhaps less direct way, namely, by increasing the communication overhead. The nature of the relationship between communication overhead and team size has been investigated by several authors. It is widely held that communication overhead increases in proportion to n^2, where n is the size of the team [6], [19], [26], [27], [35].

On deciding upon the "Total Workforce" level desired, project managers typically consider a number of factors. One important factor is the project's scheduled completion date. As part of the planning function (captured in the model's "Planning Subsystem"), management determines the workforce level that it believes is necessary to complete the project on schedule. This workforce level is referred to as the "Indicated Workforce Level" in the model. In addition to this factor, consideration is also given to the stability of the workforce. Thus, before adding new project members, management tries to contemplate the project employement time for the new members. Different organizations weigh this factor differently. In general, the relative weighing between the desire for workforce stability on the one hand and the desire to complete the project on time, on the other, is not static, but changes *dynamically* throughout the life of the project. For example, toward the end of the project there is typically considerable reluctance to bring in new people, even when the project is behind schedule. It would just take too much time and effort (relative to the time and effort that are remaining) to acquaint new people with the

mechanics of the project, integrate them into the project team, and train them in the necessary technical areas.

These managerial considerations are operationalized in the model as follows:

Workforce Level Needed

$$= \text{(Indicated Workforce Level)} * \text{(WCWF)}$$

$$+ \text{(Current Workforce)} * \text{(1-WCWF)}. \quad (1)$$

The weight factor (WCWF) is termed "*Willingness to Change WorkForce.*" It is a variable that assumes values between 0 and 1, inclusive. WCWF is itself comprised of two components, namely, WCWF-1 and WCWF-2. The first component, WCWF-1, captures the pressures for workforce stability (mentioned above) that develop as the project proceeds towards its final stages. Fig. 4(a) depicts an example WCWF-1 policy curve.

To understand what Fig. 4(a) represents, assume for the moment that the "Willingness to Change Workforce" (WCWF) is only comprised of, and is therefore equal to, WCWF-1. In the early stages of the project when "Time Remaining" is generally much larger than the sum of the "Hiring Delay" and the "Average Assimilation Delay" (which for the DE-A project were 30 and 20 working days respectively), WCWF would be equal to 1. When WCWF = 1, the "Workforce Level Needed" in (1) would simply be equal to the "Indicated Workforce Level," i.e., management would be adjusting its workforce size to the level it feels is needed to finish on schedule. The "Indicated Workforce Level" can be determined by dividing the amount of effort that management perceives is still remaining (e.g., in man-days) by the time remaining to complete the project (e.g., in days).

When the "Time Remaining" drops below 0.3 * (Hiring Dalay + Average Assimilation Delay), the particular policy curve of Fig. 4(a) suggests that no more additions would be made to the project's workforce. At that stage, WCWF equals exactly 0. The "Workforce Level Needed" in (1) would, thus, be equal to the "Current Workforce" i.e., management attempts to maintain the project's workforce at its current level. For example, for the case where the "Hiring Delay" is 30 working days and the "Average Assimilation Delay" is 20 working days, management refrains from adding new people as the "Time Remaining" drops below 15 working days (i.e., three calendar weeks). Schedule slippages at this late stage in the project would, thus, be handled through adjustments to the schedule completion date, and not through adjustments to the workforce level. (Other options might include trimming the project's deliverables, but this was infeasible in this particular case.)

When the "Time Remaining" on the project is between 0.3 and 1.5 times the sum (Hiring Delay + Average Assimilation Delay) the WCWF variable assumes values between 0 and 1. This represents a situation where management responds to schedule slippages by *partially*

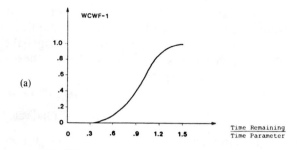

(a)

"Time Parameter" is equal to (Hiring Delay + Average Assimilation Delay)

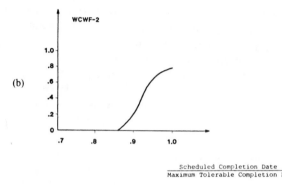

(b)

Fig. 4. The "willingness to change workforce" policy curves.

increasing the workforce level and partially extending the current schedule to a new date.

In our discussions at organizations such as NASA and MITRE, we learned that in projects involving embedded software (e.g., for weapon and space systems), serious schedule slippages could not be tolerated. In such projects software development is often on the critical path of a larger system development endeavor. Slippages in the software schedule can, thus, magnify into very costly overruns. Because of the software industry's less than impressive track record in delivering software projects on schedule, such imbedded software projects are often scheduled with some "safety factor" incorporated. For example, if some "Maximum Tolerable Completion Date" is say 100 months, and a 20 percent safety factor is used, then the project would be initially scheduled to complete in 0.80 * 100 = 80 months. If such a project, then, starts to fall behind schedule, management's reaction will depend on how close they are in violating the "Maximum Tolerable Completion Date." As long as the "Scheduled Completion Date" is comfortably below the "Maximum Tolerable Completion Date," decisions to adjust the schedule, add more people, or do a combination of both are based on the balancing of scheduling and workforce stability considerations as captured by WCWF-1. *However*, if the "Scheduled Completion Date" starts approaching the "Maximum Tolerable Completion Date," pressures develop that override the workforce stability considerations. That is, management becomes increasingly willing to "pay any price" necessary to avoid

overshooting the "Maximum Tolerable Completion Date." And this often translates into a management that is increasingly willing to keep on adding new people to the project.

The development of such overriding pressures is captured through the following formulation of the "Willingness to Change Workforce" (WCWF),

$$WCWF = MAXIMUM\ (WCWF\text{-}1,\ WCWF\text{-}2).$$

A WCWF-2 policy curve, the second component of WCWF, is depicted in Fig. 4(b). As long as "Scheduled Completion Date" is comfortably below the "Maximum Tolerable Completion Date," the value of WCWF-2 would be zero, i.e., it would have no bearing on the determination of WCWF, and consequently on the hiring decisions. When "Scheduled Completion Date" starts approaching the "Maximum Tolerable Completion Date," though, the value of WCWF-2 starts to gradually rise. Because such a situation typically develops towards the end of the project, it would be at a point where the value of WCWF-1 is close to zero and decreasing. If the value of WCWF-2 does surpass that of WCWF-1, the "Willingness to Change Workforce" (WCWF) will be dominated by WCWF-2 and, thus, the pressures not to overshoot the "Maximum Tolerable Completion Date."

Note that the above formulation of WCWF allows us to easily simulate those environments in which there are no tight time commitments. In such cases we need only to set the value of the "Maximum Tolerable Completion

Date'' to some high value. This would keep WCWF-2 always at the zero level.

It is important to realize that the variable "Willingness to Change Workforce" (WCWF) is an expression of a *policy* for managing projects. For example, the curves of Fig. 4 characterize the particular staffing policy for the DE-A project. For any specific project environment, the shapes of the WCWF policy curves can be derived on the basis of interviews with project managers as well as reviews of historical project records.

Based on the above considerations, then, management can determine the value of the "Workforce Level Needed" to complete the project. This *needed* level does not necessarily translate into an *actual* hiring goal (which is referred to in the model as the "Workforce Level Sought"). A further consideration is given to the experienced staff's ability to absorb new employees. That is, the rate of adding new project members is often restricted to that level which management feels can be adequately handled (e.g., in terms of hand-holding, orienting, training, etc.) by its pool of experienced project members.

Such a restriction is formulated in the model through the variable we call "Ceiling on New Hires." It simply equals the full-time-equivalent experienced workforce level multiplied by the limit on the number of new hires that a single full-time experienced staff member can be expected to effectively handle.

To recapitulate, the three factors: 1) schedule completion time; 2) workforce stability; and 3) training requirements, all affect management's determination of the "Workforce Level Sought." Once the determination is made, management could face one of three possible situations. First, the "Workforce Gap" between the "Workforce Level Sought" and the "Total Workforce Level" actually on hand could be zero. In this case no further staffing actions would be necessary.

A second, more common, situation is where the "Workforce Level Sought" is found to be larger than the current "Total Workforce Level." In this case, new staff will be added to the project. This, of course, takes time. While some recruits will generally be available within a short period of time from within the organization, others (especially when management is seeking special skills) will not be available for a much longer time. The delay in enlisting new software professionals is, on the average, several months long [18].

The third possibility is where the "Workforce Level Sought" is less than the project's current "Total Workforce Level," e.g., if the project is perceived to be ahead of schedule. In this case, project members will be transferred out of the project. Again, this is not an instantaneous process. It takes time to transfer people, e.g., for paper work, making transfer arrangements, etc. Such delays are captured by the model's "Average Transfer Delay" variable.

Finally, there is the effect of turnover on the project's workforce. Turnover continues, of course, to be a chronic problem for software project managers. Studies of turn-

over place the annual turnover rate at 25.1 percent [29], 30 percent [23], and even as high as 34 percent [5]. In the DE-A project, for example, the turnover rate was 20 percent.

The Model's Other Subsystems

The four primary software production activities are: development, quality assurance, rework, and testing. The development activity comprises both the designing and coding of the software. As the software is developed, it is also reviewed (e.g., using structured walkthroughs) to detect any errors. Errors detected through such quality assurance activities are then reworked. Not all errors get detected and reworked, however. Some "escape" detection until the end of development, e.g., until the testing phase. A highly aggregated depiction of the Production Subsystem is provided in Fig. 5.

How is progress measured in a software project? Our own field study findings corroborate those reported in the literature, namely, that in the *earlier phases* of software development, progress is measured in most organizations by the rate of expenditure of resources rather than by some count of accomplishments [13]. For example, a project for which a total of 100 man-months is budgeted would be *perceived* as being 10 percent complete when 10 man-months are expended; and when 50 man-months are expended it would be perceived as 50 percent complete, etc.

This surrogate for measuring project progress has some interesting implications on how management assesses the project team's productivity. When progress in the earlier phases of software development (call it time period $t1$), is measured by the rate of expenditure of resources, status reporting ends up being nothing more than an echo of the original plan. That is, "Man-Days Perceived Still *Needed* for New Tasks (MDP*N*NT) becomes, under such conditions, simply equal to the "Man-Days Perceived *Remaining* for New Tasks" (MDP*R*NT):

$$MDPRNT_{t1} = MDPNNT_{t1}$$

But "Man-Days Perceived Still Needed for New Tasks" (MDPNNT) is (implicitly if not explicitly) equal to the value of "Tasks Perceived Remaining" (TSKPRM) divided by management's notion of the project team's productivity, i.e., by the value of "*Perceived* Development Productivity" (PRDPRD). That is,

$$MDPNNT_{t1} = TSKPRM_{t1}/PRDPRD_{t1}.$$

Substituting MDPRNT for MDPNNT, we get

$$MDPRNT_{t1} = TSKPRM_{t1}/PRDPRD_{t1}$$

which leads to,

$$PRDPRD_{t1} = TSKPRM_{t1}/MDPRNT_{t1}.$$

This is an interesting result. It suggests that as project members measure progress by the rate of expenditure of resources, they, by so doing, would be *implicitly* assuming that their productivity equals "Tasks Perceived Re-

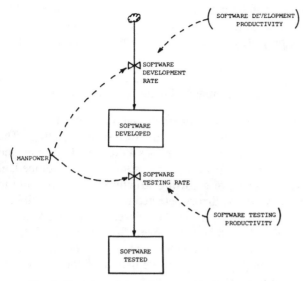

Fig. 5. Overview of the software production subsystem.

maining'' (TSKPRM) divided by the "Man-Days Perceived Remaining for New Tasks'' (MDPRNT). Notice that such an assumed value of productivity is solely a function of *future* projections (i.e., remaining tasks and remaining man-days) as opposed to being a reflection of accomplishments (i.e., completed tasks and expended resources).

This implicit notion of productivity is captured in the model by the variable "*Projected* Development Productivity'' (PJDPRD), defined as,

$$PJDPRD = TSKPRM/DMPRNT.$$

As the project advances towards its final stages, however, and accomplishments become relatively more visible, project members become increasingly more able to perceive how productive the workforce has actually been. As a result, perceived productivity ceases to be a function of projected productivity and is determined instead on the basis of actual accomplishments. That is, "Perceived Development Productivity'' approaches the value of the project team's "Actual Development Productivity'' (ACTPRD), i.e., the value of "Cumulative Tasks Developed'' (CUMTKD) divided by the value of "Cumulative Man-Days Expended'' (CUMDMD).

In the model's Planning Subsystem, initial project estimates (e.g., for completion time, staffing load, man-days, etc.) are made at the initiation of the project. These estimates are then revised, as necessary, throughout the project's life. For example, to handle a project that is perceived to be behind schedule, plans can be revised to (among other things) add more people, extend the schedule, or do a little of both. The Planning Subsystem is depicted in Fig. 6.

By dividing the value of "Man-Days Remaining'' at any point in the project, by the "Time Remaining'' a manager can determine the "Indicated Workforce Level.'' This represents the workforce size believed to be necessary and sufficient to complete the project on the currently

scheduled completion date. However, as has been explained in the Human Resource Management Subsystem, hiring decisions are not determined solely on the basis of scheduling considerations. In addition, consideration is given to the training requirements and to the stability of the workforce.

By dividing the value of the "Workforce Level Sought'' (that emerges after the above set of factors is contemplated) into the value of the "Man-Days Remaining,'' management can determine the time still required to complete the project. Once this, in turn, is known, it can be used to adjust the project's "Scheduled Completion Date,'' if necessary.

With this discussion of the model's Planning Subsystem we conclude our overview presentation of the model's structure. For the interested reader, a more detailed description of the model's structure and its mathematical formulation is provided in [1] and [2].

MODEL EXPERIMENTATION

"In software engineering it is remarkably easy to propose hypotheses and remarkably difficult to test them'' [33]. Many authors have, thus, argued for the desirability of having a laboratory tool for testing ideas and hypotheses in software engineering [31].

The computer simulation tools of system dynamics provide us with such an experimentation vehicle. Simulation's particular advantage is its greater fidelity in modeling processes, making possible both more complex models and models of more complex systems. It also allows for less time-consuming experimentation. According to Forrester [15]:

> The effects of different assumptions and environmental factors can be tested. In the model system, unlike the real systems, the effect of changing one factor can be observed while all other factors are held unchanged. Such experimentation will yield new insights into the characteristics of the system that the model represents. By using a model of a complex system, more can be learned about internal interactions than would ever be possible through manipulation of the real system. Internally, the model provides complete control of the system's organizational structure, its policies, and its sensitivities to various events.

Fig. 7 demonstrates the kinds of dynamic behaviors reproduced by the model. It depicts the model's output that resulted from simulating the behavior of the DE-A software project. The model's results conformed quite accurately to the project's actual behavior (represented by the 0 points in the figure), as is documented in detail in [1].

One interesting dynamic captured in Fig. 7 concerns the inclination *not* to adjust the project's scheduled completion date during most of the development phase. This behavior is not atypical. It arises, according to Demarco [13] because of political reasons:

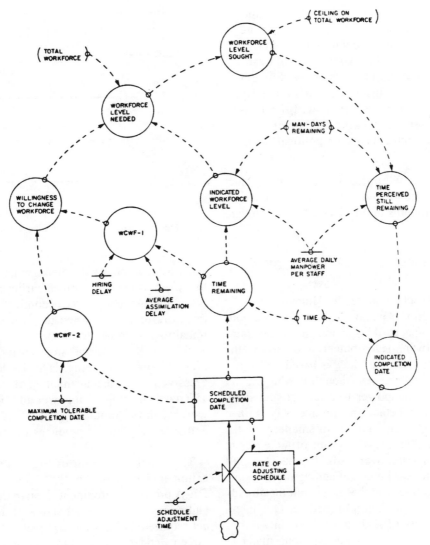

Fig. 6. The planning subsystem.

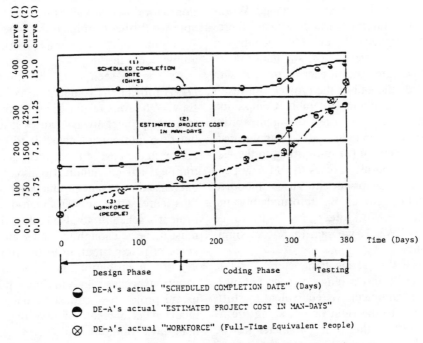

Fig. 7. Model's simulation run of the NASA DE-A software project.

Once an original estimate is made, it's all too tempting to pass up subsequent opportunities to estimate by simply sticking with your previous numbers. This often happens even when you know your old estimates are substantially off. There are a few different possible explanations for this effect: "It's too early to show slip" . . . "If I re-estimate now, I risk having to do it again later (and looking bad twice)" . . . As you can see, all such reasons are political in nature.

In the next section we will utilize the model to conduct a simulation experiment to investigate the interchangeability of people and months in the NASA DE-A software project.

APPLICABILITY OF BROOKS' LAW TO THE DE-A PROJECT

As noted in the presentation of the Human Resource Management Subsystem, several studies have demonstrated the negative impacts of communication and training overheads on software development productivity, the two insights upon which Brooks' Law is based. What has *not* yet been formally investigated though is what the *net* impact of adding new manpower to a late project is on productivity. That is, whether the productivity gained from adding new manpower is greater or smaller than the losses in productivity incurred as a result of increases in training and communication overheads. Brooks' Law, of course, implies that the *net* impact of adding more people to a late project is negative, and that as a result the already late project falls even more behind schedule. Our intent here is to test the validity of such an assumption.

As was explained in the previous section, management's policy on how to balance workforce and schedule adjustments is captured in the model through the formulation of the variable "Willingness to Change Workforce" (WCWF). By varying this variable we can, therefore, examine the impact of different manpower acquisition policies on the project's cost and duration.

Recall, WCWF-2 captures the impact of pressures to add new people towards the end of the project as a result of working under a "Maximum Tolerable Completion Date." Since we are attempting to test the applicability of Brooks' Law, we need to compare such a staffing practice to ones where management (in subscribing to the lessons of Brooks Law) stubbornly refuses to add new people in the final stages of a late project i.e., as is embodied by the WCWF-1 policy curve. By reformulating the "Willingness to Change Workforce" (WCWF) to be *solely* a function of WCWF-1, we can, therefore, simulate and test such policies.

Altering the value of the "Time Parameter" variable of Fig. 4(a), allows us to test a range of such policies. (Changing the "Time Parameter" is equivalent to shifting the WCWF-1 curve to the right or left along the X-axis.) For example, setting this time parameter to 100 working days instead of its base-case value of 50 repre-

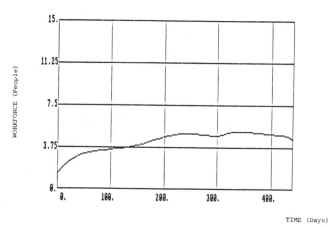

Fig. 8. Simulating DE-A with the time parameter set to 100.

sents a situation where management's reluctance to add to the workforce starts much earlier in the project. In Fig. 4(a), management starts becoming reluctant to increase the workforce level when the perceived number of days remaining to complete the project drops below $1.5 * (20 + 30) = 75$ days, and stops hiring completely when it drops below 15 working days. Under the above less aggressive policy, management starts becoming reluctant at 150 days and stops manpower additions completely at 30 working days. Simulating the DE-A project with this example staffing policy produces the workforce pattern depicted in Fig. 8.

The simulation result of Fig. 8 provides the first indication that perhaps Brooks' Law does not apply to the DE-A project environment. Notice that by refraining from adding people in the later stages of the lifecycle, the project required 440 days to complete. This is approximately three calendar months more than what was required in the base case of Fig. 1 (where more people were indeed added to the late project). By conducting further experimentation with different values of the "Time Parameter" variable we further examined the schedule consequences of a wide range of manpower acquisition policies. The results are depicted in Fig. 9.

As can be seen from the figure, the results for the DE-A project environment do not totally support Brooks' Law. What our results show is that adding more people to a late project always causes it to become more costly, but does not always cause it to complete later. The increase in the cost of the project is caused by the increased training and communication overheads, which in effect decrease the average productivity of the project team, and thus increase the project's man-day expenditures. For the project's schedule to also suffer, the drop in productivity must be large enough to render an additional person's *net cumulative* contribution to the project to, in effect, be a *negative* contribution. We need to calculate the *net* contribution because an additional person's contribution to useful project work must be balanced against the losses incurred as a result of diverting available experienced man-days from direct project work to the training of and communicating with the new staff member. And we need

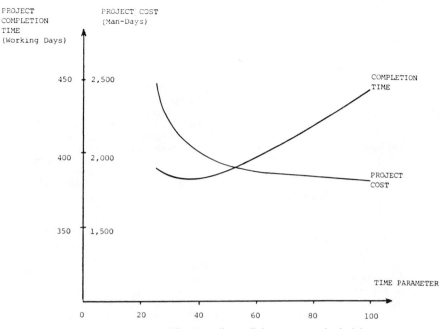

Fig. 9. Impact of different staffing policies on cost and schedule.

to calculate the *cumulative* contribution because while a new hiree's net contribution might be negative initially, as training takes place and the new hiree's productivity increases, the net contribution becomes less and less negative, and eventually (given enough training on the project) the new person starts contributing positively to the project. Only when the cumulative impact is a negative one will the addition of the new staff member translate into a longer project completion time.

The results of Fig. 9 indicate that adding manpower to a late software project does not always cause a negative net cumulative contribution to the project, and thus, does not always make the project later. The results indicate that Brooks' Law only holds when the time parameter is less than or equal to 30 working days. At that level, management would be willing to add more people up until the point where the time remaining to complete the project is less than 0.3 * 30 = 9 working days, i.e., approximately 2 weeks. That is, until the final stages of the testing phase of the project. It is at such extremely aggressive manpower acquisition policies that Brooks' Law holds in the DE-A project environment.

Summary

In this paper we reported on an ongoing research effort to study the dynamics of software project staffing. Our research vehicle is a comprehensive System Dynamics model of software project management. The model has two distinctive features. First, it is an integrative model that captures the multiple functions of software development, including both the management-type functions (e.g., planning, controlling, staffing) as well as the software projection-type functions (e.g., designing, coding, reviewing, testing). Second, we utilized the computer simulation tools of system dynamics to handle the high complexity of the resulting integrative feedback model.

Such a formal model of the software development process aids in the understanding of the process through both its formulation as well as the analysis of its behavior. The process of formulation forces explication, i.e., structural relations between variables must be explicitly and precisely defined. This, in Dubin's [14] view, is the "locus of understanding" of a theoretical model:

A (theoretical model) tries to make sense out of the observable world by ordering the relationships among "things" that constitute the (modeler's) focus of attention in the world "out there" . . . What is gained in understanding . . . is achieved by comprehending the law or laws built into the model. The locus of understanding in a scientific model is to be found in its laws of interaction. (That is, the modes of interaction among the variables of the model.)

If understanding is the intellectual outcome of a theoretical model, then prediction is its practical outcome. The model was utilized as an experimentation vehicle to study/predict the dynamic implications of staffing policies and practices on project behavior. One example was provided in the paper in which the model was used to test for the degree of interchangeability of men and months in one particular software development environment.

Appendix
The DE-A Software Project

The DE-A software project was conducted at the Systems Development Section of NASA's Goddard Space Flight Center (GSFC) at Greenbelt, MD. The basic requirements for the project were to design, implement, and test a software system that would process telemetry data and would provide attitude determination and control for NASA's DE-A satellite.

The development and target operations machines were the IBM S/360-95 and -75. The programming language was mostly Fortran. Other project statistics include:

- Project Size (in delivered source instructions) — 24 000 DSI
- Cost (for design through system testing)
  - Initial estimate — 1100 man-days
  - Actual — 2220 man-days
- Completion Time (in working days)
  - Initial estimate — 320 days
  - Actual — 380 days
- Staffing-Type Parameters:
  - Average productivity of experienced staff versus that for new hires — 2 : 1
  - Hiring delay — 1.5 months
  - Average assimilation delay — 1 month
  - Average transfer delay — 2 weeks
  - Turnover rate — 20 percent
  - Average effort committed to train new hires — 25 percent

REFERENCES

[1] T. K. Abdel-Hamid, "The dynamics of software development project management: An integrative system dynamics perspective," Ph.D. dissertation, Sloan School of Management, MIT, Jan. 1984.
[2] T. K. Abdel-Hamid and S. E. Madnick, *Software Project Management*. Englewood Cliffs, NJ: Prentice-Hall, 1988.
[3] ——, "Software productivity: Potential, actual, and perceived," *Syst. Dynamics Rev.*, 1988, submitted for publication.
[4] B. W. Boehm, *Software Engineering Economics*. Englewood Cliffs, NJ: Prentice-Hall, 1981.
[5] H. S. Bott, "The personnel crunch." In *Perspective on Information Manangement*, J. B. Rochester, Ed. New York: Wiley, 1982.
[6] F. P. Brooks, Jr. *The Mythical Man-Month*. Reading, MA: Addison-Wesley, 1975.
[7] R. Burchett, "Avoiding disaster in project control," *Data Processing Dig.*, vol. 28, no. 6, pp. 1-3, June 1982.
[8] R. G. Canning, "Managing staff retention and turnover," *EDP Analyzer*, pp. 1-13, Aug. 1977.
[9] E. Chrysler, "Some basic determinants of computer programming productivity," *Commun. ACM*, vol. 21, no. 6, pp. 472-483, June 1978.
[10] F. J. Corbato and C. T. Clingen, "A managerial view of the Multics systems development," in *Research Directions in Software Technology*, P. Wegner, Ed. Cambridge, MA: MIT Press, 1979.
[11] J. D. Cougar and R. A. Zawacki, *Motivating and Managing Computer Personnel*. New York: Wiley, 1980.
[12] E. B. Daly, "Management of software development," *IEEE Trans. Software Eng.*, May 1977.
[13] T. DeMarco, *Controlling Software Projects*. New York: Yourdon, 1982.
[14] R. Dubin, *The Organization, Management, and Tactics of Social Research*, R. O'Toole, Ed. Cambridge, MA: Schenkman, 1971.
[15] J. W. Forrester, *Industrial Dynamics*. Cambridge, MA: MIT Press, 1961.
[16] General Research Corp. (GRC), "Cost reporting elements and activity cost tradeoffs for defense system software," Santa Clara, CA, May, 1977.
[17] R. W. Jensen and C. C. Tonies, *Software Engineering*. Englewood Cliffs, NJ: Prentice-Hall, 1979.
[18] R. A. McLaughlin, "That old bugaboo, turnover." *Datamation*, pp. 97-101, Oct. 1979.
[19] H. D. Mills, "Software development," *IEEE Trans. Software Eng.*, vol. SE-2, no. 4, Dec. 1976.
[20] C. E. Oglesby and J. E. Urban, "The human resources task area," *Computer*, vol. 16, pp. 65-70, Nov. 1983.
[21] R. L. Paretta and S. A. Clark, "Management of software development," *J. Syst. Management*, Apr. 1976.
[22] R. S. Pressman, *Software Engineering: A Practitioner's Approach*. New York: McGraw-Hill, 1982.
[23] D. Richmond, "No nonsense recruitment," in *Perspectives on Information Management*, J. B. Rochester, Ed. New York: Wiley, 1982.
[24] E. B. Roberts, Ed., *Managerial Applications of System Dynamics*. Cambridge, MA: MIT Press, 1981.
[25] E. H. Schein, *Organizational Psychology*, 3rd ed. Englewood Cliffs, NJ: Prentice-Hall, 1980.
[26] R. F. Scott and D. B. Simmons, "Predicting programming group productivity—A communications model," *IEEE Trans. Software Eng.*, vol. SE-1, no. 4, Dec. 1975.
[27] M. L. Shooman, *Software Engineering—Design, Reliability, and Management*. New York: McGraw-Hill, 1983.
[28] W. R. Synnott and W. H. Gruber, *Information Resource Management*. New York: Wiley, 1981.
[29] M. R. Tanniru et al., "Causes of turnover among DP professionals," in *Proc. Eighth Annu. Computer Personnel Research Conf.*, Miami, FL, June 1981.
[30] R. C. Tausworthe, *Standardized Development of Computer Science*. Englewood Cliffs, NJ: Prentice-Hall, 1977.
[31] R. H. Thayer, "Modeling a software engineering project management system," Ph.D. dissertation, Univ. California, Santa Barbara, 1979.
[32] R. H. Thayer and J. H. Lehman, *Software Engineering Project Management: A Survey Concerning U.S. Aerospace Industry Management of Software Development Projects*, Sacramento Air Logistics Center, McClellan Air Force Base, CA, Nov. 1977.
[33] D. M. Weiss, "Evaluating software development by error analysis," *J. Syst. Software*, vol. 1, pp. 57-70, 1979.
[34] Winrow, "Acquiring entry-level programmers," in *Computer Programming Management*, J. Hannan, Ed. Pennsauken, NJ: Auerbach, 1982.
[35] M. V. Zelkowitz, "Perspectives on software engineering," *Comput. Surveys*, vol. 10, no. 2, June 1978.
[36] K. M. Bartol and D. C. Martin, "Managing information systems personnel: A review of the literature and managerial implications," *MIS Quart.*, pp. 49-70, Dec. 1982.
[37] V. R. Basili, "Improving methodology and productivity through practical measurement," lecture at Wang Inst. Grad. Studies, Lowell, MA, Nov. 1982.
[38] J. D. McKeen, "Successful development strategies for business application systems, *MIS Quart.*, Sept. 1983.

Tarek K. Abdel-Hamid (S'82-M'83) received the B.Sc. degree in aeronautical engineering from Cairo University, Cairo, Egypt, in 1972, and the Ph.D. degree in management information systems from Massachusetts Institute of Technology, Cambridge, in 1984.

He is currently an Assistant Professor of Information Systems at the Department of Administrative Sciences of the Naval Postgraduate School, Monterey, CA. Prior to joining NPS, he spent two and a half years as a senior consultant at the Stanford Research Institute. His research interests focus on software project management, system dynamics, expert simulators, and management information systems. He has authored or coauthored more than 20 papers and technical reports on these topics. His papers were published in journals such as the *Communications of the ACM, Journal of Systems & Software*, and *IEEE Software*. He is also the coauthor of a forthcoming Prentice-Hall book on software project management.

Dr. Abdel-Hamid is a member of the Association for Computing Machinery, SIM, and the IEEE Computer Society.

INFORMATION SYSTEMS PROFESSIONALS: SKILLS FOR THE 1990's

Paul H. Cheney, David P. Hale and George M. Kasper

Information Systems and Quantitative Sciences
College of Business Administration
Texas Tech University
Lubbock, Texas 79409

ABSTRACT

This paper reports the results of a survey of 79 senior information systems managers designed to determine the skill requirements needed by project managers, systems analysts/designers, and programmers in the 1990's. The respondents are senior information systems professionals representing organizations of varying size in several different industries. A total of 58 different organizations are included. Data were gathered via structured interviews and compared with similar data from 1978 and 1987. These results are used to examine the relative importance of the six skill requirement areas identified in the information systems (IS) curriculum recommended by the Association for Computing Machinery (ACM).

Introduction

The Bureau of Labor Statistics (BLS) predicts that employment in the computer industry will grow at an average annual rate of 3.7% through 1995 [2]. In fact, seven of the 10 fastest growing occupations are in the computer and electronics fields [2, p. 13]. Given the large increase in personnel needs projected for the computer industry by the BLS, along with the rapid rate of change in computer technology, and pressures to limit increases in IS budgets, organizations could find it difficult to recruit employees who have critically needed skills To meet these needs, both managers and educators must identify the critical skills needed by future IS professionals. Senior IS professionals were surveyed to identify the importance of various skills for programmers, systems analysts/designers, and project managers of the 1990's. The respondents' ratings of various IS job skills are compared with those of two previous studies [4,5] and the ACM model curriculum to identify any discrepancies.

The purpose of this paper is to identify the skills required of project managers, systems analysts/designers, and programmers in the 1990's. The predictions are based on the expert opinion of 79 information systems managers at 58 organizations of varying size. For comparative purposes, the procedure and methodology are similar to those used in both a 1978 [4] and 1987 study [5].

Following a brief summary of the curriculum recommended for college level IS programs by the ACM, the survey methodology used in this study is discussed. Next, the results are presented and compared with those of the two earlier studies. Finally, the implications for IS educators, managers, systems analysts/designers, and programmers are discussed and conclusions are presented.

ACM Curriculum

Although the 1972 [1] and 1973 [6] ACM model curriculum reports emphasize technology knowledge, they explicitly recognize the educational requirements of two types of graduates: (1) technically trained systems designers, and (2) managerially oriented information systems analysts. These reports emphasize six skill clusters: people, models, systems, computers, organizations, and society. Although the ACM report was updated again in 1982 [12], the same six basic skills continued to be considered of paramount importance (the ACM model curriculum is currently under revision). More detailed than its predecessors, the curriculum recommended in 1982 for undergraduate and graduate programs in information systems emphasizes the integration of people, management skills, and technology.

The 1982 ACM model curriculum contains the following major changes to the recommendations of the earlier reports:

* integration and increased emphasis of management and communications skills;

* inclusion of data management and data communications courses;

* inclusion of the AACSB common body of knowledge as a foundation; and

* introduction of a capstone MIS policy course.

The extent to which these recommended skills coincide with those of IS managers is unknown. To identify the skills needed by future practitioners requires surveying those currently planning and hiring for the future; that is, senior IS managers. A discussion of the survey methodology used to capture this data follows.

The Survey

The data were gathered through structured interviews. The respondents were asked questions from a prepared questionnaire, and their responses were recorded immediately. The characteristics of

Reprinted from *Proceedings 22nd Ann. Hawaii Int'l Conf. on System Sciences,* 1989, pp. 331-336. Copyright © 1989 by The Institute of Electrical and Electronics Engineers, Inc. All rights reserved.

301

the participants and the sample size of the current survey are similar to those in both the 1978 [4] and 1987 [5] reports. Table 1 presents a breakdown of the respondents in this survey by title.

Table 1. Job Titles of Respondents in this Study

Number of Respondents	Job Title
24	VP of Information Services
28	Director of Information Systems
2	Data Center Manager
15	Director of Information Systems Development
10	Manager of Technical Support

Table 2 summarizes the level of information systems experience of respondents.

Table 2. Information Systems Experience of Respondents in 1978, 1987, and 1988

Number of Respondents			Years of Data Processing Experience
1978	1987	1988	
0	15	3	0-5 years
3	16	10	5-10 years
5	10	31	10-15 years
37	15	35	over 15 years
45	56	79	Total

Table 3 presents the industries represented by respondents.

Table 3. Industries Represented by Respondents in 1978, 1987, and 1988

Number of Respondents			Industry
1978	1987	1988	
17	15	15	Manufacturing
14	16	30	Service
6	10	15	Government
5	8	10	Retailing/Wholesaling
3	7	9	Banking/Insurance

By design, the demographics of respondents were not substantially different among the three surveys.

Results

In the 1987 survey, IS managers were asked the number of employees actually working in each of several areas, whereas this survey asked managers to project their personnel needs for the year 1995.

Work Force

Table 4 compares by job category the actual work force reported by respondents in 1987 with those projected for 1995 by the current survey. These results indicate that the respondents expect continued demand for systems analysts and programmers, and an increased demand for information center personnel and data communication specialists. These projections are in accord with those of the BLS, which expect a 71.7% increase in the need for

computer programmers from 1984 to 1995. This almost doubles the population of programmers from 341,000 to 586,000.[1] Similarly, the BLS predicts a 68.7%

Table 4. Actual (1987) and Projected (1995) Work Force by Job Categories

	1987*	1995**
COBOL Programmers	11,151	6,480
FORTRAN or BASIC	300	300
PASCAL and C	2,050	4,180
Database Management	1,480	2,180
4th Generation Languages	1,105	7,401
Systems Programmers	401	600
Data Communications	401	1,400
Systems Analysts	2,840	4,150
Operators	850	400
Data Entry	330	0
Information Center Personnel	2,400	4,100

* actual employment figures
** projected employment figures

increase in the demand for systems analysts, from an estimated 308,000 to 520,000 during the same time period.[2]

Respondents expect substantial net increases in personnel requirements in all categories except COBOL programmers, FORTRAN programmers, data entry personnel, and computer operators. Consistent with the earlier surveys, the respondents' predictions for 1995 indicate a substantial demand for applications programmers and systems analysts. This coincides with the previously cited Bureau of Labor Statistics [2] forecasts. However, the need for personnel with knowledge limited to traditional high-level languages such as COBOL and FORTRAN will decrease, while the demand for workers with knowledge of more powerful procedural (Pascal, C) and non-procedural languages (4GLs) is expected to increase dramatically. The respondents also expect that the need for data entry personnel will be virtually eliminated.

The data also indicate that there will continue to be a substantial demand for database and systems programmers. The advantages of database management systems have been known for years, but the cost of converting existing applications has prevented many companies from fully utilizing this technology. Many of the firms surveyed are using a phase in/phase out approach; that is, when new systems are designed to replace existing ones, database management system (DBMS) technology is utilized, but modification of existing applications to employ DBMS technology is not actively pursued. As more

---

[1]The BLS provides three projections for 1995 employment for each occupation. The 586,000 figure represents moderate growth in the employment of programmers, ranging from a low of 559,000 to a high of 609,000 workers by 1995 [2, p. 64].

[2]The BLS expects the number of systems analysts to range from a low of 498,000 to a high of 539,000 by 1995 [2, p. 42].

software applications utilize DBMS technology, the demand for database specialists increases. Another factor affecting the demand for database specialists is the widespread use of microcomputer-based DBMSs such as dBase III Plus and Rbase 5000.

Many of the database specialists who support microcomputer-based products are located in the organizations' Information Centers or in user departments. The respondents project an increased demand for information center personnel through 1995. Because not all companies surveyed had formally chartered information centers, this category includes resident experts in functional areas.

Individuals who specialize in the use of 4GLs are in demand, and our respondents indicate that this trend will accelerate dramatically. The need for 4GL specialists appears to be tied to the movement toward using microcomputers for an increasing number of small applications. Some 4GLs such as Applied Data Research's _Empire_ and Information Builder's _Focus_ are used as development tools and are replacing procedural languages such as COBOL [8,10].[3]

Finally, the respondents report a continued and increasing demand for data communication specialists. Given the trend in most organizations to integrate their computing and communications facilities, this demand is not surprising. Such integration is motivated in part by economics, and has been facilitated by a general tendency toward distributed information systems [3,6,7,9,11]. Fifty of the 58 firms in this study have extensive distributed information systems networks.

Skills by Job Category

All three surveys (1978, 1987, 1988) recorded the respondents' perceptions of the importance of specific skills to three types of IS personnel. Senior IS managers were given a list of skills and asked to rate their importance for the:

Project Manager who coordinates the team's efforts and determines how the team's human resources should be allocated to produce the system on time and within budget;

Systems Analyst/Designer who defines the users' information needs and builds systems to generate the required information, including defining the content and structure of input forms, output reports, and files; and

Programmer who is responsible for program development and documentation.

In each of the three surveys, the activities defining each job category remained the same, however, some titles were different as they

---

[3]The numerous books by James Martin on 4GLs [10] and articles in _Computerworld_ [8,13] are only a small indication of the high level of interest business has in 4GLs.

Table 5. T-test Results Showing Significant Differences in the Value of Various Skills to Respondents. (For each skill, the first row of t-tests is based on the change from 1978 to 1987 and the second row the change from 1987 to that projected for 1995.)

Skill Area	Project Manager	Systems Analyst/ Designer	Programmer
1. Info. Gathering Techniques	2.406** 3.100*	-3.973* 1.441	-5.507* 1.004
2. Systems Design Topics	1.394 0.740	-1.170 0.901	-5.475* -4.010*
3. File Design	1.354 1.805	-1.133 3.140*	-5.794* 3.114*
4. Planning and Control of Systems Projects	1.248 2.011**	-3.951* -2.011**	-3.211* -3.001*
5. Human Relations in Systems Development	1.898 1.011	1.030 0.671	-5.637* 0.600
6. Human Factors in Equip. Design and Work Layout	-0.847 2.801*	0.012 3.111*	-3.341* 2.998*
7. Intro. Computer and Info. System Concepts	-0.042 0.601	-0.641 0.401	-0.595 -0.310
8. Applications Programming Languages	1.015 -3.814*	-2.042** -3.011*	-3.540* 1.035
9. Job Control Language	-0.486 -1.201	0.276 -0.488	-1.131 -2.011**
10. DBMS	1.402 1.041	1.865 7.140*	-0.051 6.145*
11. Operating Systems	-4.263* -3.941*	-1.741 -2.140**	-7.180* -3.101*
12. Mainframe Hardware	-3.847* -6.401*	-2.142** -4.333*	-1.913 -0.081
13. Micro/Mini Hardware	-1.939 -2.001**	-0.093 0.080	-0.781 0.040
14. Telecommunications Concepts	-2.952* 4.980*	-2.650** 7.144*	1.704 6.804*
15. Computer Security Controls and Auditing	-5.959* 3.801*	-2.341** 4.900*	-2.723* 1.800
16. Software Package Analysis	-4.328* 3.881*	4.218* 7.100*	2.403** 2.080**
17. Computer Operations	-2.080** 0.433	5.183* -1.047	1.771 0.444
18. Legal Aspects of Computing	-5.107* 2.001**	2.039** 3.853*	-2.745* 2.011**
19. Computer Simulation	3.531* 5.130*	4.608* 2.011**	2.723* 2.001**
20. Statistical Decision Theory	4.005* 6.145*	5.802* 4.001*	1.883 2.141**

* alpha = .01; ** alpha = .05

reflected existing norms. For example, in 1978 project managers were known as data center managers and systems analysts/designers were called systems analysts.

In the three surveys, respondents were asked to rate the importance of each skill on a scale of 1 to 5, with 1 meaning "not useful" and 5 meaning "essential". The reported skill categories are identical or nearly identical to those used in all three studies. To determine whether or not the skills required by IS professionals have changed significantly, differences in the mean responses between the three studies are compared using t-tests. Critical values are calculated using pooled sample variances, which adjust variances by sample size. Two-tailed t-tests with alphas of .01 and .05 were used to determine critical values. Within job categories, t-tests were computed on the difference between the mean of the skill area for 1978 and 1987, and 1987 and those projected for 1995. Significant positive t-values indicate that a skill is or is expected to increase in importance, significant negative t-values suggest that the skill is or is expected to decrease in importance, and non-significant changes indicate that the current skill level is or is expected to remain the same. These results are presented in Table 5.

The results presented in Table 5 indicate that the current and future Introductory Computer and Information Systems Concepts skill level is appropriate for all three job categories. However, the value of Operating Systems skills has decreased and is expected to decrease in importance for all categories, whereas Mainframe Hardware knowledge is expected to be less valuable for both project managers and systems analysts/designers in the future, but is expected to remain at its current skill level for programmers. With the exception of project managers, Planning and Control of Systems Project skills are and are expected to be less valuable for systems analysts/designers and programmers. Similarly, Systems Design Topics are and are expected to be less valuable skills for programmers, but retain their current level of importance for project managers and systems analysts/designers.

The need for ever increasing skill in Computer Simulation and Statistical Decision Theory is evident by the consistently significant positive coefficients across all job categories. While the value of Software Package Analysis decreased for project managers during the 1978-1987 time frame, its value increased for both programmers and systems analysts/designers and is expected to increase for all job categories in the future.

The most dramatic changes have occurred in the perceived value of Telecommunications Concepts, Computer Security Controls and Auditing, and Legal Aspects of Computing. These skills are not only expected to be very valuable in the future, but in many cases these represent complete reversals from that perceived in the 1978-1987 comparison.

Project Manager. The results reveal that Information Gathering Techniques, Computer Simulation, and Statistical Decision Theory skills are and are expected in the future to be valuable to project managers. Conversely, Operating Systems, and Mainframe Hardware are perceived to be significantly less valuable for project managers now and in the future. Compared with the 1978-1987 results, dramatic positive reversals in perceived value are expected in the future for Telecommunications Concepts, Computer Security Controls and Auditing, Software Package Analysis, and Legal Aspects of Computing skills. Those skills that are expected to be less valuable in the future than they were in the past are Application Programming Languages and Micro/Mini Hardware, while Planning and Control of System Projects and Human Factors in Equipment Design and Work Layout are expected to be more valuable skills in the future than they have been in the past.

Systems Analyst/Designer. The results reveal that Software Package Analysis, Legal Aspects of Computing, Computer Simulation, and Statistical Decision Theory skills are and are expected in the future to be valuable to systems analysts/designers. Conversely, Planning and Control of System Projects, Application Programming Languages, and Mainframe Hardware are perceived to be significantly less valuable for systems analysts/designers now and in the future. Compared with the 1978-1987 results, dramatic positive reversals in perceived value are expected in the future for Telecommunications Concepts and Computer Security Controls and Auditing skills. The skill that is expected to be less valuable in the future than it was in the past is Operating Systems knowledge, while File Design, Human Factors in Equipment Design and Work Layout, and Database Management Systems are expected to be more valuable skills in the future than they have been in the past.

Programmer. The results reveal that Software Package Analysis, Legal Aspects of Computing and Computer Simulation skills are and are expected in the future to be valuable to programmers. Conversely, Systems Design Topics, Planning and Control of Systems Projects, and Operating Systems, are perceived to be significantly less valuable for programmers now and in the future. Compared with the 1978-1987 results, dramatic positive reversals in perceived value are expected in the future for File Design, Human Factors in Equipment Design and Work Layout, and Legal Aspects of Computing skills. The skill expected to be less valuable in the future than it was in the past is Job Control Language knowledge, while Telecommunications Concepts and Statistical Decision Theory are expected to be more valuable skills in the future than they have been in the past.

Discussion

It must be emphasized that project managers, systems analysts/designers, and programmers did not rate the importance of these skills in their work; instead it was senior information systems managers involved in planning, hiring, training, and supervising these personnel who rated the importance of these skills for all job categories. As a result, it is possible that systems analysts/designers or programmers could have answered these questions differently. However, as a practical matter, the perceptions of senior IS managers concerning job category skill requirements is the most meaningful, because their judgment is ultimately the most important criteria in the planning and hiring cycle.

In general, by 1995 the respondents expect knowledge of telecommunications concepts, file and database design, human relations, and human factors to be increasingly important skills. The continuing importance of telecommunications concepts is rooted in developments in data communications, office automation, and the supporting networks. Based upon post-survey debriefings, file design was interpreted by our respondents to mean database design, which explains the increase in the importance of this skill. Computer security controls and auditing is also viewed as being an increasingly important skill. This indicates that the warnings concerning the dangers of lax computer security are being heeded. The increase in importance of telecommunications, file design, human factors and relations, and computer security skills as a group parallel the increasing demand for end-user computing.

Discussed below are the skill requirements of each of the three professional categories. Comparisons among the 1978, 1987, and 1995 projects are reviewed to identify emerging trends and needs.

Project Manager

Information Gathering Techniques are valued more and Computer Operations skills are valued less by IS managers in 1987 than they were in 1978. Both of these shifts may represent the fact that those questioned in 1978 were more concerned with scheduling and computer operations than are the 1987 respondents. The information requirements analysis demands of today's application domains may explain why project managers consider Information Gathering Techniques more valuable than did their predecessors, and why the value of this skill is expected to continue to increase through the mid-1990's.

One of the most interesting results concerns the declining importance of several technically oriented skills (i.e., Operating Systems, Applications Programming Languages, Mainframe Hardware, and Micro/Mini Hardware). Either no significant change or a decline in the importance of these skills is expected for project managers. Perhaps project managers are being viewed more as managers and less as technicians. This may also reflect a division of labor and maturity within modern IS departments.

The increased emphasis on both Computer Simulation and Statistical Decision Theory is equally interesting. The demand for increasing skills in these areas may reflect the emphasis on decision support systems (DSS) and expert systems (ES) in today's organizations. Consistent with the emergence of these technologies, Software Package Analysis is also projected to increase in importance by 1995. This is not surprising; the movement toward purchasing rather than custom building

software products has been the trend for two decades and has increased in the 1980's with the proliferation of personal computers. The respondents predict that this trend will continue.

Systems Analyst/Designer

The trend for systems analysts/designers is toward increased knowledge of people and problem-solving skills, and away from developing application software. As the purchase of packaged software technology becomes the norm, Software Package Analysis is and is expected to become a valuable skill for systems analysts/designers. Consistent with the role of using technology to find solutions, Database Management Systems skills are also viewed as being increasingly more important now and in the future.

Programmer

Telecommunication Concepts and Database Management Systems skills showed the largest increases in importance for future programmers. This result reflects an increased emphasis on networking, distributed processing systems, and utilization of DBMS. As the division of labor among computer personnel has increased, many basic skills are no longer the direct responsibility of computer programmers; this includes Operating Systems knowledge. Perhaps this is the result of new operating systems and application development languages that decrease the need for such skills.

Conclusions

Both the 1995 projections and the 1987 survey results confirm the importance of many of the skills recommended in the 1982 ACM model curriculum [12]. In general, the respondents indicate that managerial and human factors skills have increased in importance, especially for project managers and systems analysts/designers. The need for increased knowledge in technical skill areas is expected to decrease in value. This may suggest that the respondents view the role of both systems analysts/designers and project managers as increasingly managerial in nature, requiring planning, control, and human relations skills, whereas the technical knowledge is perceived as being the domain of technical specialists. This may also reflect that understanding the managerial process is essential to appreciate increasingly complex corporate applications.

The recommended inclusion of database management systems and data communications courses is supported by the findings. Both database management systems and telecommunication skills are expected to be significantly more valuable skills for systems analysts/designers in the future.

The ACM model curriculum recommendation to include the AACSB common body of knowledge is indirectly supported by the findings. While most of the AACSB common body of knowledge is not specific to IS professions, skill areas common to the ACM model curriculum, the AACSB common body of knowledge, and this study are Legal Aspects of Computing, Computer

Simulation, and <u>Statistical Decision Theory</u>. In all cases, the value of these skill areas is expected to increase for IS professionals.

There was no direct evidence regarding the usefulness of an MIS policy class as a capstone course. However, the findings suggest that several important skill areas that may have been overlooked are expected to be increasingly valuable. These include <u>Planning and Control of Systems Projects</u> and <u>Computer Security Controls and Auditing</u>; topics that normally would be covered in an Information Resource Management course. Although the results do not confirm the importance of this specific course, the perceived importance and lack of curriculum coverage of these topics suggests the need for such a course within the IS curriculum.

Collectively, the results show a shift from centralized, mainframe to distributed, micro-based systems, and from procedural to non-procedural languages. This is indicative of the emergence of end-user computing. Based on the survey results, the skills needed to support this trend include: software package analysis, database management systems, telecommunications, human relations, human factors, computer simulation, computer security, and statistical decision theory.

References

1. Ashenhurst, R. L. (ed.) Curriculum Recommendations for Graduate Professional Programs in Information Systems: A Report of the ACM Curriculum Committee on Computer Education for Management. <u>Communications of the ACM</u>, 15, 5 (May 1972), 363-98.

2. Bureau of Labor Statistics. <u>Occupational Projections and Training Data</u>. Bulletin 2251, Washington, D.C.: U. S. Government Printing Office, 1986.

3. Cash, James I., Jr., McFarlan, F. Warren, and McKenney, James L. <u>Corporate Information Systems Management: The Issues Facing Senior Executives</u>. 2nd ed. Homewood, IL: Irwin, 1988.

4. Cheney, Paul H., and Lyons, Norman R. Information System Skill Requirements: A Survey. <u>MIS Quarterly</u>, 4, 1 (March 1980), 35-43.

5. Cheney, Paul H. and Lipp, A. Information Systems Skill Requirement: 1978 and 1987. unpublished working paper, University of Georgia, #27, 1988.

6. Couger, J. Daniel. (ed.) Curriculum Recommendations for Undergraduate Programs in Information Systems. <u>Communications of the ACM</u>, 16, 12 (December 1973), 727-49.

7. Frost, Halsey. Time for a change--MIS expands its business role. <u>Computerworld Focus</u>, 22, 09A (March 2, 1988), 19 & 22.

8. Kolodziej, Stan. The fate of 4GLs. <u>Computerworld Focus</u>, 22, 05A (February 3, 1988), 25-28.

9. McFarlan, F. Warren and McKenney, James L. The information archipelago--governing the new world. <u>Harvard Business Review</u>, 61, 4 (July-August 1983), 91-99.

10. Martin, James and Leben, James. <u>Fourth-Generation Languages</u>. Vol. III. <u>4GLs From IBM</u>. Englewood Cliffs, NJ: Prentice-Hall, 1986.

11. Munro, Malcolm C., Huff, Sid L.,and Moore, Gary. Expansion and Control of End-User Computing. <u>Journal of Management Information Systems</u>, 4, 3 (Winter 1987-88), 5-27.

12. Nunamaker, Jay F., Couger, J. Daniel, and Davis, Gordon B. (eds.) Information Systems Curriculum Recommendations for the 80s: Undergraduate and Graduate Programs--A Report of the ACM Curriculum Committee on Information Systems. <u>Communications of the ACM</u>. 25, 11 (November 1982), 781-805.

13. Stevens, Lawrence. Cost control dominates in new MIS hiring season. <u>Computerworld</u>, 22, 7 (February 15, 1988), 95 & 100.

THE NET NEGATIVE PRODUCING PROGRAMMER

by G. Gordon Schulmeyer

Taking a poor performer off a team can be more productive than adding a good one [6].

We've known about net negative producing programmers (NNPPs) since the early 1960s. Almost all projects have NNPPs: people who insert enough spoilage to exceed the value of their production. It's an important issue but difficult to confront. Most development managers do not handle negative aspects of their programming staff well. This article discusses how to recognize NNPPs and how to take remedial actions to ensure a project's success.

Researchers have found a wide range in programmer performance, from a low of a 5:1

to a high of 100:1. This means that programmers at the same level, with similar backgrounds and comparable salaries, might take from 1 to 100 weeks to complete the same tasks [22].

In studies conducted by Bill Curtis, the ratio of programmer performance that repeatedly appeared was 22:1 [5]. This was both for source lines of code produced and for debugging times, which include both defect detection rate and defect removal efficiency [5]. The NNPP also produces a higher instance of defects in the work product.

Figure 1 depicts the consequences of NNPPs. This negative production does not merely apply to extreme cases. In a team of 10, you can expect as many as 3 people with a defect rate high enough to qualify them as NNPPs. With a nor-

mal distribution of skills, the probability that there is not even 1 NNPP out of 10 is virtually nil. If you are unfortunate enough to work on a high-defect project (density of from 30 to 60 defects per thousand lines of executable code), fully half your team may be NNPPs [6].

John Gardner, in *No Easy Victories* [9], suggested that "An excellent plumber is infinitely more admirable than an incompetent philosopher." If society scorns excellence in plumbing because it is a humble activity and accepts shoddiness in philosophy because it is exalted, "neither its pipes nor its theories will hold water" [15]. In our context, if we substitute "programmer" for "philosopher," either the computer program won't run or the NNPP will be so slow he or

"The Net Negative Producing Programmer", by G.G. Schulmeyer from *American Programmer*, Vol. 5, No. 6, June 1992, pages 12-19. Reprinted with permission.

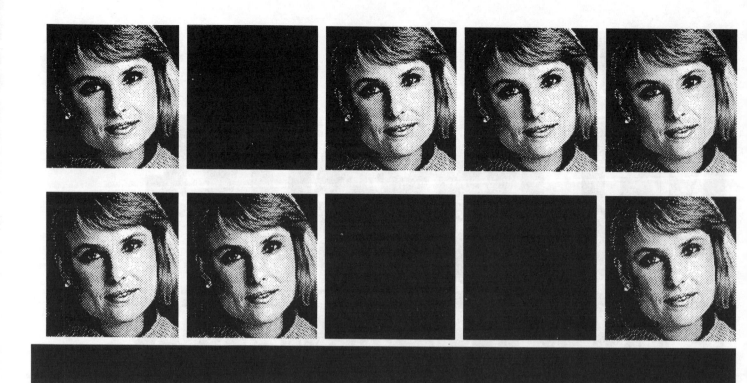

she will thwart the project's success.

Bill Curtis has suggested that the discovery of multiple NNPPs across multiple projects throughout an organization is evidence of a poor hiring or selection process within the organization [5]. Thus, the management failure may not lie at the project level but rather at the enterprise level. Keep this is mind while considering the remedial actions proposed later in this article.

RECOGNIZING NNPPs

Table 1 illustrates the significant differences between manufacturing and software development. Such differences set programmers apart and obscure recognition of the NNPP.

A model of programmer behavior would help us recognize NNPPs. Such models must be able to account for at least these basic programmer tasks:

★ *Composition:* writing a program.

★ *Comprehension:* understanding a given problem.

★ *Debugging:* finding errors in a given program.

★ *Modification:* altering a given program to fit a new task.

★ *Learning:* acquiring new programming skills and knowledge.

In addition, the model must be able to describe these tasks in terms of the *cognitive structure* that the programmer possesses or comes to possess in memory and the *cognitive processes* involved in using this knowledge or in adding to it [22]. Certainly, the programmer tasks of composition, debugging, modification, and learning can be measured fairly easily to determine programmer differences. The *cognitive structure* (comprehension) is not measurable as such but manifests itself in the *cognitive processes* (composition, debugging, modification, and learning).

METRICS

The people orientation of companies has a tough side. *In Search of Excellence* tells us that the excellent companies are measurement happy and performance oriented, but this toughness is borne of mutually

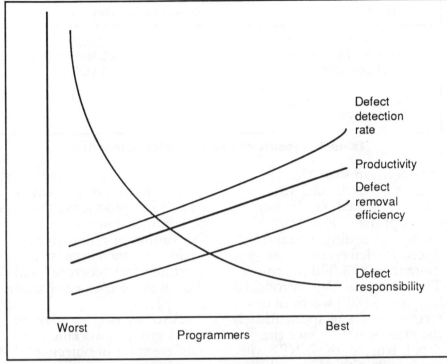

Figure 1: Programmers' efficiency and effectiveness (adapted from DeMarco [6])

high expectations and peer reviews [18].

Most activities associated with software development lend themselves to a measurement program, but little measurement has been done by the programming community. For

	Manufacturing	Software Development
Input quality	Uniform	Highly variable
Input/product characteristics	Uniform	Unique, different
Process characteristics	Repetitive	Creative
Control action	Well defined	Ambiguous
Output quality	Measurable	Not measurable
Interplay of measurement and control	None	Significant

Table 1: Software development differences (taken from Christenson [4])

whatever reason, programmers and their managers don't record information concerning software defects. Two possible reasons are lack of time and a disinclination to ponder the less attractive aspects of what to do about NNPPs [8].

To recognize NNPPs, we must measure. Of specific measurement interest is how programmers balance productivity versus defect generation, as well as the programmer's defect detection rate and defect removal efficiency.

For productivity versus defect generation, a look at the metrics at the individual level would help (see Table 2).

It is much more difficult to capture defect detection rates and defect removal efficiency during debugging and testing than it is to evaluate productivity versus defect generation. To remedy the situation, a software configuration control board could track software problem reports, identifying the individual uncovering the defects and dating the problem hand-off to an individual and dating the resolution of that problem. But be very careful that the vast differences of the seriousness of problems revealed on software problem reports are not ignored.

Though it is difficult to identify the NNPP through these metrics, it *can* be done. But questions of legality and ethics must be considered. The delicacy of measuring one-person projects is especially sensitive in Europe. Some countries prohibit the measurement of an individual worker's performance, either because of national law, as in Sweden, or because the software staffs are unionized and such measurements may violate union agreements, as in Germany [14].

Ethically, it may be inappropriate to weed out NNPPs based on metrics because

> we have not measured long enough to be certain of the accuracy of our measurements.
>
> we do not know *which of the measures* or what combination of metrics correlates best with the behavior we want to encourage.
>
> we feel that such a use would lead to distortion of the data, and we depend on the measurements to give us insight into the entire development process. [11]

The basic fear is that we will pick the wrong thing to measure or that whatever we pick cannot be measured consistently or accurately [11].

Legal and ethical concerns argue for a published protocol regarding the use of the metric data. The purpose of the protocol is to allay the legitimate worries about misuse of the data. The underlying philosophy of the protocol must be that data collected on an individual basis can be used only for the *benefit* of the individual.

Upon finding that a given project worker is an NNPP, the

Productivity	Defect Generation
Document pages per hour	Defects per 100 pages
Lines of PDL* per hour	Defects per 1000 lines of PDL
LOC† per hour	Defects per 1000 LOC
*Program design language. †Lines of code.	

Table 2: Productivity versus defect generation

measurer can share the data with that NNPP and with no one else: "Fred, you're rather defect prone. Over four months of coding, you introduced 79 defects that cost more than $53,000 to remove. The average worker introduced less than $2600 worth of defects while doing approximately the same work." Once the data is trusted, the NNPP will use it to maximize his or her contribution to the effort. One's own self-esteem is far greater motivation than any that software management could apply [6].

REASONS FOR NNPPs

Our understanding of NNPPs can be enhanced if we explore some of the driving reasons for their performance. A fairly recent study of 250 heterogeneous subjects examined four of the most frequently named causes of poor performance: lack of job satisfaction, lack of identification with and involvement in the organization for which the programmer works, belief that professional behavior will rarely result in reward, and the programmer's own lack of a sense of professionalism [7].

A person with a negative attitude toward productivity is usually less productive than is a person with a positive attitude. Pressuring for productive behavior may merely cause the person to feel "coerced" and thus increase the negative attitude [2].

Also, we may be unaware that a group is working toward a different set of objectives than its manager expects. Consequently, unless we take precautions to see that all the objectives are communicated and continue to be communicated, we should not be surprised when the program does not meet schedules or runs inefficiently or uses too much storage.

There is, however, a certain danger in communicating objectives: objectives can change estimates! Experimentally, after it was found that instructions for objectives affect performance, the estimates given by each programmer were checked. The programmers had estimated number of batch runs and number of elapsed days to complete each project; a comparison of their actual and estimated runs and days is shown in Table 3.

Those who were instructed to finish as quickly as possible were motivated to be far more conservative in their estimates of time to completion; they actually performed much better than their estimates and better than the other group, even though the other group had been much more optimistic in its estimating.

Software managers should take a long, hard look at this table before they establish the goals for their next project. If a goal is set explicitly, there are two effects: programmers work toward the goal at the possible expense of another goal, and programmers will be far more conservative (or accurate) in estimating how well they will meet the goal. Estimates on goals not emphasized will probably be completely unreliable, both because they are not made carefully and because they are not important enough to resist being sacrificed to other goals [24].

REMEDIAL ACTIONS

Now that we have seen how to recognize NNPPs through metrics and have uncovered some reasons for their poor performance, we need to focus on some of the remedial actions possible for NNPPs. No longer are steps to ignore, deny, or blame others acceptable. We must move to the top steps of problem solving, as shown in Figure 2, by assuming responsibility and finding solutions. This aphorism in *The One Minute Manager* can provide guidance to the software manager's rehabilitation of the NNPP: "Everyone is a potential winner; some people are disguised as losers; do not let appearances fool you" [3].

The model of programmer behavior discussed earlier provides some insight into potential remedial actions. The *cognitive processes* of composition, debugging, modification, and learning, when measured, give positive identification of the NNPP, which puts "strength" in the software manager's hands to deal with the issues.

When one or more of your people goes off course or does a bad job, you *must* let them know it and take immediate re-

medial action. One way of avoiding major disasters is to subdivide the job sufficiently and have enough checkpoints so that missing one is a signal, not a catastrophe [17]. Some other remedial actions are counseling, reassignment, or dismissal.

COUNSELING

The Hawthorne experiment researchers suggested that a supervisor could best counsel an employee if the supervisor followed these five rules:

1 Listen patiently to what the employee has to say before making your comments.

2 Refrain from criticizing or offering hasty advice.

3 Never argue while counseling.

4 Give your undivided attention to the employee while the employee is talking.

5 Look beyond the mere words of what the employee says; listen to perceive something deeper than what appears on the surface [1].

A significant aspect of counseling the NNPP is the correct use of performance appraisal, or better, performance management. Susan Webber has provided some new insights into software performance management [23]. A key element is appropriate consequences of

	Runs		Days		
	Estimated	Actual	Estimated	Actual	% Late
Efficient program	22	69	48	76	75
Fast programming	39	29	68	65	25

Table 3: Effect of environment on estimating (taken from Weinberg [24])

the programmer's actions. Although appropriate consequences are a critical ingredient in effective performance management, five additional factors are involved: behaviors and results, measurement, feedback, goals and subgoals, and positive reinforcement. Often the poor performance of the NNPP is a result of one or more of these major time-wasters: management by crisis, attempting too much, personal disorganization, lack of self-discipline, inability to say no, procrastination, leaving tasks unfinished, socializing, or incomplete information [16]. If identified quickly, this type of behavior can be stopped, thus turning around the poor performance of NNPPs.

A specific example of a successful implementation of software performance management has been offered by Webber. She writes that system test groups have the objective "of writing and executing effective test suites and are reinforced for finding defects. Alternatively, design groups have the pinpoints of writing code that can be executed without defects and for effectively correcting defects that are found by the system test groups" [23]. Be sure that the objectives are intended and that they are unambiguous.

One key result metric for a design group is the backlog of problems it has to resolve. Performance management has been successfully applied to defect backlog. As a result of one application of performance

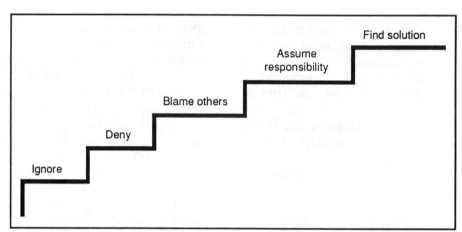

Figure 2: Stages of problem solving (taken from Grove [12])

management, a 21 percent improvement in productivity in this area was attained. In addition, rather than the objections usually raised when individual performance is measured, the programmers made positive comments about the performance management and its implementation. The experience of these programmers with performance management has resulted in an association of metrics with positive consequences [23].

REASSIGNMENT

The problems of the NNPP are often remedied by a scrupulous adherence to the principle of trying alternatives before resorting to dismissal. This is especially true when the difficulty is caused by carelessness or complacency (an unmistakable warning will often suffice to snap them out of their lethargy) or by incompatibility between the supervisor and the employee (in which case a simple reassignment sometimes works wonders) [10].

No one need be embarrassed when reassigned to a task that makes optimal use of his or her strengths. For instance, a poor coder is given debugging duties or a poor tester is given coding or documentation duties. Even NNPPs who are temporarily chastened to learn that all their testing and diagnostic skills barely made up for a high defect insertion rate will know (once assigned properly) that their prior low value to the project was mostly due to management failures rather than their own [20].

Reassignments are easier for Japanese managers who are willing to go along with a change if it contributes to any of the following goals: making the job easier or safer, making the job more productive, improving product quality, or saving time and cost. This is in sharp contrast to the Western manager's almost exclusive concern with the cost of the reassignment and its economic payback [13]. Typically, because economic payback is high

with these NNPP reassignments, they readily fulfill the Western manager's criterion.

Job satisfaction may be enhanced at all programmer skill levels by using both performance management and job enrichment techniques [21]. This job enrichment for a NNPP moves away from reassignment as such but allows creativity on the part of the software manager to focus on specific aspects of the NNPP's assignment.

DISMISSAL

Because termination is very costly for the organization and potentially a matter for legal action by the NNPP, it must be the last resort. Table 4 provides the software manager with a way to measure the influences of various alternatives to termination.

If counseling and reassignment don't work, then the organization may be best served by firing the NNPP.

CONCLUSION

There are probably NNPPs on your project. I hope this article helps you recognize the NNPPs and suggests useful remedial actions you can take to improve the situation.

REFERENCES

1 Bittel, Lester R. *What Every Supervisor Should Know*, 2nd ed. New York: McGraw-Hill, 1968.

2 Blake, Robert R., and Jane S. Mouton. *Productivity: The Human Side*. New York: AMACOM, 1981.

3 Blanchard, Kenneth, and Spencer Johnson. *The One Minute Manager*. New York: Berkley Books, 1981.

4 Christenson, D. A., et al. "Statistical Methods Applied to Software." In G. Gordon Schulmeyer and James I. McManus, *Total Quality Management for Software*. New York: Van Nostrand Reinhold, 1992.

5 Curtis, Bill. "Managing the Real Leverage in Software Productivity and Quality." *American Programmer*, Vol. 3, nos. 7–8 (July–August 1990), pp. 4–14.

6 DeMarco, Tom. *Controlling Software Projects*. Englewood Cliffs, NJ: Yourdon Press/Prentice Hall, 1982.

7 Dunn, Robert H. *Software Quality: Concepts and Plans*. Englewood Cliffs, NJ: Prentice Hall, 1990.

8 Dunn, Robert H. "The Quest for Software Reliability." In G. Gordon Schulmeyer and James I. McManus, *Handbook of*

Instructions: Insert + for positive influences, – for negative influences.	Probability of Success	Time and Resources Required	Endorsement by Superior	Temporary/ Permanent Results	Reflection on Managerial Capabilities
Rehabilitate the subordinate					
Change how you feel about NNPPs					
Restructure the job					
Restructure the situation					
Demote NNPPs					
Transfer NNPPs					

Table 4: Influences of alternatives to termination (adapted from Roseman [19])

Software Quality Assurance. New York: Van Nostrand Reinhold, 1987.

9 Gardner, John. *No Easy Victories.* New York: Harper & Row, 1968 (out of print).

10 Gellerman, Saul W. *The Management of Human Relations.* New York: Holt, Rinehart and Winston, 1966.

11 Grady, Robert B., and Deborah L. Caswell. *Software Metrics: Establishing a Company-Wide Program.* Englewood Cliffs, NJ: Prentice Hall, 1987.

12 Grove, Andrew S. *High Output Management.* New York: Random House, 1983.

13 Imai, Masaaki. *Kaizen: The Key to Japan's Competitive Success.* New York: Random House, 1986.

14 Jones, T. Capers. *Applied Software Measurement: Assuring Productivity and Quality.* New York: McGraw-Hill, 1991.

15 Longstreet, William. "Executive Exchange—Seize the Opportunity for Qualitivity." *Industry Week,* January 25, 1982.

16 Mackenzie, Alec. *The Time Trap.* New York: AMACOM, 1990.

17 Metzger, Philip W. *Managing a Programming Project.* Englewood Cliffs, NJ: Prentice Hall, 1973.

18 Peters, Thomas J., and Robert H. Waterman, Jr. *In Search of Excellence: Lessons from America's Best-Run Companies.* New York: Harper & Row, 1982.

19 Roseman, Edward. *Confronting Nonpromotability: How to Manage a Stalled Career.* New York: AMACOM, 1977.

20 Schulmeyer, G. Gordon. *Zero Defect Software.* New York: McGraw-Hill, 1990.

21 Schulmeyer, G. Gordon. *Computer Concepts for Managers.* New York: Van Nostrand Reinhold, 1985.

22 Shneiderman, Ben. *Software Psychology: Human Factors in Computer and Information Systems.* Boston: Little, Brown, 1980.

23 Webber, Susan. "Performance Management: A New Approach to Software Engineering Management." *American Programmer,* Vol. 3, nos. 7–8 (July–August 1990), pp. 64–71.

24 Weinberg, Gerald M. *The Psychology of Computer Programming.* New York: Van Nostrand Reinhold, 1971.

G. Gordon Schulmeyer, CDP, has over 30 years of software management and development experience with special emphasis on software quality concepts. He is the manager of software engineering at Westinghouse Electronic Systems Group, where he was previously manager of software quality engineering.

His publications include Total Quality Management for Software *(Van Nostrand Reinhold, 1992),* Handbook of Software Quality Assurance, *2nd ed. (Van Nostrand Reinhold, 1992),* Zero Defect Software *(McGraw-Hill, 1990), and* Computer Concepts for Managers *(Van Nostrand Reinhold, 1985).*

He can be reached at Westinghouse Electronic Systems Group, P.O. Box 746, Mail Stop 893, Baltimore, MD 21203 (410/765-3830; fax 410/765-9435).

Appraising MIS Personnel: Techniques To Make It Work In Your Organization

By Lockwood Lyon, CDP, CSP

Doing performance appraisals of MIS professionals competently and fairly can be downright impossible. The lack of good job descriptions, a highly technical environment and a widely skewed salary structure make it difficult for managers to do employees justice. Small wonder that employees don't look forward to appraisals, and managers don't like doing them.

Performance appraisals (or performance reviews) must satisfy several of the company's needs. They help determine employee compensation, assist in monitoring performance improvement, guide career development and provide documentation for hire/fire decisions. With all this riding on a single document, appraisals must be impartial, unbiased and equitable.

Here's how to make employees look forward to their yearly reviews, along with some advice on how to prepare for them yourself.

Webster's New World Dictionary defines appraise as, "... to judge the quality or worth of (something)." An appraisal, therefore, is a judgement of the quality or worth of your employee's results.

To appraise your employees, you must first review the events during the appraisal period. Then, you must summarize the goals set and results achieved. After gathering the facts, you judge the employee's performance.

Many new employees are unaware of these attributes of performance reviews. This lack of knowledge may make it difficult for them to understand the review process, and may cause anxiety.

Briefly, a performance review is a set of measurements made during a specific period, including a judgement of these measurements. This judgement is then used as a basis for further action. Here's how each of these attributes relate to their particular situation.

• **Review of a period** - Work efforts extend over time. Results occur at points in time and change over time. A performance review is a review of a period of results, not just a status report of results to date. It should cover the entire review period and contain examples of results achieved. This means that an employee's review is more than a simple "where they are now." It relates where they came from to how they got there. In addition, it tells whether or not they are learning and improving their skills and knowledge.

• **Ongoing, not one-time** - Performance consists of day-to-day communications, formal meetings, status reports and other activities. These developments occur over time, not just at the end of the year. This means that a performance review takes an entire year to complete. Every day some events happen, however small, which are part of performance. You may give employees feedback regarding their work. Their co-workers may assist them with a project. They may finish several tasks early, or complete a project well under budget. In effect, the performance review is a continuous process, happening every minute of every day.

• **Emphasis on measurement, not judgement** - The major portion of any performance review should concentrate on the observed facts. This is the measurement process. Only after all the measurements have taken place should the judging process begin. It is important to separate the act of measuring from that of appraising. This prevents judgements of some behaviors or results from clouding other judgements. It also provides an organized agenda for the review meetings with your employee.

How to Prepare

There are several types of performance review forms and procedures that companies use. Each has its own specific strengths and weaknesses.

Use the following descriptions as a guide to find the correct appraisal type for your company. Follow the recommendations for that type to help you to prepare for the appraisal meeting.

• **Management by objectives.** With this kind of review the manager and subordinate meet at the beginning of the review period and set objectives. These objectives are for the coming review period: the manager and employee set them together.

There are disadvantages to this method. Setting objectives can be very difficult. For example, one of your employees is a sales representative. You and she agree that her primary objective is to "increase sales by 10 percent." Does this mean 10 percent more products or 10 percent greater revenue?

Another disadvantage is setting the difficulty level of the objectives. Easy objectives aren't challenging: impossible or unreasonable objectives unfairly penalize employees. In both cases, appraisals may give an inaccurate picture of employee performance.

To prepare for this type of review, monitor your employee's progress toward objectives carefully during the year. Pay particular attention to circumstances beyond their control that make it difficult or impossible for them to achieve their goals.

Have employees document these events in regular status reports for you. At the end of the year, have them summarize their progress toward their objectives.

Sometimes you must revise an objective. Unexpectedly tough competition may make it impossible for you to reach sales goals. An economic downturn may cause your company to revise its corporate goals.

You should be receptive to changing or revising employees' objectives if there is a good reason - especially if it will affect their performance appraisal.

• **The easy review.** This form of review requires the manager to write prose or essay answers to certain questions. It is time-consuming and tiresome. A manager unskilled in written communication may have difficulty in rating employees correctly.

Managers have difficulty answering

essay questions with definite statements, unless they are extremely pleased with an employee's performance. In the absence of specific guidelines, the review is highly subjective. The final rating may be a function of your writing skill, not your employee's actual performance.

Give yourself a break by requiring your employees to report their results in prose form. Have them break down their work by project and by tasks within each project. Have them describe each project with several sentences. Have them describe each task with a short sentence.

Don't let them simply summarize completion of a project with "project complete." Have them write a few sentences describing the tasks completed and whether they were on time, early or late. Have them finish with a summary of the total work required for the project, and note anything they learned.

• **Rating scales.** This is the most common form of performance review. Behaviors or results are grouped into several categories. Managers then rate employees with a numerical score in each category.

This format of review is easy to fill out. A manager's ratings, however, may easily become subjective or biased. Managers sometimes let ratings on one scale affect other ratings. Also, numerical scales mean different things to different people.

For example, suppose you are rating an employee in a category titled "Written Communications." Your rating is a five on a scale of zero to five.

What does this mean? Did the employee surpass all expectations? Did they perform better than all others in your department? Than others in your industry? Did they do the minimum expected, but nothing more?

You can prepare for this type of review by discussing the procedure with each employee at the beginning of the review period. Explain what each of the categories covers, and what the numerical rating scales mean. Give examples of how you would rate certain results.

It is also very important that you and your employees agree on the standards for comparison. Will you compare them with others in your department, or with others having the same job in your company? Get agreement on this at the beginning of the review period.

• **Critical incidents.** This type of review is similar to the essay form. It requires managers to justify their recommendations by citing "critical incidents" during the review period.

The manager considers the employee's typical behavior in reference to a number of important factors. As with the essay, the manager describes the employee's performance in his or her own words. However, the description must be of a critical incident, an example of behavior that is clearly indicative of good or bad performance.

This takes time, and requires good communications skills on the part of the manager. It requires you to keep a complete and detailed log of such incidents throughout the year.

You can have your employee assist you by preparing a summary of the critical incidents in advance. Have them do this by summarizing each incident when it happens and preparing a brief status report on the matter.

After documenting the incident, have them review it verbally with you. Ask for their opinion about how they acted or reacted. Was their behavior acceptable? Were there other alternatives that they could have considered?

Review how the incident affected their work and whether it helped them to improve their knowledge or skills. Making a mistake may be embarrassing; not learning from the experience can be costly.

After the Appraisal

After all appraisal documents have been filled out, reviewed and approved, management can concentrate on the judgement portion of the process. Here, we concentrate on the purposes for appraisal and how best to use the information gathered.

• **Employee compensation.** The performance appraisal document is probably the single most important item used in determining appropriate employee compensation. Regrettably, raises and bonuses usually occur more than a year after the events that warranted them. This makes it difficult for employees to correlate rewards (or punishments) with performance. This predicament is sometimes compounded by economic downturns, which force employers to cut back on personnel costs.

Managers can lessen the negative effects of these situations by giving formal appraisals more often. Such mini-appraisals can then become the basis for giving employees raises on a semi-annual or quarterly basis. This system ties rewards more closely to performance - employee anticipation of rewards in the near future can boost productivity. The effects of economic downturns or seasonal business cycles on employees is also reduced. Instead of waiting until the economy (or business) recovers and then waiting an additional year for their appraisal, quarterly raises give employees the incentive to be more productive.

• **Performance improvement.** Appraisals are sometimes used as vehicles for improving employee performance. This is usually reserved for employees whose performance is either below normal or unacceptable. In these cases the appraisal document forms a starting point. Employee behaviors and critical incidents are summarized and compared against company standards. The supervisor and employee then discuss the evaluation and develop an action plan. The items on this plan then become the employee's goals for the next appraisal period.

• **Career development.** Many companies have developed entire performance appraisal systems that integrate into their career development programs. This permits employers to manage their supervisor's spans of control and lets companies plan ahead for future business expansion. Such systems typically match employee achievements and accomplishments with job descriptions to support promotion decisions.

In this environment the roles of the supervisor and employee during the appraisal process are geared toward employee development rather than compensation. Companies will typically implement this system with a rating scale appraisal form, and require a certain minimum score before promoting an employee.

The best way to prepare for a performance review is to begin on the very first day of the review period. Make sure your employee understands how you will conduct the review meetings and what they will cover. Make sure you and your employee agree on the basis of comparison.

Give your employee copies of the review form and have them fill one out every so often to review with you.

Status reports are critical. Have employees fill them out in detail, paying particular attention to critical incidents, completed tasks and estimates of remaining work. Have employees add a short list of tasks that they will finish in the next few weeks.

Keep a log of employee's progress during the review period. Use the log and status reports to create "mini-reviews" for their benefit. Doing this will help them overcome anxieties they may have about the appraisal process.

Keeping good records and monitoring progress carefully is good advice for any manager. It will help both you and your employees look forward to performance appraisal.

Lockwood Lyon, CDP, CSP, is a consultant with Compuware Corp. in Farmington Hills, MI. He is co-author of the ACP, CSP and CDP Review Manuals and has held the position of education director for the DPMA Detroit Chapter.

Chapter 7
Direction Advice

To resolve to make your meaning plain, even at the cost of some trouble to yourself, is more important than any other single thing.

— Ernest Gowers

Overview

Direction deals with people and the interpersonal aspects of management. It requires telling people what to do, empowering them to do it, monitoring them to ensure they do it, and stepping in to help when they need you. To provide proper direction, managers need to know how to communicate, motivate, and lead individuals and teams. They must know what turns people on and what doesn't. They need to build consensus and synergy to get the job done.

This chapter contains six papers on the topic of direction. The first of these, by Hopen, deals with overcoming communications problems. This paper describes the process scientifically in terms of six basic elements: source, message, channel, receiver, feedback, and noise. It then goes on to provide some very useful suggestions on how to manipulate these elements to improve the management of the communications process.

The next paper, by Bochenski, describes environments that accommodate the development of software products by geographically dispersed teams who are linked together through some form of communications network. Although the emphasis of the article is on workstations and tools, there are flashes of insight offered about the management approaches used to control work groups' performance. More is needed on this topic. Hopefully, suitable papers will appear in time for my fifth edition of this tutorial.

The third paper, by DeMarco and Lister, provides a revealing look at the effects of the workplace on programmer performance. A benchmarking exercise was run to examine the effects of the workplace using 166 programmers. The authors' findings based on this exercise refute the perception that the workplace has limited effect on productivity.

The fourth article, by Couger, looks further at the topic of motivation. It argues that the ability to pursue interesting and meaningful work is the primary motivator for software professionals. This is not unexpected. Nor is the suggestion to break the work tasks further to identify the skill, variety, autonomy, and significance of the work contained within them. Use of work as a motivator has been practiced for years.

The fifth article, by Shannon, is on empowerment. This is the buzzword in management circles today. Empowerment suggests change. Those empowered become the change agents. They work with their peers and create the climate that enables change to occur naturally. They become the leaders and help the firm realize its potential.

In the final paper, Bushardt, Duhon, and Fowler discuss the paradoxes of staff assignment and the myths of delegation. The paper uses wit to convey substance. It examines the authority-responsibility paradoxes that exist in firms and comments on their inability to meet their managers' hierarchy of needs. The authors make some striking observations and useful recommendations.

References

Recommended readings include DeMarco and Lister's book on the behavior of people (Reference 7 in the Bibliography) and Tom Peters' book on excellence in organizations (Reference 21). For those who don't have time to read Peters' book, I suggest getting the tape. His thoughts on skunks will keep you entertained as you drive to and from work. If you live in the Los Angeles area as I do, you will have plenty of time to listen.

The Process of Communicating

Understanding and controlling communication variables can increase comprehension and decrease problems.

**by
Deborah L. Hopen**

W**E ARE BORN WITH A NEED TO COM-**municate, but our ability to communicate effectively is learned. Even though we spend as much as 75% of our lives involved in some form of communication, we are seldom as successful as we desire. In fact, it is apparent throughout the business world that excellent communicators are quite rare. The comment "We're having a communication problem" is heard frequently and indicates the difficulty of obtaining quality communication.

To be successful in business, communication must be managed and continuously improved just like any manufacturing or service process. Six primary variables and their interactions provide a framework for the communication process. When the process is understood, communication can be improved and variability reduced.

The primary variables

Communication is defined as the process of sending and receiving messages. The sender stimulates meaning in the mind of the receiver by means of a message conveyed using symbols, and the receiver responds either mentally or physically to the message. This definition points out the six primary variables in the process shown in Figure 1: source, message, channel, receiver, feedback, and noise.[1]

The source is the originator of the communication message. Sources might be individuals, groups, committees, teams, or even an entire company. The source has a significant effect on the informational or persuasive value of the message by controlling the style and delivery.

The message is the idea or feeling that the source communicates. Messages can be conveyed either verbally or nonverbally and frequently in both manners. Verbal messages are composed of words and phrases and depend on organization. Nonverbal messages include facial expressions, tone of voice, and attitude.

The channel is the actual means of conveying the symbols. There are two primary channels: the audible, verbal path using air waves and the visual, nonverbal path using light waves. Although hearing and sight are the main senses used in communicating, the other senses can also affect the communication process. Appearance and physical contact are often a factor in setting the environment. Generally, these other senses become most important when they negatively affect the process.

Communication is more likely to be successful when multiple channels are used to carry the message. Gestures and visual aids are frequently used to reinforce the audible message. Control of the channel is critical to successful communication. However, group size is a major factor in channel selection—more channels can be used in one-on-one exchanges because of physical proximity.

There is strong interaction among the source, message, and channel. Different combinations can produce widely divergent meanings. A simple example will demonstrate how these variables can work in harmony to provide clarification or in conflict to create confusion.

Almost daily, two associates will pass in the office hall. One questions, "How are you?" and the other responds, "Fine." If the words are accompanied by a smile and a cheerful conversation is initiated, the intended message is reinforced. If, on the other hand, the words are delivered in a quivering voice and the person

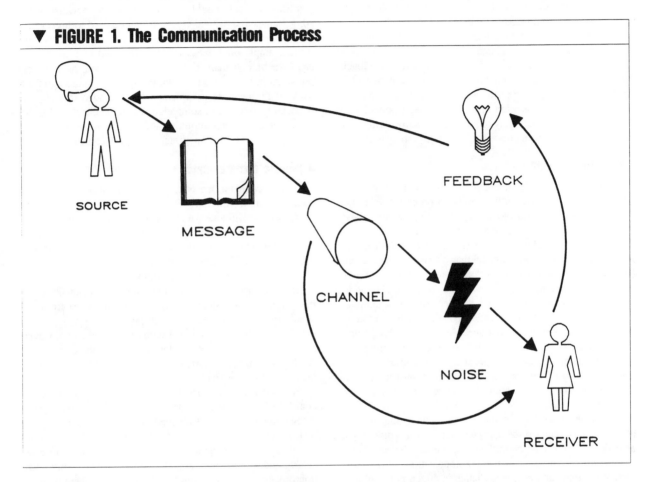

▼ FIGURE 1. The Communication Process

SOURCE

MESSAGE

CHANNEL

NOISE

FEEDBACK

RECEIVER

keeps his eyes downcast, the signals disagree and the message is distorted. Obviously, even a simple message can be miscommunicated because interpretation depends on the receiver's judgment. Regardless of whether the receiver is an individual or a group, the message is decoded by translating the channels into meaning. Technically, communication is complete as soon as decoding occurs, but effective communication is judged by the receiver's demonstrated understanding. This need for confirmation leads to the last two process variables, feedback and noise.

Feedback begins when the original receiver becomes the source and responds to the original source. Unfortunately, feedback is not always possible. Mass media and printed material offer the source very little reinforcement because the receiver is disconnected in time and place; therefore, feedback will be delayed and limited at best.

In-person communication is better suited to feedback. Larger groups can inhibit response because individuals feel feedback must be limited to a format and content that is acceptable within the group's norms; the need for maintaining security as a

member of the group might constrain the individual members. In smaller groups, feedback can be actively solicited by questioning the receiver, which will establish an interactive mode. Feedback is the only method of gauging the quality of the communication. It checks the meaning of the message.

In many circumstances, the source, message, and channel are effectively combined and the receiver is eager to offer feedback. This situation seems to be ideal for establishing quality communication, yet something might go awry and the communication process is not completed successfully. Often, external factors, called noise, inhibit communication. Sensory distractions of all types surround us and interfere with communication. In less than a second, physical noise can interrupt the receiver's attention.

Physical noise is not the most difficult obstacle to overcome, however. Deep in the mind of the receiver are internal perceptions and experiences that the source often cannot recognize. Successful communication depends on the use of clear, vivid, and emphatic language that is appropriate in the mind of the receiver. This relationship is the same as any customer-

supplier relationship. The quality of the communication process must be judged by the customer (the receiver)—not the supplier (the source). Therefore, communication must be carefully tailored to meet the needs of the receiver—language, style, channel, and a multitude of other options.

By now it is clear that the communication process is as complex as most manufacturing and service processes. The need to control the source, message, channel, receiver, feedback, and noise is much more important than is generally accepted. Insufficient time is spent planning for communication and improving the communication process. Although poor-quality communication is frequently observed, problem-solving tools are rarely employed to resolve communication issues.

Listening is a skill

Interactive communication requires control of a second process: listening. Hearing is the ability to process transmitted sound waves; it is a neurological process. On the other hand, listening involves making sense out of what is heard.[2]

Good listening takes time, effort, and energy. Indeed, active listening can be more stressful than active speaking. Listening skills are improved and effort is reduced if a listening posture is maintained. The receiver should sit upright and focus his eyes on the source, avoiding hypnotized stares and physical rigidity. The receiver should actively weigh and deeply consider each part of the message. He should withhold until comprehension is complete, which requires controlling both judgmental and emotional responses. It is important to listen for intent rather than content. The receiver must try to concentrate on the mental picture the source is painting and ignore the semantics.

On an individual level, communication can be improved by testing against uniform standards. Content, organization, style, and delivery must be controlled to persuade the receiver.

The content of any effective communication must clearly define the topic and purpose. Changing direction or subjects is a major communication problem. Likewise, drifting from the topic at hand is detrimental to interactive communication because it disrupts the receiver's train of thought and the pattern of communication.

Whereas the topic and purpose form the skeleton, ideas must be completely developed for communication to succeed. A brief introduction should be followed by the body of thought and summarized in a conclusion. Keeping communication organized helps the receiver connect the pieces of the message to form a total image.

Style and delivery are also critical. Appropriate language and attitude, a relational approach, and pleasant articulation greatly enhance communication.

In the book *How to Get Your Point Across in 30 Seconds*, Milo Frank advocates limiting each message to 30 seconds, since the attention span of the human mind has been estimated at 30 seconds. As each segment of time passes, the likelihood of successfully communicating the intended message decreases. Although 30 seconds might seem too short to adequately develop content, clear and concise points are much

more effective. Actually, the average speaker would find it difficult to continuously fill a 30-second period.[3]

Business communication should be monitored and continuous improvement should be encouraged. A checklist of the six variables and critical elements can be used to prepare for communication. When the communication process is controlled, ample time exists for decoding and interpreting because the brain is many times faster than speech. After careful preparation, the source must speak, then stop to listen to feedback. If the receiver is informed or persuaded, the process is effective; otherwise, some element on the checklist has not been met. A speaker should evaluate progress regularly, adjust accordingly, and integrate successful approaches.

A precise communicator

Frank recounts a tale of an expertly planned and executed communication process:[4]

"Charlie was in love with a charming young woman named Ava. She was in love with Charlie, but so far he had been unable to persuade her to marry him. Then one day he invited her to lunch at the Los Angeles Coliseum.

"In the center of the playing field was a small table and two chairs. A maitre d' showed them to the table, a captain seated them, and a waiter stood behind each chair. Apart from this small oasis, the Coliseum was empty.

"The table was elegantly set with crystal and china. Caviar and champagne were served, followed by a souffle and salad. As they waited for dessert, Charlie directed Ava's attention to the far end of the field.

"In a prearranged signal, he raised his glass, and the scoreboard flashed the words, 'Darling Ava, will you marry me?'

"She immediately said yes, and they are now living happily in Los Angeles."

This message took quite a bit of preparation, but the receiver clearly understood the intent! By monitoring the communication process and controlling the elements associated with the six variables (source, message, channel, receiver, feedback, and noise), the quality of communication can be greatly improved. The sender can be confident that the receiver will be informed or persuaded as intended; the process will more consistently yield the desired results.

References

1. Rudolph Verderber, *The Challenge of Effective Speaking* (Belmont, CA: Wadsworth Publishing Company, Inc., 1973), pp. 3-9.

2. Rudolph Verderber, *The Challenge of Effective Speaking*, pp. 11-15.

3. Milo O. Frank, *How to Get Your Point Across in 30 Seconds* (New York: Pocket Books, 1986), pp. 14-15.

4. Milo O. Frank, *How to Get Your Point Across in 30 Seconds*, pp. 119-120.

Deborah L. Hopen is vice president of quality assurance for the Personal Care Products Division of Weyerhaeuser Company, Tacoma, WA. She is a senior member of ASQC and a Certified Quality Engineer.

WORKGROUP GOALS PUSH GROUPWARE BOUNDARIES

Networking demands drive multiuser software tools; Case, project management, DBMS get team-oriented

By Barbara Bochenski

s groupware evolves from a young niche market to a more broad-based category of software, the term itself may become an anachronism. With the demand for networking capabilities, more users will be working in groups. And they will be using tools that, to date, have not been categorized as groupware. These include computer-aided software engineering (Case), project management and DBMS tools.

"Groupware won't be a useful term very long," said Esther Dyson, editor of the New York-based *Release 1.0* and president of EDventure Holdings, Inc., "since it won't distinguish one product from another."

Dyson, host of the annual PC Forum, is credited with coining the term "groupware." She defines groupware as software that helps people work together more effectively. In addition, this software must be "aware" that it has more than one user. For example, Notes from Lotus Development Corporation, Cambridge,

Bochenski is a high-tech freelance writer and DP professional who lives in Bellevue, Wash. She has over 28 years experience in data processing, performing a wide range of consulting and data processing services.

Mass., allows different groups of users to share information in distributed document databases, and provides communications and conferencing tools.

According to Dyson, numerous network-based applications will eventually have groupware features. The '90s, she said, will be the decade of interconnected systems and people.

Today, applications considered to

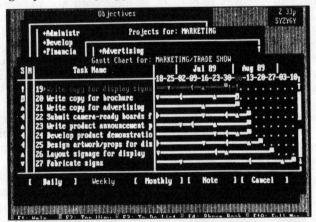

ORDER FROM CHAOS. *Syzygy, a project management groupware product from Information Research, helps groups set objectives, organize work, and manage and track progress. Syzygy includes a work outlining tool and built-in Gantt chart capability. Individuals can track their own progress with personal "to-do" lists.*

be groupware involve functions such as group scheduling, calendaring, electronic mail and group editing. Groupware packages run on a local-area network. According to the Market Intelligence Research Company, Mountain View, Calif., groupware was expected to have a 6% share of the LAN market in 1990.

Groupware has somewhat of an

identity problem, however. Users do not look to buy groupware specifically. They want software that helps them solve a particular problem or achieve a business goal, such as editing a document, managing a project, obtaining approvals or tracking events. It just happens that many people need to contribute to the final product.

"People don't call us and say, 'I'm interested in groupware,'" said Scott Kammeraad, vice president of Information Research Corporation in Charlottesville, Va. The company markets Syzygy, a successful project management groupware product.

Frequently, however, a tool that solves a problem, and helps everyone in the group, has an edge over competitive products.

More and more software will have this capability. "The second generation of groupware is workgroup computing," said John Dunkle, vice president of Workgroup Technologies in Hampton, N.H.

As perceptions change about groupware, applications software will benefit from features that facilitate group interaction. Dyson cited Case as an example.

According to Dyson, "IBM's Repository is a foundation—potentially—for groupware. The Repository can be just a database; you can build non-

DYSON

groupware with it. But it can also be considered an application-specific tool for building groupware."

"IBM's Repository is related to groupware," added Fred Luconi, president and CEO of Index Technology, a Case software developer in Cambridge, Mass.

Today, most people do not think of Case tools as groupware. But many industry analysts are predicting that Case will become an important part of workgroup computing software.

"Case has been defined too minimally in the past," said Vaughn Merlyn. "We'll see it expanded in the future." Merlyn, a noted Case analyst, speaker and consultant, is chairman of Case Research Corporation in Bellevue, Wash.

"Today, most Case tools are single-user oriented. However, second-generation Case tools are moving from single- to multiuser capabilities," said Merlyn.

"Case has to support groups," said Index Technology's Luconi. He said that software engineering by its nature is a group process. "The problem that Case is attacking is team-oriented. The need to support a team was always there," he explained, "but the advent of LAN technology made it possible." With the growing installation of LANs, the necessary infrastructure became available.

Luconi believes industry will see more attention on Case as a group process as a result of IBM's AD/Cycle and Repository.

"AD/Cycle did two major things," said Luconi. "It validated Case, and it emphasized the importance of a methodology." According to Luconi, because of AD/Cycle, users no longer question if they should use Case, but rather, they question when and how they should use it.

"The innovation of Excelerator, [a Case product from Index], was an integrated data dictionary," said Luconi. "The innovation of IBM's

Repository is that same concept, but now on an enterprise-wide basis. And an integrated dictionary is contributed to by a group of people.

"The focus of all this is 'groupware,'" he said. "It's just not called that." Luconi warns, however, that most existing PC-based software has been designed with a single user in mind.

"It's fallacious," he said, "to think that if you just link single-user software together with LANs, that will be enough to help groups." He said the software has to be designed to help groups.

Luconi said that 4Front, Index Technology's newest Case offering, "was designed from the start as a group activity."

4Front emphasizes the importance of having a formal application development methodology to support the use of Case tools.

"With AD/Cycle, a new wave of customers came in," said Luconi. "These customers said that Case tools are best used by teams that already have a methodology. However, they said it was important to have both a methodology and a Case tool aligned and integrated.

"4Front does that," Luconi added. "Before, methodology and Case tools existed separately. Now they are integrated."

Lynn Tompkins, 4Front product manager, explained that "4Front takes the methodology out of the book and puts it into the work breakdown structure in Excelerator." Now, people can see a list of their tasks in Excelerator, as well as have the tools available to perform these tasks.

"Then you link in 4Front's project management," said Tompkins. "Now that everyone knows what to do, you can find out if they are doing it on time."

"Project work is a group activity," said Luconi. "So, both the methodology and the tool have to be structured

LUCONI

to let work be subdivided and then recomposed."

Dyson said that groupware features appeared in some of the early Case tools. "Nastec's Life Cycle Manager was one of the first groupware products," she said. Nastec/Transform Logic Corporation is based in Scottsdale, Ariz.

MERLYN

According to Merlyn of Case Research, the next decade will see Case tools evolve toward workgroup computing.

"There have been a lot of interesting breakthroughs with the JAD [joint application development] concept," said Merlyn. Originated by IBM, the JAD concept uses group technologies to achieve its goals.

"JAD gets users who know the application problems together with technical people in a team-oriented workgroup," said Merlyn. "There have been some interesting research projects in JAD. For example, flip charts and white boards used to be the communication vehicle.

"As an experiment, a recent JAD project took place in a conferencing environment with a PC in front of each participant. Instantly, each person could anonymously vote on issues involved in the process," said Merlyn.

Other innovations have been introduced as well. "These are examples of real groupware technology," said Merlyn. "JAD and Case tools should support that kind of environment."

He added, "Products like Index Technology's 4Front shows vendors are aiming in the right direction."

As evidence that the concept of groupware is broadening, two leading vendors in this category of software—Lotus and Information Research—actually shun the term "groupware."

Lotus' Brownell Chalstrom, director of telecommunications and networking, said, "I never use the term 'groupware.' I don't like the label. I call Notes a group communication product."

Information Research no longer uses the term groupware.

"There isn't a good clean definition of groupware that means anything to buyers," Kammeraad of Information Research explained. He said because of confusion in the market, buyers who perceive a tool as groupware are sometimes hesitant to make a purchase decision.

Kammeraad believes that software can facilitate group work in two ways. First, it can help people share the work on the product itself. Such tools may send a document from person to person for their review and comments.

"Everyone is working on the same object. The object itself is the focus of interest. So that is one path for groupwork products to take," he said.

"The second path is where our product Syzygy fits: a tool that facilitates the process of managing the work. It provides a structure where I, as a participant, can get a status report and see who has completed what tasks, what needs to be completed and who else is involved in it. It helps me look at the work flow from a management view rather than looking at the actual work product itself.

"Syzygy means the alignment or opposition of two or more objects in space," Kammeraad explained. "We were looking for a term that had a sense of ducks in a row, organization or creating order from chaos. So that's the visual image that the word is meant to bring to mind."

Ray Davey, president of Professional Resource Inc., a consulting firm in Minneapolis, uses Syzygy on a three-PC LAN to track projects. Davey and a project team of 25 members installed a 70 file-server system for a large consumer foods company.

"In-house, we use it to track sales and client contacts as well as employee assignments and skill bases," said Davey. "At our client site, it is used for 75 to 80 different objectives." An objective, or folder, is the top level in a hierarchical organization of goal-oriented information.

"There are a myriad of applications

DAVEY

that Syzygy can be used for," said Bill Saxon, vice president of Clearview International, Ltd., a recently formed private cable television company in Bellevue, Wash. Syzygy has a number of features that Saxon can use in developing his projects and growing his company. For example, he is installing Syzygy to track the projects involved in building cable television systems, ranging from marketing and investor contact activities to project management.

Saxon is using a planning or work outlining vehicle—a major tool within Syzygy—that helps define what needs to be done. Other tools provide feedback and tracking regarding the status of that work.

Also, Saxon and his company plan to benefit from Syzygy's ability to develop a better understanding of how things get done within a group.

"[Syzygy is] a good work planning tool," said industry commentator Dyson.

In building a database to use the product in-house, Information Research personnel asked themselves how they got work done.

"You start with a little model," said Kammeraad. "It's very much an incremental approach." For example, Kammeraad said they looked at the sales function, and organized that part of the work map by prospects and customers. Then they looked at existing customers for whom they provide technical support, and organized the data for them.

"All of that gets rolled up into one work map that gives you this overall picture or atlas of what the status of an entire group or organization is," he said. "I can boot my computer and see what's happening within Information Research through Syzygy."

"Typically, the people who are buying Syzygy are people who have a lot of projects going on simultaneously," said Kammeraad. In addition, each

participant on the project can look at the Syzygy work map and see what their role is and how it fits into the overall picture. Individuals can see their own view of the project by listing their own "to-do" list.

"Syzygy offers the efficiency of quickly monitoring, measuring and reporting the productivity of a few people or an entire organization while enhancing the true meaning of communications," said Saxon.

Many corporate Syzygy users note the reduction in meetings that need to be held. Saxon said that a meeting can be an ineffective tool compared to Syzygy. "The ability to get things done in a meeting depends on the leader's ability," he said. "Syzygy is an efficient tool compared to the inefficient tools—like meetings—that we use so often."

SAXON

Saxon was also impressed with Syzygy's built-in Gantt chart features. Professional Resource's Davey also likes that feature. He uses it to match client requirements with consultant availability.

"Because of the built-in Gantt features," said Davey, "we're able to take a look across all of our accounts and say, 'Give me a Gantt chart showing what the resource end-dates are, when a consultant will be completing an assignment and when I have a new requirement coming up.' It allows me to produce a map of all the resources and client orders and see how we can put it all together."

AN OPEN DISCUSSION

Another product designed for groups is Lotus' Notes.

"We found that communication needs fall into four categories," said Lotus' Chalstrom. "First, there are the one-to-one personal communications. This is just one person talking to another person," said Chalstrom.

He described the second category as many-to-one. This is used when

Office Automation Products Help Groups

E-mail, word processing, office environments evolving

Many early groupware products were related to office automation, electronic mail, scheduling and group authoring. While the notion of groupware is expanding, many office automation applications continue to evolve, offering increasingly valuable groupwork functions.

Office automation products supporting group-related features range from extended word processing, scheduling and activities management to broad-based environments such as IBM's OfficeVision, Hewlett-Packard's New-Wave and AT&T's Rhapsody.

NewWave from Hewlett-Packard, Cupertino, Calif., is a comprehensive office system environment that permits the integration of systems and applications from multiple vendors. It provides a consistent graphical user interface across applications, decision support features, information services and communications capabilities.

Rhapsody is a series of workflow tools that AT&T, Morristown, N.J., is making available for numerous environments, including New-Wave.

According to Esther Dyson, host of the annual PC Forum and credited with coining the term "groupware," NewWave lends itself to the groupware capabilities of Rhapsody.

"NewWave is a potential foundation for groupware," said Dyson. "Rhapsody takes NewWave and provides a tool for building workflow systems."

Dyson compared IBM's OfficeVision, an SAA-compatible family of office products, to NewWave in this context because groupware can be built on top of either. "OfficeVision has facilities for sharing information," said Dyson, "but it does not know anything about work flowing from one person to another."

Dyson points out that some of the office automation environments are group utilities, rather than tools for building groupware. "They're very useful group utilities," said Dyson, but they lack workflow features.

Vendors with standalone word processing packages are busy building

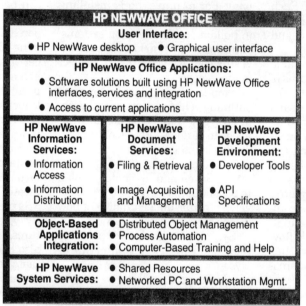

OFFICE SYSTEM INTEGRATION. *HP's NewWave office system environment allows the integration of systems and applications from multiple vendors. In addition to a user interface, NewWave includes office applications, information services, document services, development environment, object-based applications integration and system services.*

group-related functions into their software. Wordperfect Office 3.0 from WordPerfect Corporation, Orem, Utah, is an office and business automation package that provides electronic mail, calendar and scheduling services. Office 3.0 also includes a calculator, notebook, file manager, macro/program editor and menu interface.

The product provides gateway support for the Action Technologies/Novell Message Handling Service (MHS) gateway. Through MHS, Office 3.0 users can communicate with a variety of electronic-mail systems. WordPerfect Office also provides cross-platform communication between PCs and Macintosh computers.

WordPerfect Office 3.0's calendar services let users set times, descriptions and alarms for appointments. An Auto-date function helps establish repeating appointments, to-do items and memos by date and formula calculations. Personal calendars can be used to coordinate meetings. The Scheduler maintains the confidentiality of each personal calendar to display available times people may meet.

While all electronic mail is by its nature "shared," E-mail that is considered groupware has some "intelligence" and takes on a more active nature.

Dyson said, "'Intelligent' E-mail treats messages not as strings of text to be transmitted, indexed, stored and retrieved, but rather as active agents or objects that can trigger responses from other agents."

The Coordinator from Action Technologies, Alameda, Calif., is an example of "smart" electronic mail. The Coordinator integrates E-mail, individual scheduling and activities management into what the vendor calls Conversation Management. The product includes the company's MHS, which Novell incorporates into all of its LANs.

Users can classify messages in The Coordinator into categories, such as "products," "marketing" or "service," and then view and summarize their activities by category.

Dyson said she has talked to customers who found the system far more useful than they expected. "One [said the product] gradually began to replace meetings, clarifying the interactions and allowing more time for accomplishing things and

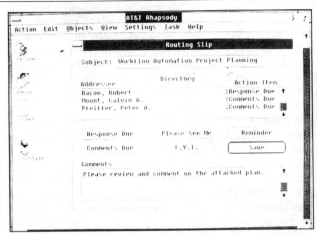

MANAGING WORKFLOW. *The Task Manager application of AT&T's Rhapsody uses workflow automation to help workgroups complete business tasks. Based on instructions provided by the user, Task Manager automatically assigns action items, distributes documents, collects comments, tracks progress against due dates and sends out reminders.*

less time for running the process."

ForComment from Access Technology, Natick, Mass., is a group document review product purchased from Broderbund Software, San Rafael, Calif. The document's author controls the master document, sets up a distribution list and establishes review deadlines. When the document is ready for review, the author sends it with the distribution list.

"ForComment gives you two windows," said Carl Schwarcz, vice president of research and development. "The top window shows the document being reviewed. The bottom window shows comments and reviews from others who have already seen the document.

"If you agree with their comments, you can indicate that, and the group can quickly move toward consensus. If you disagree, you can indicate that with the earlier comments," added Schwarcz.

WORKGROUP MOTIVATION

"The motivation for the product," Schwarcz said, "was that most of us in corporations work in groups.

"But you have to chase people around and prod them for input," he continued. "The situation gets a lot more complicated when both the East Coast and West Coast or international offices are involved."

Schwarcz said eliminating repetitive corrections is another benefit.

"When 10 people review a document, all of them may realize the liability clause is wrong," he said. If they were each reviewing their own paper copy, each one of them would take the time to note the error.

"ForComment, is intended to speed this up," he said. "Since subsequent reviewers see that the first reader indicated the problem with the liability clause, they are free to save their time for other comments."

FileNet from FileNet Corporation, Costa Mesa, Calif., incorporates group-related functions into a document-image processor. It is one of the earliest groupware systems, according to Dyson.

"FileNet," said Dyson, "combines image processing with a component called Work-Flo, that can be programmed to know who gets the image and what they do to it and who gets it next. They've sold it as image processing, not as groupware.

"And it shows one of the facets of workflow processing," she said. "That is, the system doesn't have any knowledge necessarily of the work that gets done. In this context, it doesn't understand what's in the images. However, the images are displayed to people who do understand [their] content. They fill in data fields which the system manages.

"The point is that the system understands the flow of work from one person to another, rather than the content of the work," said Dyson.

Together, from Coordination Technology, Inc. (CTI), Trumbull, Conn., is still in development. The product was designed by CTI cofounder Dr. Anatol Holt and based on the study of organized human behavior. Together uses the metaphor of a physical office. The first thing a user might see on screen is a hallway indicating different people's office doors.

The software organizes group activities into "centers" that are similar to the physical places where such activities take place.

CTI demonstrated a DOS version of Together in 1988, and showed an OS/2 version at the PC Expo in June 1990. A market version will not be available until July 1991.

"In the future," said Dyson, "I think you're going to have something like a spreadsheet for groupware.

"People will be able to design their own processes, probably using templates, forms, menus, diagrams and

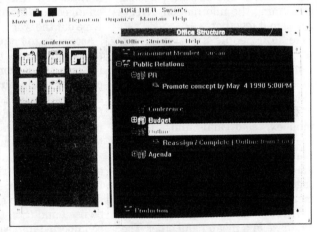

METAPHOR OF AN OFFICE. *Still in development, Together from Coordination Technology is based on a study of organized human behavior. "Look and launch" reports will display all actions and activities in an office, allowing users to view their work at a glance and check priorities.*

simple macro languages," she said. "At present, most groupware tools are at the level of financial planning languages before spreadsheets."

Dyson said it is important to have spreadsheet-level groupware development tools. "Then," she added, "individual users can define their own processes for their work-groups." ❏

—Barbara Bochenski

tracking sales or a project. Third is one-to-many—something that many people use or read. An example of this is a news feed, newspaper or even program documentation.

REACHING OUT TO MANY

"Finally, there is a many-to-many communication need," explained Chalstrom. "The source of information is many diverse people and the destination of the information is also many diverse people. And they are probably the same two sets."

According to Chalstrom, Notes is designed to solve all four problems. Giving a many-to-many example, he said there might be a group of 30 people interested in LAN technology. Since they are all on an E-mail system, they create a group distribution list. Whenever any one of them wants to say something about LAN technology, the item is sent to everyone on the distribution list.

"It's sort of an open discussion," said Chalstrom. "No one person is creating the information, no one person is consuming the information. Everyone is in it together."

He said people are simulating many-to-many communication with E-mail. However, the drawback to E-mail is that it does not order the individual messages.

"They're all jumbled together in my mailbox," said Chalstrom. "Also, if Joe sends a message on Friday and Mary sends a reply to it on Tuesday, I may have already deleted Joe's message. Therefore, Mary's reply won't mean anything to me."

With Notes, messages go into a database in a meaningful order. The message may be associated with a certain subtopic, or it may be attached as a response to a particular comment. The point is that there is organization to it.

"People are increasingly trying to do this kind of thing with E-mail and calling it computer conferencing. We do it with an organized database and call it a Notes discussion," Chalstrom explained.

According to Chalstrom, the underlying notion of Notes is a document database that is distributed.

Notes has received some criticism. For example, Notes is not strong in providing access to external mail systems. Another weakness is that it has no tool for automating big data-transfer jobs—like using terminal emulation to pull data from a mainframe.

Lotus answers this criticism by saying that Notes was not designed to provide extensive capabilities in one specific area. Rather, it was intended to answer a lot of different needs.

Notes requires a fairly powerful PC hardware/software configuration. A 286 with a couple of megabytes of RAM is considered by some as the minimum acceptable hardware platform for a Notes workstation. While the workstations can run under Windows 3.0 or OS/2, OS/2 is the better choice—and is the recommended approach for the Notes server. This need for power, however, does not seem to deter Notes' customers. (See sidebar on page 79.)

Another criticism is a potential overwriting problem. If two users on a network made simultaneous changes to a document, one could wipe out the work of the other.

According to Lotus, there are several ways to control this. For example, the original author of the document can have sole authority to make changes to the actual document. Other users would just be permitted to make comments and attach them to the original document.

"Notes was not intended as a group authoring tool," said Chalstrom. If that is needed for an application, he said that a group authoring tool can be used and then the document can be imported into Notes.

VENDORS DEFINING TERMS

As the concept of groupware expands, many vendors are referring to numerous LAN-based products as "groupware." Some vendors, however, are careful to define their terms when referring to groupware or group-facilitating capabilities.

Bruce Halverson, manager of communications and training for the Distributed Systems Division of Unisys in Blue Bell, Pa., said, "One could define groupware as PC-LAN software

that is designed to run on a LAN, as opposed to standalone software. According to that definition, all the software for the Unisys Ctos family would be considered groupware, because every application you write in a Ctos environment is network aware."

In 1988, Unisys acquired Convergent Technologies Inc., developer of the Ctos operating system.

"However, you could narrow that definition to those software components that help a group become more productive," said Halverson. "Falling into that category under Ctos would be Ctos Mail and Office Organizer, which has a calendaring and scheduling component to it. In our Unix group, we have a package called Office Procedures which allows you to route documents in a very specific fashion."

This is when Dyson's distinctions about groupware are helpful. The fact that a product can simply be used by a group of people does not make it groupware, Dyson said. It should be aware that individuals in a group are using it and help facilitate their use of the application.

Bob Pinkerton, director of marketing for Saros Corporation, a LAN software developer in Bellevue, Wash., sees the trend toward groupware as a gradual process.

He said there is a huge investment in single-user software, and that existing files and documents currently fit only into that environment. Therefore, it is prohibitive to suddenly introduce a groupware product as a replacement.

With their network-based product, Fileshare, Saros is tying single-user systems into their distributed file-server network architecture.

"Using Fileshare," said Pinkerton, "the standalone application basically becomes a network-smart application because we take care of the network back end.

"For example, when a file is opened in a word processor that was written for a single-user environment, that open command interacts with our code, which is network-smart and knows that the documents now live on a server. The save commands are

Groupware Grows on Users

Notes gaining fans at Price Waterhouse

"We can't install Notes as fast as people want it," said Sheldon Laube, national director of information technology for Price Waterhouse in New York. Notes is a groupware product from Lotus Development Corporation, Cambridge, Mass.

Price Waterhouse plans to increase Notes usage from the current 2,000 users to as many as 13,000 within the next two years.

"Notes is transforming the way we do business," he said. "We use Notes in a variety of ways, but the real value of Notes, to us, is in sharing—on a global basis—information that our professionals need to serve their clients.

"We use Notes as our information repository," he explained. "It is turning into a corporate knowledge bank. People around the world are using it to store, retrieve and manage practice information."

Practice information is the term Price Waterhouse uses for opinions, letters, memos, proposals, contracts, hot tips, news items and other pieces of information that have to do with the firm's professional business.

"This has given us tremendous value in being able to share information as solutions are developed anywhere in the globe," said Laube.

"You can think of Notes as a conferencing bulletin board system," he said. "It's different from E-mail, because with E-mail you send something to someone and it just sits there. It's not broadcast, either. With broadcast, you send it to a lot of people. We don't want to send something to specific people. We want to make it available for a lot of people to see."

Instead of checking a mailbox filled with messages, Notes users can look up what they need "in a retrieval sort of way," according to Laube. "That is much more effective for people to use."

With a bulletin board system, Laube explained, people who may not be on a distribution list can access the information. Readers can also attach comments to a document without altering the original.

Notes maintains various catalogs of databases. There are also subject, word and category searches available. "Using Notes views, you can get multiple indices into the data," said Laube.

Price Waterhouse intends to have the entire firm using Notes. The firm is also installing copies of Notes within some clients' offices, "so they can tap into our expertise directly," said Laube.

For example, clients will be able to access a customer support database for a software product that Price Waterhouse sells to help customers do corporate tax returns. The entire customer service system is done in Notes.

"Customers can put in bug reports after checking to see if someone has already reported that bug." They can also get bulletins on the latest software releases, Laube explained. He said Price Waterhouse uses Notes to respond to requests for help with the software and refers other customers to that tip.

New releases of the software are put on the bulletin board, and customers can download them to their own equipment.

Laube said the firm is continually finding new uses for Notes.

"The beauty of it is that the various people participating can be anywhere in the world. You can have a 'virtual team' serve a client," he said.

"People in our company are extremely enthusiastic about Notes," said Laube. "It is giving our people a much broader range of expertise than might have been available to them otherwise. It is definitely helping our professionals serve their clients better," he said.❑

—*Barbara Bochenski*

intercepted the same way. The user does not have to be aware of any of this. However, they are now able to use files across the whole network."

Halverson believes it is important to find ways to introduce sharing and groupware functions into existing applications to preserve the current software investment.

FOUNDATION FOR GROUPWARE

Dyson said, "Fileshare enables a lot of people to share files over a network and is frequently a foundation for groupware. Someone can write routines about who gets what files and how they might move through the organization."

Some interesting perspectives on the changing definition of groupware come from Dr. Richard Hackathorn, vice president of technology for Micro Decisionware, Inc., of Boulder, Colo.

"Workgroups will be the critical architectural element of information systems in the 1990s," he said. Hackathorn defines a workgroup as a group of persons whose workflow is tightly coupled. The workgroup may or may not be the same as an organizational unit, such as a department.

"Workgroup computing will replace end-user computing as a focus for the enterprise," he said. A workgroup manager will develop local databases and workgroup applications. "The sharing of information across the enterprise will be the most critical function for supporting workgroups," said Hackathorn.

"LAN server-based systems are becoming the intra-workgroup mechanism for data sharing," he said. "However, workgroups are isolated in the enterprise. They are LAN-locked."

He said enterprises will encounter problems deploying LAN-based workgroup technology, unless users have easy access to data outside their workgroup and MIS can manage data across the corporation.

John Quinlan, president of Micro Decisionware, said, "A majority of large companies' MIS directors are recognizing these facts and are working now to accommodate the future reality."■

PROGRAMMER PERFORMANCE AND THE EFFECTS OF THE WORKPLACE

Tom DeMarco and Tim Lister

The Atlantic Systems Guild
353 W. 12th Street
New York, NY 10014 USA

Abstract

Wide variation in programmer performance has been frequently reported in the literature [1, 2, 3]. In the absence of other explanation, most managers have come to accept that the variation is due to individual characteristics. The presumption that there are order-of-magnitude differences in individual performance makes accurate cost projection seem nearly impossible.

In an extensive study, 166 programmers from 35 different organizations, participated in a one-day implementation benchmarking exercise. While there were wide variations across the sample, we found evidence that characteristics of the workplace and of the organization seemed to explain a significant part of the difference.

Keywords: Management Issues, Productivity, Programmer Workplace.

1. Introduction

It is common wisdom that there is a huge variation in individual performance rates among programmers. Sackman, Erikson and Grant [1], for example, reported differences of as much as 25:1 in the time required for a given programming task. Boehm [2] reported that the cost driver derived from individual characteristics of team members was nearly twice as large as the second largest driver. And Augustine [3] observed that more than 50% of the work is typically done by 20% of the people.

While most programmers and managers accept that there are such variations, few have any idea where they themselves stand on the performance scale. Evidence that a particular person performed in the upper ten percentile across the industry would lead to elation; placement in the lower 10 percentile would lead to despondency — *but neither would cause great surprise.* Software developers (and the organizations they work for) remain largely ignorant of their own capacities.

The issue of performance variation is further complicated by the suspicion that high and low performers tend to cluster in different organizations. In [4], Putnam indicated success in ascribing a *technology factor* to organizations in order to explain their varying capacity. The technology factor was empirically derived, based on past performance. Once set for an organization, it was surprisingly constant across different projects and different teams. The usefulness of Putnam's technology factor implies that the wide differences in performance may be more a function of corporate culture and the workplace than of inherent individuality.

If there are large differences between organizations, managers cannot afford to remain ignorant of where they stand. If the differences can be even partially explained by remediable characteristics of the environment and the workplace, then those characteristics deserve to be a major focus of our productivity improvement effort.

2. The Coding War Games: A Public Benchmarking Exercise

The 1984 Coding War Games were conceived as an opportunity for individuals to find out how they performed relative to a sample of their peers. A further objective was to test hypotheses about the effect of the workplace.

The exercise was run according to the scheme of [5] as an open competition. Each organization submitted one or more competition pairs, each pair made up of two volunteer implementors. The two members of each pair performed the same one-day implementation task, working to the same specification. They were encouraged to compete with each other as well as with the rest of the sample. They worked at their own workspace (office, cubicle, terminal room, etc.), during normal working hours. They used the normal languages, machines and development facilities provided by their organizations. The two members of each pair worked in the same language and used the same support environment.

A total of 166 programmers from 35 organizations participated in the 1984 games. Characteristics of the participants are described in Figures 1 and 2.

The exercise was implementation of a program to a rigid specification. The program involved syntactic and semantic edits on an input stream of calendar dates, followed by computation of day-intervals between specified dates as much as 8 centuries apart. The average program built in compliance with this specification was 220 lines long. Two thirds of the programs were between 133 and 297 lines in length. The average COBOL program was 237 lines. The specification called for on-line operation, but there was an alternative for batch operation which was used by approximately 5% of the pairs.

The project was organized in such a way that there were two well-defined milestones: 1) Clean compile/ready for test, and 2) All work complete. The entire sample was divided at the beginning into two "rounds." Both rounds used the same exercise, but they used slightly variant test procedures. Round One programmers did no testing on their own code; each coder completed and desk-checked his/her program and, after producing an acceptable clean compile, then gave it to the other pair member to test. Round Two programmers ran the exercise with the more familiar procedure of coding and then testing their own code. Because the different testing approaches gave a slightly different meaning to the Milestone 1, data from the two rounds was compiled separately. Round One was composed of the first 100 entrants.

After programmers had completed their own testing, they ran a pre-set acceptance test provided in sealed form with the instruction kit. The acceptance test consisted of ten sample inputs. Participants recorded the outputs on a form which was returned to the organizers for analysis. The acceptance tests were designed to measure coherency, accuracy, precision, robustness and edit efficiency of the programs.

Reprinted from *Proceedings of the 8th Int'l Conf. Software Engineering*, 1985, pp. 268-272. Copyright © 1985 by The Institute of Electrical and Electronics Engineers, Inc. All rights reserved.

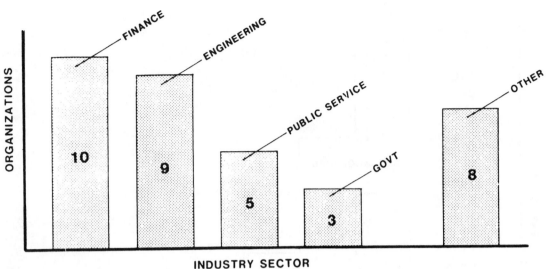

Figure 1. Participants by Industry Sector

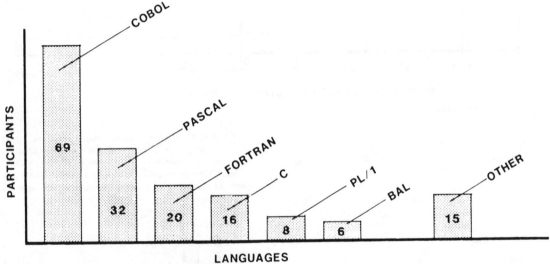

Figure 2. Participants by Language

During the exercise, participants kept rigorous track of time spent. They noted periods of work, type of work, periods of interruption and nature of each interruption. All this time data was recorded on a form supplied and returned to the organizers.

Each participant filled out an extensive questionnaire designed to determine measurable characteristics of the workplace and environment as well as the individual's subjective attitude toward these factors.

3. Programmer Performance Across the Sample

Figure 3 shows how participants performed (how much work time they used) in reaching Milestone 1. There is indeed a considerable difference across the sample: The variation from best to worst is a factor of 5.6 to 1. Average performance was 2.1 times slower than the best. The half above the median outperformed the half below the median by 1.9 to one.

While variation over the entire group was pronounced, there was very little variation within each pair. Consider these results:

● The overall fastest performer was paired with the second fastest.
● The overall slowest performer was paired with the second slowest.
● Of the thirteen participants that did not finish the exercise, all but three were paired with other non-finishers.

The two members of each pair were arbitrarily coded Red and Blue at the beginning of the exercise. The performance of one pair member turned out to be a strong predictor of the performance of the other. This is shown in Figure 4, where Red performance is plotted against Blue. Each point on the graph represents one pair's joint performance. (The x-coordinate gives Blue and the y-coordinate gives Red.) A point on the 45 degree line would indicate a pair in which the two participants performed identically. The correlation coefficient between Red and Blue performance was 0.79.

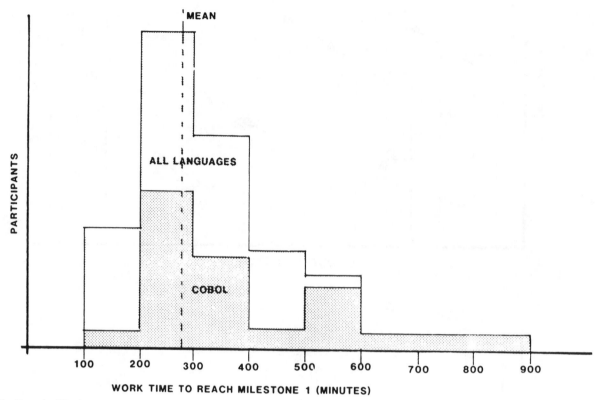

Figure 3. Spread of Performance

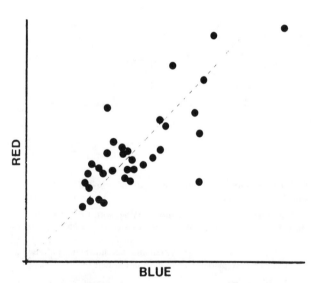

Figure 4. Correlation Between Teammates (Round One Data)

The marked grouping of points around the 45 degree line suggests that characteristics of the workplace and corporate culture (which are constant for the two members of each pair) may explain much of the overall variation in programmer performance. The difference within a pair is an indication of truly individual performance capacity. For the average pair in the sample, the difference between the two performers was a factor of 1.21 to one. For 80% of the pairs, performance of the two members was within 34% of each other.

Figure 5 shows the quality of the resultant programs as judged by a sample of five key acceptance tests. Though they were not allowed to debug their programs at all, more than one third of Round One participants produced a program that passed the major tests of coherency, functionality and accuracy on its first run.

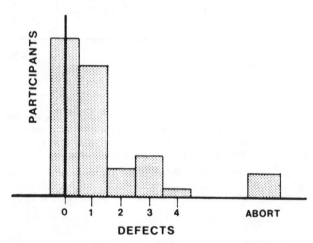

Figure 5. Spread of Defect Counts

Figure 6 shows the relationship (actually, the lack of relationship) between time to reach the milestone and number of defects. There appeared to be no quality penalty for rapid performance: Faster than median performers had fewer defects than slower than median performers, and those who performed in the top 25% in terms of time to reach the milestone had an average defect density 30% lower than that of the rest of the sample.

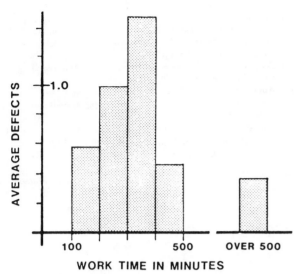

Figure 6. Speed vs. Defects

4. Characteristics of the Programmer Workplace

It may be impossible to quantify the illusive concept of "corporate culture," and difficult to improve it substantially. But this need not be true of the programmer's workplace and its surrounding environment. In this section, we shall set out observed characteristics of the workplace and in the next section we shall show how such characteristics were correlated to performance.

The environmental questionnaire that each participant filled out asked for both objective data about the workplace (how much space, what provisions for privacy etc.) and subjective assessment by the participant ("Does your office space make you feel appreciated?"). From data taken from all 160 respondents, the following picture emerges of the prototypical programmer workplace:

PROGRAMMER WORKPLACE
(AVERAGES FROM THE SAMPLE)

Dedicated space:	63 square feet
Enclosure:	cubicle walls (78%)
Cubicle height:	5 feet
Dedicated terminal:	60%

There were substantial variations in these characteristics across the sample. Figure 7, for example, shows the variation in dedicated floor space.

A rather grim picture of the workplace emerges from the subjective assessments by participants:

QUESTION	PERCENT OF RESPONDENTS
Is your workplace acceptably quiet?	58% No
Is there sufficient privacy?	61% No
Do people often interrupt you needlessly?	62% Yes
Is it difficult or impossible to work effectively in your workplace from 9-5?	41% Yes
Does your workplace make you feel appreciated?	51% No
Is your workplace at work as pleasant as your workplace at home?	54% No

Reading through the respondents' free-form comments about the environment is a distressing experience. Many programmers appear to be continually frustrated in attempts to work. They are plagued by noise and interruption, and pessimistic that the situation will ever be improved. The data recorded about actual interruptions supports the view that the so-called "work-day" is made up largely of frustration time. Reproduced below is a portion of one typical time-sheet from the exercise:

WORK PERIOD FROM – TO	TYPE OF WORK	WHAT INTERRUPTION CAUSED THE END OF THIS WORK PERIOD?
2:13 - 2:17	Coding	Phone call
2:20 - 2:23	Coding	Boss stopped in to chat
2:26 - 2:29	Coding	Question from colleague
2:31 - 2:39	Coding	Phone call
2:41 - 2:44	Coding	Phone call

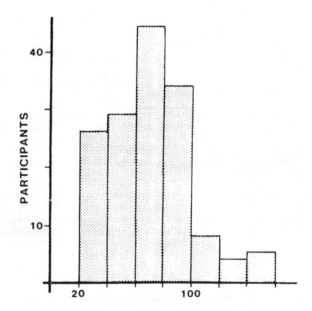

DEDICATED SPACE
(SQUARE FEET / PERSON)

Figure 7. Variation of Dedicated Floor Space

5. Effects of the Environment on Performance

In order to detect any correlation between environment and performance, we divided the set of finishers into four groups based on performance. Average performance of those in the upper 25% was 2.6 times better than that of those in the lower 25%. We then compared environmental factors recorded by the top 25% of performers to those of the lower 25%. A sample of results is presented below:

ENVIRONMENTAL FACTOR	TOP 25%	BOTTOM 25%	ALL
Dedicated floor space	78 sqft.	46 sqft.	63 sqft.
Acceptably quiet workspace	57% yes	29% yes	42% yes
Acceptably private workspace	62% yes	19% yes	39% yes
Can you silence your phone?	52% yes	10% yes	29% yes
Can you divert your calls?	76% yes	19% yes	57% yes
Do people often interrupt you needlessly?	38% yes	76% yes	62% yes
Does your workspace make you feel appreciated?	57% yes	29% yes	45% yes

We concluded that the two groups work in significantly different environments. The top performers are in fairly generous space that manages to protect them from at least some distractions. The telephone interruption problem has been addressed to the point that most people know their phones will be picked up by a clerical worker if ignored. The space is relatively pleasant and a culture of interrupt consciousness has evolved. People have relatively long periods of interrupt-free work.

The bottom 25% work in tiny cubicles — eight of this group reported dedicated space of 40 square feet or less! The phones ring until answered and cannot be diverted. There is little or no interrupt consciousness, with managers among the worst offenders. (One participant wrote, "My boss switches his secretary's phone to me when she's out.") People are forced to work in short periods of time between interrupts.

There is a danger here of confusing cause and effect. We have implied, for instance, that better (quieter) workspace may result in higher productivity. But it may be that high productivity has been rewarded by more floor space. Hence the best performers may have gravitated naturally to the more commodious and thus quieter space. To investigate this possibility, we analyzed three organizations that had submitted nine or more teams each. Within each of these organizations we found little or no variation in the main environmental factors. The best performers from each of the companies worked in more or less the same floor space and same noise level as the worst performers.

As a further control, one organization had 18 programmers take part in the exercise, working in their normal workplace while another six worked in a specially contrived "clean room" environment, free from most interruptions and noise. The clean room group out-performed their peers by 40% in the time required to reach the milestone.

Whether a better workplace causes higher productivity or higher productivity workers gravitate toward organizations with a better workplace should be of little concern to the software manager. Either argues for more concentration on the physical environment in which programmers (try to) work.

6. Summary: The Case for Improving the Programmer Workplace

In spite of widespread productivity consciousness, our industry has tended to ignore the effect of the workplace. The typical productivity manager considers changes to the physical characteristics of the workplace to be outside his/her charter. Our findings imply that the productivity charter should be widened: Environmental factors such as noise, privacy and interruptibility may be keys to substantial productivity improvement. For example, changing the workplace at a given company from that of typical of a "lower-25% performer" to that of an "upper-25% performer" offers the potential of a 2.6 to one improvement in the time to perform a complex programming activity.

REFERENCES

[1] Sackman, H., W.J. Erikson and E.E Grant. Exploratory Experimental Studies Comparing Online and Offline Programming Performance." *Communications of the ACM*, Vol. 11, No.1 (January, 1968), pp 3-11.

[2] Boehm, B.W. *Software Engineering Economics*. Englewood Cliffs, N.J.: Prentice-Hall, 1981.

[3] Augustine, N.R. "Augustine's Laws and Major System Development Programs." *Defense Systems Management Review, 1979*, pp 50-76.

[4] Putnam, L.H. "A General Empirical Solution to the Macro Software Sizing and Estimating Problem." *IEEE Transactions on Software Engineering*, Vol. SE-4, No. 4, July 1978, pp 345-361.

[5] DeMarco, T. *Controlling Software Projects: Management, Measurement and Estimation*. New York: Yourdon Press, 1982.

Motivating IS Personnel

BY J. DANIEL COUGER

"There is a critical need to motivate not only the top performers but all employees, particularly in an environment of stabilizing growth, slower promotion, and increased levels of maintenance of older systems."

As the computer industry matures, a growing concern for IS executives is the need to maintain motivation. This is indicated by the quote above, which was culled from a nationwide study of IS chiefs at 80 companies that set out to determine the key human resources issues that concern IS executives for the future. Among other concerns expressed in the survey are the needs to develop better measures of performance, to define skill requirements for the future IS environment, and to prepare a strategy for transferring IS tasks to users.

Some of the things that used to provide natural motivation are no longer present in the industry. Time was when people with computer skills were scarce, and they earned high salaries and rapid promotions. Today, with growth stabilizing, salary increases are moderating and promotions come more slowly.

Ten years ago, DATAMATION published the results of several studies concerning IS professionals and motivation. Robert Zawacki and I conducted one of these studies, which focused on what job factors made IS professionals' jobs meaningful for them (see "What Motivates Dp Professionals," Sept. 1978, p. 116). Our study was based on the core job dimension theory of motivation, which was developed by Richard Hackman of Yale University and Greg R. Oldham of the University of Illinois.

Another study examined the psychological factors characteristic of IS professionals and what motivated them (see "Who is the Dp Professional?" Sept. 1978, p. 125), and was based on the two-factor theory of motivation developed by academic researcher Fred Herzberg in the 1950s. Herzberg's two-factor theory of motivation separated job motivators from job demotivators, thereby establishing a variety of factors that influence a worker's sense of satisfaction. These include the work itself, opportunity for achievement, opportunity for advancement, pay and benefits, recognition, increased responsibility, quality of supervision, interpersonal relations, job security, work conditions, and company policies (see "A Decade's Difference").

With the passage of 10 years and all the attendant changes in the IS world, I undertook to repeat these studies. Some things changed very little, others showed significant differences. The findings dovetail in an interesting way with the motivational concerns of IS executives.

Most seminars on motivation tend to focus on how to "psyche up" employees—that is, how to motivate them externally. But, at best, such an approach deals with symptoms, not causes. The results of my most recent study of 1,800 analysts and programmers, however, hold good news for managers: the number one motivating factor for IS personnel is the work itself.

Today's IS workers don't need a cheerleader—you can concentrate on improving their jobs instead.

Sound easier said than done? Not necessarily. A systematic approach to improving the job using the core job theory of motivation has been successful in the IS departments at a variety of companies, including Hartford Insurance Co., IBM, Standard Oil, Owens Corning Fiberglass, the U.S. Labor Department, and the City of Colorado Springs.

What Motivates Workers

The job core theory was arrived at by Hackman and Oldham after analyzing 30 job variables. They found that the five job variables most sensitive to motivation were skill variety, task identity, task significance, autonomy, and feedback from the job itself (see "Core Job Theory Model of Motivation"). In other words, these are the aspects of the work itself found to be most important in motivating workers.

The presence of these five key variables contributes to an employee's feeling of meaningfulness from his work, responsibility for its outcome, and knowledge of the results of his work. Thus, by addressing these factors, you can enhance a job's motivating potential.

Maintenance work may represent the most difficult job enhancement challenge facing IS managers. It has been called "an uninteresting, necessary evil," but in most IS departments it consumes more than 50% of the labor budget and that percentage is growing each year as new applications are implemented. It is interesting to note that many companies have sought to improve motivation of maintenance personnel by changing the name of the activity. One company has even adopted the title retrofit engineer for this work.

Such a palliative merely attempts to disguise the symptom—it does not address its cause. A new title will motivate maintenance workers for only a day or so, because the work itself has not changed. The nature of the job must be enhanced to increase motivation.

By using the framework of the five core job dimensions, maintenance work can be analyzed for ways of enhancing it:

Skill variety. Assign a variety of tasks where use of skills is constrained by the design of the system being maintained.

Task identity. Identify how the modules being maintained relate to the system as a whole and how that system relates to the company's set of systems. Also, making it possible to complete the whole maintenance task—from user interaction to producing workable code—will enhance task identity.

Task significance. Provide maintenance personnel with an opportunity to work directly with users in order to recognize the importance of their work.

Autonomy. Mutually set goals with maintenance personnel, then allow them to accomplish the work without close supervision.

Feedback from the job. Establish mechanisms to enable employees to track their progress.

Periodic analysis of a job to ensure that it maintains its challenge will ensure that motivation is sufficient to the level of productivity you desire. Much depends, however, on who holds the job—not every worker needs the same degree of growth and challenge. Employees with high growth needs want "rich" jobs, that is, jobs that fulfill the five core job dimensions to a high degree.

Employees' growth needs can be determined by evaluating the degree to which they are goal-oriented, ambitious, capable of perspective (able to separate the important from the less important), interested in further education/training, self-starters, internally motivated, confident, in need of recognition, assertive, inquisitive, and systematic.

An employee's need for social inter-

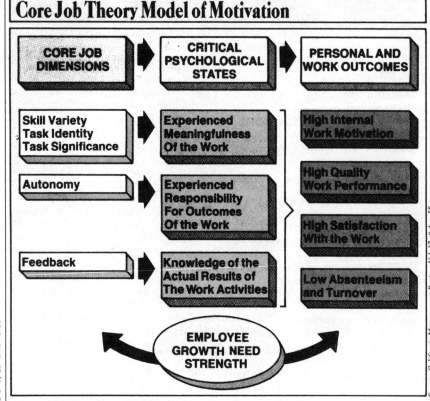

Core Job Theory Model of Motivation

CORE JOB DIMENSIONS	CRITICAL PSYCHOLOGICAL STATES	PERSONAL AND WORK OUTCOMES
Skill Variety / Task Identity / Task Significance	Experienced Meaningfulness Of the Work	High Internal Work Motivation
Autonomy	Experienced Responsibility For Outcomes Of the Work	High Quality Work Performance
Feedback	Knowledge of the Actual Results of The Work Activities	High Satisfaction With the Work
		Low Absenteeism and Turnover

EMPLOYEE GROWTH NEED STRENGTH

Source: California Management Review, Vol. 17, # 4, p. 58.

Chart by Catherine Francis

action is another significant characteristic. In 1978, our research revealed that analysts and programmers had a low need for social interaction, although they had a high need for growth. In fact, their growth needs were higher and their social needs were lower than any of the 500 occupations measured by Hackman and Oldham (they did not survey IS occupations). Their social need strength was only 4.2 on a scale of seven, compared with 5.5 for most other occupations. My continuing research on other job types within the computer field shows the social need to be equally low for all professional computer job types. Perhaps this factor is one reason for ill-defined requirements for applications. People with less need for interaction will not naturally seek contact with users as much as people with a higher social need.

For example, network designers have a social need strength that is no higher than that of software engineers and AI designers. Although it is rare for social need to change, people can change their behavior. When employees perceive they need to acquire such interactive skills, they are motivated to do well in training courses on group dynamics and communication.

Motivation Is Harder for Big Companies

Research has shown that big companies have greater difficulty in motivation than smaller companies. When a company has more than 200 analysts and programmers, managers must work harder to keep the job's motivating potential at a proper level. Not only are the project teams larger, there are more levels of management through which to communicate. There is a negative effect on all five job dimensions. Providing task identity—relating an individual's work to the whole—is more difficult when personnel are several levels away from top management and where they are not in as close contact with the user. The same is true for task significance and feedback. Big companies tend to have more policies and procedures, reducing the feeling of autonomy on the part of the employee. Often, the jobs are more specialized, reducing skill variety.

Executives at larger companies are recognizing this problem and have acted to counter it by formal training on motivation. A number of seminar offerings are available on this topic. However, in evaluating those offerings, you should ensure that a substantial amount of seminar time is devoted to techniques for analyzing the job's motivating potential (in the framework of the five core job dimensions) and to techniques to determine the strength of employee need to grow.

Using this approach, managers can ensure that jobs are matched to individual employee growth need. It doesn't take an inordinate amount of time—in fact, when measured against the potential for improvement of productivity, the time investment is quite small. Thereafter, the analysis would be required every six months or so, or whenever the job changes or a different employee is assigned. ■

J. Daniel Couger is distinguished professor of computer and management science at the University of Colorado.

Empowerment: The Catchword of the '90s

A leader's guide to establishing empowerment in organizations

by Wayne C. Shannon

IN RECENT YEARS, THE WORD "EMPOWERment" has come alive in business organizations committed to a participative climate and a quality improvement culture. The more organizations have become involved in employee participation, the more I've been asked for a clearer definition of empowerment and some helpful hints on how to make it happen. Empowerment, like quality, has about as many definitions as there are users of the term. Like we've learned with quality, if you want to make empowerment happen, you have to agree on a common definition. My definition is "the personal potential of employees and the cultural climate for employees to co-create a workplace they personally believe in and thrive in."

Let's break this definition into its parts. Empowerment:
- is the function of two variables: potential and opportunity.
- is the process of people working together to co-create quality of work life and work output.
- touches us at our core, allowing us to co-create something we personally believe in.

Empowerment's variables

Let's look at the variables: potential and opportunity. Potential means your ability to choose certain empowering behaviors in your daily routine. When you do these things, you maximize your personal potential to feel and be empowered to the degree that you can bring about that reality from the inside out. There are five potentials:

1. Being positive. You have a choice. You create your own reality. Being negative is self-defeating (you don't get what you want, or if you do, it's at a great price). Being positive is self-affirming and the odds work in favor of win-win outcomes.

2. Being proactive. Are you a fan in the stands or on the playing field? Where do you want to be? Watching the parade or in the parade? Are you part of the problem or part of the solution? Do you fix the blame or fix the problem? It's all a matter of taking full responsibility for yourself, your job, and your career.

3. Being participative. Very simply, cooperate internally and compete externally. Be a team player and a contributor.

4. Being productive. This means doing the right things and doing things right. As a manager, you want to have goals and not mistake sheer activity for desired results.

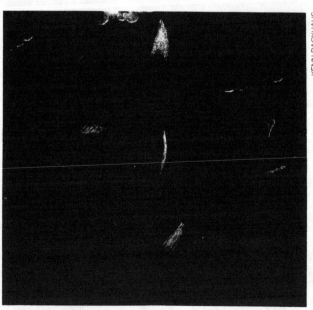

KENN BACKHAUS

5. Being a pioneer. As a leader, you have to show the way by taking risks, being a continuous learner, allowing yourself and others to fail, and moving outside your comfort zone and being vulnerable.

What these five potentials boil down to, as discussed by Peter Block in his book *The Empowered Manager*, is seeing yourself as a force for change and improvement and behaving accordingly. Block goes on to say, "It's easy and seductive at times to experience a sense of pessimism about the organization ever becoming the kind of place we wish it to be. It seems that other people and forces are driving the business, not us, and that our survival is, in fact, in someone else's hands. How do we go about changing a culture that involves thousands of people, most of whom, from a distance, seem quite satisfied with things the way they are?"

On the other hand, if not the leaders of an organization, who can promote full empowerment for employees? I believe Marvin Weisbord put it best in his book *Productive Workplaces* when he said "Changing our workplace is inevitably bound up with changing ourselves."

As a leader, do you model the five potentials and encourage these behaviors in others? The potential is in each of us. It is like a seed ready to be planted in soil—the soil is the organizational climate that you can create and sustain.

The second variable of empowerment is opportunity. Five opportunities have to occur before empowerment can take place. These opportunities are guides for relating to your employees:

1. Talk with employees. Communicate *and* listen. Encourage two-way, honest, open, frequent communication. The more informed employees are, the more secure and motivated they will be.

2. Train employees. An empowering culture is built on the bedrock of continuing education in every form imaginable. If an employee doesn't know what to do, how to do it right, or most important, why it is done a certain way and what difference it makes, don't expect him to feel or act empowered.

3. Team employees. No one has found a technological alternative to cooperation when it comes to building a positive work climate. Teams promote cooperation and raise the concept to a higher level. Some might call it synergy. I call it co-creation. Teams make it possible for people to participate in decision making and implementation that directly affects them. Teams help all members of the organization feel responsible for co-creating a workplace they can believe in and thrive in.

4. Trust employees. Believe in the process of co-creating. It is a very powerful organizational motivator. Support team decisions even if they aren't the outcomes you had in mind. Trust teams with information and allow them to fail. Encourage a team approach to every problem-solving effort. Trust teams to care about the welfare of the company. The results will amaze you and far surpass your expectations.

5. Thank employees. Find people doing things right. Recognize efforts as well as results by finding ways to frequently and creatively say thank you. Share the glory in every way possible. Give frequent specific performance feedback (good news as well as bad).

Potential setbacks

You might, at some point, discover an empowered person in an unempowered workplace (good seed, unhealthy soil). You can also have a disempowered person in an empowered workplace (unhealthy seed, good soil). But when people step up to their self-empowering potential and their company works hard to create the most supportive environment for empowerment, the combination is dynamic and powerful.

Some have defined luck as those occasions when preparation and opportunity meet; i.e., luck is not a function of chance, but of intent. Similarly, full empowerment is a function of developed potential and environmental support. In other words, when fully realized potential meets fully supportive opportunity, you have an empowered work force and workplace.

The leader's role

To reiterate, leaders have to be concerned with empowerment. They have to measure up to the five potentials and act as a model for employees, encouraging them to model themselves after the five potentials too. Leaders also have to create an environment in which the five opportunities can exist.

There is no magical way for leaders to empower themselves and others. It all boils down to simple behavioral changes. When they are in place and working, there is a magical consequence—the co-creation of organizations and workplaces we can all believe in.

Bibliography

Block, Peter, *The Empowered Manager* (San Francisco, CA: Jossey-Bass Inc., 1987).

Weisbord, Marvin R., *Productive Workplaces* (San Francisco, CA: Jossey-Bass Inc., 1987).

Wayne C. Shannon is a senior consultant in quality improvement systems for Dobbs International Services, Inc., Memphis, TN. He has a master's degree in counseling/personnel services from Memphis State University, TN. Shannon is a member of ASQC.

Management Delegation Myths and the Paradox of Task Assignment

Stephen C. Bushardt, David L. Duhon, and Aubrey R. Fowler, Jr.

The delegation process is an integral part of the manager's job. In Peter Drucker's classic definition, management is defined as "accomplishing tasks through others." The delegation process involves assigning tasks to others, providing them with the authority needed to execute those tasks, and then holding them accountable for the results. In delegating, it is generally recognized that authority can be passed from one managerial level down to another but that managers do not, thereby, reduce their own accountability. Managers remain responsible for their own actions and the actions of their subordinates. Others have referred to this phenomenon as "the principle of absoluteness of responsibility" (Koontz and O'Donnel 1976). The idea that a superior cannot escape, through delegation, responsibility for the activity of subordinates is fundamental to the theory of delegation, at least as taught in our business schools and espoused in our textbooks.

The other major tenet of effective delegation is the idea that authority must be delegated commensurate with the responsibility to be exacted. This has been referred to as the "principle of parity of authority and responsibility" (Koontz and O'Donnel 1976). Simply stated, it means one must have enough authority to carry out the job for which one will be held responsible.

The purpose of this article is to examine these two myths and their transference from the theory of management to the practice of management as parts of the delegation process. Both concepts are integral to the theory of delegation and are often repeated by practicing managers as part of the "Holy Grail" of effective management. However, both myths have little substance with regard to the practice of management, at least

among American managers.

Assigning tasks to others appears to be the most straightforward component of the delegation process. Unfortunately, assigning tasks is enmeshed in a paradox of conflicting anticipations by managers and subordinates with respect to needs and expectations. A reexamination of the delegation process is particularly relevant today as environmental uncertainty increases and more organizations adopt a decentralized structure.

> To get the most out of its employees, management must learn to put aside its myths and solve its paradoxes.

MYTH #1: AUTHORITY = RESPONSIBILITY

The "principle of parity of authority and responsibility" receives a prominent place in the management literature but only lip service by most practicing managers. The reality is that most managers are charged with responsibility while lacking the authority needed to carry it out. For example, supervisors are responsible for managing their employees, obtaining productivity from them, ensuring a reasonable level of turnover and absenteeism, and acting as the initial contact in employee grievances and complaints. However, most supervisors have no authority over hiring and little over dismissal. This function is performed by the personnel department or by managers higher in the organization. Supervisors generally have little authority over

Reprinted from *Business Horizons*, March/April 1991, pages 37-43. Copyright © 1991 by the Foundation for the School of Business at Indiana University. Used with permission.

subordinates' wages or benefits, and even work assignments are often specified in the union contract and work rules or by personnel procedures.

The reality of responsibility exceeding authority is not limited to supervisory level personnel; it is common throughout the management hierarchy. For example, the marketing manager is responsible for developing a highly effective marketing program for a company's product. The reality is that the marketing manager generally has limited input into product design, little control of product quality, and a limited advertising budget. However, once the product is introduced into the market, the marketing manager may very well be held responsible if the product fails.

Similar discrepancies between authority and responsibility exist throughout organizations. Evidence suggests that the gap between responsibility and authority tends to increase as one ascends the hierarchy. The higher one's level in the organization, the more responsibility one is charged with relative to the authority that one is granted.

An example from the American political experience serves to illustrate. The President is

given the responsibility for maintaining a healthy U.S. economy. However, he actually has little authority or control over what happens to the economy during his tenure in office. He has only indirect authority over money supply and interest rates. While responsible for government spending, he must share authority with Congress over programs and budgets. This gap between responsibility and authority has been particularly frustrating to more than one occupant of the Oval Office. President Jimmy Carter could do little to control the runaway inflation and double-digit unemployment he encountered. Even though his party was in control of the executive and legislative branches, his authority as "President" allowed him to do little. Nevertheless, voters held him personally accountable on election day in 1980.

Bushardt, Fowler, and Fuselier (1988) suggest that the violation of the "parity of responsibility and authority" tends to enhance organizational effectiveness, rather than detract from it. They suggest that effective managers meet their responsibility with limited authority by using personal power to fill the "gap." Personal power assumes the form of expertise, charisma, persuasion, obligation, and membership in informal groups. The reliance on personal power to meet responsibility offers a number of benefits to the organization that would be unavailable if the "principle of parity of responsibility" were actually used in practice.

When managers rely on personal power to meet responsibility, they are encouraged to develop their skills at communication, interpersonal relations, leadership, and basic management, thereby encouraging employee development. The process also provides a form of job enrichment by converting a routine job into one that is challenging and leads to opportunities for subordinates to exercise their creative abilities. Furthermore, since the gap between authority and responsibility increases as one ascends the hierarchy, it gives lower-level managers an opportunity to hone their skills in preparation for greater challenges and helps higher management identify those ready for promotion.

Another primary benefit of not following the principle of "parity of responsibility and authority" is hierarchical integration. The process fosters cooperation between individuals and groups as the interdependency of organizational responsibilities is brought down to a personal level. The process of creating personal power encourages managers to develop an understanding of the problems of others and a willingness to assist others in return for the assistance they receive. The result is a greater understanding of the organization as a whole and an organization that can more quickly respond to environmental change. The creation of personal power to meet responsibility is an important means by which organic organizations achieve integration.

Jimmy Carter's inability to get Congress, the Federal Reserve, and the bureaucracy to move to correct economic problems can be contrasted to Ronald Reagan's uncanny ability to accomplish much of his agenda. Both had the same amount of authority (in fact, Carter may have had more since the Democratic Party controlled Congress), yet Reagan was much more successful. The main difference between the two presidents involved the ability to use personal power and communication skills to meet the responsibility gap and make up for the lack of real authority.

MYTH #2: THE ABSOLUTENESS OF RESPONSIBILITY

The principle of "the absoluteness of responsibility" is touted as an unshakable tenet of leadership. Under this principle, when a task is delegated to another, the original delegator remains responsible for the task as responsibility can not be delegated. When del-

egating a task, managers, at least in theory, do not reduce their own accountability. Top management remains accountable for all actions taken by subordinates and in turn the subordinates are also accountable. This is much more myth than reality as practiced by current American management. More often than not, managers refuse to take responsibility for actions of subordinates if such action is severely detrimental to the image of the organization or the career of the manager.

Managers and politicians are fond of saying, "I take full responsibility," while in reality they are taking evasive action to assure that they are not held accountable. Numerous examples of this "passing the buck" phenomenon can be cited, but three prominent cases illustrate our point.

No one is sure exactly what happened at My Lai during the Vietnam War. However, the result of the investigation was that Lieutenant William Calley was held personally accountable and higher-level officers in large part avoided responsibility. Accountability was basically limited to the lowest-level manager with authority. Higher-level officers were quick to attempt to distance themselves from the actions of the soldiers and Lt. Calley.

In 1988 Texaco paid Pennzoil $3 billion to settle the Getty Oil lawsuit. Pennzoil had been awarded $11 billion by the courts because of Texaco's illegal interference with Pennzoil's attempts to purchase Getty Oil. Texaco's loss of the lawsuit, and subsequent appeals of the largest settlement in history, led to settlement out of court. Texaco's poor decisions in this episode led to the sale of billions of dollars worth of assets, a reduction of business activity, loss of revenues, stockholder lawsuits, a tarnished image, and even bankruptcy for a period. However, not a single member of Texaco's management team was fired or otherwise penalized for the debacle. Texaco's consistent management position was that they did nothing wrong and therefore had nothing for which to apologize. However, their decisions almost led to the loss of the entire company.

In the case of the recent oil spill in Alaska, the responsibility has tended to center on the captain of the Exxon ship, the Valdez. Exxon CEO Lawrence Rawl, while agreeing to pay the tab where necessary, has essentially avoided personal accountability. In an interview with *Fortune* in May he said, "I've felt personally very responsible for doing everything that I can—and I can do a heck of a lot within this company. One is to make sure that we do all that is humanly possible to get this thing cleaned up promptly. It's our problem the ship was on the rock. It's our problem the oil was spilled" (Nulty, 1989). The firm as a collective "our" is responsible, not the CEO as the one with authority. It seems as though CEO Rawls feels responsible for the cleanup but not as responsible for the actual accident. The ship's captain, in the American tradition, has attempted to fix responsibility and accountability on the unlicensed mate who was actually on the bridge and piloting the ship. As we follow the outcome of this tragic episode, it is quite probable that ultimate blame and responsibility will be placed and end with the lowest level of authority possible, in this case Captain Joseph Hazelwood. His attempt to pass along the blame to one of his subordinates will probably not succeed.

In common parlance, the phenomenon is often known as passing the buck. Regrettably, in the U.S. this phrase has become synonymous with the delegation process. The level of accountability tends to be directly proportional to the distance one is from the front lines. Apparently, this phenomenon is far more characteristic of the American management culture than the Japanese or Korean management culture. Three examples illustrate this point.

In August 1985 a Japan Air Lines 747 jumbo jet crashed into a mountain and 520 people perished. The primary cause of the accident was the rupture of the aft pressure bulkhead, which disabled all steering controls. After the crash investigation, Boeing issued an official statement admitting that repairs it had made on the bulkhead were faulty and that the failure of the bulkhead was the immediate cause of the crash. Boeing suggested, however, that the fault of the crash was more properly the failure of JAL to properly inspect Boeing's repair, and the pilot's inappropriate response to the emergency. Soon after the crash the following events occurred.

1. Yasumoto Takagi, JAL's president at the time of the crash, resigned as a symbol of sorrow.

2. JAL subsequently suffered a 10 percent drop in business. Tokuo Yamashita, head of the Japanese Ministry of Transportation, lost his job because of it. (JAL is partly Government owned.)

3. Susumu Yamaji, Takagi's successor at JAL, also resigned because of JAL's poor performance.

4. A Ministry of Transportation safety inspector who had inspected Boeing's repair committed suicide.

5. A JAL employee assigned to aid victims' families committed suicide.

6. Boeing's CEO, T.A. Wilson, sent personally signed letters of apology to each of the families. (McDermott, 1987)

Another example in Japan involved a young sumo wrestler who struck his teacher. The young sumo wrestler was held accountable for his actions by being moved back a step in the rankings, and the teacher was held accountable for his student breaking decorum by being fined.

The sumo wrestling board who held the others accountable felt responsible as well and reduced their own pay for several months.

Finally, during the Seoul Olympics in 1988, the Korean Boxing Federation was terribly embarrassed by the actions of one of its boxers and some of the Federation's officials. Protesting an apparently poor decision, a Korean boxer refused to leave the ring for several hours after his loss. His handler and a Federation official physically accosted the referee and judge and had to be restrained. Quite a melee broke out and Olympic boxing was disrupted for several hours. Kim Seung-Youn, President of the Korean Amateur Boxing Federation, resigned in embarrassment over the incident. The principle of the absoluteness of responsibility was followed.

Contrast this event with the frequent misadventures in American collegiate athletics in which those in charge seem not to feel any sense of responsibility for a player's behavior. For instance, recently it almost took an act of the Oklahoma legislature to get the Oklahoma Sooner's football coach Barry Switzer to resign. Despite the fact that his program was on NCAA probation, players had been convicted of criminal acts, and his quarterback had just been picked up for drug distribution, Coach Switzer maintained he was only the coach and should not be held responsible for the personal actions of a few of his players. In fact, when he finally resigned he still did not accept responsibility for his program's problems, but said it was because he was tired of all the hassle associated with denying and avoiding responsibility. In the United States, accountability tends to be exacted at the lowest level the general public and the stakeholders will allow— and avoided if at all possible.

In summary, then, Myth 1 states that authority and responsibility should be equal, and Myth 2 states that responsibility is absolute, that it cannot be passed on to others. These myths are not rigorously followed in the real world of managers and subordinates (particularly in the United States). Less obviously, there is a relationship between these myths and their application. In essence, organizations create jobs in which there is greater responsibility than authority but—possibly in recognition of the theoretical unfairness of that situation—choose not to hold responsible job holders accountable for their failures.

If we view responsibility as an a priori obligation to perform and accountability as a post priori evaluation of and reaction to performance quality, then we find that the reality of responsibility in both magnitude and absoluteness is much more nebulous than theory suggests. In reality the managerial network operates such that responsibility where performance is acceptable is sticky; it adheres to those who have the a priori obligation to manage that performance. However, where performance is weak or unacceptable, responsibility loses adhesion and slides down the hierarchy to the lowest possible level of accountability. In practice individuals are quick to accept praise for jobs well done while passing on blame for poor performance. Organizations accept this reality rather than giving their members sufficient authority to carry out responsibilities that would then necessitate strict accountability for both successes and failures.

THE PARADOX OF TASK ASSIGNMENT

In addition to Myths 1 and 2, managers must also learn to deal with a paradox associated with the delegation of authority to subordinates enabling them to carry out their responsibilities. Delegation involves assigning tasks to subordinates and generally depends on a contingency approach. Others suggest that specificity in assigning tasks depends on the nature of each task, the subordinates' level of development, and the leaders' capabilities (Koontz and O'Donnel, 1976). Hersey and Blanchard (1972) in their life cycle approach to leadership suggest that task specificity by the leader should be contingent on the followers' task-relevant maturity, defined as their willingness to do and knowledge about the task. In essence, the leader should specify the expected results for individuals who have low maturity levels and tend to be the low performers. On the other hand, the leader should use broad policies and guidelines for individuals with high maturity who are high performers. The use of ambiguity for these individuals allows them to use their creativity and produce results that exceed the demands placed on them by the manager. A manager who is supervising a number of employees is likely to specify tasks appropriate for the average subordinate—which provides the higher performer a lower standard than he or she would have set for him or herself.

Employees are likely to bring a very different perspective to the delegation process. David McClelland (1961), in his need theory of motivation, suggests that individuals with a high need to achieve prefer specific goals as a means of receiving feedback on their performance. Individuals with a low need to achieve tend not to place the same value on the goals. This suggests that the high performers are likely to prefer a higher level of specificity in the task assignment relative to low performers in job-related situations. The preferred task structure by high performers is likely to center on expected outcomes as opposed to specifics of how to do the task.

The process can be viewed from a behavioral perspective. The high performer is seeking a positive reinforcer. Specificity is the clearest path

Figure
Specificity Versus Ambiguity: Conflicting Expectation

to that goal. On the other hand, low performers are hoping to avoid negative outcomes as opposed to seeking positive outcomes. A low performer can successfully avoid negative outcomes by either working under ambiguous task expectations or increasing performance. Barring some positive incentive to perform at a higher level, the easier alternative is to work under ambiguous expectations, making the judgement of performance less precise and in all likelihood less rigorous.

The **Figure** illustrates the paradox of delegation. This paradox results from the rational behavior of both subordinates and managers pursuing their own best interests. High-performing subordinates are likely to prefer that the results be specified because of their confidence in exceeding the manager's expectations. The high-performing subordinates are likely to impose higher standards of performance on themselves than would the manager. From this standpoint the manager may serve his interest best through the use of ambiguity. The low performer is likely to prefer that results be nonspecific or ambiguous, as this allows a greater probability of escaping accountability. To prevent the low performers from escaping accountability and to ensure at least some minimum of performance, the manager should specify his expectations. This phenomenon is likely to be more noticeable in situations where rewards are directly tied to performance. High performers would prefer specific performance standards, confident of their ability to meet and exceed those standards and therefore guarantee receipt of rewards. Low performers would prefer less specific standards so they might maintain eligibility for rewards on subjective evaluation not directly associated with their productivity.

As is the case with any paradox, this one can create confusion on the part of those affected by it. Therefore, it is important that the paradox be reduced or eliminated to create congruency between superior and subordinate expectations. A reduction of the paradox with regard to high-level performers comes through the application of Maslow's higher order needs concept to employee expectations (Maslow 1968). In essence, we need to ask why the employee would prefer specific standards given the relationship of such standards to the employee's satisfaction of needs. At the peak of Maslow's needs hierarchy is the need for self actualization, with the need for esteem immediately below it. If the employee is motivated primarily by esteem needs, the paradox would hold: the meeting of specific performance standards would provide a clear measure of performance allowing others to recognize the employee's personal achievements and providing a clear basis for a feeling of achievement. However, if the primary motivation for the employee were the satisfaction of the need for self actualization, which theoretically doesn't occur until esteem is satisfied, the employee would be much more likely to accept nonspecific expectations, allowing greater opportunity for personal growth and self fulfillment as the employee is allowed to define the boundaries and expectations associated with job performance.

Therefore, if managers of high-performing employees would first concentrate on the employees' esteem-related needs by deferring their desire for ambiguity and providing specific objectives, the employees would soon satisfy those needs and be ready for a relaxation of specificity as the need for self actualization begins to dominate. Regarding the Hersey/Blanchard life cycle approach to leadership, managers should utilize an SIII style for high performing employees desiring specific task assignments, with a gradual change to less specificity and an SIV style as the employees' task-related maturity increases. This eventually reduces and may completely eliminate the paradox.

The theory of needs hierarchy also is applicable to employees' exhibiting lower performance levels. Here, the conflict is between needs related to the middle of that hierarchy. The lower performers recognize that they may be involuntarily separated from the organization, thereby interrupting the satisfaction of their needs for security and affiliation. Since there may be obvious reasons for such separation where clear, specific performance standards are established, the weaker employee would prefer greater ambiguity in standards with a resulting decrease in separation threat. To help alleviate this part of the paradox a manager should be specific at a level clearly within the weak performer's capability. Thus, job security and the related failure to satisfy the need for affiliation are not threatened. In addition, there should be an ascending scale of performance standards that offers progressively greater rewards and addresses the esteem needs of employees. As time passes and the employee gains confidence and shows improvement in performance, the minimum standard can be raised, not as a threat to continued employment, but to avoid the employee's backsliding to lower productivity levels. The employee, realizing that performance is possible, should not feel threatened by increased minimums. In effect, the manager is moving from an SI to an SII leadership style for less productive, less mature employees within the life cycle approach to leadership.

It is also beneficial to recognize the linkage between the paradox and the myths previously discussed. High performers recognize that a more specific assignment is likely to carry more specific authority, thereby helping equate authority to responsibility and avoiding imbalance problems. Managers of high performers, on the other hand, may recognize the beneficial impact of the imbalance on employee development and, confident of the high performer's abilities, prefer to use ambiguity with its uncertain authority to induce greater breadth and rapidity in employee development.

Conversely, poorer performers uncertain of their ability to succeed may wish to avoid clear authority and therefore prefer ambiguous assignments. This allows them greater opportunity to excuse their performance by claiming lack of authority and therefore lessened accountability.

High performers can accept specific responsibility without undue concern for being held accountable for failure, since they do not expect to fail. Poorer performers, however, do not expect to succeed and would therefore prefer ambiguity so responsibility is unclear and the likelihood of being held accountable is reduced. High performers focus on the rewards accruing from success; low performers focus on the penalties associated with failure to succeed. Generally it is easier to succeed where standards are specific and harder to fail where standards are non-specific.

Management, whether at the supervisory or strategic level, is a difficult and challenging activity. As the management profession builds a theoretical base upon which to develop a better understanding of the practice of management, it is wise to note that even the most logical, highly developed, and widely accepted theoretical constructs are, at best, representations of reality rather than reality itself. This paper has explored several examples, both myth and paradox, where theory and reality differ and where theory conflicts with itself. The astute reader is likely to recognize other instances where such differences occur. A major key to effective management is recognizing the value of understanding theory and its limitations while operating in the world of reality. ❐

References

J. Arnow, "W.L. Lyons Brown, Jr.: Chairman & CEO, Brown Form, Inc." *Sky Magazine*, September 1984, p. 48.

A.G. Bedeian, *Management* (New York: Holt, Rinehart and Winston, Inc., 1986).

S.C. Bushardt, A. Fowler, Jr., and E.P. Fuselier, "Delegation, Authority, and Responsibility: The Myth and the Reality," *Akron Business and Economic Review*, *19*, 1 (1988): 71-78.

D. Caruth and T. Pressley, "Key Factors in Positive Delegation," *Supervisory Management*, July 1984, pp. 6-11.

T.B. Green, "Communications: Some Uncoventional Thoughts on Understanding Behavior," *Academy of Management Journal*, *16*, 3 (1973): 525-526.

R.W. Griffin, *Management* (Boston: Houghton Mifflin Co., 1984).

E. Gustkey, "Boxing Ends Where it Began: In Controversy," *Los Angeles Times*, October 2, 1988.

P. Hersey and K.H. Blanchard, *Management of Organizational Behavior: Utilizing Human Resources* (Englewood Cliffs, N.J.: Prentice-Hall, 1972).

R.J. House, "A Path-Goal Theory of Leader Effectiveness," *Administrative Services Quarterly*, September 1971, pp. 321-338.

Alexander Kendrick, *The Wound Within* (Boston: Little-Brown & Co., 1974).

H. Koontz and C. O'Donnell, *Management: A Systems and Contingency Analysis of Managerial Functions* (New York: McGraw-Hill, 1976).

R. Maidment, "Ten Reasons Why Managers Need to Know More About Delegation," *Supervisory Management*, August 1984, pp. 8-11.

A.H. Maslow, *Toward a Psychology of Being* (New York: Van Nostrud, 1968).

D.C. McClelland, *The Achieving Society* (Princeton, NJ.: Van Nostrand, 1961).

T. McDermott, "Boeing, JAL Wage Court Battle Over 'Blame' for Crash of 747," *Seattle Times*, April 9, 1987.

P. Nulty, "The Future of Big Oil," *Fortune*, May 8, 1989, pp. 46-50.

G.R. Salancik and J. Pfeffer, "Who Gets Power—And How They Hold On To It: A Strategic-Contingency Model of Power," *Organizational Dynamics*, Winter 1977, pp. 3-21.

S. Savary, "Ineffective Delegation: Symptom or Problem," *Supervisory Management*, June 1985, pp. 27-33.

A.E. Schwartz, "The Why, What, and to Whom of Delegation," *Management Solutions*, June 1987, pp. 31-38.

S. Sherman, "Who's in Charge at Texaco Now," *Fortune*, January 16, 1989, pp. 68-74.

W.B. Sherwood, "Developing Subordinates: Critical to Managers and their Organizations," *Personnel*, January-February 1983, pp. 46-52.

R. Telander and R. Sullivan, "You Reap What You Sow," *Sports Illustrated*, February 27, 1989, pp. 20-26.

Stephen C. Bushardt is a professor of management, and **David L. Duhon** is an assistant professor of management, both at the University of Southern Mississippi, Hattiesburg. **Aubrey R. Fowler, Jr.** is a visiting professor of management at Murray State University, Kentucky.

Chapter 8
Visibility and Control

Design engineers will fiddle and tinker forever. If you let them alone, you are guaranteed to have schedule slippages and cost problems. Nothing will come out of the end of the pipe unless you push it out.

— J. Ronald Fox, *Arming America*

Overview

Control is the process of making things happen in an ordered manner or according to plan. The basic control process involves setting standards, measuring performance against these standards, identifying deviations, and taking corrective action. Control requires managers to take action at the right times, so things get done when they are supposed to. Feedback from the control process points out what action is needed and when. New or adjusted plans may be warranted, as situations dictate, to deal with antiquated plans.

This chapter provides eight papers on the subjects of visibility and control. It touches on the topics of software inspections, configuration management, quality assurance, and software verification and validation. It describes how we can use the considerable progress we have made in these fields to improve process, product, and project control.

This chapter is closely aligned with Chapter 9 on risk management and Chapter 10 on metrics and measurement. While these techniques contribute to control, they are disciplines of their own regard, worthy of separate coverage. That is why we have treated them separately.

The first paper, by Rook, is a survey article on project control. It sets the stage for the articles that follow by discussing background, motivation, and industry trends relative to management control. It introduces the reader to the topics of configuration management, quality assurance, verification and validation, and metrics and measurement, and describes how they can be used to improve visibility and control throughout the life cycle. It discusses the relationships between planning, estimation, measurement, and control. It emphasizes that software is manageable and that there are techniques that can be used to improve the probability of being successful. It stresses the need for quantification and for contingency planning. It is thorough and upbeat in its coverage of this important topic.

The next two papers talk about software configuration management. The first paper, by Bersoff, is a tutorial that describes the four basic elements of configuration management: configuration identification, change control, status accounting, and configuration audit. This paper was included because it clearly and concisely summarizes the fundamentals of configuration management. The second paper, by Bersoff and Davis, is more profound. It investigates the impact of different life cycle models on the processes we use to control changes to product baselines. It is perceptive in its observations. It suggests changes that need to be made to deal with new life cycle paradigms and development methods. The advanced manager will appreciate the insight it provides, especially in the areas of rapid prototyping and spiral development.

The fourth and fifth papers focus on the topic of software quality assurance. The paper by Frewin and Hatton investigates two ways to improve software quality. The first approach concentrates on specifying, measuring, and demonstrating quality. It requires you to specify and plan your quality program. The second approach is testing. Collecting, analyzing, recording, and using error data provide the feedback you need to determine whether you are realizing your specified quality goals.

The next paper, by Hon, examines Bellcore's buyer quality assurance program. It explains what Bellcore did to ensure that its telecommunications products meet the expectations and needs of its client base. The article focuses on measurement and minimizing defects. Its metrics approach and orientation are close to the consumer.

The next two papers talk about software inspections. In the first paper, Ackerman, Buchwald, and Lewski describe what an inspection is and contrast it with other forms of reviews (walk-throughs, peer reviews, etc.). The paper was selected because it stresses basics and is tutorial in nature. The second paper, by Russell, describes how Bell-Northern Research used inspections to find critical errors early in an ultralarge software development. This paper concludes that although inspections are labor intensive, their ability to remove software defects efficiently makes them very worthwhile.

The final paper, by Wallace and Fujii, discusses software verification and validation. This tutorial explains what "V&V" is all about, why it is done, when it is done, and what it does for you and *to* you. As with inspections, the costs of verification and validation are justified by their potential to eliminate costly defects early in the life cycle.

The paper makes an effort to introduce the reader to tools and techniques used as verification and validation are applied in practice.

References

The text that stands out on the topic of project control was authored by DeMarco (Reference 6 in the Bibliography). The Berlack book (Reference 1) on software configuration management is a useful basic text, as are the Schulmeyer books on software quality (References 26 and 27). Whitgift (Reference 32) should be consulted if you need software tools to put configuration management concepts into action. The Freedman and Weinberg book on walk-throughs and other forms of reviews (Reference 9) is a classic, as is Youll's book on making software development activities visible (Reference 33).

Controlling software projects

by Paul Rook

"Controlling Software Projects," by P. Rook from *Software Engineering Journal*, Vol. 1, No. 1, Jan. 1986, pages 7-16. Copyright © 1986 Institution of Electrical Engineers, reprinted with permission.

In recent years the software industry has seen the increasing imposition of structure and discipline on technical development activities in an attempt to improve the efficiency of software development and the reliability of the software produced. The clear emphasis in the modern approach to software engineering is to focus attention on the overall development process and the co-ordination of all aspects of software development. This paper examines the principles of managing and successfully controlling software development from a software engineering basis.

1 Introduction

The management of a large software development is a complex and intrinsically difficult task: a large software system is itself very complex and its production may involve hundreds of man-years of skilled effort with correspondingly large budgets.

Nearly every software development project is faced with numerous difficulties. When a project is successful it is not because there were no problems but because the problems were overcome. Many of the problems are technical but often the critical ones are managerial. Software development depends on documentation and communication — it is only structured if a structure is imposed and controlled. Everything that is done right in software development is done early — there is very little opportunity for catching up when things are discovered to be going wrong later in the development.

There is much discussion about comparisons between managing software development and managing hardware development. There are genuine differences between hardware and software, as follows:

- Software has no physical appearance.
- Few software quality metrics exist.
- Software has much higher complexity than hardware.
- It is deceptively easy to introduce changes into software.
- Effects of software change propagate explosively.
- Software includes data as well as logic.
- Software development makes very little use of pre-existing components.

However, in many important ways software development is like hardware development and ought to be managed and controlled using very similar techniques to those used in hardware engineering development. The genuine dissimilarities listed above are the very factors which make an engineering approach much more critical for software development.

Contributing to the difficulties of software management is the much publicised view of the programmer as the unbridled genius, whose creative process will be stifled by any of the recommended project management controls, design standards and programming standards.

Forced to contend with this view is the software manager, often a recently promoted analyst or programmer who has worked on projects managed as a collection of creative artists doing their independent thing. Management's job in these projects was to try, somehow, to steer this collection of individualists in a common direction so that their products would accomplish the project goals, be able to interface with each other, be finished within the project cost and schedule constraints, and, with a little luck, come reasonably close to accomplishing what the customer had in mind for the software. Such a software manager has been well grounded in how a project should not be managed, but has had little exposure or training in the use of effective software management techniques.

2 Structuring software development

To tackle these problems, the software industry has seen the increasing imposition of discipline on technical development activities in an attempt to improve the reliability of software development. Thus we have seen, in turn, the techniques of structured programming, structured design and structured analysis.

Structured programming provides rules for choosing the building blocks for programs. Structured design helps the designer to distinguish between good and bad designs. Structured analysis assists in the production of a specification that is correct and consistent and can be determined to be complete. The introduction in turn of each of these three techniques has thrown up problems which have been introduced through lack of discipline in the earlier stages of the development process.

In addition to this stage by stage attack on the problems of development, it is clear that all activities will have problems unless the goals of each activity are clearly stated and set within the context of the structure for the whole project.

The clear emphasis in the modern approach to software engineering is to focus attention on the overall development process. This is the aim of structured software development, which breaks down the project into a series of distinct phases, each with well defined goals, the achievement of which can be verified, ensuring a sound foundation for the succeeding phase. It also breaks down the work to be performed into a series of discrete manageable packages, and creates the basis for the appropriate organisational structure. This allows overall planning of 'how' the software is going to be developed as well as considering 'what' is going to be developed as the product.

3 Computer-based tools

An equally important development has been the introduction of computer-based tools to assist with specific tasks. The earliest tools were concerned with the production of code. These have been followed by tools which assist, for example, specification, design, estimating, planning, documentation and configuration management. In fact tools are now available to support most of the software development activities.

The right tools assist in increasing productivity and visibility of work achieved, provide a source of data for future proposal preparation, estimation and project planning, and maintain continuity between projects. They also provide automated testing and reduce iteration of work and thus aid improved quality. Tools are especially useful in detecting errors early, when they are less expensive to correct, thus leading to a more successful software project and product.

Although tools alone will not ensure success, the selection and installation of the right set of tools is seen to be necessary for an effective software development project.

4 The management of complexity

Thus the key to the management of the complex task of large software development is twofold:

• reducing complexity by imposing a structure on to the process
• using computer-based tools to make the remaining complexity more tractable.

5 Software development methodology

In planning how to develop the software, it is the responsibility of project management to ensure that a coherent system of methods and tools is chosen, integrated and supported.

However, differences in organisation structures, applications and existing approaches make it impractical to prescribe a single scheme that can be universally followed. Methods, tools, management practices or any other element of the total development environment cannot be chosen without considering each element in its relationship to the other parts of the development system.

Software engineering has introduced the term 'software development meth-

odology' to describe a systematic set of procedures followed from the original conception of a system through the specification, design, implementation, operation and evolution of the software in that system. A methodology not only includes technical methods to assist in the critical tasks of problem solving, documentation, analysis, design, coding, testing and configuration management, but also includes management procedures to control the development process and the deployment of the technical methods.

The management and technical aspects of the methodology support and gain strength from each other: the technical methods provide the basis needed for effective managerial control, while the management procedures provide the organisation and resources which enable the technical development to proceed effectively. Tools support the methodology and provide the information needed by project management.

6 Project control

The software development process is inherently subject to risks which are manifested as financial failures (time scale overrun, budget overrun) and technical failures (failure to meet requirements, over/under-engineered). The sources of risk can be placed in three main categories:

• perturbations (requirement changes, detection of problems, errors and failures)
• personnel (wrong people available, too many/too few people available)
• project environment (undefined methodology, unknown quality, errors

detected late, inadequate control, technical skill, support and visibility).

If the project is to be successful, then potential risks must be identified, and eliminated or controlled. A control system for a project is based on the usual principle of establishing suitable feedback loop(s) to ensure that the controlled system is oriented to its objective. The objective of a software development project is to produce the correct product on time and to budget.

Fig. 1 illustrates, in a simplified form, a project control system for software development. Technical development is what is controlled and project management is the controller. Estimating is a prerequisite for control, and a number of feedback loops are set up which operate via status and progress reports to compare actual progress with the plans based on the estimates.

The feedback loops operate directly from the technical development and also from the quality and configuration management systems. Fig. 1 illustrates a continuous process, as indicated by the inner product loop of feedback of intermediate development products to the activities of technical development. The quality and configuration management systems operate continuously in the development process, not only on the products finally delivered to the customer.

While the inner loop represents the work on the product, the outer feedback loops represent the basis for control. Control consists of obtaining information to make decisions and ensuring timely detection and correction of errors, thus controlling time scale and budget and minimising technical risks.

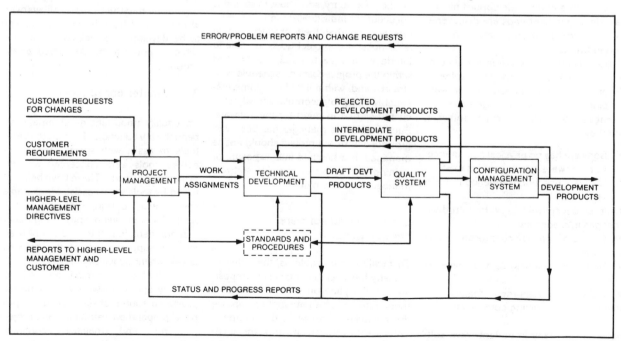

Fig. 1 Basic operation of a project control system

The upper control loops represent inevitable paths for changes, which the project manager must control through appropriate procedures, such as a change control board. The lower control loops represent the monitoring system established by the project manager to obtain information on which to make decisions and to be able to check that the consequences of those decisions are carried through and have the intended effects.

For the project to be successfully controlled the lower control loops must dominate the upper control loops. This is achieved by establishing sufficient strength in the lower loops and also by constraining the upper loops.

The operation of project control illustrated in Fig. 1 depends on an organisation with clearly defined responsibilities and disciplines related to the four functions shown — project management, technical development, quality system and configuration management system.

7 Project management

The establishment of the project environment, obtaining the personnel and dealing with perturbations (see the sources of risk listed in the previous Section) are the responsibility of the project manager. The responsibility also includes the software development methodology used on the project. In some cases a standard methodology will be available, together with the appropriate support

facilities. In other cases the project manager will have to select and establish a methodology specifically for the project. In either event, project management has the final responsibility of ensuring (or confirming) the suitability of the methodology for the project and defining precisely the details of its application.

Software development techniques such as formal specification, structured design, stepwise refinement, structured programming and correctness proofs are examples of progress in software engineering in recent years. These techniques, together with documentation standards, test methods, and configuration management and quality assurance procedures, address elements of the software development process.

The methods selected must be matched to the characteristics of the development, the imposed schedules and other operational considerations. Once selected, the methods must be implemented and controlled.

However, careful selection of software development techniques does not in itself guarantee success. Success or failure is primarily determined by the approach to project management. No matter how sophisticated the design and programming techniques, a systematic approach to project management is essential.

Project management deals with planning, defining and assigning the work to the technical development teams, monitoring status and progress, making decisions, re-planning and reporting on

the project to higher-level management and the customer.

Fig. 2 shows project management, expanded from the single box of Fig. 1, as a set of interacting processes. While the diagram is rather simplistic it does illustrate the fact that control of the project depends on the quality of information that these processes generate and the use made of it.

7.1 Decision making

The most important aspect of project management consists of making decisions (or ensuring that decisions are made), which includes making sure that timely technical decisions are made on the product as well as making the more obvious project decisions. Responsibility for decisions rests with the project manager. While he can, and must, appropriately delegate authority and decision making, he cannot avoid ultimate responsibility for customer relationship, specification, correctness of design and implementation, quality, use of allocated resources and staff, meeting time scale and budget, standards and procedures, anticipation and resolution of problems and ultimate delivery and acceptance of the product.

7.2 Planning

The planning process includes the activities of planning, scheduling, budgeting and defining milestones. This is based

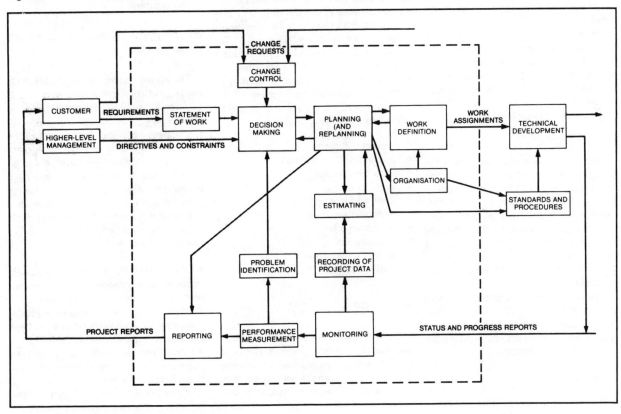

Fig. 2 The processes of project management

349

on the work breakdown structure (WBS) produced by the work definition process. It depends on estimating, with reference to the recorded project database derived from previous projects (and earlier stages of the current project), and, of course, is based on the input of the customer or system requirements and management constraints.

The project manager produces a project plan (to be publicly viewed and reviewed), which shows estimates, deliverable inter-relationships and timing dependencies, and the allocation of resources to produce deliverables. It is accompanied by definition of the project organisation and the standards and procedures to be used in technical development.

It is important for the project plan to be dynamic. Through the normal processes of iterative analysis, design and implementation changes, resource problems, customer or environment changes and estimation errors, the project plan will require updating and revision. Storable copies of each version of the project plan should be kept in the project history file together with the reasons for revision.

7.3 Work definition

The work definition process relies on a method of doing the work in order to be able to define the detailed work packages (the lowest level of the WBS) which are the basis for the planning process. For software development this is based on the tasks defined by the matrix of activities and phases of the life cycle model shown in Fig. 5.

These work packages define a series of products for project work and management. The WBS not only requires management and customer concurrence on the specification of the product but also requires agreement on the methodology to be used for the project.

7.4 Monitoring

The monitoring process involves measuring actual performance and handling minor schedule and resource requirements revisions that can be accommodated by the team. This process is also related to quality assurance through technical reviews and walkthroughs, and is used to maintain the project data file, which provides updated information for estimating.

Based on written reports and meetings, the monitoring process involves evaluation of expected progress in deliverables against actual progress and provides the basis for project reporting.

7.5 Reporting

The reporting process stores, analyses and filters information of project progress fed to it by the monitoring process. It compares actual with expected performance, and yields relevant information for the project teams, management and customer.

The project manager reviews the status, progress and problems identified as a foundation for decisions, which closes the loop of internal project control.

There is also an outer loop which depends on reports to the customer and higher-level management.

The information for management should be a filtered subset of the information needed by the project manager when tracking progress within the project. The information needed by management is to answer the questions: 'Is the project on schedule?', and if not, 'Can the team handle the schedule stoppage within its own area of responsibility, or does management need to do something to help the project return to an in-control state?'

The information on measured achievement must be presented effectively to management and the customer so that project progress can be approved at critical points and the correct decisions made.

8 The life cycle model

In order to structure the software development project it is necessary to define the development process — in other words, to adopt some model of the process as an expansion of the technical development function shown in Fig. 1. A model which defines phases in the development of a software product is referred to in software engineering as a 'life cycle model'.

There are numerous life cycle models in use and described in the literature, the specific phases and names varying in detail from one model to another.

Any modern model should be easy to relate to the following phases:

- project initiation
- requirement specification
- structural design
- detailed design
- code and unit test
- integration and test
- acceptance test
- maintenance
- project termination
- product phase-out.

8.1 Baselines

Each development phase is defined in terms of its outputs, or product. The products of each phase represent the points along the development path where there is a clear change in emphasis, where one definition of the emerging product is established and is used as the basis for the next derived definition. As such, they are the natural milestones of the development progression and offer objective visibility into that progression.

To transform this visibility into effective management control, a software development methodology based on the life cycle model uses the concept of baselines. A 'baseline' established at any stage in the development process is a set of information constituting the definition of the product at that stage.

The completion of each phase is determined by the satisfactory review of the defined products of that phase by development personnel, other project and company experts and, in many cases, customer and user personnel. These products then form the baseline for the work in the next phase. The products of the next phase are then measured and verified against previous baselines before themselves forming a new baseline. In this way confidence in project progress is progressively built on successive baselines.

The process is illustrated in the form of a V-diagram in Fig. 3. In this diagram the rectangular boxes represent the phases and the oval boxes represent the baselines. The form of the diagram shows the symmetry between the successive decomposition of the design and the building of the product by successive stages of integration and test. Each design phase is verified against the previous baseline. Each integration phase is verified against the corresponding design or specification baseline on the other side of the diagram.

8.2 Practical application of the life cycle model

The above description of the life cycle model and its representation in Fig. 3 could be interpreted as suggesting that no phase can be considered complete, and the following phases started, until all the prescribed documents have been completed to specified standards. Although the intended rigour of such an approach is commendable, it is quite unrealistic to interpret the life cycle model in such a simplistic way, particularly on large-scale software developments. For example, in a real software project:

- Exploratory work on a subsequent phase is usually required before the current phase can be completed (for example, design investigation is almost invariably required before it can be stated that a user requirement can be met).
- Problems encountered in a later phase may involve re-working the products of earlier phases — failure to recognise this leads to earlier documentation becoming inaccurate and misleading.
- The user's perceived requirement

may not remain constant during a protracted software development process, and it may be necessary to consider changed requirements and consequent design changes during later phases.

● The project plan may call for incremental development, with different increments of the product in different phases of development.

The concept of distinct phases of software development, representing the achievement of certain defined states in the development of the product, can be regarded as a device, imposed by project management to cope with complexity and improve visibility.

In practice, on a large-scale project, the precise breakpoints between the project phases are not easy to define clearly and depend to some extent on project management decision. Because completely rigid phase control is impractical, status and risk analysis at milestones is particularly important. This can only be obtained from a system of technical reviews.

However, once this reality is recognised, it does not lead to the conclusion that the life cycle model is impractical. Having escaped the simplistic interpretation, the life cycle model does represent a realistic recognition of what is actually involved in the technical work of software development.

Phases do indeed have to be imposed by project management; they will not happen of their own accord. The definitions and concepts in the life cycle model represent the best current understanding of software development methodology — gained from experience in applying software engineering to development projects.

These definitions are the worked-out basis for real control of software development, but that control has to be explicitly planned, based on an implemented methodology actually used by the development staff, and actually applied. It does not happen naturally, as is apparent from the response from some projects that the life cycle model does not correspond to reality. Project management has to *make* its version of the life cycle model realistic.

8.3 Software development life cycle phases

Listed below are the baseline outputs of each phase of the software development life cycle:

● *Project initiation phase:* A validated system architecture, founded on a design study with basic hardware-software allocations, and an approved concept of operation including basic human-machine allocations. A top-level project

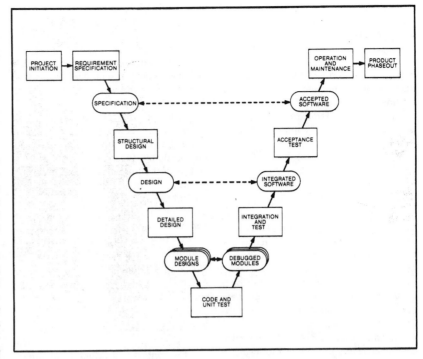

Fig. 3 The stages in software development confidence

plan, with milestones, resources, responsibilities, schedules and major activities. Defined standards and procedures.
● *Requirement specification phase:* A complete, validated specification of the required functions, interfaces and performance for the software product. A detailed project plan.
● *Structural design phase:* A complete, verified specification of the overall hardware-software architecture, control structure and data structure for the software product, along with such other necessary components as draft user's manuals and test plans.
● *Detailed design phase:* A complete, verified specification of the control structure, data structure, interface relations, sizing, key algorithms and assumptions for each program component.
● *Code and unit test phase:* A complete, verified set of program components.
● *Integration and test phase:* A properly functioning software product.
● *Software acceptance test phase:* An accepted software product handed over to the customer.
● *Maintenance phase:* A fully functioning update of the software product. This goal is repeated for each update, which follows the complete development sequence each time.
● *Project termination phase:* A completed project history document comparing estimates and plans with actual development schedule and costs as a contribution to the accumulated database of experience.
● *Product phase-out:* A clean transition of the functions performed by the product to its successors (if any).

9 Software development work

In the same way that the progress of a software development project may be partitioned into a number of discrete phases, so may the technical work involved be divided into a number of clearly identified 'activities'.

A close parallel has been deliberately adopted between the names assigned to the project phases and the technical activities, respectively. This means that, in most cases, the name of a development phase, structural design, for example, indicates the principal activity taking place within that phase. This is not to say that structural design is the only activity taking place during the structural design phase.

Conversely, not only must significant initial structural design work be performed prior to the structural design phase, but also there must be a continuing activity to deal with updates to the design during subsequent phases.

Similarly, although coding a module does not properly commence before the completion of the detailed design of that module, some programming activities must be performed during the earlier phases, such as planning coding methods and facilities, the acquisition and installation of tools and, in some cases, exploratory investigations into algorithms and operations.

Errors detected in the integration phase will require code and unit test activity even though the phase of that name has been completed.

In general, all activities continue across all phases of the project, although the emphasis shifts from activity to activity as the project proceeds from phase to phase. It follows that, in a large software development, each activity should be staffed by a distinct group of people, whose numbers might expand and contract as the emphasis of the project changes but whose existence is identifiable from project start to project end. This is illustrated in the example shown in Fig. 4.

9.1 Technical control

Since the technical activities are performed by members of a number of teams, it is vital to ensure the overall technical correctness of the product, which can be distinguished from such concerns as schedule, budget, organisation, staffing etc. which are solely the responsibility of project management. This concern with technical matters is referred to as 'technical control'.

Technical control is regarded as part of technical development (see Fig. 1) and is defined as the continuous process of making certain that what is being produced is technically correct, coherent and consistent.

It includes planning ahead for all the necessary modelling and testing. Its role is strategic in that it makes certain that the overall technical integrity of the product is not lost in the tactics of the individual technical activities. It requires an overall technical authority but does not necessarily imply managerial authority over the development staff. When sub-contractors are involved in the project, the activity of technical control becomes even more important in co-ordinating the technical aspects of all the work between the sub-contractors and the integrity of the sub-contract products.

Primary examples of technical control are the maintenance of the integrity of the design in the presence of changes following the completion of the structural design phase, and test planning. Test planning is a strategic activity from the very start of the project which defines and co-ordinates all the test methods, tools and techniques to be used throughout the life cycle. It also identifies critical components that need the most testing, what test data is required, and when it is to be prepared.

While it can be seen to be difficult to separate the two activities of project management and technical control and it is reasonable on very small projects for the project manager to undertake both activities, on large projects such a combination of roles is very rarely workable. Firstly, it is rare to find people who combine both the strong management talent and strong technical talent necessary for large projects. Secondly, and more

importantly, on a project of even a reasonable size, each activity is necessarily a full-time job, or more.

It is hard for the project manager to delegate the project management tasks to allow time for technical work. It is impossible for the technical controller to delegate technical control duties without compromising the conceptual integrity of the product. It is sometimes possible to run a project with the technical control exercised by the senior manager in charge of the project and almost all project management tasks delegated to a second-in-command. It is much more usual for the project manager to be in command, with the technical controller having the technical authority. In this case it is important that the technical controller does have enough authority for decisions without being in management line above all the project teams.

9.2 Quality system

In the context of product development the word 'quality' is defined as the degree of conformance of the product to its stated requirements, i.e. 'fitness for purpose'. This definition is applied to the intermediate products of the development as well as to the final product. The development process is fundamental to the ability of the project to produce products of acceptable quality. Quality is built into the product by the activities of the software development staff as a continuous process of building the product to the specified quality.

Quality is everybody's responsibility — it cannot be added by any testing or control on the products of phases. Such testing and quality control activities do, however, provide early warning of problems; changes can be made at much lower cost than in the later stages of development, provided, as always, that proper change control procedures are followed.

The quality system comprises two distinct activities: verification, validation and test (VV&T), and quality assurance (QA).

9.3 Verification, validation and test

The terms are defined as follows:

- *Verification:* To establish the correspondence between a software product (documentation or code) and its specification — 'Are we building the product right?'
- *Validation:* To establish the fitness of a software product for its operational mission — 'Are we building the right product?'
- *Testing:* The actual running of code to produce test results.

VV&T is checking the correctness of the products of each phase (baselines) and is performed by the software development staff. The activity should, as far as possible, be carried out by staff within the project organisation, but not by the originators of the work. For this reason it is the only development activity which may be the responsibility of a series of different teams as the project proceeds through the life cycle phases.

9.4 Quality assurance

Quality asssurance (QA) is checking the correctness of the procedures being followed, i.e. whether the development staff are following the intended procedures (in all their work, not just the VV&T activities). This is carried out by QA staff either from a separate QA department or from staff assigned to QA work within the project. The checking of procedures is backed by audits (spot checks) of the quality (and conformance to standards) of the products to find out if the procedures are effective. Generally the QA staff provide an independent voice on all quality issues, especially on the setting up of standards and procedures at the beginning of the project (i.e. 'how' the project will develop the 'what' defined in the requirement specification). The responsibilities of the QA staff are:

- advising on standards and procedures
- monitoring the procedures actually employed on the project
- auditing and certifying the quality of products achieved.

9.5 Configuration management system

The successful realisation of a software product requires the strictest control over the defining, describing and supporting documentation and the software code constituting the product. It is inevitable that the definition will be subject to continuous pressure for change over the life cycle of the product, to correct errors, introduce improvements and respond to the evolving requirements of the marketplace. Configuration management provides the disciplines required to prevent the chaos of uncontrolled change.

A comprehensive approach to configuration management requires:

- clear identification of software items and documents, and their successive versions and editions
- definition of the configuration of software products, and their related configuration items
- physical control over the master files

of software code and documentation
- control of the introduction of changes to these files by a change control board and a set of change procedures
- maintenance of a system of configuration records, reflecting the definition of products in the field.

The output of each development phase should be verified and validated against the relevant preceding baselines. Configuration management disciplines ensure that all necessary corrections are introduced before this output, in turn, is baselined and that only up-to-date definitions of baselines are used by subsequent phases. The configuration management system should be able to react to the time scales needed by different phases of the project.

Once a baseline has been formally established its contents may only be changed by the operation of the formal change control process. This has the following advantages:

- No changes are made thereafter without the agreement of all interested parties.
- The higher procedural threshold for change tends to stabilise the product.
- There is always available a definitive version of the product, or of any of the controlled intermediate products (baselines).

9.6 Documentation

The output of each phase of the whole software development project consists entirely of documentation or of documentation and code. Furthermore, during the design phases, documents are the sole means by which the successive stages of the design process are recorded, and against which each phase is validated. So much of the output of a software project is in the form of documentation that it is impossible to separate the scheduling of the documentation constituting the baselines from that of the project as a whole. Therefore careful attention to the planning, structure, content, preparation, presentation and control of documentation is vital.

Documentation produced by the software development process may:

- define the software product in terms of requirement and design specifications
- describe the product to the customer or to current or future members of the development team
- support the product in the field in the form of the user's manual, operator's manual and maintenance manual.

9.7 Software development model

Having discussed all the activities of a software development project, the full list of ten activities covering all the management and technical work can be defined as follows:

- *Project management:* Project level management functions. Includes project level planning and control, contract and sub-contract management, customer interface, cost/schedule performance management, management reviews and audits, and includes acquisition of management tools.
- *Technical control:* Responsibility for the technical correctness and quality of the complete product. Responsibility for maintaining the integrity of the whole design during the detailed design, programming and testing phases. Specification, review and update of integration test and acceptance test plans and procedures. Acquisition of requirements and design verification and validation tools. Acquisition and support of test drivers, test tools and test data.
- *Requirement specification:* Determination, specification, review and update of software functional, performance, interface and verification requirements, including acquisition of requirements analysis and specification tools. Development of requirement specification level defining and describing documentation. A continuing responsibility for communication between customer requirements and the technical development.
- *Structural design:* Determination, specification, review and update of hardware-software architecture, software design and database design, including acquisition of design tools. Development of structural design level defining documentation.
- *Detailed design:* Detailed design of individual computer program components. Development of detail design level defining documentation. When a signifi-

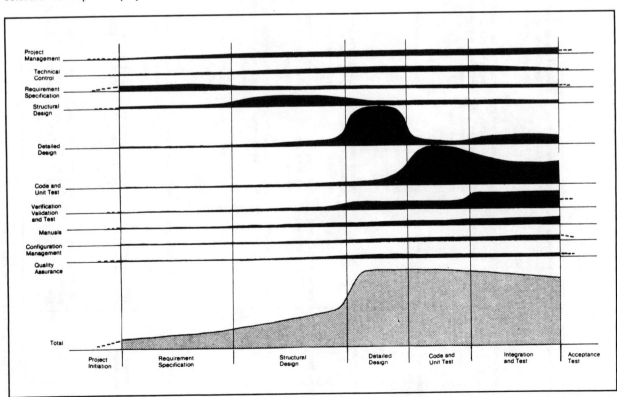

Fig. 4 Software development teams

Activity \ Phase	Project initiation	Reqmnt specification	Structural design	Detailed design	Code and unit test	Integration and test	Acceptance test	Maintenance
Project management	project estimating, planning, scheduling, procedures, organisation etc.	project management, project planning, contracts, liaison etc.	project management, status monitoring, contracts, liaison etc.	project management, status monitoring, contracts, liaison etc.	project management, status monitoring, contracts, liaison etc.	project management, status monitoring, contracts, liaison etc.	project management, status monitoring, contracts, liaison etc.	support management, status monitoring, contracts, liaison etc.
Technical control	technical strategy, technical plans, technical standards	system models and risk analysis, acceptance test plan, acquire V and V tools for reqmnts and design, top-level test plan	design quality, models and risk analysis, draft test plans, acquire test tools	design integrity, detailed test plans, acquire test tools	design integrity, detailed test plans, install test tools	design integrity, support test tools, monitor testing	design integrity, support test tools, monitor acceptance	design integrity, risk analysis, test plans
Requirement specification	analyse requirements, determine user needs	analyse existing system, determine user needs, integrate document and iterate requirements	update requirements	update requirements	update requirements	update requirements	update requirements	determine user needs and problems, update requirements
Structural design	design planning	develop basic architecture, models, prototypes	develop structural design, models, prototypes	update design	update design	update design	update design	update design
Detailed design	identify programming methods and resources	prototypes of algorithms, team planning	models, algorithms investigation, team planning	detailed design, component documentation	update detailed design	update detailed design	update detailed design	detailed design of changes and enhancements
Code and unit test	identify programming methods and resources	identify programming tools, team planning	acquire programming tools and utilities, team planning	integration planning	code and unit test	integrate software, update code	update code	code and unit test of changes and enhancements
Verification validation and test	V and V requirements	V and V specification	V and V structural design	V and V detailed design, V and V design changes	V and V top portions of code, V and V design changes	perform product test, V and V design changes	perform acceptance test, V and V design changes	V and V changes and enhancements
Manuals	define user's manual	outline portions of user's manual	draft user's, operator's manuals, outline maintenance manual	draft maintenance manual	full draft users and operator's manuals	final users, operators and maintenance manuals	acceptance of manuals	update manual
Configuration management	CM plans and procedures	CM plans, procedures, identify CM tools	CM of requirements, design, acquire CM tools	CM of requirements, design, detailed design, install CM tools, set up library	CM of requirements, design, code, operate library	CM of requirements, design, code, operate library	CM of requirements, design, code, operate library	CM of all documentation, operate library
Quality assurance	QA plans, project procedures and standards	standards, procedures, QA plans, identify QA tools	QA of requirements, design, project standards, acquire QA tools	QA of requirements, design, detailed design	QA of requirements, design, code	QA of requirements, design, code, testing	QA of requirements, design, code, acceptance	QA of maintenance updates

Fig. 5   Project tasks by activity and phase

cant number of staff are involved, this activity includes team level management functions.

- *Code and unit test:* Code, unit test and integration of individual computer program components, including tool acquisition. When a significant number of staff are involved, this activity includes team level management functions.
- *Verification, validation and testing:* Performance of independent requirements validation, design verification and validation, integration test and acceptance test, including test reports.
- *Manuals production:* Development and update of product support documentation — user's manual, operator's manual and maintenance manual.
- *Configuration management:* Product identification, operation of change control, status accounting, and operation of program support library.
- *Quality assurance:* Consultancy on the choice of project standards and procedures, monitoring of project procedures in operation, and quality audits of products.

10 The complete software development model

Fig. 5 shows a matrix of the ten activities for eight software development phases. Tasks corresponding to the specific work of an activity in a phase are shown. The tasks can be sub-divided, where relevant, to sub-systems and modules of the product.

These tasks then provide the basis for the work breakdown structure for estimating, planning and assignment of work to the development team. Thus the principles of software development methodology are unified into a single model for software development project control. In fact the matrix of tasks can be considered as a slice through a cube, as shown in Fig. 6.

Having derived the matrix of tasks and already noted that the documentation system (specification and design documents) corresponds to the work of software development, we can now briefly consider the remaining slices in the cube.

10.1 Techniques and tools

Earlier in this paper it was emphasised that one of the important elements of a modern approach to software engineering is the selection of appropriate techniques and the use of computer-based tools. The careful selection and implementation of such tools is crucial to the objective of improving control and raising productivity and product quality. Mechanisation of software development processes, where practicable, in addition to increasing efficiency, encourages consistent process quality.

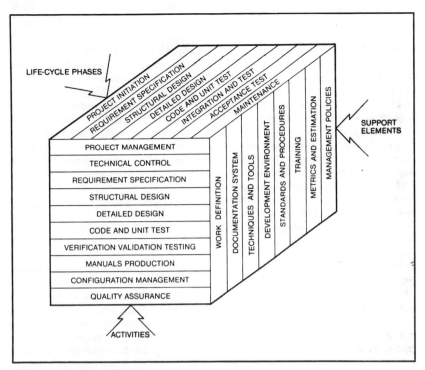

Fig. 6 The software development model

Any suggested technique or set of techniques and the supporting tools can be matched against the model to test how complete an integrated project support environment (IPSE) is provided to support all the tasks in the matrix.

This type of model provides an additional benefit: as techniques and tools are changed or improved from project to project their impact on the development process and product quality can be identified and evaluated.

10.2 Development environment

Development environment is intended to cover all aspects of the computer environment underlying the tools: namely the matters of operating system, database and file facilities, workstations, networking and mainframe computers.

10.3 Standards and procedures

A software development team can only operate effectively when each member knows the answers to the basic questions regarding the job:

- What is expected of me?
- Why is it expected?
- How do I do what is expected?
- What must I produce?
- How will my product be evaluated?
- What tools are available to me?
- What training is available to me?

A set of development procedures and standards improves communications and reduces the probability of misinterpretations among developers. Verification and validation are much easier to implement and more effective when the product is created in accordance with standards.

The model represented by the cube gives us the basis for a set of standards and procedures that are complete and non-redundant if they cover every cubicle in the cube. This is just the same method as for identifying a complete set of tools. If any standard or procedure is missing then there is a hole in the cube. Standards and procedures should be brief and to the point — they need not be bulky and complicated. In fact the cube defines a structure which can simplify the presentation of the standards and procedures documents. If everything in the cube is covered then the software development team know how they are going to develop the product.

10.4 Training

Training is vital to the success of the programming environment. Having a defined technique is useless unless every member of the team knows how to use the technique. Training should be provided not only on the techniques and tools but on all the support elements.

10.5 Metrics and estimation

We need objective metrics on both the process and the generated products (including all intermediate products for all phases). Measurements provide the immediate benefit of refining the development plan and the long-term benefit of characterising the effectiveness of the current development methodology. Whatever the measurement, it must be defined before development begins.

Collection of data, according to the activities and phases of the model, provides the basis for estimating future projects. In turn, running the project according to the model provides the means of collecting such data and the motivation to use it to succeed in controlling successful projects. All such data collection, metrics, analysis, estimation, planning and project control are much more effective when suitable computer-based tools are used.

10.6 Management policies

Management policies define the life cycle phases and the job functions. They are descriptions of what should be performed by each job function in every life cycle phase. These descriptions may be called a methodology, a corporate policy, an instruction or a procedure. Whatever they are called they must be in place at the beginning of a software development project if the project is to be managed with a high chance of successful completion on time, within budget and with a product which operates correctly to the satisfaction of the customer organisation.

11 Conclusion

The major reason for the slow evolution of software project management over the past two decades is the persistent view that programming is an art, rather than a science. This view lingers and has contributed to delays in the development of a well defined, well structured software management methodology. The problem persists despite the great advances in computer hardware technology, the introduction of software engineering, and the definition of new development approaches, such as design decomposition, structured design, structured programming, hierarchical input-output definition and team management concepts.

These factors foster the perspective in business and project management that software management must continuously evolve and change to keep up with advances in software development technology. Yet these conclusions are seldom applied to management of the rapidly advancing electronics field. Since hardware development projects, in the midst of phenomenal technology advances, can be managed in a disciplined, systematic manner based on past decades of project management experience, why should it be assumed that software projects cannot?

Software engineering recognises both technological and managerial aspects. Improvements in the technology of software development have reached the point where the major issues have been identified and considerable progress has been made in addressing these issues. Practical working tools to support improved software production are commonly available and a firm methodology for technical software development is well defined.

Published papers over the last ten years show that software development is manageable and software productivity can be significantly improved for the benefit of the business. The common denominators in the successes reported are firstly that they are usually the better developers of software making even greater improvements, and secondly that they are backed by management commitment.

Given that making software engineering methodology really work is always difficult, it follows that success depends on more than just the wish to improve control and productivity of software development: management support and the willingness to invest is necessary in order to obtain the due return on the investment.

The technical methods, tools and disciplines are the basis for the production of reliable software, on time and within budget, but it is also necessary to have an overall management framework which allows senior management to understand, and project managers to control, large software developments. The increasing complexity of the large software systems being developed and advances in software technology and tools mean that there will be a continuing evolution in technical software development, but the primary basis for the control of software development will continue to be the principles outlined in this paper.

P. E. Rook is Software Development Manager with GEC Software Ltd., 132–135 Long Acre, London WC2E 9AH, England.

Elements of Software Configuration Management

EDWARD H. BERSOFF, SENIOR MEMBER, IEEE

Abstract—Software configuration management (SCM) is one of the disciplines of the 1980's which grew in response to the many failures of the software industry throughout the 1970's. Over the last ten years, computers have been applied to the solution of so many complex problems that our ability to manage these applications has all too frequently failed. This has resulted in the development of a series of "new" disciplines intended to help control the software process.

This paper will focus on the discipline of SCM by first placing it in its proper context with respect to the rest of the software development process, as well as to the goals of that process. It will examine the constituent components of SCM, dwelling at some length on one of those components, configuration control. It will conclude with a look at what the 1980's might have in store.

Index Terms—Configuration management, management, product assurance, software.

INTRODUCTION

SOFTWARE configuration management (SCM) is one of the disciplines of the 1980's which grew in response to the many failures of our industry throughout the 1970's. Over the last ten years, computers have been applied to the solution of so many complex problems that our ability to manage these applications in the "traditional" way has all too frequently failed. Of course, tradition in the software business began only 30 years ago or less, but even new habits are difficult to break. In the 1970's we learned the hard way that the tasks involved in managing a software project were not linearly dependent on the number of lines of code produced. The relationship was, in fact, highly exponential. As the decade closed, we looked back on our failures [1], [2] trying to understand what went wrong and how we could correct it. We began to dissect the software development process [3], [4] and to define techniques by which it could be effectively managed [5]-[8]. This self-examination by some of the most talented and experienced members of the software community led to the development of a series of "new" disciplines intended to help control the software process.

While this paper will focus on the particular discipline of SCM, we will first place it in its proper context with respect to the rest of the software development process, as well as to the goals of that process. We will examine the constituent components of SCM, dwelling at some length on one of those components, configuration control. Once we have woven our way through all the trees, we will once again stand back and take a brief look at the forest and see what the 1980's might have in store.

Manuscript received April 15, 1982; revised December 1, 1982 and October 18, 1983.

The author is with BTG, Inc., 1945 Gallows Rd., Vienna, VA 22180.

SCM IN CONTEXT

It has been said that if you do not know where you are going, any road will get you there. In order to properly understand the role that SCM plays in the software development process, we must first understand what the goal of that process is, i.e., where we are going. For now, and perhaps for some time to come, software developers are people, people who respond to the needs of another set of people creating computer programs designed to satisfy those needs. These computer programs are the tangible output of a thought process—the conversion of a thought process into a product. The goal of the software developer is, or should be, the construction of a product which closely matches the real needs of the set of people for whom the software is developed. We call this goal the achievement of "product integrity." More formally stated, product integrity (depicted in Fig. 1) is defined to be the intrinsic set of attributes that characterize a product [9]:

- that fulfills user functional needs;
- that can easily and completely be traced through its life cycle;
- that meets specified performance criteria;
- whose cost expectations are met;
- whose delivery expectations are met.

The above definition is pragmatically based. It demands that product integrity be a measure of the satisfaction of the real needs and expectations of the software user. It places the burden for achieving the software goal, product integrity, squarely on the shoulders of the developer, for it is he alone who is in control of the development process. While, as we shall see, the user can establish safeguards and checkpoints to gain visibility into the development process, the prime responsibility for software success is the developer's. So our goal is now clear; we want to build software which exhibits all the characteristics of product integrity. Let us make sure that we all understand, however, what this thing called software really is. We have learned in recent times that equating the terms "software" and "computer programs" improperly restricts our view of software. Software is much more. A definition which can be used to focus the discussion in this paper is that software is information that is:

- structured with logical and functional properties;
- created and maintained in various forms and representations during the life cycle;
- tailored for machine processing in its fully developed state.

So by our definition, software is not simply a set of computer programs, but includes the documentation required to define, develop, and maintain these programs. While this notion is not very new, it still frequently escapes the software

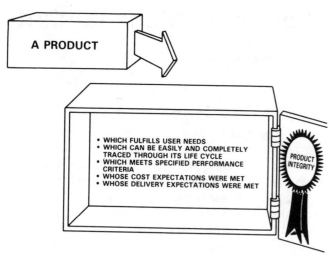

Fig. 1. Product integrity.

development manager who assumes that controlling a software product is the same as controlling computer code.

Now that we more fully appreciate what we are after, i.e., to build a software product with integrity, let us look at the one road which might get us there. We have, until now, used the term "developer" to characterize the organizational unit responsible for converting the software idea into a software product. But developers are, in reality, a complex set of interacting organizational entities. When undertaking a software project, most developers structure themselves into three basic discipline sets which include:

- project management,
- development, and
- product assurance.

Project management disciplines are both inwardly and outwardly directed. They support general management's need to see what is going on in a project and to ensure that the parent or host organization consistently develops products with integrity. At the same time, these disciplines look inside a project in support of the assignment, allocation, and control of all project resources. In that capacity, project management determines the relative allocation of resources to the set of development and product assurance disciplines. It is management's prerogative to specify the extent to which a given discipline will be applied to a given project. Historically, management has often been handicapped when it came to deciding how much of the product assurance disciplines were required. This was a result of both inexperience and organizational immaturity.

The development disciplines represent those traditionally applied to a software project. They include:

- analysis,
- design,
- engineering,
- production (coding),
- test (unit/subsystem),
- installation,
- documentation,
- training, and
- maintenance.

In the broadest sense, these are the disciplines required to take a system concept from its beginning through the development life cycle. It takes a well-structured, rigorous technical approach to system development, along with the right mix of development disciplines to attain product integrity, especially for software. The concept of an ordered, procedurally disciplined approach to system development is fundamental to product integrity. Such an approach provides successive development plateaus, each of which is an identifiable measure of progress which forms a part of the total foundation supporting the final product. Going sequentially from one baseline (plateau) to another with high probability of success, necessitates the use of the right development disciplines at precisely the right time.

The product assurance disciplines which are used by project management to gain visibility into the development process include:

- configuration management,
- quality assurance,
- validation and verification, and
- test and evaluation.

Proper employment of these product assurance disciplines by the project manager is basic to the success of a project since they provide the technical checks and balances over the product being developed. Fig. 2 represents the relationship among the management, development, and product assurance disciplines. Let us look at each of the product assurance disciplines briefly, in turn, before we explore the details of SCM.

Configuration management (CM) is the discipline of identifying the configuration of a system at discrete points in time for the purpose of systematically controlling changes to the configuration and maintaining the integrity and traceability of the configuration throughout the system life cycle. Software configuration management (SCM) is simply configuration management tailored to systems, or portions of systems, that are comprised predominantly of software. Thus, SCM does not differ substantially from the CM of hardware-oriented systems, which is generally well understood and effectively practiced. However, attempts to implement SCM have often failed because the particulars of SCM do not follow by direct analogy from the particulars of hardware CM and because SCM is a less mature discipline than that of hardware CM. We will return to this subject shortly.

Quality assurance (QA) as a discipline is commonly invoked throughout government and industry organizations with reasonable standardization when applied to systems comprised only of hardware. But there is enormous variation in thinking and practice when the QA discipline is invoked for a software development or for a system containing software components. QA has a long history, and much like CM, it has been largely developed and practiced on hardware projects. It is therefore mature, in that sense, as a discipline. Like CM, however, it is relatively immature when applied to software development. We define QA as consisting of the procedures, techniques, and tools applied by professionals to insure that a product meets or exceeds prespecified standards during a product's development cycle; and without specific prescribed standards, QA entails insuring that a product meets or

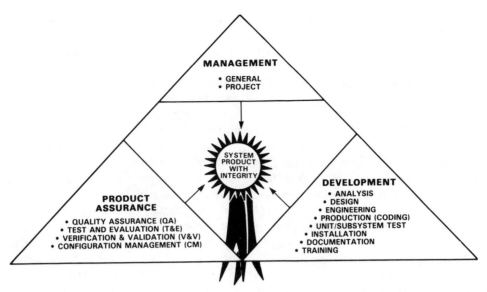

Fig. 2.   The discipline triangle.

exceeds a minimum industrial and/or commercially acceptable level of excellence.

The QA discipline has not been uniformly treated, practiced or invoked relative to software development. First, very few organizations have software design and development standards that compare in any way with hardware standards for detail and completeness. Second, it takes a high level of software expertise to assess whether a software product meets prescribed standards. Third, few buyer organizations have provided for or have developed the capability to impose and then monitor software QA endeavors on seller organizations. Finally, few organizations have been concerned over precisely defining the difference between QA and other product assurance disciplines, CM often being subservient to QA or vice versa in a given development organization. Our definition of software given earlier suggests still another reason for the software QA discipline being in the same state as SCM so far as its universal application within the user, buyer, and seller communities. Software, as a form of information, cannot be standardized; only structures for defining/documenting software can be standardized. It follows that software development techniques can only be meaningfully standardized in relation to information structures, not information content.

The third of the four product assurance disciplines is validation and verification (V&V). Unlike CM and QA, V&V has come into being expressly for the purpose of coping with software and its development. Unlike QA, which priniipally deals with the problem of a product's adherence to pre-established standards, V&V deals with the issue of how well software fulfills functional and performance requirements and the assurance that specified requirements are indeed stated and interpreted correctly. The verification part of V&V assures that a product meets its prescribed goals as defined through baseline documentation. That is, verification is a discipline imposed to ascertain that a product is what it was intended to be relative to its preceding baseline. The validation part of V&V, by contrast, is levied as a discipline to assure that a product not only meets the objectives specified through baseline documentation, but in addition, does the right job.

Stated another way, the validation discipline is invoked to insure that the end-user gets the right product. A buyer or seller may have misinterpreted user requirements or, perhaps, requirements have changed, or the user gets to know more about what he needs, or early specifications of requirements were wrong or incomplete or in a state of flux. The validation process serves to assure that such problems do not persist among the user, buyer, and seller. To enhance objectivity, it is often desirable to have an independent organization, from outside the developing organization, perform the V&V function.

The fourth of the product assurance disciplines is test and evaluation (T&E), perhaps the discipline most understood, and yet paradoxically, least practiced with uniformity. T&E is defined as the discipline imposed outside the development project organization to independently assess whether a product fulfills objectives. T&E does this through the execution of a set of test plans and procedures. Specifically in support of the end user, T&E entails evaluating product performance in a live or near-live environment. Frequently, particularly within the miliatry arena, T&E is a major undertaking involving one or more systems which are to operate together, but which have been individually developed and accepted as stand-alone items. Some organizations formally turn over T&E responsibility to a group outside the development project organization after the product reaches a certain stage of development, their philosophy being that developers cannot be objective to the point of fully testing/evaluating what they have produced.

The definitions given for CM, QA, V&V, and T&E suggest some overlap in required skills and functions to be performed in order to invoke these disciplines collectively for product assurance purposes. Depending on many factors, the actual overlap may be significant or little. In fact, there are those who would argue that V&V and T&E are but subset functions of QA. But the contesting argument is that V&V and T&E have come into being as separate disciplines because conventional QA methods and techniques have failed to do an adequate job with respect to providing product assurance, particularly for computer-centered systems with software components. Management must be concerned with minimizing the application of excessive and redundant resources to address the overlap of these disciplines. What is important is that all the functions defined above are performed, not what they are called or who carries them out.

THE ELEMENTS OF SCM

When the need for the discipline of configuration management finally achieved widespread recognition within the software engineering community, the question arose as to how closely the software CM discipline ought to parallel the extant hardware practice of configuration management. Early SCM authors and practitioners [10] wisely chose the path of commonality with the hardware world, at least at the highest level. Of course, hardware engineering is different from software engineering, but broad similarities do exist and terms applied to one segment of the engineering community can easily be applied to another, even if the specific meanings of those terms differ significantly in detail. For that reason, the elements of SCM were chosen to be the same as those for hardware CM. As for hardware, the four components of SCM are:

- identification,
- control,
- auditing, and
- status accounting.

Let us examine each one in turn.

Software Configuration Identification: Effective management of the development of a system requires careful definition of its baseline components; changes to these components also need to be defined since these changes, together with the baselines, specify the system evolution. A system baseline is like a snapshot of the aggregate of system components as they exist at a given point in time; updates to this baseline are like frames in a movie strip of the system life cycle. The role of software configuration identification in the SCM process is to provide labels for these snapshots and the movie strip.

A baseline can be characterized by two labels. One label identifies the baseline itself, while the second label identifies an update to a particular baseline. An update to a baseline represents a baseline plus a set of changes that have been incorporated into it. Each of the baselines established during a software system's life cycle controls subsequent system development. At the time it is first established a software baseline embodies the actual software in its most recent state. When changes are made to the most recently established baseline, then, from the viewpoint of the software configuration manager, this baseline and these changes embody the actual software in its most recent state (although, from the viewpoint of the software developer, the actual software may be in a more advanced state).

The most elementary entity in the software configuration identification labeling mechanism is the software configuration item (SCI). Viewed from an SCM perspective, a software baseline appears as a set of SCI's. The SCI's within a baseline are related to one another via a tree-like hierarchy. As the software system evolves through its life cycle, the number of

branches in this hierarchy generally increases; the first baseline may consist of no more than one SCI. The lowest level SCI's in the tree hierarchy may still be under development and not yet under SCM control. These entities are termed design objects or computer program components (see Fig. 3). Each baseline and each member in the associated family of updates will exist in one or more forms, such as a design document, source code on a disk, or executing object code.

In performing the identification function, the software configuration manager is, in effect, taking snapshots of the SCI's. Each baseline and its associated updates collectively represents the evolution of the software during each of its life cycle stages. These stages are staggered with respect to one another. Thus, the collection of life cycle stages looks like a collection of staggered and overlapping sequences of snapshots of SCI trees. Let us now imagine that this collection of snapshot sequences is threaded, in chronological order, onto a strip of movie film as in Fig. 4. Let us further imagine that the strip of movie film is run through a projector. Then we would see a history of the evolution of the software. Consequently, the identification of baselines and updates provides an explicit documentation trail linking all stages of the software life cycle. With the aid of this documentation trail, the software developer can assess the integrity of his product, and the software buyer can assess the integrity of the product he is paying for.

Software Configuration Control: The evolution of a software system is, in the language of SCM, the development of baselines and the incorporation of a series of changes into the baselines. In addition to these changes that explicitly affect existing baselines, there are changes that occur during early stages of the system life cycle that may affect baselines that do not yet exist. For example, some time before software coding begins (i.e., some time prior to the establishment of a design baseline), a contract may be modified to include a software warranty provision such as: system downtime due to software failures shall not exceed 30 minutes per day. This warranty provision will generally affect subsequent baselines but in a manner that cannot be explicitly determined *a priori*. One role of software configuration control is to provide the administrative mechanism for precipitating, preparing, evaluating, and approving or disapproving all change proposals throughout the system life cycle.

We have said that software, for configuration management purposes, is a collection of SCI's that are related to one another in a well-defined way. In early baselines and their associated updates, SCI's are specification documents (one or more volumes of text for each baseline or associated update); in later baselines and their associated updates, each SCI may manifest itself in any or all of the various software representations. Software configuration control focuses on managing changes to SCI's (existing or to be developed) in all of their representations. This process involves three basic ingredients.

1) Documentation (such as administrative forms and supporting technical and administrative material) for formally precipitating and defining a proposed change to a software system.

2) An organizational body for formally evaluating and

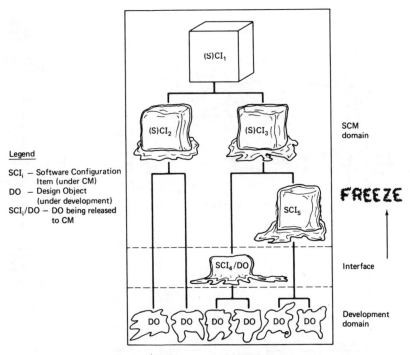

Fig. 3.   The development/SCM interface.

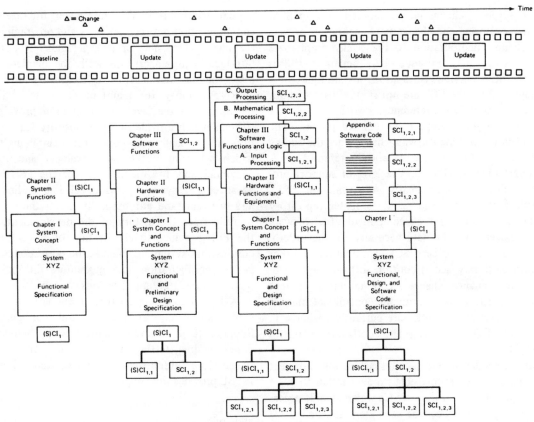

Fig. 4.   SCI evolution in a single document.

approving or disapproving a proposed change to a software system (the Configuration Control Board).

3) Procedures for controlling changes to a software system. The Engineering Change Proposal (ECP), a major control document, contains information such as a description of the proposed change, identification of the originating organization, rationale for the change, identification of affected baselines and SCI's (if appropriate), and specification of cost and schedule impacts. ECP's are reviewed and coordinated by the CCB, which is typically a body representing all organizational units which have a vested interest in proposed changes.

Fig. 5 depicts the software configuration control process.

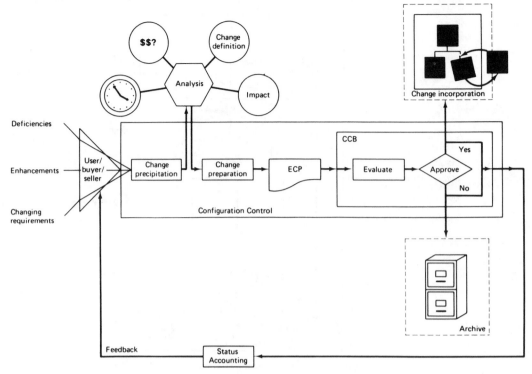

Fig. 5. The control process.

As the figure suggests, change incorporation is not an SCM function, but monitoring the change implementation process resulting in change incorporation is. Fig. 5 also emphasizes that the analysis that may be required to prepare an ECP is also outside the SCM purview. Note also from the figure how ECP's not approved by the CCB are not simply discarded but are archived for possible future reference.

Many automated tools support the control process. The major ones aid in controlling software change once the coding stage has been reached, and are generically referred to as program support libraries (PSL's). The level of support provided by PSL's, however, varies greatly. As a minimum, a PSL should provide a centralized and readily available repository for authoritative versions of each component of a software system. It should contain the data necessary for the orderly development and control of each SCI. Automation of other functions, such as library access control, software and document version maintenance, change recording, and document reconstruction, greatly enhance both the control and maintenance processes. These capabilities are currently available in systems such as SOFTOOL's change and configuration control environment (CCC).

A PSL supports a developmental approach in which project personnel work on a common visible product rather than on independent components. In those PSL's which include access controls, project personnel can be separately assigned read/write access to each software document/component, from programs to lines of code. Thus, all project personnel are assured ready access to the critical interface information necessary for effective software development. At the same time, modifications to various software components, whether sanctioned baselines or modules under development, can be closely controlled.

Under the PSL concept, the programmer operates under a well-defined set of parameters and exercises a narrower span of detailed control. This minimizes the need for explicit communication between analysts and programmers and makes the inclusion of new project personnel less traumatic since interface requirements are well documented. It also minimizes the preparation effort for technical audits.

Responsibility for maintenance of the PSL data varies depending on the level of automation provided. For those systems which provide only a repository for data, a secretary/librarian is usually responsible for maintaining the notebooks which will contain the data developed and used by project personnel and for maintenance of the PSL archives. More advanced PSL systems provide real time, on-line access to data and programs and automatically create the records necessary to fully trace the history of the development. In either case the PSL provides standardization of project recordkeeping, ensures that system documentation corresponds to the current system configuration, and guarantees the existence of adequate documentation of previous versions.

A PSL should support three main activities: code development, software management, and configuration control. Support to the development process includes support to design, coding, testing, documentation, and program maintenance along with associated database schema and subschema. A PSL provides this support through:

• storage and maintenance of software documentation and code,
• support to program compilation/testing,
• support for the generation of program/system documentation.

Support to the management of the software development process involves the storage and output of programming data such as:

• collection and automatic reporting of management data related to program development,

362

- control over the integrity and security of the data in the PSL,
- separation of the clerical activity related to the programming process.

PSL's provide support to the configuration control process through:

- access and change authorization control for all data in the library,
- control of software code releases,
- automatic program and document reconstruction,
- automatic change tracking and reporting,
- assurance of the consistency between documentation, code, and listings.

A PSL has four major components: internal libraries in machine-readable form, external libraries in hardcopy form, computer procedures, and office procedures. The components of a PSL system are interlocked to establish an exact correspondence between the internal units of code and external versions (such as listings) of the developing systems. This continuous correspondence is the characteristic of a PSL that guarantees ongoing visibility and identification of the developing system.

Different PSL implementations exist for various system environments with the specifics of the implementation dependent upon the hardware, software, user, and operating environment. The fundamental correspondence between the internal and external libraries in each environment, however, is established by the PSL librarian and computer procedures. The office procedures are specified in a project CM Plan so that the format of the external libraries is standard across software projects, and internal and external libraries are easily maintainable.

Newer PSL systems minimize the need for both office and computer procedures through the implementation of extensive management functionality. This functionality provides significant flexibility in controlling the access to data and allocating change authority, while providing a variety of status reporting capabilities. The availability of management information, such as a list of all the software structures changed to solve a particular Software Trouble Report or the details on the latest changes to a particular software document, provides a means for the control function to effectively operate without burdening the development team with cumbersome procedures and administrative paperwork. Current efforts in PSL refinement/ development are aimed at linking support of the development environment with that of the configuration control environment. The goal of such systems is to provide an integrated environment where control and management information is generated automatically as a part of a fully supported design and development process.

Software Configuration Auditing: Software configuration auditing provides the mechanism for determining the degree to which the current state of the software system mirrors the software system pictured in baseline and requirements documentation. It also provides the mechanism for formally establishing a baseline. A baseline in its formative stages (for example, a draft specification document that appears prior to the existence of the functional baseline) is referred to as a "to-be-established" baseline; the final state of the auditing process conducted on a to-be-established baseline is a sanctioned baseline. The same may be said about baseline updates.

Software configuration auditing serves two purposes, configuration verification and configuration validation. Verification ensures that what is intended for each software configuration item as specified in one baseline or update is actually achieved in the succeeding baseline or update; validation ensures that the SCI configuration solves the right problem (i.e., that customer needs are satisfied). Software configuration auditing is applied to each baseline (and corresponding update) in its to-be-established state. An auditing process common to all baselines is the determination that an SCI structure exists and that its contents are based on all available information.

Software auditing is intended to increase software visibility and to establish traceability throughout the life cycle of the software product. Of course, this visibility and traceability are not achieved without cost. Software auditing costs time and money. But the judicious investment of time and money, particularly in the early stages of a project, pays dividends in the latter stages. These dividends include the avoidance of costly retrofits resulting from problems such as the sudden appearance of new requirements and the discovery of major design flaws. Conversely, failing to perform auditing, or constraining it to the later stages of the software life cycle, can jeopardize successful software development. Often in such cases, by the time discrepancies are discovered (if they are), the software cannot be easily or economically modified to rectify the discrepancies. The result is often a dissatisfied customer, large cost overruns, slipped schedules, or cancelled projects.

Software auditing makes visible to management the current status of the software in the life cycle product audited. It also reveals whether the project requirements are being satisfied and whether the intent of the preceding baseline has been fulfilled. With this visibility, project management can evaluate the integrity of the software product being developed, resolve issues that may have been raised by the audit, and correct defects in the development process. The visibility afforded by the software audit also provides a basis for the establishment of the audited life cycle product as a new baseline.

Software auditing provides traceability between a software life cycle product and the requirements for that product. Thus, as life cycle products are audited and baselines established, every requirement is traced successively from baseline to baseline. Disconnects are also made visible during the establishment of traceability. These disconnects include requirements not satisfied in the audited product and extraneous features observed in the product (i.e., features for which no stated requirement exists).

With the different point of view made possible by the visibility and traceability achieved in the software audit, management can make better decisions and exercise more incisive control over the software development process. The result of a software audit may be the establishment of a baseline, the redirection of project tasking, or an adjustment of applied project resources.

The responsibility for a successful software development project is shared by the buyer, seller, and user. Software auditing uniquely benefits each of these project participants. Appropriate auditing by each party provides checks and balances over the development effort. The scope and depth of the audits undertaken by the three parties may vary greatly. However, the purposes of these differing forms of software audit remain the same: to provide visibility and to establish traceability of the software life cycle products. An excellent overview of the software audit process, from which some of the above discussion has been extracted, appears in [11].

Software Configuration Status Accounting: A decision to make a change is generally followed by a time delay before the change is actually made, and changes to baselines generally occur over a protracted period of time before they are incorporated into baselines as updates. A mechanism is therefore needed for maintaining a record of how the system has evolved and where the system is at any time relative to what appears in published baseline documentation and written agreements. Software configuration status accounting provides this mechanism. Status accounting is the administrative tracking and reporting of all software items formally identified and controlled. It also involves the maintenance of records to support software configuration auditing. Thus, software configuration status accounting records the activity associated with the other three SCM functions and therefore provides the means by which the history of the software system life cycle can be traced.

Although administrative in nature, status accounting is a function that increases in complexity as the system life cycle progresses because of the multiple software representations that emerge with later baselines. This complexity generally results in large amounts of data to be recorded and reported. In particular, the scope of software configuration status accounting encompasses the recording and reporting of:

1) the time at which each representation of a baseline and update came into being;

2) the time at which each software configuration item came into being;

3) descriptive information about each SCI;

4) engineering change proposal status (approved, disapproved, awaiting action);

5) descriptive information about each ECP;

6) change status;

7) descriptive information about each change;

8) status of technical and administrative documentation associated with a baseline or update (such as a plan prescribing tests to be performed on a baseline for updating purposes);

9) deficiencies in a to-be-established baseline uncovered during a configuration audit.

Software configuration status accounting, because of its large data input and output requirements, is generally supported in part by automated processes such as the PSL described earlier. Data are collected and organized for input to a computer and reports giving the status of entities are compiled and generated by the computer.

THE MANAGEMENT DILEMMA

As we mentioned at the beginning of this paper, SCM and many of the other product assurance disciplines grew up in the 1970's in response to software failure. The new disciplines were designed to achieve visibility into the software engineering process and thereby exercise some measure of control over that process. Students of mathematical control theory are taught early in their studies a simple example of the control process. Consider being confronted with a cup of hot coffee, filled to the top, which you are expected to carry from the kitchen counter to the kitchen table. It is easily verified that if you watch the cup as you carry it, you are likely to spill more coffee than if you were to keep your head turned away from the cup. The problem with looking at the cup is one of overcompensation. As you observe slight deviations from the straight-and-level, you adjust, but often you adjust too much. To compensate for that overadjustment, you tend to overadjust again, with the result being hot coffee on your floor.

This little diversion from our main topic of SCM has an obvious moral. There is a fundamental propensity on the part of the practitioners of the product assurance disciplines to overadjust, to overcompensate for the failures of the development disciplines. There is one sure way to eliminate failure completely from the software development process, and that is to stop it completely. The software project manager must learn how to apply his resources intelligently. He must achieve visibility and control, but he must not so encumber the developer so as to bring progress to a virtual halt. The product assurers have a virtuous perspective. They strive for perfection and point out when and where perfection has not been achieved. We seem to have a binary attitude about software; it is either correct or it is not. That is perhaps true, but we cannot expect anyone to deliver perfect software in any reasonable time period or for a reasonable sum of money. What we need to develop is software that is good enough. Some of the controls that we have placed on the developer have the deleterious effect of increasing costs and expanding schedules rather than shrinking them.

The dilemma to management is real. We must have the visibility and control that the product assurance disciplines have the capacity to provide. But we must be careful not to overcompensate and overcontrol. This is the fine line which will distinguish the successful software managers of the 1980's from the rest of the software engineering community.

ACKNOWLEDGMENT

The author wishes to acknowledge the contribution of B. J. Gregor to the preparation and critique of the final manuscript.

REFERENCES

[1] "Contracting for computer software development—Serious problems require management attention to avoid wasting additional millions," General Accounting Office, Rep. FGMSD 80-4, Nov. 9, 1979.

[2] D. M. Weiss, "The MUDD report: A case study of Navy software development practices," Naval Res. Lab., Rep. 7909, May 21, 1975.

[3] B. W. Boehm, "Software engineering," *IEEE Trans. Comput.*, vol. C-25, pp. 1226–1241, Dec. 1976.

[4] *Proc. IEEE* (Special Issue on Software Engineering), vol. 68, Sept. 1980.

[5] E. Bersoff, V. Henderson, and S. Siegel, "Attaining software product integrity," *Tutorial: Software Configuration Management*, W. Bryan, C. Chadbourne, and S. Siegel, Eds., Los Alamitos, CA, IEEE Comput. Soc., Cat. EHO-169-3, 1981.

[6] B. W. Boehm et al., *Characteristics of Software Quality*, TRW Series of Software Technology, vol. 1. New York: North-Holland, 1978.

[7] T. A. Thayer, et al., *Software Reliability*, TRW Series of Software Technology, vol. 2. New York: North-Holland, 1978.

[8] D. J. Reifer, Ed., *Tutorial: Automated Tools for Software Eng.*, Los Alamitos, CA, IEEE Comput. Soc., Cat. EHO-169-3, 1979.

[9] E. Bersoff, V. Henderson, and S. Siegel, *Software Configuration Management*. Englewood Cliffs, NJ: Prentice-Hall, 1980.

[10] ——, "Software configuration management: A tutorial," *Computer*, vol. 12, pp. 6–14, Jan. 1979.

[11] W. Bryan, S. Siegel, and G. Whiteleather, "Auditing throughout the software life cycle: A primer," *Computer*, vol. 15, pp. 56–67, Mar. 1982.

[12] "Software configuration management," Naval Elec. Syst. Command, Software Management Guidebooks, vol. 2, undated.

Edward H. Bersoff (M'75–SM'78) received the A.B., M.S., and Ph.D. degrees in mathematics from New York University, New York.

He is President and Founder of BTG, Inc., a high technology, Washington, DC area based, systems analysis and engineering firm. In addition to his corporate responsibilities, he directs the company's research in software engineering, product assurance, and software management. BTG specializes in the application of modern systems engineering principles to the computer based system development process. At BTG, he has been actively involved in the FAA's Advanced Automation Program where he is focusing on software management and software configuration management issues on this extremely complex program. He also participates in the company's activities within the Naval Intelligence community, providing senior consulting services to a wide variety of system development efforts. He was previously President of CTEC, Inc. where he directed the concept formulation and development of the Navy Command and Control System (NCCS), Ocean Surveillance Information System (OSIS) Baseline now installed at all U.S. Navy Ocean Surveillance Centers. He also served as Experiment Director for the Joint ARPA, Navy, CINCPAC Military Message Experiment. This test was designed to examine the usefulness of secure, automated message processing systems in an operational military environment and to develop design criteria for future military message processing systems. Prior to joining CTEC, Inc., he was Manager of Engineering Operations and Manager of FAA Operations for Logicon, Inc.'s Process Systems Division. He joined Logicon from the NASA Electronics Research Center. He has taught mathematics at universities in Boston, New York, and Washington, DC. His technical contributions to the fields of software requirements and design range from early publications in computer architecture, reliability and programming languages, to more recent publications in software quality and configuration management. A textbook entitled *Software Configuration Management* (Prentice-Hall) represents the product of three years of research in the field by Dr. Bersoff and his colleagues.

Dr. Bersoff is a member of AFCEA, American Management Association, MENSA, and the Young Presidents' Organization.

Edward H. Bersoff and
Alan M. Davis

Impacts of Life Cycle Models on SOFTWARE

"Impacts of Life Cycle Models on Software Configuration Management," by E.H. Bersoff and A.M. Davis from *Communications of the ACM*, Vol. 34, No. 8, Aug. 1991, pages 104-117. Copyright © 1991 by the Association for Computing Machinery, Inc., reprinted with permission.

The replacement of horse-drawn carriages with automobiles had a profound effect on the blacksmith's role in personal transportation. Similarly, the replacement of the conventional waterfall model of software development with alternative life cycle models [1, 12] such as prototyping, reusable software and automated software synthesis is likely to have a profound effect on the role

In all of these cases, there is a need for some organization to ensure that all parties know how to request a change, that a change is necessary, that all affected parties agree with the change, that all parties are informed of the impending change, and that there is a record of all changes made, who made them, when they were made, and why they were made. Regardless of what this organization is called, it is performing the function of SCM.

SCM organization because (1) it was too slow, (2) the work was error-prone, and (3) its practitioners were sometimes not the best-quality people. If project managers needed an up-to-the-minute status of the current baseline or to-be-established baseline, they would more likely ask the system developers (who at least were closer to the problem) than the SCM organization which was bogged down with red tape and paper work.

CONFIGURATION
Management

of software configuration management (SCM).

The purpose of SCM is to manage change throughout the software development process [4, 5]. Change is a very natural and intrinsic aspect of that process. For example, change occurs:

- during software creation, when the software requirements specification is agreed to by all parties and is "baselined,"
- during software development, when the software design, or the code, or the test plans are completed and are added to the software requirements specification as part of the package that will eventually become the final product,
- during software development or later enhancement, when it is determined that the requirements have changed (due either to a new need or to a new perception of need), and
- during software development or later enhancement, when a "bug" is detected in the software requiring a "fix" to the design or the code or the test plans.

Software configuration management has evolved considerably over the past decade. As recently as 10 years ago, for example, the discipline of SCM was still in the dark ages. It was often performed by individuals who had failed at other assignments. It was performed by using hundreds of copies of forms piled high on desks and filed away in metal filing cabinets. Processing a change request to an existing baseline might have taken days of poring through those files. To make matters worse, project managers often could not rely on the

More recently, with the advent of lower-cost computing and such automated change control systems as the change and configuration control system (CCC) [33] and the change management system (CMS) [16], the discipline of configuration management has the prospect of being both efficient and respected as an engineering discipline. Online systems have greatly reduced the amount of paper necessary. They enable SCM personnel to report accurate and timely information about the status of any requested change to any baseline to the project managers.

SCM practices, however, vary widely across the industry. Some organizations still maintain configurations primarily with paper. Some unenlightened SCM shops think software is just a *part* and deserves just a *part number*. They do not appreciate the fine grain of software, its inherent complexity, its degree of volatility, or the subtle and complex relationships that must be understood and recorded prior to making any change to it. There are, however, SCM organizations practicing modern SCM using automated tools. Such organizations

- *Maintain their baselines using an automated CM system.* By using electronic media rather than paper to store the official baselines (i.e., the software requirements, design, code, tests and all associated documentation), it is easier to make and keep track of changes to those baselines.

- *Maintain all or most of their forms on electronic media.* There is a need to report (1) discrepancies between the product's requirements and the product's behavior, (2) new requirements, (3) a recommended change to a baseline. Rather than report these on paper, which results in a proliferation of file cabinets, it makes more sense to maintain these on electronic media.

- *Maintain all cross-references among baselines (both vertically and horizontally).* Correspondence (i.e., vertical cross-references) must be maintained between requirements and design components that satisfy them, between design components and code, between test plans and everything else. In addition, correspondence (i.e., horizontal cross-references) must be maintained among individual requirements to show their hierarchical relationships or their interdependencies. The same is true among design components.

- *Maintain all cross-references among baselines, change to those baselines, and forms requesting or authorizing those changes.* An electronic request for a change should be cross-referenced to the actual change in the baselines resulting from that request.

- *Automatically route forms from person to person with electronic sign-off.* After a customer files a change request (be it a discrepancy report or a request for a new feature) electronically, it should be automatically routed to the appropriate party for handling.

Once approved by the configuration control board (CCB), the approval should be routed automatically to the development organization [11].

- *Provide reminders to individuals with action items.* For example, when logging on to his/her computer, the chairperson of the CCB should automatically see a list of outstanding action items for the CCB.

- *Provide status to each individual at appropriate levels of abstraction and venue.* Project managers, vice presidents, individual development engineers, quality assurance personnel, and configuration management specialists each have individual needs. The view they receive of the overall process and its status should be tailored to these needs.

As SCM continues to evolve, so does software engineering. Although SCM has recently entered a new phase of evolution through the use of automated tools, software engineering methodology is now entering an entirely new phase of its evolution. In particular, software development has traditionally followed what is typically called a *waterfall model* (a term coined by Royce [32]), shown in Figure 1 (adapted from [18]). In the waterfall model, system requirements and system design result in the definition of major software subsystems called computer software configuration items (CSCIs). The CSCI then evolves through a series of phases: software requirements, preliminary design, detailed design, coding, unit testing, integration testing, and software system testing. At the completion of each phase, a set of documents and executable products is produced by the engineering organization. Those documents and products are then baselined by SCM. These are typically called the functional, allocated, and product baselines [4].

This waterfall model has survived for a long time. The software industry however, is now tackling

problems that the waterfall model cannot handle. These are complex problems, which means their requirements are not well known at the beginning of the development process, their requirements are constantly in a state of flux, and once deployed, the systems continue to undergo constant change. Consequently, when these systems are built they cost much more and are created much later than predicted, and do not satisfy real users' needs.

To address this situation, the software engineering industry is experimenting with a wide variety of new models for software development including various kinds of prototypes, reusable software components, and automated software synthesis. Software practitioners and researchers all over the world are exploring the effects of these new models on cost, schedule, and user satisfaction. They appear to offer a great deal of promise. SCM as practiced today, however, may not work under these new models of software development. The purpose of this article is to explore some of the effects these new models will have on SCM.

Summary of Software Configuration Management

In small projects, the dominant aspect of SCM is the detailed recording of the who, what, and when of each change made. See Babich [3] for a thorough discussion of this type of SCM. To accomplish this, most projects use source code control systems, exemplified by Unix's SCCS [31], DEC's CMS [16], and SofTool's CCC [33]. It is possible to use these tools in a mode in which they record any changes made, when they were made, and who made them. They also store resulting baselines in an efficient manner, by storing selected baselines and their deltas, rather than storing every minor perturbation as a full baseline. With this capability, one can (1) find out who made what change and when, (2) undo any change made, and (3) reconstruct any past version.

In larger system developments, communication and control become the dominant factors of managing change. There must be a set of well-defined procedures for reporting problems with the product, recommending changes or enhancements to the product, ensuring that all parties with an interest in a change are consulted prior to the decision being made to incorporate it, and ensuring that all affected parties are informed of the schedules associated with each change to the product. As part of these procedures, there usually are forms to be filled out, routing lists to obtain concurrence, and CCBs to provide forums for discussion. In addition, the status accounting function, which in small projects amounts to simply recording "who made what change when" becomes considerably more complex. In particular, large projects need to cross-reference a change to a request for change (i.e., record the "why"), and to cross-reference the change to other affected parts of the product. Here again, automated systems are taking root due to the need to record, track, and analyze volumes of data, and to maintain complex cross-references between large documents. Modern DBMSs have proven helpful. Some SCM tools also provide the ability to tailor the user interface and to provide CM-specific features automatically [11, 20]

The trend in both small and large developments is toward more automation of the SCM function. Thus there is more widespread use of electronic forms, automatic cross-referencing among forms and multiple representations of the product, and automatic routing of forms for approval.

There are four types of activities associated with SCM [4]: *software configuration identification,* which identifies all software components, subsystems, systems, and baselines with a unique nomenclature; *software configuration control,* which creates and enforces procedures for

the orderly creation of and subsequent changes to baselines; *software configuration status accounting,* which maintains records of all SCM activities to facilitate re-creation and orchestration of all baselines and changes; and *software configuration auditing,* which checks that each to-be-established baseline possesses the appropriate technical relationship to existing baselines.

New Life Cycle Models and SCM Problems

New life cycles offer alternatives to the traditional waterfall model. These include reusable software, throwaway prototypes, evolutionary prototypes, operational prototypes, automated software synthesis from requirements and many others (see surveys in [1, 2, 12]). The following subsections will define each approach, justify it as a viable alternative to the waterfall, highlight the associated technical, management, and engineering problems, and explore the associated configuration management problems and challenges.

Reusable Software

In the hardware creation process, designers rarely design new systems at the gate level. When designing new printed circuit boards, designers select prefabricated integrated circuits from catalogs provided by chip manufacturers. These ICs may contain as many as a few million gates. Similarly, designers of integrated circuits do not design at the gate level; designers select from libraries of standard gate arrays or standard cells that have been previously designed.

In the software creation process, developers design and code new systems right down to high-level language instruction, rarely using higher-level components that have been previously designed and tested, often reinventing the same logic over and over again. At a recent informal search of Purdue University's library system [17], over 50 sorting programs were found, a dozen of which implemented the same algorithm.

Software reuse is the process of incorporating into a new product any of the following: previously tested code, previously proven designs, previously developed requirements specifications, or previously used test plans and procedures. Figure 2 shows the resulting change to the software development life cycle. The net effect of reusing software is the same as for hardware: (1) greatly reduced development time, (2) greatly reduced development cost, and (3) increased reliability because the reused components have already been "shaken down."

There are a number of engineering problems associated with reusing software:

- Not enough is known about creating or recognizing a potentially reusable component (although hardware engineers seem to have solved this problem years ago).
- Once reusable components have been created, not enough is known about cataloging and retrieving them from a repository efficiently. Some progress, however, has been made in this regard [19, 26, 34].
- Once components have been created, catalogued, and retrieved, not enough is known about how to compose complex systems from those components. In integrated circuits, all standard cells are the same width, with commonly located power and ground buses so they all fit together perfectly. This is not so for software.

There are also management problems associated with reusing software:

- How are software developers motivated to reuse components when they believe they can build better ones?
- How are government contractors motivated to reuse software? If they reduce their costs on a cost reimbursable contract, they lower their revenues.

Some of the most difficult problems associated with software reuse are the SCM problems:

- On a typical project, software is organized into large subsystems called computer software configuration items (CSCIs) by the U.S. Department of Defense [18]. Software evolution is managed by controlling changes to each of these CSCIs. Each of the rela-

tively small components in a reusable component library, however, has a life unto itself. Does SCM need to manage every component as if it were a CSCI?

- Components may be reused many hundreds of times. At first glance, it seems unreasonable to maintain a list of pointers from reusable components to every

system using them. A chip manufacturer does not have a list of every system utilizing its chips. But without such a list in the software case, a change or a fix cannot be managed or promulgated.

- Each system reusing a particular component may have tailored it for particular needs (note that this is not usually the case in

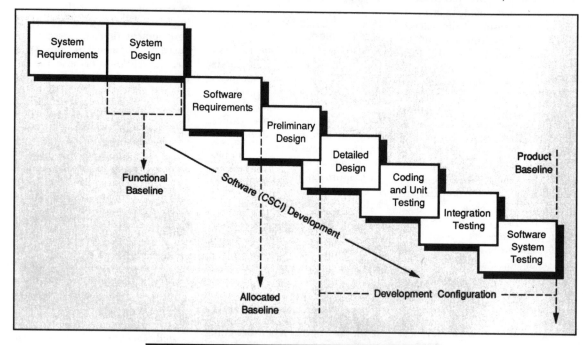

FIGURE 1
Waterfall Model of the Software Development Life Cycle

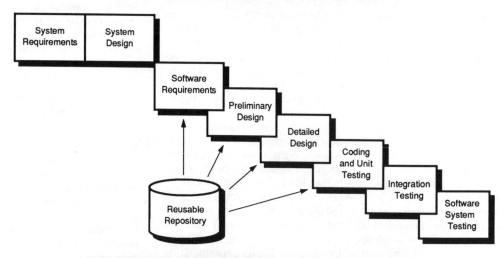

FIGURE 2
Software Reuse Model of the Software Development Life Cycle

hardware). Is it possible to manage (1) a change or a fix to the component in the library, and (2) all viable but tailored versions of components?

• What configuration control procedures handle multiple authors each "owning" a tailored version of the same component? Furthermore, what happens when person A finds a bug in person B's reusable component? Perhaps ownership (or authorship) disappears as soon as a component is accepted into the reuse library.

In short, the traditional concepts of configuration identification, configuration control, and configuration auditing practices do not seem to work well for reusable software. The following paragraphs address software configuration management from the perspectives of (1) the reusable component repository, (2) the creation of a new baseline utilizing reusable components, and (3) the modification of an existing baseline utilizing reusable components.

SCM exists because changes to software must be controlled and managed in order to produce and maintain successful software products. The control and management of changes to the software components in a reusable repository, however, are even more critical to software product success. Assuming that a particular reusable component is being used by just one product, the effect of a change to that component is identical to that of any change to any component and should undergo all the usual configuration management checks and balances. If that component is being used in multiple products, effects of uncontrolled change are obviously far more devastating. One solution to this SCM problem is to maintain the repository components the same way that a public library maintains its collection of books, namely, to keep a record of every party that has checked out an item. Then, whenever a change to a reusable component is proposed, a

change request is put through the CCBs of each product using that component. An alternative is the creation of a special CCB that controls changes to the repository only. All changes proposed to the components in the repository must be approved by this CCB only. Any change approved by this CCB results in a new equally viable version of the existing still viable component, never a replacement for it. This ensures that change cannot adversely affect users. Notices should be sent *after the fact,* however, to all CCBs responsible for products using the affected component. These CCBs can then evaluate the change and determine whether or not to upgrade. Of course, the repository CCB should explain the reason for the change; the decision of the product CCBs would probably be influenced by whether the change is a bug-fix or an enhancement. The net effect is identical to conducting multiple product CCBs where some CCBs choose to adopt and others choose to reject the change, but is far more expedient. One disadvantage is the possible proliferation of versions of any one component, and need to either

1. notify all users of any version of a component whenever any one version changes, or
2. keep track of which version of a component every user is using.

Creation of any new baseline— whether it be functional, allocated, developmental, or product—that uses components from a reusable repository is one of the few cases in which hardware configuration management (HCM) principles apply directly to software configuration management. A HCM organization typically maintains parts lists, hierarchies resulting from subassemblies, and current version numbers of any part currently being used. For software systems reusing software components, SCM maintains a similar parts list for each baseline. Some entries on the list correspond to custom product-

specific parts (i.e., new software), while others correspond to reused components or customized reused components. From a SCM perspective, new software is treated just like any other software, and reused components are treated just like hardware parts. Customized reused components are treated as two cross-referenced components: a base component (i.e., the reused component) and a delta to the base component (corresponding to the local customizations made to the repository component). From a SCM perspective, the base component is treated just like a hardware part, and the delta is treated just like other software.

Once a baseline has been established following this procedure, changes to it follow conventional software and hardware CM practices. Product CCBs meet regularly to approve, prioritize and schedule all changes. Causes for these changes are identical to those on any software product: repairs to the existing product, enhancements to the product's capability, or an evolution of the baseline (e.g., from allocated to developmental). Change to the baseline, however, can be of a variety of types:

• a change to custom (i.e., not reused) software is treated by SCM just like any change to software.
• an agreement to replace one reused component with another results in SCM making the corresponding change to the parts list. Note that it is irrelevant whether the replacement is a totally different component or a new viable version of the previous one.
• an agreement to customize a reused component causes the development organization to create a new delta of custom code, and SCM to place the new software under control and to add it to the product's parts list.
• change to a delta of a reused component is treated by SCM just like any change to software.

Throwaway Prototypes

For products that require manufac-

With an increase in the number of software products not satisfying user needs, prototyping has become quite popular.

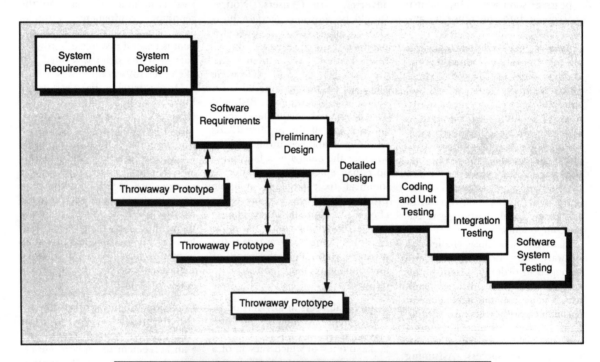

FIGURE 3
Throwaway Prototyping Model of the Software Development Life Cycle

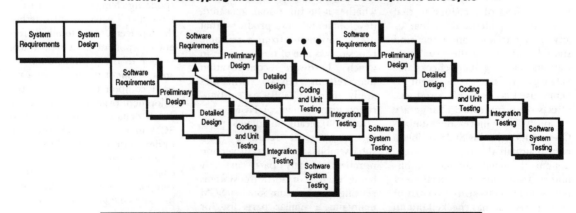

FIGURE 4
Evolutionary Prototyping Model of the Software Development Life Cycle

COMPUTING
PRACTICES

turing, much product cost lies in tooling up and running the factory. Prototypes are used in these industries to test out usability, practicality, or manufacturability of a product prior to full-scale manufacturing. In software, there is no corresponding manufacturing process. The most expensive, risky, and time-consuming task is the one-time design and implementation. Thus, prototyping would only be helpful in software if it could somehow reduce costs or risks associated with design and implementation [7].

Throwaway software prototypes are software programs created in a quick-and-dirty manner, used to validate presumed requirements, to gain experience necessary to uncover new requirements, or to validate a possible design; *and* are discarded once they fulfill their purpose [21]. Figure 3 shows how throwaway prototypes affect software development. The net effects are

1. greatly reduced risk of building a product which does not satisfy user needs [12],
2. reduced development costs due to less change during development, and
3. increased probability of project success due to enhanced communication between developer and user.

There are few engineering problems with the use of throwaway prototypes. There are numerous approaches available to construct them, including

1. using languages that facilitate very rapid (though relatively difficult-to-maintain) products such as BASIC, Lisp, APL and SNOBOL,
2. reusing software components from a previously populated repository,
3. using tools available to assist in rapid creation of user interfaces such as IBM's Structured Programming Facility (SPF), DEC's Forms Management System

(FMS), Interactive Development Environment's RAPID [35], and just about any 4th-generation language [25, 27].

Most problems with throwaway prototypes are related to management:

- How can costs be kept down with a throwaway prototype? Software developers involved in throwaway prototyping occasionally find it difficult to declare their product ready for customer inspection, and instead want to continue to play with it.

- How to respond to customers who say: "I just love that prototype. Can you add a few more lines of code and make it a production quality system?" The problem with this, of course, is that *quality and robustness cannot be retrofit into software.*

There are few unique SCM challenges associated with throwaway prototypes. The appropriate level of SCM is about the same as for small development efforts. One may use an automated code management system that tracks all changes to code by date, time, and programmer. Of course, if code from a reusable software component repository is being used, the SCM practices relating to that repository described in the previous section apply. SCM problems arise when throwaway prototypes are combined with evolutionary prototypes to create what we call *operational prototypes* to be addressed later.

Evolutionary Prototypes

With an increase in the number of software products not satisfying user needs, prototyping has become quite popular. With skyrocketing software development costs, some people have turned to prototyping as a way to reduce costs. They argue "if you have a way of producing working software so quickly, then why not deploy the prototype and make it operational? That way we end up with much

lower development costs." The fallacy is that software protypes created in a *quick* fashion are also *dirty.* A throwaway prototype cannot be simply deployed and expected to provide reliable service. Although some developers are still claiming practicality in this approach, most realize that for a prototype to survive in an operational environment and undergo the many changes that will occur to it, it must be built in a different manner than the quick and dirty throwaway prototype [12, 22].

Evolutionary prototypes are high-quality programs used to validate presumed requirements, to gain experience required to uncover new requirements, or to validate a possible design; *and* are repeatedly modified and redeployed whenever new information is learned. Figure 4 shows how evolutionary prototyping affects software development. The net effects are:

1. greatly reduced risk of building a product that does not satisfy user needs, and
2. increased probability of project success resulting from enhanced communication between developer and user.

Note how different throwaway and evolutionary prototyping are. In throwaway prototyping, only those parts of the system that are *not* well understood are built. (After all, why waste time building something that serves no purpose and which will then be discarded?) In evolutionary prototyping, those parts of the system that *are* well understood are built first, so you can continue to develop on a solid foundation. Each increment is slightly more risky than the preceding one, but the experience with preceding versions has provided enough insight into the problem to make a risky endeavor much less so. Another big difference is in quality: Throwaway prototypes are built with little or no robustness; evolutionary prototypes must have all quality built in up front or they will

373

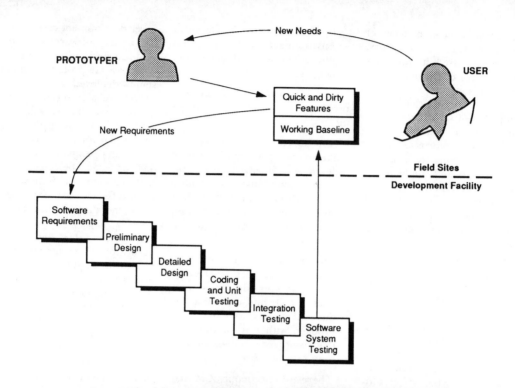

FIGURE 5

Operational Prototyping Model of the Software Development Life Cycle

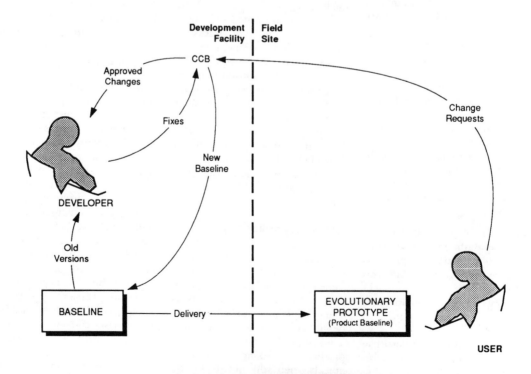

FIGURE 6

"Normal" Configuration Control Process

not be able to withstand the necessary levels of use and modification. Note that you cannot build a prototype, and then later decide if it is to be discarded or not. You *must* decide initially, or resources may be wasted building quality into something to be discarded, verifying the wrong features, trying to retrofit quality, or trying to maintain a schedule of planned enhancements on top of a shoddy foundation.

There are engineering and management problems associated with evolutionary prototyping:

- Appropriate levels of quality and documentation for an evolutionary prototype are unknown. If it is treated as a throwaway, there will be insufficient levels. If it is treated as a full-scale development, there will be sufficient, but probably unnecessarily high, levels. If any new increment results in a dead end, and has to be backed out, resources will have been wasted building in that quality level. A middle-of-the-road position is needed to reduce risk yet achieve sufficient quality. One solution is a set of evolutionary prototyping standards and guidelines. Another solution is the operational prototype, to be described in the next section.
- How is feedback from users about the use of the evolutionary prototype obtained in a timely manner, so that it can be incorporated into the next iteration? This problem may also be solved with the operational prototype.
- As experience is gained and the evolutionary prototype incorporates more requirements, each new feature becomes more and more risky. How can these new changes be incorporated in a low-risk, rapid fashion? Like the previous two problems, this problem is also solved with the operational prototype.
- Building software to accommodate large numbers of major changes is an unknown art. Some answers are: information hiding [29], low intermodule coupling

[36], high module cohesion [36], object-oriented development [8, 9], and sound documentation practices. The total answer is not known.

There are also configuration management problems associated with evolutionary prototyping. By its very nature, evolutionary prototyping thrusts SCM into the heart of the development process. In fact, all the SCM challenges of a standard life-cycle development become magnified:

- Configuration identification is challenged: there will inherently be many viable, in-use variants of all components that require identification by purpose, feature-mix, and baseline.
- Configuration control is probably the most challenged: It is almost guaranteed that there will be, at any one time, multiple versions of all baselines deployed (all of which are viable), multiple new versions under development (i.e., the next two or three versions may all be under development simultaneously), and multiple teams of developers. How are these changes planned, orchestrated, and controlled? How can all the parties interested in those changes, all of whom possess disparate goals, be coordinated?
- Configuration status accounting is challenged simply by the need to adequately inform all project participants of status of a multivariate product in several simultaneous stages of development and deployment.
- Configuration auditing is challenged by rapidly changing baselines, and the need to ensure timely promulgation of audit results that may dramatically impact any of several other-in-use and developmental baselines.

The solution to these challenges lies in judicious use of proven SCM practices, not in the creation of new ones. Evolutionary prototyping is not as much a brand-new life-cycle model as a lower-risk acceleration

of the conventional waterfall model. The only recommended change to the conventional SCM process is to populate the CCB with individuals with an extremely clear understanding of the full family of evolutionary prototypes underway. This ensures sensible decision making concerning simultaneous changes being proposed on a single component being readied for multiple future releases.

Operational Prototypes

Operational prototyping [6, 15] combines the best of throwaway and evolutionary prototyping. As shown in Figure 5, it works like this:

- A stable base is constructed using sound software engineering principles. It incorporates only those features that are well known, understood, and agreed on. This is the first step of evolutionary prototyping. When completed, this stable base of software is officially baselined by SCM.
- This version is now deployed at users' operational field sites. At each site, an expert prototyper is commissioned to observe the system in operation.
- As users use the system, they will understandably uncover problems. More importantly, as users gain experience, they will think of new features that would be helpful in the fulfillment of their assigned duties. Instead of forcing users to make phone calls or to write their comments, users need only talk to the ever-present prototyper.
- When users stop using the system (e.g., at night in a conventional operation), the prototyper constructs a quick-and-dirty implementation of desired changes on top of the working baseline.
- When new-feature implementation is complete, users experiment with the modified system to ensure that the prototyper understood the need correctly, and the requested feature really is what is needed.
- Over the course of a few days or

weeks, a collection of these temporary, quick-and-dirty changes are made to the operational baseline. Eventually, the prototyper departs the field site with those changes and returns home.

- Back at home, features incorporated by these quick-and-dirty changes are merged with others from other sites and analyzed. Although site-generated code is discarded, features they implemented are now properly engineered into a new baseline, following well-defined and accepted engineering and SCM practices.

- Finally, as these features are bundled into new versions of soft-

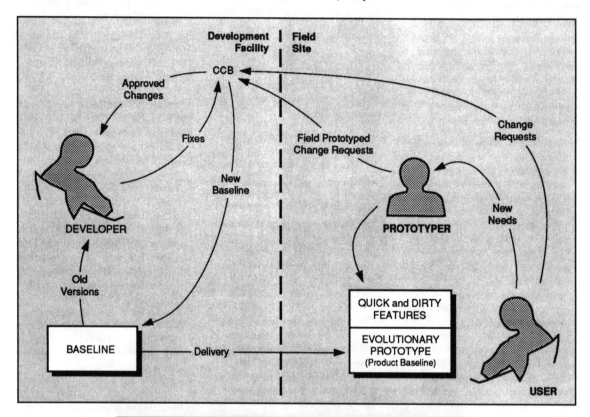

FIGURE 7
Configuration Control Process Modified for Operational Prototyping

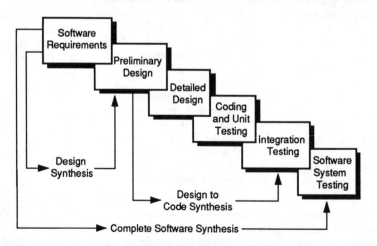

FIGURE 8
Automated Software Synthesis Model of the Software Development Life Cycle

ware, new releases are baselined and redeployed with on-site prototypers, just as before, and the process repeats.

Note that this approach solves most of the problems associated with the two earlier prototyping techniques. In particular, its use ensures a stable, quality controlled product; the ability to gain immediate user feedback without unnecessary effort by users; and the ability to provide users with rapid incorporation into the product of their expressed desires for immediate validation. Unfortunately, there are three new sets of problems:

1. People management. It takes a unique individual to serve as the on-site prototyper. That person must work well with customers, understand the application, be an extremely effective prototyper, and be willing to travel for extended periods of time if the customer site is remotely located. Such individuals are hard to find.
2. The disposition of quick-and-dirty changes made at the site. If these changes are left at the site, they may prove to be unreliable and may even adversely affect the rest of the system. This is particularly problematic if the system is deployed in a truly operational mode. On the other hand, if taken away, users may become irate because a feature is being removed that they have grown to rely on.
3. The third set of problems relate to SCM.

SCM problems can be examined from three perspectives:

1. evolutionary prototype serving as the stable base,
2. throwaway prototypes being written in the field, and
3. customers and users.

The evolutionary prototype is developed using conventional techniques with its major components being identified as CSCIs. As with any conventional development, the

functional baseline is created and put under configuration control when initial system-level requirements are approved. On approval, the software requirements specification is put under configuration control as part of the allocated baseline. On completion of system-level testing, the product baseline is created to help control changes to the design, code, test and user products and their associated documentation. The software is then fielded with knowledge that the baseline is under control. As problems are reported in the field, they undergo the "normal" process of configuration control. Change Requests (CRs) are written, reviewed, approved, categorized into requirements change vs. bug, prioritized and their fixes scheduled for later releases. See Figure 6. So far, everything about evolutionary prototyping concerning SCM is identical to conventional development.

Prototypers in the field are making their local changes using only *small project* SCM, i.e., a tool may automatically maintain a trace of what changes to the code are being made by whom and when. As prototypers return home from the field, they carry with them a set of patches on electronic media, and in their heads they carry a set of modified requirements that correspond to the new or modified features realized by those patches. These enhancements must be funneled into the SCM process of the developing evolutionary prototype. The easiest way to do this is to initiate change requests for each change made in the field, as shown in Figure 7. A new entry must be included on the standard CR form to clearly indicate this as a proposed change to software functionality that has already been field tested as a prototype at site x. The normal configuration control process can now merge these with the other two types of change requests, i.e., those corresponding to bugs being reported, and those corresponding to functionality enhancement requests that have not been prototyped.

All these change requests are evaluated by a CCB composed of developers and customers based on benefit to customer and cost and schedule impacts; then they are prioritized and packaged into scheduled to-be-built releases. Obvious priority must be given to those originating from the fielded prototypes since the customer has already "tasted" these enhancements.

Automated Software Synthesis

Automated software synthesis means automating software development. The following are typical cases of automated software synthesis, as shown in Figure 8.

- Users and/or software developers write a formal requirements specification, and a software tool is used to translate requirements into operational software. For database applications, this technology is widely available today in fourth-generation languages [25, 27]. For other applications, technology is generally available, but primarily in research institutions [30]; requirements languages that must be used are either too cumbersome or too formal for common use at this time, and the resulting software tends not to satisfy performance constraints.
- Users and/or software developers write a formal requirements specification, and a software tool is used to automatically generate the high-level design; then software engineers complete development by more conventional means. As in the first case, this technology is currently available, but requirements languages are too formal and the resulting designs are far from optimal.
- Users and/or software developers

    1. perform a high-level design, usually as hierarchies of data-flow diagrams (e.g., see [37]) showing movement of data and control through the system, or as hierarchies of hypothetical machines such as statecharts (e.g., see [23]),
    2. specify algorithms for the exe-

cution of each primitive function, usually as Structured English, decision tables, decision trees, finite state machines, etc., and then

3. use a software tool to simulate or generate a majority of low-level code. This type of software synthesis is the easiest to use today, and is available from the vendors of many CASE tools (e.g., [24, 35]).

In all three scenarios, software is being developed at a higher level than that of a high-level programming language, and software tools are used to automatically generate necessary lower-level instructions. The potential effects of this process on software development costs and schedules are significant. The biggest problems are technical:

- What specification language should be used? It must be formal enough to enable software synthesis but readable enough for customers who understand an application but who may not be trained computer scientists [10]. Surveys of available specification languages can be found in [13, 14].
- Can real users ever be expected to write or read specifications? [28]
- Will performance of the resulting systems ever be adequate? The answer to this will eventually be yes. Early users of any high-level language, however, have complained that their software has run too slowly.

The best way to understand SCM implications of software synthesis is to study how we perform SCM today on systems written in high-level languages. The software is written and maintained in the high-level language, even though the software running on the computer is really machine language. SCM manages most changes at the high level. The only SCM responsibility with respect to the machine code is to ensure a correspondence between every compiled version of

machine code with an identifiable baselined source configuration. In software synthesis, SCM must manage all changes to software at the level from which synthesis occurred—usually the requirements level. SCM's involvement with lower-level versions of software is limited to maintaining correct correspondence between these versions and identifiable versions of the allocated baseline.

Summary

Changes necessary to the discipline of software configuration management to accommodate the radical changes being made to the software development process have been discussed. In some cases, changes to SCM were straightforward or even nonexistent. In other cases, changes were significant. As software costs continue to skyrocket, and more resources are spent on systems that do not satisfy user needs, more widespread use of reusable software and all kinds of prototyping will be seen. As the problem continues to escalate, automated software synthesis will become more practical, and brand new yet-to-be-invented alternatives to the waterfall life cycle will appear. Software engineers bear the responsibility of learning all these techniques. Software management bears the responsibility of embracing these new life cycles to help control costs and to better assist customers. Software configuration management personnel must find ways to manage new types of changes to software development. If we do not learn to manage change, we will become its victims, not its beneficiaries.

Acknowledgment

The authors would like to thank Hassan Gomaa for his helpful comments on an earlier version of this manuscript. **C**

References

1. Agresti, W. *Tutorial: New Paradigms for Software Development.* IEEE Computer Society, Washington, D.C., 1986.

2. Alexander, L. and Davis, A. Selection criteria for software development life cycle models. Masters Thesis, George Mason University, Fairfax, Va. 1990. In *Proceedings of the IEEE Computer Software and Applications Conference* (Washington, D.C.), IEEE Comput. Soc., 1991.

3. Babich, W. *Software Configuration Management.* Addison Wesley, Reading, Mass., 1986.

4. Bersoff, E. et al., *Software Configuration Management.* Prentice Hall, Englewood Cliffs, N.J., 1980.

5. Bersoff, E. Elements of software configuration management. *IEEE Trans. Softw. Eng. 10,* 1 (Jan. 1984), 79–87.

6. Bersoff, E. and Davis, A. Some thoughts on acquisition strategies for C³I systems. *SIGNAL* (1991).

7. Boehm, B. A spiral model of software development and enhancement. *IEEE Comput., 21,* 5 (May 1988), 61–72.

8. Booch, G. Object Oriented Development. *IEEE Trans. Softw. Eng. 12,* 2 (Feb. 1986), 211–221.

9. Coad, P. and Yourdon, E. OOA—*Object Oriented Analysis.* Prentice Hall, Englewood Cliffs, N.J., 1989.

10. Davis, A. The design of a family of applications-oriented requirements languages. *IEEE Comput. 15,* 5 (May 1982), 21–28.

11. Davis, A. Customized automated configuration management. STARS Business Practices Workshop, Nov. 1985.

12. Davis A. et al. A strategy for comparing alternative software development life cycle models. *IEEE Trans. Softw. Eng. 14,* 10 (Oct. 1988), 1453–1461.

13. Davis, A. A comparison of techniques for the specification of external system behavior. *Commun. ACM 31,* 9 (Sept. 1988), 1098–1115.

14. Davis, A. *Software Requirements: Analysis and Specification.* Prentice Hall, Englewood Cliffs, N.J., 1990.

15. Davis, A. Operational prototyping: The POST story submitted to *IEEE Softw.,* 1991.

16. Digital Equipment Corporation. VAX DEC/CMS Reference Manual. Maynard, Mass., Nov. 1984.

17. DeMillo, R. Observing reusable Ada software components—techniques for recording and using operational histories. AIRMICS Project Review, Fairfax, Va., Feb. 1, 1989.

18. Department of Defense. *Military Standard: Defense System Software Development,* DOD-STD-2167A, Washington, D.C., Feb. 1988.

19. Freeman, P. *IEEE Tutorial: Software Reusability.* Washington D.C.: IEEE Computer Society Press, 1987.

20. Fricker, S. Configuration management using the change and configuration control (CCC) 2.0 environment. Second Annual CCC Users Group (Mar. 1985).

21. Gomaa, H. and Scott, D. Prototyping as a tool in the specification of user requirements. *IEEE Fifth International Conference on Software Engineering* (Mar. 1981).

22. Gomaa, H. Software prototypes - Keep them or throw them away?. Inf. Tech. State-of-the-Art Report on Prototyping, Pergamon Press, London, 1986.

23. Harel, D. Statecharts: A visual formalism for complex systems. *Sci. Comput. Prog. 8* (1987), North-Holland, 231–274.

24. Harel, D. et al. STATEMATE: A working environment for the development of reactive systems. *IEEE 10th International Conference on Software Engineering* (Apr. 1988).

25. Horowitz, E. et al. A Survey of Application Generators. *IEEE Softw., 2,* 1 (Jan. 1985), 40–54.

26. Incorvaia, A. and Davis, A. Case studies in software reuse. IEEE COMPSAC '90, IEEE Computer Society Press, Washington, D.C., 1990.

27. Martin, J. *Fourth Generation Languages.* Prentice Hall, Englewood Cliffs, N.J., 1986.

28. Orr, K. User focused system development needs planning and design. *FUTURES(S),* 1987, 5–7.

29. Parnas, D. On the criteria to be used in decomposing systems into modules. *Commun. ACM 15,* 12 (Dec. 1972), 1053–1058.

30. Partsch, H. and Steinbruggen, R. Program transformation systems. *ACM Comput. Surv., 15,* 3 (Sept. 1983), 199–236.

31. Rochkind, M. The source code control system. *IEEE Trans. Softw. Eng. 1,* 12 (Dec. 1975), 364–370.

32. Royce, W. Managing the development of large software systems: Concepts and techniques. *WESCON,* Aug. 1970; reprinted in *Ninth International Conference on Software Engineering,* Washington, D.C.. IEEE Computer Society Press, 1987, pp. 328–338.

33. SofTool Corporation. Change and Configuration Control (CCC) User's Manual. Goleta, Calif., 1988.

34. Vogelsong, T. Remarks made during interview by A. Davis and A. Incorvaia, Arlington, Virginia: U.S. AIRMICS RAPID Project, July 27, 1989.

35. Wasserman, A. Extending state transition diagrams for the specification of human-computer interaction. *IEEE Trans. Softw. Eng. 11,* 8 (Aug. 1985), 669–713.

36. Yourdon, E. and Constantine, L. *Structured Design.* Prentice Hall, Englewood Cliffs, N.J., 1979.

37. Yourdon, E. *Modern Structured Analysis.* Prentice Hall, Englewood Cliffs, N.J., 1989.

CR Categories and Subject Descriptors: D.2.9 [**Software Engineering**]: D.2.m [**Software Engineering**]: Miscellaneous

Additional Key Words and Phrases: Life cycle models, process models prototyping, reusable software, software configuration management, software engineering, software management

About the Authors:
ALAN M. DAVIS is a professor of software systems engineering at George Mason University in Fairfax, Virginia. He was previously a vice president at BTG, Inc., and a director of the Software Technology Center at GTE Laboratories. **Author's Present Address:** George Mason University, Center for Software Systems Engineering, School of Information Technology and Engineering, Fairfax, VA 22030-4444.

EDWARD H. BERSOFF is the president and founder of BTG, Inc., a northern Virginia-based company involved in the development and integration of computer-based solutions for a wide variety of complex real-time applications. In 1989 he was named KPMG Peat Marwick mid-Atlantic High Technology Entrepreneur of the Year. **Author's Present Address:** BTG, Inc., 1945 Old Gallows Road, Vienna, VA 22182.

This research is supported in part by the Commonwealth of Virginia Center for Innovative Technology Grant #STC-87-002 and the U.S. Army Institute for Research in Management Information and Computer Sciences (AIRMICS)/Martin Marietta Energy Systems Contract #19K-CR588C.

Quality management — procedures and practices

by G. D. Frewin and B. J. Hatton

This paper presents a discussion of the need for better quality management, followed by descriptions of what the authors currently consider to be the two most effective instruments of its achievement; these are the project (or product) quality plan and its associated test plans. Finally, there is a discussion of the use of the quality plan and test plans beyond their initiating projects, followed by a summary and some thoughts on future work. A brief set of references is appended, mainly as an indication of the starting point for the concepts and procedures described in the rest of this paper.

1 Introduction

The definition of the term 'quality' which has been adopted by the British Standards Institution and a number of other national and international bodies states that:

'Quality is the totality of features and characteristics of a product or service which bear on its ability to satisfy a given need.'

A quality failure, or defect, is thus the presence in a product or service of a feature or characteristic which creates dissatisfaction in given circumstances. Defects can arise from several causes, starting with a failure to perceive and specify the customer's real needs, proceeding through failures to translate the specification into a conforming design and/or to maintain that conformity throughout the development processes, and culminating in a product which cannot be demonstrated to meet its specification.

The situation might be controllable if there were only one specification, and a standard route through product development. However, in reality, it is rarely possible for either a user or a developer to have sufficient understanding and control of his circumstances to enable the colla-tion of a specification which will remain valid throughout a product's development and use. Neither is it usually possible for a developer to be able to put together a sequence of processes in which every one of the several different transformations between specification and end product can be proved to be exactly equivalent either to each other or to the specification.

Hence real specifications and developments tend to progress irregularly, with returns to stages which had once been considered complete and with the possibility of significant changes to the first specification being required at almost any point in the development process or in-service life.

In this difficult and changing environment, the basic aims of quality management are the prevention of errors, the detection and removal of faults which contrive to occur, and the demonstration of conformance between intermediate representations of a product and between final product representations, their functionality and performance, and their specifications. In addition, there is a responsibility to assist in the improvement of processes, procedures, tools and enabling mechanisms (such as training, standards and user-awareness) in such a way that the achievement of desired qualities becomes progressively more effective and efficient, throughout the organisation.

Our own initial interest in this area of work arose from the desire to improve both the quality of software produced in our own projects and the experience of working in those projects. That is, we were concerned to find procedures, methods and tools which were satisfying to work with, consistently produced the required results, and were sufficiently predictable, controllable and cost-effective to meet project management objectives as well as quality management objectives.

In studying the literature we found that, in comparison with other areas of software development, little work has been done towards improving software quality management procedures, and it was our view that investigations into this subject would benefit the software industry in general. Subsequently we have become involved in the Alvey Test Specification and Quality Management project and believe that the working procedures and tools to manage and measure software quality, which will ultimately be recommended as an outcome of that project, will be of benefit to a wide range of people concerned with the reliable development and procurement of software with qualities which are as required.

The provision of a detailed quality plan for every project and a formal test plan for every product have been brought into the Test Specification and Quality Management project as the initial basic instruments by which the methods of constraining and enhancing quality-affecting factors are presented for consideration and guidance during a software development project.

We believe that all sizes and types of

project will benefit from following a detailed quality plan; however, the need to follow such a plan increases with the size, value and importance of the project.

2 Costs and benefits associated with managing — and failing to manage — software quality

2.1 Failing to manage software quality

Costs of failing to manage software quality include unnecessarily expensive and/or long-running projects, and the immediate and long-term effects of having dissatisfied customers. In addition to this, there are less easily quantified items, such as:

- staff disaffection, leading to loss of efficiency and/or loss of the staff themselves — among other reasons, this state can be caused by a project's lack of success, lack of apparent purpose, and/or emphasis on procedures and standards which are not seen by staff as being useful
- the formation of low expectations for productivity (which will be reflected in estimates and achievements in future)
- low appreciation of the technical and administrative ability of management, and consequent difficulties in achieving acceptance and implementation of procedures, plans, assessments etc.
- a failure to record software activities in such a way that they can contribute to future improvements.

Short-term cost savings (which could be regarded by the short-sighted as benefits) can be made if quality management is not considered — for example by ignoring the consequences of failing to ensure that each task should result in products of usable quality or that every clause of the specification should be accompanied by the definition of a demonstration that the clause has been satisfied. These examples could lead to the project spending no effort on product and process assurance, and could reduce the time spent in testing. However, if the project goes through to completion, the inevitable and costly consequences are always greater than any short-term benefit to project schedules and plans — and no manager can afford to snatch this kind of relief unless he is convinced that the project will be cancelled before the chickens come home to roost.

2.2 Getting a grip on quality management

Quality management may appear expensive in the short term — procedures must be devised and tested, tools obtained and integrated, and staff must be encouraged and instructed to apply the new methods properly. However, real benefits and improved results should be apparent within an encouragingly short time of implementing the procedures. Indeed, actively bad management may be needed to avoid benefits. Although expenses and bad reactions tend to make themselves obvious, while benefits usually need to be actively sought, with sensible planning, recording and analysis there should be little difficulty in obtaining and demonstrating real improvement well within the course of a single project, or the life time of a single product.

The following list gives examples of the impact of improving and measuring software quality through quality management procedures:

- Known and predictable product reliability enables the software user to plan and schedule activities accurately.
- Predictable reliability can be vital in software which controls, for example, nuclear reactors, aeroplanes and medical diagnoses.
- From a producer's point of view, higher-quality software:
    - □ minimises the risk of legal/financial repercussions due to damage caused by faulty software
    - □ enhances his reputation within the marketplace.
- From the customer's point of view, his business will not suffer because of the use of an unreliable software product.
- Both producers and customers want software to be produced more cheaply and reliably. Implementing quality management procedures will reduce costs by:
    - □ ensuring that the customer is involved throughout specification and development, and is always clear on what is and what is not part of his new system — this means that any differences of concept or requirement are made manifest at the earliest possible point, and that there is a good match between release and acceptance criteria
    - □ less time being spent throughout the software life cycle on correcting faults and re-testing
    - □ the automation of testing and the design of products which are more 'testable', making the maintenance and updating of software easier, more reliable and less time consuming.
- For everyone concerned it is important to create products in the shortest possible time and which can be demonstrated to meet the customer's needs. Development methods which lead to a greater proportion of initially 'correct' products lead to lower development costs and higher customer satisfaction, which in turn lead to more competitive production.

Some producers may feel that, since they produce satisfactory software already, altering their quality management procedures will not benefit them in any way. This is not necessarily the case. They may, in fact, be producing higher-quality software than is actually required, or producing it more slowly, thereby wasting their own time and effort and charging customers more than is necessary. This situation can only be avoided by having the ability to specify and demonstrate the required qualities accurately and repeatedly.

3 Software quality management overview

3.1 Basic elements of software quality management

The basic elements can be stated briefly as consisting of specification, planning, defect prevention, defect correction, measurement, demonstration and control of the qualities of a product and of the project which develops that product. Each of these aspects is considered briefly below; an abstract and general view of the nature of software development is presented in Fig. 1. The model of the process has been presented purely as a basis for discussion in this paper, and it is fully accepted that there are many other alternative models in use which are more faithful to particular situations.

This paper is mainly concerned with the planning and control of the activities from analysis to release, inclusive, and it is suggested that it is prudent to ensure that each of the tasks in these periods is predicted, or undertaken to a moderate degree of detail, at the opening of the project in order to reach a sufficiently reliable position on the project's and product's feasibility in good time. Thus it is recommended that each of the standard sections of a quality plan, and the higher levels of the test plans, should always be drafted and agreed in principle before the analysis phase is opened — and that the arrival of any disturbing surprises or shocks in the later, formal creation of those documents should be regarded as a matter for serious concern.

3.2 The specification of required qualities

A specification will define the functions which the product must perform and qualities which must be present either in particular functions or in the product as a whole. For example, a function might be specified as doing certain things in a given time or to a given accuracy, while the entire product might be specified as having the qualities of ease of use or of being relatively simple to port between different supporting systems.

It is obvious that the example of a functional item specification just given would be straightforward to develop and demonstrate, with the main problems being concerned with practical details, while the quality specification for the whole product would present difficulties in interpretation, achievement, measurement and demonstration. It is an important aspect of quality management that specifications should be analysed into their constituent propositions — 'this function will calculate the result of this algorithm to an accuracy of four decimal places', 'this product will be easy to use' — and that for each one the feasibility and methods of achievement and demonstration be documented and agreed.

The specification roles and responsibilities of the technical and managerial development staff, and of the corresponding staff with the customer or user, should be documented and formally agreed in the project's quality plan, as should the general description of the methods and controls to be used in achieving the specified product. Precise details of process controls and product demonstrations appear in the test plan.

It is obvious that there must be an agreed and effective way of dealing with ambiguous or impossible aspects of a specification at the earliest possible point in a project. Continuing the example given above, 'easy to use' might be built into a product by way of an intensive prototyping and review process applied to all aspects of the user interfaces with the system, and demonstration might be agreed to have been made after a period of trial use of the completed product in which not more than a given number of wrong usages and requests for help were made.

Early translation of ambiguous 'quality' statements into detailed processes for achievement, demonstration and acceptance enables more accurate project planning and costing and reduces the chance of awkward misunderstandings at later project stages.

In addition to product aspects specified for a given customer or user, there may be others which are either required or assumed to meet local standards, general standards or local convenience. For instance, traceability between the specification and intermediate products is unlikely to concern the user but is of great importance to a developer, who may have to reconstruct either the product or the project at some point. Similarly, the practice of re-using parts of products requires certain standards for the design, documentation and control of all parts. Aspects of a specification which are not special to the particular product may either be represented in the main specification (and thus flow into the quality plan in the normal way) or may be called on by the

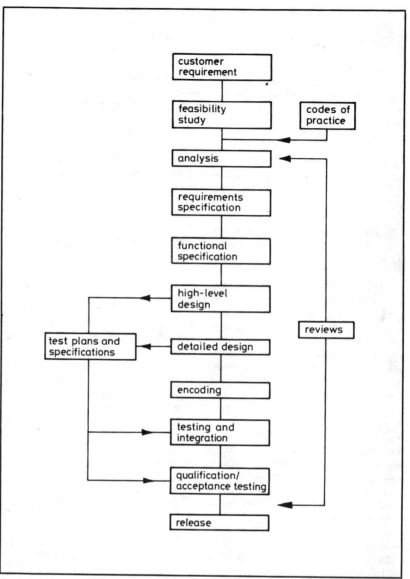

Fig. 1 A software development process

quality plan as standards or codes of practice to be applied during the project.

3.3 Planning a controlled achievement of required qualities

The phrase 'controlled achievement' has been used above. This means that there is not only a possible and known process by which elements of a specification can be instantiated, but that the process is such that it can be tested at intermediate points to indicate whether it is working as expected, either in general or for a particular element of the specification. This is an area which has not yet been adequately researched or served by appropriate concepts, models and metrics. While reviews and inspections, made against suitable checklists and fully followed up and recorded, are very useful in controlling the creation of general qualities and specific functionality, there is little support for anyone needing to engineer their processes more closely.

3.4 Defect prevention and defect containment

If defects can be prevented from occurring, the effort applied to their detection, removal and management will be reduced. While an effective prevention programme can thus reduce the overall costs of quality management, it should never be used as a reason for dismissing the need for such management: faults will always be with us, and it will always be an asset to be able to increase confidence in the belief that a process or a product has few if any faults — without a full quality management programme, there can be no such confidence.

It is important in defect prevention and reduction to limit the freedom of an error to propagate through the development, i.e. to prevent as many as possible of the faults which occur from leaving the process in which they were born in the products of that process, and therefore potentially affecting other processes and products adversely. The measures taken to limit faults are collectively known as defect containment, and they are principally found in product design (where interactions between design elements can be consciously limited) and in the design of the development process (where the natural propensities of one step in the process to result in faults of a particular kind can be used to tailor the detection procedures at the end of the process for maximum efficiency and security).

3.5 Defect detection

In spite of the defect prevention measures taken in the analysis and design stages it is likely that some residual defects will be present after them, in all but trivial programs. Thus defect detection and removal techniques must also be used. Review techniques (including 'inspections' and animations) and testing are the two main methods currently employed: for safety both types should be applied in every case, since they each tend to disclose a different profile of faults.

The cost of removing a defect increases rapidly with the extent of progress between its creation and discovery [1]. As defects may be created at any stage from the formulation of requirements to coding, and as the output from one stage forms the specification for the next, it follows that the output of each stage must be carefully reviewed and checked for correctness and any required modifications made before the next stage is commenced.

The importance of carrying out these reviews carefully and using personnel of adequate competence cannot be overstressed. Experience suggests that this is the most cost-effective method of uncovering specification, design and coding defects. Failure to perform such reviews or to act on their findings has often led to inadequate product quality.

All software must be tested by program execution in a controlled environment against defined test specifications and carefully chosen test data. There are a number of testing strategies which can be employed, but 'bottom-up' testing is probably the most widely applied and accepted [2]. The degree of testing to be applied should be defined in the project quality plan.

The testing should initiate execution of every statement at least once and exercise all interfaces. However, it will generally be impossible to test all combinations of paths, and hence the tests and input data must be carefully chosen so that the successful execution of the aggregate of tests implies a very high probability that the program is correct.

Clearly each defect found must be elim-

inated. On the other hand, each defect removed creates a new program, and an adequate selection of tests must be repeated (regression testing) to give confidence that no new defects have been introduced. All defects found should also be recorded and analysed: a high incidence of defects found during development in one part of the software may be a pointer to poor reliability, and re-design of that part should be considered.

When all unit and integration testing has been successfully completed, it is strongly advocated that a separate qualification or acceptance test be run before release to the customer (in the instance of there being an outside customer). This should cover all demonstrable aspects of the requirements specification and ideally should be run in the target environment. The customer should be invited to prepare or agree the qualification test specification and witness the running of the tests. On the successful completion of these tests the product can then be released to the customer.

3.6 Measuring quality (or qualities)

Quality can only be managed if it can be specified and measured unambiguously and consistently, i.e. if there are both precise and accepted words to describe the qualities of interest and the complementary concepts, metrics and other instruments by which they can be quantified. As we currently lack adequate provisions for both the quantitative and qualitative specification of software qualities, we must for the moment deal as best as we can with quality indicators which are either or both indirect and imprecise. Consequently we need to apply the most powerful procedures which we can find for specification by example or by demonstration [3]. This has led to an emphasis on the inclusion of descriptions of acceptable demonstrations with qualitative elements of a product's specification, and to an early and intensive pre-occupation with the creation and acceptance of all levels of test plans.

Examples of our present problems include even such apparently obvious qualities as the size or 'density' of a program. 'Density' has been used here to indicate the intensity of logical operations within a program, and is related to the essential complexity of the tasks being performed and to the way in which the design and development of the program has acted to reduce or to enhance that complexity. There are no standard measures for either program attribute, and, more seriously, there are no demonstrably valid relationships between 'size' and 'density' and more important properties such as a program's innate capacity

for being understood, or amended or interfaced to other programs and systems. There are 'demonstrable' relationships between size and structural features and costs, or errors, but there are no known causal relationships [4].

There are several aspects of the nature of a completed program, and of its behaviour when in use, which are important to its users. These aspects include reliability of operation, ease of use (or 'user-friendliness'), ease of maintenance and portability. Although there are rudimentary theories and models of the way in which a program's design and development affect these qualities, and hence the beginnings of an engineering science by which they may be measured, predicted and controlled, there seems to be no reason to suppose that this area of research and development will be in a position to supply the needs of software buyers and builders in the near future.

3.7 Quality demonstration

It is not enough to specify qualities which are required to be present in a product, and to devise a development process which puts them there — for acceptability their presence must be demonstrated. As has been pointed out above (in Sections 3.6 and 3.2), this means that the maker and receiver must mutually agree, and probably mutually perform, demonstrations of those qualities. These demonstrations necessarily have to wait until near the end of the development, and for their peace of mind both parties would like reliable early indications of whether the qualities will or will not be present in the final product in the required degree.

Depending on the nature of the product, its intended use and the processes used in development, it may be possible to obtain these early indications, either directly (by prototyping or a phased delivery) or indirectly (by counting or measuring events and attributes found in early stages of development).

Although both direct and indirect methods must be treated with caution, they are the best currently available, and should contribute to the quality and test plans. Some of the disadvantages are as follows:

- *Prototyping:* Modes of use, workloads and interaction with both the manual and computing environment all tend to change once a product is in full operation. Thus a satisfactory prototype may not translate into an acceptable product.
- *Phased delivery:* As well as having the disadvantages of prototyping, the partial deliveries encourage working methods which make full use of whatever is currently in hand. This often leads to ingenious interim solutions to compensate for the parts which are not yet available, and

then to subsequent non-standard use of the full system. Together these mean that neither the parts nor the whole should be judged by standards laid down at the start of the project, and that the release and acceptance plans should be reviewed and revised for each delivery.

• *Indirect quality indications:* While these can give a fairly accurate general expectation about a product (for instance, products with a complex design structure and/or an unstable development environment can be predicted to be of poorer operational quality than ones which are simple and from a stable situation), there is at present insufficient theory or evidence to enable reliable inferences to be drawn.

3.8 Controlling quality during product design and development

The Sections above have discussed our deficient situation with respect to specifying, measuring and demonstrating the qualities of a software product. Given this, the only responsible thing for a quality manager to do is to choose tools and methods which have good reputations, and to seek for direct and indirect controls throughout product design and development. While no one of the controls might be reliable in itself, or be related to all the qualities of interest, the use of several different measures and indicators should at the very least enable a more informed choice of controls in future projects, and can be expected to give better results than no controls at all.

By making quality and test plans and following them closely, and by enhancing their value by integrating these activities across several projects, a good measure of local predictability and control should be achieved — even if the underlying reasons are not yet clear.

3.9 Future developments

The advent of new, advanced methods or techniques (here we have in mind specification languages, design languages, automated 'pseudo-code' interpretation, automated source code generation) should not prevent or avoid the requirements for planned and controlled defect prevention and detection since, although the defects may be fewer and of less severity, some will certainly still exist.

No new methods or techniques should be adopted generally unless suitable means are also introduced — at the same time — to ensure that appropriate defect prevention, and defect detection and repair, are possible in the new environments that these methods or techniques will create, and that the resultant products are of at least the same quality as that achieved with the best of current practice.

4 The roles and contents of the quality plan

4.1 Introduction to the quality plan

It is becoming more common for the better organised procurers of software to ask for a quality plan as part of the contractual package, and for suppliers — especially those working to fixed prices — to have some form of overall quality plan for all their developments. There are thus several general-purpose, and company-specific, standards (or models) of quality plans available [5], and we should perhaps justify the production of another. Without presenting a comparison and assessment of all the other versions known to us, we can only give qualitative reasons for suggesting that our version is worth consideration by readers — briefly, they are that:

• the version has been applied successfully in a range of different projects: it is not bound to any particular method of development, product type or customer/ user organisation

• the version has been found to be largely compatible with US and UK standards (or proposals for standards), and we believe the differences from those standards to be in favour of our version, with its greater generality and flexibility

• because our aims include the improvement of our software engineering, the plan asks for data collection beyond that strictly necessary for any one project — there is a higher-level plan (not given here for reasons of space) which is concerned with the re-usability and integration of all quality plans and the information collected under them (see Section 6.1 for a discussion of this topic).

4.2 The role of quality plans

The quality plan brings quality objectives together with the means by which they are to be achieved, the controls which will assure that the processes and their results are in line with objectives, and the organisation and the administration which will support and relate all the activities and intentions of the plan.

Each quality plan should contain a scheme for the collection, analysis and application of project data. While the collection of information to serve management purposes is usually routine, and quality records will be kept to support statements on the character of the delivered product, more sophisticated data usages can often be found which can identify areas of risk in the project or product, help locate reasons for the deviations and predict long-term outcomes.

Quality plans and quality records there-fore provide the guidelines for carrying out and controlling at least the following:

• development processes
• documentation management
• design evaluation
• re-use of parts
• product testing
• data collection and interpretation
• acceptance and release processes.

4.3 The contents of a quality plan

A quality plan identifies the method of working to be used throughout a project (including an indication of the relevant standards and guidelines to be used) in order to achieve the agreed quality of the product; i.e. included in the quality plan are descriptions of the procedures to be used to enable adequate quality specification, defect detection, defect prevention, controlled correction etc.

The following sections are normally included in a quality plan:

• *Introduction to the quality plan:* The introduction to the quality plan should contain:

☐ a statement of which project it relates to

☐ a statement of the agreed quality of the product(s), expressed as technical requirements

☐ a list of deliverables (software items, support documentation etc.) and any quality requirements for them

☐ a statement of intent to outline the methods, practices and tools to be used to achieve the agreed quality of the product

☐ a statement of the target environment (for example hardware, operating system, other software)

☐ a statement of how (and by whom) product release and delivery will occur.

• *Description of the project:* This section provides a very brief overview of the purpose and aims of the project, including a description of the work involved. Quality objectives for the product should be emphasised here. Reference should be made to other documents, in particular the project plan, which provide a more detailed description of specific aspects of the project, for example the project contract (this includes a statement on the situation concerning ownership, copyright and royalties), requirements specifications, technical specifications, corporate quality guide, project plan, design plan, test plan.

• *Documentation structure and production:* This section indicates how the documents will relate to one another and what the naming and/or numbering system will be. Reference should be made to the project plan for a list of all documents which will be produced throughout the project, including identification of the user manuals. Information should be included on which documents must be reviewed and approved before production of others can commence. For example, certain testing activities may have to take place before further documents can be produced or reviewed.

- *Project organisation and responsibilities:* This section includes a statement of staff responsibility for:

  ☐ adherence to quality control procedures
    ☐ quality approval
    ☐ the quality of each deliverable
    ☐ meeting requirements
    ☐ product maintenance
    ☐ product support
    ☐ user training
    ☐ acceptance of the product
    ☐ attending reviews of both software and documentation.

Note that the project plan also provides details of the structure of the project team, along with staff skills and availability.

- *Codes of practice:* The standards and guidelines to be used throughout the development of the product should be listed. This section provides a more detailed description of the standards and guidelines to be used than does the corresponding section in the project plan.

- *Quality control:* This section provides an outline of the working procedures which will be implemented in order to ensure that the product is initially correct (as opposed to quality assurance procedures which trigger retrospective correction). Where a corporate quality guide exists, this section covers the interactions between quality control at the group level and that within the project, as well as those peculiar to the project. Quality control procedures include:

  ☐ identification of any special checking or design procedures which will help to ensure that a certain level or measure of quality is attained
  ☐ indication of when and where procedural audits, documentation audits, code inspections and document reviews should be held
  ☐ indications of what data should be collected on products and processes (for example, details of faults found at each review and at each test attempt, and the effort used in the repair of each fault) — there should also be an indication of how data should be interpreted and what actions should result
  ☐ an outline of any field trial arrangements
  ☐ identification of any quality metrics to be captured.

Reference should be made to the relevant documentation on quality control procedures.

- *Quality assurance:* This section outlines the procedures for analysing pieces of work after they have been completed,

i.e. retrospective checking which will trigger any necessary correction to ensure that a product attains a given level or measure of quality. The following quality assurance procedures should be defined:

  ☐ at which stages of the project the work and progress will be reviewed and what form the reviews (and inspections) will take, for example meetings, written comments
  ☐ how to ensure that certain procedures are addressed
  ☐ which reports and plans should be produced at which stages of the project
  ☐ the required levels of testing for various aspects of the product, i.e. what to check for when trying to establish that testing has been successfully completed
  ☐ the responsibility for and procedures for quality audits and at what stages and frequency they should be held.

Reference should be made to the relevant documentation on quality assurance procedures.

- *Test approach·* The quality plan provides an indication of which parts of the product will be tested and of what the testing method will be in order to ensure the required levels of testedness.

Reference should be made to the test plan which provides details of the testing activities and their organisation. The test plan defines the scope, the assessment criteria, the assessment techniques (these include an assessment of testing techniques to decide which would be most suitable, and assessment of test results to draw some conclusion about the quality of the product), the resources and the schedule of the testing activities.

- *Configuration management:* This section defines the following:

  ☐ the methods to be used for the identification, control, release and version numbering systems of the product
  ☐ change request and fault report mechanisms to be used throughout the project
  ☐ how source code will be stored and archived
  ☐ who will be responsible for adherence to the agreed configuration management procedures (for example the software librarian).

Note

A section on configuration management may be found in either or both of a project plan and the quality plan for that project, since the activities and responsibilities include tasks ranging from pure administration to the technical assessment of the quality, and hence status, that any product or sub-product should have.

Administration — i.e. identification, authorisation, recording and documentation — may be regarded as a management function, while evaluation of the

fitness of any one item for inclusion under configuration control (and hence its availability for use in building products and sub-products) is one requiring technical processes, evaluation and judgment, and falls quite clearly in the area of the quality plan. Whether the range of activities is placed entirely in one plan or divided between them, there must be at least a cross-reference to ensure that the full range of the activity is always appreciated, and preferably either a summary or a full quotation of the entry, in the secondary plan.

5 The roles and contents of test plans

5.1 Introduction to formal test plans

The test plans are created as a subsection, or as an associated document, to the quality plan, although as they are progressively detailed and expanded their lower levels eventually become project documents in their own right [6]. Their essential aim is that all testing activities (including those used for controlling the process of development, and in indicating the progress of the project) are expected, are manageable and are managed. In the literature of software testing, the emphasis is often more on the mechanics of testing existing items than on ensuring that all relevant items *are* tested, and that the testing is purposeful and informative. For a discussion of the consequences of failing to get a tight grasp on testing see Ref. 7.

5.2 The role of the test plan and test results within a project

The fundamental role of a test plan is to give instructions about how and when to proceed with testing throughout the project, and about what use to make of the results from each testing activity. However, both a test plan and the corresponding test results have additional roles to play in supporting project management, beyond those immediately concerned with controlling and reporting on the project's schedule of tests. Examples of the roles of test plans and test results within a project follow:

- *The uses of test plans in the management and planning of resources and environment:* When managing and planning resources for a project, the test plan should offer assistance in:

  ☐ monitoring the testing activities of a project
  ☐ scheduling and organising project resources to ensure that products are ready for testing at the planned times, and that tested products are ready to be

handed on (or placed under configuration management) as expected

☐ recognition of the need to re-schedule activities and resources, as a consequence of qualities disclosed during testing.

Test plans should also supply information to the personnel responsible for providing the environments required for the testing activities. The test plan should provide a picture of the hardware and software support needed throughout the project, enabling their timely provision.

• *The role of test plans in ensuring the testability of the design and the code:* The test plan should provide a medium for communication between the designer of a product and the designer of the tests of that product, so that details of the design of the product will assist, rather than hinder, the testing of the product. Programs should be both designed and coded in a way that is consistent with the expected methods of testing of the system, as outlined in the test plan. When a code item is under review, consideration must be given to the requirements, the design, the detailed implementation and the associated test set (which is, itself, created from the — already tested — requirements, design and implementation).

• *Test plans used as a guide for those performing testing:* Test plans should act as a guide for those performing testing. The test plan should enable all testing activities to be seen in the context of the full test schedule, rather than as independent actions. It is possible that staff carrying out testing could meet with difficulties in following the specified range and sequence of tests (owing to time pressures, faults in product areas on which other areas depend, equipment failure, lack of resources, lack of special facilities etc.). In such a case, decisions on the nature and sequence of alternative paths through the testing task should be made in the light of both the complete testing plan and the present project priorities. For example, there are circumstances in which full testing of a limited set of product elements will be preferred to a less than full level of testing across all elements.

• *Test plans used as an input to quality assurance and quality control procedures:* Test plans can provide reference materials for independent quality control and quality assurance staff who will need schedules of required actions and outcomes in order to audit a project's progress and achievements. Plans relating to the acceptance and release of a product should also include evidence of quality as shown by the testing methods and their recorded results.

• *The re-use of test cases (the test cases having been detailed in the test plan) in several phases of one project:* Within a particular project a set of test cases will be refined and used frequently throughout the software life cycle — for example, as guides to refining the specification and requirements and to product design and design reviews, coding and code reviews. If testing by reviews, prototyping and animation is to start early in the life cycle, then test cases must be specified as early as the requirements, specification and design phases of that software life cycle. All these early phases will be tested by sets of examples which define the required functions of the product. The sets of examples are the initial versions of test cases which may be refined and re-used throughout the project.

• *The use of test results to decide on an appropriate course of action following a testing activity:* Test results can be used to suggest an appropriate course of action to take either during the testing activity or when it is complete. The test plan should contain, for each testing activity, a statement of what specifically should be tested for, and what the acceptable limits are for the 'number of errors found' for each set of test results. After each testing activity an analysis of the test results will indicate which of several courses of action should be taken. Thus different actions would be required depending on whether the actual number of errors found is lower than, equal to or higher than the expected number. For a further discussion of the interpretation of test results see Refs. 2 and 8.

5.3 The contents of a test plan

A test plan is a document which details the testing activities of a project and the organisation of those activities, and which will be used to establish that the software product satisfies the requirements as stated in a requirements document. In addition, the plan outlines the techniques used at each stage of the project to detect and correct defects.

The test plan defines the scope, the assessment criteria, the assessment techniques, the resources and the schedule of the testing activities of a project. It will be updated and refined throughout the project as more information becomes available about the details of the testing yet to be performed and the results of that which has been completed. Examples of this updating include the addition of new items to be tested (as the result of re-design or new requirements) and the extension of test sets as items progress from their high-level design to detailed design and implementation.

A project's test plan is intended to provide a basis for identifying what to test, when to perform the test, how to perform the test, how to assess the results and finally what to infer from the assessment of the results.

The following sections should be included in a test plan:

• *An introduction:* This is a summary of the software items and software features to be tested. It provides:

☐ an outline of the structure of the test plan, i.e. what sections it will contain and whether it will be a single document or several related documents.

☐ a description of the approach to testing (methods and tools to be used throughout the project)

☐ a description of how a particular approach to testing a specific part of the project is to be decided on

☐ a report on any constraints which outside factors impose

☐ a statement on whether the test plan is to be updated throughout the project. It may be that a particular testing method can only be decided on when that part of the project is complete (for example what sort of code analysis will take place?).

The introduction to a test plan should refer to its associated quality plan, which describes the overall approach to testing to be used throughout the project, and may also define constraints which will affect the testing activities of the project.

• *Test items:* This section should either identify all test items (software items which are the object of testing) or provide means of recognising them as they arise during the development process. The identification should include version/revision levels. As the skeleton test plan is to be produced as soon as possible — for example after requirements definition — then:

☐ initially only the user's (and some aspects of the project manager's) views will be known, and hence the test plan can only deal with these at this stage

☐ as more detail becomes known additional items will have to be included in the test plan.

Hence the test criteria will change from the user's view to the implementation view (from a black-box view to a white-box view) and the test plan must reflect this change, and subsequent changes, as more white-box detail becomes available.

Reference should be made to the following relevant documents: requirements specification, project specification, design, user guide, operating instructions, installation guide and incident reports relating to test items (where 'no errors found' will be stated if the case).

All items are identified which are to be specifically excluded from testing. A statement should be made as to why they are to be excluded and supporting documentation should be provided.

- *Functions to be tested:* This section attempts to identify all software functions and combinations of software functions to be tested. It also identifies the testing method and associated tests for each function and combination of functions.
- *Functions not to be tested:* This section identifies all the functions and combinations of functions which will not be tested and gives reasons why.
- *Non-functional testing:* This section identifies all non-functional tests to be carried out on the system — for example does the system perform adequately under stress, are the security precautions adequate, are requirements such as specified mean time between failures satisfied, what acceptance and installation testing will be required?
- *Approach to testing:* A general statement about the parts of the product to be tested and the testing strategy which will be used to ensure the required levels of testedness will already have been made in the quality plan. The strategy and constraints outlined in the quality plan are based on both general and particular constraints such as warranties, specifications and contracts. The test plan gives a more detailed description of the testing activities, techniques and tools.

  This section specifies the major activities, techniques and tools which are used to test each group of functions or function combinations. The testing approach will be described in sufficient detail to permit identification of the major testing tasks and estimation of the time required to do each one.

  The techniques are identified which will be used to measure the effectiveness of the testing process, i.e. how it will be determined that a given degree of testedness has been achieved. Also any minimum requirements will be specified as far as test effectiveness is concerned.
- *Constraints affecting the test approach:* This section identifies the constraints which will affect the approach to testing. Constraints include:
  - □ availability of items to be tested
  - □ time limits
  - □ financial resources
  - □ number of available staff
  - □ particular skills of staff
  - □ hardware resources
  - □ machine availability
  - □ relevant software and hardware tools available
  - □ product design
  - □ relationship with the customer (or quality assurance department)
  - □ product type
  - □ difficulty in predicting output — see the section on testing systems with unknown outputs in Ref. 9.
- *How the approach to testing will be tailored in view of the identified constraints:* This section specifies how the

resources available for testing will be most effectively used (bearing in mind the minimum requirements for test effectiveness), indicating which strategies have been chosen and why.
- *Organisation of testing activities:* This provides a description of how the testing activities will be organised:
  - □ to make optimum use of the available resources
  - □ to overcome any problems associated with accomplishing any very large, time-consuming testing activities (including analysis of large volumes of test results).

  A statement is also made as to how re-testing after fault correction will be dealt with.
- *Pass/fail criteria for items under test:* This section specifies the criteria to be used to determine whether each test item has passed or failed testing.
- *Procedures and facilities for updating the test plan throughout the duration of the project:* The following procedures and facilities are specified:
  - □ the parts of the test plan which may be updated throughout the project
  - □ procedures for updating the test plan, for example any authorisation required, version control, whether updating part of a test plan is allowed after that part has been used in the test procedure etc.
  - □ any tools available to help with updating.
- *Test deliverables:* This section identifies the deliverable documents produced during the testing activities of the project, for example:
  - □ test plan(s)
  - □ test design specifications
  - □ test case specifications
  - □ test logs
  - □ test incident reports
  - □ test summary reports
  - □ test input data and test output data (actual and intended)
  - □ test tools (for example module drivers and stubs).

  Documents which are inputs to or outputs from particular phases of testing should be recorded as such.
- *Testing tasks:* This section identifies and specifies the set of tasks necessary to prepare for and perform testing. Also, special skills required are identified — for example, final product testing may need to involve staff who are typical of the end user, and who may therefore need to be specifically *unskilled* in some sense.
- *Environmental needs:* This section specifies the necessary and desired properties of the test environment, for example:
  - □ hardware
  - □ communications and system software
  - □ mode of usage (for example stand alone)
  - □ other software or supplies needed to support the test
  - □ level of security which must be provided for the test facilities, system software and proprietary components such as software, data and hardware
  - □ special test tools needed
  - □ other needs (for example provision of office space).
- *Testing responsibilities:* This section identifies who is responsible for the following aspects of testing:
  - □ designing and managing
  - □ providing test items
  - □ providing environmental needs.
- *Staffing and training needs:* This section specifies how many staff with what level of skill are required. It defines what training is required to provide the necessary skills.
- *Scheduling of testing activities:* An initial estimate is provided of the time required to perform each testing task. The availability, and restrictions on use, of each resource (facilities, tools and staff) are specified. Taking into account the overall time scale of the project, a list of testing milestones and the start and end dates for each testing task are specified. The required level of quality to be achieved must also be stated.
- *Contingency plans:* This section specifies contingency plans to be carried out in the event of delayed delivery of test items (for example increase night shift working to meet the delivery date).

6 Re-usability of quality management plans, procedures and results

6.1 Re-use and integration of quality plans

The creation of a quality plan has benefits beyond those immediately apparent as relating to the nature and performance of the product built under its direction. By devising and agreeing these plans, the patterns of authority, responsibility and information flows within the project team and in its interfaces with its environment — including the duties and privileges of customers — are set out and are made clear to all concerned. This organisation can be instrumental in preventing expensive and time-consuming misunderstandings during the project and at release/acceptance time. In addition, the level of planning appropriate to these documents makes it simple to pick out and evaluate any needs for special training and special tooling, and to predict the effects of changes or failures during the project.

When quality plans are integrated between projects, common support facilities can be planned, and information applied for multiple purposes, even more effectively than when plans are made only for individual projects. Although some elements of each plan must be made specific to the quality needs and other circumstances of the project in hand, conceptually and practically there will be many areas which are common and can be considered together. These considerations might include the potential for shared use of facilities, re-use of parts and plans, and the application of lessons learnt from one situation to the avoidance of problems in others.

Thus integration of quality plans includes the selective re-use of methods and procedures (to reduce re-invention and to benefit by experience), the harmonisation of goals and measurements, the provision of support tools and services, and the extraction from project and product records of indications of what works and what should be avoided. The integration of quality plans helps to gain local control of the development situation (environment, methods, tools etc.), to progressively refine that control, to promote efficiency, and in time perhaps to contribute to the better general understanding of software products and processes.

Study of the opening specifications, quality plans and outcomes, and in-service records of previous products is a valuable resource in:

- settling on mutually acceptable (and understood) forms of characterisation in specifications
- finding workable and effective forms of control during development
- defining and implementing demonstrations of achievement
- devising workable and meaningful schemes of description and measurement for use in recording and reporting both the development and its final results
- devising workable and meaningful schemes to control, record and report in-service performance and maintenance activities.

The integration of quality plans, i.e. their treatment as a single body of information related to all the projects undertaken in a development area, includes:

- the application of all available and relevant data to the estimation and planning of projects, both in administrative and technical terms
- the application of all available and relevant data to the re-estimation and planning of on-going projects, both in administrative and technical terms
- the intensive use of project data, supported by data from previous and contemporary projects, in managing the

project, its products and the processes and means being used
- the selective re-use of methods and procedures (to reduce re-invention and to benefit by experience)
- the harmonisation of goals and measurements across projects
- rationalisation of the provision of support tools and services
- the extraction from project and product records of indications of what works and what should be avoided.

This integration is intended as a means of gaining local control, progressively refining that control, promoting efficiency and, in time, contributing to general research and understanding.

In order to be effective, integration of quality plans requires careful management, both technically and administratively. In particular, the differences between products and between projects, and the rates of change in hardware and software environments, mean that the interpretation and application of recorded information cannot become routine but must always be the subject of intensive technical scrutiny.

6.2 The roles of test plans and test results in subsequent projects

In addition to their roles within a specific project, test plans and their associated test results can be a useful general resource applied over many projects. For example, information from one project can be used to achieve more realistic scheduling and expectations for quality achievement for subsequent projects. Examples of the uses of test plans and test results, through a range of projects, are as follows:

- *Test plans and test results used as an input to project management, including resource planning and scheduling:* By keeping a record of the testing activities and corresponding test results throughout a project, a 'test history' can be produced for each project. The test history states exactly which testing activities were performed at each stage of the project and what results were observed. The test history can then be compared with the test plan, and as a conclusion to the test history a list of guidelines can be produced for what can reasonably be expected in terms of quality and productivity in future projects.

An assessment of the in-field use of a product in conjunction with an assessment of its test history can provide information to help in the refinement, in future projects, of the following:
  - □ development processes
  - □ selection of suitable types of test
  - □ test plans

  - □ quality plans
  - □ cost and resource estimates
  - □ testing methods
  - □ quality control procedures
  - □ choice of tools
  - □ scheduling
  - □ planning
  - □ design.

The idea of 'learning lessons' from previous projects and refining working methods between individual projects can be extended to be part of an organisation's working strategy. In this situation a company has an established method of collection, review and application of the lessons learnt by each project into all subsequent projects. This method of working helps to avoid projects suffering from problems which have already been solved: it may also avoid projects being able to obtain only those tools and services which can be justified within their individual budgets — since justification across several projects may result in better tools and better results for them all. For example, it is more effective to procure test beds, test analysers, simulators and other special testing-related tools as a resource for several projects, thereby spreading the benefits and the cost.

- *The re-use of the format of the test plan from one project to another:* Once the format, contents list and major and minor section headings of a test plan have been designed and established for one project, then the document can serve as a useful proforma for other projects — provided that actual testing experience has been applied to the initial version in order to remove any points of difficulty.

The outline of contents and headings should provide a useful guide to what should be in the test plan and should minimise re-thinking and re-organising the plan for other projects. Some sections of the plan (for example testing methods, test cases and test result analysis) may actually be re-usable for other, very similar, projects.

- *The use of test results to identify 'fault-prone modules':* Test results can be used to identify product elements showing a greater than average level of fault occurrence (i.e. 'fault-prone modules'). A proportion of the project effort could be reserved for their revision, by re-design or by re-coding, at the end of the project; see Refs. 2 and 10.

- *The use of test results to identify modules of greater than average complexity:* Test results can assist in the identification of product elements of greater than average 'complexity', so that these can be set aside for review etc. ('complexity' can be measured in several ways, one of which is by the use of coverage analysers — elements of the product for which the test coverage is found to be low after passing through the normal testing procedures can be diagnosed as 'of high complexity').

- *The use of test results to assess the effectiveness of testing procedures:* Test results can be used to assess the effectiveness of the standard testing procedures being used within a project, by randomly selecting a small number of modules for a period of additional intensive testing subsequent to their 'normal' testing. Observation of the number of faults disclosed by this additional testing, interpreted relative to the number of faults found by the standard testing, gives a rough estimate of the effectiveness of the project's standard testing procedures. It can also give some indication of the wisdom of releasing the product without further testing.

7 Summary and future directions

To summarise, we feel that there is a need for better quality management for products throughout the software industry, both in terms of improving the quality management procedures available and of implementing the procedures more widely. We currently consider that the two most effective instruments in the achievement of quality management are the project quality plan and its associated test plans. It is envisaged that future developments will lead to production of these documents being automatic and standard, throughout the software development field — they may be part of the automated development environment; i.e. production of the documents will be an expected standard procedure for all developments, and their physical production will be aided by their interactive building up by way of computer-guided discussions both within the development team and between them and their customers or users — rather than being a separate, stand-alone activity. The user and the quality manager and his team will provide relevant information throughout the life of the project when prompted by the system, and the system will produce a standard, up-to-date and complete set of documents.

Other possible future work in the area of software quality management includes research into and development of appropriate concepts, models and metrics for the controlled achievement of required qualities, and also the development of methods or techniques such as specification languages, design languages, automated pseudo-code interpretation and automated source code generation. In summary, the objective should be a set of methods, procedures and tools aimed at improving the quality of software products, which are easy to use, produce the required results consistently and are sufficiently predictable, controllable and cost effective to meet both project management and quality management objectives.

8 Acknowledgments

This work was supported by the Alvey Directorate as part of the Test Specification and Quality Management project (project reference: ALV/PRJ/SE/031).

9 References

1 BOEHM, B. W.: 'Software engineering economics' (Prentice-Hall, 1981)
2 MYERS, G. J.: 'The art of software testing' (Wiley Interscience, 1979)
3 BOEHM, B. W., BROWN, J. R., KASPAR, H., LIPOW, M., MACLEOD, G. J., and MERRIT, M. J.: 'Characteristics of software quality' (North-Holland, 1978)
4 KAFURA, D., and CANNING, J.: 'A validation of software metrics using many metrics and many resources'. Unpublished manuscript, 1985
5 'Software quality assurance plans'. IEEE Standard 730, 1983
6 'Software test documentation'. IEEE Standard 829, 1984
7 EVANS, M. W.: 'Productive software test management' (Wiley, 1984)
8 BASILI, V. R., and DOERFLINGER, C. W.: 'Monitoring software development through dynamic variables'. Proceedings of IEEE Computer Society International Computer Applications Conference (COMPSAC), 1983
9 HENNELL, M. A., and HEDLEY, D.: 'Testing in difficult situations'. Alvey Test Specification and Quality Management Project Document, Version 1, Feb. 1985
10 FAGAN, M. E.: 'Design and code inspections to reduce errors in program development', *IBM Systems Journal*, 1976, **15**, (3)

G. D. Frewin and B. J. Hatton are with Standard Telecommunication Laboratories Ltd., London Road, Harlow, Essex CM17 9NA, England.

Assuring Software Quality through Measurements: A Buyer's Perspective

Samuel E. Hon III

Bell Communications Research, Inc. (Bellcore), Piscataway, New Jersey

The acquisition of quality software is one of the major challenges that faces buyers of software systems in this decade. In the past, accomplishing this objective has been a struggle, mainly due to the lack of effective software quality measurements. To address this problem for the Bellcore Client Companies (BCCs),* Bellcore Quality Assurance Engineering, Software (QAES) has developed and implemented at their direction comprehensive buyer software quality assurance programs that focus on resolving the underlying problems associated with developing quality software. These programs are founded on identifying the risks and managing impacts to BCC quality through measurement and analysis. This paper discusses Bellcore QAES's buyer software quality assurance approach and explores the measurements that help assure that telecommunications systems meet BCCs needs and expectations. In conclusion, the paper discusses how the measures can be applied by all buyers and vendors, challenges facing the application of quality measurements in the future, and how these challenges can be successfully approached and overcome.

1. "THE CHALLENGE"

The acquisition of "quality software"[†] has been a struggle and a painful experience for many buyers over the past several years. Victims of poor-quality software have included both large (Department of Defense [DoD]) and small (general public) volume buyers. We are constantly reading stories, for example, about major weapon systems being canceled after several years of development or large, unexplained discrepancies in bank balances due to poor-quality software. A recent report by T. C. Jones confirms the struggle to produce quality software by doc-

umenting horrifying figures concerning large software development projects: *25%* of the software systems initiated were canceled; *less than 1%* of completed systems are finished on time, within budget, and according to user requirements; and the average large system is finished *over a year* late and costs *twice as much* as the original estimate [1]. Buyers can no longer afford to accept the risks and penalties associated with procurement of poor-quality software. Buyers must initiate efforts to assist their software vendors in identifying and managing these risks. Only then can buyers be assured of acquiring software that meets their needs and expectations.

The question that must be answered by buyers of software is "What can we do to prevent our software projects from becoming another statistic in T. C. Jones's studies?" The DoD, the largest procurer of software in the United States (from Figure 1, approx. 15 billion $ a year), believes that the major problem with government-sponsored software development projects is managerial, rather than technical, in nature. Other recent views on the subject of software quality agree [2, 3]. To address this problem, the DoD has initiated several projects that deal with the issue of software quality. Of particular note are the efforts of the Software Engineering Institute (SEI) in the area of process maturity [4]. These initiatives, along with the fact that software expenditures in the United States grow at an approximate rate of 12% per year (Figure 1), have prompted buyers to focus on their methods and techniques for "software acquisition management" or "buyer quality assurance."

2. "THE PROBLEM"

To allow for the identification (visibility) of risk and subsequent management (control) of that risk, comprehensive buyer software quality assurance (SQA) programs are focusing on solving the underlying problems associated with acquiring quality software—*the lack of*

Address correspondence to Samuel E. Hon III, 6 Corporate Place, PYA-1K270, Piscataway, NJ 08854.

* Bellcore Client Companies (BCCs) is a collective reference to all owner-clients and non-owner clients.

[†] From a buyer's perspective, "quality software" is defined as software that (1) meets all buyer requirements, (2) performs in a reliable manner, (3) is delivered on time, and (4) is within budget.

0164-1212/90/$3.50

Reprinted by permission of the publisher from "Assuring Software Quality through Measurements: A Buyer's Perspective", by S.E. Hon III, *Journal of Systems and Software,* Vol. 13, No. 2, October 1990, pages 117-130. Copyright 1990 by Elsevier Science Publishing Co., Inc.

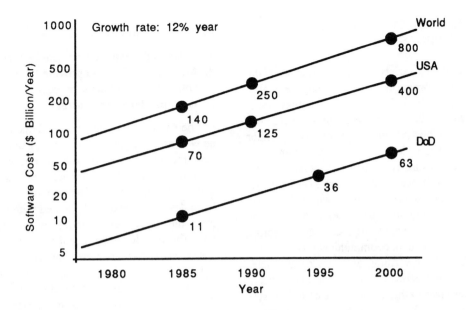

Figure 1. Software cost trends [5].

visibility and control over the software development process. These programs provide buyers with ongoing assurance that vendors are successfully meeting quality objectives and buyer requirements.

Lack of visibility and control by buyers and vendors alike can be attributed to many causes. Two predominant causes are the lack of quality standards and comprehensive quality measurement programs. Much progress has been made in the effort to define quality standards and requirements, including the development of DoD Standards 2167/2168 [6, 7] and Bellcore's TR-TSY-000179.‡ However, a successful quality measurements program awaits further development. Two famous quotes summarize the key role of measurements, one from Lord Kelvin:

> When you can measure what you are speaking about, and express it in numbers, you know something about it; but when you cannot measure it, when you cannot express it in numbers, your knowledge is of a meager and unsatisfactory kind.

and another from Tom DeMarco:

> You can't control what you can't measure.

To this end, software buyers are continually striving to develop and implement measures that provide objective evidence that they are getting good value for their money. They want a quantified approach to "buyer software quality assurance." Recent efforts to address this concern have come from the Air Force Systems Command [8, 9], IEEE [10], and Bellcore [11–13]. The latter, Bellcore Quality Assurance Engineering, Software's (QAES) Software Surveillance Measurements Program for telecommunications systems will be further described in this paper.

3. QUALITY ASSURANCE OF TELECOMMUNICATIONS SYSTEMS

Since divestiture of the AT&T company in 1984, the responsibility for sustaining high-level software quality and services has become a major challenge for the BCCs. Together, the BCCs spend over $1 billion on software purchases annually. The increase in software control of telecommunications systems has contributed greatly to this level of software procurement. And, because network operation and support are becoming increasingly dependent on software control, poor quality has the potential to adversely affect not only operations, cost, and revenue, but the effectiveness of the services provided to the public. Avoidance of these potential ill effects has become a major objective of the BCCs. In 1984, Bellcore QAES was established to assist the BCCs in attempting to assure the quality of the software they purchase.§ The systems and methodologies used to develop and administer these quality assurance functions are described by Pence [14].

---

‡ TR-TSY-000179 "Software Quality Program Requirements" documents Bellcore's mature view of generic software quality program objectives that vendors should strive to achieve in developing software for the Bellcore Client Companies (BCCs).

§ Bellcore does not make recommendations concerning BCC procurement decisions. Bellcore only provides quality information to BCCs to assist them in making their individual procurement decisions.

4. THE BELLCORE QAES SOFTWARE SURVEILLANCE PROGRAM

Bellcore QAES offers a variety of services that assist the BCCs in evaluating, procuring, and assuring the quality of the software used in their telecommunications businesses [15]. One of these services, Software Surveillance, monitors established quality programs at vendor facilities in order to provide the BCCs with ongoing confidence that their software systems will continually meet requirements. Surveillance programs are necessary because of the dynamic telecommunications environment in which the BCCs operate. Businesses as well as the individual consumer are eager for increased flexibility and functionality in their telecommunications systems. Features such as call forwarding, 800 service, and integrated services digital network (ISDN) require frequent software updates (two to three times a year) to key systems in the telecommunications network. These changes affect the network as well as systems that support BCC operations (provisioning, maintenance, billing, testing, etc.). Accordingly, the risk of introducing poor-quality software into the network increases and thus necessitates an emphasis on long-term "buyer" software QA programs.

The objective of Bellcore QAES's surveillance program is to develop "cooperative" relationships that cause vendors to focus on (1) implementing methods and techniques to improve control of software development; (2) improving the effectiveness of the underlying processes used to develop and support software, thus improving the level of quality achieved by those processes; and (3) understanding the needs and requirements of the BCCs. A major component of this program is the establishment and implementation of a comprehensive quality measurement program. Software quality measures, or metrics, are the key to controlling and improving quality in software systems. Previous work by T. Capers Jones [16] and Barry Boehm [17] provide some insight into the historical problems of developing quality software and how measurements hold the key to better understand and resolve these problems. To this end, Bellcore QAES has researched, developed, and implemented a comprehensive set of software quality measures that allows Bellcore QAES analysts to measure a vendor's accomplishments toward quality goals and objectives. These measures can

be grouped into three categories as follows:

1. Assure adequate vendor quality control
2. Minimize defects (improving the effectiveness of the software development process)
3. Optimize buyer satisfaction

The surveillance program implements these measures as well as a program of monitoring and analysis to provide the BCCs with ongoing confidence that software they are purchasing meets their needs and expectations. The following sections describe measurements that have been developed and implemented within these groups to meet the objectives of acquiring quality software systems for the telecommunications network. Specific measurements shown are representative of programs implemented for network switching systems. Because system technology, criticality of function, and complexity influence software life cycles and system-specific quality, reliability, and support requirements, measurement programs will vary. However, buyers should insist on comprehensive vendor measurement programs to achieve the objectives of quality control, defect minimization, and customer satisfaction as described in this paper.

4.1 Assure Adequate Vendor Quality Control

One of the objectives of a software surveillance program is to assure that vendors adequately control their software development processes. Quality control is accomplished by implementing a software life-cycle process that incorporates management "hooks" (milestones) that allow measurement and assessment of quality and development progress. There are a number of possible life cycles available for use in industry today. Therefore, for purposes of example, Figure 2 depicts a typical life cycle, the waterfall model, showing milestones and criteria.

Many failures in software development result from beginning a subsequent set of life-cycle activities on "immature" software from a previous phase (i.e., software that has not successfully completed all of its quality objectives). This greatly increases the risk that quality problems will go undetected and will propagate into

Figure 2. Typical software life cycle with milestone criteria.

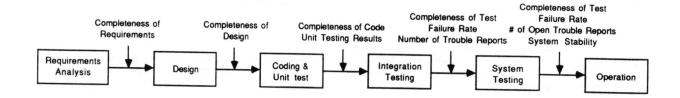

the later phases of the life cycle. The results are additional costs incurred by avoidable rework, schedules lengthened to fix problems, and the increased risk of problems entering undetected into a buyer's operational environment. To avoid these scenarios, measures have been implemented in the surveillance program to track the accomplishment of milestone criteria. These include:

Requirements, design, coding and unit test-phase measurements
- Phase deliverable completion
- Number of open corrective action requests
- Review coverage

Test-phase measurements
- Test coverage
- Number of test cases executed and passed
- Number of trouble reports
- Number of open trouble reports by severity
- Trouble report initiation rates
- Product-specific quality, reliability, and stability measures

Requirements, design, coding, and unit test-phase measures. Measures of "phase deliverable completion," "open corrective action requests," and "review coverage" identify and track the extent to which development and quality activities have been applied and completed on individual software deliverables. These measures provide visibility to buyers and vendors about the progress of software development and can indicate difficulties or problems that may hamper the accomplishment of quality objectives.

Figures 3 and 4 provide examples of measures regarding the completion of "requirements analysis" activities (e.g., development and review of functional specifications [FSs]). Project management is concerned with the overall software systems progress against project milestones and schedules. Therefore, Figure 3 provides development progress information by tracking the percentage of FSs that have been developed, reviewed, and approved for subsequent design. For purposes of quality control, Figure 4 tracks the completion of individual FS reviews and the resolution of corrective action requests.

In the example presented, a milestone date of March 13 was scheduled and criteria for completion of FSs was established at 95%. However, on March 13 only 79% of the FSs were actually approved for subsequent design (i.e., the FS had been reviewed, all outstanding corrective action items are resolved, and the FS is baselined in accordance with the vendor's configuration management practices). Figure 4 provides additional details concerning the number of actual FSs reviewed and corrective action request still outstanding. Specifically, on March

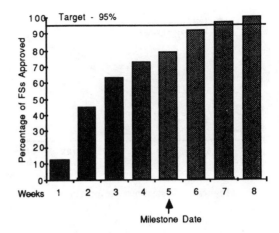

Figure 3. Functional specifications approved.

13, 33 FSs (of 39 planned) had been reviewed and 17 corrective action requests remained opened. These measures indicate a failure to meet planned development milestones and could be highlighting a potential problem in completing "requirements analysis" objectives.

With this visibility into the development process, controls can now be implemented to ensure that quality is not jeopardized and problems are identified and resolved. This can be accomplished through vendor milestone review meetings, during which the possible causes of poor performance (as indicated by measurements) are identified and investigated. Once the causes have been identified, buyer risks can be assessed and plans to manage and reduce these risks can be developed by the vendor. This scenario contributes significantly to the successful development of software systems. In the above example, the vendor's investigations concluded

Figure 4. Functional specifications reviewed and number of open corrective actions.

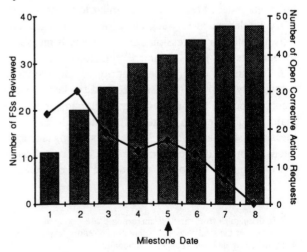

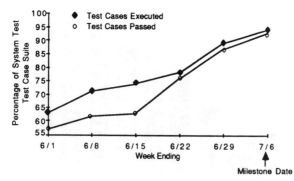

Figure 5. System test performance.

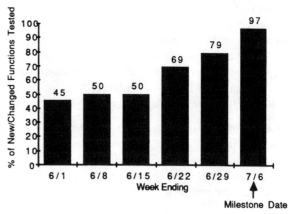

Figure 6. System test coverage.

that initial project planning did not take into account the complexity and size of the software project. In light of this scheduling problem, the surveillance program scrutinized further vendor efforts to ensure accomplishment of all planned quality activities. Furthermore, subsequent life-cycle phases were reviewed and adjusted, as required. For the "design" and "coding and unit testing" phases, similar measures are implemented.

Test-phase measures. During the testing phases of the development cycle, executed and passed test cases, test coverage, product performance indicators, and failure information can be measured and tracked to control the success and completion of the testing process. Figures 5 and 6 show the completeness of system testing ¶ by tracking the number of test cases executed and passed, as well as the level of coverage of the test cases executed. Coverage can be measured by structure, functions, or paths depending on the vendor's quality program. Bellcore's software quality program requirements specify only that a vendor must measure test coverage, but does not specify the method of measurement. Figure 6 shows coverage measured by the percentage of functions tested. Measurements similar to Figures 5 and 6 are implemented to track the progress of regression tests as well. For regression tests, coverage is measured by percentage (%) of "planned" functions tested.

Indicators of quality and maturity of the produced software system can be measured and tracked through trouble report initiation rates (Figure 7), number of open major trouble reports (Figure 8), and product-specific measures such as stability.** Vendors, using accumulated historical data can compare a previous release's "rate to maturity" to the rate of the current release.

This can provide insight into the progress of the testing effort and will lead to the prompt detection of specific problems in attaining a mature software system. Criteria for completing the "system test" phase are shown in Table 1.

Here again, quality criteria are established to ensure that software products attain a level of maturity and quality acceptable for transition to the next phase of the life cycle, in this case, customer site installation. The actual results can now be compared to the required objectives and any deviations can be scrutinized. In this example, the test cases and functions not tested were analyzed and the open major problems were reviewed by the vendor to determine their impact on the buyer. After analysis, the vendor determined that the impact of the two open major problems could have impact on the buyer's operations. Plans were developed to resolve and validate these issues before turnover of the system to the buyer.

In conclusion, measures associated with assuring adequate vendor quality control can benefit buyers and vendors. Quality measurements highlight problem areas so vendors can scrutinize software development to identify the quality risks to the buyer. Once these risks are known, timely and effective actions can be taken to manage and prevent them from affecting the quality of the buyer's software.

4.2 Minimize Defects—Improving the Effectiveness of the Software Development Process

The previous section described measurements that are implemented to ensure the timely completion of quality objectives. These measure the completion of life-cycle

---

¶ To distinguish from the "system testing phase," system testing is that portion of the total "system testing phase" effort devoted specifically to testing new and changed functionality.

** Stability index, as used here, is a composite measure of critical performance and reliability characteristics of a telecommunications switching system over a defined period of time.

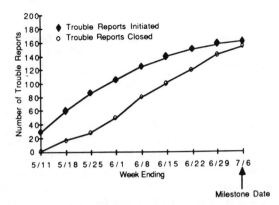

Figure 7. Number of trouble reports initiated and closed.

Table 1. System Test-Phase Criteria

Deliverables	Required	Actual
System testing		
Executed	100.0%	99.0%
Passed	95.0%	98.0%
Regression testing		
Executed	100.0%	100.0%
Passed	95.0%	98.0%
Stability index	97.5%	98.0%
No. of open trouble reports	<200	178
Trouble report rate	Decreasing	Decreasing
Open major problems	None	2

activities but do not address the quality of the activities themselves. For instance, the completion measures of functional specifications (FSs) do not measure the effectiveness of the "requirements analysis" process nor the quality of the actual FSs developed. The objectives of the measurements and methods described in this section are to measure, control, and improve the effectiveness of software development activities, thus minimizing defects during the development process. The surveillance program specifies methods and measures to help vendors detect and correct process problems that promote software defects. These measures also provide information for vendors to use in quality planning and improvement activities.

A development process can be characterized by its capability to produce quality software. Components of this capability are an established and implemented methodology, process standards, tools and techniques, and people who operate within the defined process. According to the concepts of "statistical quality control," the process will consistently produce software of a known quality

level when external influences (people and project complexity, size and schedule) are constant. Therefore, if a vendor determines the quality capability of the process, then measuring its outputs (software development artifacts) can highlight quality problems associated with personnel[††] and project-specific characteristics. This process is called the "real-time" program for minimizing defects. Since the quality achievable by the established process is not "ideal" (i.e., it produces some defects), a "long-term" program identifies the root causes of defects and determines how they can be detected and prevented to minimize defects in future releases.

Minimizing defects—the "real-time" approach. Reviews of software development artifacts (e.g., requirements specifications, design documentation, and source code) and testing results provide measurable evidence about the effectiveness of the implemented software development process, that is, specific information about the type and quantity of defects produced. This information can be used by vendors to determine the capability of the process to produce quality software. Once the capability is quantified, measurements that highlight significant deviations can reveal problems with personnel or a process's ability to effectively develop software to certain project-specific characteristics.

In addition to detecting problems, historical information gathered at this level can identify software components that should be scrutinized during subsequent quality activities. For example, if a module has a significantly higher density of logic errors detected during code inspection, the module could warrant a rewrite or more detailed testing in later stages of the development cycle.

Figure 8. Number of open trouble reports.

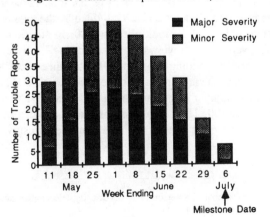

[††] Measurements proposed and used by Bellcore are not used to measure individual performance, capability, or capacity. Issues concerning personnel refer to adequate training and/or force required to perform the job.

Table 2. Average Numbers and Types of Defects Detected during Code Inspections

	Documentation	Data definition	Logic	Interface	Total
Total defects	338	143	415	104	1000
Avg defects/subsystem	7	3	8	2	20
Avg defects/module	2	1	2	<1	5

Specific measurements used in "real time" to minimize defects include:

- Average number of defects detected (in modules and subsystems) by reviews (by type)
- Historical system, subsystem, and module fault densities
- Number of defects detected during reviews

Tables 2 and 3 represent a vendor's efforts to collect, organize, and depict defect relationships according to types and software structure. These relationships, when compared to current code inspection defect information, can highlight possible problem areas. For example, based on Table 2, coding defects can be expected from each subsystem and module on an average of 20 and 5, respectively. Although based on averages, this information is easily collected and used by software engineers and managers to identify general areas for improvement. During a code inspection, 38 logic defects were detected in module A6yy (Table 3). A historical review of this module would provide more information about defect history and the relative significance of 38 defects. Assuming that no history of logic defects was revealed, analysis would be undertaken to discover the probable cause of "19-times-the-average" (from Table 2) increase in logic defects. Possible causes may include inadequate personnel training, poor standards, nonadherence to standards, module complexity, or an increase in new/changed lines of code (LOC). If, for example, module complexity is determined to be the cause, scrutiny of this module during later activities of the development cycle can be carried out and possible redesign scheduled for the next release.

This type of analysis for all life-cycle phases allows vendors to focus on the products of the development process. Relevant information about software defects facilitates smarter assessments and decisions concerning the quality of software. This in turn allows vendors to identify problems early in the development process so they can be managed and resolved efficiently. Measurements similar to those shown in Tables 2 and 3 are also established for requirement and design reviews and testing efforts.

Minimizing defects—a "long-term" approach. In a telecommunications environment, software-controlled systems typically evolve over long periods of time, and their software programs are "updated" several times annually. Under this scenario, a BCC enters into long-term commitments with vendors to provide software enhancements to systems that must change with operational and subscriber[‡‡] needs. The BCC expects vendors to implement programs that improve on the quality of previous software releases. Therefore, measures assist vendors in identifying the causes of software defects to limit the possibility of these problems reoccurring.

The key to any long-term approach to quality improvement is the collection of comprehensive defect data. Information about the defect type, its origin, the mechanism used for detection, and defect severity (based on impact to the buyer) are required to isolate ineffective processes and detection mechanisms. Bellcore QAES has developed an approach for collecting and analyzing the introduction and detection of software defects throughout the life cycle [18]. Table 4 shows which data is collected and how it can be grouped to identify life-cycle phases that produce a significant number of errors. Data arranged in this manner can also determine the effectiveness of vendor's detection processes.

Defects found during reviews and testing are classified according to the phase detected (x axis) and originated (y axis). For example, a "requirements" defect discovered during vendor testing would be grouped under D15 in Table 4. After defect data are accumulated, simple calculations will determine the percentage of total defects attributable to certain phases of the life cycle and the effectiveness of phase defect detection efforts. For example, the percentage of total defects attributable to "requirements" is calculated as the total number of "requirements" defects (D1X) divided by the total number of defects (DX) multiplied by 100. In addition, the effectiveness of "reviews of requirements" can be determined by dividing the number of "requirements" defects found during "reviews of requirements" (D11) by the total number of "requirements" defects (D1X) multiplied by 100. These relationships are used to determine the development phases and detection mechanisms that

---

[‡‡] A subscriber is a person or business using telecommunications services provided by a BCC.

Table 3. Module History

Subsystem	Release	Module	Documentation	Data definition	Logic	Interface	Total
A5	5	A5x	2	2	1	0	5
A6	5	A6y	5	2	3	0	10
A6	5	A6yy	2	6	38	7	53
A6	5	A6yx	0	2	2	1	5
A6	5	A6yyx	12	9	2	3	26

are ineffective in minimizing defects, warranting further scrutiny. Methods to determine root causes pinpoint specific procedures and processes that are failing. Once these are isolated, preventive actions can be taken.

Working in conjunction with vendors, Bellcore QAES developed a phase defect initiation/detection chart, populated with historical defect data. Using historical benchmark data (2 to 1 ratio of design vs. coding errors and 2 defects per thousand lines of new/changed code), vendors compare achievements in software quality to their past performance. Results can highlight areas that require improvement. Using a measure of fault density before and after software release, effects of process improvements on software quality are noted. Specific successes in implementing quality improvement techniques are documented in Figure 9.

The efforts described in this section minimize software defects during development. This is extremely important for both buyers and vendors since it is well documented that (1) the later a problem is detected in the life cycle, the more costly it is to fix; (2) it is probable that later quality activities (especially testing) will be shortened if additional time is required to correct and verify problems that could have been detected during earlier quality activities; and (3) detecting and preventing more problems early in the life cycle decreases the opportunity for them to proliferate in a customer environment. To avoid the ill effects of software defects a buyer's QA program should employ measurements and methods that minimize software defects in "real time" and for the "long term."

4.3 Optimize Buyer Satisfaction

Optimizing buyer satisfaction involves (1) identifying software quality, reliability, and support characteristics that are important to the buyer; (2) establishing measurements that quantify and track these characteristics; and (3) implementing methods and techniques to analyze these measures in order to identify areas that require improvement. To accomplish these tasks, a set of buyer SQA measurements identifies, quantifies, and tracks the key *quality and reliability* characteristics of software operational performance and *buyer support* functions. These measures highlight the effectiveness of a vendor's software development and support processes in (1) providing reliable software consistent with buyer needs, (2) minimizing software defects, and (3) providing support to buyers.

Quality and reliability measures. Measurement and analysis of key quality and reliability indicators quantify and assess a vendor's capability to (1) collect and define buyer requirements, (2) design software consistent with the buyer's reliability objectives of the buyer, and (3) validate buyer-specific requirements to ensure proper performance in an operational environment. In addition, measurements of operational defects will quantify how well a vendor achieves the goal of "minimizing defects" during the development process. Information derived from these measures can be used to positively affect software quality and reliability in future releases.

Table 4. Phase Detection Effectiveness Chart

Defect point of origin	Life-cycle phase defects found					Total phase defects	Percent phase defects	Phase detection effectiveness
	Internal detection							
	Req	Design	Code	Test	Operation			
Requirements	D11	D12	D13	D14	D15	D1X	D1X/DX * 100	D11/D1X * 100
Design	—	D22	D23	D24	D25	D2X	D2X/DX * 100	D22/D2X * 100
Coding	—	—	D33	D34	D35	D3X	D3X/DX * 100	D33/D3X * 100
Test	—	—	—	D44	D45	D4X	D4X/DX * 100	D44/D4X * 100
Total defects	—	—	—	—	—	DX	—	—

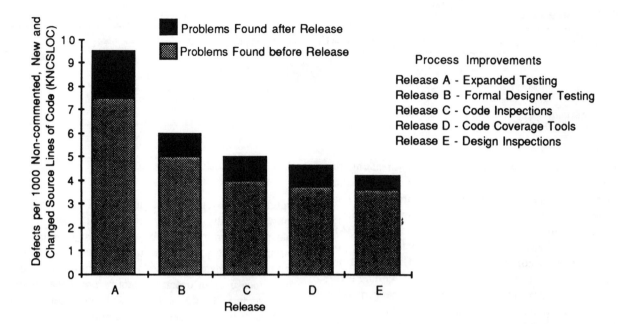

Process Improvements

Release A - Expanded Testing
Release B - Formal Designer Testing
Release C - Code Inspections
Release D - Code Coverage Tools
Release E - Design Inspections

Figure 9. Defects per KNCSLOC before and after five releases.

Quality and reliability measures include:

- Number and duration of system outages due to software failure
- Number of customer trouble reports (CTRs)
- CTR cause analysis
- Patch statistics

In the telecommunications industry, there are stringent quality and reliability requirements on systems that provide services to the general public. Key quality and reliability attributes specify allowable system outages[§§] and duration of system downtime[¶¶] caused by software failure during a given time period (Figures 10, 11). These key attributes affect buyer costs and revenue and therefore must be tracked and minimized.

Figure 10 highlights monthly buyer-reported outages on a particular software system. Sudden rises in the numbers indicate new releases and installations of software generics, for example, during the months of April and August. As time progressed, the April release reached a state of maturity, indicated by the steady downward trend in outages. This scenario would be expected at the introduction of a new, unproven release of software. In contrast, the trend following the August release is constant and does not indicate that a similar state of maturity was reached. This particular trend is not healthy and warrants a detailed analysis of the causes of outages for the August software release. Resulting in-

formation could be used to restrict deployment of certain software releases and development of future releases until a stable maturity level is achieved. Downtime (Figure 11) measures the extent of the software system outages in minutes. Since this measure is closely coupled with outages, the same trends are evident.

Measures of customer trouble reports (CTRs) (Figures 12, 13), especially the percentages of critical CTRs, indicates the presence of critical software problems that adversely affect the ability of a BCC to provide effective, continuous service to its subscribers. Figure 12 shows the rates of CTR initiation that demonstrate the maturity of released software. Comparison with future releases will show trends in improvement or degradation. As in the case of outages and downtime, reaction

Figure 10. Number of outages.

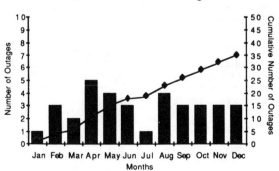

[§§] Outage is defined as a loss of capability or functionality or decreased capacity of switching systems.
[¶¶] Downtime is a measure of the duration of a specific outage.

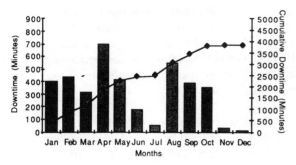

Figure 11. Duration of downtime (minutes).

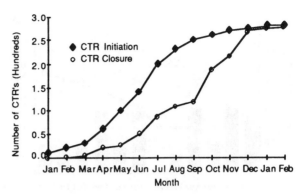

Figure 12. CTR initiation and closure rates.

to indications of poor quality can include restricting on further release and enhancement of this software. Root-cause analysis of CTRs (Figure 13) shows causes of the problems that are reaching a field environment. This reveals process deficiencies that are contributing to poor-quality software. This information, as well as the efficiencies of the testing processes to detect defects, can be used by vendors to improve the effectiveness of their software development processes and thus optimize buyer satisfaction.

Patching*** software is commonly practiced to fix operational problems quickly. Although patching provides a means of fast support in resolving operational problems, patches are themselves causes of software quality and reliability problems that result in buyer dissatisfaction. BCC personnel apply and verify patches to software systems, and every patch requires administrative time on the part of BCC maintenance personnel. This process introduces opportunities for problems to arise. In addition, vendors must provide strict control over the administration of patches to ensure that they are corrected or successfully applied to later releases and that future design and coding efforts take into account the patched area. Many patches often result in a loss of control and increased probability of problems being introduced, due to these administrative tasks. In general, patches should be minimized.

Measures of patches depicted in Figures 14 and 15 identify the trends in a buyer operational environment. Vendors can use these trends as indicators of maturity and stability to react to poor performance in the patching area by reissuing software at appropriate times. The reissue should have resolved all patches to date in source code, thus minimizing patches applied to particular releases. Although the "band-aid" solution to this quality

problem does not remove the underlying cause, it can provide a means to control potential ill effects that large areas of patches can exert on software performance and patch administration.

Patches are also used to resolve problems found in the later stages of the development cycle. Since delivery schedules and quality are two very important conditions of a buyer's software acquisition, it is necessary to patch software defects found in the later stages of the development cycle, instead of fixing source code. The time to fix, check, and test fixes realized in source code increases the risk of delaying software delivery. And when schedule is deemed important by buyers, fixes in source code run the risks of quality checks not adequately being performed and testing becoming less effective. As both scenarios result in buyer dissatisfaction, patches become necessary but must be controlled and limited. Therefore, measures of the number and size of patches applied during the later stages of the development cycle and those propagated from previous releases should be kept. The buyer's aim in interpreting this data is to fewer and smaller patches applied to purchased software.

Figure 13. CTR root-cause analysis.

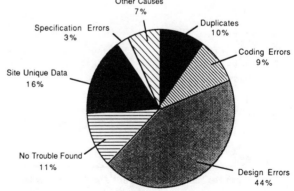

*** A patch is an interim fix, usually coded in a language other than that of the original source code, applied to a production baseline through means outside the full life-cycle development process.

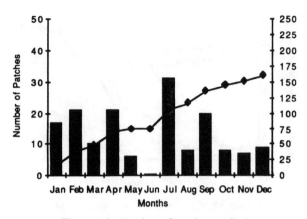

Figure 14. Number of patches applied.

The surveillance measures described in this section facilitate identification, measurement, and trending of the software quality and reliability characteristics that are important to BCCs. These deserve close attention from vendors. In addition to using these measurements to control the effects of poor quality, analysis methods and techniques can identify and eliminate the causes of problems. This can ensure that future releases will not be affected by faulty development and support processes. Through the reduction of software defects (which result in major system outages and downtime, poor performing software, and patches), buyer satisfaction will be optimized.

Buyer support measures. In addition to requiring quality and reliability from their software systems, buyers also expect the problems that do occur to be resolved in a timely manner. They also expect assistance for users of the system, to facilitate understanding of its operation. Buyers need quick responses to their inquiries

Figure 15. Size of patches applied (in bytes).

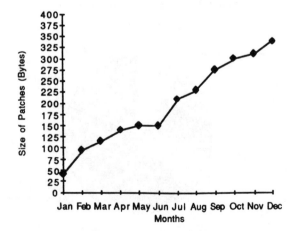

and do not want trouble reports open for long periods of time. Therefore, the objective of these surveillance measures is to depict the level of support currently provided by vendors and to highlight trends in vendor support that are direct indicators of customer dissatisfaction. Specific measures include:

- Customer services response time
- Number of open customer trouble reports
- Site distribution of open fault reports
- Aging of open customer trouble reports (by severity)
- Time-to-correct (MTTC) customer trouble reports

Figure 16 charts the time taken by a vendor's customer services group to respond to inquiries from the BCCs. Inquiries take the form of assistance requests, acknowledgment of trouble report disposition, and schedule commitments to resolve open trouble reports. Vendors are required to set specific time objectives for responding to severity 1, 2, and 3 inquiries reported. This chart indicates the degree to which those support requirements are achieved.

Measures of the number, average age, and site distribution of open trouble reports highlight the effectiveness of a vendor's processes to provide timely resolution to customer trouble reports (CTRs). Vendors are required to establish criteria for the resolution of all CTRs reported based on the trouble's impact to buyer operations and service. These measures reflect a vendor's commitment and capability to resolve CTRs. Figures 17 and 18 are examples of measures of the average age of open trouble reports. In this example, the average age has steadily increased from April to January. Of particular note is the rapid increase in age of severity 1 CTRs to over 155 days. These measures indicate that the vendor is having difficulty in supporting this volume of CTRs and field sites.

The added visibility provided through these measurements caused the vendor to scrutinize the software support system to isolate the reasons for this poor performance and to plan for improvement.

A final measure worth noting involves tracking the time required to resolve operational problems. Figure 19 depicts how long buyers wait for correction to reported problems by problem severity. Vendors are expected to establish objectives for the resolution of critical problems, and this measurement is designed to track the achievement of those objectives.

The measurements described in this section identify, measure, and provide quantitative information to vendors about critical characteristics that contribute to buyer satisfaction. These measures concentrate on assuring

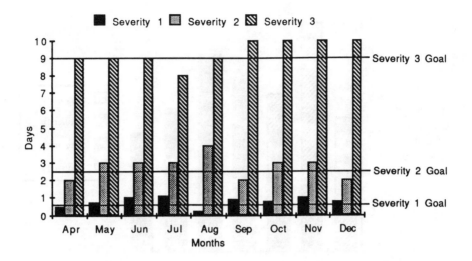

Figure 16. Customer support response time.

that (1) buyer requirements are met; (2) impacts of poor quality on buyer operations are known and tracked; and (3) vendors identify poor performance and take the appropriate corrective and preventive actions

4.4 Future Challenges

In the area of telecommunications, the BCCs have benefited, vendors have benefited, and the overall quality of BCC networks and operations are stable or improving due to the quality emphasis described above. However, hurdles still remain that restrict the application of measurements in software development. These include (1) developing efficient and effective implementation strategies for measurements, (2) researching and developing predictive measures of quality, and (3) improving communication about measurements.

To be effective, the measures must be integral to the vendor's own process. Bellcore QAES and its clients re-

quire a minimal set of measurements, but if they are not deemed beneficial and adapted by vendors, they will be unsuccessful. Measures must be used to improve present operations, not to appraise individual performance. This necessitates that measurement goals by clearly defined and communicated. Measures have to be integrated into the process so that problems are detected, results are analyzed, and resolutions are provided in a timely and efficient manner that eliminates problem causes. This will ensure that additional pressure is not exerted to simply detect problems, thus clouding the true objectives of the testing effort. For these reasons, Bellcore QAES has developed a strategy which it strives to actualize with vendors; this is shown in Figure 20. Here, the quality measurements for control and minimization of defects are integrated into the development process.

During software artifact reviews, defect data can be extracted and used in conjunction with defect history and product-specific characteristics to direct future quality efforts (quality planning). Tracking the completion of all

Figure 17. Average age of all open trouble reports.

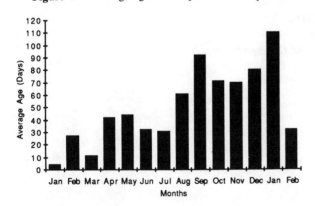

Figure 18. Average age of open trouble reports (by severity).

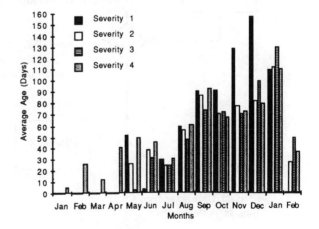

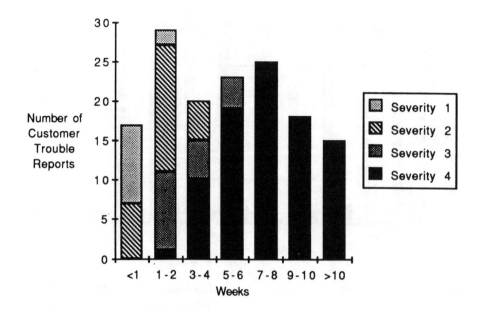

phase reviews and resolution of open-action items measure phase completeness and helps ensure the accomplishment of quality objectives (quality control). Fault history and the collection and analysis of defect data resulting from artifact reviews pinpoint processes that need improvement (quality improvement). This integration allows for the most efficient and effective application of quality principles.

In addition, the next few years will see the continuous pursuit of better measures, better application of measures, and the development of predictive measures of quality. The attainment of reliable, quantitative predictive measures will further promote the ability of the BCCs to acquire quality software. Bellcore QAES is

Figure 19. Time to correct CTRs (by severity).

continuously working with telecommunications vendors who compare and analyze internal measures (before release) against operational measures (after release) to identify for good, reliable predictors of operational quality.

Our last challenge, and perhaps the most important, is communication. A significant number of vendors are still without good measures of software quality. This is unfortunate, and is the primary reason for the many

Figure 20. The fully integrated measurement process.

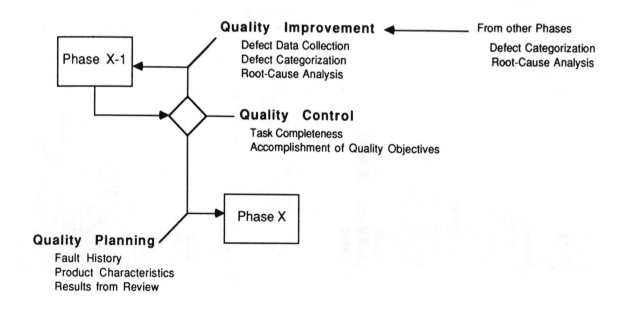

stories about poor software quality in the literature today. Vendors already using quality measurements should communicate their measures, application, and resulting successes to others in the industry in order to elevate state-of-the-art measurement to all developers of software. This will result in greater benefits for both buyers and vendors alike.

4.5 Conclusion: "The Global Application"

I have just described the methods and measurements associated with assuring quality software from a buyer's perspective. Although specific characteristics of the telecommunications environment were presented, the measures and techniques can be applied with the same success *globally* to any situation where a buyer-vendor relationship exists. Additionally, the measures described help achieve software quality and thus benefit any organization that develops software. Buyers should continuously monitor vendors to ensure that they implement programs that minimize the number and severity of defects caused during the development process and improve operational performance and support. These objectives will be fostered if buyers communicate their need for improved quality and if they promote the development of comprehensive software QC and QA programs supported with comprehensive quality measurements. Through this preventive behavior, buyers can optimize their own satisfaction.

ACKNOWLEDGMENTS

I would like to acknowledge Vince Dowd, who provided much of the founding work in software quality measurements for telecommunication systems on which this paper is based. Additionally, I thank Ron Braun, Brian Casey, Susan Einbinder, Randy Greene, Brian Handspicker, and Jim Roberts for their insights and ideas that contributed to the development of this paper. Finally, special thanks to Sal Pasquariello and Lorlee Wagnecz for their valued editorial comments on the initial versions of this paper.

REFERENCES

1. T. C. Jones, *Programming Productivity*, McGraw-Hill, New York, 1986.
2. R. H. Dunn, Software Quality Assurance: A Management Perspective, *Quality Progress*, July 1988, pp. 52–56.
3. R. B. Grady, Measuring and Managing Software Maintenance, *IEEE Software*, September 1987, pp. 35–45.
4. W. S. Humphrey and W. L. Sweet, A Method for Assessing the Software Capability of Contractors, Technical Report SEI-87-TR-23, Software Engineering Institute, Pittsburgh, PA, September 1987.
5. B. W. Boehm, Improving Software Productivity, *IEEE Computer*, September 1987, pp. 43–57.
6. DOD-STD-2167A, Defense System Software Development, April 29, 1988.
7. DOD-STD-2168, Defense System Software Quality Program, April 29, 1988.
8. Software Management Indicators, Air Force System Command, AFSCP 800-43, January 1986.
9. Software Quality Indicators, Air Force System Command, AFSCP 800-14, January 1987.
10. Draft Guide for the Use of Standard Measures to Produce Reliable Software (P982), IEEE, May 1987.
11. V. T. Dowd, Bellcore Software Surveillance Metrics, Bellcore Technical Memorandum TM-TSY-011569, April 15, 1988.
12. Software Surveillance Quality Measurement Guidelines, Bellcore Software Quality Assurance, Issue 4, July 1988.
13. Bellcore Technical Advisory TA-TSY-000929, Reliability and Quality Measurements for Large Telecommunications Systems, Draft, Issue 1, September 1988.
14. J. L. Pence, The System and Methodologies of Bell Communication Research, Inc.'s Quality Assurance Function, IEEE Global Telecommunications Conference, Conference Record, Volume 3, pp. 1114–1119.
15. T. Kalisz and J. W. Bischoff, Analysis of Software Quality from a User's Perspective, IEEE Global Telecommunications Conference, Conference Record, Volume 3, pp. 1448–1452.
16. T. C. Jones, Programming Productivity.
17. B. W. Boehm, *Software Engineering Economics*, Prentice-Hall, Englewood Cliffs, New Jersey, 1981.
18. V. T. Dowd, Bellcore Software Surveillance Metrics.

Software Inspections: An Effective Verification Process

A. Frank Ackerman

A. Frank Ackerman, *Institute for Zero-Defect Software*
Lynne S. Buchwald, *Qualitech*
Frank H. Lewski, *AT&T Bell Laboratories*

Properly applied, software inspections rival testing in defect detection and correction but cost less time and effort. This article explains what inspections are and how to perform them.

Afundamental of a good verification and validation program is that verification steps must be performed throughout the software-development effort. Traditionally, reviews and walkthroughs at different points in the development have been used to do so. But, in the past 13 years, several development organizations have replaced or supplemented traditional reviews and walkthroughs with software inspections. For V&V purposes — the detection and correction of defects (faults, failures, and other deficiencies resulting from nonconformance to standards or requirements) early in the development process — software inspections have been found to be superior to reviews and walkthroughs.

The first published description of the inspection process appeared in a 1976 paper[1] by its inventor, Michael E. Fagan. Since the publication of this initial paper, the Fagan inspection process (or variations of it) has been presented in many papers, books, and reports.[2,3] Without exception, all these reports claim that the use of software inspections improves product quality, as well as the productivity and manageability of the development process.

We have been involved with software inspections since 1981. On the whole, our experience has been consistent with the results reported in the literature. Still, we find few papers on the topic and much misunderstanding about the process and how to apply it. This article is an attempt to clarify what software inspections are, to explain how you can use them to improve both your process and your product, and to summarize what is known about their effectiveness.

What inspections are

The software-inspection process as it was defined by Fagan involves the interplay of five elements:

- six well-defined inspection steps

Reprinted from *IEEE Software*, Vol. 6, No. 3, May 1989, pp. 31-36. Copyright © 1989 by The Institute of Electrical and Electronics Engineers, Inc. All rights reserved.

(planning, overview, preparation, meeting, rework, and follow-up),

• four well-defined inspection roles (moderator, recorder, reader, and producer),

• the formal collection of process and product data,

• the product being inspected, and

• a supporting infrastructure.

In this article, "product" means the intermediate, development product, not the final product delivered to the customer. This development product is also known as the work product.

Inspection steps. Although most of the time and energy of an inspection is focused on the inspection meeting, the other five steps are essential for effective defect detection and correction. Two are often underused: overview and preparation.

The purpose of the overview is to bring all the inspectors to the point where they can easily read and analyze the inspection materials. A half-hour or hour presentation by the producer can often save the other inspectors two or three hours each in achieving the desired level of understanding of the inspection materials.

The preparation step lets the inspectors thoroughly understand the product so each can participate fully in the meeting. In the preparation step, the inspectors should first review the checklist for that type of inspection. They should also study the ranked distribution of defect types found by recent inspections. Inspectors should note how much time they spend in preparation; the moderator will collect this data and sum it to provide the total preparation time that went into each meeting. You use this information to assess the overall effectiveness of inspection in an organization.

Inspection roles. Creating software is a highly individualistic intellectual activity. Each software component is typically the work of one person or of a team of two or three people. In a sense, each piece of software is its own unique world. To effectively inspect a software product for defects, the inspection team must penetrate this world and discover its secrets. This is most easily done by those who are creating

similar worlds. Thus, the selection of inspectors for a software product is often constrained to a handful of other developers working on similar or interfacing components.

The reader role is the least understood and the one most likely to be missing in an organization's inspection process. The purpose of the reader is to focus the inspection team's attention sharply on the details of the materials being inspected. To do this, the reader paraphrases and summarizes each section of the material. Where design or code logic is especially complex, the reader should be prepared to lead the group in acting out the logic

---

In a sense, each piece of software is its own unique world. To effectively inspect a software product for defects, the inspection team must penetrate this world and discover its secrets. This is most easily done by those creating similar worlds.

---

with selected test cases. It may also be appropriate for the reader to prepare special exhibits to help the team keep all the relevant information together.

One of the most common questions asked by those who have not experienced a software inspection is "Why must the producer be present?" The answer is that if the producer is not present, the inspection team may spend too much effort trying to understand the product. Also, the presence of the producer enhances the communication from the other inspectors to the producer about the defects that must be fixed. When training inspectors, we always include a practice inspection. Rarely is the producer present at this practice inspection and, inevitably, at its conclusion the need for the producer's presence is obvious.

In our training courses, we find that the role of the reader is the hardest to explain, so we aren't surprised to find that some organizations use a process that does not include this role, that combines it with the moderator, or that assigns it to the producer. However, we often hear of organizations who later change their process by defining the reader as a separate role.

Data collection. The collection and analysis of data lies at the heart of the inspection process. The primary uses of this data are immediate process control and long-term process improvement. Although many organizations, for practical reasons, do not collect all of the data listed below, there is general agreement that these data should be collected for each inspection:

• the date the product was distributed for inspection,

• the date of the meeting,

• the date the rework was complete,

• whether this was an initial inspection or a reinspection, and the type of inspection it was,

• the identity of the product inspected,

• the size of the material inspected,

• the name of the moderator,

• the number of inspectors,

• whether an overview was held,

• the preparation time,

• the meeting duration,

• the number of defects of each type and severity found by the inspection, and

• the disposition (pass, rework, or reinspect) decided on by the inspection team.

If the staff hours used for rework is also collected, you can estimate the effectiveness of inspections versus testing.

Product. One characteristic that sets inspections apart from less formal examinations is the use of explicit entry criteria, which define when an inspection may begin. An inspection does not continue beyond the planning stage until the moderator verifies that the specified entry criteria have been met. Examples of entry criteria are:

• The existence of inspected predecessor products. For example, a detailed design document should not be inspected until an inspected (and reworked) high-level design is available.

• Conformance to pro forma standards. It can be useful to require that products be specially formatted for inspection. For example, you might require that the document to be inspected be run off with line numbers.

• Satisfaction of automated checks. Examples include spelling and grammar checks for text documents and error-free-compilation and complexity checks for code.

Supporting infrastructure. Inspections cannot occur spontaneously. They must be planned or supported by an individual or organization with the responsibility for them. We call this job the "software inspections coordinator." Its tasks include

• learning about inspections and convincing the project to try them,

• determining where inspections should be used on the project,

• creating and documenting the project-specific inspection procedures in an inspections manual,

• organizing training in the inspection process and keeping documentation and training up-to-date,

• collecting inspection data for the project's inspection database,

• issuing reports based on the information in the database, and

• analyzing the data in the database, comparing project results with those reported elsewhere, and making recommendations for process improvements.

You may apply inspections to more than one type of product. Typical products are requirements specifications, design documents, code listings, test plans, and test-case specifications. You may also apply inspections to hardware specifications and designs.[4] For each of these types of inspections, the project-inspection documentation must specify the inspection entry criteria, the job functions that should be represented at the inspection meeting, the recommended preparation rate, the recommended inspection rate, the type of defects to be inspected for and how they can be found, and the inspection exit criteria.

The definition of the types of defects to be sought in each type of inspection is an important part of the inspection infra-

structure. These definitions focus the inspection meeting sharply on defect detection and keep it from wandering into questions of style or alternative designs. Also, the inspection-preparation checklist should be keyed to the defined defects and should provide suggestions on how and where to find defects of each type. Figure 1 gives some examples of defect types for a requirements inspection.

In addition to typing defects, you should also note their severity. Different organizations use different severity definitions, but two levels — major and minor — are usually sufficient. One important use of severity is to distinguish defects that will not affect execution from those that will. This distinction is important when you compare the effectiveness of inspections with testing, since only those defects that offset execution will be detected during testing.

Fagan also requires that defects be classified as missing, wrong, or extra. This classification provides additional information that you can use for process improvement, but it also adds additional complexity to the process. We do not know of any organization that has used missing, wrong, or extra data to quantitatively demonstrate an improvement in its devel-

opment process.

Based on our experience, most organizations use an inspection process that is very similar to the one originally defined by Fagan. This similarity probably exists because most of the successful programs we know about are part of IBM or were initiated by people who had some direct contact with the IBM procedures.

Essential characteristics. In practice, each organization that implements software inspection varies the process. Whatever the variation, we believe the essential characteristics of software inspections — as opposed to other types of reviews — are a set of technical examinations

• performed by knowledgeable peers,

• of an explicit, completed product,

• at which the producer is present and participates,

• whose primary purpose is to find defects in a completed product so they may be corrected before they contaminate later activities,

• used routinely and according to some plan,

• supported by infrastructure elements,

• carried out with specific roles and following a specific set of steps,

• conducted by at least three people,

Completeness
1. Are all sources of input identified?
2. What is the total input space?
3. Are there any "don't care" sets in the input space?
4. Is there a need for robustness across the entire input space?
5. Are there any timing constraints on the inputs?
6. Are all types of outputs identified?
7. What is the total output space?
8. Are there any timing constraints on the outputs?
9. Are there sets that are in both the input space and the output space? Is there any state information?
10. What are all the types of runs?
11. What is the input space and the output space of each type of run?
12. For each type of run, is an output value specified for each input value?
13. Is the invocation mechanism for each run type defined? Are initial states defined?
14. Are all environmental constraints described?
15. Are sample input/output examples provided where appropriate?
16. Are all necessary performance requirements described?
17. Should reliability requirements be specified? Is an operational profile specified?

Ambiguity
1. Are all special terms clearly defined?
2. Does each sentence have a single interpretation in the problem domain?
3. Is the input-to-output mapping clearly defined for each type of run?

Consistency
1. Do any of the designated requirements conflict with the descriptive material?
2. Are there any input states that are mapped to more than one output state?
3. Is a consistent set of quantitative units used? Are all numeric quantities consistent?

Figure 1. Sample defect types for a requirements-inspection checklist.

one of whom (usually called the moderator) is responsible for the effectiveness of the examination, and

• that produce consistent data that can be used for project management, quality control, and process improvement.

We require *all* of these elements for a review to qualify as an inspection.

Inspection metrics. Once you've implemented an inspection process, how do you judge its effectiveness? Useful generic metrics for evaluating and comparing inspection programs include

• the average preparation effort per unit of material,

• the average preparation rate per unit of material,

• the average examination effort per unit of material,

• the average explanation rate per unit of material,

• the average number of defects found per unit of material,

• the average staff-hours spent per defect,

• the average number of major defects found per unit of material, and

• average staff-hours spent per major defect.

The most commonly used units for inspected materials are thousand lines of source code and thousand lines of noncomment source code. For requirements and design inspections, page counts and line counts are also used. You can convert these units to equivalent lines of code when a project ends by relating the total number of pages or lines produced to the total number of lines of code in the final product.

What are typical values for these metrics? Is there any consistency in these values across organizations and across projects? The following is a sample of values from the literature and from private reports:

• The development group for a small warehouse-inventory system used inspections on detailed design and code. The results for detailed design were 3.6 hours of individual preparation per thousand lines, 3.6 hours of meeting time per thousand lines, 33.7 defects found per thousand lines, 1.0 hours per defect found, 7.1 major defects found per thousand lines,

and 4.8 hours per major defect found. The results for code were 7.9 hours of preparation per thousand lines, 4.4 hours of meetings per thousand lines, 42.2 defects found per thousand lines, and 1.2 hours per defect found.

• A major government-systems developer[5] reported the following average results from inspections on more than 562,000 lines of detailed design: 5.76 hours of individual preparation per thousand lines, 4.54 hours of meetings per thousand lines, 17.88 defects found per thousand lines, and 0.58 hours per defect found. The same developer reported the following average results from inspection on 249,000 lines of code: 4.91 hours of individual preparation per thousand lines,

---

A major government contractor reported that their code-inspection data showed a surprising consistency over different applications and languages. Indeed, there is surprising consistency industry-wide.

3.32 hours of meetings per thousand lines, 12.25 defects found per thousand lines, and 0.67 hours per defect found.

• Two quality engineers from a major government-systems contractor[6] reported that their code-inspection data showed a surprising consistency over different applications and programming languages: eight to 12 defects found by inspections per thousand lines of new code and three to five staff-hours per major defect detected by inspections.

Given the great variety of applications and development environments in these and other efforts, there is a surprising consistency in the results. From detailed microcode to high-level business applications, from small engineering groups to large data-processing shops, there is general agreement that the use of inspections

improves the quality of the final product.

The data also shows that, while inspections do not eliminate testing, they can significantly reduce the testing effort because inspections are from two to 10 times more efficient at defect removal than testing. Furthermore, regardless of the application or the language, you can expect inspections to find from seven to 20 major defects per thousand noncomment lines of source code and to find major defects at a cost of one to five staff-hours.

Inspection experience

To be effective, you must apply inspections to a substantial portion of a product. The best strategy is to apply inspections to all documents of a given type (such as all design descriptions or all new or modified code). Inspections can therefore take up a noticeable part of the project's time. Estimates range from 4 to 15 percent. How can you justify this expense? There are two answers.

1. Inspections improve quality. If everything else in the development process remains the same, the use of inspections will result in a higher quality product. This is especially true if you use inspections at various development stages, such as at system definition and system implementation. Using inspections at various stages will help you catch defects in later stages that have slipped through inspections at earlier stages.

The literature contains many claims for improved product quality based on the use of inspections, but these claims are only rarely quantified. Sometimes, relative quality-improvement figures are given. Two claims of improvement are:

• After the introduction of inspections, a large computer manufacturer reported that the number of defects found in released code was reduced by two thirds.[7]

• A major aerospace contractor that has a rigorous and comprehensive inspection program reported an after-release defect rate of less than 0.11 defects per thousand lines of source code.[8]

2. Inspections improve productivity. Along with improved quality, substantial productivity gains have also been reported. Such gains are possible for two reasons.

First, the longer a defect remains in a

product, the more costly it is to remove it. One large telecommunications firm has said that each software fault that must be corrected after the product is delivered costs $10,000. Such a sum can pay for a lot of inspection hours.

Second, except for reviews and walk-throughs, the only other widely applicable technique for detecting and eliminating software defects is testing. If inspections can detect and eliminate faults more cheaply than testing, they can be used to improve productivity and to shorten development schedules.

Inspection versus testing. Can inspections in fact detect and eliminate faults more cheaply than testing? For most development organizations, the answer is yes.

Our experience and that reported in the literature supports this:

• On a 6,000-line IBM business application, inspections found 93 percent of all defects discovered.[7]

• Rework at the design and coding levels is 10 to 100 times less expensive than if it is done in the last half of the development process.[1]

The basic trade-off behind these claims is the average amount of effort expended to detect and eliminate a defect during inspection versus the average effort during testing. Although it is easy to collect data during inspection that will yield an average for the number of hours required to detect a major defect, it is harder — and less precise — to collect data on the rework effort. The usual procedure is to collect this data during follow-up by asking the producer to estimate the effort spent in eliminating the defects uncovered by the inspection.

A further problem is that inspections and testing each detect different types of defects with different efficiencies. One way to address this problem is to try to classify the defects found at an inspection into minor defects and major defects. Major defects should be caught by testing. With this distinction in mind, consider the following reports on inspection defect detection and elimination efficiency:

• A banking computer-services firm that tried out inspections kept statistics on unit testing of some of the programs inspected and found that it took 4.5 hours to eliminate a defect by unit testing compared to 2.2 hours by inspection, according to data the firm supplied us.

• An operating-system development organization for a large mainframe manufacturer reported that the average effort involved in finding a design defect by inspections is 1.4 staff-hours compared to 8.5 staff-hours of effort to find a defect by testing, according to data the organization supplied us.

• A large switching-system project found that defects found in inspections cost an average of 10 times less to eliminate than defects found during development but outside inspections and reviews.[4]

Inspection has certain attributes that might account for these reports. At an inspection meeting, the product under examination is being considered in toto

---

Can you conclude that inspections can replace testing? In general, the answer is no. They can reduce the cost and schedule of testing, but they do not eliminate it.

— the entire input space, the entire output space, and the relationships between them are under continual scrutiny. While the inspection team may occasionally consider an isolated point in the input space and step through a program or detailed design to check that this input point results in the required output, it does so only to gain an understanding of the whole input space or some large subset.

In this sense, an inspection is like mathematics: It deals abstractly with entire classes rather than concretely with individual elements, as testing does. While an inspection requires preparation and meeting time, testing also requires preparation time to design and prepare test cases and to set up and take down test configurations.

When deciding whether to use code inspections, it is important that you consider this test-preparation time and the flexibility and speed with which tests can be selected, executed, and analyzed. Another consideration is the amount of effort involved in isolating and correcting the faults underlying the failures uncovered by testing. In testing, faults tend to be corrected one by one. In inspection, all the defects discovered and listed at the meeting can be corrected in a single rework pass.

Can you therefore conclude that inspections can replace testing? In general, the answer is no. Inspections can replace — and have replaced — testing at the unit level, but beyond that their effect is to reduce testing cost and schedule, not eliminate testing.

Other benefits. The regularity of inspection, combined with the fact that both process and product quality data is collected from each inspection, means that inspections give project management more definite and more dependable milestones than less formal review processes. The data collected by inspections can also be a key ingredient in making judgements about quality-improvement proposals. Christenson and Huang[9] provide an excellent example of how inspection data can be used to diagnose and cure quality problems.

Survey. Because Fagan's original paper on inspections and the later reports in the literature are almost unanimously agreed that inspections are effective, it would be useful to know to what extent software inspections are used both nationally and internationally, how much inspection processes vary and what effects these variations have, and whether there is a consistent set of organizational, managerial, and technical factors that accompany successful and unsuccessful inspection programs.

A comprehensive, scientific study of these questions is obviously beyond the scope of a few people acting privately, but we thought we might conduct a preliminary survey. By soliciting the cooperation of our clients and by tapping into our professional networks, we tried to contact all the English-speaking software-development organizations we could find that were using or had used a peer-review process that fell within our definition of a inspection.

We prepared an extensive interview form and an accompanying organization/project data sheet. Although we expected that many of those surveyed would not be able to give us any quantitative results, we were disappointed to find that they would tell us very little, if anything, unless they had published something on their use of inspections. We were therefore left only with the clients we had worked with or with contacts they referred us to.

We were sensitive to the proprietary issues involved and were willing to take whatever steps required to ensure confidentiality, but we usually met a blank wall when we stepped outside our immediate circle of clients.

Still, we were able to obtain some information on the use of inspections in 15 organizations. The data we obtained is generally consistent with the results cited above, but its narrow scope disappointingly limited our ability to answer the questions we posed.

Most organizations that have used inspections have found them to have significant benefit. In fact, one of our interviewees told us that she did not want to discuss her organization's use of inspections because they were a competitive advantage in bidding for software contracts! Of the organizations that have established rigorous and routine inspection processes, none reported that it later dropped inspections because they were ineffective or inefficient. In fact, several organizations were planning to extend inspections.

Inspections are a very useful tool. If more could be discovered and published about how to initiate and use inspections, the whole software industry could benefit. We suggest that a government agency like the US Commerce Dept.'s National Institute of Standards and Technology sponsor a comprehensive study. With the proper sponsorship, a cooperative approach could be taken that could benefit everyone. ❖

Acknowledgment
We gratefully acknowledge the help of John C. Kelly of the Jet Propulsion Laboratory in pointing out additional sources of information on inspections.

References
1. M.E. Fagan, "Design and Code Inspections to Reduce Errors in Program Development," *IBM Systems J.*, Vol. 15, No. 3, 1976, pp. 182-211.
2. A.F. Ackerman, P.J. Fowler, and R.G. Ebenau, "Software Inspections and the Industrial Production of Software," in *Software Validation*, H.L. Hausen, ed., Elsevier, Amsterdam, 1984, pp. 13-40.
3. T. Gilb, *The Principles of Software-Engineering Management*, Addison-Wesley, Reading, Mass., 1987.
4. P.J. Fowler, "In-Process Inspections of Products at AT&T," *AT&T Technical J.*, March/April 1986, pp. 102-112.
5. J.H. Dobbins, "Inspections as an Up-Front Quality Technique," in *Handbook of Software Quality Assurance*, G.G. Schulmeyer and J.I. McManus, eds., Van Nostrand Reinhold, New York, 1987, pp. 137-177.
6. R.D. Buck and J.H. Dobbins, "Application of Inspection Methodology in Design and Code," in *Software Validation*, H.L. Hausen, ed., Elsevier, Amsterdam, 1984, pp. 41-56.
7. M.E. Fagan, "Advances in Inspections," *IEEE Trans. Software Eng.*, July 1986, pp. 744-751.
8. "Application for the National Aeronautics and Space Administration Excellence Award for Quality and Productivity," tech. report, IBM Federal Systems Div., Houston, 1986.
9. D.A. Christenson and S.T. Huang, "Code-Inspection Management Using Statistical Control Limits," *Proc. Nat'l Comm. Forum*, Nat'l Comm. Forum, Chicago, 1987, pp. 1095-1101.

A. Frank Ackerman is a coauthor of another article in this issue. His biography appears on p. 27.

Lynne S. Buchwald is president of Qualitech, a Brooklyn, N.Y., consulting firm specializing in software engineering and quality assurance. She has more than 12 years of experience in software development and software-engineering technology transfer and training, most recently concentrating in the areas of development methodologies and CASE tools.

Buchwald received a BA in linguistics from Trinity College and an MA in ancient near-Eastern languages from the University of Pennsylvania. She is a member of ACM and IEEE.

Frank H. Lewski is a member of the technical staff of the Quality Methods Group at AT&T Bell Laboratories. Since 1986, he has provided training and consulting in software engineering, including inspections, to more than 25 internal development projects.

Lewski received a BS in computer science from Pennsylvania State University and did graduate work in computer engineering at Syracuse University. He is a member of IEEE.

Address questions about this article to Ackerman at Institute for Zero-Defect Software, 200 Runnymede Pkwy., New Providence, NJ 07974.

Reprinted from *IEEE Software*, Vol. 8, No. 1, January 1991, pp. 25-31. Copyright © 1991 by The Institute of Electrical and Electronics Engineers, Inc. All rights reserved.

Experience with Inspection in Ultralarge-Scale Developments

GLEN W. RUSSELL, *Bell-Northern Research*

◆ *Code inspection, now 14 years old, is labor-intensive and low-tech. But overcoming resistance to its use pays off with faster detection of more errors.*

The basic principle of inspection is quite simple — you systematically examine interim work products to detect errors as early as possible. But despite documented benefits,[1-4] organizations are often reluctant to introduce software inspection.[5]

Part of the problem is the perception that inspections cost more than they are worth. Inspections are obviously labor intensive, and the payback may not be immediately obvious. The process also requires that a designer's work be exposed to a very detailed group review. Thus both management and designers may resist inspections. (The box on p. 26 is an overview of how inspection works.)

But inspections can be very cost-effective and highly beneficial, even when scaled up for ultralarge projects. Here I present quantitative results based on a 1988 study of inspection of 2.5 million lines of high-level code at Bell-Northern Research.

The data represent one of the largest published studies in the industry and confirm that code inspection is still one of the most efficient ways to remove software defects. In the box on pp. 28-29, I describe how to successfully introduce inspections in large-scale production environments.

CODE INSPECTIONS AT BNR

Bell-Northern Research is the research and development subsidiary of Northern Telecom, a supplier of fully digital switching networks and business communication products. By 1988, BNR project teams had written over 15 million lines of code, most in modern, high-level languages.

This software forms the basis of such telecommunications products as DMS-

SIMPLE BUT POWERFUL IDEA

Michael Fagan developed inspection at IBM and publicized it in a now-famous 1976 article.[1] (Fagan recently published an update.[2])

Originally developed for general-purpose verification, inspection can be applied to any well-defined work product such as requirements and design documents, test plans, hardware logic, and of course code. Here I show how the technique applies to code.

A code inspection is a formal, explicit examination conducted by a trained team of peer developers whose primary objective is to detect errors in the code. The team paraphrases the code, line by line, to express source-statement functionality. Several characteristics distinguish the process from other less formal reviews.

Roles. *Each inspection team member has a well-defined role.*

The moderator chairs the inspection meetings and logs all discovered defects. He must ensure that the participants work as a team, follow the correct process, and stick to paraphrasing code. The challenge is to keep the proceedings objective, professional, and friendly, and to avoid needless criticism. Under these conditions, project teams are likely to view the process as a constructive, valuable step in writing software.

Inspectors are knowledgeable peer designers who paraphrase the code line by line. To be effective they should attend an overview meeting, read requirements and design documents, and thoroughly read the code before the inspection meetings. Inspectors must understand the design context and the base system on which the code is built.

The code author participates as a silent observer who does not paraphrase any code. Because of his familiarity with the software, the author may paraphrase too quickly for the others to follow. And he is more likely to express what he intended rather than what he actually implemented. The author also must not preempt the team from deciphering the software, unless the team requests specific explanations.

Purpose. *A code inspection has a single purpose: to detect as many errors as possible. The objective is error detection, not error correction.*

When the team finds errors, the moderator records the defect location and severity on a summary form. The inspectors do not try to fix the error. Repairing code during the meetings greatly slows inspection. It also leads to inferior quick fixes and encroaches on the designer's responsibilities. Good moderators diligently prevent any attempt at redesign.

Technique. *The team uses a systematic examination process — paraphrasing — to detect errors. Paraphrasing is the essence of inspection and the focal point of the meetings. An inspector verbally expresses the meaning of one or more lines of code, at a higher level than the literal source text.*

The code reader must continuously decide how many lines to express at once, but generally never more than two or three lines. If the code is complex, he may read just part of a line.

Paraphrasing is very demanding — the maximum rate should never exceed 150 lines an hour, and each meeting should last no longer than two hours.

Inspections are distinct from such reviews as code walk-throughs, code browsing, "giving the code to another designer to look over," and desk checking. In general, these approaches proceed through the code too quickly to detect a significant number of errors, lack focus on a single objective, and do not benefit from team synergy.

In contrast, during a code inspection well-prepared experts analyze the code line by line, using a precise paraphrasing technique.

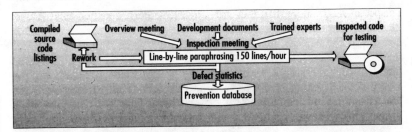

FIGURE A. THE CODE-INSPECTION PROCESS.

References

1. M.E. Fagan, "Design and Code Inspections to Reduce Errors in Program Development," *IBM Systems J.*, No. 3, 1976, pp. 184-211.
2. M.E. Fagan, "Advances in Software Inspections," *IEEE Trans. Software Engineering*, July 1986, pp. 744-751.

---

100 digital switches, Meridian SL-1 PBXs, and DPN packet-switching systems.

From 1978 to 1986, code inspections spread informally to most major software projects at BNR. However, their use was largely a matter of local policy, decided by individual developers and project managers.

Nevertheless, by 1984 inspections were well established in key projects whose gains in quality and productivity attracted senior managers' attention. Code inspections seemed to be enhancing development. Thus, in 1986, the technique became standard in nearly all BNR software developments.

QUANTIFYING BENEFITS

BNR has collected a very large set of statistics on code inspection. This substantial database clearly shows that inspection is a cost-effective way to eliminate defects.

Cost/benefit. The graph in Figure 1 is based on data collected from inspections carried out in developing the DMS family of digital switching products. In 1988, this very large, embedded, real-time software system contained more than 10,000,000 lines of high-level source code.

The graph shows results from 2.5 million lines of code inspected for eight software releases over a two-year interval. For each release, the graph shows the number of defects found per man-hour of effort invested in inspections.

Each bar in the graph is divided into major errors (those affecting operations), minor errors (those not affecting operations), and commentary errors. Major errors are serious defects that would prevent or significantly degrade the product's normal functions. Minor errors would not compromise essential product operation, but would still be seen by the customer as a fault. Commentary errors represent inadequate or incorrect code comments.

Excluding comments, inspections of these 2.5 million lines of code yielded between 0.8 and 1 defect per man-hour. The effort hours include all activities for all participants involved with inspections — including preparation time, overview pre-

sentations, and the inspection meetings. Thus the graph shows the effort cost of finding defects by inspection.

These results are consistent with data from other large BNR software projects. The implication is that if you apply inspections seriously, with adequate preparation and at the recommended pace, you can find approximately *one defect for every man-hour invested*. As I show later, this is two to four times faster than detecting code errors by execution testing.

Here's some more perspective on this data. Statistics collected from large BNR software projects show that each defect in software released to customers and subsequently reported as a problem requires an average of 4.5 man-days to repair. Each hour spent on inspection thus avoids an average of 33 hours of subsequent maintenance effort, assuming a 7.5-hour workday.

This is a major return on investment. It not only cancels inspection's original cost, but also provides a sizable saving in effort over the total project life cycle. Best of all, customers see higher quality in the delivered product.

Inspection pace. Inspection effectiveness is directly related to the *paraphrasing rate* — the speed at which the source-code statements are examined. Using the same 2.5 million lines of code, Figure 2 plots the defects per thousand lines of source code discovered at inspection paces ranging from 150 to 750 lines of code per hour. (Inspection pace was computed from the meeting duration and number of inspected lines reported by the inspection teams.)

The slower paces yield the most impressive results. Inspections that proceed near the BNR-recommended rate of 150 lines of code per hour detect the most errors — about 37 defects per thousand lines of code, excluding comments. Those carried out at around 750 lines of code per hour detect the fewest defects, fewer than eight defects per thousand lines of code, excluding comments.

In 1986, Capers Jones published data suggesting that the defect density of software ranged from 49.5 to 94.6 defects per thousand lines of code for the five systems he studied.[6] On the basis of these results

and internal BNR data, I estimate that 37 defects per thousand lines of code may represent up to 80 percent of all defects in the code.

Inspection versus testing. Even designers who support inspections often carry out basic code testing because they think this is a fast way to clean up the simple errors.

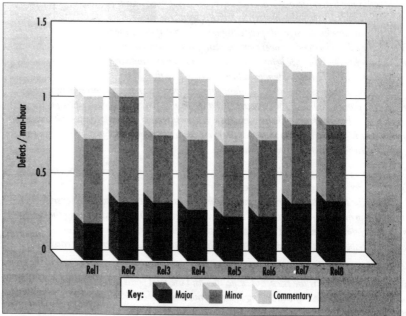

FIGURE 1. DEFECTS FOUND PER MAN-HOUR INVESTED IN THE TOTAL INSPECTION PROCESS. THE EIGHT PRODUCT RELEASES INCLUDE MORE THAN 2.5 MILLION LINES OF HIGH-LEVEL INSPECTED CODE.

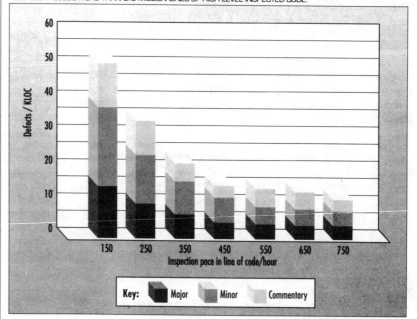

FIGURE 2. DEFECTS DETECTED PER THOUSAND LINES OF CODE VERSUS INSPECTION PACE, EXPRESSED IN LINES OF CODE PER HOUR. (THESE RESULTS ARE FROM THE INSPECTIONS GRAPHED IN FIGURE 1.)

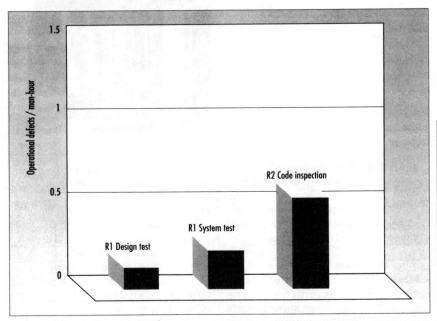

FIGURE 3. DETECTION EFFICIENCY: FORMAL DESIGNER AND SYSTEM TESTING COMPARED WITH CODE INSPECTION. RELEASE 1 AND RELEASE 2 WERE COMPARABLE, BUT RELEASE 1 WAS NOT INSPECTED.

But which technique is more efficient at finding defects?

To investigate this question, BNR studied inspection and test efficiency using two comparable software releases developed during 1986 and 1987 for a large packet-switching system.

The first release, labeled Release 1 in Figure 3, included 300,000 lines of new or changed high-level source code. The code was not inspected, but fault and test-effort data were collected for the standard quality-assurance program.

Release 2 coincided with the general introduction of inspections and was used

HOW TO INTRODUCE CODE INSPECTION

Attempts to change a development process inevitably encounter resistance. While most objections to code inspection are unfounded, you must anticipate and address them all or inspection will not catch on. The issues are much more related to developers and their culture than to methodology. Here are obstacles you will probably encounter and how to overcome them.

Image problem. *Inspection is decidedly "low tech." It involves a lot of meticulous, painstaking, manual work. Many designers would much rather test the code by executing it. Moreover, finding errors with test monitors and debuggers appears faster than group examination. (In the main article, I disprove the common notion that dynamic testing is more efficient than inspection for finding defects.)*

The process also doesn't appeal to corporate managers who may prefer technological "silver bullets." Inspections lack the advanced image of computer-aided software design workstations. However, inspections are available now. Computer-aided software design is pretty much still a promise or at the research stage.

Fuzzy definitions. *Despite the extensive literature, development teams often have only a vague understanding of inspection. Informal reviews, walk-throughs, and desk checking are commonly equated with a true inspection.*

It is hard to persuade teams to adopt the correct process when they feel they already use the technique. However, only a team code inspection delivers the productivity gains discussed here and elsewhere in the literature.

Successful introduction requires that both managers and developers clearly understand the exact procedure. Thus education and training are important to distinguish the genuine practice from practices with similar-sounding names that do not deliver comparable benefits.

Time factor. *Inspections require a lot of people and time. The investment is fairly reasonable relative to the overall development cycle.*

Nevertheless, it still translates into weeks, not days.

Thus, an important first step is to quantify the cost and establish a realistic set of planning guidelines, so developers can accommodate the process in the project plan from the beginning. Effective inspection can't be a last-minute addition.

BNR uses a simple scheduling formula to determine the elapsed time for the total process. Any organization can develop similar guidelines. The formula is based on thousands of lines of source code (kLOC) and incorporates Fagan's recommendations for inspection pace, meeting duration, and frequency:[1]

elapsed time (in days) = $3 \times n$ kLOC

Here n is an estimate of how many thousands of lines of code will be inspected.

The formula includes time for preparing the source code, attending a code overview, participating in the actual inspection meetings, and reinspecting 10 to 20 percent of the code after reworking. Multiplying this figure by the number of people on the inspection team gives the total inspection effort in man-days.

For example, a 20 KLOC program being inspected by a four-person team (including the code author) would require 60 days or 12 weeks of elapsed time for preparation, overview, and inspection. The process would consume a total of 48 man-weeks of effort.

In isolation, this figure may seem unacceptably large — a full man-year. However, in large real-time projects involving millions of lines of code, the average designer produces 3,000 to 5,000 lines of code a year. Thus our 20,000-line example would require 4 to 6.7 man-years to develop. In this context, 48 man-weeks is 1.5 to 2.5 percent of the total effort — certainly a significant but not an unreasonable component.

Demand for proof. *When you introduce inspections, someone will demand up-front evidence that the process is worth the effort.*

Published industry results seldom serve as proof; skeptics reject the data because of the study's size or nature. Staff may refuse to accept

to test the technique. It included 180,000 lines of new or changed code. Both systems were similar in functionality and development.

Figure 3 shows the defects found per man-hour invested. There are two Release 1 bars — one for faults detected per man-hour for formal designer testing, the other for system testing. The Release 2 bar shows results for the complete inspection process.

For these two large releases, inspections were two to four times more efficient at finding errors than either formal designer testing or system testing. If non-execution errors such as code optimizations and noncompliance to standards are

included, the difference is even larger.

In general, these results agree with those in other published studies.[7] Depending on the test environment's complexity, code inspection can be up to 20 times more efficient than testing.

Distinct processes. The difference in detection efficiencies is related to a fundamental difference between the two processes. As Figure 4 shows, inspections find defects by direct examination. Usually when a team finds an error, the solution is self-evident. The code author can repair defects simply by editing the source code.

Contrast this with the typical product-

testing environment shown in Figure 5. A well-designed test plan turns up product faults (as opposed to software defects). However, fault symptoms do not directly reveal the underlying code defects.

A great deal of debugging and deductive thinking usually go into uncovering code errors from the observed symptoms. Debugging can be quite time consuming, particularly when the fault is intermittent or hard to reproduce.

Given this analysis, you should inspect software to clean it up before the more complex and indirect test stage. Testing then becomes more productive because you find fewer faults to debug.

---

inspections until a significant in-house trial "proves" that the process really pays off. However, collecting statistically meaningful data is impossible until many project teams agree to do inspections.

The solution to this impasse is decisive management willing to gamble that inspections will work. A certain amount of good will and faith also comes in handy. BNR required an assessment of effectiveness after a year of extensive application. Reports then provided the concrete in-house data needed for continued support.

Selling inspection. *Often an organization's concerns simply reflect a natural resistance to change. You need an innovative and aggressive approach to overcome this inertia and generate the commitment needed for sustained success.*

BNR used a creative, high-profile advertising campaign aimed directly at project teams. The goal was to persuade this group that inspections really do work. Instead of focusing on benefits for the corporation, the campaign addressed an obvious question: "As a member of a busy project team, what's in this for me?" The answer was equally direct: "Inspections simply make your life a lot easier."

The campaign consisted of a sequence of two posters and an information flyer. This material unfolded as a progressive "tease" campaign, designed to attract attention first and then focus interest on inspection's benefits.

The first poster depicted a solitary, frustrated designer, struggling late at night in an obviously unproductive debugging session. The image was captioned "...a better way?"

This was followed a week later by a second poster showing the same designer working productively with others in an inspection meeting. The revised caption — "...a better way!" — emphasized that inspections were indeed a more predictable approach to detecting defects.

This was very much a hard-sell approach. But the change warranted the campaign: It had to persuade hundreds of developers to adopt a generally unpopular process. The publicity provided a good start.

Training. *To train designers BNR developed a comprehensive self-study video course. Video was chosen because it shows precisely and unambiguously how to conduct effective inspection meetings. Also, BNR management wanted to train hundreds of staff across multiple sites in about two months, a time frame in which an instructor/classroom approach would have been unworkable. Video has the further advantage of being a permanent, on-demand resource, available as needed for future training.*

BNR's inspection course is a stand-alone, self-paced instruction program with a 75-minute video and a supporting workbook. In about a half a day the course provides the basic skills and enough training to start applying the technique to the current assignment.

The tape covers the meeting process, team roles, error reporting, planning guidelines, and paraphrasing, with a demonstration of good paraphrasing technique. The workbook gives an example program for practice.

Perhaps the liveliest part of the video is a series of staged inspection meetings. Students first see a "bad" meeting, where poor attitudes and practices cause the entire process to disintegrate. This is followed by a "good" meeting. The same people now use a professional team approach. They apply paraphrasing effectively and focus on error detection to bring about a successful inspection meeting.

The training program started with BNR senior managers, who attended a session using the same material distributed to the development teams. Managers learned about what was required from their staffs and about process and scheduling. For distribution through the organization, senior designers introduced the material and acted as local experts and champions.

Most training was completed within two months. The technique is now well established.

REFERENCE

1. M.E. Fagan, "Design and Code Inspections to Reduce Errors in Program Development," *IBM Systems J.*, No. 3, 1976, pp. 184-211.

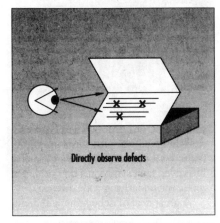

FIGURE 4. INSPECTIONS FIND DEFECTS BY DIRECT OBSERVATION, AND THE SOLUTIONS ARE OFTEN SELF-EVIDENT.

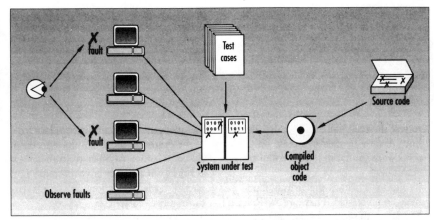

FIGURE 5. TESTING FINDS DEFECTS BY INDIRECT OBSERVATION. DEBUGGING A FAULT TO UNCOVER THE UNDERLYING DEFECT CAN BE VERY TIME CONSUMING.

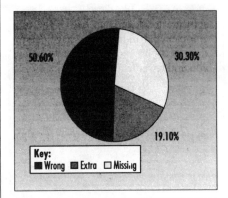

FIGURE 6. PERCENTAGE OF DEFECTS FOUND IN INSPECTION ARISING FROM WRONG, EXTRA, AND MISSING STATEMENTS.

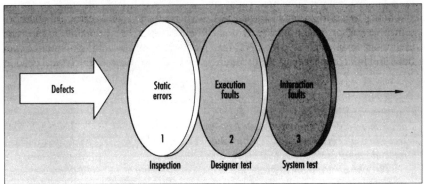

FIGURE 7. INSPECTION AND TESTING ARE COMPLEMENTARY BECAUSE EACH TECHNIQUE UNCOVERS DIFFERENT TYPES OF ERRORS. THE STEPS SHOULD BE APPLIED IN THE ORDER SHOWN.

Discouraging pretesting. There are two other good reasons for not testing before inspections.

Inspection relies on a motivated team committed to finding the most defects possible. Testing before meetings makes the code partially operational, creating the impression that it is in some sense correct. Inspection seems redundant, and the team loses motivation.

When pretesting is extensive, another factor comes into play. The code author now has invested a lot of time in this version of the software and is considerably less receptive to optimizations that would require major reworking. Such improvements would alter an already-stable program image and require previous testing to be repeated.

Synergistic techniques. My point is not that inspections can or should replace testing. Both techniques are essential in producing high-quality software. When inspection is combined with testing, error detection is much broader because inspection tends to find errors difficult to uncover in testing.

Figure 6 classifies the defects reported for the 2.5 million lines of inspected code according to whether they arose from wrong, extra, or missing statements.

Extra and missing statements account for almost 50 percent of all errors found by the inspection process. Extra statements are more likely to be found only in inspections; it's almost impossible to find superfluous code through testing. Even missing statements are difficult to detect in testing, since omissions are often related to infrequent failure paths that are difficult to create in the product under test.

On the other hand, dynamic testing is better for finding problems related to execution, timing, traffic, transaction rates, and system interactions. It provides the ultimate check by verifying the software in actual use. Figure 7 shows inspections and testing as complementary filters to detect most software defects.

Michael Fagan introduced inspection as a general approach to verification that can be applied to any documented work product with well-defined completion criteria.

It can be used throughout development, from requirements specification through test planning. Thus the technique is likely to endure for some time, despite ongoing evolution in development technology.

As the industry moves toward more automated computer-aided design environments, systematic inspection will be especially appropriate for verifying the formalized specifications and designs that these tools produce. Designers will use the technique to inspect the formal capture of software architectures instead of code.

The technique is already finding new applications. For example, BNR successfully introduced inspections to hardware developments in late 1988, after a year and a half of research and pilot trials. The major challenge was to devise an appropriate way to paraphrase circuit schematics.

In hardware inspection meetings, the traditional roles of moderator, inspectors, and designer stay the same. But the team also includes a manufacturing test engineer to address testability and a software representative to cover the hardware/software interface. Also, BNR has established new planning and scheduling guidelines based on the circuit's size.

Hardware inspections were launched using a high-profile publicity campaign and training video. Data collected to date suggest that the detection efficiency of the new process is comparable with that of code inspection.

So far the technique has uncovered errors difficult to find in circuit simulation (the equivalent of software unit testing). Hardware inspections also appear to speed up and streamline simulation. The technique applies equally well to printed circuit packs and application-specific integrated circuits. ◆

REFERENCES

1. M.E. Fagan, "Advances in Software Inspections," *IEEE Trans. Software Engineering*, July 1986, pp. 744-751.

2. A.F. Ackerman, P.J. Fowler, and R.G. Ebenau, "Software Inspections and the Industrial Production of Software," in *Software Validation*, H.L. Hausen, ed., Elsevier, Amsterdam, 1984, pp. 13-40.

3. R.D. Buck and J.H. Dobbins, "Application of Software Inspections Methodology in Design and Code," in *Software Validation*, H.L. Hausen, ed., Elsevier, Amsterdam, 1984, pp. 41-56.

4. W.L.G. Koontz, "Experience with Software Inspections in the Development of Firmware for a Digital Loop Carrier System," *IEEE Int'l Conf. Comm. '86 Conf. Record*, IEEE, New York, 1986, pp. 1188-1189.

5. A.F. Ackerman, L.S. Buchwald, and F.H. Lewski, "Software Inspections: An Effective Verification Process," *IEEE Software*, May 1989, pp. 31-36.

6. T.C. Jones, *Programming Productivity*, McGraw-Hill, New York, 1986, p. 172.

7. P.J. Fowler, "In-Process Inspections of Work-products at AT&T," *AT&T Technical J.*, March/April 1986, p. 106.

ACKNOWLEDGMENTS

The successful large-scale introduction of code inspections at BNR involved many people. However, most of the credit for ongoing success must certainly go to the hundreds of committed software developers throughout BNR, who have the challenge of carrying out the process every day.

Glen Russell is manager of the development productivity group at the Network Switching Systems division of Bell-Northern Research in Ottawa, Canada. His professional interests include applying navigation, browsing, and reengineering technology to improve designer productivity on large, mature software systems.

Russell received a BS in physics from St. Francis Xavier University and an MS in electrical engineering from the University of New Brunswick.

Address questions about this article to Russell at BNR Ltd., PO Box 3511, Station C, Ottawa, Ontario, Canada K1Y 4H7.

Software Verification and Validation: An Overview

Dolores R. Wallace, *National Institute of Standards and Technology*
Roger U. Fujii, *Logicon*

Properly applied throughout the life cycle, verification and validation can result in higher quality, more reliable programs. This article introduces the V&V method and standards to support it.

Verification and validation is one of the software-engineering disciplines that help build quality into software. V&V is a collection of analysis and testing activities across the full life cycle and complements the efforts of other quality-engineering functions. This overview article explains what V&V is, shows how V&V groups' efforts relate to other groups' efforts, describes how to apply V&V, and summarizes evaluations of V&V's effectiveness. The box on p. 11 describes standards and guidelines for planning and managing a V&V effort.

What is V&V?

V&V comprehensively analyzes and tests software to determine that it performs its intended functions correctly, to ensure that it performs no unintended functions, and to measure its quality and reliability. V&V is a systems-engineering discipline to evaluate software in a systems context. Like systems engineering, it uses a structured approach to analyze and test the software against all system functions and against hardware, user, and other software interfaces.

Verification involves evaluating software during each life-cycle phase to ensure that it meets the requirements set forth in the previous phase. Validation involves testing software or its specification at the end of the development effort to ensure that it meets its requirements (that it does what it is supposed to). While "verification" and "validation" have separate definitions, you can derive the maximum benefit by using them synergistically and treating "V&V" as an integrated definition.

Ideally, V&V parallels software development and yields several benefits:

• It uncovers high-risk errors early, giving the design team time to evolve a comprehensive solution rather than forcing a makeshift fix to accommodate development deadlines.

• It evaluates the products against system requirements.

• It gives management continuous and

Reprinted from *IEEE Software*, Vol. 6, No. 3, May 1989, pp. 10-17. Copyright © 1989 by The Institute of Electrical and Electronics Engineers, Inc. All rights reserved.

comprehensive information about the quality and progress of the development effort.

• It gives the user an incremental preview of system performance, with the chance to make early adjustments.

The V&V tasks in Table 1 are the minimum tasks for the development phases required by ANSI/IEEE Std 1012-1986, *Standard for Software Verification and Validation Plans*. The V&V standard specifies minimum input and output requirements for each V&V task. A V&V task may not begin without specific inputs, and is not completed until specific outputs are completed.

You can tailor a V&V effort by adding or deleting tasks to or from the minimum set. Table 2 lists some optional V&V tasks and considerations that you might use to assign the tasks to your V&V group. You can apply these tasks to different life-cycle models by mapping the traditional waterfall phases to the new model. Examples include variations of the traditional waterfall, Boehm's spiral development,[1] rapid prototyping, and evolutionary development models.

Where V&V fits in

Because V&V should occur throughout the life cycle, applying it involves many groups. Furthermore, V&V and other groups complement each other's software-quality responsibilities:

• The software-development group builds the product to satisfy the established quality and performance requirements. The group relies on its quality-assurance group, systems engineers, requirements analysts, designers, programmers, testers, data-management and configuration-management specialists, documentation specialists, and others.

• The quality-assurance group verifies that the development process and products conform to established standards and procedures. Using reviews, audits, inspec-

V&V standards and guidelines

The concepts of V&V emerged in the late 1960s and 1970s as the use of software in military and nuclear-power systems increased. Initially, individual programs' standards addressed the need for V&V. Then government and industry began to develop V&V standards so they would have a specification of this methodology for contract procurements and for monitoring the technical performance of V&V efforts. Today's V&V standards and guidelines serve large, heterogeneous communities and are applicable to many types of software. They include:

• Federal Information-Processing Standards Publication 101, *Guideline for Life-Cycle Validation, Verification, and Testing of Computer Software*,

• FIPS Pub. 132, *Guideline for Software Verification and Validation Plans*, which adopts ANSI/IEEE Std 1012-1986, the *Standard for Software Verification and Validation Plans*,

• the US Air Force's AFSC/AFLC 800-5, *Software Independent Verification and Validation*,

• the American Nuclear Society's ANS 10.4, *Guidelines for the Verification and Validation of Scientific and Engineering Computer Programs for the Nuclear Industry*, and

• the NASA Jet Propulsion Laboratory's JPL D-576, *Independent Verification and Validation of Computer Software: Methodology*.

Table A shows you how to develop a V&V effort based on the strength of the guidance in these standards and guidelines.

Table A.
Planning V&V with guidance from V&V documents.

Activity	Procedure	Guidance
Scope the V&V effort	Criticality assessment	AFSC 800-5
	Organization	AFSC 800-5, ANS 10.4
	Cost estimation	AFSC 800-5
Plan the V&V effort	Planning preparation	FIPS 132/IEEE 1012, ANS 10.4, FIPS 101
	Objectives	FIPS 132/IEEE 1012, FIPS 101, ANS 10.4, JPL D-576
	General V&V task selection	all
	Minimum, required	FIPS 132/IEEE 1012
	Optional	FIPS 132/IEEE 1012
	Criticality levels	FIPS 101, AFSC 800-5
	Test management	FIPS 132/IEEE 1012
	Test types	FIPS 132/IEEE 1012, FIPS 101, JPL D-576
	Objectives	FIPS 132/IEEE 1012
	Documentation	FIPS 132/IEEE 1012
	Coverage	FIPS 101, FIPS 132/IEEE 1012, ANS 10.4
	Planning	all
	Planning V&V for maintenance	ANS 10.4, FIPS 132/IEEE 1012
Manage the V&V effort	V&V management tasks	FIPS 132/IEEE 1012
	Reporting	FIPS 132/IEEE 1012, ANS 10.4

Table 1.

Table 1.
Minimum set of recommended V&V tasks.

Phase	Tasks	Key issues
Concept	Concept-documentation evaluation	Satisfy user needs; constraints of interfacing systems
Requirements definition	Traceability analysis	Trace of requirements to concept
	Requirements validation	Correctness, consistency, completeness, accuracy, readability, and testabililty; satisfaction of system requirements.
	Interface analysis	Hardware, software, and operator interfaces
	Begin planning for V&V system testing	Compliance with functional requirements; performance at interfaces; adequacy of user documentation; performance at boundaries
	Begin planning for V&V acceptance testing	Compliance with acceptance requirements
Design	Traceability analysis	Trace of design to requirements
	Design evaluation	Correctness, consistency, completeness, accuracy readability, and testability ; design quality.
	Interface analysis	Correctness, consistency, completeness, accuracy readability, and testability; data items across interface
	Begin planning for V&V component testing	Compliance to design; timing and accuracy; performance at boundaries
	Begin planning for V&V integration testing	Compliance with functional requirements; timing and accuracy; performance at stress limits
Implementation	Traceability analysis	Trace of source code to design
	Code evaluation	Correctness, consistency, completeness, accuracy, readability, and testability; code quality
	Interface analysis	Correctness, consistency, completeness, accuracy, readability, and testability; data/control access across interfaces
	Component test execution	Component integrity
Test	V&V integration-test execution	Correctness of subsystem elements; subsystem interface requirements
	V&V system-test execution	Entire system and at limits and user stress conditions
	V&V acceptance-test execution	Performance with operational scenarios
Installation and checkout	Installation-configuration audit	Operations with site dependencies; adequacy of installation procedure
	V&V final-report generation	Disposition of all errors; summary of V&V results

tions, and walkthroughs, it acts as a formal check and balance to monitor and evaluate software as it is being built.

• The systems-engineering group ensures that the product satisfies system requirements and objectives. It uses techniques like simulation to gain reasonable assurance that the requirements are satisfied.

• The configuration-management and data-management groups monitor and control the program versions and data during product development, using techniques like formal audits, change-control records, requirements traceability, and sign-off records. The user organization must provide assurance that the software satisfies user requirements and operational needs. Typically, it uses techniques like formal design reviews and acceptance testing.

• Like the systems-engineering group, the V&V group is responsible for verifying that the product at each life-cycle phase satisfies quality attributes (like correctness) and that at each phase it satisfies the requirements of the previous phase. The V&V group is also responsible for validating that the software satisfies system requirements and objectives.

While its activities are directed at the software, the V&V group must also consider how the software interacts with the system, including hardware, users, other software, and other external systems. The V&V group maintains its own configuration- and data-management functions on program, data, and documentation received from the development team to ensure that V&V discrepancy reports are made against controlled documents and to repeat V&V tests against controlled

Table 2.
Optional V&V tasks and suggested applications.

Tasks	M	C	R	D	I	T	X	O	Considerations
Algorithm analysis	□	□	■	■	■	■	□	■	Numerical and scientific software using critical equations or models
Audit performance									When the V&V group is part of the quality-assurance or user
Configuration control	□	□	□	□	■	■	■	■	group, for large developments to help quality-assurance or
Functional	□	□	□	□	■	■	■	■	f or user-group staff audits
In-process	□	□	■	■	■	■	■	■	
Physical	□	□	□	□	□	■	■	■	
Audit support									When the V&V group is part of a systems-engineering group or
Configuration control	□	□	□	□	■	■	■	■	is independent, for large software developments
Functional	□	□	□	□	■	■	■	■	
In-process	□	□	■	■	■	■	■	■	
Physical	□	□	□	□	□	■	■	■	
Configuration management	■	■	■	■	■	■	■	■	When the V&V group is part of the user group
Control-flow analysis	□	□	■	■	■	□	□	□	Complex, real-time software
Database analysis	□	□	■	■	■	■	□	■	Large database applications; if logic is stored as parameters
Dataflow analysis	■	□	■	■	■	■	□	■	Data-driven real-time systems
Feasibility-study evaluation	□	■	□	□	□	■	■	■	High-risk software using new technology or concepts
Installation and checkout test	□	□	■	■	■	■	■	■	When the V&V group is part of the systems-engineering or user group
Performance monitoring	□	□	□	□	■	□	□	□	Software with changeable man-machine interfaces
Qualification testing**	□	□	■	■	■	■	■	■	When the V&V group is part of the systems-engineering or user group
Regression analysis and testing	□	□	■	■	■	■	■	■	Large, complex systems
Reviews support									When the V&V group is part of the systems-engineering or user group
Operational readiness	□	□	□	□	□	□	■	■	
Test readiness	□	□	□	□	■	■	□	■	
Simulation analysis	□	□	□	■	■	■	□	■	No system-test capability or the need to preview the concept for feasibility or the requirements for accuracy
Test certification	□	□	□	□	□	■	■	■	For critical software
Test evaluation	□	□	■	■	■	■	■	■	When the V&V fgroup is part of the quality-assurance or user group
Test witnessing	□	□	□	□	□	■	■	■	When the V&V group is part of the quality-assurance, user, or systems-engineering group
User-documentation evaluation	□	■	■	■	■	■	■	■	Interactive software requiring user inputs
V&V tool-plan generation	■	□	□	□	□	□	□	□	When acquiring or building V&V analysis and test tools
Walkthroughs									When the V&V group is part of the quality-assurance or systems-engineering group, for large software developments to staff walkthroughs
Design	□	□	□	■	□	□	□	■	
Requirements	□	□	■	□	□	□	□	■	
Source code	□	□	□	□	■	□	□	■	
Test	□	□	□	□	■	■	■	■	

*Phase codes: M=management, C=concept, R=requirements, D=design, I=implementation, T=test, X=installation/checkout, and O=operations/maintenance
**Test plan, test design, test cases, test procedures, and test execution

software releases.

The V&V group's documentation evaluation and testing are different from those conducted by other groups. The quality-assurance group reviews documents for compliance to standards and performs a logical check on the technical correctness of the document contents. The V&V group may perform in-depth evaluations by activities like rederiving the algorithms from basic principles, computing timing data to verify response-time require-ments, and developing control-flow diagrams to identify missing and erroneous requirements. The V&V group may suggest more optimal approaches.

The V&V group's testing is usually separate from the development team's testing. In some cases, the V&V group may use development test plans and results and supplement them with additional tests.

A major influence on the responsibilities of a V&V group and its relationship to other groups is to whom the V&V group

reports. There are four ways to organize a V&V effort:

• Independent. The traditional approach is that the V&V group is independent of the development team and is called "independent V&V" or "IV&V." In this relationship, the V&V group establishes formal procedures for receiving software releases and documentation from the development group. The V&V group sends all its evaluation reports and discrepancy reports to both the user and development groups. To maintain an unbiased technical viewpoint, the V&V group does not use any results or procedures from the quality-assurance or systems-engineering groups.

The independent V&V group's tasks are oriented toward engineering analysis (like algorithm analysis and control-flow and dataflow analysis) and comprehensive testing (like simulation). The objective is to develop an independent assessment of the software's quality and to determine whether the software satisfies critical system requirements.

The advantages of this approach are detailed analysis and test of software requirements, an independent determination of how well the software performs, and early detection of high-risk software and system errors. The disadvantages are higher costs and additional development interfaces.

• Embedded in the system-engineering group. When the V&V group is embedded in the systems-engineering group, its tasks are to review the group's engineering analyses (like algorithm development, sizing, and timing) and testing (like test evaluation and review of the adequacy of the development test-planning document). In some instances, the V&V group may be the independent test team for the systems-engineering group, sharing its data. The V&V group's results are reviewed and monitored by the systems-engineering and quality-assurance groups. An independent V&V group reporting to the systems-engineering group is another form of this organizational approach.

The advantages to using systems-engineering personnel in the V&V tasks are minimum cost to the project, no system learning for the staff, and no additional development interfaces. A disadvantage is the loss of objective engineering analysis.

• Embedded in the quality-assurance group. When the V&V group is embedded in the quality-assurance group, its tasks are monitoring, auditing, and reviewing content (through tasks like audit performance, audit support, test witnessing, walkthrough support, and documentation review). In these tasks, the V&V group works as part of the quality-assurance group and maintains its relationship to the systems-engineering and other development groups in the same way that the quality-assurance group does.

The advantages of embedding the V&V group in the quality-assurance group are low cost to the project and the entry of V&V analysis capabilities into reviews, audits, and inspections. A disadvantage is the loss of independent systems analysis and testing.

• Embedded in the user group. When the V&V group is embedded in the user group, its tasks are an extension of the user group's responsibilities. Its tasks are configuration-management support of products under development, support of formal reviews, user-documentation evaluation, test witnessing, test evaluation of the development test-planning documents, and user-testing support (like user-acceptance testing and installation and checkout testing). As an extension of the

---

V&V should focus on identifying and eliminating the high risks a project is likely to encounter. V&V management must define and use methods of risk management.

---

user group, the V&V group would receive formal software deliverables and provide comments and data to the development's project management that distributes the information to its own development team.

An advantage of this approach is the strong systems-engineering and user perspectives that can be brought to bear on the software during development. The disadvantages are loss of detailed analysis and test of incremental software (because these incremental versions typically are not formal deliverables) and loss of error detection and feedback to the development group (because of the constraints caused by the frequency of formal product deliverables). If the user group has an independent V&V group reporting to it,

these disadvantages can be overcome — but the price is an additional development interface.

Applying V&V

V&V tasks span the entire development effort, and several of these tasks affect the selection of development techniques and tools. The V&V group's management plans the V&V process, coordinates and interprets its performance and quality, reports discrepancies promptly to the development group, identifies early problem trends and focuses its activities on them, provides a technical evaluation of the product's performance and quality at each major program review, and assesses the full effects of proposed product changes. The group's management produces a V&V plan, task reports, phase summary reports, a final report, and a discrepancy report.

Boehm and Papaccio[2] have reported that Pareto analysis (which shows that 20 percent of the problems cause 80 percent of the rework costs) applies to software and have recommended that V&V "focus on identifying and eliminating the specific high-risk problems to be encountered by a software project." Part of the V&V management activities is to define and use methods to address these problems of rework and risk management.

One method for reducing rework costs is to provide early delivery of information (like draft portions of incremental documents) and software builds to the V&V group. (A software build represents a basic program skeleton containing portions of the full software capabilities. Each successive build integrates additional functions into the skeleton, permitting early software deliveries to the V&V group in an orderly development process.) Based on discrepancy or progress reports, program managers can make the technical and management decisions to refocus the V&V and development groups onto the product's problem areas.

Another method is criticality analysis, which can reduce high-risk problems. You perform it at the beginning of a project to identify the functions and modules required to implement program functions or to identify quality requirements whose failure would cause a safety or security

Table 3.
Matrix of selected V&V issues and V&V techniques and tools.
Gray rows are techniques described in the text.

hazard or a large financial or social loss. You usually identify and trace these through a block or control-flow diagram of the system and its software; each block or control-flow box represents a system or software function (module).

You repeat the analysis for each lifecycle phase to observe whether the implementation details shift the emphasis of the criticality. You can combine the criticality analysis with the cross-reference matrix of Table 1 to identify which V&V techniques are needed for a project.

Techniques. There are many V&V techniques that you can use. But how do you know which ones to use at each phase? Table 3 matches 41 techniques against some of they V&V issues they address. Which phases you apply these techniques to depends on each project's characteristics and V&V objectives.[3] Among the table's 41 techniques are five likely, nonexclusive techniques (highlighted in gray) for determining the feasibility of a software concept and its requirements:

• Requirements parsing separates the desired performance requirements from other requirements data.

• Analytical modeling assesses the desired performance capability.

• Simulations of the proposed operating environment let you execute test data to determine whether the resulting performance matches the desired performance.

• Criticality analysis identifies the critical functions and their distribution in the system architecture.

• Test-data generation defines the performance limits of the proposed system requirements. You can verify predicted performance by using simulation to execute the test scenario.

A forthcoming report[4] will include the full matrix on which Table 3 is based.

Testing. V&V test activities span many phases, from requirements through installation and checkout. V&V testing activities continue into the operations and maintenance phase to address any changes made to the software after initial delivery.

A comprehensive test-management approach recognizes the differences in ob-

Techniques and tools	Acceptance tests	Bottlenecks	Environment interaction	Execution characteristics	Execution support	Feasibility	Portability	Processing efficiency	Requirements evaluation	System-performance prediction
Algorithm analysis	□	□	□	□	□	□	□	■	□	■
Analytical modeling	□	■	■	□	□	■	□	■	■	■
Assertion generation	□	□	□	□	□	□	□	□	□	□
Assertion processing	□	□	□	□	□	□	□	□	□	□
Cause-effect graphing	□	■	□	□	□	□	□	□	□	□
Code auditor	□	□	□	□	□	□	■	■	□	■
Comparator	□	□	□	□	□	□	□	□	□	□
Control-flow analyzer	□	■	□	□	□	□	□	□	□	■
Criticality analysis	■	□	□	□	□	■	□	□	■	□
Cross-reference generator	□	□	□	□	□	□	□	□	□	□
Database analyzer	□	□	□	□	□	□	□	□	□	□
Dataflow analyzer	□	■	□	□	□	□	□	□	□	■
Design-compliance analyzer	□	□	□	□	□	□	□	□	□	□
Execution-time estimator	□	■	□	□	□	□	□	□	□	■
Formal review	□	□	□	□	□	□	□	□	□	□
Formal verification	□	□	□	□	□	□	□	□	□	□
Functional testing	□	□	□	□	□	■	□	□	□	■
Inspections (Fagan)	□	□	□	□	□	□	□	□	□	□
Interactive test aids	□	□	□	□	□	□	□	■	□	□
Interface checker	□	□	□	□	□	□	□	□	■	□
Metrics	□	□	□	□	□	□	□	■	■	□
Mutation analysis	□	□	□	□	□	□	□	□	□	□
Program-description-language processor	□	□	□	□	□	□	□	□	□	□
Peer review	□	□	□	□	□	□	□	□	□	□
Physical-unit testing	□	□	□	□	□	□	□	□	□	□
Regression testing	■	□	□	□	□	□	□	□	□	□
Requirements parsing	■	□	■	□	□	■	□	□	■	□
Round-off analysis	□	□	□	□	□	□	□	□	□	□
Simulations	□	□	■	■	■	□	□	□	□	■
Sizing	□	□	□	□	■	□	□	□	□	□
Software monitors	□	■	■	■	■	□	□	■	□	■
Specification base	■	□	□	□	□	□	□	□	■	■
Structural testing	□	□	□	■	□	□	□	□	□	□
Symbolic execution	□	□	□	□	□	□	□	□	□	□
Test drivers	■	□	■	■	■	□	□	□	□	□
Test-coverage analyzer	□	□	□	■	□	□	□	□	□	□
Test-data generator	■	■	■	■	■	■	□	■	■	■
Test-support facilities	■	□	■	■	□	□	□	■	□	□
Timing	□	■	□	□	□	□	□	■	□	□
Tracing	■	□	□	□	□	□	□	□	□	□
Walkthroughs	□	□	□	□	□	□	□	□	□	□

jectives and strategies of different types of testing. Each of four test-planning activities — component, integration, system, and acceptance testing — produces test-plan, test-design, test-case, and test-procedure documents:

• Component testing verifies the design and implementation of software units, modules, or subelements.

• Integration testing verifies functional requirements as the software subelements are integrated, directing attention to internal software interfaces and external hardware and operator interfaces.

• System testing validates the entire program against system requirements and performance objectives.

• Acceptance testing validates the software against V&V acceptance criteria, defining how the software should perform with other completed software and hardware.

V&V system testing uses a laboratory environment in which some system features are simulated or performed by hardware or software that will not be in the final user environment. Acceptance testing uses the operational environment.

In addition to testing against system and software requirements, effective testing requires a comprehensive understanding of the system. You develop such understanding from systematically analyzing the software's concept, requirements, design, and code.

V&V testing includes structural (white-box) testing that requires knowledge of internal software details. It is effective when probing for errors and weaknesses to reveal hidden faults in regions where some test cases for functional (black-box) testing can produce "correct" output despite internal errors.

Another V&V test technique is to develop test cases that violate software requirements. This approach is effective at uncovering basic design-assumption errors and unusual operational-use errors. These types of errors escape initial detection because they are obscure or so simple that you fail to design for them. V&V test planning is as effective for detecting errors as test executions are for uncovering software faults.

Operations and maintenance. For each software change made in the operations and maintenance phase, you repeat all development V&V activities in Table 1 to ensure that nothing is overlooked. You should add or delete V&V activities to address the type of software change made, but take care in doing so because small changes may have subtle but significant side effects. In many cases, an examination of the proposed software change shows that the V&V group must repeat its activities on only a small part of the prod-

uct. Some V&V activities, like concept-documentation evaluation, may require little or no effort to verify a small change.

How effective is V&V?

Two studies that evaluated the effectiveness of V&V used different data and reported on different factors. While they can't be directly compared, the studies do provide insights on V&V's effectiveness.

One 1982 study by McGarry[5] reported that V&V was *not* an effective approach on three projects at the Software Engineering Laboratory at the National Aeronautics and Space Administration's Goddard Space Flight Center. In the study, three flight-dynamics projects ranging in size from 10,000 to 50,000 lines of code were selected. A V&V group was involved in re-

---

A comprehensive test-management approach recognizes the differences in objectives and strategies of different types of testing.

---

quirements and design verification, separate system testing, and validation of consistency from start to finish. The project lasted 18 months and used an average of 1.1 people, peaking at three people. Results included:

• Productivity of the development groups was the lowest of any previously monitored SEL project (due to the cost of the V&V interface).

• Rates of errors found early in the development cycle were better than usual.

• The V&V effort found 2.3 errors per thousand lines of code.

• The cost of fixing all discovered errors was no less than in any other SEL project.

• The software's reliability (defined as the error rate during acceptance and maintenance and operations) was no different from other SEL projects.

However, a 1981 study by Radatz[6] for the Air Force's Rome (N.Y.) Air Development

Center reported that V&V *was* effective for four large independent V&V projects ranging from 90,000 to 176,000 lines of code. The projects were real-time command-and-control, missile-tracking, and avionics programs, as well as a time-critical, batch trajectory-computation program. The projects took from 2.5 to four years to develop. Two projects started using V&V at the requirements phase; two others started at the coding phase. The V&V groups used five to 12 people per project. Results included:

• Errors were detected early in the development — 50 percent to 89 percent were detected before development testing began.

• Many discrepancies (1,259) were reported — an average of more than 300 per program.

• The V&V effort found an average of 5.5 errors per thousand lines of code.

• More than 85 percent of the errors affected reliability and maintainability.

• Programmer productivity improved (as measured by subtracting the time required to evaluate the V&V error reports from the programming time saved by the programmers' not having to find the error). The savings per error was 1.3 to 6.1 hours of programmer time and more than seven minutes of computer time.

• For the projects starting at the coding phase, the savings from early error detection were 20 to 28 percent of independent V&V costs. For the projects starting at the requirements phase, the savings from early error detection were 92 to 180 percent of independent V&V costs.

These studies showed that V&V can improve quality, cause more stable requirements, cause more rigorous development planning (at least to interface with the V&V group), catch errors earlier, promote better schedule compliance and progress monitoring, make project management more aware of interim quality and progress, and result in better criteria and results for decision making at formal reviews and audits.

But V&V has several negative effects: It adds 10 to 30 percent to the development cost, requires additional interfaces between project groups, can lower developer productivity if programmers and engineers spend time explaining the system to V&V-analysts when trying to resolve invalid anomaly reports, adds to the documentation requirements if the V&V group is receiving incremental program and documentation releases, requires the sharing of computing facilities and classified data with the V&V group, and increases the paperwork to provide written responses to the V&V group's error reports and other V&V data requirements.

As the Radatz study showed, you are more likely to recover V&V costs when you start using it early in the requirements phase. You should consider the interface activities between development and V&V groups for documentation, data, and software deliveries an inherently necessary step to evaluate intermediate development products. This is a necessary by-product of doing what is right from the outset. The cost of the development interface is minimal, and sometimes nonexistent, when the V&V assessment is independent of the development group.

To offset unnecessary costs, the V&V group must organize its activities to focus on the software's critical areas so it can uncover critical errors and thus significantly save development costs. The V&V group must use criticality analysis to identify critical areas and it must scrutinize each discrepancy report before release to ensure that no inaccurate information is released so the development group will not waste time on inaccurate or trivial reports.

To eliminate the need for the development group to train the V&V group, you must select a V&V staff that is experienced and knowledgeable about the software and its application. When V&V engineers and computer scientists reconstruct the details and idiosyncrasies of the software to reconfirm the correctness of the product's engineering and programming assumptions, they often find subtle errors. They gain detailed insight into the development process and an ability to spot critical errors early.

Finally, the number of discrepancies detected in software and the improvement in documentation quality resulting from error correction suggest that V&V costs are offset by the resulting more reliable and maintainable software. In many application areas, the costs of V&V are offset by either increased reliability during operation or by reduced maintenance when additions or changes are made. Many companies rely on their software systems for their daily operations. For them the costs of system or data loss outweigh the costs of preventing the losses. ❖

Dolores R. Wallace is project leader for software quality and safety at the National Computer Systems Laboratory at the US National Institute of Standards and Technology (formerly the National Bureau of Standards). Her research interests include software V&V, acceptance, testing, management, quality assurance, and safety.

Wallace received an MA in mathematics from Case Western Reserve University. She is secretary for ANSI/IEEE Std 1012-1986, *Standard for Software Verification and Validation Plans*, and co-chairman of the IEEE P1059 working group to develop a guide for V&V plans. She is a lecturer for the IEEE standards seminar on software V&V. She is a member of ACM and the IEEE Computer Society.

Roger U. Fujii is the manager of the Systems Technology Operation at Logicon in San Pedro, Calif. His organization performs V&V on critical US Army and Air Force systems. He has also led the software nuclear-safety analysis on several missile and weapons systems. His research interests include software V&V, simulation, artificial intelligence, and expert systems.

Fujii received a BS in engineering mathematics and an MS in electrical engineering and computer science from the University of California at Berkeley. He is chairman of the US JTC1/SC7 Technical Activities Group and had been chairman of ANSI/IEEE Std 1012-1986, *Standard for Software Verification and Validation Plans*. Fujii is the principal instructor for the IEEE standards seminar for software V&V. He is a member of the IEEE Computer Society and ACM.

Address questions about this article to Wallace at National Institute for Standards and Technology, Technology Bldg., Rm. B-266, Gaithersburg, MD 20899.

References

1. B.W. Boehm, "A Spiral Model of Software Development and Enhancement," *Computer*, May 1988, pp. 61-72.

2. B.W. Boehm and P.N. Papaccio, "Understanding and Controlling Software Costs," *IEEE Trans. Software Eng.*, Oct. 1988, pp. 1462-1467.

3. P.B. Powell, "Software Validation, Verification, and Testing Technique and Tool Reference Guide," NBS Special Pub. 500-93, Nat'l Inst. Standards and Technology, Gaithersburg, Md., 1982.

4. D.R. Wallace and R.U. Fujii, "Software Verification and Validation: Its Role in Computer Assurance and Its Relationship with Software Project-Management Standards," NIST Special Pub., Nat'l Inst. Standards and Technology, Gaithersburg, Md., to be published, 1989.

5. F. McGarry and G. Page, "Performance Evaluation of an Independent Software Verification and Integration Process," Tech. Report SEL 81-110, NASA Goddard Space Flight Center, Greenbelt, Md., Sept. 1982.

6. J.W. Radatz, "Analysis of IV&V Data," Tech. Report RADC-TR-81-145, Rome Air Development Center, Griffiss AFB, N.Y., June 1981.

Chapter 9
Risk Management

Take calculated risks. That is quite different from being rash.
— George Patton

Overview

This chapter contains two papers on the topic of risk management. Risk in this context refers to those factors, both technical and managerial, that are threats to success and/or a major source of problems on software-intensive projects. For example, volatile requirements, feature creep, gold plating, and the loss of key personnel are normal risks that need to be guarded against on most developments. Risk management is the process of identifying these threats, analyzing them, quantifying their effects, and implementing plans that counteract their negative effects.

The first paper, by Boehm, provides a tutorial on the basics of software risk management. It starts by identifying the fundamental concepts, processes, tools, and techniques associated with the discipline. It then takes the reader step by step through the risk assessment and control processes, using realistic examples whenever possible to illustrate the "how-to's" of getting the job done. Throughout, the article discusses the merits and demerits of various risk management tools and techniques. As with most Boehm articles, it is prescriptive in its recommendations and constructive in its criticisms.

The second paper, by Bell, uses the space shuttle as an illustrative case study on risk management. This example is but one of six cases taken from the original article that Bell uses to identify the limits of current risk management techniques. The article provides a chronology for the Challenger disaster, describes the risk analyses that were conducted, and summarizes the lessons learned from them. Although not a pure software example, the shuttle clearly illustrates the politics of risk and the need to force management to place more emphasis on risk assessments in their decision-making processes.

References

The June 1989 issue of *IEEE Spectrum* is devoted to understanding and managing risk. As already noted, the shuttle example that I have included in this edition of the tutorial is but one of this issue's six risk management case studies. The others are well worth reading.

The most comprehensive book on the topic of risk management that I have seen is the compilation of papers prepared by Boehm (Reference 3) and issued again by the IEEE. I would suggest the Marciniak and Reifer text (Reference 17) for those interested in acquisition management risks.

Reprinted from *IEEE Software*, Vol. 8, No. 1, January 1991, pp. 32-41. Copyright © 1991 by The Institute of Electrical and Electronics Engineers, Inc. All rights reserved.

Software Risk Management: Principles and Practices

BARRY W. BOEHM,
Defense Advanced Research Projects Agency

◆ *Identifying and dealing with risks early in development lessens long-term costs and helps prevent software disasters.*

It is easy to begin managing risks in your environment.

Like many fields in their early stages, the software field has had its share of project disasters: the software equivalents of the Beauvais Cathedral, the *HMS Titanic*, and the "Galloping Gertie" Tacoma Narrows Bridge. The frequency of these software-project disasters is a serious concern: A recent survey of 600 firms indicated that 35 percent of them had at least one runaway software project.[1]

Most postmortems of these software-project disasters have indicated that their problems would have been avoided or strongly reduced if there had been an explicit early concern with identifying and resolving their high-risk elements. Frequently, these projects were swept along by a tide of optimistic enthusiasm during their early phases that caused them to miss some clear signals of high-risk issues that proved to be their downfall later.

Enthusiasm for new software capabilities is a good thing. But it must be tempered with a concern for early identification and resolution of a project's high-risk elements so people can get these resolved early and then focus their enthusiasm and energy on the positive aspects of their product.

Current approaches to the software process make it too easy for projects to make high-risk commitments that they will later regret:

◆ The sequential, document-driven waterfall process model tempts people to overpromise software capabilities in contractually binding requirements specifications before they understand their risk implications.

◆ The code-driven, evolutionary development process model tempts people to say, "Here are some neat ideas I'd like to put into this system. I'll code them up, and if they don't fit other people's ideas, we'll just evolve things until they work." This sort of approach usually works fine in some well-supported minidomains like spreadsheet applications but, in more complex application domains, it most often creates or neglects unsalvageable high-risk elements and leads the project down the path to disaster.

At TRW and elsewhere, I have had the good fortune to observe many project managers at work firsthand and to try to understand and apply the factors that distinguished the more successful project managers from the less successful ones. Some successfully used a waterfall approach, others successfully used an evolutionary development approach, and still others successfully orchestrated complex mixtures of these and other approaches involving prototyping, simulation, commercial software, executable specifications, tiger teams, design competitions, subcontracting, and various kinds of cost-benefit analyses.

One pattern that emerged very strongly was that the successful project managers were good *risk managers*. Although they generally didn't use such terms as "risk identification," "risk assessment," "risk-management planning," or "risk monitoring," they were using a general concept of risk exposure (potential loss times the probability of loss) to guide their priorities and actions. And their projects tended to avoid pitfalls and produce good products.

The emerging discipline of software risk management is an attempt to formalize these risk-oriented correlates of success into a readily applicable set of principles and practices. Its objectives are to identify, address, and eliminate risk items before they become either threats to successful software operation or major sources of software rework.

BASIC CONCEPTS

Webster's dictionary defines "risk" as "the possibility of loss or injury." This definition can be translated into the fundamental concept of risk management: risk exposure, sometimes also called "risk im-

pact" or "risk factor." Risk exposure is defined by the relationship

$$RE = P(UO) * L(UO)$$

where RE is the risk exposure, P(UO) is the probability of an unsatisfactory outcome and L(UO) is the loss to the parties affected if the outcome is unsatisfactory. To relate this definition to software projects, we need a definition of "unsatisfactory outcome."

Given that projects involve several classes of participants (customer, developer, user, and maintainer), each with different but highly important satisfaction criteria, it is clear that "unsatisfactory outcome" is multidimensional:

♦ For customers and developers, budget overruns and schedule slips are unsatisfactory.

♦ For users, products with the wrong functionality, user-interface shortfalls, performance shortfalls, or reliability shortfalls are unsatisfactory.

♦ For maintainers, poor-quality software is unsatisfactory.

These components of an unsatisfactory outcome provide a top-level checklist for identifying and assessing risk items.

A fundamental risk-analysis paradigm is the decision tree. Figure 1 illustrates a potentially risky situation involving the software controlling a satellite experiment. The software has been under development by the experiment team, which understands the experiment well but is inexperienced in and somewhat casual about software development. As a result, the satellite-platform manager has obtained an estimate that there is a probability P(UO) of 0.4 that the experimenters' software will have a critical error: one that will wipe out the entire experiment and cause an associated loss L(UO) of the total $20 million investment in the experiment.

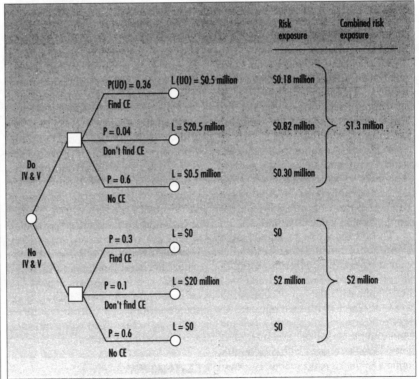

FIGURE 1. DECISION TREE FOR WHETHER TO PERFORM INDEPENDENT VALIDATION AND VERIFICATION TO ELIMINATE CRITICAL ERRORS IN A SATELLITE-EXPERIMENT PROGRAM. L(UO) IS THE LOSS ASSOCIATED WITH AN UNSATISFACTORY OUTCOME, P(UO) IS THE PROBABILITY OF THE UNSATISFACTORY OUTCOME, AND CE IS A CRITICAL ERROR.

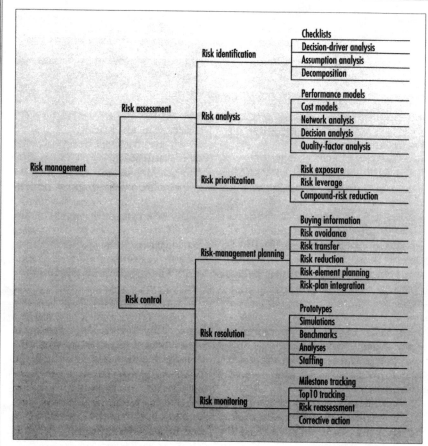

FIGURE 2. SOFTWARE RISK MANAGEMENT STEPS.

The satellite-platform manager identifies two major options for reducing the risk of losing the experiment:

♦ Convincing and helping the experiment team to apply better development methods. This incurs no additional cost and, from previous experience, the manager estimates that this will reduce the error probability P(UO) to 0.1.

♦ Hiring a contractor to independently verify and validate the software. This costs an additional $500,000; based on the results of similar IV&V efforts, the manager estimates that this will reduce the error probability P(UO) to 0.04.

The decision tree in Figure 1 then shows, for each of the two major decision options, the possible outcomes in terms of the critical error existing or being found and eliminated, their probabilities, the losses associated with each outcome, the risk exposure associated with each outcome, and the total risk exposure (or expected loss) associated with each decision option. In this case, the total risk exposure associated with the experiment-team option is only $2 million. For the IV&V option, the total risk exposure is only $1.3 million, so it represents the more attractive option.

Besides providing individual solutions for risk-management situations, the decision tree also provides a framework for analyzing the sensitivity of preferred solutions to the risk-exposure parameters. Thus, for example, the experiment-team option would be preferred if the loss due to a critical error were less than $13 million, if the experiment team could reduce its critical-error probability to less than 0.065, if the IV&V team cost more than $1.2 million, if the IV&V team could not reduce the probability of critical error to less than 0.075, or if there were various partial combinations of these possibilities.

This sort of sensitivity analysis helps deal with many situations in which probabilities and losses cannot be estimated well enough to perform a precise analysis. The risk-exposure framework also supports some even more approximate but still very useful approaches, like range estimation and scale-of-10 estimation.

RISK MANAGMENT

As Figure 2 shows, the practice of risk management involves two primary steps each with three subsidiary steps.

The first primary step, risk assessment, involves risk identification, risk analysis, and risk prioritization:

♦ Risk identification produces lists of the project-specific risk items likely to compromise a project's success. Typical risk-identification techniques include checklists, examination of decision drivers, comparison with experience (assumption analysis), and decomposition.

♦ Risk analysis assesses the loss probability and loss magnitude for each identified risk item, and it assesses compound risks in risk-item interactions. Typical techniques include performance models, cost models, network analysis, statistical decision analysis, and quality-factor (like reliability, availability, and security) analysis.

♦ Risk prioritization produces a ranked ordering of the risk items identified and analyzed. Typical techniques include risk-exposure analysis, risk-reduction leverage analysis (particularly involving cost-benefit analysis), and Delphi or group-consensus techniques.

The second primary step, risk control, involves risk-management planning, risk resolution, and risk monitoring:

♦ Risk-management planning helps prepare you to address each risk item (for example, via information buying, risk avoidance, risk transfer, or risk reduction), including the coordination of the individual risk-item plans with each other and with the overall project plan. Typical techniques include checklists of risk-resolution techniques, cost-benefit analysis, and standard risk-management plan outlines, forms, and elements.

♦ Risk resolution produces a situation in which the risk items are eliminated or otherwise resolved (for example, risk avoidance via relaxation of requirements). Typical techniques include prototypes, simulations, benchmarks, mission analyses, key-personnel agreements, design-to-cost approaches, and incremental development.

♦ Risk monitoring involves tracking the project's progress toward resolving its risk items and taking corrective action where appropriate. Typical techniques include milestone tracking and a top-10 risk-item list that is highlighted at each

weekly, monthly, or milestone project review and followed up appropriately with reassessment of the risk item or corrective action.

In addition, risk management provides an improved way to address and organize the life cycle. Risk-driven approaches, like the spiral model of the software process,[2] avoid many of the difficulties encountered with previous process models like the waterfall model and the evolutionary development model. Such risk-driven approaches also show how and where to incorporate new software technologies like rapid prototyping, fourth-generation languages, and commercial software products into the life cycle.

SIX STEPS

Figure 2 summarized the major steps and techniques involved in software risk management. This overview article covers four significant subsets of risk-management techniques: risk-identification checklists, risk prioritization, risk-management planning, and risk monitoring. Other techniques have been covered elsewhere.[3,4]

Risk-identification checklists. Table 1 shows a top-level risk-identification checklist with the top 10 primary sources of risk on software projects, based on a survey of several experienced project managers. Managers and system engineers can use the checklist on projects to help identify and resolve the most serious risk items on the project. It also provides a corresponding set of risk-management techniques that have been most successful to date in avoiding or resolving the source of risk.

If you focus on item 2 of the top-10 list in Table 1 (unrealistic schedules and budgets), you can then move on to an example of a next-level checklist: the risk-probabil-ity table in Table 2 for assessing the probability that a project will overrun its budget. Table 2 is one of several such checklists in an excellent US Air Force handbook[5] on software risk abatement.

Using the checklist, you can rate a project's status for the individual attributes associated with its requirements, personnel, reusable software, tools, and support environment (in Table 2, the environment's availability or the risk that the environment will not be available when needed). These ratings will support a probability-range estimation of whether the project has a relatively low (0.0 to 0.3), medium (0.4 to 0.6), or high (0.7 to 1.0) probability of overrunning its budget.

Most of the critical risk items in the checklist have to do with shortfalls in domain understanding and in properly scoping the job to be done — areas that are generally underemphasized in computer-science literature and education. Recent

Risk item	Risk-management technique
Personnel shortfalls	Staffing with top talent, job matching, team building, key personnel agreements, cross training.
Unrealistic schedules and budgets	Detailed multisource cost and schedule estimation, design to cost, incremental development, software reuse, requirements scrubbing.
Developing the wrong functions and properties	Organization analysis, mission analysis, operations-concept formulation, user surveys and user participation, prototyping, early users' manuals, off-nominal performance analysis, quality-factor analysis.
Developing the wrong user interface	Prototyping, scenarios, task analysis, user participation.
Gold-plating	Requirements scrubbing, prototyping, cost-benefit analysis, designing to cost.
Continuing stream of requirements changes	High change threshold, information hiding, incremental development (deferring changes to later increments).
Shortfalls in externally furnished components	Benchmarking, inspections, reference checking, compatibility analysis.
Shortfalls in externally performed tasks	Reference checking, preaward audits, award-fee contracts, competitive design or prototyping, team-building.
Real-time performance shortfalls	Simulation, benchmarking, modeling, prototyping, instrumentation, tuning.
Straining computer-science capabilities	Technical analysis, cost-benefit analysis, prototyping, reference checking.

TABLE 2.
QUANTIFICATION OF PROBABILITY AND IMPACT FOR COST FAILURE.

Cost drivers	Probability		
	Improbable (0.0-0.3)	Probable (0.4-0.6)	Frequent (0.7-1.0)
Requirements			
Size	Small, noncomplex, or easily decomposed	Medium to moderate complexity, decomposable	Large, highly complex, or not decomposable
Resource constraints	Little or no hardware-imposed constraints	Some hardware-imposed constraints	Significant hardware-imposed constraints
Application	Nonreal-time, little system interdependency	Embedded, some system interdependencies	Real-time, embedded, strong interdependency
Technology	Mature, existent, in-house experience	Existent, some in-house experience	New or new application, little experience
Requirements stability	Little or no change to established baseline	Some change in baseline expected	Rapidly changing, or no baseline
Personnel			
Availability	In place, little turnover expected	Available, some turnover expected	Not available, high turnover expected
Mix	Good mix of software disciplines	Some disciplines inappropriately represented	Some disciplines not represented
Experience	High experience ratio	Average experience ratio	Low experience ratio
Management environment	Strong personnel management approach	Good personnel management approach	Weak personnel management approach
Reusable software			
Availability	Compatible with need dates	Delivery dates in question	Incompatible with need dates
Modifications	Little or no change	Some change	Extensive changes
Language	Compatible with system and maintenance requirements	Partial compatibility with requirements	Incompatible with system or maintenance requirements
Rights	Compatible with maintenance and competition requirements	Partial compatibility with maintenance, some competition	Incompatible with maintenance concept, noncompetitive
Certification	Verified performance, application compatible	Some application-compatible test data available	Unverified, little test data available
Tools and environment			
Facilities	Little or no modification	Some modifications, existent	Major modifications, nonexistent
Availability	In place, meets need dates	Some compatibility with need dates	Nonexistent, does not meet need dates
Rights	Compatible with maintenance and development plans	Partial compatibility with maintenance and development plans	Incompatible with maintenance and development plans
Configuration management	Fully controlled	Some controls	No controls
Impact			
	Sufficient financial resources	Some shortage of financial resources, possible overrun	Significant financial shortages, budget overrun likely

initiatives, like the Software Engineering Institute's masters curriculum in software engineering, are providing better coverage in these areas. The SEI is also initiating a major new program in software risk management.

Risk analysis and prioritization. After using all the various risk-identification checklists, plus the other risk-identification techniques in decision-driver analysis, assumption analysis, and decomposition, one very real risk is that the project will identify so many risk items that the project could spend years just investigating them. This is where risk prioritization and its associated risk-analysis activities become essential.

The most effective technique for risk prioritization involves the risk-exposure quantity described earlier. It lets you rank the risk items identified and determine which are most important to address.

One difficulty with the risk-exposure

TABLE 3.
RISK EXPOSURE FACTORS FOR SATELLITE EXPERIMENT SOFTWARE.

Unsatisfactory outcome	Probability of unsatisfactory outcome	Loss caused by unsatisfactory outcome	Risk exposure
A. Software error kills experiment	3-5	10	30-50
B. Software error loses key data	3-5	8	24-40
C. Fault-tolerant features cause unacceptable performance	4-8	7	28-56
D. Monitoring software reports unsafe condition as safe	5	9	45
E. Monitoring software reports safe condition as unsafe	5	3	15
F. Hardware delay causes schedule overrun	6	4	24
G. Data-reduction software errors cause extra work	8	1	8
H. Poor user interface causes inefficient operation	6	5	30
I. Processor memory insufficient	1	7	7
J. Database-management software loses derived data	2	2	4

quantity, as with most other decision-analysis quantities, is the problem of making accurate input estimates of the probability and loss associated with an unsatisfactory outcome. Checklists like that in Table 2 provide some help in assessing the probability of occurrence of a given risk item, but it is clear from Table 2 that its probability ranges do not support precise probability estimation.

Full risk-analysis efforts involving prototyping, benchmarking, and simulation generally provide better probability and loss estimates, but they may be more expensive and time-consuming than the situation warrants. Other techniques, like betting analogies and group-consensus techniques, can improve risk-probability estimation, but for risk prioritization you can often take a simpler course: assessing the risk probabilities and losses on a relative scale of 0 to 10.

Table 3 and Figure 3 illustrate this risk-prioritization process by using some potential risk items from the satellite-experiment project as examples. Table 3 summarizes several unsatisfactory outcomes with their corresponding ratings for P(UO), L(UO), and their resulting risk-exposure estimates. Figure 3 plots each unsatisfactory outcome with respect to a set of constant risk-exposure contours.

Three key points emerge from Table 3 and Figure 3:

♦ Projects often focus on factors having either a high P(UO) or a high L(UO), but these may not be the key factors with a high risk-exposure combination. One of the highest P(UO)s comes from item G

(data-reduction errors), but the fact that these errors are recoverable and not mission-critical leads to a low loss factor and a resulting low RE of 7. Similarly, item I (insufficient memory) has a high potential loss, but its low probability leads to a low RE of 7. On the other hand, a relatively

low-profile item like item H (user-interface shortfalls) becomes a relatively high-priority risk item because its combination of moderately high probability and loss factors yield a RE of 30.

♦ The RE quantities also provide a basis for prioritizing verification and vali-

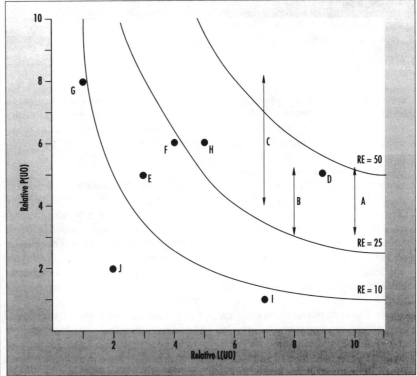

FIGURE 3. RISK-EXPOSURE FACTORS AND CONTOURS FOR THE SATELLITE-EXPERIMENT SOFTWARE. RE IS THE RISK EXPOSURE, P(UO) THE PROBABILITY OF AN UNSATISFACTORY OUTCOME, AND L(UO) THE LOSS ASSOCIATED WITH THAT UNSATISFACTORY OUTCOME. THE GRAPH POINTS MAP THE ITEMS FROM TABLE 3 WHOSE RISK EXPOSURE ARE BEING ASSESSED.

1. Objectives (the "why")
   ◆ Determine, reduce level of risk of the software fault-tolerance features causing unacceptable performance.
   ◆ Create a description of and a development plan for a set of low-risk fault-tolerance features.
2. Deliverables and milestones (the "what" and "when").
   ◆ By Week 3.
      1. Evaluation of fault-tolerance options
      2. Assessment of reusable components
      3. Draft workload characterization
      4. Evaluation plan for prototype exercise
      5. Description of prototype
   ◆ By Week 7.
      6. Operational prototype with key fault-tolerance features.
      7. Workload simulation
      8. Instrumentation and data reduction capabilities.
      9. Draft description, plan for fault-tolerance features.
   ◆ By Week 10
      10. Evaluation and iteration of prototype
      11. Revised description, plan for fault-tolerance features
3. Responsiblities (the "who" and "where")
   ◆ System engineer: G.Smith
      Tasks 1, 3, 4, 9, 11. Support of tasks 5, 10
   ◆ Lead programmer: C.Lee
      Tasks 5, 6, 7, 10. Support of tasks 1, 3
   ◆ Programmer: J.Wilson
      Tasks 2, 8. Support of tasks 5, 6, 7, 10
4. Approach (the "how")
   ◆ Design-to-schedule prototyping effort
   ◆ Driven by hypotheses about fault-tolerance-performance effects
   ◆ Use real-time operating system, add prototype fault-tolerance features
   ◆ Evaluate performance with respect to representative workload
   ◆ Refine prototype based on results observed
5. Resources (the "how much")
   $60K — full-time system engineer, lead programmer, programmer
      (10 weeks)∗(3 staff)∗$2k/staff-week)
   $0 — three dedicated workstations (from project pool)
   $0 — two target processors (from project pool)
   $0 — one test coprocessor (from project pool)
   $10K — contingencies
   $70K — total

FIGURE 4. RISK-MANAGEMENT PLAN FOR FAULT-TOLERANCE PROTOTYPING.

dation and related test activities by giving each error class a significance weight. Frequently, all errors are treated with equal weight, putting too much testing effort into finding relatively trivial errors.

◆ There is often a good deal of uncertainty in estimating the probability or loss associated with an unsatisfactory outcome. (The assessments are frequently subjective and are often the product of surveying several domain experts.) The amount of uncertainty is itself a major source of risk, which needs to be reduced as early as possible. The primary example in Table 3 and Figure 3 is the uncertainty in item C about whether the fault-tolerance features are going to cause an unacceptable degradation in real-time performance. If P(UO) is rated at 4, this item has only a moderate RE of 28, but if P(UO) is 8, the RE has a top-priority rating of 56.

One of the best ways to reduce this source of risk is to buy information about the actual situation. For the issue of fault tolerance versus performance, a good way to buy information is to invest in a prototype, to better understand the performance effects of the various fault-tolerance features.

Risk-management planning. Once you determine a project's major risk items and their relative priorities, you need to establish a set of risk-control functions to bring the risk items under control. The first step in this process is to develop a set of risk-management plans that lay out the activities necessary to bring the risk items under control.

One aid in doing this is the top-10 checklist in Figure 3 that identifies the most successful risk-management techniques for the most common risk items. As an example, item 9 (real-time performance shortfalls) in Table 1 covers the uncertainty in performance effect of the fault-tolerance features. The corresponding risk-management techniques include simulation, benchmarking, modeling, prototyping, instrumentation, and tuning. Assume, for example, that a prototype of representative safety features is the most cost-effective way to determine and reduce their effects on system performance.

The next step in risk-management planning is to develop risk-management plans for each risk item. Figure 4 shows the plan for prototyping the fault-tolerance features and determining their effects on performance. The plan is organized around a standard format for software plans, oriented around answering the standard questions of why, what, when, who, where, how, and how much. This plan organization lets the plans be concise (fitting on one page), action-oriented, easy to understand, and easy to monitor.

The final step in risk-management planning is to integrate the risk-management plans for each risk item with each other and with the overall project plan. Each of the other high-priority or uncertain risk items will have a risk-management plan; it may turn out, for example, that the fault-tolerance features prototyped for this risk item could also be useful as part of the strategy to reduce the uncertainty in items A and B (software errors killing the experiment and losing experiment-critical data). Also, for the overall project plan, the need for a 10-week prototype-development and -exercise period must be factored into the overall schedule, to keep the overall schedule realistic.

Risk resolution and monitoring. Once you have established a good set of risk-management plans, the risk-resolution process consists of implementing whatever prototypes, simulations, benchmarks, surveys, or other risk-reduction techniques are called for in the plans. Risk monitoring ensures that this is a closed-loop process by tracking risk-reduction progress and applying whatever corrective action is necessary to keep the risk-resolution process on track.

Risk management provides managers with a very effective technique for keeping on top of projects under their control: *Project top-10 risk-item tracking.* This technique concentrates management atten-

tion on the high-risk, high-leverage, critical success factors rather than swamping management reviews with lots of low-priority detail. As a manager, I have found that this type of risk-item-oriented review saves a lot of time, reduces management surprises, and gets you focused on the high-leverage issues where you can make a difference as a manager.

Top-10 risk-item tracking involves the following steps:

♦ Ranking the project's most significant risk items.

♦ Establishing a regular schedule for higher management reviews of the project's progress. The review should be chaired by the equivalent of the project manager's boss. For large projects (more than 20 people), the reviews should be held monthly. In the project itself, the project manager would review them more frequently.

♦ Beginning each project-review meeting with a summary of progress on the top 10 risk items. (The number could be seven or 12 without loss of intent.) The summary should include each risk item's current top-10 ranking, its rank at the previous review, how often it has been on the top-10 list, and a summary of progress in resolving the risk item since the previous review.

♦ Focusing the project-review meeting on dealing with any problems in resolving the risk items.

Table 4 shows how a top-10 list could have worked for the satellite-experiment project, as of month 3 of the project. The project's top risk item in month 3 is a critical staffing problem. Highlighting it in the monthly review meeting would stimulate a discussion by the project team and the boss of the staffing options: Make the unavailable key person available, reshuffle project personnel, or look for new people within or outside the organization. This should result in an assignment of action items to follow through on the options

chosen, including possible actions by the project manager's boss.

The number 2 risk item in Table 4, target hardware delivery delays, is also one for which the project manager's boss may be able to expedite a solution — by cutting through corporate-procurement red tape, for example, or by escalating vendor-delay issues with the vendor's higher management.

As Table 4 shows, some risk items are moving down in priority or going off the list, while others are escalating or coming onto the list. The ones moving down the list — like the design-verification and -validation staffing, fault-tolerance prototyping, and user-interface prototyping — still need to be monitored but frequently do not need special management action. The ones moving up or onto the list — like the data-bus design changes and the testbed-interface definitions — are generally the ones needing higher management attention to help get them

Risk item	Monthly ranking			Risk-resolution progress
	This	Last	No. of months	
Replacing sensor-control software developer	1	4	2	Top replacement candidate unavailable
Target hardware delivery delays	2	5	2	Procurement procedural delays
Sensor data formats undefined	3	3	3	Action items to software, sensor teams; due next month
Staffing of design V&V team	4	2	3	Key reviewers committed; need fault-tolerance reviewer
Software fault-tolerance may compromise performance	5	1	3	Fault-tolerance prototype successful
Accommodate changes in data bus design	6	—	1	Meeting scheduled with data-bus designers
Test-bed interface definitions	7	8	3	Some delays in action items; review meeting scheduled
User interface uncertainties	8	6	3	User interface prototype successful
TBDs in experiment operational concept	—	7	3	TBDs resolved
Uncertainties in reusable monitoring software	—	9	3	Required design changes small, successfully made

TABLE 4.
PROJECT TOP-10 RISK ITEM LIST FOR SATELLITE EXPERIMENT SOFTWARE.

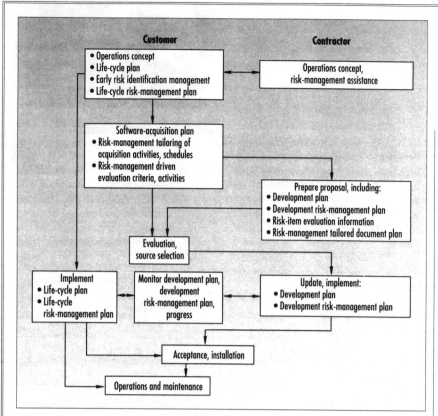

- Operations concept
- Life-cycle plan
- Early risk identification management
- Life-cycle risk-management plan

Operations concept, risk-management assistance

Software-acquisition plan
- Risk-management tailoring of acquisition activities, schedules
- Risk-management driven evaluation criteria, activities

Prepare proposal, including:
- Development plan
- Development risk-management plan
- Risk-item evaluation information
- Risk-management tailored document plan

Evaluation, source selection

Implement
- Life-cycle plan
- Life-cycle risk-management plan

Monitor development plan, development risk-management plan, progress

Update, implement:
- Development plan
- Development risk-management plan

Acceptance, installation

Operations and maintenance

FIGURE 5. FRAMEWORK FOR LIFE-CYCLE RISK MANAGEMENT.

resolved quickly.

As this example shows, the top-10 risk-item list is a very effective way to focus higher management attention onto the project's critical success factors. It also uses management's time very efficiently, unlike typical monthly reviews, which spend most of their time on things the higher manager can't do anything about. Also, if the higher manager surfaces an additional concern, it is easy to add it to the top-10 risk item list to be highlighted in future reviews.

IMPLEMENTING RISK MANAGEMENT

Implementing risk management involves inserting the risk-management principles and practices into your existing life-cycle management practices. Full implementation of risk management involves the use of risk-driven software-process models like the spiral model, where risk considerations determine the overall sequence of life-cycle activities, the use of prototypes and other risk-resolution techniques, and the degree of detail of plans and specifications. However, the best implementation strategy is an incremental one, which lets an organization's culture adjust gradually to risk-oriented management practices and risk-driven process models.

A good way to begin is to establish a top-10 risk-item tracking process. It is easy and inexpensive to implement, provides early improvements, and begins establishing a familiarity with the other risk-management principles and practices. Another good way to gain familiarity is via books like my recent tutorial on risk management,[3] which contains the Air Force risk-abatement pamphlet[5] and other useful articles, and Robert Charette's recent good book on risk management.[4]

An effective next step is to identify an appropriate initial project in which to implement a top-level life-cycle risk-management plan. Once the organization has accumulated some risk-management experience on this initial project, successive steps can deepen the sophistication of the risk-management techniques and broaden their application to wider classes of projects.

Figure 5 provides a scheme for implementing a top-level life-cycle risk-management plan. It is presented in the context of a contractual software acquisition, but you can tailor it to the needs of an internal development organization as well.

You can organize the life-cycle risk-management plan as an elaboration of the "why, what, when, who, where, how, how much" framework of Figure 4. While this plan is primarily the customer's responsibility, it is very useful to involve the developer community in its preparation as well.

Such a plan addresses not only the development risks that have been the prime topic of this article but also operations and maintenance risks. These include such items as staffing and training of maintenance personnel, discontinuities in the switch from the old to the new system, undefined responsibilities for operations and maintenance facilities and functions, and insufficient budget for planned life-cycle improvements or for corrective, adaptive, and perfective maintenance.

Figure 5 also shows the importance of proposed developer risk-management plans in competitive source evaluation and selection. Emphasizing the realism and effectiveness of a bidder's risk-management plan increases the probability that the customer will select a bidder that clearly understands the project's critical success factors and that has established a development approach that satisfactorily addresses them. (If the developer is a noncompetitive internal organization, it is equally important for the internal customer to require and review a developer risk-management plan.)

The most important thing for a project to do is to get focused on its critical success factors.

For various reasons, including the influence of previous document-driven management guidelines, projects get focused on activities that are not critical for their success. These frequently include writing boilerplate documents, exploring intriguing but peripheral technical issues, playing politics, and trying to sell the "ultimate" system.

In the process, critical success factors get neglected, the project fails, and nobody wins.

The key contribution of software risk management is to create this focus on critical success factors — and to provide the techniques that let the project deal with them. The risk-assessment and risk-control techniques presented here provide the foundation layer of capabilities needed to implement the risk-oriented approach.

However, risk management is not a cookbook approach. To handle all the complex people-oriented and technology-driven success factors in projects, a great measure of human judgement is required.

Good people, with good skills and good judgment, are what make projects work. Risk management can provide you with some of the skills, an emphasis on getting good people, and a good conceptual framework for sharpening your judgement. I hope you can find these useful on your next project.   ♦

REFERENCES

1. J. Rothfeder, "It's Late, Costly, and Incompetent — But Try Firing a Computer System," *Business Week*, Nov. 7, 1988, pp. 164-165.
2. B.W. Boehm, "A Spiral Model of Software Development and Enhancement," *Computer*, May 1988, pp. 61-72.
3. B.W. Boehm, *Software Risk Management*, CS Press, Los Alamitos, Calif., 1989.
4. R.N. Charette, *Software Engineering Risk Analysis and Management*, McGraw-Hill, New York, 1989.
5. "Software Risk Abatement," AFSC/AFLC pamphlet 800-45, US Air Force Systems Command, Andrews AFB, Md., 1988.

Barry W. Boehm is director of the Defense Advanced Research Project Agency's Information Science and Technology Office, the US government's largest computer/communications research organization. In his previous position as chief scientist for TRW's Defense Systems Group, he was involved in applying risk-management principles to large projects, including the National Aeronautics and Space Administration's space station, the Federal Aviation Administration's Advanced Automation System, and the Defense Dept.'s Strategic Defense Initiative.

Boehm received a BA in mathematics from Harvard University and an MA and PhD in mathematics from UCLA.

Address questions about this article to the author at DARPA ISTO, 1400 Wilson Blvd., Arlington, VA 22209-2308.

SPECIAL REPORT:

The space shuttle: a case of subjective engineering

Trudy E. Bell   Senior Editor
Karl Esch   Contributing Editor

Culture and policy within NASA set its priorities: for 20 years it resisted probabilistic risk analysis, and so failed to collect statistical data

"Statistics don't count for anything," declared Will Willoughby, the National Aeronautics and Space Administration's former head of reliability and safety during the Apollo moon landing program. "They have no place in engineering anywhere." Now director of reliability management and quality assurance for the U.S. Navy, Washington, D.C., he still holds that risk is minimized not by statistical test programs, but by "attention taken in design, where it belongs." His design-oriented view prevailed in NASA in the 1970s, when the space shuttle was designed and built by many of the engineers who had worked on the Apollo program.

"The real value of probabilistic risk analysis is in understanding the system and its vulnerabilities," said Benjamin Buchbinder, manager of NASA's two-year-old risk management program. He maintains that probabilis-

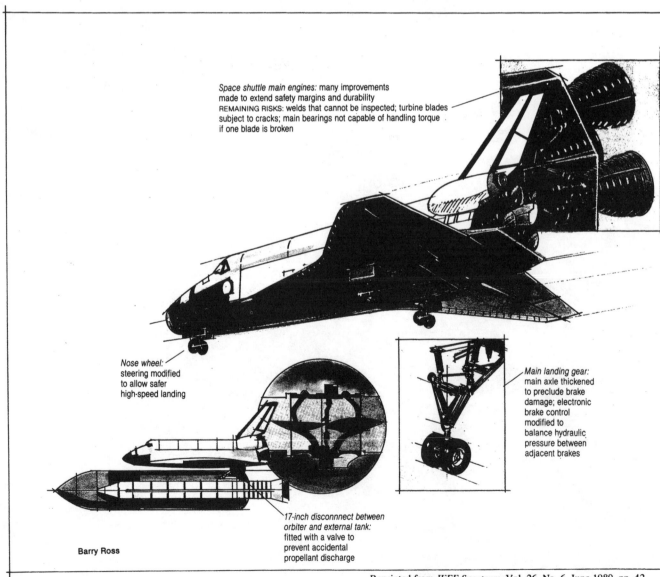

Space shuttle main engines: many improvements made to extend safety margins and durability
REMAINING RISKS: welds that cannot be inspected; turbine blades subject to cracks; main bearings not capable of handling torque if one blade is broken

Nose wheel: steering modified to allow safer high-speed landing

17-inch disconnnect between orbiter and external tank: fitted with a valve to prevent accidental propellant discharge

Main landing gear: main axle thickened to preclude brake damage; electronic brake control modified to balance hydraulic pressure between adjacent brakes

Barry Ross

Reprinted from *IEEE Spectrum*, Vol. 26, No. 6, June 1989, pp. 42-46. Copyright © 1989 by The Institute of Electrical and Electronics Engineers, Inc. All rights reserved.

tic risk analysis can go beyond design-oriented qualitative techniques in looking at the interactions of subsystems, ascertaining the effects of human activity and environmental conditions, and detecting common-cause failures.

NASA started experimenting with this program in response to the Jan. 28, 1986, Challenger accident that killed seven astronauts. The program's goals are to establish a policy on risk management and to conduct risk assessments independent of normal engineering analyses. But success is slow because of past official policy that favored "engineering judgment" over "probability numbers," resulting in NASA's failure to collect the type of statistical test and flight data useful for quantitative risk assessment.

This Catch 22—the agency lacks appropriate statistical data because it did not believe in the technique requiring the data, so it did not gather the relevant data—is one example of how an organization's underlying culture and explicit policy can affect the overall reliability of the projects it undertakes.

External forces such as politics further shape an organization's response. Whereas the Apollo program was widely supported by the President and the U.S. Congress and had all the money it needed, the shuttle program was strongly criticized and underbudgeted from the beginning. Political pressures, coupled with the lack of hard numerical data, led to differences of more than three orders of magnitude in the few quantitative estimates of a shuttle launch failure that NASA was required by law to conduct.

Some observers still worry that, despite NASA's late adoption of quantitative risk assessment, its internal culture and its fear of political opposition may be pushing it to repeat dangerous errors of the shuttle program in the new space station program.

NASA's preference for a design approach to reliability to the exclusion of quantitative risk analysis was strengthened by a nega-

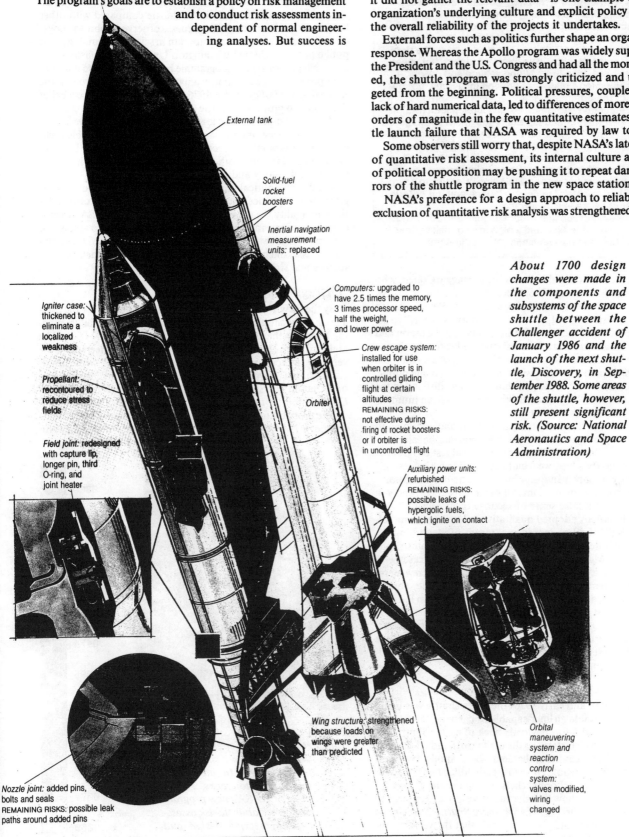

External tank

Solid-fuel rocket boosters

Inertial navigation measurement units: replaced

Computers: upgraded to have 2.5 times the memory, 3 times processor speed, half the weight, and lower power

Crew escape system: installed for use when orbiter is in controlled gliding flight at certain altitudes
REMAINING RISKS: not effective during firing of rocket boosters or if orbiter is in uncontrolled flight

Orbiter

Igniter case: thickened to eliminate a localized weakness

Propellant: recontoured to reduce stress fields

Field joint: redesigned with capture lip, longer pin, third O-ring, and joint heater

Auxiliary power units: refurbished
REMAINING RISKS: possible leaks of hypergolic fuels, which ignite on contact

Wing structure: strengthened because loads on wings were greater than predicted

Nozzle joint: added pins, bolts and seals
REMAINING RISKS: possible leak paths around added pins

Orbital maneuvering system and reaction control system: valves modified, wiring changed

About 1700 design changes were made in the components and subsystems of the space shuttle between the Challenger accident of January 1986 and the launch of the next shuttle, Discovery, in September 1988. Some areas of the shuttle, however, still present significant risk. (Source: National Aeronautics and Space Administration)

tive early brush with the field. According to Haggai Cohen, who during the Apollo days was NASA's deputy chief engineer, NASA contracted with General Electric Co. in Daytona Beach, Fla., to do a "full numerical PRA [probabilistic risk assessment]" to assess the likelihood of success in landing a man on the moon and returning him safely to earth. The GE study indicated the chance of success was "less than 5 percent." When the NASA Administrator was presented with the results, he felt that if made public, "the numbers could do irreparable harm, and he disbanded the effort," Cohen said. "We studiously stayed away from [numerical risk assessment] as a result."

"That's when we threw all that garbage out and got down to work," Willoughby agreed. The study's proponents, he said, contended " 'you build up confidence by statistical test programs.' We said, 'No, go fly a kite, we'll build up confidence by design.' Testing gives you only a snapshot under particular conditions. Reality may not give you the same set of circumstances, and you can be lulled into a false sense of security or insecurity."

As a result, NASA adopted qualitative failure modes and effects analysis (FMEA) as its principal means of identifying design features whose worst-case failure could lead to a catastrophe [see "Managing Murphy's law," pp. 24–27]. The worst cases were ranked as Criticality 1 if they threatened the life of the crew members or the existence of the vehicle, Criticality 2 if they threatened the mission, and Criticality 3 for anything less. An R designated a redundant system [see "How NASA determined shuttle risk," opposite]. Quantitative techniques were limited to calculating the probability of the occurrence of an individual failure mode "if we had to present a rationale on how to live with a single failure point," Cohen explained.

The politics of risk

By the late 1960s and early 1970s the space shuttle was being portrayed as a reusable airliner capable of carrying 15-ton payloads into orbit and 5-ton payloads back to earth. Shuttle astronauts would wear shirtsleeves during takeoff and landing instead of the bulky spacesuits of the Gemini and Apollo days. And eventually the shuttle would carry just plain folks: nonastronaut scientists, politicians, schoolteachers, and journalists.

NASA documents show that the airline vision also applied to risk. For example, in the 1969 *NASA Space Shuttle Task Group Report*, the authors wrote: "It is desirable that the vehicle configuration provide for crew/passenger safety in a manner and to the degree as provided in present day commercial jet aircraft."

Statistically an airliner is the least risky form of transportation, which implies high reliability. And in the early 1970s, when President Richard M. Nixon, Congress, and the Office of Management and Budget (OMB) were all skeptical of the shuttle, proving high reliability was crucial to the program's continued funding.

OMB even directed NASA to hire an outside contractor to do an economic analysis of how the shuttle compared with other launch systems for cost-effectiveness, observed John M. Logsdon, director of the graduate program in science, technology, and public policy at George Washington University in Washington, D.C. "No previous space programme had been subject to independent professional economic evaluation," Logsdon wrote in the journal *Space Policy* in May 1986. "It forced NASA into a belief that it had to propose a Shuttle that could launch all foreseeable payloads...[and] would be less expensive than alternative launch systems" and that, indeed, would supplant all expendable rockets. It also was politically necessary to show that the shuttle would be cheap and routine, rather than large and risky, with respect to both technology and cost, Logsdon pointed out.

Amid such political unpopularity, which threatened the program's very existence, "some NASA people began to confuse desire with reality," said Adelbert Tischler, retired NASA director of launch vehicles and propulsion. "One result was to assess risk in terms of what was thought acceptable without regard for verifying the assessment." He added: "Note that under such circumstances real risk management is shut out."

'Disregarding data'

By the early 1980s many figures were being quoted for the overall risk to the shuttle, with estimates of a catastrophic failure ranging from less than 1 chance in 100 to 1 chance in 100 000. "The higher figures [1 in 100] come from working engineers, and the very low figures [1 in 100 000] from management," wrote physicist Richard P. Feynman in his appendix "Personal Observations on Reliability of Shuttle" to the 1986 *Report of the Presidential Commission on the Space Shuttle Challenger Accident*.

The probabilities originated in a series of quantitative risk assessments NASA was required to conduct by the Interagency Nu-

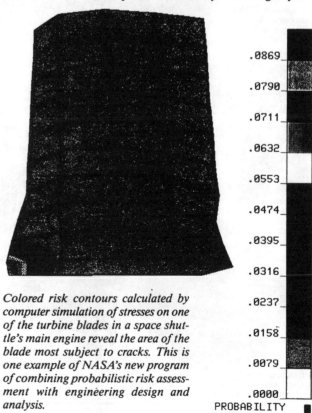

.0869

.0790

.0711

.0632

.0553

.0474

.0395

.0316

.0237

.0158

.0079

.0000

PROBABILITY

Colored risk contours calculated by computer simulation of stresses on one of the turbine blades in a space shuttle's main engine reveal the area of the blade most subject to cracks. This is one example of NASA's new program of combining probabilistic risk assessment with engineering design and analysis.

clear Safety Review Panel (INSRP), in anticipation of the launch of the Galileo spacecraft on its voyage to Jupiter, originally scheduled for the early 1980s. Galileo was powered by a plutonium-fueled radioisotope thermoelectric generator, and Presidential Directive/NSC-25 ruled that either the U.S. President or the director of the office of science and technology policy must examine the safety of any launch of nuclear material before approving it. The INSRP (which consisted of representatives of NASA as the launching agency, the Department of Energy, which manages nuclear devices, and the Department of Defense, whose Air Force manages range safety at launch) was charged with ascertaining the quantitative risks of a catastrophic launch dispersing the radioactive poison into the atmosphere. There were a number of studies because the upper stage for boosting Galileo into interplanetary space was reconfigured several times.

The first study was conducted by the J. H. Wiggins Co. of Redondo Beach, Calif., and published in three volumes between 1979 and 1982. It put the overall risk of losing a shuttle with its spacecraft payload during launch at between 1 chance in 1000 and 1 in 10 000. The greatest risk was posed by the solid-fuel rocket boosters (SRBs). The Wiggins author noted that the history of other solid-fuel rockets showed them as undergoing catastrophic launches somewhere between 1 time in 59 and 1 time in 34, but that the study's contract overseers, the Space Shuttle Range Safety Ad Hoc Committee, made an "engineering judgment" and "decided that a reduction in the failure probability estimate was warranted for the Space Shuttle SRBs" because "the historical data includes motors developed 10 to 20 years ago." The Ad Hoc Committee therefore "decided to assume a failure probability of 1×10^{-3} for each SRB." In addition, the Wiggins author pointed out, "it was decided by the Ad-Hoc Committee that a second probability should be considered . . . which is one order of magnitude less" or 1 in 10 000, "justified due to unique improvements made in the design and manufacturing process used for these mo-

tors to achieve man rating."

In 1983 a second study was conducted by Teledyne Energy Systems Inc., Timonium, Md., for the Air Force Weapons Laboratory at Kirtland Air Force Base, N.M. It described the Wiggins analysis as consisting of "an interesting presentation of launch data from several Navy, Air Force, and NASA missile programs and the disregarding of that data and arbitrary assignment of risk levels apparently per sponsor direction" with "no quantitative justification at all." After reanalyzing the data, the Teledyne authors concluded that the boosters' track record "suggest[s] a failure rate of around one-in-a-hundred."

When risk analysis isn't

NASA conducted its own internal safety analysis for Galileo, which was published in 1985 by the Johnson Space Center. The Johnson authors went through failure mode worksheets assigning probability levels. A fracture in the solid-rocket motor case or case joints—similar to the accident that destroyed Challenger—was assigned a probability level of 2; which a separate table defined as corresponding to a chance of 1 in 100 000 and described as "remote," or "so unlikely, it can be assumed that this hazard will not be experienced."

The Johnson authors' value of 1 in 100 000 implied, as Feynman spelled out, that "one could put a Shuttle up each day for 300 years expecting to lose only one." Yet even after the Challenger accident, NASA's chief engineer Milton Silveira, in a hearing on the Galileo thermonuclear generator held March 4, 1986, before the U.S. House of Representatives Committee on Science and Technology, said: "We think that using a number like 10 to the minus 3, as suggested, is probably a little pessimistic." In his view, the actual risk "would be 10 to the minus 5, and that is our design objective." When asked how the number was deduced, Silveira replied, "We came to those probabilities based on engineering judgment in review of the design rather than taking a statistical

---

How NASA determined shuttle risk

At the start of the space shuttle's design, the National Aeronautics and Space Administration defined risk as "the chance (qualitative) of loss of personnel capability, loss of system, or damage to or loss of equipment or property." NASA accordingly relied on several techniques for determining reliability and potential design problems, concluded the U.S. National Research Council's Committee on Shuttle Criticality Review and Hazard Analysis Audit in its January 1988 report *Post-Challenger Evaluation of Space Shuttle Risk Assessment and Management*. But, the report noted, the analyses did "not address the relative probabilities of a particular hazardous condition arising from failure modes, human errors, or external situations," so did not measure risk.

A failure modes and effects analysis (FMEA) was the heart of NASA's effort to ensure reliability, the NRC report noted [see "Managing Murphy's law," pp. 24–27]. An FMEA, carried out by the contractor building each shuttle element or subsystem, was performed on all flight hardware and on ground support equipment that interfaced with flight hardware. Its chief purpose was to identify hardware critical to the performance and safety of the mission.

Items that did not meet certain design, reliability and safety requirements specified by NASA's top management and whose failure could threaten the loss of crew, vehicle, or mission, made up a critical items list (CIL).

Although the FMEA/CIL was first viewed as a design tool, NASA now uses it during operations and management as well, to analyze problems, assess whether corrective actions are effective, identify where and when inspection and maintenance are needed, and reveal trends in failures.

Second, NASA conducted hazards analyses, performed jointly by shuttle engineers and by NASA's safety and operations organizations. They made use of the FMEA/CIL, various design reviews, safety analyses, and other studies. They

considered not only the failure modes identified in the FMEA, but also other threats posed by the mission activities, crew-machine interfaces, and the environment. After hazards and their causes were identified, NASA engineers and managers had to make one of three decisions: to eliminate the cause of each hazard, to control the cause if it could not be eliminated, or to accept the hazards that could not be controlled.

NASA also conducted an element interface functional analysis (EIFA) to look at the shuttle more nearly as a complete system. Both the FMEA and the hazards analyses concentrated only on individual elements of the shuttle: the space shuttle's main engines in the orbiter, the rest of the orbiter, the external tank, and the solid-fuel rocket boosters. The EIFA assessed hazards at the mating of the elements.

Also to examine the shuttle as a system, NASA conducted a one-time critical functions assessment in 1978, which searched for multiple and cascading failures.

The information from all these studies fed one way into an overall mission safety assessment.

The NRC committee had several criticisms. In practice, the FMEA was the sole basis for some engineering change decisions and all engineering waivers and rationales for retaining certain high-risk design features. However, the NRC report noted, hazard analyses for some important, high-risk subsystems "were not updated for years at a time even though design changes had occurred or dangerous failures were experienced." On one procedural flow chart, the report noted, "the 'Hazard Analysis As Required' is a dead-end box with *inputs* but *no output* with respect to waiver approval decisions."

The NRC committee concluded that "the isolation of the hazard analysis within NASA's risk assessment and management process to date can be seen as reflecting the past weakness of the entire safety organization."—*T.E.B. and K.E.*

data base, because we didn't feel we had that."

After the Challenger accident, the 1986 presidential commission learned the O-rings in the field joints of the shuttle's solid-fuel rocket boosters had a history of damage correlated with low air temperature at launch. So the commission repeatedly asked the witnesses it called to hearings why systematic temperature-correlation data had been unavailable before launch.

NASA's "management methodology" for collection of data and determination of risk was laid out in NASA's 1985 safety analysis for Galileo. The Johnson space center authors explained: "Early in the program it was decided not to use reliability (or probability) numbers in the design of the Shuttle" because the magnitude of testing required to statistically verify the numerical predictions "is not considered practical." Furthermore, they noted, "[e]xperience has shown that with the safety, reliability, and quality assurance requirements imposed on manned space-flight contractors, standard failure rate data are pessimistic."

"In lieu of using probability numbers, the NSTS [National Space Transportation System] relies on engineering judgment using rigid and well-documented design, configuration, safety, reliability, and quality assurance controls," the Johnson authors continued. This outlook determined the data NASA managers required engineers to collect. For example, no "lapsed-time indicators" were kept on shuttle components, subsystems, and systems, although "a fairly accurate estimate of time and/or cycles could be derived," the Johnson authors added.

One reason was economic. According to George Rodney, NASA's associate administrator of safety, reliability, maintainability and quality assurance, it is not hard to get time and cycle data, "but it's expensive and a big bookkeeping problem."

Another reason was NASA's "normal program development: you don't continue to take data; you certify the components and get on with it," said Rodney's deputy, James Ehl. "People think that since we've flown 28 times, then we have 28 times as much data, but we don't. We have maybe three or four tests from the first development flights."

In addition, Rodney noted, "For everyone in NASA that's a big PRA [probabilistic risk assessment] seller, I can find you 10 that are equally convinced that PRA is oversold.... [They] are so dubious of its importance that they won't convince themselves that the end product is worthwhile."

Risk and the organizational culture

One reason NASA has so strongly resisted probabilistic risk analysis may be the fact that "PRA runs against all traditions of engineering, where you handle reliability by safety factors," said Elisabeth Paté-Cornell, associate professor in the department of industrial engineering and engineering management at Stanford University in California, who is now studying organizational factors and risk assessment in NASA. In addition, with NASA's strong pride in design, PRA may be "perceived as an insult to their capabilities, that the system they've designed is not 100 percent perfect and absolutely safe," she added. Thus, the character of an organization influences the reliability and failure of the systems it builds because its structure, policy, and culture determine the priorities, incentives, and communication paths for the engineers and managers doing the work, she said.

"Part of the problem is getting the engineers to understand that they are using subjective methods for determining risk, because they don't like to admit that," said Ray A. Williamson, senior associate at the U.S. Congress Office of Technology Assessment in Washington, D.C. "Yet they talk in terms of sounding objective and fool themselves into thinking they are being objective."

"It's not that simple," Buchbinder said. "A probabilistic way of thinking is not something that most people are attuned to. We don't know what will happen precisely each time. We can only say what is likely to happen a certain percentage of the time." Unless engineers and managers become familiar with probability theory, they don't know what to make of "large uncertainties that represent the state of current knowledge," he said. "And that

is no comfort to the poor decision-maker who wants a simple answer to the question, 'Is this system safe enough?' "

As an example of how the "mindset" in the agency is now changing in favor of "a willingness to explore other things," Buchbinder cited the new risk management program, the workshops it has been holding to train engineers and others in quantitative risk assessment techniques, and a new management instruction policy that requires NASA to "provide disciplined and documented management of risks throughout program life cycles."

Hidden risks to the space station

NASA is now at work on its big project for the 1990s: a space station, projected to cost $30 billion and to be assembled in orbit, 220 nautical miles above the earth, from modules carried aloft in some two dozen shuttle launches. A National Research Council committee evaluated the space station program and concluded in a study in September 1987: "If the probability of damaging an Orbiter beyond repair on any single Shuttle flight is 1 percent— the demonstrated rate is now one loss in 25 launches, or 4 percent—the probability of losing an Orbiter before [the space station's first phase] is complete is about 60 percent."

The probability is within the right order of magnitude, to judge by the latest INSRP-mandated study completed in December for Buchbinder's group in NASA by Planning Research Corp., McLean, Va. The study, which reevaluates the risk of the long-delayed launch of the Galileo spacecraft on its voyage to Jupiter, now scheduled for later this year, estimates the chance of losing a shuttle from launch through payload deployment at 1 in 78, or between 1 and 2 percent, with an uncertainty of a factor of 2.

Those figures frighten some observers because of the dire consequences of losing part of the space station. "The space station has *no* redundancy—*no* backup parts," said Jerry Grey, director of science and technology policy for the American Institute of Aeronautics and Astronautics in Washington, D.C.

The worst case would be loss of the shuttle carrying the logistics module, which is needed for reboost, Grey pointed out. The space station's orbit will subject it to atmospheric drag such that, if not periodically boosted higher, it will drift downward and within eight months plunge back to earth and be destroyed, as was the Skylab space station in July 1979. "If you lost the shuttle with the logistics module, you don't have a spare, and you can't build one in eight months," Grey said, "so you may lose not only that one payload, but also whatever was put up there earlier."

Why are there no backup parts? "Politically the space station is under fire [from the U.S. Congress] all the time because NASA hasn't done an adequate job of justifying it," said Grey. "NASA is apprehensive that Congress might cancel the entire program"— and so is trying to trim costs as much as possible.

Grey estimated that spares of the crucial modules might add another 10 percent to the space station's cost. "But NASA is not willing to go to bat for that extra because they're unwilling to take the political risk," he said—a replay, he fears, of NASA's response to the political negativism over the shuttle in the 1970s.

The NRC space station committee warned: "It is dangerous and misleading to assume there will be no losses and thus fail to plan for such events."

"Let's face it, space is a risky business," commented former Apollo safety officer Cohen. "I always considered every launch a barely controlled explosion."

"The real problem is: whatever the numbers are, acceptance of that risk and planning for it is what needs to be done," Grey said. He fears that "NASA doesn't do that yet." ◆

In addition to the sources named in the text, the authors would like to acknowledge the information and insights afforded by the following: E. William Colglazier (director of the Energy, Environment and Resources Center at the University of Tennessee, Knoxville) and Robert K. Weatherwax (president of Sierra Energy & Risk Assessment Inc., Roseville, Calif.), the two authors of the 1983 Teledyne/Air Force Weapons Laboratory study; Larry Crawford, director of reliability and trends analysis at NASA headquarters in Washington, D.C.; Joseph R. Fragola, vice president, Science Applications International Corp., New York City; Byron Peter Leonard, president, L Systems Inc., El Segundo, Calif.; George E. Mueller, former NASA associate administrator for manned spaceflight; and Marcia Smith, specialist in aerospace policy, Congressional Research Service, Washington, D.C.

Chapter 10
Metrics and Measurement

Exact scientific knowledge and methods are everywhere, sooner or later to replace rules-of-thumb.
— Frederick Taylor

Overview

As the software field has matured, considerable progress has been made in the field of software measurement. By collecting, analyzing, and using measurement data, software engineers can now construct modern feedback systems that enable them to determine status, track progress, analyze trends, and ensure success. In addition, these systems can be used to improve estimating capabilities and implement tighter control, when warranted.

Software metrics refer to standards of measurement used to quantify specific aspects of a software process, product, and project. Process metrics quantify attributes of the development/maintenance process and its environment (defect rate, productivity, etc.). Product metrics quantify some attribute of the software product (size, complexity, quality, etc.) under investigation. Project metrics quantify development status and progress.

This chapter contains five papers on metrics and measurement topics. In the first paper, Grady looks at the work products of the software development process and proposes metrics based on their generation and the availability of data. He investigates tools and looks at ways to present results to various target audiences. His advice is based on his years of experience in implementing the concepts he preaches.

The second paper, by Andersen, shows the insight that can be provided when software engineering data is captured on a large project. The metrics and measurement program can help optimize your software process because problems with it can be identified and corrected promptly. In addition, lessons learned in metrics data collection, analyses, and reporting are summarized and recommendations made for improving problem-solving abilities.

In the third paper, Ehrlich, Lee, and Molisani provide a case study in applied software reliability measurement. They discuss their use of metrics and reliability goals during the testing phase of their RMS-D1 software. For those interested, the article contains some tutorial material on software reliability models. However, its primary goal is to show how reliability models can be used productively to reduce overall test time and costs.

The fourth paper, by Pfleeger and McGowan, suggests a set of metrics compatible with the process maturity framework recommended by the SEI. The authors also briefly identify the steps that should be taken to implement a responsive metrics program at each of the five levels of the SEI framework.

The final paper, by Grady, illustrates the use of the "goal-question-metric" for defining a software maintenance measurement program. By orienting metrics toward answering management's questions, a cost-effective measurement program can be implemented quickly and with minimum pain. Grady goes on to show how the dual goals of minimizing defects and maximizing customer satisfaction were quantified. Specific metrics and reports are also specified in this paper.

References

The two references that I would recommend include the Camp book on benchmarking (Reference 5 in the Bibliography) and the Grady and Caswell book (Reference 11) on establishing a metrics program. For those interested in metrics for acquisition management, the Marciniak and Reifer text (Reference 17) is recommended.

Work-Product Analysis: The Philosopher's Stone of Software?

Robert B. Grady, Hewlett-Packard

There is no magical way to transform typical development efforts into high-quality ones. But applying metrics to work-product analysis can greatly improve your products' quality.

I t is an age-old dream to achieve perfection. An example from early times is the mythical philosopher's stone sought by alchemists to transform base metals into gold. In recent times, we have developed tools that have helped us achieve highly complex yet highly reliable hardware. But, so far, the philosopher's stone for transforming ordinary software into easy-to-maintain, highly reliable software has been more difficult to find.

One attribute of software that makes it more difficult than hardware to produce with high quality is captured in its name. Unlike hardware, software components and designs are largely unconstrained by physical bounds. By contrast, the evolution of hardware components has been artificially constrained by the "hard" physical limits of packaging. There has been a natural migration of circuits that once fit on parts of a printed circuit board to fit onto chips, and this has aided the creative process by providing at least one limit on the introduction of complexity at each evolutionary step.

With software, we have no such constraints, and the greatest challenge of software-project management is to limit the various intermediate and final products to the levels of complexity that are really necessary. This has led to the introduction of a wide variety of methods and life-cycle models to decompose problems in logical ways that include intermediate steps where we can test whether the right thing is produced the right way.

Work products and metrics

Figure 1 is a simplified version of the traditional waterfall model of the life cycle. It shows examples of work products supported today by software tools that produce outputs of the life-cycle phases. (A work product is an intermediate or final output of software development that describes the design, operation, manufacture, or test of some portion of a deliver-

Reprinted from *IEEE Software*, Vol. 7, No. 2, March 1990, pages 26-34.
Copyright © 1990 by The Institute of Electrical and Electronics Engineers, Inc. All rights reserved.

able or salable product. It is not the final product.) There are at least four ways that these work products encourage better standards for software components:

• Each work product follows some form of standard representation that guarantees a degree of common terminology. Training engineers in their use encourages the use of the best practices and helps eliminate past problems.

• Tool support allows automated checks and immediate feedback to engineers. This feedback most commonly takes the form of error messages and warnings.

• Common terminology simplifies inspections of work products by other team members. Inspections expose some defects that the automated checks cannot detect.

• The tools can also generate metrics and sometimes create numerical figures of merit (or goodness). Both engineers and managers use the metrics to track progress. Unlike the automated checks that clearly identify defects, the figures of merit suggest the *probabilities* of defects occurring.

Software metrics. A software metric defines a standard way of measuring some attribute of the software-development process. Metrics can be primitive (directly measurable or countable, like counting lines of code) or computed (like noncomment source statements per engineer per month).[1]

People in the software field have experimented with metrics for virtually every form of work product since the earliest lines-of-code metric and various later attempts to analyze code complexity.

As new methods to represent specifications and designs have appeared, metrics have informally — and then more formally — appeared for each of them. For example, function points followed Hierarchical Input-Process-Output diagrams,[2] bang/design weight followed structured analysis/structured design.[3] (Bang and design weight are measures of functionality derived from dataflow-diagram and structure-chart representations of software.) And as computer power increased, people even created tools to classify the readability of textual documents.[4]

Why is it that we need to attach numbers to these fragments of intellectual activity?

It is human nature for project managers (and many developers I know, as well) to want to be in control. Just as the new methods generally provide a greater sense of

---

Like the rest of us, managers want to know if they are heading in the right direction at the right speed.

---

control, numeric values attached to these methods also strengthen that feeling.

A manager's three primary objectives during development are to

• measure progress,

• provide project visibility for management review, and

• ensure success.

Like the rest of us, managers want to know if they are heading in the right direction at the right speed, and they want to know when they have successfully reached their destination.

Recognizing these general objectives, it becomes easier to see how metrics naturally derive from the methods we use. Take, for example, the lines-of-code metric. Very early in the days of software development, rules of thumb evolved like "People can code an average of eight lines of code per day." We needed such crude rules to achieve the objectives of measuring progress and providing visibility. Later, we measured many projects and many associated project variables, and we applied statistical techniques to improve our initial crude rules.

We've seen this evolution repeated for other work products and metrics with varying degrees of success. Often, success depended on the different ways that engineers and managers used the tools.

Engineering interface

In the past, engineers have expressed little need for metrics data, largely because the data was meaningful mostly for a project, not for an individual engineer. The engineers needed timely data tuned

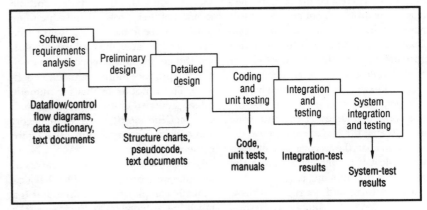

Figure 1. Waterfall development model with sample work products.

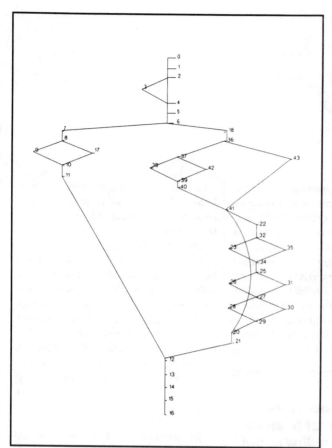

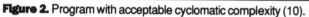

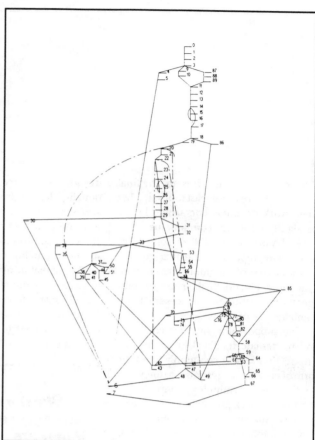

Figure 2. Program with acceptable cyclomatic complexity (10).

Figure 3. Program with high cyclomatic complexity (26).

to the problem at hand while they were trying to solve that problem.

Code complexity. Consider the acceptance of one metric over time. In a 1976 article,[5] Tom McCabe described a metric of cyclomatic complexity. It is derived from an analysis of potential paths through source code. Since then, several studies have correlated the McCabe metric with the probability of defects. One of these concluded that modules with complexity values greater than 10 were much more defect-prone than those with lower values,[6] while another determined that a complexity value of 14 correlated better.[7] However, other studies showed that defects correlated almost as well with code size.[8] Because the McCabe metric was derived from code, the acceptance of the metric was slow. It hardly seemed worth the extra effort of computing it.

At Hewlett-Packard, we repeated these studies of code size, complexity metrics, and defects with similar results. More recently, however, we have used commercially available tools that not only provide the metric values but also a graphical representation of the analyzed code. The re-

sults have been much better. Hewlett-Packard engineers responded more readily to the visual image of complexity than they had to just the numeric value.[9]

The primary reason for this seems to be that the graph gives them information in a more useful form. A single number tells them only that they have a problem. The graph, and its cross-references to their source code, helps them understand the location of their problem and what some steps might be to fix it. The graphs excite managers, because their availability during the coding phase encourages engineers to produce more maintainable software. This is not to say that the numeric values produced by the tools are ignored: The McCabe metric provides managers and engineers a simple numerical figure of merit.

Figures 2 and 3 show two examples of modules from one product. One has a cyclomatic complexity of 10; the other is a much less acceptable 26. Engineers take pride in more structured-looking graphs. They know that at inspection a graph like the one in Figure 3 will be difficult to explain to their peers and, indeed, is undoubtedly more error-prone, difficult to

test, and difficult to maintain than the one in Figure 2. Unfortunately, the code in question was created before the tools we now use were widely available.

Design complexity. The challenge to the engineer is that the complexity identified in one work product often interacts with the complexity in another.

For example, consider the flow graph in Figure 3. It represents the logic contained in the top box of the structure chart in Figure 4. One approach to reducing the cyclomatic complexity is to move parts of the module of Figure 3 to other modules, but this could easily increase the structural complexity of the total system.

The metric of design weight[3] also helps quantify the results of proposed changes. It is derived from the dataflow tokens at a module's boundary, as well as the control-flow tokens.

This more global perspective complements the strictly modular one of the McCabe metric. Figure 4 gives the design-weight value of 654.55, which was computed by a Hewlett-Packard tool for the module in question, as well as the values of the modules with which it communicates.

444

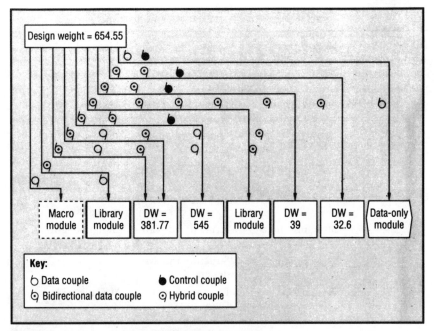

Figure 4. Structure chart with design-weight analysis.

Our experience with design weight is not as advanced as with the McCabe metric. Initial investigations suggest that values of design weight greater than 200 potentially lead to complex code, a fact that is borne out by this real example. Even without knowing a magic number for design weight, a developer can see from the relative values shown in Figure 4 that it would be much better to move some of the code into a new module or to move code to the modules with weights of 39 or 32.6 than to the ones with much greater weights.

The design decisions illustrated in this example are choices that engineers face daily. The advantage of these graphical tools and metrics is that they provide additional information to support the gut feelings of the engineer so decisions will be made more effectively.

In addition, the two views in this example illustrate a more general paradigm of a conceptual view of a problem accompanied by a numerical figure of merit. Having these two views helps the engineer finish part of a design for a product that will be more reliable and easier to maintain.

Testing. Consider another metric example that occurs later in the life cycle, during unit test. During testing, an internal Hewlett-Packard tool called a path-flow analyzer tells developers how well their tests cover all the potential paths in their programs.

Path coverage is measured by using a program that automatically inserts statements into a product's precompilation source code. These statements increment counters during testing to provide a histogram of code execution. The reports of the path-flow analyzer tell an engineer which parts of code were tested and how often they were tested. Combining this ability with a well-planned testing strategy helps us effectively validate software.

Figure 5 shows a typical report from the analyzer. Once again, the attractiveness of the tool to developers is a key to its success. One developer wrote, "It is psychologically motivating to the programmer in that it gives instant feedback by way of the summary report that produces the final percentage value. After working to design and debug a large piece of software, I look forward to the final exercising of the code

```
Summary Path Flow Report

Report for memdiag

Procedure Name          # Times      Existing     Number of     Percent of
                        Invoked      Paths        Paths Hit     Paths Hit

File: print.c
  collect_range         391905             9             9         100.0
  mystrncmp                 72             6             6         100.0
 *print_MA_table            0             21             0           0.0
  print_MC_table             7            34            28          82.4
  print_literal           3476             3             3         100.0
  print_msg                712            13             8          61.5
  print_page_listing         9            12            11          91.7
  print_page_summary         2            10             6          60.0
  print_prompt              30            15            14          93.3
  print_range_status         3            44            24          54.5
  print_ranges              17             7             5          71.4
  print_test_pages      408304            12            12         100.0
  user-collect_range     16348            11            10          90.9
  valid_response           194             5             5         100.0
                        ━━━━━━          ━━━━          ━━━━          ━━━━
                        821079           202           141          69.8
```

Figure 5. Typical path-flow analysis report.

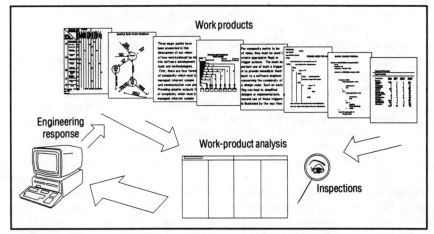

Figure 6. Work-product analysis configured to the engineers' needs.

Table 1.
Engineering work products, tools, and metrics.

Phase	Work product	Tools	Metrics
Specification/ requirements	Text	Writing analysis	Flesch-Kincaid readability
	Spreadsheet	Quality function deployment	Weighted customer needs
	Prototype	Fourth-generation languages	———
	Dataflow diagrams	Structured analysis	Bang
Design	Text	Writing analysis	Flesch-Kincaid readability
	Structure charts	Structured design	Design weight, fanout-squared
	Data dictionary	Structured analysis/ design	———
	Pseudocode	Program-design language	McCabe
Implementation	Code	Compilers, complexity analysis	Lines of code, McCabe
	Unit tests	Code coverage	Percent coverage
	Manuals	Writing analysis	Flesch-Kincaid readability
	Performance tests	Ad hoc	Execution times

Table 2.
Timeliness of metrics data.

Primary user	Use of data	Optimum timing
Engineers	Understand and change work products	Seconds to minutes
Project manager	Identify trends and potential problem areas	Hours
Project manager	Adjust schedule	Weeks
Project manager, program manager	Adjust plans, revise estimates	Months

with the analyzer. It's a challenge to find ways to push the percentage up, and it has helped me to find bugs within my code that had not previously surfaced."

The use of this tool doesn't end at unit test. It has played an important role in Hewlett-Packard system and integration testing for more than five years.

Work-product analysis. Figure 6 shows the process of work-product analysis during development. The work products represent the graphical and textual outputs of various life-cycle steps all the way from analysis of customer requirements through testing. Computers analyze these outputs for the responsible engineers, and other engineers inspect these outputs. The feedback

is timely and specific, and the complete working framework encourages well-documented, quality products.

Table 1 summarizes some of the tools and metrics available today and the development phases to which they apply. It includes work products for prototypes and data dictionaries because they are widely used today, although they represent two cases where metrics research has been very limited (and so no metrics are shown).

Automated work-product-analysis tools provide the benefits of standard terminology, automated checks and feedback, inspection aids, metrics, and numerical figures of merit. These benefits help both developers and managers of projects. However, the management approach to them

all — and to the metrics particularly — must be nonthreatening if the tools are to be used successfully.

Management interface

There is a delicate balance between data used by engineers and the same data used by project managers. Unless the same data is used and interpreted under the same ground rules by both engineers and project managers, you run the risk of distorting the idea of data as a helper and perverting it into data as a weapon.

It is the job of project managers to achieve the goals of measuring progress, providing visibility for management reviews, and ensuring success in a nonthreatening way. Their activities include

- estimating,
- planning,
- scheduling, and
- tracking.

One of the greatest promises of CASE is the automated delivery of metrics to the project manager. Data that is often too difficult and time-consuming to obtain is crucial for making good decisions. Table 2 shows the relationships among the users of various metrics, how they use the data, and the most favorable timing availability of the data.

The table is a continuum of time that varies from real-time feedback to engineers as they represent designs in various forms to much longer sampling periods that are more appropriate to tracking and managing the activities of large teams. This helps you understand why the most commonly available automated project-management tools — PERT programs and estimation tools — provide little support for project managers when schedules become tight and when they must convince others that the project is on track. These tools have update intervals of weeks or months, and it is difficult to keep their data current.

Project-trend indicators are much more effective in alerting managers that events on a PERT chart need to change or that estimates are incorrect because of poor assumptions. This is when metrics are an invaluable supplement to these other tools for project managers. The integration of project-milestone data and the data from various work-product-analysis tools into a

PROJECT MANAGEMENT STATUS TABLE

MODULE	FUNCTION	RESP. ENG.	STATUS	EST. NCSS	ACTUAL NCSS	CURRENT COMPLEXITY	DEFECTS	TEST COVERAGE
DISPLAY		D.C.	Test	390	442		8★	55
	MATCH				73	8	6★	96
	GETUSERSTRING				100	42★		100
	GETADDEDIT				64	25★	2★	32
	GETMAININPUT				56	5		45
	GETDELETEINPUT				53	7		60
	GETONELINE				36	11		100
	GETPLOTMENU				60	8		25
ARC		M.G.	Design Insp.	60	0	72	4★	0
SUM		M.G.	Coding	100	209★	15★	3★	0
CRL		S.B.	Design	215	0	236★	1	0
SUB		D.D.	Test Done	250	1279★	10	4	85

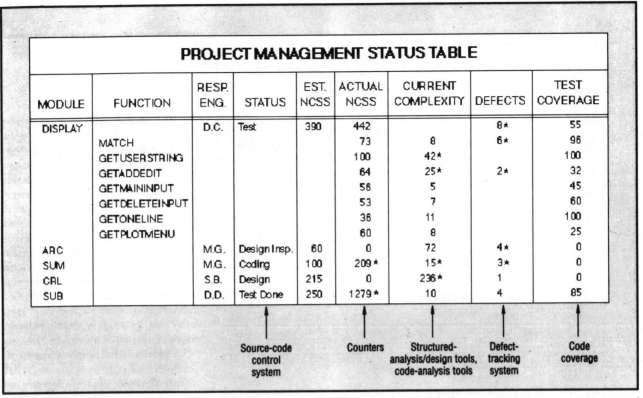

Annotations (bottom of table, by column):
- STATUS → Source-code control system
- ACTUAL NCSS → Counters
- CURRENT COMPLEXITY → Structured-analysis/design tools, code-analysis tools
- DEFECTS → Defect-tracking system
- TEST COVERAGE → Code coverage

Figure 7. Example screen from a project-management status table. The annotations on the bottom of the figure would not be part of the table's screen display.

convenient, accessible summary for project managers will provide a powerful capability for managing more effectively.

Figure 7 shows an example of such a summary, which we call a project-management status table, as it might appear on a project manager's terminal.[1] It consists of data from a combination of work-product-analysis tools, source-control tools, defect-tracking tools, and weekly reports by software engineers. Items shown with asterisks beside them violate boundary conditions that were predefined (by the project manager). These alert the project manager to potential problems as they develop.

For example, the actual noncomment source statements ("NCSS" in the screen) for the module Sum are more than twice the original estimate. Why was the estimate off by so much? This might be a signal that the design was misunderstood or is changing. Some of the other flagged conditions shown in this example include design weights greater than 200, McCabe complexities greater than 14, and defect densities greater than 10.

Without the various tools to determine the data shown here and without a way to consolidate the data into an interface like the one shown in the figure, you can understand how difficult it is today for project managers to know the true status of a project and for them to make timely decisions. It is just not practical to manually gather all the data in a timely fashion. And without the data, project managers are operating with blindfolds on.

Figure 8 illustrates how the same sources of work-product analysis and inspections shown in Figure 6 provide tracking feedback to project managers — and do so as effectively as they do for engineers.

Project managers use this data to make decisions that ultimately affect project schedules, plans, and estimates. The power is in the range of data automatically available from these new tools. This is data that the technically rooted project manager has always known was available but has never had the time and resources to obtain.

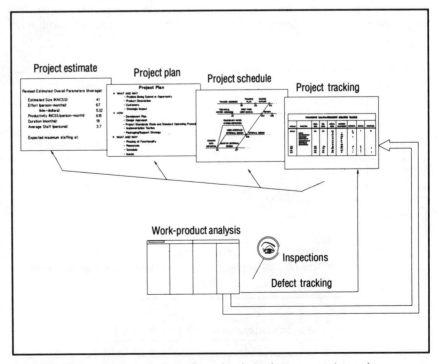

Figure 8. Work-product analysis configured to the project manager's needs.

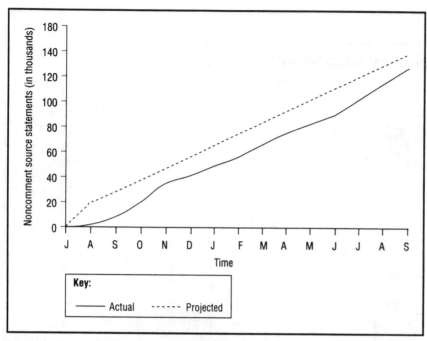

Figure 9. Plot of code generation against time. This graph, like those in Figures 10 and 11, is based on actual project data and shows the value of such graphs in providing engineers and project managers feedback about the project.

Public interface

For the same reasons that engineers want to be in control of their work products, the project manager will want the project-management status table to be relatively private. The manager is probably the only person who can correctly interpret what might appear to be an excessive number of boundary violations without a lot of research. On the other hand, the data in the status table must be accessible on a per-engineer basis, or else the engineers might perceive it as a threat. Engineers must know the boundary-condition values ahead of time. And the system should also probably notify them some time before the status table receives its periodic update.

Why would engineers perceive a project-management status table as a threat? Our experience at Hewlett-Packard shows that engineers don't mind quality-criteria targets and the collection of data to achieve their goals as long as they participate in setting those goals and agree with them.

But when data collection and interpretation are hidden from them, they will wonder whether the ground rules have changed without their being informed.

A project manager can also derive various trends from stored data and present them publicly. These are useful to both the team and to others who need regular reassurance, like senior management and customers. Some of the graphs in this section's figures are automated by-products of the tools that support a status table. Others are derived from a combination of that data and other data that the project manager must learn by being in close touch with the development team and its activities. (The graphs in this section are all real graphs from actual projects.)

Unfortunately, when the graphs were drawn, an automated status table did not exist. This cost the project managers extra effort and time for data collection, analysis, and presentation.

The first graph, shown in Figure 9 and adapted from the book *Software Metrics: Establishing a Company-Wide Program,*[1] is simply a plot of engineering effort against project deliverables. Is the effort being spent in proportion to estimates? This is what you look at when you plot code generation against time.

There are other measures that you can use to plot effective engineering effort besides code, including percentage of weighted functionality complete, bang, design weight, and function points. Graphs of each of these measures are effective in showing progress, since they show actual effort against planned effort. Of course, their success depends heavily on the accuracy of a projected end point.

Graphs of effort versus time are generally by-products of work-product-analysis tools. A necessary complement to these graphs comes from a defect-tracking system, although defects are all too often accurately tracked only *after* product release, not before. The most natural time to require accurate reporting of defect data before release is after formal testing begins. Despite people's sensitivity about making mistakes, engineers today more readily accept that accurate defect reporting for system-level and integration-level testing is necessary to coordinate the change efforts of many engineers.

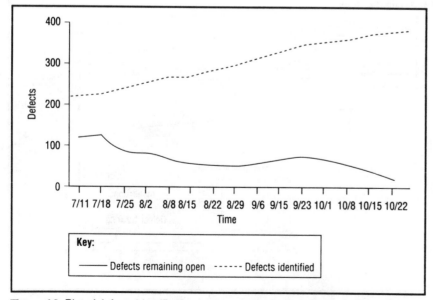

Figure 10. Plot of defects identified and defects remaining open against time.

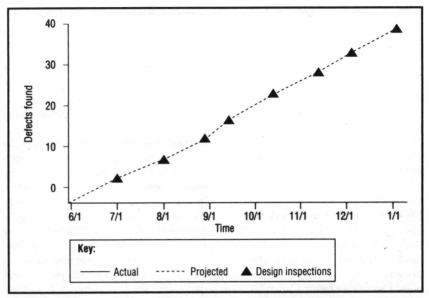

Figure 11. Plot of projected defects and projected design inspections. The plot is for a project with an expected size of 50,000 noncomment source statements and an estimated 72 design defects, 55 percent of which will be found in eight inspections. Determining such a plot before working on actual code both helps make inspections an integral part of development and helps begin systematic defect tracking as early as possible.

Nevertheless, reporting defects is labor-intensive, and project managers must be ready to devote their energy to encouraging the need for timely recording of accurate defect information. This is particularly necessary when the development team must double as the testing team. An automated defect-tracking system is an important cornerstone of an integrated development environment, and plots of its data can provide several trends that project managers may want to monitor.

One trend that is highly useful to project teams is a graph of defects against time. An example is shown in Figure 10. Such graphs are easily generated when an automated defect-tracking system is available. These graphs show both the trend of defects discovered and the trend of defects that remain unfixed (open). In the later stages of a project, these trends are just as important as the trends of effort versus estimates are during the earlier stages.

Perhaps the most difficult time for a project manager is the period early in a project when no code or prototypes yet exist. During this creative period in a project, it is very difficult to quantify progress, because it often alternates between slow and rapid as engineers overcome conceptual blocks. Thus, plotting design metrics can be frustrating.

An alternative way of looking at progress during this period is to calculate the number of design defects that you *expect* to find during inspections and to plan and plot the inspections (design reviews) necessary to find these defects. Figure 11 shows an example. The estimated number of design defects and the time to find them during inspections are based on historical data. I have described these more fully elsewhere.[10]

Inspections can act as a catalyst for the team to remove conceptual blocks, because even informal inspections encourage clarification of issues and discussion of different approaches. The purpose of the plot is to encourage holding the inspections on a predetermined schedule. You must take care to ensure that the team understands and agrees with this type of scheduling, and you must be flexible enough to postpone some formal inspections and to replace them with informal ones. Defects are not formally reported during *informal* inspections.

This example is an unusual one, but it illustrates two points about work-product analysis and project management. First, it emphasizes that inspections remain an integral part of work-product analysis. It will be a long time before we eliminate them. Second, it emphasizes how useful it is to begin systematic defect tracking as early as possible. Such tracking normally starts after formal testing begins. In this case, formal inspections really represent the first appearance of *formal* testing in the development process.

The idea in Figure 11 of graphing defects over time is not particularly different from the approach used in Figure 10 — it is simply done at a different period of the development process.

How do these three real-life examples compare with the alternatives that past project managers used without the benefits that recent tools and environments provide? Figure 12 compares automated and manual tracking and reporting methods.

Common methods of displaying progress in the past included a PERT chart and reports of percentage completion. PERT charts suffer without up-to-date data from

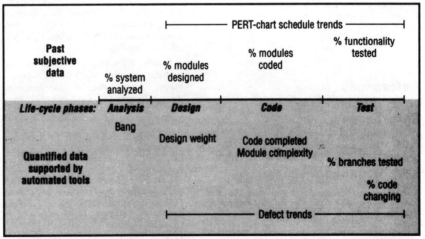

Figure 12. Comparing automated and manual tracking and reporting methods. The top half shows information that has often driven past decisions. The bottom half shows typical information now available to drive decisions. In both cases, the information is lined up with the relevant parts of the life cycle.

the programming environment. Reporting percentage completion also has its weaknesses: Perhaps no other words are as capable of striking terror in the hearts of project managers as "I'm 90-percent done." (It sometimes seems as if programs are 90-percent done for months.) And yet, without measurable work products, we depend totally on subjective guesses of completion. The best results will occur when PERT charts and completion estimates are backed up by the solid data and trends that metrics supply.

The examples in Figure 12 of metrics supported by automated tools must continue to evolve as our development methods continue to change and improve. They already offer substantial clarity over past subjective methods, however, in quantifying and showing progress.

The complexity of developing software and of the organizations required to develop and support it continue to increase. Work-product-analysis tools help measure and control development complexity, and data from these tools can be brought together to reduce the complexity of project management. Unlike the past manual use of some of these methods, the tools used today finally provide a sense of control to developers and managers alike.

Perhaps these tools and environments are like the mythical philosopher's stone that would turn lead into gold. The ability to do automated work-product analysis certainly holds promise for helping engineers recognize and reduce unnecessary complexity and for managers to receive more timely feedback about progress and quality.

Our experience at Hewlett-Packard with work-product-analysis tools and data in real projects shows that the combination of tools, methods, and metrics results in improved product reliability and more maintainable software.

Whether the evolution of these tools will proceed far enough to reverse the long-term trend of increased complexity and help eliminate process steps without sacrificing high quality remains to be seen.

But one thing does seem clear: The automation that we are seeing provides solid data to plot measurable trends for project managers. These trends have never been readily available in the past. This alone will help managers make better, more informed decisions. Even if we don't yet have a software philosopher's stone, perhaps we have uncovered some philosopher's pebbles. ❖

Acknowledgments

I thank Jan Grady, Debbie Caswell, and Fred Schurkus for their timely and helpful suggestions during this article's development.

References

1. R. Grady and D. Caswell, *Software Metrics: Establishing a Company-Wide Program*, Prentice-Hall, Englewood Cliffs, N.J., 1987, pp. 4, 31, 216.

2. A.J. Albrecht, "Measuring Application-Development Productivity," *Proc. Joint Share/ Guide/IBM Application-Development Symp.*, Share, Chicago, 1979, pp. 83-92.

3. T. DeMarco, *Controlling Software Projects*, Yourdon Press, New York, 1982, pp. 80, 106.

4. J.W. Losa, J. Aagard, and J.P. Kincaid, "Readability Grade Levels of Selected Navy Technical-School Curricula," Tech. Report TAEG-TM-83-2, Naval Training Analysis and Evaluation Group, Orlando, Fla., Feb. 1983.

5. T. McCabe, "A Complexity Measure," *IEEE Trans. Software Eng.*, Dec. 1976, pp. 308-320.

6. T.J. Walsh, "A Software-Reliability Study Using a Complexity Measure," *Proc. Nat'l Computer Conf.*, AFIPS Press, Montvale, N.J., 1979, pp. 761-768.

7. R. Rambo, P. Buckley, and E. Branyan, "Establishment and Validation of Software Metric Factors," *Proc. Int'l Soc. Parametric Analysts Seventh Ann. Conf.*, Int'l Soc. Parametric Analysts, Germantown, Md., 1985, pp. 406-417.

8. B. Curtis, S.B. Sheppard, and P. Milliman, "Third-Time Charm: Stronger Prediction of Programmer Performance by Software Complexity Metrics," *Proc. Fourth Int'l Conf. Software Eng.*, CS Press, Los Alamitos, Calif., 1979, pp. 356-360.

9. W. Ward, "Software Defect Prevention Using McCabe's Complexity Metric," *Hewlett-Packard J.*, April 1989, pp. 64-69.

10. R. Grady, "Dissecting Software Failures," *Hewlett-Packard J.*, April 1989, pp. 57-63.

Robert B. Grady is the manager of development-environment methods at Hewlett-Packard's Development Environment Lab. He has managed development projects for compilers, measurement and control systems, firmware, and manufacturing automation and information systems. His research interests include software tools, development environments, management methods, and metrics.

Grady received a BS in electrical engineering from the Massachusetts Institute of Technology and an MS in electrical engineering from Stanford University. He is a member of the IEEE Computer Society.

Address questions about this article to Grady at Development Environment Lab, Hewlett-Packard, 19447 Pruneridge Ave., Cupertino, CA 95014-9974.

The use of software engineering data in support of project management

by Ole Andersen

Based on software metrics data from a large (19 working-years) software development project, a number of analyses have been carried out. The results reveal the causes for cost overruns, show how effort planning can be refined during development, and identify a relationship between the quality of the design documents and the effort consumed for their production. This gives an insight into the development process and establishes norms for interpreting metrics values obtained in future projects. In this way, it is a first step for a company towards increasing its software development process maturity level.

1 Introduction

The main activities of software project managers include planning, estimating, tracking and decision making. It is a characteristic of a mature engineering discipline that the end-product quality level is planned, reliable project plans are made, progress is tracked on a detailed level, and estimates and decisions can be made, based on well documented experience with previous successful projects.

This situation is not usually found in the relatively new discipline of software engineering. One reason is that, over the years, software engineering has adapted to a rapid technological development. This, together with the fact that the end product is intangible, has led to a situation where many software development projects are carried out in an *ad hoc* fashion and very often fail to meet their success criteria.

For software development, the important management parameters are project cost and duration, and product quality. Measurements of cost and calendar time are fairly easy. Control of these parameters is often attempted and is possible within limits, although most managers have difficulties predicting project cost and duration. Discussion of the quality of the end product starts with defining the relevant quality factors and their measurement units. However, the next steps of predicting, at the start of the project, the

expected end-product quality factor levels, and controlling progress towards specified quality factor levels during the project, are not usually attempted.

To improve the present state of affairs, it is necessary, during a software development project, to collect data that describe the various production processes, as well as the resulting partial and intermediate products. Thereby, the technical achievements, as well as the overall project status and progress, can be assessed. By analysing the data, a quantitative basis for decisions can be established, with results improving as norms for interpreting measurement values become available from finished projects.

When selecting data and analyses for use in a project, or across projects in an organisation, the emphasis should be on data that are simple and easy to collect and analyses giving results that can easily be understood. The benefits of introducing a software metrics programme will then include

- improved tracking and control of a development project;
- early identification of atypical measurement values, which may indicate a previously undiscovered problem;
- an accumulated set of data describing completed projects, for use in planning and estimation of future projects;
- the possibility of optimising the software development process, since the problem areas can be identified and the results of changes to the existing process can be documented.

The last three points require that norms for measurement values are available and, in many cases, such norms must be derived from data collected during previous projects.

This paper will describe a number of data analyses, together with the conclusions that may be drawn from their results. The analyses are performed on a very comprehensive data set collected during a 19-working-year software development project. The analyses demonstrate how the experience can help the company to improve project planning and monitoring, through the establishment of company norms and by introducing specific changes to the development process.

2 Monitoring of software development

The work reported here is one result of a concerted effort to improve the prediction, monitoring and assessment of soft-

"The Use of Software Engineering Data in Support of Project Management," by O. Andersen from *Software Engineering Journal*, Vol. 5, No. 6, Nov. 1990, pages 250-256. Copyright © 1990 Institution of Electrical Engineers, reprinted with permission.

ware product quality. This was undertaken as part of the ESPRIT project REQUEST (REliability and QUality of European Software Technology). In the area of software quality, work has concentrated on developing COQUAMO (COnstructive QUAlity MOdel) [1].

The original idea of COQUAMO was to transfer the approach that had been successfully applied in COCOMO (COst MOdel) [2] to the field of software quality. COQUAMO has now been developed into three models, the first of which is a predictive model for software quality (using an approach similar to that of COCOMO) to be applied in the early phases of development. The second part consists of a monitoring model for use during the project, and the third part is a quality assessment model for the later stages in the development.

Introduction of the monitoring model [3] as part of COQUAMO enables it to support the natural activities of a project manager during a software development project. In this way, software metrics are utilised in software project control activities, based on the general project control procedure of setting quantitative targets, measuring against these targets and responding to deviations. The approach aims to work at a more detailed level and include more metrics than other software metrics programmes [4] and [5].

In support of the development of COQUAMO, large-scale data collection and storage have been carried out for software metrics data as part of REQUEST [6]. For the monitoring model, this allows significant metrics and relationships to be identified. In-depth analyses have been carried out for a number of project data sets, with the aims of developing the model and investigating the assumptions behind it, as well as investigating the possibilities for automating the analyses of project data.

One set of analyses has been based on the ideas of using anomalies [7], i.e. atypical metric values, to detect the deviations that, at an early stage, may indicate potential quality problems [8]. This paper shows how detailed analyses of data from a large software development project may be used to support general project management, by establishing quantitative norms, and how they may also be used to improve the software development process in a company.

Collection and analysis of software engineering data from just one project allow initial norms to be established. These can be used to support planning, as well as interpretation of data, in subsequent projects. The data collected from these projects may then be used to check, refine and expand the set of norms.

To begin with, the empirical foundation for the norms is naturally weak, since they are based on the information extracted from one project. It is, however, an advantage to utilise this quantified experience as support in the next project, rather than continuing a purely qualitative approach. As data become available from more projects, the initial assumptions concerning relationships between parameters can be verified and the uncertainties of numerical values can be reduced. In addition, the coverage of the norms can be expanded, and gradually this will lead to a set of company norms, in which the project manager can have confidence, and which will help managers of future projects to learn from the experience gained in previous projects.

This process does not follow a strict scientific approach, of first establishing a number of hypotheses, then collecting a statistically sufficient number of datasets and finally verifying or rejecting the hypotheses based on data analyses. In a commercial environment, the attitude will be to analyse the first available data set, draw conclusions from (or base decisions on) the results of the analyses and then introduce changes to optimise the development process.

The description below is concerned with the first step a company must take in order to introduce a quantitative basis for the management of software development projects. This includes the collection of a first data set, which describes one of the company's own projects, together with a number of analyses of the data, leading to the establishment of a first set of norms for software engineering data.

3 The product and the development process

The software development project from which data were obtained can be characterised in the following way.

- *The product:* the software product is a real-time information system for use in a highly integrated, but geographically widespread, environment. Requirements for total system reliability are very high, since the consequences of severe faults are critical. It was developed for one customer, consists of four subsystems and has a total (all inclusive) size of 73 000 lines of code.
- *The process:* the development process followed an in-house software development handbook prescribing a life-cycle, documentation level and V & V activities, corresponding to a standard third-generation development

Table 1 Summary of task categories

Category	Plan man-hours	Number of tasks	Overrun man-hours	Number [2,6[tasks	Overrun [2,6[%	Number [0.8,1.2] tasks
Unplanned	0	21	5455	—	—	—
S	855	23	565	7	98	1
A	1909	23	203	3	270	6
L	2626	17	1341	5	104	3
VL	5965	19	374	1	114	5

For the unplanned tasks, as well as for the tasks in the four categories, the Table shows the total planned effort in man-hours, the number of tasks of each kind and the total overrun of effort in man-hours. For each category, the number of tasks where the ratio actual man-hours/planned man-hours is >=2, as well as the overrun caused by these tasks in percentage of the total overrun for the category, are shown. The last column gives the number of tasks in each category where the actual effort is within ±20% of the planned value.

approach. In practice, this was followed fairly strictly. This was the case, despite the fact that it was the first time the project group had followed the already existing development handbook, which was well tested in use by other development groups. The development was based on detailed plans, with effort allocated to tasks in the range of 20–600 man-hours and follow-up supported by an extensive data collection. The code was written in a high-level dedicated application language and supported by dedicated tools, as well as host and target environments.

● *The personnel:* all developers were involved in most of the project, and the majority had several job functions. The average experience among the developers in the application area and in the software development was fairly high.

● *The project:* the project was carried out by 20–25 developers from one department at one site, delivering a total of 19 working years within a calendar time of two years. The period covered the activities from analysis until the product was released to the customer. The delivery took place on time, and the total cost ($-$overrun) was kept within acceptable limits.

● *The organisation:* the company has an experience of many (>20) years in the development of systems in the application area.

4 The data and data collection

A large amount of data was collected as an integrated part of the development process and the project management. This was supported by existing administrative procedures and viewed by all involved as a necessity for successful project management. The following data items were among those made available to REQUEST, subject to the condition that the identity of the provider remains undisclosed for commercial reasons:

☐ planned and actual effort for each development and inspection task broken down, so that the planned task effort is in the range of 20–600 man-hours;

☐ size of documents (pages);

☐ number of errors detected by inspection of documents.

Information was made available so that it was possible to link the effort consumed to produce a specific document or module to its size, the effort consumed by V & V activities (inspections), as well as the number of errors detected.

5 Data analyses and results

Results are presented below from a number of analyses which have been chosen so as to focus on the establishment of company norms. The norms can be used to interpret measurements made in future projects, and further data from these can then be used to check and improve the norms. Furthermore, some of the analyses give an insight into the development process and show how the process may be optimised. The analyses include

● *detailed comparisons between planned and actual effort for tasks occurring up to the end of coding* (see Section 5.1). The results are used to highlight the sources of significant overruns in expenditure, when compared to the planned cost, and to determine how this can be avoided in future projects.

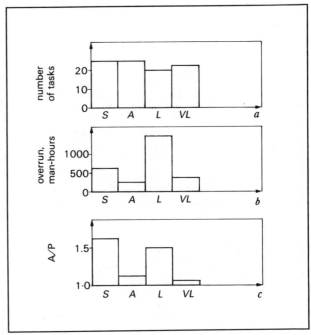

Fig. 1 Effort overrun for planned tasks
a The number of tasks in each of the four categories of effort planned for the tasks
b The total overrun in man-hours over the planned effort, observed for all tasks in each category
c The ratio between the total actual and planned efforts (A/P) in each category

● *comparisons of different activities within one phase and across phases* (see Section 5.2). This allows sets of activities for which the effort consumptions are mutually related to be identified. This, in turn, allows plans to be refined during future projects.

● *comparisons of the complexity of document-producing tasks and the quality of the resulting documents* (see Section 5.3). In future projects, the identified relationship can be used to evaluate the documents produced, the inspection procedure, or to plan or evaluate results of individual inspections.

All of the analyses are concerned with issues that may vary from company to company. For example, the activities which have mutually related efforts may not be the same in different companies. This depends on the lifecycle used, the availability of internal standards and the strictness with which such standards are adhered to. It is therefore necessary for each company to go through the process of establishing their own norms, based on data describing their own projects, rather than relying on industry averages extracted from the literature. Only in this way is it possible to arrive at detailed norms that, in the given environment, give relevant management support.

5.1 Planned and actual effort

Analysis of the relationships between the effort planned and actually occurring for development tasks will enable the company to improve the evaluation of similar plans prepared in future projects. They may learn how to limit the number of unplanned tasks, as well as the total overrun occurring in the planned tasks.

For each task, from the start of high-level design until the end of coding, the effort planned, as well as that actually

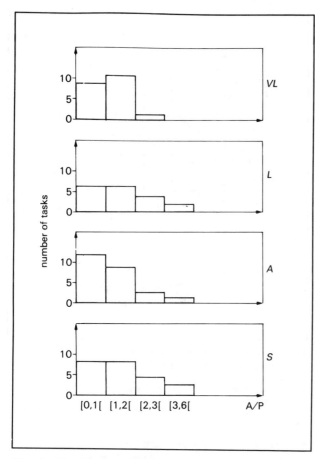

Fig. 2   Distribution of tasks in each of the four categories S, A, L and VL, according to the ratio between actual and planned effort (A/P)

consumed, is available in man-hours for all four subsystems. Planning was done in an empirical fashion, with effort allocation to each task based on consultations between the project manager and the task leader. The plan, which was made before finishing the high-level design, included 82 tasks out of the 103 tasks which were planned or actually did occur in these phases. Of the tasks originally in the plan, five were later found to be superfluous and two (inspection) tasks were not carried out.

The tasks included, for each subsystem, the production of

☐ high-level design
    subsystem design
    interface design
    user manual
    test specification
    test design
☐ detailed design
    module design
    test design
☐ coding
    module code

as well as the inspection of each document (except the test design documents) and the module code.

In Fig. 1 the tasks are shown categorised according to their planned size.

- S = small (1–50 man-hours)
- A = average (51–100 man-hours)

- L = large (101–200 man-hours)
- VL = very large (201–600 man-hours)

excluding the tasks not originally included in the plan. The categories have been chosen so that the number of tasks (Fig. 1a) in each is roughly the same. Figs. 1b and c show the overrun in man-hours observed for all the tasks in each category, as well as the relative overrun in units of the total planned effort for the category.

Fig. 2 shows the distribution of tasks in each of the four categories used in Fig. 1, according to the ratio between actual and planned effort (A/P = actual man-hours/planned man-hours):

☐   [0,1[: $0 < = A/P < 1$
☐   [1,2[: $1 < = A/P < 2$
☐   [2,3[: $2 < = A/P < 3$
☐   [3,6[: $3 < = A/P < 6$

The unplanned tasks are shown in Table 1, together with the tasks in the four categories. For each task category, the planned man-hours, the number of tasks and the overrun in man-hours observed in each category are shown. Furthermore, the Table contains, for each of the task categories, the number of tasks where $A/P > = 2$ (i.e. those which cost twice the planned effort or more), together with the overrun caused by these tasks as a percentage of the total overrun recorded in the category, and the number of tasks where $0.8 < = A/P < = 1.2$. Of these well planned tasks, there are a total of 15 where 8 have $A/P < = 1$ and 7 have $A/P > 1$, with the symmetry around 1 supporting the statement that the efforts were indeed well estimated.

The data illustrate the relative importance of the two causes for deviations between actual and planned effort for the project as a whole.

- Approximately 20% of the tasks carried out were not included in the original plan. This caused an overrun of 5455 man-hours or close to 30% of the total costs.
- For the tasks that did appear in the plan, with a total planned effort of 11355 man-hours, an overrun of 2483 man-hours or 22% was recorded.

The majority of the unplanned tasks were concerned with either the test design documents (none of which were included in the original plan [approx. 2000 man-hours]) or the production of graphical documentation of the design (approx. 3300 man-hours). Omission of the test design documents from the plan was caused by the fact that the development group was following the development handbook for the first time. They were therefore not familiar with the requirements for early test planning. This shortcoming of the project plan can be easily avoided in future projects.

The reason why a number of design tasks were omitted from the plan is that the planning was based on the assumption that a specific design method could be applied. When it later became clear that this was not possible, a fallback was necessary to the use of a more traditional and complicated method.

There is no general way in which to avoid a situation where assumptions concerning the basic design approach do not hold. Decisions regarding the way to perform the design are based on an analysis of the system and software requirements, and the effort invested in such an analysis should be weighed against the cost incurred if incorrect decisions are made.

With regard to the planned tasks, the largest total overrun in man-hours is seen in the L (101–200 man-hours) category of tasks, and the next largest in the S (1–50 man-hours) category. In both cases, the relative overrun is more than 50% of the planned effort. Only small overruns were recorded in the other two categories, both in absolute and relative terms.

In addition, the S and L categories show the largest number of tasks with an actual effort of more than twice the planned level and the smallest number of well planned tasks with the actual effort within ±20% of the planned level. The overrun in the S and L categories corresponds to the amount that is recorded for the tasks where the actual effort is larger than twice the planned level. This is also the case in the VL category, but it is hardly significant with only one task showing such an overrun in the category.

The *a priori* credibility of planned effort values therefore depends on the category in which it falls. In the S and L categories there is a larger risk that a given task has been underestimated by a significant fraction. The underestimation is seen to give rise to the largest overruns, not only in relative terms but also on an absolute scale, in the S and L categories, when compared to the A and VL tasks. If these underestimated tasks can be identified early in the process and re-estimated, the planned effort in the two categories will be very close to reflecting the actual effort needed.

Two different strategies must therefore be applied in the short-term to reduce the uncertainty of the effort estimates for the tasks in the plan.

☐ When the planned effort for a task falls in the S or L categories, it must be carefully reviewed to ensure that no gross underestimation has been made.

☐ For tasks in the A and VL categories the easiest approach is to increase the estimates by 5–10% to cover for the slight underestimations that occur for such tasks.

It should also be considered if the estimation process is carried out so as to induce the developers to estimate the 'minimum time to complete', rather than the actual size of the task. If this is the case, a long-term response to the planning difficulties must include a change in attitude to the planning process and possibly also training in the estimation process.

An attempt to identify a pattern of which tasks display the large overruns does not give a clear picture. The 11 module coding tasks were the ones most consistently showing large overruns (80% total — in agreement with the old adage of making an estimate of coding time and then doubling it), and the company could therefore consider emphasising the reviewing of the coding task effort allocations, taking experience values into account.

5.2 Relationships between activities

By establishing a set of experience values for expansion ratios (e.g. the ratios between the efforts used in producing the high-level design, the detailed design and the code) it is possible to create a basis for revision of effort allocations during future projects in those cases where overruns occur in the early phases.

The actual effort used in the phases of high-level design, detailed design and coding for the production of the design descriptions, test specifications, test designs and module code have been used in Table 2. The Table contains the

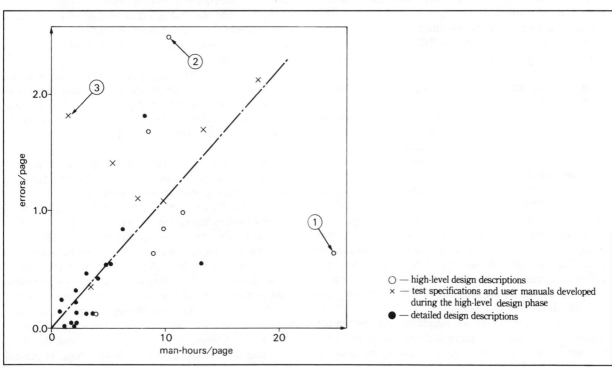

Fig. 3 Scatterplot of errors/page found in inspections against production effort man-hours/page for the majority of documents from the two design phases

The line is based on a least-square fit to all the points, except the three pronounced outliers marked 1, 2 and 3, with no constraints that it should pass the origin

Table 2 ·Summary of expansion ratios

Ratio	Sub1	Sub2	Sub3	Sub4	Total
DD/HLD	0.68	0.89	1.44	0.27	0.73
CODE/DD	1.23	0.85	0.92	0.95	1.00
CODE/(HLD + DD)	0.50	0.40	0.54	0.20	0.42
TP/(HLD + DD)	0.31	0.24	0.15	0.21	0.24

The ratios between the total effort used for production of the high-level design documents (HLD), the detailed design documents (DD), the module code (CODE) and the test plans (TP), including test specifications and test design documents from both design phases. The ratios are calculated for each of the four subsystems (Sub1, Sub2, Sub3, Sub4), as well as for the system as a whole.

'expansion ratio' between actual effort in detailed design (DD) and high-level design (HLD), between code (CODE) and detailed design, and between code and the total design effort (HLD + DD), for each of the four subsystems, as well as for the total system. Furthermore, the Table contains the total actual effort used for test planning (TP, i.e. specification and design) in the two design phases, in relation to the total design effort (HLD + DD) for the subsystems and the total system.

A relatively large variation is seen for the ratio DD/HLD, whereas this is less pronounced for the CODE/DD ratio. One cause of the variation is that a serious deficiency was detected at the inspection of the high-level design of subsystem 4 (Sub4), causing a substantial effort to be used for a total redesign of this subsystem. Another cause seems to be that the level of design details to be included in the high-level design documents, as described in the software development handbook. has not been interpreted in the same way for all four subsystems.

When comparing the coding effort to the total design effort for each subsystem (CODE/(HLD + DD)), the variation is less, except for subsystem 4 where this ratio is also affected by the redesign. This ratio, however, is insensitive to the point of transition between high-level and detailed design.

In the comparison of the ratios between test planning and total design effort (TP/(HLD + DD)), subsystem 4 does not show a large deviation. This reflects the fact that, when the high-level design had to be changed, so did the test specification and test design documents.

If the company, in future projects, strengthens the definitions of the content of high-level and detailed design documents, the expansion ratios can be used to support the initial planning activity, as well as revisions of the plan during development. Assuming that an overrun (caused by the task being larger than anticipated, rather than by design faults) is recorded for the high-level design, the expansion ratios can be used to re-estimate the effort for the test planning, detailed design and coding.

Until this change of design standards has been implemented, the ratio between coding and total design effort can be used in the same way. This is of less value, however, than using the DD/HLD and CODE/DD ratios, since the total design effort becomes available at a later time than the high-level design effort, causing responses to overruns to be less effective.

5.3 Document complexity and quality

A detailed analysis of the production process has been performed for documents from the design phases, and a relationship established between production process parameters and the quality of the produced documents, measured as the number of errors found by inspections. For the majority of documents produced in the high-level and detailed design phases, the following three measures are available:

- effort (man-hours) consumed in the production of the document;
- document size in pages;
- total number of errors found during inspections.

Fig. 3 shows a scatter plot which, for each document,· displays errors per page against the effort consumed to produce one page, thereby normalising out effects caused by the mere size of the documents. The Figure also shows the least-square line fitted to all data points, excluding the three most pronounced outliers (1, 2, 3) detected by visual inspection. The line was not constrained to pass through the origin.

The trend of the data leads to the interpretation that a large effort per page for a document from the design phases implies that the task of producing the document was a complex one, and the document therefore contains a relatively large number of errors. This interpretation is supported by the background information relating to the documents causing the outliers (the numbers refer to Fig. 3)

□ 1: this document contains the high-level design of the subsystem which is the corner-stone of the entire system. The designer has taken extra time to arrive at a good design, and consequently fewer errors were found.

□ 2: this was the first interface design to be produced and inspected. The large number of errors are indicative of the ensuing discussion about the right level of detail to aim for in such documents.

□ 3: this was the first test specification to be produced and inspected. As a result, it was realised that the task of test planning was far greater than anticipated and that it required the production of test design documents, which, so far, had not been included in the project plan.

The general trend is observed for all the documents from the design phases, although they are of different type and their size is measured in primitive units. A first assumption would be that the number of pages is too simple a measure to be involved in the capture of the complexity of tasks as different as the production of design descriptions, user manuals and test specifications. However, no pattern related to document type has been identified for the documents, as can be seen from the different markings used for three kinds of documents in Fig. 3. The only exception is that documents from the high-level design phase tend to have a larger value of the man-hours/page than those from the detailed design phase. This is in agreement with the expectation that tasks in the high-level design phase, in general, are more complex than those involved in the detailed design.

It should be noted that the trend seen in Fig. 3 need not be valid for all companies. The trend depends on the way the task breakdown is performed and on the management follow-up on plans, assuming the same inspection procedure for all documents. A large number of tasks showing large values of man-hours/page and a correspondingly small number of errors/page could result from costly gold-plating of the documents. On the other hand, a large number of documents with low man-hours/page values and high number of errors/page indicate that the necessary care was not applied in the corresponding task.

The knowledge that the relationship between man-hours/page and errors/page is as shown in Fig. 3 can, in future projects, be used for

• planning of inspections when a document has been produced and the man-hours/page is known. Maximum effort may be allocated to the inspection of complex documents, i.e. those with a large value of man-hours/page, and the participants in such reviews selected with care.
• assessment of inspection efficiency, by comparing the number of errors found to the norm.
• assessment of documents, by comparing the effort consumed for the document production to the norm.

Concerning the two last points, it should be noted that, with regard to outliers in two-dimensional plots, there is generally no indication of whether the outlier is caused by one or other parameter having an atypical value. The identification of an outlier merely focuses the project management's attention on, for example, a given document. It is then up to the manager to decide, among a number of possible causes, the reason for the anomaly.

6 Conclusion

Collection and analysis of software metrics data, even from just one software development project, will provide a company with an improved insight into their development process. This insight will develop further as more data sets become available and they are used to check and improve the initial norms. The analyses of the data may indicate that the underlying part of the process is performed in an acceptable way. In such cases, the data may be used as norms within the company for planning of future projects, or so that data values from future projects can be compared to the norms.

An example is the trend seen in Fig. 3. When the average effort required to produce one page in a document is influenced by the complexity of writing the document, the higher error rates recorded for high values of man-hours/page are acceptable, and the trend may be used as a norm as described above.

On the other hand, the analyses may reveal problems with an aspect of the development process and possibly may also point to the cause of the problems. In such cases, the increased insight may be used to plan and implement changes to the development process, and to document the impact of the changes by repeating the analyses on data from projects carried out under the changed conditions.

As an example, the tasks in categories S and L on Fig. 1 may be considered. The severe overruns seen for these tasks indicate that the effort allocation should be improved to avoid gross underestimations for some tasks (i.e. the planning process must be changed), rather than to continue using the same planning process and then increase the planned values by 50–60%.

The data, analyses and results presented here will, in a future project, provide important guidance on how to

☐ plan the required effort with confidence;
☐ refine the effort allocation during the development;
☐ assess the produced documents and inspection results.

By collecting and analysing a detailed data set, the company has taken a first step towards increasing their software development process maturity level [9], and ultimately, their productivity and end-product quality. The description of the data collection and analysis can therefore serve as an example of the activities that many companies must undertake in the near future, in order to build up quantitative support for project management, in the form of norms for interpreting data from future projects.

7 Acknowledgments

This paper is based on results obtained in REQUEST Subproject 1. The author wishes to thank the many contributors to the general approach and ideas outlined above: Poul Grav Petersen, Susanne Klim, Johanne Schmidt, Jens Heile Heilesen, ElektronikCentralen, Denmark; Stephen Linkman, Lesley Pickard, Niall Ross, STC Technology, UK; Peter Mellor, The City University, UK; and Barbara Kitchenham, National Computing Centre, UK. The work has been supported by the EEC ESPRIT programme (Grant ESP/300) and the Danish Council of Technology (Grant 840563.0).

8 References

[1] PETERSEN, P.G.: 'Software quality: The COnstructive QUAlity MOdelling System' in Directorate General XIII (Eds.): 'ESPRIT '86: Results and Achievements' (Elsevier Science Publishers B.V., North-Holland, 1987)
[2] BOEHM, B.W.: 'Software engineering economics' (Prentice-Hall Inc., 1981)
[3] KITCHENHAM, B.A., and WALKER, J.G.: 'A quantitative approach to monitoring software development', Soft. Eng. J., 1989, 4, (1), pp. 2–13
[4] GRADY, R.B., and CASWELL, D.L.: 'Software metrics: establishing a company-wide program' (Prentice-Hall Inc., 1987)
[5] DUNCAN, A.S.: 'Software development productivity tools and metrics'. Proc. 10th Int. Conf. on Software Engineering, Singapore, April 1988, pp. 41–48
[6] DALE, C.: 'The REQUEST database for software reliability and software development data' in Directorate General XIII (Eds.): 'ESPRIT '87: achievements and impact (Elsevier Science Publishers B.V., North-Holland, 1987)
[7] DOERFLINGER, C.W., and BASILI, V.R.: 'Monitoring software development through dynamic variables'. IEEE Trans., 1985, SE-11, (9), pp. 978–985
[8] KITCHENHAM, B.A., ANDERSEN, O., and KLIM, S.: 'Interpreting software metrics data: a case study'. REQUEST document R1.10.3, 1989
[9] HUMPHREY, W.S., and SWEET, W.L.: 'A method for assessing the software engineering capability of contractors'. Software Engineering Institute Technical Report CMU/SEI-87-TR-23, 1987

The author is with ElektronikCentralen, Venlighedsvej 4, DK-2970 Horsholm, Denmark.

The paper was first received on 2nd January and in revised form on 19th March 1990.

Applying Reliability Measurement: A Case Study

Willa K. Ehrlich, **S. Keith Lee**, and **Rex H. Molisani**, *AT&T Bell Laboratories*

An appropriately based reliability model can both save testing time and let you target the degree of reliability your final product will have.

In the face of changing markets and aggressive competition, many companies are discovering that the key to long-term competitive advantage is improving customer satisfaction. In terms of software-quality measurement, this implies using customer-oriented metrics to measure how fit the product is for use.

One aspect of quality that can be related directly to the customer perspective is reliability, which is the probability of failure-free program execution (like a reliability of 0.92 for eight hours of execution). Although reliability is intimately related to faults, it is not necessarily proportional to fault content.

For example, some faults may be virulent, causing failures at a high rate, while other faults may be innocuous, causing failures very infrequently. Thus, a measure of quality based on departures from requirements during dynamic program execution is especially meaningful to software-system users.[1]

Test dilemma. Reliability applies to the development process as a criterion for determining when to stop testing. The realities of large-scale industrial software production are that systems are

- developed that contain tens of thousands or even millions of lines of code,
- produced by large teams of developers, and
- situated in several locations.

These realities dictate that software engineers need to formulate precise criteria for system release. However, one of the most difficult problems in testing is knowing when to stop. If testing stops too early, many bugs remain and the development organization incurs the cost of later fault removal, the cost of operational failures, and losses due to customer dissatisfaction. If testing continues, there is the cost of testing effort and delayed product introduction.

One strategy for deciding whether to continue testing or to stop is to determine a reliability level or rate of failure occurrence

Reprinted from *IEEE Software*, Vol. 7, No. 2, March 1990, pages 56-64.

acceptable to the customer. The system's reliability is monitored throughout the system test. The system is released to the field only when the measured reliability is at or above this objective. The box on p. 60 describes two probabilistic models used in this approach.

We applied this reliability-measurement approach to test-failure data collected on Remote Measurement System-Digital 1, a large telecommunications testing system developed at AT&T Bell Laboratories, that had already gone through system test and been released to the field. The RMS-D1 failure data, which consisted of command-response errors versus commands executed, had been routinely collected by the system-test organization during testing.

The testing phase analyzed — the load test — was an operational-profile-driven test in which a controlled load was imposed on the system reflective of the system's busy-hour usage pattern. We found that it is feasible to apply the reliability-measurement approach in real time — to systems actually undergoing system test — given a controlled load-test environment.

System and test environment

To apply the reliability-measurement approach to an actual software system, it is important to understand both the system's architecture and the test phase of its development.

RMS-D1. RMS-D1 is a transmission-measurement system for remote testing of special-service circuits that are connected through a digital cross-connect system. RMS-D1 accesses a circuit directly via a 1.544-Mbit Digital Service-Level 1 facility without the need for either additional access hardware or digital-to-analog conversion equipment. As Figure 1 shows, RMS-D1 provides centralized circuit testing by letting testers at a special-services center

access and directly test digitized circuits in a distributed network.

We analyzed RMS-D1 Release 2, which provided additional test capabilities needed with a network operations system, the Switched Access Remote Test System.

Software components. The initial release of RMS-D1 contained hardware and software to perform digital testing of dataphone digital services using pseudorandom pattern generation and measurement. (These services were typically implemented with stand-alone equipment in the central office, but they are increasingly being integrated as a subrate digital capability in the digital cross-connect system.) Circuit testing was performed on a channel basis

from a digital DS-1 access. Most of the software was written in high-level languages (C and PL/M). More than 50 engineers, who were divided into four groups at the same location, designed the hardware, software, and testing functions.

RMS-D1 Release 2 augmented the hardware and software with voice-band and voice-band-data measurements from the same DS-1 access point. The new hardware generated and measured analog signals using digital-signal processors. Digital-signal-processor code was written in assembly language with controlling software in C and PL/M. Because of this distinct functionality, much of the system-control software was either new or rewritten, with a resulting code size of 275,000 lines.

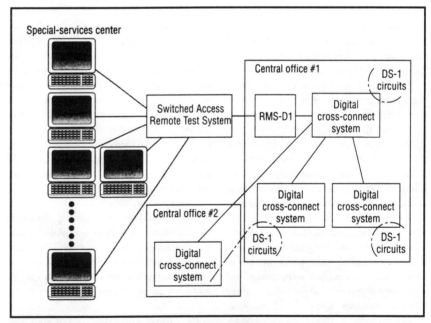

Figure 1. The RMS-D1 operational environment, including special-services-center circuit testers, Switched Access Remote Test System central controller, the remote measurement system, and digital cross-connect system. Testing can be performed between two separate central offices.

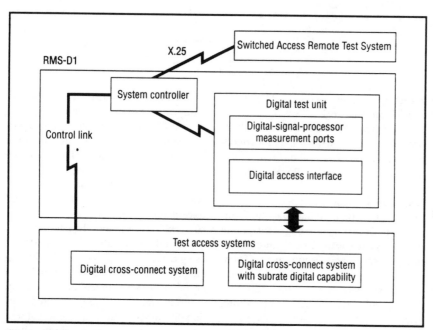

Figure 2. The RMS-D1 system architecture. This architecture embodies digital measurement technology and complete transmission and signaling capability; it is software-configurable.

Architecture. RMS-D1 is a distributed system. Its basic building blocks are the system controller and the digital test unit. Figure 2 shows the RMS-D1 architecture.

The system controller is an AT&T 3B2/400 running Unix System V with applications software. It interprets testing and access commands from a central controller (SARTS processor), performs digital-cross-connect-system access and control through a DS1 network, allocates testing resources, controls the test system's measurement resources, and administers the test system.

The digital test unit is a stand-alone cabinet, located with the digital cross-connect system, that measures signaling and transmission for digital, voice-band, and voice-band-data circuits. Software-controlled digital-signal-processor algorithms measure the transmissions. You can add measurement capabilities by modifying the software. One system controller can control as many as three digital test units.

Test process and environment. The RMS-D1 system-test phase consisted of many testing activities (including functional, regression, load, and stress), with different objectives and strategies for each.

Because the best candidates for reliability-model application are system-wide tests in which input conditions reflect field usage,[2] we selected only the load-test phase to apply the reliability-measurement approach. Load testing detects failures following prolonged system use in the expected user mode. Such testing acts as an amplifier of faults not noticeable in single cycles of features or not noticeable without interaction among features.

In our testing,

• the RMS-D1 system-test group did stand-alone load testing without the SARTS's central controller and

• the RMS-D1 and SARTS test groups jointly load-tested the system from end to end using an SARTS machine.

Tester scripts. For both types of load testing, command mixtures were based on load-test scenarios representing the RMS-D1 operational profile. (We modified the testing profiles as features were added to the system.) Each test script contained a list of commands to control the operation of RMS-D1, the digital cross-connect system, and

test circuits. We executed multiple scripts and multiple copies of scripts within a session to simulate several simultaneous users. Typical sequences of circuit-testing commands in a tester script included

• accessing a digital-cross-connect-system circuit monitor,

• setting up a local telephone monitor for a circuit,

• setting the circuit signal in the testing direction to the off-hook state,

• determining the incoming signaling states,

• transmitting a test tone,

• measuring frequency and level of incoming tone,

• removing tone and measuring residual circuit noise,

• sending a timed tone sequence to activate a loop-back and measure attenuation distortion, return loss, envelope-delay distortion, and transient measurement, and

• deactivating the loop-back and then releasing the circuit access.

RMS-D1 responded to these testing commands with measured circuit parameters or by completing normally if no measurement parameters applied.

Test configuration. Figure 3 shows the system-test configuration for both test environments.

The test configuration for stand-alone testing (Figure 3a) consisted of a test driver simulating an SARTS (the dynamic test system), system controller, digital test unit, digital-cross-connect-system software simulator, and test-circuit hardware simulator to simulate network configurations providing a test-access facility (a DS-1 signal) to the digital-test unit.

The test configuration for end-to-end testing (Figure 3b) consisted of an SARTS driver simulating testers (a test-point position simulator or controller), an SARTS central controller (a Digital Equipment Corp. VAX 11/780), system controller, digital test unit, and digital cross-connect system.

Failure definition. We defined load-test failures in terms of both incorrect command responses and error messages. (The RMS-D1 application software generated the error messages in response to testing commands.) The SARTS or the software simu-

460

lator used in the stand-alone test configuration recorded these errors. A preprocessing routine (a Unix shell program) reported errors; it distinguished normal command responses with valid measurement parameters from abnormal command responses containing either invalid measurement parameters or failure codes.

Abnormal command responses could indicate total system failure (like an RMS-D1 system crash, where reinitialization is required), partial RMS-D1 system failure (like a failure of an application process resulting in the loss of system messages or invalid measurement results), or isolated system failure (like a failure of an application process or subsystem that interfered with the work of a restricted group of users). However, we did not distinguish such failure-severity levels in our analysis because severity levels had not been recorded during load testing.

Fault correction. AT&T developers repaired faults causing application-generated error messages and abnormal command responses as quickly as possible so software corrections would be included in the next formal test version of the system. System testers functionally tested each internal release and then used regression testing to assure that no additional faults arose from our code fixes.

We ran load tests only after the release successfully passed these tests. Each load test ran for an average of eight hours at a rate of more than 1,200 commands per hour. The number of load-test sessions conducted on an formal test version varied, averaging five load tests. We analyzed 19 formal system-test releases in the study reported here

Reliability modeling

To document the value of using the reliability-measurement approach techniques during the RMS-D1 load test, we analyzed reliability for *historical* RMS-D1 Release 2 load-test data (which was collected between May 1987 and November 1987). The intent of this analysis was to evaluate the predictive validity of the reliability-measurement approach using a product that had already gone through system test.

The analysis entailed fitting the exponential nonhomogeneous Poisson process

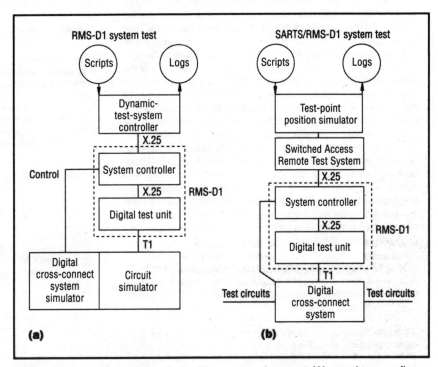

Figure 3. The RMS-D1 Release 2 system-test environment. We used two configurations: **(a)** one that simulated the Switched Access Remote Test System's central controller and **(b)** one that simulated multiple special-services-center testers. For both configurations, we performed system-wide testing for extended periods with command mixtures based on expected field activity.

model at several points during RMS-D1 Release 2 load test and validating the accuracy of the model's predictions.

We selected the exponential process model because it applies to a wide range of execution environments used in testing large and complex industrial software systems. At AT&T, this model had been applied to other development projects with considerable success.

The exponential process model assumes that faults contribute about equally to overall failure intensity, so the repair of each fault likewise contributes equally to the overall failure intensity.

Strategy. To use the reliability-measurement approach as a criterion for ending system test, you must first establish a failure-intensity objective. Because RMS-D1 Release 2 had already completed system test, we used a hypothetical (but realistic) failure-intensity objective of 0.010 failures per commands executed.

To establish the exponential process model's predictive accuracy, our next step was to statistically fit the model over six intervals in the RMS-D1 load test. For each interval, we obtained model-parameter estimates and used them to generate the model's fitted failure counts for each interval. We also used model fitting for a particular interval to predict future failure behavior, as well as the additional test time required to attain the failure-intensity objective.

We used model fitting over two consecutive intervals to assess model stability. Our rationale was that if the exponential process model was a stable model, the failure-intensity curve derived from early load-test failures should be similar to the failure-intensity curve based on a larger set of load-test failures. Thus, by fitting the exponential process model at several points during load test, we could evaluate model stability as well as the accuracy of the model's predictions.

Software-reliability measurement

A widely accepted definition of software reliability is the probability that a program performs its defined purpose satisfactorily (without failure) over a specified time in a particular execution environment. The execution environment is known formally as the "operational profile," which is defined in terms of sets of possible input values and their probabilities of occurrence. Failures are assumed to occur probabilistically over time according to a certain rate of failure occurrence (failure intensity). Failure intensity relates directly to reliability or the probability of failure-free program performance over some time.[1]

In one important class of reliability models, the number of failures observed in the time interval $(0,t)$ is assumed to be generated by a Poisson process (the probability that exactly y failures will be observed by time t is given by a Poisson probability distribution).

If the assumptions of a Poisson process are satisfied, a homogeneous Poisson process — a constant-failure-intensity model — characterizes an executing program's failure behavior during field operations, in between field releases, caused by the absence of debugging and fault correction. By contrast, a *non*homogeneous Poisson process model with a decreasing failure intensity function — a reliability-growth model — applies when corrections are made in response to failures, like during system test.

Example models. For example, in one reliability-growth model, the exponential nonhomogeneous Poisson process model or failure intensity, $\lambda(t)$, is expressed through parameters as a family of exponentially decreasing functions over time,

$$\lambda(t) = \lambda_0 \exp\left(-\frac{\lambda_0}{v_0}t\right)$$

so the mean cumulative number of failures, $\mu(t)$, increases exponentially to an asymptote with time:

$$\mu(t) = \int_0^t \lambda(s)\,ds = v_0\left[1-\exp\left(-\frac{\lambda_0}{v_0}t\right)\right]$$

In another reliability-growth model,[2] the logarithmic nonhomogeneous Poisson process model, failure intensity is a family of inverse linear functions with respect to time:

$$\lambda(t) = \frac{\lambda_0}{\lambda_0\theta t+1}$$

such that the expected cumulative number of failures is a logarithmic function of time:

$$\mu(t) = \int_0^t \lambda(s)\,ds = \frac{1}{\theta}\ln(\lambda_0\theta t+1)$$

Figure A presents an example of a reliability-growth nonhomogeneous Poisson process model, the exponential nonhomogeneous Poisson process model used in the study reported in the main text. The failure intensity (rate of failures) decreases exponentially with execution time, while the expected cumulative number of failures increases exponentially to an asymptote with time.

Example application. Figure B shows how you can apply the reliability-measurement approach during system test.

Assume that a project is in system test and a reliability objective, in terms of a rate of failure occurrence, has been established. The project is using a certification approach to testing software in which testers statistically select and present test cases to quantify the system's reliability from the customers' point of view.[3] Failure data on execution time is collected in the form of number of failures occurring per unit of time.

If you plot the observed failure rate as a function of cumulative execution time since start of system test (see Figure B), you can statistically fit a reliability model to the data points and then plot the fitted failure-intensity curve. You can then plot the fitted failure-intensity curve to answer the following questions:

• What is the estimated failure intensity at this point in system test?
• Is the estimated failure intensity less than or equal to the failure-intensity objective? (If so, the system can be released.)
• If the estimated failure intensity exceeds the objective, how much additional test resources must be expended to attain the objective?

References

1. H. Ascher and H. Feingold, *Repairable Systems Reliability: Modeling, Inference, Misconceptions, and Their Causes*, Marcel Dekker, New York, 1984.
2. J.D. Musa, A. Iannino and K. Okumoto, *Software Reliability: Measurement, Prediction, Application*, McGraw-Hill, New York, 1987.
3. P.A. Currit, M. Dyer and H.S. Mills, "Certifying the Reliability of Software," *IEEE Trans. Software Eng.*, Jan. 1986, pp. 3-11.

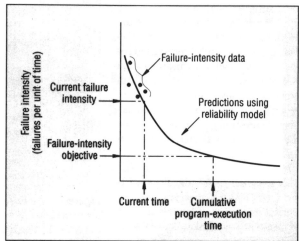

Figure A. A reliability-growth model based on an exponential nonhomogeneous Poisson process model in which the instantaneous rate of failure occurrence or failure intensity decreases exponentially with program-execution time while the expected cumulative number of failures increases exponentially to an asymptote with execution time.

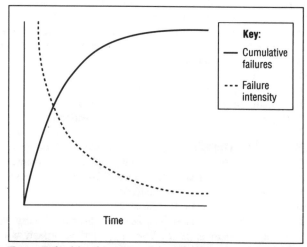

Figure B. Applying the exponential-process-based model to system test. A release criteria has been specified in terms of a certain failure-intensity (reliability) objective and failure data is collected against execution time. An exponential process model is fit to observed failure rates. The fitted model is then used to estimate failure intensity as well as additional execution time required to attain the failure-intensity objective.

The model-fitting strategy was to

- establish a (hypothetical) failure-intensity objective (0.010 error messages per command executed),
- fit our exponential process model at 25, 50, 60, 70, 80, and 100 percent of the way into load testing,
- get estimates of exponential-process-model parameters,
- generate a predicted-reliability curve,
- determine the exponential process model's adequacy, and
- determine the exponential process model's predictive power.

Data collected. The RMS-D1 load-test failure data we analyzed was the number of abnormal command responses attributed to code executing on the system controller versus the number of commands executed per load-test session for both stand-alone and end-to-end testing.

We did not differentiate abnormal command responses documenting total, partial, and isolated RMS-D1 system failures in the reliability modeling because these data had not been collected initially. We eliminated from the count command responses reflecting invalid external conditions, test-configuration set-up problems, and simulator-induced problems.

We then expressed the adjusted failure counts as a function of cumulative adjusted commands.

Model fitting. We used maximum-likelihood estimation to estimate the exponential process model's parameters. We then used these parameter estimates to generate the model's fitted failure counts (the expected cumulative number of failures as a function of time) and the instantaneous rate of failure occurrence.

To determine the model's adequacy, we used regression analysis to directly fit the failure-intensity function. We first expressed the exponential process model in linear form $y = \beta_0 + \beta_1 t$ by transforming the exponentially decreasing failure-intensity function (see the box on p. 60 for mathematical descriptions) to

$$\log(\lambda(t)) = \log\lambda_0 - \frac{\lambda_0}{v_0} t$$

Because fault correction did not occur

in each of the 19 internal test releases, we could model failure behavior in such an interval as a *homogeneous* Poisson process. You can directly estimate the constant failure rate λ for an internal test release as $\hat{\lambda} = n_0 / t_0$, where n_0 is the number of failures during the testing of the internal system release and t_0 is the number of commands executed when testing that internal release. Because fault correction takes place between any two consecutive formal test versions, the estimated failure rate $\hat{\lambda}$ varies from internal test release to internal test release and can be modeled by

$$y = \log(\hat{\lambda}) = \log\lambda_0 - \frac{\lambda_0}{v_0} t$$

The quantity t is the cumulative command usage. You can then get least-squares estimates of β_0 and β_1 by regressing the estimated transformed failure intensities on t. You can then evaluate the explained variation in the estimated transformed failure-intensity values (the R^2 "goodness of fit" value).

Because the variances of the transformed failure intensities are not equal (for example, failure intensity based on longer test intervals will have less variation than that based on shorter test intervals), the ordinary least-squares estimation formula does not apply, so you must amend the least-squares procedure.[3] Therefore, we weighted the estimated transformed failure-intensity values by quantities inversely proportional to their variances and then applied a regression analysis.

By applying standard regression methods, we were able to examine the adequacy of the exponential reliability-growth model in describing RMS-D1's rate of failure occurrence. We fit the exponential nonhomogeneous Poisson process model at six intervals during RMS-D1

load testing: at 25-percent (230,297 commands executed), 50-percent (464,537 commands), 60-percent (586,198 commands), 70-percent (646,088 commands), 80-percent (779,114 commands), and 100-percent (945,773 commands) completion of the load test.

Results

Figures 4 through 9 show both the fitted cumulative failure counts for the exponential process model, together with the observed failure counts, and the failure-intensity curve versus the time curve for each of the six intervals analyzed.

Preliminary analysis indicated that the exponential process model provided a better fit to RMS-D1 load-test data than the logarithmic process model (another reliability-growth model described in the box on p. 60). Thus, the proportion of variation in the transformed failure intensities that could be explained by an exponential process model was higher (R^2 equaled 0.6611) than that explained by the logarithmic process model (R^2 equaled 0.2702). This supports our decision to consider only the exponential process model.

25 percent into test. Figure 4 shows the results of applying the exponential process model to failures observed from the start of RMS-D1 load test to where a fourth of the load-test commands have been executed (after 11 internal releases). The exponential process weighted least-squares regression analysis yielded an R^2 of 0.0522, indicating that the model does not accurately describe the observed failure data.

At 25 percent into system testing, the model indicates that the estimated failure intensity is 0.100 failures per command executed (Figure 4b), so, given a failure-intensity objective of 0.010 failures per com-

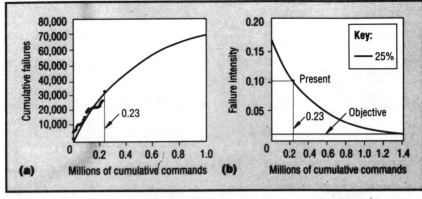

Figure 4. Applying the exponential nonhomogeneous Poisson process model to RMS-D1's load test when **(a)** a fourth of the commands have been executed. **(b)** At 25 percent into load test, the estimated failure intensity is 0.110 failures per command executed.

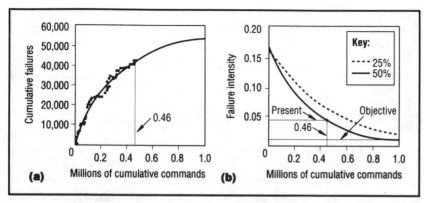

Figure 5. Applying the exponential process model to RMS-D1's load test when **(a)** half the commands have been executed. **(b)** At 50 percent into load test, the estimated failure intensity is 0.040 failures per command executed.

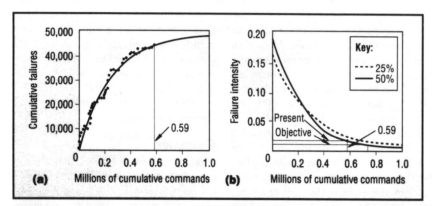

Figure 6. Applying the exponential process model to RMS-D1's load test when **(a)** 60 percent of the commands have been executed. **(b)** At 60 percent into load test, the estimated failure intensity is 0.019 failures per command executed. Also at this point, the model's predictive accuracy became acceptable.

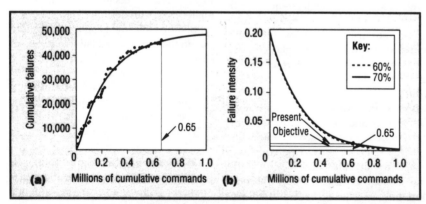

Figure 7. Applying the exponential process model to RMS-D1's load test when **(a)** 70 percent of the commands have been executed. **(b)** At 70 percent into system test, the estimated failure intensity is 0.015 failures per command executed.

mand, the exponential process model would dictate that the RMS-D1 product remain in system test, with a total testing effort of 1.39 million commands (with corresponding debugging) from start of load test required to meet the product-reliability objective.

50 percent into test. Figure 5 shows the results of fitting the exponential process model to failures found when half the load-test commands have been executed (after 13 internal releases). The R^2 value is 0.4451, indicating that the model has improved in descriptive adequacy.

Half way into system test, the exponential process model yielded an estimated failure intensity of 0.040 failures per command executed (the solid curve in Figure 5b). Because the estimated failure intensity is greater than the objective (0.010 failures), a reliability-measurement-approach release criteria would dictate that, if this were being performed in real time, RMS-D1 remain in system test so additional program execution and debugging could occur. It predicts a test effort of 0.94 million commands to attain the objective of 0.010 failures per command.

The dashed failure-intensity-versus-time curve shown in Figure 5b represents the failure-intensity curve derived from 25 percent of the data. Clearly, the two curves differ, which is due to differences in the fitted model parameters. In addition, the earlier predicted test expenditure (1.39 million commands) is clearly different from the current predicted test expenditure of 0.94 million commands. These results indicate lack of predictive validity of the model based on the 25-percent data. You might expect this, considering that we were so early in the test process when we analyzed the first period.

60 percent into test. Figure 6 shows the results of fitting the exponential process model to when 60 percent of the commands have been executed (after 15 internal releases). The R^2 value is 0.5417, indicating that the exponential process model provides a reasonably adequate fit to the data. The estimated failure intensity is 0.019 failures per command executed (the solid curve in Figure 6b), so again the release criteria would require that RMS-D1 remain in system test.

The failure-intensity curve derived midway into system test (the dashed curve in Figure 6b) approximates the failure-intensity curve derived at 60 percent into system test. The estimated total test effort required to achieve the failure-intensity objective derived at 50 percent into test (0.94 million commands) corresponds more closely to the current estimate (0.74 million commands) than the preceding model fitting.

70 percent into test. At 70 percent into system test (after 16 internal releases), the estimated failure intensity is about 0.015

failures per command executed (the solid curve in Figure 7b), implying that the system-test organization is approaching the hypothetical failure-intensity objective. The R^2 value is 0.5818. The failure-intensity curve derived at 60 percent into system test (the dashed curve in Figure 7b) is virtually identical to the failure-intensity curve derived at 70 percent into system test.

In addition, the earlier estimate of total test effort to achieve the failure-intensity objective of 0.01 failures per command executed — 0.74 million commands — agrees with the current estimate of 0.74 million commands. These findings are encouraging, since they indicate that the exponential process model possesses both descriptive adequacy and predictive capability 60 percent of the way into test.

80 percent into test. Figure 8 shows the results of exponential process model at 80 percent into load test (after 18 internal releases). The R^2 value is 0.6161, indicating a relatively good model fit. The reliability model gives an estimated failure intensity of 0.009 failures per command executed (the solid curve in Figure 8b), implying that the system-test organization had achieved the hypothetical failure-intensity objective. Thus, the RMS-D1 product could now be released to the field given the 0.010 reliability release criteria.

The failure-intensity curve derived at 70 percent into system test (the dashed curve in Figure 8b) is indistinguishable from the exponential-process-model curve derived 80 percent into load test. In addition, the earlier estimate of total test effort (0.74 million commands) required to achieve the failure intensity matches the current estimate of 0.74 million commands.

Test completion. Figure 9 shows the results of applying the exponential process model to all the RMS-D1 load-test failure data (after all 19 internal releases). The R^2 value is 0.6611, implying that the model possesses descriptive adequacy. The estimated failure intensity at end of system test (the solid curve in Figure 9b) is 0.004 failures per command executed.

In terms of the failure-intensity objective of 0.010 failures per command executed, RMS-D1 Release 2 clearly exceeded this reliability objective when released by the sys-

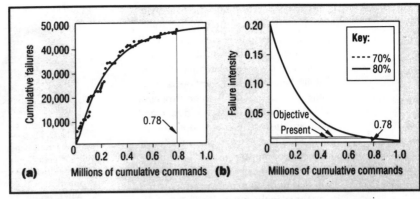

Figure 8. Applying the exponential process model to RMS-D1's load test when **(a)** 80 percent of the commands have been executed. **(b)** At 80 percent into system test, the estimated failure intensity is 0.009 failures per command executed — less than the 0.010 target for release from testing.

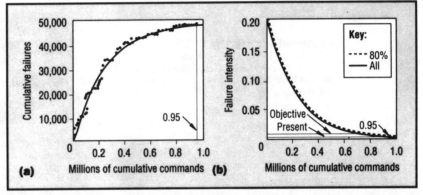

Figure 9. Applying the exponential process model to **(a)** the entire RMS-D1 load test.**(b)** At end of system test, the estimated failure intensity is 0.004 failures per command executed.

tem-test organization. Also, you would expect that when RMS-D1 was released to the field, it would have a failure intensity of 0.004 failures per command executed. (Field data was not available to us.)

In terms of the predictive validity of the exponential process model, the failure-intensity curve is virtually indistinguishable from the failure-intensity curve derived at the 80-percent point in system test (the dashed line in Figure 9b). In addition, the estimated test effort — 0.74 million commands — required to attain the failure-intensity objective also agreed with the 80-percent estimate. These findings attest to the descriptive adequacy and predictive capability of the exponential process model.

Our study shows that an exponential process model had predictive validity for RMS-D1 Release 2 as early as 60 percent into system test. We believe this work has two major implications for software development.

First, for projects that are trying to *use* customer-based metrics, it is possible to

monitor and measure quality from the customer's point of view by analyzing failure occurrences during a controlled type of testing like load testing. Thus, you can apply the reliability-measurement approach in real time if you test in a controlled environment.

In fact, we successfully applied the reliability-measurement approach in real time to an AT&T Bell Laboratories network-management system, which monitors a telemetry network. We tested this system in a controlled environment consisting of a command mix and alarm rate characteristic of the system's typical busy hour.

Second, this work indicates the need to extend the reliability-measurement approach to customer environments *not* being tested in the system laboratory. Most system testing is performed in an environment designed to simulate actual field conditions. Although such a test model is equipped for testing different field configurations, it is impractical to implement and test *all* possible usage patterns.

For software systems that are not tested

against a specific customer's field environment, it is conceivable that the reliability experienced in this field environment will differ from that measured during test. Thus, we still need a way to relate or transform reliability behavior under a test operational profile into the reliability to be expected when the program is released and executed under an alternative (field) operational profile, without actually testing the software in this environment.

Extending the reliability-measurement approach to customer environments not being tested in the system laboratory is extremely desirable because it would let software engineers estimate — during testing — reliability under different usage patterns without incurring the cost of retesting the system in these different environments. ❖

Acknowledgments

We thank Harvey Cohen, Audrey Curtis, Howie Gittleson, Harvey Lieber, Jim McDonald, and Vince Peck for their support and help with this work.

References

1. J.D. Musa, "Tools for Measuring Software Reliability," *IEEE Spectrum*, Feb. 1989, pp. 39-42; correction, April 1989, p. 8.

2. W.K. Ehrlich and T.J. Emerson, "Modeling Software Failures and Reliability Growth During System Testing," *Proc. Ninth Int'l Conf. Software Eng.*, CS Press, Los Alamitos, Calif., 1987, pp. 72-82.

3. N.R. Draper and H. Smith, *Applied Regression Analysis*, second ed., John Wiley & Sons, New York, 1981.

Willa K. Ehrlich is a technical staff member at AT&T Bell Laboratories. She has studied software measurement and reliability for several large development projects, including transmission measurement, network management, and real-time operating systems. Her research interests include the effect of test strategy on software-reliability measurement and the use of formal methods for requirements specifications.

Ehrlich received a PhD in psychology from the University of Minnesota.

S. Keith Lee is a technical supervisor at AT&T Bell Laboratories. He has worked on systems engineering and product quality for customer-premise equipment and software quality for operations-systems products. His work interests include planning and implementing software-quality technologies.

Lee received a BS in physics from Chinese University of Hong Kong, an MA in physics from City College of New York, and a PhD in statistics from the University of Minnesota.

Rex H. Molisani is a technical staff member in the Network Services Assurance Laboratory at AT&T Bell Laboratories, where he has designed hardware and software for local-access functions of the RMS product line. His work interests include system testing and quality assurance.

Molisani received a BE in electrical engineering from Cooper Union University and an MS in electrical engineering from Cornell University. He is a member of the IEEE.

Address questions about this article to Ehrlich at AT&T Bell Labs, Crawford Corner Rd., Holmdel, NJ 07733-1988.

Software Metrics in the Process Maturity Framework

Shari Lawrence Pfleeger and Clement McGowan

The Contel Technology Center's Software Engineering Laboratory (SEL) has as one of its goals the improvement of software productivity and quality throughout Contel Corporation. The SEL's Process and Metrics Project addresses that goal in part by recommending metrics to be collected on each software development project throughout the corporation. This article suggests a set of metrics for which data are to be collected and analyzed, based on a process maturity framework developed at the Software Engineering Institute. Metrics are to be implemented step by step in five levels, corresponding to the maturity level of the development process. Level 1 metrics provide a baseline for comparison as improvements are sought. Level 2 metrics focus on project management. At the third level, metrics measure the products produced during development, while level 4 metrics capture characteristics of the development process itself to allow control of the process. Finally, the feedback loops of level 5's process metrics permit the metrics to be used to change and improve the development process.

1. INTRODUCTION

Dozens, if not hundreds, of software metrics are described in the software engineering literature [1]. The metrics chosen for a particular project play a major role in the degree to which the project can be controlled, but deciding which metrics to use is difficult. We can evaluate the purpose and utility of each metric only in light of the needs and desires of the development organization. Thus, we should collect data and analyze software metrics in the broad context of the software development process and with an eye toward understanding and improvement. It is for this reason that we at the Contel Technology Center's Software Engineering Laboratory have chosen a process maturity framework in which to place software metrics. Originating at the Software Engineering Institute, process maturity [2] describes a set of maturity levels at which an organization's development process takes place. Only when the

development process possesses sufficient structure and procedures does it make sense to collect certain kinds of metrics.

Thus, rather than recommend a large (and probably unwiedly) set of metrics to collect for each project throughout an organization, we recommend that metrics be divided into five levels, where each level is based on the amount of information made available by the development process. As the development process matures and improves, additional metrics can be collected and analyzed. In turn, the new information derived from the metrics allows the process to be controlled and enhanced. Thus, metrics collection begins at maturity level 1, moving on to the other levels only when dictated by a process that can support it.

This article explores the idea of process maturity and explains how process maturity levels are integrated naturally with metrics collection. We give examples of metrics at level, and we describe how the process and metrics program is working at Contel to improve the quality of our software.

2. PROCESS MATURITY LEVELS

The concept of process maturity is based on the notion that some development processes provide more structure or control than others. In effect, as certain characteristic process problems are solved by process methods and tools (e.g., configuration management), the process matures and can focus on other problems. Thus, maturity provides a framework in which to depict the several types of processes and to evaluate what kinds of metrics are best suited for collection in each type. The metrics, in concert with a variety of tools, techniques, and methods, are used to improve the process, increase the maturity level, and allow additional metrics collection to take place.

Figure 1 depicts the five levels of process and their characteristics. Assessing or determining the level of process maturity is the first step in deciding what metrics to collect.

Address correspondence to Shari Lawrence Pfleeger, Contel Technology Center, 15000 Conference Center Drive, P.O. Box 10814, Chantilly, VA 22021-3808.

© Elsevier Science Publishing Co., Inc.
655 Avenue of the Americas, New York, NY 10010

Reprinted by permission of the publisher from "Software Metrics in the Process Maturity Framework", by S.L. Pfleeger and C. McGowan, *Journal of Systems and Software*, Vol. 12, No. 3, July, 1990, pp. 255-262. Copyright 1990 by Elsevier Science Publishing Co., Inc.

Level	Characteristics	Metrics to Use
5. Optimizing	Improvement fed back to process	Process + feedback for changing process
4. Managed	Measured process (quantitative)	Process + feedback for control
3. Defined	Process defined, institutionalized	Product
2. Repeatable	Process dependent on individuals	Project
1. Initial	Ad hoc	Baseline

Figure 1. Process maturity levels related to metrics.

2.1 Level 1: Initial Process

The first level of process is termed *initial* and is characterized by an ad hoc approach to the software development process. That is, the inputs to the process are ill-defined, the outputs are expected, but the transition from inputs to outputs is undefined and uncontrolled. Similar projects may vary widely in their productivity and quality characteristics, because of lack of adequate structure and control. For this level of process maturity, the collection of metrics is difficult. Preliminary "baseline" project metrics should be gathered at this level to form a basis for comparison as improvements are made and maturity increases. The degree of improvement can be demonstrated in part by comparing new project measurements with the baseline ones. For example, initial measurements can be made of product size and staff effort, to determine a baseline rate of productivity; this rate can be compared with similar rates on subsequent projects. However, rather than concentrate on metrics and their meanings, the developers using a level 1 process should focus on imposing more structure and control on the process itself.

2.2 Level 2: Repeatable Process

The second process level, called *repeatable*, identifies inputs, outputs and, constraints. The requirements act as input, the code is output, and typical constraints are budget and schedule limits. The process is repeatable in the same way that a subroutine is repeatable: Proper inputs produce proper outputs, but we have no visibility into how the outputs are produced. Figure 2 depicts a repeatable process as an SADT diagram, where the incoming arrow on the left shows the input, the outgoing arrow on the right the output, and the arrow from the top the control or constraints. For example, the requirements may be the input to the process, with the software system as output. The control arrow represents constraints, such as schedule, budget, tools, standards, and other management control directives.

Only project-related metrics make sense at this level, since the activities within the actual transition from input to output are not available to be measured. Figure 3 illustrates the types of measures that make sense by associating measurable characteristics with each arrow. Notice that an additional arrow has been placed below the box to represent the personnel working on the project. Thus, for a repeatable process, we can measure the amount of effort needed to develop a system, the duration of the project, the size and volatility of the requirements, and the overall project cost, for example. The output can be measured in terms of its physical or functional size, and the resources used to produce that output can be viewed relative to size to compute productivity.

At Contel, we recommend that development organizations at the repeatable level include the following types of measures (the italicized metrics are examples of measures at this level; the metrics are defined and explained

Figure 2. SADT diagram of repeatable process.

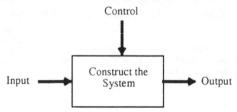

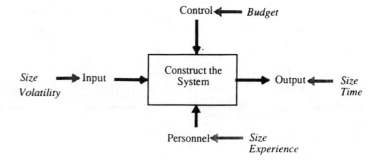

Figure 3. Measures for a repeatable process.

in detail in a technical report [3]):

- Software Size
  Noncommented source lines of code
  Function points
  Object and method count
- Personnel Effort
  Actual person-months of effort
  Reported person-months of effort
- Requirements Volatility
  Requirements changes

Several additional metrics may be desirable, depending on the characteristics of the project and the needs of project management. Many studies of project cost indicate that relevant technical experience and employee turnover can have a significant impact on overall project cost. Thus, the following items can be added to the level 2 metrics set at the discretion of management.

- Experience
  With domain/application
  With development architecture
  With tools/methods
  Overall years of experience
- Employee turnover

2.3 Level 3: Defined Process

The third process maturity level is called *defined*, because the activities of the process are clearly defined with entry and exit conditions, as depicted in Figure 4.

This additional structure means that we can examine the input to and output from each well-defined functional activity performed during development. That is, the intermediate products of development are well-defined and visible. This characteristic of the process allows us to measure characteristics of the intermediate products. Thus, the box of Figure 2 can be decomposed to view the activities necessary to construct the final system. Figure 4 describes three typical activities: design, build parts, and assemble. However, different processes may be partitioned into more distinct functions or activities. Figure 5 is an example of a simplified diagram suggesting the details of input, output, and control for each activity in a defined process.

Because the activities are delineated and distinguished from one another, the products from each activity can be measured and assessed, as shown in Figure 6. In particular, project managers can look at the complexity of each product. That is, we can examine the complexity of the requirements, design, code, and test plans, and assess the quality of the requirements, design, code, and testing.

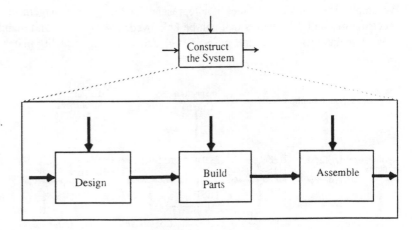

Figure 4. SADT diagram of defined process.

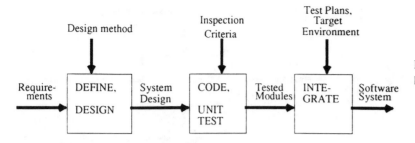

Figure 5. Example of a particular defined process.

In terms of complexity, we suggest that the following items be measured for a defined process:

- Requirements complexity
  Number of distinct objects and actions addressed in requirements
- Design complexity
  Number of design modules
  Cyclomatic complexity
  McCabe design complexity
- Code complexity
  Number of code modules
  Cyclomatic complexity
- Test complexity
  Number of paths to test
  If object-oriented development, number of object interfaces to test

One perspective from which to view the quality of the products is examination of the number of faults in each product and the density of defects overall. In addition, we can assess the thoroughness of testing. Thus, our recommended quality metrics include:

- Defects discovered
- Defects discovered per unit size (defect density)
- Requirements faults discovered
- Design faults discovered
- Code faults discovered
- Fault density for each product

We emphasize that this set does not represent the full spectrum of quality measures that can be employed. Issues of maintainability, utility, ease of use, and other aspects of quality software are not addressed by defect counts. However, defect analysis is relative easy to implement, and it provides a wide spectrum of useful information about the reliability of the software and the thoroughness of testing.

An additional product metric may be desirable. When customer requirements dictate that significant amounts of documentation be written (as often happens on government contracts), the number of pages of documentation may be a desirable measure to track and correlate with effort or duration. Thus, the set of product metrics may also include:

- Pages of documentation

2.4 Level 4: Managed Process

The *managed* process is the fourth level of maturity. Here, feedback from early project activities (e.g., problem areas discovered in design) can be used to set priorities for later project activities (e.g., more extensive review and testing of certain code). Because activities can be compared and contrasted, the effects of changes in one activity can be tracked in the others. In a managed process, the feedback determines how resources are deployed; the basic activities themselves do not change. As shown in Figure 7, this level allows measurements to be made across activities. For example, we can measure and evaluate the effects of major process factors such as reuse, defect-driven testing, and configuration management. The measures collected are used to control and stabilize the process, so that productivity and quality match expectations.

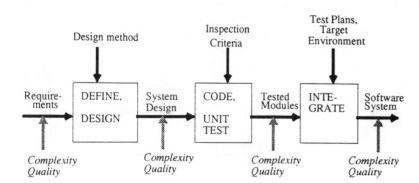

Figure 6. Measures for a particular defined process.

470

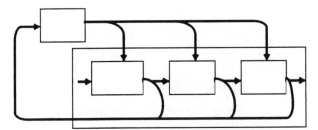

Figure 7. SADT diagram of managed process.

Figure 8 illustrates how a particular managed process might took. Metrics are used in feedback loops to report on the number of design defects and on the number and types of problems encountered with specific versions of the system. Then, project management uses the metrics information to make decisions about course corrections.

If the maturity of the process has reached the managed level, then process-wide metrics can be collected and analyzed. These metrics reflect characteristics of the overall process and of the interaction among major activities in the process, as shown in Figure 9. A distinguishing characteristic of a managed process is that the software development can be carefully controlled. Thus, a major characteristic of the recommended metrics is that they help management control the development process.

We recommend that the following types of data be collected for a managed process. In some cases, the actual metrics must be defined and analyzed to suit the development organization.

Process type. What process model is used in development? For example, the waterfall, prototype, and transformational development paradigms are very different. In concert with other product and process characteristics, the type of process may correlate highly with certain positive or negative consequences.

Amount of producer reuse. How much is designed for reuse? This measure includes reuse of requirements, design modules, and test plans as well as code. By de-

signing components for reuse, one project group may benefit from the effort of another group. Effort in understanding, creating, and testing code can be minimized, thus making the project easier to control. Furthermore, future projects can benefit from the reuse of components produced here.

Amount of consumer reuse. How much does the project reuse components from other projects? This measure includes reuse of requirements, design modules, and test plans as well as code. By using tested, proven components, effort can be minimized and quality can be improved.

Defect identification. How and when are defects discovered? Knowing whether defects are discovered during requirements reviews, design reviews, code walkthroughs, and reviews, integration testing or acceptance testing will tell us whether those process activities are effective.

Use of defect density model for testing. To what extent does the number of defects determine when testing is complete? Many organizations have no overall defect goals for testing the product. Thus, there is no way to judge the quality either of the testing or of the code. The use of defect density models has been shown to control and focus testing, as well as to increase the quality of the final product.

Use of configuration management. Is a configuration management scheme imposed on the development process? Configuration management and change control work to afford management a great deal of control over the development process. Traceability links can be used to assess the impact of alterations in some or all development activities or products.

Module completion over time. At what rates are modules being completed? Although ostensibly a prod-

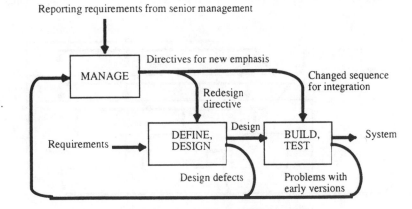

Figure 8. Example of a managed process.

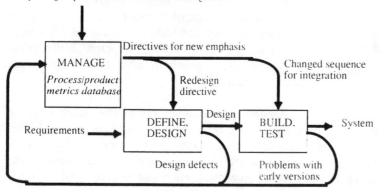

Reporting requirements from senior management

MANAGE
Process/product metrics database

Directives for new emphasis

Changed sequence for integration

Redesign directive

Requirements

DEFINE, DESIGN

Design

BUILD, TEST

System

Design defects

Problems with early versions

Distribution of defects, productivity of tasks, plans vs. actuals, resource allocation

Figure 9. Measures in a managed process.

uct metric, the rate at which modules are identified, designed, coded, tested, and integrated reflects the degree to which the process and development environment facilitate implementation and testing. If the rate is slow, the process may need improvement.

All of the process metrics described above are to be used in concert with the metrics discussed in earlier sections. Relationships can be determined between product characteristics and process variables to assess whether certain processes or aspects of the process are effective at meeting productivity or quality goals. The list of process measures is by no means complete. It is suggested only as an initial attempt to capture important information about the process itself.

2.5 Level 5: Optimizing Process

An *optimizing* process is the ultimate level of process maturity; it is depicted in Figure 10. Here, measures from activities are used to change and improve the process. This process change can affect the organization and the project as well. Results from one or more ongoing or completed projects may lead to a refined, different development process for future projects. In addition, a project may change its process before project completion, in response to feedback from early activities. The spiral model of development is such a process [5].

This dynamic tailoring of the process to the situation is indicated in the figure by the collection of process boxes labeled $T_0, T_1, \ldots, T_n$. At time T_0, the process is as represented by box T_0. However, at time T_i, management has the option of revising or changing the overall process. For example, the project manager may begin development with a standard waterfall approach. As requirements are defined and design is begun, metrics may indicate a high degree of uncertainty in the requirements. Based on this information, the process may change to one that prototypes the requirements and the design, so that we can resolve some of the uncertainty before substantial investment is made in implementation of the current design. In this way, an optimizing process gives maximum flexibility to the development. Metrics act as sensors and monitors, and the process is not only under control but is dynamic, too.

Studies by the Software Engineering Institute of 113 software development projects report that 85% of those surveyed were at level 1, 14% were at level 2, and 1% were at level 3. That is, none of the development projects had reached levels 4 or 5: the managed or optimizing levels. Based on these results, and the highly unlikely prospect of finding a level 5 project, our recommendations for initial metrics include only the first four levels.

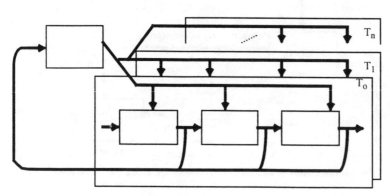

T_n

T_1

T_0

Figure 10. SADT diagram of optimizing process.

3. STEPS TO TAKE IN USING METRICS

Metrics are most useful only when implemented in a careful sequence of process-related activities. These activities lay the groundwork for effective project management by evaluating the needs and characteristics of development before identifying the appropriate metrics to collect. The typical development organization should take the following steps:

Assess the process. Working with a set of guidelines or with a process and metrics team, determine the level of process maturity desired (for a proposed project) or implemented (for an ongoing one).

Determine the appropriate metrics to collect. Once the process maturity level is known, decide which metrics to collect. For example, if level 2 is indicated by the process level, but the ongoing project currently collects no metrics data at all, then level 1 metrics may be suggested as a starting point, with level 2 metrics to be added at a later time.

Recommend metrics, tools, techniques. When the types of metrics are determined, identify tools and techniques to be used on the project. Choose these tools and techniques with the overall goals of the project in mind. Whenever possible, implement automated support for metrics collection and analysis as part of the project development environment. It is essential that metrics collection and analysis not impede the primary development activities; thus, metrics collection and analysis should be as unobtrusive as possible.

Estimate project cost and schedule. Having determined the process level and selected the development environment, estimate the cost and schedule of the project. By using measures implemented at levels 1 or 2, continue to monitor the actual cost and schedule during development.

Collect appropriate level of metrics. Oversee the collection of metrics.

Construct project data base. Design, develop and populate a project data base of metrics data. This data base can be used for analysis, where appropriate. Track the value of metrics over time, as recommended by Schultz [4] and others, to determine trends and to understand how project and product characteristics change.

Cost and schedule evaluation. When the project is complete, evaluate the initial estimates of cost and schedule for accuracy. Determine which of the factors may account for discrepancies between predicted and actual values.

Evaluate productivity and quality. Make an overall assessment of project productivity and product quality, based on the metrics available.

Form a basis for future estimates. Finally, incorporate the project metrics in a corporate or organizational metrics data base. This larger data base can provide historical information as a basis for estimation on future projects. In addition, the data base can be used to suggest the most appropriate tools and techniques for proposed projects.

We are following these steps today at Contel. As a result of our process and metrics program, a large Ada development project is collecting complexity information using automated tools. A tool development project using Objective C is counting objects and methods to track the size of the project; defects and their severity levels are also being monitored to assess the level of product quality. Likewise, satellite and telephone operations development groups are looking at a process maturity-based metrics approach to aid decisions about productivity and quality. Eventually, our corporate metrics data base will allow project managers to make decisions based on evidence from previous, similar projects.

4. EXPECTED BENEFITS

The increased understanding of the process and the control of the project offered by a process maturity approach outweigh the effort needed to capture, store, and analyze the information required. Objective evaluation of any new technique, tool, or method is impossible without quantitative data describing its effect. Thus, the use of metrics in a process maturity framework should result in

- enhanced understanding of the process.
- increased control of the process.
- a clear migration path to more mature process levels.
- more accurate estimates of project cost and schedule.
- more objective evaluations of changes in technique, tool, or method.
- more accurate estimates of the effects of changes on project cost and schedule.

REFERENCES

1. S. D. Conte, H. E. Dunsmore, and V. Y. Shen, *Software Engineering Metrics and Models*, Benjamin-Cummings, Menlo Park, California, 1986.
2. Watts Humphrey, *Managing the Software Process*, Addison-Wesley, Reading, Massachusetts, 1989.
3. Shari Lawrence Pfleeger, *Recommendations for an Initial Set of Metrics*, Contel Technology Center Technical Report CTC-TR-89-017, Chantilly, Virginia, 1989.
4. Herman P. Schultz, *Software Management Metrics*, Mitre Technical Report M88-1-ESD-TR-88-001, Bedford, Massachusetts, 1988.
5. B. W. Boehm, A Spiral Model of Software Development and Enhancement," *IEEE Computer*, May 1988.

Measuring and Managing Software Maintenance

Robert B. Grady, *Hewlett-Packard*

An effective way to improve software quality is to set measurable goals and then manage your projects to achieve those goals. Hewlett-Packard has developed some methods to do just that.

Why does it take so many people to support software systems? Software development has evolved rapidly in the short time that computers have existed. With most products, such evolution is accompanied by the creation of replacement products and the obsolescence of old ones. However, the nature of software products is that they change and evolve *frequently*. Today, better design and implementation methods lead to higher initial software quality than in the past, but the quality of older products that have undergone continuous change is often poor. Because we cannot economically replace all our old software, we must find better ways to manage needed changes. Until we do, software maintenance will continue to represent a large investment — and software quality will *not* improve.

Management patterns

Many organizations responsible for the evolution of software systems seem to operate constantly in a reactive mode, fighting the flames of the most recent fire. Behind the visible sense of urgency, though, three primary strategic elements appear to control the actions of managers:

- minimizing defects,
- minimizing engineering effort and schedule, and
- maximizing customer satisfaction.

In a broad sense, the ultimate objective of all three approaches is customer satisfaction. This article specifically discusses their relationships to the maintenance of delivered software. Maintenance includes fixing defects, enhancing product features or performance, and adapting to new hardware or external software. Of course, the items above are not unique to the maintenance phase. Managers know that a consolidated strategy must be pursued, although shifting priorities among the items is sometimes more frequent during maintenance than during initial product development. The following examples illustrate this argument.

Minimizing defects: (1) Besides fixing defects, engineers investigate the causes of defects. (2) Before a major new enhancement is attempted, the number of defects in the part of the product to be enhanced is reduced to a minimum. (3) The original

Reprinted from *IEEE Software*, Volume 4, Number 9, September 1987, pages 35-45. Copyright ©1987 by The Institute of Electrical and Electronics Engineers, Inc. All rights reserved.

development engineers continue to be responsible for fixing defects and making product enhancements for at least six months after product release and before moving on to other product development.

Minimizing engineering effort and schedule: (1) Resources are removed from maintaining/enhancing activities and assigned to new-product development (minimize effort). (2) Resources are removed from development to perform maintaining/enhancing activities (minimize schedule). (3) Extended work times are used to complete an enhanced version in an unalterable schedule. (4) The amount of time taken to make fixes or run tests becomes so critical that shortcuts become necessary.

Maximizing customer satisfaction: (1) After initial product deliveries, development-team members visit customer sites to train, observe operations, and isolate defects. (2) Special patches and workarounds are quickly found for defects and installed for individual customer installations. (3) Work on some defects is deferred to create an enhancement for one key customer.

Business pressures. If you look at an organization that is starting to get involved with software products, it frequently will try to capture a market by working closely with customers to define their product needs completely and correctly the first time and by following up with quick responses to problems. Its initial success depends heavily on customer satisfaction. As its products become accepted in the market, it tries to increase its advantage by maximizing the quality of all its product releases and by gradually improving them with enhancements and improved hardware and software connections.

On the other hand, when competitive products exist, pressures build to create unique features or new products. Organizations are forced to balance engineering effort and schedules between new development and maintenance, and trade-offs are often made to decrease the maintenance effort in favor of new development.

Thus business pressures encourage organizations to emphasize different strategic elements to remain competitive. These pressures influence product fea-

tures, product quality, timeliness, and the ability to satisfy all these needs more economically than the competition. Table 1 summarizes the major characteristics of these strategic elements.

Metrics. Project measurements are a powerful way to track progress toward goals. Such metrics are frequently displayed in high-level management presentations. For example, the number of defects outstanding or the time to respond to defects are frequently cited when discussing postrelease software. The rate of generating code or product features is often tracked for prerelease software. Without such measures for managing software maintenance, it is difficult for any organization to understand whether it is successful, and it is difficult to keep from frequently changing strategy. It is in the best interests of both managers and engineers responsible for software maintenance to help provide the data needed to choose the best balance among available strategies.

The metrics included in this article were summarized by Hewlett-Packard's Software Metrics Council at its October 1986 meeting using a measurement and evaluation paradigm described by Victor Basili, Dieter Rombach, and David Weiss.[1-3] (The four-year-old council has 20 software managers and engineers from 15 HP divisions and supports many types of software. They identify key software metrics and promote their use through HP's divisions.) The complete HP list contains five goals, 31 questions, and 35 metrics (see the box on p. 38).

Collection and analysis of this metric data does *not* depend on any specific process of maintenance or development.

Minimizing defects

The following graphs and methods are successfully used to minimize defects. They help identify how many defects exist, what the trend is, where and when defects occur, and what the defects' underlying causes are. Although their thrust is fixing defects during maintenance, the information they provide also helps managers when making decisions about enhance-

ments and adaptive changes (to surrounding hardware and software). The metrics are

- count of prerelease defects,
- count of postrelease defects,
- count of remaining critical and serious defects,
- count of defects sorted by module and cause,
- noncomment source-code statements (NCSS),
- percentage of branches covered during test, and
- calendar time by phase.

Defect categories. Figure 1 shows a bar chart that addresses three important questions about postrelease quality and how to maximize engineers' effectiveness during maintenance.[4] In this example (and in later ones), the questions' numbers are the same as those in the box on p. 38. Defect analysis indicated that three of the 13 modules (24 percent of the code) accounted for 76 percent of the defects reported before release. This could have meant that these modules had simply been tested more thoroughly than the others. Six months after release, though, a similar analysis was performed using data reported by customers, and the results were that the same three modules accounted for a similar portion of the defects.

This information helped managers formulate a more thorough plan to test the three modules and long-term plans to rewrite the error-prone modules. Until then, the team was wise to exercise caution when considering enhancements to those modules, since their design was relatively unstable or complex. Defect categorization is a powerful tool to help identify where work must be done and to predict where you can expect more defects to appear.

Another effective way to examine defect data is to analyze causes of defects. By identifying common causes of defects, you can take steps to limit the possibility of these problems occurring again.

One organization at HP performed such an analysis[4] and found that more than one third of their defects were caused by a poor understanding of their users' interface requirements. They responded by

Table 1.
Major strategic elements of software maintenance.

	Minimize defects	Minimize engineering effort and schedule	Maximize customer satisfaction
Major business factor	Hold/increase market share	Competitive pressures forcing new-product development or cost control	Attempt to capture market share
When least effective	When product features are not competitive or reasonable market is not held	When single product is primary source of revenue	Late in the life of a product
Characteristic features	Analysis and removal of sources of defects	Focus on balancing resources between maintenance and new development	Customer communication, quick response
Most visible metrics	Defect categorization by module, cause, type, and severity; size; branch coverage	Calendar time, engineering effort, defects	Product metrics, defects, time
Group most likely to drive strategy	Lab or quality organization; customer support as catalyst	Division or company management	Lab during initial development, customer support later
Potential drawbacks if focus is too restricted	Defects may be fixed that are not cost-effective; modules may not be rewritten that should be	Defect backlog can become unmanageable	Process of developing products may not improve

changing their process to focus more specifically on user-interface design (such as technical design reviews and evolutionary prototypes reviewed by representative customers; Grady and Caswell[4] give a more complete discussion of their analysis).

Figure 2 shows three categories of defects before and after release for four successive releases of the same product after the organization had changed its user-interface design process. It shows that the organization now has few design errors. The percentage of defects found after release also dropped from 25 percent of the total for the first two releases to less than 10 percent in the third and to zero in the fourth. While they were not completely successful in removing all sources of defects, they did improve their process so that the defects did not reach customers.

Another way to monitor defects is to plot a weekly graph that shows cumulative defect and enhancement requests along with similar graphs of the unresolved defects. Such trends help indicate project

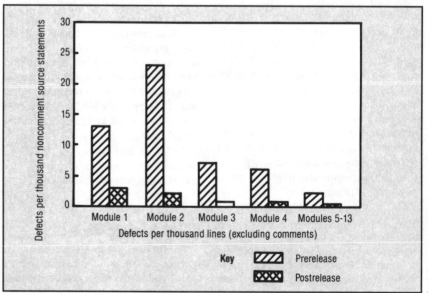

Figure 1. Defect analysis by code module. Addresses questions 13 (what are high-leverage opportunities during preventive maintenance?), 16 (what is the postrelease quality of each module?), and 26 (what can I predict will happen after release based on prerelease metrics?). (The questions are detailed in the box on p. 38.)

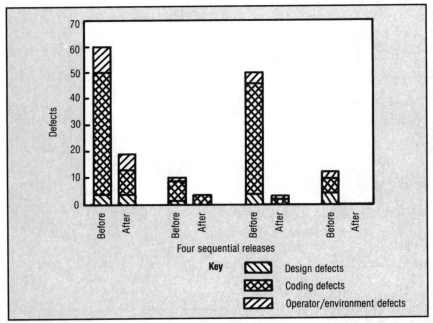

Figure 2. Number of defects found before and after release. Addresses questions 18 (what are we doing right?) and 28 (what defects are getting through?).

progress and expected completion. For large systems, the rate of change in these trends may be more important than the trends themselves because it shows the product's stability. Figure 3 shows the rates of change of both the incoming defects and the defects fixed for part of one large HP system. HP's experience has proven that products whose defect-status slopes did not decline had poor quality after release.

The defect data can also be combined with a weekly staffing profile to calculate the average time needed to fix a defect.

Branch coverage. During a product's maintenance cycle, one primary concern is

Maintenance goals, questions, and metrics

The metrics defined by the HP Software Metrics Council were derived using a measurement and evaluation paradigm that says that goals lead to questions that lead to metrics that supply answers to the questions (see references 1-3 in the main text). To the extent that the questions are a complete set, and to the extent the metrics satisfactorily answer the questions, you can learn if the goals are met.

This section is organized by the primary goals that must be accomplished. With each goal, there is a brief discussion of who is most likely to ask the questions. While discussing these metrics, the council identified four major individuals or groups who are most likely to ask the questions in their areas: top management, project management, customer engineers (this category includes all individuals responsible for dealing directly with customers), and process managers. While "process manager" is not an official job title at HP, someone at most divisions is identified as holding that responsibility for software maintenance.

A fifth group likely to ask these questions is the quality-assurance staff. Because they frequently act as the voice of a conscience, they are likely to ask questions in all areas, so they are not explicitly noted in the following list.

The metrics listed here are not precisely defined and should be considered general approaches to measurable feedback.

Goal: Maximize customer satisfaction. The group most likely to ask questions about customer satisfaction is that responsible for dealing with customers. There is some overlap with other groups. For example, question 6 concerns everyone, and project managers usually will ask question 7.
1. *What are the attributes of customer satisfaction?*
2. *What are the key indicators of customer satisfaction?*
3. *What are the factors resulting in customer satisfaction?*
4. *How satisfied are customers?*
5. *How do you compare with the competition?*
   • Survey data.
6. *How many problems are affecting the customer?*
   • Incoming defect rate.

• Open critical and serious defects.
• Break/fix ratio.
• Postrelease defect density.
7. *How long does it take to fix a problem (compared to customer expectation and compared to commitment)?*
   • Mean time to acknowledge problem.
   • Mean time to deliver solution.
   • Scheduled versus actual delivery.
   • Customer expectation (by severity level) of time to fix.
8. *How does installing the fix affect the customer?*
   • Time customer's operation is down.
   • Customer's effort required during installation.
9. *How many customers are affected by a problem? And how much are they affected?*
   • Number of duplicate defects by severity.

Goal: Improve the maintenance/enhancement process. This goal is almost equally shared by project managers and process managers. The primary difference between the two groups lies in the scope of the questions. Project managers will ask the questions with a much narrower view, with the emphasis on optimizing the performance of their particular project.
10. *Where are the resources going? Where are the worst rework loops in the process?*
    • Engineering months by product/component/activity.
11. *What are the total life-cycle maintenance and support costs for the product (and how distributed by time and organization)?*
    • Engineering-months by product/component/activity.
    • Engineering-months by corrective, adaptive, and perfective maintenance.
12. *What development methods affect maintenance costs?*
    • Prerelease records of methods and postrelease costs.
13. *What are high-leverage opportunities for preventive maintenance?*
    • Defect categorization.
    • Code stability.
14. *Are fixes effective? Are unexpected side effects created?*
    • Break/fix ratio.

to ensure that new defects are not introduced. An effective way to check this is to maintain suites of test programs that are continually updated as products change and improve. Figure 4 illustrates one of several ways needed to verify the tests' completeness. It shows two levels of branch-coverage limits and the data for one part of an HP product.

Branch coverage is measured by using a program that automatically inserts statements into the product's precompilation source code. These statements increment counters during testing to provide a histogram of what code parts were executed and what parts were not. In the example, you

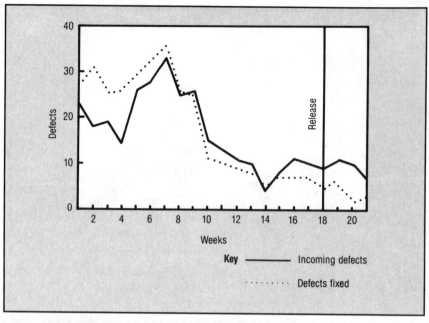

Figure 3. Project defect status. Addresses questions 20 (how do we know when to release?) and 22 (how long does it take to fix a defect?).

15. *How maintainable is the product as changes occur? When do I give up and rewrite?*
- Incoming problem rate.
- Defect density.
- Code stability.
- Complexity.
- Number of modules changed to fix one defect.
16. *What is the postrelease quality of each module?*
- Defect density, critical and serious defects.
17. *What will process monitoring cost and where are the costs distributed?*
- Engineering-hours and cost.
18. *What are you doing right?*
- Error-detection effectiveness (ratio of prerelease defect density to postrelease defect density).
- Break/fix ratio.
19. *What are key indicators of process health, and how are you doing?*
- Release schedules met, trends of defect density, and serious and critical defects.

Goal: Make maintenance more predictable. Everyone is interested in schedules. Other than question 20, though, every group has its own view of what is important.
20. *How do you know when to release?*
- Predicted defect detection based on prerelease records and postrelease defect densities.
- Branch coverage.

21. *What will the maintenance requirements be?*
- Code stability, complexity, and size.
- Prerelease defect density.

22. *How long does it take to fix a defect historically? With new processes? With resource changes? With complexity and severity variations? For each activity in process?*
- Calendar time and process and module records.
23. *Where are the bottlenecks?*
- Queue time.

24. *How can you predict cycle time, reliability, and effort?*
- Calendar time.
- Engineering time.
- Defect density.
- Number of defects to fix.
- Break/fix historical averages.
- Code stability.
- Complexity.
- Number of lines to change.

Goal: Improve prerelease development. This goal belongs to the process manager.
25. *How effective is the development process in preventing defects?*
- Postrelease defect density.
26. *What can I predict will happen after release, based on prerelease metrics?*
- Correlations between prerelease complexity, defect density, stability, FURPS, and postrelease defect density; ability to easily make changes; and customer survey results.
27. *What practices yield the best results?*
- Correlations between prerelease practices and customer satisfaction metrics.
28. *What defects are getting through? What caused those defects?*
- Defect categorization.

Goal: Minimize maintenance cost. This goal belongs to top management, although the questions are sometimes indirectly heard from other groups.
29. *How much do the maintenance-phase activities cost?*
- Engineering time and cost.
30. *What are the major cost components? What factors affect the cost?*
- Engineering-months by product/component/activity.
31. *How do costs change over time?*
- Track cost components over entire maintenance life cycle.

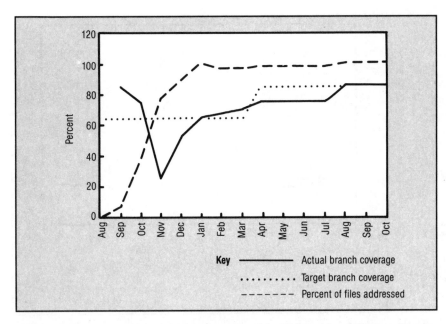

Figure 4. Branch coverage. Addresses question 20 (how do we know when to release?).

can see how the goals for coverage and the actual coverage get higher over time. This graph represents composite data during integration-level testing of all components. Unit-level testing is performed earlier in the process, and the goal for unit-level coverage is 100 percent.

Top-management presentation. The graphs presented so far are most useful for project managers. The next two help summarize the status of product maintenance for top managers. The first graph deals with measuring customer satisfaction. Fig-

ure 5 is an example of data that receives monthly management attention in HP because it summarizes how many unfixed critical and serious problems customers see.[4] (The data shown is not current, and it is normalized so the actual number of defects is not reflected.)

The second graph (Figure 6) shows the postrelease defect density for the first 12 months after release for one division's products. Better than any other visual representation, this graph summarizes whether all the other efforts to reduce defects are having a permanent, positive

effect. The figure shows some progress toward higher quality at release in the past year and a half for product line 2. There are no recent data points for the other two product lines that would indicate whether they made such progress.

You can see how these last two graphs complement the earlier graphs by providing top-management views that are consistent with the focus of minimizing defects.

These six illustrations came from different projects, entities, and times. Measuring any one or two of them is useful, but the best results are achieved by tracking them all. Fortunately, the amount of data to collect is not a great burden. Many managers track such data as numbers instead of graphs, and on a daily basis this minimizes their effort. On the other hand, graphs are helpful when it is important to *see* a trend.

Minimizing engineering effort and schedule

A common management focus is minimizing engineering effort and completion time. For many projects, this focus is the most effective way to serve all the customers' needs. One set of metrics particularly applies to this focus in the maintenance phase. Like some defect-categorization examples in the previous section, the effort and time data in the following examples must be supplemented by analysis of detailed data and specific actions to make improvements in costly areas. The metrics here are

 • engineering-months by product/component/activity,
 • engineering-months by defects/enhancements,
 • defect and enhancement request counts,
 • counts of remaining critical and serious defects,
 • calendar time by phase and activity, and
 • code stability (percent of code changed).

Completion rates. Figures 7 and 8 illustrate two views of engineering and calendar time in the maintenance of two products. The first shows the actual times to fix various defects versus the estimated

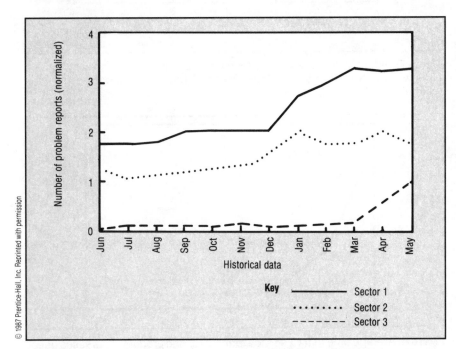

Figure 5. Unresolved critical and serious problem reports (software quality by sector). Addresses question 6 (how many problems affect the customer?).

times.[4] The advantage of this type of representation over the one shown in Figure 3 is that it gives you some feel for the data dispersion (calculating average fix times from the data in Figure 3 doesn't). This figure shows the average time it takes to respond to defects in engineering-hours. It also shows that the predicted time to fix defects was reasonably accurate for estimates of six hours or under, but higher estimates were not as accurate.

One important variable not included in Figure 7 is the percentage of *effective* hours available (not including non-project-related efforts). In this case, the average number of effective hours available pushed the estimated time to fix closer to 4 than to 2.71. The manager of this product line uses this data to estimate schedules more accurately, to measure how effective new tools or training are, and to shorten schedules by providing an environment with a higher percentage of effective hours (even if only temporarily).

On the other hand, Figure 8 shows fix times in calendar time (from when an engineer is first assigned to a defect until the corrected code is tested and returned to a control library) rather than in engineering-hours. This form of tracking is useful during maintenance as a mechanism to focus on the release schedule for a product update. The figure shows the results of a concentrated effort at one HP division to drastically reduce the time to get product updates through the release process.

The steps that they took (and are still taking) are a model for process improvement. First, they set a fixed cycle time for updates that went to customers. The order in which defects were fixed was set by the marketing group that dealt with customers. Next, they created a sign-off form that specified the steps needed to fix each defect (quick fixes and workarounds were handled separately from this process). This form also captured the amount of engineering time spent for each step. From this data, they learned what the breakdown of time was for each task. These times were compared to each task's effectiveness. Last, they introduced one major process change per update cycle so they could monitor their overall effectiveness.

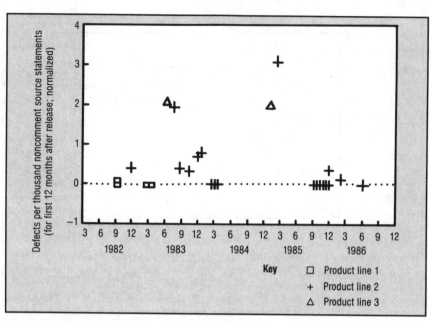

Figure 6. Software quality (postrelease defect density). Addresses question 25 (how effective is development in preventing defects?).

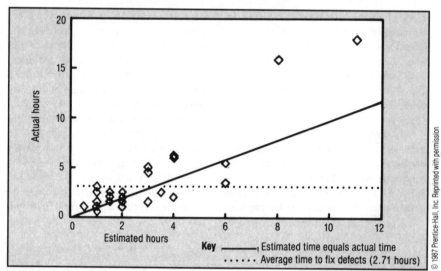

Figure 7. Defect fix times (estimated versus actual time). Addresses questions 22 (how long does it take to fix a defect?) and 24 (how can we predict cycle time, reliability, and effort?).

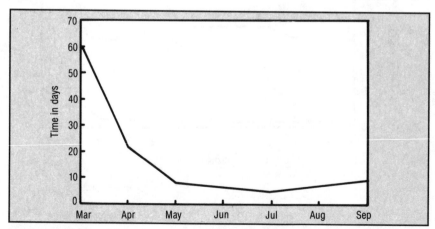

Figure 8. Average time to fix a service request for one product. Addresses questions 22 (how long does it take to fix a defect?) and 24 (how can we predict cycle time, reliability, and effort?).

For example, it may have taken an engineer half a day to unit-test a change. They found that few defects turned up during unit test if design reviews were conducted before the changes were made and that these defects were successfully caught by defect-specific tests. As a result, they eliminated the unit tests.

When you use the approaches shown in the Figures 7 and 8, remember that not all maintenance activities are corrective. The effort and time characteristics of changes made to improve products can be quite different from the those for defect fixes. For tracking purposes, it is convenient to treat enhancements either as major changes (in terms of time and effort) with most of the characteristics of new designs or as minor changes to be grouped with defect fixes. Generally, only minor enhancements are allowed for some period after initial product release, and major enhancements begin to become a predominant cost only after incoming defects have stabilized.

Complexity. For large software systems, a strategic focus on minimizing effort and schedule must take into account the effect of overall complexity. Some years ago, Belady and Lehman proposed a law of software development that said, "The entropy of a system increases with time unless specific work is executed to maintain or reduce it."[5] Figure 9 shows increasing entropy for one large software product, OS/360, in the form of the fraction of modules handled for each new release over almost 10 years' time. The larger the percentage of modules changed, the greater the probability that new defects will be introduced and that more testing will be required to complete the job. At the 3000-day point, it appears that a major effort was undertaken to control the number of modules changed for an update.

Looking at the percentage of modules affected is just one of several metrics that characterize maintainability. It is important to also look at incoming defect rates, individual module stability and complexity, test coverage, and other factors to isolate the areas of the product that are the largest contributors to overall maintenance costs.

Cost trade-offs. Managers seek information on cost trade-offs between methods that might be applied to new development or maintenance. HP has improved quality in recent years by applying effective software-engineering methods to products during initial development. These methods include structured analysis and design, the use of prototypes for products with extensive user interactions, design and code inspections, branch-coverage analysis, testing-prediction models, and statistical quality-control techniques.

The next example, analysis of engineering time, demonstrates the potential value of these methods, whether they are used during initial development or during maintenance. Table 2 shows the relative amounts of time needed to fix defects as a function of when the defects were introduced for two products.

The first thing you can see is that the average times to find and fix defects are substantially more than the four hours discussed in the Figure 7 example. That example represented the early maintenance records of a relatively small product (10,000 noncomment source-code statements). The data in Table 2 is from two very large, mature software products. The effects of defects on their maintenance is also very large.

When you become aware of the potential downstream costs of as much as two engineering-months for each design defect, the motivation to train engineers to use design reviews effectively becomes high. Similarly, the motivation to use other defect-prevention methods also becomes high. Only by tracking and analyzing engineering costs by different activities can you learn the facts to make the most cost-effective decisions for your maintenance situation.

The most common top-level graphic view that supports a focus on minimizing engineering effort and schedule is the project PERT chart. The primary metric it tracks is time. Some automated PERT packages also allow input of engineering-hours and associated work-breakdown reports. Another metric graphed at HP is the mean time to fix critical and serious known problems. It is similar to Figure 8, but it includes all the time seen by customers — not just the time used by the lab.

A major goal in the maintenance phase is to *balance* responsiveness to customer needs against the need to minimize overall engineering resources that do not create new sources of revenue.

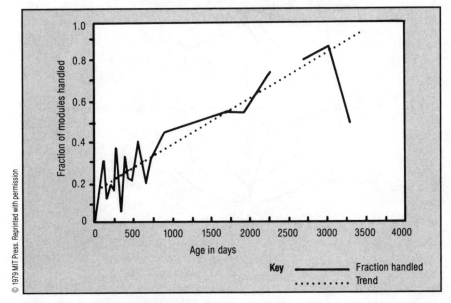

Figure 9. OS/360 modules handled as a function of system age. Addresses question 15 (how maintainable is the product as changes occur? when do I give up and rewrite?).

Maximizing customer satisfaction

Maximizing customer satisfaction is easiest to pursue when the product team has close ties to customers. Examples are small-volume products or products used only by customers in the same company. For other products, it is necessary to provide very efficient communication links from the customers through the various layers of a sales and support organization to get the data and feedback needed.

In some ways, overemphasizing this focus can result in a short-term viewpoint if the following examples are not supplemented by other measures to make more permanent process and product changes. On the other hand, the effective use of surveys on which this strategic focus depends is a very powerful tool to positively affect later product generations. The metrics here are

- survey data,
- counts of unresolved critical and serious defects,
- calendar time by phase and activity (emphasis on times customers experience problems),
- defect and enhancement request counts, and
- break/fix ratio (count of defects introduced versus count of defects fixed).

Quality attributes. Figure 10 shows how one Japanese company displays quality. It combines a view of defect status (correctness) with a stronger product (as opposed to process) focus[6] than in the previous figures. This diagram was used during the initial development of a product, and several metrics were selected for each product attribute to derive the percentages.

For products in the maintenance phase, you can learn effective measures for some of these attributes through well-constructed customer surveys. By responding to these customer needs with product enhancements, a company not only improves its market position, it also makes an important statement to customers of ongoing commitment to serving their needs.

One HP group has developed several guidelines for creating such surveys:

- Define what the goals are for the survey, what questions must be answered, how the data will be analyzed, and how results will be presented. State or graph sample conclusions.
- Test the survey and your method of data analysis before sending it out.
- Ask questions that require simple answers, preferably quantitative or yes/no.
- Keep surveys short (preferably one page).
- Don't send surveys with other material so they won't get lost in the shuffle.
- Make them very easy to return (for example, a fold-and-seal, prestamped form).

Product-quality attributes that should

Table 2.
Engineering-time versus defects for two software projects.

Phase introduced	Project 1 % defects introduced	Average fix time*	Project 2 % defects introduced	Average fix time*
Investigation	—	—	3	575
Design	20	315	15	235
Implementation	75	80	65	118
Test	5	46	17	74
Total	100	125	100	140

*Time includes finding and fixing (units are engineering-hours). Defects were fixed mainly during implementation and test phases.

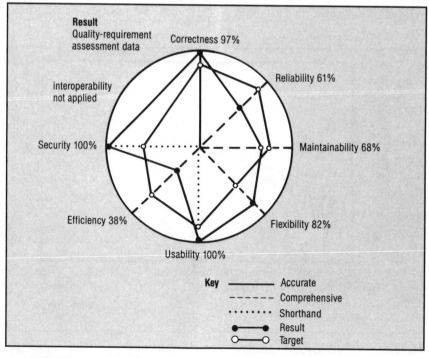

Figure 10. Example of displaying quality. Addresses question 3 (what are the factors resulting in customer satisfaction?).

be considered are contained in a model of quality features, called FURPS, which is commonly used in HP.[4] (The letters stand for the categories modeled: functionality, usability, reliability, performance, and supportability.) Each category contains several measurable attributes. You should formulate at least one question from each category when preparing customer surveys. The presentation method in Figure 10 is useful because it allows all the major FURPS components to be displayed in one chart. This helps raise awareness of the importance of balance and completeness when setting goals and measuring progress against the goals.

Other sources of quality-attribute measurements are sales followups, direct visits by designers to customer sites, and direct measurements of a product in the labs.

Responsiveness. Another key factor of customer satisfaction is responsiveness to concerns. For example, the two categories of HP defect reports that represent the problems of most concern to customers are "serious" and "critical." When customers experience these problems, they expect a timely response. Figure 11 shows how one division at HP has represented data and weighted it to ensure that activities' priorities are rated appropriately. A site is placed on "alert" status when a serious or critical problem is encountered. If no workaround is found quickly, the site is placed on "hot" status by the field organization. The graph in Figure 11 shows the results of improved responsiveness by the division.

Similar graphs help control maintenance activities for a product line or customer relationship. For example, a goal can be set for response time to resolve critical and serious problems with any key customer account. This provides a much tighter coupling between setting customer expectations and achieving customer satisfaction. The key point is to establish the desired metric and consistently measure the appropriate part of the process.

While Figure 11 addresses the most important defects visible to customers, it is also important to deal with all the other defects that are day-to-day nuisances (not serious or critical, just annoying). The graph of the average time to fix service requests in Figure 8 is a useful way to monitor all the defects. Optimizing the average time to fix a service request, as well as minimizing the problem resolution indexes in Figure 11, helps ensure that there is some balance between responsiveness to problems that have no workarounds and those that do.

Focusing on customer satisfaction can lead to well-accepted, successful products. On the other hand, managers will be most successful in the long term by supplementing this focus with some of the process-related methods from the other emphases (minimizing defects and minimizing engineering effort and schedule).

Controlling software maintenance costs requires that an organization have a strategy for maintenance (whether or not it is explicitly stated) and that the primary characteristics of the strategy and the most effective measures of its success be understood. Software metrics provide measurable pictures of progress in meeting the organization's goals.

Figure 12 shows a simplified dataflow diagram of maintenance that summarizes relevant data for three strategic elements. The metrics mainly involve detailed defect information. They also include size and complexity data from automated counters, engineering effort and time information collected manually, and information from customer surveys performed mainly by marketing and support personnel. Because the model only addresses data sources, it does not depend on any particular process for maintenance. On the other hand, evaluating the data provides useful checks against any of the three focuses, and the model provides a framework for data that supports better decisions. Conscientious use of this model will help achieve a proper balance between the equally important goals of customer satisfaction and development control.

There are several factors to remember when considering which focus you might emphasize. Software metrics can only be *part* of a successful overall plan for development improvement. The metrics selected will help manage a business for many years, so they must be carefully cho-

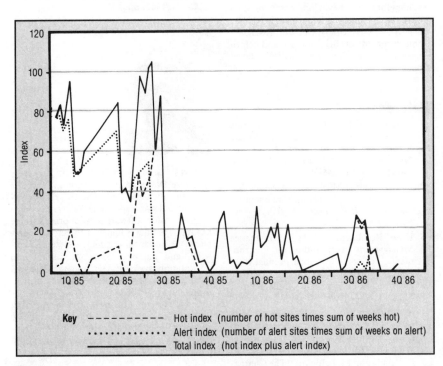

Figure 11. Division software-problem resolution index. Addresses question 19 (what are key indicators of process health and how are we doing?).

483

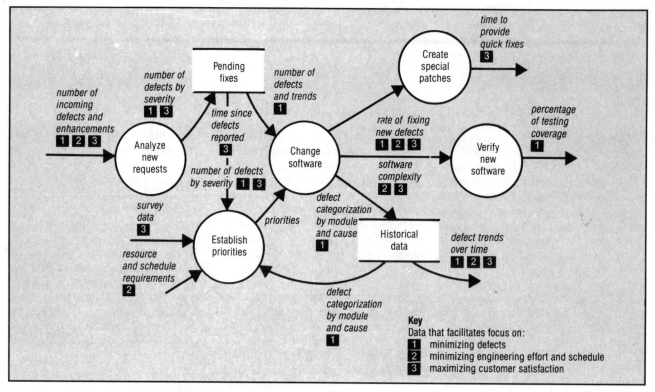

Figure 12. Sources of software maintenance-management information.

sen. No matter what strategy you pursue, you can effectively execute that strategy only if you understand the necessary product and process attributes. That understanding *requires* software metrics.

The focus on minimizing defects is directed most completely to long-term improvement. The focus on maximizing customer satisfaction and the focus on minimizing engineering effort and schedule both serve important purposes driven by immediate business needs. If the initial set of metrics is selected carefully, you can start with a short-term focus and evolve into a long-term strategy.

Project managers today seldom take the time to analyze data for more than one or two of the views presented here. And yet they could make better decisions if they did spend the time. There is a strong need for more complete automation of the data collection, analysis, and presentation process than is generally available. Such automation would include comparison of data against preset limits and automatic generation of exception reports, as well as many of the views shown earlier. Until such a complete system is available, subsets of the methods described here are effective and can be used immediately by software managers to achieve higher quality software. ⬦

Acknowledgments

I would like to express my continued appreciation to the HP Software Metrics Council for its commitment and efforts that formed the basis for the successes of our program. Chuck Sieloff, Brian Sakai, Ken Oar, Bob Horenstein, Vic Langford, Dick Levitt, and Susan Muldoon all provided valuable data for this article. I particularly thank Jan Grady, Debbie Caswell, and John Burnham for their patience and helpful suggestions regarding this article's development.

References

1. V. Basili and H.D. Rombach, "Tailoring the Software Process to Project Goals and Environments," *Proc. Ninth Int'l Conf. Software Eng.*, CS Press, Los Alamitos, Calif., 1987, pp. 345-357.

2. V. Basili and D.M. Weiss, "A Methodology for Collecting Valid Software Engineering Data," *IEEE Trans. Software Eng.* Nov. 1984, pp. 728-738.

3. H.D. Rombach, "Using Maintenance Management in an Industrial Environment," presentation incorporated into Tech. Report TR-1764, Computer Science Dept., Univ. of Maryland, College Park, Md., 1987.

4. R. Grady and D. Caswell, *Software Metrics: Establishing a Company-Wide Program*, Prentice-Hall, Englewood Cliffs, N.J., 1987, pp. 88, 110, 123, 124, and 159.

5. L. Belady and M. Lehman, "The Characteristics of Large Systems," in *Research Directions in Software Technology*, P.
Wegner, ed., MIT Press, Cambridge, Mass., 1979, pp. 106-142.

6. T. Sunazuka, M. Azuma, and N. Yamagishi, "Software Quality Assessment Technology," *Proc. Eighth Int'l Conf. Software Eng.*, CS Press, Los Alamitos, Calif., 1985, pp. 142-148.

Robert B. Grady works in Hewlett-Packard's Software Development Technology Lab. He previously managed the HP Software Engineering Lab and was responsible for establishing a company-wide software metrics program. He has managed development projects for compilers, measurement and control systems, firmware, and manufacturing automation and information systems. His research interests include software tools, development environments, and metrics.

Grady received a BS in electrical engineering from the Massachusetts Institute of Technology and an MS in electrical engineering from Stanford University. He is a member of the Computer Society of the IEEE.

Grady can be contacted at Hewlett-Packard, PO Box 10350, Palo Alto, CA 94303-0867.

Chapter 11
Software Engineering Technology Transfer

The real problem is not whether machines think but whether men do.
— B. Frederic Skinner, *Contingencies of Reinforcement*

Overview

Software technology is in a rapid state of change. Advanced concepts like domain engineering, object-oriented methods, rapid prototyping, and visual languages offer hope to those trying to increase software productivity, reduce cost, and improve quality. Yet it is a fact that most software shops do not use the state of the art in their state of the practice. There are many reasons for this state of affairs. Some are economic, others are social. Yet something must be done to quicken the introduction of technology, so we can reap the benefits of technology quicker. Which technologies should I bank on and how can I take full advantage of them? What mechanisms can I use to transfer these technologies and what are the costs and benefits? These and similar questions are addressed in the four papers that make up this chapter.

The first paper, by Shaw, discusses the prospects for an engineering discipline for software where science replaces art and software development becomes based on a mature, stable, and theoretical foundation. The paper characterizes other engineering disciplines (chemical, etc.) and shows how software can learn from them as it evolves from craft to scientific practice. Many interesting ideas are offered on how to make this future transition. The paper is sound and provocative in its appeals for rigor.

The second paper, by DeMarco and Lister, reports the results of a series of performance benchmarks conducted in the mid-1980s to evaluate the relative productivity of 392 primarily business programmers from 79 organizations. The benchmarks confirm that improvements have been made in the state of the practice. Yet many of the hypotheses tested against these data yield results counter to expectations. The article seems to confirm some of Shaw's observations. It too emphasizes the need to add more rigor to the software design and coding processes.

The third paper, by Barnes and Bollinger, focuses on software reuse. It distinguishes between what it takes to achieve broad-scope rather than ad hoc reuse. It identifies the costs involved and quantifies the potential rewards. It discusses the barriers to reuse as it describes strategies for overcoming them. The article concludes by making an appeal for automation-based reuse with life cycle paradigms, processes, methods, and tools engineered to provide the incentives needed to make reuse practical in most firms.

The final paper, by Babcock, Belady, and Gore, describes a new approach to technology transfer that was developed as a product of the Microelectronics and Computer Technology Corporation's Software Technology Program. This approach fosters collaboration instead of relying on more traditional transfer-and-feedback mechanisms. The paper summarizes MCC's experiences to date with its new technology transfer process model. It makes specific recommendations as it describes how to minimize risk using collaborative approaches that get both the researchers and shareholder organizations to buy into high-quality product prototypes.

References

There are several good texts on the topic of organizational change and technology management. The Edosomwan book (Reference 8 in the Bibliography) is a good book to start with. For those interested in Japanese change concepts, the Imai book on Kaizen (Reference 15) and the Ouchi discussion of Theory Z (Reference 20) are musts. Because of its humor, I favor Weinberg's text, which is full of insight and wisdom (Reference 31).

Prospects for an Engineering Discipline of Software

Reprinted from *IEEE Software*, Vol. 7, No. 6, November 1990, pages 15-24. Copyright © 1990 by The Institute of Electrical and Electronics Engineers, Inc. All rights reserved.

Mary Shaw, *Carnegie Mellon University*

> *Software engineering is not yet a true engineering discipline, but it has the potential to become one. Older engineering fields suggest the character software engineering might have.*

The term "software engineering" was coined in 1968 as a statement of aspiration — a sort of rallying cry. That year, the North Atlantic Treaty Organization convened a workshop by that name to assess the state and prospects of software production. Capturing the imagination of software developers, the NATO phrase "software engineering" achieved popularity during the 1970s. It now refers to a collection of management processes, software tooling, and design activities for software development. The resulting practice, however, differs significantly from the practice of older forms of engineering.

What is engineering?

"Software engineering" is a label applied to a set of current practices for development. But using the word "engineering" to describe this activity takes considerable liberty with the common use of that term. The more customary usage refers to the disciplined application of scientific knowledge to resolve conflicting constraints and requirements for problems of immediate, practical significance.

Definitions of "engineering" abound. Although details differ, they share some common clauses:

• *Creating cost-effective solutions* ... Engineering is not just about solving problems; it is about solving problems with economical use of all resources, including money.

• *... to practical problems* ... Engineering deals with practical problems whose solutions matter to people outside the engineering domain — the customers.

• *... by applying scientific knowledge* ... Engineering solves problems in a particular way: by applying science, mathematics, and design analysis.

• *... to building things* ... Engineering emphasizes the solutions, which are usually tangible artifacts.

• *... in the service of mankind.* Engineering not only serves the immediate customer, but it also develops technology and expertise that will support the society.

Engineering relies on codifying scientific knowledge about a technological problem domain in a form that is directly useful to the practitioner, thereby providing answers for questions that commonly occur in practice. Engineers of ordinary talent can then apply this knowledge to solve problems far faster than they otherwise could. In this way, engineering shares prior solutions rather than relying always on virtuoso problem solving.

Engineering practice enables ordinary practitioners so they can create sophisticated systems that work — unspectacularly, perhaps, but reliably. The history of development is marked by both successes and failures. The successes have often been virtuoso performances or the result of diligence and hard work. The failures have often reflected poor understanding of the problem to be solved, mismatch of solution to problem, or inadequate follow-through from design to implementation. Some failed by never working, others by overrunning cost and schedule budgets.

In current software practice, knowledge about techniques that work is not shared effectively with later projects, nor is there a large body of development knowledge organized for ready reference. Computer science has contributed some relevant theory, but practice proceeds largely independently of this organized knowledge. Given this track record, there are fundamental problems with the use of the term "software engineer."

Routine and innovative design. Engineering design tasks are of several kinds. One of the most significant distinctions separates routine from innovative design. Routine design involves solving familiar problems, reusing large portions of prior solutions. Innovative design, on the other hand, involves finding novel solutions to unfamiliar problems. Original designs are much more rarely needed than routine designs, so the latter is the bread and butter of engineering.

Most engineering disciplines capture, organize, and share design knowledge to make routine design simpler. Handbooks and manuals are often the carriers of this organized information. But current nota-

tions for software designs are not adequate for the task of both recording and communicating designs, so they fail to provide a suitable representation for such handbooks.

Software in most application domains is treated more often as original than routine — certainly more so than would be necessary if we captured and organized what we already know. One path to increased productivity is identifying applications that could be routine and developing appropriate support.

The current focus on reuse emphasizes capturing and organizing existing knowledge of a particular kind: knowledge expressed in the form of code. Indeed, subroutine libraries — especially of system calls and general-purpose mathematical

---

Given our track record, there are fundamental problems with the use of the term "software engineer."

---

routines — have been a staple of programming for decades. But this knowledge cannot be useful if programmers do not know about it or are not encouraged to use it. Furthermore, library components require more care in design, implementation, and documentation than similar components that are simply embedded in systems.

Practitioners recognize the need for mechanisms to share experience with good designs. This cry from the wilderness appeared on the Software Engineering News Group, a moderated electronic mailing list:

"In Chem E, when I needed to design a heat exchanger, I used a set of references that told me what the constants were ... and the standard design equations. ...

"In general, unless I, or someone else in my [software-] engineering group, has read or remembers and makes known a solution to a past problem, I'm doomed to recreate the solution. ... I guess ... the critical difference is the ability to put together little pieces of the problem that are relatively well known, without having to gen-

erate a custom solution for every application. ...

"I want to make it clear that I am aware of algorithm and code libraries, but they are incomplete solutions to what I am describing. (There is no *Perry's Handbook for Software Engineering*.)"

This former chemical engineer is complaining that software lacks the institutionalized mechanisms of a mature engineering discipline for recording and disseminating demonstrably good designs and ways to choose among design alternatives. (*Perry's Chemical Engineering Handbook*, published by McGraw-Hill, is the standard design handbook for chemical engineering; it is about four inches thick and printed in tiny type on 8.5″ × 11″ tissue paper.)

Model for the evolution of an engineering discipline. Historically, engineering has emerged from ad hoc practice in two stages: First, management and production techniques enable routine production. Later, the problems of routine production stimulate the development of a supporting science; the mature science eventually merges with established practice to yield professional engineering practice. Figure 1 shows this model.

The exploitation of a technology begins with craftsmanship: A set of problems must be solved, and they get solved any which way. They are solved by talented amateurs and by virtuosos, but no distinct professional class is dedicated to problems of this kind. Intuition and brute force are the primary movers in design and construction. Progress is haphazard, particularly before the advent of good communication; thus, solutions are invented and reinvented. The transmission of knowledge between craftsmen is slow, in part because of underdeveloped communications, but also because the talented amateurs often do not recognize any special need to communicate.

Nevertheless, ad hoc practice eventually moves into the folklore. This craft stage of development sees extravagant use of available materials. Construction or manufacture is often for personal or local use or for barter, but there is little or no large-scale production in anticipation of resale. Community barn raisings are an example of this stage; so is software written by application experts for their own ends.

At some point, the product of the technology becomes widely accepted and demand exceeds supply. At that point, attempts are made to define the resources necessary for systematic commercial manufacture and to marshal the expertise for exploiting these resources. Capital is needed in advance to buy raw materials, so financial skills become important, and the operating scale increases over time.

As commercial practice flourishes, skilled practitioners are required for continuity and for consistency of effort. They are trained pragmatically in established procedures. Management may not know why these procedures work, but they know the procedures *do* work and how to teach people to execute them.

The procedures are refined, but the refinement is driven pragmatically: A modification is tried to see if it works, then incorporated in standard procedure if it does. Economic considerations lead to concerns over the efficiency of procedures and the use of materials. People begin to explore ways for production facilities to exploit the technology base; economic issues often point out problems in commercial practice. Management strategies for controlling development fit at this point of the model.

The problems of current practice often stimulate the development of a corresponding science. There is frequently a strong, productive interaction between commercial practice and the emerging science. At some point, the science becomes sufficiently mature to be a significant contributor to the commercial practice. This marks the emergence of engineering practice in the sense that we know it today — sufficient scientific basis to enable a core of educated professionals so they can apply the theory to analysis of problems and synthesis of solutions.

For most disciplines, this emergence occurred in the 18th and early 19th centuries as the common interests in basic physical understandings of natural science and engineering gradually drew together. The reduction of many empirical engineering techniques to a more scientific basis was essential to further engineering progress. And this liaison stimulated fur-

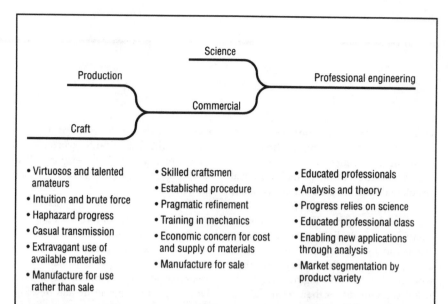

- Virtuosos and talented amateurs
- Intuition and brute force
- Haphazard progress
- Casual transmission
- Extravagant use of available materials
- Manufacture for use rather than sale

- Skilled craftsmen
- Established procedure
- Pragmatic refinement
- Training in mechanics
- Economic concern for cost and supply of materials
- Manufacture for sale

- Educated professionals
- Analysis and theory
- Progress relies on science
- Educated professional class
- Enabling new applications through analysis
- Market segmentation by product variety

Figure 1. Evolution of an engineering discipline. The lower lines track the technology, and the upper lines show how the entry of production skills and scientific knowledge contribute new capability to the engineering practice.

ther advances in natural science. "An important and mutually stimulating tie-up between natural and engineering science, a development [that] had been discouraged for centuries by the long-dominant influence of early Greek thought, was at long last consummated," wrote historian James Kip Finch.[1]

The emergence of an engineering discipline lets technological development pass limits previously imposed by relying on intuition; progress frequently becomes dependent on science as a forcing function. A scientific basis is needed to drive analysis, which enables new applications and even market segmentation via product variety. Attempts are made to gain enough control over design to target specific products on demand.

Thus, engineering emerges from the commercial exploitation that supplants craft. Modern engineering relies critically on adding scientific foundations to craft and commercialization. Exploiting technology depends not only on scientific engineering but also on management and the marshaling of resources. Engineering and science support each other: Engineering generates good problems for science, and science, after finding good problems in the needs of practice, returns workable solutions. Science is often not driven by the immediate needs of engineering; however, good scientific problems often follow from an understanding of the problems that the engineering side of the field is coping with.

The engineering practice of software has recently come under criticism for lacking a scientific basis. The usual curriculum has been attacked for neglecting mathematics[2] and engineering science.[3] Although current software practice does not match the usual expectations of an engineering discipline, the model described here suggests that vigorous pursuit of applicable science and the reduction of that science to practice *can* lead to a sound engineering discipline of software.

Examples from traditional engineering. Two examples make this model concrete: the evolution of engineering disciplines as demonstrated by civil and chemical engineering. The comparison of the two is also illuminating, because they have very different basic organizations.

Civil engineering: a basis in theory. Originally so-called to distinguish it from military engineering, civil engineering included all of civilian engineering until the middle of the 19th century. A divergence of interests led engineers specializing in other technologies to break away, and today civil engineers are the technical experts of the construction industry. They are concerned primarily with large-scale, capital-intensive construction efforts, like buildings, bridges, dams, tunnels, canals, highways, railroads, public water supplies, and sanitation. As a rule, civil-engineering efforts involve well-defined task groups that use appropriate tools and technolo-

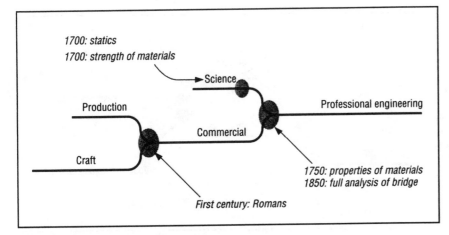

Figure 2. Evolution of civil engineering.

gies to execute well-laid plans.

Although large civil structures have been built since before recorded history, only in the last few centuries has their design and construction been based on theoretical understanding rather than on intuition and accumulated experience. Neither the artisans of the Middle Ages nor of the ancient world showed any signs of the deliberate quantitative application of mathematics to determine the dimensions and shapes that characterizes modern civil engineering. But even without formal understanding, they documented pragmatic rules for recurring elements. Practical builders had highly developed intuitions about statics and relied on a few empirical rules.

The scientific revolution of the Renaissance led to serious attempts by Galileo Galilei, Filippo Brunelleschi, and others to explain structures and why they worked. Over a period of about 200 years, there were attempts to explain the composition of forces and bending of a beam. However, progress was slowed for a long time by problems in formulating basic notions like force, particularly the idea that gravity could be treated as just another force like all the others. Until the basic concepts were sorted out, it was not possible to do a proper analysis of the problem of combining forces (using vector addition) that we now teach to freshmen, nor was it possible to deal with strengths of materials.

Around 1700, Pierre Varignon and Isaac Newton developed the theory of statics to explain the composition of forces and Charles Augustin de Coulomb and Louis Marie Henri Navier explained bending with the theory of strength of materials. These now provide the basis for civil engineering. By the middle of the 18th century, civil engineers were tabulating properties of materials.

The mid-18th century also saw the first attempts to apply exact science to practical building. Pope Benedict ordered an analysis of St. Peter's dome in 1742 and 1743 to determine the cause of cracks and propose repairs; the analysis was based on the principle of virtual displacement and was carried out precisely (although the model is now known to fail to account properly for elasticity). By 1850, it was possible for Robert Stephenson's Britannia Tubular Bridge over the Menai Strait between Wales and England to be subjected to a formal structural analysis.

Thus, even after the basic theories were in hand, it took another 150 years before the theory was rich enough and mature enough to have direct utility at the scale of a bridge design.

Civil engineering is thus rooted in two scientific theories, corresponding to two classical problems. One problem is the composition of forces: finding the resultant force when multiple forces are combined. The other is the problem of bending: determining the forces within a beam supported at one end and weighted at the other. Two theories, statics and strength of materials, solve these problems; both were developed around 1700. Modern civil engineering is the application of these theories to the problem of constructing buildings.

"For nearly two centuries, civil engineering has undergone an irresistible transition from a traditional craft, concerned with tangible fashioning, towards an abstract science, based on mathematical calculation. Every new result of research in structural analysis and technology of materials signified a more rational design, more economic dimensions, or entirely new structural possibilities. There were no apparent limitations to the possibilities of analytical approach; there were no appar-

ent problems in building construction [that] could not be solved by calculation," wrote Hans Straub in his history of civil engineering.[4]

You can date the transition from craft to commercial practice to the Romans' extensive transportation system of the first century. The underlying science emerged about 1700, and it matured to successful application to practice sometime between the mid-18th century and the mid-19th century. Figure 2 places civil engineering's significant events on my model of engineering evolution.

Chemical engineering: a basis in practice. Chemical engineering is a very different kind of engineering than civil engineering. This discipline is rooted in empirical observations rather than in a scientific theory. It is concerned with practical problems of chemical manufacture; its scope covers the industrial-scale production of chemical goods: solvents, pharmaceuticals, synthetic fibers, rubber, paper, dyes, fertilizers, petroleum products, cooking oils, and so on. Although chemistry provides the specification and design of the basic reactions, the chemical engineer is responsible for scaling the reactions up from laboratory scale to factory scale. As a result, chemical engineering depends as heavily on mechanical engineering as on chemistry.

Until the late 18th century, chemical production was largely a cottage industry. The first chemical produced at industrial scale was alkali, which was required for the manufacture of glass, soap, and textiles. The first economical industrial process for alkali emerged in 1789, well before the atomic theory of chemistry explained the underlying chemistry. By the mid-19th century, industrial production of dozens of chemicals had turned the British Midlands into a chemical-manufacturing district. Laws were passed to control the resulting pollution, and pollution-control inspectors, called alkali inspectors, monitored plant compliance.

One of these alkali inspectors, G.E. Davis, worked in the Manchester area in the late 1880s. He realized that, although the plants he was inspecting manufactured dozens of different kinds of chemicals, there were not dozens of different

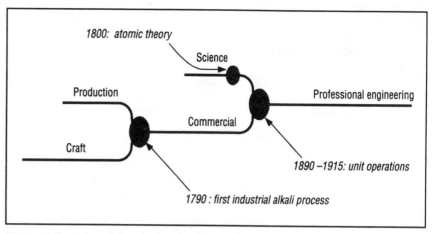

Figure 3. Evolution of chemical engineering.

procedures involved. He identified a collection of functional operations that took place in those processing plants and were used in the manufacture of different chemicals. He gave a series of lectures in 1887 at the Manchester Technical School. The ideas in those lectures were imported to the US by the Massachusetts Institute of Technology in the latter part of the century and form the basis of chemical engineering as it is practiced today. This structure is called *unit operations;* the term was coined in 1915 by Arthur D. Little.

The fundamental problems of chemical engineering are the quantitative control of large masses of material in reaction and the design of cost-effective industrial-scale processes for chemical reactions.

The unit-operations model asserts that industrial chemical-manufacturing processes can be resolved into a relatively few units, each of which has a definite function and each of which is used repeatedly in different kinds of processes. The unit operations are steps like filtration and clarification, heat exchange, distillation, screening, magnetic separation, and flotation. The basis of chemical engineering is thus a pragmatically determined collection of very high-level functions that adequately and appropriately describe the processes to be carried out.

"Chemical engineering as a science ... is not a composite of chemistry and mechanical and civil engineering, but a science of itself, the basis of which is those unit operations [that] in their proper sequence and coordination constitute a chemical process as conducted on the industrial scale. These operations ... are not the subject matter of chemistry as such nor of mechanical engineering. Their treatment is in the quantitative way, with proper exposition of the laws controlling them and of the materials and equipment concerned in them," the American Institute of Chemical Engineers Committee on Education wrote in 1922.[5]

This is a very different kind of structure from that of civil engineering. It is a pragmatic, empirical structure — not a theoretical one.

You can date the transition from craft to commercial practice to the introduction of the LeBlanc process for alkali in 1789. The science emerged with the British

chemist John Dalton's atomic theory in the early 19th century, and it matured to successful merger with large-scale mechanical processes in the 1890s. Figure 3 places chemical engineering's significant events on my model.

Software technology

Where does software stand as an engineering discipline? For software, the problem is appropriately an engineering problem: creating cost-effective solutions to practical problems, building things in the service of mankind.

Information processing as an economic force. The US computer business — including computers, peripherals, packaged software, and communications — was about $150 billion in 1989 and is projected to be more than $230 billion by 1992. The packaged-software component is projected to grow from $23.7 billion to $37.5 billion in this period, according to the Data Analysis Group's fourth-quarter 1989 forecasts. Services, including systems integration and in-house development, are not included in these figures.

Worldwide, software sales amounted to about $65 billion in 1989. This does not include the value of in-house development, which is a much larger activity. World figures are hard to estimate, but the cost of in-house software in the US alone may be in the range of $150 billion to $200 billion.[6] It is not clear how much modification after release (so-called "maintenance") is included in this figure. Thus, software is coming to dominate the cost of information processing.

The economic presence of information processing also makes itself known through the actual and opportunity costs of systems that do *not* work. Examples of costly system failures abound. Less obvi-

ous are the costs of computing that is not even tried: development backlogs so large that they discourage new requests, gigabytes of unprocessed raw data from satellites and space probes, and so on. Despite very real (and substantial) successes, the litany of mismatches of cost, schedule, and expectations is a familiar one.

Growing role of software in critical applications. The US National Academy of Engineering recently selected the 10 greatest engineering achievements of the last 25 years.[7] Of the 10, three are informatics achievements: communications and information-gathering satellites, the microprocessor, and fiber-optic communication. Two more are direct applications of computers: computer-aided design and manufacturing and the computerized axial tomography scan. And most of the rest are computer-intensive: the Moon landing, advanced composite materials, the jumbo jet, lasers, and the application of genetic engineering to produce new pharmaceuticals and crops.

The conduct of science is increasingly driven by computational paradigms standing on equal footing with theoretical and experimental paradigms. Both scientific and engineering disciplines require very sophisticated computing. The demands are often stated in terms of raw processing power — "an exaflop (10^{18}) processor with teraword memory," "a petabyte (10^{15}) of storage," as one article put it[8] — but the supercomputing community is increasingly recognizing development, not mere raw processing, as a critical bottleneck.

Because of software's pervasive presence, the appropriate objective for its developers should be the effective delivery of computational capability to real users in forms that match their needs. The dis-

Table 1.
Significant shifts in research attention.

Attribute	1960 ± 5 years: programming any-which-way	1970 ± 5 years: programming-in-the small	1980 ± 5 years: programming-in-the-large
Characteristic problems	Small programs	Algorithms and programming	Interfaces, management system structures
Data issues	Representing structure and symbolic information	Data structures and types	Long-lived databases, symbolic as well as numeric
Control issues	Elementary understanding of control flows	Programs execute once and terminate	Program assemblies execute continually
Specification issues	Mnemonics, precise use of prose	Simple input/output specifications	Systems with complex specifications
State space	State not well understood apart from control	Small, simple state space	Large, structured state space
Management focus	None	Individual effort	Team efforts, system lifetime maintenance
Tools, methods	Assemblers, core dumps	Programming language, compilers, linkers, loaders	Environments, integrated tools, documents

tinction between a system's computational component and the application it serves is often very soft — the development of effective software now often requires substantial application expertise.

Maturity of development techniques. Our development abilities have certainly improved over the 40 or so years of programming experience. Progress has been both qualitative and quantitative. Moreover, it has taken different forms in the worlds of research and practice.

One of the most familiar characterizations of this progress has been the shift from programming-in-the-small to programming-in-the-large. It is also useful to look at a shift that took place 10 years before that, from programming-any-which-way to programming-in-the-small. Table 1 summarizes these shifts, both of which describe the focus of attention of the software research community.

Before the mid-1960s, programming was substantially ad hoc; it was a significant accomplishment to get a program to run at all. Complex software systems were created — some performed very well — but their construction was either highly empirical or a virtuoso activity. To make programs intelligible, we used mnemonics, we tried to be precise about writing comments, and we wrote prose specifications. Our emphasis was on small programs, which was all we could handle predictably.

We did come to understand that computers are symbolic information processors, not just number crunchers — a significant insight. But the abstractions of

algorithms and data structures did not emerge until 1967, when Donald Knuth showed the utility of thinking about them in isolation from the particular programs that happened to implement them.

A similar shift in attitudes about specifications took place at about the same time, when Robert Floyd showed how attaching logical formulas to programs allows formal reasoning about the programs. Thus, the late 1960s saw a shift from crafting monolithic programs to an emphasis on algorithms and data structures. But the programs in question were still simple programs that execute once and then terminate.

You can view the shift that took place in the mid-1970s from programming-in-the-small to programming-in-the-large in much the same terms. Research attention turned to complex systems whose specifications were concerned not only with the functional relations of the inputs and outputs, but also with performance, reliability, and the states through which the system passed. This led to a shift in emphasis to interfaces and managing the programming process.

In addition, the data of complex systems often outlives the programs and may be more valuable, so we learned that we now have to worry about integrity and consistency of databases. Many of our programs (for example, the telephone switching system or a computer operating system) should *not* terminate; these systems require a different sort of reasoning than do programs that take input, compute, produce output, and terminate. In systems

that run indefinitely, the sequence of system states is often much more important than the (possibly undesirable) termination condition.

The tools and techniques that accompanied the shift from programming-any-which-way to programming-in-the-small provided first steps toward systematic, routine development of small programs; they also seeded the development of a science that has matured only in the last decade. The tools and techniques that accompanied the shift from programming-in-the-small to programming-in-the-large were largely geared to supporting groups of programmers working together in orderly ways and to giving management a view into production processes. This directly supports the commercial practice of development.

Practical development proceeded to large complex systems much faster than the research community did. For example, the Sage missile-defense system of the 1950s and the Sabre airline-reservation system of the 1960s were successful interactive systems on a scale that far exceeded the maturity of the science. They appear to have been developed by excellent engineers who understood the requirements well and applied design and development methods from other (like electrical) engineering disciplines. Modern development methodologies are management procedures intended to guide large numbers of developers through similar disciplines.

The term "software engineering" was introduced in 1968 to name a conference convened by NATO to discuss problems of software production.[9] Despite the label, most of the discussion dealt with the challenge of progressing from the craft stage to the commercial stage of practice. In 1976, Barry Boehm proposed the definition of the term as "the practical application of scientific knowledge in the design and construction of computer programs and the associated documentation required to develop, operate, and maintain them."[10] This definition is consistent with traditional definitions of engineering, although Boehm noted the shortage of scientific knowledge to apply.

Unfortunately, the term is now most often used to refer to life-cycle models, routine methodologies, cost-estimation techniques, documentation frameworks, configuration-management tools, quality-assurance techniques, and other techniques for standardizing production activities. These technologies are characteristic of the commercial stage of evolution — "software management" would be a much more appropriate term.

Scientific basis for engineering practice. Engineering practice emerges from commercial practice by exploiting the results of a companion science. The scientific results must be mature and rich enough to model practical problems. They must also be organized in a form that is useful to practitioners. Computer science has a few models and theories that are ready to support practice, but the packaging of these results for operational use is lacking.

Maturity of supporting science. Despite the criticism sometimes made by software producers that computer science is irrelevant to practical software, good models and theories *have* been developed in areas that have had enough time for the theories to mature.

In the early 1960s, algorithms and data structures were simply created as part of each program. Some folklore grew up about good ways to do certain sorts of things, and it was transmitted informally. By the mid-1960s, good programmers shared the intuition that if you get the data structures right, the rest of the program is much simpler. In the late 1960s, algorithms and data structures began to

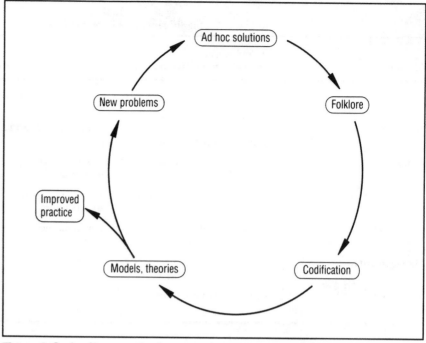

Figure 4. Cycle of how good software models develop as a result of the interaction between science and engineering.

be abstracted from individual programs, and their essential properties were described and analyzed.

The 1970s saw substantial progress in supporting theories, including performance analysis and correctness. Concurrently, the programming implications of these abstractions were explored; abstract-data-type research dealt with such issues as:

• Specifications: abstract models and algebraic axioms.

• Software structure: bundling representation with algorithms.

• Language issues: modules, scope, and user-defined types.

• Information hiding: protecting the integrity of information not in the specification.

• Integrity constraints: invariants of data structures.

• Composition rules: declarations.

Both sound theory and language support were available by the early 1980s, and routine good practice now depends on this support.

Compiler construction is another good example. In 1960, simply writing a compiler at all was a major achievement; it is not clear that we really understood what a higher level language was. Formal syntax was first used systematically for Algol-60, and tools for processing it automatically (then called compiler compilers, but now called parser generators) were first developed in the mid-1960s and made practical

in the 1970s. Also in the 1970s, we started developing theories of semantics and types, and the 1980s have brought significant progress toward the automation of compiler construction.

Both of these examples have roots in the problems of the 1960s and became genuinely practical in the 1980s. It takes a good 20 years from the time that work starts on a theory until it provides serious assistance to routine practice. Development periods of comparable length have also preceded the widespread use of systematic methods and technologies like structured programming, Smalltalk, and Unix, as Sam Redwine and colleagues have shown.[11] But the whole field of computing is only about 40 years old, and many theories are emerging in the research pipeline.

Interaction between science and engineering. The development of good models within the software domain follows this pattern:

We engineers begin by solving problems any way we can. After some time, we distinguish in those ad hoc solutions things that usually work and things that do not usually work. The ones that do work enter the folklore: People tell each other about them informally. As the folklore becomes more and more systematic, we codify it as written heuristics and rules of procedure. Eventually, that codification becomes crisp enough to support models and theories, together with the associated mathematics. These can then help improve practice,

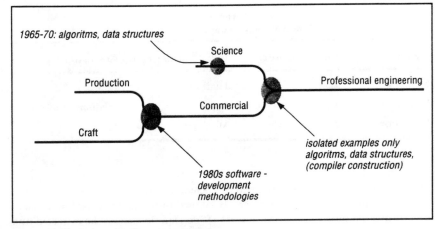

Figure 5. Evolution of software engineering.

and experience from that practice can sharpen the theories. Furthermore, the improvement in practice let us think about harder problems — which we first solve ad hoc, then find heuristics for, eventually develop new models and theories for, and so on. Figure 4 illustrates this cycle.

The models and theories do not have to be fully fleshed out for this process to assist practice: The initial codification of folklore may be useful in and of itself.

This progression is illustrated in the use of machine language for control flow in the 1960s. In the late 1950s and the early 1960s, we did not have crisp notions about what an iteration or a conditional was, so we laid down special-purpose code, building each structure individually out of test and branch instructions.

Eventually, a small set of patterns emerged as generally useful, generally easy to get right, and generally at least as good as the alternatives. Designers of higher level languages explicitly identified the most useful ones and codified them by producing special-purpose syntax. A formal result about the completeness of the structured constructs provided additional reassurance.

Now, almost nobody believes that new kinds of loops should be invented as a routine practice. A few kinds of iterations and a few kinds of conditionals are captured in the languages. They are taught as control concepts that go with the language; people use them routinely, without concern for the underlying machine code.

Further experience led to verifiable formal specifications of these statements' semantics and of the programs that used them. Experience with the formalization in turn refined the statements supported in programming languages. In this way, ad hoc practice entered a period of folklore and eventually matured to have conventional syntax and semantic theories that

explain it.

Where is software? Where, then, does current software practice lie on the path to engineering? It is still in some cases craft and in some cases commercial practice. A science is beginning to contribute results, and, for isolated examples, you can argue that professional engineering is taking place. (Figure 5 shows where software practice fits on my model.)

That is not, however, the common case. There are good grounds to expect that there will eventually be an engineering discipline of software. Its nature will be technical, and it will be based in computer science. Although we have not yet matured to that state, it is an achievable goal.

The next tasks for the software profession are

• to pick an appropriate mix of short-term, pragmatic, possible purely empirical contributions that help stabilize commercial practice and

• to invest in long-term efforts to develop and make available basic scientific contributions.

The profession must take five basic steps on its path to becoming a true engineering discipline:

Understand the nature of expertise. Proficiency in any field requires not only higher order reasoning skills but also a large store of facts together with a certain amount of context about their implications and appropriate use. Studies have demonstrated this across a wide range of problem domains, including medical diagnosis, physics, chess, financial analysis, architecture, scientific research, policy decision making, and others, as Herbert Simon described in the paper "Human Experts and Knowledge-Based Systems" presented at the 1987 IFIP Working

Group 10.1 Workshop on Concepts and Characteristics of Knowledge-Based Systems.

An expert in a field must know about 50,000 chunks of information, where a chunk is any cluster of knowledge sufficiently familiar that it can be remembered rather than derived. Furthermore, in domains where there are full-time professionals, it takes no less than 10 years for a world-class expert to achieve that level of proficiency.[11]

Thus, fluency in a domain requires content and context as well as skills. In the case of natural-language fluency, E.D. Hirsch has argued that abstract skills have driven out content; students are expected (unrealistically) to learn general skills from a few typical examples rather than by a "piling up of information"; and intellectual and social skills are supposed to develop naturally without regard to the specific content.[12]

However, Hirsch wrote, specific information is important at all stages. Not only are the specific facts important in their own right, but they serve as carriers of shared culture and shared values. A software engineer's expertise includes facts about computer science in general, software design elements, programming idioms, representations, and specific knowledge about the program of current interest. In addition, it requires skill with tools: the language, environment, and support software with which this program is implemented.

Hirsch provided a list of some 5,000 words and concepts that represent the information actually possessed by literate Americans. The list goes beyond simple vocabulary to enumerate objects, concepts, titles, and phrases that implicitly invoke cultural context beyond their dictionary definitions. Whether or not you agree in detail with its composition, the list and accompanying argument demonstrate the need for connotations as well as denotations of the vocabulary.

Similarly, a programmer needs to know not only a programming language but also the system calls supported by the environment, the general-purpose libraries, the application-specific libraries, and how to combine invocations of these definitions effectively. The programmer must

Table 2.
Cost distributions for the thee ways to get a piece of information.

Method	Infrastructure cost	Initial-learning cost	Cost of use in practice
Memory	Low	High	Low
Reference	High	Low	Medium
Derivation	Medium-high	Medium	High

be familiar with the global definitions of the program of current interest and the rules about their use. In addition, a developer of application software must understand application-area issues.

Simply put, the engineering of software would be better supported if we knew better what specific content a software engineer should know. We could organize the teaching of this material so useful subsets are learned first, followed by progressively more sophisticated subsets. We could also develop standard reference materials as carriers of the content.

Recognize different ways to get information. Given that a large body of knowledge is important to a working professional, we as a discipline must ask how software engineers should acquire the knowledge, either as students or as working professionals. Generally speaking, there are three ways to get a piece of information you need: You can remember it, you can look it up, or you can derive it. These have different distributions of costs, as Table 2 shows.

Memorization requires a relatively large initial investment in learning the material, which is then available for instant use.

Reference materials require a large investment by the profession for developing both the organization and the content; each student must then learn how to use the reference materials and then do so as a working professional.

Deriving information may involve ad hoc creation from scratch, it may involve instantiation of a formal model, or it may involve inferring meaning from other available information. To the extent that formal models are available, their formulation requires a substantial initial investment. Students first learn the models, then apply them in practice. Because each new application requires the model to be applied anew, the cost in use may be very high.[13]

Each professional's allocation of effort among these alternatives is driven by what he has already learned, by habits developed during that education, and by the reference materials available. Today, general-purpose reference material for software is scarce, although documentation for specific computer systems, languages,

and applications may be extensive. Even when documentation is available, however, it may be underused because it is poorly indexed or because developers have learned to prefer fresh derivation to use of existing solutions. The same is true of subroutine libraries.

Simply put, software engineering requires investment in the infrastructure cost — in creating the materials required to organize information, especially reference material for practitioners.

Encourage routine practice. Good engineering practice for routine design depends on the engineer's command of factual knowledge and design skills and on the quality of reference materials available. It also depends on the incentives and values associated with innovation.

Unfortunately, computer-science education has prepared developers with a background that emphasizes fresh creation almost exclusively. Students learn to work alone and to develop programs from scratch. They are rarely asked to understand software systems they have not written. However, just as natural-language fluency requires instant recognition of a core vocabulary, programming fluency should require an extensive vocabulary of definitions that the programmer can use familiarly, without repeated recourse to documentation.

Fred Brooks has argued that one of the great hopes for software engineering is the cultivation of great designers.[14] Indeed, innovative designs require great designers. But great designers are rare, and most designs need not be innovative. Systematic presentation of design fragments and techniques that are known to work can enable designers of ordinary talent to produce effective results for a wide range of more routine problems by using prior results (buying or growing, in Brooks's terms) instead of always building from scratch.

It is unreasonable to expect a designer or developer to take advantage of scientific theories or experience if the necessary information is not readily available.

Scientific results need to be recast in operational form; the important information from experience must be extracted from examples. The content should include design elements, components, interfaces, interchange representations, and algorithms. A conceptual structure must be developed so the information can be found when it is needed. These facts must be augmented with analysis techniques or guidelines to support selection of alternatives that best match the problem at hand.

A few examples of well-organized reference materials already exist. For example, the summary flowchart of William Martin's sorting survey[15] captured in one page the information a designer needed to choose among the then-current sorting techniques. William Cody and William Waite's manual for implementing elementary mathematical functions[16] gives for each function the basic strategy and special considerations needed to adapt that strategy to various hardware architectures.

Although engineering has traditionally relied on handbooks published in book form, a software engineers' handbook must be on line and interactive. No other alternative allows for rapid distribution of updates at the rate this field changes, and no other alternative has the potential for smooth integration with on-line design tools. The on-line incarnation will require solutions to a variety of electronic-publishing problems, including distribution, validation, organization and search, and collection and distribution of royalties.

Simply put, software engineering would benefit from a shift of emphasis in which both reference materials and case studies of exemplary software designs are incorporated in the curriculum. The discipline must find ways to reward preparation of material for reference use and the development of good case studies.

Expect professional specializations. As software practice matures toward engineering, the body of substantive technical knowledge required of a designer or developer continues to grow. In some areas, it has long since grown large enough to require specialization — for example, database administration was long ago separated from the corresponding programming. But systems programming has been resistant to explicit recognition of professional specialties.

In the coming decade, we can expect to see specialization of two kinds:

• internal specialization as the technical content in the core of software grows deeper and

• external specialization with an increased range of applications that require both substantive application knowledge and substantive computing knowledge.

Internal specialties are already starting to be recognizable for communications, reliability, real-time programming, scientific computing, and graphics, among others. Because these specialties rely critically on mastery of a substantial body of computer science, they may be most appropriately organized as postbaccalaureate education.

External specialization is becoming common, but the required dual expertise is usually acquired informally (and often incompletely). Computational specializations in various disciplines can be supported via joint programs involving both computer science and the application department; this is being done at some universities.

Simply put, software engineering will require explicit recognition of specialties. Educational opportunities should be provided to support them. However, this should not be done at the cost of a solid foundation in computer science and, in the case of external specialization, in the application discipline.

Improve the coupling between science and commercial practice. Good science is often based on problems underlying the problems of production. This should be as true for computer science as for any other discipline. Good science depends on strong interactions between researchers and practitioners. However, cultural differences, lack of access to large, complex systems, and the sheer difficulty of understanding those systems have interfered with the communication that supports these interactions.

Similarly, the adoption of results from the research community has been impeded by poor understanding of how to turn a research result into a useful element of a production environment. Some companies and universities are already developing cooperative programs to bridge this gap, but the logistics are often daunting.

Simply put, an engineering basis for software will evolve faster if constructive interaction between research and production communities can be nurtured. ❖

Acknowledgments

This article benefited from comments by Allen Newell, Norm Gibbs, Frank Friedman, Tom Lane, and the other authors of articles in this special issue. Most important, Eldon Shaw fostered my appreciation for engineering. Without his support, this work would not have been possible, so I dedicate this article to his memory.

This work was supported by the US Defense Dept. and a grant from Mobay Corp.

References

1. J.K. Finch, *Engineering and Western Civilization*, McGraw-Hill, New York, 1951.

2. E.W. Dijkstra, "On the Cruelty of Really Teaching Computing Science," *Comm. ACM*, Dec. 1989, pp. 1,398-1,404.

3. D.L. Parnas, "Education for Computing Professionals," *Computer*, Jan. 1990, pp. 17-22.

4. H. Straub, *A History of Civil Engineering: An Outline from Ancient to Modern Times*, MIT Press, Cambridge, Mass., 1964.

5. F.J. van Antwerpen, "The Origins of Chemical Engineering," in *History of Chemical Engineering*, W.F. Furter, ed., American Chemical Society, Washington, D.C., 1980, pp. 1-14.

6. Computer Science and Technology Board, National Research Council, *Keeping the US Computer Industry Competitive*, National Academy Press, Washington, D.C., 1990.

7. National Academy of Engineering, *Engineering and the Advancement of Human Welfare: 10 Outstanding Achievements 1964-1989*, National Academy Press, Washington, D.C., 1989.

8. E. Levin, "Grand Challenges to Computational Science," *Comm. ACM*, Dec. 1989, pp. 1,456-1,457.

9. *Software Engineering: Report on a Conference Sponsored by the NATO Science Committee, Garmisch, Germany, 1968*, P. Naur and B. Randell, eds., Scientific Affairs Div., NATO, Brussels, 1969.

10. B.W. Boehm, "Software Engineering," *IEEE Trans. Computers*, Dec. 1976, pp. 1,226-1,241.

11. S.T. Redwine et al., "DoD-Related Software Technology Requirements, Practices, and Prospects for the Future," Tech. Report P-1788, Inst. Defense Analyses, Alexandria, Va., 1984.

12. E.D. Hirsch, Jr., *Cultural Literacy: What Every American Needs to Know*, Houghton Mifflin, Boston, 1989.

13. M. Shaw, D. Giuse, and R. Reddy, "What a Software Engineer Needs to Know I: Vocabulary," tech. report CMU/SEI-89-TR-30, Carnegie Mellon Univ., Pittsburgh, Aug. 1989.

14. F.P. Brooks, Jr., "No Silver Bullet: Essence and Accidents of Software Engineering," *Information Processing 86*, pp. 1,069-1,076.

15. W.A. Martin, "Sorting," *ACM Computing Surveys*, Dec. 1971, pp. 147-174.

16. W.J. Cody, Jr., and W.M. Waite, *Software Manual for the Elementary Functions*, Prentice-Hall, Englewood Cliffs, N.J., 1980.

Mary Shaw is a professor of computer science at Carnegie Mellon University, where she has been on the faculty since 1971. From 1984 to 1987, she was chief scientist at the Software Engineering Institute, with which she still has a joint appointment. Her primary research interests are programming systems and software engineering, particularly abstraction techniques and language tools for developing and evaluating software.

Shaw received a BA in mathematics from Rice University and a PhD in computer science from Carnegie Mellon University. She is a member of the IEEE Computer Society, ACM, New York Academy of Sciences, and Sigma Xi. She also serves on the National Research Council's Computer Science and Technology Board, IEEE Technical Committee on Software Engineering, and IFIP Working Group 2.4 (System Implementation Languages).

Address questions about this article to the author at Computer Science Dept., Carnegie Mellon University, Pittsburgh, PA 15213-3890; Internet shaw@cs.cmu.edu.

SOFTWARE DEVELOPMENT: STATE OF THE ART VS. STATE OF THE PRACTICE

Tom DeMarco and Tim Lister
The Atlantic Systems Guild
353 W. 12th St.
New York, NY 10014

ABSTRACT: The state of the art of software development has changed considerably from the folkloric approaches of the 1950s and 60s. But has the state of the practice kept up? A commonly held (rather cynical) view is that the great revolutions associated with the names of Dijkstra, Wirth, Mills, Hoare, Parnas, Myers and others might as well not have happened for all the effect they had on the practice of the average developer.

During the years 1984 through 1987, the authors conducted a series of performance benchmarking exercises to allow individuals and organizations to evaluate their relative productivity. The emphasis of the benchmarks was on speed of program construction and low defect rate. A side-effect of the exercise was that nearly 400 programmers wrote the same program (they all wrote to the same specification) and sent in listings of these programs along with their questionnaires, time logs, and test results. This afforded an opportunity to assess design and coding practice of a wide sample of developers.

KEYWORDS: Empirical study, program design, software development methodology, software measurement.

1. BACKGROUND

Both individuals and the organizations they work for are aware of a distressing ignorance of how their effectiveness compares to that of their peers and competitors. Beginning in 1984, we offered both the opportunity to take part in a kind of "implementation bakeoff," called *Coding War Games* to help them assess their relative productivity. These exercises were run according to the following rules:

- ❏ developers took part in pairs; the two individuals of each pair competed with each other as well as with other pairs in the exercise

- ❏ all participants wrote the same program to the same specification

- ❏ after design, coding, desk-check and compilation, pair members exchanged programs for testing; development was thus conducted using a clean-room approach, as described in [1]; programs were not repaired at any point—defects reported included all the defects present at the end of desk-check

- ❏ after their own tests, developers ran our predefined tests on the product

- ❏ submissions sent to us were identified by a code number drawn by the individual at the beginning of the exercise; only the individual knew his/her code; results were conveyed back to participants by code number, thus assuring confidentiality

(A summary of findings from the 1984 and 1985 Coding War Games is presented in [2].)

Over the period of the experiment, we had 392 individuals take part in the Coding Wars. Participants came from 79 different organizations. We divided the participants by language used into seven communities. The relative proportions by language are shown in Figure 1:

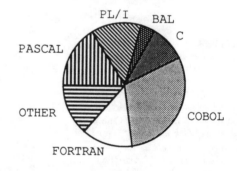

Figure 1: Participants by Language Community

There were 118 COBOL programmers, and 50 in the group called "OTHER." Included under OTHER were Ada, Modula-2, Forth, Cybil, Mapper, MUMPS, Jovial, APL and some languages that we couldn't identify at all.

©1989 ACM 0270-5257/89/0500/0271$00.75

Recommended by: Anthony Wasserman

"Software Development: State of the Art vs. State of the Practice," by T. DeMarco and T. Lister from *Proc. 11th Int'l Conf. Software Engineering*, 1989, pages 271-275. Copyright © 1989 by the Association for Computing Machinery, Inc., reprinted with permission.

A distinguishing characteristic of our sample is the fact that participants were curious about how good they were. In addition, they were solicited through announcements in various journals, and through seminars and conferences, thus proving that they could read, or worked for organizations with non-zero training and travel budgets. Aside from these admitted biases, the sample seemed normal to us. Individuals came from all kinds of organizations: financial, service, engineering, university and public sector. There were participants from the U.S., the United Kingdom and Denmark. They were all professional programmers, ranging in experience from one to 16 years.

To determine if the improved state of the art of software development is indeed reflected in the practice, we examined the listings submitted by language. We counted executable statements and declarations, modules, subroutine invocations, pathological connections, module size, variable locality, and coupling. In addition, we attempted to assess module binding strength. Not all analyses were performed on all language groups.

2. HYPOTHESES TO TEST

We selected seven indications of good modularization and programming technique, as reflected in the literature. Each of these was formulated into a positive hypothesis, asserting that the technique was reflected in practice. Then we analyzed participants' code to confirm or refute each hypothesis. The seven hypotheses were:

1. Developers divide programs into modules of manageable size.
2. Developers attempt to maximize locality of data.
3. Developers attempt to maximize module binding strength.
4. Developers attempt to practice data hiding.
5. Developers can use clean room methods to develop zero-defect products.
6. Developers practice structured coding.
7. Organizations with strongly enforced design methodologies achieve meaningful convergence of design from individual to individual.

3. THE RESULTS: AN ASSESSMENT OF THE STATE OF THE PRACTICE

It is possible that the task of wading through 300 plus listings of the same program causes severe damage to the human judgmental capacities. If that is not the explanation, then we must conclude that the state of modularization and programming technique is surprisingly respectable. This is exactly the opposite of what we expected to find. Based on an initial scan of a subset of the data, we were convinced we would be writing a paper demonstrating that the state of the practice was utterly uninfluenced by the state of the art. (Such a paper might have been more amusing.) Five of the seven hypotheses were confirmed. The details are presented below:

- HYPOTHESIS 1 (USE OF SMALL MODULES): CONFIRMED

In all of the following, we use the word *module* to mean a closed subroutine with a single identifier by which the unit can be activated as a whole.

By the middle seventies, the case for small modules was already being made persuasively in the literature (see [3 and 4], for example). But hearsay evidence implied that the state of the practice even ten years later was a module of 500 lines or more. This is complicated by an early "modularization" act performed by the manager at the time of job assignment. These allocations are usually of at least 500 lines, and also called modules. But do developers then implement these as undivided monoliths, or subdivide them further, out of respect for the principle of small modules?

Our sample indicated a strong preference for subdivision into small modules. The average module was 23 statements. In an analysis of 200 COBOL and Pascal programs, we found only 55 that had even a single module that exceeded a page of listing (the limit proposed by Mills).

Use of small modules paid off handsomely. When we analyzed the records of those 55 developers who allowed large modules (one or more), we found that they had been substantially outdone by those who exhibited a more serious respect for small modules. The no-large-module subset had 38% fewer defects and was nearly twice as likely to pass the aggregate test of functionality (referred to below as the *acid test*) included in our test set.

When we divided the sample into quartiles based on speed and accuracy, we found an increasing number of long module users in the poorer quartiles:

Performers in:	
1st quartile —	21% had long module(s)
2nd quartile —	31% had long module(s)
3rd quartile —	36% had long module(s)
4th quartile —	47% had long module(s)

- HYPOTHESIS 2 (MAXIMUM LOCALITY): PARTIALLY CONFIRMED

Locality analysis was performed only on the Pascal subset.

As a coarse metric of locality, we looked at the percentage of all variables that were defined so as to be visible in only one module. (The metric is coarse because variables that are truly local to the main-line module are nonetheless visible to subordinate modules under the scoping rules of Pascal.) We defined a *locality factor* as the count of local variables divided by the count of all variables. Locality factors varied from 0 (all variables visible to all modules) to .96 (only 4% of variables visible outside of defining module). The average locality was .51. Only 12% of the sample had a locality factor of less than .20. Developers were clearly making an effort to keep as many variables as possible local to their defining modules.

Emphasis on high locality paid off: 1st quartile performers had average locality factors nearly 25% higher than 4th quartile performers. The subset of programs with higher than median locality had 63% fewer errors than programs with lower than median locality.

- HYPOTHESIS 3 (STRONG MODULE BINDING): CONFIRMED

The idea that a module ought to be strongly connected within and loosely connected to its exterior comes to us from [4, 5, and 6]. The tightness of connection within is called *binding strength*. Most writers on the subject describe functional binding (all elements of the module act to achieve a single function) as the strongest.

There was one algorithm in the benchmark problem that gave a natural opportunity for functional binding. We looked at the COBOL, Pascal and Fortran subsets to see how many developers seized the opportunity and encapsulated the algorithm in its own module. More than three quarters of all the programs analyzed did encapsulate the algorithm, giving good evidence that programmers are mindful of binding strength.

Those who did hit upon the functionally bound module were nearly twice as likely to pass the acid test of correctness. Those who did not hit upon the functionally bound module were four times as likely to end up in the 4th performance quartile (based on speed and accuracy) as in the 1st.

- HYPOTHESIS 4 (DATA HIDING): NOT CONFIRMED

The principle of data hiding as a basis for modularization is presented in [7], and more recently in [8]. There was a clear opportunity in the Coding War problem to encapsulate and thus conceal an awkward data structure. A modular design that takes advantage of this opportunity yielded a slightly better readability, in our opinion. Yet none of the subset of programs analyzed did encapsulate the data structure.

Our assessment on this point is weak because the awkward data structure was not *very* awkward. Had it been more unwieldy, perhaps more developers would have tried to conceal it within a module. All we have found is a lack of evidence that programmers are looking aggressively to hide complexity.

- HYPOTHESIS 5 (CLEAN ROOM METHODS): WEAKLY CONFIRMED

The term *clean-room development*, first coined by Harlan Mills, implies a development process that emphasizes correct initial program construction, rather than cycles of coding and repair. In its most common form developers either code or test, but not both; those who write the code have had the last chance to save their honor (avoid defects) when they announce the product is ready for test. The Coding War Games required a total separation of code and test.

After a controlled experiment on the use of clean-room methods, Selby, Basili and Baker reported in [9] that 86% of participants had complained of missing the satisfaction of testing their own code, but 81% nonetheless said they would use the method again. And resultant product quality was excellent.

Our findings were similar. The most frequent comment from participants was objection to clean-room procedures. However, more than one third of all participants did deliver zero-defect products, even without the opportunity to test and repair. The exercise was small, but not trivial. It involved an average length of 163 Pascal statements or 234 COBOL statements. The fact that clean-room novices could perform so well in this mode is an encouraging sign.

- HYPOTHESIS 6 (USE OF STRUCTURED CODING): CONFIRMED

A frequently repeated horror story among consultants is that the 1970s never happened at such-and-such corporation, where spaghetti-bowl coding is the invariant rule. Our sample gave little evidence of this (perhaps apocryphal) effect. Programs were mostly well structured and sensibly indented to call attention to control subordination.

There was more goto use than we might have expected. In the Pascal subset, for example, fully 21% of the programs had goto statements. We looked at each incident of goto use to understand the developers rationale for this possible violation of structured programming technique. Of the 105 goto statements analyzed, the vast majority were emergency exits or loop exits, in keeping with the disciplined use of gotos suggested by Knuth and Zahn [10 and 11]. Fewer than 4% of the programs could be judged "unstructured."

The COBOL subset was slightly less pure in its use of structured programming. The average program had 11 subroutine invocations and 8 gotos. Again, the gotos were mostly used to implement sensible structured programming constructs not directly supported by the language.

- HYPOTHESIS 7 (CONVERGENCE OF DESIGN): REFUTED

An argument for strong, centrally enforced Methodology is that any two developers would be inclined to come up with the same design for a given specification.

One company, known for its almost religiously imposed Methodology, had 16 participants in the 1987 Games. All had been trained in "The Methodology." There was no sign at all of convergence of design concept among the 16. Their programs had as few as 4 and as many as 23 modules with an even distribution between the extremes. They didn't even code in a very similar style (from 0 to 17 gotos, a nearly 3-1 variation in total program length).

4. ANOMALIES DETECTED EN ROUTE

In looking over the code, we observed three pronounced patterns that, though they do not pertain precisely to the theme of this paper, seemed worth noting.

The first was a surprising variation in program length. For those who hope to treat length as an indication of function size, the variation of nearly ten-to-one across a sample of programs in the same language and written to the same specification is truly daunting. Figure 2, presented below, shows the variation in program length for the COBOL community.

The observed variation is bound to raise questions about our counting standard. For the record, we performed a syntax-directed count of executable and declaration statements, excluding comments and blank lines. We defined total length as the sum of executable statements and declaration statements. To achieve some uniformity between languages, we did not count braces in C or BEGINs and ENDs in other languages. All counts were conducted to a written standard.

Since we had so many programmers who hit upon the same functionally bound module, we used that module as the basis for a detailed analysis of varying length. All the modules analyzed were functionally identical. The count of statements, however varied for this single tiny module by a factor of eight. When we counted lines instead of statements, the variation was greater. This seemed like an ideal opportunity to experiment in the use of some of the Halstead metrics [13]. We computed Halstead's length, vocabulary and volume for a subset of the modules. Each of the

Halstead metrics succeeded to some degree in damping out the variation. Consider the maximum divided by the minimum for different ways of assessing the module's size:

SIZE MEASUREMENT	MAX/MIN
STATEMENT COUNT	8.00
HALSTEAD'S LENGTH	1.73
VOCABULARY	1.59
VOLUME	1.94

The second pattern observed was the variation in the number of variables used. In the Pascal community, for example, the average number of variables used was 20. But some programmers used as few as 7 and others as many as 42. Those who used more variables had proportionately longer programs.

The third pattern was that those who wrote more verbose programs took longer to do the work and had a higher defect rate than those who wrote spare programs. This would not have been thought an anomaly at all in the 1970s. But current conventional wisdom is that spare programs might be tighter and so harder to deal with. Our data indicates otherwise.

5. USE OF CWG RAW DATA

Such a large sample of programs written to the same specification appears to be unique. We propose to make copies of the raw data available gratis to researchers who request them. The data is in the form of Macintosh-format Excel diskettes.

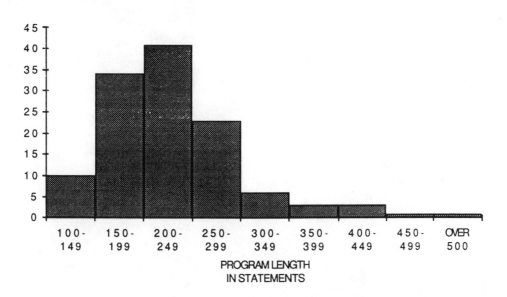

Figure 2.: Distribution by Program Length (COBOL only)

REFERENCES

1. Dyer, M., R.C. Linger and H.D. Mills, "Cleanroom Software Engineering," *IEEE Software*. September, 1987.

2. DeMarco, T., and T. Lister, "Programmer performance and the effects of the workplace." *IEEE Proceedings , 8th International Conference on Software Engineering,* Silver Spring, MD: IEEE Computer Society. 1985.

3. Mills, H.D., "Top Down Programming in Large Systems," in R. Rustin, ed., *Debugging Techniques in Large Systems,* Englewood Cliffs, NJ: Prentice-Hall. 1971.

4. Myers, G.J., *Reliable Software Through Composite Design*. New York: Petrocelli/Charter. 1975.

5. Stevens, W., G.J. Myers and L.L. Constantine, "Structured Design," *IBM Systems Journal*. Vol. 13, No. 2. May, 1974.

6. Yourdon, E. and L.L. Constantine, *Structured Design*. Englewood Cliffs, NJ: Prentice-Hall. 1979.

7. Parnas, D.L., "On the Criteria to Be Used in Decomposing Systems into Modules." *Communications of the ACM*, Vol. 15, No. 12. December, 1972.

8. Booch, G., *Software Engineering with Ada*. Menlo Park, CA: The Benjamin Cummings Publishing Company. 1983.

9. Selby, R.W., V.R. Basili and F.T. Baker, "Cleanroom Software Engineering: An Empirical Evaluation." *IEEE Transactions on Software Engineering*. September, 1987.

10. Knuth, D.E., "Structured Programming with go to Statements." R.T. Yeh, Ed., *Current Trends in Programming Methodology*. Englewood Cliffs, NJ: Prentice-Hall. 1977.

11. Zahn, C.T., "A Control Statement for Natural Top-Down Structured Programming." *Symposium on Programming Languages*. Paris, France. 1974.

12. Halstead, M.H., *Elements of Software Science*. New York: American Elsevier. 1977.

Reprinted from *IEEE Software*, Vol. 8, No. 1, January 1991, pp. 13-24. Copyright © 1991 by The Institute of Electrical and Electronics Engineers, Inc. All rights reserved.

Making Reuse Cost-Effective

BRUCE H. BARNES, *National Science Foundation*
TERRY B. BOLLINGER, *Contel Technology Center*

◆*Software reuse must be recognized as having the same cost and risk features as any financial investment.*

This article suggests analytical approaches for making good reuse investments.

There has been quite a bit of debate in the last few years on the merits of software reuse. One reason for this continuing debate has been a question of scope: Should software reuse be defined narrowly in terms of one or a few specific methods (such as libraries of scavenged parts), or should it be defined broadly so it includes widely differing methods and processes?

The question of scope is important, since it really asks whether the concept of software reuse provides any major insight into the software-development process. A narrow definition implies that reuse is simply another development technique that, like many other techniques, is helpful in some contexts and inappropriate in many others. A broad definition implies that reuse incorporates one or more general principles that should be recognized and addressed ex-

plicitly in the software-development process.

We believe that reuse is in fact one of the fundamental paradigms of development and that, until it is better understood, significant reductions in the cost of building large systems will simply not be possible. We base this assertion primarily on our belief that:

The defining characteristic of good reuse is not the reuse of software per se, but the reuse of human problem solving.

A SCARCE RESOURCE

By "human problem solving," we mean those nonrepetitive, nontrivial aspects of software development and maintenance that cannot easily be formalized or automated using current levels of expertise. Unlike many other hardware and software resources used in development,

human problem solving cannot readily be multiplied, multiplexed, accelerated, or enhanced. Problem solving thus shares many of the characteristics of precious metals in the materials-processing industry: It must be used judiciously, replaced by less expensive resources when possible, and recovered for further use whenever feasible.

If human problem solving is viewed as a scarce resource then the three techniques of judicious use, replacement, and recovery correspond fairly closely to project planning, automation, and reuse:

• Good planning reduces the loss of human problem solving by minimizing redundant and dead-end work, by enhancing communication of solutions among developers, and by helping development groups select environments that support worker productivity.

• Automation is the classic process of tool building, in which well-understood work activities such as the conversion of formulas into assembly code are replaced with less costly automated tools such as compilers.

• Reuse multiplies the effectiveness of human problem solving by ensuring that the extensive work or special knowledge used to solve specific development problems will be transferred to as many similar problems as possible. Reuse differs from judicious planning in that it can actually amplify available problem-solving resources, just as automation can amplify the effect of well-understood, formally defined work activities.

Broad-spectrum reuse. If the key feature of effective software reuse is the reuse of problem-solving skills, it follows that reuse should not be restricted to source code. Any work product that makes problem solutions readily accessible to later projects is a good candidate for reuse. (A

> Problem solving shares many characteristics of precious metals. It must be used judiciously, replaced by less expensive resources when possible, and recovered for further use whenever feasible.

work product is any explicit, physical result of a work activity in the development and maintenance process.)

Examples of potentially reusable work products are requirements specifications, designs, code modules, documentation, test data, and customized tools.

This idea of *broad-spectrum* reuse[1] is particularly important because it has the potential to reduce costs substantially. It can reduce costs because reusing an early work product can greatly increase the likelihood of reuse of later work products developed from it.

For example, although reusing code modules from a custom database system can certainly reduce costs, reusing the system's overall functional specification could lead to the reuse of the entire set of designs, code modules, documentation, test data, and associated user experience that were developed from that specification. The chances of cost-effective reuse are much higher, both because more work products are reused and because the effort needed to adapt and integrate those work products into a new environment is greatly diminished.

Curiously, informal reuse of early work products is actually very common, but it often is not recognized because it masquerades as code-level reuse. Informal reuse of early work products occurs primarily when highly experienced developers use their familiarity with the functionality and design of a code module set to adapt those modules to new, similar uses.[2]

This powerful form of reuse is feasible only when developers can use their familiarity with early work products to zero in on the code modules that were derived from those products. The fact that these early work products may reside entirely within the developers' memories does not diminish their importance. Indeed, such situations point out the importance of au-

tomated support for reuse early in the life cycle. You need only have those developers retire or quit to discover how inefficient true code-level reuse is by comparison!

Reuse and automation. Thinking of effective software reuse as problem-solving reuse provides a good general heuristic for judging a work product's reuse potential. For example, modules that solve difficult or complex problems (like hardware-driver modules in an operating system) are excellent reuse candidates because they incorporate a high level of problem-solving expertise that is very expensive to replicate.

In contrast, a set of Unix date-and-time routines that differ only in their output formats are generally poor reuse candidates. You can program such format variants easily in Unix by using a stream editor such as Sed to modify the output of the standard date-and-time function. This approach is very flexible, and it requires little problem-solving skill beyond specifying the desired output formats and familiarity with a standard Unix tool. Trying to anticipate all the possible variants of date-and-time formats would in effect place a costly reuse technique (building a large library of variants) in direct competition with an existing automated method (generating variants by directly specifying output formats).

This example leads to a general rule: *Reuse should complement automation, not compete with it.*

Automation and reuse are complementary in that automation tries to transfer as much work as possible to the computer, while reuse tries to make the most efficient use of work activities that cannot be fully automated.

Automated problem solving may one day help reduce the need for the human variety, but until that day arrives, software reuse offers a practical, high-potential approach to stretching the critical development resource of human problem solving.

REUSE AS AN INVESTMENT

If reuse is a vital component of the development process, what then is the best approach to understanding it and increasing its efficiency? First and foremost, we must recognize that reuse has the same cost and risk characteristics as any financial investment. Figure 1 illustrates why reuse should be viewed as an investment and introduces the reuse-investment relation.

Reuse-investment relation. The left side of this relation, the producer side, represents all the investments made to increase reusability. Reuse investments are any costs that do not directly support the completion of an activity's primary development goals but are instead intended to make one or more work products of that activity easier to reuse. For example, labor hours devoted specifically to classifying and placing code components in a reuse library are a reuse investment, since those hours are intended primarily to benefit subsequent activities.

Reuse investments should not be confused with the costs of making software maintainable, since maintainability costs are an integral part of building deliverable products. Instead, the completion of maintenance investments is the starting point for reuse investments. This distinction is particularly important because maintenance technology overlaps extensively with reuse technology. The threshold between these two costs is best defined in terms of global objectives, rather than in terms of specific technologies.

The right side of the reuse-investment relation, the consumer side, shows the cost benefits accrued as a result of earlier reuse investments. For each activity that applies reuse, the benefit is simply a measure in dollars of how much the earlier investment helped (or hurt) the activity's effectiveness.

To calculate the reuse benefit, you must first estimate the activity's cost without reuse and compare that to its cost with reuse. For example, if an activity placed several reusable components in a library, a subsequent activity would estimate its reuse benefit by comparing total development costs without reusing those components to total development costs when the reusable components are fully exploited.

You find the *total reuse benefit* by esti-

mating the reuse benefit for *all* subsequent activities that profit from the reuse investment, even if those activities occur in the distant future. It is vital that you include all activities that benefit from a reuse investment, because it is this total benefit that determines the maximum level of reuse investment that you can apply economically to a set of work products.

In short, reuse investment is cost effective only when

$$R < B$$

where R is the total reuse investment and B is the total cost benefits. B is in turn defined as

$$B = \sum_{i=1}^{n} b_i = \sum_{i=1}^{n} [e_i - c_i]$$

where b_i is the benefit from reuse investment for activity i, e_i is the estimated cost of activity i without exploiting reuse, c_i is the cost of activty i when reuse investment is exploited, and n is the number of activities affected by the investment.

If an early estimate of the total reuse benefit indicates that it will be very small, you should make only a very limited investment in reuse technologies (beyond those needed to meet maintenance requirements). If estimates indicate that the total benefit will be very great, you should make substantial investments in advanced reuse technologies.

In either case, the failure of a development group to acknowledge the constraints of the reuse-investment relation could be disastrous from a cost perspective. After all, of what use is a very impressive, very advanced suite of reusable software if no one ever gets around to reusing it?

Producers and consumers. In Figure 1, activities that work to increase the reusability of work products are called reuse producer activities and activities that seek to reduce costs through reuse of work products are called reuse consumer activities. We intentionally used terminology with strong commercial implications because the underlying processes behind software reuse and commercial software marketing are strikingly similar.

Vendors of commercial software achieve net cost benefits only when their products are purchased (reused) enough times to cover development costs, just as reuse producers achieve a net benefit only when their work products are reused enough times to cover investment costs. Most reuse producers (vendors) and reuse consumers (buyers) differ from their commercial counterparts primarily in that the transfer of products between them takes place within a single company or project, rather than across company or organiza-

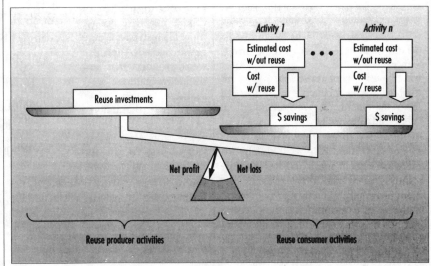

FIGURE 1. REUSE-INVESTMENT RELATION.

tional boundaries.

The producer/consumer reuse model is rich in both managerial and technical implications. One obvious managerial implication is that organizations that fail to provide some form of payback incentives to producer projects are unlikely to succeed at reuse, since producers will, in effect, be penalized for making overhead expenditures that do not directly contribute to their development project.

Indeed, it is likely that one of the most significant inhibitors of reuse in the software industry is a lack of incentive strategies to encourage coordinated reuse investments. Without such incentives, reuse becomes a scavenger hunt, where each reuse customer must bear the full cost of finding, understanding, and modifying work products to meet his needs.

Scavenging is an extremely inefficient form of reuse because it duplicates reengineering costs each time the product is reused. Well-planned investments made up front by producers can make it much easier for consumers to find, understand, and customize the parts they need. Also, reuse producers can build in reusability, which avoids the significantly more costly task of reengineering reusability into existing work products.

MAKING REUSE COST-EFFECTIVE

Another way to express the reuse-investment relation is to define a *quality-of-investment measure*, Q, which is simply the ratio of reuse benefits to reuse investments:

$Q = B/R$

where R is the total reuse investment and B is the total cost benefits resulting from reuse investment.

The Q measure is just another way of saying, "Try to get the most for your money." If Q is less than 1 for a reuse effort, there was a net financial loss; if Q is significantly greater than 1, the reuse investment provided good returns.

In the case of commercial products, Q can become very large due to the many reuses (sales) afforded by commercial marketing. The commercial-marketing comparison again points out an important issue: Reuse investments are most likely to

pay off when they are applied to high-value work products. Applying expensive reuse technologies to low-value work products is not at all likely to produce reuse winners, although in some cases such a strategy may result in particularly spectacular failures.

If the key to making reuse cost-effective is to increase the Q measure, how is such an increase best accomplished? The variables in the reuse-investment relation suggest three major strategies for increasing Q:

♦ Increase the level of reuse.

♦ Reduce the average cost of reuse.

♦ Reduce the investment needed to achieve a given reuse benefit.

We have developed ways to implement these strategies, and in the process we uncovered a few surprising implications about how reuse is closely linked to the general problem of developing high-quality software.

INCREASING REUSE

The first strategy for increasing Q is to increase the level of consumer reuse. However, the likely level of consumer reuse for a work product depends strongly on the product's intrinsic value. Components that incorporate a high level of unique expertise are far more likely to have a large reuse market than are weak products that lack distinctive features.

Increasing the number of actual instances of reuse thus should be viewed primarily as an analysis task, to identify the relative merit of investing in a set of work products. By performing such an analysis early in development, you can avoid low-value investments and more accurately determine the potential of high-value products.

Reuse instances. A *reuse instance* occurs

> One of the most significant inhibitors of reuse is a lack of incentive. Without incentives, reuse becomes a scavenger hunt, where each reuse customer must bear the full cost of finding, understanding, and modifying work products.

whenever a work product is actually reused in a subsequent development activity. Due to the strong (roughly linear) dependence of Q on the overall level of reuse, if you have low expectations for the number of reuse instances, you should keep the average level of reuse investment per unit of code low. But if you expect many reuse instances, the project may merit much more extensive reuse investments per unit of code.

In estimating reuse instances, an important first step is simply to ask questions. Often, if you ask the specifiers and architects of a new system to make an order-of-magnitude guess of the number of reuse instances (one? 10? 1,000?), they can do so with little difficulty. Even such rough approximations can help you avoid costly overinvestments.

Reuse and competition. The process of estimating reuse instances for a software component is linked to the much broader problem of understanding the commercial software market. This is because all forms of reuse are essentially competitive: Any group that wants to reuse software must decide whether to take that software from a corporate reuse library or buy it. If the quality of library software is low, if it requires extensive adaptation, or if it is poorly documented, it is entirely possible that a similar commercial product with an initially higher cost could in the long run prove to be less costly than the equivalent "free" software.

This means that reuse investors should be careful not to inflate instance estimates with reuse opportunities that are real but that are likely to be filled by products from other sources. As an extreme example, very few developers should seriously consider making a custom file system reusable, since this would place them in direct competition with a very advanced commercial market for database-management systems. A realistic estimate of the number of reuse instances in this case should be very low, perhaps zero.

You can greatly reduce the risks of mistakenly competing with external markets if you apply the principle that good software reuse is actually good problem-solving reuse. Most companies are particularly skilled in one or more problem-solving areas, which gives them important competitive advantages. A company that builds software for the National Aeronautics and Space Administration may have special expertise in flight-dynamics algorithms, for example. If a persistent need for this type of expertise is expected, the company might well find it profitable to build reusability into its flight-dynamics software. A rule of thumb summarizes such situations:

Build reusable parts for local expertise; buy reusable parts for outside expertise.

Variants analysis. Estimating reuse instances is the simplest form of a more general type of analysis that we call *variants analysis*. Variants analysis is to reusable software what requirements analysis is to traditional once-only software. Its objective is to quantify requirements for reuse investment up front, just as requirements analysis attempts to quantify requirements for functionality up front.

As in reuse-instance estimation, variants analysis in its simplest form consists simply of asking questions — explicitly examining how future development or maintenance efforts may use updated or altered versions of the current project's functional requirements.

More elaborate forms of variants analysis require a structured format to record such information. By analogy with requirements specifications, these repositories of information about likely future variants are called variants specifications.

Variants specifications. A variants specification is a requirements specification extended to include the best available information on how the activity's work products are likely to be reused.

To help designers translate these specifications into reusable products, they are stated in terms of product variants — functional variations of the primary product. Product variants can be described in many ways, ranging from explicit descriptions of multiple products to parameterized, generic requirements.

Unlike a requirements specification, a variants specification tries to describe an objective that is inherently heuristic — it must express a set of best guesses as to which of a potentially infinite range of product variants is most likely to be needed in the future.

This likelihood of use can be described in terms of a probability percentage, which may range from 100 percent for products that are specifically required as part of the product delivery, through moderate values (10 percent) for variants that are fairly good reuse candidates, to potentially very low values (0.01 percent) for product variants that are not likely to be needed but that could be very valuable if they are ever actually reused.

You can also use such likelihood-of-use percentages to set priorities, where a 100-percent rating would indicate a customer requirement that must be met to fulfill contractual obligations, while lower ratings would determine the relative value of variants.

Because variants specifications describe sets of software products, you can make them as simple or as elaborate as you want. If you describe only one product (all requirements have 100-percent priority), the variants specification is identical to a (simplistic) requirements specification. Better is a group of variants specifications that correspond to a typical requirements specification.

Although requirements specifications are not usually viewed in terms of reuse, they normally contain some variants requirements phrased in terms of modularity and portability. For example, a requirement that a product must be portable across Digital Equipment Corp., IBM, and Sun computers is a variants requirement, because it says in effect that there is a very high probability that the customer will reuse (port) the product to one or more environments.

Reuse, maintenance, and good design. Besides reusability, there is another intriguing reason explicit variants analysis could be a useful addition to the development process.

A key feature of a well-designed architecture is that it be easy to maintain, since such systems are more likely to have a long useful life span and less likely to be expensive to support. However, software maintenance is itself a form of reuse-with-replacement, in which new variants of entire systems are created and then substituted for the original systems.

From this perspective, the problem of creating a well-designed system is fundamentally a problem of anticipating its most likely variants and of applying design techniques that will ensure that the most likely variants will also be the least expensive to build during maintenance — in other words, variants analysis. Current design approaches apply general rules that, while they usually result in designs that support the necessary variants, lack the specificity provided by an explicit variants analysis.

If variants analysis is in fact a hidden dimension of good software design, then a better understanding of how to build highly reusable software could simultaneously lead to a more quantitative understanding of what makes a particular design "good" or "bad." It would also imply that good design may be a more relative concept than is generally recognized. A design that supports long-term maintenance very

> **Creating a well-designed system is fundamentally a problem of anticipating its most likely variants and of applying design techniques that will ensure that the most likely variants will also be the least expensive to build during maintenance.**

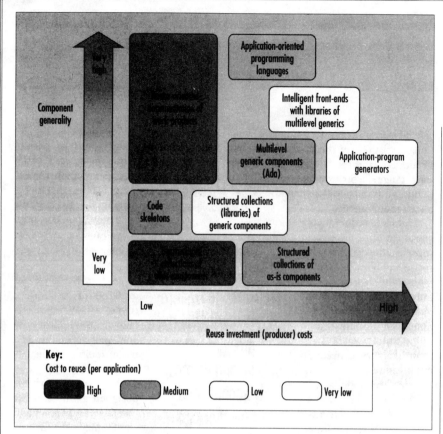

Key:
Cost to reuse (per application)

(black) High	(gray) Medium
(white) Low	(white) Very low

FIGURE 2. COST-BASED SELECTION OF REUSE TECHNOLOGIES. COMPONENT GENERALITY REFERS TO THE NUMBER OF READILY AVAILABLE VARIATIONS OF A PART; PRODUCER COST IS THE TOTAL COST OF MAKING PARTS READILY AVAILABLE TO LATER DEVELOPERS.

well in one corporate environment could simultaneously be badly mismatched to the long-term needs of a different corporate environment.

REDUCING COST

The second technique for increasing the investment-quality measure Q is to reduce the average cost of reusing work products by making them easy and inexpensive to reuse. Just as commercial vendors try to make their packages easy to adapt to the environments of many customers, reuse producers need to encourage reuse of their products by making them easy to find, adapt, and integrate into new systems.

How much a reuse producer can invest in such efforts will depend both on expected levels of reuse and the availability of appropriate reuse technologies. Reducing the cost of reuse thus depends to a large degree on selecting technologies that adequately support the needs of reuse customers while constraining reuse investment costs to acceptable levels.

Classifying reuse technologies by cost. To se-

lect reuse technologies on the basis of cost versus power, you first must compare them in these terms. Figure 2 shows some ballpark approximations of how various code-specific reuse technologies compare in terms of costs versus power.[3] (Comparable sets of reuse technologies for non-code work products such as designs and requirements specifications do not yet exist. This is a curious deficiency, since the development of such broad-spectrum reuse technologies may eventually prove to be a profitable enterprise.) The diagram has three dimensions: reuse investment costs, component generality, and cost to reuse.

Reuse investment costs. The reuse investment cost is the total cost to the producer to make parts readily available for reuse. Comparing technologies along this dimension alone will help eliminate major classes of reuse technologies as too costly. For example, program generators (exemplified by operating-system Sysgen programs) are very powerful and easy to use but require large investments.[4] You can justify such investments only if you anticipate many potential reuse instances, such

as is true for operating-system installations.

Component generality. The component-generality dimension introduces the concept of the relative power of a reuse technology, expressed in terms of how many variations of a part can readily be obtained by applying that technology. Generality measures how well a particular technology can cover the needs of an application area. Because very few parts can be reused without some modification, a technology that provides large suites of easy-to-reuse, predefined variants greatly increases the total number of reuse opportunities.

But building generality into reusable parts tends to be expensive and labor-intensive. While Ada's generic procedures are undeniably more flexible and reusable than conventional Fortran-like procedures, they are also significantly harder to build.

Generative methods are an extreme example of component generality. In effect, these methods allow the synthesis of reusable parts from application-specific languages in much the same way that compilers allow the synthesis of object-code modules from higher level languages. Although generative methods provide high levels of generality and ease of use, they require extensive analysis and preparation. Their high investment cost thus makes them appropriate only when you anticipate very many reuse instances.

Cost to reuse. The cost to reuse is the total cost to the reuse consumer of finding, adapting, integrating, and testing a reusable component. In the simplest cases, you can minimize the cost to reuse by identifying a plausible level of reuse investment and choosing the corresponding reuse technology that has the lowest cost to reuse.

Thus, if a reuse producer group has identified the need for a moderate level of reuse investment and has adequately characterized the likely reuse instances, it might choose to use Ada generics, for example, to implement its reusable components.

The key phrase, however, is "adequately characterized." The problem is

that the generality of Ada generics is comparatively low, because they primarily substitute data types rather than modify functionality. If future reuse instances are poorly characterized, this means that highly specific generalizations could easily miss the target of actual future needs. Alternately, the total costs of generalization could become excessive as the developers try to use an overly restrictive technique to cover a very broad range of conceivable reuse instances.

REDUCING INVESTMENT COSTS

The prospect of overextending a reuse technology brings up the third strategy for increasing the Q measure: reducing investment costs. Just as a reuse technology that is not general enough can be unduly expensive for reuse consumers, a technology that is either overextended or more general than necessary can result in excessive costs to the reuse producer.

What you need is a way to analyze the information provided by variants analysis more carefully, so the level of generality provided by reuse technologies will match future expected needs.

The starting point for this matching is the concept of *instance spaces*, which let you define the generality level of reusable components more precisely. The instance space of a component or other work product is the full set of variants that can be retrieved at reasonable cost (defined as less than the equivalent full development cost) by a reuse consumer.

Figure 3 shows an instance space for an Ada generic component. An important feature of an instance space is that it makes no difference whether a specific instance of a part is actual (a part in a library) or virtual (a potential but as-yet-unrealized instantiation). Because they abstract out the issue of whether a part is physical, instance spaces let you compare highly diverse reuse technologies such as code libraries and generative methods.

Instance-space abstraction also takes manual methods into account, since they can be classified as having very large instance spaces (people can program nearly anything in time) but high consumer costs (programming is more expensive than, say,

building new procedures with Ada generics).

Matching generality to needs. In variants analysis, you characterize consumer needs in terms of product variants. Characterizing variants this way lets you compare the results of variants analysis to the instance spaces of generalized components or work products.

Figure 4 shows such a comparison, including the three groups of instances that normally result from an intersection of variants and instance spaces. These three groups are labeled in terms of how they are perceived by reuse consumers: extensive-adaptation instances, moderate- to minimal-adaptation instances, and unused instances.

♦ Extensive-adaptation instances are actually accessed and used by consumers, but they are so difficult to adapt that the cost benefits are negligible or possibly even negative. These instances represent lost opportunities where a reusable part could have provided cost benefits, but its generalization failed to anticipate the needs of the consumer adequately.

♦ Moderate- to minimal-adaptation instances represent significant cost benefits to one or more customers. In these cases, the part was generalized so it was easy to retrieve and adapt.

♦ Unused instances are a large category that, while they should be expected in any application, should be controlled by reuse producers to prevent overinvestment. Many low-cost unused instances are

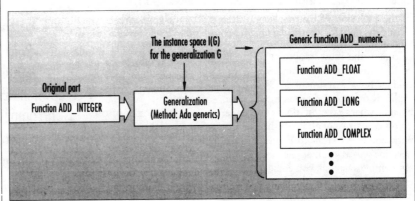

FIGURE 3. INSTANCE SPACES.

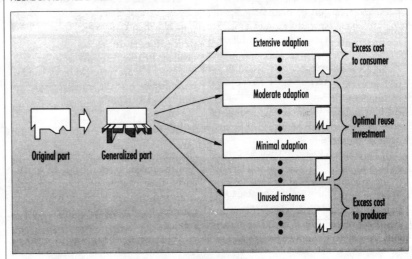

FIGURE 4. COST OBJECTIVES IN BUILDING HIGHLY REUSABLE SOFTWARE.

generally acceptable and even desirable as insurance, but many unused instances created with expensive technologies could easily result in reuse-investment losses.

Comparing instance spaces to variants analysis works best when the product is relatively small. Otherwise, the size of the instance space becomes so large that it becomes impractical to directly characterize the moderate- to minimal-adaptation instances.

Even for small components, the instance spaces are typically so large that they are better handled by specifying characteristics than by explicitly enumerating all possible instances. Thus, you would characterize the moderate- to minimal-adaptation instance space for the Ada generic example of Figure 3 by specifying key constraints, such as the potential need for any legal scalar variant of the routine, the exclusion of matrix-algebra variants, and the need for a particular range of computational accuracies.

Again, the most important reason to perform such characterizations is to encourage reuse investment decisions based explicitly on expected needs, instead of on habit or what's easiest to do. For example, if you could firmly establish that the generic addition routine in Figure 3 would never be reused in any applications requiring complex algebra, you could avoid the extra expense of generalizing that routine to include complex addition. Conversely, if the routine was part of a larger package for which conversion to matrix algebra was plausible, the extra effort to add hooks for such conversion might be worthwhile.

Mixing reuse technologies. You need not pick just one reuse technology for a set of components. In fact, it is more likely that the best and most economical coverage of consumer needs will be provided by two or more reuse technologies.

The reason for this is related to risk reduction. In most cases, you will be able to describe likely consumer variants only in broad terms. While you may be able to state firmly that there will be many instances of reuse within a broad set of variants, you may not know where in that set those instances will fall. Ada generics are a simple example of this situation, since they

involve cases where the need for new data types is well established but the exact definition of those data types cannot be known until the consumer actually needs a new routine.

Such late-binding situations are best covered by reuse technologies that provide a high level of generality, but they are relatively costly to the consumer. An example of such a technology is reuse-oriented documentation, which amounts to simply ensuring that the results of variants analysis are embedded as documentation throughout a development effort's work products.

On the other hand, instances that are very good candidates for reuse should be handled using technologies that pass the lowest possible cost to the reuse consumer. Moving costs to the producer for such sure-bet cases is nearly always appropriate, since the developer of a system can usually generalize its work products far more cheaply than later reuse consumers can reengineer them.

In these cases of certain reusability, it may be inappropriate to invest in large amounts of costly generality, because the target reuse instances are already well characterized. An extreme example is a reuse variant that is fully specified and is 100-percent certain to be needed. In this case, the ideal reuse strategy would be to build the reuse instance at the same time the primary product is built.

REUSE STRATEGIES

Although instance spaces help represent the diversity and quality of reusable parts, they rapidly become intractably large and difficult to characterize as the complexity of reusable components increases.

What we need is a way to introduce modularity into the design of reusable systems so the instance-space size can be

made more tractable. Modular reuse strategies should take a divide-and-conquer approach that supports both the design of new, highly reusable systems and the analysis of existing, potentially reusable systems.

The starting point is to recognize that you can view reuse (and development) as the construction of new systems by combining two forms of functionality:

♦ Invariant functionality, which is the set of components (or component fragments) that are used without change. Mathematical routines are common examples. By definition, invariant functionality alone cannot create a new system, since it lacks the customization needed to meet a new set of requirements.

♦ Variant functionality, which is the set of new functionality (software) that must be added to customize invariant components. Variant functionality may be as simple as a set of arguments passed to a parameterized package, or as complex as full, from-scratch, new-system development.

Mixing variant and invariant functionality. Regardless of how simple or complex a system is, it will always contain some mix of these two functionality types. Invariant functionality provides the kernel of functionality around which new systems are constructed; variant functionality provides the novel functionality that lets a system address a new set of needs.

The objective of reuse-intensive development is not to do away with the variant component, since that would, in effect, prevent any new needs from being addressed. The objective of effective reuse-intensive development is the creation of invariant components that help focus the development of variant functionality into very precise, succinct statements of the differences between the old and new systems.

Paradoxically, then, reuse-intensive

> Paradoxically, reuse-intensive development is best accomplished by focusing more on how to change software effectively than on how to keep it from changing.

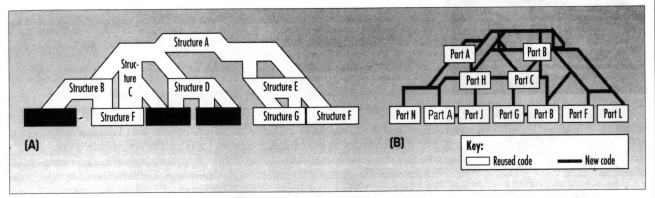

FIGURE 5. FUNDAMENTAL REUSE STRATEGIES. (A) ADAPTIVE REUSE; (B) COMPOSITIONAL REUSE.

development is best accomplished by focusing more on how to change software effectively than on how to keep it from changing. Well-focused mechanisms for expressing variant functionality will do far more to keep large sections of code invariant than will arbitrary attempts to build around existing code components.

The concept of variant and invariant functionality can readily be extended to noncode work products by analyzing how they can be built by combining baseline components of various sizes and types. As with executable code, the objective in building, say, a highly reusable system specification is to develop a set of baseline components that support concise, succinct descriptions of how new specifications differ from existing ones. Technologies such as hypertext are being applied toward this type of objective,[5] but far more work on characterizing the features of "good" variant and invariant components of noncode work products must be done.

Two fundamental strategies. If reusable systems are always constructed from some mix of invariant and variant functionality then the way in which they are combined is an important criterion for evaluating a system's reuse characteristics. This observation leads immediately to the definition of two broad, complementary reuse strategies, which are shown in Figure 5:

♦ Adaptive reuse uses large frame structures as invariants and restricts variability to low-level, isolated locations within the overall structure.[6] Examples include changing arguments to parameterized modules, replacing low-level I/O modules, and altering individual lines of code within modules. Adaptive reuse is similar to maintenance in that both try to isolate changes to minimize their system-wide impact.

♦ Compositional reuse uses small parts as invariants and variant functionality as the glue that links those parts.[7,8] Examples include constructing systems from parts in a reuse library and programming in high-level languages. As its name implies, compositional reuse is similar to conventional programming, in which individual functions of moderate complexity are composed according to some grammar to create new, more powerful functions.

Differences. In terms of cost and component-generality characteristics, adaptive and compositional reuse are strikingly different. For example, because adaptive reuse tries to keep most of the overall structure invariant, it tends to be application-specific and comparatively inflexible, but it helps keep both producer and consumer reuse costs under control.

By contrast, compositional reuse can be very flexible if the initial set of reusable components is sufficiently rich and generalized. However, constructing such a generalized component set (such as the functions in an application-specific language) can be very expensive for the reuse producer. Also, consumer costs for compositional reuse tend to rise rapidly as the complexity of the constructed software increases; when compositional reuse is extended too far, it begins to look more and more like conventional programming.

Coverage level. For compositional reuse, we make a further distinction based on the coverage level of part sets. Coverage level refers to the ability of a set of parts to address an application area without forcing the consumer to use a lower level language such as Ada or Cobol. There are two major coverage types:

♦ Full-coverage sets are sufficiently rich and complete to let you solve new problems within a well-defined application area using only those reusable parts. Examples of full-coverage sets include application-specific languages and abstract data types implemented with Ada packages.

♦ Partial-coverage sets provide representative parts that act as examples of the component types needed to solve problems in an application area. However, partial-coverage sets are not sufficiently generalized to let you solve all problems in that application area without resorting to the use of lower level languages. A library is a good example of a partial-coverage set, because the parts in it usually are neither highly generalized nor complete in their coverage of a problem area.

Partial-coverage sets are likely to be much less expensive to produce, but they are also more likely to be expensive to reuse because the parts they contain are hard to understand, modify, and test.

Combining strategies. By themselves, neither adaptive nor compositional reuse strategies are general enough to cover the full range of potentially reusable structures. However, the structured combination of these two approaches creates hybrid strategies much broader in coverage. Figure 6 shows the two major hybrid approaches.

♦ Full-coverage hybrid reuse uses an adaptive framework to keep overall costs down and "bubbles" of full-coverage compositional sets at key locations to provide flexibility.

Unix's Termcap package demonstrates this concept nicely, even though it was not designed as a reuse technology. With Termcap, you build drivers for new terminal types using interface descriptions written in the special-purpose Termcap language. These interface definitions are actually examples of compositional reuse, since the Termcap language allows ready access to (reuse of) a complex suite of general-purpose driver routines. Because you can handle hardware variations with a specialized minilanguage that strongly encapsu-

lates such variations, you can transfer (adaptively reuse) higher level programs that use Termcap among systems with few or no changes.

♦ Partial-coverage hybrid reuse is very similar to the full-coverage hybrid, but it allows the bubbles to be either full-coverage or partial-coverage — they need not be fully generalized for handling the problem area they address.

Many types of maintenance are equivalent to partial-coverage hybrid reuse, since they are based on localized modification of components that have never been fully generalized.

Cutting costs. Partial-coverage hybrid reuse provides the best overall framework for defining the divide-and-conquer approach that is our motive for exploring reuse strategies. Partial-coverage hybrid reuse keeps the overall structure invariant, so producers can focus on smaller, more precisely defined problem areas. Reuse investments in those problem areas then can produce minilanguage sets that permit the flexibility consumers need.

When variants analysis indicates a need for extensive generalization (Termcap's terminal-interface problem, for example), producers can invest in expensive technologies such as application-specific languages or program generators. When needs are clearly identified but full generalizations are not justified due to poor characterizations or limited numbers of expected reuse instances, producers can provide partial-coverage sets such as local-

ized libraries.

It is the ability to combine such techniques within the partial-coverage hybrid framework that makes it a good strategy for keeping producer costs in check.

REUSE AND PARAMETERIZATION

When we say that highly generalized parts define minilanguages for solving specialized problems, we don't mean to imply that these languages are true general-purpose languages — they are not. But designers use them in a way similar to general-purpose languages. Thus, sets of reusable graphics routines are a minilanguage for constructing and modifying diagrams; libraries of mathematical routines are minilanguages for dealing with mathematical problems.

From this perspective, good sets of reusable parts should possess the same general characteristics of expressive power and ease of composition that are the hallmarks of good programming languages.

Producers and consumers can further reduce reuse costs by designing appropriate, well-structured minilanguages. While this language design is identical to the task of generalizing parts, the language-design perspective places a much stronger emphasis on the integration of parts. The minilanguages that result should define clear and succinct problem solutions through the composition of a relatively small number of objects and operators.

The design of optimal minilanguages can be assisted by recognizing a curious

equivalence that has significant consequences. The equivalence is this:

All parameterizations can be interpreted as minilanguages, and all minilanguages can be interpreted as parameterizations.

Parameters as programs. At first glance, the statement that parameterizations and languages are in some way equivalent seems outlandish, particularly if it encompasses data parameterizations. After all, what does the passing of two complex numbers to a Fortran subroutine for complex division have to do with expressing a problem in a minilanguage?

Actually, quite a bit. A Fortran complex-division subroutine is a formal system for solving problems in a very small, very precisely defined domain: division of complex numbers. There are only two terms in this domain's minilanguage, which may be paraphrased as "define the dividend to be (value)" and "define the divisor to be (value)."

These terms are "coded" with a simple positional notation, but the semantic interpretation implied by the paraphrased versions most definitely must be met to obtain valid results.

Ironically, such routines are not usually thought of as defining small languages precisely because of their effectiveness: They are very succinct and directly address the key variability (new data values) needed to solve problems in their domains. In Ada, you can make this equivalence more obvious through the use of named parameters that help preserve such

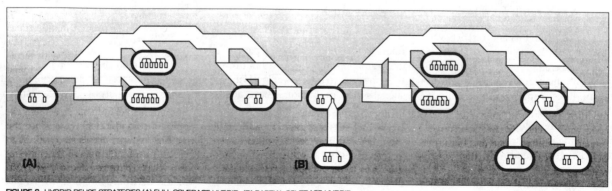

FIGURE 6. HYBRID REUSE STRATEGIES. (A) FULL-COVERAGE HYBRID; (B) PARTIAL-COVERAGE HYBRID.

semantic implications.

Programs as parameters. Looking at the equivalence from the other side, you can view a compiler as a formal system for interpreting program parameter values. Like any other parameter, a program consists of a string of binary data that has a specific meaning when passed to the formal system (compiler) for which it was constructed.

The key way in which a program differs from a traditional set of parameter values is that instead of defining a problem solution in terms of many relatively independent terms, a program uses comparatively few highly interrelated terms.

There is no rigid boundary between low-complexity schemes in which parameters are fairly independent and high-complexity cases in which they are highly interrelated. For example, some application-specific languages such as database-report generators often provide ways to specify common "programs" (reports) with very simple, parameter-like specifications.

Also, conventional parameterization schemes may include language-like features to reduce the number of necessary parameters. For example, many Unix tools such as Grep and Sed use parameterizations that range in complexity from the passing of simple flags for commonly needed variants of their functionality to the passing of complicated, program-like character strings for customizing their behavior in very specific ways.

Limits of parameterization. Figure 7 shows that extreme parameterization does not necessarily lead to a more understandable or reusable system, since extreme parameterization is functionally equivalent to developing a highly generalized minilanguage.

Very high levels of parameterization tend to approach what we call the Turing limit, the point at which the parameterization becomes so extensive that it is comparable in power to a general-purpose language. "Turing" refers to the fact that a fully generalized minilanguage permits construction of any desired program, and thus is akin to a Turing machine. At best, a

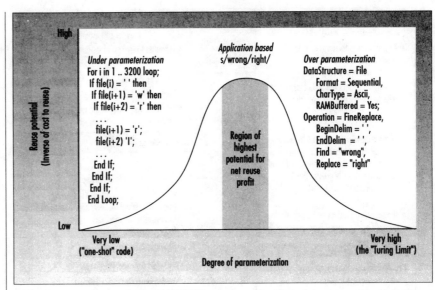

FIGURE 7. LIMITS OF PARAMETERIZATION IN REUSE.

parameterization scheme that has reached the Turing limit will be as complex as a general-purpose language, and it could easily be far more complex.

At that point, the reuse potential of a component effectively becomes nil, since it would probably be easier and less costly to redevelop the component in the original language.

As Figure 7 shows, the best payoff in parameterization comes from finding combinations of parameters that cover common application variabilities while simultaneously requiring the least possible specification efforts from consumers. Just as many manufacturing disciplines have developed sets of complementary parts that can be adjusted and combined to produce wide ranges of useful products, good software-parameterization schemes should provide versatile tool kits of options by which the needs of later consumers can be succinctly specified.

Options that are very likely to be needed should be made as simple to specify as possible, while increasingly less likely variations should be made to require proportionally larger specification efforts. At the lower end of this domain-specificity continuum is the language itself, in which variations with very low priorities can be coded directly.

WHAT'S NEXT?

We need consistent, broad-spectrum methodologies that integrate reuse analysis and development methods across the development life cycle.

In fact, life-cycle integration is likely to be one of the key factors that makes reuse truly effective. After all, if the first thing developers see in their programming environments are compilers, the first thing they will be tempted to do is to write code. If the first thing they see are lists of existing parts that may match their needs, the first thing they will be tempted to do is reuse. Put more colloquially, if you want to lose weight you should put the healthy food at the front of the fridge and the junk food at the back.

Reuse-oriented automation. Figure 8 shows the broad structure of a tool that would use instance spaces as the basis for presenting reusable components to reuse consumers[9] and that would implement separation concepts similar to those of Vic Basili and Dieter Rombach's reuse factory.[10]

The idea is to deemphasize how reusable parts are retrieved or created and emphasize the cost of retrieving them. Incorporating cost issues at such a fundamental level would let the system take a much

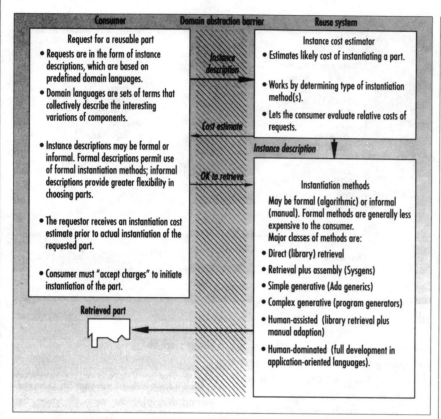

Consumer | Domain abstraction barrier | Reuse system

Request for a reusable part

- Requests are in the form of instance descriptions, which are based on predefined domain languages.
- Domain languages are sets of terms that collectively describe the interesting variations of components.

- Instance descriptions may be formal or informal. Formal descriptions permit use of formal instantiation methods; informal descriptions provide greater flexibility in choosing parts.

- The requestor receives an instantiation cost estimate prior to actual instantiation of the requested part.

- Consumer must "accept charges" to initiate instantiation of the part.

Instance description

Cost estimate

OK to retrieve

Retrieved part

Instance cost estimator

- Estimates likely cost of instantiating a part.

- Works by determining type of instantiation method(s).

- Lets the consumer evaluate relative costs of requests.

Instance description

Instantiation methods

May be formal (algorithmic) or informal (manual). Formal methods are generally less expensive to the consumer.
Major classes of methods are:

- Direct (library) retrieval
- Retrieval plus assembly (Sysgens)
- Simple generative (Ada generics)
- Complex generative (program generators)
- Human-assisted (library retrieval plus manual adaption)
- Human-dominated (full development in application-oriented languages).

FIGURE 8. REUSE ABSTRACTION: SEPARATING REQUESTS FROM METHODS.

For some time, reuse has suffered from an image problem. Anyone who has ever gone to an auto salvage yard to pick up a spare part for his old car "knows" what reuse is, and the image that it thus invokes is not altogether favorable.

The theme we most want to convey is that reuse is not a trivial concept. As a mechanism for preserving and guiding the use of that most expensive of resources, human creativity and ingenuity, software reuse is a field that merits careful attention both from managers interested in the bottom line and from researchers interested in better understanding that most curious of symbiotic relationships, the one that exists between humans and computers. ◆

more active role in making reuse decisions. For example, consumers who reuse early work products such as specifications or designs would receive cost quotes that would indicate the strong relative cost advantages for their selections. This type of "shop around" approach would encourage reuse consumers to select development paths that make the best possible use of existing work products.

References

1. M.D. Lubars, "Wide-Spectrum Support for Software Reusability," in *Software Reuse: Emerging Technology*, Will Tracz, ed., CS Press, Los Alamitos, Calif., 1988, pp. 275-281.
2. V.R. Basili and H.D. Rombach, "Towards a Comprehensive Framework for Reuse: A Reuse-Enabling Software Evolution Environment," Tech. Report CS-TR-2158, Dept. of Computer Science, Univ. of Maryland, College Park, Md., Dec. 1988.
3. T. Biggerstaff and C. Richter, "Reusability Framework, Assessment, and Directions," *IEEE Software*, March 1987, pp. 41-49.
4. F.J. Polster, "Reuse of Software through Generation of Partial Systems," *IEEE Trans. Software Eng.*, March 1986, pp. 402-416.
5. L. Latour and E. Johnson, "Seer: A Graphical Retrieval System for Reusable Ada Software Modules," *Third Int'l Conf. Ada Applications and Environments*, IEEE, Piscataway, N.J., May 1988, pp. 105-113.
6. P.G. Bassett, "Frame-Based Software Engineering," *IEEE Software*, July 1987, pp. 9-16.
7. M.A. Simos, "The Domain-Oriented Software Life Cycle: Towards an Extended Process Model for Reusability," in *Software Reuse: Emerging Technology*, Will Tracz, ed., CS Press, Los Alamitos, Calif., 1988, pp. 354-363.
8. M. Lenz, H.A. Schmid, and P.F. Wolf, "Software Reuse through Building Blocks," *IEEE Software*, July 1989, pp. 34-42.
9. T. Bollinger and B.H. Barnes, "Reuse Rules: An Adaptive Approach to Reusing Ada Software," *Proc. Artificial Intelligence and Ada Conf.*, George Mason Univ., Fairfax, Va., 1988, pp. 14-1–14-8.
10. V.R. Basili and H.D. Rombach, "The TAME Project: Towards Improvement-Oriented Software Environments," *IEEE Trans. Software Eng.*, June 1988, pp. 758-773.

Bruce H. Barnes is deputy director of the division of computer and computation research at the National Science Foundation. His main research interest is software research.

Barnes received a BS, MS, and PhD in mathematics from Michigan State University. He is a member of the American Mathematics Society, IEEE Computer Society, and ACM.

Terry B. Bollinger is a senior member of the technical staff at the Contel Technology Center. He works in the software-engineering laboratory on applied software research topics ranging from reuse and software maintenance to cost-oriented modeling of software processes.

Bollinger received a BS and MS in computer science from the University of Missouri at Rolla. He is a member of the IEEE.

Address questions about this article to Barnes at Division of Computer and Computation Research, NSF, 1800 G St. NW, Washington, D.C., 20550; Internet bbarnes@note.nsf.gov, or Bollinger at Contel Technology Center, 15000 Conference Center Dr., Chantilly, VA 22021-3808; Internet terry@ctc.contel.com.

The Evolution of Technology Transfer at MCC's Software Technology Program: From Didactic to Dialectic

James D. Babcock, Laszlo A. Belady, and Nancy C. Gore

Software Technology Program
Microelectronics and Computer Technology Corporation

Abstract

MCC's Software Technology Program (STP) has a dual mission: to create tools and methodologies to assist development teams in the design of large, complex, distributed software systems, and to ensure the widespread diffusion of these technologies within STP shareholder organizations. STP has developed a comprehensive set of traditional technology transfer methods; while these methods allow us to successfully communicate research results to shareholder receptors, they have spurred little actual use of released technology. We recently reevaluated our approach to technology transfer and discovered how it can better be accomplished—by fostering collaboration as its chief agent, rather than by depending on traditional transfer-and-feedback mechanisms. This paper describes the evolution of this new approach and presents some of the results of our collaborative experiences to date.

INTRODUCTION

The software engineering community is increasingly concerned with the problem of technology transfer. There is a growing awareness that while many innovative program-design methodologies have been developed in recent years, few of these innovations are being widely used within actual software development environments [11]. The suggestion often arises that the success of the discipline of software engineering itself will depend at least as much on discovering and implementing effective technology transfer strategies as on creating new design technology [1, 11].

MCC has grappled with this issue since its inception in 1983. Three years ago, then-CEO Bobby Inman called technology transfer the "weakest link in the chain" and mused that the real premium would now be on "the speed of transferring technology from lab to production line" [3]. The question *How will they do it?* is one that has been on the minds of many people at MCC—and certainly a prime concern for the shareholder companies who sponsor MCC's research—throughout the life of the consortium.

In an ongoing attempt to address this question, MCC's Software Technology Program (STP) has developed and refined a number of communication- and education-oriented methods for technology transfer, such as review sessions, workshops, and video conferences. While these activities effectively convey information and research results to a fairly wide shareholder audience, in and of themselves they tend to lead to only sporadic use of STP technologies on real development projects. We have recognized that our goal of widespread diffusion requires a new approach to technology transfer and an expanded methodology for achieving it.

As a result of this reassessment, we have adopted a view of technology transfer that is closely tied to the collaborative model of research—a model prescribed early in STP's life to increase the responsiveness of STP research to shareholder needs. Just as collaboration is a key to successful *research* in an industrial consortium, so is it the chief catalyst for the effective *transfer* of that research. Indeed, STP/shareholder collaboration is indistinguishable from technology transfer, which is itself an inseparable part of the research agenda.

The validity of this claim is born out by the results of STP's collaborative experience so far, and this paper provides an account of these results based on the increasingly numerous and extensive STP/shareholder collaborative projects that have evolved over the past year or so. But first, we flesh out a bit of the overall context within which our discovery has occurred.

Reprinted from *Proceedings of the 12th Int'l Conf. Software Engineering,* 1990, pp. 290-299. Copyright © 1990 by The Institute of Electrical and Electronics Engineers, Inc. All rights reserved.

Recommended by: John Musa

AN HISTORICAL OVERVIEW

Founded in early 1985, the Software Technology Program has as its mission the creation of tools and methodologies that will assist development teams in the design of large, complex, distributed software systems. STP chose to focus on the early, informal phases of design and aims to support such processes as requirements analysis, project coordination, cooperation within and among groups, and design simulation and recovery.

Readers who are interested in a thorough account of specific research areas and accomplishments should consult [6] and [13]. For our purposes here, it suffices to note that all along, the Program's stated commitment has been to problem-driven research. Beginning with a major field study early on to pinpoint problems in 19 large shareholder development projects spanning nine different companies [5], we have consciously attempted to discover shareholder needs and concerns and to address them through our research. As prototypes have been released, we have supported their use by shareholders and have actively solicited and incorporated feedback. Field studies will continue to provide additional information about the design process and about how our tools might support it.

Technology Transfer Methods

Hand-in-hand with STP's commitment to problem-driven research has been its technology transfer effort, coordinated full-time by a management-level staff member (Jim Babcock, an author of this paper) to ensure that research results and activities are thoroughly communicated to shareholders and that paths for feedback remain open. The mechanisms for achieving technology transfer are shown in Figure 1.

Shareholders have responded favorably to these technology transfer activities and artifacts, perceiving them as thorough and instructive. We have also been encouraged by shareholders' acceptance of the Technology Transfer Lab and by their eagerness to use it. Indeed, if the quality of these methods or the shareholder feedback they generate is any indication, then we can claim that STP has been quite successful in communicating and transferring its research results.

STAC (Software Technology Advisory Committee) reviews

The STAC consists of individuals who represent the shareholder organizations that depend on STP for long–range technological guidance and assistance. There have been two to four comprehensive STAC reviews a year, and STAC members also participate in other activities in this list.

TeleSTACs

Since the cost in both time and money of sending large numbers of designers and developers to Austin for STP reviews is prohibitive, we have sponsored three wide–area video conferences (in 1987, 1988, and 1989). 20-25 sites have participated for an audience of 600, and we distribute videotapes following a TeleSTAC to reach an audience twice or three times that size.

PTAB (Program Technology Advisory Board) reviews

Senior technical leaders from the shareholder companies meet four times a year in Austin for a one–day management–oriented review of STP activities. PTAB members evaluate STP's research progress and report on its overall status.

Shareholder "Days"

Fairly large groups (of 40–80) from a single shareholder company come to Austin for the company's yearly shareholder day, during which attendees interact informally with STP researchers and managers to learn about STP's research activities.

Technical reports

Technical reports (TRs) are the traditional vehicle for communicating research ideas and for reporting on early, mid-stream, and final results. Over the past four years, STP has published over 275 high-quality TRs, produced by a population of about 40 professional researchers. This corpus includes videotapes as well as written documents.

Transfer workshops

As research progresses in response to shareholder needs, prototypical "spin-offs" inevitably occur. We have formalized the release of these spin-offs in workshops, during which researchers describe the technology in depth, demonstrate its use, conduct lab exercises, deliver software tapes and documentation, and so on. STP has conducted six of these transfer workshops in the past three years.

Technology Transfer Laboratory

STP has provided workstations, office and conference space, and a printer in part of its Austin facility to host groups of shareholders who want to work on long or short-term design and development projects in cooperation with STP researchers. The Technology Transfer Lab was established in 1988 and has been the site of a variety of projects. Currently, a shareholder group is occupying space in the Lab to build a software development platform to be used by over 2,000 of their company's developers.

Figure 1. Technology Transfer Methods

We must, however, apply a different yardstick, for in terms of technology transfer, STP's major commitment is to *usher the technologies into widespread use on actual, profit-generating shareholder design and development projects*. The degree to which we honor this commitment is the ultimate measure of our success. Our technology transfer methods and activities, valuable though they may be for communication and education, have in four years contributed little toward that goal; in and of themselves, they have spurred only a few, relatively unsustained instances of shareholder use. While we will continue to employ them frequently and with vigor, our experience suggests that given the nature and extent of our commitment, "communication" and "education" are accessory, not central, to the main business of technology transfer.

STP prototypes. This model was created not just to assist us in planning for transfers, but for public consumption as well: it has appeared in at least five workshop announcements, in a myriad of letters to shareholders, and in many of our technology transfer presentations.

The development of this process model arose through STP's experience with its first transfer of a prototype in early 1987. The prototype had been developed very quickly, with little thought to its eventual transfer, by researchers working toward generalized design representation models. When the time came, STP created thorough documentation and called a release workshop. This rather haphazard process resulted in very little shareholder use of the system, for a number of reasons: the code was unstable; the workshop, while (again) informative and thorough,

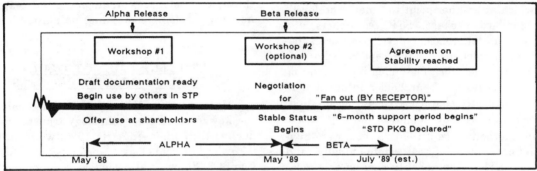

Figure 2. STP's First Technology Transfer Process Model (Example)

Toward the latter half of 1988, we began asking ourselves *why* these high-quality, well-executed activities were failing to produce the result we sought. If the methods were effective, and we believed they were, then what had we failed to consider? What would empower us both to communicate our research results *and* to catalyze their diffusion? If it was more than a simple matter of discovering new methods and techniques for technology transfer—as we suspected it might be—then what features of the overall *process* itself might we change? Was a major shift in perspective required? Might we need to be looking at things in an entirely new way?

Our recognition of the role of collaboration in technology transfer constitutes just such a shift in perception. Before we describe this new view and present some of its results, we sketch one more piece of the background within which the movement toward collaboration has occurred.

Technology Transfer Process Model

Figure 2 reproduces what has been the STP technology transfer process model, which we developed in 1987 and which, we believed, described (and prescribed) a workable, effective process for transferring

offered little training in opportunities for actually applying the technology in real design work; the required workstation environments were at that time in short supply in shareholder organizations; and—last but by no means least—there had been no *effective widespread* use by STP'ers themselves during development of the technology, much less shareholder collaboration prior to the release.

We designed the technology transfer process model to address these problems and, we hoped, to increase the likelihood that future STP releases would be more successful. The model prescribes both STP-internal and shareholder use of a prototype fairly early in its lifecycle, at the time of the Alpha release, and it helps to ensure an agreed-upon level of stability before the technology is deemed ready for "fanning out" into shareholder environments.

But like the technology transfer methods we described earlier, the process model proved insufficient to the task of achieving widespread industrial application of STP technology in shareholder development organizations. In fact, the model itself reveals some important clues as to why our efforts have tended in the past to be less than wholly successful. For perhaps more powerfully than any other artifact of

STP's technology transfer experience to date, it offers a perfect window through which to view a landscape of unexamined assumptions and beliefs—the landscape of STP's whole technology transfer *gestalt*, if you will, until recently. A brief overview of these assumptions and beliefs reveals that they were, in important respects, not only insufficient to but actually *at odds with* our ultimate commitment to bring about the diffusion of STP technology.

First, there is the assumption that technology transfer is essentially a linear process; acts of "transfer" occur in major chunks, at markers on the time continuum, when shareholders attend workshops and receive software and documentation. Moreover, the "technology" in this model is an artifact—a piece of software, a prototype or spin-off—which is offered for use at a predefined point in time and which at another point in time is "declared" a stable standard package. STP researchers and their target users (shareholder developers) are separated by a middleman (the receptor) who—not STP—is responsible for disseminating ("fanning out") the technology. STP/shareholder interaction in the model is explicitly characterized by "negotiation" and "agreement"—by the language of *trans*action rather than interaction, as if the two sides were buying and selling a piece of real estate. Finally, and most tellingly, STP's responsibility ends in this model when the sale is made, even though the seller does throw in a six-month "warranty" of sorts.

To the extent that we have been working within a background of assumptions such as these, it is really no wonder that STP's overall technology transfer effort has met with less than astounding success. We have wanted for the technology to be put to use, but our model for the process has prescribed agreed-upon "stability," rather than "robustness" or "usability," as the criterion for letting a prototype go. As a result, the research has tended at times to stop when the prototypes are, as a rule, not robust enough to be applied, or even tested, in real work situations. As one STP researcher recently put it, "we often get messed up by little things" when working from this model: people don't like the user interface, for example; or they have a different flavor of Unix; or (perhaps not such a little thing) they have a real job to do and don't have the time or money to acquire new workstations, third-party software, or, in one great leap, a whole new way of doing something, no matter how innovative.

THE MOVEMENT TOWARD A COLLABORATIVE PROCESS

The road toward our discovery of collaboration as the key to successful technology transfer took a productive turn when, in early 1989, we identified what we call the technology transfer "gap," illustrated in Figure 3. Figure 3 also conveys a notion of the role of collaboration in moving STP research forward and, at the same time, in achieving technology transfer.

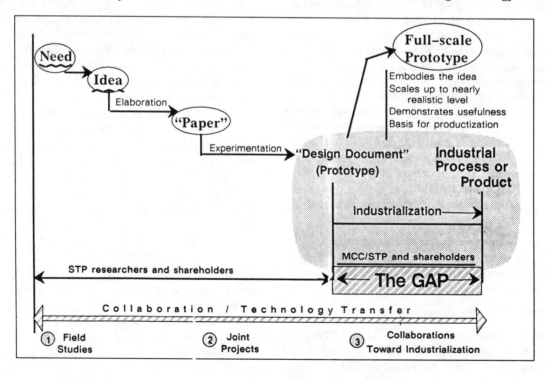

Figure 3. The Technology Transfer Gap and the Three Major Types of TT Activities

In this view, STP's responsibility extends beyond the release of STP prototypes, to bridging the gap through what we call "industrialization." This is achieved when either of the following two events has occurred:

- An STP technology is fully integrated into a comprehensive design application or process used by shareholder designers to create profit-generating products. Domain-specific knowledge must be wrapped around the STP tool for this to be the case.

- The technology has been the basis for a "productization" that has generated profit for a shareholder company. In other words, the shareholder has turned an STP technology into a product in its own right.*

Our visualization of the gap, along with our identification of the two conditions for its closure, transformed what had been an enormous, endlessly perplexing problem—the problem of technology transfer—into an arena of opportunity. For once we had established this concrete vision of the desired outcome, we could focus more clearly on how to bring it about. No longer was "technology transfer" merely the act of passing on a prototype as though it were a baton in a footrace. We saw clearly that our original commitment had all along necessitated that we join in on the latter part of the race as well, because only through working with shareholders throughout the process could we effect technology transfer as we had ourselves defined it.

Which brings us to a key point. If the collaborative effort of industrialization is to begin in earnest—if we are to realize our ultimate goal—then the shareholders have to recognize the *opportunity* for industrialization in the first place. And for this to occur, an STP tool must *by the time of its release as a prototype* demonstrate a higher degree of "fit" than our technologies have tended to achieve so far. It must be not just released, but *transferred* from STP's environment to that of our shareholders. And this requires collaboration not just during the effort at industrialization, but *throughout the research cycle.*

Already, numerous collaborative projects are becoming integral to the design and development of STP prototypes. Researchers are traveling frequently to shareholder sites, and shareholders to Austin, to work together in applying STP technologies to actual design problems; there is also an increasingly noticeable collaborative flavor to workshops and other transfer-oriented events at STP. While the players in a collaboration will change as a technology moves from creation and into industrialization, the basic nature of the collaborative relationship will not. We assert that the dynamics of this relationship are having a profound impact on our ability to transfer our research results. It is what will, we believe, ultimately propel STP's technology transfer agenda to success.

THE COLLABORATIVE RELATIONSHIP: OBSERVATIONS AND EXPERIENCES

As our discussion so far suggests, STP's commitment to collaboration represents more a fundamental shift in attitude than movement toward a new "process model" of technology transfer. As collaborative relationships between STP researchers and shareholders take hold and continue to evolve, it becomes increasingly clear that *activities we previously distinguished as "research" and "technology transfer" are not wholly separate and distinct. We are beginning to see that the person-to-person interaction at the heart of collaborative work gives rise to a dynamic field of interplay wherein two things happen simultaneously and interdependently: an idea, a methodology, or a tool is transferred to a shareholder, and there is a rearrangement, however subtle, in the direction of the research itself.*

Because a collaboration is driven essentially by people in interaction, and not by a set of predefined steps and functions, the outcome of a particular project cannot be wholly predicted. If we are committed to creating, evolving, and transferring STP technology in partnership with shareholders, we cannot say that technology X will be created by date Y and it will look exactly like Z (at which point we will invite shareholders to Austin for a workshop in which the new technology is "transferred" with a tape, a user's manual, and the solicitation of feedback). In fact, the dependence for technology transfer on predicted research outcomes and planned transfer activities has only served to widen the gap between STP and its shareholders. Particularly when little or no collaboration has occurred during the research, a "transfer" only points out (painfully, at times) the lack of a fit between what is often brilliantly innovative technology and the development environments in which it will, presumably, be used and applied.

It is far too early to evaluate the success or failure of the collaborative experiment at STP. Nonetheless, we have derived a number of observations from

---

* There is currently a set of eight options for achieving industrialization, options that include such things as shareholders contracting with an MCC support organization or assigning a design and development team to Austin for a period of weeks or months. A complete list of these options is not appropriate here; what is important to note is that all of them depend on a high level of collaboration to find and implement industrialization solutions.

our experience so far, observations about how this experiment is leading us—and in many respects our shareholders as well—toward a different understanding of what constitutes the creation and transfer of new software design technology.

The Shareholder as Seminarian

The graduate-level university seminar is a useful analogy for both describing and fostering the collaborative situation. Such a seminar typically follows a two-way path, through which a great deal of learning and discovery occurs on both sides. New ideas evolve over the course of a term, as students apply them to their own research and as the teacher discovers how such applications can take place.

Collaboration between STP and its shareholders appears to parallel this model in key respects. The researcher presents an idea or technology and offers suggestions for making use of it in the software design process; as it is actually being used, the shareholders contribute insights about the idea's real value (or lack thereof) to their immediate situation and provide suggestions for its refinement; and through several iterations of this interactive process, the idea evolves into something that is both innovative from a research perspective and useful in a real-world development environment.

The experience of researchers and shareholders participating in STP's VERDI project is a useful example. VERDI (a Visual Environment for Raddle Design and Investigation) [7] is a graphically oriented system for using Raddle, a high-level design language, to create and simulate the design of distributed systems. After the Alpha version was released in early 1988, two of STP's distributed systems researchers visited a number of shareholder development sites to talk with developers and learn how the design of "real-world" distributed systems had been performed in past years. STP also began to collaborate with a group of shareholder developers who wanted to use VERDI to produce and maintain the design of a cellular telephone algorithm. One of the key realizations that evolved was that in order for VERDI to be useful, it would have to simulate not just how a system would process single transactions, but how it would process, say, a thousand transactions simultaneously. The researchers realized that large-system performance modeling capabilities were critical, and thus the collaboration reordered the priorities on their research agenda.

This example also illustrates an important way in which an industrial research consortium is able to go beyond the university model. The opportunity to collaborate with shareholder developers allows us

continuously to profit from practical tests of the ideas—and, perhaps more importantly, to learn from ongoing conversations with the developers about their work. In the collaborative "seminar" in which research ideas are tested in a development environment, the "teacher" and "student" roles become interchangeable. As shareholders respond to the research ideas and attempt to apply them, they offer information that is key both to the process of refining a particular technology and to setting new research priorities. In a very real sense, what happens in this interaction is the mutual exchange of intellectual excitement and new knowledge [9]. From our perspective, the process is more akin to "listening" than "educating," a distinction that has been made in previous discussions of the collaborative relationship [10].

Effects on a Technology's Evolution

Technology transfer research suggests that a product or a technology that has evolved through a process of incremental improvement has an increased chance of enjoying successful transfer and widespread diffusion [1, 10, 12]. Observers have noted the ubiquity of this incremental model for R&D and manufacturing in Japan, whose success in creating and diffusing new technology is widely known. While STP did not consciously and explicitly set out to evolve our ideas and prototypes incrementally, our experience suggests that this process seems to be a natural outgrowth of the collaborative relationship. Indeed, we have noticed that the earlier in a project's life a collaboration is set into motion, the more incremental and evolutionary its progress tends to be, in two key respects. First, a series of relatively small, incremental improvements to the technology gradually increases its "fit" within an existing shareholder development environment. At the same time, the researchers discover new, often unanticipated directions for improving its usefulness in solving real shareholder problems. It is perhaps in these instances that the collaborative dialectic will have its greatest impact on the overall direction of STP's research and technology transfer.

An Incremental Process of Technology Improvement. That collaboration tends to foster the incremental, evolutionary growth of a technology can be illustrated through a look at STP's DESIRE project [2], which is creating a design recovery methodology allowing users to organize and display large collections of code and to recover designs for future reuse. Aiming for a "quick test" [10] of the ideas, STP recently packaged a group of tools we thought would be useful in implementing the methodology and released the system as a very early prototype. In a "call for experimentation," shareholders were encouraged to bring their own code and were told that they would receive an opportunity to collaborate with STP researchers on a real-world test of the DESIRE methodology. Essentially, the DESIRE team ran the workshop as an extended lab exercise, except that the data upon which the lab tests were performed—in most cases, very large collections of code—was not hypothetical but from the shareholders' own development shops.

The tests were deemed a success, in that there emerged proof that DESIRE would work—but that is not the point here. Rather, the point is that at an early stage in the creation of a technology, shareholders were called into a collaborative relationship, and a fairly significant incremental improvement to DESIRE has occurred as a result of what researchers learned at the workshop alone. (The improvement is a facility that explains to the user why the system has clustered a set of modules in a certain way.) The workshop occurred in May, 1989, and the half-dozen collaborations to which it gave rise are just now getting underway, so it is too early to say with certainty that such incremental improvements will continue to characterize the system's evolution. The DESIRE researchers, however, are explicitly committed to this being the case; they intend to modify the system's tools in cooperation with shareholders, with whom they will be working closely throughout the life of the project. This "refinement through collaboration," as a member of the DESIRE team put it, will occur as the experiment begun at the workshop is allowed to grow.

The workshop experiences also offered a related insight that bears reiteration here. Incremental improvement as a natural outgrowth of collaborative work is separate and distinct from the traditional process of soliciting and incorporating "feedback." The word "feedback" itself (which, incidentally, used to figure prominently in STP's technology transfer presentations) connotes precisely the kind of dichotomy—between producer and user, provider and recipient—that tends to evaporate in the space of collaborative action. Collaboration leads to the mutual discovery of real problems that need to be addressed, rather than to a sense that one side is providing a technology and the other evaluating its usability.

Readjustments in Research Directions. Just as the technology changes the design process in a shareholder environment, so does its use within that environment change the technology and redirect its future. The researcher enters the collaborative partnership with a fairly concrete research agenda and then, through working with shareholders to see how the technology can serve the real work of a software design project, often discovers that a rearrangement of emphases and priorities is in order.

The VERDI project's decision to address the performance modeling issue, which we described earlier, is one example of how collaborative interaction tends to affect the course of STP research. The DESIRE team had a similar experience. They had designed a tool that analyzed static code, but collaborations during the DESIRE workshop emphasized that dynamic-analysis capabilities were required for realistically large collections of code. The researchers had been committed to researching and implementing a dynamic-analysis tool at some unspecified later date; after the workshop this concern had moved to the top of the priority list, and there were a number of other rearrangements as well.

Another extensive STP/shareholder collaboration, between the Design Journal project and a shareholder software development team, has been underway since 1988. Communicating almost weekly with STP's Design Journal researcher, who also has made several trips to the development site, the developers have used the IBIS (Issue Based Information System) methodology [8] to capture the rationale for a design of a major new kitchen display system. The researcher has noted that his purpose here is "to allow the research to be driven by the needs of the developers," and the collaboration has, indeed, redirected the Design Journal research in significant ways. For example, it emerged that the IBIS methodology and its implementation tool, gIBIS (for graphical IBIS) [4], lacked a way to flag action items as design decisions were made, and this then became a primary research topic for STP. Similarly, the shareholder collaboration made it clear that several planned AI features would really serve little purpose, and the AI research was tabled as a result.

A Redefinition of "Technology"

Earlier in this paper, we noted that according to STP's latest technology transfer process model, our involvement ends when the "deliverable" (the prototype) is released, and it is supposed to magically fit into the shareholder environment because we have receptors, communicate well, give good workshops, package well, and so on. The model tends to foster a concomitant assumption on the part of the shareholders—that the "technology" in "technology transfer" is a robust, product-quality prototype, which they can use immediately and which STP will support for six months. So it has surprised and frustrated shareholders to receive technology that is, for whatever reasons, unusable in their environments.

The collaborative relationship is nudging both parties away from these assumptions. There is a growing awareness that a collaborative interaction is itself an act of technology transfer, giving rise to an expanded definition of "technology" to include ideas, suggestions, slightly different ways to approach a problem, and, most importantly, *the mindset required to successfully conduct collaborative work.* One of the researchers put it this way recently: "In this project, the collaboration *is* the deliverable." With industrial project teams growing ever larger and more diverse, it is the collaborative mindset that will drive the production of software in the 1990s and beyond; we do, indeed, consider it to be one of our key deliverables.

RISKS AND IMPLICATIONS

A commitment to collaborative interaction as the primary catalyst for technology transfer, and the decision to foster and depend on it rather than on a rigid process model, packs a number of risks that we are already aware of and (no doubt) many that will become apparent as the collaborative experiment continues.

First, the collaborative dialectic requires that STP come to terms with a new kind of tension between the long-term research agenda and the need to offer short-term results. If the research manager adopts the applied industrial research method of continuous interaction between researchers and developers—in other words, of "getting our hands dirty"—it is *inevitable* that continuous spin-offs will occur, even if there have been no plans to produce them. Not only are these spin-offs the fuel that encourages continued funding of long-term research, but they also fuel new research directions, which in turn spur new collaborations. While we welcome this process—are, in fact, encouraging it—there is a question whether it will ultimately detract us from pursuing the new ideas and avenues that make initial research breakthroughs possible. We do not know how this tension will eventually be resolved, but we do suggest that it is important for a research organization in our position to manage it well and to strive for a balance between the long and short term.

Collaboration makes things far more complex in several other ways as well. When we put out a call for experimentation on a particular technology, any of over 75 individual shareholder development organizations might respond, and the idiosyncratic nature of a respondent's existing culture, its unique needs and problems, can create consequences that are large indeed. For if the technology changes the organization by subtly but fundamentally altering its way of doing business, so also does the organization change the technology in equally fundamental ways, and according to variables as uncontrollable and as diverse as a manager's preference for a certain scheduling system or a project leader's personality.

Researchers and shareholders alike must take into account the significant implications of this unpredictability. Earlier in this paper, we noted that one of the *benefits* of collaboration is that it redirects the research in evolutionary, needs-driven ways; a potential *down side* is that these changes occur in response to the needs of the collaborating shareholder organization, and whether other shareholders will also benefit is necessarily an open question. Similarly, if a technology's use, even in the arena of experimental collaboration, requires changes to the organization that are revolutionary, that greatly alter its existing processes and culture, then the technology will quite probably be rejected and not used at all. A more incremental, evolutionary organizational change, on the other hand, helps ensure that subtle changes to the new technology are healthy—that it will likely be able to accommodate the cultures of other organizations as well and can be transferred successfully to the wider shareholder community.

From the perspective of shareholder developers and their managers, the collaborative enterprise carries yet another dimension of risk. For there might ensue an unavoidable mismatch between the goals of the collaboration and the schedule—even the ultimate mission—of the shareholder project, regardless of how subtle and evolutionary an organizational change is required. This can happen even when a new technology initially seems eminently applicable to a given project. There are no guarantees but that in the end, the time and money spent in collaboration will have served merely to deviate or disrupt the project and done nothing to advance it. Management can minimize this risk—by organizing around people and their needs, by eschewing rigid process models and work schedules—but it must also be accepted and taken into account.

In a similar but slightly different vein, the oft-cited "Not Invented Here" syndrome is one to which collaborating researchers and shareholders alike may well be prone, with unavoidable implications. From the shareholder perspective, a collaborative project might serve to point up the fact that the goals of an STP research effort are actually quite similar to those of a shareholder project; while this might serve to *enlarge* the collaboration to include this similar project, it could also evoke sufficient competitiveness to put the entire collaborative relationship at risk.

In terms of NIH from the research perspective, we have defined as integral to the collaborative relationship that the STP researcher allow his or her research agenda to evolve in response to shareholder needs and concerns. As this occurs, the research prototype itself—be it an idea, a tool, a methodology—begins perhaps to acquire a nature quite different from that of the pure and pristine abstraction originally conceived in the research lab. For one thing, a collaboration will almost always take place on the platforms already in deployment in industrial environments; it cannot ordinarily use state-of-the-art advancements coming out of other research labs, such as multiprocessor or multimedia systems, high speed networks, logic programming languages, and the like. The point is that even regardless of the platforms for collaboration, visions of the breakthrough paper, the accolades from the academic set, may recede as the commitment to meeting real industrial needs lends a decidedly more workaday flavor to the research.

This has professional implications that may well be unavoidable as collaborative work becomes ever more inextricably woven into the fabric of STP's overall research agenda. But we suggest that these implications represent at least as much an arena of opportunity as one of breakdown. If the necessity of technology transfer places collaboration near the heart of the industrial research effort, and we assert that it does, then what opens up is a new set of issues for a given research project to pursue. The researcher can begin to explore how the hypothetical world of "pure" research corresponds, or not, with the actual world of industrial development; how the diverse factors at play in the collaborative field interact to produce a successful transfer, or fail to do so; how to ensure that a research prototype is received as more than merely a toy that won't scale up to the work of product design and development. As questions such as these appear on the research agenda, surely the fabric of that agenda only becomes richer, more complex, and even more conducive to results that interest a growing interdisciplinary audience.

CONCLUSIONS

STP's experience with collaboration is still relatively new. But while the results of STP/shareholder collaborations cannot, at this point, be quantitatively measured and analyzed, there is observable evidence that collaborations revitalize our research and that they empower STP's shareholders to affect the directions of that research. We believe that the collaborative dialectic will usher STP research results into widespread industrial application within our shareholder organizations. Collaboration is indistinguishable from technology transfer, and only through fostering and nurturing collaborative relationships throughout the life of STP will our technology transfer effort succeed.

ACKNOWLEDGEMENTS

For their many insightful observations during conversations about the subject of this paper, the authors wish to thank the following STP researchers: Michael Begeman, Jeff Conklin, Mike Graf, Gail Rein, Vincent Shen, Baldev Singh, and Dallas Webster. We would especially like to acknowledge Susan Gerhart, Colin Potts, Leigh Power, and Zvi Weiss for their thoughtful and insightful reviews. Mostly, we thank the MCC/STP shareholders for their willingness to participate with us in this experiment and for their invaluable ongoing contributions toward making it all work.

REFERENCES

[1] Babcock, J. and Scacchi, W. "Understanding Software Technology Transfer," MCC Technical Report STP-3010-87, 1987.

[2] Biggerstaff, T. "Design Recovery for Maintenance and Reuse," *IEEE Computer*, vol. 22, no. 7, July 1989, pp. 36-410.

[3] Botkin, J. and Dimancescu, D. *The New Alliance: America's R&D Consortia,* Ballinger Publishing, 1986.

[4] Conklin, J. and Begeman, M. "gIBIS: A Hypertext Tool for Exploratory Policy Discussion," *ACM Transactions on Office Information Systems*, vol. 6, no. 4, October 1988, pp. 303-331.

[5] Curtis, B., Krasner, H., and Iscoe, N. "A Field Study of the Software Design Process for Large Systems," *Communications of the ACM,* vol. 31, no. 12, November 1988, pp. 1368-1387.

[6] Gerhart, S. "The MCC Software Technology Program," *Proceedings of the World Computer Congress*, IFIP Congress 1989, pp. 803-889.

[7] Graf, M. "VERDI: A Visual Environment for the Design of Distributed Systems," in *Visual Programming and Visual Languages*, ed. R. Korphage, Plenum Press, 1987.

[8] Kunz, W. and Rittel, H. "Issues as Elements of Information Systems," Working Paper No. 131, Institute of Urban and Regional Development, University of California at Berkeley, 1970. (See also Rittel, H. "APIS: A Concept for an Argumentative Planning Information System," Working Paper No. 324, Institute of Urban and Regional Development, University of California at Berkeley, 1980.)

[9] Marks, P. "Whither MCC?" Memo posted in an STP-internal newsgroup, July 1988.

[10] Peters, T. *Thriving on Chaos: Handbook for a Management Revolution*, Alfred A. Knopf, 1987.

[11] Raghaven, S. and Chand, D. "Diffusing Software Engineering Methods," *IEEE Software*, vol. 6, no. 4, July 1989, pp. 81-90.

[12] Rogers, E. *Diffusion of Innovations*, 3rd edition, MacMillan and Co., 1983.

[13] Yourdon, E. "Ed Yourdon's Observations on the American Software Scene," *The American Programmer*, vol. 2, no. 5, May 1989, pp. 2-11.

Chapter 12
Support Material

This chapter completes the volume by reprinting the following two IEEE standards, which are provided for reference purposes:

· ANSI/IEEE Std 1058.1-1987, *Standard for Software Project Management Plans*. This standard describes the format and contents of a software project management plan.

· IEEE Std P1074, *Standard for Developing Software Life Cycle Processes*. This standard provides the set of activities that constitute the mandatory processes for the development and maintenance of software, whether stand-alone or part of a system.

The following other IEEE standards serve as useful reference sources for those performing software management functions:

· IEEE Std 610.12-1990, *Standard Glossary of Software Engineering Terminology.*

· ANSI/IEEE Std 730-1989, *Standard for Software Quality Assurance Plans.*

· ANSI/IEEE Std 828-1983, *Standard for Software Configuration Management Plans.*

· ANSI/IEEE Std 829-1983, *Standard for Software Test Documentation.*

· ANSI/IEEE Std 830-1984, *Guide to Software Requirements Specifications.*

· ANSI/IEEE Std 983-1986, *Guide for Software Quality Assurance Planning.*

· ANSI/IEEE Std 1012-1986, *Standard for Software Verification and Validation Plans.*

· ANSI/IEEE Std 1028-1988, *Standard for Software Reviews and Audits.*

· ANSI/IEEE Std 1042-1987, *Guide to Software Configuration Management Planning.*

· ANSI/IEEE Std 1063-1987, *Standard for Software User Documentation.*

These and other standards can be obtained from any IEEE office or by calling the IEEE order desk at (800) 678-4333. IEEE Std P1074 (draft) maps all these standards to the activities of the software development and maintenance process.

IEEE Standard for Developing Software
Life Cycle Processes

Sponsor

**Software Engineering Standards Subcommittee of the
Technical Committee on Software Engineering of the
IEEE Computer Society**

Approved September 26, 1991

IEEE Standards Board

Abstract: The set of activities that constitute the processes that are mandatory for the development and maintenance of software, whether stand-alone or part of a system, is set forth. The management and support processes that continue throughout the entire life cycle, as well as all aspects of the software life cycle from concept exploration through retirement, are covered. Associated input and output information is also provided. Utilization of the processes and their component activities maximizes the benefits to the user when the use of this standard is initiated early in the software life cycle. This standard requires definition of a user's software life cycle and shows its mapping into typical software life cycles; it is not intended to define or imply a software life cycle of its own.

Keywords: project management process, project monitoring and control process, software development process, software implementation process, software installation process, software life cycle, software life cycle model process, software life cycle process, software maintenance process, software operation and support process, software post-development process, software pre-development process, software quality management process, software requirements process, software retirement process, software system allocation process

Reprinted from *IEEE Standard for Developing Software Life Cycle Processes,* IEEE Std 1074-1991. Copyright © 1992 by The Institute of Electrical and Electronics Engineers, Inc. All rights reserved.

Library of Congress Cataloging in Publication Data

Institute of Electrical and Electronics Engineers, Inc., the.
    IEEE standard for developing software life cycle processes / sponsor, Software Engineering Standards Subcommittee of the Technical Committee on Software Engineering of the IEEE Computer Society.
      p.   cm.
    "Approved September 26, 1991, IEEE Standards Board."
    "IEEE Std 1074-1991."
    Includes index.
    ISBN 1-55937-170-6
    1. Computer software—Development—Standards—United States. 2. Software maintenance—Standards—United States. I. IEEE Computer Society. Software Engineering Standards Subcommittee. II. IEEE Standards Board. III. Title
QA76.76.D47I545 1992
005.1'021873—dc20
                                91-41510
                                CIP

Foreword

(This Foreword is not a part of IEEE Std 1074-1991, IEEE Standard for Developing Software Life Cycle Processes.)

This Foreword is intended to provide the reader with some background into the rationale used to develop this standard. This information is being provided to aid in the understanding and usage of the standard. The Foreword is nonbinding.

Purpose

This is a standard for the Processes of software development and maintenance. This standard requires definition of a user's software life cycle and shows mapping into typical software life cycles, but it is not intended to define or imply a software life cycle of its own. This standard applies to the management and support Processes that continue throughout the entire life cycle, as well as all aspects of the software life cycle from concept exploration through retirement. Utilization of these Processes, and their component Activities, maximizes the benefits to the user when the use of this standard is initiated early in the software life cycle.

Software that has proceeded past the initialization phase when this standard is invoked should gradually comply with the standard.

This standard was written for any organization responsible for managing and developing software. It will be useful to project managers, software developers, quality assurance organizations, purchasers, users, and maintainers. Since it was written to consider both software and its operating environment, it can be used where software is the total system or where software is embedded in a larger system.

Terminology

The words *shall, must,* and the imperative form identify the mandatory (essential) material within this standard. The words *should* and *may* identify optional (conditional) material. As with other IEEE Software Engineering Standards, the terminology in this document is based on IEEE Std 610.12-1990, IEEE Standard Glossary of Software Engineering Terminology (ANSI). To avoid inconsistency when the Glossary is revised, the definitions are not repeated in this document. New terms and modified definitions are included, however.

History

Work on this standard began in August 1984. A total of 15 meetings produced the draft submitted for ballot in January 1990. Two additional meetings were held to resolve comments and negative ballots, and the document was resubmitted for recirculation in February 1991.

Participants

This standard was developed by a working group consisting of the following members who attended two or more meetings, provided text, or submitted comments on more than two drafts of the standard:

David J. Schultz
Chair

John W. Horch
Vice Chair

Dennis E. Nickle
Secretary

Jean A. Gilmore
Group Leader

Art Godin
Group Leader

Lynn D. Ihlenfeldt
Group Leader

Robert W. Shillato
Group Leader

Joseph J. Guidos,* David W. Burnett
Configuration Managers

Michael Buckley
Editor

Joe Albano	Carolyn Harrison	Denis Meredith
Tom Antczak	Peter Harvey	Manijeh Moghis
Susan Burgess	Eric Hensel	Richard Morton
David Burrows	Denise Holmes	Gerry Neidhart
Dan Chang	George Jackelen	Brian Nejmeh
Paul Christensen	Linell Jones	Hans Schaefer
Raymond Day	Laurel Kaleda	Isaac Shadman
Marvin Doran	Phil Keys	Kelley Stalder
Mike Ellwood	Tom Kurihara	David Taylor
Arden Forrey	Bill Mar	Leonard Tripp
John Graham	Darrell Marsh	George Tucker
Daniel Gray	Leroy May	Odo Wang
Rob Harker		Richard Werling

*Deceased

Contributors

The following individuals also contributed to the development of the standard by attending one meeting or providing comments on one or two drafts:

Scott Allen	Jim Hughes	Jeff Pattee
Kathleen Alley	Suzana Hutz	Virgil Polinski
Robert Baris	Ron Hysom	P. A. Rhodes
Dwight Bellinger	Phyllis Illyefalvi	Bill Romstadt
H. Ronald Berlack	Corbin Ingram	Benson Scheff
William Blum	Ramon Izbinsky	Richard Schmidt
Robert Both	Tom Jepson	David Schwartz
Fletcher Buckley	Jia Yaoliang	Carl Seddio
John Chihorek	Allen Jin	Paul Sevcik
Geoff Crellin	David Johnson	Randy Shipley
M. A. Daniels	Richard Karcich	Kimberly Steele
Geoffrey Darnton	E. Klamm	Karen Steelman
Leonard DeBaets	Rick Kuhn	Jim Stoner
Ingrid deBuda	Stephan Lacasse	Wayne Sue
Kristin Dittmann	F. C. Lim	Ann Sullivan
Gary Driver	Ben Livson	Daniel Teichroew
Susan East	Theresa Mack	Russell Theisen
Leo Egan	Karen Mackey	Donna Thomas
Violet Foldes	Stan Magee	George Tice
Roger Fujii	John Marciniak	R. Van Tilburg
Michael Garrard	Richard McClellan	Graham Tritt
Yair Gershkovitch	Neal Mengel	Dolores Wallace
Ole Golubjatnikov	Rocco Novak	Valerie Winkler
Jim Harkins	George O'Connell	Grady Wright
James Heil	John Patchen	Fred Yonda
Cheng Hu		Lin Zucconi

Acknowledgments

Participants in the working group were individually supported by their employers with travel expenses and working days. This support does not constitute or imply approval or endorsement of this standard. These organizations were:

Abbott Critical Care	Lockheed Aircraft Service Co.
ARINC, Inc.	Martin Marietta
Apollo Computer Inc.	MUMPS Development Committee
AT&T Bell Laboratories	NCR Corp.
AT&T Technologies	Naval Air Development Center
Bell Canada	Northern Telecom Canada Ltd.
Bellcore	Northrop Electronics Div.
Bell Northern Research, Inc.	Northrop Aircraft Div.
Boeing Computer Services	Perkin-Elmer
Burnett Associates	Quality Assurance Institute
Computer Sciences Corp.	Singer Link
Digital Switch Corporation	Tandem Telecommunications Systems, Inc.
E. I. Dupont de Nemours & Co.	Tektronix
E-Systems, Inc.	Teledyne Brown Engineering
Eastman Kodak Co.	Teledyne Controls
Hewlett Packard	Texas Instruments
Honeywell, Inc.	The Horch Company
IBM	U. S. Air Force
Institute for Defense Analyses	U. S. Dept. of Transportation
Jet Propulsion Laboratory	Unisys
Litton Aero Products	3M

The following organizations hosted working group meetings in their respective cities:

AT&T Bell Laboratories, Columbus, OH	Martin Marietta, Orlando, FL
Bellcore, Piscataway, NJ	NCR Corp, San Diego, CA
Boeing Computer Services, Seattle, WA	Northrop Electronics, Hawthorne, CA
Computer Sciences Corp., Silver Spring, MD	Northern Telecom, Ottawa, Ont.
E-Systems, Inc., Salt Lake City, UT	Tektronix, Beaverton, OR
Eastman Kodak Company, Rochester, NY	Teledyne Brown Engineering, Huntsville, AL
Hewlett Packard, San Jose, CA	Travelers Companies, Hartford, CT
Honeywell, Inc., Phoenix, AZ	Unisys, Eagan, MN
IEEE Computer Society, Dallas, TX	

AT&T Bell Laboratories provided word processing support. Bellcore and Computer Sciences Corporation assisted with mailings. The X3K1 Logical Flow Project provided technical coordination.

Suggestions for the improvement of this standard will be welcome. They should be sent to the Secretary, IEEE Standards Board, Institute of Electrical and Electronics Engineers, P. O. Box 1331, Piscataway, NJ 08855-1331.

IEEE Standard for Developing Software Life Cycle Processes

1. Introduction

1.1 Scope. This standard provides the set of Activities that constitute the Processes that are mandatory for the development and maintenance of software, whether stand-alone or part of a system. (Non-software Activities, such as hardware development and purchasing, are outside of the scope of this standard.) This standard also provides associated Input and Output Information.

For convenience, Activities are listed and described under specific Processes. In practice, the Activities may be performed by persons whose organizational titles or job descriptions do not clearly convey that a Process is part of their job. The Process under which an Activity is listed in this standard may be transparent in practice.

This standard does not prescribe a specific software life cycle model (SLCM). Each using organization must map the activities specified in the standard into its own software life cycle (SLC). If an organization has not yet defined an SLC, it will be necessary for them to select or define one before attempting to follow this standard. Further, this standard does not presume the use of any specific software development methodology nor the creation of specific documents.

For software already developed, it is recommended that these requirements, or a subset thereof, be applied. The existence of this standard should not be construed to prohibit the imposition of additional or more stringent requirements where the need exists, e.g., critical software.

Compliance with this standard is defined in 1.5.1.

1.2 References. No other publications are required for use of this standard. However, a list of other IEEE standards, which may be consulted for additional guidance, is given in the Bibliography in Section 8. Although this standard does not require adherence to any other IEEE standard, knowledge of principles and concepts described in the standards listed in the Bibliography would be helpful.

1.3 Definitions and Acronyms

1.3.1 Definitions. The definitions listed here establish meanings within the context of this standard. Definitions of other terms used in this document can be found in IEEE Std 610.12-1990 [1].[1]

Activity. A constituent task of a Process. *See:* **task.**

analysis. Examination for the purpose of understanding.

anomaly. Any deviation from requirements, expected or desired behavior, or performance of the software.

contractual requirements. Customer-imposed performance, logistics, and other requirements and commitments governing the scope of software development, delivery, or support.

customer. The person, or persons, who pay for the product and usually (but not necessarily) decide the requirements. In the context of this document the customer and the supplier may be members of the same organization. [5]

data base. A collection of data fundamental to a system. [22]

---

[1]The numbers in brackets correspond to those of the bibliographic references listed in Section 8.

evaluation. Determination of fitness for use.

external. An Input Information source or Output Information destination that is outside the control of this standard, and therefore may or may not exist.

function. A specific purpose of an entity or its characteristic action. [22]

installation. The period of time in the software life cycle during which a software product is integrated into its operational environment and tested in this environment to ensure that it performs as required. [1]

Mapping. Establishing a chronological relationship of the Activities in this standard according to a selected SLCM.

methodology. A body of methods, rules, and postulates employed by a discipline.

owner. A single point of contact, identified by organization position.

problem. The inability of a system or component to perform its required functions within specified performance requirements. [1]

Process. A function that must be performed in the software life cycle. A Process is composed of Activities.

product. Any output of the software development Activities; e.g., document, code, model.

quality management. That aspect of the overall management function that determines and implements the quality policy. (ISO 9000)

quality policy. The overall quality intentions and direction of an organization as regards quality, as formally expressed by top management. (ISO 9000)

revision. A controlled item with the same functional capabilities as the original plus changes, error resolution, or enhancements.

software life cycle (SLC). A project-specific, sequenced mapping of Activities.

software life cycle model (SLCM). The skeleton framework selected by each using organization on which to map the Activities of this standard to produce the software life cycle.

software quality management. That aspect of the overall software management function that determines and implements the software quality policy.

software quality policy. The overall quality intentions and direction of an organization as regards software quality, as expressed by top management.

software system. Software that is the subject of a single software project.

supplier. The person, or persons, who produce a product for a customer. In the context of this document, the customer and the supplier may be members of the same organization. [5]

task. The smallest unit of work subject to management accountability. A task is a well-defined work assignment for one or more project members. Related tasks are usually grouped to form Activities. [17]

unit. A logically separable part of a program. [1]

user. The person, or persons, who operate or interact directly with the system. [5]

1.3.2 Acronyms. The following acronyms appear within the text of this standard:

CASE   Computer-Aided Software Engineering
I/O   Input/Output
PR&RP   Problem Report and Resolution Planned Information
SCMP   Software Configuration Management Planned Information
SDD   Software Design Description
SLC   Software Life Cycle
SLCM   Software Life Cycle Model
SPMP   Software Project Management Planned Information
SQA   Software Quality Assurance
SRS   Software Requirements
SVVP   Software Verification and Validation Planned Information

1.4 Organization of This Document. The organization of this standard provides a logical approach to the development, operation, and maintenance of software. The detailed requirements of this document are organized into 17 Processes, which are comprised of a total of 65 Activities. The Processes and their Activities are described in six major sections. Table 1 depicts this organization.

Table 1
Organization of the Standard

Section	Title	Processes
2	Software Life Cycle Model Process	Software Life Cycle Model
3	Project Management Processes	Project Initiation Project Monitoring and Control Software Quality Management
4	Pre-Development Processes	Concept Exploration System Allocation
5	Development Processes	Requirements Design Implementation
6	Post-Development Processes	Installation Operation and Support Maintenance Retirement
7	Integral Processes	Verification and Validation Software Configuration Management Documentation Development Training

All of a Process' required actions are specified in its constituent Activities. Each Activity discussion has three parts:

(1)   Input Information, which lists information that is to be used by the Activity, and its source.
(2)   Description, which details the actions to be performed.
(3)   Output Information, which lists the information that is generated by the Activity, and its destination.

Where information flows between Activities, it can be traced from its original Activity to the receiving Activity through the Input and Output Information tables.

As mentioned above, all Processes are mandatory. Activities, however, are categorized as mandatory[2] or "If Applicable."[3] "If Applicable" Activities are marked "If Applicable" in the Activity title. All other Activities are mandatory. Each "If Applicable" Activity contains an explanation of the cases to which it will apply (e.g., 5.2.4, Design Data Base, applies when the software product contains a data base).

1.5 Use of This Standard. To facilitate the understanding and use of a standard of this magnitude, this section provides additional information.

1.5.1 Applicability. This standard applies to software development and maintenance projects.

This standard can be applied to commercial, scientific, and military software. Applicability is not restricted by size, complexity, or criticality of the software. This standard considers both the software and its context.

It is recognized that a project may be too small, in terms of schedule, budget, risk, nature, or use of software to be developed, used, and maintained, to warrant total application of the standard. In such cases, selected Activities may be applied even though compliance with this standard may not be claimed. This may also apply when only purchased software is involved.

A large project may be subdivided into smaller manageable projects, and this standard applied to each of the smaller projects and then to the whole. Similarly, some projects may be of long duration, and may be delivered in multiple versions or releases; it may be helpful in some cases to treat the development of each successive version as a separate project with its own life cycle.

1.5.2 Compliance. Compliance with this standard is defined as the performance of all mandatory Activities. Some mandatory Activities may occur in different instances (e.g., performing tests at various levels); compliance with this standard means the complete performance of each instance of the mandatory Activity. The standard does not specify instances of any Activity.

The performance of an Activity or an instance thereof is complete when all Input Information has been processed, and all Output Information has been generated. This may require several iterations of an Activity or instance.

All Input and Output Information are not required for a given occurrence of an iterative Activity. The presence of sufficient Input Information to permit processing by the Activity to begin constitutes the entry criterion, and the creation of any Output Information is a sufficient exit criterion.

This standard does not impose the order in which Activities must be performed. However, an order must be established by executing the Activities defined in Section 2 and the Activity in 3.1.3.

In some cases, certain Input and Output Information may not be required for completion of an Activity. These are indicated as "External" to the SLC and may not exist. To the extent that they exist, they must be processed by affected Activities.

This standard prescribes the *processes* of the software life cycle, not the *products* of that life cycle. Therefore, the standard does not require the completion of specific documents. The information generated by Activities, listed in the Output Information tables, may be collected into documents in any manner consistent with the selected SLCM.

In the event that this standard is contractually imposed, and one or more subcontractors are involved in the project, it is recommended that the requirements of this standard be imposed on the subcontractors.

---

[2]The term "mandatory" as used in this standard is synonymous with the term "essential."

[3]The term "if applicable" as used in this standard is synonymous with the terms "conditional" and "optional."

1.5.3 Intended Audience. This standard cannot be implemented by a single functional group within a development organization. Mapping this standard's Activities into an organization's SLCM, and coordinating these Activities with existing development and support methodologies and standards, require specific expertise and authority within the organization.

After mapping is complete, the Activities in Sections 3–7 are ready for execution. These Activity descriptions are directed to the functional specialist most likely to be performing them (e.g., the Requirements and Analysis Activities assume a basic familiarity with analysis techniques).

1.5.4 Process and Activity Relationships

1.5.4.1 Project Management Processes. There are three Processes in this section: the Project Initiation Process, the Project Monitoring and Control Process, and the Software Quality Management Process. The Project Initiation Process consists of those Activities that create and maintain the project framework. The Activities within the Project Monitoring and Control Process and the Software Quality Management Process are performed throughout the life of the project to ensure the appropriate level of project management and compliance with the mandated Activities.

1.5.4.2 Development-Oriented Processes. These are the Processes that must be performed before, during, and after the development of the software. The Pre-Development Processes are Concept Exploration and System Allocation. Development Processes include Requirements, Design, and Implementation. Finally, the Post-Development Processes include Installation, Operation and Support, Maintenance, and Retirement.

1.5.4.3 Integral Processes. This section includes those Processes that are necessary to ensure the successful completion of a project, but are not Development Processes. The Integral Processes are Verification and Validation, Software Configuration Management, Documentation Development, and Training. All of these Processes contain two types of Activities:

(1) Those that are performed discretely and are therefore mapped into an SLCM.
(2) Those that are performed in the course of completing another Activity. These are invoked Activities and will not be mapped into the SLCM in every instance.

Many Activities invoke, or call like a subroutine, appropriate Integral Process(es). This is an intuitive method of getting a task, such as the evaluation or production of a document, done without specifying an exact control flow within this standard.

To track the flow of a product into, through, and back from an Integral Process, there are generic sources and destinations listed in the Input and Output Information tables called "Creating Process." Within the Integral Process that is invoked, the Activity that first receives the product has a generic Input Information whose source is Creating Process. This product passes through one or more Activities of that Integral Process, then is returned to the invoking Activity through an Activity's Output Information, whose destination is Creating Process. An example of this flow is shown in Fig 1, which illustrates how one Activity within the Design Process invokes the Integral Processes. This figure will be easier to follow if it is compared directly with 5.2.7, "Perform Detailed Design." The order of Invoked Processes in the figure differs from that in 5.2.7.

The invoked Process is specified in the text by the name of the Process and the number of the first Activity to be performed within that Process [e.g., Verification and Validation (7.1.4)].

1.5.4.4 Use of I/O Tables. The Input Information to and Output Information from each Activity are listed in tables that accompany the Activity descriptions. As a convention of this document, Input and Output Information names are always capitalized in the text.

The I/O tables show the flow of Information through the Activities. The pertinent Information is listed in the left-hand column. The source or destination of the Information (both Process and Activity) is shown in the right-hand columns. The Information names were chosen, where possible, to suggest the titles of documents commonly used in the software industry. The Information names also frequently relate to the documents described in the standards listed in Section 8. Some of these Information items are represented in the text by acronyms that were deliberately chosen to suggest the commonly used names of the corresponding documents.

External Input Information sources and External Output Information destinations are outside the scope of this standard. External Input Information may or may not exist, and if it does not exist, it is not required. When an External Input does exist and is therefore used, it is presumed to include any associated documentation. External output destinations also may or may not exist. External sources and destinations are not necessarily Processes, and no corresponding Activities are shown in the I/O tables.

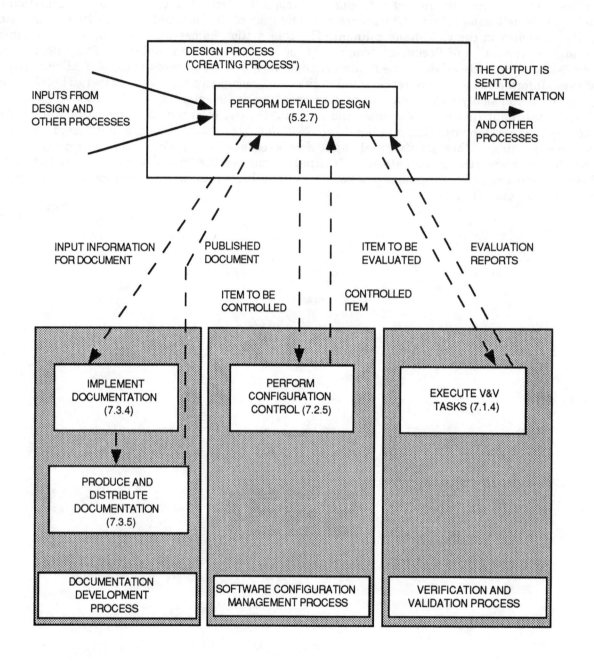

Fig 1
Example of Invoked Processes

In most cases, the Input Information and Output Information columns of the tables designate the specific information that enters or exits the Activity. However, since many Activities have Output Information whose destination is Retain Records (3.2.6), the various Input Information to Retain Records is collected under the term "Original Records." The corresponding Process and Activity columns refer simply to Originating Process and Originating Activity. Figure 2 depicts the conceptual flow of Input Information and Output Information into and out from an Activity, respectively.

1.5.5 Getting Started. Before beginning a project that will use this standard, the Activities need to be reviewed for applicability to a specific project and organized into a time sequence appropriate to that project. To perform that time sequencing, an SLCM must be chosen or developed and Activities mapped into the SLCM. This mapping is discussed in Section 2 and the mapping Activity in 3.1.3. Examples are given in Appendix A.

This mapping produces a temporal "road map" called the Software Life Cycle (SLC) used to follow this standard throughout the project. The mapped Activities must be initiated in their designated sequence.

1.5.6 Additional Considerations

1.5.6.1 Organizational Independence. This standard does not presume or dictate an organizational structure for a software project. Therefore, it is neither implied nor required that Activities within a Process be performed by the same organizational entity, nor that an organizational entity's involvement be concentrated in only one Process. To ensure that all Activities are assigned to an appropriate organizational entity, the concept of Activity Ownership is described in the Activity in 3.1.3.

1.5.6.2 Combining Documents. The Information developed in this standard, as shown in the Output Information tables, may carry generic names similar to those used in other IEEE standards. This does not imply that the format and content specified in other IEEE standards must be followed, nor that this information must be packaged into documents in any particular manner.

Combination of documents into a single document is acceptable as long as understanding is not compromised.

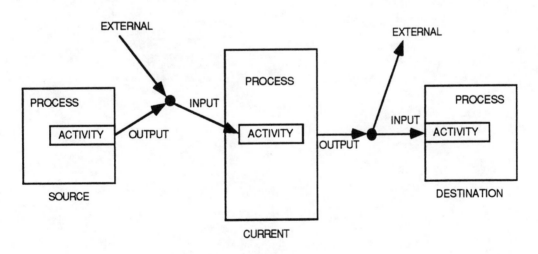

Fig 2
Information Flow

2. Software Life Cycle Model Process

2.1 Overview. Many variables affect an organization's selection of a software life cycle model (SLCM). While this standard neither dictates nor defines a specific software life cycle (SLC) or its underlying methodologies, it does require that an SLCM be chosen and used.

This Process provides the Activities required to identify candidate SLCMs and select the SLCM to be used by other Activities in the standard.

This standard includes the specification of the non-time-ordered set of "Mandatory" Activities that must be incorporated into an SLCM. An SLCM (e.g., Rapid Prototyping) defines a specific approach to producing software. It specifies a time-ordered set of Activities (including all of the "Mandatory" Activities identified in this standard), which is to be used as the basis for mapping the Activities of this standard. An SLCM may also propose standards for the performance of the Activities or the deliverables produced during the project.

The SLC (defined for a project by the Activity in 3.1.3) is the time-ordered set of Activities or instances of Activities to be performed. This set is to be mapped into a selected SLCM. The SLC also identifies specific responsibilities for each Activity. While the same SLCM may be valid for several projects, each project must define its own SLC.

Once an SLCM is selected, there are two additional required actions:

(1) Mapping the Activities described in this standard into the chosen life cycle (3.1.3).
(2) Identifying and documenting the standards and controls that govern the SLC (3.1.5).

Figure 3 illustrates this progression from this standard to a project-specific SLC.

Section 1.5, "Use of This Standard," provides background information necessary for the successful understanding and application of this material. It should be read prior to proceeding further in this section.

2.2 Activities List

(1) Identify Candidate Software Life Cycle Models
(2) Select Project Model

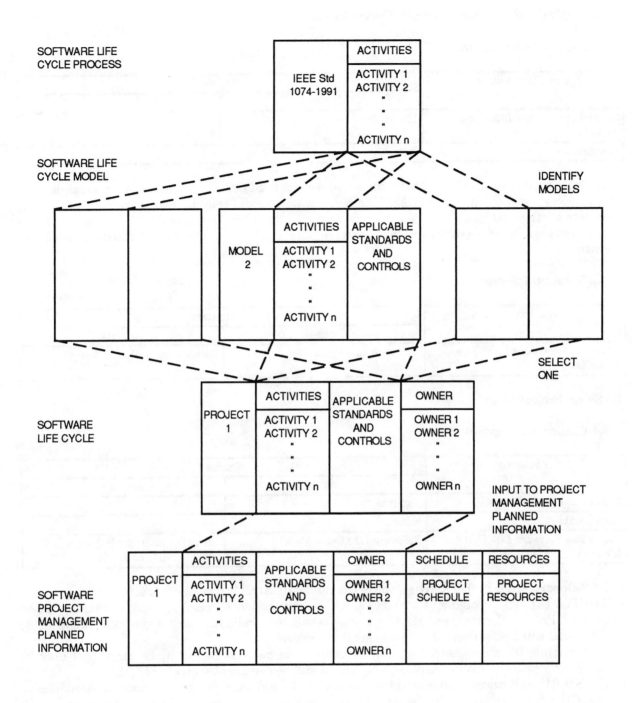

Fig 3
Software Life Cycle Relationships

2.3 Identify Candidate Software Life Cycle Models

2.3.1 Input Information

Input Information	Source	
	Process	Activity
Available Software Life Cycle Models)	External	
Constraints	External	

2.3.2 Description. In this Activity, the set of Available SLCMs and applicable Constraints shall be considered and Candidate SLCMs identified. A new model may be constructed by combining elements of other SLCMs.

Maintenance is an iteration of the Software Life Cycle, and the SLCM must support this iteration.

2.3.3 Output Information

Output Information	Destination	
	Process	Activity
Candidate Software Life Cycle Model(s)	Software Life Cycle Model	Select Project Model (2.4)

2.4 Select Project Model

2.4.1 Input Information

Input Information	Source	
	Process	Activity
Historical Project Records	External	
Constraints	External	
Candidate Software Life Cycle Model(s)	Software Life Cycle Model	Identify Candidate Software Life Cycle Models (2.3)

2.4.2 Description. In this Activity, one of the candidate SLCMs from 2.3.2 is selected for use.

Based on the type of product (interactive, batch, transaction processing, etc.), Constraints, and Historical Project Records, an SLCM analysis shall be conducted, and a decision made as to which model will best support the management of the project.

It is possible for an organization to have more than one SLCM, but only one model may be selected for a project. It is not necessary to have a single, organization-wide SLCM.

The SLCM shall provide the necessary framework for software projects to map the Activities to produce the SLC (as shown in Fig 3). The mapping effort is specified in the Project Initiation Process, Map Activities to Software Life Cycle Model (3.1.3).

2.4.3 Output Information

Output Information	Destination	
	Process	Activity
Selected Software Life Cycle Model	Project Initiation	Map Activities to Software Life Cycle Model (3.1.3)

3. Project Management Processes

These are the Processes that initiate, monitor, and control software projects throughout the software life cycle (SLC).

3.1 Project Initiation Process

3.1.1 Overview. This Process contains those Activities that create the framework for the project. During this Process, the SLC is created for this project, and plans for managing the project are established. Standards, methodologies, and tools needed to manage and execute the project are identified and a plan prepared for their timely implementation.

Section 1.5, "Use of This Standard," provides background information necessary for the successful understanding and application of this material. It should be read prior to proceeding further in this section.

3.1.2 Activities List

(1)   Map Activities to Software Life Cycle Model
(2)   Allocate Project Resources
(3)   Establish Project Environment
(4)   Plan Project Management

3.1.3 Map Activities to Software Life Cycle Model

3.1.3.1 Input Information

Input Information	Source	
	Process	Activity
Contractual Requirements	External	
Selected Software Life Cycle Model	Software Life Cycle Model	Select Project Model (2.4)
Statement of Need	Concept Exploration	Refine and Finalize the Idea or Need (4.1.7)

3.1.3.2 Description. The Activities identified in this standard shall be mapped into the selected SLC Model (SLCM). Mapping involves establishing the chronological relationship of the Activities in this standard according to the selected SLCM. It may be necessary to use the Contractual Requirements and the Statement of Need to accomplish this mapping. Appendix A provides several examples of such mappings. Appendix B is a template for adding additional project-specific information, such as document titles and applicable standards, to the mapped Activities.

The use of certain software development methods defines the execution of some Activities to be automated. Compliance with this standard must be demonstrated by mapping those automated Activities into the appropriate points within the SLCM.

Each Activity shall be assigned a single "owner." An owner is a single point of contact, and is identified by organizational position. Ownership is assumed by the person currently filling that position. Each owner has the responsibility and authority to control and complete the Activity within the planned schedule and budget. In addition, each owner is accountable for the quality of the Activity outputs. If Activities are to be performed by multiple organizations, the owning organization and position of the owner shall be identified. In the case of multiple instances of an Activity, an owner for each instance shall be identified.

The resulting map of the Activities to be performed, with their corresponding owners, is the SLC for this project. All "If Applicable" Activities that do not apply to this project shall be identified and explained in the List of Activities Not Used.

3.1.3.3 Output Information

Output Information	Destination	
	Process	Activity
Software Life Cycle	Project Initiation	Allocate Project Resources (3.1.4)
		Establish Project Environment (3.1.5)
		Plan Project Management (3.1.6)
List of Activities Not Used	Project Monitoring and Control	Retain Records (3.2.6)

3.1.4 Allocate Project Resources

3.1.4.1 Input Information

Input Information	Source	
	Process	Activity
Historical Project Records	External	
Resources	External	
Statement of Need	Concept Exploration	Refine and Finalize the Idea or Need (4.1.7)
Software Life Cycle	Project Initiation	Map Activities to Software Life Cycle Model (3.1.3)
System Functional Software Requirements	System Allocation	Decompose System Requirements (4.2.5)

3.1.4.2 Description. Resource Allocations shall be identified at the Software Life Cycle's Activity level. Resources to be allocated include personnel, equipment, space, etc. Available Historical Project Records and the Statement of Need may provide valuable insight into Resource Allocation.

3.1.4.3 Output Information

Output Information	Destination	
	Process	Activity
Resource Allocations	Project Initiation	Establish Project Environment (3.1.5)
		Plan Project Management (3.1.6)
	Project Management and Control	Analyze Risks (3.2.3)

3.1.5 Establish Project Environment

3.1.5.1 Input Information

Input Information	Source	
	Process	Activity
Methodologies	External	
Standards	External	
Tools	External	
Software Library	External	
Purchased Software	External	
Contractual Requirements	External	
Analysis of Risks	Project Monitoring and Control	Analyze Risks (3.2.3)
Software Life Cycle	Project Initiation	Map Activities to Software Life Cycle Model (3.1.3)
Defined Metrics	Software Quality Management	Define Metrics (3.3.4)
Collection and Analysis Methods	Software Quality Management	Define Metrics (3.3.4)
Resource Allocations	Project Initiation	Allocate Project Resources (3.1.4)
Statement of Need	Concept Exploration	Refine and Finalize the Idea or Need (4.1.7)

3.1.5.2 Description. The needs of the project for procedural and technological Tools, Methodologies, and Standards shall be defined. Approaches to these needs shall be identified and evaluated. These approaches could include automated and nonautomated tools, modeling and prototyping methodologies, environment simulators, test beds, and software libraries. Selection criteria for Tools and Methodologies should include resource, schedule, safety, and security considerations, and the project requirements defined in the Statement of Need and Analysis of Risks. The project standards shall include requirements, design, coding, test, and documentation standards.

After evaluating the approaches, a set of Tools, Methodologies, Standards, and reusable or Purchased Software shall be selected to provide the Project Environment, considering the Input Information.

The selected tools shall be acquired or developed and installed for use in project Activities. The owner of this Activity shall ensure that applicable personnel are familiar with the Tools, Methodologies, and Standards selected for the project.

For assistance in identifying applicable standards, [9] should be consulted.

Prior to distribution of the Project Environment, the Training Process (7.4.4) shall be invoked.

3.1.5.3 Output Information

Output Information	Destination	
	Process	Activity
Project Environment	Project Initiation	Plan Project Management (3.1.6)

3.1.6 Plan Project Management

3.1.6.1 Input Information

Input Information	Source	
	Process	Activity
Contractual Requirements	External	
Software Life Cycle	Project Initiation	Map Activities to Software Life Cycle Model (3.1.3)
Resource Allocations	Project Initiation	Allocate Project Resources (3.1.4)
Project Environment	Project Initiation	Establish Project Environment (3.1.5)
Contingency Planned Information	Project Monitoring and Control	Perform Contingency Planning (3.2.4)
Project Management Reported Information	Project Monitoring and Control	Manage the Project (3.2.5)
Preliminary Statement of Need	Concept Exploration	Identify Ideas or Needs (4.1.3)
Recommendations	Concept Exploration	Conduct Feasibility Studies (4.1.5)
Statement of Need	Concept Exploration	Refine and Finalize the Idea or Need (4.1.7)

3.1.6.2 Description. Project management planning requires collection and synthesis of a great deal of information into a coherent and organized Software Project Management Planned Information (SPMP) based on the SLC. This Activity shall initially define and subsequently update the SPMP using the Input Information. This Activity shall detail the project organization and assign responsibilities. Standards, methodologies, and tools for configuration management, quality assurance, verification and validation, training, documentation, and development shall be specified. This Activity shall apportion the project budget and staffing, and define schedules, using the applicable Input Information. It also shall define procedures for scheduling, tracking, and reporting, and shall address considerations such as regulatory approvals, required certifications, user involvement, subcontracting, and security.

This Activity shall include planning for support, problem reporting, and retirement. Support planning shall include methods for supporting the software in the operational environment. Problem Reporting and Resolution Planning Information shall include, at a minimum, defining a method for logging, routing, and handling problem reports; categories of severity; and the method for verifying problem resolution. Retirement Planned Information shall address issues such as probable retirement date, archiving, replacement, and residual support issues.

As new or revised Input Information is received in this Activity, project plans shall be updated and further project planning shall be based upon these updated plans.

Additional guidance for SPMPs can be found in [17].

Prior to distribution of the SPMP, the following Processes shall be invoked:

(1) Verification and Validation (7.1.4)
(2) Software Configuration Management (7.2.5)
(3) Documentation Development (7.3.4)

3.1.6.3 Output Information

Output Information	Destination	
	Process	Activity
Problem Reporting and Resolution Planned Information	Project Monitoring and Control	Manage the Project (3.2.5)
		Analyze Risks (3.2.3)
		Implement Problem Reporting Method (3.2.7)
Retirement Planned Information	Project Monitoring and Control	Manage the Project (3.2.5)
	Retirement	Notify User (6.4.3)
		Conduct Parallel Operations (If Applicable) (6.4.4)
		Retire System (6.4.5)
Software Project Management Planned Information	Most Processes	Most Activities
Support Planned Information	Project Monitoring and Control	Analyze Risks (3.2.3)
		Manage the Project (3.2.5)
	Operation and Support	Maintain Support Request Log (6.2.5)
		Operate the System (6.2.3)
		Provide Technical Assistance and Consulting (6.2.4)

3.2 Project Monitoring and Control Process

3.2.1 Overview. Monitoring and control is an iterative Process of tracking, reporting, and managing costs, schedules, problems, and performance of a project throughout its life cycle. The progress of a project is reviewed and measured against project milestones established in the Software Project Management Planned Information (SPMP).

Section 1.5, "Use of This Standard," provides background information necessary for the successful understanding and application of this material. It should be read prior to proceeding further in this section.

3.2.2 Activities List

(1) Analyze Risks
(2) Perform Contingency Planning
(3) Manage the Project
(4) Retain Records
(5) Implement Problem Reporting Method

3.2.3 Analyze Risks

3.2.3.1 Input Information

Input Information	Source	
	Process	Activity
Procurement/Lease Data	External	
System Constraints	External	
Historical Project Records	External	
Support Planned Information	Project Initiation	Plan Project Management (3.1.6)
Resource Allocations	Project Initiation	Allocate Project Resources (3.1.4)
Software Project Management Planned Information	Project Initiation	Plan Project Management (3.1.6)
Problem Reporting and Resolution Planned Information	Project Initiation	Plan Project Management (3.1.6)
Transition Impact Statement (If Applicable)	Concept Exploration	Plan System Transition (If Applicable) (4.1.6)
Statement of Need	Concept Exploration	Refine and Finalize the Idea or Need (4.1.7)
Software Interface Requirements	Requirements	Define Interface Requirements (5.1.4)
Software Requirements	Requirements	Prioritize and Integrate Software Requirements (5.1.5)
Software Design Description	Design	Perform Detailed Design (5.2.7)
Integration Planned Information	Implementation	Plan Integration (5.3.7)
Analysis Reported Information	Verification and Validation	Collect and Analyze Metric Data (7.1.5)
Test Planned Information(s)	Verification and Validation	Plan Testing (7.1.6)
Test Summary Reported Information	Verification and Validation	Execute the Tests (7.1.8)

3.2.3.2 Description. Because risk management often involves trade-offs between many factors, risk analysis is an iterative Activity performed throughout a project's life. This analysis shall consider project risks, including technical, economic, operational support, and schedule risks.

Factors that may impair, prevent, or require technical trade-offs for accomplishing the technical objectives of the project or product shall be identified and analyzed. Technical factors may include such items as real-time performance, safety considerations, security considerations, implementation considerations, testability, and maintainability. Analytical approaches for technical risk assessment may include static and dynamic modeling and simulation, prototyping, independent reviews, and audits.

Cost, resource factors, earnings, liabilities, or other economic measures involved in the project shall be identified and analyzed. The objective of this analysis is to identify potential economic opportunities, losses, and trade-offs. Analytical approaches for economic risk assessment may include financial analysis, such as return on investment and possible incentive and penalty contract clauses.

Operational and support risk analysis shall determine the probability that the delivered software will meet the user's requirements. Operational and support requirements such as interoperability, security, performance, installability, and maintainability shall be considered. Both completeness of, and conformance to, these requirements shall be analyzed.

Cost, resource, technical, and other requirements shall be evaluated for their impact on project schedule. This analysis should consider project interdependence and the effect of schedule adjustments. Analytical approaches for schedule risk assessment may include critical path analysis and resource leveling techniques.

3.2.3.3 Output Information

Output Information	Destination	
	Process	Activity
Analysis of Risks	Project Initiation	Establish Project Environment (3.1.5)
	Project Monitoring and Control	Perform Contingency Planning (3.2.4)
	Requirements	Define and Develop Software Requirements (5.1.3)
	Verification and Validation	Plan Verification and Validation (7.1.3)

3.2.4 Perform Contingency Planning

3.2.4.1 Input Information

Input Information	Source	
	Process	Activity
Analysis of Risks	Project Monitoring and Control	Analyze Risks (3.2.3)
Analysis Reported Information	Verification and Validation	Collect and Analyze Metric Data (7.1.5)

3.2.4.2 Description. This Activity shall define alternative actions in the event that a given risk materializes, using the Input Information. Contingency Planned Information shall include resource planning and the establishment of trigger conditions that would invoke a contingency action. Contingency actions may include consideration of revised requirements, delay, or cancellation of the project.

3.2.4.3 Output Information

Output Information	Destination	
	Process	Activity
Contingency Planned Information	Project Initiation	Plan Project Management (3.1.6)
	Project Monitoring and Control	Manage the Project (3.2.5)

3.2.5 Manage the Project

3.2.5.1 Input Information

Input Information	Source	
	Process	Activity
Problem Reporting and Resolution Planned Information	Project Initiation	Plan Project Management (3.1.6)
Retirement Planned Information	Project Initiation	Plan Project Management (3.1.6)
Software Project Management Planned Information	Project Initiation	Plan Project Management (3.1.6)
Support Planned Information	Project Initiation	Plan Project Management (3.1.6)
Contingency Planned Information	Project Monitoring and Control	Perform Contingency Planning (3.2.4)
Software Quality Management Planned Information	Software Quality Management	Plan Software Quality Management (3.3.3)
Quality Improvement Recommendations	Software Quality Management	Identify Quality Improvement Needs (3.3.6)
Integration Planned Information	Implementation	Plan Integration (5.3.7)
Installation Reported Information	Installation	Install Software (6.1.5)
Evaluation Reported Information	Verification and Validation	Execute Verification and Validation Tasks (7.1.4)
Analysis Reported Information	Verification and Validation	Collect and Analyze Metric Data (7.1.5)
Test Planned Information(s)	Verification and Validation	Plan Testing (7.1.6)
Test Summary Reported Information	Verification and Validation	Execute the Tests (7.1.8)
Status Reported Information	Software Configuration Management	Perform Status Accounting (7.2.6)
Feedback Data	Operation and Support	Operate the System (6.2.3)

3.2.5.2 Description. Throughout the life cycle, the progress of the project shall be reviewed and measured against the established milestones and budget in the plan(s) (i.e., predicted and planned progress versus actual progress, and budgeted versus actual expenditures). Project tracking and reporting includes analyzing the Input Information, collecting other pertinent data, and monitoring project Activities. Anomalies may result. Risk management procedures must be implemented to control risk.

This Activity also encompasses the day-to-day management of the project needed to ensure successful project completion. Information collected within this Activity is used to improve the performance of the project.

Prior to distributing the Project Management Reported Information, the Verification and Validation Process (7.1.4) should be invoked.

3.2.5.3 Output Information

Output Information	Destination	
	Process	Activity
Project Management Reported Information	Project Initiation	Plan Project Management (3.1.6)
	Project Monitoring and Control	Retain Records (3.2.6)
	External	
Anomalies	Project Monitoring and Control	Implement Problem Reporting Method (3.2.7)

3.2.6 Retain Records

3.2.6.1 Input Information

Input Information	Source	
	Process	Activity
Documentation Retention Standards	External	
Original Records	Originating Process	Originating Activity
Software Project Management Planned Information	Project Initiation	Plan Project Management (3.1.6)
Software Configuration Management Planned Information	Software Configuration Management	Plan Configuration Management (7.2.3)
Documentation Planned Information	Documentation Development	Plan Documentation (7.3.3)
Published Document	Documentation Development	Produce and Distribute Documentation (7.3.5)

3.2.6.2 Description. This Activity accepts the original project documentation and records from each originating Process. The records shall be retained in accordance with the SPMP, Software Configuration Management Planned Information, and any external document retention standards. Input Information documentation becomes part of the Historical Project Records of the organization. Uses for these records may include project audits, future project planning, and corporate accounting.

3.2.6.3 Output Information

Output Information	Destination	
	Process	Activity
Historical Project Records	External	

3.2.7 Implement Problem Reporting Method

3.2.7.1 Input Information

Input Information	Source	
	Process	Activity
Anomalies	External	
	Creating Process	
Controlled Item	Software Configuration Management	Perform Configuration Control (7.2.5)
Problem Reporting and Resolution Planned Information	Project Initiation	Plan Project Management (3.1.6)

3.2.7.2 Description. This Activity accepts Anomalies from any source and prepares a problem report. The problem report shall contain information as specified in the Problem Reporting and Resolution Planned Information (PR&RP). Possible problem solutions may be suggested by the problem reporter. Problems may be resolved through corrections or enhancements (as defined in the PR&RP). Corrections are documented in the Correction Problem Reported Information for further consideration. Enhancements may be documented in the Enhancement Problem Reported Information and are possible candidates for new projects. A Report Log shall be maintained to assure that all problems are tracked until they are resolved and the resolution has been approved.

This Activity shall also analyze the problem including the Controlled Item, the problem report, and the Report Log to make the following determinations:

(1) What the anomalies are.
(2) Source and cause of product or process problem.
(3) Product(s) or process(es) presumed to contain the error, including documentation.
(4) Problem severity.
(5) Course of corrective action.

Problem reports that originate from an Activity not included in this standard are noted as resolved within this Activity and forwarded for appropriate action to the responsible authority.

This Activity shall monitor the problem correction efforts performed by the responsible Process, shall determine (according to the PR&RD) that the implementation of the solution by the responsible Process has been completed, and shall then record the resolution of the problem in the Resolved Problem Reported Information. The Resolved Problem Reported Information shall be distributed as specified in the Problem Reporting and Resolution Planned Information.

Further information related to this Activity may be found in [15].

The Resolved Problem Reported Information should be made available to the Process or external source that reported the problem.

Prior to distribution of a Problem Reported Information or the Report Log, the Software Configuration Management Process (7.2.5) should be invoked.

3.2.7.3 Output Information

Output Information	Destination	
	Process	Activity
Resolved Problem Reported Information	External	
	Creating Process	
	Software Quality Management	Manage Software Quality (3.3.5)
	Verification and Validation	Execute Verification and Validation Tasks (7.1.4)
		Collect and Analyze Metric Data (7.1.5)
Report Log	Software Quality Management	Manage Software Quality (3.3.5)
	Verification and Validation	Collect and Analyze Metric Data (7.1.5)
Enhancement Problem Reported Information	Concept Exploration	Identify Ideas or Needs (4.1.3)
	Verification and Validation	Collect and Analyze Metric Data (7.1.5)
Correction Problem Reported Information	Maintenance	Reapply Software Life Cycle (6.3.3)
	Verification and Validation	Collect and Analyze Metric Data (7.1.5)

3.3 Software Quality Management Process

3.3.1 Overview. An important role of Software Quality Management is to address the planning and administration of the Software Quality Assurance (SQA) program. It further addresses such concerns as client satisfaction (which transcends adherence only to established technical requirements), and internal quality improvement programs. The responsibilities, functions, obligations, and duties of an SQA program are properly a constituent part of all Activities in the Software Life Cycle, and thus are interspersed into each Activity as appropriate. Software Quality Management is the methodology used in this standard for tying the SQA responsibilities together with other Quality concerns. The Activities of this Process span the entire Software Life Cycle (SLC).

Section 1.5, "Use of This Standard," provides background information necessary for the successful understanding and application of this material. It should be read prior to proceeding further in this section.

3.3.2 Activities List

(1) Plan Software Quality Management
(2) Define Metrics
(3) Manage Software Quality
(4) Identify Quality Improvement Needs

3.3.3 Plan Software Quality Management

3.3.3.1 Input Information

Input Information	Source	
	Process	Activity
Software Project Management Planned Information	Project Initiation	Plan Project Management (3.1.6)
Defined Metrics	Software Quality Management	Define Metrics (3.3.4)
Collection and Analysis Methods	Software Quality Management	Define Metrics (3.3.4)

3.3.3.2 Description. A Software Quality Management program shall be initiated and documented.

It shall include a Software Quality Assurance program, which may be documented separately.

The goals of the Software Quality Management program are to identify SQA actions, describe supplier quality requirements, address client satisfaction, and provide for the identification of quality improvement needs.

Overall quality objectives are derived using the organizational guidelines and contractual requirements from the Software Project Management Planned Information.

The program information shall include the Software Quality Management organization and responsibilities, and the tools, techniques, and methodologies to implement the program.

The goals and standards to be applied to the project shall also be identified.

The goals are further expanded into quality objectives and milestones in the Software Quality Management Planned Information.

Further information related to this Activity may be found in [2] and [8].

Prior to distribution of the Software Quality Management Planned Information, the following Processes shall be invoked:

(1) Verification and Validation (7.1.4)
(2) Software Configuration Management (7.2.5)
(3) Documentation Development (7.3.4)

3.3.3.3 Output Information

Output Information	Destination	
	Process	Activity
Software Quality Management Planned Information	Project Monitoring and Control	Manage the Project (3.2.5)
	Software Quality Management	Define Metrics (3.3.4)
		Manage Software Quality (3.3.5)
		Identify Quality Improvement Needs (3.3.6)
	Verification and Validation	Plan Verification and Validation (7.1.3)
		Collect and Analyze Metric Data (7.1.5)

3.3.4 Define Metrics

3.3.4.1 Input Information

Input Information	Source	
	Process	Activity
Software Quality Management Planned Information	Software Quality Management	Plan Software Quality Management (3.3.3)
Software Project Management Planned Information	Project Initiation	Plan Project Management (3.1.6)

3.3.4.2 Description. The metrics required for the project, based on the Software Project Management Planned Information, shall be defined. Metrics should be applied to the products of the project and to the processes that affect the project. The metrics shall be used throughout the SLC. For each Defined Metric, Collection and Analysis Methods shall be specified.

Further information related to this Activity may be found in [6], [7], [16], and [19].

Prior to the distribution of Defined Metrics, the Verification and Validation Process (7.1.4) shall be invoked.

3.3.4.3 Output Information

Output Information	Destination	
	Process	Activity
Defined Metrics	Software Quality Management	Manage Software Quality (3.3.5)
		Plan Software Quality Management (3.3.3)
	Project Initiation	Establish Project Environm't (3.1.5)
	Verification and Validation	Collect and Analyze Metric Data (7.1.5)
Collection and Analysis Methods	Software Quality Management	Plan Software Quality Management (3.3.3)
		Manage Software Quality (3.3.5)
	Verification and Validation	Collect and Analyze Metric Data (7.1.5)
	Project Initiation	Establish Project Environm't (3.1.5)

3.3.5 Manage Software Quality

3.3.5.1 Input Information

Input Information	Source	
	Process	Activity
Report Log	Project Monitoring and Control	Implement Problem Reporting Method (3.2.7)
Resolved Problem Reported Information	Project Monitoring and Control	Implement Problem Reporting Method (3.2.7)
Software Quality Management Planned Information	Software Quality Management	Plan Software Quality Management (3.3.3)
Defined Metrics	Software Quality Management	Define Metrics (3.3.4)
Collection and Analysis Methods	Software Quality Management	Define Metrics (3.3.4)
Quality Improvement Recommendations	Software Quality Management	Identify Quality Improvement Needs (3.3.6)
Analysis Reported Information	Verification and Validation	Collect and Analyze Metric Data (7.1.5)
Post-Operation Review Reported Information	Retirement	Retire System (6.4.5)

3.3.5.2 Description. Using the listed Input Information, this Activity implements the provisions of the Software Quality Management Planned Information. Based on the Software Quality Management Planned Information quality objectives and milestones, progress shall be measured and reported in Project Quality Assessments.

3.3.5.3 Output Information

Output Information	Destination	
	Process	Activity
Project Quality Assessments	Verification and Validation	Execute Verification and Validation Tasks (7.1.4)

3.3.6 Identify Quality Improvement Needs

3.3.6.1 Input Information

Input Information	Source	
	Process	Activity
Software Project Management Planned Information	Project Initiation	Plan Project Management (3.1.6)
Software Quality Management Planned Information	Software Quality Management	Plan Software Quality Management (3.3.3)
Software Verification and Validation Planned Information	Verification and Validation	Plan Verification and Validation (7.1.3)
Evaluation Reported Information	Verification and Validation	Execute Verification and Validation Tasks (7.1.4)
Analysis Reported Information	Verification and Validation	Collect and Analyze Metric Data (7.1.5)
Test Planned Information(s)	Verification and Validation	Plan Testing (7.1.6)
Training Planned Information(s)	Training	Plan Training Program (7.4.3)

3.3.6.2 Description. This Activity identifies needs for quality improvements and outputs the Quality Improvement Recommendations in accordance with the Software Quality Management Planned Information. This is accomplished by using the Input Information. These recommendations shall include their impact on the quality of the software delivered. In addition, applicable tools, techniques, and methods for implementation of these recommendations should be identified.

3.3.6.3 Output Information

Output Information	Destination	
	Process	Activity
Quality Improvement Recommendations	Project Monitoring and Control	Manage the Project (3.2.5)
	Software Quality Management	Manage Software Quality (3.3.5)
	External	

4. Pre-Development Processes

These are the Processes that must be performed before software development can begin.

4.1 Concept Exploration Process

4.1.1 Overview. A development effort is initiated with the identification of an idea or need for a system to be developed, whether it is a new effort or a change to all or part of an existing application. The Concept Exploration Process examines the requirements at the system level, producing a Statement of Need that initiates the System Allocation or Requirements Process. The Concept Exploration Process includes the identification of an idea or need, its evaluation and refinement, and, once boundaries are placed around it, generation of a Statement of Need for developing a system.

Section 1.5, "Use of This Standard," provides background information necessary for the successful understanding and application of this material. It should be read prior to proceeding further in this section.

4.1.2 Activities List

(1) Identify Ideas or Needs
(2) Formulate Potential Approaches
(3) Conduct Feasibility Studies
(4) Plan System Transition (If Applicable)
(5) Refine and Finalize the Idea or Need

4.1.3 Identify Ideas or Needs

4.1.3.1 Input Information

Input Information	Source	
	Process	Activity
Changing Software Requirements	External	
Customer Requests	External	
Ideas from Within the Development Organization	External	
Marketing Information Sources	External	
User Requests	External	
Enhancement Problem Reported Information	Project Monitoring and Control	Implement Problem Reporting Method (3.2.7)
Maintenance Recommendations	Maintenance	Reapply Software Life Cycle (6.3.3)
Feedback Data	Operation and Support	Operate the System (6.2.3)

4.1.3.2 Description. An idea or a need for a new or modified system is generated from one or more of the sources identified in the table above. Input Information to the Preliminary Statement of Need shall be documented, outlining function and performance needs. Changing Software Requirements may come from legislation, regulations, national and international standards, maintenance, etc.

Prior to distribution of the Preliminary Statement of Need to other Activities, the Verification and Validation Process (7.1.4) may be invoked.

4.1.3.3 Output Information

Output Information	Destination	
	Process	Activity
Preliminary Statement of Need	Project Initiation	Plan Project Management (3.1.6)
	Concept Exploration	Formulate Potential Approaches (4.1.4)
		Conduct Feasibility Studies (4.1.5)
		Plan System Transition (If Applicable) (4.1.6)
		Refine and Finalize the Idea or Need (4.1.7)

4.1.4 Formulate Potential Approaches

4.1.4.1 Input Information

Input Information	Source	
	Process	Activity
Development Resources and Budget	External	
Market Availability Data	External	
Resource Information	External	
Preliminary Statement of Need	Concept Exploration	Identify Ideas or Needs (4.1.3)

4.1.4.2 Description. Using Resource Information, budget data, and availability of third party software products, Potential Approaches shall be developed based upon the Preliminary Statement of Need and any data pertinent to the decision to develop or acquire the system. The Formulate Potential Approaches Activity shall also produce the constraints and benefits with regard to development of the software. The Constraints and Benefits should include all aspects of the life cycle.

Prior to release of Constraints and Benefits and Potential Approaches, the following Processes may be invoked:

(1) Verification and Validation (7.1.4)
(2) Software Configuration Management (7.2.5)

4.1.4.3 Output Information

Output Information	Destination	
	Process	Activity
Constraints and Benefits	Concept Exploration	Conduct Feasibility Studies (4.1.5)
		Refine and Finalize the Idea or Need (4.1.7)
Potential Approaches	Concept Exploration	Conduct Feasibility Studies (4.1.5)
		Refine and Finalize the Idea or Need (4.1.7)

4.1.5 Conduct Feasibility Studies

4.1.5.1 Input Information

Input Information	Source	
	Process	Activity
Preliminary Statement of Need	Concept Exploration	Identify Ideas or Needs (4.1.3)
Constraints and Benefits	Concept Exploration	Formulate Potential Approaches (4.1.4)
Potential Approaches	Concept Exploration	Formulate Potential Approaches (4.1.4)

4.1.5.2 Description. The feasibility study shall include the analysis of the idea or need, Potential Approaches, and all life cycle Constraints and Benefits. Modeling and prototyping techniques may be considered. In conducting the feasibility study, there may be a need to decide whether to make or buy the system, in part or in total. Justification for each Recommendation shall be fully documented and formally approved by all concerned organizations (including the user and the developer).

Prior to the distribution of the Recommendations, the Verification and Validation Process (7.1.4) may be invoked.

4.1.5.3 Output Information

Output Information	Destination	
	Process	Activity
Recommendations	Project Initiation	Plan Project Management (3.1.6)
	Concept Exploration	Plan System Transition (If Applicable) (4.1.6)
		Refine and Finalize the Idea or Need (4.1.7)
	System Allocation	Analyze Functions (4.2.3)

4.1.6 Plan System Transition (If Applicable)

4.1.6.1 Input Information

Input Information	Source	
	Process	Activity
Retirement Planned Information	External	
Preliminary Statement of Need	Concept Exploration	Identify Ideas or Needs (4.1.3)
Recommendations	Concept Exploration	Conduct Feasibility Studies (4.1.5)

4.1.6.2 Description. This Activity is applicable only when an existing system (automated or manual) is being replaced with a new system. The transition shall be planned and documented in accordance with the Retirement Planned Information of the system being replaced, Preliminary Statement of Need, and recommended solutions. Transition strategies and tools shall be part of the Transition Planned Information. A Transition Impact Statement shall also be produced.

Prior to distribution of the Transition Planned Information, the following Processes may be invoked:

(1) Verification and Validation (7.1.4)
(2) Software Configuration Management (7.2.5)
(3) Documentation Development (7.3.4)

4.1.6.3 Output Information

Output Information	Destination	
	Process	Activity
Transition Impact Statement	Project Monitoring and Control	Analyze Risks (3.2.3)
Transition Planned Information	Concept Exploration	Refine and Finalize the Idea or Need (4.1.7)
	Installation	Plan Installation (6.1.3)

4.1.7 Refine and Finalize the Idea or Need

4.1.7.1 Input Information

Input Information	Source	
	Process	Activity
Preliminary Statement of Need	Concept Exploration	Identify Ideas or Needs (4.1.3)
Constraints and Benefits	Concept Exploration	Formulate Potential Approaches (4.1.4)
Potential Approaches	Concept Exploration	Formulate Potential Approaches (4.1.4)
Recommendations	Concept Exploration	Conduct Feasibility Studies (4.1.5)
Transition Planned Information (If Applicable)	Concept Exploration	Plan System Transition (If Applicable) (4.1.6)

4.1.7.2 Description. The idea or need shall be refined by analyzing the Preliminary Statement of Need, the Potential Approaches, Recommendations, and Transition Planned Information (If Applicable). An approach shall be selected and documented that refines the initial idea or need.

Based upon the refined ideas or needs, a Statement of Need shall be generated that identifies the software idea, need, or desire, the recommended approach for its implementation, and any data pertinent to a management decision concerning the initiation of the described development effort.

Prior to distribution of the Statement of Need, the following Processes may be invoked:

(1) Verification and Validation (7.1.4)
(2) Documentation Development (7.3.4)

4.1.7.3 Output Information

Output Information	Destination	
	Process	Activity
Statement of Need	Project Initiation	Map Activitieso Software Life Cycle Model (3.1.3)
		Allocate Project Resources (3.1.4)
		Establish Project Environment (3.1.5)
		Plan Project Management (3.1.6)
	Project Monitoring and Control	Analyze Risks (3.2.3)
	System Allocation	Analyze Functions (4.2.3)
		Develop System Architecture (4.2.4)

4.2 System Allocation Process

4.2.1 Overview. The System Allocation Process is the bridge between Concept Exploration and the definition of software requirements. This Process maps the required functions to software and hardware.

The Statement of Need forms the basis for the analysis of the system, resulting in system requirements. This definition determines the inputs to the system, the processing to be applied to the inputs, and the required outputs. The software and hardware operational functions are also identified in these definitions.

The architecture of the system must be developed during the System Allocation Process. The system functions are derived from system requirements, and the hardware, software, and operational requirements are identified. These requirements are analyzed to produce System Functional Software Requirements and System Functional Hardware Requirements. The hardware, software, and operational interfaces must be defined and closely monitored. The hardware requirements analysis is not discussed in this document since it is beyond the scope of this standard.

Section 1.5, "Use of This Standard," provides background information necessary for the successful understanding and application of this material. It should be read prior to proceeding further in this section.

4.2.2 Activities List

(1) Analyze Functions
(2) Develop System Architecture
(3) Decompose System Requirements

4.2.3 Analyze Functions

4.2.3.1 Input Information

Input Information	Source	
	Process	Activity
Recommendations	Concept Exploration	Conduct Feasibility Studies (4.1.5)
Statement of Need	Concept Exploration	Refine and Finalize the Idea or Need (4.1.7)

4.2.3.2 Description. The Statement of Need and Recommendations for solution shall be analyzed to identify the functions of the total system. Once the functions have been defined, they are delineated in the Functional Description of the System and used to develop the system architecture and identify the hardware and software functions.

Prior to the distribution of the Functional Description of the System, the following Processes shall be invoked:

(1) Verification and Validation (7.1.4)
(2) Software Configuration Management (7.2.5)

4.2.3.3 Output Information

Output Information	Destination	
	Process	Activity
Functional Description of the System	System Allocation	Develop System Architecture (4.2.4)
		Decompose System Requirements (4.2.5)
	Requirements	Define Interface Requirements (5.1.4)

4.2.4 Develop System Architecture

4.2.4.1 Input Information

Input Information	Source	
	Process	Activity
Project Environment	Project Initiation	Establish Project Environment (3.1.5)
Statement of Need	Concept Exploration	Refine and Finalize the Idea or Need (4.1.7)
Functional Description of the System	System Allocation	Analyze Functions (4.2.3)

4.2.4.2 Description. The Statement of Need and the Functional Description of the System shall be transformed into the System Architecture, using the methodology, standards, and tools established by the organization. The System Architecture becomes the basis for the Design Process and the determination of the hardware and software functions.

4.2.4.3 Output Information

Output Information	Destination	
	Process	Activity
System Architecture	System Allocation	Decompose System Requirements (4.2.5)
	Design	Perform Architectural Design (5.2.3)

4.2.5 Decompose System Requirements

4.2.5.1 Input Information

Input Information	Source	
	Process	Activity
Functional Description of the System	System Allocation	Analyze Functions (4.2.3)
System Architecture	System Allocation	Develop System Architecture (4.2.4)

4.2.5.2 Description. The system functions documented in the Functional Description of the System shall be divided according to the System Architecture to form software requirements, hardware requirements, and the system interfaces. The System Interface Requirements define the interfaces that are external to the system and the interfaces between configuration items that comprise the system. Note that the hardware requirements go to an external destination since they are beyond the scope of this standard. The decomposition of the system may result in requirements for more than one project. Each software project shall be managed individually.

Prior to distribution of the requirements produced by this Activity, the following Processes shall be invoked:

(1)   Verification and Validation (7.1.4)
(2)   Software Configuration Management (7.2.5)
(3)   Documentation Development (7.3.4)
(4)   Training (7.4.4)

4.2.5.3 Output Information

Output Information	Destination	
	Process	Activity
System Functional Hardware Requirements	External	
System Functional Software Requirements	Project Initiation	Allocate Resources (3.1.4)
	Requirements	Define and Develop Software Requirements (5.1.3)
		Define Interface Requirements (5.1.4)
System Interface Requirements (If Applicable)	Requirements	Define and Develop Software Requirements (5.1.3)
		Define Interface Requirements (5.1.4)
	External	

5. Development Processes

These are the Processes that must be performed during the development of a software product.

5.1 Requirements Process

5.1.1 Overview. This Process includes those Activities directed toward the development of software requirements. In the development of a system containing both hardware and software components, the Requirements Process follows the development of total system requirements, and the functional allocation of those system requirements to hardware and software. For a system involving only software development, this effort begins once the Statement of Need is completed.

Section 1.5, "Use of This Standard," provides background information necessary for the successful understanding and application of this material. It should be read prior to proceeding further in this section.

5.1.2 Activities List

(1) Define and Develop Software Requirements
(2) Define Interface Requirements
(3) Prioritize and Integrate Software Requirements

5.1.3 Define and Develop Software Requirements

5.1.3.1 Input Information

Input Information	Source	
	Process	Activity
Installation Support Requirements	External	
System Constraints	External	
Project Environment	Project Initiation	Establish Project Environment (3.1.5)
Software Project Management Planned Information	Project Initiation	Plan Project Management (3.1.6)
Analysis of Risks	Project Monitoring and Control	Analyze Risks (3.2.3)
System Functional Software Requirements (If Applicable)	System Allocation	Decompose System Requirements (4.2.5)
System Interface Requirements (If Applicable)	System Allocation	Decompose System Requirements (4.2.5)

5.1.3.2 Description. The first Activity in this Process, defining the software requirements, is iterative in nature. Whether the software development constitutes the entire project or is part of a system (hardware and software), software requirements, including constraints, shall be generated from Input Information documents and the results of modeling, prototyping, or other techniques.

Using the above Input Information, the developer shall analyze the software requirements to determine traceability, clarity, validity, testability, safety, and any other project-specific characteristics. The use of a comprehensive methodology is recommended to ensure that requirements are complete and consistent. Techniques such as structured analysis, modeling, prototyping, or transaction analysis are helpful in this Activity. When needed, the requirements for a data base shall be included in the requirements.

The Preliminary Software Requirements shall include consideration of System Constraints such as timing, sizing, language, marketing restrictions, and technology.

Further information related to this Activity may be found in [5].

Prior to the distribution of the Preliminary Software Requirements and Installation Requirements, the following Processes shall be invoked:

(1) Verification and Validation (7.1.4)
(2) Software Configuration Management (7.2.5)
(3) Documentation Development (7.3.4)

5.1.3.3 Output Information

Output Information	Destination	
	Process	Activity
Preliminary Software Requirements	Requirements	Prioritize and Integrate Software Requirements (5.1.5)
		Define Interface Requirements (5.1.4)
	Verification and Validation	Plan Testing (7.1.6)
Installation Requirements	Installation	Plan Installation (6.1.3)

5.1.4 Define Interface Requirements

5.1.4.1 Input Information

Input Information	Source	
	Process	Activity
System Constraints	External	
Software Project Management Planned Information	Project Initiation	Plan Project Management (3.1.6)
Preliminary Software Requirements	Requirements	Define and Develop Software Requirements (5.1.3)
Functional Description of the System (If Applicable)	System Allocation	Analyze Functions (4.2.3)
System Functional Software Requirements (If Applicable)	System Allocation	Decompose System Requirements (4.2.5)
System Interface Requirements (If Applicable)	System Allocation	Decompose System Requirements (4.2.5)

5.1.4.2 Description. All user, software, and hardware interfaces shall be defined using the applicable Input Information. These interfaces shall be defined either as requirements or as constraints and shall be reviewed by all involved parties.

The user interface is critical in determining the usability of the system. The user interface definition shall specify not only the information flow between the user and the system but also how a user goes about using the system. For a complex interactive system, user interface definition may be a separate document.

The Software Interface Requirements shall specify all software interfaces required to support the development and execution of the software system. Software interfaces may be affected by System Constraints including operating system, data base management system, language compiler, tools, utilities, network protocol drivers, and hardware interfaces.

Prior to the distribution of the Output Information, the following Processes shall be invoked:

(1) Verification and Validation (7.1.4)
(2) Documentation Development (7.3.4)
(3) Software Configuration Management (7.2.5)

5.1.4.3 Output Information

Output Information	Destination	
	Process	Activity
Software Interface Requirements	Project Monitoring and Control	Analyze Risks (3.2.3)
	Requirements	Prioritize and Integrate Software Requirements (5.1.5)
	Design	Design Interfaces (5.2.5)
	Implementation	Create Operating Documentation (5.3.6)

5.1.5 Prioritize and Integrate Software Requirements

5.1.5.1 Input Information

Input Information	Source	
	Process	Activity
Preliminary Software Requirements	Requirements	Define and Develop Software Requirements (5.1.3)
Software Interface Requirements	Requirements	Define Interface Requirements (5.1.4)

5.1.5.2 Description. The functional and performance requirements shall be reviewed and a prioritized list of requirements shall be produced, addressing any tradeoffs that may be needed. The organization of the emerging Software Requirements shall be reviewed and revised as necessary. While completing the requirements, a particular design shall not be imposed (i.e., design decisions are made in the Design Process). The Software Requirements shall describe the functional, interface, and performance requirements. It shall also define the required operational and support environments.

Further information related to this Activity may be found in [5].

Prior to distribution of the Software Requirements, the following Processes shall be invoked:

(1) Verification and Validation (7.1.4)
(2) Software Configuration Management (7.2.5)
(3) Documentation Development (7.3.4)

5.1.5.3 Output Information

Output Information	Destination	
	Process	Activity
Software Requirements	Project Monitoring and Control	Analyze Risks (3.2.3)
	Design	All Activities (5.2)
	Implementation	Create Test Data (5.3.3)
		Plan Integration (5.3.7)
	Verification and Validation	Plan Testing (7.1.6)
		Develop Test Specification(s) (7.1.7)
	Training	Plan Training Program (7.4.3)

5.2 Design Process

5.2.1 Overview. During the Design Process, major decisions are made that determine the structure of the system. The objective of the Design Process is to develop a coherent, well-organized representation of the software system that meets the Software Requirements.

The Design Process maps the "what to do" of requirements specifications into the "how to do it" of design specifications. At the architectural design level, the focus is on the functions and structure of the software components that comprise the software system. At the detailed design level, the emphasis is on the data structures and algorithms that are used within each software component.

The Perform Architectural Design and Perform Detailed Design Activities are usually carried out in sequence because detailed design is derived from the architectural design. They differ from each other in the level of design detail. Other Design Process Activities may be carried out in parallel with these Activities.

Section 1.5, "Use of This Standard," provides background information necessary for the successful understanding and application of this material. It should be read prior to proceeding further in this section.

5.2.2 Activities List

(1) Perform Architectural Design
(2) Design Data Base (If Applicable)
(3) Design Interfaces
(4) Select or Develop Algorithms (If Applicable)
(5) Perform Detailed Design

5.2.3 Perform Architectural Design

5.2.3.1 Input Information

Input Information	Source	
	Process	Activity
Software Project Management Planned Information	Project Initiation	Plan Project Management (3.1.6)
System Architecture	System Allocation	Develop System Architecture (4.2.4)
Software Requirements	Requirements	Prioritize and Integrate Software Requirements (5.1.5)

5.2.3.2 Description. The Perform Architectural Design Activity transforms the Software Requirements and the System Architecture into high-level design concepts. During this Activity the software components constituting the software system and their structures are identified. Purchased software and the contents of the software libraries (as referenced in the SPMP) may influence the architectural design. Techniques such as modeling and prototyping may be used to evaluate alternative designs if called for in the SPMP.

By the end of the Perform Architectural Design Activity, the design description of each of the software components shall have been completed. The data, relationships, and constraints shall be specified. In addition, all internal interfaces (among components) shall be defined. This Activity shall create the Software Architectural Design Description.

Prior to distribution of the Software Architectural Design Description, the following Processes shall be invoked:

(1) Verification and Validation (7.1.4)
(2) Software Configuration Management (7.2.5)
(3) Documentation Development (7.3.4)

5.2.3.3 Output Information

Output Information	Destination	
	Process	Activity
Software Architectural Design Description	Design	Perform Detailed Design (5.2.7)

5.2.4 Design Data Base (If Applicable)

5.2.4.1 Input Information

Input Information	Source	
	Process	Activity
Project Environment	Project Initiation	Establish Project Environment (3.1.5)
Software Requirements	Requirements	Prioritize and Integrate Software Requirements (5.1.5)

5.2.4.2 Description. The Design Data Base Activity applies when a data base is to be created as a part of the project. This Activity shall specify the information structure outlined in the Software Requirements and its characteristics within the software system. The Design Data Base Activity involves three separate but dependent steps: conceptual data base design, logical data base design, and physical data base design. Techniques such as data dictionary, data base optimization, and data modeling may be considered. Requirements are molded into an external schema that describes data entities, attributes, relationships, and constraints. The various external schemas are integrated into a single conceptual schema. The conceptual schema is then mapped into an implementation-dependent logical schema. Finally, the physical data structures and access paths are defined. The result of this Activity is to generate the Data Base Description.

Prior to distribution of the Data Base Description, the following Processes shall be invoked:

(1) Verification and Validation (7.1.4)
(2) Software Configuration Management (7.2.5)
(3) Documentation Development (7.3.4)

5.2.4.3 Output Information

Output Information	Destination	
	Process	Activity
Data Base Description	Design	Perform Detailed Design (5.2.7)

5.2.5 Design Interfaces

5.2.5.1 Input Information

Input Information	Source	
	Process	Activity
Software Interface Requirements	Requirements	Define Interface Requirements (5.1.4)
Software Requirements	Requirements	Prioritize and Integrate Software Requirements (5.1.5)

5.2.5.2 Description. The Design Interfaces Activity shall be concerned with the interfaces of the software system contained in the Software Requirements and Software Interface Requirements. This Activity shall consolidate these interface descriptions into a single Interface Description of the software system.

5.2.5.3 Output Information

Output Information	Destination	
	Process	Activity
Interface Description	Design	Perform Detailed Design (5.2.7)

5.2.6 Select or Develop Algorithms

5.2.6.1 Input Information

Input Information	Source	
	Process	Activity
Software Requirements	Requirements	Prioritize and Integrate Software Requirements (5.1.5)

5.2.6.2 Description. This Activity is concerned with selecting or developing a procedural representation of the functions specified in the Software Requirements for each software component and data structure. The algorithms shall completely satisfy the applicable functional and/or mathematical specifications. To the extent possible, the use of existing algorithms should be considered.

Prior to distribution of the Algorithm Descriptions, the following Processes shall be invoked:

(1) Verification and Validation (7.1.4)
(2) Software Configuration Management (7.2.5)

5.2.6.3 Output Information

Output Information	Destination	
	Process	Activity
Algorithm Descriptions	Design	Perform Detailed Design (5.2.7)

5.2.7 Perform Detailed Design

5.2.7.1 Input Information

Input Information	Source	
	Process	Activity
Software Project Management Planned Information	Project Initiation	Plan Project Management (3.1.6)
Software Requirements	Requirements	Prioritize and Integrate Software Requirements (5.1.5)
Software Architectural Design Description	Design	Perform Architectural Design (5.2.3)
Data Base Description (If Applicable)	Design	Design Data Base (If Applicable) (5.2.4)
Interface Description	Design	Design Interfaces (5.2.5)
Algorithm Descriptions	Design	Select or Develop Algorithms (5.2.6)

5.2.7.2 Description. In the Perform Detailed Design Activity, design alternatives shall be chosen for implementing the functions specified for each software component. By the end of this Activity, the data structure, algorithm, and control information of each software component shall be specified. The Software Design Description (SDD) contains the consolidated data for all of the above Input Information. The details of the interfaces shall be identified within the SDD.

For further information on this topic, see [12].

Prior to distribution of the SDD, the following Processes shall be invoked:

(1) Verification and Validation (7.1.4)
(2) Software Configuration Management (7.2.5)
(3) Documentation Development (7.3.4)

5.2.7.3 Output Information

Output Information	Destination	
	Process	Activity
Software Design Description	Project Monitoring and Control	Analyze Risks (3.2.3)
	Implementation	Create Test Data (5.3.3)
		Create Source (5.3.4)
		Create Operating Documentation (5.3.6)
		Plan Integration (5.3.7)
	Verification and Validation	Plan Testing (7.1.6)
		Develop Test Specification(s) (7.1.7)
	Training	Develop Training Materials (7.4.4)

5.3 Implementation Process

5.3.1 Overview. The Activities completed during the Implementation Process result in the transformation of the Detailed Design representation of a software product into a programming language realization. This Process produces the source code, data base (if applicable), and the documentation constituting the physical manifestation of the design. In addition, the code and data base are integrated. Care must also be taken during the Implementation Process to apply the appropriate coding standards.

The output of this Process must be the subject of all subsequent testing and validation. The code and data base, along with documentation produced during previous Processes, are the first complete representation of the software product.

Section 1.5, "Use of This Standard," provides background information necessary for the successful understanding and application of this material. It should be read prior to proceeding further in this section.

5.3.2 Activities List

(1)   Create Test Data
(2)   Create Source
(3)   Generate Object Code
(4)   Create Operating Documentation
(5)   Plan Integration
(6)   Perform Integration

5.3.3 Create Test Data

5.3.3.1 Input Information

Input Information	Source	
	Process	Activity
Software Requirements	Requirements	Prioritize and Integrate Software Requirements (5.1.5)
Software Design Description	Design	Perform Detailed Design (5.2.7)
Source Code (If Applicable)	Implementation	Create Source (5.3.4)
Data Base (If Applicable)	Implementation	Create Source (5.3.4)
Test Planned Information(s)	Verification and Validation	Plan Testing (7.1.6)
Test Requirements	Verification and Validation	Develop Test Requirements (7.1.7)

5.3.3.2 Description. Using the Software Requirements, the Software Design Description (SDD), and the Source Code (when required), Test Data shall be generated. The Test Planned Information(s) describe the test environment. Test Requirements define the type of test data to be used. To support the testing effort, test Stubs and Drivers may be generated at this time for each item to be tested. The test drivers allow the execution of software tests on an individual or integrated basis. Test Data may be loaded for use in testing the data base.

Further information may be found in [10].

5.3.3.3 Output Information

Output Information	Destination	
	Process	Activity
Stubs and Drivers (If Applicable)	Implementation	Perform Integration (5.3.8)
Test Data	Verification and Validation	Execute the Tests (7.1.8)

5.3.4 Create Source

5.3.4.1 Input Information

Input Information	Source	
	Process	Activity
Software Project Management Planned Information	Project Initiation	Plan Project Management (3.1.6)
Software Design Description	Design	Perform Detailed Design (5.2.7)

5.3.4.2 Description. The Source Code, including suitable comments, shall be generated using the project environment, as found in the Software Project Management Planned Information (SPMP) and the Software Design Description. If the software requires a Data Base, then the Data Base utilities may need to be coded. If Source Code is going to be used to create test data, the Source Code shall be made available to the Create Test Data Activity (5.3.3).

5.3.4.3 Output Information

Output Information	Destination	
	Process	Activity
Data Base (If Applicable)	Implementation	Create Test Data (5.3.3)
		Generate Object Code (5.3.5)
Source Code (If Applicable)	Implementation	Create Test Data (5.3.3)
Source Code	Implementation	Generate Object Code (5.3.5)

5.3.5 Generate Object Code

5.3.5.1 Input Information

Input Information	Source	
	Process	Activity
Data Base (If Applicable)	Implementation	Create Source (5.3.4)
Source Code	Implementation	Create Source (5.3.4)

5.3.5.2 Description. The code shall be grouped into processable units. (This will be dictated by selected language and design information.) All assembly language units shall be assembled and all high-level language units compiled into Object Code. Syntactically incorrect code, identified by the assembler or compiler output, shall be reworked until the source code can be processed free of syntactical errors. These units shall be debugged. If a Data Base is coded, it too shall be debugged.

Prior to distribution of the software, the following Processes shall be invoked:

(1) Verification and Validation (7.1.4)
(2) Software Configuration Management (7.2.5)

5.3.5.3 Output Information

Output Information	Destination	
	Process	Activity
Corrected Data Base (If Applicable)	Implementation	Perform Integration (5.3.8)
Corrected Source Code	Implementation	Perform Integration (5.3.8)
Object Code	Implementation	Perform Integration (5.3.8)

5.3.6 Create Operating Documentation

5.3.6.1 Input Information

Input Information	Source	
	Process	Activity
Software Design Description	Design	Perform Detailed Design (5.2.7)
Software Interface Requirements	Requirements	Define Interface Requirements (5.1.4)
Documentation Planned Information(s)	Documentation Development	Plan Documentation (7.3.3)

5.3.6.2 Description. This Activity shall produce the software project's operating documentation from the SDD and the Software Interface Requirements in accordance with the Documentation Planned Information. The Operating Documentation is required for installing, operating, and supporting the system throughout the life cycle.

For further information, [21] may be used.

Prior to distribution of the documents listed below, the following Processes shall be invoked:

(1) Verification and Validation (7.1.4)
(2) Software Configuration Management (7.2.5)
(3) Documentation Development (7.3.4)

5.3.6.3 Output Information

Output Information	Destination	
	Process	Activity
Operating Documentation	Installation	Distribute Software (6.1.4)

5.3.7 Plan Integration

5.3.7.1 Input Information

Input Information	Source	
	Process	Activity
Software Project Management Planned Information	Project Initiation	Plan Project Management (3.1.6)
Software Requirements	Requirements	Prioritize and Integrate Software Requirements (5.1.5)
Software Design Description	Design	Perform Detailed Design (5.2.7)
Test Planned Information(s)	Verification and Validation	Plan Testing (7.1.6)

5.3.7.2 Description. During the Plan Integration Activity, the Software Requirements and the SDD are analyzed to determine the order of combining software components into an overall system. The project environment, as defined in the SPMP, shall be considered when planning integration. The integration methods shall be documented in the Integration Planned Information. The Integration Planned Information shall be coordinated with the Test Planned Information(s) and they may be combined.

Prior to distribution of the Integration Planned Information, the following Processes shall be invoked:

(1) Verification and Validation (7.1.4)
(2) Software Configuration Management (7.2.5)
(3) Documentation Development (7.3.4)

5.3.7.3 Output Information

Output Information	Destination	
	Process	Activity
Integration Planned Information	Project Monitoring and Control	Analyze Risks (3.2.3)
		Manage the Project (3.2.5)
	Implementation	Perform Integration (5.3.8)
	Verification and Validation	Plan Testing (7.1.6)

5.3.8 Perform Integration

5.3.8.1 Input Information

Input Information	Source	
	Process	Activity
Stubs and Drivers (If Applicable)	Implementation	Create Test Data (5.3.3)
Corrected Data Base (If Applicable)	Implementation	Generate Object Code (5.3.5)
Corrected Source Code	Implementation	Generate Object Code (5.3.5)
Integration Planned Information	Implementation	Plan Integration (5.3.7)
System Components	External	
Software Project Management Planned Information	Project Initiation	Plan Project Management (3.1.6)
Object Code	Implementation	Generate Object Code (5.3.5)
Tested Software	Verification and Validation	Execute the Tests (7.1.8)

5.3.8.2 Description. This Activity shall execute the Integration Planned Information. This is accomplished by appropriately combining the Corrected Data Base, Corrected Source Code, Object Code, and Stubs and Drivers, as specified, into Integrated Software. Other·necessary Object Code, from the project environment as defined in the SPMP, shall also be integrated. If a system includes both hardware and software components, the system integration may be included as part of this Activity.

Prior to software integration and the distribution of the Integrated Software, the following Processes shall be invoked:

(1) Verification and Validation (7.1.4)
(2) Software Configuration Management (7.2.5)

5.3.8.3 Output Information

Output Information	Destination	
	Process	Activity
Integrated Software	Verification and Validation	Execute the Tests (7.1.8)

6. Post-Development Processes

These are the Processes that must be performed to install, operate, support, maintain, and retire a software product.

6.1 Installation Process

6.1.1 Overview. Installation consists of the transportation and installation of a software system from the development environment to the target environment. It includes the necessary software modifications, checkout in the target environment, and customer acceptance. If a problem arises, it must be identified and reported; if necessary and possible, a temporary "work-around" may be applied.

During the Installation Process, the software to be delivered is installed, operationally checked out, and monitored. This effort culminates in formal customer acceptance. The scheduling of turnover and customer acceptance is defined in the Software Project Management Planned Information (SPMP).

Section 1.5, "Use of This Standard," provides background information necessary for the successful understanding and application of this material. It should be read prior to proceeding further in this section.

6.1.2 Activities List

(1)   Plan Installation
(2)   Distribute Software
(3)   Install Software
(4)   Accept Software in Operational Environment

6.1.3 Plan Installation

6.1.3.1 Input Information

Input Information	Source	
	Process	Activity
Software Project Management Planned Information	Project Initiation	Plan Project Management (3.1.6)
Installation Requirements	Requirements	Define and Develop Software Requirements (5.1.3)
Transition Planned Information (if applicable)	Concept Exploration	Plan System Transition (4.1.6)
Operating Documentation	Implementation	Create Operating Documentation (5.3.6)

6.1.3.2 Description. The tasks to be performed during installation shall be described in Software Installation Planned Information. The Installation Requirements and the other Input Information shall be analyzed to guide the development of the Software Installation Planned Information. This Planned Information, the associated documentation, and the developed software shall be used to install the software product.

Prior to distribution of the Software Installation Planned Information, the following Processes shall be invoked:

(1) Verification and Validation (7.1.4)
(2) Software Configuration Management (7.2.5)
(3) Documentation Development (7.3.4)
(4) Training (7.4.4)

6.1.3.3 Output Information

Output Information	Destination	
	Process	Activity
Software Installation Planned Information	Installation	Distribute Software (6.1.4)

6.1.4 Distribute Software

6.1.4.1 Input Information

Input Information	Source	
	Process	Activity
Operating Documentation	Implementation	Create Operating Documentation (5.3.6)
Software Installation Planned Information	Installation	Plan Installation (6.1.3)
Data Base Data	External	
Tested Software	Verification and Validation	Execute the Tests (7.1.8)
Software Project Management Planned Information	Project Initiation	Plan Project Management (3.1.6)

6.1.4.2 Description. During this Activity, the Tested Software with necessary Data Base Data, Operating Documentation, and Installation Planned Information shall be packaged onto their respective media as designated in the SPMP. The Packaged Software is distributed to the appropriate site(s) for installation. The Installation Planned Information is distributed as appropriate to the site(s) to facilitate the installation efforts. The Packaged Operating Documentation shall be available for operation of the system.

Prior to distribution of the Output Information, the following Processes shall be invoked:

(1) Software Configuration Management (7.2.5)
(2) Verification and Validation (7.1.4)
(3) Documentation Development (7.3.4)

6.1.4.3 Output Information

Output Information	Destination	
	Process	Activity
Packaged Operating Documentation	Operation and Support	Operate the System (6.2.3)
Packaged Installation Planned Information	Installation	Install Software (6.1.5)
Packaged Software	Installation	Install Software (6.1.5)

6.1.5 Install Software

6.1.5.1 Input Information

Input Information	Source	
	Process	Activity
Packaged Installation Planned Information	Installation	Distribute Software (6.1.4)
Packaged Operating Documentation	Installation	Distribute Software (6.1.4)
Packaged Software Installation	Installation	Distribute Software (6.1.4)
Data Base Data	External	

6.1.5.2 Description. The packaged software and any required Data Base Data shall be installed in the target environment according to the procedures in the Software Installation Planned Information. This may include tailoring by the customer. The Installation Reported Information shall document the installation and any problems encountered.

6.1.5.3 Output Information

Output Information	Destination	
	Process	Activity
Installation Reported Information	Project Monitoring and Control	Manage the Project (3.2.5)
Installed Software	Installation	Accept Software in Operational Environment (6.1.6)

6.1.6 Accept Software in Operational Environment

6.1.6.1 Input Information

Input Information	Source	
	Process	Activity
User Acceptance Planned Information	External	
Test Summary Reported Information	Verification and Validation	Execute the Tests (7.1.8)
Installed Software	Installation	Install Software (6.1.5)

6.1.6.2 Description. The software acceptance shall consist of analysis of the Test Summary Reported Information(s) according to the User Acceptance Planned Information to assure that the Installed Software performs as expected. When the results of the analysis satisfy the requirements of the User Acceptance Planned Information, the Installed Software System is accepted by the User.

Prior to completion of accepting software in the operational environment, the following Processes should be invoked:

(1)   Verification and Validation (7.1.4)
(2)   Software Configuration Management (7.2.5)

6.1.6.3 Output Information

Output Information	Destination	
	Process	Activity
Customer Acceptance	External	
Installed Software System	Operation and Support	Operate the System (6.2.3)
	Retirement	Conduct Parallel Operations (If Applicable) (6.4.4)

6.2 Operation and Support Process

6.2.1 Overview. The Operation and Support Process involves user operation of the system and ongoing support. Support includes providing technical assistance, consulting with the user, and recording user support requests by maintaining a Support Request Log. Thus the Operation and Support Process may trigger Maintenance Activities via the ongoing Project Monitoring and Control Process, which will provide information re-entering the software life cycle (SLC).

Section 1.5, "Use of This Standard," provides background information necessary for the successful understanding and application of this material. It should be read prior to proceeding further in this section.

6.2.2 Activities List

(1) Operate the System
(2) Provide Technical Assistance and Consulting
(3) Maintain Support Request Log

6.2.3 Operate the System

6.2.3.1 Input Information

Input Information	Source	
	Process	Activity
Packaged Operating Documentation	Installation	Distribute Software (6.1.4)
Support Planned Information	Project Initiation	Plan Project Management (3.1.6)
Installed Software System	Installation	Accept Software in Operational Environment (6.1.6)

6.2.3.2 Description. During this Activity, the Installed Software System shall be utilized in the intended environment and in accordance with the operating instructions. Feedback Data are collected for product and documentation improvement and system tuning. The user shall analyze the Feedback Data and identify System Anomalies (which include desired enhancements). System Anomalies are reported.

Prior to the distribution of the Output Information, the following Processes shall be invoked:

(1) Verification and Validation (7.1.4)
(2) Software Configuration Management (7.2.5)

6.2.3.3 Output Information

Output Information	Destination	
	Process	Activity
System Anomalies	Project Monitoring and Control	Implement Problem Reporting Method (3.2.7)
Operation Logs	External	
Feedback Data	Project Monitoring and Control	Manage the Project (3.2.5)
	Concept Exploration	Identify Ideas or Needs (4.1.3)

6.2.4 Provide Technical Assistance and Consulting

6.2.4.1 Input Information

Input Information	Source	
	Process	Activity
Request for Support	External	
Support Planned Information	Project Initiation	Plan Project Management (3.1.6)

6.2.4.2 Description. This Activity applies after the user has accepted the software. The support function shall include providing responses to the user's technical questions or problems. A Support Response is sent to the Maintain Support Request Log Activity so that feedback can be provided to other Processes.

6.2.4.3 Output Information

Output Information	Destination	
	Process	Activity
Support Response	Operation and Support	Maintain Support Request Log (6.2.5)
	External	

6.2.5 Maintain Support Request Log

6.2.5.1 Input Information

Input Information	Source	
	Process	Activity
Support Planned Information	Project Initiation	Plan Project Management (3.1.6)
Support Response	Operation and Support	Provide Technical Assistance and Consulting (6.2.4)

6.2.5.2 Description. This Activity shall record support requests in the Support Request Log. Methodology regarding management of this Activity shall be identified in the Support Planned Information. Anomalies that are reported shall be reported also to the Project Monitoring and Control Process. Prior to release of the Support Request Log, the Verification and Validation Process (7.1.4) shall be invoked.

6.2.5.3 Output Information

Output Information	Destination	
	Process	Activity
Anomalies	Project Monitoring and Control	Implement Problem Reporting Method (3.2.7)
Support Request Log	Verification and Validation	Execute Verification and Validation Tasks (7.1.4)

6.3 Maintenance Process

6.3.1 Overview. The Maintenance Process is concerned with the resolution of software errors, faults, and failures. The requirement for software maintenance initiates software life cycle (SLC) changes. The SLC is remapped and executed, thereby treating the Maintenance Process as iterations of development.

Section 1.5, "Use of This Standard," provides background information necessary for the successful understanding and application of this material. It should be read prior to proceeding further in this section.

6.3.2 Activities List

(1)   Reapply Software Life Cycle

6.3.3 Reapply Software Life Cycle

6.3.3.1 Input Information

Input Information	Source	
	Process	Activity
Software Project Management Planned Information	Project Initiation	Plan Project Management (3.1.6)
Correction Problem Reported Information	Project Monitoring and Control	Implement Problem Reporting Method (3.2.7)

6.3.3.2 Description. The information provided by the Correction Problem Reported Information and the current Software Project Management Planned Information (SPMP) shall result in the generation of Maintenance Recommendations. These Maintenance Recommendations will then enter the SLC at the Concept Exploration Process to improve the quality of the software system.

6.3.3.3 Output Information

Output Information	Destination	
	Process	Activity
Maintenance Recommendations	Concept Exploration	Identify Ideas or Needs (4.1.3)

6.4 Retirement Process

6.4.1 Overview. The Retirement Process involves the removal of an existing system from its active support or use either by ceasing its operation or support, or by replacing it with a new system or an upgraded version of the existing system.

Section 1.5, "Use of This Standard," provides background information necessary for the successful understanding and application of this material. It should be read prior to proceeding further in this section.

6.4.2 Activities List

(1)   Notify User
(2)   Conduct Parallel Operations (If Applicable)
(3)   Retire System

6.4.3 Notify User

6.4.3.1 Input Information

Input Information	Source	
	Process	Activity
Retirement Planned Information	Project Initiation	Plan Project Management (3.1.6)

6.4.3.2 Description. This Activity shall be the formal notification to any user (both internal and external customers) of an operating software system that is to be removed from active support or use. This notification can take any of several forms as appropriate for the individual environment. It is important that all users of the outgoing system be made aware that it will become unsupported. The actual dates of the removal of support are to be clearly specified and must allow time for current users to make whatever arrangements are necessary to respond to this notification. Included in the user notification should be one or more of the following:

(1)   Description of the replacement system including its date of availability.
(2)   Statement as to why the system is not being supported.
(3)   Description of possible other support.

Prior to the distribution of the Official Notification, the Documentation Development Process (7.3.4) shall be invoked.

6.4.3.3 Output Information

Output Information	Destination	
	Process	Activity
Official Notification	Project Monitoring and Control	Retain Records (3.2.6)
	External	

582

6.4.4 Conduct Parallel Operations (If Applicable)

6.4.4.1 Input Information

Input Information	Source	
	Process	Activity
Transition Planned Information (for the replacing system)	External	
Retirement Planned Information	Project Initiation	Plan Project Management (3.1.6)
Installed Software System	Installation	Accept Software in Operational Environment (6.1.6)

6.4.4.2 Description. If the outgoing system is being replaced by a new system, this Activity may apply. This Activity shall involve a period of dual operation utilizing the retiring system for official results, while completing the preparation of the new system for formal operation. It is a period of user training on the new system and validation of the new system. The Retirement Planned Information, as well as the Transition Planned Information, may be used to provide information to conduct parallel operations for the replacing system.

While conducting this Activity, the following Processes shall be invoked:

(1) Verification and Validation (7.1.4)
(2) Software Configuration Management (7.2.5)
(3) Training (7.4.4)

6.4.4.3 Output Information

Output Information	Destination	
	Process	Activity
Parallel Operations Log	Project Monitoring and Control	Retain Records (3.2.6)

6.4.5 Retire System

6.4.5.1 Input Information

Input Information	Source	
	Process	Activity
Retirement Planned Information	Project Initiation	Plan Project Management (3.1.6)

6.4.5.2 Description. This Activity shall consist of the actual removal and archiving of the retiring system from regular usage according to the Retirement Planned Information. It may be spread over a period of time and take the form of a phased removal, or it may be the simple removal of the entire system from the active software library. Prior to the retirement, users must have been notified of the event. Any preparations for the use of a replacement system should have been completed. The Post-Operation Review Reported Information is generated at this time. The Retire System Activity must be documented in Archive Reported Information.

Prior to the final distribution of the Post-Operation Review Reported Information and Archive Reported Information, the following Processes shall be invoked:

(1) Verification and Validation (7.1.4)
(2) Software Configuration Management (7.2.5)
(3) Documentation Development (7.3.4)

583

6.4.5.3 Output Information

Output Information	Destination	
	Process	Activity
Post-Operation Review Reported Information	Project Monitoring and Control	Retain Records (3.2.6)
	Software Quality Management	Manage Software Quality (3.3.5)
Archive Reported Information	External	

7. Integral Processes

These are the Processes needed to successfully complete project Activities. These Processes are utilized to ensure the completion and quality of project functions.

7.1 Verification and Validation Process

7.1.1 Overview. The Verification and Validation Process includes planning and performing both Verification and Validation tasks. Verification tasks include reviews, configuration audits, and quality audits. Validation tasks include all phases of testing. These Verification and Validation tasks are conducted throughout the software life cycle (SLC) to ensure that all requirements are satisfied. This Process addresses each life cycle Process and product.

Section 1.5, "Use of This Standard," provides background information necessary for the successful understanding and application of this material. It should be read prior to proceeding further in this section.

7.1.2 Activities List

(1) Plan Verification and Validation
(2) Execute Verification and Validation Tasks
(3) Collect and Analyze Metric Data
(4) Plan Testing
(5) Develop Test Requirements
(6) Execute the Tests

7.1.3 Plan Verification and Validation

7.1.3.1 Input Information

Input Information	Source	
	Process	Activity
Software Project Management Planned Information	Project Initiation	Plan Project Management (3.1.6)
Analysis of Risks	Project Monitoring and Control	Analyze Risks (3.2.3)
Software Quality Management Planned Information	Software Quality Management	Plan Software Quality Management (3.3.3)

7.1.3.2 Description. This Activity shall be responsive to the Software Project Management Planned Information and the Software Quality Assurance (SQA) Planned Information by identifying Processes and Process Output Information to be verified and validated. The purpose and scope of the verification and validation task shall be defined for each Process and all Process Output Information. The planning shall include developing schedules, estimating resources, identifying special resources, staffing, and establishing exit or acceptance criteria. Verification and validation methods to be considered in this planning Activity include audits (e.g., functional and physical configuration, compliance), reviews (e.g., design, code, document), prototyping, inspection, formal proof, analysis, and demonstration. Special attention should be given to minimizing technical risks and verifying requirements traceability. This planning shall be documented in the Software Verification and Validation Planned Information (SVVP).

Because of the importance of testing in the Verification and Validation Process, this standard addresses testing Activities separately. Test planning and execution may be included in the Verification and Validation Planning and Execution Activities.

Further information on verification and validation planning may be found in [2], [3], [4], [6], [7], [8], [12], [13], [14], [15], and [16].

Prior to distribution of the SVVP, the following Processes shall be invoked:

(1) Verification and Validation (7.1.4)
(2) Documentation Development (7.3.4)
(3) Software Configuration Management (7.2.5)

7.1.3.3 Output Information

Output Information	Destination	
	Process	Activity
Software Verification and Validation Planned Information	Software Quality Management	Identify Quality Improvement Needs (3.3.6)
	Verification and Validation	Execute Verification and Validation Tasks (7.1.4)
		Plan Testing (7.1.6)

7.1.4 Execute Verification and Validation Tasks

7.1.4.1 Input Information

Input Information	Source	
	Process	Activity
Item(s) to Be Evaluated	Creating Process	
Resolved Problem Reported Information	Project Monitoring and Control	Implement Problem Reporting Method (3.2.7)
Project Quality Assessments	Software Quality Management	Manage Software Quality (3.3.5)
Support Request Log	Operation and Support	Maintain Support Request Log (6.2.5)
Software Verification and Validation Planned Information	Verification and Validation	Plan Verification and Validation (7.1.3)
Basis or Bases for Evaluation	External	
	Creating Process	

7.1.4.2 Description. This Activity shall include performing the tasks specified in the SVVP using the Input Information. Results shall be provided in Evaluation Reported Information. Anomalies identified during the performance of these tasks shall be reported.

Further information related to this Activity may be found in [2], [3], [8], [12], [13], and [14].

Prior to distribution of Evaluation Reported Information, the following Processes shall be invoked:

(1) Documentation Development (7.3.4)
(2) Software Configuration Management (7.2.5)

7.1.4.3 Output Information

Output Information	Destination	
	Process	Activity
Evaluation Reported Information	Project Monitoring and Control	Manage the Project (3.2.5)
	Software Quality Management	Identify Quality Improvement Needs (3.3.6)
	Verification and Validation	Collect and Analyze Metric Data (7.1.5)
	Creating Process	
Anomalies	Project Monitoring and Control	Implement Problem Reporting Method (3.2.7)

7.1.5 Collect and Analyze Metric Data

7.1.5.1 Input Information

Input Information	Source	
	Process	Activity
Support Personnel Reported Information	External	
User Input Information	External	
Metric Data	Originating Process	Originating Activity
Correction Problem Reported Information	Project Monitoring and Control	Implement Problem Reporting Method (3.2.7)
Enhancement Problem Reported Information	Project Monitoring and Control	Implement Problem Reporting Method (3.2.7)
Report Log	Project Monitoring and Control	Implement Problem Reporting Method (3.2.7)
Resolved Problem Reported Information	Project Monitoring and Control	Implement Problem Reporting Method (3.2.7)
Software Quality Management Planned Information	Software Quality Management	Plan Software Quality Management (3.3.3)
Defined Metrics	Software Quality Management	Define Metrics (3.3.4)
Collection and Analysis Methods	Software Quality Management	Define Metrics (3.3.4)
Evaluation Reported Information	Verification and Validation	Execute Verification and Validation Tasks (7.1.4)

7.1.5.2 Description. This Activity collects Evaluation Reported Information, Problem Reported Information, and project-generated Metric Data, as stated in the Software Quality Management Planned Information. The data shall be analyzed using defined methodologies. This Activity shall identify improvements in both quality and requirements as a result of Support Personnel and User Input Information. Analysis Reported Information shall be generated describing the results of metrics validation and analysis, defect trend analysis, and the user's view analysis.

Further information related to this Activity may be found in [6], [7], [15], and [16].

Prior to distribution of the Analysis Reported Information, the following Processes should be invoked:

(1) Verification and Validation (7.1.4)
(2) Software Configuration Management (7.2.5)
(3) Documentation Development (7.3.4)

7.1.5.3 Output Information

Output Information	Destination	
	Process	Activity
Analysis Reported Information	Project Monitoring and Control	Analyze Risks (3.2.3)
		Perform Contingency Planning (3.2.4)
		Manage the Project (3.2.5)
	Software Quality Management	Manage Software Quality (3.3.5)
		Identify Quality Improvement Needs (3.3.6)

7.1.6 Plan Testing

7.1.6.1 Input Information

Input Information	Source	
	Process	Activity
Software Project Management Planned Information	Project Initiation	Plan Project Management (3.1.6)
Preliminary Software Requirements	Requirements	Define and Develop Software Requirements (5.1.3)
Software Requirements	Requirements	Prioritize and Integrate Software Requirements (5.1.5)
Software Design Description	Design	Perform Detailed Design (5.2.7)
Integration Planned Information	Implementation	Plan Integration (5.3.7)
Software Verification and Validation Planned Information	Verification and Validation	Plan Verification and Validation (7.1.3)

7.1.6.2 Description. This Activity shall identify the overall scope, approach, resources, and schedule of the testing tasks over the entire SLC and document them in Test Planned Information(s). The Test Planned Information(s) shall define the generic levels of testing and the basic test environment and structure needed to support required levels of testing. Each Test Planned Information shall identify the items to be tested, the requirements to be tested, and the test pass-or-fail criteria based on the Software Requirements and the Software Design Description (SDD) (as soon as available). The Test Planned Information(s) shall identify test coverage criteria, the tools and approaches being applied, the environmental needs, the testing tasks to be performed, the organizational structure, the management controls and reporting procedures, and the risks and contingencies.

The Test Planned Information(s) shall be coordinated with, and may be combined with, the Integration Planned Information and SVVP.

Further information related to this Activity may be found in [4], [10], [12], and [18].

Prior to distribution of the Test Planned Information(s), the following Processes shall be invoked:

(1) Verification and Validation (7.1.4)
(2) Software Configuration Management (7.2.5)
(3) Documentation Development (7.3.4)

7.1.6.3 Output Information

Output Information	Destination	
	Process	Activity
Test Planned Information(s)	Project Monitoring and Control	Analyze Risks (3.2.3)
		Manage the Project (3.2.5)
	Software Quality Management	Identify Quality Improvement Needs (3.3.6)
	Implementation	Create Test Data (5.3.3)
		Plan Integration (5.3.7)
	Verification and Validation	Develop Test Requirements (7.1.7)
		Execute the Tests (7.1.8)

7.1.7 Develop Test Requirements

7.1.7.1 Input Information

Input Information	Source	
	Process	Activity
Software Requirements	Requirements	Prioritize and Integrate Software Requirements (5.1.5)
Software Design Description	Design	Perform Detailed Design (5.2.7)
Test Planned Information(s)	Verification and Validation	Plan Testing (7.1.6)

7.1.7.2 Description. Test Requirements for each generic level of testing shall be developed to refine the test approach from the Test Planned Information(s) to item-specific test procedures used for test execution. The Test Requirements shall define what is to be tested, the data to be used in testing, expected results, the test environment components, and the procedures to be followed in testing. Information from the SRS, the SDD, and the Test Planned Information(s) is used to generate the Test Requirements.

Further information related to this Activity may be found in [4] and [10].

Prior to distribution of the Test Requirements, the following Processes shall be invoked:

(1) Verification and Validation (7.1.4)
(2) Software Configuration Management (7.2.5)
(3) Documentation Development (7.3.4)

7.1.7.3 Output Information

Output Information	Destination	
	Process	Activity
Test Requirements	Implementation	Create Test Data (5.3.3)
	Verification and Validation	Execute the Tests (7.1.8)

7.1.8 Execute the Tests

7.1.8.1 Input Information

Input Information	Source	
	Process	Activity
Test Environment Components	External	
Test Data	Implementation	Create Test Data (5.3.3)
Integrated Software	Implementation	Perform Integration (5.3.8)
Test Planned Information(s)	Verification and Validation	Plan Testing (7.1.6)
Test Requirements	Verification and Validation	Develop Test Requirements (7.1.7)

7.1.8.2 Description. This Activity shall configure the Test Environment Components as required by the Test Requirements. Each test shall be conducted on the Integrated Software using Test Data as defined in its associated Test Requirements and in accordance with the Test Planned Information(s).

This Activity could be iterative, with several instances performed during the software's life. Not all Input Information and Output Information are required for a given iteration; the presence of any Input Information is sufficient as an entry criterion, and the creation of any Output Information is a sufficient exit criterion.

Based on comparison of actual results with expected results, according to the pass-fail criteria, a pass-fail determination shall be made and recorded in a test log. Each anomalous event that occurs during execution which requires further investigation shall be reported. The impact on the validity of the test should also be noted.

Test Summary Reported Information shall summarize the results of a test based on its Test Requirements and test log. Tested Software is that software which has successfully passed all tests at the appropriate level and met the specified criteria and requirements. Tested Software may then be further integrated with other software or sent for installation.

Further information related to this Activity may be found in [4] and [10].

Prior to distribution of the Output Information from this Activity, the following Processes shall be invoked:

(1) Verification and Validation (7.1.4)
(2) Software Configuration Management (7.2.5)
(3) Documentation Development (7.3.4)

7.1.8.3 Output Information

Output Information	Destination	
	Process	Activity
Test Summary Reported Information	Project Monitoring and Control	Analyze Risks (3.2.3)
		Manage the Project (3.2.5)
	External	
Tested Software	Implementation	Perform Integration (5.3.8)
	Installation	Distribute Software (6.1.4)
Anomalies	Project Monitoring and Control	Implement Problem Reporting Method (3.2.7)

7.2 Software Configuration Management Process

7.2.1 Overview. Software Configuration Management the items in a software development project and provides both for control of the identified items and for the generation of Status Reported Information for management visibility and accountability throughout the software life cycle (SLC). Items to be managed are those defined in Software Configuration Management Planned Information (SCMP). Examples to be considered for inclusion in the SCMP are code, documentation, plans, and specifications. Configuration audits, if required by the Project, should be addressed in the Verification and Validation Process. The Software Configuration Management approach for a given project should be compatible with the Configuration Management approach being used on associated systems.

Section 1.5, "Use of This Standard," provides background information necessary for the successful understanding and application of this material. It should be read prior to proceeding further in this section.

7.2.2 Activities List

(1) Plan Configuration Management
(2) Develop Configuration Identification
(3) Perform Configuration Control
(4) Perform Status Accounting

7.2.3 Plan Configuration Management

7.2.3.1 Input Information

Input Information	Source	
	Process	Activity
Contract Deliverable List	External	
Software Project Management Planned Information	Project Initiation	Plan Project Management (3.1.6)
Configuration Identification	Software Configuration Management	Develop Configuration Identification (7.2.4)

7.2.3.2 Description. This Activity shall plan and document specific software configuration management organizations and responsibilities, procedures, tools, techniques, and methodologies in an SCMP. The SCMP shall also describe how and when such procedures are to be performed.

Overall software configuration management objectives are derived using internal guidelines as well as contractual requirements from the Software Project Management Planned Information (SPMP).

Further information related to this Activity may be found in [3] and [14].

Prior to distribution of the Planned Information, the following Processes shall be invoked:

(1) Verification and Validation (7.1.4)
(2) Documentation Development (7.3.4)

7.2.3.3 Output Information

Output Information	Destination	
	Process	Activity
Software Configuration Management Planned Information	Project Monitoring and Control	Retain Records (3.2.6)
	Software Configuration Management	Develop Configuration Identification (7.2.4)
		Perform Configuration Control (7.2.5)
		Perform Status Accounting (7.2.6)

7.2.4 Develop Configuration Identification

7.2.4.1 Input Information

Input Information	Source	
	Process	Activity
Software Project Management Planned Information	Project Initiation	Plan Project Management (3.1.6)
Software Configuration Management Planned Information	Software Configuration Management	Plan Configuration Management (7.2.3)

7.2.4.2 Description. This Activity shall define a Configuration Identification that includes project baseline definition, titling, labeling, and numbering to reflect the structure of the product for tracking. The SCMP identifies those configuration items to be addressed by the Configuration Identification. The identification shall support the software throughout the SLC, and shall be documented in the SCMP. The Configuration Identification shall also define the documentation required to record the functional and physical characteristics of each Configuration Item.

A series of baselines shall be established as the product moves from initial idea to the maintenance phase as required by the SPMP.

Further information related to this Activity may be found in [3] and [14].

7.2.4.3 Output Information

Output Information	Destination	
	Process	Activity
Configuration Identification	Software Configuration Management	Plan Configuration Management (7.2.3)

7.2.5 Perform Configuration Control

7.2.5.1 Input Information

Input Information	Source	
	Process	Activity
Items to Be Controlled	Creating Process	
Software Configuration Management Planned Information	Software Configuration Management	Plan Configuration Management (7.2.3)

7.2.5.2 Description. This Activity controls the configuration of products. Changes to controlled products shall be tracked to assure that the configuration of the product is known at all times. Each baseline shall be established and all subsequent changes tracked relative to it. All items specified in the SCMP are subject to this change management discipline. The history of changes to each configuration item shall be maintained throughout the SLC for status accounting.

Changes to Controlled Items shall be allowed only with approval of the responsible authority. This may result in establishment of a formal software configuration control board. Controlled Items shall be maintained in a software library.

Further information related to this Activity may be found in [3] and [14].

7.2.5.3 Output Information

Output Information	Destination	
	Process	Activity
Change Status	Software Configuration Management	Perform Status Accounting (7.2.6)
Controlled Item	Creating Process	
	Project Monitoring and Control	Implement Problem Reporting Method (3.2.7)

7.2.6 Perform Status Accounting

7.2.6.1 Input Information

Input Information	Source	
	Process	Activity
Software Configuration Management Planned Information	Software Configuration Management	Plan Configuration Management (7.2.3)
Change Status	Software Configuration Management	Perform Configuration Control (7.2.5)

7.2.6.2 Description. This Activity shall include the receipt of Change Status from the Perform Configuration Control Activity and the preparation of Status Reported Information that reflects the status and history of controlled items. Status Reported Information may include such data as number of changes to date for the project, number of releases, and the latest version and revision identifiers.

Further information related to this Activity may be found in [3] and [14].

Prior to the distribution of the Status Reported Information, the following Processes shall be invoked:

(1)   Verification and Validation (7.1.4)
(2)   Documentation Development (7.3.4)

7.2.6.3 Output Information

Output Information	Destination	
	Process	Activity
Status Reported Information	Project Monitoring and Control	Manage the Project (3.2.5)
	External	

7.3 Documentation Development Process

7.3.1 Overview. The Documentation Development Process for software development and usage is the set of Activities that plan, design, implement, edit, produce, distribute, and maintain those documents needed by developers and users. The purpose of the Documentation Development Process is to provide timely software documentation to those who need it, based on Input Information from the invoking Processes.

This Process covers both product- and procedure-oriented documentation for internal and external users. Examples of internal users include those who plan, design, implement, or test software. External users may include those who install, operate, apply, or maintain the software.

The Documentation Development Process occurs over various phases of the software life cycle (SLC) depending on the individual document and the timing of its development. Typically there will be multiple documents, each at different stages of development.

The Documentation Development Process has Activities that must be performed concurrently with the software development or usage. Since the software is seldom stable during development or testing, this requires effective communication and timely response between the software personnel and documentation personnel.

7.3.2 Activities List

(1)   Plan Documentation
(2)   Implement Documentation
(3)   Produce and Distribute Documentation

7.3.3 Plan Documentation

7.3.3.1 Input Information

Input Information	Source	
	Process	Activity
Contractual Requirements	External	
Project Standards	Project Initiation	Establish Project Environment (3.1.5)
Software Project Management Planned Information	Project Initiation	Plan Project Management (3.1.6)

7.3.3.2 Description. In this Activity, information such as the Software Project Management Planned Information (SPMP) product descriptions, schedules, and resource constraints shall be assimilated to create a consistent and disciplined approach to achieving the required documentation. The approach shall identify required documents, document production schedules and delivery schedules, and documentation standards. Responsible organizations, information sources, and intended audiences shall be defined for each document. The approach shall be documented in the Documentation Planning Information. The Documentation Planning Information shall include resource allocations for this Activity.

Additional guidance for the development of user documentation can be found in [21].

Prior to distribution of the Documentation Planning Information, the following Processes shall be invoked:

(1)   Verification and Validation (7.1.4)
(2)   Documentation Development (7.3.4)

The Software Configuration Management Process (7.2.5) should also be invoked.

7.3.3.3 Output Information

Output Information	Destination	
	Process	Activity
Documentation Planned Information	Project Monitoring and Control	Retain Records (3.2.6)
	Implementation	Create Operating Documentation (5.3.6)
	Documentation Development	All Activities (7.3)

7.3.4 Implement Documentation

7.3.4.1 Input Information

Input Information	Source	
	Process	Activity
Input Information for Document	Creating Process	
Project Environment	Project Initiation	Establish Project Environment (3.1.5)
Documentation Planned Information	Documentation Development	Plan Documentation (7.3.3)

7.3.4.2 Description. This Activity includes the design, preparation, and maintenance of documentation. Those documents identified in the Documentation Planned Information shall be defined in terms of audience, approach, content, structure, and graphics. Arrangements may be made with word or text processing and graphics facilities for their support of implementation.

Input Information shall be used to produce the document, including related graphics. This involves extensive use of information sources, close communication with the responsible subject matter experts, and utilization of word or text processing and graphics tools.

Following a documentation review, any changes shall be incorporated to produce a technically correct document. Format, style, and production rules shall be applied to produce a final document.

Prior to distribution of the Document, the following Processes should be invoked:

(1)   Verification and Validation (7.1.4)
(2)   Software Configuration Management (7.2.5)

7.3.4.3 Output Information

Output Information	Destination	
	Process	Activity
Document	Documentation Development	Produce and Distribute Documentation (7.3.5)

7.3.5 Produce and Distribute Documentation

7.3.5.1 Input Information

Input Information	Source	
	Process	Activity
Documentation Planned Information	Documentation Development	Plan Documentation (7.3.3)
Document	Documentation Development	Implement Documentation (7.3.4)

7.3.5.2 Description. This Activity shall provide the intended audience with the needed information collected in the document, as specified in the Documentation Planned Information. Document production and distribution may involve electronic file management, paper document reproduction and distribution, or other media handling techniques.

7.3.5.3 Output Information

Output Information	Destination	
	Process	Activity
Published Document	Project Monitoring and Control	Retain Records (3.2.6)
	Creating Process	
	External	

7.4 Training Process

7.4.1 Overview. The development of quality software products is largely dependent upon knowledgeable and skilled people. These include the developer's technical staff and management. Customer personnel may also have to be qualified to install, operate, and maintain the software. Training is therefore essential for developers, technical support staff, and customers. It is essential that Training Planned Information be completed early in the software life cycle, prior to the time when personnel would be expected to apply required expertise to the project. Plans for customer training should be prepared and reviewed with the customer.

Section 1.5, "Use of This Standard," provides background information necessary for the successful understanding and application of this material. It should be read prior to proceeding further in this section.

7.4.2 Activities List

(1) Plan the Training Program
(2) Develop Training Materials
(3) Validate the Training Program
(4) Implement the Training Program

7.4.3 Plan the Training Program

7.4.3.1 Input Information

Input Information	Source	
	Process	Activity
Applicable Information	External	
Skills Inventory	External	
Project Environment	Project Initiation	Establish Project Environment (3.1.5)
Software Project Management Planned Information	Project Initiation	Plan Project Management (3.1.6)
Software Requirements	Requirements	Prioritize and Integrate Software Requirements (5.1.5)
Training Feedback	Training	Implement the Training Program (7.4.6)
		Validate the Training Program (7.4.5)

7.4.3.2 Description. This Activity shall identify the needs for different types of training and the categories of people requiring training for each need. Customer and project documents shall be reviewed along with existing personnel inventories. This information is used to produce documented Training Planned Information. Implementation schedules shall also be generated and resources allocated to the training program. Implementation schedules, resource allocations, and training needs shall be specified in the Training Planned Information.

Prior to distribution of the Training Planned Information, the following Processes shall be invoked:

(1)   Verification and Validation (7.1.4)
(2)   Software Configuration Management (7.2.5)
(3)   Documentation Development (7.3.4)

7.4.3.3 Output Information

Output Information	Destination	
	Process	Activity
Training Planned Information	Software Quality Management	Identify Quality Improvement Needs (3.3.6)
	Training	All Activities (7.4)

7.4.4 Develop Training Materials

7.4.4.1 Input Information

Input Information	Source	
	Process	Activity
Applicable Documentation	External	
	Creating Process	
Project Environment	Project Initiation	Establish Project Environment (3.1.5)
Software Design Description	Design	Perform Detailed Design (5.2.7)
Training Planned Information	Training	Plan Training Program (7.4.3)

7.4.4.2 Description. This Activity shall consist of identification and review of all available materials that appear pertinent to the training objectives. Included in the Develop Training Materials Activity shall be the development of the substance of the training, training manual, and materials to be used in presenting the training, such as outlines, text, exercises, case studies, visuals, and models.

Prior to distribution of the Training Manual and Training Materials, the following Processes shall be invoked:

(1)   Verification and Validation (7.1.4)
(2)   Documentation Development (7.3.4)

The Software Configuration Management Process (7.2.5) should also be invoked.

7.4.4.3 Output Information

Output Information	Destination	
	Process	Activity
Training Manual	Training	Validate Training Program (7.4.5)
Training Materials	Training	Validate Training Program (7.4.5)

7.4.5 Validate the Training Program

7.4.5.1 Input Information

Input Information	Source	
	Process	Activity
Training Planned Information	Training	Plan Training Program 7.4.3)
Training Manual	Training	Develop Training Materials (7.4.4)
Training Materials	Training	Develop Training Materials (7.4.4)

7.4.5.2 Description. This Activity shall consist of presenting the training to a class of evaluators using the preliminary training manual and materials. The evaluators shall assess the training presentation and materials in detail. The purpose is to evaluate the effectiveness of the delivery and the validity of the material presented. Lessons learned in the test of the training program shall be incorporated into the material prior to a general offering. All training manuals and materials shall be evaluated and, if necessary, updated at this time.

Prior to distribution of Updated Training Manuals and Materials, the following Processes shall be invoked:

(1) Verification and Validation (7.1.4)
(2) Documentation Development (7.3.4)

The Software Configuration Management Process (7.2.5) should be invoked.

7.4.5.3 Output Information

Output Information	Destination	
	Process	Activity
Updated Training Manual	Training	Implement Training Program (7.4.6)
Updated Training Materials	Training	Implement Training Program (7.4.6)
Training Feedback	Training	Plan Training Program (7.4.3)

7.4.6 Implement the Training Program

7.4.6.1 Input Information

Input Information	Source	
	Process	Activity
Staff Participants	External	
Students	External	
Training Planned Information	Training	Plan Training Program(7.4.3)
Updated Training Manual	Training	Validate Training Program (7.4.5)
Updated Training Materials	Training	Validate Training Program (7.4.5)

7.4.6.2 Description. This Activity shall ensure the provision of all necessary materials, arrange the locations and facilities for training, assign instructors and, if necessary, train them. Included in this Activity shall be the enrolling of students and monitoring of the course effectiveness.

Lessons learned and information needed for updating the materials for the next training cycle shall be fed back into the beginning of the Training Process.

7.4.6.3 Output Information

Output Information	Destination	
	Process	Activity
Trained Personnel	Creating Process	
Training Feedback	Training	Plan Training Program (7.4.3)
Updated Skills Inventory	External	

8. Bibliography

The IEEE standards listed below and other subsequent standards should be consulted when using this document. However, compliance with this standard neither requires nor implies compliance with the listed standards. Table 2 provides a cross reference of specific Activities to other IEEE standards.

[1] IEEE Std 610.12-1990, IEEE Standard Glossary of Software Engineering Terminology (ANSI).[4]

[2] IEEE Std 730-1989, IEEE Standard for Software Quality Assurance Plans (ANSI).

[3] IEEE Std 828-1990, IEEE Standard for Software Configuration Management Plans (ANSI).

[4] IEEE Std 829-1983, IEEE Standard for Software Test Documentation (ANSI).

[5] IEEE Std 830-1984, IEEE Guide to Software Requirements Specifications (ANSI).

[6] IEEE Std 982.1-1988, IEEE Standard Dictionary of Measures to Produce Reliable Software (ANSI).

[7] IEEE Std 982.2-1988, IEEE Guide for the Use of IEEE Standard Dictionary of Measures to Produce Reliable Software (ANSI).

[8] IEEE Std 983-1986, IEEE Guide for Software Quality Assurance Planning (ANSI).

[9] IEEE Std 1002-1987, IEEE Standard Taxonomy for Software Engineering Standards (ANSI).

[10] IEEE Std 1008-1987, IEEE Standard for Software Unit Testing (ANSI).

[11] IEEE Std 1012-1986, IEEE Standard for Software Verification and Validation Plans (ANSI).

[12] IEEE Std 1016-1987, IEEE Recommended Practice for Software Design Descriptions (ANSI).

[13] IEEE Std 1028-1988, IEEE Standard for Software Reviews and Audits (ANSI).

[14] IEEE Std 1042-1987, IEEE Guide to Software Configuration Management Planning (ANSI).

[15] P1044, Standard for Classification of Software Errors, Faults, and Failures.[5]

[16] P1045, Standard for Software Productivity Metrics.

[17] IEEE Std 1058.1-1987, IEEE Standard for Software Project Management Plans (ANSI).

[18] P1059, Guide for Software Verification and Validation.

---

[4]IEEE publications are available from the Institute of Electrical and Electronics Engineers, Service Center, 445 Hoes Lane, P.O. Box 1331, Piscataway, NJ 08855-1331, USA.
[5]References [15], [16], [18], [19], and [20] are authorized standards projects that were not approved by the IEEE Standards Board at the time this document went to press. The latest drafts of the documents are available from the IEEE Service Center.

[19] P1061, Standard for a Software Quality Metrics Methodology.

[20] P1062, Recommended Practice for Software Acquisition.

[21] IEEE Std 1063-1987, IEEE Standard for Software User Documentation (ANSI).

[22] ANSI Technical Report, American National Dictionary for Information Processing, X3/TR-1-77, September 1977.

Table 2
Cross Reference of IEEE Standards and Authorized Standards Projects

Activities (Paragraph Numbers) / Referenced IEEE Standards and Authorized Standards Projects	Applicability of Standards								
	1.3.1	3.1.5	3.1.6	3.2.7	3.3.3	3.3.4	5.1.3 5.1.5	5.2.7	5.3.3 5.3.5
[1] 610.12-1990	X								
[2] 730-1989					X				
[3] 828-1990									
[4] 829-1983									
[5] 830-1984	X						X		
[6] 982.1-1988						X			
[7] 982.2-1988						X			
[8] 983-1986					X				
[9] 1002-1987		X							
[10] 1008-1987									
[11] 1012-1986									
[12] 1016-1987									
[13] 1028-1988									
[14] 1042-1987									
[15] P1044				X					
[16] 1045						X			
[17] 1058.1-1987	X		X						
[18] P1059									
[19] P1061						X			
[20] P1062									
[21] 1063-1987									

Activities (Paragraph Numbers) Referenced IEEE Standards	5.3.3 5.3.5	5.3.6	7.1.3	7.1.4	7.1.5	7.1.6	7.1.7 7.1.8	7.2.3 7.2.4 7.2.5 7.2.6	7.3.3
Applicability of Standards									
[1] 610.12-1990									
[2] 730-1989			X	X					
[3] 828-1990			X	X				X	
[4] 829-1983			X			X	X		
[5] 830-1984									
[6] 982.1-1988			X		X				
[7] 982.2-1988			X		X				
[8] 983-1986			X	X					
[9] 1002-1987									
[10] 1008-1987	X					X			
[11] 1012-1986			X	X		X	X		
[12] 1016-1987									
[13] 1028-1988			X	X					
[14] 1042-1987			X	X				X	
[15] P1044			X		X				
[16] P1045			X		X				
[17] 1058.1-1987									
[18] P1059						X			
[19] P1061									
[20] P1062									
[21] 1063-1987		X							X

Appendixes

(These Appendixes are not a part of IEEE Std 1074-1991, IEEE Standard for Developing Life Cycle Processes, but are included for information only.)

Appendix A
Mapping Software Life Cycle Processes to Various Examples of Software Life Cycles

This Appendix demonstrates the mappings of the Activities in this standard to four different software life cycles (SLCs). This Appendix is not intended to be comprehensive. Many other SLCs are possible, for example, small development, quick reaction, and the spiral model. The SLCs presented here are examples only, and the user of this document is not required to select any of these SLCs.

Table A1 demonstrates a mapping of Activities to an eight-phase SLC.

Table A2 demonstrates a mapping of Activities to a five-phase SLC.

Table A3 demonstrates a mapping of Activities to an SLC that uses prototyping to establish requirements and design.

Table A4 demonstrates a mapping of Activities to an SLC that includes a theoretical, highly automated software development mode.

Section 1.5, "Use of This Standard," provides background information necessary for the successful understanding and application of this material. It should be read prior to proceeding further in these Appendixes.

Table A1
Software Life Cycle Example Based on Eight Phases

Concept Exploration (CE)
Design (DE)
Test (TE)
Operation and Maintenance (OM)

Requirements (RQ)
Implementation (IM)
Installation and Checkout (IN)
Retirement (RT)

Activities	CE	RQ	DE	IM	TE	IN	OM	RT
SOFTWARE LIFE CYCLE PROCESS								
Identify Candidate SLC Models	X							
Select Project Model	X							
PROJECT MANAGEMENT PROCESSES								
Project Initiation Process								
Map Activities to SLC Model	X							
Allocate Project Resources	X	X	X	X	X	X	X	X
Establish Project Environment	X	X	X					
Plan Project Management	X	X						
Project Monitoring and Control Process								
Analyze Risks	X	X	X	X	X	X		
Perform Contingency Planning		X	X	X	X	X		
Manage the Project	X	X	X	X	X	X	X	X
Retain Records	X	X	X	X	X	X	X	X
Implement Problem Reporting System		X	X	X	X	X	X	X
Software Quality Management Process								
Plan Software Quality Management	X	X	X					
Define Metrics		X	X					
Manage Software Quality	X	X	X	X	X	X	X	X
Identify Quality Improvement Needs	X	X	X	X	X	X	X	X
PRE-DEVELOPMENT PROCESSES								
Concept Exploration Process								
Identify Ideas or Needs	X							
Formulate Potential Approaches	X	X						
Conduct Feasibility Studies	X	X	X	X	X	X	X	X
Plan System Transition (If Applicable)	X	X						X
Refine and Finalize the Idea or Need		X						
System Allocation Process								
Analyze Functions		X	X					
Develop System Architecture		X	X					
Decompose System Requirements		X						

Activities	CE	RQ	DE	IM	TE	IN	OM	RT
DEVELOPMENT PROCESSES								
Requirements Process								
Define and Develop Software Requirements		X	X					
Define Interface Requirements		X	X					
Prioritize and Integrate Software Requirements		X	X					
Design Process								
Perform Architectural Design			X					
Design Data Base (If Applicable)			X					
Design Interfaces			X					
Select or Develop Algorithms		X	X					
Perform Detailed Design			X					
Implementation Process								
Create Test Data			X	X				
Create Source			X	X				
Generate Object Code			X	X				
Create Operating Documentation			X	X				
Plan Integration			X					
Perform Integration				X	X			
POST-DEVELOPMENT PROCESSES								
Installation Process								
Plan Installation					X			
Distribute Software						X		
Install Software						X		
Accept Software in Operational Environment						X		
Operation and Support Process								
Operate the System							X	
Provide Tech. Asst. & Consult.							X	
Maintain Support Request Log							X	
Maintenance Process								
Reapply Software Life Cycle							X	
Retirement Process								
Notify User							X	X
Conduct Parallel Operations (If Applicable)								X
Retire System								X

Activities	CE	RQ	DE	IM	TE	IN	OM	RT
INTEGRAL PROCESSES								
Verification and Validation Process								
Plan Verification and Validation	X	X	X					
Execute V&V Tasks	X	X	X	X	X	X	X	X
Collect and Analyze Metric Data		X	X	X	X	X	X	X
Plan Testing		X	X	X				
Develop Test Requirements			X	X				
Execute the Tests				X	X	X		
Software Configuration Management Process								
Plan Configuration Management		X	X					
Perform Configuration Identification		X	X	X	X			
Perform Configuration Control			X	X	X	X	X	X
Perform Status Accounting			X	X	X	X	X	X
Documentation Development Process								
Plan Documentation		X	X					
Implement Documentation		X	X					
Produce and Distribute Documentation				X	X			
Training Process								
Plan the Training Program		X	X					
Develop Training Materials			X	X	X			
Validate the Training Program					X	X		
Implement the Training Program						X		

Project Initiation (PI)   Concept Development (CD)
Definition and Design (DD)   System Development (SD)
Installation and Operation (IO)

Activities	PI	CD	DD	SD	IO
SOFTWARE LIFE CYCLE PROCESS					
Identify Candidate SLC Models	X				
Select Project Model	X				
PROJECT MANAGEMENT PROCESSES					
Project Initiation Process					
Map Activities to SLC Model	X				
Allocate Project Resources	X	X	X	X	X
Establish Project Environment	X	X	X		
Plan Project Management	X	X			
Project Monitoring and Control Process					
Analyze Risks	X	X	X	X	X
Perform Contingency Planning		X	X	X	X
Manage the Project	X	X	X	X	X
Retain Records	X	X	X	X	X
Implement Problem Reporting System		X	X	X	X
Software Quality Management Process					
Plan Software Quality Management	X	X	X		
Define Metrics		X	X		
Manage Software Quality	X	X	X	X	X
Identify Quality Improvement Needs	X	X	X	X	X
PRE-DEVELOPMENT PROCESSES					
Concept Exploration Process					
Identify Ideas or Needs	X				
Formulate Potential Approaches	X	X			
Conduct Feasibility Studies	X	X			
Plan System Transition (If Applicable)	X	X			
Refine and Finalize the Idea or Need		X			
System Allocation Process					
Analyze Functions		X	X		
Develop System Architecture		X	X		
Decompose System Requirements		X			

609

Activities	PI	CD	DD	SD	IO
DEVELOPMENT PROCESSES					
Requirements Process					
Define and Develop Software Requirements		X	X		
Define Interface Requirements		X	X		
Prioritize and Integrate Software Requirements		X	X		
Design Process					
Perform Architectural Design			X		
Design Data Base (If Applicable)			X		
Design Interfaces			X		
Select or Develop Algorithms		X	X		
Perform Detailed Design			X		
Implementation Process					
Create Test Data			X	X	
Create Source			X	X	
Generate Object Code			X	X	
Create Operating Documentation			X	X	
Plan Integration			X		
Perform Integration				X	
POST-DEVELOPMENT PROCESSES					
Installation Process					
Plan Installation				X	
Distribute Software					X
Install Software					X
Accept Software in Operational Environment					X
Operation and Support Process					
Operate the System					X
Provide Tech. Asst. & Consult.					X
Maintain Support Request Log					X
Maintenance Process					
Reapply Software Life Cycle					X
Retirement Process					
Notify User					X
Conduct Parallel Operations (If Applicable)					X
Retire System					X

Activities	PI	CD	DD	SD	IO
INTEGRAL PROCESSES					
Verification and Validation Process					
Plan Verification and Validation	X	X	X		
Execute V&V Tasks		X	X	X	X
Collect and Analyze Metric Data		X	X	X	X
Plan Testing			X	X	
Develop Test Requirements			X	X	
Execute the Tests			X	X	X
Software Configuration Management Process					
Plan Configuration Management		X	X		
Perform Configuration Identification		X	X	X	
Perform Configuration Control			X	X	X
Perform Status Accounting			X	X	X
Documentation Development Process					
Plan Documentation		X	X		
Implement Documentation			X	X	
Produce and Distribute Documentation				X	X
Training Process					
Plan the Training Program		X	X		
Develop Training Materials			X	X	
Validate the Training Program				X	X
Implement the Training Program					X

Concept Exploration (CE)   Prototyping (PT)
Implementation (IM)   Test (TE)
Installation and Checkout (IN)   Operation and Maintenance (OM)
Retirement (RT)

Activities	CE	PT	IM	TE	IN	OM	RT
SOFTWARE LIFE CYCLE PROCESS							
Identify Candidate SLC Models	X						
Select Project Model	X						
PROJECT MANAGEMENT PROCESSES							
Project Initiation Process							
Map Activities to SLC Model	X						
Allocate Project Resources	X	X	X	X	X	X	X
Establish Project Environment	X	X					
Plan Project Management	X	X					
Project Monitoring and Control Process							
Analyze Risks	X	X	X	X	X		
Perform Contingency Planning		X	X	X	X		
Manage the Project	X	X	X	X	X	X	X
Retain Records	X	X	X	X	X	X	X
Implement Problem Reporting System		X	X	X	X	X	X
Software Quality Management Process							
Plan Software Quality Management		X					
Define Metrics		X					
Manage Software Quality	X	X	X	X	X	X	X
Identify Quality Improvement Needs	X	X	X	X	X	X	X
PRE-DEVELOPMENT PROCESSES							
Concept Exploration Process							
Identify Ideas or Needs	X						
Formulate Potential Approaches	X	X					
Conduct Feasibility Studies	X	X					
Plan System Transition (If Applicable)	X	X					X
Refine and Finalize the Idea or Need		X					
System Allocation Process							
Analyze Functions		X					
Develop System Architecture		X					
Decompose System Requirements		X					

Activities	CE	PT	IM	TE	IN	OM	RT
DEVELOPMENT PROCESSES							
Requirements Process							
Define and Develop Software Requirements		X					
Define Interface Requirements		X					
Prioritize and Integrate Software Rqmts.		X					
Design Process							
Perform Architectural Design		X					
Design Data Base (If Applicable)		X					
Design Interfaces		X					
Select or Develop Algorithms		X					
Perform Detailed Design		X					
Implementation Process							
Create Test Data		X	X				
Create Source		X	X				
Generate Object Code		X	X	X			
Create Operating Documentation		X	X				
Plan Integration		X					
Perform Integration			X	X			
POST-DEVELOPMENT PROCESSES							
Installation Process							
Plan Installation				X			
Distribute Software					X		
Install Software					X		
Check out Software in Operational Envnmt.					X		
Operation and Support Process							
Operate the System						X	
Provide Tech. Asst. & Consult.						X	
Maintain Support Request Log						X	
Maintenance Process							
Reapply Software Life Cycle						X	

Activities	CE	PT	IM	TE	IN	OM	RT
Retirement Process							
Notify User						X	X
Conduct Parallel Operations (If Applicable)							X
Retire System							X
INTEGRAL PROCESSES							
Verification and Validation Process							
Plan Verification and Validation		X					
Execute V&V Tasks		X	X	X	X	X	X
Collect and Analyze Metric Data		X	X	X	X	X	X
Plan Testing		X	X				
Develop Test Specifications		X	X				
Execute the Tests			X	X	X		
Software Configuration Management Process							
Plan Configuration Management		X					
Perform Configuration Identification		X	X	X			
Perform Configuration Control		X	X	X	X	X	X
Perform Status Accounting		X	X	X	X	X	X
Documentation Development Process							
Plan Documentation		X					
Implement Documentation		X	X				
Produce and Distribute Documentation				X	X		
Training Process							
Plan the Training Program		X					
Develop Training Materials		X	X	X			
Validate the Training Program				X	X		
Implement the Training Program					X		

Table A4
Software Life Cycle Example Based on an Operational Specification[*]

System Requirements (SR) Operational Specification (OS)
Transformed Specification (TS) Delivered System (DS)

Activities	SR	OS	TS	DS
SOFTWARE LIFE CYCLE PROCESS				
Identify Candidate SLC Models	X			
Select Project Model	X			
PROJECT MANAGEMENT PROCESSES				
Project Initiation Process				
Map Activities to SLC Model	X			
Allocate Project Resources	X	X	X	X
Establish Project Environment	X	X		
Plan Project Management	X			
Project Monitoring and Control Process				
Analyze Risks	X	X	X	X
Perform Contingency Planning	X	X	X	X
Manage the Project	X	X	X	X
Retain Records	X	X	X	X
Implement Problem Reporting System		X	X	X
Software Quality Management Process				
Plan Software Quality Management	X	X		
Define Metrics	X	X		
Manage Software Quality	X	X	X	X
Identify Quality Improvement Needs	X	X	X	X
PRE-DEVELOPMENT PROCESSES				
Concept Exploration Process				
Identify Ideas or Needs	X			
Formulate Potential Approaches	X			
Conduct Feasibility Studies	X	X		
Plan System Transition (If Applicable)	X			X
Refine and Finalize the Idea or Need	X			
System Allocation Process				
Analyze Functions	X	X		
Develop System Architecture	X	X		
Decompose System Requirements	X			

[*] As defined in the IEEE Tutorial, "New Paradigms for Software Development," by William W. Agresti.

Activities	SR	OS	TS	DS
DEVELOPMENT PROCESSES				
Requirements Process				
Define and Develop Software Requirements	X	X		
Define Interface Requirements	X	X		
Prioritize and Integrate Software Requirements	X	X		
Design Process				
Perform Architectural Design		X		
Design Data Base (If Applicable)		X		
Design Interfaces		X		
Select or Develop Algorithms	X	X		
Perform Detailed Design		X		
Implementation Process				
Create Test Data		X	X	
Create Source		X	X	
Generate Object Code		X	X	
Create Operating Documentation		X	X	
Plan Integration		X		
Perform Integration			X	
POST-DEVELOPMENT PROCESSES				
Installation Process				
Plan Installation			X	
Distribute Software				X
Install Software				X
Check out Software in Operational Environment				X
Operation and Support Process				
Operate the System				X
Provide Tech. Asst. & Consult.				X
Maintain Support Request Log				X
Maintenance Process				
Reapply Software Life Cycle				X
Retirement Process				
Notify User				X
Conduct Parallel Operations (If Applicable)				X
Retire System				X

Table A4
Software Life Cycle Example Based on an Operational Specification *(Continued)*

Activities	SR	OS	TS	DS
INTEGRAL PROCESSES				
Verification and Validation Process				
Plan Verification and Validation	X	X		
Execute V&V Tasks	X	X	X	X
Collect and Analyze Metric Data	X	X	X	X
Plan Testing		X	X	
Develop Test Specifications		X	X	
Execute the Tests			X	X
Software Configuration Management Process				
Plan Configuration Management	X	X		
Perform Configuration Identification	X	X	X	
Perform Configuration Control		X	X	X
Perform Status Accounting		X	X	X
Documentation Development Process				
Plan Documentation	X	X		
Implement Documentation		X	X	
Produce and Distribute Documentation			X	X
Training Process				
Plan the Training Program	X	X		
Develop Training Materials		X	X	
Validate the Training Program			X	X
Implement the Training Program				X

Appendix B
Software Project Management Tailoring Template

The Software Project Management Tailoring Template is designed to assist project managers in identifying project-critical deliverables and assuring their completion as needed.

This template may be used to assist in the project-specific mapping of information into the required project documentation.

Table B1
Software Project Management Tailoring Template

SOFTWARE PROJECT MANAGEMENT TAILORING TEMPLATE			
Process or Activity Name	Section	Output Information	Mapped Deliverables or Activities
PROCESS GROUP **Process** Activity		Required Output Information	
SOFTWARE LIFE CYCLE PROCESS	2		
Identify Candidate SLC Models	2.3	Candidate SLC Model(s)	
Select Project Model	2.4	Selected SLC Model	
PROJECT MANAGEMENT PROCESSES	3		
Project Initiation	3.1		
Map Activities to SLC Model	3.1.3	Software Life Cycle	
		List of Activities Not Used	
Allocate Project Information	3.1.4	Resource Allocations	
Establish Project Environment	3.1.5	Project Environment	
Plan Project Management	3.1.6	Problem Reporting & Resolution Planned Info.	
		Retirement Planned Info.	
		Software Project Management Planned Info.	
		Support Planned Info.	
Project Monitoring and Control	3.2		
Analyze Risks	3.2.3	Analysis of Risks	
Perform Contingency Planning	3.2.4	Contingency Planned Info.	
Manage the Project	3.2.5	Project Management Reported Info.	
		Anomalies	
Retain Records	3.2.6	Historical Project Records	
Implement Problem Reporting Method	3.2.7	Resolved Problem Reported Info.	
		Report Log	
		Enhancement Problem Reported Info.	
		Corrections Problem Reported Info.	

SOFTWARE PROJECT MANAGEMENT TAILORING TEMPLATE			
Process or Activity Name	Section	Output Information	Mapped Deliverables or Activities
Software Quality Management	3.3		
Plan Software Quality Management	3.3.3	Software Quality Management Planned Info.	
Define Metrics	3.3.4	Defined Metrics	
		Collection and Analysis Methods	
Manage Software Quality	3.3.5	Project Quality Assessments	
Identify Quality Improvement Needs	3.3.6	Quality Improvement Recommendations	
PRE-DEVELOPMENT PROCESSES	**4**		
Concept Exploration	**4.1**		
Identify Ideas or Needs	4.1.3	Prelim. Statement of Need	
Formulate Potential Approaches	4.1.4	Constraints and Benefits	
		Potential Approaches	
Conduct Feasibility Studies	4.1.5	Recommendations	
Plan System Transition (If Applicable)	4.1.6	Transition Impact Statement	
		Transition Planned Info.	
Refine and Finalize the Idea or Need	4.1.7	Statement of Need	
System Allocation	**4.2**		
Analyze Functions	4.2.3	Funct'l Description of System	
Develop System Architecture	4.2.4	System Architecture	
Decompose System Requirements	4.2.5	Funct'l Hardware Rqmts.	
		Funct'l Software Rqmts.	
		System Interface Requirements (If Applicable)	
DEVELOPMENT PROCESSES	**5**		
Requirements	**5.1**		
Define and Develop Software Rqmts.	5.1.3	Prelim. Software Rqmts.	
		Installation Rqmts.	
Define Interface Requirements	5.1.4	Software Interface Rqmts.	
Prioritize and Integrate Software Rqmts.	5.1.5	Software Rqmts.	

SOFTWARE PROJECT MANAGEMENT TAILORING TEMPLATE			
Process or Activity Name	Section	Output Information	Mapped Deliverables or Activities
Design	**5.2**		
Perform Architectural Design	5.2.3	Software Architectural Design Description	
Design Data Base (If Applicable)	5.2.4	Data Base Description	
Design Interfaces	5.2.5	Interface Description	
Select or Develop Algorithms	5.2.6	Algorithm Descriptions	
Perform Detailed Design	5.2.7	Software Design Description	
Implementation	**5.3**		
Create Test Data	5.3.3	Stubs and Drivers (If Applicable)	
		Test Data	
Create Source	5.3.4	Data Base (If Applicable)	
		Source Code	
Generate Object Code	5.3.5	Corrected Data Base (If Applicable)	
		Corrected Source Code	
		Object Code	
Create Operating Documentation	5.3.6	Operating Documentation	
Plan Integration	5.3.7	Integration Planned Info.	
Perform Integration	5.3.8	Integrated Software	
POST-DEVELOPMENT PROCESSES	**6**		
Installation	**6.1**		
Plan Installation	6.1.3	Software Installation Planned Info.	
Distribute Software	6.1.4	Packaged Operating Docs.	
		Packaged Software	
		Packaged Installation Planned Info.	
Install Software	6.1.5	Installation Reported Info.	
		Installed Software	
Accept Software in Operational Envrmt.	6.1.6	Installed Software System	
		Customer Acceptance	

SOFTWARE PROJECT MANAGEMENT TAILORING TEMPLATE			
Process or Activity Name	Section	Output Information	Mapped Deliverables or Activities
Operation and Support	**6.2**		
Operate the System	6.2.3	System Anomalies	
		Operation Logs	
		Feedback Data	
Provide Tech. Asst. & Consult.	6.2.4	Support Response	
Maintain Support Request Log	6.2.5	Anomalies	
		Support Request Log	
Maintenance	**6.3**		
Reapply Software Life Cycle	6.3.3	Maintenance Recommendations	
Retirement	**6.4**		
Notify User	6.4.3	Official Notification	
Conduct Parallel Operations	6.4.4	Parallel Operations Log	
Retire System	6.4.5	Post-Operation Review Reported Information	
		Archive Reported Info.	
INTEGRAL PROCESSES	**7**		
Verification and Validation	**7.1**		
Plan V&V	7.1.3	Software V&V Planned Info.	
Execute V&V Tasks	7.1.4	Evaluation Reported Info.	
		Anomalies	
Collect and Analyze Metric Data	7.1.5	Analysis Reported Info.	
Plan Testing	7.1.6	Test Planned Info.	
Develop Test Requirements	7.1.7	Test Requirements	
Execute the Tests	7.1.8	Test Summary Reported Info.	
		Tested Software	
		Anomalies	

SOFTWARE PROJECT MANAGEMENT TAILORING TEMPLATE			
Process or Activity Name	Section	Output Information	Mapped Deliverables or Activities
Software Configuration Management	**7.2**		
Plan Configuration Management	7.2.3	Software Config. Management Planned Info.	
Develop Configuration Identification	7.2.4	Config. Identification	
Perform Configuration Control	7.2.5	Change Status Controlled Item	
Perform Status Accounting	7.2.6	Status Reported Info.	
Documentation Development	**7.3**		
Plan Documentation	7.3.3	Documentation Planned Info.	
Implement Documentation	7.3.4	Document	
Produce and Distribute Documentation	7.3.5	Published Document	
Training	**7.4**		
Plan the Training Program	7.4.3	Training Planned Info.	
Develop Training Materials	7.4.4	Training Manual	
		Training Materials	
Validate the Training Program	7.4.5	Updated Training Manual	
		Updated Training Materials	
		Training Feedback	
Implement the Training Program	7.4.6	Trained Personnel	
		Training Feedback	
		Updated Skills Inventory	

Appendix C
Process Interrelationships

Figure C1 in this Appendix shows the interrelationships between the Processes. The boxes in Fig C1 are Processes; the directed lines show the flow of input and output information between Processes. The Management Processes are grouped in the center of the figure, with the Development-Oriented Processes arranged around them.

This figure does not attempt to show Process invocations. All the directed lines to and from the Invoked Processes represent explicit information passed between those Processes.

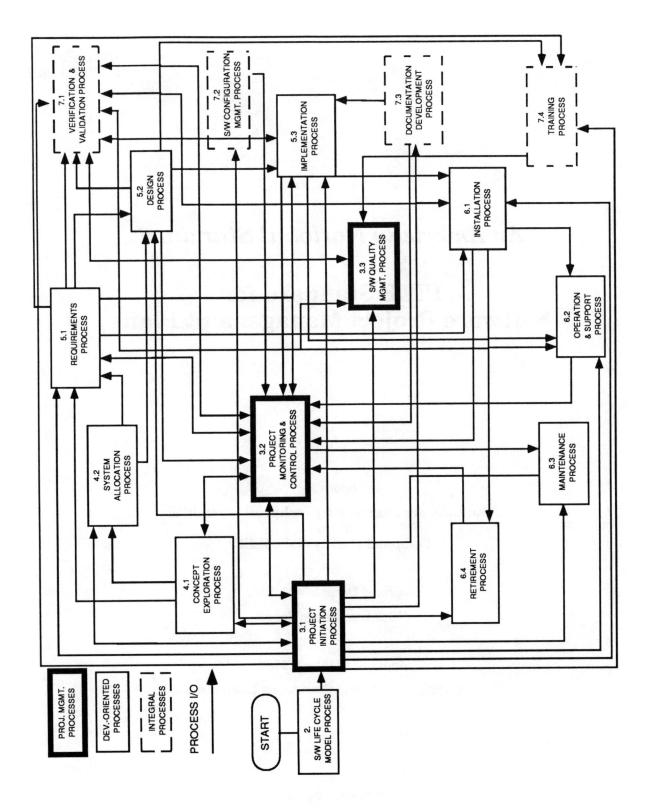

Fig C1
Process Interrelationships

An American National Standard

IEEE Standard for
Software Project Management Plans

Sponsor

**The Software Engineering Technical Committee
of the
Computer Society of the IEEE**

Approved December 10, 1987

IEEE Standards Board

Approved October 6, 1988

American National Standards Institute

The Software Engineering Standards Subcommittee comprised the balloting committee that approved this document for submission to the IEEE Standards Board, and at the time of balloting was composed of the following persons:

A. F. Ackerman
Richard L. Aurbach
Motoei Azuma
H. J. Barnard
J. Behm
H. Ronald Berlack
Michael A. Blackledge
Giles Bracon
J. Joseph Brandt
Kathleen L. Briggs
A. Winsor Brown
F. Buckley
L. J. Call
H. Carl
John W. Center
John Chihorek
T. S. Chow
J. K. Chung
Won L. Chung
Antonio M. Cicu
Judith Clapp
Peter Coad, Jr.
François Coallier
Christopher M. Cooke
Richard Cotter
T. Daughtrey
Peter Denny
F. M. Discenzo
David A. Dobraiz
David Doty
Einar Dragstedt
William Dupres
Albert D. DuRee
Mary Eads
L. E. Egan
W. D. Ehrenberger
Steven R. Eisen
Walter Ellis
Caroline Evans
Richard E. Fairley
David W. Favor
Joan Feld
John Fendrich
Glenn S. Fields
Violet Foldes
T. Foote-Lennox
Joel Forman
Julian Forster
Richard C. Fries
F. K. Gardner
L. B. Gardner

David Gilperin
Shirley Gloss-Soler
J. G. Glynn
Andrej Grebenc
Victor Guarnera
Lawrence M. Gunther
David A. Gustafson
J. A. Haksi
Jeffrey Hickey
John W. Horch
Cheng Hu
Laurel V. Kaleda
Harry Kalmbach
Daniel E. Klingler
Shaye Koenig
Joseph A. Krupinski
Joan Kundig
T. Kurihara
Lak Ming Lam
John B. Lane
Robert A. C. Lane
G. Larsen
F. C. Lim
Bertil Lindberg
B. Livson
Austin Maher
Paulo Cesar Marcondes
Nicholas Marselos
Roger Martin
John McArdle
J. A. McCall
R. McDowell
Manijeh Moghis
Charles S. Mooney
Gary D. Moorhead
D. D. Morton
G. T. Morun
Hiranobu Nagano
Geraldine Neidhart
Dennis Nickle
Wilma M. Osborne
Michael T. Perkins
W. E. Perry
John Petraglia
Donald J. Pfeiffer
I. C. Pyle
Thomas S. Radi
Salim Ramji
Jean-Claude Rault
Meir Razy
Donald Reifer

Patrick A. Rich
R. San Roman
John C. Rowe
Margaret Rumley
Julio G. Sanz
Steven Schach
Wolf A. Schnoege
Norman Schneidewind
David Schultz
Gregory D. Schumacker
Leonard W. Seagren
Gerard P. Shabe
Robert Shillato
David Siefert
William J. Singer
Jacob Slonim
H. M. Sneed
V. Srinivas
G. Wayne Staley
Franklin M. Sterling
Mary Jane Stoughton
W. G. Sutcliffe
Michael H. Taint
Richard H. Thayer
Paul U. Thompson
Terrence L. Tillmans
Valentin Tirman
G. R. Trebble
C. L. Troyanowski
William S. Turner, III
Robert Urling
David Usechak
Thomas E. Vollman
Dolores R. Wallace
John P. Walter
Dale R. Webdale
Charles J. Wertz
Peter J. Weyman
Allan Whitaker
Gary L. Whitten
Andrea S. Williams
Patrick J. Wilson
W. Martin Wong
Dennis L. Wood
Paul R. Work
Nancy Yavne
Natalie C. Yopronka
Leon Young
Donald Zelenu
Hugh Zettel
Peter Zoll

When the IEEE Standards Board approved this standard on December 10, 1987, it had the following membership:

Donald C. Fleckenstein, *Chairman*   **Marco W. Migliaro,** *Vice Chairman*

Andrew G. Salem, *Secretary*

James H. Beall
Dennis Bodson
Marshall L. Cain
James M. Daly
Stephen R. Dillon
Eugene P. Fogarty
Jay Forster
Kenneth D. Hendrix
Irvin N. Howell

Leslie R. Kerr
Jack Kinn
Irving Kolodny
Joseph L. Koepfinger*
Edward Lohse
John May
Lawrence V. McCall
L. Bruce McClung

Donald T. Michael*
L. John Rankine
John P. Riganati
Gary S. Robinson
Frank L. Rose
Robert E. Rountree
William R. Tackaberry
William B. Wilkens
Helen M. Wood

*Member emeritus

Foreword

(This Foreword is not a part of IEEE Std 1058.1-1987, IEEE Standard for Software Project Management Plans.)

Purpose

This standard specifies the format and contents of software project management plans. It does not specify the exact techniques to be used in developing project plans, nor does it provide examples of project management plans. Each organization that uses this standard should develop a set of practices and procedures to provide detailed guidance for preparing and updating software project management plans based on this standard. These detailed practices and procedures should take into account the environmental, organizational, and political factors that influence application of the standard.

Not all software projects are concerned with development of source code for a new software product. Some software projects consist of a feasibility study and definition of product requirements. Other projects terminate upon completion of product design, and some projects are concerned with major modifications to existing software products. This standard is applicable to all types of software projects; applicability is not limited to projects that develop operational versions of new products. Application of this standard is not limited by project size. Small projects may require less formality in planning than large projects, but all components of this standard should be addressed by every software project.

Software projects are sometimes component parts of larger projects. In these cases, the software project management plan may be a separate component of a larger plan or it may be merged into the system level project management plan.

Overview

This standard contains three sections. Section 1 defines the scope of the standard and provides references to other IEEE standards that should be followed when applying this standard. Section 2 provides definitions of terms that are used throughout the standard. Section 3 contains an overview and a detailed specification of the standard, including required components that must be included, and optional components that may be included in project plans based on this standard. The sequence of project plan elements presented in Section 3 does not imply that project plans should be developed in the order of presentation. In most instances, project plans based on this standard will be developed by repeated iteration and refinement of the various elements in the plan.

Audience

This standard is intended for use by software project managers and other personnel who prepare and update project plans and monitor adherence to those plans.

Evolution of Plans

Developing the initial version of the software project management plan should be one of the first activities to be completed on a software project. As the project evolves, the nature of the work to be done and the decomposition of work will be better understood. The project management plan must be updated periodically to reflect the evolving situation. Thus, each version of the plan should be placed under change control, and each version should contain a schedule for subsequent updates to the plan.

Terminology

This standard follows the IEEE Guide to Standards Development. In particular, the words shall, must, and the imperative form identify mandatory material within the standard. The words should, might, and may identify optional material.

History

The project authorization request for development of this standard was approved by the IEEE Standards Board on December 13, 1984. Modification of the authorization request was approved in September, 1986. Ten meetings were held within the United States and internationally between September, 1984, and September, 1986. These meetings produced the draft submitted for balloting in December, 1986.

Contributors

This standard was developed by the Software Project Management Plans Working Group of the Software Engineering Standards Subcommittee of the Computer Society of the IEEE. The following individuals contributed to the development of this standard:

Richard H. Thayer, *Chairman*   **Richard E. Fairley,** *Co-Chairman*
Gary L. Whitten, *Secretary*

Steering Committee

Ronald L. Atchley	Hosein Fallah	Robert F. Metz
H. Jack Barnard	Richard Johansson	Patrick A. Rich
François Coallier	Kari Kansala	Hans Schaefer

Working Group

Bakul Banerju	Galwin Ferwin	Robert Poston
George J. Bozoki	Cheng Hu	David Schultz
V. Churchill	John A. King	Robert Shillato
Peter Coad	Thomas M. Kurihara	Daniel Solis
P. I. Davis	F. C. Lim	George Spidel
Raymond Day	Richard W. MacDonald	Richard Van Tilburg
T. Debling	Roger Martin	Delores Wallace
J. Deleo	Randy Paddock	David Weiss
Ake Dovstram	Francoise Perrodeau	Lauri Werth
R. Ferreol		Janusz Zalweski

Supporting Organizations

The following organizations provided support for development of this standard:

AT&T Bell Laboratories	National Bureau of Standards
AT&T Information Systems	NCR Corporation
Bell Canada	Programming Environments, Inc.
California State University, Sacramento	Standard Telecommunications Labs
Center for Industrial Research, Norway	System Development Corporation
Compagnie D'Informatique Militaire, France	Technical Research Centre of Finland
Computer Sciences Corporation	Teleindustrier AB, Sweden
Goodyear Atomic Corporation	U.S. Department of Commerce
Hughes Aircraft Company	U.S. Department of Transportation
Institute of Atomic Energy, Poland	U.S. Naval Research Laboratories
Intercon Systems Corporation	University of Nevada, Las Vegas
Lockheed Missiles & Space Co.	University of Texas, Austin
Mirror Systems, Inc.	Wang Institute of Graduate Studies

IEEE Standard for
Software Project Management Plans

1. Scope and References

1.1 Scope. This standard prescribes the format and content of software project management plans. A software project management plan is the controlling document for managing a software project; it defines the technical and managerial processes necessary to satisfy the project requirements.

This standard may be applied to all types of software projects. Use of this standard is not restricted by the size, complexity, or criticality of the software product. This standard is applicable to all forms of product delivery media, including firmware, embedded systems code, programmable logic arrays, and software-in-silicon. This standard can be applied to any and all segments of a software product lifecycle.

This standard identifies the minimal set of elements that shall appear in all software project management plans. In order to conform to this standard, software project management plans must adhere to the format and content for project plans specified in the standard. However, users of this standard may incorporate other elements by appending additional sections or subsections to their project management plans. In any case, the numbering scheme of the required sections and subsections must adhere to the format specified in this standard. Various sections and subsections of a software project management plan may be included in the plan by direct incorporation or by reference to other plans and documents.

This standard for software project management plans incorporates and subsumes the software development plans described in ANSI/IEEE Std 729-1983 [1][1] and ANSI/IEEE Std 730-1984 [2].

---

[1]The numbers in brackets correspond to those of the references in 1.2.

1.2 References. The standards listed here should be consulted when applying this standard. The latest revisions shall apply.

[1] ANSI/IEEE Std 729-1983, IEEE Standard Glossary of Software Engineering Terminology.[2]

[2] ANSI/IEEE Std 730-1984, IEEE Standard for Software Quality Assurance Plans.

[3] ANSI/IEEE Std 828-1983, IEEE Standard for Software Configuration Management Plans.

[4] ANSI/IEEE Std 829-1983, IEEE Standard for Software Test Documentation.

[5] ANSI/IEEE Std 983-1986, IEEE Guide for Software Quality Assurance Planning.

[6] ANSI/IEEE Std 1012-1986, IEEE Standard for Software Verification and Validation Plans.

2. Definitions

The definitions listed here establish meanings within the context of this standard. Definitions of other terms that may be appropriate within the context of this standard can be found in ANSI/IEEE Std 729-1983 [1].

activity. A major unit of work to be completed in achieving the objectives of a software project. An activity has precise starting and ending dates, incorporates a set of tasks to be completed, consumes resources, and results in work products. An activity may contain other activities in a hierarchical manner.

---

[2]ANSI/IEEE publications are available from the Sales Department, American National Standards Institute, 1430 Broadway, New York, NY 10018; or from the IEEE Service Center, 445 Hoes Lane, P.O. Box 1331, Piscataway, NJ 08855-1331.

baseline. A work product that has been formally reviewed and agreed upon, and that can be changed only through formal change control procedures. A baseline work product may form the basis for further work activity(s).

customer. The individual or organization that specifies and accepts the project deliverables. The customer may be internal or external to the parent organization of the project, and may or may not be the end user of the software product. A financial transaction between customer and developer is not necessarily implied.

project agreement. A document or set of documents agreed to by the designated authority for the project and the customer. Documents in a project agreement may include some or all of the following: a contract, a statement of work, system engineering specifications, user requirement specifications, functional specifications, the software project management plan, a business plan, or a project charter.

project deliverables. The work product(s) to be delivered to the customer. The quantities, delivery dates, and delivery locations are specified in the project agreement.

project function. An activity that spans the entire duration of a software project. Examples of project functions include project management, configuration management, quality assurance, and verification and validation.

review. A meeting at which a work product or a set of work products is presented to project personnel, managers, users, customers, or other interested parties for comment or approval.

software project. The set of all project functions, activities, and tasks, both technical and managerial, required to satisfy the terms and conditions of the project agreement. A software project may be self-contained or may be part of a larger project. A software project may span only a portion of the software product lifecycle.

software project management. The process of planning, organizing, staffing, monitoring, controlling, and leading a software project.

software project management plan. The controlling document for managing a software project. A software project management plan defines the technical and managerial project functions, activities, and tasks necessary to satisfy the requirements of a software project, as defined in the project agreement.

SPMP. Software project management plan.

task. The smallest unit of work subject to management accountability. A task is a well-defined work assignment for one or more project members. The specification of work to be accomplished in completing a task is documented in a work package. Related tasks are usually grouped to form activities.

work package. A specification for the work to be accomplished in completing an activity or task. A work package defines the work product(s), the staffing requirements, the expected duration, the resources to be used, the acceptance criteria for the work products, the name of the responsible individual, and any special considerations for the work.

work product. Any tangible item that results from a project function, activity, or task. Examples of work products include customer requirements, project plan, functional specifications, design documents, source and object code, users' manuals, installation instructions, test plans, maintenance procedures, meeting minutes, schedules, budgets, and problem reports. Some subset of the work products will form the set of project deliverables.

3. Software Project Management Plans

The individual or organization responsible for a software project shall also be responsible for the software project management plan (hereafter referred to as the SPMP). This section of the standard describes each of the essential elements of a SPMP. These elements shall be ordered in the sequence of sections and subsections prescribed in Table 1.

Table 1
Software Project Management Plan Format

Title Page
Revision Chart
Preface
Table of Contents
List of Figures
List of Tables

1. Introduction
   1.1 Project Overview
   1.2 Project Deliverables
   1.3 Evolution of the SPMP
   1.4 Reference Materials
   1.5 Definitions and Acronyms

2. Project Organization
   2.1 Process Model
   2.2 Organizational Structure
   2.3 Organizational Boundaries and Interfaces
   2.4 Project Responsibilities

3. Managerial Process
   3.1 Management Objectives and Priorities
   3.2 Assumptions, Dependencies, and Constraints
   3.3 Risk Management
   3.4 Monitoring and Controlling Mechanisms
   3.5 Staffing Plan

4. Technical Process
   4.1 Methods, Tools, and Techniques
   4.2 Software Documentation
   4.3 Project Support Functions

5. Work Packages, Schedule, and Budget
   5.1 Work Packages
   5.2 Dependencies
   5.3 Resource Requirements
   5.4 Budget and Resource Allocation
   5.5 Schedule

Additional Components

Index

Appendices

The ordering of SPMP elements presented in Table 1 is not meant to imply that the sections and subsections must be developed in that order. The order of presentation is intended for ease of use, not as a guide to the order of preparing the various elements of a SPMP. The sections and subsections of a SPMP may be included by direct incorporation or by reference to other plans and documents.

Detailed descriptions of each section and subsection in a SPMP are presented in sections 3.1 through 3.5 of this standard. Certain additional components may be included in a SPMP. Additional components are described in section 3.6.

Each version of a SPMP based on this standard shall contain a title and a revision notice sufficient to uniquely identify the document. Revision information may include the project name, version number of the plan, date of release, approval signature(s), a list of pages that have been changed in the current version of the plan, and a list of version numbers and dates of release of all previous versions of the plan.

The preface of a SPMP based on this standard shall describe the purpose, indicate the scope of activities, and identify the intended audience for the SPMP. A Table of Contents, and lists of the Figures and Tables in the SPMP shall be included in every SPMP, as indicated in Table 1.

3.1 Introduction (Section 1 of the SPMP). This section of the SPMP shall provide an overview of the project and the product, a list of project deliverables, the plan for development and evolution of the SPMP, reference materials for the SPMP, and definitions and acronyms used within the SPMP.

3.1.1 Project Overview (1.1 of the SPMP). This subsection of the SPMP shall provide a concise summary of the project objectives, the product to be delivered, major work activities, major work products, major milestones, required resources, and master schedule and budget. The project overview shall also describe the relationship of this project to other projects, as appropriate. This overview shall not be construed as an official statement of product requirements. Reference to the official statement of product requirements shall be provided in this subsection of the SPMP.

3.1.2 Project Deliverables (1.2 of the SPMP). This subsection of the SPMP shall list all of the items to be delivered to the customer, the delivery dates, delivery locations, and quantities required to satisfy the terms of the project agreement. This list of project deliverables shall not be construed as an official statement of project requirements.

3.1.3 Evolution of the SPMP (1.3 of the SPMP). This subsection of the SPMP shall specify the plans for producing both scheduled and unscheduled updates to the SPMP. Methods of disseminating the updates shall be specified. This subsection shall also specify the mechanisms used to place the initial version of the SPMP under change control and to control subsequent changes to the SPMP.

3.1.4 Reference Materials (1.4 of the SPMP). This subsection of the SPMP shall provide a complete list of all documents and other sources of information referenced in the SPMP. Each document should be identified by title, report number, date, author, and publishing organization. Other sources of information, such as electronic files, shall be identified in an unambiguous manner using identifiers such as date and version number. Any deviations from referenced standards or policies shall be identified and justifications shall be provided.

3.1.5 Definitions and Acronyms (1.5 of the SPMP). This subsection of the SPMP shall define, or provide references to the definition of all terms and acronyms required to properly interpret the SPMP.

3.2 Project Organization (Section 2 of the SPMP). This section of the SPMP shall specify the process model for the project, describe the project organizational structure, identify organizational boundaries and interfaces, and define individual responsibilities for the various project elements.

3.2.1 Process Model (2.1 of the SPMP). This subsection of the SPMP shall define the relationships among major project functions and activities by specifying the timing of major milestones, baselines, reviews, work products, project deliverables, and sign-offs that span the project. The process model may be described using a combination of graphical and textual notations. The process model must include project initiation and project termination activities.

3.2.2 Organizational Structure (2.2 of the SPMP). This subsection of the SPMP shall describe the internal management structure of the project. Graphical devices such as hierarchical organization charts or matrix diagrams may be used to depict the lines of authority, responsibility, and communication within the project.

3.2.3 Organizational Boundaries and Interfaces (2.3 of the SPMP). This subsection of the SPMP shall describe the administrative and managerial boundaries between the project and each of the following entities: the parent organization, the customer organization, subcontracted organizations, or any other organizational entities that interact with the project. In addition, the administrative and managerial interfaces of the project support functions, such as configuration management, quality assurance, and verification and validation shall be specified in this subsection.

3.2.4 Project Responsibilities (2.4 of the SPMP). This subsection of the SPMP shall identify and state the nature of each major project function and activity, and identify the individuals who are responsible for those functions and activities. A matrix of functions and activities versus responsible individuals may be used to depict project responsibilities.

3.3 Managerial Process (Section 3 of the SPMP). This section of the SPMP shall specify management objectives and priorities; project assumptions, dependencies, and constraints; risk management techniques; monitoring and controlling mechanisms to be used; and the staffing plan.

3.3.1 Management Objectives and Priorities (3.1 of the SPMP). This subsection of the SPMP shall describe the philosophy, goals, and priorities for management activities during the project. Topics to be specified may include, but are not limited to, the frequency and mechanisms of reporting to be used; the relative priorities among requirements, schedule, and budget for this project; risk management procedures to be followed; and a statement of intent to acquire, modify, or use existing software.

3.3.2 Assumptions, Dependencies, and Constraints (3.2 of the SPMP). This subsection of the SPMP shall state the assumptions on which the project is based, the external events the project is dependent upon, and the constraints under which the project is to be conducted.

3.3.3 Risk Management (3.3 of the SPMP). This subsection of the SPMP shall identify and assess the risk factors associated with the project. This subsection shall also prescribe mechanisms for tracking the various risk factors and implementing contingency plans. Risk factors that should be considered include contractual risks, technological risks, risks due to size and complexity of the product, risks in personnel acquisition and retention, and risks in achieving customer acceptance of the product.

3.3.4 Monitoring and Controlling Mechanisms (3.4 of the SPMP). This subsection of the SPMP shall define the reporting mechanisms, report formats, information flows, review and audit mechanisms, and other tools and techniques to be used in monitoring and controlling adherence to the SPMP. Project monitoring should occur at the level of work packages. The relationship of monitoring and controlling mechanisms to the project support functions shall be delineated in this subsection of the SPMP (see 3.4.3).

3.3.5 Staffing Plan (3.5 of the SPMP). This subsection of the SPMP shall specify the numbers and types of personnel required to conduct the project. Required skill levels, start times, duration of need, and methods for obtaining, training, retaining, and phasing out of personnel shall be specified.

3.4 Technical Process (Section 4 of the SPMP). This section of the SPMP shall specify the technical methods, tools, and techniques to be used on the project. In addition, the plan for software documentation shall be specified, and plans for project support functions such as quality assurance, configuration management, and verification and validation may be specified.

3.4.1 Methods, Tools, and Techniques (4.1 of the SPMP). This subsection of the SPMP shall specify the computing system(s), development methodology(s), team structure(s), programming language(s), and other notations, tools, techniques, and methods to be used to specify, design, build, test, integrate, document, deliver, modify or maintain or both (as appropriate) the project deliverables. In addition, the technical standards, policies, and procedures governing development or modification or both of the work products and project deliverables shall be included, either directly or by reference to other documents.

3.4.2 Software Documentation (4.2 of the SPMP). This subsection of the SPMP shall contain either directly or by reference, the documentation plan for the software project. The documentation plan shall specify the documentation requirements, and the milestones, baselines, reviews, and sign-offs for software documentation. The documentation plan may also contain a style guide, naming conventions and documentation formats. The documentation plan shall provide a summary of the schedule and resource requirements for the documentation effort. ANSI/IEEE Std 829-1983 [4] provides a standard for software test documentation.

3.4.3 Project Support Functions (4.3 of the SPMP). This subsection of the SPMP shall contain, either directly or by reference, plans for the supporting functions for the software project. These functions may include, but are not limited to, configuration management [3]; software quality assurance [2] and [5]; and verification and validation [6]. Plans for project support functions shall be developed to a level of detail consistent with the other sections of the SPMP. In particular, the responsibilities, resource requirements, schedules, and budgets for each supporting function shall be specified. The nature and type of support functions required will vary from project to project; however, the absence of a software quality assurance, configuration management, or verification and validation plan shall be explicitly justified in project plans that do not include them.

3.5 Work Packages, Schedule, and Budget (Section 5 of the SPMP). This section of the SPMP shall specify the work packages, identify the dependency relationships among them, state the resource requirements, provide the allocation of budget and resources to work packages, and establish a project schedule.

3.5.1 Work Packages (5.1 of the SPMP). This subsection of the SPMP shall specify the work packages for the activities and tasks that must be completed in order to satisfy the project agreement. Each work package shall be uniquely identified; identification may be based on a numbering scheme and descriptive titles. A diagram depicting the breakdown of activities into subactivities and tasks (a work breakdown structure) may be used to depict hierarchical relationships among work packages.

3.5.2 Dependencies (5.2 of the SPMP). This subsection of the SPMP shall specify the ordering relations among work packages to account for interdependencies among them and dependencies on external events. Techniques such as dependency lists, activity networks, and the critical path method may be used to depict dependencies among work packages.

3.5.3 Resource Requirements (5.3 of the SPMP). This subsection of the SPMP shall provide, as a function of time, estimates of the total resources required to complete the project. Numbers and types of personnel, computer time, support software, computer hardware, office and laboratory facilities, travel, and maintenance requirements for the project resources are typical resources that should be specified.

3.5.4 Budget and Resource Allocation (5.4 of the SPMP). This subsection of the SPMP shall specify the allocation of budget and resources to the various project functions, activities, and tasks. An earned value scheme may be used to allocate budget and resources, and to track expenditures and resource utilization.

3.5.5 Schedule (5.5 of the SPMP). This subsection of the SPMP shall provide the schedule for the various project functions, activities, and tasks, taking into account the precedence relations and the required milestone dates. Schedules may be expressed in absolute calendar time or in increments relative to a key project milestone.

3.6 Additional Components. Certain additional components may be required. These may be included by appending additional sections or subsections to the SPMP. However, the numbering scheme for the required sections and subsections must adhere to the format specified in this standard. Additional items of importance on any particular project may include subcontractor management plans, security plans, independent verification and validation plans, training plans, hardware procurement plans, facilities plans, installation plans, data conversion plans, system transition plans, or the product maintenance plan. If present, additional components must be developed in a format and to a level of detail consistent with the required sections of the SPMP.

3.6.1 Index. An index to the key terms and acronyms used throughout the SPMP is optional, but recommended to improve usability of the SPMP.

3.6.2 Appendices. Appendices may be included, either directly or by reference, to provide supporting details that could detract from the SPMP if included in the body of the SPMP.

Glossary of Management Terms

This glossary defines key terms used in this tutorial. By design, it is neither complete nor comprehensive. That would be impossible to accomplish because of the breadth of the field. Instead, it was developed to explain terms which may be new or foreign to our more technical readers.

The approximate 120 entries in the glossary are arranged alphabetically. An entry may consist of a single word, such as management, or a phrase, such as configuration management. Phrases are given in their natural order (project management) instead of being reversed (management, project). Terms are spelled out prior to placing their acronyms or abbreviations in parenthesis. If a term has more than one commonly accepted definition, several explanations may be listed. Ordering for these listings is random and does not convey preference. Where necessary, examples and notes have been included to clarify definition of terms.

The source for most definitions is the following two IEEE documents:

1. IEEE Standard Glossary of Software Engineering Terminology, Institute of Electrical and Electronics Engineers, 1983.

2. Glossary of Software Engineering Terminology, ANSI/IEEE Std 610.12-1990, Institute of Electrical and Electronics Engineers, 1990.

In those cases where a definition is taken from another source, the reference is cited in brackets "[ ]" following the entry. A list of these references is included at the end of this glossary.

Definitions

Acceptance: In acquisition management, the official act by which the customer accepts transfer, title, and delivery of any item specified as part of the contract.

Acceptance criteria: The criteria a system or component must satisfy in order to be accepted by a user, customer, or other party.

Acquisition management: The management of third parties who generate products or perform services under contract.

Activity: A major unit of work to be completed in achieving the goals of a software project. An activity has precise starting and ending dates, incorporates a set of tasks to be done, consumes resources, and results in work products. An activity may contain other activities arranged in a hierarchical manner.

Allocation: In management, the process of allotting resource budgets to performing organizations.

Allocated baseline: In configuration management, the initial approved specifications governing the development of configuration items that are part of a higher level configuration.

Application: A system which provides a set of services which solve some type of user problem [1].

Asset: Units of information of current or future value to a software development which can be capitalized or depreciated over a multiple year time period to recoup its cost [1].

Audit: An independent examination of a work product or set of work products to assess compliance with specifications, standards, contracts, or other criteria.

Authority: In project management, the right to give direction and allocate resources (staff, schedule, etc.). This right should be commensurate with responsibility.

Baseline: A work product that has been formally reviewed and agreed upon and that can be changed only through formal change control procedures. A baseline work product may form the basis for further work activity(s).

Benchmark: In management, an industry-wide or organizational standard against which performance measurements or improvement comparisons are made.

Budget: In management, a statement of expected results expressed in numerical terms [2].

Build: An operational version of a software product which includes a specified subset of the capabilities provided by the final product.

Collaborative development: A development process characterized as a cooperative team effort that often crosses organizational or geographic boundaries [2].

Commitment: An obligation to expend resource at some future time, such as a purchase order or travel authorization, which is charged against a budget although it has not yet been paid.

Computer Aided Software Engineering (CASE): The use of computers to aid in the software engineering process. May include the application of tools to software design, requirements tracing, code production, testing, document generation, and other software engineering activities.

Configuration Management (CM): A discipline applying technical and administrative direction and surveillance to identify and document both the functional and physical characteristics of a configuration item, control changes to these characteristics, record and report change processing and implementation status, and verify compliance with requirements.

Contingency: In management, an amount of design margin, time, or money used as a safety factor to accommodate future growth and uncertainty.

Controlling: Those management activities conducted to determine whether or not progress is being made according to plan. Control involves measuring, monitoring and acting on information obtained throughout the development to correct deviations, focus resources, and mitigate risk.

Costing: In management, the process of developing a cost estimate for an item, task, or activity. Costing and pricing are separate by related activities typically done by different people.

Cost-benefit analysis: Management tradeoffs normally conducted to determine whether or not the benefits which accrue to alternatives are worth the costs involved.

Cost center: An organization to which control over resources has been assigned and to which budgets and profitability goals have been made.

Computer Software Configuration Item (CSCI): An aggregation of software that is designated for configuration management.

Critical path: In a network diagram, the longest path from start to finish or the path which doesn't have any slack, thus the path corresponding to the shortest time in which the project can be completed.

Critical Path Method (CPM): In project management, a technique used to determine the critical path through a cost or schedule network diagram.

Customer: The individual or organization that specifies and accepts the project deliverables. The customer may be internal or external to the parent organization and may or may not be the end user of the software product. A financial transaction between customer and developer is not necessarily implied.

Deliverable: The end product or service which is specified by and delivered to a customer or user.

Delivery: Release of a system or component to its customer or user.

Design review: A process or meeting during which the system, hardware, or software design is presented to project personnel, managers, customers, users, or other interested parties for comment or approval.

Directing: Those management activities conducted to energize, motivate, and guide personnel to achieve organizational goals.

Domain: A set of problems with similar requirements for which a corresponding set of similar software systems (a program family) might be developed. As an example, an inventory system is within the manufacturing domain [1].

Domain analysis: The software system engineering discipline that identifies, acquires, organizes, and models information within a problem domain and produces requirements for reusable components.

Domain engineering: The construction of components, methods, and tools and their supporting documentation to solve the problems of system development/maintenance by the application of the knowledge in the domain model and software architectures [1].

Earned value: In project management, a technique used to assess progress and budgetary performance using milestone completions. Actuals and projections are compared to earned value to compute trends and variances.

Education: The communication of knowledge to interested parties. Quite different from training where the aim is developing those skills and abilities needed to perform a job [2].

Error: (1) The difference between the computed, observed, or measured value or condition and the true, theoretically correct, or specified value or condition, (2) An incorrect step, process or data definition, (3) An incorrect result, (4) A human action which produces an incorrect result.

Feedback: In management, the acquisition of that information needed to ascertain status or progress.

Forecasting: In management, the prediction of future events. Forecasts differ from estimates in terms of the means used to derive them and their accuracy. For example, an estimate of the area of a curve is quite different from a market forecast.

Functional baseline: In configuration management, the initial approved technical documentation for a configuration item.

Functional organization: An organization form that groups people by skill or specialty (such as software or hardware engineering) in one department, reporting to a single manager.

Independent Verification & Validation (IV&V): Verification and validation of a software product by some organization that is technically, managerially, and financially independent of the development organization.

Indicators: In management, a device which identifies a prescribed state of affairs relative to managerial or financial performance.

Inspection: A formal evaluation technique in which software products are examined in detail by a person or group other than the author to detect faults, violations of standards, and other problems.

Leadership: In management, the ability to influence the behavior of others and focus it towards accepted goals.

Legacy: Reusable software developed on one program that has potential for use on another program. For example, algorithms developed on one program may be candidates for another if similar equipment is employed and the algorithms were designed to be reused [1].

Leveling: In management, the process of adjusting schedules to smooth out the staffing curves.

Life cycle: The period of time that starts when a software product is conceived and ends when that product is retired from use.

Line organization: That part of the functional organization to which the authority for performing a task has been delegated.

Management: Getting things done through the work of other people.

Management reserve: In project management, resources set aside for contingency purposes.

Manager: The person charged with the job of planning, organizing, staffing, directing, and controlling the activities of others.

Matrix organization: A combination of functional and project forms of organization where the line is responsible for providing skills and the project is responsible for budgets and programmatic performance.

Measurement: In project management, the process of collecting, analyzing, and reporting metrics data useful in assessing status, progress, and trends.

Metric: A quantitative measure of the degree to which a system, process, or component possesses a given attribute. For example, error density is an indicator of software reliability.

Milestone: A schedule event for which some project member or manager is held accountable and that is used to measure progress.

Monitoring: In management, keeping constant surveillance over and track of what is actually happening on a project.

Motivation: In management, the act of influencing the behavior of others through the combined use of incentives and rewards.

Object: An element of the software Work Breakdown Structure (WBS) derived using the criteria of information hiding and abstraction. An object typically maintains complete internal knowledge of its own state and reveals hidden information through a set of services or methods. A primitive object consists of some data, a group of operations on that data, and a mechanism for selecting an operation given a command [2].

Organizing: Those management activities conducted to structure efforts that involve collaboration and communication so that it is effectively performed.

Ownership: In management, the degree to which an individual or group buys into plans established to which they are performing against.

Performance: In management, a measure of a manager's ability to achieve goals and realize forecasts.

Planning: Those management activities conducted to establish future courses of action at all levels of the organization. At the top, plans tend to be strategic. At lower levels, plans are more tactical. At both levels, plans establish the baselines against which progress is measured.

Policy: General statements or understandings developed at a corporate level to channel thinking and decision making.

Position: In management, the specific role an individual plays within an organization.

Power: In management, the perceived ability of one person to influence the actions of others.

Practice: A preferred course of action for getting a job done.

Pricing: In management, the process of determining how much to charge a customer or user for products or services. Costing and pricing are separate activities. Organizations can price services at less than their cost and still make a profit.

Procedure: Guides to action that provide a structure for the activity to be accomplished.

Process: A series of steps, actions, or activities ordered to bring about a desired result [1].

Process management: The direction, control, and coordination of the work performed to develop a product or perform a service.

Process maturity: A relative assessment of an organization's ability to achieve its goals through the technical and managerial processes it uses to develop its products and services.

Product baseline: In configuration management, the approved technical documentation (including, for software, the source code) defining a configuration item during the production, operation, maintenance, and logistics support phases of its life cycle.

Productivity: In economics, productivity is defined as the ratio of output to input so that the efficiency and effectiveness with which resources (personnel, equipment, facilities, etc.) are used to produce output of value can be calculated.

Product: The output of a process. Can be a either deliverable or something used internal to a project.

Program Evaluation and Review Technique (PERT): A form of the critical path method devised by the Navy which uses probabilistic estimates to compute the quickest way through the network.

Program Manager (PM): A person who manages several aligned projects.

Project: An organized undertaking which uses human and physical resources, done once, to accomplish a specific goal.

Project leader: A person who is tasked with supervising a part of a project.

Project management: The system of management established to focus resources on achieving project goals. In actuality, project management is the art of creating the illusion that any outcome is the result of a series of predetermined, deliberate acts when, in fact, it was luck [3].

Project manager: A person who is held responsible for planning, controlling, and directing project activities. Many times, these responsibilities involve coordinating and integrating activities across functional units.

Project organization: The form of organization in which all of the people working on the project report to the project manager.

Quality: The totality of features and characteristics of a product or service that bears on its ability to satisfy given needs or customer requirements.

Quality Assurance (QA): A planned and systematic pattern of all actions necessary to provide adequate confidence that the item or product conforms to established technical requirements.

Rapid prototyping: A type of prototyping in which emphasis is placed on developing prototypes early in the life cycle to permit early feedback and analysis in support of the development process.

Receivables: Those products generated in one phase to form the basis of development in another phase of the life cycle.

Requirement: A condition or capability needed by a user to solve a problem or achieve an objective.

Resources: In management, the time, staff, capital, and money available to perform a service or build a product.

Resource management: The identification, estimation, allocation, and monitoring of the means used to develop a product or perform a service.

Responsibility: In management, responsibility infers obligation, not authority to perform a task. In other words, responsibility relates to duties, both real and imaginary, that one feels obliged to perform.

Reusable: The ability of or extent to which a software component can be reused across multiple applications. To be meaningful, the software property "reusable" must be measurable [2].

Reusable Software Component (RSC): Life cycle products that are created during the software development process that are needed to operate, maintain, and upgrade deliverable systems during their lifetime and that have potential for reuse. The components may include, but are not limited to: requirements, architectures, designs, algorithms, source and object code, tests, tools, and document fragments. Components may be textual, graphical, or both. They are usually stored in electronic media [2].

Reuse: The activity associated with using a Reusable Software Component developed by one program on either another program and/or within a different release on the same program. To occur, reuse must be shown to have taken place in some quantifiable manner [2].

Reuse Engineering: Those engineering activities performed to develop and/or use Reusable Software Components. The key elements of a software reuse program include: a well-defined process, supportive standards and guides, meaningful reviews, metrics, mature methods, and tools that are part of the Software Engineering Environment [2].

Review: A process or meeting during which a work product, or set of work products, is presented to project personnel, managers, customers, users, or other interested parties for comment.

Risk: Refers to those factors, both technical and managerial, that are threats to success and/or major sources of problems.

Risk management: The process of identifying, analyzing, quantifying, and developing plans to eliminate risk before it does any harm on a project.

Rules: Specific actions that you are required to take without respect to the situation.

Schedule: The actual calendar time budgeted for accomplishing the goals established for the tasks at hand.

Scheduling: The process of allocating and interrelating tasks to the schedule. This activity is like figuring out a jigsaw puzzle especially when many of the tasks need to be done in parallel. Some form of network, like a PERT chart, usually is extremely helpful in the conduct of the process.

Software: Computer programs, procedures, rules, and possibly associated documentation and data pertaining to the operation of a computer system.

Software Development Library (SDL): A software library which contains computer readable and human readable information relevant to a software development effort.

Software development methodology: The overall approach selected to manage the development of software. Hopefully, an integrated set of methods supported by mature standards, practices, and tools will be used.

Software Engineering Environment (SEE): The hardware, software, and firmware used to perform a software development effort. Typical elements of a SEE include computer equipment, compilers, assemblers, operating systems, debuggers, simulators, test tools, documentation tools, and database managers.

Software Reuse Library (SRL): Part of the Software Engineering Environment (SEE) used for storage and maintenance of reusable components that have the real potential for reuse on multiple development efforts [2].

Spiral development: A software development process in which activities — normally requirements analysis, architectural design, implementation, and testing — are performed iteratively until the software is completed.

Staff: Those skilled persons assigned to an organization who are available to perform tasks.

Staffing: Those management activities conducted to acquire, develop, and retain staff resources for the organization.

Standard: Mandatory requirements employed and enforced to force a disciplined and uniform approach to software development; that is, mandatory conventions and practices are in fact standards.

Task: In project management, the smallest unit of work subject to management accountability. A task contains a well-defined work assignment for one or more project members. The specification of work needed to complete a task is documented in a work package. Related tasks are usually grouped to form activities.

Total Quality Management (TQM): A modern philosophy of management where quality becomes the primary concern and goal in system development.

Tracking: In project management, the process of identifying cost and schedule variances by comparing actuals to projections.

Training: The planned development of skills and abilities needed by personnel to perform their jobs.

Uncertainty: In management, the degree of entropy associated with the information used to make a decision.

Validation: The process of evaluating a system or component at the end of the development process to determine whether or not it satisfies specified requirements.

Verification: The process of evaluating a system or component to determine whether or not the products of a given development phase satisfy the conditions imposed at the start of that phase.

Walk-through: A review process in which the developer leads one or more members of the software team through a segment of design or implementation to uncover errors, violations of standards, and other problems.

Work Breakdown Structure (WBS): A family tree that organizes, defines, and graphically illustrates the products, services, or tasks necessary to achieve project objectives.

Work instructions: Step-by-step procedures devised to be followed that perform a specific task. They are much more detailed than procedures.

Work package: A specification of the work to be accomplished in completing a function, activity, or task. A work package defines the work product(s), the staffing needs, the expected duration, the resources to be used, the acceptance criteria for the work products, the name of the responsible individual, and any special considerations for the work.

References

1. D.J. Reifer, *Joint Integrated Avionics Working Group Glossary of Reuse Terms,* RCI-TN-438A, Revision 1, 26 February 1990.

2. D.J. Reifer, *Software Jargon Unraveled,* RCI-TR-014, Prepared for Texas Instruments, Revision 1, 7 October 1988.

3. H. Kerzner, *Project Management for Executives,* Van Nostrand Reinhold, New York, N.Y., 1982.

Annotated Software Management Bibliography

This short bibliography provides the reader with a list of references on software management-related topics. Entries were selected based upon their readability and practicality. The list is aimed at providing the reader with references which will help them perform their managerial tasks.

H.R. Berlack, *Software Configuration Management,* John Wiley & Sons, New York, N.Y., 1992. This book provides a comprehensive and complete discussion of the topic of software configuration management. The topics of configuration identification, change control, status accounting, library management, and configuration auditing are discussed simply and with a focus on implementation. A special section on automation is provided

B.W. Boehm, *Software Engineering Economics,* Prentice-Hall, Englewood Cliffs, N.J., 1981. This classic text discusses the issues, experiences, and methods used within the field of software cost estimation and life cycle management. It goes on to describe the COnstructive COst MOdel (COCOMO) software estimation model and the factors, constraints, and mathematical formulas upon which it is based. It shows how the model can be used to generate resource inputs to help managers plan and control their projects.

B.W. Boehm, *Software Risk Management,* IEEE CS Press, Los Alamitos, Calif., 1989. This recent collection of papers was assembled to introduce the reader to the topic of risk management: its fundamentals, its processes, and its resolution mechanisms. The book provides a well organized, pragmatic, and comprehensive treatment of this important topic. Its case studies and annotated bibliography add to its depth and breadth. The tutorial contains a lot of material that would be difficult to obtain through other means. Well worth acquiring and reading.

F.P. Brooks, Jr., *The Mythical Man-Month: Essays on Software Engineering,* Addison-Wesley, Reading, Mass., 1975. This well-written monogram discusses the problems and pitfalls that beset the author as he managed the development of the IBM 360 operating system. Although somewhat dated, this classic is well-written and full of sound advice. It holds the distinction of being the software text that has supposedly sold the most copies.

R.C. Camp, *Benchmarking,* ASQC Quality Press, Milwaukee, WI, 1989. This book is about benchmarking, the continuous process of measuring products, services, and practices against the toughest competitors or those companies recognized as industry leaders. It is important because it provides practical guidance to change agents working within software organizations to set realistic, but aggressive goals for process and quality improvement. The book is readable, enjoyable and enlightening.

T. DeMarco, *Controlling Software Projects,* Yourdon Press, New York, N.Y., 1982. This book's message is that measurement is an inseparable part of the planning and control process. It stresses the need to define metrics and establish a measurement program. It advocates that the measurement and estimation be linked to improve project planning and control.

T. DeMarco and T. Lister, *Peopleware,* Dorset House, New York, N.Y., 1987. Another DeMarco classic which challenges the myth that technology is the cornerstone of productivity. The book focuses on people and human behavior. It makes you think about the things that you need to do to enable your people to work together more effectively. The presentation is witty and entertaining. The advice provided is practical as is the book's theme — work smarter, not harder. Well worth your time.

J.A. Edosomwan, *Integrating Innovation and Technology Management,* John Wiley & Sons, New York, N.Y., 1989. This book is about managing innovation, change, and technology transfer. It surveys current practices and looks at management's role in stimulating creativity. This book is an idea generator. After you read it, don't be surprised if its notions stay with you for many days. It is well written and provides numerous real-life examples and case studies.

D.P. Freedman and G.M. Weinberg, *Handbook of Walkthroughs, Inspections and Technical Reviews*, (Third Edition), Little, Brown and Company, Boston, Mass., 1982. This handbook discusses the topic of technical reviews and the mechanics of successfully conducting them. It provides answers to the questions: "What do I do to get ready for a review?"; "Who do I invite?"; "How do I conduct the review?"; and "How do I interpret the results?". The book is well written, easy to use, and insightful.

T. Gilb, *Principles of Software Engineering Management,* Addison-Wesley, Reading, Mass., 1988. This book provides practical management guidelines for the key success factors in software engineering. Its emphasis is quality and its focus evolutionary methods. Proven principles form a foundation which were developed to help practitioners overcome deadline pressures and deliver high quality products on-time and within budget.

R.B. Grady and D.L. Caswell, *Software Metrics: Establishing a Company-Wide Program,* Prentice-Hall, Englewood Cliffs, N.J., 1987. This is the most readable book I've encountered on the topic of metrics and measurement. It describes how the authors sold, developed, implemented, and continued to improve a metrics program within Hewlett-Packard. It is insightful and extremely pragmatic in its views. It provides many aids including briefing charts that were used, metrics definitions, and checklists. A must for those venturing forth into the realm of software metrics and measurement.

H. Dines Hanson, *Up and Running,* Yourdon Press, New York, N.Y. 1984. This monograph describes how structured techniques were used to make an electronic bond system project a success. It shows how good software engineering and management methods can be combined to create a framework that allows a manager to assess the progress of the project and the quality of the products that it is producing throughout the development.

W.S. Humphrey, *Managing the Software Process,* Addison-Wesley, Reading, Mass., 1989. This text provides practical guidelines for assessing and improving the processes used for software development and maintenance. It uses a five level layered maturity model as an evaluation framework. Key technical and management practices associated with each level are noted along with the criteria to determine how good they are. Methods and actions needed to establish control over and improve the process are also provided.

P.L. Hunsaker and A.J. Alessandra, *The Art of Managing People,* Prentice-Hall, Englewood Cliffs, N.J., 1980. This book discusses people and how to deal with them under different situations. It emphasizes the need for interaction and discusses modern techniques for effective listening, questioning, projecting, and problem solving. The book states things simply and has some profound messages.

M. Imai, *Kaizen,* McGraw-Hill, New York, N.Y., 1986. Those intrigued by Japanese management successes are referred to this text which explains how to put sixteen Kaizen principles (just-in-time, quality first, zero defects, quality deployment, etc.) to work under a variety of situations. Communications is enhanced by the over 100 examples, 15 case studies, and 50 illustrations used within the work.

H. Kerzner, *Project Management for Executives,* Van Nostrand Reinhold Company, New York, N.Y., 1982. Using a hands-on approach to management, this text answers typical questions posed by executives about the systems, practices, standards, tools, and organizational forms used to implement the concepts of project management. All facets of project management are thoroughly explained including approaches that can be used to assess performance and develop skills on the parts of its practitioners. Anyone who reads this book could profit from its breadth and depth of coverage.

J.J. Marciniak and D.J. Reifer, *Software Acquisition Management,* John Wiley & Sons, New York, N.Y., 1990. This book describes management practices used by organizations who acquire software systems contractually for their users. Using a buyer versus seller model, it covers the entire acquisition life cycle from competitive award until system retirement. It explains the contractual and legal aspects of the cycle and provides readers with tips on how to maintain visibility and control over those third parties who develop software under contract.

D. McGregor, *The Human Side of Enterprise,* McGraw-Hill, New York, N.Y., 1960. Another of the classic texts on management. This book discusses Theory X versus Theory Y, which is important because it serves as the basis for understanding motivation theory. It identifies those items under a manager's control which can be used to motivate software professionals. Theory Z (see Reference 20 by Ouchi) extends McGregor's theory with a more modern team-oriented view of management. Try to read this one first as it sets the stage for the other.

P.W. Metzger, *Managing a Programming Project* (Second Edition), Prentice-Hall, Englewood Cliffs, N.J., 1981. This textbook describes how classical project management techniques can be related to software life cycle processes to generate visible products that satisfy user requirements. The book emphasizes the practical by providing many checklists and outlines for deliverables. Tasks and products are described in detail and related to project management techniques in this easy to understand and use volume. Although somewhat dated, the book is still useful and worth reading.

W. Ouchi, *Theory Z: How American Business Can Meet the Japanese Challenge,* Addison-Wesley, Reading, Mass., 1981. Another management classic that is worth reading. This book discusses how American firms could learn from the Japanese to make their work environments more socially attractive and to motivate their employees to greater productivity. The book compares US and Japanese employer roles and attitudes and shows how they can be combined to create a humanistic philosophy of management directed towards mutually beneficial common goals within both cultures.

T.J. Peters and R.H. Waterman, Jr., *In Search of Excellence,* Harper & Row, New York, N.Y., 1982. This classic, which advocates a return to the basics of management, advances strategies which firms could follow to be successful. Some of its messages to managers include: "have a bias for action"; "be close to your customer"; "keep a lean, but mean staff"; "employ a hands-on, value-driven style"; and "achieve productivity improvement by providing your key producers with the means to excel". If you have not read a Peters book, this one would be a good one to start off with.

L.H. Putnam and W. Meyers, *Measures for Excellence: Reliable Software On Time and Within Budget,* Prentice-Hall, Englewood Cliffs, N.J., 1991. This text discusses the issues, experiences and challenges involved in estimating the cost, duration, and quality of software developments. A very detailed treatment of the popular SLIM cost estimation model is provided along with an explanation of the philosophies upon which it was built. Many useful suggestions are offered relative to collecting cost and productivity data and analyzing it. Well written and perceptive.

M.D. Rosenau, Jr., *Successful Project Management,* Lifetime Learning Publications, Belmont, Calif., 1981. A very well-written text for the beginner on the topics of planning and control. A step-by-step recipe for project management is provided along with examples of where it works and where it doesn't. Well organized and supported by numerous examples and good illustrations.

T.A. Rullo, *Advances in Computer Programming Management,* Vol. 1, Heyden & Sons, Philadelphia, Penn., 1980. Another collection of papers that discusses the many aspects of software engineering management. Unfortunately, it tries to do this in an ad hoc manner. As a result, it is somewhat disjointed. Many of the papers tend to be theoretical, although they seem full of common sense.

C.M. Savage, *5th Generation Management,* Digital Press, Maynard, Mass., 1990. This text advocates replacing current management thinking with a new set of principles based upon peer-to-peer networking, integrative processes, concurrent engineering, and virtual task forces to empower teams of concerned individuals to achieve technological flexibility and market agility. An important work that harmonizes an organizational philosophy based upon people with marketplace tendencies.

G.G. Schulmeyer and J.I. McManus, *Handbook of Software Quality Assurance,* Van Nostrand Reinhold Company, New York, N.Y., 1987. This handbook clearly explains all aspects of software quality assurance from management through tools and techniques, including those peculiar to the quality like Pareto analysis and statistical quality controls. It is straightforward and perceptive, especially with regards to industry trends. In addition, it describes interfaces with related disciplines like configuration and reliability management.

G.G. Schulmeyer, *Zero Defect Software,* Van Nostrand Reinhold Company, New York, N.Y., 1990. This book argues for the application of statistical inspection and control principles for progressive software error detection, reduction and elimination. It challenges conventional wisdom by advocating a new approach for software quality assurance. For those interested in Total Quality Management (TQM) for software, reading this text is a must.

P.C. Semprevivo, *Teams in Information Systems Development,* Yourdon Press, New York, N.Y. 1980. This monograph presents a thorough approach to organizing, structuring, evaluating, and improving team performance when building information systems. Guidelines presented throughout the text are useful as are the checklists provided to help put them into action. The emphasis of the book on the people aspects of productivity is to be commended.

M. Spiner, *Elements of Project Management,* Prentice-Hall, Englewood Cliffs, N.J., 1981. This textbook describes the fundamentals of PERT/CPM (Program Evaluation and Review Technique/Critical Path Networks) in a simple, but effective manner. The book is short, focused, and readable. It illustrates the effective use of PERT/CPM networks for planning, scheduling, and control through simple examples.

R. Thomsett, *People and Project Management,* Yourdon Press, New York, N.Y., 1980. This monograph is a well-written, nicely illustrated, thought provoking treatise on the interface between people and methods within a project management environment. The book is good reading, but is too short and provides too little detail. It is hard to put the concepts recommended into practice in most operational settings.

G.M. Weinberg, *The Secrets of Consulting,* Dorset House, New York, N.Y. 1985. This witty and insightful text provides advice on how to deal with people. It is down to earth and full of pointers on change and change management. Its underlying premise is that a software consultant is really a change agent. It uses memorable rules, laws, and principles to show the path to success under often trying circumstances.

D. Whitgift, *Methods and Tools for Software Configuration Management,* John Wiley & Sons, New York, N.Y., 1991. This book discusses the concepts, principles and practices of software configuration management with emphasis on the role of software tools. All of the functions are illustrated using examples or case studies. The DSEE (Domain Software Engineering Environment) second generation environment from HP (Hewlett-Packard) is used as an extended example to discuss how release management and version control are done in practice.

D.P. Youll, *Making Software Development Visible,* John Wiley & Sons, New York, N.Y. 1990. This book discusses the concepts, principles, and practices of software configuration management with emphasis on the role of software tools. All of the functions are illustrated using examples or case studies. The DSEE (Domain Software Engineering Environment) from Hewlett-Packard and the Rational CMVC (Configuration Management and Version Control) environment are used as extended examples to show how release management and version control are done in practice using state-of-the-art tools.

Author Biography

Donald J. Reifer holds a BS in electrical engineering from New Jersey Institute of Technology, an MS in operations research from the University of Southern California, and the Certificate in Business Management from the University of California at Los Angeles. He is an internationally recognized expert in the fields of software engineering and management, with over 23 years of experience in both industry and government. He has successfully managed large projects, served on source selections, wrote winning proposals, and led project recovery teams.

While affiliated with TRW, he was the Deputy Program Manager for Global Positioning Satellite (GPS) verification and validation projects. As a Software Director with the Aerospace Corporation, he managed over $800 million in software contracts for the Space Transportation System (Space Shuttle) Directorate. As a Project Leader at Hughes Aircraft, he managed several major weapons system developments. Currently President of RCI, a software consulting firm, he directs efforts aimed at helping Fortune 500 firms and government agencies to effectively manage large software projects, organizations, and technology introduction.

Over the past ten years, he has developed software productivity and quality improvement strategies for use worldwide. He has also helped to create successful product and marketing strategies for other high technology firms. He has conducted market surveys, worked with investment firms, and served as a software advisor to executives throughout industry.

He is the author of over 100 papers and four books on software engineering and management topics. He is a Senior Member of the IEEE Computer Society and a member of the Association for Computing Machinery and International Society of Parametric Analysts. He is active professionally and serves as an Editor for the *Journal of Systems and Software*. He is an ACM national lecturer and a past member of the Board of Directors of the Ada Software Alliance. His many honors include being listed in Who's Who in the West, the NASA Distinguished Service Medal, and the Hughes Aircraft Company Masters Fellowship.

BEST SELLERS

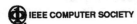 

PUBLISH WITH IEEE COMPUTER SOCIETY PRESS

TODAY'S COMPUTER SCIENCE PROFESSIONALS ARE TURNING TO US TO PUBLISH THEIR TEXTS

BENEFITS OF IEEE COMPUTER SOCIETY PRESS PUBLISHING :

- ❑ **Timely publication schedules**
- ❑ **Society's professional reputation and recognition**
- ❑ **High-quality, reasonably priced books**
- ❑ **Course classroom adoption**
- ❑ **Open options on the type and level of publication to develop**
- ❑ **Built-in mechanisms to reach a strong constituency of professionals**
- ❑ **Peer review and reference**

Enjoy the personal, professional, and financial recognition of having your name in print alongside other respected professionals in the fields of computer and engineering technology. Our rapid turnaround (from approved proposal to the published product) assures you against publication of dated technical material, and gives you the potential for additional royalties and sales from new editions. Your royalty payments are based not only on sales, but also on the amount of time and effort you expend in writing original material for your book.

Your book will be advertised to a vast audience through IEEE Computer Society Press catalogs and brochures that reach over 500,000 carefully chosen professionals in numerous disciplines. Our wide distribution also includes promotional programs through our European and Asian offices, and over-the-counter sales at 50 international computer and engineering conferences annually.

IEEE Computer Society Press books have a proven sales record, and our tutorials enjoy a unique niche in today's fast moving technical fields and help us maintain our goal to publish up-to-date, viable computer science information.

Steps for Book Submittals:

1- Submit your proposal to the Editorial Director of IEEE Computer Society Press. It should include the following data: title; your name, address, and telephone number; a detailed outline; a summary of the subject matter; a statement of the technical level of the book, the intended audience, and the potential market; a table of contents including the titles, authors, and sources for all reprints; and a biography.

2- Upon acceptance of your proposal, prepare and submit copies of the completed manuscript, including xerox copies of any reprinted papers and any other pertinent information, and mail to the Editorial Director of IEEE Computer Society Press.

3- The manuscript will then be reviewed by other respected experts in the field, and the editor-in-charge.

4- Upon publication, you will receive an initial royalty payment with additional royalties based on a percentage of the net sales and on the amount of original material included in the book.

We are searching for authors in the following computer science areas:

ADA	LOCAL AREA NETWORKS
ARCHITECTURE	OPTICAL STORAGE DATABASES
ARTIFICIAL INTELLIGENCE	PARALLEL PROCESSING
AUTOMATED TEST EQUIPMENT	PATTERN RECOGNITION
CAD / CAE	PERSONAL COMPUTING
COMPUTER GRAPHICS	RELIABILITY
COMPUTER LANGUAGES	ROBOTICS
COMPUTER MATHEMATICS	SOFTWARE ENGINEERING
COMPUTER WORKSTATIONS	SOFTWARE ENVIRONMENTS
DATABASE ENGINEERING	SOFTWARE MAINTENANCE
DIGITAL IMAGE PROCESSING	SOFTWARE TESTING AND
DISTRIBUTED PROCESSING	VALIDATION
EXPERT SYSTEMS	AND OTHER AREAS AT THE
FAULT-TOLERANT COMPUTING	FOREFRONT OF
IMAGING	COMPUTING TECHNOLOGY !

Interested ?

For more detailed guidelines please contact:

Editorial Director, c/o IEEE Computer Society Press, 10662 Los Vaqueros Circle, Los Alamitos, California 90720-1264.